RICHARD MILHOUS
NIXON
THE INVINCIBLE QUEST

RICHARD MILHOUS
NIXON
THE INVINCIBLE QUEST

CONRAD BLACK

Quercus

First published in Great Britain in 2007 by Quercus

Quercus
21 Bloomsbury Square
London
WC1A 2NS

Originally published in Canada by McLelland & Stewart Ltd., Toronto

A CIP catalogue record for this book is available from the British Library

ISBN 10: 1 84724 209 X

ISBN 13: 978 1 84724 209 9

Unless otherwise noted, all photos courtesy of the Nixon Presidential Materials Project, National Archives and Records Administration, College Park, Maryland.

The lyrics from Camelot on page 455. Music and lyrics by Alan Jay Lerner and Frederick Loewe. © 1960 Warner Bros., Inc. All Rights Reserved. Warner Bros. Publications U.S. Inc., Florida.

Typeset in Electra by M&S, Toronto
Printed and bound in Great Britain by Clays Ltd, St Ives plc

10 9 8 7 6 5 4 3 2 1

www.quercusbooks.co.uk

To Barbara.
Through good and bad times, she has been magnificent.
No man could ask more and few could have received so much.
She is beyond praise and criticism.

Contents

Acknowledgments

My wife, Barbara, has been a constant and patient encouragement in this book, from the first occasions when we both met with Richard Nixon, through the composition of it in very distracting circumstances, as I prepared at the same time to deal with serious judicial problems. Without her encouragement, it could not have been written. My agent, Michael Levine, has performed prodigies well beyond what an author has any right to expect from an agent. Doug Pepper of McClelland & Stewart, Anthony Cheetham and Richard Milbank (of Quercus), Peter Osnos and Clive Priddle of Public Affairs, and my old friends George (Lord) Weidenfeld and Morton L. Janklow have been indispensable and often tireless in advancing it to publication. Bill Whitworth, an editor of astounding virtuosity, diplomacy, patience, and stamina, has done as much to make this book publishable as he did for my life of Franklin D. Roosevelt, in a much shorter time. Elizabeth Kribs and her team at M&S, including Heather Sangster, Alex Schultz, and Trena White, have made a great further contribution to polish the manuscript and remove or soften some of my less felicitous tendencies as a writer. Thank you also to Terra Page (typesetter), Scott Richardson (designer), and Scott Sellers (publicist) of M&S. Robert Nedelkoff of the Nixon Presidential Materials Project in College Park, Maryland, has been selfless, tireless, and invaluable in providing access to original documents and arranging photographs. He has shown Job-like patience in receiving telephone calls at home at odd hours, and Samaritanly goodwill in assisting in many vital areas. My very valued and resourceful colleague, Joan Maida, who has worked with me in many things with unfailing ingenuity and good humor for more than fifteen years, has been, yet again, a tremendously efficient and thoughtful collaborator. Adam Daifallah and Edward Saatchi carried out extensive and vital research for me in the latest available material in the vast Nixon and related archives. Among those who have helped and encouraged me from the official Nixon camp are Dimitri Simes of the Nixon Center and John H. Taylor of the Nixon Library and Birthplace. Margaret MacMillan, another friend of many years and an outstanding historian, has been extremely helpful, especially in directing me to some of her sources for her excellent recent book on President Nixon's visit to China. Among those who have read parts of the manuscript and made valuable suggestions about it, apart from some already named, are Ronald Genini, Edward L. Greenspan, Alexander Haig, Roger Hertog, George Jonas, Andrew Roberts, Brian Stewart, Peter White, Ken Whyte, and Ezra Zilkha. I tried to incorporate all of their suggestions and am grateful to all of them.

PART I

—

The Meteoric Rise

1913–1953

Chapter One

One of the Common People
1913–1945

— I —

RICHARD MILHOUS NIXON was one of America's greatest political leaders, and probably its most controversial president. He was both brilliant and strangely awkward, but ultimately and uniquely indestructible. And in his perseverance he made many of his countrymen awkward also, throughout a very long career, and after. He would not go away, and lingers yet.

Like much about Richard Nixon, the circumstances of his early years were nondescript. They were not as modest as those of some presidents, though they were certainly modest. There was almost nothing picturesque about them, little levity, but no degeneracy either; no careening, drunken, abusive adults about, none of the romance of the frontier, and not quite, in southern California around the First World War, the full proverbial wholesomeness of traditional, small-town America.

Life was real and life was earnest in the Quaker community of his childhood twenty miles from Los Angeles, which was just about to arise as a colossal and garish city that would influence the world. Young Richard listened to the distant train whistles and the roar of the steam engines in the night, "the sweetest music I've ever heard,"[1] and dreamt of the wider world. There was often the scent of citrus groves in the air, but the harsh life of the great ranches and farms and migrant workers, the hucksterism of this early phase of the great trek to California from the East and the Midwest, blended uneasily with the Quakerism of the Nixons and their neighbors. There was

3

little that seemed permanent or even durable, and almost no nearby trace of the long Spanish history in Southern California. Los Angles and its surroundings were just becoming a catchment for the demographic driftwood of America, as New York long had been for Europe.

And there was nothing to suggest that serious, diligent, well-scrubbed little Richard Nixon would incite the political passions of the United States as no one else has, for more than forty years, or that he would change the history of the world. But, of course, he did.

In Richard Nixon's youth, the population of Southern California would grow very quickly, and be recognized as some sort of laboratory for America. Bertrand Russell, an unlikely visitor, called it the "ultimate segregation of the unfit," and Upton Sinclair, the crusading novelist and radical 1934 candidate for governor of California, thought it a paradise of swindlers. The film industry arose and recorded, refracted, foretold human drama and comedy, and dispensed its images of American life to the whole world. Southern California became a precursor of public tastes in many fields, evanescently recruiting vast swaths of America and the world to its fashions and tastes, and repelling many by its insubstantial brazenness.

Richard Milhous Nixon was born close by this surging Babylon on January 9, 1913, to Quaker parents in a Quaker town, Whittier, named after one of America's leading poets and most illustrious Quakers, John Greenleaf Whittier.

The Quakers, the Society of Friends, had departed the existing Christian churches in seventeenth-century England, rebelling against the political and religious feuding of the time. The English Reformation seesawed back and forth from the Roman Catholic apostate Henry VIII and his Papist (Mary) and Protestant (Elizabeth) daughters, through Cromwell's Puritan Commonwealth, to the officially self-proclaimed Glorious Revolution of 1688. George Fox had started the Society of Friends, taking the name from Christ's assertion that his "friends" were those who did as he "commanded" (John 15:14). Fox founded an unstructured, quietist church, espousing simple dress and tastes, abstinence, temperance, asceticism, and many prophetic secular causes. These included pacifism and abolition of capital punishment, slavery, and racial discrimination. It was a contemplative church, where divine inspiration would come to the quiet seeker of it. They were good and courageous and idealistic, if somewhat unworldly, and unexciting people.

William Penn brought the Quakers to what became Pennsylvania in 1682, and by the American Revolution a century later, there were fifty thousand of them in the American colonies. The Friends moved west with the rest of the population, establishing communities across the country as the United States spread steadily toward the Pacific.

Richard Nixon's Quaker heritage came from his mother's family, the Milhouses. They had come from the German principalities to England in the seventeenth century and changed their name from Milhausen. They fought with Cromwell in the English Civil War against the Anglo-Catholic King, Charles I. Cromwell rewarded them with land in Ireland, a country Cromwell, for all his Puritanism, suppressed with a severity that must have helped propel the Milhouses into the arms of the Quakers. They emigrated to Pennsylvania in 1729. In 1854, Richard Nixon's great-grandparents, Joshua and Elizabeth Milhous, joined the move westward and decamped from Pennsylvania to Indiana. Joshua Milhous was the model for the protagonist of the novel *Friendly Persuasion*, written by another great-grandchild, Richard Nixon's cousin, Jessamyn West. Elizabeth Milhous was a famous preacher, whom Richard Nixon well remembered from her later years, including one occasion when she related the miracle of the loaves and fishes with such exuberance that she showered the congregation with her lunch of sardine sandwiches.[2]

At the end of the 1880s, Richard Nixon's grandparents, Franklin and Almira Milhous, moved to California. They brought with them their daughter, Hannah, Richard's mother, born in 1885 and named after an aunt and the biblical mother of Samuel. They joined the colony in Whittier, incorporated in 1887, for which occasion the town adopted a bit of doggerel the poet had written for his grandnephew:[3]

> A life not void of pure intent,
> With small desert of praise or blame,
> The love I felt, the good I meant,
> I leave thee with my name.

In a tiny foretaste of what would summarize much of Southern California's future, as historian Roger Morris wrote in his fine history of Richard Nixon's early years, what enveloped the Milhous family in Whittier was a "dusty mix of piety and profiteering."[4] This mélange of Low Church

5

Christianity and sleazy commercial dealings would be an important component of the heritage bequeathed by circumstances to Richard Milhous Nixon.

Whittier itself suffered at the hands of California land speculators, "men of no conscience, smooth oily tongued professional land sharks."[5] In 1888 there was a bust in land prices, which fell by about 90 percent in Whittier as the population thinned out from a thousand to about four hundred.

The Friends set up their meeting house, and municipal ordinances banned the sale of alcoholic beverages, dance halls, and theaters. One of the earliest inhabitants was Lou Henry, daughter of a local banker, who eventually became Mrs. Herbert Hoover. Franklin and Almira Milhous were joined in Whittier, as the years passed, by two of Franklin's brothers and two of his sisters, and by his mother. Their evening dinners were very well attended, not only by relatives but by the servants (usually African-Americans, Mexicans, or Indians), who sat with their employers, and even by indigent passersby that Almira invited to join them. This too was part of Richard Nixon's heritage – an absence of racial, religious, and economic prejudice, and a respect for everyone, regardless of their financial and social standing. There were participatory scriptural readings before dinner.

Hannah Nixon was a quiet but strong-minded, gentle person, who had a religious apotheosis at a Quaker evangelical meeting when she was fifteen, three years after her family moved to Whittier.

The first Nixons came to America from Ireland in 1731 and settled in Delaware, moving later to Pennsylvania, and in 1853 to Ohio. Richard Nixon's great-grandfather volunteered to take the place of a wealthy man in the Grand Army of the Republic during the Civil War and gave his life for Lincoln and the Union at Cemetery Ridge, on the third day of the Battle of Gettysburg, in 1863. Richard Nixon's grandfather, Samuel Brady Nixon, was named after a man who, when about to be burned by Indians, seized a papoose and threw it into the conflagration stoked up to consume him, so distracting his executioners that he escaped, running several miles, naked, to elude his pursuers.

The seventeen-year-old Samuel B. Nixon, whose mother died a few months after her husband was killed at Gettysburg, struggled to maintain the family homestead, but it was eventually gaveled down to creditors at a sheriff's sale, and the young family was parceled out among relatives. Samuel Nixon resettled near Richland, Ohio, married, and had five children. The middle child, Francis Anthony Nixon, Richard Nixon's father, was born in 1878. Samuel's wife was afflicted with tuberculosis, which would take a heavy toll on her family, and for two years they moved to West Virginia, and then through the Carolinas and Georgia, in search of a salubrious climate, while Sam worked at odd jobs. Nothing availed and they returned to Ohio, where Richard Nixon's grandmother died in 1886, aged thirty-four.

Again the Nixon family, in its poverty and bereavement, was dispersed among relatives. Samuel Nixon remarried in 1890 and gathered his family again, but Frank Nixon did not get on with his stepmother, who scolded and thrashed him. He went to school only for a few months, when he was thirteen, and his education was very rudimentary. As a teenager he worked in a brick works and raised his own potatoes, and earned a reputation as a dapper dresser, having smarted under the insults of his classmates for the penury of his wardrobe. In 1896, he encountered the Republican presidential candidate and governor of Ohio, William McKinley, who complimented Nixon on his fine-looking horse.[6]

He was a rough and ready man, fearless and belligerent. He struck out for Colorado while still in his teens, and worked on a sheep farm, in a railway yard and a glass factory, as a telephone installer and an electric company repairman, and finally as a carpenter, becoming very skilled.

He returned to Ohio, to Columbus, and worked for the municipal streetcar company. After five years he was promoted to motorman, and suffered frostbitten feet in the winter, as the motormen were in open, unheated cabs, while passengers and conductors traveled in stove-heated comfort. Frank Nixon, rebuffed both by management and his union in his efforts to get the streetcar cabs heated or enclosed, supported a candidate for state senator who promised to provide a legislated solution. Frank organized motormen and others behind the candidate, campaigning tirelessly for him out of hours, despite exhausting work days, and the candidate was elected and pushed through the law. Frank Nixon, who had shown great pluck and ingenuity, quit before he was fired and moved with another motorman to California. He would start again, having known nothing, as he later said, "but struggle and hardship."

With a letter of introduction from an officer of the Columbus Motormen's union, he became a streetcar driver on the run from Long Beach to Whittier, and moved into a Quaker boarding house in Whittier. His fellow roomers brought him to their church, and here, at a staid

Valentine's Day festivity in the Christian Endeavor room of the Whittier Friends' Meeting House, Frank Nixon met Hannah Milhous. It was love at first sight, augmented in Frank's case by the loneliness of a newcomer far from home, and in Hannah's by the omnipresence of her numerous family and especially her overbearing father.

The Milhouses, despite their Quakerism, were not above an affectation to social superiority and looked down on Frank Nixon as a rough-at-the-edges drifter. This impression was heightened when Frank was fired by Pacific Electric as a streetcar driver soon before his wedding, for hitting an automobile at a level crossing. But Frank quickly got another job, as a foreman at one of the large local citrus ranches, and he appeased a major Milhous concern by becoming a Quaker.

Frank Nixon and Hannah Milhous were married in a Quaker ceremony in Whittier on June 2, 1908, and moved into a staff cottage on the ranch where Frank worked. After a few months, with Hannah expecting their first child, Frank again retired his job. They moved in with Hannah's family, and Frank worked for his father-in-law in his plant and tree nursery. This was an awkward arrangement, but while it lasted the couple's first child, Harold Samuel Nixon, named after a pre-Norman English king and Frank Nixon's father, was born, in June 1909.

After a brief foray two hundred miles up-country to try to operate an orange grove on a parcel of Frank Milhous's land, Frank and Hannah Nixon returned and Frank planted a lemon grove on a ten-acre plot he bought on kinfolk terms from his father-in-law at Yorba Linda, fifteen miles from Whittier. At the back of this plot, Frank Nixon used his carpentering skills to build a very simple clapboard bungalow beside the Anaheim ditch, an irrigation and water collection channel.

This little house would become a national historic site, for here Richard Milhous Nixon was born on the cold ninth of January in 1913. He emerged weighing a formidable eleven pounds, with a strong voice and an almost full head of black hair and dark eyebrows, an instant miniature of what he would famously become. (A newborn, tiny version of the adult Richard Nixon is a startling concept.) He was named after Richard the Lion-Heart, brave crusader and king of England from 1189 to 1199.

Richard Nixon was a relatively placid child, serious and studious, and interested in everything. Though not at all effeminate, he liked to play with dolls when he visited families who had little girls. The Nixons kept producing sons; twenty-two months after Richard, Francis Donald Nixon was born. Richard's first memory was of falling off a horse-drawn buggy, driven by his mother, when it turned a sharp corner. One of the wheels inflicted a long but shallow cut in the middle of Richard's head, which required extensive stitching. This caused him to brush his hair straight back, unparted, which he did for the rest of his life, and as a youth it gave him a slightly unfashionable appearance.

Frank Nixon pursued his living first as an orange- and then a lemon-grove owner and operator. The countryside was rolling hills and foothills, turning in the east to the Santa Ana Mountains, and beyond them the taller San Bernardinos. There were sagebrush, cactus, and luxuriant wildflowers, but a lot of semi-desert – soil generally too dry to be ideal for citrus fruit. Duststorms occurred occasionally in the summer, and in winter there were usually a few descents into freezing temperatures.

An astonishing amount of pompous surmise and malicious fiction has been written and portrayed in film about Richard Nixon's upbringing. His mother, though reserved, was affectionate and devoted. His father, though noisy and irascible, was conscientious and not excessively severe. Frank appears to have had the confidence normal for the time in the corrective powers of corporal punishment, but rarely to have had occasion to apply it to Richard. The most frequent cause of such incidents was the boys' inability to avoid swimming or wading in the Anaheim ditch – or, more grandly, canal – which flowed invitingly by their house through the hot summer, but playing in which was forbidden by law, as well as by parents concerned by its swift current.

Richard Nixon was a rather self-contained little boy, with a round face and big, dark eyes. He enjoyed good health, despite a bout of pneumonia when he was four. He was always well turned out and never misbehaved in the presence of adults. The Nixon family revolved around Hannah, who deeply loved her children, never raised her voice, and instilled her religious faith in her husband and sons. While it was a desperately serious environment, it was stable and emotionally solid. "No one projected warmth and affection more than my mother did," Richard recalled. "But she never indulged in the present day custom, which I find nauseating, of hugging or kissing her children or others for whom she had great affection."[7] Henry Kissinger's famous rhetorical question of sixty years later – "Can you imagine what this man could have done if he had ever been loved?" – was probably well-intentioned amateur analysis, but it was mistaken. Richard Nixon was always loved by his parents, and by his own family. His personality had some serious foibles, but a noticeable absence of affection from those from whom he most needed it was not the source of them.

Though the Nixons were not prosperous, their means were adequate, their needs few, and Frank fairly steadily bettered his lot by dint of hard work, decade after decade. But in these early days, while the lemon trees slowly grew to full size, Frank had to deploy some of his many secondary skills to supplement his income and meet bills. The Nixon family diet, with its principal staple of cornmeal, was very monotonous. But by 1918, Frank had a tractor and an automobile, and Hannah had some china dishes. She made the children's clothes herself, and they were handed down from Harold to Richard to Donald and, after 1918, on to Arthur Burdg, the Nixons' fourth son. (Arthur was also named after a famous old English king; Burdg was grandmother Milhous's maiden name.)

They were able to hire a helper to take care of the children, whom Hannah would not tolerate to be called a "hired girl" by her sons. She was to be referred to as their "friend," who was helping them.[8] The three boys slept in a semi-attic. The house had only one other bedroom, a modest parlor, a dining room and kitchen, and one bathroom, and was heated by a single stove. There was no upholstered furniture and minimal decoration.

Frank Nixon loved to argue about politics and the Bible, and became a very popular Sunday school teacher, flamboyantly taking the Quaker youth of Whittier all the way through the scriptures. He was an animated and thorough teacher with flair, and a human interest in individual students.

Richard Nixon went to the little wooden Yorba Linda school, entering Grade One in the autumn of 1919, when he was a few months short of his seventh birthday. He sometimes went barefoot, but carried shoes and socks in a paper bag, and always wore a starched white shirt, black bow tie, and knee pants. He never rumpled or dirtied his clothes, and his mother visited the school early on to admonish the teacher never to call her son anything except Richard. "Dick" was not acceptable. Richard got on well and was such an apt student that he skipped forward to Grade Three in his second year. In later life, he gave his mother credit for this, for teaching him to read before he set foot in a school.[9] His prodigious memory, which would become famous, revealed itself early, as he routinely memorized prose passages and poems and recited them for prizes at school and at his church. The Nixon family read poems and stories aloud after dinner, and the family took a daily newspaper and the *Saturday Evening Post, Ladies' Home Journal,* and *National Geographic.* But there were no books in the home. (Jessamyn West did find there, hidden away, in 1919, a pamphlet on sex education.)

By 1920, Richard Nixon, under his father's influence, was already interested in politics, and already a Republican. Frank Nixon considered Woodrow Wilson a fuzzy-minded idealist and William Jennings Bryan, the three-time unsuccessful Democratic presidential candidate, a wild-eyed radical. He believed the Republicans the party of self-help and rugged individualism and Wilson an international busybody. Hannah, truer to Quaker pacifism than her husband, was impressed by Wilson's quest for a League of Nations and a durable world peace. In 1920, a rare election in which three of the four candidates for national office ultimately became president, Frank and Richard were delighted that the Republicans, Warren Harding and Calvin Coolidge, defeated the Democrats, James M. Cox and thirty-eight-year-old Franklin D. Roosevelt, by a wide margin. (Both presidential candidates were from the Nixons' native state of Ohio.)

Hannah, who had had more access to rudimentary culture than her husband, detected a musical talent, and specifically an aptitude for the piano, in Richard. The family had an elementary upright piano, and Hannah forced Richard to practice, against his wishes, every afternoon. He never learned to read music, but he did memorize a good many pieces of classical music and rendered them with confidence and often with gusto, without consulting the score, which would have been incomprehensible to him.

Yorba Linda grew rapidly, and there were soon many young people for Richard to play with. He blended well into the group, though always retaining, as he would his entire life, the standoffish manner and odd formality of dress that amused humorists and caricaturists decades later. And he spent an inordinate amount of time reading. Harold and Donald Nixon were playful, gregarious boys. Richard got by, but was more serious and very bookish. Where his social qualities seemed to emerge most unselfconsciously was in the affection and interest he always showed for his little brother Arthur. He played with him as a baby and pushed him around the neighborhood in an improvised pram, an adapted children's wagon. Arthur grew up a quiet and serious child, like Richard, less affable than Harold and Donald.

By late 1919, Frank Nixon's inability to afford the fertilizer needed to encourage his lemon trees in the semi-arid ground caused him to give up being a lemon farmer. He moved on to the next in the succession of California's get-rich resources, oil, which was pumped at many places in the area. He became a field worker for Union Oil. At the same time, Hannah took a job in the local Sunkist lemon packinghouse – work regarded as being above that done by the mainly Mexican pickers in the groves. Hannah was a sorter and packer, and sometimes brought Richard or Donald with her to act as sweepers. Richard found it literally nauseating work, because the sound and movement of the lemon-packing machinery aggravated his motion sickness. Richard and Donald also worked in the summers of 1920 and 1921 as pickers in the bean fields, twelve hours for one dollar, and Richard acquired a life-long revulsion for string beans.

In May 1922, Frank Nixon sold the little house he had built in Yorba Linda, and his failed lemon grove with its stunted trees, for less than he had paid his father-in-law for it, and, with a Milhous guarantee for a five-thousand-dollar loan, set up a gas station on Whittier Boulevard in East Whittier. Frank believed that his father-in-law had lied to him about the condition and prospects of the Yorba Linda lemon grove, and Richard dutifully adhered to his father's line that his grandfather had misled and exploited him.[10]

The Milhous reservations about Frank Nixon as a rough and abrasive man had not much abated, other than with Hannah, and there arose against it a Nixon view that the Milhouses were condescending snobs and exploiters. Hannah straddled this schism with the implacable and silent dignity of a devout Quaker. There were frequent family gatherings at the Milhous home in Whittier, which most of the Nixons found excruciating. Frank dodged them when he could.

It is not the case, as has often been claimed, including by Richard Nixon, that oil was ever discovered on Frank Nixon's land, though he did look at possible gas station locations where oil was subsequently discovered. These were difficult years for young Richard Nixon, and he did not look back on them with much pleasure, other than his respect for the strong characters of his parents; he had a tendency to exaggerate the stark, Dickensian realities of their existence: income had to match expenses or disaster impended. All the family worked hard, every day.

— II —

Henry Kissinger recounted in the second volume of his official memoirs a trip he took with President Nixon in 1970 by car from Los Angeles to Yorba Linda to Whittier. As he walked around the little house where he was born, Nixon shouted that the Secret Service contingent and a press car had to leave them. It seemed to Kissinger, in passages that he drew on many years later for his eloquent eulogy of Nixon, that Nixon was more comfortable back in the simple, inauspicious world he came from than in the mighty and storied realms he then inhabited. It seemed that it was all a series of accidents that had thrust Nixon upwards in public life. Kissinger reflected: "What extraordinary vehicles destiny selects to accompany its designs."[11] (Undoubtedly so, but Kissinger was as illustrative of this truth as Nixon was.) He believed that Nixon had accepted the apparently hopeless initial Republican nomination for a congressional seat because "he had nothing better to do." It was also what Nixon had long been determined to do.

By the time he put in for that nomination, and long before, Nixon had settled on a political career, probably by the time he was reading about the 1920 election. What seemed to please and relax him that summer day in 1970 was the contemplation of how far he had come and how much he had achieved, whatever the war protesters, who then, just after the Cambodia incursion in 1970, were surging through the streets of many cities, might think of it.

Nixon did not consider his remarkable rise to the summit of modern history to be a series of accidents. He considered it a triumph of his will-power, intermittently blessed and facilitated by the God he worshipped, but whose omnipotence and unpredictability frightened him. Some combination of a fierce determination to better his lot and a piercing fear, a terror, that he was aspiring to too much, was already perceptible in Nixon as a boy, and it became more disruptive to his equanimity as he aged, until all was reconciled in his brilliant final years. Only Nixon could resolve it, in the serenity that can come to some people only after immense tumult. His tumult would be immense.

Whittier was a metropolis compared with Yorba Linda, despite the enforced reticence of the Quakers. (When there was an impromptu dance at the high school at the end of 1919 celebrating the return of First World War veterans, the school principal had been excoriated from the pulpit and by the school board.)[12] The earth was richer and the botany less scrubby than at Yorba Linda. Walnut and olive trees, as well as fruit trees, abounded. Whittier College had a fine hillside campus, and the town, by California standards, had a deserved air of durability. In the spring, the perfumed scent of orange blossoms was overpowering.

Where Yorba Linda was a raw subdivision, with people attracted from all over to try their hands at some aspect of the citrus business, Whittier had more of the instances of an American city, including a Mexican district, Jimtown. The Mexicans were day laborers in Whittier, but retired to Jimtown, or even to the seething Gomorrah of Los Angeles, at night. In nearby Anaheim, the municipal swimming pool was drained and refilled after the one day of the week when Mexicans were allowed into it.[13]

Frank Nixon again built the family home, adjacent to his gas station. The boys' bedroom was above the garage, reached by an outside staircase. This became a sort of clubhouse, and there were social gatherings with musical accompaniment from Richard on the piano, and other diversions. The straitened circumstances of Yorba Linda had given way to a few up-holstered chairs and antimacassars.

Frank Nixon had finally, in his early forties, found a commercially winning formula. There was no other gas station for miles around, and the automobile was a proliferating novelty, especially in such a mobile, socially fluid place as Southern California. Frank offered a whole line of automotive products, tires and so forth, and as a person with high craft skills and consid-erable mechanical experience he mastered minor repairs. Soon local farmers began leaving produce with Frank Nixon to be sold to passersby.

His integrity was conceded by everyone and his service station swiftly was transmuted into a general store. Both Frank and Hannah Nixon were indulgent with shoppers who were financially distressed. They granted credit easily, would not hear of discriminating against African-Americans, Mexicans, Indians, Roman Catholics, or, as far as there were any in Whittier, Jews. They even, at Richard's very strong urging, declined to expose a shoplifter and allowed her discreetly to repay, over a generous period, the balance owed for what she had taken.

The threads of the Nixons' lives were oddly united when Frank bought the old Friends' church, as the Quakers moved to a larger one, and turned that into a general store. Soon Hannah, a talented cook, especially of favored American fruit pies, was selling baked goods, and Frank stocked a wide range of wares, even Hannah's knitted goods. Frank added butchering to his long line of talents, and became the quintessential versatile shopkeeper, working in an apron. The Nixon boys helped out in the store and gas station, and, like that of most of the country, the family's standard of living began to rise through the twenties.

Frank Nixon engaged most customers in political debate, which was a popular feature of his emporium for those who enjoyed his boisterous personality, but many sought out Hannah or one of the older boys at the cash register so as not to have an acrimonious and prolonged exchange with Frank. Frank had read Ida Tarbell's 1904 attack on the near monopoly exercised by John D. Rockefeller's Standard Oil Company, and he refused to sell Standard products. This may be taken as the beginning of Richard Nixon's long, and heartily reciprocated, skepticism about the Rockefeller family.

Frank Nixon preached more flamboyantly than ever to his Sunday school classes. Politically, he departed the Republicans for the Progressives in 1924, when senators Robert M. La Follette of Wisconsin and Burton K. Wheeler of Montana ran a national campaign against Calvin Coolidge's Republicans and the bitterly divided Democrats (split between the anti-Prohibitionists led by the Roman Catholic governor of New York, Alfred E. Smith, and the Prohibitionists led by future California senator, and Woodrow Wilson's son-in-law, William G. McAdoo). La Follette came third, but carried Wisconsin and took almost 20 percent of the country-wide vote. (The Democratic nominee, John W. Davis, took as his vice-presidential nominee Charles Bryan, the brother of three-time presidential candidate William Jennings Bryan.)

Richard Nixon was an outstanding student and moved effortlessly through the school system. For Grade Seven, in order to pursue piano studies more ambitiously, Richard moved two hundred miles to stay with Hannah's sister, Jane Beeson, who had studied at the Indianapolis Conservatory of Music and gave him lessons every day. He walked a mile and a half to the Sunnyside School, and added violin lessons to his piano studies. These, still based entirely on rote, as it became almost a matter of pride to him not to learn how to read music, broadened into Chopin, Brahms, Bach, and other sophisticated composers. He returned to Whittier in June 1925 and to the East Whittier elementary school in September.

The Nixons continued to have a stable and normal family life. Much has been made of a letter Richard wrote his mother when he was ten, subscribing himself "your good dog, Richard." Read in context, it was a humorous effort at ingratiation, and the fantastic imputations of the boy's derangement, neurotic personality, and abuse by his mother are nonsense. Hannah showed it decades later to an interviewer as "just another sign of her son's intelligence."[14]

The Nixons' was, for a time, a happier house than the more cramped homestead in Yorba Linda had been. But in July 1925, the first of several dark shadows fell over the family with the inexplicable illness of the littlest of them, Arthur. He came down with constant headaches, indigestion, lack of appetite, listlessness, and fatigue. The doctor was called after a few days, and Arthur was moved into the main house. The first time Richard saw his father cry was after a medical visit during which Frank was told that his son might not survive. There has never been a satisfactory medical explanation of Arthur's ailment, but officially it was a result of encephalitis or tubercular meningitis, possibly provoked by a schoolyard stone-throwing accident.

Prayer meetings were held for Arthur in the Friends' church in Whittier. The illness was inexorable, and the little boy died on August 19, 1925, aged six. He was buried near his grandfather, Franklin Milhous. Richard "slipped into a big chair and sat staring into space, silent and dry-eyed in the undemonstrative way in which, because of his choked, deep feeling, he was always to face tragedy."[15] He wasn't dry-eyed for long. "For weeks after Arthur's funeral, there was not a day that I did not think about him and cry. For the first time, I learned what death was like and what it meant." Hannah thought that Richard redoubled his determination to make his parents proud of him. "Now his need to succeed became even stronger."[16]

An important part of American history was presaged in his valedictory address to the East Whittier elementary school. He had been president and "outstanding member" of the Grade Eight class, and wrote a little piece about himself in which he said he would graduate from Whittier High School and Columbia University law school, then enter politics "so that I might be of some good to the people."

Richard said that his father "half-believed that Arthur's death represented some kind of divine displeasure" at the family's commercial preoccupations, and he closed his gas station and general store on Sundays forever. With Frank taking the lead, the family's religious devotions became more fervent than before. He arose in the contemplative Quaker sessions where the congregation was invited to speak of their religious insights. The Nixons attended four services on Sunday, and another during the week. Richard Nixon started to play the piano at church services. Frank also began to frequent the great evangelists of Los Angeles. He took his sons to hear Billy Sunday, who gesticulated wildly and roared against the evils of drink, sexual dissolution, and gambling, and held vast audiences spellbound by the power and exertions of his fire-and-brimstone sermons.

Another great evangelist in the mid-twenties was Aimee Semple McPherson. Originally from Ingersoll, Ontario, Canada, she fetched up in Los Angeles in the early twenties, almost penniless, but already an experienced touring evangelical. As Sister Aimee, she started to pull radio audiences for her claims of divine revelation, and in 1924 founded her own radio station. In these days before any regulation of the airwaves, her technique was to start broadcasting at the bottom of the dial and gradually alter her station's wavelength, going right across the dial, poaching listeners as she went, and concluding with a colossal market share. She prospered so greatly she was able to build the five-thousand-seat Angelus Temple. A fetching woman, exiguously dressed, she sang well, accompanied by full orchestras and choirs, and conducted faith-healings and morality plays in which she chased a satanic beast around the stage with a pitchfork. They were splendid entertainments, but her fortunes began to decline when she was accused, though in 1927 exonerated of the charge, of staging her own kidnapping.

Frank also took the Nixons to see Aimee's great, and slightly less exotic, rival, Robert Shuler of the Trinity Methodist Church. He eventually had an even larger radio audience than Sister Aimee, and terrorized Los Angeles politicians he judged to be morally deficient, driving a mayor and several other prominent officials from office. Another radio revivalist, who conducted crusades in Africa and Asia on motorcycles, was Paul Rader. It was at one of his meetings in Los Angeles in 1926 that the thirteen-year-old Richard Nixon went through a public conversion and spiritual reawakening.

His older brother, Harold, did not take to this pious regime quite as convincingly. A carefree, easygoing, amiable lad, Harold liked girls and parties and a rebuilt Ford Model T. His parents decided that he was insufficiently God-fearing and sent him off to evangelist Dwight L. Moody's spartan and fire-breathing Mount Hermon School for Boys, in rural Massachusetts, in the autumn of 1926. Frank was now prosperous enough to afford such a luxury, but Harold was not a natural candidate or happy arrival at such a place.

Richard, who had comported himself a good deal more soberly, was sent to a nearby high school, Fullerton Union. Given the restraints under which he had been raised, it was a wonder that Richard Nixon was progressing through his teens as a well-adjusted young man, despite the inexpressible sadness of Arthur. The Nixons were now economically in the middle class and Richard was an excellent student, socially awkward but serviceable, in a loving if perfervidly pious family.

Richard now went to school on the school bus, which he disliked because of the lack of cleanliness and body odor of many of the students. This became so bothersome to him that in 1927 he moved to live during the week with an aunt in Fullerton, returning to Whittier to work in the store on Friday evening and Saturday. He was always well turned out in neatly pressed gray flannels, and brushed his teeth so strenuously that it was a substitute for mouthwash.

He was a very strong student, who worked while his classmates relaxed. He studied with fierce determination, forcing himself to succeed whether he possessed any liking or aptitude for the subjects or not. He did like English and history and did not find it burdensome to commit large swatches of famous prose or historic facts to memory. But even in geometry, he applied himself until he knew enough to do well, despite his intense lack of interest in the subject.

He forced himself to become a capable public speaker, overcoming his innate shyness by writing out what he considered, after meticulous redrafting, an excellent speech, committing it entirely to memory, and then practicing rendering it in as natural a way as he could simulate. It was laborious, but, as with much that he achieved in his life, his doggedness and implacability brought success. His forensic efforts were assisted by his generally goodnatured debates with his loquacious and outspoken father. As Richard grew and learned, he became a steadily worthier challenger in argument for Frank, and rather than these exchanges being contentious, they tended to bring the two closer together.

Richard had played soccer at East Whittier. At Fullerton, he changed to football and developed what was to become a lifelong passion for the sport. He was now, as he never had been before and would not be as an adult, a somewhat full-figured young man, being about five feet, seven inches in height and carrying a weight of about a hundred and fifty pounds. He turned out for every practice, but was only on the B team and saw little action. He wasn't fast or well-coordinated, but he was game and fearless, and never gave up. He had an encyclopedic knowledge, then and always after, for football statistics.

Richard was not a boy who had an early interest in girls. His painful shyness was accentuated by a lack of familiarity with females: he had no sisters and wasn't close to his female cousins, and his mother didn't fill the void; whatever her other virtues, there was nothing girlish about Hannah.

It was less than six months after Harold was shipped off to Dwight Moody's seminarian boot camp that the next gruesome shadow came down on the Nixon family. Harold was sent home in April 1927 with a chest condition that was feared, accurately, to be tuberculosis. A heartbreaking drama ensued, with little doubt of the outcome, protracted though it would be. The inexorable, gradual decline of Harold Nixon would go on for nearly five years.

Frank would not consider a public clinic, as this would make him a dependent of the state. He again stretched his personal resources to send his eldest son to an expensive sanatorium in the San Gabriel Mountains. From here, after a few months, Harold was moved to a rural cabin with supposedly salubrious air. Harold had several remissions but ignored medical advice. He was an amateur aviator and indulged himself in this activity, which was dangerous to tubercular cases, and even took a job spraying citrus groves with insecticide, a very unhealthy occupation for anyone with any pulmonary condition. A year after his return from school, Harold was taken in tow by Hannah and they went to Prescott, Arizona, counting on dry desert air and Hannah's strict watchfulness to protect Harold from his own careless exuberance.

Prescott was an air spa, and a tourist attraction because of its Wild West entertainments. But there was a discreet community for sufferers of tuberculosis and asthma. Hannah rented a cabin and took in three other tubercular young men, caring for them all as thoroughly as for Harold. Everything had to be repeatedly sterilized, many times a day, as no one knew how the disease was transmitted, and Hannah had no assistance lugging groceries for five up the hill from town. Frank, Richard, and Don remained in Whittier but traveled the four hundred miles to Prescott at least once a month in Frank's 1924 Packard (a luxury car, albeit a used one). It was a fourteen-hour trip each way. Relatives minded the store as the Nixons faced this new emergency with their customary courage and stoicism.

Richard spent the summers of 1928 and 1929 in Prescott and contributed to the family income with a variety of jobs, including janitor in a posh country club, plucking chickens in a poultry shop, and serving very successfully and even lucratively as a barker at Prescott's Wild West carnival in July. Prescott, apart from the tubercular sections, was a wealthy town, and Richard Nixon had perhaps his first up-close glimpse of rich people, just as the fabulously wealthy decade of the twenties wound noisily to a spectacular climax.

Needed in his father's business, Richard moved in September 1928 back from Fullerton Union to Whittier Union, which his parents had considered morally unsuitable for Richard and Harold two years before. Richard would now embark on a more onerous regime than he had ever imagined, but he bore up under it once again, uncomplainingly. He became the vegetables manager of his father's business, and got up every morning at 4 A.M., drove (which he was licensed to do at age fifteen) in a dilapidated truck into the Seventh Street market in Los Angeles, and selected, haggled for, and brought back the produce, then washed and displayed it, before putting in a full school day.

Richard never complained and did his job with great skill, but as with many other things that he had to do in his youth, he hated it and never after drove "by a vegetable stand without feeling sorry for the guy who picks out the rotten apples."[17] Under these influences, Richard Nixon developed a concern for his weight and diet that never deserted him. His weight would be almost constant, and not at all excessive, from his late teens into his eighties.

To pitch in at the business and maintain his fine academic standing, Richard reluctantly gave up the orchestra and football and came home in the afternoons and studied whenever there was a lull in customers for food and automobile service. In 1929 his father bought his two resident sons an old Ford to make the school run.

He did maintain his interest in debating and in 1929 won a Whittier oratorical contest sponsored by the *Los Angeles Times*. He would have a long and complicated relationship with this newspaper, starting with his unsuccessful application for a job there as an office boy in 1924. His theme in the oratory contest was the limit of rights, and he endorsed Lincoln's assertion that there can be "no individual rights against the best interests of society." This was to have some interesting echoes in his own career. He won the same contest again in 1930, with an even more impassioned invocation of America's

"incomparable Constitution." He even ascribed to the Constitution's cura-
tive powers for emulators, purporting to find the "amazing" rise of Latin
America illustrative of the peerless exportability of the American system.
Latin America was, of course, a cesspool of corruption, despotism, and back-
wardness, and it is not clear whether Nixon believed any of what he was
saying on the subject or was merely exploiting the unworldly chauvinism of
his audience.

He was brought up in the belief that America was a divinely blessed
country that had discovered and proclaimed the secret of successful self-
government. He would discover relatively early in his adult life the limits of
public tolerance and clean government within America, and in the world
the impotence of the good example. And he would apply these lessons to
American public and foreign policy when finally able to do so. These, and
not the irony of his early enthusiasm for the safeguards of the Constitution
(as some of his detractors have claimed), were the real omens of his collegiate efforts at political oratory.

Richard Nixon's success in the *Times* oratory contest was the principal
factor that caused the Whittier Union faculty and senior class to run him
against the faculty-approved candidate of the junior class for the position of
student body president, in the spring of 1929. Nixon appeared to be the
favorite, but the race was shaken up by the rare Whittier phenomenon of an
unofficial third candidate, a fine athlete and captain of the basketball team.
Nixon was cast as a machine politician and the junior class candidate as a
sort of patsy for the senior candidate. He was not a natural or relaxed campaigner, and his chief opponent, the grassroots renegade Robert Logue, was.
Indeed, Logue was all that Nixon was not: tall, attractive to women, a fine
athlete, and a good student to whom everything appeared to come easily. He
won election by a good majority, having not seemed especially to want it,
almost accepting a spontaneous draft of students who were tired of having
their executive selected for them by "bosses." It was, in several respects, an
object lesson for the young Nixon.

He was never under the illusion that he was particularly popular, other
than in small groups that got to know him well. He was always wary of a type
of person who seemed naturally graceful and lucky, and he thought the
world was frequently unjust, as such felicitous people kept popping up to over-
turn what he had worked with great self-discipline to achieve. In later years
and higher offices, some would think this paranoia, but it was a realistic appre-

ciation of his limitations and of the caprices of electoral life. At his elementary school, he was selected by an electorate whose criteria for election he could easily address. As he prepared to leave secondary school, it was already more complicated.

Nixon knew well enough the fears and ambitions of the average person, and he could project his own ordinariness of circumstance. He sometimes seemed dogmatic or humorless, but rarely pompous. But lacking the quality of natural attraction was what made him vulnerable as a candidate and even as an office-holder embroiled in controversy, and was what made his ultimate attainments in his chosen career so astounding. He was vulnerable, but ultimately unstoppable. In the vortex between these two qualities there would be great drama and national controversy many years later, and for a whole generation.

Nixon never acknowledged that the Whittier Union setback hurt him, but it could not fail to have been humiliating. The rest of the senior class slate won; it was a personal rejection, very clearly, by the great majority of his peers. It was a little like Franklin D. Roosevelt's not being named a full prefect at his prestigious private school by his legendary rector, Dr. Endicott Peabody. Roosevelt claimed to his parents that the honor had been rendered meaningless by nepotism, as Peabody had appointed his own nephew. But in fact Roosevelt, who was much more the natural politician than Nixon but in small groups was undermined by his own charm – so facile that, before he became a powerful man, it appeared somewhat dishonest – was also deeply offended.[18]

As a consolation prize for Nixon, the faculty exercised its right to name him student body general manager. For the first of many times, Nixon used a position to do favors for people, to get mundane tasks, cumulatively important, done properly. He sold advertising in the yearbook and positioned himself to be helpful to many students in many ways. Here he was very efficient and ultimately much better appreciated than when he had been perceived as a lackey of the faculty overreaching for the highest post in student government.

In an even more spectacular and embarrassing fiasco than the election, Nixon played Aeneas in a reenactment of Virgil's *Aeneid*, which the school ambitiously staged on the two thousandth anniversary of the birth of Rome's greatest poet. Nixon had an ill-fitting costume and was completely unrehearsed apart from his lines, and the love scene with Dido, involving an energetic and prolonged embrace, replete with passionate dialogue, brought down the house in brickbats and catcalls. It was a horrifying experience, but it got Nixon over his initial embarrassment and into an innocent and long-running romance with Dido, Ola Florence Welch.

She was a very popular, attractive girl, the daughter of Whittier's deputy chief of police. Thanks to Ola, Nixon, who now called himself Dick, concluded high school in a blaze of glory. After a month-long fever – during which his mother, who was back in Whittier to have yet another child at the age of forty-five, had his course work sent over from the school – Nixon graduated third in a class of 207. He seemed a popular enough youth, after all, not gregarious, but well adjusted and well appreciated, and happy in the manner of doting teenagers.

The Nixons' fifth son, Edward Calvert, was born in May 1930. Hannah and Harold would be back and forth between Whittier and Prescott for nearly three more years. All the other boys Hannah had cared for in Prescott gradually were worn down by their tuberculosis and died. Harold fought gamely on, cheerful but fatalistic.

There is nothing to support the claims of those who purport to find in the collegiate Dick Nixon a monster in the making. His upbringing had been rather joyless; he had had to work very hard and his father was difficult. It was a relentlessly serious life and nothing came easily to him. But he was a good student, a good worker in a wide range of challengingly dull jobs; he was very responsible, and had got on well with his classmates in the end.

The Harvard Club of California rated him the "best all-round student" at Whittier Union. This comported an invitation to apply for a tuition grant to Harvard. Nixon claims in his memoirs that there also was a prospect of a similar scholarship from Yale. Instead he went to Whittier College, where his mother had attended (but didn't finish, as marriage and a brief time as a school teacher, which didn't require a degree, intervened). Frank Milhous had left each of his grandchildren a $250 bequest for university tuition, and this would effectively defray all the costs of higher learning in Whittier.

The reason Nixon always gave for passing on Harvard and Yale was that Harold's illness, a new child in the family, and the requirement for him to be an alternate head of the family business to his father, prevented him from going three thousand miles away and generating substantial expenses. This is plausible, and his parents, who thought Harold had been led morally astray by Whittier Union high school, were probably not enchanted at the thought of bundling off the seventeen-year-old Richard to such sophisticated places, so far away, at the final spike of the Jazz and Prohibition Age.

His life might have been a little less charged with fears and resentments of the Eastern establishment if he had accepted such an honor. When Nixon did come to grips with the empowered alumni of the Ivy League in the great law firms and corporations of the East, it was always an uneasy arrangement. Harvard or Yale, and wherever he had gone in graduate school, might have given him a less fearful and abrasive insight into that milieu and forged him some relationships that would have made the peaks of his career less lonely, and his many successes easier for him to celebrate.

Already, in the spring of 1930, as the Great Depression started to settle on America, it was possible to predict an interesting career for Richard Nixon. But it would have been difficult to predict for him an easy pursuit of happiness. He celebrated his graduation from high school with a holiday with cousins in the Grand Canyon.

— III —

Whittier College was a pleasant hillside campus, and continued the Quaker tradition of the founder and the namesake. A furled flag in honor of the college's dead of the First World War stood next to a furled flag in honor of the conscientious objectors in the same conflict. There was a mandatory chapel hour each day. The curriculum was varied, and the academic standards were reasonably rigorous. The spirit of the college was tolerant up to a point, but very Christian and very staid. The most famous former faculty member up to this time had been the playwright Maxwell Anderson, author of the pacifistic 1924 Broadway production *What Price Glory?* The process of evolution was accepted in the curriculum.

There were four hundred students in the college, only about ten from outside California. There were a few African-American and Japanese-American students. They were treated correctly, although town ordinances prevented such people from being homeowners.

Instead of sororities or fraternities, there were "literary societies," which performed the same function. There were four for women and only one for men, the Franklins, whom Nixon considered from the outset of his freshman year to be unrepresentative snobs. His desire for public office, interest in the mechanics of politics, and awareness of his own limitations as a natural politician gave him from this time onward a sense of other peoples' vulnerabilities, and an idea of how to exploit political opportunities in almost any situation. He was already an astute and lonely operator. He was elected president of the freshman class with 90 percent of the votes.

When he was not approached by the Franklins, he quickly accepted an invitation to be a charter member of a new group, called the Orthogonians (meaning square-shooters). This was largely a collection of football players who were not academic enough to make it as Franklins, and they calculated that they needed a serious student, if not a cunning nerd, to help organize their alternative society. Nixon was the perfect founding president of the group and got them off to a good start. Their toe-curlingly sophomoric motto was "Beans, Brains, Brawn, and Bowels," as if they were a manufacturer of laxatives for athletes. Their animal was the unheroic wild boar, and their club slogan, more interestingly, was Voltaire's anti-clerical exhortation "*Ecrasons l'Infame,*" or "Crush the Infamous."

An outrageous initiation was conceived, which Nixon and the other founders evaded. The initiates were made to eat rancid meat. Hazing was a fact of campus life. Candidates for the Glee Club, including Nixon, had to strip naked and have their bottoms paddled. Candidates for the Orthogonians were also stripped naked, and were left to return to their homes in the dead of night dressed only in underwear. Nixon did not dissent from the imposition of this harsh juvenilism, though he didn't like it. He was laid up for a week after joining the Glee Cub, and Frank wanted to sue the club.[19]

The Orthogonians soon adopted as campus adviser the college's football coach, Wallace "Chief" Newman, replacing the English lecturer who originally held the position but found the "Beans and Brawn" group less than convivial. Newman, a partial North American Indian from the La Jolla Reservation and a tough leader of the football team, would be a lifelong friend and strong formative influence on Richard Nixon. Their relations would flower despite Nixon's ineptitude as a football player and would endure all the tumult of Nixon's unique career. They would be friends to the end.

Here again is a slight parallel to Franklin D. Roosevelt's relations with Dr. Peabody. Roosevelt had craved more recognition from Peabody than the Doctor was happy to give to him as a thrusting schoolboy. But Peabody ceased to withhold it as Roosevelt achieved and retained the nation's highest office. Newman was not prepared to exaggerate Nixon's athletic prowess while he was at Whittier. But he admired Nixon's determination and was happy to be his friend as Nixon followed the same path as Roosevelt, and after.[20]

Chief Newman was a large and swarthy man who had been a star football player at the University of Southern California. He came to Whittier in 1929, attracted some good football talent, and made the small college a greater football force than its numbers could normally assure. He was a tough coach, sparing in congratulation and consolation, who told his players they had to be "angry, terribly angry" about losing. "I think that I admired him more and learned more from him than from any man I have ever known outside my father," Nixon would write in his memoirs.[21]

Nixon was such a dedicated player there was great affection for him on the team and among its fans. He was not talented, but gave it all he could and never shrank from the terrible pounding he received in practice and when he got into games. (He said that his "only athletic trophy" was a porcelain bridge he got after taking an elbow in the mouth in a basketball game.) Toward the end of football games that weren't close, regardless of which team was winning, a chant would go up in the stands: "We want Nixon, Put Nixon in." He became a folk hero, as improbable athletes do (the British national ski-jumper Eddie "the Eagle," the erratic baseball pitcher known in the nineties as "Wild Thing," and so forth). A huge ovation would greet his appearance in the game, and his teammates would try to make him look good, setting him up for yardage gains or touchdowns.

Nixon became more jocular in his university days than at any other time. In March 1931 he staged a pretended coup d'état for the benefit of the college newspaper, *Quaker Campus*, purporting to abolish chapel and impeach the student body president. It was a popular lark. He studied English, French, European history, algebra, and, in something of an irony, journalism. He had an active extracurricular and social life, but studied as much as was necessary to be on top of all subjects, frequently until after one o'clock in the morning. He still arose at 4 A.M. to drive into Los Angeles, buy vegetables, and come back and wash them and set them out. As an adult, he was not a sound sleeper, and as a teenager he seemed able to get by on only a few hours of sleep most nights. His campus days were overwhelmingly purposeful. He never appeared to have a spare minute and was always between classes, clubs, sports, or campus hobbies.

He took up as a debater where he had left off at high school and had a distinguished career as a collegiate debater. Frank let the Whittier debating team drive all over California in his Packard to debate with other universities in the early thirties. Here Richard Nixon acquired some of the phrases he would make tiresomely familiar decades later: "Let me make one thing perfectly clear," etc. This tendency to repetition of the banal, and his slightly jerky physical gestures, caused caricaturists, as well as his opponents, to underestimate him. He was a crafty debater, sometimes pulling out what was really a blank piece of paper and claiming to quote an authoritative source. Though in debating as in other spheres, Richard Nixon was more concerned with winning than with sportsmanship, as Chief Newman counseled, there is no evidence from this or subsequent stages of his career that he was completely unscrupulous; he was merely cynical at the margins. But this would lead to serious public relations problems in the real world.

Richard was back in Prescott in the summer of 1932 with his mother and Harold and little Edward. It was a punishing time for all the Nixons. Frank and Donald held the fort in the business, which continued to be profitable even as the Depression worsened, since Frank was selling only essential goods, with carefully shaved margins and only family labor. The family had two cars and a truck, and Richard did not have to rent a dinner jacket for college formal evenings – he owned one, a criterion separating the bourgeoisie from the working class in the thirties. If Harold could have been saved by more expensive medical treatment, the Nixons would have managed it.

Frank Nixon had hard-scrabbled a long way economically for a man who attended school only for a few months and whose parents had been destitute. But the United States, the great promised land that had gained the admiration, or at least the curiosity, of the whole world and had attracted millions of the oppressed and deprived of other countries from their proverbially teeming shores, was on the verge of economic collapse. For the first time since the Civil War, there were machine-gun emplacements at the entrances and corners of the great public buildings of Washington for Franklin D. Roosevelt's inauguration on March 4, 1933.

The unemployment rate was over 30 percent, and there was no direct federal relief, and little help from most of the states. Nearly half the homes and farms of America were encumbered by mortgages and subject to seizure and the eviction of their occupants, sixty million people, at almost any time. Most of the farms of the country were uneconomical in a time of huge farm surpluses and massive dumping into foreign markets. The banking system had collapsed, and the New York Stock Exchange and Chicago Grain Exchange were closed *sine die* on Inauguration Day. As the wife of a prominent Federal Reserve trustee (and mother of Richard Nixon's eventual nemesis and finally admirer, Katharine Graham), Agnes Meier, wrote in her diary, "Hoover is leaving office to the sound of crashing banks."[22]

Herbert Hoover, a man who had administered European relief programs with great distinction after the First World War and was a very respected secretary of commerce in the Harding and Coolidge administrations, had no idea how to deal with the Great Depression. His policy prescription was the worst that could have been imagined: tax increases, a shrunken money supply, higher tariffs. And no direct relief for the unemployed or the poor. The American people threw Hoover out to bring in Roosevelt in November 1932. In America's greatest crisis since the Civil War, its greatest president since Lincoln emerged. For a time, even Frank Nixon was an FDR supporter. The underlying Republican majority that had existed since Lincoln's first election, and which had won fourteen of the last eighteen presidential elections, was dissolved. The country was entering a new political cycle. No one, not even Richard Nixon in his most ambitious thoughts, could imagine he, the overworked and over-serious younger son of angry, noisy Frank Nixon, would help bring the Republicans back to the White House after twenty years, and in the country's next great crisis, half a generation after that, would introduce a new cycle of restored Republican governance.

When Harold asked for a trip into the San Bernardinos early in 1933, Frank bought a primitive house-trailer and they set off, but had to return after three days because of Harold's condition. On March 6, 1933, Harold asked Richard to take him to a hardware store so they could buy a cake mixer for their mother's forty-eighth birthday, which was the following day. On her birthday, Harold asked for his mother and told her that although he wanted more than he could say to get well again, "This is the last time I will see you until we meet in heaven." Then he died, leaving Richard, summoned home from the college, to find the same undertaker who had removed Arthur and, his parents sobbing uncontrollably, to give his mother the birthday present he and Harold had bought. No one who has not experienced such sadness can judge the impact these premature deaths had on Richard Nixon. No one who was not fiercely determined would have persevered through all the travails he did. To some extent, he occasionally intimated, he was fighting a battle for all the Nixons, who he felt had been so wronged in life and death.* [23] Harold was buried beside Arthur and their grandfather, Frank Milhous.

Whittier was not a great center of learning by international standards, and the library only had about twenty thousand books, but it offered a good grounding to those who were there to learn. Nixon had a very animated history professor, Paul Smith, who entertained less beatific versions of the motives and actions of the country's founding fathers than had been taught in high school. One of the principal texts was co-authored by Samuel E. Morison and Henry Steele Commager (the latter would be one of Nixon's most belligerent and inflexible critics at the climax of his career). Nixon developed a taste for historical biography that he never lost, slogging through John Hay and John Nicolay's ten-volume life of Abraham Lincoln. Nixon did not become a qualified historian at Whittier, but had a vast interest in the subject and steadily absorbed it all his life.

Nixon had no exposure at Whittier to the physical or social sciences, and his canvass of English and French literature was fairly cursory, but it at least gave him a taste for them. Exploration of philosophy was extremely rudimentary.

Of the extracurricular activities, apart from football, Nixon's greatest interest was in drama. This must have helped him overcome his shyness, a condition that afflicts many people who pursue public careers, and it assisted in making his public speaking more animated. He learned how to pitch and modulate his voice, affect a full range of emotions, and even induce false tears. (There is no evidence that he ever had recourse to this last skill in his future career.) This too was a field for which Nixon had a natural aptitude, and his professor thought he might have made it as a full-time actor had that been his ambition.

He continued to be a rigorously practicing Quaker, and some of his friends thought that might ultimately be his career. There is no question of Nixon's religious sincerity, then or subsequently, but as with acting, religion dovetailed with his political ambitions. The tendency to invoke divine

---

* Many years later, the youngest Nixon brother, Edward, asked Richard to describe their deceased brothers. The older brother "broke down completely" and left the room. "He just decided to sink those tragedies deep in his mind and never to talk about them again."

inspiration or at least God-fearing piety in enunciating public policy was very widespread at this time, and the United States generally expected such flourishes from its politicians. From William Jennings Bryan seizing the Democratic leadership in 1896 by warning (the Republicans), "You shall not press down upon the brow of labor this crown of thorns; You shall not crucify mankind upon a cross of gold," to Theodore Roosevelt stalking out of the Republican Convention in 1912 and asseverating, "We stand at Armageddon and we fight for the Lord," to Woodrow Wilson concluding his war-message in 1917, "God helping her [America], can do no other," to Franklin D. Roosevelt, who was about to drive the money-changers "from their high seats in the temple," at his first inauguration, religion and politics were often blended, and not always very scrupulously.

Hannah Nixon urged upon Richard the life of a clergyman or even missionary, but "he didn't exactly respond favorably."[24] For all his campus enthusiasms, he never joined the Whittier religious society, one of the most frequented clubs at the college. With the senior class, he took a course called "the Philosophy of Christian Reconstruction," taught by Dr. J.H. Coffin. It was a challenging presentation of science and revealed Christianity and caused Richard Nixon to consider and durably settle his views.[25] It is clear from essays Nixon wrote that he had fairly conventional Christian views; he believed in God, self-help, the Commandments, the integrity of family and marriage, but he was not deterministic or even, despite frequent religious observance, fervent. He believed in the supernatural powers of Jesus and in at least the concept of resurrection, and he accepted the process of evolution. America was a uniquely blessed country, but no intelligent person who saw the exploitation of unskilled labor and the antics of commercial sharpers at the expense of the unwary in Southern California, as Richard Nixon did, could imagine that America was a morally unoffending country. Nixon had a religion that he clung to and that helped him through many dark nights. He had no notion of proselytizing anyone to a quantum step upward in the perfectibility of the nature of man. He left such extravagant fantasies to the atheistic left.

The relationship between Richard Nixon and Ola Florence Welch flourished, despite differences of politics and personality. The Nixons were militant Republicans and opposed any relief for the unemployed, even though there were now huge numbers of hopeless derelicts in Los Angeles and other large cities. Ola was an enthusiastic Democrat, with a deep admiration for Roosevelt (inaugurated three days before Harold's death in March 1933), and, like many students in all eras, was gently, and rather ingenuously, socialistic. They managed this, especially as Frank warmed to FDR, but more of a problem were some of Richard's unutterably gauche social miscues, especially his habit of arriving in his car in front of Ola's family's house and announcing his presence and desire for her to come out by honking the horn until she did. He knew her parents did not care for him, and this was his way of avoiding them. It was counterproductive.

She was vivacious and liked to dance, and he was still rather moody, reticent, and a very reluctant dancer, despite his musical talents. Ola was very popular and widely admired, and Richard in person was gentle and thoughtful and intelligent. Like many early romances, it was to some extent the attraction of opposites, and in those times of restraint and in that most circumspect place, their relations never approached the borders of chastity. She, like generations of American voters, learned to overlook his minor abrasions. "Most of the time," she later said, "I just couldn't figure him out."[26]

At Whittier College, Richard Nixon had been aiming at the position of student president, the office that had eluded him at Whittier Union. Stung, perhaps, by the recurrent charge through most of his career that he was, as Lyndon Johnson would famously claim, a "chronic campaigner," Nixon recalled that "in college, political battles as such never appealed to me, but I always seemed to get dragged into them to run for some office or another."[27] It was one of the anomalies of Nixon's personality that he never admitted that he was resistless against the possibility of election, from the age of twelve on, until there were no more offices to seek.

He steadily built his political position at Whittier College. At the end of his first year, he managed to be elected as student council member-at-large. This was a clever choice of route upwards, as there was no defined opponent and he was thus enabled to excel as a councilor. This he shortly did, when some Whittier students caused a collegiate scandal by painting the front of Occidental College on the eve of a big football game between the two, and then muddying the waters by then similarly desecrating their own campus. What they actually painted was innocuous, and they admitted their prank forthrightly, but there was great outrage, as well as the threat of expulsion of the students involved and of Whittier from the athletic conference. Nixon championed the students before the faculty, administration, and student council. Presaging his great talents as an advocate in weightier matters, though only eighteen, he struck upon the device that the students and the college would have the same fate – that expelling the students would be taken as an admission of collective unworthiness by Whittier and would shame the college, cause its banishment from the athletic conference, and result in a serious loss of community athletic grants and student applications. His reasoning prevailed after a discussion of several hours, and he was justly lionized by his fellow students.

He took another vote-winning initiative in 1933, as chairman of the annual bonfire committee. A considerable bonfire was habitually topped off by the chairman contributing, usually from an improper provenance, an outdoor privy. It was a manifestation of the innocent, boosterish scatology of the place and time that Richard Nixon added a cubit to his stature by finding, for the first time in the history of the annual bonfire, a four-hole privy with which he crowned the fire.

Less to his advantage, but much to his credit, Nixon, who never evinced the slightest traditional racial prejudice, sponsored a black student as a member of the Orthogonian Society. There was nothing in this for him; he liked the student and was anti-segregationist. In this, he doubtless owed much to his Quaker heritage. Again, he was successful.

Nixon prepared his own elevation by helping to arrange a complete division of electoral spoils between the Franklins and the Orthogonians. With the two societies voting en bloc, they could alternate student offices in a way that was designed to allow Nixon to serve as president in his final year after an unopposed election. He had again end-run the caprices of electoral politics by a machine electoral fix, while shoring up his own popularity by performing well and thoughtfully in the positions to which he had been elected. It was vintage, methodical Nixon.

As so often happened to Richard Nixon, the unpleasantly unexpected occurred; he was rarely a very lucky politician, which is one of the reasons for his tendency to be morose. A popular, relaxed, attractive, athletic candidate leapt in at the last minute, with some editorial support from the campus newspaper. This development, unlike a similar one four years before, found the Nixon political apparatus more prepared, and Nixon the political tactician was four years cleverer. He waited until late in the campaign and then published his advocacy of the permission for on-campus dances. This was the sort of tactical masterstroke that he would regularly produce in more serious elections. There was a heavy turnout, and although the breakdown of the votes was never revealed, Nixon won and spent his final year at Whittier as president of the students.

Further, Nixon followed through on his promise and successfully championed the amendment of campus rules to allow for dances, convincing his elders that this would be preferable to having dances take place in morally dubious bars and hotels in neighboring communities (since the Town of Whittier was as priggish as the college) or even, as was in fact usually the case, in the festering metropolis of Thirties Los Angeles, world capital of unrepentant wickedness. It was well known to his friends that he wanted a political career, but the greatest ambition Nixon would admit to at this point was to be a congressman. It is impossible that his ambitions, even at this early date, would stop there.

He graduated from Whittier College second in a senior class of eighty-five, in the spring of 1934 aged twenty-one. He did not smoke or drink, was probably a virgin, was a devout churchgoer, and was an upright, resourceful, determined young man, with a very nice girlfriend, whom, it was generally assumed, including by both of them, he would eventually marry. His background was unrelievedly ordinary, but he had already risen above it. He had made the most of a modest education, determined on a political career, and already had acquired many of the arts necessary to make a success of his ambitions. As his father had spent the twenties boot-strapping himself up from penury, Richard Nixon, spurred by the tragic deaths of two of his brothers, had made through his teens, as Chief Newman might put it, a lot of yardage. The college's annual, *Acropolis*, featured Nixon: "After one of the most successful years the college has ever witnessed, we stop to reminisce, and come to the realization that much of the success was due to the efforts of Richard Nixon. Always progressive and with a liberal attitude, he has led us through the year with flying colors."[28] The Orthogonians thought he would be president of the United States.[29]

— IV —

In May of 1934, Nixon had already been granted a $250 scholarship to Duke University Law School, in Durham, North Carolina. Now, without a heavy illness in the family, and Frank Nixon's business still doing well, and Hannah back at home, he would finally spread his wings. He took Donald with him to Duke, as Donald had dropped out of Whittier Union two years before and it was hoped that Richard's influence would get him through and on the road to university. It didn't work; Don went to school in Greensboro, but did not make a success of it and returned to Whittier before the academic year was out.

Once again, Richard Nixon found himself thrust back into penury. His tuition was paid for, but he did not have the money for campus residence and lived in boarding houses for about five dollars a month, with his clothes in the trunk he had brought, and wearing the same purple sweater every day. He supplemented his income with a thirty-five-cent-an-hour payment for work in the Duke law library through a National Youth Administration program for unemployed youth. This was one of many workfare programs (a word Nixon would himself invent thirty-five years later) Roosevelt set up to get the seventeen million unemployed out of breadlines and earning incomes, however modest. He also drove the invalid wife of one of his law professors on occasion, earning a little more to add to the thirty-five dollars per month his parents sent him, and the odd bonus from his grandmother Almira Milhous.

Duke had been incorporated and its buildings erected just ten years before with a forty-million-dollar endowment from the estate of tobacco magnate James Buchanan Duke. But it had been built to a grand, European, medieval standard, entirely from stone, with a profusion of spires and turrets and stained glass. It was a fine campus and a fine faculty, and Duke set out by its scholarship program to produce a talented and success-ful group of alumni as soon as possible. There were forty-four starting law students in Richard Nixon's year, and half of them were on tuition scholar-ships, as he was.

Liberated from having to drive every morning to Los Angeles to buy and wash and display vegetables, Nixon was able to alleviate his fears of increased scholastic competition by a relentless regime of study. One of the senior students assured him after a few months that he would be fine because he had "an iron butt" and could sit endlessly in the library. Nixon himself was never too worried or preoccupied to give a helping hand to other students. One who dropped out, penniless and dispirited, attracted Nixon's sympathy as he sat dejectedly on the library steps. Nixon introduced himself, inquired into the young man's problem, and gave him such an inspiriting lecture that he went back to his native Ohio, struggled through to qualify as a teacher, then became a school principal in Cincinnati, and always credited Nixon for his success, for his kind words to a "confused, homesick, and frightened young man."[30]

At Duke, he helped a severely handicapped student up and down the main stairway of one building every day; his polio-afflicted classmate, Fred Cady, would wait for him and Nixon never failed him. "He never smiled, though he had a very nice smile, and a great deal to smile about. When he allowed himself to smile, he could light up a room. He had good straight, gleaming white teeth, with nice crinkles around his eyes. In repose his heavy jowls sagged and added years to his appearance, but when he smiled the jowls lifted up, dimples appeared, and what had been a slightly sinister appearance, became a glowing one."[31]

Richard Nixon had an intense year with little pleasure, aside from a Christmas trip with Donald to New York City, his first visit and an inspiring experience. But he came third in his class, of which 40 percent did not get through at all, and had a comparatively relaxed summer in Whittier, apart from his irritation and sadness that the lovely Ola had taken up with someone else. With his usual tenacity, Richard called upon her and wrote to her, but she courteously declined his attentions and married the rival in 1936. In later years, Nixon would downplay the strength of his feelings for Ola, and she never spoke ill of him, while allowing that the man she did marry was "more fun."

Frank drove his son and a friend back to Duke in September 1935. Roosevelt had got to grips with the Depression; unemployment was down from 33 percent to about 23 percent, and of those, about half were in work-fare programs, building public works, roads, parks, power dams, and canals, or occupied in conservation or specialized projects. Almost all the rest were receiving unemployment insurance, as a comprehensive social security system had been launched. The Nixons noticed as they drove across the country that the human landscape of America had begun to change. The breadlines and soup kitchens and indigents selling apples and traveling across the country in boxcars had almost disappeared.

Roosevelt had thrown out the failed hypocrisy of Prohibition, and the speakeasies and other appurtenances of the twenties went with it. The entire banking system, which had been on the verge of complete collapse less than three years before, had been reconstructed, and deposits were guaranteed by the federal government. All forms of agriculture now were subsidized to roll back production to useful levels so that prices would rise to a point where farmers could make both ends meet. The government had refinanced all the country's home and farm mortgages that were in danger of default, and the atmosphere, in emulation of the irrepressible president, was decidedly optimistic. The extreme parties of left and right had fallen back, a trend that was assisted by the assassination of Louisiana governor Huey P. Long, a rollicking populist demagogue, who died from gunshot wounds as the Nixons drove from California to North Carolina.

Richard Nixon had a more varied and confident academic year in 1935–1936. He worked in the law school clinic, which seconded him to the local prosecutor's office, and gained what would prove invaluable experience at techniques of research and inquisition. He also was asked to write for the law school journal, *Law and Contemporary Problems*. This was disinterested recognition from the faculty, and, after some trepidation, buoyed his self-confidence. He lived in a rented cottage with three divinity students. One of them was married, and his wife cooked and washed for them all. In the summer of 1936, Nixon remained at Duke, he told his parents, to permit him to write his piece for the law journal, though it may have been to avoid being in Whittier when Ola Florence Welch married another man.

He and two friends became so concerned about their anticipated grades that one night, seeing the transom window above the dean's door open, they boosted up one of them, who let his comrades in, and they rummaged around and found that they had all passed satisfactorily. They replaced everything, took nothing, damaged nothing, and committed no indiscretions. Yet some Nixonophobes have suggested that this was a foretaste of felonious behavior, and of a propensity for office break-ins.[32]

In July 1936, Nixon went with a friend to Washington and Baltimore. It was his first view of the capital, and he was much interested in the great buildings and monuments, but he particularly enjoyed seeing a promising rookie for the Yankees, Joe DiMaggio, hit a home run at Griffith Stadium.

In the autumn of 1936 and for his final year at Duke, he moved in with two friends in a cabin, heated by a wood stove, in the Duke Forest. It had neither running water nor electricity, and it was as spartan accommodation as Richard Nixon had ever had, but it was cheap; they christened it Whippoorwill Manor, and greatly enjoyed themselves. It was the poverty of spartan youth and not of failure or oppression, and many students lived in similar quarters in the Duke Forest, so it was not at all depressing.

Once again, after he became acclimatized to where he was, Richard Nixon got on well with his mates. He was called Gloomy Gus, not because he was dejected, but because he was practical and dour of appearance with his dark and jowly features and persistent beard, and he tended to bring others down to earth with a humorous abruptness. Nixon became so demonstrative and noisy at Duke football games, he was part of the crowd attraction. He lost himself completely in the games and shouted uninhibitedly until he was hoarse. It was presumably more of a psychological displacement for him even than whatever motivates most sports fans to identify so strongly with the outcome of sporting matches.

True to his previous pattern, Nixon, without appearing to most people to have ardently sought the office, consented to run for the presidency of his law school bar association in 1936 for the 1937 year. He stood for election with his handicapped friend, Fred Cady, running with him as secretary, on a platform of promising to get the bar to focus on employment prospects for law graduates. It was hardly an original theme in the thirties, but it worked, and they were easily elected, giving Nixon student office at all four levels of his formal education, from Grade Eight to law school. The election gave him a physical office on campus, which enabled him to wash and change there, rather than in the howling and primitive discomfort of Whippoorwill Manor.

There weren't many girls in the law faculty, and Nixon didn't seem to be much involved with other departments of the university, so he had no romantic life in his Duke years that anyone remembers. Johnny Long and Les Brown, who went on to great success in the big band era, were Duke undergraduates then, and Nixon sometimes attended their performances, but mainly he studied.

In the spring of 1937, he suddenly stood up on a picnic table at a class celebration and improvised a hilarious talk on social security, praising the values of insecurity in an absurdly pompous, mock-professorial way. It was an unprecedented and probably unique effort, and reduced his friends to helpless laughter. But he rarely was so spontaneous and was generally thought to be intelligent and kind, but reserved and wary; a puzzle, as he would remain.

Richard Nixon did strenuously dissent from the prevailing Southern disparagement of African-Americans. He was shocked at the endemic bigotry of the South, but he developed some sympathy he had not felt before for the South's sense of victimhood after the defeat by the North and the corrupt and repressive occupation of the South by the Union Army and the infamous carpetbaggers. This was still verdant in the mind of every Southerner sixty years later, even to Nixon's contemporaries.

Nixon and two of his friends were back in New York at Christmas 1936, seeking employment after graduation. Though well-regarded, Duke's was a new law school and there was huge demand for places in the great New York firms. Richard Nixon cooled his heels unsuccessfully at Sullivan & Cromwell, where John Foster Dulles was the managing partner.[*][33] He would be back, twelve years later, and the reception would be much warmer.

They went to plays and to the Metropolitan Opera House, but Nixon got no job offers. In February 1937, Nixon, in his law student presidential role at Duke, received J. Edgar Hoover's assistant, who was recruiting for the FBI. He put in for a position, but again without success. And again, he would be back in touch with Hoover eventually, but not as a supplicant.

His entire family, including his indomitable eighty-eight-year-old grandmother, Almira Milhous, drove east for his graduation, and they all crowded back into Frank's car for the long trip home. Nixon had done well at Duke, but he had not made a breakthrough in permanent friendships, or in developing a more relaxed personality and becoming more comfortable with himself.

Richard Nixon had passionately hoped to escape Whittier and was dejected to find himself, after his prodigies at Duke University and his efforts at job-hunting in New York and at the FBI, back where he started. As head of the Duke student bar association, he had organized a publicity effort for all graduates, using the university's office to send out stories and photographs to the local newspapers of all graduates. Whittier responded and as a result Nixon was at least something of a local celebrity, when he reluctantly returned.

Hannah Nixon had already made overtures to an old Milhous friend, Thomas Bewley, a local lawyer. Bewley, a Whittier College alumnus, inquired of Nixon's history professor if it would be a "mistake" to offer Richard Nixon a position in his firm, and received the ineffably Quakerish response that it "would not be a mistake." Bewley then phoned the Nixon store and home repeatedly for four weeks, but elicited no response from the

---

[*] Nixon would claim to Jonathan Aitken that Dulles himself interviewed him, though that was not the first version of his visit to Sullivan & Cromwell.

sullen young Richard, back in his old stuffy upstairs bedroom as if his years of work and self-denial in rooming houses and Whippoorwill Manor had been for nothing.

With Bewley still calling in messages every few days, Nixon tried again with the FBI, in Los Angeles, and then decided to take the California bar examination. He started studying late and was worried, as he often was throughout his life, by the thought of failing. A cousin remonstrated with him about his rudeness in not replying to Bewley, and he did meet with the lawyer. After he was rejected again by the FBI, "for lack of aggressiveness," and passed the bar examinations in September 1937, he joined Wingert and Bewley, in the top (sixth) floor of Whittier's tallest building, the Bank of America building, at the end of the year.

Whittier had remained an insular, pious, priggish place, where an effort at unionization by Mexican citrus workers was violently suppressed in the early thirties. Jimtown was almost razed by management vigilantes and scabs. Roosevelt's assisted work plans were at first rejected, until the virtues of federal funds for sewer improvements were at last recognized.

Wingert and Bewley acted for local oil companies and handled wills and other non-contentious matters. It wasn't much of a litigation firm and did not touch criminal matters. It represented almost all the principal commercial figures of the town and its surroundings, and would serve Nixon well as a launching pad for his political career. Bored though he was with the work, Nixon applied himself with his inevitable diligence and was the first person in each morning, rarely left for lunch, and put in long hours. At Duke, his standard breakfast had been a Milky Way chocolate bar. While he lived under Hannah's roof, he got a more nutritious start to the day, but often continued that custom for his lunches as a young lawyer.

Nixon's first significant case was a disaster that would haunt him for years. He acted for a woman who was owed money by her aunt and uncle, and obtained a two-thousand-dollar lien on their house in consideration of the debt. When the court eventually ordered the sale of the house to cover the debt, Nixon bid the quantum of the debt owed his client without inquiring whether there were other charges on the house. There were, and the holders of those claims appeared and Nixon and Bewley's client effectively remained unsecured. Bewley was able to arrange another judicial sale and bid a nominal sum, but was outbid, effectively removing the security of the firm's client, who sued the firm. Bewley, who was the chief defendant, settled the original $2,000 claim for $4,800, a sizable sum to a small law firm in 1938. But that was not the end of it; the original litigants came back to court and dragged it out until 1942. Bewley manfully accepted responsibility for the errors of his firm. Nixon paid the price of inexperience, but his hostile biographers have endlessly excavated the case to claim that it foretold duplicity and dishonesty. It did not, but it may have been the last occasion when Nixon showed less than his usual extreme suspicion of the motives of almost everyone.

Despite this fiasco, Nixon was quickly and durably respected as a barrister and a solicitor. Thorough in preparation and a skillful court tactician and cross-examiner, Nixon soon established himself as one of the county's most capable lawyers. He could not handle divorce cases, because he did not have, said Bewley, the necessary "bedside manner," and by his own admission he was severely embarrassed by women's confessions of sexual misconduct.[34]

— v —

Whatever Nixon's awkwardness with women, nature took its course and imposed an implacable romantic desire on him in 1938. He agreed to appear in a Community Players production of *The Dark Tower*, by George S. Kaufman and Alexander Woollcott, ostensibly to drum up legal business. He found himself playing opposite a striking young woman who taught shorthand at night school at Whittier Union. Patricia Ryan was a slender golden redhead with high cheekbones, bright brown eyes, and a dignified, even proud, but not haughty, poise and bearing. She was reserved but pleasant, and was a very attractive and stylish woman by metropolitan standards, and certainly by the norms of Whittier. Nixon pressed his attentions on her and, before she had even agreed to a date, told her he was going to marry her. He had to have taken a direct hit from Cupid's arrow for such a reserved young man to set out his stall so early and directly.

Patricia Ryan was born Thelma Catherine Ryan on March 16, 1912, ten months before Richard Nixon, in the clapped-out copper mining town of Ely, Nevada. She had had a considerably more difficult upbringing than Richard Nixon did. Her father, William, was an improvident Irish-American whaler and prospector, who left his family in Connecticut in his teens and prospected in Alaska, the Philippines, Borneo, and the Western states, never with success. He was forty-six when his daughter Thelma was born. His wife, Kate Halberstadt Ryan, was born in Hesse, Germany, and was brought to the United States when she was ten. She first married a successful mining engineer, and had a son and a daughter, but was widowed when her husband drowned trying to rescue flood victims. She had two sons with Will Ryan, and then Thelma (Patricia), and a year after her birth they gave up the mining country and moved to the dusty, poor, unyielding rural town of Artesia, ten miles from Whittier.

They grew alfalfa, Will drank heavily, and there were terrible scenes that gave their daughter a lifelong aversion to arguments. He was a lapsed Roman Catholic and his wife was a Lutheran tempted by Christian Science, but there wasn't much religion in their children's upbringing. Education in Artesia, a town of five hundred without paved roads or street-lighting, was not much more than the three R's and a bit of debating and drama. Thelma was a member of the drama club, the Nightwalkers. The whole Ryan family worked in the fields, struggling with the unremitting soil. Mrs. Ryan died in January 1926, before her daughter's fourteenth birthday, a victim of liver cancer. Thelma had washed her each evening in her last months, when she lived in the house of a local doctor who could alleviate her pain only with morphine. In 1928, her father was diagnosed with tuber-culosis and Thelma took over the nursing of him too, performing tasks similar to those undertaken by Hannah Nixon with her eldest son starting a year later. Will Ryan returned to Catholicism shortly before he died in May 1930, and was buried in the cemetery at Whittier, beside his wife and not far from Arthur Nixon and Frank Milhous.

Because she was born the day before St. Patrick's Day and her father had called her "Patrick's babe" (her friends called her Buddy), she dropped the name Catherine and took, and used, the name Patricia. Will Ryan left nothing but his poor farm and some worthless oil shares, and Pat, at eigh-teen, became the real head of the family. She rented out the farm to Japanese-American farmers and went to work as a cleaning lady in a bank branch in Artesia. All her life she painfully remembered the jibes of school-mates when they saw her at her menial work.

Pat's first escape from the drudgery and poverty of her youth came when relatives in Connecticut engaged her to chauffeur an elderly couple east from California in their car and then stay with the relatives. Her principal recollection of the long trip was the endless clicking noise the owner of the car made with his teeth throughout the day as they traversed the continent.

She remained in New York for two years, working for an aunt, a nun who was the head of the X-ray and pharmacy unit at the Sisters of Charity's Seton Hospital. She lived in the nuns' residence next to the hospital and worked as a secretary and technical assistant, and became very popular with the sisters and the patients.

She stayed weekends with her family in Connecticut. She spent a lot of time with young tuberculosis sufferers and toured around New York with them, trying to put some happiness in their lives. She later recalled these six months with the young patients as "the most haunting of my life."

Pat got to know New York well, traveled through New England and to Washington, and attended grand occasions, including an address of President Roosevelt's at the Waldorf Astoria. She was, from all accounts and pictures, a beautiful young woman, thirty pounds heavier than in her somewhat gaunt later days in public life. She was ardently courted by some of the young doctors, and came to find living in a nunnery a bit confining. When her brother Tom offered to help her financially to go to the University of Southern California, she leapt at the chance and took a bus back to Los Angeles, via Niagara Falls, in the summer of 1934. She moved into an apartment with her two brothers, got a $270 scholarship, and worked at campus jobs to supplement her income. She proceeded through her courses without difficulty. As one faculty member recalled the poised young woman, "She stood out from the empty-headed, over-dressed little sorority girls of that era like a good piece of literature on a shelf of cheap paperbacks."

Although she had won a screen test contest when she lived in Manhattan, she did not follow it up, but back in Los Angeles she became an extra at RKO and MGM. In 1935, she spoke one line in *Becky Sharp*, which was edited out, though she can be glimpsed fleetingly. The uncertainty of an actress's life, and her unwillingness to advance her career on the casting couch, caused her to lose interest in a life in films.

She worked in the upmarket Los Angeles department store Bullock's at Christmas 1935, and developed a disdain for the pretensions and insensitivities of the idle rich that she never lost.[35] These working experiences helped her to adopt education as her university major, and she graduated with honors in the spring of 1937, qualified as a secondary school teacher in commercial subjects. She had registered as an independent voter; her parents had been Democrats.

Casting about for a suitable position, she applied as a teacher at Whittier Union, and was enthusiastically engaged to teach typing, bookkeeping, stenography, and basic business methods, starting in September 1937. After New York and Los Angeles, Whittier, though a metropolis compared with Artesia, was a severe change. It was an intensely self-obsessed community, and a glamorous young woman did not swim like a fish in the sea of dowdy Whittierites. But Pat had developed a formula for dealing with older people who might feel themselves upstaged by a young person: she was outwardly deferential, courteous, and unaffected, neither standoffish nor effusive, showing the self-possession she had had since her childhood, but inwardly she was disdainful of self-important people.

When she became a prominent public person with her husband, she was widely disparaged by his critics as a rather wooden figure, a colorless Stepford wife, or, at best, Betty in the movie send-up of the fifties, *Pleasantville*. But she was a person of high intelligence and strong character, and her critics were rarely her peers. Few women in American history have had a greater challenge in retaining their dignity through tremendous upheavals than she faced in her public life, and she would bear up under heavy travails with exceptional fortitude.

She got on well at Whittier Union and was something of a counselor to the girls, being closer to them in age and attitude than the other, more elderly, and less fashion-aware teachers. She departed for Los Angeles every weekend, staying with her half-sister, and conducted an active social life with friends from her USC days.

It was at this point, in early 1938, that Pat encountered the dark, brooding, ambitious, and instantly besotted Richard Nixon. He laid siege to her, dropping by unannounced at her apartment, and not always being admitted, writing her poems, and even a song. He was decisive, and, as in all things, he was persistent. He took to chauffeuring her back and forth to Los Angeles on weekends, but began Sundays with a rousing performance at the college-age Quaker Sunday school, where he was a worthy successor to Frank in his flamboyance and persuasiveness.

Despite his youthful eminence, Nixon continued to live in cramped quarters in his parents' house and to fill in at the store, serving customers and delivering groceries, even after he became a full partner in his law firm and his name was added to that of the firm, in 1939.

At this time Richard Nixon launched his first commercial venture, and, as he came to believe to be the probable destiny of most of his initial efforts, this too was a disaster. There was a surplus of oranges in 1938, and Nixon went with others into the business of freezing orange juice. They founded a company called Citra-Frost, with Nixon as president and counsel. The problem was that they set out to freeze the juice, not a concentrate, and never puzzled out the technical problem. Nixon pitched in, cutting and squeezing oranges after hours, working his heart out to try to save the company. The final gamble was to package the juice in plastic bags, but a refrigerated boxcar of these plastic bags burst, destroying the entire inventory, and Citra-Frost failed.

Nixon lost his own small savings, but aroused resentment in investors that endured a long time.[36] This sad episode seemed to cure Nixon of the desire to try to strike it rich. He convinced himself that he wasn't particularly interested in money, but more likely he resigned himself to not having the natural pecuniary intuition. In this he was like Franklin Roosevelt, who poured inherited money into an endless sequence of hare-brained schemes in the twenties, from a passenger dirigible company to an attempted lobster cartel to talking vending machines, which malfunctioned so often that guards had to be hired to protect the machines from shortchanged customers.[37]

Nixon opened a branch of the law firm in the nearby town of La Habra, in the back of a derelict hardware store. La Habra was claimed by Robert Ripley's *Believe It or Not* to be a national leader in churches per capita.[38] It was, if anything, even sleepier than Whittier. Nixon's law practice did not flourish there either, but he had already fastened on a new method of elevating himself out of the adhesive tedium of his origins. Without a citrus business to consume his time and savings, he prepared for politics by plunging into the service-club circuit. There was no plethora of riveting or worldly speakers in Whittier and La Habra, and Richard Nixon was a relatively cosmopolitan character. He joined Kiwanis, the local bar, chambers of commerce, alumni associations, and businessmen's clubs, and campaigned for friends in at least one service club national convention (unsuccessfully),[39] making extensive connections and becoming a very sought-after luncheon and dinner speaker.*

---

* Between 1937 and 1940, he became president of the Whittier College and Duke alumni associations and of the Whittier 20-30 Club, chairman of the Habra Kiwanis Club, and program chairman of the Junior Chamber of Commerce.

The torrid pursuit of Pat Ryan continued and she became less resistant and coy. They often went to Los Angeles for dinner and to nightclubs and led a double life between L.A. nights and workaday Whittier, including Nixon's roles as the Whittier Sunday school teacher and assistant city attorney who managed to drive out the town's one bar. There was one particularly riotous trip to Topsy's strip joint in East Los Angeles, when a customer singed famous stripper Betty Roland's bare behind with his ciga-rette.[40] Pat was impressed by Richard's endless and thoughtful attentions, and found his voice melodious and solicitous. He was, despite the decades of subsequent effort by the caricaturists, a fine-looking man of the dark and enigmatic kind, and he had a burning ambition. Above all, they were both exceptional people in a very dreary place, and they were both determined to break out of it and get on in the world.

Richard introduced Pat to his parents. She found Frank "blustery and inarticulate," but became popular with Hannah by getting up at 5 A.M. to help her bake her locally popular pies, one of the best profit centers in the Nixon store. They never became particularly intimate, and Hannah con-vinced herself that Pat was chasing Dick.[41] At first, Pat was more enthused about Dick's Irish setter, King, than about King's owner; and she prevailed upon Nixon to have porcelain replace gold in the visible dental work at the front of his mouth.[42]

Richard proposed many times and finally succeeded in March 1940 at Dana Point, on a rocky peak above the San Clemente Beach between Los Angeles and San Diego. They were married at the Mission Inn at Riverside, California, on June 21, 1940. Pat, to Hannah's delight, had officially become a Quaker and there was a Quaker service presided over by the president of Whittier College (of which Dick Nixon, as he was now widely known, had been elected a trustee at the impressive age of twenty-six). Pat would not have a church wedding, because she was, in fact, an agnostic. The principal wedding presents were starting dinnerware from Pat's brothers and a china dinner service from Frank and Hannah. They used them all through their marriage.[43] There were fewer than two dozen guests, only immediate family, including the now ninety-one-year old Almira Milhous, and a very few friends. (In Europe, France capitulated to Germany the next day, leaving the British and their newly elevated leader, Winston Churchill, to face the mighty Nazi war machine almost alone.) The newlyweds left at once on their honeymoon in Mexico in Pat's Oldsmobile, with two hundred dollars, mostly hers, since Citra-Frost and the acquisition of an engagement ring had depleted Richard's savings. Pat paid for most of the Oldsmobile and part of the ring. To save money, Dick had taken a bus to Michigan, bought the car, and driven it back to California.[44] They took baskets of canned goods from the Nixon store to economize on restaurant bills (which were very cheap in Mexico anyway). It was a happy, carefree time; they returned when their money ran out, via the great Boulder Dam (renamed after Herbert Hoover in the post-Roosevelt era).[*] [45]

They lived first in Long Beach, twenty miles of often-congested road from Whittier, where they both worked and he was still ambitious politically, trying to straddle between their ambition and their origins. In a pattern they would maintain throughout their more than fifty years of married life, they moved twice again within a few months, settling for a time in a unit of Frank's, rent-free, near the East Whittier school. Frank, who had maintained his carpentering skill, built homes on lots that he bought, and sold them at a handsome profit, with the country finally moving out of depression under the impulse of huge rearmament expenditures, as war threatened and then broke over East Asia and Western Europe. The young Nixons were not thinking much about the war or the world.

— VI —

Richard Nixon knew, well before he graduated from Whittier College in 1934, that he wanted to be a politician. One of the great riddles of his life was why he chose a career for which he seemed not to have a natural aptitude, but in fact in many ways he had a great aptitude for it. To the end of his days, though warm with impersonal and amorphous crowds, he tended to be shy and not at all easy with individuals. Though he was a competent raconteur, and often had a very fast wit, as well as a flair for the quip and the good phrase – especially, as years passed, the vulgar phrase – and he had a sonorous and versatile voice, he was rarely at ease or able to put others at ease. Unlike other contemporaries who would rise to the heights of

---

[*] Nixon noted that "even in the anti-clerical Mexico of that period, the churches were usually the cleanest and most attractive places to visit." He and Pat were startled when they attended a concert by the Mexican Symphony Orchestra, and a work by U.S. composer Aaron Copland was booed by the audience.

American politics, he was not a graceful, elegant, naturally charming, or facile young man, or even a plain vanilla young gentleman of the Ivy League type. Richard Nixon, as he was acutely aware, was different.

But that he was different from other American leaders at a comparable stage in their lives did not mean that he was not a man of great political gifts, even by the time he left Whittier. Because he was not confident of his ability to cajole or charm or at least legitimately persuade, as required, almost anyone he met, he designed his career around his strengths and weaknesses. Being, because of his shyness, an outsider, at least until he was thoroughly integrated into a group, he judged the susceptibilities of others with the observant keenness of a wary pugilist. Because he was not flamboyant or overpowering, he addressed ordinary people in a way that reminded them of themselves. And when he did not feel obliged to be devious, he had great and natural, even inborn, empathy for the disadvantaged and was very generous to the unfortunate. He demonstrated this throughout his life, with no ulterior motive.

Even when he achieved positions too exalted for general attention to the less fortunate, his heart and his thoughts, as a policy-maker, a vote-seeker, and as a man, were always for those who had little, who struggled, who had been shortchanged. To some degree he identified with them as one who, though favored with high intelligence and opportunity, had known the sorrow of family tragedy and the loneliness of isolation and chronic insecurity. These feelings were not always obvious to the public, but they equipped Richard Nixon to be a more effective judge of the public good, and of the sensibilities of many.

From collegiate days on, he was a shrewd and tireless political organizer. He had an unusually early and thorough experience of the responsibilities of basic administration, and he knew that for any enterprise to work, there was a great number of details that had to be addressed. He also knew that most people had no mind for such things, and that many who did not were grateful for those who did. He approached this side of politics from all points: he would assure that any task was properly organized, retaining control of it, and earning the gratitude of the beneficiaries.

And although he would never become a great orator like Franklin D. Roosevelt or Ronald Reagan, or quite as fast on his feet with the press as John Kennedy or Bill Clinton, he was a good and effective public speaker and was never, even in the worst moments, unable to deal with the press.

He was massively informed and never groped to remember a fact or an answer. Though he refined them, his speaking and debating techniques seem to have been those he learned and practiced in high school.

He tended to perspire under intense lighting, and used certain clichés that gave ammunition to satirists, but at the public-speaking requirements of great office, he would, in the modern era, be surpassed among American leaders only by Roosevelt, Kennedy, and Reagan, and equaled only by Clinton.

So it is not the case that Richard Nixon forced himself to succeed in a field much harder for him than others would have been. There was no other occupation that interested him as much, or that he would have tackled more successfully. He had problems with opponents who were effortlessly charming, but he encountered them only three times: Robert Logue for the student presidency of Whittier Union in 1929, John F. Kennedy for the presidency of the United States in 1960 (when he almost won and was possibly robbed), and Pat Brown for the governorship of California in 1962 – a race he should never have entered and lost because of international events. He came back strongly from all of those setbacks.

By 1940, through his constant presence on the lunch and dinner speaking circuit, Richard Nixon had begun to focus more narrowly on political office. If he couldn't get into a major New York law firm, couldn't get into the FBI, and didn't have the gift of making money, he would move forward his political ambitions and wait for the return of the Republican hour. Roosevelt had so shattered the Republican Party that it faced a colossal rebuilding job, although it finally made substantial gains in the off-year elections of 1938, after four straight drubbings at the polls through the Great Depression.

After he became an assistant city attorney in Whittier, Nixon tried, but failed, to oust the incumbent city attorney in La Habra. He began giving a good deal of advice to city councilors and aldermen. This was a reversion to the grassroots organization that he had first mastered at Whittier Union in his teens. He had his eye on a state assembly seat then held by an aging Republican who was thought to be considering retirement.

His stock speech, delivered to any gathering of more than a handful of people within a wide radius of Whittier, and almost every night when he was not pursuing Pat, was an attack on Roosevelt's attempt to pack the Supreme Court. This was a pretty hackneyed theme by 1940, since the court-packing bill had been introduced in 1937 and abandoned after a few months. The Supreme Court had struck down much of Roosevelt's New Deal legislation, but after this assault it became more careful, and in the three years since 1937, Roosevelt had named five of the nine justices. But it was an easy speech for Nixon to recite, made him sound learned and constitutionally upright, and left no doubt of his Republican leanings. He could be seen in the not-overcrowded firmament of promising potential Republican legislators. This particular effort was stillborn, because the incumbent state assemblyman decided to remain, but Nixon had made a mark.

Dick Nixon had his first taste of national politics in that election year. Franklin D. Roosevelt broke a tradition as old as the Republic when he sought a third term. His hokey method of doing so was to claim to wish to retire, profess to be too busy with the war emergency to go to the convention in Chicago, have the keynote speaker read a letter in which he said that delegates should feel free to support any candidate – i.e., including him – and then leave it to the Chicago Democratic machine to stampede the delegates, who did not, in any case, need much guidance in that decision. He even earnestly declared that as he had urged the Congress to conscript young men to ensure America was adequately armed to deter aggression, he wondered if he had the right to desert his post, as if continued occupation of the White House could be compared to the induction of draftees into boot camp.

A week before the Republican convention, Roosevelt had recruited Hoover's secretary of state, Henry L. Stimson, and the Republicans' 1936 candidate for vice president, Frank Knox, as secretary of war and secretary of the navy in his administration, putting the armed forces into Republican hands as the campaign began. This was a brilliant tactical move, because it would blunt the Republicans' ability to attack Roosevelt on the peace issue. The Republican convention opened wide the schism between the Midwestern conservative bedrock of the Republican Party and the more liberal and international East Coast establishment, which had a precarious standing with the voters but controlled a great deal of money and media influence.

Roosevelt was accepting renomination only because of the war, and he pledged to keep America out of the conflict by arming it to the teeth to ensure its deterrent strength, and by arming the democracies against the war-making dictators, Hitler and Mussolini. The Republican isolationists wanted to avoid any possible involvement in the war, and the more extreme advocates of this view claimed to be unable to detect any appreciable moral distinction between the two great rivals, Hitler and Churchill.

The leaders of the main Republican factions were men who would play important roles in Nixon's future political life, Ohio senator Robert A. Taft, leader of the conservative isolationists, and New York's crime-busting district attorney, Thomas E. Dewey, of the more liberal Eastern bloc of the Republican Party. In fact, Taft personally ended up endorsing Roosevelt's assistance to Britain and Canada, and Dewey was rather ambivalent on international issues, but the political complexions of the factions they headed were more predictable.

In a rare phenomenon, especially for the Republicans, a nearly genuine draft developed for a fusion candidate, Wendell Willkie, originally of Indiana but now a New York utilities executive. Willkie was a relatively liberal Republican and supported Roosevelt's aid to the democracies, but the Republican heartland was much more comfortable with him, as a Midwesterner, than with the unregenerate and rather desiccated Easterner, Dewey. Willkie had never held elective office, but he was a robust populist intellectual, a great bear of a man, and a stirring speaker. As he agreed with Roosevelt's foreign policy, he was reduced to claiming that despite what he said, Roosevelt would plunge the nation into war. "They [the young men of the nation] are already almost at the boats," he shouted throughout the campaign.

Roosevelt professed to be too preoccupied to campaign, though he reserved the right to enter the fray later, and he set out on a tour of munitions plants and training facilities, which had the same effect as a campaign trip. As Willkie grew hoarse trying to frighten the electorate with the specter of Roosevelt pushing the country into war, Roosevelt held his fire until two weeks before the election and then gave a memorable series of speeches in major cities of the East. "I cannot say that this is an unpleasant duty; I am an old campaigner and I enjoy a good fight." He hung isolationism – which he implicitly represented as pro-Nazi – and all the evils of the vividly remembered Depression around the necks of the Republicans with his habitual oratorical virtuosity.[*] To the anxious parents of war-age youth he said, "I have said this before, and I

---

[*] In his quadrennial Madison Square Garden address, October 28, 1940, he concluded a recitation of Republicans who had what he considered primitive voting patterns with congressmen "Martin, Barton, and Fish," leaving it, after the first reference to them, to the crowd to shout out the names. Martin and Barton would play a role in Nixon's political future.

will say it again and again and again: your sons will not be sent into any foreign wars."

Willkie made a gallant effort, but Roosevelt was the greatest vote-getter and partisan tactician in the country's history. Near the end of the campaign he turned his returning, pro-fascist ambassador to Britain, Joseph Kennedy, who was expected to endorse Willkie, back into a partisan of his, allegedly by offering to help Kennedy's sons in their political careers. Then he read letters from a rabbi, a Protestant clergyman, and New York's Roman Catholic archbishop, Francis J. Spellman, as he announced over the radio the country's first peacetime conscription in its history, which Roosevelt, using Revolutionary War parlance, called a "muster." Spellman said, "It is better to have force and not need it than to need it and not have it. . . . We must have a peace that is not a choice between slavery and death."[46] The Roman Catholic leadership, which had some ability to influence its thirty million coreligionists, gave all that it had for the president; he could not have asked for more. Willkie cut Roosevelt's 1936 plurality from eleven million to five million votes and ran him a close race in many states, but the president was invincible.

Even before the election, won on the promise of peace through strength, Roosevelt had started extending American territorial waters from three to 1,800 miles, and soon after the election he commanded the U.S. Navy to attack any German ship on detection. He also put through his Lend-Lease measure, which offered the British anything they wanted, including 26,000 airplanes, on the theory that they would return what they were "loaned." As he famously told the press, it was like lending a neighbor a garden hose if his house were on fire. And he embargoed oil and scrap iron to Japan, forcing that country either to desist from its invasion of China and Indochina or attack to the south, as it imported 85 percent of its petroleum and required the scrap for about 70 percent of its steel production. This was an idiosyncratic definition of neutrality, but it was brilliant statesmanship, on the heels of inspired electoral politics.

Richard Nixon watched all this closely. He noted Roosevelt's wiles, and he noted the fissiparous nature of his own inherited and chosen party. He was already devising a strategy of advocating various points dear to both major groups in the Republican Party and becoming an inter-factional bridge.

The Republicans had been founded by Lincoln and others eighty-five years before to fight slavery and secessionism, and had coasted on Lincoln's coattails for the balance of the nineteenth century. Theodore Roosevelt, an accidental president as a result of the assassination in 1901 of Frank Nixon's old hero, William McKinley, invented progressive Republicanism. The struggle between the original Roosevelt and the original (William Howard) Taft in 1912 led to the election of the Democrat Woodrow Wilson in 1912. The conservative Republicans were back with Harding, Coolidge, and Hoover in the twenties, and had been electorally exterminated by Roosevelt and the Depression. It was now a battered, disoriented party, and Willkie, having no elected office, quickly melted away as a public force and was friendlier with Roosevelt than with the Republican barons of the East or the Midwest.

While he started to think in national political terms, Nixon also devised a new campaign for himself. The man who had married Dick and Pat, William Mendenhall, had come under fire as president of Whittier College because he had slowed the reforms of his predecessor, Walter Dexter, the president with whom Nixon had worked as an undergraduate. It was a miniature Roosevelt-Taft breach, and Nixon canvassed the other trustees, making himself conspicuously available. Mendenhall faced down the trustees for a time, and Nixon never overtly opposed him. Mendenhall was forced out in 1943, but by that time Nixon was literally thousands of miles away. As with the incumbent state assemblyman, Nixon was restlessly seeking an office, though the presidency of Whittier College would only have been a stepping stone.

Nixon had already begun campaigning for the state assemblyman post again, as well as for the city attorney's post in La Habra. In May 1941, he got himself elected president of the Association of Northern Orange County Cities, a group of nine municipalities comprising most of the targeted state assembly district, and president of the Young Republicans. He was just twenty-eight, and his ambitions could not be contained indefinitely. His wife gave him a ceramic knight on a charger as a birthday present, and would generally encourage, at least in the early years, his political ambitions, even though she joined him in trying to mislead posterity by saying there was "no talk of politics" before the war.[47]

Between them, they were making nearly five thousand dollars per year. In 1940, half the men and two thirds of the working women in the United States earned less than one thousand dollars per year. In a country of 132 million, only 48,000 taxpayers made more than twenty-five hundred dollars per year, which was perhaps fifteen to twenty times as much in the purchasing power of sixty-five years later.[48] The young Nixons had risen swiftly out of poverty, Pat with no help from her improvident and deceased parents. And they celebrated their first anniversary by motoring to New Orleans and taking a Caribbean cruise. The shipboard part was not a howling success, because Dick was a terrible sailor and was confined to his cabin with seasickness most of the time, a condition aggravated by the odor of bunker fuel from the nearby engines. The ship was a tired tramp steamer of the United Fruit Company.

The visual highlight, unfortunately not recorded in photographs, was a costume party that the men attended in drag – "Dick as a Grecian lady . . . sheet, turban, brooch, bosom, etc." The ship docked at Colon, Panama, which Pat judged to be "the most immoral spot in the world,"[49] and then in Havana, where Nixon wondered about opening a law office, such was his desperation to emancipate himself from Whittier. Pat had already given Whittier Union notice that she would not be back in the fall. Nixon would regale audiences many times with his indelible recollection of having had "oysters Rockefeller" for dinner when they disembarked at New Orleans.

While they were on their cruise, they learned that Germany had invaded the Soviet Union. Nixon had not, until now, given much thought to foreign affairs, though he later said that he had favored the republicans in the Spanish Civil War, because of a press campaign against Franco, and had initially preferred Chamberlain's policy of appeasement of the dictators to Churchill's robust attitude.

Richard Nixon's character, ambitions, talents, and techniques were pretty well settled by the time he left Duke in 1937. But he had not really had the opportunity to think much about the world, or develop what would prove an historic gift for foreign policy. He was about to broaden his horizons.

— VII —

The Nixons finally made their escape from Whittier. They did this through classmates at Duke who had gone to Washington to work in the Office of Price Administration (OPA), an amorphous effort of Roosevelt's to accelerate war preparations while restraining inflation. He was hired for $3,200 per year, and began as a tire pricing and rationing regulator. Between the time Nixon accepted a general offer and then went to work, the country was plunged into war by the Japanese attack at Pearl Harbor on December 7, 1941, and Hitler and Mussolini's spontaneous declarations of war on the United States three days later. Hannah Nixon was relieved that Dick was going to a civilian government position and not to war, adhering always to her Quaker beliefs. Dick and Pat drove five days through often difficult weather, arriving in Washington on Dick's twenty-ninth birthday, January 9, 1942.

The OPA was a chaotic organization, wrestling with impossible administrative problems, and would have collapsed in shambles and probably corruption if there had not been a national spirit of sacrifice and determination to win the war. There were many talented people in the administration of it who would not normally be in the public sector. The forceful and fearless Leon Henderson, something of a crony of both Franklin and Eleanor Roosevelt, was at the head of the vast agency. Among Nixon's intelligent contemporaries in the OPA were economist and future Federal Reserve chairman Arthur Burns, Canadian-born economist John Kenneth Galbraith, civil rights lawyer and Democratic insider Joseph Rauh, and future Harvard Sovietologist Merle Fainsod. (Once Nixon was president, Galbraith used to send him invitations to OPA reunions, but never received a response.) Nixon's supervisor at OPA was Thomas Harris, later one of the senior in-house lawyers of the American Federation of Labor and Congress of Industrial Organizations (AFL-CIO).

Nixon's first assignment was less absurd than it sounded, because the United States imported almost all its rubber from places that the Japanese were about to occupy or interdict, and there had to be an instant and overwhelming effort at conservation and redirection to military use. Roosevelt ordered the cessation of all retail sales of tires, the retreading, as necessary, of tires for civilian use, and a reduced speed limit to extend the life of tires. (Nixon would take note of all these measures and use some of them thirty years later when confronting an oil shortage.)

Nixon's organizational talents and general zeal and efficiency made him very effective from the first, and his natural sympathy for ordinary people and small businessmen made him an excellent human face for the bureaucracy, trying to assist the public in adjusting to sharply changed conditions. He wiped out the correspondence backlog within a few weeks. He designed an intricate new system for receiving and processing and responding to correspondence, down to licking stamps and envelopes, and, as

always with Nixon's endeavors of this kind, it was successful and appreciatively noted by higher-ups.[50]

In March 1942, after just two months at the OPA, he was promoted to the
uneuphonious post of acting chief of interpretations in the Rubber Branch.
Despite the absurd bureaucratese, this was an important position, especially
for a man in his twenties, and Nixon devised a new flowchart to deal with
these responsibilities. He became the OPA's resident expert at dealing
with the agency's voluminous correspondence, and devised new systems for
other branches, including gasoline and sugar. He was praised by his super-
visors: "splendid . . . bright . . . great capacity for work . . . a real plugger," etc.[51]
In the summer he received a full-grade promotion and a 20 percent pay raise,
and became acting chief of the entire Rationing Coordination Unit. Almost
everything was rationed, and in a wartime civilian population of over
120 million people, this was an important and onerous job.

The Nixons took a brief driving vacation to Charleston in April, with a
stop to show Pat the campus at Duke. Nixon became a sort of itinerant
troubleshooter, going to problem areas personally and taking charge, setting
up in Boston for a week in June 1942. He took Pat on this trip too, and
managed a few days off near Kennebunkport. It was very pleasant, but like
millions of young couples all over the world, they would expect few replica-
tions of such carefree leisure for several years.

On returning from Boston, or other field trips, he would work even
harder than usual to clear up what had accumulated in his absence. Another
comprehensive report that he had written, streamlining and grouping
together all the regulations governing automobiles (tires, gasoline, etc.), was
left for consideration while he was in Boston. When he returned, he found
that it had fallen victim to bureaucratic envy and backbiting, and some of its
proposals had already been appropriated and put forward by others.

Nixon had already decided to leave the OPA and join the navy. He could
certainly have dodged the war if he had wished, as he had a double exemption. He was excused as a cradle Quaker with two Quaker parents and a
Quaker education through to his undergraduate degree. And as an OPA executive, he was in a draft-immune position. Nixon found the work uncongenial,
though important, and he resented the meddlesome fervor of federal officials,
which he thought bordered on sadistic harassment of ordinary people.

The whole administration, from the president down, was very preoccupied to avoid war profiteering, which had been invoked by the isolationists

in the thirties as one of the motives for entering the First World War. Nixon was opposed to anyone ripping off the country for private gain or overcharging the taxpayer as the nation fought for its life and thousands of young Americans died most weeks in combat in the armed forces. But he resented the efforts of leftist colleagues to badger small businessmen to reduce their profits. Most of the OPA lawyers came from professional backgrounds and had no sympathy or regard for small businessmen. Richard Nixon, of course, had an entirely different formation and perspective.

In his memoirs, Nixon records that one of his superiors told him to request a staff, and then it would be possible to promote him. When Nixon said he didn't need a staff, he was advised that he could do without a promotion too. He wrote of the OPA and other regulators they they "were obsessed with their own power . . . and seemed to delight in kicking other people around."[52] He transformed his brief sojourn in the OPA into a sort of non-elective *Mr. Smith Goes to Washington* odyssey. He never forgot the nature of the federal civil service, and the will to dominate and restrict and interfere that he saw there. This too would be the stuff of a lot of good political oratory over many years.

There may have been also a political consideration. Since Nixon had his heart set on a career in politics, he would have reasoned that sitting out the war in the office that rationed everything, including profits, and, for millions of people, incomes, would not be a great postwar vote winner. The United States has always liked veterans politically, and lionized war heroes. In all but two of the fifteen presidential elections from 1824 to 1880, at least one of the major parties had put up a candidate best known as a senior military officer (including presidents and generals, Jackson, W.H. Harrison, Taylor, and Grant). A postwar candidate whose campaign photograph depicts him in a uniform has a public relations and oratorical advantage. An endless number of reflections can begin "When I was in the air force," or "when I was on Corregidor," or whatever. (Nixon's specialty was "I learned in the foxholes of the South Pacific . . ." – a considerable liberty, though unlike Lyndon Johnson, Joseph McCarthy, and others, he did not glamorize his war service.)

Most likely, Nixon was influenced chiefly by patriotism. He loved his country, he hated the Nazis, and was as livid as all Americans at the unprovoked attack on Pearl Harbor and throughout the Western and Central Pacific, and he wanted to serve because it was the right thing to do. As a lawyer and government regulatory administrator, he could reasonably assume that he would be an officer candidate, and had no reason to doubt that he could have a successful tour in the armed forces. He had begun to feel out of place in a Washington swarming with uniformed men. And Pat later said, "I would have felt mighty uncomfortable if Dick hadn't done his part."[53]

He chose the navy, though the reason is not obvious, since he was, as his Caribbean holiday the year before had demonstrated, prone to sea-sickness. Being a Californian, he may have thought of the navy as the senior service, and the scuttlebutt in his milieu in Washington was that the navy needed lawyers for seagoing administrative tasks in the larger ships, especially aircraft carriers.

Richard Nixon said good-bye to his wife at Washington's Union Station on August 17 entrained for Providence, Rhode Island, and at nearby Quonset Point joined the Naval Officer Candidate School. It was a two-month course, and Nixon found the physical training rigorous and the navigation instruction a challenge, but he tucked into it with his usual unflinching self-discipline. Obligatory target practice, at which he was unsuccessful, was the first time he had ever held a gun. Nixon got on well and even helped one of his friends make his bed every day.[54] He corresponded faithfully with Pat, who addressed him affectionately in their delightfully romantic and tasteful exchanges as "Plum." They even managed a two-day rendezvous in New York. Pat had joined the OPA five days after Dick had left Washington, becoming an assistant business analyst.

Lieutenant Nixon had requested "ships and stations" as a work category in the navy. But there was something in the character and ineluctable destiny of Richard Nixon that would make a dashing posting difficult to obtain. Even if he were already accustomed to such disappointments, he was astounded to be posted on graduation to an initial-pilot-training airfield in Ottumwa, Iowa, with only 225 men, and, as he wrote in his memoirs, "a runway that stopped abruptly in the middle of a cornfield." Pat gave up her new OPA job and they were together again, in a modest off-base apartment. This was more pedestrian, after working in the shadows of the United States Capitol in an important position, than Nixon could have imagined, but he was a dogged man, and he and his wife had learned long before that the path to their ambitions was blocked by the banal and the implausible as well as by more conventional adversity. (It remains a mystery why the navy was operating an airstrip in landlocked Iowa, but Nixon guessed it was a patronage gift to an Iowa congressman.) At least he had a crisp officer's uniform in the world's largest navy.

This rustication lasted seven months. Pat worked as a bank teller and "didn't care much for those coffee socials with navy wives."[55] Dick then liberated them from the bowels of Iowa and moved a good deal closer to the combat zone. He responded to a notice asking for applications for sea duty, and was ordered to report to San Francisco in May 1943 for reassignment to the South Pacific. His mother and his grandmother, the ageless (ninety-three in fact) Almira, were disappointed at his abandonment of greater principles. His parents and brothers and his law partner, Tom Bewley, saw Pat and him off at the station in Los Angeles, and after two weeks in a small hotel in San Francisco, he finally did take leave of his wife and sailed on May 31, 1943, on the *President Monroe* for Espiritu Santo, in the New Hebrides. Pat could not face Whittier, and remained in San Francisco, becoming a corresponding secretary with the Office of Civilian Defense and later working for the Kafkaesque-titled Committee for Congested Production Areas, and then, also in San Francisco, like a homing pigeon, for the OPA as a price economist, the Nixons' third tour with this ubiquitous bureaucracy.

There were nine officers in the same shipboard room, with triple bunks, and one of them, but not Nixon, was constantly seasick. He wrote Pat a letter each day, although they would all be delivered at once, and spent his waking hours playing poker. His cabin mate, James Stewart, taught him how to play, and the strategy never to bid unless he believed, on the odds and his reading of the other players, that he had a winning hand. This would be a great revenue source for Nixon; he proved a remarkably adept player, quiet, expressionless, always calculating odds, and shrewdly judging the nature of the other players. He started to win on the *President Monroe*, and continued to throughout his time in the Pacific. (Stewart said Nixon didn't smoke or drink, read the Bible a lot, and told him he had never slept with anyone except Pat.)[56]

Even in the South Pacific, Nixon wasn't catapulted into a role that created an obvious opportunity for heroism. He was naval passenger control officer for the South Pacific Air Transport Command, which was technically under the direction of the U.S. Marines. It was an important logistical operation, moving marines forward and around General Douglas MacArthur's

Southwest Pacific theater. The tide of battle had turned in this region with the repulse of the Japanese at Guadalcanal, a bitter and often desperate struggle that raged for almost eight months before the Japanese were finally forced off the island, in the Solomons group north of Australia, in February 1943.

This was the end of the Japanese threat to Australia, and after the great American naval victory at Midway in June of 1942, and as Roosevelt's colossal naval and aircraft rearmament program stoked up, MacArthur and Admiral Chester Nimitz in the Central Pacific theater were able to bypass Japanese islands and move relatively swiftly northwest from the Solomon Islands and due west from Midway, island-hopping toward the Philippines and the home islands of Japan. As the Japanese were driven out of Guadalcanal, the British finally defeated the Germans in Egypt, the Russians snapped shut their great trap at Stalingrad, and the Americans and British took over French North Africa. By the time Nixon got to the New Hebrides, the Russians had defeated the Germans in the great tank battle of Kursk and forced the Wehrmacht into permanent retreat, the British and Americans had expelled the enemy from Africa and captured Sicily, and Mussolini had been deposed and imprisoned and then rescued and set up as a puppet leader in German-occupied northern Italy. In the first seven months of 1943, the Germans had lost over a million soldiers, killed or captured, the Italians had collapsed, and the Americans had established decisive naval superiority in the Pacific.

Nixon was just behind the swiftly moving front lines, and while he didn't see much direct combat, his role was extremely important and there is no doubt that he performed excellently. He was thorough, enterprising, solicitous of the wounded and the war-weary, very popular with all the many servicemen he came in touch with, and, when necessary, physically courageous. He wasn't allowed the opportunity for a glorious war, but he did have a very admirable and useful one.

He started out supporting the logistics for the Bougainville action, the island MacArthur went to when it was decided to bypass Rabaul, where the Japanese had 250,000 soldiers who were left stranded as the lines moved past them northwestward. Nixon was only a couple of hundred miles from where Lieutenant John F. Kennedy commanded his torpedo boat against a fast Japanese nighttime resupply mission in the Blackett Strait in August 1943.

Dick and Pat wrote each other every day, and numbered the envelopes. Almost all her letters began "Dear [or Dearest] Plum." She sent him expensive (five-dollar) pajamas, parcels of books, and often kissed her letters, leaving lipstick on them. The depth of their feeling for each other was obvious and often beautifully expressed. Dick wrote an astonishing number of letters, to all his family members and his old law dean and many friends, and read every day from a family Bible he brought with him, as well as avidly devouring the books Pat sent, including works by Karl Marx and Guy de Maupassant (whom Nixon judged the greatest short story writer in any language). He moved from Espiritu Santo to New Caledonia to Guadalcanal to Villa Lavela through the fall of 1943.

Even here, close to combat, Nixon felt out of the main action and denied the possibility to excel. He watched carefully the progress of other men in publicly prominent positions, including the thirty-four-year-old president of the University of Arkansas, J. William Fulbright (later U.S. senator in 1944), and the thirty-five-year-old governor of Minnesota, Harold Stassen, whose transport as a lieutenant Nixon arranged.[57] Nixon kept a diary and was able to read so extensively because he had a good deal of idle time, when there were not emergency arrivals of wounded men from the combat islands, or overwhelming quantities of supplies moving forward. His diary included aphorisms he liked, and evidences of popular taste. Some phrases struck him as apposite in themselves (Tennyson's "The most virtuous hearts have a touch of hell's own fire in them"),[58] and some were interesting expressions of general sentiment that he would remember to pitch to when the occasion arose.

In December 1943, Nixon's request for command and to get closer to the action was granted, and he moved up to Bougainville. There were still mopping-up actions going on at the island, and these were always difficult with the Japanese, who generally preferred to be killed by their enemies than captured. Nixon was head of the air transport operation – again, a serious responsibility in a combat zone. He claimed to his wife, not altogether truthfully, that the greatest danger was the poisonous centipedes, though they were large and nasty.

In March 1944, he moved up again, to Green Island, which had been largely occupied by New Zealanders in fierce fighting. They were bombed several times by the Japanese. This was where Nixon took refuge in what he later described, a bit histrionically, as "foxholes," though he was, if anything, needlessly self-conscious about his war experiences. (This was quite a difference with the then commander-in-chief, Franklin D. Roosevelt, who on the strength of a VIP tour of the western front and to the Royal Navy's home base and the Italian high command in 1918, claimed to have seen more of the First World War than any other American.)

Nixon's most graphic view of war was watching a flak-damaged B-29, arriving from having bombed Rabaul and unable to put down its landing gear, seem to come in safely, slide down the runway, and then strike a bulldozer and blow up. "I can still see the wedding ring on the charred hand of one of the crewmen when I carried his body from the twisted wreckage," he wrote.[59]

When the traffic was heavy, Nixon, who could have confined himself to giving orders, took off his shirt, donned his pith helmet – a touch of swank (like Livingston and Stanley) and mucked in with the men to load and unload aircraft as quickly as possible. He was always ingenious and generous at finding refreshment for exhausted aircrews. Nixon commanded units of about twenty, and they were always a diverse cross-section of America, every region, economic stratum, religion, and ethnic group (except African-American, because the armed forces were not integrated).

He was known to thousands of men in transport and bomber and fighter aircrews as Nick, and his commissary was known as "Nick's" and was famous for the "coldest pineapple juice in the South Pacific." He took an exceptional interest in his men, listened to their problems, advised them on letters home, requested special leave for them, and was a beloved figure, to his own unit and well beyond it. He could find or lay hands on almost any piece of equipment, and developed an intimate knowledge of the vast logistical and supply apparatus of the Pacific war effort. He even managed to get a couple of stuffed koala bears from New Zealand, which he sent home to Pat, who kept them all her life. He was like Henry Fonda's film portrayal of the capable and thoughtful *Mr. Roberts*, his comrades would independently state many years later.[60]

Nixon's talents at poker, especially five-stud, became legendary, but not from any braggadocio of his. He played poker every free occasion, and even passed up a small dinner with Colonel Charles Lindbergh, despite his interest in celebrities, to make a pre-scheduled poker game engagement with fellow officers.[61] He famously drew a royal flush on one occasion, and, even more famously, bluffed a senior officer out of $1,500 with a pair of twos.[62] He sent some of his winnings back to his old law office to pay for the disastrous home foreclosure case with which he began his practice, and to pay back some of the investors in Citra-Frost. Richard Nixon never forgot a slight, but he did not forget a debt either.

When Nixon was ordered home for promotion, his men gave him a boisterous and heartfelt farewell party. He returned to the United States with two battle stars and a ringing citation of commendation from his commanding officer. He flew to Guadalcanal, then Midway, then Pearl Harbor. At Midway, in the middle of the night, he took advantage of the stop to go for a stroll and looked at the military cemetery adjacent to the airfield, with row on row of dead young men, and reflected on "the ultimate futility of war and the terrible reality of the loss that lies behind it."[63] He went by ship from Pearl Harbor to San Diego, and had a joyous reunion with Pat at the San Diego airport, where she had flown to meet him. Pat ran "fifty yards at breakneck speed and threw her arms around me."[64]

He had three weeks' leave, spent mainly in Whittier, where he gave service club and church luncheon speeches about his war experiences, while Pat returned to her job in San Francisco. He appeared to his Whittier friends to be more affable and relaxed and confident than they remembered him. He made himself conspicuously available to Republican notables in Orange County for the congressional nomination to run against five-term congressman Jeremiah "Jerry" Voorhis.

Nixon resumed his naval career as base administrative officer of the Alameda Naval Air Station. He would later disparagingly describe himself as "chief janitor." A note from the base commander – "Lieutenant Nixon, has my desk been dusted this morning?" – particularly incensed him, though it greatly amused his wife.[65] In January 1945, Nixon was transferred back to Philadelphia, and then to New York, to negotiate the termination of war contracts. They lived in small, short-lease apartments and in New York frequented the Metropolitan Opera House. They learned of President Roosevelt's death while dining in a restaurant in Philadelphia, and Nixon had his first glimpse of a man he would come to know very well, the Allied commander in Western Europe, General Dwight D. Eisenhower, as the general's tickertape parade passed beneath Nixon's twentieth-story office window on Church Street in lower Manhattan, in May.

Nixon was promoted lieutenant commander in October 1945, and received a warm letter of commendation from the secretary of the navy, James V. Forrestal, for "meritorious service, tireless effort and devotion to country."[66] He closed out his naval service with more legal work unwinding war purchase contracts, in Middle River, Maryland, just east of Baltimore on Chesapeake Bay. He agreed to stay on in the navy until New Year's Day,

1946, and corresponded with the unofficial elders of the Republican Party in the Whittier area about the congressional nomination. This was another trial balloon like his effort to become the state assemblyman, or the president of Whittier College, but in the first case he was hoping the incumbent would retire, and in the second that the incumbent (who had married him a few months before) would be forced out. Neither event occurred until two years later, when Nixon was away. There was no nominee against Voorhis, and the previous Republican candidate had been completely lackluster. Someone had to run against him, and Richard Nixon, almost thirty-three, was a much more prepossessing figure, especially in uniform and combat decorations, than had been the ambitious but hesitant youth of five years before, prior to his and America's great trial of war.

— VIII —

Franklin D. Roosevelt had died on the verge of military victory. His much-evolved New Deal, which started with huge emergency unemployment relief projects and eliminated unemployment with an immense defense production preparedness program and peacetime conscription, concluded with his GI Bill of Rights, which turned most of America's working class into a middle class. Posthumously, this was one of Roosevelt's greatest accomplishments; for five years after the Second World War, about half the university students enrolled in the United States had their tuition paid by the U.S. government. Hundreds of thousands of veterans received interest-free loans to set up businesses or buy farms.

While Roosevelt's death was untimely in terms of trying to force Stalin to live up to his Yalta commitments for the promotion of democracy in Eastern Europe, in some respects, as one who had led the country through two of the greatest crises in its history, the Great Depression and the Second World War, it was opportune. As his great associate, Winston Churchill, said in his official eulogy in the British Parliament, "What an enviable death was his! He had brought the country through the worst of its perils and the heaviest of its toils. Victory had cast its sure and steady beam upon him. In the days of peace he had broadened and stabilized the foundation of American life and union. In war he had raised the strength, might, and glory of the great Republic to a height never attained by any nation in history."[67]

63

This was true, but Roosevelt had done nothing to prepare his chosen successor, Harry S Truman, to take in hand all the threads of government, and after fifteen years of economic and military struggle, the country was in no mood for continued rationing and the oppressive spirit of collective sacrifice. The controls were pretty well eliminated by the end of 1945 (by contrast, rationing in Britain continued into the fifties), and the peacetime economy absorbed the demobilized servicemen well without an early spike in inflation. Yet industrial disputes abounded, as labor felt it had been short-changed, the public quickly tired of any waiting lines and shortages, and Truman, a plainspoken, natty, smallish man with a Missouri twang, was a startling contrast to the patrician and overpowering personality of his predecessor. Problems of availability of housing, new cars and appliances, and a lack of variety of food, as well as the nerve-wracking discussion of the power of atomic weapons and the swiftly rising tensions with the Russians, and most of all the sense that it was time for a change and that Truman was not up to his great task, depressed the popularity of the Democrats.

It was not long before the most fantastic fears and recriminations were bandied about concerning the Russians and communism. At a strategic level, it soon became clear that Stalin had shredded the Yalta agreement. Truman moved to assist anti-communist forces in Greece and to reinforce Turkey. Churchill, now British opposition leader, speaking in Fulton, Missouri, in 1946, spoke of an "Iron Curtain" between "Stettin in the Baltic and Trieste in the Adriatic."

A unique combination of factors quickly conjoined to make anti-communism a fiery tonic for American voters. The administration, recognizing the Soviet threat to Western Europe and the strength of the Chinese Communists in the civil war in that country, was prepared to stoke up anti-communist sentiment to ensure political support for what was soon identified as a policy of containment of the Soviet Union and international communism. The Republicans were even more offended by communists than the Democrats, and had the added bonus of being able to accuse Roosevelt and his entourage of having been duped by Stalin.

This malicious historical revisionism was abetted by the disgruntlement of the British imperialists, out of office and watching helplessly as the Labour government of Clement Attlee sloughed off large chunks of the Empire: India, Pakistan, Burma, Ceylon, Palestine. The British Tories around Churchill (who was personally quite careful about what he said and wrote about Roosevelt) had great credibility in the world after their outstanding bravery and perseverance in the war, and suggestions that the U.S. administration had been too friendly with Russia were warmly received and amplified in the United States by the Republicans.

The facts were a good deal more complicated. Roosevelt had not wished to demarcate occupation zones in Germany before the war ended, because he correctly judged that the Germans would resist a good deal more fiercely in the East than in the West and that the Western Allies had a chance to occupy almost all the country, including Berlin. The British voted with the Russians at the European Advisory Commission (EAC) to divide pre-war Germany into three nearly equal occupation zones. This was a considerable triumph for British diplomacy, because they had many fewer divisions engaged in the theater than the Americans and Russians and had been afraid that the occupation zones would be proportionate to forces deployed in Germany.

This division of postwar Germany was made in February 1944, four months before the Normandy landings, about which the British civilian and military leaders were a good deal less optimistic than the Americans. The occupation zones were imposed on the 1939 map of Germany, because the EAC (the American and Russian ambassadors to Britain and the third-ranking official in the British Foreign Office) were not informed of the secret agreement at the Teheran Conference in December 1943 that the western borders of the U.S.S.R. and Poland would both be moved two hundred miles to the west. This effectively delivered Poland to Russian occupation, but, coupled with the physical flight of eight million Germans westward to escape the Russian armies, it brought Germany from Central Europe into Western Europe.

Churchill himself had explicitly signed over Romania, Hungary, and Bulgaria to the Russians, and had split Yugoslavia with them and taken Greece for the British sphere of influence, when he visited Stalin in October 1944. These arrangements reflected military realities, but they had nothing to do with Roosevelt, who requested that no such agreements be made.

In the weeks after Roosevelt's death (on April 12, 1945), as the American, British, Canadian, and French armies poured into and through Germany, Churchill beseeched Truman to take Berlin. Truman referred the matter to the chairman of the Combined Allied Military Chiefs, General George

C. Marshall, who consulted the theater commander, General Dwight D. Eisenhower. Eisenhower took the position that he would naturally carry out orders, but did not see why Western Allied soldiers should be lost taking territory that was committed by the EAC agreement to Russian occupation. This was a reasonable view, but less explicable is Eisenhower's professed lack of interest in taking Berlin, which he expressed directly to Stalin on March 31 (he was authorized to communicate directly with the Soviet high command). Another unexplained issue in Eisenhower's career was his failure to take Prague, and at least the Bohemian part of Czechoslovakia.

Eisenhower was very concerned not to blunder into direct conflict with the vast Soviet military forces as the Allies approached each other, squeezing the dying Nazi regime between them. Eisenhower had a considerable regard for his ability to negotiate with the Russians, based on his visit to Stalin just before he returned to his hero's welcome in the United States. He had proved his qualities as a soldier-diplomat dealing with such testy comrades as British Field Marshal Montgomery, an anti-American gamecock; the imperious and inflexible Free French leader, General Charles de Gaulle, and the bombastic but effective U.S. Third Army commander, General George S. Patton. There is, in some of Eisenhower's reflections, then and subsequently, the hint that he felt he could have done a better job of working things out with his wartime Russian comrades-in-arms than did Roosevelt and Truman and their entourages. None of these historic personalities were self-effacing egos.

Roosevelt had hoped that an atomic monopoly in America's hands, the prospect of durably pacifying Germany, a country the Soviet leadership naturally feared (this was the only reason he entertained his Treasury secretary Henry Morgenthau's absurd plan for the pastoralization of Germany), and the inducement of massive economic assistance might persuade Stalin to honor his commitments to democracy in Eastern Europe. Stalin swiftly disabused Truman.

Churchill quickly rewrote history, consigning the Soviet occupation of Eastern Europe to the vortex between a dying Roosevelt and an inexperienced Truman. Eisenhower wrote his war memoirs and confined himself to the German zonal agreement, ducking his strategic lack of interest in Berlin and not mentioning Prague. Truman, when his time came, implicitly blamed the failure to take Berlin on Eisenhower. Churchill, Eisenhower, and Truman all knew better than to try to take the Yalta Myth of a Roosevelt capitulation too far, and observed an uneasy truce of the memoirists, sparing each other and Roosevelt direct attack.

But in this historical standoff and increasingly frenzied international atmosphere, the mischief-makers were free to operate, and the Republicans soon had a group of wild conspiracy theorists as their most vocal spokesmen, claiming a Red fifth column was lurking everywhere and communism was like a virus that could strike down the innocent of America in their beds, or could infect them almost through their breakfast cereal. There were Reds under the bed and lurking behind every bush that wasn't already burning. There would be a sequence of events, especially the Soviet development of an atomic bomb, revelations of extensive Russian espionage activity, the blockade of West Berlin, necessitating its supply by air, and the Communist takeovers of Czechoslovakia and China, that inflamed hysterical anti-communist sentiment in the United States.

Richard Nixon was not slow to grasp the potential for this line of attack, though he was always careful to stay well clear of the most rabid imputations of treason to distinguished Democrats. Others, who should have known better, were not so careful. The Roman Catholic hierarchy's chief authority on communism in America, Father John Cronin of Georgetown University, warned that the fifth column (a phrase of Franco's junta associate, General Emilio Mola, in the Spanish Civil War) was numerous and active throughout the United States. The head of the American Chamber of Commerce, John J. Sullivan, declared in 1946 that "we will have to set up . . . firing squads in every . . . city and town in the country . . . and liquidate the Reds and Pink Benedict Arnolds."[68] There would soon be radio and television programs suggesting that anyone's neighbor or relative could be, and might well be, a communist agent. A febrile atmosphere was created as the wartime goodwill between the Soviet Union and the West evaporated in a few months. This rising Cold War militancy was useful to help keep America's guard up and come completely out of isolation, but it was an insalubrious political climate for all other purposes.

Harry Truman, whom the Republicans underestimated, rose quickly to the Russian danger, but was rather casual about concerns over domestic communism. He rightly believed that no significant number of Americans would serve the Soviet Union to the detriment of their own country.

In 1945 Nixon had only a hint of some of this, but without the anti-Red tide having nearly crested, he sensed that the Republican hour, after four consecutive defeats at the hands of Roosevelt, and eight straight defeats in congressional elections, was coming, and that he could catch history at its turning. He was braced by the camaraderie he had enjoyed in the navy, alarmed by what he had seen of the regulatory mentality at the OPA, and fortified by some of the deep thinking he had done in the South Pacific about the tragedy of war and how America could take its place in the world.

Politically, California was, as in all things, a complicated place, with thousands of people flowing into the state every week, and a mecca to all the most exotic and extreme varieties of American political eccentricity. The longtime king of California politics, Senator Hiram W. Johnson, had died on the day of the release of the atomic bomb on Hiroshima, August 6, 1945, after twenty-eight years as U.S. senator from California, following six years as governor. He had been Theodore Roosevelt's running mate as Progressive candidate for vice president in 1912, when they bolted from the bosses of the Taft-dominated Republicans. He is at least folklorically credited with delivering California, by a narrow margin, and thereby the election, to Woodrow Wilson in 1916, because he felt he had been slighted by the Republican candidate, Charles Evans Hughes.

Johnson had been an FDR supporter while Roosevelt was using Western Progressives to overcome Southern Democrats and conservative Republicans to put his New Deal measures through. But Johnson was a raving isolationist, who publicly claimed that Hitler had "got the better" of his exchange with Roosevelt in 1939 (when Roosevelt had asked Hitler to forswear any aggressive designs on thirty countries in Europe and the Middle East[69]). By this time, Roosevelt had ditched the isolationists and was relying on Southern Democrats, who had a strong pro-British and -French tradition going back to the Civil War, and favored a strong defense as a matter of principle, to put his rearmament program through. Roosevelt thus managed the strategic coup of completing the rout of one enemy, unemployment and Depression, by preparing to defeat the next enemy, and arming to face the aggressive foreign dictators.

Roosevelt referred to Johnson sarcastically in his election addresses of 1940 – and a year later, after Pearl Harbor, when Johnson came to the White House, a correspondent wrote that he saw him "stalk across the little stone stage of the portico, and all the ghosts of isolationism seemed to stalk with him."[70] He had been a progressive governor and senator in his time, but, politically speaking, the name died before the man.

The governor of California, as of 1942, and political strongman of the state, was the sturdy and almost bipartisan liberal Republican Earl Warren. When Johnson died, Warren named William Knowland, the son of Warren's great patron and owner of the *Oakland Tribune*, Joseph Knowland, to fill Johnson's unexpired term in the Senate. Bluff, hearty, and uncomplicated, William Knowland had the booming confidence of inherited position, and benefited from the patronage of the much more substantial and esteemed Warren. These two and Nixon would play a minuet for control of the California Republican Party and the power it conferred nationally. For a time, all would seem to win. In the end, Warren was twenty-two years older than Nixon, and Knowland a good deal less intelligent and motivated, but they would all make some history.

As Richard Nixon set out on his quest for a congressional seat in his usual methodical manner, claiming to be drafted by the leading Republicans in his district while in fact ardently wooing them, he felt a seismic change coming. Sixteen of California's twenty-five congressional seats were held by Democrats, elected in wartime, in November 1944, on the magic carpet of Roosevelt's coattails, a week after the Battle of Leyte Gulf (the greatest naval victory since Trafalgar). Many must by now be vulnerable.

Nixon's old patron and landlord, Whittier's premier financier and man of influence, Herman Perry, local head of the Bank of America, started touting Nixon as the local congressional candidate in September 1945. He wrote Nixon "to ask if you would like to be a candidate for Congress on the Republican ticket in 1946. Jerry Voorhis expects to run. Registration is about fifty-fifty. The Republicans are gaining. Please airmail me your response if you are interested."[71] Dick and Pat discussed it for two days and concluded on his part that it was exactly what he wanted to do, and on hers that it was the best passport out of the rubesville environment that she had spent more than fifteen years trying to escape. Nixon telephoned Perry (airmail being insufficiently expressive of the keenness of his ambition) on October 1, 1945, to say he was "honored" and wished to run. He and Pat were concerned not to spend their ten thousand dollars of savings accumulated during the war from her many consecutive jobs and his poker winnings, and Perry implied that if Nixon was the one, he could assure the money. Herman Perry and his friends were becoming awfully tired of Jerry Voorhis.

Horace Jeremiah Voorhis was in many ways an admirable public servant. He was an evangelical Episcopalian, from a wealthy Midwestern family, who after he graduated from Yale became a factory worker and a YMCA relief officer in Germany, and operated an orphanage in Wyoming. He married a social worker and at the end of the storied Twenties, in whose hedonistic spirit he had never participated, he and his father consecrated much of the family's fortune to the Voorhis School for homeless boys near Pomona, twelve miles from Whittier. He ran the school himself, taught and coached the boys, took a graduate degree at Claremont College close by, and helped turn some of the smaller ranches into cooperatives, trying to improve working conditions and giving them a better chance against the giant ranches that dominated the area.

Voorhis subscribed to muckraking author Upton Sinclair's End Poverty in California (EPIC) campaign for governor against incumbent Frank Merriam in 1934. The core of Sinclair's program was that the state should buy or rent California's unused manufacturing capacity and allow the unemployed to produce for their own needs there. As economics, it was nonsense, but it aroused huge alarm in all monied and bourgeois circles of the state. Sinclair was sandbagged by the combined efforts of the big film studios – who ran extensive newsreels of shifty people with un-American profusions of facial hair and East European accents, endorsing Sinclair as the Soviet candidate – and other large industries; the Republicans joined with the conservative Democrats. A huge war chest was built up for Merriam. Louis B. Mayer led the informal resistance to Sinclair. He organized a virtual press boycott and a cascade of phony polls showing a Merriam landslide, and even arranged for a splinter candidate to divide Sinclair's vote. Merriam won by 260,000 votes, with the third candidate taking about 300,000. It was a textbook case in how to win an election by the lowest means short of physical intimidation of campaign workers and massive tampering with the ballots.[72]

Voorhis had been so disgusted by the EPIC debacle that he defected from the Socialist Party and became an orthodox Democrat and in 1936 secured the nomination of that party for the Twelfth District, which included Whittier, as well as his own school. It was not a difficult race, because Roosevelt carried forty-six of the forty-eight states, and swept California with 67 percent of the vote and a plurality of 930,000.

Jerry Voorhis was a conscientious and hardworking congressman, championing the interests of the migrant workers and the many poor people in the district as best he could. The Republicans got into the habit of putting up inept reactionaries and tyros against him, with the result that Voorhis was reelected with the national Democratic majority four times through 1944 and became somewhat complacent about his incumbency. Not only was the national, postwar mood changing; the demographics of his district were changing. Poverty was alleviated and middle class suburbs spread into the district. In 1941, redistricting had stripped out the heavily labor areas that had voted overwhelmingly for Voorhis. And after 1945, Roosevelt was gone from the leadership of his party. Most important, there was a chance that the unsuspecting Voorhis would be facing a candidate unlike any he had faced before.

The Roosevelt administration had sought out Voorhis to be a moderating influence on the witch-hunting House Un-American Activities Committee, generally known as HUAC. The chairman was a Red-baiting Texas congressman, Martin Dies, a protégé of Roosevelt's first vice president, John N. Garner, and his long-serving House Speaker, Sam Rayburn. But Dies in 1937 had attacked Frank Murphy, the governor of Michigan and future attorney general and Supreme Court justice, whereupon Roosevelt canceled federal public works contracts in his district. When Dies revealed this to the press, who raised it at one of FDR's informal press conferences, the president replied, "Ho hum."[73] Dies's antics were among the reasons that when Roosevelt went for a third term he didn't take Garner with him. Roosevelt could generally prevent HUAC from getting out of control, but by 1946 he was gone and the Red Scare was flaming up to a tremendous conflagration. Dies was still there and the administration Democrats had no idea what a firestorm was coming. In these circumstances, Jerry Voorhis had a lot hanging out, and Richard Nixon, if given the opportunity, would make the most of it. Influential columnist Drew Pearson wrote that Voorhis was "so kindly and altruistic, he defeats his own purposes."[74]

Where Voorhis had been particularly effective, in revealing and causing the cancellation of a sweetheart lease by Standard Oil of the Elk Hills oil reserve in California, in May 1943, he had served the public interest, but in a way that wasn't obvious to the average voter. He did seriously arouse the oil companies, who had the means to be a financial influence in California elections.

For good measure, Voorhis had attacked the large insurance companies as monopolies, antagonized the oil companies again by militating against transfer to the states of offshore oil rights (because the states were deemed more indulgent of the oil companies than the federal government), large land developers over assisted housing, utilities by his sponsorship of public power and rate reductions, newspaper publishers and large advertising agencies over tax issues, and the mighty film studios by invariably supporting their underpaid employees in labor disputes.

He also attacked the Bank of America for buying up smaller banks, though there was no absence of banking competition in California. This was again striking close to home, because the Bank of America, founded by A.P. Giannini and built up initially as a bank for Italian-Americans, had been discriminated against by the San Francisco Federal Reserve and assisted by the intervention of Roosevelt personally in the banking crisis of 1933. The Bank was pro-Roosevelt and vice versa. Voorhis was getting into very deep water, and he went even further when he tendered a bill to strip the profit out of the Federal Reserve System and give it to the government's general revenues. This was seen as a swipe at the congressional establishment and the administration, and a potential blow to the stability of the banking system, which had wobbled so badly just a decade before.

For all of these political, demographic, and specific reasons, Jerry Voorhis was much less invulnerable in his district than he imagined. On October 2, 1945, Nixon wrote back to Herman Perry, the day after their phone call, "I feel very strongly that Jerry Voorhis can be beaten, and I'd welcome the opportunity to take a crack at him." He promised "an aggressive, vigorous campaign."[75]

One of Herman Perry's Republican friends, Roy Day, set up what he called the Committee of 100, an organization of reasonably representative Twelfth District Republicans determined to find the best candidate and get him (presumably) nominated with a minimum of internecine squabbling. The rich suburbs of San Marino, Whittier, and the rural San Gabriels were all represented more or les according to the size of their populations. It was a hapless group of lackluster people that they interviewed, and everyone seemed to assume that Voorhis was very strongly installed in his district. There was a brief attempt to attract General George S. Patton, who was from the district, but he had no interest (and died soon after in a road accident). Day next went after the former Whittier College president, Walter Dexter, who seemed to be ready to take the plunge, but he died four days before meeting Day's committee.[76]

Had he survived, there would probably have been a contest with Nixon, which Dexter would presumably have won, but Nixon would at least have been the heir apparent, whether Dexter won or lost against Voorhis, whose local manager was assuring him at this point that there was no visible threat to him.

In his haste to get to California, Nixon got someone with whom he was negotiating a navy contract termination to use his firm's priority card in buying a trans-continental air ticket, and such tickets were hard to come by at this time. He paid the ticket buyer back a week later, but some have professed to find in this the first signs of a penchant for unethical conduct in politics; this is a fairly prissy and hair-shirted interpretation.

On November 2, Nixon met in the University Club of Los Angeles with Perry and Day and a group of influential Twelfth District businessmen: a large automobile dealer, an insurance broker, a rancher – not industrialists, but captains of industry by the standards of Whittier and San Marino. Nixon made a very good impression. He was obviously highly intelligent, motivated, and an attractive candidate apparently in sympathy with their desire for less government, lower taxes, and a hard line with international communism and militant domestic labor unions. There were more work hours lost to strikes in 1946 than in any other year in American history, and inflation was at 20 percent.

Nixon and the other candidates were formally interviewed later that night and Nixon came through as "an electrifying personality."[77] Nixon made this favorable impression despite invoking his rather overworked formula of speaking for veterans, as he had "talked to many of them in the foxholes." Navy lieutenants weren't normally in foxholes; as the word implied, they were single-occupancy shelters, and conversation at such times tended not to be discursive. Nixon dove into a trench a couple of times under Japanese air attack on Guadalcanal and elsewhere, but it is unlikely that even he discussed politics on those occasions.

One of those who was very impressed was Murray M. Chotiner, already a well-known California Republican organizer, who had been ordered out of Governor Warren's office for suggesting that Warren should remember political favors. Chotiner was a believer in the school of winning elections by attacking the enemy. He would prove uninhibited and ingenious in these rough political arts. Less satisfactory was Pat's lunch with the Republican ladies, one of whom criticized her nail polish.[78]

Nixon was formally nominated on December 1 by Day's committee to enter the Republican primary, with fifty-three of seventy-seven votes at the meeting. Roy Day telephoned him at 2 A.M. to advise him, and he and Pat remained up all night talking about this new venture.[79] The *Los Angeles Times* began touting him as an outstanding candidate, and a potential candidate for higher offices. The publisher and proprietor of the *Times*, Norman Chandler, was a conservative Republican, and his brother-in-law, John T. Garland, was a member of Day's committee. Nixon determined to visit Republican House leader Joe Martin (one of those mocked by Roosevelt in his "Martin, Barton, and Fish" jibe) to start to develop a line of attack against Voorhis's voting record (eleven months before the election).

Voorhis would claim that he had met Nixon once before, in 1940 or 1941, and to have been very coldly received by him.[80] It is not clear that this meeting was quite as Voorhis describes it, since Nixon did not remember it as particularly frosty. He recalled: "He [Voorhis] was highly idealistic. . . . He impressed everyone there and if I had voted in 1936, which I did not, I would have voted for him."[81]

On December 4, 1945, Nixon wrote Day: "I am really hopped up about this deal and I believe we can win."[82] Nixon also got one of his fellow officers who knew Harold Stassen, the young Minnesota governor Nixon had met in Bougainville, to write to Stassen and say that Nixon was interested in rounding up liberal votes for the Republicans. Within a few days of his first nomination, Nixon started to put in place a method he would use for nearly fifty years to balance the liberal and conservative Republicans, the heirs of the old Theodore Roosevelt and Taft wings of the Republican Party (currently represented by Stassen and by President Taft's son, the Republican Senate leader, Robert A. Taft). It was a tightrope that he never fell off, accident-prone though he was in some other respects.

Chapter Two

Into the Arena
1945–1950

— I —

IN JANUARY 1946, Dick and Pat Nixon again drove across the country, and again moved in with his parents until they found another home. Pat was eight months pregnant, and their daughter Patricia (always known as Tricia) was born uneventfully on February 21. Jerry Voorhis's staff studied the local press for birth, death, and marriage announcements, and on observing the Nixon birth notice sent Nixon a copy of the government pamphlet *Baby Care*, in which Voorhis wrote, "Congratulations! I look forward to meeting you in public."[1] Nixon replied, invoking the one meeting they had had, which Voorhis had found so disagreeable. Voorhis replied to this in April, predicting a "clean, open, above board" campaign and expressing the hope that they could arrange some joint public meetings or debates, as Nixon preferred. This was a mad proposal, presumably based on the assumption, without research, that Nixon would be no more formidable than the ciphers who had preceded him as Republican candidates against the congressman.

Nixon tried to recruit other campaign managers, but they declined, leaving Roy Day in place, although Nixon thought him under-qualified for the position. In practice, then and subsequently, he ran his own campaign. The Twelfth District contained 300,000 people in about four hundred square miles, with thirty-two communities. San Marino and South Pasadena, suburbs of Los Angeles, were steadily encroaching on the citrus groves. Apart from these rich fringes of the sprawling metropolis of Los Angeles, the

75

Twelfth was middle-class, middle-aged, middle in all things, with small cities and towns dispersed among agricultural areas. There was no interesting urban center, not a great deal of higher education, and nothing exotic except the lion farm at El Monte, which supplied the film industry.

Democrats led Republicans 49 percent to 46 percent in registration, but that was an heirloom from the Roosevelt era. Many more were now in fact independent voters, and many newcomers had not registered. Nixon had spent a lot more time in the district than Voorhis had, since 1936, despite his absences in the Office of Price Administration and the navy.

Nixon tore off into the district giving set speeches to service clubs. His official kickoff was at a women's club in Pomona, with an audience of four hundred on Lincoln's birthday, February 12, 1946. Roy Day became a little carried away, introducing Nixon as possibly a future president of the United States. A few days later, Nixon told the Pomona Kiwanis Club, after giving a rather learned review of the brutalities of seven centuries of Russian history, "We owe it to the world to hold the line for the growth of democratic ideals, to show how well our own democracy works here and to sell our ideas to the rest of the world and to the Russian people."[2] It was an amazingly substantial address for such a modest audience.

In April, the three Nixons moved into Dick and Pat's eleventh home together, near Whittier College, which Herman Perry had got for them. The house was never free from the serious distractions of the piercing sound and pungent smell of the mink that their next-door neighbors were raising as a side occupation. Pat had a helper for Tricia and quickly took over the campaign office. She found that the matrons of San Marino reminded her of the mindless, feckless, wealthy women she had had to wait on at the Bullock's department store in Los Angeles. Again, she had to give up smoking in public and practice innocuous conversation. She was particularly irritated when there was a forced entry at their campaign office and a stock of campaign pamphlets was stolen. (In vastly more publicized circumstances many years later, she would acidly comment, "No one seemed to mind when they broke into our campaign office.")

John H. Hoeppel, the Democratic congressman Voorhis had unseated in 1936, who had been sent to prison for taking bribes and had a deep grudge against the incumbent, offered his services to Nixon: for "$400 or $500" he would file in the Democratic primary and throw all the muck he could find against Voorhis. He wanted a civil service job from Nixon if he won. Nixon referred it to Roy Day, who referred it to his committee, which declined, but Hoeppel ran anyway, as a Prohibitionist. Voorhis subsequently claimed that Day had paid Hoeppel's filing fee, but this has never been substantiated. It would not, in any case, have been a dishonorable thing to do by the standards of hardball California politics.

Murray Chotiner, who would go into American political history arm-in-arm with Nixon as his early guru and the *ne plus ultra* of devious but effective electoral politics, was engaged as the head of public relations of the campaign. Chotiner had, at the age of nineteen, worked on Herbert Hoover's unsuccessful reelection campaign in 1932, had kicked around a number of campaigns since, including his own unsuccessful run for the state assembly in 1938, and had been banned from Earl Warren's campaign for reelection because Warren was scandalized by Chotiner's cynicism and requests for recognition of campaign services. Chotiner's continuing business was as a bail-bond lawyer, with a rather down-market clientele. He was co-manager of Knowland's campaign for reelection also. Chotiner confected a method of energizing the Nixon campaign, by deliberately confusing two similar-sounding organizations with some overlapping directors, and decrying an endorsement of Voorhis by one of them, while claiming, in effect, that they were the same organization.

The Political Action Committee of the Congress of Industrial Organizations, or CIO PAC, was a militant labor lobbying and political support group that apparently had some communist sympathizers in it and was still rather pro-Soviet Union. The National Citizens Political Action Committee, or NC PAC, was a left-liberal group that shared many directors with the CIO PAC but called only for "conciliatory diplomacy" with the U.S.S.R. It wasn't communist, but in the atmosphere that was starting to prevail, it was pretty woolly. Actors Melvyn Douglas and Ronald Reagan were members. Voorhis had received the endorsement of NC PAC but not CIO PAC, but Chotiner caused stories to be planted around the district to express alarm about the unspecific PAC endorsement of Voorhis. In fact, the distinction, in policy terms, though not in the sphere of public relations, was a subtle one.

Newspapers in the district ran expressions of concern about the "PAC" endorsement of Voorhis in the last week of April. Voorhis was only officially informed of the NC PAC endorsement on May 17. He sent some clarifying letters to a couple of newspapers, but did not recognize the danger of this issue. Nixon caught fire and spruced up his now rather tired stump speech. He developed a new mélange of conservative and liberal proposals: private sector job creation, slum clearance, and improved medical care, and support for the United Nations (which in its early days was stuffed with Latin American banana republics and friendly British dominions, and had a built-in majority for the Anglo-Americans). He railed at the political lackeys in diplomatic postings, and was already starting to pour scorn on the State Department as an anthill of incompetence led by degenerate "snobs in striped pants," but not (yet) of treason. Voorhis's local advisers attended some of Nixon's meetings and warned the congressman that Nixon was a dangerous candidate: "You will have the fight of your life to beat him," one of his trusted agents warned.[3]

The Nixon campaign secured the editorial support of local small news-papers and free sheets, often by having sympathetic advertisers take out ads in exchange for pro-Nixon stories and comment, or paying for the ads them-selves on that basis, and then getting a whole or partial rebate from the putative advertiser. This was another imaginative Chotiner flourish, and it resulted in a great deal of local press support. Voorhis was allegedly frozen out of some of the more partisan pro-Nixon papers. In May 1946, Nixon made a deferential visit to the journalistic powerhouse of Southern California, the *Los Angeles Times*. He was received by the principal politi-cal writer, Kyle Palmer, who liked Nixon and explicitly supported him, though he referred to him later as a "serious, determined, rather gawky young fellow who was out on a sort of giant-killer operation." However, he later said it wasn't long before "we began to realize that we had an extraor-dinary man on our hands."[4] After a few weeks, Nixon was back, and Palmer introduced him to the proprietor, Norman Chandler. *Times* support was steadily amplified, as Chandler and Palmer increasingly thought that Nixon might actually rid them of Voorhis.

In a formula he would often repeat, Nixon claimed no lack of regard for Voorhis personally, but portrayed him as a tax- and regulation-mad govern-mental authoritarian. Money poured into the Nixon campaign. On primary day, June 4, Nixon won the Republican primary two to one against Voorhis (both men filed under both parties), but Voorhis outpolled Nixon among Democrats by five to one, and led him overall 56 percent to 44 percent. This was still a significant improvement on two years before. Only 38 percent of eligible voters came out to vote in the primaries, so it was difficult to calculate the real depth of the drift toward the Republican candidate in the Twelfth District. The final campaign expense figures never came out, but Nixon clearly heavily outspent Voorhis, who did not return to his district until September, after two weeks in hospital in Utah for surgical removal of hemorrhoids. When he did get back to the Twelfth District, he was still convalescing and not in best form. He later good-naturedly wrote, "I was not really ready for the fray but the fray was ready for me."[5]

Although Nixon set out to rally his campaign workers to what he called a "win complex,"[6] he was, as was the usual cycle with him, momentarily downcast that he had not run ahead of Voorhis, and darkly contemplated an aborted political career. He and Pat took a brief holiday in the Canadian Rockies, and he came back physically energized but obsessed that he had only three months to overcome a substantial lead held by a five-term incumbent. As would also prove typical, Pat was a powerful source of encouragement. Strong and reasoned, neither saccharine nor a mere cheerleader, she reassured him that he was off to a good start and that it was all to play for. This was before the concept of "peaking too early," and Nixon assumed that he was twelve full points behind and would have to take drastic measures to close it up.

Roy Day was retired to fundraising and Nixon brought in Harrison McCall, a politically experienced and prosperous Republican structural engineer, as campaign manager. Chotiner was now so heavily engaged in Knowland's reelection campaign that he had to be supplemented in the public relations direction of the Nixon campaign. There was friction between Chotiner and Pat Nixon, who, not without reason, and being fundamentally more confident than her husband, considered Chotiner's methods unnecessarily cynical and apt to taint her husband's reputation. (As usual, Pat, one of the unjustly unsung heroines of American political history, was right.)

Whatever Nixon personally thought, his primary performance was adequate to inspire a number of sizable contributors with the possibility of seeing off Voorhis, who was hostile to almost every substantial commercial interest in the Twelfth District. There was plenty of room for Nixon to be comparatively desirable to all of those interests without his failing to advocate better working and social conditions for the unskilled. Money flowed in increasing amounts into the Nixon campaign, where it was directed – in accord with the candidate's fanatical determination to have a successful political launch, and the shadowy Chotiner's usual electoral ethos – into a strident assault on Voorhis's moderation and even patriotism. Nixon was careful not to take money personally, but was not overly discriminating about who contributed to his campaign, as long as no favors were attached to contributions.

In August, Herbert Hoover, the seventy-two-year-old former president, came to California, and having heard good things about Nixon, including from his wife, who had been a trustee with him on the Whittier College board, met with Nixon. Hoover and his son confirmed the good reports they had heard about the young candidate and assured him that the campaign would not cost him anything.

It is surprising, at first thought, that Hoover retained any influence, so unsuccessful had he been as president, but he remained a symbol to all who resented the Roosevelt expansion of government and tax increases. What were remembered now were not Hoover's theory that the unemployed fared well selling apples, or the "Hoovervilles," as Roosevelt called the vast improvised slums that arose for the drifting unemployed in every large American city, or the deflationary measures that aggravated the Depression, or his isolationism prior to Pearl Harbor. Hoover was the only living ex-president and he had been a distinguished distributor of aid to refugees after the First World War. He was seen as a statesman of the conservative Republicans, efficient yet compassionate. His support was useful to Nixon, in 1946 and after.

Nixon continued to apply his talents at ideological diversity, and had met with Harold Stassen when he came to California in May. Stassen got one of his California fund-raisers to help Nixon, and Nixon gave unspecific promise that if he was successful in his election he could provide access for Stassen to the big California delegation at the 1948 Republican convention. Nixon's views were in many respects closer to Stassen's than to Hoover's, but he developed techniques of packaging his opinions on each issue that avoided sharp divisions. Thus he was for every liberal domestic goal, provided that the private sector, not the government, accomplished it (medical care, better housing, etc.), and he was a strong internationalist, but the United States had to end the appeasement of the Russians and the general foreign policy incompetence of the current administration.

Nixon would request a return visit by Stassen to speak in his favor, but this was vetoed by Earl Warren, who also declined to rebut Voorhis's insinuation that he was the governor's preferred candidate in the Twelfth

District. This opened up a feud between Nixon and Warren that would be carried on for decades, to the highest offices in the nation.

Nixon's formal campaign kickoff was in August in Arcadia, and his host was someone who had deserted Voorhis because of the congressman's failure to get his son into West Point. Nixon would take support almost wherever he could find it. Voorhis was grossly overconfident about his ability to defeat Nixon in a debate, and before he had even returned to his district, a joint appearance had been arranged for September 20. The previous Republican candidate had been so inept and disorganized that Voorhis had had to introduce his opponent at such meetings, a task he graciously accomplished. Voorhis was a ponderous and rambling speaker, but amiable in manner, self-confident, and well-liked in his own district. He still had no idea what sort of opposition awaited him when he recovered sufficiently from his hemorrhoidal problems to face his electors.

Before the agreed meeting could take place, an unrepresentatively liberal group in South Pasadena had convoked, for September 13, an all-candidates' meeting. Knowland and his opponent, Will Rogers Jr., named proxies (Chotiner for Knowland), and the real target of interest for the conveners were the state assembly candidates. But Voorhis didn't feel he could decline the invitation of such loyal supporters, so he accepted, and so did Richard Nixon; they would provide the only direct exchange between candidates on this evening. (Earl Warren had been nominated by both parties for reelection as governor and was virtually unopposed.) Nixon managed to arrange to speak last, on grounds of previous commitments, and attended several Voorhis appearances in the preceding week, incognito, to take his opponent's measure. Nixon prepared for the debate for three days.

The September 13 meeting took place in the South Pasadena High School auditorium. Nixon had arranged for planted questions and largely packed the hall, putting bunches of vocal supporters front, back, and at each side, "diamonding" the house. An ostensibly independent Nixon front organization passed out to the arriving audience a two-page flyer that was called "Facts About Jerry Voorhis," in which the candidate was identified as a Socialist Party member up to 1934, and a socialist at heart still. The PAC endorsement was played up. Voorhis used his fifteen minutes in an undisciplined, engaging stream of consciousness about how to make the postwar world, and especially Southern California, a better place. Nixon entered just when Voorhis finished, shook hands with his opponent, received great (pre-arranged) applause, and began speaking, apparently with complete spontaneity. Nixon spoke clearly and fairly rapidly and railed against shortages and irresponsible labor and management practices, taking on the Australian-born and allegedly communist longshoremen's union leader Harry Bridges, who was then threatening to shut down the harbors of the West Coast in a strike.

The questions began with a planted Nixon query about Voorhis being an ex-socialist, and about his fuzzy money supply ideas, which elicited, as had been intended, an incomprehensible answer. Next came a Voorhis-planted question about Nixon's making false charges that Voorhis had been endorsed by the CIO PAC. Nixon pulled from his pocket a copy of the NC PAC resolution of support, advanced toward Voorhis with long strides and belligerently uplifted chin, and asked him to comment. Voorhis had come partway to meet Nixon and then wandered back to his place and read the document amid considerable tumult in the hall. He hesitantly stated that it was a different organization. Nixon was ready for that; he recited the names of the interlocking directors and said, "It's the same thing, virtually, when they have the same directors." Nixon played all his roles, undergraduate actor and debater, righteous Quaker, poker player.

Posterity has made much of Nixon's alleged sleazy practice in deliberately confusing the voters with these two organizations. In fact, the CIO, which would soon be united with the American Federation of Labor and had been directed for many years prior to 1940 by John L. Lewis of the United Mine Workers, was not a communist organization. Nor was Sidney Hillman, the recently deceased head of the Amalgamated Clothing Workers and of the CIO PAC, whom the Republicans had mythologized as a virtual agent of chaos of the Kremlin's. (Hillman had been a Roosevelt supporter, whom FDR indulged at times, though he didn't much like labor leaders and could never get it straight which union Hillman headed and which was led by David Dubinsky [Garment Workers].) As has been mentioned, there was not a great deal, in policy and advocacy terms, to choose between the two PACs, though there was a perception that the CIO was farther to the left and it was an aggressive union.

What Nixon and Chotiner did was mischievous, but not worse than that, and if Voorhis had not been so complacent, he would not only have planted a question about it, but been ready with a strong rejoinder. Instead, he was ineffectual and the house, half-packed by Nixon, clearly went over to the Republican candidate. The questions resumed, and Nixon gave sharper, more articulate replies than his opponent. The evening ended when former congressman John Hoeppel, very drunk despite being the Prohibition candidate, stumbled forward and asked Voorhis about his support for communists in the Spanish Civil War. The meeting descended into farce and contumely. It was a decisive victory for Nixon.

In the aftermath of this debacle, Voorhis asked NC PAC to take back its "qualified endorsement." This had the reverse effect of what had been intended. At the next debate, September 20 in Whittier before two hundred veterans, Voorhis was precise and plausible, and when Nixon raised the NC PAC endorsement, Voorhis said that he could not be held responsible for those who gave him unsolicited endorsements. The debate was probably a draw and Voorhis gave a good account of himself, but it was a much less well publicized occasion, with a much smaller audience.

Chotiner challenged Voorhis, on Nixon's behalf, to five more debates, and two were agreed as they tuned up the Red smear. The Nixon camp leaked to the friendly local press "six pro-Soviet votes" by Voorhis in Congress. All the votes were for Lend-Lease shipments to the U.S.S.R. to assist in the battle against the Nazis, as the administration had requested, and received bipartisan support. But they were implicitly presented as more sinister. This tactic wasn't directly traceable to Nixon, but there wasn't much doubt about who was setting the tone of the campaign. Nixon, in a formulation that became extremely tedious, droned near the end of the stock campaign speech, "I do not question the motives of my opponent in voting the PAC line in Congress."

Nixon also made a lot out of the opening of a CIO political office in the district. (The CIO hadn't even endorsed Voorhis, though they would certainly have preferred him to Nixon, and while it was an aggressive union and had some communist members, it wasn't unpatriotic.) Nixon literature began to associate Voorhis with the quasi-communist congressman from East Harlem, Vito Marcantonio, and with the left-liberal Los Angeles congresswoman Helen Gahagan Douglas. None of this was illegal or grossly unethical by rough-and-tumble political standards, but it was pretty tawdry at times and did attract a lot of eventual sympathy for the bumbling, gentlemanly, absentminded plodder, Voorhis, a man full of good intentions but completely out of tune with the abrasive politics of a Red-baiting era.

J. Edgar Hoover gave a speech in San Francisco to the American Legion in September 1946 saying that there were "at least 100,000 communists . . . at large in the country,"[7] many of them in places of influence, and that even the churches had been infiltrated. This was nonsense, but Hoover had cultivated his public image and was taken seriously on such matters by most people.

Nixon's diligent research unearthed the fact that of 132 bills sponsored by Voorhis in the past four years, only one had been adopted, and that was one that "transferred the activities affecting domestic rabbits from one federal department to another."[8] This was technically true, but was an outrageous mislabeling of the act in question. Nixon would go on to the well-tried line that "one had to be a rabbit to get effective representation in this congressional district." Voorhis finally researched his own record, late in the campaign, and the 132 bills came down to only twenty-seven roll calls. His supposedly "subversive" or "pro-Russian" votes had nothing to do with Russia and concerned school lunches, conservation, foreign aid, oil prices, the poll tax, Lend-Lease, veterans' housing, and a vote not to exclude insurance companies from some anti-trust regulations. These were not particularly controversial votes, and the incumbent and his staff seemed to forget that he had sponsored the "Voorhis Act" in 1940, requiring the registration of communists. It took Voorhis until very late to respond to Nixon's preposterous charges at all.

Holders of licenses to sell liquor were warned, again by an apparently unaffiliated organization, about Voorhis's plan to hand out grain for international food aid, which would allegedly short-supply the liquor companies, and bartenders and others who came in frequent touch with the public were invited to militate against a vote for Voorhis.[9] A bartender about to serve a thirsty man could be a persuasive political canvasser.

The next debate between the candidates was at the academic complex at Claremont College. Voorhis's supporters were finally out in strength and prevented the mob humiliation of their candidate, but Nixon won the debate, partly by reciting a plan for preventing strikes in the public sector that Voorhis recognized only after the fact as having been lifted from proposals he had made in a bill he himself had introduced. Nixon then had the effrontery to take Voorhis aside privately and "bawl the hell" out of him for referring to him as Lieutenant Commander Nixon, supposedly to drive off the enlisted men, who would resent an officer.[10] Nixon was so offended that thereafter he pointedly referred to Voorhis as someone who had not served in the war. President Roosevelt had in fact forbidden war service by congressmen, thus preserving, inter alia, Lyndon B. Johnson for the home front.

The Nixon-Chotiner bag of tricks was quite innovative. Grocers and butchers were encouraged, when out of anything, to put signs in their windows reading "No Meat [or whatever] See Your Congressman." It was alleged that Herman Perry's Bank of America made volunteer work for Nixon a condition of employment in some branches. The Nixon campaign headquarters had a lot of small appliances in its window, such as toasters, which had not been manufactured in the United States for years because of war requirements, and people were told that the campaign would telephone heavily throughout the district and that those who answered their telephones "Vote for Nixon" would be offered a free appliance. Many people answered their telephones accordingly, but not many toasters were handed out.

There were allegations, which have been largely accepted by many historians ever since, that the Nixon campaign was associated with anti-Semitic activities linking Voorhis to questionable Jewish interests, and that it was even in league with the Ku Klux Klan, although Nixon publicly became a member of the National Association for the Advancement of Colored People in Monrovia, California, in the midst of the campaign. These allegations are not substantiated and are not believable, and indicate the irrational hostility that persisted toward Nixon for many years.[11] It is also alleged that the Nixon campaign sponsored a random telephone canvass of the district, anonymously advising respondents that Voorhis was a communist. There may have been some of this, but it is unlikely that Nixon approved it, or that it changed many votes.

The final debate was in the San Gabriel Civic Auditorium on October 28 in front of fifteen hundred people. Voorhis opened with an attack on monopoly and a pitch for greater social benefits, and Nixon replied with his opposition to excessive regulation, taxation, and interference with the genius of the private sector. Nixon did emphasize his support of the Truman administration's emerging hard line against Soviet Communism. The Republican slogan throughout the country was "Had Enough?" and Nixon pitched to that sentiment, envisioning the returning veteran, the victim of shortages, the white-collar worker hoping for a long-delayed raise. Neither candidate made a serious error, but Nixon was much the more effective debater and speaker.

Voorhis had never before had to fight a serious election, having just stood as Roosevelt's man, and he had no idea how to wage a toe-to-toe battle with a determined adversary. According to the *San Gabriel Sun*, Voorhis "pauses, breathes heavily, adjusts his glasses nervously with both hands," etc.[12] Voorhis supporters started heckling Nixon in the last days with bullhorns and there were some disorderly scenes. Voorhis finally accused Nixon of being financed by the oil companies, which brought an angry response from Nixon's supporters. The *Los Angeles Times* loyally reported the inconceivable canard that Nixon's total campaign expenses had been $370, compared with $1,000 for Voorhis. A moron let loose in the Twelfth District to see the billboards and look at the newspapers would notice that the Nixon campaign was spending a lot of money.

On election night the Nixons had dinner with Roy Day. Voorhis led in the earliest returns, as the hand-counted ballots came slowly in, and Nixon was initially despondent. He pulled even at about 9 P.M., and his lead grew steadily after that. Reversing the primary result, Nixon won 57 percent of the vote, a margin of about sixteen thousand, and took twenty-nine of the district's thirty-two municipalities, including Voorhis's home town, San Dimas. It was a country-wide sweep, as the Republicans gained control of both houses of the Congress for the first time in eighteen years. The rabidly Republican *Chicago Tribune* called it the greatest victory for the Republicans since Appomattox.[13] The Republicans ran well across California, and Knowland was easily reelected. Voorhis decamped to Chicago and became a leader in cooperative and lay Episcopalian activities, disillusioned with politics.

Nixon made a gracious victory speech and then responded to an invitation to come to the *Los Angeles Times*. He and Pat, his parents, and brother Don and his wife went to the suite of Norman Chandler in the *Times* building. The whole Nixon party asked for glasses of milk and then Nixon followed Mrs. Chandler toward the kitchen and asked for a double bourbon. He did not want his parents to see him take a drink, any more than he had wanted them to know that the bartenders of their district had been brainwashing their clienteles on his behalf. The Nixons went on to the Committee of 100 party at the Huntington Hotel in Pasadena. Nixon played the piano, and his supporters removed the trousers of one of his fund-raisers and threw them up on to a chandelier.[14]

Nixonographers portrayed this first campaign as a citizens' crusade in which Nixon, to pay campaign expenses, had to sell the suit he had bought to be able to get out of uniform, and Pat had to sell Will Ryan's almost worthless ranch. In fact, Herman Perry and Herbert Hoover were as good as their word: Nixon did not spend any of his own money. Though the initial acknowledgement was, as the *Times* had reported, of only $370 of expenses, filings with the secretary of state of California showed Nixon campaign expenses of $17,774, and less than $2,000 for Voorhis, and money spent on front or supportive organizations in the interest of the Nixon campaign might have doubled that. This was a prodigious sum for a congressional election in 1946.

A great mythology has grown around this campaign. It was expensive, but Nixon did not subsequently sell favors or vote otherwise than he had indicated he would while campaigning, and he did not personally accept a cent. It was a messy campaign, but Voorhis, though anti-communist, was a moderate socialist at heart and this was now out of favor in the Twelfth District, and in the country generally.

Politics is a rough occupation, and Voorhis had led a sheltered life. He should have seen Nixon coming and responded more effectively and promptly to his attacks. It was not an edifying example of clarity of political debate at its best, but it wasn't the infamous prostitution of the political process that Nixon-haters have sold to a drooling posterity, either.

Herman Perry gathered his banking friends together and told them that he would not live to see it but that most of them would one day be Dick Nixon's guests in the White House. The Nixons' friends Jack and Helene Drown set a bottle of sherry aside for the day the Nixons took up residence there. Privately, Nixon made no secret of his ambitions, though he was naturally very circumspect publicly. Dick and Pat went for a brief motoring vacation in Mexico, leaving his parents to take care of Tricia and bring her to Washington. Frank Nixon had thoughtfully packed the congressman-elect's car for him, and when the young couple reentered the United States, customs officials required that it be completely unpacked. Nixon never mentioned that he was a congressman-elect, which would have spared him this travail, because he did not want to seem to be throwing his weight around.

— II —

They arrived in Washington in early December, and stayed in the venerable Mayflower Hotel. There were problems finding a house in Washington, since almost all housing construction had stopped during the war and the shortage for young families was acute. Frank and Hannah arrived with Tricia in time for the installation of the new Congress on January 2, 1947, and the hotel altered its normal policy and permitted a crib in her parents' room.

Nixon was now well out of the poverty trap, with no debts, savings of almost fifteen thousand dollars (at least twenty times as much in the money of sixty years later), and sundry assets, as well as the support of wealthy friends.

Voorhis, after agonizing over it for some time, sent Nixon a very gentlemanly letter, recalling "most poignantly" his arrival as a congressman-elect ten years earlier, and promising any assistance Nixon thought he might be able to give. He added, "I have refrained, for reasons I am sure you will understand, from making any references to the circumstances of the campaign recently conducted in our district. It would only have spoiled the letter."[15] This message made the circuit from Washington to Whittier and back to the Mayflower, and Nixon responded in person, by materializing unannounced in Voorhis's office. Their conversation was cordial, but Nixon concluded on the discordantly presumptuous note of asking for Voorhis's congressional district mailing list, which the outgoing congressman declined to give him. Voorhis did write in his memoirs that they parted "as personal friends" and predicted that Nixon would be "fairly conservative" but a "good" member of the House of Representatives.

The Republicans came rolling overconfidently into Washington. They assumed that they were just the first wave of a sea change that would push back much of the New Deal. Like Herbert Hoover, they still thought that the Roosevelt presidency was aberrant, a product of the infelicitous combination of an economic depression for which the Republicans were blameless and the demagoguery and political flimflammery of Roosevelt, a consummate trickster. They were convinced that Truman was a lame duck, serving out Roosevelt's term but clearly not up to being president and unlikely even to be reselected by his own party. They set about unwinding the mutations of the New Deal with a grim sense of stamping out a flickering epidemic, sanitizing the capitol and fumigating or otherwise exterminating bacteria.

In the scramble for House committee seats, Nixon at first wanted Judiciary, but was advised that that would be unavailable to a freshman, so he asked for and received Education and Labor, which would be at the forefront of the Republican assault on the labor unions. He had received some national recognition for knocking off a prominent incumbent, and had some powerful backers, including the former president, so he started ahead of many of the new intake.

Nixon had also sought a seat on the House Un-American Activities Committee (HUAC), and had arranged for the new Speaker, Joe Martin (whom he had called upon a year earlier to get some pointers on how to embarrass Voorhis), to be lobbied by a group of wealthy California political contributors in favor of Nixon's HUAC candidacy. Nixon was deemed to be a good lawyer, had earned some gratitude from the leadership by getting rid of Voorhis, and was thought to be intelligent and sensible enough to be a restraining influence on HUAC's witch-hunting instincts but alert and sound enough on the anti-communist issues to work with the senior members. Nixon had avidly sought this position, because he recognized that scorching out communists was likely to be a political growth stock, and he knew what a group of bigoted, simplistic Red-baiters had infested HUAC up to then.

In his memoirs, Nixon claimed that he had gone on to HUAC reluctantly, "because of [its] dubious reputation," but in fact he ardently sought the seat but skillfully disguised it. Politically, it could have been the kiss of death.[16] But the way he approached it, that was unlikely. Martin did not even put his meeting with Nixon's wealthy California backers on his calendar, so wary was he of seeming to be influenced by moneyed interests.[17]

On the Education and Labor Committee, Nixon was from the start in the forefront of the move to roll back the legal position of organized labor. With great fanfare he went in February 1947 to Scranton, Pennsylvania, where he purported to canvass unionized miners and factory workers and find them concerned about the democracy, financial integrity, and tendency to physical violence of their unions. This is not implausible, since American labor had committed many excesses and benefited beyond what the Roosevelt administration had intended from some New Deal measures.

At the start of the Roosevelt administration, the objective had been to raise prices and incomes, conventional inflation not based on simple debasement of the currency. Roosevelt and his advisers were trying to ensure that demand increased, pulling profits and employment up behind it. To this end, the National Industrial Recovery Act, the core of the first New Deal, tolerated cartels and price-fixing by companies, and, on the side of the employees, encouraged collective bargaining, not so much out of love of labor unions but to improve wages and reduce the work week, generating, it was hoped, more jobs and more demand.

In 1935, Senator Robert Wagner of New York put through a bill further assisting collective bargaining with what amounted to a closed shop. Roosevelt was ambivalent about it, and was distrustful of labor leaders generally, but signed the bill to conserve his political constituency. With the Supreme Court decision in 1936 that the NIRA was unconstitutional, the toleration of cartels ended and there was an official imbalance of legal force between the unions and companies that was largely invisible during the war, when both sides generally behaved sensibly. By 1947, all the Republicans and most of the Democrats had real reservations about the conduct of many of the labor leaders; there were too many strikes, too much labor violence, too little democracy in the unions, too much labor corruption, and too many extreme leftists among some of the union executives.

In 1947 the Republicans set out to repeal Wagner and give the nation a right-to-work law. It is not unlikely that a great many unionized workers agreed with this, because the unions had seriously abused their positions. The Democrats were not going to the wall for them. In the thirties, management abuse of employees had been a substantial problem, and corruption and irresponsibility on the part of labor leaders, though hardly unknown, was objectively a lesser evil. By 1947, facts and perceptions had changed.

Nixon was one of the principal authors of the Taft-Hartley Act, which repealed the closed shop, banned secondary boycotts and sympathy strikes, restricted picketing, regulated union political contributions, and provided for an eighty-day "cooling off period" before strikes could occur in designated strategic industries. Nixon intervened importantly in the debate, assuring the House that with this legislation, "the fate of millions of workers . . . would not be settled in the sumptuous quarters of a labor baron in the Carlton Hotel, not in some smoke-filled room."[*] He claimed it was a pro-labor bill, and rhetorically asked if the American workers objected to "the right to speak freely in their union meetings . . . to vote freely in democratic elections for their officers . . . to the fact that we have attempted to control violence, mass picketing and other abuses, which all good union

---

[*] The original smoke-filled room was the one in the Blackstone Hotel in Chicago, where the Republican bosses selected Warren Harding as their 1920 presidential candidate.

leaders have decried? . . . I submit to this house that the man who goes out on strike and has more to lose, should decide whether to strike or not." He had already developed a weakness for hyperbole, which would cause him many problems: "I see no difference whatever between the dictatorial practices of labor and those of Hitler and Mussolini." [18]

Taft-Hartley passed the House 308 to 107, which indicates that almost half the Democrats deserted their union allies. Nixon received great credit as a co-author of the legislation, and wrote a summary of Taft-Hartley for the *Congressional Record* in July 1947 entitled "The Truth About the New Labor Law." Hundreds of thousands of copies were distributed by the Republican Party throughout the country, and hundreds of Republican candidates used it as their basic source in defending the legislation in their states and districts. Nixon's role in the legislation was an almost unprecedented triumph for a freshman congressman, and it helped bring him to national prominence in his first few months in Washington. He would retain and add to that status for nearly two whole generations.

Nixon had given his maiden speech in the House on February 18, 1947, just after his return from his fact-finding mission to Scranton. He used the occasion to give himself a flying start in HUAC matters, calling for a vote of contempt of Congress against Gerhart Eisler, a longtime communist who had been in and out of the United States for fifteen years and had had a volcanic exchange with HUAC two weeks before. Nixon slightly exceeded his allotted ten minutes but spoke fluently and without histrionics, and was credited with making a fine legal argument. His motion passed, and Eisler was sentenced to a year in prison; he later jumped bail while his conviction was on appeal and returned a hero to East Germany (whose puppet Stalinist government would declare the next year that it had "lost confidence in the people").

Little noticed in Nixon's speech was a theme he had first sounded in one of the *Los Angeles Times* oratory contests in 1929, when he was only sixteen – the view that freedom of speech and expression did not extend to advocacy of the destruction of that freedom. Generally, the United States and other advanced English-speaking countries have held freedom of expression to be absolute, except for sedition, treason, extreme defamation, and offenses to public morals. The advocacy of dictatorship or despotism is generally considered to be an acceptable, if unrepresentative, use of the freedom of speech in the United States, as in Britain and Canada.

While Nixon's Eisler speech was an impressive and successful indict-ment, it took certain liberties with the facts, in the manner of an indictment, as opposed to an objective presentation. Eisler was not really, as Nixon alleged, "a seasoned agent of the Communist International . . . [whose role was] to direct and mastermind the political and espionage activities of the Communist Party in the United States."[19] Eisler had been taken out of the HUAC hearing two weeks before, not because he refused to answer the committee's questions, which would be the ground for a contempt citation such as Nixon's, but because, claiming to be a political prisoner, he insisted on making an opening statement. The committee would not permit this until he was questioned. Nor was there any evidence, as Nixon claimed to the House, that Eisler had had anything to do with the massive Gouzenko espionage ring recently uncovered in Ottawa, Canada. FBI records ulti-mately indicated that the Bureau, in a frequently repeated pattern, had used the HUAC and friendly elements of the press to end-run the Justice Department, to which the FBI was officially subordinate. But J. Edgar Hoover was such a power in Washington that he was subordinate only to the president, and not always even to him. Eisler was not the spymaster Nixon and the FBI implied, but a lower-level Soviet informant.

HUAC in 1947 was, apart from Nixon, a singularly undistinguished group. J. Parnell Thomas of New Jersey, narrow-minded, histrionic, and generally rather limited, was the chairman. More competent was Karl E. Mundt, Republican of South Dakota, an educated man whose sole purpose on the committee appeared to be the hunt for subversives, as if he were engaged in the permanent sport of pursuing an anonymous quarry. He was smarter than his perpetual masquerade as a hayseed indicated, but he was a political grandstander with no sense of responsibility. The other Republican, apart from Nixon, was John McDowell, a cipher, who owned a small newspaper in his district in Pennsylvania.

The ranking Democrat, John Rankin of Mississippi, was a vintage Southern redneck, a bigot and an ignoramus. Considerably smarter was F. Edward Hebert of Louisiana, a junior sidekick of the late Huey P. Long, and a friend of Long's son Russell (who would serve nearly forty years in the Senate). He was the clever, somewhat courtly, and more egalitarian type of Southern politician, but he had great difficulty resisting the general stam-pede to turn HUAC into a magic carpet for the publicity-seeking of its members and an outlet for sensational and completely unfounded allegations of subversion lurking everywhere. The other Democrat, John Wood of Georgia, an ex-Klansman, was a malignant nonentity. George Reedy, United Press HUAC reporter and twenty years later President Lyndon Johnson's press secretary, thought, possibly without exaggeration, that apart from Nixon, they were "the worst collection of people that have ever been assembled in the entire history of American politics."[20] (Reedy recognized Nixon's merit and intelligence but found both Nixon and his wife strangely stiff and unspontaneous, though there could be some retrospective partisanship in this.[21])

It is fantastic, sixty years later, to imagine that the United States had such a preposterous congressional committee, with such an Orwellian name, and so dangerously, malevolently composed. It began investigating fascist influences in the thirties, swung toward communism in the late-thirties, and built to a fiery coruscation of smearing and persecuting in the late-forties and early-fifties, before blowing up like a dreadful, self-destroying meteor. As it was still gaining in speed and visibility, Richard Nixon briefly lent it some legitimacy, and took from it great momentum for himself.

The HUAC staff was a rag-tag of ex-communists and former FBI agents, mainly fugitives from the espionage version of the rubber-gun brigade, still recovering from shell shock. The chief investigator, Robert Stripling, was almost uneducated legally, and had advanced through the years from being a document filer for the former chairman, Martin Dies, dedicated to HUAC but without any perspective on what the higher purposes or consequences of the actions of the committee were. HUAC's chief fixer was a fervent ex-communist (and ex-manager of the *Daily Worker*), Benjamin Mandel. He was an almost mindless zealot, but he engaged the informers in the demimonde that provided the committee its leads, and managed, in his fashion, relations with the press and the FBI, receiving and planting leaks, destroying reputations without any due process, and operating at the seamy margin of congressional prerogatives in this fetid time.

Nixon's detractors would claim that exposure to these people infected him for the balance of his career with a weakness for using sleazy people in underhanded schemes. This is not a sustainable case. He was careful in how he used the committee and he never returned to association with such people, though a few of them bore a slight resemblance to some of the doubtful characters that arose twenty-five years later in the lower echelons of the Watergate affair. Nixon had little to do with the later group, and this was a coincidence, not an enduring addiction.[22]

When the Education and Labor Committee, not to be left behind, held hearings on whether there was a communist element in the 1941 Allis-Chalmers strike in Wisconsin, Nixon was impressed by the probing questions of Milwaukee congressman Charles J. Kersten. He asked Kersten for some help with his HUAC activities after buttonholing Kersten in the lobby of the Mayflower Hotel. Kersten was a strong Roman Catholic who drew most of his information from the anti-communist specialists of the Roman Catholic hierarchy, and introduced Nixon to them: Monsignor Fulton J. Sheen and Father John Cronin.

Sheen was at that time about to become the American director of the Pontifical Society for the Propagation of the Faith, and Cronin was a Ph.D. whom Nixon had probably met during the war when Cronin was on Baltimore's Rationing Board, and who was now the assistant director of the National Catholic Welfare Conference. He had been active in Catholic unions during the war and was appalled at reports he received, which he passed on to his superiors and to the FBI, of strongarm communist union activity. He developed an interchange of information between the FBI and the Roman Catholic Church throughout the country, and was thus at the source of a general exchange of counter-subversive intelligence. Cronin also had input from the State Department's security unit, and from HUAC's Mandel, so he was in some respects the best qualified anti-communist in the country. This was before Sheen became a national figure with a television program for his flamboyant discussions of the Gospel and reception of the conversions of the famous. Sheen was closer to the Church leaders, especially New York's Francis Cardinal Spellman, than Cronin, but Cronin was closer to the FBI. Both were valued informants of Kersten, and Cronin, especially, became a vital source for Nixon.

This gave Nixon, almost from the start, a better channel of information than HUAC possessed, because all HUAC had was its Keystone Kops, jolly-hockey-sticks staff, and tactically planted leads from the FBI designed to upstage the Justice Department or mislead the press, while Nixon was getting the real feed from the FBI and the vigilant Roman Catholic anti-communist brigades. Cronin worked with the China Lobby, alarmed at the deterioration of the anti-communist side in the Chinese civil war, and determined to agitate for increased aid to Chiang Kai-shek, the Chinese

Nationalist leader. Cronin, Mandel, and others, including future Nixon biographer Ralph de Toledano, founded the magazine *Plain Talk* as a rallying point for the like-minded.

Cronin had a large swath of entire FBI files, so intimate had he become with his sources and recipients. He showed Nixon a great deal of material, in which suspected communists in or formerly in government were clearly identified, including *Time* magazine assistant editor Whittaker Chambers, and former State Department official and head of the Carnegie Endowment for International Peace, Alger Hiss.

This combination of detailed and relatively high-quality intelligence, and the power of an important congressional committee otherwise in the hands of a group of witch-hunting yokels, gave Nixon a potentially very strong position from which to exercise leverage on the fury of events, as the anti-Red tide steadily rose. He would be ready, and his time was not far off.

Although Cronin's information was better than the scraps and squealings from lowlife informants that HUAC largely lived on, it was far from infallible. Cronin produced his "The Problem of American Communism in 1945: Facts and Recommendations" for the bishops and selected other leaders. He named John J. McCloy, who had been assistant secretary of war and was about to become high commissioner in Germany, Congressional Librarian Archibald MacLeish, and *New York Herald Tribune* Washington bureau chief Bert Andrews, as among four hundred prominent "pro-Soviet" people. All would prove as dedicated Cold Warriors as Nixon. Cronin calculated that almost two thirds of American communists were Jews (a finding that may not have been accurate, was not particularly relevant because of the small numbers of American communists, and in any case did not do wonders for Catholic-Jewish relations in the United States). Interestingly, Cronin estimated the African-American proportion of American communists at 14 percent, only slightly above their share of the entire U.S. population.

The anti-communist atmosphere steadily intensified. On March 12, 1947, President Truman, following the advice of Republican senator Arthur H. Vandenberg to "scare the hell out of the American people," told the Congress that the United States had to help the anti-communist faction in the Greek Civil War, and the Turks, as a matter of absolute national interest in a worldwide struggle with tyranny. The president said the world was threatened by the totalitarian governments and that "nearly every nation must choose," and the United States must "support free peoples."[23] The measure passed without significant opposition. The British had been propping up the non-communist Greek government for two years, but on February 21 they informed the State Department that the communists would prevail if the United States didn't assist the Greek government in the civil war in that country. This prompted Truman to act.

The inimitable J. Edgar Hoover appeared at HUAC and conferred an avuncular pep talk: He compared communism to a disease in an epidemic stage and said that there were more communists per capita in the United States than there had been in Russia at the time of Lenin. This was almost certainly untrue, and in any case irrelevant, as Russia was a war-ravaged society where the vast mass of people had been trodden down under the degenerating Romanov absolute monarchy for centuries. Russia was a tinderbox. Also, communism in 1917 was led by Russians and was to some extent a patriotic movement, despite its universalist pretensions. American communism in the 1940s was led by nonentities taking their orders from Stalin. The about-to-be-famous Red-hunter Senator Joseph R. McCarthy didn't even know that Earl Browder was the American Communist Party leader. Hoover claimed, on skimpy historic and current evidence, that in Russia in 1917 there was one communist for every 2,777 people, and that in the United States there was one communist for every 1,814 people.[24] This would have meant 800,000 American communists, which was probably twenty times the real number, and of which most were passive malcontents, not a rich crop of Lenins, Trotskys, and Stalins. Hoover's was the sort of statement that could be assured of firing the excitable imaginations of HUAC members and staff, as the director intended.

Nixon had not met Hoover before and asked if there was a particular area of acute communist infiltration. Hoover pointed to radio, universities, and the motion picture industry. Hoover was well aware of Nixon's excellent anti-subversive background, but was probably not aware of how much indirect access Nixon had to the Bureau's files. Theirs would be a long and jejune relationship, leading all the way to Nixon's generous eulogy of Hoover at a state funeral a quarter of a century later.

HUAC obligingly followed the FBI director's advice and zeroed in on Hollywood. Nixon was not directly involved in the preparation of what would be one of HUAC's most publicized moments, a showdown with a group of defiant leftist screenwriters, known as the Hollywood Ten, one of whom would call the whole episode "the time of the toad."[*] [25] Nixon did allow that it was time to "throw the fear of God into Hollywood." When the subcommittee held massively publicized hearings in Los Angeles in October 1947, he attended and put some questions, including asking Jack Warner how many "anti-communist" films Warner Brothers had done. Warner replied that one was in progress. Nixon did go to the outer limits of what was acceptable questioning by a responsible congressman by asking what was the impact of showing the film version of John Steinbeck's *The Grapes of Wrath* (for which book more than anything else, Steinbeck won the Nobel Prize for Literature) abroad. The book and the film lauded Roosevelt's New Deal, but this was hardly communism, and the fact that there were distressed conditions and millions of destitute people in the United States in the early thirties was hardly a self-flagellating revelation to the world, nor a condition unique to America, much less an incitement to consider the virtues of communism.

The fatuous grandstanding of HUAC, added to the glitz of Hollywood, produced an astonishing spectacle. The opening witnesses spoke with dignity. Novelist Ayn Rand spoke of the Soviet Union she fled in 1926: "It is almost impossible to convey to a free people what it is like to live in a total-itarian dictatorship. . . . It is in a way good that you cannot even conceive of what it is like. . . . They try to live a human life, but, you understand, it is totally inhuman. Try to imagine what it is like if you are in constant terror from morning till night and at night you are waiting for the doorbell to ring, where you are afraid of anything and everybody, living in a country where human life is . . . less than nothing, and you know it. You don't know who or when is going to do what to you because you may have friends who spy on you, where there is no law [nor] any rights of any kind."

Four prominent actors appeared: Adolphe Menjou, Robert Taylor, Gary Cooper, and the head of the Screen Actors Guild, Ronald Reagan. Menjou surprised many by saying that he was born in Pittsburgh, describing J. Edgar Hoover as "a close personal friend," warning about the porosity

---

[*] The ten were Alvah Bessie, Herbert Biberman, Lester Cole, Edward Dmytryk, Ring Lardner Jr., John Howard Lawson, Albert Maltz, Samuel Ornitz, Adrian Scott, and Dalton Trumbo. Dmytryk became a friendly witness; Lardner and Trumbo confessed to being ex-communists. Bertolt Brecht would have made it eleven, but he departed the jurisdiction (and was certainly a communist, though by this time not a very enthusiastic one).

of the Mexican border (which was prescient, but not because of subversion), and preaching the virtues of compulsory military service. Robert Taylor drew great applause by calling for the abolition of the Communist Party in the United States and the expulsion of all communists, though he acknowledged that he was not sure of the legalities of this. Gary Cooper was more guarded, but allowed that communism wasn't "on the level." Ronald Reagan gave a more detailed and knowledgeable description of some of the techniques of the Hollywood left, but resisted recourse to more coercive measures: "Sir, I detest, I abhor their philosophy . . . but at the same time I never as a citizen want to see our country . . . urged, by either fear or resentment of this group, [to the point] that we ever compromise with any of our democratic principles through that fear or resentment. I still think that democracy can do it." He was already cooperating with the FBI. This was Nixon's first meeting with Reagan; their relations would be generally cordial as their careers meandered through the decades to the shared elder statesmanship of ex-presidents.[26] There were some spectacular confrontations with other, less cooperative witnesses, but not involving Nixon, who stayed away from most of those sessions.

Nixon did move the motion, as he had with Eisler, to cite the Hollywood Ten for contempt of Congress, but they had refused outright to answer questions, unlike Eisler, who was prepared to respond if he had been allowed to make an opening statement. It was an unsavory business, but Nixon skirted the worst aspects of it. As HUAC, Hoover, and large parts of the media whipped up the anti-communist fervor, Hollywood, thoroughly cowed and very concerned about box office, began producing a great many anti-communist films, ranging, as had the anti-Nazi films of a decade before, from the meritorious to the juvenile.

— III —

Nixon put in his usual long hours, with a staff of two women and a male assistant, Bill Arnold, who had worked on his campaign. He would not have been Nixon if he did not chafe at the relative lack of influence inflicted by the seniority system, to which he responded by co-founding the Chowder and Marching Society of fifteen freshman or junior Republican congressmen, who shared conviviality and gossip and tried to vote as a bit of a bloc. Among the members who went on to higher offices were future senators

Kenneth Keating, Caleb Boggs, and Norris Cotton, future party chairman Thruston Morton, and, in 1949, future president Gerald Ford.

Another future president that Nixon encountered early, as the correspondingly junior Democratic member of the Education and Labor Committee, was the thirty-year-old John F. Kennedy of Massachusetts. They debated Taft-Hartley before a hundred and fifty people in the steel-making town of McKeesport, Pennsylvania, in the spring of 1947. It was generally agreed that Nixon won the debate, though Kennedy was more popular with the labor-dominated audience, more relaxed, better dressed, and more photogenic. Kennedy was astounded at the seriousness, diligence, and general lack of *joie de vivre* of Nixon, though he respected his drive, intelligence, and pleasant personality. Nixon liked Kennedy, and detected his intelligence, as well as the demons of his overbearing father, of the need to take the place of a brother who died in the war, and of a sexual drive verging on satyriasis. Nixon was impressed, and eventually intimidated, by Kennedy's ability to project at his best, and conceal from the public his several shortcomings. Nixon did get on well with Joseph Kennedy, the family patriarch, a former fascist sympathizer, unsuccessful ambassador to Britain, and unscrupulous businessman, who bankrolled his sons' political careers. John Kennedy and Richard Nixon were running from different fears but toward the same distant prize. Their collision would be one of the epic chapters of American history.

Yet another future president Nixon met often, part of the congressional establishment after just ten years as a congressman, was Lyndon B. Johnson of Texas. Big, demonstrative, and mercurial, endlessly in motion, wheeling and dealing, Johnson was already a genius at the congressional arts, the most assiduous student of legendary and long-serving (though not at the moment) Speaker Sam Rayburn. Johnson would regard Nixon as too sober, too much a loner, and too fanatically motivated for his own advancement to be a clubbable congressman, while Nixon considered Johnson a shady, self-serving, dominatingly vital force. There was not much warmth in their relations for many years, but no absence of respect either.

Nixon had good relations with the working press and received a good deal of favorable attention from early on in his days in Washington. He was a ready source for reporters and had an advantage, as the press was always ready to distinguish him from the racists and posturers who made up most of the rest of HUAC. He encouraged this distinction, and constantly briefed against his sillier and more sinister colleagues. Bert Andrews, of the *New York Herald Tribune*, whom Cronin had identified as "pro-Soviet," was one of those with whom Nixon struck up a good functioning, but not personal, relationship.

As he had promised, Nixon voted a pretty conservative line. He favored tax cuts and less government, abolition of the poll tax, which effectively restrained African-Americans from voting, acceptance of European immigrants, and foreign aid to governments that were not Soviet-dominated. He unreservedly supported the administration on increased defense appropriations and a muscular anti-communist foreign policy. He was a protean, almost chameleon-like, politician; he retained the support of the reactionary conservatives, while distinguishing himself to the press and the moderates from the reactionaries. He favored liberal goals as long as the private sector achieved them, and anathematized the far left, but never questioned, and even defended, the motives of those on the left whose policies he opposed, except for the occasional sacrificial offering like Gerhart Eisler. All the time, he took care of his district very meticulously.

On the strength of his exemplary launch in Congress, he was chosen to be a member of the Herter Committee, which was to conduct research in Europe and report to the House on the advisability of Secretary of State George C. Marshall's proposal of a couple of months before of a generous aid plan for the economic and social reconstruction of Europe. State Department Soviet specialist George F. Kennan had drawn up an outline for economic assistance to Europe. Assistant Secretary of State Dean Acheson brushed it up, and General Marshall proposed it at a Harvard commencement address on June 5. He stressed that it was directed against no country, but only against "hunger, poverty, desperation and chaos." The U.S.S.R., technically eligible, refused Marshall Plan aid for itself and the East European countries it was occupying. This clearly revealed the different ambitions for Europe of the United States and the Soviet Union.[27] Nixon was the youngest member of the group, which, unlike HUAC, was composed exclusively of serious, intelligent, and hardworking people, and he was the only congressman in the group from a Pacific Coast state.

Nixon made his first visit to the presidential Oval Office in July, as Mr. Truman received four Republican congressmen and made a bipartisan appeal. (He had been to a White House reception on the day of his maiden speech, February 18, but not in the Oval Office.) He found the president sincere, friendly, straightforward, humorous, and lacking all pomposity.

When Nixon departed for England with the Herter Committee on the great British liner *Queen Mary*, his family again came to see him off. Herman Perry had written him a warning not to be swayed by Truman and Marshall and not to approve giving the European mendicants a cent.[28] The party disembarked at Southampton on September 2, and was received by British prime minister Clement Attlee and his senior colleagues. Nixon joined the southern subcommittee and visited Greece and Italy. He met a young Greek woman whose breast had been amputated by communists in torturing her, and in Trieste saw a young man blown up by a communist-launched grenade. In Rome, Nixon interviewed a communist labor leader, Giuseppe Di Vittorio, who gave such uniform answers to Nixon's questions that the congressman felt he had proof that "communists throughout the world owe their loyalty not to the countries in which they live but to Russia." (This was a view that he eventually saw did not apply to East Asia.) Nixon drew other conclusions, especially that the ruling elites of Europe had largely capitulated to the communists, and that communists only understood force and could not be reasoned with on any other basis. On their return, fourteen of the Herter Committee's seventeen members, including Nixon, supported the Marshall Plan. The influence of the committee was decisive, and the Marshall Plan, one of the greatest triumphs of American states-manship in history, was passed overwhelmingly by the Congress.

This was the last stand of the isolationists. Nixon detected that while the committee had voted 14 to 3 and the House as a whole quite lopsidedly for the administration's plan, there remained some persuading to be done in the Twelfth District, where Marshall aid smacked of the sort of mindless altruism his constituents might have expected from Voorhis. His own polls indicated 75 percent opposition in his district.[29] Nixon began writing op-ed pieces describing his trip and the Soviet threat he encountered and sent them to all the local newspapers. He returned to the district in late October and again at the beginning of December, and embarked on a whirlwind speaking tour (fifty separate speeches in the district in a few days on the first visit) to bring his constituents around. He was able to assure them that his district's oranges would be in the food packages to Europe.

His constituents were uniformly anti-communist, and he encouraged this sentiment to prevail over their frugality, isolationism, and xenophobia.

It did not take long before humanitarian considerations merged with the national interest and militant hostility to the Red aggressors. Nixon, and events, converted the people of the Twelfth District. The communist takeover of Czechoslovakia in February 1948 helped build the already solid strength of anti-communism over isolationism in the United States, and Nixon added to his own stature, and spoke his mind, when he co-sponsored, with Kersten, a House resolution offering military aid to any non-communist Central European country requesting it (there were none, but it resonated well). Such a policy, if acted on, could have been useful in Hungary in 1956. In foreign policy matters Nixon was intelligent and principled from the start.

Nixon built from this success into a carefully constructed reelection strategy. He would again, as was then the California custom, cross-file in both primaries, holding the Republicans with his incandescent anti-communism, and fishing after the Democrats' votes by running as a nonpartisan patriot and candidate of good government, and on his constituency record. Father John Cronin had been his principal, behind-the-scenes sponsor in having Nixon named by the National Junior Chamber of Commerce one of "America's outstanding young men." This was the sort of wholesome, consensual image that played to his new bipartisan strategy. Party names were de-emphasized. Nixon was not running against any incumbent or known quantity in the primaries, he was just boosting himself as a dynamic young American.

It took the Democrats until April 12, six weeks before the primary, to put up a candidate, thirty-one-year-old former Voorhis assistant Stephen Zetterberg, who declined to cross-file, considering it hypocritical. Margaret Porter, a leftist who had followed former vice president Henry Wallace out of the Democratic Party and into the Progressive Party, essentially an alliance of fellow travelers advocating reconciliation with Moscow, also was running for the Democratic nomination. Voorhis warned Zetterberg that although his ancestry was Swedish, there would be some anti-Semitic comment and gave him a box of names of former campaign helpers. This, he said, was what remained of the Democratic machine in the Twelfth District.

Nixon fell on icy steps in February while carrying Tricia and broke his left elbow protecting the baby, and was lionized by the press for his exemplary fatherhood. In the light of the great advantage Kennedy would have over him in the support of the press twelve years later, it is easy to forget what a generous launch with the national press Nixon enjoyed.

He was fortunate to escape criticism on a couple of issues in early 1948. He resolved a long-standing dispute about construction of a dam near El Monte, one of the three municipalities that had voted for Voorhis in 1946. El Monte did not want the dam, which would flood several hundred farms, but more populous communities that would be served by it, did. The leader of the local opposition was an evangelical clergyman, Dan Cleveland, pastor of the Church of the Barn, which would be flooded out by the project. Nixon was visited by former Democratic national committeeman Ed Pauley, who favored the dam and was an important local Democratic fund-raiser, and a compromise emerged. The dam site was moved almost two miles, sparing 10 to 20 percent of the farms, as well as the Reverend Cleveland's church, and everyone hailed the victory of good sense. Cleveland, a Democrat, endorsed Nixon, and Pauley raised money for him. The dispossessed of El Monte, according to Nixon's account, were better compensated than had originally been proposed and the majority of people affected were pleased. It still bore the earmarks of a questionably cynical arrangement.

More dodgy was the Condon affair. The HUAC chairman, J. Parnell Thomas, convalescing in Walter Reed Army Hospital with gastrointestinal problems, summoned reporters and attacked Dr. Edward Condon, the director of the National Bureau of Standards, as a menace to atomic security. Condon was a distinguished scientist of leftist but not communist views. Thomas said that the FBI had determined that Condon, who had worked on the Manhattan Project, which developed the atomic bomb, had been in contact with someone "alleged to have engaged in espionage activities with the Russians." Thomas omitted to quote the next line from the FBI document, which had been illegally obtained, which cleared Condon of any such activity. HUAC demanded the Condon security file and President Truman declined, stating that no such files would be handed over, and ordering that any such requests or subpoenas received in any department should be referred to the White House. Nixon grandstanded for a few weeks on the rights and prerogatives of Congress, implying a Truman cover-up, and sent W. Averell Harriman, then the commerce secretary, a telegram that Nixon gave to the press before it was delivered to the addressee, demanding the release of the FBI Condon letter.

As Nixon started to see the more responsible press reaction to this lynching of Condon, who had demanded unsuccessfully to be heard by HUAC, he started to hedge. Nixon claimed only to be trying to find the truth, in an attitude of complete neutrality, and wrote labored explanations of his impartiality to a number of prominent academics. This time, in contrast to his behavior in the Hollywood Ten affair, Nixon was incautious and reflexively demagogic until he understood the issues better, and then scurried out of sight, ultimately describing the treatment of Condon (by his committee) as "shameful."[30]

Nixon was more concerned with rummaging through the administration's files than with Condon, and he did desist quickly, but his initial impulse was, to say the least, injudicious. He made a small contribution to HUAC's record of, in the words of the *New York Times*, "more than a year of baseless rumor-mongering." A man of Nixon's talents and ambitions, and in many respects principles as well, should not have been so involved in grubby, abusive demagogy. The discussion of executive privilege and the subpoena rights of Congress against the executive would arise with bitter irony twenty-five years later, when Nixon would be on the other side of the issue. The fact situations would be distinguishable, but in neither case would Nixon's performance be very creditable.

Nixon led the House move to force the registration of the Communist Party and its front groups in May 1948. Even critics of the measure acknowledged that Nixon handled the debate with tact, courtesy, and fairness. The bill, which became known as Mundt-Nixon, defined the Communist Party and affiliated organizations as seeking the imposition of totalitarian government, required registration of them for that reason, and required the attorney general to designate any other such organizations, which would then have to be registered. It was nonsense, in that declaring an organization in advance to be a totalitarian conspiracy was disrespectful of traditional standards of due process. Supporters both claimed and denied that it effectively banned the Communist Party (which J. Edgar Hoover had recommended against as impractical). In a radio debate on May 17, Harold Stassen asserted his support of Mundt-Nixon as the de facto banning of the CP, and Thomas E. Dewey quoted Mundt as saying that it did not ban the CP. It was demeaning for the Republican Party and for the country to be reduced to such foolishness. When Mundt-Nixon got to the Senate, Robert Taft and others would not bring it forward because of its unconstitutionality.

Nixon had conducted himself admirably, and had run his flag to the top of the anti-communist mast, but he had still co-sponsored a shabby bit of posturing. It must be said that his stance was consistent; he never believed that freedom should be available to those who wished to use their freedom to destroy a free society. That such freedom *should not* be available to opponents of a free society is the traditional view of some other enlightened democracies, including France, but has never been the legitimate stance of the United States, which traditionally draws the line at attempted violent overthrow of the government or betrayal of it to a foreign power. The U.S. Communist Party, in its ambitions, was borderline on both counts but was never formally accused, much less convicted, of either.

Nixon returned to his district on the weekend before the primary vote, and was delighted to find CIO pickets at a rally of his for seven hundred people in El Monte. Nixon began by recounting the perils and travails of his twelve-hour flight from Washington, with a fire scare and unscheduled stops. He then regaled the crowd by reading from the pamphlets handed out at the door by the CIO and rebutting their allegations. Nixon made a major effort with the Democrats, running personally rather than emphasizing party. There were various organizations styling themselves, in effect, as Democrats for Nixon, and blanketing the district with pro-Nixon mailings addressed to "Fellow Democrats."

Nixon did win effective reelection on May 22, as he was acclaimed on the Republican side and defeated Zetterberg by five thousand votes on the Democratic side. More than half the California members of Congress were thus reelected, but it was still an achievement for a freshman congressman running where his opponents had held office fairly effortlessly until two years before. Nixon attended the Republican convention in Philadelphia in June, where Dewey won easily and chose Warren as his running-mate. Nixon had a fairly positive opinion of the presidential candidate, but not of his vice presidential choice. But he did not join in the general Republican euphoria that 1946 had announced their return and that disposing of Truman was a mere formality awaiting its pre-fixed calendrical moment.

Since Nixon did not have to campaign himself, he was free to build up a bank of goodwill by speaking on behalf of other Republicans around the country. He was a swiftly moving thirty-five-year-old, but before taking his career any further, he drove his wife to the hospital on the evening of July 4, where Pat was delivered of their second daughter, Julie. He had been an inattentive husband and rather formulaic father – fifteen or twenty minutes a night making Tricia giggle and lisp words, and then back to work. Pat was a stoical wife, but not an infinitely pliant one, and she made it clear she wanted something a little more interesting. Dick promised another Caribbean cruise in the fall. But neither the election campaign nor the Nixons' relaxed holiday would come off exactly as foreseen.

— IV —

A grand jury had been sitting for over a year in the Foley Square courthouse in New York considering the allegations of communist subversion from FBI informers and the responses of government officials. The Justice Department was apparently not pressing hard for indictments, as, despite the notorious malleability of grand juries, which were set up as a constitutional protection but had long since degenerated into a rubber stamp for prosecutors, no charges had been laid.

The inevitable J. Edgar Hoover, his well-rounded shadow long over the Capitol (and long to remain there), was becoming irritated at the lack of enterprise of the Justice Department and concerned about the credibility of his Bureau. He sent his unofficial agent for leaks and lobbying, FBI assistant director Louis Nichols, around to the Senate Investigations Subcommittee and HUAC to deliver supposedly confidential information and incite hearings, in the light of the feeble response of the Justice Department. This was a gross, but not untypical, abuse of the FBI's institutional integrity and the rights of individuals involved, and an exploitation of the partisan differences between the White House and the congressional majorities. (Given Hoover's egregious behavior and Truman's fearlessness, it is surprising that the president did not fire Hoover instead of General MacArthur.)

Truman summoned Congress back to session for August, to illustrate to the voters what he considered the "do-nothing" propensities of the Republicans. Armed with Nichols's indiscretions, HUAC went happily back into action like nasty little elves. They summoned Elizabeth Bentley, "the blond Mata Hari," a Vassar alumna who had been the lover and messenger of a Soviet spymaster in the United States during the war but thought better of it after his death and confessed everything voluntarily to the FBI. Through hearsay and without corroboration, she implicated a number of people, including the assistant secretary of the Treasury, Harry Dexter White. Uncertain what to do for an encore to Bentley, HUAC staff chief Robert Stripling grasped from the leaked FBI files the name of an assistant editor of *Time* magazine, Whittaker Chambers. Chambers was subpoenaed for the next day, August 3, leaking the fact only to the HUAC Hearst reporters, as the most lobotomously anti-communist journalists of all. (The eighty-five-year-old ogre of American publishing, William Randolph Hearst, magnificent yet incorrigibly irresponsible, veteran of a hundred political wars and a financial crisis in his seventies because of his extravagant art collecting, was still dictating this anti-Red line from his splendid castle at San Simeon, California.)

Chambers would be one of the remarkable personalities who became briefly prominent in unfolding early Cold War history. Nixon judged him "one of the most disheveled looking persons" he had seen. Others were more graphic. Chambers was obese, furtive, somewhat unhygienic, and had a mouth that the eminent man of letters Lionel Trilling described as "a devastation of empty sockets and blackened stumps." He was forty-seven, sometimes almost inaudible, but eerily self-possessed and very articulate. He had been a seedy, prowling homosexual, as well as a communist, in the thirties but lost faith in Marx and Stalin and became an evangelical Quaker and a faithful husband and good father, bearing, as one contemporary put it, "the conscience of Raskolnikov and the mission of Jesus Christ."[31] He was also a prodigious intellectual, and his translation in 1927 of the German novel *Bambi*, by Felix Salten, was judged an outstanding work of scholarship.

After the Nazi-Soviet Pact of August 1939, Chambers tried to interest the U.S. government in his story of espionage, and met with Adolf Berle, a former brain-truster of Roosevelt's, at that point an adviser awaiting a new assignment. Chambers told of espionage conducted to obtain an American bomb-sight device and plans for new battleships, and the direct transmission of secret cables from the U.S. embassy in Moscow. Under questioning from Berle, he identified two middle-level State Department officials, Donald and Alger Hiss, as Soviet spies.

The story has survived, against all odds, that Berle advised Roosevelt of this a few weeks later, in the midst of a croquet game, and that Roosevelt, considering it yet another effort to discredit his administration as being riddled with communist loyalty risks, invited Berle to tell his informant "to go fuck himself." The wheelchair-bound Roosevelt was not known to play much croquet, and there is no other allegation of his having used that expression. It comes from an interview Ladislas Farago, who is not altogether reliable and would not necessarily know what Roosevelt and Berle said to each other, had with Fawn Brodie, who on anything to do with Nixon is more a mythmaker than a historian. So it is very improbable, but the thought of the suave, mellifluous, and patrician president indirectly urging such unseemliness on the infinitely rumpled Chambers, a man bedraggled in body and soul, is too diverting to be allowed to die.[32]

As Chambers pulled himself together at the end of the thirties, he went to work for *Time*, and presented his story to HUAC in 1939 and 1940. Dies, the malicious charlatan chairman, as dishonest as Parnell Thomas but a good deal more intelligent, soaked it for a few headlines without blowing Chambers's cover, and then let the story go. The newly minted anti-communist Whittaker Chambers was not to be foiled so easily by the tenebrous thickets of Washington officialdom; he wanted to get something important off his chest and he was going to do it, with the conviction of a troubled soul seeking the confessional.

He contacted HUAC's Benjamin Mandel, an ex-communist himself and a more ethical person than the sleazy pre-Nixon politicians he served on HUAC. The FBI finally interviewed Chambers in May 1942, but did not find his comments very noteworthy or even believable. The entire administration was as casual as the president, and the follow-up on Chambers and others' leads about Soviet espionage was, as a Truman official finally put it, "a rotten, lousy bumbling operation," but it wasn't the cover-up Nixon and his Republican colleagues were getting ready to claim.[33]

Alger Hiss rose in the State Department during the war and was finally assistant secretary for international organizations. Much has been made of Hiss's presence at the Yalta Conference, and the more lurid Republican Red-baiters would claim that he played a Mephistophelean role with Roosevelt there. In fact, his only contribution was to oppose giving the U.S.S.R. three seats in the UN General Assembly, advice that was ignored. The Soviet ambassador to the UN and future foreign minister and president, Andrei Gromyko, recommended Hiss as UN secretary general.[34]

After the Gouzenko espionage case arose in Canada in 1945, and U.S.-U.S.S.R. relations deteriorated, the FBI and others finally started to take the subject seriously. Hiss was wire-tapped and subjected to close physical surveillance for two years. Hoover suggested to Truman's second secretary of state, James F. Byrnes, that Hiss be eased out of the department, but that public hearings that would reveal the Bureau's sources be avoided. Resorting to his usual methodology when an administration official did not follow his advice, Hoover then leaked inflammatory but impersonal accounts of security problems to broadcaster Walter Winchell.

His noisy agitation achieved the FBI director's immediate (and reasonable) goal of getting Hiss out of government. On the recommendation of James Reston of the *New York Times* and Bert Andrews of the *Herald Tribune* and others, Hiss became head of the Carnegie Endowment for International Peace, a blue chip New York international foundation. He had fenced with the rumors and denunciations, having gone voluntarily to the FBI to deny them after Byrnes spoke to him about Hoover's intervention in 1946. He gave the same assurances to the influential Republican foreign policy expert, author of the Japan Peace Treaty and future secretary of state, John Foster Dulles, chairman of Carnegie trustees.

Hiss was covering off his establishment patrons, but his accusers kept returning to the attack. Cronin and Mandel caused a detailed allegation of treason to be published in *Plain Talk* in December 1947, with scant impersonality, although Hiss was not actually named. The Hiss story was widely circulated before Chambers revealed it to HUAC – and Richard Nixon, through John Cronin and FBI files, and leaks from the newly formed Central Intelligence Agency, knew a great deal more about Chambers and Hiss than the rest of the committee did, or than he let on, then or subsequently.

Cronin had explicitly told Nixon that Hiss was a communist. All Nixon's sources came from one original wellspring, Whittaker Chambers, but Nixon didn't know that. Chambers had been denouncing Hiss for nine years to everyone from President Roosevelt (via Berle and regardless of whether there was any croquet) through the FBI and thus Cronin and Winchell to HUAC. To Nixon, in the summer of 1948, there seemed to be plenty of corroboration for Chambers, but Chambers had been in an echo chamber, and was really corroborating himself.[35]

Whittaker Chambers, after being sworn in at a HUAC hearing, read an opening statement recounting his efforts to lift the rock on communist activity in America, and then started to name names. Karl Mundt, no allegory of condign judicature but a serious improvement on the still ailing Parnell Thomas, was in the chair. At the mention of individuals, he adjourned the committee to reconvene in a larger room with the press in attendance. HUAC had been starved for real revelations for a long time and this might revive its half-interred credibility.

Chambers began again. His implausible appearance seemed to lend credence to his mumbled eloquence. He led the hushed room through his defection a decade before, and gave the names of active communists, including Lee Pressman, a junior New Dealer and general counsel of the Congress of Industrial Organizations, and the blockbuster, Alger Hiss, the mention of whose name sent reporters scrambling to the telephones. Chambers had told his wife that as he departed the communists (keeping a revolver within easy reach for over a year), he was leaving "the winning side for the losing side" but would rather die in freedom "than live under communism." He concluded that his appearance at HUAC would "darken my effort to integrate myself into the community of free men. But that is a small price to pay if my testimony helps to make Americans recognize at last that they are at grips with a secret, sinister, and enormously powerful force whose tireless purpose is their enslavement."

With this, his voice broke, and there was silence in the crowded committee room. It was an electrifying and impenetrably sincere performance. The buffoonish, dangerously reckless, and ludicrously named committee had finally hit the jackpot, and only Richard Nixon among its members knew much of the facts and had earned the stature to do anything with them. Nixon was relatively quiet, while other members interjected inanities, such as Rankin's statement that it was a good thing for Hiss that the Carnegie Endowment was located in New York, because such a thing would not be tolerated in Mississippi.

Nixon's statement in his memoirs that this was the first time he had heard of Hiss or his brother was untrue. It is an important component of the official Nixon line that he knew nothing more than what was adduced before the committee and that he risked everything in betting on Chambers over Hiss. This is partially true, as Nixon didn't know that Chambers was really Hiss's sole accuser. Nor did he know, however confident he was at times of Chambers's honesty – and Chambers did not always inspire as much confidence as on this first appearance before him – that the checkered and shambling Chambers would prevail over the elegant and extremely well-connected Hiss. Chambers had himself been involved in espionage, though he tried to duck this aspect of his confession for a long time, and the committee indulged him, deliberately or otherwise. Nixon was perhaps about to gamble almost as much as he would claim, his whole political career, but not altogether knowingly. He thought he had a surer thing than he did.

Hiss asked HUAC to hear his defense, after being badgered by reporters telephoning his home, and he appeared on August 5. It was a boffo performance, a startling superficial contrast to Chambers's, but not surpassing it in credibility. Hiss was tall and well-dressed and spoke with crisp confidence, good humor, and a slight condescension. He had overcome the suicide of his father, sister, and one brother, and had not had many social or economic advantages in his Baltimore youth. At Harvard Law School, he became a protégé of Roosevelt's senior jurisconsult, subsequent Supreme Court justice Felix Frankfurter, and then clerk to Justice Oliver Wendell Holmes. Like a lot of bright young lawyers, he was cycled through the lower and middle echelons of a number of government activities in the thirties, and was an aide to Woodrow Wilson's son-in-law, Francis B. Sayre, then assistant secretary of state.

Hiss became friendly with a number of young men who would go on to great public eminence, including Dean Acheson and Adlai Stevenson, then assistant secretaries of state and the navy. He also had the knack of impressing his elders, such as the crusty Dulles, no man of the left and no great admirer of the Roosevelt entourage. When Hiss finally left State, his place was taken by Dean Rusk, yet another future secretary of state (under presidents Kennedy and Johnson). Hiss was rather dominated by his temperamental and radically socialistic wife, an unstable faddist in many things, and, like Chambers and Nixon, in an odd coincidence, a Quaker. (With all the allegations about of sinister societies and sects, it was astonishing, and probably because of Nixon, that the Quakers did not become at least the momentary subject of national paranoia.)

In January 1949, a Pennsylvania Quaker wrote Nixon, Chambers, and the Hisses: "Friends, stand still in the Lord. Judge not." Chambers, only, replied: "I must lay bare the sin of the world and the century. Perfidy and terror are the works of the age which has resolved to live without God – therefore the confession that I have to make is a confession of perfidy and terror."[36] This was the ultimate invincibility of Chambers, apart from the fact that he was telling the truth: he launched a mortal accusation under the guise of a penitent confession.

Alger Hiss made a good impression in his appearance at HUAC on August 5, 1948. Nixon asked early on who had suggested that Hiss come to

Washington. Hiss replied, "Is it necessary? There are so many witnesses who use names rather loosely before your committee." Nixon insisted, and Hiss mentioned Frankfurter. Nixon said to a journalist after the session, "He was rather insolent to me; frankly, I didn't like it." Nixon did not smile throughout Hiss's rather facile appearance, in which he made a number of witty comments, played to the obviously favorable gallery, and elicited the anger of some members against *Time* magazine, Chambers's employer, for what Rankin called "smear attacks" against HUAC. Hiss also fired a subtle shot across Chambers's bow, by referring disapprovingly to allegations of espionage, a subject Chambers had tried to keep his own distance from in his testimony. This was a warning that Chambers could bring such a charge down on himself. Hiss should have known that a partisan HUAC would arrange immunity for Chambers to get Hiss, if that was what was required.

When he was asked if he recognized Chambers from a photograph, not having recognized his name, Hiss said the person in the picture looked "like a lot of people" and that he could mistake him for the acting committee chairman, the pudgy Mundt. Nixon recorded that Hiss's "friends . . . from the Washington social community . . . broke into a titter of delighted laughter." Nixon thought Hiss "much too careful a witness . . . and too mouthy."[37] In fact, Nixon was convinced from all he had been given by Cronin and his other sources that Hiss was lying about not knowing Chambers, and he had asked Mandel to call Chambers and find out if there were any other names by which Hiss might have known him. Mandel returned with an answer as the hearing was breaking up.

Hiss had won on the day, and even Rankin congratulated him. The rest of HUAC, like the traditional bully, started to lose its nerve. Mundt said that the committee had been taken in by Chambers and suggested they try to salvage their credibility by finding another issue. He and others blamed the staff for allowing them to be ambushed. Hebert said they should "wash our hands" of it and ask the attorney general to figure out which of Hiss and Chambers was telling the truth. Apart from being cowardly, it was a nonsensical idea; all Hiss had really done was deny knowing Chambers from his photograph and dispute Chambers's uncorroborated recollections. Attorney General Tom Clark could not do much with that, and as a Democrat he would not have much incentive to do anything with it.

But Nixon knew it had been only a skirmish. Apart from what he already had known of Hiss, he had some seriously considered views about security risks in public life. He had sought membership on HUAC for his own advancement, but also because it was concerned with the national interest. His colleagues were mere posturers. Nixon also had a visceral dislike of the elitist affectations of the long-ruling federal leftist apparat. He carefully hid his determined hostility to Hiss and the extent of his prior briefings, but he was stalking a big target, who was perhaps more over-confident than ever.

Not only the committee members were waffling. The press, which had lapped up what Chambers had had to say, now wobbled back to Hiss. President Truman lambasted HUAC the morning of the Hiss appearance and took up a phrase from a reporter's question, dismissing the hearings as a "red herring." It was a good line, and the president's denunciation of HUAC's pursuit of civil servants was also justified. But the hearings would not be taking place at all if he had not summoned Congress back to Washington in the steamy summer just to demonstrate its inefficacy under Republican leadership, and to delay the start of the election campaign.

Alger Hiss shored up his own position by writing a self-congratulatory yet obsequious letter to John Foster Dulles, his chairman at the Carnegie Endowment. Dulles was the presumed secretary of state if Dewey was elected, and Hiss told him the incumbent undersecretary, Dean Acheson, who was expected to replace General Marshall if Truman was reelected, had helped him with his defense.[38] Hiss was not so cozy with the powerful Republicans, who were generally expected to win the 1948 election. Dulles, whose brother Allen, a senior intelligence officer, had got to know and appreciate Nixon when briefing the Herter Committee, cautiously acknowledged Hiss's letter but told his colleagues that they should await the outcome of the HUAC hearings before taking a position on Hiss. Dulles fluctuated a little in the ensuing days, and Nixon and Congressman Kersten called on him at the New York Republican headquarters in the Roosevelt Hotel (named after Theodore, not Franklin) on August 11, and gave the Dulles brothers and future Democratic Treasury secretary C. Douglas Dillon the Chambers subcommittee testimony. Foster Dulles read it, pondered it for a minute, and said that there was no doubt that Chambers had known Hiss, and that Nixon must see the investigation through to the end.

Nixon rallied the committee by warning them that they would commit political suicide if they folded now. He also attacked Hiss's slickness as a witness, and said that it wasn't clear that he was truthful and that Chambers was not. He had not definitively denied that he had known Chambers, and was coy about it. They knew Chambers had been a communist, so if Hiss knew him, he might have known him in that role. Stripling, the chief investigator, who was a far from inspired occupant of his position, opined that there was a "prima facie perjury" somewhere, which alone gave them reason to go on.[39] And he added that the malicious comments about Chambers being an alcoholic, a homosexual, and a mental case were the sort of slanders communists usually engage in. Thus was Chambers's credibility partially rebuilt.

This was fairly thin reasoning, as Stripling's generally was, but Nixon brought his ill-assured colleagues back from under the committee room table by adopting a suggestion of Mandel's: a subcommittee would question Chambers closely about intimate details of his knowledge of Hiss, then question Hiss on the same points and determine which of them they thought was being truthful. This was agreed. Nixon was relieved, but reflected that he had taken up the defense of the deservedly shabby reputation of HUAC and taken on the president and the press. These odds would have been more daunting if he had not known a great deal more about the facts than any of them did. (And Truman should have been better informed; his FBI director was panting to tell him more. Hoover was insubordinate and lawless at times, but he was on top of American communists like a leopard, even though he grossly exaggerated their number and significance.)

— v —

Nixon called on Christian Herter, who told him that the consensus in the State Department was that Hiss was innocent, and that he personally thought Chambers had misled HUAC. Nixon adopted the same technique he had used in the Condon affair and said that he was personally neutral and just wanted to find out which of Chambers and Hiss was lying, and that HUAC had a duty to do so. Herter had to agree with that, which snuffed out any chance of a full revolt against HUAC by Republican congressmen. As one eminent historian put it: "It was the artful position Nixon took throughout the case with the crucial, ever self-protective figures of the eastern establishment – most notably the Dulles brothers – who found HUAC's inquisitions at once farcical and menacing, aggravating and politically useful."[40]

Nixon also intensified communications with Cronin. Hoover was in the fight almost as deeply as Nixon was, as the failure of the grand jury to indict any subversives made HUAC the last stop for the FBI's credibility also, and had attracted the mirthful derision of the president. If Hiss was not nailed by Nixon, as seemed likely, and Truman was reelected, as seemed unlikely in August 1948, Hoover might finally be out. Hoover authorized an open artery of intelligence to Cronin, who had pretty well enjoyed and reciprocated it for years, and Cronin passed on everything he heard directly to Nixon.

The new subcommittee (Nixon, McDowell, Hebert) arranged to meet Chambers on Saturday morning, August 7, in the Foley Square courthouse in New York. Nixon was thoroughly prepared, being "determined . . . [to be] . . . at least as well prepared as the witnesses themselves" from now on.[41] It was a tense session with, as Chambers wrote, Mandel hovering "over me with disquieting solicitude."[42] Chambers quickly drew back into the running in the credibility sweepstakes, as far as Nixon and the HUAC insiders were concerned, by rattling off descriptions of the Hiss homes and child and cocker spaniel and car ten years before, the nicknames Hiss and his wife used for each other, Hiss's pastime of bird-watching, and his sighting of the rare and splendid (and soon to be famous) prothonotary warbler. His descriptions of Hiss and his family members were vivid, though in fact inaccurate in some respects (he underestimated Hiss's height by several inches) but confidently stated. Chambers, in answer to a question of Nixon's, instantly said that he was prepared to take a lie-detector test.

The HUAC group, reinvigorated, returned to Washington, and the next week the committee heard other witnesses named by Elizabeth Bentley, most notably Harry Dexter White. White won the admiration of the packed chamber by rebutting the returned Parnell Thomas's tasteless comments about White's cardiological condition. However, when he referred to HUAC's "Star Chamber proceedings," Nixon curtly assured him that where star-chambers had not allowed for self-defense and produced judgments without deliberation, the committee wanted White's version of events and would be thoughtful and thorough. White subsided, clearly put in his place.

On August 9, Nixon had driven to Chambers's farm in Maryland and grilled him again, personally, while they gently swayed in rocking chairs on Chambers's porch. Nixon put new questions to Chambers about his credibility, and was reassured when Chambers pointed out that he could have no possible motive, other than sincere anti-communism, to jeopardize his career and life and family. When Nixon mentioned that he, Nixon, was a Quaker, Chambers said that he and his wife were too, and that so was the wife of Alger Hiss. Then he recalled that at home Mrs. Hiss addressed Alger in "the plain language" – i.e., "thee, thine, thou." This resonated with Nixon, whose mother did the same at home, but not in front of strangers. Nixon was reassured about the solidity of the witness upon whom his career now depended. Chambers, for his part, thought Nixon "the kindest of men" and said his "somewhat martial Quakerism sometimes amused and always heartened me." Chambers's children called him "Nixie, the kind and the good, about whom they will hear no nonsense."[43] Nixon even brought his parents to meet Chambers once.

Nixon called upon the violently anti-communist chairman of the Senate Investigations Subcommittee, Homer Ferguson, and asked for one of his ablest staff members to review the testimony HUAC had taken from Hiss and Chambers. Ferguson, a rabid Republican who wanted to embarrass the administration in an election year, sent over William P. Rogers, whom Nixon had met at the Naval Officer Training school at Quonset, Rhode Island, in 1942. Rogers was an affable and competent protégé of Thomas E. Dewey, and would work closely with Nixon, off and on, for more than twenty years. They complimented each other, as Nixon was driven and highly intelligent, but personally awkward and often insecure, and Rogers was relaxed, gracious, confident, but not excessively ambitious or remarkably intelligent. Nixon gave him the material and the Herter speech of impartiality. Rogers reported back that Chambers was clearly believable. Wisconsin congressman Charles Kersten said the same when Nixon shared the material with him the following day. Then Nixon and Kersten visited the Dulleses in New York.

The next eminence on whom Nixon tried out Chambers's August 7 testimony was Bert Andrews, Washington bureau chief of the *New York Herald Tribune*. Andrews had been severely critical of HUAC but had also criticized Hiss for what he mistakenly thought to be his role in granting the U.S.S.R. three UN General Assembly seats. (He was unaware that Roosevelt had arranged the same right for the United States but he and Truman had not exercised it.) Andrews read Chambers's testimony, and it was arranged that he and Nixon would visit Chambers on Sunday, August 15. Hiss was summoned to meet the committee on the following day. Nixon and Stripling visited Chambers for a confidence-building session on Saturday,

August 14, and Nixon was back the following day with Andrews. Chambers was convincing on both occasions, identifying photographs of houses the Hisses had lived in more than a decade before, and not hesitating on matters of fine detail. Back in Washington, Andrews warned Nixon that although he believed Chambers, HUAC was composed, apart from Nixon, of such incompetent scoundrels they would inadvertently vindicate Hiss if Nixon did not keep control of the committee.

Andrews, Nixon, and the FBI, through leaks to columnists the Bureau considered reliable, were gradually staging a media comeback, which was already perceptible when Alger Hiss returned to the committee on August 16. There was no longer any pretense of following seniority or alternating questioners. Nixon took over the interrogation as the only person competent to do so. Thomas assured Hiss of the confidentiality of an executive session, but since he and the other side had been leaking floods of material to the media for the last ten days, Hiss knew how much confidence to place in that arrangement.

Nixon frankly stated that there were conflicts in the testimony between Hiss and Chambers and that the committee wanted to get to the bottom of it. Hiss denied he had been a part of an underground organization or activity, or that he had known "Carl," which had been identified as Chambers's name at the time. Hiss said he would like to see the person to be sure if he had known him or not, though he now found his photograph "not completely unfamiliar."

Nixon assured Hiss that there would be no embarrassment to Hiss's stepson, Timothy Hobson, who had been discharged from the navy for homosexuality and was undergoing psychiatric treatment and did not have any relationship with his mother or stepfather at the time. Hiss complained of the damage to his reputation and the public humiliation he had suffered, and accused the committee of being biased in favor of Chambers. He referred to newspaper reports of Nixon spending the weekend at Chambers's farm. Nixon, although he had been there for several hours on Saturday and again on Sunday, said, "That is quite incorrect. . . . I can say, as you did a moment ago, that I have never spent the night with Mr. Chambers." This was a bit slippery.

The exchange quickly became very snappish, as Hiss objected that Nixon was just trying to arm Chambers, and complained that Chambers should not be believed because he was a confessed communist and traitor, although he had not, in fact, confessed to anything resembling treason. Hebert made his principal intervention, saying that "stool pigeons" were the core of police work and that many saints were reformed sinners. This exchange was played up in the press and was damaging to Hiss. Hiss remembered that he had someone stay in his house in the thirties, named "George Crosley," whom he identified as having had a "strikingly dark wife." Nixon, having met Esther Chambers, knew this was the person, and that therefore Chambers was almost certain to be telling the truth. Hiss was still outwardly confident, but his fate was almost sealed.

After Hiss had referred to Crosley's (i.e., Chambers's) bad teeth, Nixon continued with questions about Hiss's car. Again, Chambers's version of events rang true. Hiss alternated between vagueness and precision in a way that reduced his credibility as the day progressed, and unlike Chambers, he declined to take a lie-detector test. McDowell, who had been on the subcommittee that questioned Chambers, asked if Hiss had ever seen a prothonotary warbler. Hiss leapt into the trap and rhapsodized about the "gorgeous bird." It was agreed that Hiss would meet Chambers face to face on August 25, and after the most sanctimonious assertions from Thomas, Hebert, and Nixon that they had taken an oath of secrecy and would abide by it, promises to which Hiss attached the credence they deserved, the hearing was terminated.

In the press the next day, leaks crested to a point where the Old Testament commended the building of an ark. And three days after Parnell Thomas (who had emerged from his stay in hospital to seize his share of HUAC's publicity) had mocked Harry Dexter White's cardiological condition, White died of a coronary. To counteract negative publicity that HUAC had hounded him to death, Nixon brought forward the Hiss-Chambers confrontation to August 17. This was a logistical challenge, but as they frantically telephoned around for Chambers, he came by intuition to the HUAC office, where Stripling greeted him "with a somewhat bird-like stare" and credited him with psychic powers. They entrained at once for New York, went to the Commodore Hotel, to a room decorated with Audubon bird prints,[44] and called Hiss to invite him, without warning as to the purpose, to join them at five-thirty that afternoon.

Hiss arrived, professed to have just learned of, and been shocked by, White's death, made his now customary and well-founded complaints about the indiscretions of the committee, and heard the usual unctuous disclaimers. The earnest, but unworldly, McDowell agreed with Hiss and made the usual promise to fire the staff member responsible. Nixon had Chambers brought in and asked Hiss if he knew him. On request, Chambers said the words that would be emulated in titles and scripts of countless Red Scare television dramas into the fifties: "My name is Whittaker Chambers." Hiss went through the farce of asking him to speak louder and open his mouth so he could inspect his teeth. He even asked the nature of the dental work he had had done since the thirties and the name of his dentist. Nixon later expressed his difficulty in keeping a "straight face" and felt the "comedy has gone far enough."

Hiss asked Chambers if he had used the name "George Crosley," and Chambers replied, probably dishonestly, on two occasions, "Not to my knowledge."[45] Nixon walked Chambers through more of his recollections of his acquaintance with Hiss, and Hiss declared that he could now identify Chambers as George Crosley, technically embracing the truth more fully than, on this issue, was Chambers. Hiss belligerently invited Chambers to make his allegations of Hiss's communist activities without the privilege against defamation actions afforded by committee testimony. The session ended after nearly two hours with the usual false promises of confidentiality (though not from Nixon himself) and a sharp exchange between Hiss and Thomas. Hiss had had a very bad day.

Nixon spent the evening telephoning the press and dictating the story without even bothering to put it on background. He asked the staff member Donald Appell to spend the night in his suite in the Commodore Hotel, because he did not want to be alone there.[46] He was now seeking identification as the person who had cracked the Hiss case. Nixon spoke to the *Herald Tribune*'s Andrews for over three hours. Chambers had dinner with his employer, *Time* co-founder and controlling shareholder Henry R. Luce, son of a missionary in China, who compared Chambers to the person Christ cured of blindness. Hiss collected his wife at Grand Central Station, because Nixon would be interviewing her the next day, and was so jarred by the telephone calls he received when he got home inviting him to comment on Nixon's revelations that he called a press conference for midnight and told the press that he was not a communist.

Priscilla Hiss was quiet and apparently timid, and asked to "affirm" in Quakerese, rather than be sworn. Nixon treated her with exquisite courtesy, in her husband's presence, and they thanked each other for their civility.

Nixon later felt that he had lost an opportunity to put tough questions, and had been beguiled by the witness.

Hiss's world started to disintegrate. Dulles suggested he resign from the Carnegie Endowment. Nixon was achieving enormous celebrity, but Chambers was flagging. Nixon confirmed the original August 25 confrontation as a public hearing and Chambers wondered if he could go through it. Nixon argued that the Justice Department wanted to indict him right away, to take the heat off Hiss, and that Chambers could escape that only by winning the public-opinion battle with Hiss in a public confrontation. Chambers agreed, because he liked and trusted Nixon, but felt, he wrote, like "a very small creature, skirting the shadows of encircling powers that would not hesitate to crush me impersonally as a steamroller crushes a bug."[47]

Nixon interviewed Lee Pressman of the CIO and others, and accused Truman to the press, only ten weeks before the election, of deliberately "obstructing an investigation which is absolutely essential to the security of each and every person in this country."[48] He was now conducting what amounted almost to round-the-clock press briefings. He took over direct control of the HUAC staff and made sure that they and he were ready for August 25, though he followed Andrews's advice and took a sleeping pill a couple of nights before and awakened rejuvenated "for the most important test I had had up to that time." On August 23, HUAC staff found a motor vehicle transfer certificate that proved that Hiss's old Ford (with "a sassy little trunk") had been given to a Communist Party member, William Rosen, in 1936.

The day was excruciatingly hot; the committee room was crammed as if with sardines. Alistair Cooke referred in the *Manchester Guardian* to "the darkly handsome Mr. Nixon. . . . the most watchful of all committeemen, straining at the leash." The HUAC transcript has Hiss qualifying his answers with "as I recall" or "to the best of my recollection" 198 times. He wasn't sure about having given Chambers his car. Nixon asked, "How many cars have you given away in your life, Mr. Hiss?" Hiss had made such an issue of Chambers's teeth that Nixon asked, "Didn't you ever see Crosley with his mouth closed?"[49]

Chambers was eloquent and persuasive. "I do not hate Mr. Hiss. We are close friends, but we are caught in a tragedy of history. Mr. Hiss represents the concealed enemy against which we are all fighting. . . . I have testified against him with remorse and pity, but in a moment of history in which this nation now stands, so help me God, I could not do otherwise." It was a lurid combination of soul-wrenching political and patriotic struggle, legitimate, acute national security concerns, fierce partisan combat, and unmitigated hucksterism and low farce. As is usually the case when such forces conjoin in the United States, and as happened more in the career of Richard Nixon than of anyone else in the country's history, it was gripping, but also pathetic and, at times, sickening.

The nine-and-a-half-hour session was a disaster for Hiss. He attempted condescension and told Nixon, "I attended Harvard Law School. I believe yours was Whittier." This was a terrible mistake, and Duke was nothing to be embarrassed about.[50] Some of the most influential newspapers, particularly the *New York Times* and the *Washington Post*, thought that the grilling of Hiss was so much more severe than the questioning of Chambers that there was a partiality issue. But 80 percent of Americans thought that HUAC should continue its investigation. Even Truman (who was pledged to get rid of HUAC if he was reelected with a Democratic Congress) stopped making snide puns about it and told the Justice Department to find out which of the two protagonists was telling the truth.

Nixon had become a national celebrity, but was enervated by the intensity of the last few weeks. When Chambers arrived for a supplementary executive session, he brought his son, whom Nixon introduced to the press as "Mr. Hiss's young son."[51] Chambers went on the radio program *Meet the Press* and was roughly handled, though he took it with resigned dignity. He was invited to take up the Hiss challenge to repeat his charges without an immunity to prosecution for slander, and did so, saying Hiss had been a communist and "may still be one." Hiss sued Chambers on September 27, under goading in the press but despite cautionary advice from Dulles and his own lawyers. Chambers, so unprepossessing in person, but a formidable wordsmith, commented that he did not think Hiss could "use the means of justice to defeat the ends of justice." Hiss raised the damages claimed from fifty thousand to seventy-five thousand dollars.[52] Congress adjourned and one of the nation's more memorable presidential election campaigns began.

— VI —

Nixon and his wife took a few days' holiday at Ocean City, Delaware, and he wrote Dulles on September 7, with a blind copy to Andrews, who had departed Washington with the Dewey campaign, outlining HUAC's progress and including suggestions of how the Republicans could make use of its findings. In his covering note to Andrews, which he assumed would be verbally transmitted to Dewey and Dulles, Nixon urged that Hiss be removed from the Carnegie Endowment. This was no legitimate concern of his, and was a vindictive attempt to inflict gratuitous harm on Hiss and to meddle where he had no rightful place.

Nixon made the point to Dulles that he was aware from HUAC research that Hiss had misled the Carnegie trustees about his past when he was engaged by them. This was a not overly subtle promise to get Carnegie off the hook with the committee and with his media allies if Dulles and the others acted promptly to put Hiss over the side.

Nixon claimed to Dulles that his initial bias, if any, had been in favor of Hiss, because, he falsely wrote, he and Alger and Donald Hiss had many mutual friends. As so often in politically charged prosecutions, for that was what Nixon was conducting, the survival of one protagonist meant the demise of the other, and Nixon attacked Hiss however he could, having conducted a press assault after he had sworn under oath to maintain confidentiality about HUAC's executive session proceedings.

In his letter to Dulles, Nixon wrote that they had discovered that the Soviet embassy had given Elizabeth Bentley two thousand dollars, and urged that the administration be attacked for not deporting alien communists and tolerating the infiltration of too many dubious foreigners. "I realize that there would be some difficulty in making a political issue out of this because of the danger of alienating certain minority groups," he wrote with some understatement.

He asked Dulles to tell Dewey he could allege this on the hustings and suggested that Dewey propose the removal of Fifth Amendment rights in national security cases and for federal employees. This was an outrageous idea, as it involved not just the right not to testify against oneself but the requirement of a grand jury indictment, the avoidance of being tried twice for the same offense, the guarantee of due process, and the sanctity of private property against uncompensated seizure. Nixon blandly assured Dulles that "some restrictions on the defense in such cases would certainly meet with popular approval at this time."

Nixon deserves great credit for perseverance and even courage in the Hiss affair, but he also showed an unbecoming zeal, and gave Dewey and

Dulles advice (which they fortunately ignored) that would have been an assault on the civil liberties of Americans, and on the entire concept of the rule of law. Having given lip service to avoidance of carrying the anti-communist crusade to the point of shrinking the freedom Americans enjoyed, he proposed just that, and not out of passion for national security, only for political gain in an election campaign. It was this sense that Nixon at key points might lack moderation, and on fundamental principles be without scruple, that worried many of his countrymen and has tainted his reputation – excessively, in fact, since these inclinations were aberrant, and he did not act on them when he had the opportunity.

Four months later, at a conference at Dartmouth College, Nixon attacked Attorney General Clark's proposal to legalize wiretapping in serious espionage cases as far too drastic.[53] This was a much less draconian measure than the partial vacation of Fifth Amendment rights he proposed to Dulles and Dewey, and was academic anyway, since the Justice Department and the FBI wiretapped whenever they wanted to, and the issue was admissibility of evidence, not illegal telephone intercepts themselves. It would also prove ironic, given Nixon's later enthusiasm for, or at least toleration of, telephone intercepts.

Dulles replied with unusual exuberance, thanking Nixon for his "sound suggestions," and declared himself "very glad" that Nixon understood the blamelessness of the trustees. This was not Dulles's finest hour either, as he circulated Nixon's letter to some of the trustees, but not to those closest to Hiss. Hiss had rallied his influential supporters with a round of encouraging letters, while Dulles had already begun sending self-serving memos to file explaining that he had not known Hiss well. One new trustee who declined to rush to judgment, and failed to see how someone could be destroyed just on the allegations of one other person, was General Dwight D. Eisenhower, now the president of Columbia University. As Republican chairman and future Senate leader Congressman Hugh Scott put it, Dewey thought it "degrading to suspect Truman personally of being soft on Communism." Besides, it was nonsense. Truman had protected Greece and Turkey and Iran and West Berlin, proclaimed a policy of containment, enhanced atomic weapons development, and required loyalty oaths of federal employees. He was the foremost of Cold Warriors, and it remains a mystery why Nixon went as far as he did attacking the president personally on this issue, apart from the rankest opportunism.[54]

Another unseemly trait of Nixon's at this time, for one who was so unrestrained at press manipulation, was his extreme sensitivity to press criticism. When Drew Pearson asserted that Nixon had allowed the real estate developers of California to write a statement for him supporting their opposition to public housing, Nixon became unnaturally indignant. Nixon's position on the subject was consistent throughout his career and there is no reason to believe that he was influenced by contributions from developers, but as he was accusing Harry Truman, a distinguished president and a formidable non-communist, of mollycoddling "commies," most recently by preventing J. Edgar Hoover from testifying before HUAC,[55] he could have been less thin-skinned, and less self-important. Like many people who have enjoyed a honeymoon with the media, he would adjust with difficulty to the nastiness of much of the press. Later in his career, Nixon would have a legitimate grievance against the media, but he never learned to shrug it off, as most successful public figures do.

Nixon spent most of September campaigning for Republicans around California, retailing the line that a Republican administration would not be afraid to uncover "skeletons in the closet" when exposing subversives, while Truman would. Nixon discovered on his return to Washington that Louis Nichols, his chief direct contact with the FBI, had complained about Nixon's self-serving claims of credit for the Hiss case. He was particularly irritated at a report that Nixon had said that HUAC had achieved more in unmasking communists in the United States in three days than the FBI had in eight years. Nixon phoned Nichols and professed the utmost support for the FBI, and especially for the pharaonic Hoover. He said that he had been misquoted, and had compared HUAC to the Justice Department, not the FBI. Nichols wrote up a memo of the conversation and concluded that he was "impressed with Nixon's attitude." Hoover's deputy director and frequent companion (a controversial arrangement), Clyde Tolson, wrote on the memo that Nixon was a headline-seeker who "plays both ends against the middle." Hoover wrote on it "I agree" (with Tolson).[56]

Behind the majestic facades of Washington's monumental federal buildings, the public interest was being pursued by some with an infelicitous combination of egomania, cynicism, contempt for the public's intelligence, and personal and national paranoia. Fortunately, Truman, and even, up to a point Dewey, conducted themselves relatively responsibly. But Truman had ignored the loyalty and security issues for too long, and they became very combustible. If the Justice Department had prosecuted anyone in two years of grand jury hearings, Hoover would not have felt it necessary to collude with the president's enemies in the Congress, and HUAC would not have been so prominent.

In filling a vacuum, Nixon amplified an issue that was not completely fraudulent. Communist influence in the State Department, and even in Hollywood, was a reasonable matter of public concern, and if the administration had not treated the issue as a joke it would not have been so recklessly exploited by unworthy men. Nixon showed a good deal more moderation in these matters than some of his Republican colleagues would, and has often been unfairly labeled an extremist. He was honored at the *Herald Tribune* forum and explained the procedures he had insisted on for HUAC meetings to protect witnesses: full defense, their own witnesses, the right to question other witnesses, and no television coverage. Whatever his failings, Nixon was a force for comparative moderation.

He generally did the right thing in the end, and showed by his agonizing that he was a conscientious man, if not a lockstep Quaker, but he had some lapses of judgment and taste on the way through. Few of these, in the hard world of politics, could be described as ethical failings, and they were more understandable in a young man who had progressed so rapidly from obscurity to international prominence. But they scarred him and his reputation, during his career, and into his posterity.

Nixon campaigned in October 1948 in nine states for the Republicans. He wrote a campaign column for the *Whittier News* that was syndicated around the state, and reported from Minnesota on a promising Democratic candidate for senator, the mayor of Minneapolis, Hubert H. Humphrey.[57] Nixon demonstrated his precocity, as a thirty-five-year-old running for a second two-year term, by telling his staff and intimates when he returned from his tour, "We're losing this thing – we're throwing it away."[58]

Truman had integrated the armed forces and given some support to civil rights for African-Americans, a cause that Roosevelt had announced many times in his last four years in office was coming, and must come. With this, a block of Southern Democrats walked out of the party and ran Governor Strom Thurmond of South Carolina for president, calling themselves Dixiecrats. Henry Wallace, Truman's predecessor as vice president (possibly Roosevelt's most insane personnel decision), was so upset at

Truman's hard line with the Russians that he bolted and consented to be nominated by a socialist, left-liberal coalition of interests, seizing the standby third party label, Progressive, used by Theodore Roosevelt in 1912 and Robert La Follette in 1924. This splintering contributed to the glacial serenity of Republican confidence.

Nixon saw through it at once. He said that he nowhere saw any Republican enthusiasm, that Dewey was taking the voters for granted, and that Warren, as vice presidential nominee, was utterly useless. Truman was "giving 'em hell" and making tremendous inroads, warning that the Republicans were reactionary enemies of the working families of America. Situated between Thurmond and Wallace, he was clearly a centrist and generated great personal respect by his unflagging underdog campaign, frequently beginning his speeches, "I'm Harry Truman; I work for the government and I'm trying to keep my job." Who could not identify with this, especially compared with the imperious and little Dewey, whom TR's daughter, Alice Roosevelt Longworth, a patroness of the Nixons, unforgettably described, fierce Republican though she was, as "the bridegroom on the wedding cake"? Like Nixon himself, "Dewey always displayed the overly sober mien of a . . . man to whom success has come too soon." (His air of desiccation persisted despite his habit of drinking three quarts of water each day.)[59]

Though Nixon was unimpressed by Dewey and disliked Warren, he was a loyal Republican. What was more worrisome than the presidential campaign was that instead of building on their 1946 victory, the Republican congressional party was in danger of being dumped back into opposition, as Truman flailed at the "do-nothing eightieth Congress." Nixon's fears were justified. After his own huge victory came in, polling 25,000 more than the combined major party totals of two years before and defeating his nearest opponent, the Progressive candidate in the Twelfth District, by 123,000 votes, he and Pat went to the Republican headquarters in Los Angeles. People were still confidently claiming that the Midwest and Far West would put Dewey over. Nixon demurred quietly to only a few people, saying that it was an unmitigated disaster.

Truman led Dewey by two million votes, won safely enough, and brought both houses of Congress in behind him for the Democrats. Roosevelt and Truman had now won five consecutive terms and nine of ten Congresses. Apart from the Civil War and its aftermath, when the South

couldn't really participate in presidential elections, no such record of electoral success by one party had been achieved since the days of Andrew
Jackson. Truman was greeted by half a million people when he returned
to Washington from Missouri, a larger crowd even than had cheered his
illustrious predecessor when he returned to the capital after his three
reelections. Nixon described himself as "a 'comer' with no place to go."[60]

Nixon's friend Charles Kersten was defeated in Wisconsin, as was
HUAC member John McDowell. The abysmal outgoing chairman, Parnell
Thomas, was indicted for fraud, repeatedly exercised his Fifth Amendment
rights, and was eventually imprisoned. The attorney general prepared a bill
for the returning Democratic congressional leaders abolishing HUAC.
Truman referred to HUAC publicly as a "defunct" committee. Stripling
announced he was leaving to return to Texas.

Chambers had told the Manhattan grand jury in October that he knew of
no one conducting espionage, and rumors were that the Justice Department
had insufficient evidence to charge Hiss or Chambers with perjury. But
if Chambers lost the slander case to Hiss, he might well be indicted.
Chambers's depositions in the Hiss slander case in Baltimore went where
HUAC had not: Chambers had been more or less expelled from Columbia,
had been a pornographer, had stolen books from the New York Public
Library, and had written false affidavits. There was an informal understanding that homosexuality would be left out of it, as Hiss did not want his
stepson exposed.

However, the other informal arrangement, about espionage, broke
down. Chambers became so incensed at the aggressive questioning that he
accused Hiss of having been a Soviet spy in the thirties. On November 16,
after Hiss's lawyers had reduced Esther Chambers to tears with their questions, Whittaker Chambers produced documents that he had stashed with
relatives for over a decade: cables from Roosevelt's ambassadors in Paris,
Rome, Vienna, and elsewhere, other State Department cables, and a War
Department paper, most given the highest security classification. These
were almost all copies allegedly typed by Priscilla Hiss. There were also
some notes by Alger Hiss. Chambers described how these documents were
given over to the Russians.

Hiss told his own lawyer, William Marbury, that his notes were innocuous and that he had not seen the typed pages before. Marbury did not

believe him and warned him that he was likely to be indicted and might be convicted. On December 1, Nicholas Vazzana, a young lawyer who assisted the counsel assigned by *Time* to advise Chambers, who had been present at the November 17 revelations, arrived at the HUAC office and told Nixon and Stripling about them, after being reluctant at the outset. He was under a formal threat of contempt of court, but paid no more attention to that than Nixon and the other HUAC members had to their oaths of secrecy. Nixon was so startled that he asked Vazzana if he should go, as long promised to his wife, on his Caribbean cruise the next day. The young man pointed out that it was not his place to advise on that. Vazzana left and Nixon took a call from Andrews, who had heard the mounting rumors about the Chambers papers. Jerry Kluttz had hinted in the *Washington Post* at a Chambers bombshell in the Hiss slander case. Nixon decided to drive out to Chambers's farm.

Nixon and Stripling attended upon Chambers, and Nixon asked if he had "dropped a bombshell" in his deposition. He had, he allowed, but declined, under court order, to share it with Nixon, portentously adding that "it was nothing compared to the second bombshell," and that he had conserved a copy of the first, as well as the fresh material, "in case they tried to suppress the first." Nixon was horrified that the Justice Department had had this material for two weeks.

"You keep that second bombshell. Don't give it to anybody except the committee," said Nixon. Chambers, a shy man and deliberate speaker, turned slowly toward Nixon and told him, straight on, with direct eye contact, "You will understand this. When I testified before the committee last August I wanted to expose the communist conspiracy, but I did not want to destroy the individuals involved. I sat for a whole day in meditation. But after my testimony, they spread stories that I was insane, and that I was a pervert. Then they called in my wife and were very tough with her. It made me angry. I know as a Quaker I must never act in anger. So I sat another day, and I came to the conclusion that the only thing to do was to tell everything I knew, to spare no one."[61]

Nixon, who had asked for the first bombshell without success, did not ask for the second, and Chambers asked, intriguingly, if they had a good photographic technician. He must have known that a congressional committee could have all the expertise it needed, but this was a teaser. It worked, and on the drive back to Washington Nixon and Stripling guessed at what he had. There is no dispute up to this point between Chambers, Nixon, and

Stripling about what had been said on this trip, but Stripling didn't think Chambers really knew what he had kept in reserve, an absurd opinion, and Nixon didn't think he had anything. Both were mistaken.[62]

Nixon went to his office and spoke to Louis Nichols of the FBI, telling him most of the day's developments, and the fact that Chambers had a good deal of documentation that the Justice Department did not have. Nixon said he would subpoena all of this, and he urged Nichols not to tell Justice, because the attorney general would only try to block the exposé in progress. Nichols recommended to Hoover that nothing be done except request information from Justice. Hoover agreed with Nichols. Andrews, whom Nixon had also phoned, urged him to have HUAC issue a general subpoena for documentation on Chambers, which Nixon then ordered. Nixon and his wife then, obligingly, took their vacation. In fact, Stripling had already prepared a subpoena and had had it signed by Speaker Joe Martin. (A fact to which Tom Wicker, in his generally friendly life of Nixon, *One of Us*, attaches inexplicable significance.)[63]

— VII —

Stripling, whom Nixon had phoned from the railway station and then from the train itself, as he and Pat made their way to New York to catch their ship, called Chambers and asked him to come to the HUAC offices, and when he did so pressed a subpoena into his hand. Chambers had already transferred five strips of developed and undeveloped microfilm and a note, his ultimate vindication, wrapped in wax paper, to a pumpkin in his back yard that he hollowed out for the purpose. These were the about-to-be immensely famous "pumpkin papers." Chambers had to give other testimony to another committee in Washington, and when he had finished, returned to the HUAC offices and then set out for home, with two of Stripling's staff in a following car. Chambers, once home, marched about his pumpkin patch a bit in the late autumn gloom, committee agents in tow, located the magic pumpkin, and handed the agents the concealed contents. He also gave them copies of the papers he had handed over in his Baltimore deposition.

Andrews had already wired the shipboard Nixon that something earth-shaking was afoot. Stripling's agents went over the pumpkin papers with him the next day, finally examining the microfilm in a locked and darkened washroom, and then sending it to a Veterans Administration photographic expert for development/enlargement. When it was returned, they found that they had a hundred and thirty-six pages of State Department and Navy Department secret files, clearly linked to Hiss, which Chambers was prepared to swear had been given to the agents of the U.S.S.R., as well as the Baltimore deposition documents already in the hands of the Justice Department. Stripling shared the information with Andrews. Both of them cabled Nixon, who was having dinner with his wife at the captain's table of the S.S. *Panama*, asking him to return at once as a matter of national urgency. Nixon read Stripling's message to the table and Pat threw up her hands resignedly and said, "Here we go again."

The chameleon-like Andrews (of the *Herald Tribune*) helped Mundt, over the telephone in South Dakota, to issue an adequately portentous statement, and Nixon asked for arrangements to be made to return him to Washington. Stripling, who had thought he was leaving a dying committee, prevailed upon the Coast Guard to rendezvous with the *Panama* in a cove in the Bahamas with a seaplane and return the congressman to Miami. The dutiful Pat was left to make her return solo from the next scheduled port of call. Nixon sat in the copilot's seat on the way back, and gave the swarming press a broad hint of what was coming even before he had completed the transfer between planes after reaching the mainland. Nixon knew nothing of the pumpkin papers when asked about them, and as he flew back to Washington wondered again if they "had a crazy man on our hands." Clerk of the House William "Fishbait" Miller later reported that Nixon told him the day he left on his vacation that he expected to be recalled because of startling developments. Questions have been raised about why James Forrestal, now the secretary of defense, approved Stripling's request that a plane be sent for Nixon and how the press knew when he was landing,[64] but Forrestal could hardly have refused and the press has its sources, possibly Nixon's own office in this case.[65]

Stripling collected Nixon at the airport and described the contents of the pumpkin papers. He had already consulted FDR's former assistant secretary of state, Sumner Welles, about code-breaking as a result of this espionage, and had received an alarmist and (as it turned out) exaggerated report. Nixon looked briefly at the documents and then told the massed press at the HUAC doors that he had "conclusive proof of the greatest treason conspiracy in this nation's history." He claimed that the committee had in its possession stolen and traitorously transmitted secret documents three feet thick when stacked. In fact, they were about an inch thick, and since there had been little treason proven in American history, the claim, even if it had been true, was not so impressive.

Nixon also learned that the Justice Department was about to indict Chambers, and he launched an impassioned defense of his informant, warning that any attempt to discredit him by the administration would be seen as just an attempt to whitewash themselves and the traitors who had been allowed to fester in the long Roosevelt-Truman era. Nixon sat up all night reading the microfilm. Much of it was rather banal (how to paint State Department fire extinguishers, etc.), but most of it would have been of interest to the Kremlin: cables on economic relations with Germany, and on Sino-Japanese affairs. The embattled Hisses were now to stage almost their last stand on the question of whether these cables had been copied on their typewriter.

Nixon met a huge scrum of journalists on the morning of December 6. From this session came the famous pictures of Nixon looking at the microfilm recovered from the pumpkin. Unfortunately, no journalist had the presence of mind to bring a pumpkin and add it as a prop, though the pictures were hokey enough as it was. Some of them showed Nixon with a magnifying glass, like Sherlock Holmes, squinting at the film (which would have been ineffectual, because the film could not be read without a projector).

Another tense, private drama occurred when a reporter asked about the emulsion date on the microfilm; i.e., when it had been developed. After the press had departed, Stripling asked for an official of Eastman Kodak to come over at once. When he arrived, he telephoned to the company headquarters in Rochester, New York, and, after waiting a couple of minutes for the information, informed the group that the film had been manufactured in 1945. Nixon, thunderstruck, and unprepared for another plunge of the roller coaster, exclaimed, "Oh my God. This is the end of my political career." He then tried to blame everything on the young lawyer, Vazzana, who pointed out that he knew nothing of any microfilm and had confined himself to the Baltimore material.

Stripling telephoned Chambers, finding him in his lawyer's office, and handed the phone to Nixon. Chambers affirmed that the film was developed in 1938, and when Nixon told him the company said it had only been manufactured in 1945, Chambers replied, "Impossible." When pressed, he said, "I can't understand it. God must be against me." Nixon shouted that "you had better have a better answer than that," adding that the subcommittee was coming to New York and would see him at the Commodore Hotel at nine that night. Chambers, cracking under the tension, felt deserted by his last and greatest ally, and went out into Wall Street to plan his suicide. He did not wish to go on.

Nixon called a press conference and predicted to Stripling the greatest eating of crow in the history of the Capitol. It would have been embarrassing, to be sure, if the film had been fake, and the pumpkin aspect would have been mercilessly exploited by Nixon's enemies. But he still could have brought Hiss down with the Baltimore material, and brought Chambers down for falsifying evidence. It would have been a farcical debacle, of the kind that intermittently threatened Nixon throughout his career, and that such a retrograde enterprise as HUAC invited.

But the roller coaster abruptly turned up again; the Eastman Kodak man phoned back and said that there had been a mistake. He told Stripling, who took his call, that the film had been manufactured in 1937. Stripling let out a piercing rebel yell, arousing curiosity among the reporters already congregating next door. Stripling started leaping on the furniture and dancing around the room with a dragooned and mystified Nixon, no great dancer under the best of circumstances. Nixon thoughtfully commented, not about himself but about his informant, "Poor Chambers. No one believes him at first." He tried to reach Chambers, to set his mind at ease and "tell him of my regrets at what I had said earlier."[66] Nixon went ahead with the press briefing that, three minutes before, he had expected to be almost his (long-to-be-delayed) "last press conference," and told reporters that they had checked and confirmed the emulsion date, illustrating their thoroughness.

After dismissing a Justice Department delegation that came to demand that HUAC refrain from interviewing any more witnesses and hand over any material it had, Nixon reconvened the press and blasted Truman and Clark as not to be trusted to conduct their own investigation. Richard Nixon called, ironically as the decades would prove, for a "special prosecutor." He was on balance correct that Clark and Truman could not be trusted to handle this, and a special prosecutor intelligently chosen would have been preferable to HUAC, a gang of buffoons except for Nixon, unless returning Speaker Sam Rayburn strengthened its membership and rewrote its mission and procedures. Even Nixon, as we have seen, was irrationally militant at times.

When the subcommittee arrived at Penn Station in New York, on the way to the 9 P.M. meeting with Chambers, its proceedings descended to a new, subterranean level of absurdity. They were met by a U.S. attorney trying to prevent them from questioning Chambers and laying claim to the pumpkin microfilm. An itinerant and very public shouting match occurred as they were driven through the streets in speeding taxis from the station platform to the Commodore Hotel, with HUAC and Justice Department officials hurling threats back and forth between and within the vehicles, while the press rode along in some of the taxis and cars alongside. At the hotel, Stripling, who as the hour of his departure from the committee approached, developed a greater (and completely unforeseen) talent for comedy than he ever had for investigation, threw open a window and screamed down to perplexed passersby on the sidewalk, "We might as well let them hear all about it." (This may have been the inspiration for the great comic success in the next few years of Jackie Gleason's television portrayal in *The Honeymooners* of a bus driver escalating arguments with his wife [Audrey Meadows] by opening the window and screaming amusing insults at her to the neighbors.)

The HUAC-Justice dispute was resolved by the committee's giving over copies of all its material and continuing to interview witnesses even if they were under grand jury subpoena, as Chambers was. No one really pretended any more to be much interested in stopping the leaks they were all sworn to avoid and in which they all garrulously engaged.

Chambers had spent the afternoon preparing to end his life. He bought two tins of cyanide insecticide and put them in a locker at Penn Station, missing by only a few minutes the traveling HUAC-Justice-press circus when it rolled through. He had had occasion to telephone his lawyer in the afternoon to tidy up details before committing suicide, and was told of the mistake about the date of manufacture of the film. He felt deserted and let down by Nixon and Stripling and intended to make an end of it anyway. When he met Nixon and the others at the Commodore, he gave useful evidence to HUAC, adding espionage details and the flourish of a Russian spymaster giving Bukhara rugs to Hiss, the late Harry Dexter White, and another communist agent, Julian Wadleigh.

That night, Chambers went to his mother's house on Long Island, wrote a note asserting the truthfulness of his testimony about Hiss, and tried to do away with himself by asphyxiation from the fumes of the cyanide. It didn't work; he was revived to consciousness by his own vomiting, which quickly brought his mother, who scolded him as a "quitter." Pathetic though it was, and unknown to the public at the time, this episode added to the inanity of the proceedings. But the emerging fact of the communist espionage of Hiss and the others was a serious matter, even if the manner of its elucidation decidedly was not.

Nixon held a midnight press conference in the Commodore Hotel lobby, repeating that the administration was trying to throttle and discredit his witness (who was at the time busily engaged in trying to gas himself to death) by indicting him. Nixon kept up this warning against the indictment of Chambers throughout the week, and his concerns were well-founded. Nixon's minuet with the FBI continued, as he refused to give it a copy of the pumpkin papers but told senior FBI agents he encountered how great was his admiration for the Bureau and for Hoover.[67] Hoover continued to regard Nixon as an unreliable opportunist. He was, but Hoover was a pretty self-interested and high-handed chief of police too.

Nixon tried, most of the time, to maintain some decorum, and in mid-December visited the distinguished undersecretary of state, Robert A. Lovett, and laid out all the facts in the Hiss case. It was a private and secret visit, and he asked that Lovett advise the president of the details. Lovett was impressed, with the facts revealed and with Nixon himself. Discretion was maintained, on both sides, about the conversation, and Truman stopped the "red herring" series of dismissive remarks, as almost the entire press now saluted Nixon's efforts. This was earned praise, as Nixon had single-handedly mined the Chambers source, and his revelations were important. Nixon was now extremely famous and was the featured subject of a Gridiron Club skit, in the presence of Truman and the whole executive, legislative, and judicial leadership, shortly before Christmas. Nixon dissuaded HUAC from the insane project of trying to prove that Roosevelt's confidant, Harry Hopkins, had sent uranium to Stalin, and from investigating communist influence on schoolbooks.[68]

Chambers and Hiss were now both constantly before the grand jury, which was to wind up on December 15. Andrews, whose friendship with Nixon was far from indefectible, ran a story on December 11 about the fiasco over the date of the film and put Nixon in an indifferent light for being panicky and abusive to Chambers. The Justice Department, which had shown no more integrity than HUAC or the FBI in these matters and less competence, sent HUAC a message demanding testimony on the emulsion date issue to ascertain the reliability of the pumpkin papers, undeterred by the fact that Justice did not at that point have them. Nixon had wanted to be called before the grand jury and seized this as his opportunity.

He took it upon himself, quite appropriately, to function as a committee of one, dismissing John Rankin's claims to collegiality. With two aides, and carrying a shiny new briefcase as a decoy, one of the escorts actually bringing the pumpkin films, Nixon attended upon the grand jury in New York on December 13. He was delayed arriving from Washington by a train wreck on the tracks ahead of him.

Nixon was a powerful witness. The prosecutors had him brought before a judge elsewhere in the Foley Square courthouse to resolve his refusal to hand over the microfilm. Nixon explained to the judge that the pumpkin papers belonged now to the House of Representatives and one congressman alone could not dispose of the property of Congress. A compromise was reached in which Nixon would take the microfilm back to Washington and allow the FBI the following day to look at it and within a reasonable time return it to Nixon as agent for the House of Representatives. Nixon testified at length to the grand jury about the salient facts of the case. He was widely acclaimed, both for his stance on the documentary evidence issue, and for his testimony on the facts.

Nixon's appearance was undoubtedly influential in getting the grand jury to vote unanimously (the well-regarded historian Roger Morris wrote that it was by a margin of only one) to indict Alger Hiss for perjury. By now, the Justice Department was in two minds about Hiss. The administration, now barely a month away from reinauguration, would have liked to be done with the whole affair. But there was another school of thought in the Justice Department: that if Hiss were indicted it would stop the administration's being a punching bag for the leaks and harassments of Nixon and Hoover, and the Truman administration could take credit for prosecuting. Hiss's offenses had been so long before, the administration would not be damaged by them. Up to the end, prosecutors were threatening to indict Hiss's wife if he did not plead guilty. He refused.

Nixon claimed complete vindication in the indictment, although that had been wrung from the grand jury in politically questionable circumstances, and as if there were no presumption of innocence. Just before the indictment, the Carnegie Endowment had put Hiss on three months' paid leave. Dulles now moved to dispense with him completely. One of the State Department witnesses late in the grand jury's activities, Lawrence Duggan, jumped out of a sixteenth-story window. Mundt, Nixon, and Stripling held a press conference and Mundt had the abominable taste, after denouncing the deceased as a communist and being asked what other public officials he thought were communists, to say, "We'll name them as they jump out of windows."[69]

In the afterglow of his apparent victory, Nixon apologized for Mundt's comment and acknowledged, when interviewed on network radio by Andrews, that the committee's treatment of Dr. Edward Condon was "unfair." There was a relative hiatus until the Hiss trial in June and July of 1949. Chambers confessed to the FBI his homosexual past, and the Bureau lost no time leaking it to the press (although it would be unhelpful to their case against Hiss). Nixon admirably dissuaded the press from going with it, and convinced them that it was a smear tactic by the Justice Department. The prosecutors also questioned Hiss about his stepson's activities, which alerted the Hiss camp not to get into such questions about Chambers. In acting as effectively as he had, Nixon fully redeemed himself from his brief rage at Chambers over the emulsion date of the microfilm, which had brought on Chambers's attempted suicide.

The Hiss trial produced the coruscation such an intense and complicated and vulgar drama required. Hiss's lawyer, Lloyd Paul Stryker, pulled out all the stops that weren't already at full volume: Chambers, a "furtive, deceptive, liar, blasphemer [as if the population of America eschewed blasphemy], communist conspirator . . . thug . . . moral leper," should be preceded, as in medieval times, by someone warning, "Unclean! Unclean!"

Nixon was more thorough than ever, even preparing a dossier on the Truman-appointed federal judge, Samuel H. Kaufman. Nixon, Mundt, and Hebert prevailed upon Pat McCarran, Democratic senator from Nevada, to tell Kaufman, according to Louis Nichols's report to the inevitable J. Edgar Hoover, that he hoped it would not be necessary for the Senate Judiciary Committee to look into "how the judge functions in the Hiss-Chambers case." This was an outrageous tampering with the judge, but was fairly consistent with the standards of disinterested conduct and the quest for condign justice throughout this appalling melodrama.

Nixon contacted the chief prosecutor, Thomas Murphy, through

Victor Lasky of the *New York World-Telegram*. Nixon wrote up a full "Memorandum on Hiss Testimony Before Committee," which didn't tell Murphy much that he needed to know. Lasky was not Nixon's only channel. He advised Nichols, FBI deputy director, that a certain witness probably had a "guilt complex" at the thought that Hiss might get off, and that he could therefore be unusually useful.[70] Hoover ordered that the witness be interviewed again, but nothing came of it.

Nixon was an impatient, intimately involved bystander. As it came down to the wire, Nixon and the HUAC staff began to be overtly pre-occupied by the verdict. There was nothing improper in any of this, but when the jury reported it was unable to reach a decision, four jurors un-shakable in not-guilty verdicts, Nixon went over the top and demanded an inquiry into the judge's "fitness to serve on the bench." He also accused the jury foreman of pro-Hiss bias, a charge supported by some jurors. Truman defended Kaufman.[71]

The new Democratic majority on HUAC now rallied in support of the judge and the administration, and Nixon showed one of his worst traits, self-righteous hypocrisy. He, who had had no possible motive except political advancement in HUAC matters, po-facedly stated that administration spokesmen "unable to defend Judge Kaufman's conduct . . . are attempting to turn the case into a political issue which it is not." If it wasn't, then what was politician Nixon doing commenting on it at all?[72]

— VIII —

The government prepared to reaccuse Hiss. Isaac D. Levine, a prominent behind-the-scenes anti-communist and HUAC collaborator, met with Lloyd Stryker, Hiss's lawyer, and Allen Dulles, brother of Hiss's former employer, and walked him through a lot of evidence that Murphy was not able to introduce. Hiss wanted someone less histrionic than Stryker, and by mutual agreement Stryker withdrew from the case. Felix Frankfurter, who had given character evidence for Hiss, was lobbied intensely. He was not present at the second trial.

By the time the second trial began in November 1949, China had been taken over by Mao Tse-tung and Chou En-lai, and the U.S.S.R. had tested an atomic bomb, obliging Truman to announce that the United States would develop a hydrogen bomb. The North Atlantic Treaty Organization had been set up. The Truman administration did not allay public concern by urging all American families to dig a bomb shelter. International concerns about communism had spiked to new levels of hostility. While the trial was in progress, the atomic espionage of Klaus Fuchs became known. Soon after it ended, the allegations against Julius and Ethel Rosenberg and other alleged atomic spies came down. The euphoria of victory in the Second World War had given way to bitter recriminations and paranoia with astonishing speed. Kaufman was succeeded on the bench by Henry W. Goddard, a Warren Harding Republican who slept regularly during proceedings and was known to and admired by some of the jurors.

The most important aspect of the second trial was the typewriter that Priscilla Hiss had allegedly used to retype the cables revealed by Chambers in the Baltimore deposition. If the typewriter could be authoritatively matched to other Hiss correspondence of the time, it would be determining. This would be more of a technical and scientific evidence trial. There remains a good deal of controversy about the rigor of the prosecution's case on this issue. What the government thought to be the Hiss typewriter they traced to a sale in 1927, two years before company records indicated it was manufactured. Hoover himself was reduced almost to demanding that the facts be made to conform to the prosecution's requirement. The prosecutors relied on claims by experts that the same typewriter was used for domestic Hiss purposes and to retype the Baltimore documents handed over to the Russians. They produced no sworn verification apart from expert analyses of the typed product. The defense counsel, less flamboyant and determined than Lloyd Stryker, did not press the point as he should have.

Having got away with an incomplete rendering of proof, the assistant U.S. attorney admonished the jurors, "If you think that any bit of evidence . . . material or immaterial, was manufactured, conceived, or suborned by the FBI, acquit this man. . . . The FBI ought to be told by you that they can't tamper with witnesses and evidence." The skirmishing between the Justice Department and the FBI continued right to the summations. The defense did not exploit the spirit of this generous thought. Judge Goddard was more indulgent of the government's witness list. There was never proof of the ownership of the old Ford that Hiss had supposedly given Chambers. It was only proved that Hiss had given the car to Rosen. And Chambers was an eccentric witness, who had sudden inexplicable lapses of recollection that jarred his credibility. A psychiatrist was called to attack Chambers's mental stability, and the government attacked the psychiatrist as a crank (with some reason) as well as an unethical cheat and a subversive. Alistair Cooke, an astute, if perhaps inflated, observer of American phenomena, thought it "the first public trial run of the common man's resistance to psychiatry" – an interesting perspective, but the jurors did not opine directly on this question. Despite his shabby appearance and hesitant speaking patterns, Chambers was not only eloquent, he had a sonorous voice, similar to that of his younger friend William F. Buckley. (On his distinguishedly attended eightieth birthday, in 2005, Buckley reverently quoted, as part of the conclusion of his address, from Chambers.)

On January 21, 1950, Alger Hiss was found guilty of two counts of perjury. Of course the atmosphere in which the trials had occurred was unhelpful and the second judge was incompetent, and the evidence would have been found inconclusive if the defense had not been outlawyered. That would not have happened if Hiss had stayed with Stryker. But the most important contributing element in the verdict was the almost indisputable fact that Hiss was guilty. He had been a communist and had known Chambers much better than he had acknowledged.

Nixon received the results with dignified satisfaction, claiming vindication for congressional investigations generally, "when they are accompanied by adequate staff work and fair procedure" (both of which were generally lacking in this case). When interviewed later that night on the radio by the inevitable Bert Andrews, Nixon fired a full broadside at Truman and Roosevelt: "This conspiracy would have come to light long since had there not been a definite, determined, and deliberate effort on the part of certain high officials in two administrations to keep the public from knowing the facts."[73] Congratulations poured in to Nixon, including the imperishable Herbert Hoover's happy claim that "the stream of treason that existed in our government has been exposed." This remained the orthodox Republican view of what had gone horribly wrong with the fortunes of their party in the last twenty years. On January 23, Nixon held an immense press conference and accused the administration of being negligent and cavalier about what he now called the "Red Master Plot to subvert America."

Of a higher moral order was the comment of Secretary of State Dean Acheson: "I should like to make it clear to you that whatever the outcome of the appeal . . . I do not intend to turn my back on Alger Hiss." He cited a

Biblical reference for the hard-bitten reporters (Acheson was the son of a bishop), and when they looked it up, it was "[I was] naked and ye clothed me; I was sick and ye visited me; I was in prison and ye came unto me."[74] Nixon declared what he called this invocation of the Last Supper "disgusting" and whipped up a backlash to Acheson's fearless personal loyalty. He stated that "Traitors in the high councils of our own government have made sure that the deck is stacked on the Soviet side of the diplomatic tables."

The public policy of the United States was now being conducted in almost the same terms of Orwellian hyperbole as in the U.S.S.R., though more clangorously, since there was no audible opposition in Russia. Acheson offered his resignation to Truman over the controversy, and the president refused it. Truman had attended (in 1945) the funeral of his original political patron, Tom Pendergast, political boss of Kansas City, "an old friendless man who had just been released from jail," as Mr. Truman said. When put to an even more severe test than Truman and Acheson many years later, Nixon too would know something about loyalty.

Nixon sought and received agreement from the House of Representatives to address it on the Hiss case, which he did in a tour de force of about two hours on January 26, 1950, holding the packed chamber and galleries spellbound throughout his remarks. He recognized the need, as anticommunism became America's principal pastime, of reinforcing HUAC, even though it would now have a Democratic majority, and continuing to befriend the FBI as the only counterweight to an administration commanding congressional majorities that would be no less determined to defend American interests abroad than the Republicans but would be less inclined to tear its own government apart looking for Reds than Hoover and Nixon would like.

Nixon got great applause for the FBI and Hoover, although he knew their performance had been, to say the least, unimpressive. Nixon gave his colleagues a rather bowdlerized account of the case, and called for a campaign to educate the country about communism. His peroration was one that he would endlessly repeat until his party had displaced the Democrats: Five years before, 180 million people had lived under "Soviet totalitarianism" and the odds were nine to one in favor of the democratic West. Now, as the administration slept, and, implicitly, the Hiss and other subversive tumors festered and metastasized, the demographic odds were five to three against the West. Mao's takeover of China facilitated this sort of numbers game, and it was widely assumed at this time that Stalin controlled all communists, wherever and whomever they might be.

It was only eleven days after Nixon's speech in Congress that Wisconsin's Senator Joseph R. McCarthy told the astonished ladies of the Ohio County Women's Republican Club in Wheeling, West Virginia, that he had the names of 205 known communists in the State Department that the administration was tolerating to continue undisturbed in their work. This was a complete invention and marked the beginning of the most appalling and irresponsible phase of the Red Scare in America. It had worked for McCarthy in 1946, when, as a lower court judge, he had run against a scion of Wisconsin's long-governing family, Robert La Follette Jr., on the spurious ground that he had been playing into the hands of the communists.[75] McCarthy had been considering what theme to strike to get some publicity and stoke up his campaign for reelection two years later.

He took some of Nixon's phrases and metaphors and wildly contorted them, skewing the demographic imbalance with the communists to ratios that, if rendered more elegantly, could have recalled the Lays of Ancient Rome in their portrayal of the bravely outnumbered.

The Mundt-Nixon bill, forcing the registration of the Communist Party and affiliated organizations, was passed as the McCarran-Wood Act over Truman's veto, and HUAC was voted huge increases in budget and grew to have a staff of seventy-five, much to Hoover's disconcertion. The three-cornered jockeying between HUAC, the FBI, and the Justice Department escalated, with endless quarrels and alliances and exchanges, all battled out in campaigns of press leaks.

Nixon felt ever afterward that he had had a Pyrrhic victory, that while he had gained great renown and prominence from the Hiss affair, he had also earned the implacable and relentless animosity of the most powerful media and political and social elements of the liberal establishment. He might have always been an outsider because of his own foibles, but there is some truth that they looked upon him with general distrust and distaste (but not disrespect) until late in his life, when even these fires subsided. By then it would be a world much changed, in no small part because of Richard Nixon's efforts. The U.S. liberal establishment could not ultimately dispute that he had done more to de-escalate the impasse with the communist powers, and to help de-communize them, than had their own liberal champions. The leading historian of the Hiss affair, Allen Weinstein, found "no evidence that a demonic Dick Nixon participated in an effort to frame Alger Hiss."[76]

For the time being, even the highbrow left was gulled, if not cowed. Arch-liberals Richard Rovere, who called the Hiss case a "triumph of due process," and Irving Howe, who thought it a victory of "intelligent anti-communism," and Arthur Schlesinger Jr., who corresponded cordially with the dumpy little hypocrite Karl Mundt, expressed fleeting sentiments of anti-communist solidarity. But Nixon would be at war without much interruption with his domestic political foes, with no quarter given and little asked, for nearly forty years.

He was invited to give General Dwight D. Eisenhower a secret briefing on the communist issue, and did so, effectively and judiciously, in late 1949.[77] This was his first meeting with Eisenhower, and it went well. It might have been reasonably possible to foresee that these two would lead the Republican Party out of the wilderness, as Eisenhower was much discussed as a presidential candidate, and Nixon was clearly one of the very ablest card-carrying Republicans (to borrow from McCarthyite parlance). What would have required a genuine clairvoyant would be to foresee that Eisenhower and Nixon would lead their party in five of the next six presidential elections, and would profoundly change the world.

On March 12, 1951, the Supreme Court (including Hiss's patron Frankfurter) refused to hear Hiss's appeal. Nixon found this a suitable time for another release: "The decision should under no circumstances be an occasion for elation or gratification because not since the days of Benedict Arnold have the American people been the victim of such a brazen and inexplicable act of treachery by a man who commanded the faith and confidence of our highest officials." This was the usual Nixon hyperbole on the subject.[78]

Alger Hiss, impeccably dressed, majestic in his defiance of cruel events that he had largely but not entirely brought on himself, and handcuffed to an African-American fellow prisoner hiding his face under his coat, went in a penitentiary van from Foley Square courthouse to serve his more than two years in prison on March 22, 1951. He fought on for more than forty years to clear his name, getting his disbarment revoked and his pension restored, but was denied vindication by a judicial review that ignored the problems with the typewriter and other weaknesses in the original prosecutions. When the Soviet Union collapsed, the authorities in President Yeltsin's post-communist Russia said there was no record of Hiss having been a Soviet agent. Even if that was true, and it could not be verified, it was not what Hiss was convicted of; whether he was an agent or not, he had been an active communist sympathizer. There is nothing legally wrong with that either, but he was almost certainly engaged in passing secret documents to the Russians, and he did commit perjury opposite Chambers. Hiss's unstable wife divorced him. He had to work for a time as a salesman, remarried, and cobbled together his life in dignified obscurity. He wrote a couple of books and soldiered on like other old communists, such as Molotov and Spain's La Pasionaria (Dolores Ibárruri, 1895–1989), to a great age, ninety-two, dying in New York in 1996, having outlived Hoover, Chambers, and Nixon.

Both the ululations of triumph and the tragic lamentations over the Hiss case are broadly justified. It was a great victory for a thirty-seven-year-old two-term congressman. He had wounded the long-ruling Eastern establishment, shaken a long-sitting Democratic government, and shown the need to take loyalty questions in the quickly escalating Cold War with the U.S.S.R. more seriously. In procedural terms, he had been fairly responsible, when the temptations not to be so must have been great, and when the conduct of most others in prominent roles was disgraceful. Once battle was engaged and Nixon was convinced of Hiss's guilt, he bore down on him relentlessly, but apart from lobbying Dulles to deny Hiss, as his employer, the presumption of innocence, he confined himself to normal channels of legal combat, as well as doing his full part in the deluvian battle of press leaks. He retracted and publicly apologized for the excess over the Condon affair, and for his slight association with Mundt's tasteless comment about communists committing suicide.

Of course there were no gigantic internal Red plots and infestations of treason as claimed, but much of this would have been avoided if Truman and Clark had taken the issue more seriously at the outset. If they had acted preemptively and conducted, as they had the power to do, dignified private hearings without simply whitewashing everyone and making jokes about "red herrings," they would not have sent Hoover out on the warpath against them, or left such an opening for HUAC once it got into the hands of a serious political opponent in Nixon. If Truman had not summoned Congress for no good purpose back to Washington in August 1948, there never would have been any Hiss hearings, at least any that led anywhere.

And if the Keystone Kops dunderheads running the grand jury at the end of 1948 had not given Nixon the opportunity to appear, Hiss might not have been indicted at all. If Hiss had not lied under oath about knowing Chambers in his first appearance at HUAC, there would have been no cause to indict him, as the statute of limitations had cleared him on espionage. If he had not changed lawyers after the first trial, he would probably have got another hung jury, or even an acquittal.

The conspiracy of incompetence was far wider than any subversive one, and included Hoover, Clark, Hiss, Chambers, most of HUAC, and many judges and Justice Department officials. Only Nixon was never in that category. For that, as for his courage and diligence, he deserved and received great credit. In the circumstances, his pursuit of Hiss was not discreditable. Hiss was lying, he had been a loyalty risk, and he compounded his vulnerability with a provokingly disdainful attitude to Nixon personally. This was not the time, and Nixon was not the person, to turn the other cheek.

The fate of Alger Hiss is objectively sad. But he thought he could bulldoze the yokels at HUAC with his urbane establishment show of social and sartorial and epigrammatic strength. Just telling the truth would have worked much better.

The minor problem of communist infiltration in the United States would be over-attended to in public policy. The atmosphere of public discourse was needlessly embittered. The lowest mutations of political demagogues had already begun to surface. The Cold War was fairly launched, with uncertain portents. The United States was the ultimate power in the history of the nation state, despite the vagaries of parts of its political and prosecutorial system. But Europe and the Far East, where the peace had broken down in the thirties, were very vulnerable. Stalin, commanding the false mystique of communism, much of the Eurasian landmass, and an atomic arsenal, was more dangerous than Hitler had been.

Richard Nixon's star was rising quickly. He would sometimes join in partisan stridency, but for a time he generally kept clear of the more extreme forms of partisan backbiting that were now about to disturb the nation and astound the world.

Chapter Three

Vertical Ascent
1950–1952

— I —

AFTER THE IMMENSE CELEBRITY of the Hiss success, and with the anti-communist theme being hammered relentlessly by most of the country's politicians, it was natural for a man of Richard Nixon's ambitions and acute political instincts to consider moving up the ladder of office. Earl Warren was an immoveable fixture as governor of California, William Knowland was a contemporary Republican, so the logical next step was the Senate seat held by Democrat Sheridan Downey. Downey had followed a long trajectory from left to right in California politics, having run in 1934 as Upton Sinclair's candidate for lieutenant governor on the EPIC (End Poverty in California) ticket. After that campaign was sandbagged by a coalition of Republicans, conservative Democrats, and the movie studio heads, Downey ran for and won the nomination of the Democrats as U.S. senator in 1938.

In doing this, he displaced another of the Democrats' great heavy-weights, William Gibbs McAdoo, who had been Wilson's Treasury secretary and, for good measure, his son-in-law (like Alger Hiss's pre-war boss, Francis Sayre). In the twenties, McAdoo had led the Prohibitionist forces in the Democrats against the anti-Prohibition, Roman Catholic governor of New York, Alfred E. Smith. They deadlocked the Democratic convention of 1924, which chose a compromise candidate, John W. Davis, after Smith had been nominated by Franklin D. Roosevelt, who was returning to public life three years after his disabling attack of polio. McAdoo had delivered the

California delegation that started the rockslide for Roosevelt on the third ballot at the 1932 convention, beginning the long Democratic reign in the White House that was still continuing uninterrupted in 1950. McAdoo was elected U.S. senator from California in 1932, but in 1938, aged seventy-five, he lost to Downey, who ran as a reformer, but without the EPIC baggage.

Downey had been a vocal supporter of pensioners and veterans in his early years. But all unemployment was eliminated before Pearl Harbor, and Downey had become steadily more friendly with the big ranchers, oil interests, land developers, and movie studio heads, who were the financial leaders of California. The Golden State had enjoyed a return to economic boom times during and after the Second World War, and there was a steady stream to California of hundreds of thousands of people per year from all over the country, "their noses and radiators pointed toward the promised land."[1] Downey even published a book ghost-written for him called *They Would Rule the Valley*. He and his book opposed restraints on large landowners and developers in the Central Valley of California, where Downey himself had presciently become a substantial landowner himself.

In the years during and immediately following the war, as prosperity returned, the influx of newcomers to California tended to be less John Steinbeck's Okies, seeking the finest citadels of the New Deal and bearing westward likenesses of Franklin D. Roosevelt like the Infant of Prague. They tended to be conventional Southerners well to the right politically of the egalitarian EPIC group, which had believed in collective economics and the absence of complexional distinctions.

As the election year 1950 began, there was speculation about Downey's health. There was also concern that he could face a liberal Democratic challenger. He would have no difficulty bringing cross-over Republicans on to the Democratic side to retain the nomination, unless the Republican candidate was as popular as Downey with conservative voters. If he was, the danger for Downey would be either losing so many liberal votes to his Democratic rival that he lost the nomination or making an implausible move to the left that sent the conservative Democrats to the Republican challenger. The thirty-seven-year-old Richard Nixon was precisely the personification of the dangers to the reelection of the sixty-five-year-old Downey.

Nixon had been looking at this prospect all through 1949. In 1944, the Republican candidate against Downey, the lackluster Frederick F. Houser, who had lost to Voorhis in 1936, had lost by only 52 percent to 48 percent, and would have won if Downey had not been pulled in on the long coattails of Franklin D. Roosevelt, who carried the state by about half a million votes. Republican analysts thought that without Roosevelt, and given the change in the political horizon as communist and other issues intruded, and with Nixon in place of Houser and Downey six years slower, Nixon could win. He wanted to be president, and if he could get to senator, he would be within striking distance. His Twelfth District coterie wanted him to stay where he was, because they wanted a world-famous congressman, not a senator they would have to share with the rest of the state.

In April 1949, Nixon spoke to the Los Angeles County Republican Central Committee. He warned them about complacent assurances that they had lost only narrowly in the last election, something they had not managed to do in their four defeats at the hands of Roosevelt. He said that Truman had moved well to the left of where he had run, that Strom Thurmond and Henry Wallace and their Dixiecrat and liberal followers had been given a good trip to the woodshed and were back in the Democratic house, and that there was no reason to imagine that the Republicans could not be in the wilderness for a long while yet if they did not do things differently. Though he did not personalize it, Nixon felt a bitter grievance against the smugness, which amounted to defeatism, of Warren, Dewey, Taft, and the other party elders. They might be content to be noted provincial officials while their enemies ran the country and changed, even imperiled, the world. But settling for this status was not why Nixon had bustled into public life.

He enunciated a skillful program that covered all the Republican sensibilities, without painting them into the corner of reaction. He wanted reduction of government and of taxes to pay for government; a crackdown on the abuses of both management and labor, which he specified in appropriate detail; tax incentives for small business; and, little publicized subsequently, serious remedial action about civil rights and not just window dressing, which is what he accused Truman and Hubert Humphrey of producing. Nixon wanted a rollback of the socialization of services, but their assured and affordable provision through the private sector, and generalized profit sharing for unionized labor to give it a stake in the employer companies. He advocated comprehensive government-guaranteed but private-sector-provided medical insurance. He demanded a serious attack on loyalty risks in government, and the restoration of a bipartisan foreign policy pledged to a worldwide defense of the security interests of the United States. He wanted Truman to show as much determination fighting communism in Asia as in Europe.

Nixon was only a second-term congressman, but he wasn't just any two-term congressman. Except for Sam Rayburn and possibly Joe Martin, he was probably the most famous member of the House of Representatives, and he was a grayhound pawing in the slips. Following the 1948 Republican debacle, there was a sizable number of Californians who were disgusted with Earl Warren's masquerade as an allegory of good government above it all, in partisan terms, and they resolved, very publicly, that their governor was "wishy-washy and namby-pamby."[2] (Warren was not used to such lèse-majesté, and had convinced himself that the electoral disaster was Dewey's fault. It had been, but Warren had his share of it.)

Nixon met privately with some of the leading financial influences in San Francisco and Los Angeles, and engaged Murray Chotiner as manager, before more or less publicly declaring his candidacy for the Senate on May 20, 1949, eighteen months before the election. The Nixon campaign, with the usual dissembling in these matters, was called California Volunteers for Good Government. Apart from the identity of the state, and that only as a stepping-stone to the White House, the title gave no hint of its real nature or purpose. Nixon oscillated between confidence that the Democrats could be finally defeated and concern that if he and like-minded people could not get control of it, the Republican Party would continue to be a doormat for the Democrats for another twenty years. That had almost been the fate of the Democrats, from Abraham Lincoln to Woodrow Wilson (the Republicans won eleven of thirteen presidential elections from 1860 to 1908, inclusive, and lost to Wilson only when Theodore Roosevelt and Taft split the party).

He arranged to be drafted by the California Young Republicans, and then the *Los Angeles Times* quoted extensively and approvingly from a speech of his, and he arrived with much publicity in Los Angeles from Washington and spoke to the Beverly Hills Republican Women and a quick sequence of other prominent political groups.

Nixon did not manage the natural indignities of political ambition as well as some others did. Roosevelt looked and sounded apostolic, no matter what political skulduggery he was engaged in. Truman came from the other stylistic end to Roosevelt's, and seemed to treat grubby politics and the dropping of the atomic bomb all with the same directness and absence of histrionics. Dwight Eisenhower managed to seem above much of it, or at least a politician ennobled by his uniform. Adlai Stevenson and John F. Kennedy offered witticisms that were actually amusing, and were able to send the message that they would rather be doing something else without offending their audiences. When Nixon, as he toured California preparing for his Senate campaign, was asked if he was running for the Senate, he actually said, "I will pray about it." This wasn't a self-inflicted wound, but it was a lost opportunity for self-deprecation. Nixon probably had prayed about it, and not at all to his discredit, but he was certainly confident of the response to his request for divine guidance by then.

Nixon finally announced his candidacy for the Republican nomination for U.S. senator in Pomona on November 3, 1949, in an address broadcast throughout the state. He warned that the country was facing a choice between freedom and "state socialism," and that the Republicans could not win by "pussyfooting." He said, "They can call it planned economy, the Fair Deal, or social welfare. It's still the same old socialist baloney any way you slice it." He warned of an immense Democratic "slush fund" that would be deployed against them by a "clique of labor lobbyists." The only way to win was to "put on a fighting, rocking, socking campaign." In this, even his enemies would agree, he would be as good as his word.

By this time, a formidable and glamorous opponent to Downey had attacked from the left, seeking to wrest the Democratic nomination from Downey as he had taken it from McAdoo twelve years before. Helen Gahagan Douglas, actress, wife of actor Melvyn Douglas, congresswoman, national committeewoman, and friend of Eleanor Roosevelt, announced her candidacy on October 5. This doubtless assisted Nixon in his religious devotions on the subject.

Helen Douglas, forty-nine, was a New York–born, upper-income, private-school and Barnard woman who went on to the stage and enjoyed early and continuous success, in the theater, opera, and in her one film, in the title role of *She*. She married Melvyn Douglas in 1931, and was reckoned to be one of America's most beautiful women. Once installed in California, she became an ardent advocate for the migrant workers and the displaced fugitives from the Dust Bowl. John Steinbeck wrote his famous novel *The Grapes of Wrath* about such people and formed a committee to help them, which Helen Douglas happily joined. In this capacity, she met Eleanor

Roosevelt, and eventually the president, and became friendly with them. Helen Douglas had had a torrid and rather public affair with congressman and then senator Lyndon B. Johnson, from shortly after she arrived in Washington. They publicly lived together, drove to work together, and held hands even in the corridors of the Congress.[3]

She was the prototypical energetic bleeding heart, aggressively full of good intentions but somewhat impractical in her political methods. She fought Taft-Hartley but had an impeccable record in foreign policy, including voting with Nixon for the Marshall Plan, until she voted against the Truman administration on aid to Greece and Turkey. She felt that the United States must not allow its hostility to communism to drive it into support for regimes that were themselves undemocratic. It was not going to be possible to conduct the Cold War that way, but Douglas did not grasp that. (She should have listened when Franklin D. Roosevelt said of a notorious Latin American dictator, Anastasio Somoza Garcia of Nicaragua, that he was "a son-of-a-bitch, but he's our son-of-a-bitch.")

She was unambiguously anti-communist, but felt that communism posed no threat at all to the United States internally, and that abroad, the United States should only embrace countries that were reasonably democratic. She was right in the first point, and not completely mistaken in the second, but had no strategic sense and made no effort to package her views in a way not guaranteed to attract the animosity of most of her listeners. In one of her early addresses, as a congressional candidate, to an African-American church, she exclaimed, "I love the Negro people."[4] Her effusions were always well-intentioned but not always well-received.

A turn-of-the-century law had confined public-assisted irrigation in California to properties not exceeding 160 acres. Many got around this by jointly operating connected properties as if they were one, or incorporating properties and spreading the shares adequately to keep within the 160-acre limit. Downey wished to repeal the law, but Helen Douglas was a passionate retentionist. She was similarly adamant in opposing transferring control of offshore oil to the state, which was much more likely to be influenced by the oil companies than was the federal government, despite Earl Warren's occupancy of the governor's mansion.

Nixon and Warren agreed that they would run separate campaigns. Since Warren was going to do that anyway, it gave Nixon some pleasure to trek up to Sacramento and tell the governor that this was his, Nixon's, intention.

Chotiner had already begun to canvass the state's newspapers. His standard gambit was not to ask for support on the first visit but to lay out the candidate's views in the manner best-suited to attract support and then to inquire about advertising rates. Chotiner considered almost all the press, except the very largest outlets, to be for sale.

Sheridan Downey, despite a severe ulcer, ended speculation that he would retire by telling a Democratic Party dinner in Los Angeles in December 1949 that he would be running for a third term. He attacked Helen Douglas forcefully and scarcely mentioned Nixon. The Downey campaign was instantly well lubricated with oil and rancher and developer money. Douglas accused her own party of trying to strangle her financially. Downey accused her of being an extremist, and she accused Downey of being a lackey of monopolists and a part-time senator.

The California Republican Assembly (CRA), an association of party regulars, met at Pebble Beach on January 27, the day after Nixon gave his marathon speech in Congress on the Hiss case. A former candidate, Frederick Houser, now a superior court judge, had let it be known that he wanted to run again for senator. Nixon, because of Washington commitments, was unable to get to the CRA meeting, but Chotiner had persuaded the *Los Angeles Times* to write a strong endorsement of Nixon on the day the CRA would be meeting, and had had delivered to the CRA executive committee on the morning of the CRA vote a recording of Nixon's powerful speech.[5] The combined effect was as had been desired, and Nixon was endorsed unanimously by the committee. Thus was Houser disposed of. Even easier to deal with was the Los Angeles supervisor, Raymond V. Darby, who went for lieutenant governor against the incumbent Goodwin J. Knight. To get him out of the Senate race, the *Times* agreed to endorse him against Knight, but this was another put-up job, as the *Times* presented a small, tepid endorsement but plastered headlines and flattering photographs of Knight through the paper. To take the Republican nomination for U.S. senator from California, Nixon would only have to face an obscure anti-Catholic candidate and dating-agency owner who rejoiced in the name of Ulysses Grant Bixby Meyers.

Gerald L.K. Smith, the ancient plowhorse of downmarket American politics, a raving racist evangelical clergyman from Shreveport, Louisiana, and former sidekick of Huey Long and Dr. Francis Townsend, entered the California campaign in Nixon's favor. He declared that the uncoverer of Alger

Hiss would "get rid of the Jew-Communists." (After the assassination of Huey Long in 1935, Smith had publicly implied that Roosevelt was responsible for murdering Long. He tried to carry on Long's Share the Wealth campaign, but Long's entourage made a deal with Roosevelt and returned to the Democratic fold. This was known in the Roosevelt camp as "the Second Louisiana Purchase," making Smith a political orphan. He had been drifting for fifteen years.)

Nixon was careful to stay clear of the extreme Republicans; he voted with the Democrats in distributing two billion dollars' worth of food in domestic aid in March 1950, and he called for a bipartisan foreign policy and general support for the president. He suggested that Truman consult such Republicans as Dewey, Warren, Dulles, Stassen, and Eisenhower on foreign policy matters, and left the Red-baiters out. Nixon took his distance from McCarthy, saying that there should be an impartial investigation of the State Department – not by McCarthy or HUAC or any congressional committee. He de-emphasized his HUAC connection and was conspicuously absent when the new chairman, the nonentity John Wood, who had rarely raised his voice when Nixon was active on HUAC, informed the House that HUAC was assembling a blacklist of one million subversives.

On April 15, 1950, he told a press conference that only the Communist Party was profiting from McCarthy's charges.[6] Nixon also staunchly defended Dr. Robert Oppenheimer, the principal scientist on the Manhattan (atomic) Project, who had been accused of being a communist before a California legislative committee that mimicked HUAC.[7] Nixon later identified Owen Lattimore and Philip Jessop as the principal supporters in the State Department of the pro–Mao Tse-tung view of the Chinese debacle but stopped well short of calling them communists or "commie" agents.[8] (Privately he was astounded at how ignorant McCarthy was. He allegedly did not even know that the American CP leader was Earl Browder.)[9] Nixon gave a Lincoln Day address in which he said the U.S.S.R. was the ultimate version of the slave state and Britain, because of its socialism, was a half-slave state – pretty severe treatment of Clement Attlee.

The Democratic primary was still heating up, with Nixon waiting to see from which angle he should attack his opponent, when Downey's ulcer spiked up again and he withdrew from the race on March 28, 1950. His statement, which he left to a reporter to draft, said that he did not want to have to reply to the "vicious and unethical propaganda" of Helen Douglas. She didn't bother wishing him a quick recovery as he checked into Bethesda Naval Hospital; rather she accused Downey of chickening out and implied that he wasn't sick at all. This assured Downey's support for Nixon, who graciously wished the outgoing senator well. Nixon had thought all along that Douglas would be a much easier opponent than Downey, who had made many rich friends, and with whom most California voters were comfortable.

The day after Downey's withdrawal, the publisher of the quirky Los Angeles *Daily News* (much smaller than the market-leading *Times* and Hearst's *Herald-Examiner*), Manchester Boddy, threw his hat in the ring for the Democratic nomination. Boddy, a former encyclopedia salesman who had come to California in 1920 after being gassed on the Western Front in 1918, was a self-educated philosopher and literary scholar who frequently wrote columns in his often racy tabloid about Plutarch, Plato, and *fin de siècle* French novelists. Boddy had been friendly with and supportive of Douglas but hit the ground running as a primary candidate, calling her an extremist.

Helen Douglas counterattacked, but on March 30, presumably trying to move from internecine to partisan attack, she called Nixon a "demagogue" selling "fear and hysteria . . . [and] nice, unadulterated fascism." It was already known that when Nixon promised a "rocking, socking campaign," as he had when he announced in November, it was likely to be pretty rough. But when Douglas, who was no tactical genius, not content with denying that her late opponent was really unwell, opened fire on Nixon as a fascist, she was almost sure to get more than she bargained for. She went on to call Nixon a "Peewee trying to frighten people so that they are too afraid to turn out the lights."[10] Beautiful and intelligent woman as she was, had she stopped dissenting from the bipartisan, Truman-sponsored consensus on Greece and Turkey and run a moderate and tasteful campaign, she could have exploited a great deal of underdog and chivalrous sentiment if Nixon and Chotiner had tried the Red or Pink scare on her. Instead she fired the first shot at an opponent who deployed far heavier artillery with much better marksmanship than she did. The Nixon-Douglas campaign is well-remembered, but it is little remembered that Helen Douglas started the mudslinging.

At the beginning of April, Dick and Pat Nixon set out in a "woody," a paneled station wagon loaded with loudspeaking equipment and donated by a supportive car dealer, to tour the state. He stopped every ten or twenty miles and spoke from on top of or beside the car, after handing out placards to the first ten or so people to arrive. Pat would distribute little red Nixon thimbles, as they had in their first campaign four years before. Nixon claimed the mantle of Downey for himself, and said the dispute over the 160-acre limit for federal irrigation subsidies was a phony issue designed to sow division in the state. He claimed, in effect, that everybody who needed irrigation should have it, and those who needed financial assistance should have that too. Accompanying reporters got tired of it, as they always do following candidates, but Nixon always allowed for questions and always handled them adroitly.

He continued to put blue water between McCarthy and himself, repeating that the "communists profit" from excessive charges, that he was neutral about McCarthy's ever-mounting allegations, and that if they were false, McCarthy should be "forced to pay the political penalty for making false charges." He referred repeatedly to the dangers of "wild, unsubstantiated charges . . . [and] indiscriminate anti-communist name-calling." Helen Douglas repeatedly said she had "utter scorn for pip-squeaks like Nixon and McCarthy."[11] Nixon's enemies have tried to tar him with the McCarthy brush. The suggestion that they were interchangeable was not true at the start of McCarthy's rise as the self-nominated scourge of communists, and it certainly did not approach the truth as McCarthy's wild assault on perceived loyalty risks continued.

Nixon was happy to throw a certain amount of raw meat to the Red-baiters and was not prepared to allow an issue he had burnished to its present intensity to get away from him; but, having ridden the rocket to a great altitude, neither was he going to stay with it as it descended into perfidy. He called for the deportation of Australian-born fellow traveler Harry Bridges, leader of the longshoremen's union, a reasonable proposition, and laced his speeches with exhortations to preparedness against Soviet aggression. He repeatedly stated that the U.S.S.R. would unleash war if it thought that it could win, but that was nothing more than Winston Churchill and others had been saying for several years, and was almost certainly true.

Across the country, the anti-Red message was selling well. John Foster Dulles, one of the least gregarious men in modern American public life, ran for senator from New York against Roosevelt's successor (and Dewey's predecessor), as governor of New York, Herbert H. Lehman. Dulles said, "I know that he is not a communist, but I also know that the communists are in his corner." In Florida, John F. Kennedy's closest carousing companion, George

Smathers, defeated old-time New Dealer Claude Pepper in the Democratic primary, calling him the "Red Pepper." Helen Douglas called this "the dirtiest campaign" in the country. She would help to assure that that dubious honor would not stand for long.

The attacks on Helen Douglas began with the pro-Nixon press. The general line was that whether she was a communist was irrelevant, as she had been giving aid and comfort to the communists for years.[12] Nixon sailed fairly serenely through the primary. There was one joint meeting with Helen Douglas at San Francisco's Press Club. He began by reading a telegram of endorsement from Eleanor Roosevelt, which startled Douglas and astounded the audience. Nixon then acknowledged that in fact this was Mrs. Theodore Roosevelt Jr., a substantial woman in her own right and the widow of a general, Congressional Medal of Honor winner, former governor of Puerto Rico and the Philippines, and unsuccessful candidate for governor of New York (against Alfred E. Smith). Like his cousin Franklin and his father TR, her husband, too, had been assistant secretary of the navy.[13]

Helen Douglas proclaimed her loyalty to the memory of Franklin D. Roosevelt and said that those who were always crying "communist" and had reactionary political careers were fomenting communism. This was true, but she should have borrowed from some key parts of her mentor's political repertoire. When FDR was attacked as a leftist or communist, he struck back witheringly at the Republican Flat Earth Society, the "Old Guard Republicans in their entrenched positions," "the malefactors of great wealth . . . economic royalists . . . monopolists, war profiteers, class antagonists . . . who tried to thwart and block nearly every attempt that this administration made to warn our people and arm our nation" against the Nazis and the Japanese. She was like a dead ventriloquist's dummy (in drag) who was programmed to give only half of the departed master's message, and refused to be coached by capable continuators like Truman and Rayburn.

Roosevelt was never on the defensive and never took long to paint his opponents as Stone Age exploiters, snobs, crooks, and Nazi sympathizers. For good measure, he would recite their names in rhymes ("Martin, Barton, and Fish"), recalling their ill-considered congressional votes, and comment on their more insane accusations, such as that he had sent a destroyer to the Aleutian Islands to retrieve his dog: "He's a Scottie, and he has not been the same dog since." Harry Truman, though not a great orator like Roosevelt, didn't pull any punches, and showed in the 1948 campaign how effective he could be. But Helen Douglas didn't have the knack of claiming to be a victorious veteran in a war with greedy and unworthy men; she recited the great but fading name of Roosevelt, did not stay in lockstep with Truman, and tried to reason with her impatient listeners rather than serving into their faces the red-hot counterfire that would have won the argument.

Nixon had cross-filed, as he had in his previous congressional races, and he tried to put out an advertising campaign that would attract Democrats. This was a much more charged atmosphere than the one that had existed in the Voorhis and Zetterberg campaigns, and Douglas and Boddy, and the Democratic organization generally, rebuffed Nixon's blandishments. In advertisements warning Democrats not to be taken in by Nixon was born the phrase this campaign would popularize: "Tricky Dick."

— II —

The primary was on June 6. Nixon took 70 percent of the Republican vote, most of the rest divided between Douglas and Boddy, and it was not a rewarding evening for the lonesome-hearts doctor or the papaphobist whose hats were also in the Republican ring. Nixon led Douglas one million votes to 890,000, with 535,000 for Boddy. He took 22 percent of the Democrat primary vote to 13 percent of the Republican vote for Douglas. The Nixon camp was confident that most of the Boddy votes would come to them and that the race was theirs to lose. The Douglas camp felt that they had beaten off a severe attack from Boddy, having first chased out Downey, and that Nixon's lead would evaporate as their candidate put out her message. The ensuing campaign would be long remembered.

Nixon and his advisers had taken the measure of Helen Gahagan Douglas before the main event began. He had observed her in the House of Representatives. She was a guileless, forthright, brave, admirable woman who was still under the hypnotic influence of Franklin Delano Roosevelt, a master of American politics so consummate that to his admirers he appeared pristine in his methods as well as his goals. Helen Douglas would drive straight ahead, espouse her goals without any contemptible temporizing, and be easily distracted from her strengths – a sincere and attractive woman fighting bravely for principles most Americans would agree with if they were packaged correctly – to scrapping with Nixon's picadors on matters where she could not win. The Nixon camp obtained Helen Douglas's itinerary and sent questioners and hecklers to sidetrack her meetings and assure that she replied intemperately.

Though Nixon had already taken the measure of McCarthy, as a dangerous and vapid demagogue (although Whittaker Chambers had privately thrown in his lot with McCarthy), he was not going to allow McCarthy to take the communist issue for himself, especially opposite such a tempting target as Helen Gahagan Douglas. Chotiner and Nixon worked out early the little refrain that "Some have advised me not to talk about communism, but I am determined to tell the people the truth." (Most of those who so advised were afraid that if they heard Nixon's anti-Red speech one more time, they would scream or be struck dumb, or turn into a statue or at least throw up in boredom and revulsion.)

On June 24, 1950, the North Koreans attacked the South Koreans across the thirty-eighth parallel. The United States was certainly not clamoring for another war, but it had one, and it was helpful to those warning of the international communist menace. The floodgates were thrown open on the most florid permutations of the Red Scare. Nixon claimed that HUAC files contained hair-raising descriptions of what the Red fifth column would try to do to stab America in the back, poisoning the nation's food and water supply, derailing trains, seizing armories, sabotaging public utilities, and so forth. He and others offered a virtual War of the Worlds. In this sweepstakes of hysteria, the greatest tout and handicapper of all, J. Edgar Hoover, was not going to be left at the gate. He announced that 540,000 subversives were at large and active in the country. It is not clear why Hoover was allowed to get away with such outrages.

Helen Douglas again struck first, pointing out her early support for aid to South Korea and adding that Nixon had voted, with communist-backed congressman Vito Marcantonio, the American Labor Party representative from East Harlem, against aid to South Korea. Nixon had voted against the bill in question because it did not include aid to Formosa, which now styled itself Nationalist China; he did support a subsequent measure that included such aid. She also accused him of voting to cut a European aid measure in half. Nixon indignantly responded that he voted to retain the funding but make a one-year grant, rather than two. Linking Nixon to Marcantonio and trying to portray Nixon as soft on Asian communist aggression and weak on aid to Europe was playing with fire. She said, "On every key vote, Nixon stood with party-liner Marcantonio against America in its fight to defeat communism."[14]

Vito Marcantonio was the congressman from East Harlem from 1935 to 1950. He claimed to be a follower of Fiorello La Guardia and was sometimes treated as the son the mayor never had, but he was far to the left of La Guardia and did espouse an overtly pro-Russian line. He was admirably progressive in civil rights matters, an orthodox socialist in economic policy, but an outright Soviet supporter in foreign policy. He was pushed out of the Democratic Party, forced to run as an American Labor candidate, and gerrymandered out of his district, finally losing in 1950. He was fanatically devoted to the interests of his multi-ethnic constituents, who mourned him in huge numbers when he died in 1954. By 1950, he was almost everywhere branded a communist, a slight liberty with the facts, in that there is no reason to believe that he was a Soviet agent or that he favored the end of the democratic system in the United States. (For some reason, he intensely disliked Helen Douglas, but his relations with "Nicky," as he called Nixon, were cordial, and he sent him good wishes in the campaign.)[15]

The North Koreans had taken the United States completely by surprise and hurled the small American force helping the South Koreans steadily back toward the southern port of Pusan. With each reversal, alarm on the home front increased and anti-communist attitudes hardened even from where they had been. Nixon had become an anti-communist icon to respectable elements wary of McCarthy. In this campaign, he developed contacts with many wealthy contributors who would stay with him throughout his career, including California's greatest rancher, Robert Di Giorgio; Dean Witter (stock brokerage); Steve Bechtel (engineering); Walter Haas (Levi Strauss); Howard Ahmanson (insurance and savings and loan); Henry Salvatori (oil); Justin Dart (Rexall Drugs); Louis B. Mayer and other Hollywood executives, past and present, including Joseph P. Kennedy, who had not forgiven Melvyn Douglas's pro-labor agitations at the studios; and Harry F. Haldeman (automobile dealerships and father of Nixon's future chief of staff).

Money poured in in such quantities that Nixon was able to contribute some of it to other candidates in California, boot-strapping himself up as a potential rival to Earl Warren as leader of the California Republicans at a national convention if he was victorious in his Senate race. Press support remained solid, and in one of the last political acts of his eventful eighty-eight years, William Randolph Hearst directed that all aid be given to Nixon not only editorially, but in archival and research support in anti-communist matters.[16]

The Democratic leadership did their best for Helen Douglas. President Truman personally asked Sheridan Downey, whom he had known well in the Senate, to heal party wounds and support Douglas. Downey refused. Sam Rayburn strenuously urged her to do everything possible to rid the Congress of Nixon: "His is the most devious face of all those who have served in the Congress in all the years I've been here," he said.[17]

In July, Nixon was Herbert Hoover's guest at the Bohemian Grove, north of San Francisco, the ultimate hangout of the California establishment, where for a weekend men dressed in old clothes and lived in camps and urinated on the bases of the vast redwood trees, and talked business and politics. General Dwight D. Eisenhower was the club's principal guest, and he came to lunch at Hoover's camp. The consensus, in which Nixon participated, was that Eisenhower had great appeal, charm, and mystique, but it was not clear that he possessed the considered judgment to be president. (There is rarely so arch a judge of presidential qualities as someone who has been ejected from the office as Hoover had, and businessmen are usually well behind the public in evaluating presidential qualities.)

Helen Douglas was one of only twenty congressmen to vote against the McCarran-Wood bill, which updated Mundt-Nixon in forcing registration of communists and vaguely defined affiliations of communists. Her vote was an admirable position of principle, but it was, in the circumstances, handing a great deal of ammunition to her opponent. "I will not be stampeded by hysteria. Nor will I waver for political expediency."[18] The next day, the Nixon campaign finally launched its long-awaited attack on Douglas, publishing a lengthy statement accusing her of voting 353 times with Vito Marcantonio and mentioning her votes against aid to Greece and Turkey, funding for HUAC, along with other indications of her softness on communism, and quoting the *Daily Worker*'s description of her as a "hero." The Nixon statement was run extensively in the *Los Angeles Times* and received heavy coverage throughout California. The Hearst press and Manchester Boddy had described her as "pink" already, but the description "the pink lady" caught on in the Nixon-friendly press.

This was damaging, but was no more ungentlemanly than her opening references to Nixon as "Tricky Dick" and a "fascist." The Nixon campaign followed up with a widely distributed flyer on thick pink stock entitled "The Douglas-Marcantonio Record – Here is the Record!" It became universally known as "The Pink Sheet."

An analysis of the shared votes of Douglas and Marcantonio revealed that aid to Greece and Turkey and the McCarran-Wood bill were almost the only matters of any security implications on which they voted together. The other 352 votes concerned public housing, welfare measures, and similar matters, on which large sections of the House voted with them.

There was a good deal of self-righteous flummery for many years about the "mordant comment of the color of the paper," as Nixon subsequently wrote.[19] Over half a million copies of "The Pink Sheet" were distributed. Helen Douglas was the first to escalate the campaign to ad hominem imputations of political extremism; Nixon can be faulted for overachieving as he joined in the spirit of it, but not more than that. Nixon did veto circulating a further version of "The Pink Sheet" in bright red late in the campaign. Marcantonio had been hung like an albatross around Voorhis's neck in 1946, and Douglas's campaign team should have been ready for this. As it was, they never really responded.

Douglas kicked off the final round of her campaign with a radio address just after Labor Day, proclaiming grandiloquently that "the future course of the world" depended upon her winning. Nixon launched the final phase of his campaign on September 18, moving by airplane from San Diego to Los Angeles to Fresno to San Francisco and giving a state-wide radio address that was, in its way, a classic. In a reasonable and measured voice, he sanctimoniously assured his listeners that there would be no smears or name-calling (two months after "The Pink Sheet" debuted) and then gave the campaign litany. His opponent had said that "communism is no real threat," she had let down "our troops in Korea," and, inexorably: "It just so happens that my opponent is a member of a small clique which joins the notorious Communist Party-liner Vito Marcantonio of New York, in voting time after time against measures that are for the security of this country."[20]

Helen Douglas went on describing Nixon as "Tricky Dick" and accusing him of selling fascism, ensuring a uniformly base tone to the campaign, but she did not put her message across as skillfully as he did. They were supposed to have a joint meeting on September 20 in Los Angeles to discuss communism in the United States, but she remained in Washington to try to sustain Truman's veto of McCarran-Wood. In her place was the

Democratic candidate for governor against Warren, FDR's oldest son, James Roosevelt. Nixon regretted the absence of his opponent and said that she "should speak for herself so that every person in California may know just why she has followed the Communist Party line so many times." It was a clear-cut victory; Jimmy Roosevelt replicated none of the powerful leadership qualities of his father.

Interestingly, Nixon staked out, starting in his September 18 speech, a demand for "complete victory" in Korea: "I believe we should not stop at the thirty-eighth parallel unless a complete military capitulation is inflicted on the North Koreans." Obviously, if such a defeat were inflicted, there would be no reason to stop there, so he was, even at this early date, an advocate of the destruction of North Korea and an unambiguous victory. This would become a burning issue in the next few years, as some wanted to minimize the risk of war with China or the Soviet Union and save South Korea and go no further; and others wanted a decisive victory over international communism, even if it meant administering a severe military thrashing to Red China at this first opportunity. These were competing strategic visions, which Nixon himself would ultimately largely resolve. Helen Douglas didn't help herself in continuing to advocate giving Red China the Security Council seat held by Chiang. Nixon called this the last straw of appeasement toward communism.[21]

At the end of September, with great fanfare, alliances of putative Democrats began emerging in support of Nixon. While Downey retained a public silence after saying that Douglas was not qualified to be a U.S. senator, it was well-known that he was a Nixon supporter. A Field poll in early October showed Nixon leading by eight points, with a third of the voters undecided. It was still thought to be a tight race, and Nixon was constitutionally incapable of overconfidence. Both candidates performed prodigies of physical and vocal endurance.

There were two more joint meetings, both in Los Angeles, and both clear-cut Nixon victories. In the first, he decisively defeated Helen Douglas in simple debating fluency and mastery of facts. There was no incivility. And in the second, to frustrate her attempts to avoid debating him, he had claimed to be unable to make it, and then arrived unexpectedly just after she had finished speaking at what she thought was a meeting of her partisans only. Douglas stalked out and Nixon gave a powerful address to a packed house and an empty opponent's chair. She avoided the successive debating disasters of Jerry Voorhis in 1946, but for all her courage and outspokenness, she was clearly afraid of Nixon's debating skill.

Senator Joe McCarthy came to California in early October, and in an address in San Diego, cordially endorsed Nixon. He denounced Acheson and referred to the "Commicrat" Party and engaged in his usual fireworks. Nixon did not meet him on this trip and asked his friends in the press to downplay the references to himself. Nixon already knew that rhetoric as explosive as this would put McCarthy on a path to self-destruction. Douglas, however, claimed that McCarthy was stumping the state for her opponent, allegations the Republicans easily debunked.

President Truman, who reportedly found Mrs. Douglas a "nuisance," canceled plans to campaign in California, though he sent the vice president, Alben W. Barkley, Averell Harriman, and, except for Acheson, most of the cabinet. Nixon referred to them mockingly as "Mrs. Douglas's foreign legion." The only one of them who was effective was the young Senator Hubert Humphrey of Minnesota, who toiled through the interior of the state on Douglas's behalf, unlike John F. Kennedy, who, assured of easy reelection in his Boston congressional district, made a private visit in mid-campaign with no political overtones.

In the last few weeks of the campaign, before the most reliably partisan audiences, Nixon used one of his most imaginative lines, referring to his opponent as "pink down to her underwear." This not only put across the subversive allegation; in the prurient bourgeois California of 1950, it titillated the men and made Nixon seem like the king of the political locker room.

Less innocuous was the Gerald L.K. Smith anti-Semitic campaign, which made much of the fact that Melvyn Douglas's original name had been Hesselberg. Nixon expressly repudiated this support on August 31, and it is unlikely that ant-Semitism was a particularly strong political motivation in California at this time, but it added to the nasty aftertaste of the campaign. Douglas was then in a touring play that frequently attracted anti-communist pickets around the country. None of his travails can be blamed on Nixon, but it was an ugly and demeaning episode. For their part, the Douglas camp, probably without the agreement or even knowledge of the candidate, tried to put it about that Pat Nixon was a lapsed Roman Catholic. This was not true, and, in any case, in such a febrile atmosphere, not a very scorching allegation.[22]

Helen Douglas carried on gamely and tried to return Nixon's well-aimed fire. She brought out her own flyers with titles like "Expose the Big Lie" and "Thou Shalt Not Bear False Witness." The latter Nixon unctuously dismissed as sacrilege. Douglas kept referring to "Tricky Dick" as a "fascist" and to "the backwash of Republican young men in dark shirts," evoking a black-shirt image. Nixon's spokesmen replied that he wore a dark shirt as a lieutenant commander in the navy, fighting fascists. This sort of exchange did not come easily to Douglas, while Nixon and Chotiner were very expert at it. The distinction between the two was not one of moral or ethical quality; they were both mudslinging more or less full-time. The difference was that Nixon and his entourage were good at it, and Helen Douglas was a spontaneous, sincere, emotional woman who wasn't good at tactical calculation and did not have an entourage who thought in these terms.

Douglas did not pull in the film community behind her. Not only the studio bosses, but all the actors and other film personnel who were concerned about leftist inroads in Hollywood went for Nixon. Among the more prominent of these were Hedda Hopper, Irene Dunne, George Murphy (who was so ungentlemanly as to denigrate Helen Douglas as an actress), Zasu Pitts (who called Douglas "the pink lady who would allow the communists to take over our land and homes as well"), Dick Powell, June Allyson, and, discreetly, former Democrat and influential Screen Actors' Guild president Ronald Reagan.[23]

Nixon led in California newspaper endorsements by about twenty to one, and the endorsements often included partial blackouts on Douglas, and pretty unprofessionally biased choices of photographs, cut-lines, headlines, and story introductions (though Mrs. Douglas was such an attractive woman, almost any photograph of her was bound to be positive). Drew Pearson denounced the Nixon campaign, and his column ran in a number of places. Raymond Moley, disillusioned former braintruster of FDR's, writing in *Newsweek*, attacked Helen Douglas with uncharacteristic violence; dragging out the worm-eaten chestnut of solidarity with Marcantonio, Moley referred to Douglas's degree from Barnard as "a somewhat sketchy college education not too far from Marcantonio's district."[24] President Truman finally attacked the conduct of the California publishers in a White House press conference on November 3. It was too late and too distant to have any useful impact.[25]

In another revenant of 1946, and a demonstration that in politics old tricks are best, a variety of appliances was advertised as prizes if Nixon campaign workers telephoned and the residential phone was answered, "I'm for Nixon!" As usual, there were a good many more such responses than happy owners of new, free appliances.

Nixon had tried to enlist Warren after his primary victory, but Warren wasn't having it, and withheld an endorsement of Nixon almost to the end. Chotiner had Nixon operatives at Douglas's meetings and taunted her to endorse James Roosevelt. Finally, on the last weekend of the campaign, Helen Douglas, showing her amateurism, but also the courage and spontaneity that had helped make her something of a minor American political folk heroine, said, "I hope and pray that Jimmy Roosevelt will be the next governor." When this was shown to Warren, he responded that her statement "does not change my position. In view of her statement, however, I might ask her how she expects I will vote when I mark my ballot for U.S. senator next Tuesday."[26]

Nixon wound up his campaign with a speech at the Hollywood American Legion Stadium on November 2, where he arrived in a torchlight parade. Dick Powell moderated, and for the benefit of the live and radio audiences, there was a mystery acted out over the Hiss apprehension, gripping entertainment provided by Nixon's Hollywood supporters but pretty indifferent history. Nixon's speech was the usual hard-hitting late-campaign effort, long on innuendo and self-righteousness, but staying clear of full-blooded McCarthyism.

On November 6, the Red Chinese, as they were then known, officially crossed the Yalu River between China and Korea, drastically escalating the war. (They already had about two hundred thousand soldiers in North Korea, but U.S. and allied intelligence had not detected them.) This was a final, end-of-campaign illustration of the tortured state of the struggle with the worldwide Red Menace. The war in Korea had seesawed dramatically. Reduced to a southern pocket around Pusan, MacArthur made a daring amphibious landing at Seoul's port, Inchon, on September 15, captured Seoul ten days later, virtually annihilated the North Korean Army, and surged northward.

The main Chinese attack on November 25 would send the Allied forces reeling, and the peninsula became a bloody stalemate near the original demarcation between North and South Korea. MacArthur and Nixon and many others wanted to insert greater forces, especially Chiang Kai-shek's five-hundred-thousand-man Kuomintang Army, as a response to the Red

Chinese Army; attack China from the air, especially in Manchuria; smash the Red Chinese Army in Korea; and threaten use of the atomic bomb. Truman, Eisenhower, and the Joint Chiefs did not think Korea worth such a risk and expense; it was enough to salvage South Korea. This strategic disagreement between MacArthur and Truman would have a dramatic climax, and the debate would go on through the fifties, and after.

On November 7, 1950, Richard Nixon was nervous and fidgety to the end, but it was soon clear that his massive onslaught had harvested a huge majority. He won by nineteen points, nearly 700,000 votes (2,183,454 to 1,502,507) and ran ahead of almost all California Republican congressional candidates in their own districts. His majority was about 350,000 votes less than Earl Warren's over the ineffectual Jimmy Roosevelt, but Warren was seeking a third term; Nixon had the greatest senatorial majority in the country as a thirty-seven-year-old first-time candidate. He had changed the correlation of forces in the California Republican Party and henceforth Warren could no longer treat him as an insignificant and distasteful little harpy, as he had been in the habit of doing.

The Republicans picked up five Senate and twenty-eight House seats, fairly normal for off-year elections, and some of the campaigns were rougher than that in California. Everett Dirksen, winning the first of four Senate terms in Illinois, had announced he was running against Stalin. The Democratic incumbent in Maryland, Millard E. Tydings, whom Roosevelt had tried to purge as insubordinate in 1938, was defeated in part by the circulation of a doctored photograph showing him in animated conversation with the U.S. Communist Party leader, Earl Browder. Nixon's victory was widely acclaimed. Vito Marcantonio was defeated by a coalition of Republicans and Democrats in East Harlem. Herbert Hoover, Allen Dulles, Herbert Brownell, twice Dewey's presidential campaign manager, and Harold Stassen were among Nixon's congratulators. John F. Kennedy privately expressed great pleasure at Nixon's defeat of Douglas.

Downey announced his retirement from the Senate, facilitating the appointment of Nixon by Warren, giving him seniority over the other senators just elected for the first time. As an apparent quid pro quo, Nixon had agreed to support as federal judges two nominees of Downey's who had been anti–Douglas Democrats. He attended upon Warren on November 22 in Sacramento, and was confirmed as the senator-designate and elect, and was sworn in in the old Capitol chamber on December 4, 1950. Only Huey Long's son Russell, a senator from Louisiana, would be a younger member of the Senate than Nixon.

The rules governing revelation of campaign expenses were very loose and don't provide much guidance to what really happened. A consensus seems to be that Nixon spent around $1.5 million and that Helen Douglas would have spent a little less than half that. There is no doubt that Nixon's campaign was magnificently organized and skillfully executed. It was a dirty campaign, but Helen Douglas, having blundered artlessly into the denigration of her opponent, had no right to expect that her rival would be no nastier nor more effective at it than she was herself.

The great hostility to her in Hollywood was not entirely ideological, and the indifference to her of the Democratic leaders, including President Truman, a gallant man in all respects, indicates that her interpersonal skills were seriously deficient. And support for Nixon was not just because of, and probably had little to do with, his "Pink" smear campaign against her. He was a dynamic, intelligent young politician who dispatched Helen Douglas with humiliating ease when they debated, and gave promise of a great career in national politics. He had been an extremely effective congressman, was well-spoken, blended liberal goals and conservative means with great agility, and was even thought to be physically attractive, as Alistair Cooke attested (Chapter 2), in the state that put the greatest premium on such things.

It is hard not to like and admire Helen Douglas at a distance; glamorous, courageous, and principled, she fought gamely against lengthening odds, and was soundly defeated by a politician who has received little subsequent approbation. But she had made herself vulnerable, did nothing to reunite her party behind her, opened the floodgates of negative campaigning, was thoroughly disorganized, and ran a sophomoric campaign. She also had a number of rather prissy, soft-left views that were unsound in themselves and wildly out of concert with the place and times.

The legend of Nixon's unacceptable campaigning methods spread from this campaign, and magnified both the Voorhis and Alger Hiss legends. The editor of the London *Observer*, David Astor, later claimed that Nixon expressed regret about how he had conducted his campaign in 1950. Nixon denied this and never expressed such sentiments to anyone else. It must have been a misunderstanding on the part of the leftish Astor, who was later unable to recall it himself.[27] Nixon had earned widespread respect by his qualities as a winner, a congressional prosecutor, a legislator. But he was an indistinct personality, and one that it was possible to represent as slightly mechanical, almost bloodless, and therefore unpredictable and sinister. He had won an astonishing series of hard-fought victories and had gone from being a completely obscure small-town lawyer to a very prominent U.S. senator representing the second state in the country, and a power in the Republican Party, as history might be about to turn. But he had also created a large number of enemies, who, now silent or invisible, would attack him savagely if they detected he was vulnerable. They were motivated by envy, ideology, sentiment, traditional partisanship, and, in some cases, an irrational and visceral animus. He had moved so quickly, he had no obvious base of support. For the upwardly mobile, admiration is as durable, and as fleeting, as momentum.

— III —

The first noteworthy event of Richard Nixon's career as a U.S. senator was to break up an assault by Joe McCarthy on Drew Pearson in the washroom of the Sulgrave Club. This occurred on December 12, 1950, when McCarthy kneed Pearson in the groin and claimed to be testing an old Indian theory that the victim of such an attack would bleed through the eyes. Nixon settled McCarthy down and claimed to have saved Pearson's life.

It was obvious from the beginning of Nixon's time in the Senate that he did not intend for his career to stop there. He tore off around the country giving headline-winning speeches on his usual themes about subversion, but also advocating greater military strength, less economic regulation, and a major ideological counter-offensive against international communism. He demanded that containment be redefined as rolling back the communists, but was rather unspecific about this, because he wanted to avoid a general war. He was the Republican speaker most in demand in the country in 1951.

On February 1, 1951, General Dwight D. Eisenhower spoke to a joint session of Congress and urged a comprehensive rearmament of Western Europe, and discretion to the president to deploy to Europe whatever forces he chose. Eisenhower submitted to committee questions, but only Senator Taft grilled him aggressively. It was agreed that the president's deployment of four divisions to Europe was his right, but that he would return to the Senate for authorization to go beyond that. Acheson dismissed this (correctly), as of no legal effect. Truman was laying claim to the full Rooseveltian powers of the commander-in-chief. The Republican right had not thought it through. They wanted to keep American forces at home, ignore Western Europe, liberate Eastern Europe, and dictate the outcome of the Chinese civil war, and became apoplectic when Truman, Marshall, Eisenhower, and Acheson told them this was not possible. It was a primitive, nativist, reactionary group that Nixon drew on for support but was trying, in policy terms, to reorient.

On June 28, 1951, Nixon told the National Young Republican Convention in Boston that the "American people have had enough of the whining, whimpering, groveling attitude of our diplomatic representatives who talk of American's weaknesses and of America's fears rather than of America's strength and of America's courage."[28]

While Nixon was not on this occasion taking out exclusively after Dean Acheson, the secretary of state was always a tempting target, with his striped trousers and bowler hat, supercilious airs, luxuriant mustache, and slightly absurd pseudo-British accent. It also fell to him to explain why containment would work in Europe but not in China, and why, with the resources it was prepared to deploy, the United States could not simply "roll back" all the forces of adversity. Unlike the immensely esteemed General George C. Marshall (whom he succeeded in early 1949) and future secretaries of state of great public relations ability, such as Henry Kissinger, George Schultz, James Baker, and Condoleezza Rice, Acheson, though very intelligent, articulate, courageous, and sound in his views and talented in their execution, was a sitting duck for the administration's foes. It was in this session of the Senate that McCarthy crossed what ultimately proved to be his Rubicon of general toleration by accusing General George C. Marshall, one of the greatest soldiers and statesmen of American and modern world history, of "treason." Nixon always upheld Marshall, long before he was associated with Eisenhower, who was Marshall's foremost protégé.

While Nixon, as has been recorded, kept his distance from McCarthy, accusing the Truman-Acheson foreign policy of "whining, whimpering, and groveling" was preposterous. Harry Truman, fearlessly combative, and Dean Acheson, an incandescent, but relatively well-qualified snob, never whined, whimpered, or groveled, even, so far as is known, as infants. And Nixon was speaking, again, of the administration that had bundled the U.S.S.R. out of Iran and Greece, protected Turkey, West Berlin, and South

Korea, co-founded NATO, put Western Europe back on its economic and military feet, and brought Germany out of its post-Nazi purgatory and into the respectability and fellowship of the democratic West.

Nixon dragooned John Foster Dulles, who had served briefly in the Senate when Dewey named him to fill a vacancy, but had been narrowly defeated by Herbert Lehman, to join him for the fiftieth anniversary of Whittier College in March 1951. Dulles was the Republicans' leading authority on foreign policy and was friendly with Dewey and, increasingly, with Eisenhower. Though Dulles was a hard-line anti-communist, he was a convinced internationalist. Getting close to him was an astute maneuver by Nixon.

Nixon covered the other wing of the party as well, and McCarthy put him on his (McCarthy's) permanent investigations sub-committee of the Senate Committee on Expenditures. Nixon replaced Margaret Chase Smith of Maine, who had made an admirable "declaration of conscience" aimed at McCarthy, and warned against a campaign of "the four horsemen of fear, ignorance, bigotry, and smear."[29]

On April 11, 1951, the long-simmering dispute between MacArthur and Truman finally blew up when Truman sacked the five-star, much-decorated general as UN commander in Korea and governor of Japan, and terminated his military career of fifty-two years, one of the most distinguished in the country's history. MacArthur had been insubordinate and had publicly criticized the administration's war policy. When he had heard in early 1951 that Truman was contemplating opening negotiations for a truce, MacArthur made public his appraisal of the war, disparaging the Chinese Red Army and stating that they should come to terms with the UN. This enraged Moscow and Beijing and delayed the start of negotiations. Republican House Leader Joe Martin had written MacArthur asking if he thought Chiang Kai-shek's army should be thrown into the war. He replied that it should, and Martin, rather mischievously, read his letter to the House. For the commander-in-chief, this was the last straw. Civilian control of the military required that Truman resolve the dispute in favor of the president.

However, the termination was extremely abrupt treatment for one of the nation's greatest heroes, and a drastic escalation of their differences. When MacArthur had been Roosevelt's army chief of staff and they had differed, Roosevelt tamed the general with his lofty, almost aristocratic self-confidence. Truman, the natty but less exalted ex-haberdasher from Kansas City, did not have the same natural authority, nor the devious subtlety, of his predecessor, and MacArthur did not tender him the same level of personal respect. Roosevelt found MacArthur's political ambitions sinister but amateurish, and thought his personal affectations amusing, almost endearing: his elaborate speech, eccentric costume, and evident vanity. Truman bitterly resented them and was hostile to MacArthur before they had ever met.

Yet, when they did meet, on Wake Island on October 15, 1950, when it seemed the Korean War was almost won, they got on well. Truman, who was there, as Nixon later wrote, solely to shore up his own popularity,[30] thought MacArthur "a most stimulating and interesting person . . . very friendly – I might say much more so than I had expected." And MacArthur, even in the retrospect of his memoirs, thought Truman "radiated nothing but courtesy and good humor . . . He has an engaging personality, a quick and witty tongue, and I liked him from the start."[31] MacArthur had assured Truman that the Chinese would not intervene, and when they did a month later, this brief flowering rapport reverted to the negative impressions the two men had had of each other at a distance.

Vastly more important than these personal abrasions was the underlying strategic difference between them. Truman, contrary to partisan Republican cant, was the originator and, in tandem with Stalin, the chief escalator of the Cold War. But he was in favor of a defensive alliance of noncommunist states and a policy of containment against communism. MacArthur, as the general told the Congress in one of the great orations of the era, April 19, 1951, believed that "In war, there is no substitute for victory," that American and Allied soldiers could not be asked to risk or sacrifice their lives for any objective less than victory.

He further believed that wherever the communists gave aggressive battle, they had to be severely punished. He considered Korea an opportunity to suck into the peninsula and destroy the Chinese Communist army, to bomb China's industrial areas to rubble, and so to weaken the People's Republic that Chiang Kai-shek's Nationalists, who had just been chased off the mainland to Taiwan, could return. MacArthur would tell Richard Nixon in the later fifties that if he had had five hundred thousand soldiers of Chiang's army with him at the Yalu (the river that was the border between China and Korea), he would have "split China in two, and in one stroke, have changed the world's balance of power." It is not clear that Chiang's soldiers were especially battle-worthy, but under MacArthur's command and with American close air support, they would certainly have broken the stalemate in Korea, with interesting results.[32] MacArthur did not believe for an instant that Stalin would resort to nuclear war.

He tended to regard communism as a fairly unitary phenomenon, directed from Moscow, though he knew that Mao Tse-tung was no puppet like the East European satellite leaders whose countries were occupied by the Soviet Army. MacArthur was caricatured, then and subsequently. "It has been said, in effect, that I was a warmonger. Nothing could be further from the truth; I know war as few other men now living have known it, and nothing to me is more revolting," he told the cheering Congress.

There was more basis to his argument than posterity has generally conceded. A severe humiliation of Communist China could have been inflicted, at a high cost (though under MacArthur's scenario, much of this would have been in the lives of Nationalist Chinese). If the United States had been prepared to use nuclear weapons, which would have been unwise, as well as inhuman and provocative, it would have been easier, at least theoretically, to tame Red China. But not even MacArthur, at this point, was advocating that. Eisenhower would discreetly threaten this, to his and America's profit – a policy option MacArthur was accused of advocating but never did. It is unlikely that Chiang, a corrupt and largely inept Nationalist leader and generalissimo, would have politically resurrected himself, no matter what MacArthur had done to the Red Army, though his forces would have been useful in Korea. Chiang, after twenty-five years of misrule, did not have a great deal of support in China. (He fared rather better with the famous China Lobby in the United States.)

Such a course would have been a salutary lesson to the new regime in Peking and would have got rid of North Korea, which proved to have astonishing durability as a trouble-making, unreconstructed communist state. General Charles de Gaulle, a MacArthur admirer, though they did not know each other, said in a speech on April 15, 1951, that MacArthur was a "soldier whose boldness was feared after full advantage had been taken of it."[33] There was more truth to this than most American historians of the period have admitted.

The containment policy was ultimately successful, and the United States eventually developed a civilized relationship with the People's

Republic, thanks largely to Nixon, without a wider war. On balance, Truman's policy was probably correct, but the MacArthur alternative was a viable option, and at time of writing, the last word in North Korea's provocations as an enduring nuisance are not in.

MacArthur memorably concluded his remarks to the Congress: "I still remember the refrain of one of the most popular barrack ballads of that day [when he was a West Point cadet at the end of the nineteenth century], which proclaimed, most proudly, that 'old soldiers never die, they just fade away.' Now, like the old soldier of that ballad, I just fade away, an old soldier who tried to do his duty as God gave him the light to see that duty. Goodbye." It was splendid oratory, eloquently delivered, and Truman was a little harsh in judging it "a lot of damn bullshit." But the general had taken some liberties, including his false and unqualified assertion that the Joint Chiefs of Staff shared his opinions about how to conduct the Korean War. They emphatically did not.

If Truman had terminated MacArthur's career, the general had come home to massive outpourings of public goodwill, determined to return the blow and avenge himself on Truman. He did not distinguish himself in hearings before the Senate Armed Forces Committee, but he did lethal damage to Truman's standing in the country. The Los Angeles City Council ordered flags lowered and declared the city in mourning "in sorrowful contemplation of the political assassination of General MacArthur."[34] Initially, polls indicated 69 percent of Americans agreed with MacArthur rather than Truman. These numbers evened out, but Truman still suffered a mortal political wound as a result of his treatment of MacArthur. The general toured much of the country and stirred up great sympathy, and corresponding antagonism to Truman.

In the ensuing debate, Nixon clearly supported the general, and even proposed a rather fatuous bill reversing the president's recall of MacArthur, an unconstitutional usurpation of the prerogatives of the commander-in-chief. Writing thirty years later, Nixon defended his initiative by citing his explanatory speech in the Senate, which, he wrote, distributed blame fairly to the president and the general. That is a reinterpretive reading of his remarks, and says nothing about the absurdity of the Congress trying to reinstate officers whom the commander-in-chief has removed. MacArthur should not have been insubordinate; he should have carried out orders without indiscretion, or voluntarily retired. Truman should have summoned him to the West Coast and privately warned him, and if he had to pull the trigger, there would have been no harm in leaving him as governor of Japan, where his services have been universally admired. This would also have blunted the domestic political impact of MacArthur's removal. (The general was seventy-one and retirement, if decorously executed, would not have been premature.)

Nixon claimed to find the rationale for the unjust treatment of MacArthur in the "Europe-first" policy and in Truman's appeasement of Attlee's Labour government in Britain. Attlee, terrified of what China could do to Hong Kong and Malaysia, had offered to mediate U.S. withdrawal from Korea even as British forces were engaged with Americans and others in fighting the Chinese. Truman declined and said that he would rather be driven out of Korea by the Chinese, though he did not expect that to happen, than to accept the dishonorable course proposed by Attlee.

Nixon wanted to use Chiang's forces, as they were available, in Korea. He wanted strategic bombing of Red China, a naval blockade of the country, and an effort to make the UN allies put in serious forces or stop their tokenism and get out (it was technically a UN mission, voted while the U.S.S.R. was boycotting the UN and unable to veto it). Nixon and many other Republicans were exasperated with nominal allies using their presence to urge excessive caution on the United States, and especially, in this regard, with Britain. Privately, Truman and Acheson agreed with many of these concerns, but in Britain, Attlee, whom Acheson had compared to a "woodchuck chewing on a log," was about to give way to the legendary and revered Winston Churchill, leading his party to victory for the first time at the age of seventy-six. Churchill, as he had demonstrated many times in the previous forty years, was made of sterner stuff.

The Democrats replied to Nixon and other sensible Republicans that blockading China would achieve nothing, bombing it would bring in the Soviets (questionable), and that forcing the Europeans to choose so abruptly, since most of them had no Far Eastern interests, and the position of the French was ambiguous, would make Korea, as Eisenhower's replacement as chief of staff, Omar N. Bradley, said, "the wrong war in the wrong place at the wrong time against the wrong enemy." The Europeans, including the British, in a pattern that would be repeated, were irritating in their ambivalence and tepidity, but essentially General Bradley was correct.

Nixon asked, "What would be the right war?" Bradley's and Truman's unspoken answer was a geopolitical region of decisive importance – Western Europe or Japan – but not a quarter or a third of the Korean Peninsula. But the MacArthur-Nixon counter was that this would be a relatively cheap and easy way to humble the Chinese before that genie emerged from its huge bottle, and that North Korea could be a terrible nuisance, which it has been. Nixon believed an armistice would hand Formosa to Red China and give China a UN Security Council seat. He put the Republican side very effectively and Taft, as Republican Senate leader, encouraged him to speak for their party, which he did more persuasively than Taft and his senior colleagues did.

Nixon, unwavering in his support of administration policy in Europe, even managed a cordial exchange of correspondence with Averell Harriman, Truman's director of the Mutual Security Agency.[35] He joined the administration's supporters in advocating higher appropriations for NATO and for the Voice of America, and vigorously defended the president for assigning Secret Service protection to his daughter, Margaret, which some Republican legislators had criticized.[36]

The sacking of MacArthur opened wide the prospects of the Republicans. After twenty years, the country was tiring of the Democrats, and this was accentuated by a series of rather undignified scandals, to which Truman seemed relatively indifferent, although his own probity was never questioned. Beset by such embarrassments, tormented by allegations of failure in the communist issues, including tolerating loyalty risks in government, and explicitly, according to Nixon, "losing China" through the blunders of the State Department, the Democrats were finally vulnerable provided the Republicans presented believable candidates on a sensible platform. Senator Nixon, not slow to see and seek a key role for himself, would pitch in and do his part, which he could be counted on to define quite ambitiously.

A fund was set up by Herman Perry and Dana Smith and other early Whittier backers to help Nixon pay for the activities of a national politician. There has long been controversy about this money, which came on top of a senator's $12,500 salary and $75,000 for staff and other expenses. It was presented to potential contributors as irreproachable and ethically bulletproof, and there has never been a serious suggestion that Nixon personally trousered any of it himself. The argument has been over the appropriateness of financially prominent people contributing to assist Nixon in building his standing as a national figure by endless touring and speechmaking. Smith's budget in this fund for 1951 was $21,000, devoted to Christmas cards, mailings, and radio advertising. Despite frenzied efforts of Nixon's enemies, no connection has ever been made between Nixon's Senate votes or public policy positions and contributions to Nixon through this fund or otherwise.

Nixon's office grew to twelve assistants and secretaries, including the redoubtable Rose Mary Woods, who would be with him for the balance of his career. She was the ultimate devoted office wife, single, competent, and discreet, and she enjoyed and maintained an excellent relationship with Pat. Her quiet but unflagging Roman Catholicism added, over coming decades, to the mystique of her single-minded devotion to the interests of her employer. Nixon decreed that there always be a man in the office, as unannounced visitors might feel short-changed otherwise. (Women were generally considered less substantial than men as representatives of important people and organizations in these times.) He cautioned that even the "crackpots" had to be received, because after Whittaker Chambers, it was impossible to be sure whether a "crackpot" would be of no value. Nixon took rather overbearing measures to make sure that mail was answered promptly, requiring unanswered letters to be left in baskets on top of desks, and any mail unanswered after two weeks reported to him. From the early days, he was a martinet, authoritarian and slightly compulsive in his efficiency, but considerate of staff.[37]

Nixon was so dedicated to his office that on one humid Sunday afternoon in 1951, which had been long promised to his family as a picnic day, they had their picnic, in picnic clothes on a blanket, in front of his desk, in his air-conditioned office.[38]

Harry Truman, a man of impenetrable integrity personally, was a product of the Tom Pendergast machine in Kansas City, Missouri. After his haberdashery failed, Truman worked for six years to pay off all creditors. He went to law school at night, became a machine-nominated judge, and was elected U.S. senator from Missouri in 1934 and reelected in 1940. He was personally selected by Roosevelt as vice president, on the recommendation of the party chairman, Robert E. Hannegan of Missouri, in 1944, when it was determined by the president and the party elders that the erratic and faddish Henry Wallace had to be replaced in that role.

Truman had served as vice president only from January 20 to April 12, 1945, when Roosevelt died, having done nothing to prepare his chosen successor for the great burdens of office. Upon him fell the responsibility to use the atomic bomb, to discern Stalin's motives and nature and prepare the defense of Western civilization against a new enemy, and to protect American public policy from a Republican Party that had been so shattered by Roosevelt's electoral invincibility that it was inhabited largely by reactionaries and isolationists. The grandest Republican traditions of Lincoln and Theodore Roosevelt were hard to excavate from the primitivism of "Martin, Barton, and Fish." And from the antediluvian rump of dispossessed office-seekers that Nixon set out to join and reorient and energize in 1946.

Harry Truman is generally reckoned a distinguished president, but the nature of his political formation made him fairly casual about the self-indulgences of his cronies. He carried to a fault his loyalty to the people who came up with him. These were admirable traits, but they opened vulnerabilities more legitimate than his casualness about subversives in government. There was very little outright disloyalty and betrayal by government officials, despite the Hiss affair and other causes célèbres. But the incidence of improper gifts to officials, kickbacks, selective prosecutions, and blatant patronage in the Truman administration stung and irritated the sometimes dormant, but never extinguished, puritanical conscience of America.

Never one to leave a partisan opportunity unexploited, Nixon leapt to the attack over the Truman administration scandals. In 1951, he presented Senate bills to extend the statute of limitations on all offenses in the conduct of federal positions, including senators and congressmen, and to give grand juries the right to special counsel in investigations of public officeholders, and security from dismissal by federal judges. These were not completely unreasonable proposals, though the Democratic majority caused them to die with dignity. Nixon made no exception for legislators and implied, which was not an unfounded claim, that the Democrats were so long in office in both the White House that nominated judges, and the Senate that confirmed them, that partisanship had permeated the bench and the Democratic administration was signing its own expense account.

As in the House of Representatives, Nixon had no notion of sitting on his hands until he had gained some seniority. His reputation and celebrity now preceded him, and he hit the ground running as a sword-bearer for the renovation of the Republicans and the closure of the great Roosevelt-Truman ascendancy. The Democratic National Committee chairman, William Boyle, was exposed for influence peddling with Hoover and Roosevelt's Reconstruction Finance Corporation, and while the Republicans ululated about this, it came to light that there was a lesser question about the Republican National Committee chairman, Guy Gabrielson, continuing as president of the Carthage Hydrocol Corporation.

This momentarily neutralized the controversy, but Nixon, the intrepid and cunning emancipator of all traditional notions of the reticence of freshmen in all spheres, since he was in elementary school, proposed that both chairmen resign. He followed this up in the investigations subcommittee, managing to asperse the vice president, Alben Barkley, a congressional warhorse even longer in the tooth than Truman, as he had been the Democratic leader of the Senate from 1937 until he came to preside over it as Truman's vice president. Nixon said that it was unacceptable that there should be any doubt that the chairman of either party be immune to using his influence and power in exchange for personal gain.

To the public, this reinforced Nixon's image as a questing young man of pure motive, a believable bipartisan on issues of broad public sector integrity. To the Republicans, it was a factional move as well. Gabrielson was a protégé of Senator Robert A. Taft, and a close friend of Senator William Knowland, who would clearly be a rival to Nixon in any upward career move. Nixon, by his anti-communist exertions, had earned the support of a good deal of the Republican right, but he was not going to paint himself into the corner of parochialism, and endless national defeat, of the Taft right, whom Roosevelt had endlessly caricatured with great mirth and effect. (In this, FDR was carrying his cousin TR's flag as well as his own.)

And to the professional political community in both parties, Nixon was a young fox who moved forward with agility, and with utter ruthlessness, toward well-liked opponents such as Voorhis, a somewhat naive but brave woman, Helen Gahagan Douglas, and now the chairman of his own party. Such people attract a great deal more popularity among those who don't know them, as members of the public, than among those who do. Nixon had made his big play in the public arena, and had been too calculating for the clubbiness – to which, in any case, his personality was ill-suited – necessary to build loyalties among his peers. His was a high-octane, high-risk, maximum-thrust career plan. In 1951, it still seemed to be working. (The Democratic chairman retired; Gabrielson remained for another year.)

He continued to walk the tightrope on the subversion issue, excoriating the administration for softness, voting to override Truman's admirable veto of the restrictive and paranoid McCarran-Walter Act, which reaffirmed the 1924 measure that stranded many victims of the Nazis when they would have made a fine addition to the United States. In November 1951 in Boston, he warned against "indiscriminate name-calling and professional Red-baiting [that] can hurt our cause more than it can help it." He obviously was referring to McCarthy and his claque but told the press he had no one "in particular in mind."[39]

Throughout his public career, Nixon had a weakness for strange or unsavory characters. One was Nicolae Malaxa, a former pillar of the fascist Iron Guard in Romania, and then an industrialist sheltered by the communist regime in that country. Nixon helped him gain entry to the United States to build a seamless pipe factory for the oil industry in Whittier. Malaxa became a U.S. permanent resident, on Nixon's and Knowland's application (Knowland having been recruited by Nixon), but the plant was never built. Nixon never became an intimate of Malaxa's but had a rather undiscriminating approach to such people, even after the allowance for the need of a politician to help his constituents. Some critics and historians have made something of the fact that he sent in a bill to enable two contributors to his fund to drill for oil on federal land in California. Nixon did not push hard for the bill, which died. Nixon didn't lift a finger for the people who had given him a few thousand dollars, which were uncontroversially spent.

Nixon's general voting record was against price and other controls, public power, and illegal immigration; and for civil rights (against the poll tax), statehood for Alaska and Hawaii, foreign aid, and emergency food and disaster relief for India and Yugoslavia. He was in favor of the deployment of troops to Europe but voted to restrict the president's power to make treaties and foreign troop deployments without congressional approval. He was close to the Taft bloc on most domestic issues but generally voted with moderate Republicans and the administration on foreign questions.

The Nixons were prospering. Don now operated Frank's flourishing business, and Frank and Hannah retained their Maryland, Florida, and California homes. The senator sold his Whittier house and war bonds and with the proceeds paid for about half the cost of a fine new suburban house in Spring Valley, in northwest Washington. Pat, who still came in to help out in the office, indulged herself for the first time with an interior decorator. Nixon drove a comfortable new Oldsmobile, bought from the dealership of a Whittier College classmate, and supplemented his senatorial pay by about 60 percent with speaking fees. As a family, the Nixons had come a long way from the grinding poverty Frank and Pat had known as youths and from the poor but respectable circumstances of Dick's early years.

But by late 1951, Nixon's health was deteriorating, apparently as a result of tension and overwork. He did not relax well, had no hobbies or sports, and was an indifferent sleeper. Sheridan Downey, Nixon's predecessor in the Senate, had given him a book called *The Will to Live*, advice on how to counteract stress and strain, because Nixon was suffering from backaches as well as sleeplessness. Nixon visited the author, a doctor, Arnold Hutschnecker, on Park Avenue in New York. He continued to have appointments with him for four years, and stopped only when there was some danger of his being accused by the press of being under psychiatric care, although Hutschnecker was not in fact a psychiatrist but an internist specializing in psychosomatic medicine.

Florida senator George Smathers, who befriended Nixon, and was concerned at his intense nervous state, arranged for him to take a Florida vacation at the end of 1951. Here he was taken for a harbor tour by an enigmatic and rather dashing local businessman, Charles "Bebe" Rebozo. This would be the start of an unusual and permanent friendship.

— IV —

As 1952 opened, the Republicans could smell blood, though some of it was their own. They had known in their hearts they could never beat Roosevelt, and had been severely scorched by underestimating Truman. It was not clear who the Democratic nominee would be in 1952, but there was a powerful sentiment that it was time for a change, a public attitude always enhanced by scandals and, in this case, magnified by what seemed the endless war in Korea and the spectacular departure of MacArthur.

Harry Truman had written himself a memo on the fifth anniversary of his succession to Roosevelt, April 12, 1950, in which he asserted that he would not be a candidate for reelection. He wrote that he had no doubt he could be reelected, and took a swipe at Roosevelt for violating the two-term tradition. (Roosevelt was in fact indispensable to the Western world in 1940, as Truman knew, and Truman had no objections when FDR took a fourth term, bringing him in as vice president. It was unusual for Harry Truman, as honest a man as senior politicians can generally be, to engage in such hypocrisy, especially in a memo that he knew would be of great historical interest if he ever released it.)

How confident he really was of reelection is not clear. Nor is it certain that he really intended to act on the memo, rather than use it if electoral prospects deteriorated or throw it out if he decided to run after all. He read the memo to his staff in November 1951, by which time his standing in the polls had descended into the twenties. Finally, at a Jefferson-Jackson Day Democratic celebration on March 29, 1952, at the end of a typically combative speech, the president added, "I shall not be a candidate for reelection. I have served my country long, and I think efficiently and honestly. I shall not accept a renomination. I do not feel that it is my duty to spend another four years in the White House."[40]

The Republicans agreed with him. Dewey was not presentable after two defeats, the last a historic case of snatching defeat from the stomach of victory. Taft was back again in 1952, as in 1948, as in 1944, as in 1940, stolid but courageously honest and principled, "Mr. Republican," respected by all his colleagues but no great vote-getter. Earl Warren was hovering about, hoping lightning would strike him but not doing much to attract it. The great hope of the Republican moderates was Eisenhower, who was being entreated but had not publicly decided to run, though by the end of March 1952, he had gone so far as to consent to be nominated.

Taft decided every issue on the principles as he saw them. He had been an isolationist since he came to the Senate in 1938 but had supported Lend Lease in 1941. He had opposed the Nuremberg Trials as ex post facto justice meted out in suspect fashion by a tribunal that included Russians, who represented a power that had committed atrocities comparable to Germany. Though a conservative and the author of the Senate version of Taft-Hartley, he was a compassionate supporter of sensible social welfare programs. He cared tenderly for his paralyzed wife and explained with exquisite courtesy to a little girl, in front of cameras, why he would not give her an autograph.[41] Nixon was concerned that Taft took American socialists for communists, as McCarthyites tended to do, and didn't recognize that most American socialists and leftists were dedicated anti-communists. Nixon thought that Taft seriously misjudged the international situation and that, in both policy and electoral terms, he was not the right candidate. Taft had remarkable qualities, but no galvanizing appeal to voters, and was essentially an isolationist and in other policy respects was rather quirky. He was a good man but was mistaken at least half the time in major policy questions and had little ability or desire to attract large number of voters.

Nixon was approached for his support in 1951 by Tom Shroyer of the Taft camp, a committee aide and one of the authors of Taft-Hartley. Nixon was friendly but noncommittal,[42] and he let it be known that he doubted Taft could win. Besides that, Taft had virtually adopted William Knowland, and it was widely thought that Knowland would be his vice presidential candidate if Taft were nominated.

The serious possible alternative to Taft was General Dwight D. Eisenhower. He was a much more personable man than Taft, with an expressive face and pleasant smile and piercing blue eyes. Behind his masquerade as a pleasant and politically unworldly officer, he was a very astute political operator. He had been brought up in the nondescript prairie town of Abilene, Kansas, had an unremarkable time at West Point, was in a staff position in the First World War on the Western Front, and made inching progress between the wars.

When Douglas MacArthur retired as chief of staff of the army in 1935 and went to the Philippines to set up that country's army, preparatory to independence, he took Eisenhower with him as an aide. Eisenhower subsequently claimed that he had spent his time there studying "dramatics" under MacArthur. With the outbreak of war in Europe, Eisenhower returned to Washington and caught the eye of the incoming chief of staff, General George C. Marshall. He was promoted rapidly, became the Allied commander in the Torch landings in North Africa in November 1942, and in December 1943 was named supreme commander for the invasion and liberation of Western Europe. He supervised the planning of, and successfully commanded, the greatest military operation in the history of the world with the invasion of Normandy, and commanded the liberation of France and the invasion of western Germany.

As supreme Allied commander in Northwest Africa and Western Europe, he conciliated the interests of Churchill, Roosevelt, and de Gaulle, and coordinated the disparate and rivalry-riven efforts of such temperamental army commanders as George S. Patton and Field Marshal Sir Bernard L. Montgomery. He mastered the politics of both military and alliance bureaucracy. Beneath his cordial exterior, he was a man of calculation, a politician in a uniform. He did not mind being thought affable, guileless, or even syntactically incomprehensible. He knew what he wanted and, after a slow start in life, had made a howling success of everything he had done since he left the Philippines in 1939. He was impressive in person; ramrod straight, the fierce but inscrutable gaze of his pale blue eyes, well tailored, and always a razor edge on a crease and shoes polished to a mirror (typical of generals, having strong-armed young men to shine them).

He had not been partisan, though he did not care for the Democrats, and thought Roosevelt an exalted political trickster. He came to disdain Truman for his cronyism, though their relations started out well and warmed in their latter years. He once described the Democrats as "a mixture of extremes on the left, extremes on the right, with political chicanery and expedience shot through the whole business."[43] He was, in fact, rather liberal, and had no illusions about repealing most of Roosevelt's reforms. He did believe in balancing the budget, had no notion of economics except a Dickensian idea of matching spending and revenue closely, but was a determined internationalist.

He attracted, and was attracted to, successful businessmen. He liked their efficiency, organizational ability, and wealth, and especially their great deference to him. They admired and supported him, and he believed successful American business executives to be a great pool of talent, as well as conviviality. And many of them came to see him as the man who could end the Democratic monopoly of the federal government. Eisenhower cultivated the support of the leaders of American finance and industry, who showered him with favors, and he seemed to rise serenely, ineluctably, toward the presidency, as if above the political fray, in which he was, in fact, a consummate manipulator.

In his diaries, and in his memoirs, Eisenhower recounts the history of discussions of his political future. A political career was first suggested to him in June 1943, when he was in Algiers. It was raised again in the summer of 1945. He claimed a desire to retire from the military, with no hint of what he would retire to; he was only fifty-five. If not politics, what would be appropriate for so eminent a figure as Eisenhower had justly become? Eisenhower claimed that he did not wish to be army chief of staff when Truman appointed him to that position, but that Truman prevailed upon him to take the post until General Omar N. Bradley, Eisenhower's senior army group commander on the Western Front, had finished a two-year tour as head of the Veterans' Administration, a very important position as twelve million American servicemen were demobilized and were eligible for the benefits of Roosevelt's generous GI Bill of Rights. Eisenhower filled this position until 1948 and then relinquished it to Bradley.

Overtures from both parties continued throughout this time, and after Eisenhower retired and became president of Columbia University in May 1948, both parties continued to pursue him. He fended them off. But when Thomas E. Dewey ran successfully for a third term as governor of New York in 1950, he denied any further interest in the White House and said he was supporting Eisenhower for the Republican nomination in 1952. In December 1950, Truman telephoned Eisenhower and asked if he would take over the founding command of NATO. "He and I both knew that this was a thankless job," Eisenhower wrote in his diary. "But I was in complete agreement with the president that collective security arrangements for Western Europe had to be worked out in the least possible time and that America had to participate in the effort. By this time I had become deeply interested in my work at Columbia University and it was a tremendous personal disappointment to me to have to give it up."[44] (There is little evidence that he and Columbia had particularly taken to each other.)

He claimed to be about to forswear any political ambition if Taft had assured him, as he departed to take over NATO at the beginning of 1951, that he, Taft, wholeheartedly supported the alliance. Taft declined to do this, and Eisenhower promised no such abstention. He knew what Taft's answer would be; it was all part of his carefully prepared campaign to appear to be drafted, almost like General Washington (except that Washington's was sincere). He took up his NATO post but retained incessant contact with politically useful figures at home throughout his seventeen months in Paris.

Eisenhower wrote that Taft was unsure whether he supported the dispatch of four or six divisions to Europe but "repeated his refusal to make the point clear . . . [of] his support in the work for which I was called back to active duty." Eisenhower claims that he had intended, if Taft had responded positively, to tell him that he, Eisenhower, would then make a public statement that in returning to military service he unconditionally renounced any thought of ever seeking political office . . . "Of course, I did not go through with that part of my plan that would have depended upon his affirmative reply."[45]

As usual with claims of disinterest from subsequently elected figures (writing about conversations with deceased people), this is not entirely believable, especially since it lays on his chief rival for the Republican presidential nomination the responsibility for Eisenhower running at all. It invites the question of what nature of support Eisenhower was seeking and not receiving from Taft if the senator was prepared to send at least four divisions to Europe. It also raises the question of why, if he was so reluctant to throw his well-decorated hat in the ring, he didn't hint to Taft that he could secure a clear run at the White House, in which the general was not really interested, if Taft would become a little more enthusiastic about the mission Eisenhower was about to undertake. Upright man though Taft was, this bargain could not have failed to interest him.[46]

Eisenhower continued to receive appeals from both parties while in Europe, and claims to have concluded that he was probably a Republican, since he had always voted Republican and was concerned that the Democrats had won for twenty years by "spend and spend, and elect and elect . . . We were coming to the point where we looked toward a paternalistic state to guide our steps from cradle to grave."[47] Presumably, these were not piercing conscientious revelations that came to him as he commanded the organization of NATO forces from Paris at the age of sixty-two. In any case, he did not propose, then or subsequently, the repeal of any significant Roosevelt or Truman social measure, and made it clear that he was well to the left of Taft on these matters. "I still hoped and believed that someone else could lead the Republican Party much more effectively and to a better result than I could." He never made any suggestions of who that mystery leader might be, and half a century of energetic retrospection has failed to produce a plausible candidate.

The usual sequence occurred: "What impressed me more than anything else was the extent of real grassroots sentiment for me to become a candidate," etc.[48] On New Year's Day 1952, Eisenhower wrote to Truman, who had asked him, most amicably, what his intentions were. In a longhand letter, Eisenhower replied that he would not seek the presidency: "You know, far better than I that the possibility that I will ever be drawn into political activity is so remote as to be negligible."

Five days later, Massachusetts senator Henry Cabot Lodge announced the Eisenhower-for-President campaign, and the following day Eisenhower announced that he was prepared to accept the Republican nomination.

Truman, with admirable restraint, told the press he thought Eisenhower "a grand man . . . I am just as fond of General Eisenhower as I can be. I think he is one of the great men produced by World War II."[49] Astonishingly, Stephen Ambrose, a respected biographer of Eisenhower and Nixon, claimed that Eisenhower was "furious" at Lodge's action.[50]

To believe Harry Truman and Dwight Eisenhower, two of the distinguished leaders of American history, the one was as eager to quit the White House in 1953 as the other was to avoid it. Both versions strain credulity and are largely humbug. However, the champion of such posturing was FDR's orchestrated draft for a third term in 1940. Necessary though it was to the world to reelect the president who would become a supposedly neutral semi-combatant against the Nazis and the Japanese imperialists, the hokey Democratic convention in Chicago in 1940 must rank as one of the great monuments to political cynicism of American history.

Compared with Franklin Roosevelt, the leader who elevated them both (though neither liked him very much and its not clear that he much cared for them either), Truman and Eisenhower were earnest political amateurs. Compared with all of them, Nixon's rather naked ambition, and that of his most important and talented contemporaries, Kennedy, Johnson, and Reagan, would be almost refreshing. (The first three were born between 1882 and 1890, the last four between 1908 and 1917.)

Truman told his staff that the Republican bosses were showing Ike "gates of gold and silver that will turn out copper and tin."[51] Truman underestimated Eisenhower's worldliness, not to say, duplicity. The general had written to one of his army comrades: "so-called drafts . . . have been nurtured, with the full, even though undercover support of the 'victim.'"[52]

Eisenhower's political cunning would be an element of both common interest and friction with Nixon. As Ike presented himself as the reluctant hero, Nixon strove to be Mr. Clean. Eisenhower would admire Nixon's intelligence, courage, and determination but disapprove his Cassius-like appetite for power. He would affect the avuncular grandeur of the spontaneously elevated hero, but was made uneasy by Nixon's knowledge that with Eisenhower, all was not what it seemed. At the end, after Nixon had made it to the White House on his own, Eisenhower would be gratified by the success of the man he would then claim as his understudy, and Nixon would be delighted with the approbation of the soldier-statesman he would acknowledge as his mentor. Both roles were largely a fiction. It would be a tortured script with, as between these protagonists, a happy ending.

Richard Nixon had seen Dwight D. Eisenhower six times before the general declared his availability for the Republican nomination. He had looked down on the general's tickertape parade through lower Manhattan in the spring of 1945 and had seen him when Eisenhower marched with Marshall and others in the funeral cortege of General John J. Pershing, Ike's precursor as commander of the American Expeditionary forces in France in the First World War. This was in 1948. He met Eisenhower for the first time in 1948, when the general briefed Nixon and other congressmen on European security matters. They met one-on-one for the first time when Nixon gave Eisenhower a briefing on the Hiss affair and related matters in 1949. Nixon was present when Eisenhower addressed Congress in February 1951. Nixon attended a World Health Conference in Geneva in the spring of 1951, and made an official and an unofficial request to visit Eisenhower while the senator was in Europe. Eisenhower received Nixon for over an hour on the morning of May 18, 1951. Ike had promised his backers that, opposite American politicians, he would "maintain silence in every language known to man."[53]

Eisenhower was more forthcoming than that. He railed against defeatism and lamented that American opinion did not realize the gains that had been made in shaping up Western Europe to resist the communists. He impressed Nixon as the first military person the senator had met who stressed factors other than armed force; Eisenhower called for a commercial, cultural, and ideological offensive against the communists. The general had read Ralph de Toledano's *Seeds of Treason*, an admiring study of Nixon in the Hiss case. Eisenhower congratulated Nixon on getting Hiss "fairly." He later wrote admiringly of Nixon's earned reputation for "fairness . . . Not once had he overstepped the limits proscribed by the American sense of fair play. . . . He did not persecute or defame. This I greatly admired." His admiration was not altogether misplaced, but it was perhaps exaggerated. Whether it was flattery or naivety on the general's part is not clear, but he was more given to the first than the second.

Nixon came away convinced that Eisenhower should be the next president. He detected behind "a warm smile and icy blue eyes . . . a lot of finely tempered hard steel." He would soon get past the facade and to grips with what was behind it. A month after the Paris meeting, Nixon was one of a group of Eisenhower backers who met June 23-24, 1951, at Clarksboro, New Jersey, at the home of a Stassen backer, Amos J. Peaslee, to launch Stassen's campaign as a holding operation on behalf of Eisenhower. Joe McCarthy, Congressman Walter Judd, and Stassen's manager, Warren Burger, were among the participants. A paper was drawn up that Stassen signed, promising that he would not be a candidate against Eisenhower and that if Ike ran Stassen would withdraw. Dewey described Stassen, his former rival, with his usual asperity, as a "useful . . . counterirritant."

One of Eisenhower's wealthy business friends, Ellis Slater, a liquor executive, attended the Bohemian Grove in July 1951 and gave the Eisenhower message to Herbert Hoover and his friends that Taft could not win and only Eisenhower could round up enough floating votes to put the Republicans across. A week later, in the Bohemian Grove's San Francisco clubhouse, July 28, 1951, the same group of Hoover's close collaborators, Slater representing Eisenhower, and some wealthy California businessmen, met and pursued the idea of the Eisenhower nomination to the point of the vice presidency. Slater proposed Nixon, because he was young, a navy man, could bring California, had an excellent record on the communist issue, and shared Ike's internationalist views. Knowland was the only rival, and he was not thought to have any of Nixon's advantages except that he too might pull California and some younger voters generally. Slater reported his conversations to Eisenhower in Paris five days later, and Nixon's informants would certainly have advised him of the clubhouse discussion promptly. Nixon was a logical vice presidential candidate.

In the autumn of 1951, Dewey took charge of the prenatal Eisenhower campaign, set up an office in the Commodore Hotel, and put in hand a massive fund-raising effort led by John Hay Whitney that produced $4 million for the non-candidate, an unprecedentedly lavish pre-launch war chest. Southern California fund-raising was taken over by Nixon's own fund treasurer, Dana Smith. Dewey formed up an Eisenhower committee. The chairman was Henry Cabot Lodge, who was judged a perfectly adequate fig leaf for Eisenhower, but not a strategist or commanding political eminence, despite his Boston Back Bay airs and name made famous by his grandfather, Woodrow Wilson's bête-noire.

Dewey's campaign manager in his two presidential bids, Herbert Brownell, a wily New York lawyer; General Lucius D. Clay, Ike's closest army confidant and former chief occupation official in Germany; former Marshall Plan administrator Paul Hoffman; and Kansas senators Frank Carlson and Harry Darby (Kansas was Ike's native state) were in the group. One of their first challenges was to prevent the publication by General George Patton's widow of her husband's papers that revealed the torrid affair Eisenhower had had from 1943 until after the war with Kay Summersby, his attractive female British chauffeur. Lodge got Mrs. Patton's lawyer a plum appointment and headed off what in the prim postwar times could have been a public relations disaster.

California posed a special problem, because its large delegation, second only to New York's, was being held by Earl Warren, who entertained his own presidential ambitions. Warren did not want to be an overt candidate and felt that such an endeavor would require him to compromise his honor beyond what he was prepared to do. The California delegation had to be infiltrated and undermined, but not so that Warren, who ruled in Sacramento as an emperor – in his third term, like Dewey – would notice. The delegation had to respect the governor's sensibilities but be capable of being snaffled up for Eisenhower if need arose. And the need was likely, because Taft had built up a large delegate lead after more than a decade of diligent and distinguished service as Mr. Republican. Richard Nixon was an expert at this sort of Machiavellian maneuver, and he would undertake to subvert Warren's position without greatly offending him, while maintaining good relations with the Taft Old Guard, by whom he was generally well-liked in the Senate. Chotiner had discussed the vice presidency for Nixon with Dewey and Brownell, as Nixon was being entrusted with his delicate, vital, and slightly unseemly mission.[54]

Earl Warren was an impressive governor but an eccentric national politician. He took positions that were, on the whole, commendable, but he paid no attention to where the chips fell within his own party. Warren was an implacable foe of McCarthyism, a champion of civil rights who warned Republicans not to stray from the principles of Lincoln, a public supporter of Secretary of State Acheson and of Truman over MacArthur, a supporter of public utilities, and even a critic of unfocused criticism of the scandals in the Truman administration, implicitly criticizing Nixon's efforts to capitalize on them for the benefit of the Republicans. He thus managed to annoy virtually all Republicans, and it was a matter of some mystery what he was doing in that party, other than as a traditional Theodore

Roosevelt–Hiram Johnson Progressive. He was popular with the California public, as much with Democrats as Republicans, but apart from Knowland, whom he had appointed to the Senate when Hiram Johnson died, he had no friends in the higher reaches of his ostensible party. Even Knowland, though conspicuously pro-Warren, was really for Taft and hoping to be his vice presidential nominee.[55]

Chotiner, on Nixon's behalf, met with the Taft California delegates, who were itching to bolt from Warren's control and challenge him in the primary for control of California's convention delegation, on June 29, 1951, in Fresno. Chotiner was encouraging to the Taftites but did not commit Nixon to challenge Warren for control of the California delegation. In October, the Taftites moved a resolution at a California Young Republicans convention opposing any Republican candidate "who has a reputation of having given ground to creeping socialism." This was not only a clear sniping at Warren, it had more than a whiff of effulgent McCarthyism, since it attacked a reputation rather than a substantive fact. Nixon's followers joined with Warren's to defeat the motion and pass a rather sycophantic motion in favor of Warren.[56]

Warren announced his candidacy for president on November 14, 1951, and Nixon gave a rather tepid comment about Warren "certainly" being one of the "good men" possibly seeking the nomination. Nixon had said that he and Warren were "not unfriendly. We are two individuals going our own ways."[57] The following day, at a press conference in Los Angeles, Nixon claimed he had discovered as he had toured around the country that Warren had "surprisingly" strong support. He commended Warren as "completely honest" and "electable" but an unknown quantity in policy terms. Nixon then shifted gears and tried to prod Eisenhower by saying that the general "has been playing it a little too coy and people are beginning to lose some of their enthusiasm," though he would be a vote-getter.[58]

At the Republican State Central Committee meeting in San Diego on November 21, despite Nixon's public personal endorsement of Warren, the Taft and Nixon forces united to prevent an endorsement of Warren. Nixon told Taftites who were annoyed at his having joined the endorsement of Warren that he had done it for party unity, but that even if he ended up being on the Warren delegation, he would still be for Taft. Nixon was now ostensibly supporting all three candidates, including the undeclared Eisenhower, while assuring the Taft faction that he was really for them, and the Eisenhower faction that he was merely following Dewey's advice in avoiding an open party schism in working for the general inside the Warren camp, while encouraging the Taftites against Warren. Knowland, supporting Warren, but secretly ineffectually for Taft, was no more honorable than Nixon and blunderingly inept.

Warren mistrusted Nixon but had no idea what an intricate game he was playing. Taft, a guileless man, believed Nixon was a supporter with reservations, while Dewey, the tactical manager for Eisenhower, was satisfied that however devious Nixon became, he was executing a plan that in concept had been generated by Dewey himself, avenging himself for having been defeated by both Roosevelt and Truman. Nixon was deftly playing on the complacence of Warren, the trusting integrity of Taft, and the vanity and cynicism of Dewey, and behind him the self-importance and tactical political inexperience of Eisenhower himself. This gave Nixon lots of room to work in.

The California Taftites, in search of someone to head an alternate delegation opposed to Warren, after Nixon demurred, offered the honor to Herbert Hoover, Douglas MacArthur, and Joe Martin, none of whom was really a Californian and all of whom declined. They should have gone with Adolphe Menjou, who was a conservative Republican California activist. Instead they ended up with kooky-right congressman Thomas H. Werdel of Bakersfield. Nixon loyalists completely infiltrated this group, and Nixon's original benefactor, Herman Perry of the Bank of America in Whittier, even became their treasurer. Werdel would denounce Warren as "atheistic, materialistic, socialistic," with such vehemence that even the *Los Angeles Times* would come to the governor's defense.[59]

Warren was further beset by the discovery of abdominal cancer, which was successfully removed surgically, but which he unsuccessfully tried to represent publicly as an appendectomy. Warren's enemies depicted him as a terminal case, including the misanthropic Herbert Hoover.[60]

Nixon covered off another flank by calling, December 12, for an hour each, on Hoover and MacArthur; they both lived in the Waldorf Towers in New York. This was rather exalted lobbying for a thirty-eight-year-old in his first year in the Senate. Nixon had become a serious participant in a drama that involved a number of world historic American personalities, well before he had become one himself. Both men preferred Taft, and MacArthur was astounded and dismayed by the popularity of Eisenhower, whom he affected to regard as a "clerk" and "the best second lieutenant I ever had." Eisenhower thought MacArthur a vainglorious fraud addicted to "boot-lickers." (Nixon claimed in his book *Leaders*, in the chapter on MacArthur, that he met the general for the first time at Taft's funeral in 1953.[61])

At the same time, Stassen had been calling upon Eisenhower in Paris and returned excitedly claiming that the general would not run, and saying that he was rethinking his Clarksboro pledge of less than six months before. Stassen called upon Nixon and offered him the vice presidential nomination in exchange for Nixon's support with California delegates. It was only seven years since the boy wonder of the Republicans had met Nixon in the South Pacific. Nixon had refined his noncommittal answers to a high art, and did not take Stassen seriously enough to give him the most sophisticated version of his stock response.

Nixon's duplicity achieved a new depth with his assurance to the *Los Angeles Times* on February 21, 1952, that he was an unambiguous Warren supporter and that "none of the Warren delegates will be pledged to any other candidates as their second choice." Nixon had gone one better and pledged himself to Eisenhower, who had now said he would accept the nomination, as of January 7, and implied support of Taft, on the second ballot, if not the first.

— v —

Early in the new (presidential) year, Nixon resumed his strenuous speaking schedule, more than thirty such events in the first four months. He wound up a series of speeches in Honolulu in April and then took a ten-day holiday on Oahu with Pat and her friends the Drowns, genuinely relaxing and, in his case, implausibly, taking hula lessons. He told the *Hilo Tribune-Herald* that Warren might hold a hundred delegates and would "smile sweetly at both sides" and claimed that "Ike had been badly bitten by the presidential bug."[62] (This was true but was probably no better appreciated by the general for that.)

In February, some of Eisenhower's backers staged a rally for thirty thousand people in Madison Square Garden after the Friday-night prize fights. It was a rather fatuous festivity of maudlin and idolatrous laudations, but Ike and Mamie watched a film of it in their Paris residence and were moved to "a sniffle once or twice."[63] Eisenhower won the New Hampshire primary, organizationally assisted by Henry Cabot Lodge as neighboring senator, and won a big victory with a write-in ballot in Minnesota, assisted by Harold Stassen's local followers. The general's popularity was incontestable. Still, he waited for a consensus, as if it were Taft's duty simply to melt away.

To be fair to Eisenhower, he was clearly somewhat ambivalent about a presidential candidacy, in that he wanted to be president but wanted the office virtually handed to him. If Dewey had won in 1948 as he should have, he would presumably have been the candidate again in 1952, and Eisenhower would probably not have much regretted never having been a politician. But after the 1948 debacle, he was, as Nixon said, bitten by the bug, and his desire to be president was contending with his desire to seem to be reluctant. By April 1952, he was running the danger of seeming indecisive; he had not discouraged a huge groundswell in his favor, but if he didn't move soon, the whole movement could collapse, and despite popular sentiment, Taft had earned the affection of the party rank and file. Where Truman looked for decisions to make and was happy that "The buck stops here," the cautious Eisenhower left his options open until they almost foreclosed themselves. Both approaches worked for these practitioners, but they both had their hazards.

On March 22, Nixon signed the pledge of loyalty as a Warren delegate, as the California Election Code required, and swore that "I, Richard Nixon personally prefer Earl Warren as nominee . . . and hereby declare I shall, to the best of my judgment and ability, support Earl Warren." Airtight though it seemed, Nixon would interpret the oath rather idiosyncratically. More important, Nixon had bargained his signature for important concessions. He had initially declined to be a delegate, to avoid such a pledge, and Warren sent Knowland to attract him to the slate. There were several conversations, as Warren knew that an unpledged Nixon could be a serious weakness in his status as a favorite-son candidate of California. Nixon agreed only when Knowland, on the governor's behalf, agreed to allow Nixon to name at least twenty-three of the seventy delegates, a third of the total. In fact, he packed the delegation with unidentified ringers.

Nixon's adherence seemed an act of obeisance by Nixon to Warren, but the Warren native-son campaign was a hollowed-out shell before its delegates had even been identified. Nixon was able to continue to assure the Taft forces that he was still open-minded after the first ballot, and the Eisenhower camp that he was carrying out the cunning plan he and Dewey had broadly agreed. Indeed, he was carrying it out with a cynical finesse that Dewey, a rather blunt and impatient ex-prosecutor, could not have imagined or executed. Nixon now adopted the unctuous posture of seeking party unity and a civilized nominating process, because "one of [the candidates] is needed in Washington to put an end to communism, crime, and corruption."

Whatever Dewey's failings as a presidential candidate, he unlocked the key to the reluctant general. He sent a handwritten note to Eisenhower in April – given personally, coincidentally, to a TWA pilot named Nixon[64] – stating that if Eisenhower did not return and enter the race officially, the Republican Party might well turn to MacArthur. This was nonsense, since Eisenhower's supporters would not have gone to the other, more conservative general, and MacArthur would not have run against Taft. He might have accepted the vice presidency, largely to stick his thumb in Truman's eye, and would have been a scene-stealing holder of that position. Indeed, he would have made a contribution to a Taft election, and since Taft died in August 1953, MacArthur would have succeeded him as president, at the unprecedented age of seventy-three. MacArthur was a great talent, but the thought of him as president is disquieting. But Dewey's stratagem worked: to no one was the prospect of a President MacArthur more disquieting than to his former aide. Eisenhower prepared to return to the United States and enter the campaign at last.

Dewey invited Nixon to speak at the New York State Republican Party's annual dinner in early May 1952, in the grand ballroom of the Waldorf-Astoria Hotel. This was a great opportunity, broadcast nationally. Nixon rehearsed and prepared his remarks for a week, and after Dewey and liberal New York Republican senator Irving Ives had spoken briefly, Nixon filled the time slot exactly, leaving the last minute for the prodigious applause that he received. He spoke without notes and without any hesitation or grammatical problems, and it was a notable address. His themes were very familiar to him, having been his staple through his recent speaking tour: the need to avoid divisions, attract sensible Democrats, wage a "rocking, socking" campaign, and turn the (subversive) rascals out. It made a tremendous impression and Dewey was generous in his praise. Dewey told him when he finished speaking and the house rose to applaud that if he didn't "get fat" or "lose your zeal" he could be president. (Dewey had had a great grievance against his former rival, the 1940 Republican presidential nominee, Wendell Willkie, for being overweight.) Nixon went with Dewey after dinner to the governor's suite in the Commodore Hotel and met with him and Brownell and Russell Sprague, Dewey's principal aide and Republican boss in Nassau County. They met for ninety minutes before Nixon returned by train to Washington. Dewey offered to support Nixon for the vice presidency with Eisenhower. Dewey implied confidence that this was almost within his gift and that Eisenhower, if nominated, would owe the governor a great debt. Nixon said he would be "greatly honored."[65] Ten days later, at the Gridiron Dinner in Washington, Brownell took Nixon aside and confirmed that he and Dewey were supporting him as the vice presidential nominee with Eisenhower.

A few days later, Nixon had another meeting with General Lucius D. Clay, Herbert Brownell (former Republican National Committee chairman), and some fund-raisers. Nixon later wrote that these people were "sizing me up,"[66] but they were more likely talking about how to integrate Nixon's California and Texas fund-raising apparatus with Eisenhower's, and preliminary strategizing for the convention against Taft and the election beyond. Truman had withdrawn and the Democratic field was wide open. There was no obvious successor to Roosevelt and Truman. Henry Cabot Lodge told Nixon on the Senate floor that he should be the vice presidential nominee with Eisenhower, and informed Eisenhower that he had said so. Eisenhower declared himself "entirely favorable."[67]

Nixon consulted his Washington social patroness, Alice Roosevelt Longworth, Theodore Roosevelt's daughter and the widow of the last Republican House Speaker before Joe Martin. Although her own father got to be president only by succeeding the assassinated McKinley from the vice presidency, she did not think much of that position. However, she thought conservative Republicans would need Nixon to prevent Eisenhower from compounding what she considered to be the errors of her cousin, Franklin (who finally banned her from the White House in 1940 for saying she would prefer to vote for Hitler than a third term for FDR).[68]

The fix was in for Nixon, if he could bring his infiltration of Warren's supposed delegation to fruition. It was a subplot of Eisenhower's elaborate charade of replicating the popular draft of George Washington, that he professed to believe that the vice presidential selection was within the gift of the party organizers. He had seen the presidential nominees of both parties select the vice presidential candidates for at least twenty years, and especially Roosevelt's spectacular imposition of Wallace in 1940 and Truman in

1944, and cannot have been under any illusions about whose prerogative it was to make the choice. He just didn't want to be connected to an arrangement that antedated his reluctant consent to be conscripted by the nation to the White House boot camp for the commander-in-chief.

Party regulars took note of Eisenhower's great popularity, but they resented the manipulations of the twice-failed Dewey faction and had become a little tired of Eisenhower's insistence that the great Republican Party come, (private's) cap in hand, to Paris to beg the general to accept all that they had to give. Taft, the scion of a Republican presidential family, had worked heart and soul through difficult times for their party, and was supported by a greater and more eloquent, if also rather more temperamental, general than Eisenhower, who was conspicuously available to help the Republicans without George Washingtonian posturing. At the end of May 1952, with the convention only six weeks off, though polls showed Eisenhower as much as ten points ahead of Taft, the Ohio senator seemed to be leading, approximately 460 delegates to 390. Warren, whom his former ticket-mate Dewey had taken with his usual brusqueness to calling "that big dumb Swede,"[69] was under the impression he had about 100. For some time, Nixon had been on his auto-cue of declaring himself a Warren delegate, while saying how important it was to attract independent and soft Democratic voters (deferential bow to Eisenhower) and quietly telling the Taftites that he was open after the first ballot and the Eisenhowerites that he would produce astounding permutations in the Warren delegation.

To shake the Taft momentum in delegate accumulation, there needed to be a cause, a moral issue that would enable the Eisenhowerites to galvanize Republican opinion. Their man had the people and was clearly the strongest candidate, and he was being sandbagged by the Flat Earth Society within the Republican Party, which had taken to reviling Ike, to the general's considerable irritation, as a stooge of New Dealers and Reds. This was not quite the Hallelujah chorus the general had been hoping for, but it offended the average reasonable Republican and was helpful to the Eisenhower cause.[70]

The flashpoint came when the Texas Republicans chose their convention delegates at Mineral Wells on May 27. There had been a big upsurge of Eisenhower support, and a large number of new Texas Republican adherents materialized. The Taft supporters used their control of the credentials committee and other levers and simply elected their own slate to the Chicago convention, slamming the door on Eisenhower.

Brownell and Lodge erupted in moral outrage at the "theft" of the Texas delegation. It was a theft, but this was hardly unprecedented in these matters in either party. However, it was a possible theft of the entire nomination, and that was not so common, and it was not usual for someone other than a grubby politician to be both the author and the victim of such a move. Taft was Mr. Integrity, and Eisenhower had not led the Western Allies to the unconditional surrender of Nazi Germany and founded the military structure of NATO, which would prove the most successful alliance in world history, in order to be consigned to the ash heap by a handful of backwoods Texas political hucksters.

William Rogers was placed by Brownell at the head of a group of lawyers to mount a challenge at the convention, and major Madison Avenue agencies were engaged to generate a fierce public relations outcry. A Pennsylvania congressman, Hugh Scott (eventually Republican Senate leader), proposed a Fair Play resolution. This was the device for mobilizing opinion. The uncommitted delegates, especially California's, would be necessary to put it over. Among the most knowledgeable insiders, as the race came down to the wire, all eyes turned to Nixon.

As the heavy battalions formed up, Earl Warren had the uneasy sensation that his candidacy was less appreciated than he had hoped. The Werdel slate, well financed, attacked him around the state in the most inflammatory terms, which in these febrile times rarely excluded some unflattering application of the word *Red*. He might already have had some premonitions of the antlike movements of Nixon and his supporters within the California delegation. Warren's great capacity for self-righteousness had been admired in California, especially given the chicanery of many prominent California politicians, but he was playing Little League rules in a rough-house league. He excoriated his critics on the right as "scurrilous . . . venomous [participants in] a coalition of hate, backed by enormous sums of money." There was some truth to this, but they were a sideshow, and Warren's candidacy was an exercise in delusional vanity. He didn't have any real support as a presidential candidate, and instead of maximizing his influence as he could have done, he imagined that he was on the same historic plane as Eisenhower, Taft, Dewey, MacArthur, and Truman. He would make a great contribution to U.S. history yet, but not in politics, where he was now completely out of his depth. By contrast, the junior senator from California was already too clever and powerful for the small pond to which Warren tried to confine him. The brutal meritocracy of American presidential politics was separating strivers from achievers.

Warren was moved to concede that if he could not win the nomination, his delegates would be released – not a bulletin, exactly, but an acknowledgment of where events were going. Nixon followed with a statement that was, in its way, a masterpiece. He assured everyone that he was "not a rubber-stamp," noted that there appeared to be a near-deadlock between the Taft and Eisenhower forces, and that the California delegation "is in a position to name the Republican nominee for president . . . [and] holds the key to the situation." He expressed his personal respect for Werdel, but stated that the "Warren delegation is better qualified to represent California. Once Governor Warren releases the delegation, we shall be free to look over the field and select the man best qualified . . . the very strongest possible nominee." He was clinging to the fig leaf of loyalty to Warren, debunking in advance the nonsensical pretense of Warren having any chance to achieve anything for himself as a nominee, and laying claim to the title of king-maker for himself. It was a stunning feat of political leverage, giving himself in a few months a remarkable purchase on the torrent of events.

Warren, even at this late date, could have got himself in as vice president, the position for which he had been nominated four years before, if he had thrown his delegates behind either candidate. Nixon was allowed to exercise the influence he did only because of Warren's inflated notions of his own stature and prospects. As it turned out, by sheer luck, he did better than his pre-convention performance merited, but not because of any aptitude of his for presidential politics.

Neither Warren nor Thomas H. Werdel was pleased with Nixon's statement, but he had not written it for their benefit. Warren won about two-thirds of the vote in the presidential primary in California on June 3. This was well behind his primary performance running for a third term as governor two years before and a serious blow to Warren's prestige as Mr. California, when a bigoted nonentity like Werdel could take a third of the vote and sweep much of the southern part of the state. As Warren shrank, Nixon grew. Grumpy though the governor and his people were at Nixon's statement, and at his devious tactics, their position had become too tenuous for Warren to adopt his headmasterly posture toward Nixon again. Knowland had won both the Republican and Democratic primaries, an impressive showing in a presidential election year, and was touted by many as a vice presidential candidate. He was a large, confident, and hale man, but he was not particularly intelligent and, as events would prove, not a strong character. He appeared plausible enough, but he had done nothing for Eisenhower, for whom Nixon was about to try to deliver the prize.

Nixon now reached more deeply into his bag of tricks, and on June 11 his office sent out under his senatorial frank, because his fund was exhausted, twenty-three thousand letters to known California Republicans, ostensibly asking guidance for what should be done when Warren released his delegates. Nixon promised confidentiality on the answers, but news of his poll, which is what it was, leaked at once. He alone would count the vote. Warren became so aroused that Nixon agreed not to release the results, but he did not seriously discourage rumors that Eisenhower had run well ahead of Taft. Nixon, under pressure even from the *Los Angeles Times*, which thought he had gone too far with this shabby ploy, reaffirmed his fidelity to Warren.

In the Eisenhower camp, Nixon's gesture was greatly appreciated. He had done all he could while remaining outwardly loyal to Warren and without burning bridges with Taft. He spoke at the Massachusetts Republican convention in Worcester at the end of June and commended the renomination of Senator Henry Cabot Lodge, who would be running against the attractive John F. Kennedy. He told reporters that it was level pegging between Taft and Eisenhower, and that he was for Knowland for vice president. It is conceivable that Knowland believed him.

Warren and Knowland asked Nixon to be California's representative on the Platform Committee at the Chicago convention. Nixon arrived in Chicago on July 1 and began lobbying for Eisenhower, and himself. The Taftites barred Eisenhower delegates from Florida, replicating Texas, and for good measure barred the media from national committee hearings. Lodge became extremely demonstrative, and Taft had no choice but to back down on the media. The Warren delegates voted with the Eisenhowerites on the seating of the Florida delegation.

At the national governors' conference in Houston just before the Chicago convention, Dewey managed to get all twenty-three Republican governors, including Warren, to sign a statement that no contested delegates should be allowed to vote on any substantive matter at the convention. This became known as the "Houston Manifesto" and was much commented on in Chicago, where it was correctly interpreted as a victory for Eisenhower. The Taftites replicated their Texas and Florida performances by seating the Taft delegation from Georgia. With this indication of where the winds were blowing in cross-currents, Nixon took it upon himself to say to the press that the Eisenhower delegation from Texas had to be seated. He cleared this statement in advance with the general's headquarters and explained that it was a matter of the survival of the Republican Party. They could not run against Democratic "corruption" without "clean hands . . . If the Republican Party approves the Texas grab, we will be announcing to the country that we believe ruthless machine politics is wrong only when the Democrats use it."[71]

Chotiner urged Nixon on July 2 to fly to meet the train bringing the California delegation to Chicago in mid-journey, and to convince the delegates that the balance of forces had turned against Taft and that California, to retain influence, had do drop the Warren nonsense and support Eisenhower. Knowland continued to be the press favorite for the vice presidential nomination. Nixon had kept his operation completely secret from everyone except the Eisenhower insiders.

Meanwhile, as delegates and alternates dropped off with the normal attrition, the Nixon forces further packed the California delegation, Chotiner even being named an alternate, which completely scandalized Warren when he looked over the final list. Chotiner was then put in charge of political signage, transport, accommodation, and accreditation of press people. The fox was truly managing the chicken coop.

In Chicago, as the California delegation left Sacramento by train on July 3 and rode north and east toward the convention, the Taft camp had seated their delegates from Louisiana, Mississippi, and Missouri, and had a delegate lead of 510 to 414, with 132 pledged to Warren and other favorite sons and 151 being disputed. Eisenhower's idyll of an uncontested convention drafting him to lead the nation was turning into a bare-knuckle fight, as Nixon flew from Chicago to Denver to join Warren's train.

The Taft camp announced informally that it was thinking of asking MacArthur to be vice president, and that the general was not averse to such an invitation. Nixon boarded a train in Denver whose passengers, having been traveling for a day, were out of touch with what was really happening in Chicago, and began circulating a very pro-Eisenhower line. Nixon paid his respects to Warren and repeated his loyalty to the governor. Nixon then went right through the train, speaking with all the delegates and alternates and their families, and selling the Eisenhower message. The latest compromise he had conceived was that the delegation would vote for Warren on the first ballot as pledged, but would announce even before the first ballot that it would go to Eisenhower on the second ballot. He gave an impassioned statement to everyone as he went through the train that California had to vote to seat the Eisenhower supporters among the contested delegates in the interests of fairness and political democracy. Nixon's entourage following through the train behind him suggested selectively that California's reward for delivering for Eisenhower would be to name Nixon for vice president. As the train sped through the Colorado night and Warren sat in his car in mounting irritation at reports of Nixon's astounding evangelization of his delegates, Nixon completed the hijacking of his supporters. The Nixonian cat was now finally emerging from the bag, and his performance on the trip from Denver would become known as "the great train robbery."

— VI —

Warren had a jubilant greeting at Chicago's Union Station and paraded through the station at the head of several hundred well-wishers to buses that Chotiner had festooned, rather cheekily, with Eisenhower for President signs. Warren aides made frantic makeshift changes. Eisenhower loudspeakers were around the convention hall blaring "Thou Shalt Not Steal" in reference to the aggressive Taft tactics on seating delegates. Eisenhower himself arrived the same day as Warren at another railway station and attended a moving, if contrived, candle-light ceremony for the Second World War dead.

Pat Nixon and Helene Drown went to an Eisenhower reception and after a one-hour wait got to shake his hand. The general, advised by an aide that it was Nixon's wife, was especially warm, and Pat found his pale blue eyes "mesmerizing." Rockefeller cousin Winthrop Aldrich held an Eisenhower reception on his yacht in Lake Michigan, off the Chicago Midway, as Dewey, Governor John Fine of Pennsylvania, and others started to muscle votes for the Fair Play resolution.

On Sunday, July 6, the evening before the convention formally opened, William Knowland opened the caucus of the California delegates.

Knowland began with what would shortly be the hackneyed line that it was not true that he and Warren were not speaking to Nixon. He said that he had not come to Chicago to be a "bandwagon jumper," that putting through the Fair Play amendment would prevent sixty-eight Taft delegates that the National Committee had approved from voting on whether to accept more than another hundred disputed delegates, and would throw the convention automatically to Eisenhower. Knowland did not discuss the merits of the argument, but said there was right on both sides. Knowland claimed that the fair course was for California to split its vote, preserving the possibility of deadlock and victory for Warren.

There had been no agreed program for the session, but as soon as Knowland stopped, Nixon stepped forward and gave a powerful address, based on what he held to be the moral issues. He said that if the delegates simply acquiesced in what the committees did when acting in place of the whole party, there would be no need to have a convention, and the delegates would be shirking their responsibility. Further, some of the Taft delegates were installed improperly against the will of the delegate-electors in several states. This would taint the nominating process, morally hobble the party, and quite possibly, in itself, forfeit the election, because there would be no credibility to Republican claims of cleaning up government. Nixon said that any presidential candidate, including Earl Warren, would have a much harder time getting elected if encumbered by the arbitrarily chosen Taft delegates, who would give the whole process the stench of a flawed, rigged convention. "We will be announcing to the country that we believe that ruthless machine politics is wrong only when the Democrats use it," he said.[72]

Earl Warren, a conscientious if self-important man, then spoke briefly and, to the astonishment of both Knowland and Nixon, said that it was a legitimate ethical issue, that they all would have to return to the Californians who had sent them, and that everyone should vote his conscience. The delegation voted 62-8 for Fair Play. This may not have been quite as disinterested behavior by Warren as his admirers have claimed. Given the feebleness of Knowland's argument, Warren might have completely lost control of his delegation if he and Knowland had tried to impose an artificial ambiguity on the views of the delegates. The vote showed how far Lodge and Brownell and Nixon had got with their argument about the attempted suppression of democracy by the Taft faction.

Lodge had presented Eisenhower as an underdog, even as Nixon had worked the Warren train describing him as a virtual shoe-in. Depending on which version was believed, some delegates who voted for Fair Play would have thought they were leveling the playing field and improving the chances of a deadlock, and others would have thought they were getting on a bandwagon that was coming in to win anyway. Nixon had emphasized on the train that though he greatly liked and admired Taft, the Ohio senator could not win a presidential election, that he, Nixon, could not abide the thought of a sixth consecutive Republican loss in a presidential election, that it was now or never, and that Ike was the winning candidate and everyone knew it. This resonated with all serious Republicans.

Nixon reported to the Eisenhower managers that California was solid for Fair Play, that the Warren hold on California was crumbling, and that he, Nixon, had delivered the supreme prize for the general. So he had.

That night and the next morning, Knowland labored to agree a compromise. The Taft forces accepted that the disputed delegates would abstain until their status was resolved. This was presented to Lodge, who passed it on to Brownell, who rejected it. It would not have saved the day for Taft anyway, and the floor fight, with the Taft forces singing "Onward Christian Soldiers" and the Eisenhower forces using loudhailers to chant "Thou Shalt Not Steal," became acrimonious. The Eisenhower forces won, 658 to 548; California was decisive, and the effect on the morale of the Taftites was devastating.

As the Fair Play vote went through, Eisenhower met Warren for a goodwill session in the general's suite. Warren was unpleasantly startled when the gatekeeper of the suite proved to be none other than Murray Chotiner, a Wagnerian Loge figure who was starting to obsess Warren by his nemesistic ubiquity. Chotiner, who wore loud ties and clock-face cufflinks, conducted Warren to Eisenhower with a nonchalance that set the governor's teeth on edge. After a lengthy meeting, the two candidates emerged and Ike declared, "Neither Warren nor I am going to get involved with a lot of pinkos, but we're not going to be dragged back by a lot of old reactionaries either." This was rather peppy politicalese for the general; there were few pinkos to be found at this convention.

The next day, Warren mobilized his friend Paul Davis, who had been Eisenhower's vice president at Columbia, and whom Warren had been holding in reserve in a non-convention hotel. He asked Davis to call on Eisenhower at once and say that Nixon was a traitor in the Warren delegation, trying to bring the delegation to Eisenhower, and that he wished Eisenhower would order Nixon to desist. It is not clear why Warren didn't say this to Eisenhower himself when he had the chance.

There was an unspecified element of threat in this, and Davis delivered the message at once to Eisenhower in his suite at the Blackstone Hotel. Eisenhower replied in what would become a familiar manner: "Well, I'm not at all sure that his information is correct," he told Davis about Nixon. He reasserted that he thought his people were not interfering in any way in the Warren campaign (which he knew to be a complete falsehood), and said that he wanted Warren's campaign to retain its strength, and that he hoped that in the event of deadlock Warren would be the nominee. Ike added a reference to the nightmare scenario that had brought him back from Paris to receive his severely contested "acclamation": if Warren's candidacy deteriorated and there was a deadlock, MacArthur might win, and this would be a disaster. The general was giving the Dewey-Nixon script with the full authority of his military prestige and the enhanced credibility of his supposed political innocence.

Eisenhower concluded the interview by saying that he thought Nixon would make a good vice presidential nominee, completely ignoring Warren's allegation that he had been a traitor. He said that Nixon was the sort of solid, aggressive young person needed in the Republican leadership, and said that he or Warren should call him if there were any more suggestions of his campaign interfering in that of the California governor.

The night before, July 6, MacArthur had failed to electrify the delegates with his keynote speech. The usually brilliant orator got his signals crossed and gave a rather flaccid address. The letdown sense of the delegates was enhanced by Dewey and other Eisenhower supporters' telling their delegates not to applaud MacArthur, because of Eisenhower's paranoid fear of a MacArthur boom generated by his riveting talents as a public tribune.[73]

Intensive politicking continued, though Eisenhower was now in the lead. Taft offered Knowland the vice presidential nomination and, if the convention deadlocked despite Knowland's delivering the California delegation, Taft's support for the presidential nomination. Knowland was interested, but was unable to deliver what was asked of him. If he didn't hold the Californians for Warren, they would certainly go, under Nixon's influence, to Eisenhower.[74]

On Wednesday, July 9, the *Chicago Daily News* published the front-page story that Eisenhower and Nixon would be the nominees, which the newspaper's publisher, John S. Knight, approved. Nixon responded, to United Press questions, that "It's the first time I've heard of it, and I expect it will be the last."

Joe McCarthy and Everett Dirksen did a better job of stirring the delegates than MacArthur had. McCarthy gave his usual litany: "One communist [wherever] is one communist too many." Dirksen, speaking on the issue of the competing Georgia delegations, turned to Dewey, pointed at him, and exclaimed, "We followed you before and you took us down the road to defeat. Don't do this to us again." There was a tremendous demonstration and near bedlam in parts of the hall. Some Taft delegates approached the New York governor and shook their fists at him. Dewey, smiling slightly, was impassive and unimpressed, and when the tumult subsided, the convention voted by heavy margins to seat the Eisenhower delegates from Georgia and Texas. Taft called on Warren, offering anything Warren or Knowland wanted, in exchange for his support, including the vice presidency, which he confirmed MacArthur wanted. It might all have been different if only Taft had thought in these terms when he visited Eisenhower at the beginning of 1951 and Ike had asked for his support for NATO; though, as mentioned, Eisenhower's account is not entirely believable.

Stassen, too, called on Warren and suggested that they play the role of kingmakers for Eisenhower together, though he implied his own availability. Warren didn't pay much attention to this. In effect, on the eve of the voting, it was shaping up as Eisenhower-Nixon versus Taft-MacArthur, versus Warren-Stassen in the event of a deadlock, with Knowland as the man with no chair when the music stopped. Apart from Stassen, it was an impressive group of potential nominees, all of whom rendered great service in high office.

Herbert Brownell was almost constantly with Eisenhower, and by the end of the long battles for delegate selection on July 9, he and Dewey were confident enough of victory that Brownell pressed Nixon on Eisenhower. The general allegedly claimed that he thought it was up to the convention to choose the vice presidential nominee. It is unlikely he believed anything of the kind; though an indecisive man up to the point where he had to decide, he was rarely unaware of his prerogatives. Brownell consulted Chotiner about the comparative merits of Nixon and Knowland, and Chotiner naturally upheld Nixon, but did so very contemplatively and by a supposedly narrow margin in order to enhance the credibility of his answer.

While Brownell had dinner with Eisenhower on the evening of July 10 and talked about the vice presidency, Nixon, who had told his wife that the press speculation the day before was nonsense, sat up with Pat until after 4 A.M. trying to persuade her that accepting the position, which had suddenly become a live possibility, was the best thing to do. He even summoned Chotiner, whom Pat despised as an evil little hack, in his dressing gown, to make the case. Chotiner did so, pointing out that Nixon would always be the junior senator to Knowland, but that as vice president he could be president, or retire and do very well. Pat finally acknowledged that she could stand another campaign if she had to.

On Friday, July 11, the voting for the presidential nomination began just before noon and ended after thirty-five minutes. Stassen sent his manager, Warren Burger, to ask Knowland if Earl Warren, who had held California's seventy delegates, would join Minnesota in delivering the convention to Eisenhower, as it became clear during the voting that Ike was coming to the brink of victory. The vote was Eisenhower 595, Taft 500, Warren 81, Stassen 20, and MacArthur 10. Knowland could not reach Warren, so Stassen acted alone and Burger put Eisenhower over the top by switching Minnesota's 19 votes to him. He thus had 614 votes to a combined total of 592.

Eisenhower, with a trace of tears in his eyes, went to the bedroom of his suite to be with his wife, who was recovering from emergency dental work. Taft, in his suite, allowed that he was accustomed to defeat in these contests. Warren professed to be proud of being no one's "patsy." In fact, he had been a patsy; he had been complicit in the fiasco of 1948 and his candidacy in 1952 was a charade. (In one of the convention's interesting twists, either Warren or Stassen's manager, Warren Burger, would be chief justice of the country for almost all of the next thirty-four years, better consolation prizes than other losers would receive.[75]) Eisenhower graciously crossed the street to visit Taft and called him a "very great American," one of the few superlatives of the convention that was not outrageous hyperbole. Cyrus Sulzberger of the *New York Times* reported that when Eisenhower returned to his own suite and his celebrating supporters, he sat alone for a time, with his thoughts "far, far away."[76]

As the voting ended, Lodge told Nixon he was the vice presidential choice. Eisenhower confirmed this to his immediate entourage a few minutes after returning from his visit to Taft. Brownell invited a group of about thirty party elders, including Earl Warren, to meet to discuss the vice presidency. Earl Warren, finally figuring out what had happened, declined to be part of a coronation of Nixon as dauphin. Brownell said that no deals had been made, which was only true in the sense that if Nixon had been jettisoned at this point, there would not have been much he could do about it. There was a brief suggestion of Taft, but it was agreed that he would be needed in the Senate, and Sprague said that his presence would lose New York State to the Democrats. Dirksen was suggested, but after his attack on Dewey, that was out of the question. Dewey eventually proposed Nixon; there was an enumeration of good points, no demurral. Nixon it was.

Dewey dispatched someone to find Pat Nixon, to warn her to look cheerful through what was about to come. Brownell telephoned Eisenhower and Nixon. Nixon had returned to his hotel, where the air conditioner had broken on this stifling day, and he stripped down to his underwear and lay down on the bed "trying to think cool thoughts."[77] Nixon was half asleep when Brownell called and asked him to come to see Eisenhower right away, "if you want it." Nixon did not shower, shave, or put on an unwrinkled suit. The ever-ingenious Chotiner managed to get a motorcycle escort for them. Pat Nixon, Helene Drown, and Chotiner's wife were having lunch together when the news flashed across a television screen, placed in the restaurant for the delegates, that Nixon was Eisenhower's choice. Clare Booth Luce, in the press box, was surprised by "shouts of rage and disbelief" from some journalists when Nixon's name was announced as nominee.[78]

Nixon finally put a foot wrong on entering Eisenhower's suite, when he said, "Congratulations, Chief," and patted him on the shoulder. Eisenhower, stiffer than a ramrod and full of the protocol due a five-star general and twice former theater commander, looked piercingly and silently at the young senator. Nixon must have felt entitled to a little familiarity after carrying water on both shoulders for Eisenhower all through the farce of the general's supposed period of possible, and then confirmed, availability, when he was supposedly not seeking the nomination. And Nixon had had the raw task of subverting the delegation of his own state. The candidate introduced Nixon to his wife, Mamie, and said that the campaign would be a "crusade" (as Eisenhower had described the campaign in Western Europe in the title of his best-selling book on the subject). It would be a crusade "for ideals." He asked if Nixon would join him and got the instant reply: "I would be proud and happy to." Ike said that he wanted the vice presidency to be a serious position. It became clear that, as in the run-up to the nomination, Ike wanted Nixon to do the dirty work while he rose above it all. Nixon, Eisenhower said, should campaign on communism, corruption, and Korea.[79]

Eisenhower and his aides did ask Nixon to put more distance between himself and McCarthy, and get his views on Korea in conformity with Eisenhower's and not MacArthur's. Nixon effortlessly obliged by saying Truman's lassitude had spawned McCarthyism, and had made it too late to go for a full victory in Korea after eighteen months of dithering in which the Chinese had strengthened their position. Nixon's talents at improvisation were considerable.

Dewey had wished to nominate Nixon, but the bruises of the convention were too raw for that, so Knowland was asked. Deeply unenthused, Knowland agreed and gave a tepid speech. Nixon had asked blowhard McCarthyite Senator John Bricker, the 1944 vice presidential candidate against Truman, when Roosevelt was reelected over Dewey, to be seconder, but Bricker was so upset over the treatment of Taft that he declined. The governor of New Jersey, Alfred Driscoll, seconded. Governor Fine of Pennsylvania moved to make the vote unanimous. Pat made a fine entry, and Nixon gave a floor interview to legendary newsmen Edward R. Murrow and Walter Cronkite. Ike spoke again of his crusade. Nixon closed out the convention with a brief address, praising Eisenhower and Taft, bringing the greatest ovation of the entire convention for Mr. Republican. While this was happening, photographers massed at the Nixon home in Washington, rang the doorbell, rushed past the babysitter popping flashbulbs, and frightened Tricia and Julie Nixon in their beds.[80] This proved something of a foretaste of what the Nixons might expect from the media for most of the next thirty years.

It had been one of the cameo masterpieces of maneuver of American political history. Six years before, Richard Nixon was an unheard-of lawyer from the unheard-of town of Whittier, starting out on an uphill fight against a five-term congressman. Four years before, he had not even been a delegate or had a floor pass at the Philadelphia convention. Now he had been associate kingmaker to Dewey, ostensible party leader and governor of the nation's premier state, in the elevation of one of America's greatest heroes. He was almost certain to come into the second office in the nation, still only thirty-nine. Dewey's race was run; Nixon's had just begun. He had shown the artistry of a seasoned and cunning master of the political arts. And he had been instrumental in rescuing the Republican Party from the lobotomous right, which except for the aberrant Willkie moment in 1940, had controlled it almost uninterruptedly since the premature retirement of Theodore Roosevelt in 1909. For Richard Nixon, all seemed possible.

Chapter Four

The Travails of the Fox

1952–1953

— I —

NIXON'S NOMINATION was generally well-received by the press; despite Clare Booth Luce's contrary impression of the convention, he was regarded as hard-hitting enough as an anti-communist for the hard-liners, but well short of a McCarthyite by the moderates, and a man who had put himself out for the party by endlessly speaking on behalf of candidates and office-holders all around the country. Personally, he seemed dynamic and present-able, with no hint of bad habits, and had an attractive wife who came through well in her opening contacts with the national media.

Nixon stayed close to Eisenhower and met the faction heads with him, then made the rounds privately. It was too late to do much with Earl Warren, whose irritation and that of his friends was compounded by a final indignity: Chotiner had shot the logistical budget and left the governor and others to cover some of their hotel bills from their own pockets.[1] Warren and Knowland did manage to make positive public statements about Nixon, but privately made no secret of their feelings of nausea at his behavior. As the Californians grumblingly returned to the West, reports began to circu-late about financial irregularities in the Nixon campaign.

Nixon called on Taft, who was too experienced to believe in Nixon's protestations of innocence. He described Nixon as "a little man in a big hurry . . . [full of] tension and conflict."[2] This was an insightful observation, as long as "little" was loosely applied to physical matters. A few days later, Nixon went with Brownell to a baseball game in New York and when a home run was hit, Brownell was appalled that Nixon stood on a chair "waving his arms about and screaming."[3] He was always strangely phlegmatic and unpredictably excitable.

From the start, Eisenhower delegated almost all unpleasantness to Nixon, starting with trying to keep the party's honor from being violated by McCarthy, but without driving McCarthy into opposition. Nixon had given the keynote address at McCarthy's renominating convention in Milwaukee in June, and had roused the audience by referring to the "communist fifth column in America." He had promised a "fair" investigation of McCarthy's charges, which satisfied McCarthy's perfervid followers without implying that Nixon thought the charges had much merit. It was his usual acrobatic performance. McCarthy had preferred Taft to Eisenhower, and had even offered to try to raid some of Eisenhower's delegates, in company with a Washington lawyer friend of his who would be catapulted to prominence twenty years later, John Sirica.[4]

Nixon succeeded in his initial task of placating McCarthy and Taft. McCarthy thought Eisenhower was soft and preoccupied with his own public relations (he was not at all soft and his conception of himself was the essence of mental hygiene compared with McCarthy's). And Taft regarded Eisenhower as a front for New York money and a tool of those who would make the Republicans over into a look-alike copy of the Democrats. But both senators found Nixon's presence comparatively reassuring, in policy terms. Two weeks after the Chicago convention, Nixon and his wife and Chotiner, Bill Rogers, and Rose Mary Woods flew to Colorado for a relaxed meeting among the Republican candidates. The main venues for talks were to be the golf course and the fishing stream. Nixon was compelled to stand in hip waders and pay attention to Eisenhower's casting lessons. When presented with a fish net, he allegedly, but not altogether plausibly, asked, "What is this?" He caught no fish and had a pleasant talk with his leader, but it all had the uneasy air of Nixon's being deliberately made to feel awkward in front of the press.

Nixon did form an admiration for Mamie Eisenhower that would never waver. At one point, on leaving the Eisenhowers after a few drinks, he slapped a wall and exclaimed, "I really like that Mamie. She doesn't give a shit for anybody – not a shit!"[5]

The Nixons flew on to California and had an effusive homecoming at Whittier on July 28. Warren, Knowland, and Lieutenant Governor Goodwin J. Knight manfully greeted the Nixons at Los Angeles Airport, and Warren even managed to claim: "All the people of California are rejoicing at your success."[6]

A motorcade formed up and after a stop at the Ambassador Hotel went on to Hadley Field at Whittier, where Nixon had performed his prodigies of patience and endurance in his football career. Warren, Knowland, and Knight endured all this in the interests of party unity, while a marine honor guard and a reform school drill team went through their paces. Nixon, who was speaking from an improvised dais on the playing field, joked that it had taken him eighteen years "to get off the bench and on to the playing field." Nixon and his wife spent well over an hour shaking hands with many of the more than three thousand people present, including the indelible Chief Newman.

By now, the Democrats had held their convention. Adlai Stevenson, as governor of Illinois, gave the welcoming speech in the same place where the Republicans had just convened. He won the nomination with the eloquence of his remarks, beginning: "For two weeks pompous phrases marched about this landscape in search of an idea. And what they came up with was that twenty years of victory over Depression and foreign tyranny, were twenty years of defeat and despair." Stevenson, scion of a wealthy Illinois family and grandson of Grover Cleveland's second vice president, had been one of the many intelligent young men attracted to Washington in the Roosevelt administration. He had been special assistant to the secretary of the navy, as it was built up to be the greatest fleet in the history of the world, and then to the secretary of state, and adviser and alternate delegate in the U.S. delegation to the United Nations. He was elected governor of Illinois in 1948 by nearly six hundred thousand votes and had run an effective, reforming administration. He was an urbane and witty man, and while he seemed to many to be an effete temporizer, his high intellect and always sharp wit as an aphorist or quipster earned him a huge following.

In his acceptance speech, he had asked that this "cup pass from me," and had expressed admiration for Eisenhower, but said that he had been called upon to heal a terminal case "of political schizophrenia." It was eloquent, as Stevenson always was, but it was not the right note. It was too pious about the nomination, too deferential to his opponent, and not believable in claiming that the man who had received the unconditional surrender of Nazi Germany in the West could not control the Republican Party. Eisenhower was the favorite from the start, but by nature and because of the precedent, he and Nixon had none of the overconfidence of Dewey and Warren four years before.

Eisenhower had named a large Chevrolet dealer from Michigan, Arthur Summerfield, a close Nixon supporter, as party chairman, replacing Nixon's Taftite enemy, Guy Gabrielson. Nixon and Chotiner worked out with Summerfield and other professionals a campaign plan in all details before taking it to Eisenhower, still fishing and golfing in Colorado. The essence of the plan was to pull every Republican organization and affiliated entity together under the Republican National Committee, focus a full attack on the Democrats in a way that would unite all Republican factions, and use the new medium of television with unprecedented frequency and imagination. Eisenhower's popularity would be exploited to the full. The plan was accepted, and Nixon returned to California and had dinner with his own fund-raising sources, which included not only Louis B. Mayer, Justin Dart, Darryl F. Zanuck, and Joseph M. Schenck, who had supported him before, but also Walter Annenberg (*Philadelphia Inquirer*), Norman Chandler (*Los Angeles Times*), Leonard Firestone, and other magnates. Nixon was all for integrating all political organization under the umbrella of his friend Summerfield, but he would preserve his own direct access to political contributions. He sketched for these backers an uplifting picture of years of power stretching out before them.

Nixon continued to cut the political coat to fit the cloth. To Eisenhower's friend Roy Roberts of the *Kansas City Star*, he flailed away at Hiss, the "loss of 600 million people to communism" under Truman, and the need to "stencil" the Truman record on to Stevenson. These Republican orators conveniently overlooked the ineptitude of Chiang Kai-shek, as if local matters in the world's most populous country had nothing to do with the outcome of the civil war there. They also overlooked the facts that Truman had saved Greece, West Berlin, and Korea from the communists, founded the world's most ambitious alliance, which the Republican candidate had led (and had split with Taft because of his support of it), and had launched the greatest and most effective and imaginative foreign aid program in history, which Nixon had passionately supported after the Herter Committee trip to Europe. Truman had also dropped the atomic bomb and developed the hydrogen bomb, but the Republicans didn't much criticize him for that.

It had been agreed that the issues were to be communism, the endless and insufficiently energetically conducted war in Korea, corruption, and economic matters. Nixon finessed his former hawkish views on Korea and endorsed John Foster Dulles's platform promise of taking containment to mean liberation but was pretty vague and implausible about how to do it.

The same day as the interview with Roy Roberts, August 21, 1952, Nixon also authorized aides to leak to William S. White of the *New York Times* his familiar formula for distancing himself from McCarthy: he was a militant anti-communist, but unsubstantiated charges of subversion should not be made, and those that are made help the communists. Nixon knew that McCarthy was not only a destructive, but a self-destructive, force, and he knew to put himself at the head of the anti-subversive forces, but in clear dissent from the practice of reckless smears and scares. It does not, from a distance, seem to be a particularly difficult balancing act, but in execution in these times when every politician was under a loyalty microscope, it required great skill to execute.

Eisenhower had sent Nixon out to lay on the anti-communist lash and be a lightning rod for offended American liberals. As always, Nixon would do the necessary to satisfy the one remaining person to whom he had to answer, but initially, at least, he would not immolate himself beyond resuscitation doing so. The balance was between securing the loyalty of the Republican apparatus that would be there when Eisenhower retired or died without permanently alienating the independent middle of the American electorate. Roosevelt had built the modern Democratic coalition of the working class, the rural poor, Roman Catholics, Jews, African-Americans, environmentalists, and intellectuals. Because he was such a stylish and successful leader, Roosevelt also pulled a large section of the young and upwardly mobile middle class.

Nixon, in Eisenhower's name and in his own, constructed the Republican coalition of the majority of the white, largely Protestant, great socio-economic and geographic middle of America. Roosevelt took the natural majority away from the party of Lincoln during the Great Depression. Nixon would take it back when the Democrats next got into war in East Asia but for a cause less than victory. Even before the affable and almost stately Eisenhower regency began, Nixon was preparing to recreate the natural party of government. But he warned at the onset of the 1952

campaign that he did not want a "nicey-nice little powder puff duel."
"Reelecting the Democrats," he said, would be "national suicide."[7]

The leak to William White of the New York Times caused a story that announced that Eisenhower and Nixon were taking their distance from McCarthy. When questioned after the publication of the piece, Nixon said that of course he supported the reelection of his fellow Republican, McCarthy, but that neither he nor Eisenhower wished to imply that in urging someone's reelection they necessarily agreed with everything that candidate said. Eisenhower, in a technique that would later become familiar, exploited the refuge offered by confused syntax and supported McCarthy "as a member of the Republican organization" but implied that he might have employed "un-American . . . methods or procedures."

Eisenhower was specifically asked about McCarthy's attack on the general's great mentor and champion, General George C. Marshall, whom McCarthy had accused of "a conspiracy so immense . . . [and] black." He responded admirably that Marshall was "a perfect example of patriotism" and that his record of service to the nation was beyond criticism.[8] This was true and to Eisenhower's credit. Nixon followed up with an interview with U.S. News & World Report, blaming McCarthyism on Truman's bungled handling of communist infiltration of his administration.

Eisenhower and – ultimately, though less clearly – Nixon were too substantial to remain long under the same political roof as McCarthy, and the battle lines were already discernible. Eisenhower would keep his distance from the acrimony, and Nixon would steal the respectable part of the anti-communist thunder and leave McCarthy with no reputable allies or followers, while professing personal goodwill. If he could steal most of the political clothes of such an honest and intelligent man as Earl Warren, and do it as a junior senator, McCarthy, a fraudulent psychopath, would not last long against Vice President Nixon, acting in the name of a popular soldier-statesman who was a good deal cagier than his (deliberate) syntactical confusion and penchant for golf would indicate.

The press started to complain that Eisenhower had been nominated for president and had then gone fishing for the rest of the summer. It was possible that he did not understand how campaigns worked, and though Brownell was able and devoted, his credentials as manager for Dewey's two unsuccessful efforts were not necessarily persuasive.

Stevenson announced at the end of August that he had a "plan" for ending the Korean War, but that national security considerations prevented him from revealing it. Nixon tore into this as a "cruel hoax" on the fighting men in Korea and their loved ones. Nixon campaigned in New England around Labor Day and steadily turned up the heat on Stevenson personally: "a tired relic of a whole series of deals, of dubious State Department training and of leftist leaning."[9] He claimed that for every financial or national security scandal in Washington, there are ten that have not yet been uncovered. (This begged the question that if he knew this, why had they not been uncovered?) In Maine, in keeping with Nixon's habitual awkwardness, a lobster, having bitten Pat's hand, seized him by the lapel in front of cameras and had to be pried off with pliers while it hissed and its free claw snapped menacingly in Nixon's face.[10]

Eisenhower and Taft had breakfast together at Columbia University on September 12. Eisenhower assured Taft that he could have his full share of patronage, that there would be a tax limit of $60 billion, and that Dewey would not be in the cabinet. This was described by many as "the surrender of Morningside Heights." But it brought the Taft organization entirely into tandem with the main Republican Party. Taft emerged happy and supportive of the candidate. Eisenhower invited Earl Warren to visit him in Denver at the beginning of September and heard out Warren's complaints against Nixon. Eisenhower claimed to be concerned about a write-in ballot in California for MacArthur. Warren assured him this would not occur. Nixon again visited Eisenhower in Denver on September 15. Ike told him to continue his destructive attacks on the Democrats while he, the general, would more gently evince the peaceful America of tomorrow under his leadership. Nixon was used to political roughhousing, but was not enthused about getting too far out in front of Eisenhower as the Republican hit man.

Nixon was regularly describing Stevenson as "Sidesaddle Adlai," inciting the inference that there was a question about the Democratic candidate's masculinity, an outrageous reflection. On September 17, before fifteen thousand people at the Pomona railway station, Nixon declared, in reference to Korea, that "Dead Americans are live issues." He accused the administration of having "bungled us into war" and again (very spuriously) of tolerating a "communist fifth column in America."[11]

It was a powerful but dangerous tide that was bearing Nixon forward and upward in political life. He had rolled over Jerry Voorhis and Helen

Gahagan Douglas in very rough manner, and pursued Alger Hiss with a tenacity that most had admired, and that had yet offended many, who thought Hiss was, as Chambers said, "caught in a tragic moment of history." While he had made sophistical distinctions between his approach and McCarthy's, he had spoken repeatedly of Truman's having tolerated a "communist fifth column" in the country, which was nonsense. He had cast aspersions on the intelligence, courage, and patriotism of Dean Acheson – next to his predecessor General Marshall, probably the most distinguished secretary of state since John Quincy Adams, if not Thomas Jefferson. And he had attacked Adlai Stevenson as a weakling and a leftist. He had ridiculed and denigrated a very considerable incumbent president. Stevenson and Truman had millions of admirers, many of them people of great stature and influence. Nixon had pulled the rug out from under the three-term governor of California, the candidate of both the Democrats and the Republicans in his last election, and had done so before the delegates of the national party and the media of the country.

Nixon had done his best to maintain and cultivate favor with party regulars, and had spoken tirelessly around the country for members of the party executive. He had his supporters and allies, but he had accumulated a great many powerful and angry people who would be delighted to tear him down and grind him to powder if the opportunity arose. Unfortunately, it did, just as his career was reaching an astonishing crest. He had achieved his vertical career climb by taking his opponents, Voorhis, Hiss, Douglas, and to some degree Warren, by surprise, having stealthily approached, though his success was facilitated by the errors of all of them. Now, without warning, his opponents would swarm him, and produce overnight what would be the supreme crisis of his career, until he was overtaken by even graver events twenty years later.

— II —

Stories of a questionable fund for Nixon had been drifting around the Chicago convention, and in its aftermath, and had been the subject of rumor among California political media. As one reporter would say to Nixon, the convention had been a "scandal-monger's paradise," and not too much attention was paid to these reports at first.[12] Dan Green of the Los Angeles suburban weekly *Independent Review* had picked up from angry

Warren supporters a summary of Nixon's Chicago performance and the reports of improprieties in contributions to Nixon. Green published a partial exposé of Nixon's jejuneries at Chicago, and a reader phoned Green and told him about Dana Smith asking him for money for Nixon, and eventually showed Green the canceled check endorsed by Smith. Another source called Green, who continued to probe and encountered journalists from the ultra-liberal *New York Post*, quirky *Los Angeles Daily News*, and centrist *Reporter* magazine, all working on the same story. They coordinated their efforts and resolved to publish at the same time, but the general manager of the *Daily News* got cold feet and before going to press wanted conservative columnist Peter Edson of Scripps-Howard to look into it.

Edson was one of those interviewing Nixon on *Meet the Press* on Sunday, September 14, and he questioned him about the fund after the program (which had gone well for Nixon). Nixon gave his standard responses that his wife was not on the government payroll, unlike the wife of the Democratic vice presidential nominee, Senator John J. Sparkman, that he had no idea who contributed to his fund, that no favors were paid out in consideration of donations, and that the money all went to legitimate expenses. Nixon gave Smith's telephone number to Edson and invited him to call for any elaboration he wanted. Nixon thought the matter over: "such an innocent beginning to the most scarring personal crisis of my life" (up to the time he wrote these words, in 1961). Edson called Smith the next day, and shortly after, the *Post*, *News*, and *Reporter* journalists arrived together, in person, at Smith's office. To all of them Smith explained that the fund was innocuous, that contributions were restricted in size to ensure there was no appearance of Nixon's being overly beholden to any individual, and that the money was just to ensure that Nixon had what he needed to do his job: traveling, Christmas cards, etc. He became more expansive with the reporters who came in person, not realizing that he was not talking to kindred spirits, and said that "the New Deal and Fair Deal [Truman's program] were full of commies" selling big government. "Our thinking was that we had to fight selling with selling, and for that job Dick Nixon seemed to be the best salesman against socialization available. That's his gift really, salesmanship." Smith debunked Knowland and Warren, and didn't deny that he had repaid a loan for Nixon in 1950 but said that it could not have come from the fund. Smith assumed the interview had gone satisfactorily.

After the grand sendoff at the Pomona railway station on September 17, the train, the *Nixon Special*, had moved to a siding a few miles away for the night. Nixon was not concerned when he heard a story was coming, thinking it the Edson story. At midnight, a report came in to the train from L.A. party headquarters that there would be a story that might cause some problems. Nixon convened a 1 A.M. meeting with Chotiner, William Rogers, and a couple of others. Rogers and Chotiner, after Nixon had explained as much as he remembered about the fund, concluded that there was nothing to worry about. On the morning of September 18, the Edson story was published in over a hundred newspapers around the country that took the Scripps-Howard service. It was a benign piece, which referred to the Smith telephone-call explanation of the safeguards that ensured there was nothing inappropriate with the fund. The *Los Angeles Daily News* went with the Edson piece rather than their own, and the *Reporter*'s piece was a little more provocative, but still not alarming to the Nixon campaign.

It was Leo Katcher, a Warren supporter and friend (and future biographer), L.A. correspondent of the *New York Post*, who blew the lid off the controversy and rocked the campaign. Katcher found one contributor whom he quoted as saying, "We've been paying his expenses for some time now. I don't like the idea of this man being a heartbeat away from the presidency." The headline was "Secret Rich Men's Trust Fund Keeps Nixon in Style Far Beyond His Salary." The introduction revealed the existence of "a millionaires' club devoted exclusively to the financial comfort of Senator Nixon." The body of the story was less salacious, but it did state that the donors included people with interests in banking, oil, real estate, railroads, and manufacturing.

The *Nixon Special*'s first stop, at 9 A.M. on September 18, was at Bakersfield, where Tom Werdel, who had run against Earl Warren in the Republican gubernatorial primary and taken a third of the vote on a platform that Warren described with some reason as "scurrilous," was facing a hard test in the election. Werdel had not appreciated Nixon's having played footsie with the anti-Warren forces and then joining the Warren delegation. He had preferred Taft to Eisenhower, but in the circumstances of that morning, Nixon and Werdel needed each other and Nixon warmly endorsed the congressman from the rear platform of his train.

As the train pulled out, one of Werdel's aides handed Nixon a copy of a local newspaper sporting the headline "Nixon Scandal Fund." This was a

United Press story; Associated Press had not carried the story, nor had most of the country's most important newspapers. Drew Pearson ignored it. But Nixon was so shaken by the headline in front of him that Chotiner and another aide helped him to his compartment.

Nixon had recovered his composure for the next stop at Tulare, where Chotiner tried from the station pay phone to arrange that a telephone call between Nixon and Eisenhower be made when the *Nixon Special* arrived that evening at Fresno. The train started to pull out before Nixon had finished speaking and part of the crowd ran down the track after it as Nixon invited them (though presumably not as literally as they seemed to think) to "join our crusade." Nixon raged at the designated train manager, Jack Drown, for allowing the train to leave while he was still speaking, until Rogers cooled things out. But some reporters who had joined the pool at Tulare told the other journalists already on board about the Katcher story in the *Post*, and the press contingent demanded a statement from the candidate. Nixon's press assistant, James Bassett, responded by barring the press from Nixon's own car until further notice. This had the natural effect of ratcheting up the problem.

In Washington, Robert Humphreys, the public relations director of the Republican National Committee, a well-respected and fair-minded former senior editor of *Newsweek*, saw the danger at once and tried to arrange to speak to Nixon at Fresno. He also dictated a press release for Karl Mundt to give on behalf of the Republican Party. Humphreys was somewhat conversant with the fund, and he chose the now typical tenor and theme of such rebuttals: "smear tactics . . . a filthy maneuver by left-wingers, fellow travelers, and former communists."

Chotiner telephoned Humphreys from Madera, California, at 4 P.M. Eastern Time. Humphreys urged Chotiner to tell Nixon to take the offensive along the lines of the Mundt (i.e., Humphreys) statement. Humphreys telephoned Summerfield, the new party chairman, aboard Eisenhower's train, the *Look Ahead, Neighbor, Special*, which had arrived in Des Moines, Iowa. The Democratic chairman, Stephen Mitchell, had already demanded Nixon's resignation as a candidate. "Senator Nixon knows that it is morally wrong. General Eisenhower knows that it is morally wrong. The American people know that it is morally wrong," he solemnly intoned, rising quickly to the windfall opportunity for self-righteous histrionics.

The chief passenger of the *Look Ahead, Neighbor, Special* was keeping his own counsel. He had been hammering the theme of honesty in government. He would "rather not be elected president than to be elected by the help of those who have lost their sense of public morals," he had said that morning to whistle-stop audiences. Ike was proclaiming an "Honest deal." Dewey had telegraphed Summerfield that Nixon should return to New York to combat the "smear campaign." By the afternoon of September 18, less than a day into the controversy, Republican professionals could see that Eisenhower's "crusade" could become a shambles of hypocrisy and absurdity almost overnight if something was not done to reverse the sudden disintegration of Nixon's credibility, tearing Eisenhower's down with it.

Humphreys reached Summerfield, who, like Humphreys, was pro-Nixon, and appreciated what he had done to pick up the pieces after 1948, and extracted from Summerfield, without difficulty, the promise that the Eisenhower camp and the National Committee would maintain a solid front with Nixon. Faithful to this promise, Eisenhower's capable press secretary, who would become one of the world's famous people over the next eight years, James Hagerty, told the reporters accompanying him: "We never comment on a *New York Post* story."[13] Although it was founded by Alexander Hamilton, the *Post* was a rabidly liberal and partisan Democratic paper. The *Look Ahead, Neighbor, Special* conveyed General Eisenhower and his party on to Omaha, where the local newspaper billed the trust in a way that made it seem that Nixon had come into an inheritance from a kindly relative. Summerfield, Hagerty, Eisenhower's chief of staff, New Hampshire governor Sherman Adams, and the other professionals around Eisenhower told him nothing about it, so the candidate was serene, but by that evening, his entourage was becoming deeply concerned. Summerfield tried without success to contact Nixon personally. In these days before cellular telephones, with the campaigns not equipped with radio phones, the only direct contact was through the regular telephone system and when both campaign trains were stopped and a secure place could be found for the callers to confer.

Chotiner and Rogers composed a press release to give the journalists, who were now crowding on to Nixon's train at each stop. They represented the fund as indicative of Nixon's probity. "It handles postage for mail on which I do not choose to use the much-abused senatorial franking privilege. It defrays necessary travel expenses. . . . pays [for] printing speeches and documents which otherwise might have been printed at the taxpayers' expense . . . [and] extra clerical help.

"As an alternative I might have resorted to the use of tax-paid facilities, free government transportation, or I might have put my wife on the federal payroll as did the Democratic nominee for vice president. I did none of these, nor have I been accepting law fees. . . . I prefer to play completely square with the taxpayers."[14] This went out at about 4:30 P.M. Eastern Time on September 18, when the *Nixon Special* pulled into Merced and made all the news wires at once, including Associated Press's first story on the fund. It was a good counter to the Democratic chairman's demand that Nixon resign. Bassett didn't elaborate for the press and Nixon still did not speak to reporters. If Nixon had recovered his equilibrium a little more quickly, he might have nipped some of the press comment, but at least he had been heard from, if only through Chotiner and Rogers, who were pretty unflappable, as usual. Chotiner by his cynical professionalism and Rogers by his bonhomous affability and legal knowledge were good men in a crisis. They were free of Nixon's mercurial moods and inner Shakespearean fears that a dark, unstoppable destiny was afoot that could only be combated (if at all) by fearful acts of desperate courage.

Dana Smith, who had generated much of the problem by his well-intentioned candor to Katcher and the others, caused further problems by confirming to Katcher in a follow-up story, amplifying the damage of the first, that the *New York Post* story was "essentially correct." Somebody on Nixon's staff should by now have given him a tutorial on follow-up questions. On the heels of Smith's latest adaptation of the press to a confessional, including naming a number of contributors to the fund, it all started to stoke up again into the evening. Katcher claimed to have found a contributor to the fund who said that the appeal to him was based on the Nixons' need for a larger home and inability to afford a maid. Up to now, the allegations had been an irritant, but with this sort of reflection, Katcher was starting to draw blood.

Chotiner was further concerned at the silence from the *Look Ahead, Neighbor, Special.* The Nixon train had an uneventful stop at Stockton, but in the evening at Sacramento, the story caught up with him. The crowd was enthusiastic, but there was a near-boycott by political officials in the state capital (whom Warren would not have encouraged to attend), and the press were becoming more persistent. When asked about Mitchell's demand for his resignation, Nixon dismissed the whole affair as a "political smear," as he left for a brief side trip by airplane to Reno. Pat, who was finding the tension very unpleasant, told the press that she didn't discuss politics, but that she had been very impressed with the large and positive crowds all day.

Nixon was in combative mood when he got back to his train at about midnight. He summoned the press that he had kept at arm's length all day and unloaded his counterattack, which he largely maintained through the crisis. He called it "an attempted smear by the same left-wing elements which have fought me ever since I took part in the investigation that led to the conviction of Alger Hiss." He said that the matter was "completely open and above board in every respect. If they think that by such tactics they can slow up my attack against communists and corruption, they will find out differently." He would persevere against "the elements which have been selling this country down the river, until the crooks and the communists and those who defend them are driven out of Washington." He felt better having got this blast off his chest, and retired for a good sleep (in emulation of his leader, who was sleeping soundly in Omaha, still not informed of the problem).[15]

The general's entourage, led by Summerfield, Adams, and Hagerty, and Senators Carlson and Seaton, and his brother, Milton Eisenhower, concluded that they had to brief the candidate properly and did so at 8 A.M., September 19. Summerfield urged a statement supporting Nixon and saying that he had, in effect, been "cleared." The rest of the group did not think Nixon could get by with the two-paragraph statement Chotiner and Rogers had cobbled up. Adams didn't like Nixon, and the Eisenhower inner circle tended to find him slightly distasteful. His relations with Carlson and Seaton were quite good, but not close. They all treated the matter with, as one of them leaked to the *New York Times*, "the utmost seriousness."

They were right to take it seriously, but by being ambivalent about their support of Nixon, they were courting disaster. If Nixon had been forced out at this point, he would have gone back to being a U.S. senator, and would have made his return as a national candidate eventually. The general would have been made to look a political amateur, could have lost the election, or, more likely, could have won with a drastically shorn reputation as a leader and judge of men. Republican congressional election prospects would have been badly battered. Nixon had done nothing illegal or improper, on anything that had come to light; he didn't know what Dana Smith was telling contributors, and had received no money for inappropriate purposes. He would have recovered better than Eisenhower from such a debacle, and Eisenhower's entourage should have been more purposeful and less sanctimonious.

The general himself had said nothing as the briefing and debate among his advisers went on and finally asked, "But what are the facts? . . . I don't believe Dick did anything wrong." They should "wait and see." He then repaired to a corner of the railway car and wrote out a draft personal message to Nixon. He wrote that he "obviously" couldn't go beyond a statement of "personal confidence," because he knew nothing about it. "In the certainty that the whole affair comprises no violation of the highest standards of conduct, a critical question becomes the speed and completeness of your presentation of facts to the public. . . . The fact that you never received a cent in cash is of the utmost importance." He advocated the publication of all documentary evidence, all accounts, names, amounts received and paid, and details of expenses.

This was a bit rich, given the gifts Eisenhower had received from important people and the tax treatment of his war memoirs as a capital gain on the advance and royalties rather than the income tax that would normally be charged, saving him at least ten times the quantum of Nixon's fund. However, in the circumstances, there might have been some justification for such an open kimono policy. Where Eisenhower demonstrated a complete lack of political savoir faire was when he wrote to Nixon that he should consider giving all this information simultaneously to the Democratic elections chairman, Stevenson's closest ally, Illinois senator Paul Douglas, "to examine your records and make his findings public." This last was a mad suggestion. He should by now have realized that if Nixon had given the Democrats the Ten Commandments, they would construe it as proof of heinous shortcomings. Truman had already ordered the attorney general to launch a criminal investigation of Nixon's fund and ensured that this was leaked to the press.[16] He also ordered an examination of Nixon's record at the Office of Price Administration (OPA), without useful results.[17]

Eisenhower was right to take the view that Nixon had probably done nothing wrong, but he had no business asking Nixon to do more than he was prepared to do himself, and asking the Democrats to play a role in exonerating Nixon almost incites doubts about whether Ike wanted to keep his invited nominee at all. In all of the circumstances, he was probably just being cautious and was as likely to have been motivated by partisan inexperience and by confidence in Nixon as lack of it.

It is clear that Eisenhower, within a few minutes of hearing about the fund, grasped its danger to him. He was quick to see the threat, and not altogether mistaken about how to deal with it. Nixon certainly had to discharge some onus of suspicion beyond mere denials and accusations of smears. As far as anyone knew, or knows today, there was nothing in the slightest unethical about Nixon's fund, and it is illustrative of the precariousness of his position that Nixon had become a tenuous nominee, and Eisenhower had asked him to let the Democrats judge him, because of a news story by a partisan Democratic reporter of a militantly anti-Republican newspaper that was only the seventh in circulation of New York's dailies.

In Eisenhower's message to Nixon, he promised to telephone him at the earliest possibility, and then conspicuously failed to make contact as the days went eerily by. Hagerty issued the first statement in what Eisenhower intended as a series of stalls until either the facts had cleared or had mortally wounded his vice presidential candidate. Eisenhower said in his statement that he had "long admired and applauded" Nixon's "American faith and determination to drive communist sympathizers from positions of public trust . . . I believe Dick Nixon to be an honest man. I am confident that he will place all the facts before the American people, fairly and squarely." This last line blew the controversy wide open. With Eisenhower publicly demanding full disclosure, despite his refusal to do anything comparable himself, the press of the country was encouraged to go after Nixon, snapping and snarling.

Nixon awakened in Sacramento as his train set out for Marysville. At the end of his talk there, as the train started to move out, a heckler shouted, "Tell them about the sixteen thousand dollars." Nixon shouted, "Stop the train!" and responded very effectively. He said that "ever since" he had investigated communists in the United States, "the communists and left-wingers have been fighting me with every smear that [they could invent]. . . . I'm going to reveal it today for the first time. I was warned that if I continued to attack the communists and the crooks in this government that they would continue to smear me." He said that he had saved the taxpayers money because he could easily have expensed through his Senate office to the account of the federal government the sixteen thousand dollars that he received from his fund. He recounted that Sparkman had put his wife on the payroll (a particular bugbear of Nixon's that he mentioned even conversationally with inexplicable and mind-numbing frequency), although, as he pointed out, Pat had worked countless times in his office, gratis. He explained that he had never taken legal fees while he had been in Washington. He concluded by promising to go "up and down" the country, and "the more they smear, the more I'm going to expose the communists and the crooks and those that defend them until they throw them all out of Washington."

Distinguished historian Roger Morris regards this as "a singular act of stump-speech demagoguery in an American national campaign."[18] "Demagoguery" is excessive. Nixon had not taken personally any of the money from the fund. He was unaware of precisely who had donated to it, and no favors were bought through it. It is now clear that he had the cleanest finances of any of the four main party candidates for national office, and Katcher and his editor, James Wechsler, and publisher, Dorothy Schiff, were foaming-at-the-mouth liberal Democrats (compounded in Katcher's case by being an Earl Warren groupie), and their motives, though certainly having nothing to do with communism, were partisan, unrigorous, and suspect. (Communism was constantly invoked in these days; there were microscopically small numbers of communists, and infinitesimally small numbers of traitors in the United States, but the Red Bogey was abroad in the land. The uproar over the fund had more to do with vengeance by Warren and his supporters, but Nixon could hardly allege that.)

Nixon was within his rights to become as belligerent as he did; in financial terms at least, he was an honest man, and he *was* being smeared. If there had been anything wrong with the fund, Dana Smith would not have so openly and loquaciously discussed it with any journalist who turned up, in person or on the telephone. Nixon was also being attacked for having carried the battle so fiercely to Voorhis, Douglas, Hiss, and Stevenson. But if they had responded as energetically and persuasively as he just had, Voorhis would have been reelected, Douglas would have run more closely and preserved a political career, and Hiss would not have been convicted. (Stevenson might have performed marginally better than he did, but Nixon wasn't running directly against him; Eisenhower was, and barring disastrous errors, he was the man of the hour.)

Eisenhower did not know Nixon well and he can be excused for not going straight to the battlements for him. But he brought down a great deal of the horrible problems Nixon was to endure in the next few days by putting the bait directly in front of the press and demanding an unprecedented level of disclosure. Part of the problem was the lack of synchronization between the candidates. While Eisenhower's staff was determined not to disturb him, Nixon was recovering from his original recoil of mortification at the attack on him by Katcher. When Nixon had snapped out of it and was fighting back, Eisenhower first learned of the problem and overreacted. This undercut Nixon's efforts and aroused his suspicions, never hard to energize, that he was being shabbily treated by the man he had been instrumental in nominating and who had asked him to stand for the vice presidency.

The *Nixon Special* went on to Chico, California, where a crowd of eight hundred awaited, and he unlimbered his lines about fighting the communist and leftist smears. After the speech there, the train remained for half an hour while Chotiner and Nixon manned the telephones in the stationmaster's office. Nixon spoke to Seaton, and Chotiner spoke to several people on the Eisenhower train. This was the first they had heard of Eisenhower's request for total public disclosure. Chotiner waxed emphatic about how the general shouldn't require more than Nixon's word. Nixon listened to Seaton's unctuous transmission of Eisenhower's letter and rang off without really responding. He wrote that "it was clear to me that Eisenhower was not committing himself." This was the beginning of the intermittent friction between Eisenhower and Nixon that would flicker for fifteen years.

Chotiner gave Seaton a further response from Nixon that he made up as he went along, for Eisenhower's use in Kansas City that night. The statement said that Nixon was asking "for a complete accounting . . . [to refute] a deliberate smear attempt." The donors had asked and received no "special favors, consideration, or treatment," and "not one red cent was spent by me for personal use." The "legitimate political fund" was the product of "an earnest and unselfish desire . . . to support my fight against communism and corruption." Chotiner and Nixon telephoned Dana Smith and told him to prepare to release a list of donors. Smith assured them that all the records were in order and would not produce the least criticism. The donors were not especially prominent and gave the lie to the *New York Post*'s reference to a "millionaires' club." They may also (finally) have advised Smith to be a little more careful in what he volunteered to the press.

In extreme heat, and running late because of the telephone calls, the *Nixon Special* moved on to Red Bluff, where the crowd had thinned to three hundred, waiting. Nixon gave another recitation of the speech he was working up for rebuttal to the fund allegations. As the train moved northward, the crowds were small in smaller centers, but enthusiastic in their support. Nixon drew strength from what he thought of as the support of regular people. This reinforced his view that he represented legitimate democracy, popular sovereignty, and that his opponents were leftists, the effete rich, nasty, and treasonous intellectuals. The people were with him; those who mislead or exploit the people were his enemies.

It was hard in the northern hinterland of the state to keep in touch with the news. In the bigger cities, Nixon's position was more tenuous. There were news reports that Nixon was under tax scrutiny from the state controller, Thomas Kuchel, a Warren man. In the Republican headquarters in Los Angeles, there was a great influx of abusive and insulting calls demanding Nixon's withdrawal.

— III —

As General and Mrs. Eisenhower drove from the railway station in Kansas City to their hotel, they were greeted with pickets holding up such signs as "DONATE HERE TO HELP POOR RICHARD NIXON." Eisenhower read Chotiner's statement on behalf of Nixon to a crowd of ten thousand, and appended his own statement of confidence in Nixon: "When the facts are known to all of us, they will show what is right. Both he and I believe in a single standard of morality in public life."

This was pusillanimous humbug, as Eisenhower was not prepared to lay bare his own financial condition, and he could have expressed confidence that Nixon would be vindicated. Eisenhower should have said from the start that Nixon had assured him that he had behaved with complete propriety and he had no reason to doubt him, and worked out with Nixon as the days went by what level of disclosure was required. Instead, he imposed an unreasonable level of disclosure and failed to express an adequate confidence level that Nixon would be upheld. This was not only unjust to his running mate, it threatened his own position; Eisenhower was fortunate that Nixon responded as resourcefully as he did, as changing vice presidential nominees in these circumstances would not only have reduced Eisenhower's electoral plurality and moral authority, it would certainly, as has been mentioned, have drowned many Republican congressional candidates.

Both Sherman Adams in Kansas City and Herbert Brownell in New York telephoned William Knowland, in Honolulu giving a speech, and asked him to join the *Look Ahead, Neighbor, Special* as soon as possible as a potential substitute vice presidential candidate. (At Chicago, the convention had delegated to the National Committee the power to fill a vacancy if either nominee resigned, died, or became incapacitated.) The fact that there was discussion in the general's entourage about dumping Nixon was splashed about in the press, and Hagerty denied it with his customary aplomb.

The balance of Eisenhower's speech, on the now familiar themes of corruption and "bossism," in the home city of President Truman and Boss Tom Pendergast, was politely but far from spiritedly received by his audience of ten thousand.

While Ike was speaking in Kansas City, the *Nixon Special* was crossing into Oregon. On board, Chotiner and Rogers told the candidate that all he had to do was keep repulsing the critics as he was and stonewalling the press and it would blow over, that the Democrats had overreacted. Jim Bassett, who had to deal with the journalists on the train, disagreed. The reporters had been knocking on the doors in nearby whistle-stops to telephone their newspapers and get the latest scuttlebutt. They wanted a precise time for the conversation between the candidates that had been envisioned for two days, and they wanted a proper press conference with Nixon. Bassett recommended a press conference, but Nixon demurred, saying that it would just legitimize a spurious story that had received too much attention already.

They arrived in Medford, Oregon, after nine on the evening of Friday, September 19, and Chotiner learned that the *New York Herald Tribune* and the *Washington Post* would be publishing editorials the next morning asking for Nixon's resignation as vice-presidential nominee. The *Herald Tribune* wanted Nixon to offer his resignation pending the facts being ascertained and judged according to Eisenhower's "unsurpassed fairness of mind." The *Post* was more declarative, referred to some of Nixon's attacks on the ethics of others, including both former party chairmen, and wrote that Eisenhower's promises of housecleaning "will be gravely handicapped if his running mate exemplifies the unethical conduct that he is denouncing." Chotiner and Rogers decided to spare the candidate this news for the night and reconsidered the optimistic prognoses they had been exuding as their train was approaching the Oregon border. Nixon stood with fixed smile while Medford's fur-wearing "Cave Men" initiated him into their municipal booster club, at extraordinary length.

Chotiner and Rogers were frustrated in their effort to assure the candidate a good night's sleep by a reporter who asked Nixon as he walked through the train if he had any comment on the *Herald Tribune* and *Post* editorials, which he summarized when Nixon said he had not heard of them. Nixon was severely shaken. He said nothing to the reporter but returned to his compartment and considered the *Herald Tribune* a severe defection, given his friendship with the proprietary family, the Reids, and leading editorial figures such as Bert Andrews, now traveling with Eisenhower. Nixon thought that the paper would not be taking this position if it were not the view of the New York group around Eisenhower. He wrote off the *Post* as an old enemy that just happened to be behind Eisenhower on this occasion.

Chotiner had a teletype of the *Herald Tribune* editorial and showed it to Nixon, who thought that the hyperbole about his running mate's "unsurpassed fairness of mind" must have come almost verbatim from Eisenhower himself, that the senior figures of the newspaper would not write such sycophancies. Nixon was by now more angry at the Eisenhower camp for virtually cutting him loose than he was fearful about how it would end up. He told Rogers to call Dewey and Chotiner to call Seaton first thing in the morning; he would speak only to Eisenhower. Chotiner and Rogers left at two and Nixon was alone, and rather depressed. He woke up his wife, told her what was happening, and said that perhaps he should resign. Pat wouldn't hear of it. As she had done before and would do often again at critical moments, she told him that if Eisenhower wanted to get rid of him, he could, and he would then likely lose the election and Nixon would eventually be vindicated. But if he were to "crawl away, you will destroy yourself. Your life will be marred forever and the same will be true of your family and, particularly, your daughters."[19] This had the desired effect.

The next morning, Saturday, September 20, there were scores of editorials and massive comment across the country, most of it unfavorable, but only a few newspapers calling for Nixon's withdrawal or dismissal. *Time* magazine wrote that if the facts had been known, Nixon would not have been selected by Eisenhower. Bob Humphreys awakened early in Washington on September 20 and decided that the only way to salvage the Nixon candidacy and the possibility of a big Eisenhower win was to turn the furor to advantage by putting Nixon on television. He called Summerfield in Kansas City and proposed that a group of party elders be consulted about the idea, and he had selected a jury that was a sure thing, including Taft, Martin, Mundt, McCarthy, publishers Roy Roberts and John Cowles, and Congressman Charles Halleck, Martin's deputy Republican leader in the House. This group, he judged, was sure to approve the idea and the money for a national telecast. Summerfield agreed and checked with Eisenhower, and called back to say that the general agreed and wanted to add only one person, suggested by Adams – William Robinson, publisher of the *Herald Tribune*.

As Eisenhower's train conveyed him toward St. Louis on Saturday morning, Eisenhower wrote out an angry letter to Robinson about his newspaper's "hair-trigger" opinion. He was not "prepared to prejudge any man" without the facts. "I have had reason to believe [Nixon's] honesty and character. As you know, I've admired him greatly." From here his letter deteriorated somewhat into a screed that the *Herald Tribune* was preempting his judgment.

The National Committee was solid for Nixon, but the group around Brownell and Dewey in New York was hostile, especially General Lucius Clay. Yet when Eisenhower dashed through heavy rain to telephone Clay from the Jefferson City, Missouri, railway station in midmorning, Clay told him not to be stampeded and to leave it until Monday, when Brownell would join the train in Cincinnati. This reinforced Ike's natural instinct, and proved to be decisive. Humphreys, Summerfield, and Nixon himself had a relative breathing space in which to stage what Chief Newman would have called a goal-line stand.[20] Divisions opened between the professionals in the central organization and the coalition of the Dewey group, which had twice failed the party in national campaigns before, and Eisenhower's personal entourage, who were, in political terms, tinkering amateurs.

While the *Look Ahead, Neighbor, Special* was proceeding south toward St. Louis in a glum mood, the *Nixon Special* was moving north through Oregon in an even more somber spirit. Nixon thought his luxurious train "like a prison with its inexorable schedule." At Roseburg, they encountered some hecklers, though the crowd, at five hundred, was larger than had been forecast and was generally friendly. The train moved on to Eugene and encountered the first large, hostile signs: "SH-H-H! ANYONE WHO MENTIONS $16,000 IS A COMMUNIST." On the other side of the sign was "NO MINK COATS FOR NIXON – JUST COLD CASH." There were similar signs, but the great majority of the two thousand people was friendly. In fact, Nixon had long been self-conscious about his inability to afford a mink coat for his wife of twelve years, and when he had given his usual retorts, he pointed at that sign and said that he was proud not to have encumbered the taxpayers with his expenses and that his wife did not have a mink coat. But she did have "a good Republican cloth coat."

As the train pulled out, the crowd set upon the picketers, assaulted them, and tore up their signs. The police were required to prevent serious injuries. Nixon noted, not without satisfaction, that those who gave him a fair hearing were as disgusted as he was by this defamation and as determined to fight back. The spectacle of his supporters resorting to physical abatement against his critics helped to torque up his determination not to be simply dangled like one of the general's fishing flies out the back of the *Look Ahead, Neighbor, Special.*

Jim Bassett handed out to the reporters yet another summary of the official version of the facts, resuming the points Nixon was making at the whistle-stops: Smith would, "at my request," give out a full list of donors. The fund's purpose was "to permit me to carry on my fight against communism and corruption above and beyond my official duties in Washington, D.C." There had never been any concealment, personal use of funds, padding of the federal payroll, and the contributors were all "longtime supporters." Some would say that this was a contradiction of his claim that he did not know who the contributors were, but since Smith was about to reveal the names and Nixon was taking Smith's word for the nature of the donors, this is an unjustified charge.[21]

Nixon was well-received in Salem, the state capital, by the governor, Douglas McKay, and gave a speech to fifteen hundred people on the steps of the capitol that was applauded enthusiastically. There were some pickets along the route, but no incidents. Rejoining his train, Nixon and his advisers were bombarded with press rumors about the state of the argument in the Eisenhower camp. They heard of the call to Clay, though not of Clay's advice, of the recall of Knowland, and of the desertion of identified members of the *Herald Tribune* senior staff and management. Nixon's best loyalists were the Old Guard and the new Red-baiters. Herbert Hoover, Robert Taft, and Joe Martin all spoke up for him. And when Oklahoma's wealthy Democratic senator Robert Kerr, co-owner of the Kerr-McGee Oil Company, who used his Senate position to advance his economic interests through tax breaks for the petroleum industry, referred to organizing

"Bundles-for-Nixon," Joe McCarthy pointed out that Alger Hiss had had an admiring job recommendation from Adlai Stevenson.[22]

Taft was refreshing, in stating that there would be no need for favors to be extracted from Nixon in exchange for contributions, because "Those who contributed to the fund probably agreed one hundred percent with his legislative position anyway." Nixon ascribed Taft's support to his recognition that the Republican campaign could blow up if he were dumped, but Taft was not so concerned about Eisenhower losing. He almost always acted on principle (otherwise, as has been recorded, he might well have been the nominee).

Not so clear was Adlai Stevenson, who began by stating that he would not, as so many of the Republicans had been in the habit of doing, rush to judgment without the facts. Some of Nixon's traveling party thought this generous, some thought it the Democratic candidate's usual irresolution, and Chotiner thought it indicated that Stevenson himself had some complexities in his own financial arrangements. Humphreys had heard something of this and passed it on to Chotiner. They were on to something, but Stevenson's natural civility, as well as his frequent indecisiveness, may also have played a role.[23]

Frank Nixon had taken to his bed in Whittier, reduced to sobs as new bulletins came in about the perils of his son. He was angry that Dick had accepted any money at all. (Hannah was in Washington, babysitting the Nixon daughters.) Hagerty acknowledged to the press on the general's train that the mail being brought on board was running evenly for and against Nixon, and the press told him that on Eisenhower's train they had voted forty to two to dump Nixon. Such facts as these would weigh heavily in Nixon's dealings with the press through the rest of his career. He felt that on the fund issue, the reporters had turned on him and could never be trusted, with a very few individual exceptions.

Eisenhower met his traveling press contingent at 4 P.M. on Saturday, having had beer distributed to the reporters just before he arrived. He told the journalists that the Nixon affair was not a "closed incident," that he was concerned about Nixon replying to the charges without speaking to him, that his staff had made a mistake not telling him about it until Friday morning, but that although he knew Nixon "little and only briefly," he didn't believe an intelligent and promising young man would squander his career by "wrongdoing." He deployed his famous charm and persuasiveness by leaning forward and saying, "I don't care if you fellows are forty to two.

I am taking my time on this. . . . Of what avail is it for us to carry on this crusade against this business of what has been going on in Washington if we, ourselves, aren't as clean as a hound's tooth?" He said Nixon's fund had to be not only legal, but not immoral, "or else."

Eisenhower's crowds were markedly less enthusiastic as his train came down the west bank of the Missouri River toward St. Louis, though they were still polite and appreciative. Humphreys reported to Summerfield on Saturday evening that he had consulted all the party elders, and that, as expected, all except Robinson supported Nixon, and all except Robinson supported the national speech of explanation, with varying degrees of enthusiasm. Robinson had said, "I wouldn't put him on TV; I'd throw him off the ticket."[24] This episode was already hardening Nixon's dislike of the Eastern Establishment, as well as the national press. Robinson was at the confluence of both. When the *Nixon Special* arrived in Portland on Saturday evening, the press on board were starting to feel, and even felt in some cases, that they detected among the public some sympathy for Nixon, as a man whose entire career was being put at risk on the basis of unknown facts.[25] Crowds were sparse for Nixon on a damp early-autumn night in Portland. And Nixon and his wife were jostled by pickets when they arrived at their hotel. The signs were "NICKELS FOR POOR NIXON" and similar themes, more mocking than viciously hostile, and there weren't many of them, but the individual pickets were nasty and threw pennies at the Nixons.

Nixon ignored an "urgent" message from Sherman Adams and gave it to Chotiner to deal with. He would not be "fobbed off on staff aides," and didn't like Adams anyway.[26] Bassett came in the middle of Chotiner's telephone back and forth with news of Eisenhower's "hound's tooth" statement, which Nixon interpreted as meaning that if he did not completely clear himself, Eisenhower proposed to get rid of him. This probably is what Eisenhower meant, but his position wasn't that clear. He couldn't fire the candidate, and Nixon had the support of the National Committee. Nixon knew that he had not done anything with the fund that was illegal or unethical or more controversial than what Eisenhower and Sparkman and, he suspected (correctly), Stevenson had done with their own financial arrangements. In these circumstances, while Eisenhower might have forced Nixon out, Nixon could split the party and make the golden Indian summer of Ike's career a bitter harvest indeed. He was still a U.S. senator from California for another four years before he faced the voters.

Nixon ordered that all the correspondence received on his train and in his offices be examined to see what had been heard from congressional Republicans, national committeemen, and other influential party members. Among those whose written statements of support were received were Gerald Ford and Warren Burger. Their ultimate rewards for this and other acts of principle would be very great.[27] Nixon told Bassett to find out all he could from the press on both trains and asked Chotiner and Rogers to call all the accessible people around Eisenhower, whose train had now reached St. Louis and whose passengers could be got to a telephone. Nixon went to his scheduled rally and performed well before an audience of nearly two thousand at the U.S. Grant High School. If he had accepted a cent of the fund money for personal purposes, "I should never have accepted the nomination." He gave the familiar rhetorical questions and elicited the usual resounding negative answers. The audience crowded the stage and admiringly mobbed the candidate at the end. It was an uplifting session, and reinforced his conviction that the people were with him, and the enemies were the Eastern Establishment, treacherous and cowardly as they were – the Republican look-alikes as much as their Democratic role models.

This tended to accentuate the difference in perspective between the presidential and vice presidential nominees of the Republican Party. Eisenhower, through pretension and naivety, judged himself above the subtleties and nuances of American politics. He thought the New Deal too leftist, but all elements of the New Deal that he really objected to, the cartels and favoritism to labor unions, had been abandoned or declared unconstitutional by the Supreme Court more than fifteen years before. Ike was not promising to roll back anything Roosevelt had done, nor to reduce taxes. He was really exploiting his popularity as a military leader to press the usual, last-resort argument after twenty years of one party in office, that it was time for a change. To this end, he was lambasting corruption in the federal government, not that it was so widespread, and tuning up the anti-communist rhetoric a little.

He had fallen in love with the idea of a crusade, but, of course, as he intended it, it was only a slight policy change in matters of administering loyalty oaths to federal employees, and wasn't a crusade at all. To Nixon, the crusade could be a rollback of taxes and regulation at home, a decisive victory in Korea by the application of overwhelming military force as suggested by MacArthur, and the organization of a giant flying column of assistance for any state that revolted from the Soviet yoke. This would have been an interesting policy, but in the meantime, Nixon was fighting for his survival, to the amusement of his many enemies, and of the packed galleries of impersonal envy.

After receiving all the intelligence on Saturday evening from the Eisenhower camp, and from congressional respondents, who were over-whelmingly favorable to his continuing, and from the press across the country, which was wobbly but mixed, Nixon asked his closest advisers if they thought he should resign the vice presidential nomination. None thought that he should. Bassett said he had to get to the media and turn them around, and thought that possible, given the facts. Rogers told him to "fight it out."

The last and most authoritative stop short of Pat Nixon, who was the reserve backbone if all else should fail, was Chotiner. He said that the prize was the presidency, implying that Eisenhower was a caretaker and a means to an end; that the Democrats were attacking on the fund as the apparent greatest vulnerability; that if it were not that, it would be something else. They were afraid to attack the general, whom, it was suggested by Chotiner and agreed by the others, was too cowardly and naive in political terms to recognize his debt to Nixon and to see this as an attack upon himself, where Nixon would take the hit as a more assailable intermediate target.

Though Eisenhower and the political novices and Deweyite losers he listened to might buy into the bunk about the untarnishable hero, thought Chotiner, if Nixon were pushed out, the whole Eisenhower myth would come down in shards around his ears. To the loyalists, he would be the cowardly general. To the independent voters, he would be the bumbler suckered into a Nixon vice presidency in the first place. To the uncritical faithful, he would be the wrecker of party unity, the fallen idol, the com-mander in chief with no loyalty to his chief subaltern. The Nixon candidacy had to be protected in the higher interests of the country, the party, and even the Eisenhower myth, which itself had to be protected from the political imbeciles playing with dynamite around the booted feet of the general, like children pulling at crackers on Christmas morning.

A consensus emerged that Nixon must take up the Humphreys option of a national television and radio address; that Nixon could always persuade live audiences, as the last few days had shown, even with the cynical travel-ing press. Nothing less would go over the heads of the malicious speculators or galvanize the great general. Nixon had to go to the people, who would listen to reason.

Chotiner was a distasteful, disturbingly, almost hauntingly, cynical, and even sleazy political operator. Broadly, the operatic comparisons were with Wagner: Chotiner was Loge, Nixon a dark Siegfried, Eisenhower a cheerful but calculating Wotan. Nixon was being done over by an infelicitous combination of false morality (the press), political narcissism (Eisenhower), and raving partisanship (the Democrats), and he had to wrench himself loose from this vortex and evoke the issue to the electorate. Eisenhower's effort to establish himself as impartial and imperious judge was a pompous and potentially self-destructive affectation, born of his habit of command and his unfamiliarity with the unglamorous nature of boiler room American politics.

There was more telephone conversation between Chotiner and Humphreys, but Chotiner said that allotted time to the vice president should be brought forward to a national telecast and broadcast, and that if anyone at the National Committee was upset about the cost, they should reflect on the cost of launching a new vice presidential candidate and scrapping all the literature and posters extolling the perfect electability of Ike and Dick.

After thinking it through, Nixon slept soundly. At last, after four horrible days, his fate would be in his own hands. Whether the general – who had still not brought himself to telephone Nixon, though it would have been easy to do so in the last three evenings as the crisis built – liked it or not, Eisenhower's pretense to absolute Solomonic judgment of the fate of an impotent marionette of a vice presidential candidate was about to end. Just Richard Nixon alone before the American people as judge – he had not sought this evocation, but it was the next and, in a sense, logical stage in the vertical ascent of the lower-mid-market riser from Whittier.

In a strange way, Nixon was starting to draw strength from the ordeal. Sparkman, his ostensible opponent as Democratic vice presidential candidate, was a Dixiecrat cipher, a segregationist gesture by the great liberal idealist Stevenson, to a part of the country where there had never really been a two-party system. Nixon, in his time, would be instrumental in changing that.

Stevenson was "more veneer than substance," said Nixon.[28] An elegant quipster and fine intellectual speaker, he had no background in anything difficult where he was not taking instruction from strong leaders – Roosevelt, Nimitz, Forrestal, Marshall, Truman, none of whom, from all accounts, ever thought of him as a presidential runner. And Eisenhower was a much cleverer and more ambitious natural politician than he admitted. But he was clinging to the fraud of reluctant, patriotic, crusading disinterest, and he was susceptible to the fawning blandishments of dispossessed Republican office-seekers and assorted sycophants accumulated in war and peace. Nixon would slice the Gordian knot created by his enemies, leapfrog the crowded political queue, and, for the first time for a mere vice presidential candidate, speak to the whole people.

— IV —

Sunday, September 21, was another tempest-tost day. The editorial comments from around the country were running about two to one against Nixon. Large Republican contributors from around the country were about evenly divided, the East and South negative, the West and Midwest favorable to the vice presidential candidate. The *New York Times* claimed that Dana Smith's list was a "who's who" of Southern California business interests and made much of the insignificant fact that the total of the fund was not $16,000 as Nixon had himself been informed, but $18,235.[29]

The *Times*'s co-leading political writer, Arthur Krock, who had been in the pay of the sinister Joseph Kennedy for many years, piously informed his dominical readership that if the fund had been known, Nixon would not have been selected. (One wonders where Krock thought Eisenhower's money came from.) Eisenhower was "bombarded" with gratuitous advice, including from the inexhaustibly self-righteous old influence-peddler Bernard Baruch, who was as obsequious to Eisenhower as he had been to Truman, Churchill, Roosevelt, Herbert Hoover, and Woodrow Wilson. Nixon did have his supporters on the *Look Ahead, Neighbor, Special,* including one of Ike's brothers.[30] Eisenhower, as was his nature, was searching for a golden mien as a thread through the minefield. While his aerated self-importance, failure to speak to Nixon, and shilly-shallying at times were irritating and elicited shrieks of anger and frustration on the *Nixon Special,* at least the general refused to be stampeded by the lynch mob. This was a new milieu he had been thrust into, and he was feeling his way as best he could, trying to appear the decisive theater commander, crusader, and liberator, in times and facts and among people that did not lend themselves to heroic thespianism. He thought of asking seventy-seven-year-old retired

Supreme Court justice Owen Roberts to look into it, and Roberts was happily recruited on Sunday afternoon by one of Eisenhower's companions. But this was not practical, given the time constraints. Sherman Adams commissioned an immediate and lightning-fast analysis of the fund by the well-respected Los Angeles law firm Gibson, Dunn & Crutcher, and by accountants Price Waterhouse. Summerfield ordered Humphreys to join the train and assist him in repulsing the anti-Nixon forces around Eisenhower. Humphreys managed it by a very grueling, multi-stop air route to Louisville, beyond which he did not have a reservation, but refused to be budged from the aircraft. Finally, he was allowed to proceed on to St. Louis and join Summerfield.[31]

In Portland, Nixon's old friends Tom Bewley and John Riley had flown in from Whittier to encourage him, and Nixon and his wife went to the Quaker Church and returned serenely through the pickets, Nixon having found what his Quaker forebears called "peace at the center." Hundreds of favorable telegrams had come in and Nixon was photographed with them, including one from "the Aroused Citizens of Whittier," urging him to fight off his accusers. The story was leaked that the Nixon people thought there might be some hysteria aboard the *Look Ahead, Neighbor, Special*, a bit of counterfire from the beleaguered *Nixon Special*.

Nixon telephoned Dewey and got a very noncommittal response from him, and then received a lengthy telegram from the egregious Stassen urging Nixon to offer his resignation. Stassen added that if Eisenhower accepted it, Warren should be invited to be the vice presidential candidate. The entire message was so patronizing and insensitive and uninformed (with Knowland now on the Eisenhower train as reserve vice presidential nominee), it makes it clear why Stassen eventually became one of the ludicrous figures of American politics. (Stassen had been the boy wonder of the Republican Party – governor of Minnesota at thirty-one and keynote speaker at the 1940 convention. He was at this point president of the University of Pennsylvania, but later ran nine times as a self-nominated candidate for president of the United States and often for lesser offices.)

Rogers mused that Eisenhower's silence might be a calculated effort to force Nixon out. He also received a call from an unspecified well-wisher urging him to flee the Nixon campaign before he went down with it. A telegram was delivered from Nixon's mother, who was babysitting Tricia and Julie: "Girls are okay. This is to tell you we are thinking of you and know everything will be fine. Love always, Mother." With this, Nixon was overcome with emotion and tears began streaming down his face. Twenty minutes later, as on other occasions on this difficult day, he was composed but limply sprawled in an armchair, his hands hanging over the arms, close to despair.[32]

Dewey phoned back, having conducted his own canvass. He said the Eisenhower entourage was a "hanging jury," though Dewey was not and Ike himself was undecided, pulled one way by his panicked advisers and another by his innate sense of justice, with his ever-present sense of self-interest also divided. Dewey urged the national television address on him, and urged him to take it out of Eisenhower's hands and invite the viewers and listeners to make their wishes known by writing to or wiring Nixon himself, giving him a few days to measure reactions. This was very useful counsel, but Dewey then demonstrated why he had most but not all of what was necessary to make it all the way to the White House. He proposed that Nixon reveal in advance that if his support level was not 90 percent, he would offer Eisenhower his resignation. This would enable the Democrats, or the Warren faction, or possibly even the American Communist Party, to tip the balance with a telephone or postal campaign and was a mad capstone to a sensible proposal. What was the point of wrenching it out of Eisenhower's hands if it was going to be necessary to clear such a hurdle? Nixon thanked Dewey and agreed that the speech should go forward as soon as possible.

Arthur Summerfield called and said that the National Committee was solid behind Nixon and that he should not speak to the press yet. Summerfield was concerned that reports of Nixon's dejection and exasperation might lead the candidate to go into the deep end in remarks to the press, and he was just settling things down. Nixon assured him that he would defer saying anything too declarative, and he departed for a meeting at Portland's Temple Beth Israel, scheduled before the fund matters arose, to hose down any lingering thoughts that Nixon was anti-Semitic. Nixon sat through a lengthy recitation of his alleged anti-Semitic utterances, gave his good-natured and well-received refutation, and, though visibly tired, made a good impression. He returned to his hotel and had a recurrence of the sore upper back muscles that had caused him to visit Dr. Hutschnecker. A physiotherapist was found to give him a massage.

At the same time, in St. Louis, Eisenhower had gone to a private dinner where everyone wanted Nixon disembarked from the ticket. Bob Humphreys finally arrived in St. Louis after his circuitous and contentious plane ride, and Summerfield, who was fluish, took him to meet Sherman Adams on the campaign train. Every argument Humphreys raised for the retention of Nixon was rejected by Adams, but it was clear that Adams wasn't sure that he knew what to do either. Dewey's call and the weight of the (mainly anti-Nixon) New York party had tipped the scales for the national telecast and broadcast as a way of resolving the problem.

Humphreys, in what was frequently almost a shouting match with Adams, demanded to know what Adams proposed to do with all the masses of campaign material with Nixon's name on it if there were a change. Adams dismissed that as a triviality. The temperature of the conversation descended, Humphreys recalled, to "zero centigrade." (Zero Fahrenheit is thirty-two degrees colder, but Humphreys's many talents did not extend to being conversant with the metric system.) Humphreys, extremely irritated at having put himself to such discomfort getting to St. Louis to be treated in such a cavalier fashion by the granite-faced, oppressively serious Adams, then asked him how to explain to the press the failure of Eisenhower to call Nixon for sixty hours, since Ike had said that he intended to speak to him as soon as possible almost three days before. "No wonder everyone thinks there is a plot to throw Nixon off the ticket."[33] Without comment, Adams quietly picked up a telephone and ordered that a call be arranged between the candidates when Eisenhower returned from his dinner.

This came in at 10 P.M. in Portland when Nixon was on the massage table, even less clothed than he had been when Brownell had called him in his Chicago hotel to tell him that he was the vice presidential nominee. "Hello, Dick. You've been taking a lot of heat the last couple of days. I imagine it's been pretty rough." Nixon replied, "It hasn't been easy." Nixon mentioned Dewey's advocacy of a telecast, and said he was at Eisenhower's disposal. This was not as specific as Eisenhower would claim in his memoirs, where he wrote that Nixon had offered his resignation but "I flatly refused."[34] No resignation was offered or refused but "disposal" could be taken as such. "This is not my decision" was the general's response. Eisenhower might have been relieved if Nixon had announced his resignation, but Ike was not going to call for it.

Nixon said that he was "glad to take responsibility, but Eisenhower and his advisers should hear my side of the story" and cautioned Ike against "some of those people around you who don't know a damn thing about it."

Eisenhower didn't want anyone to think that Nixon had been forced off by him, but he couldn't issue a supportive statement because too many people would accuse him of "condoning wrongdoing." Eisenhower did not express even a pro forma consideration for anything except how he himself would come out of it. That this was his chief concern was natural, but a man of his diplomatic abilities might have been expected to show a little solicitude for the sensibilities of his chosen running mate. Eisenhower expected Nixon to say something, but he remained silent. Finally, after an awkward pause, Eisenhower said that the dinner he had just attended was very divided about what should be done. "I don't want to be in the position of condemning an innocent man." He urged Nixon to go ahead with the telecast and lay out everything from his financial affairs since he entered politics.

After a pause, Nixon asked, "General, do you think that after the television program that an announcement could then be made one way or another?" Eisenhower waffled inexplicably: "Hoping no announcement necessary . . . maybe . . ." etc. Nixon, with the cobralike strike with which he often seized the initiative, discarded the comparative standing of his illustrious interlocutor and his own parlous condition and sharply responded, "General, I just want you to know that I don't want you to give any consideration to my personal feelings." (He need have had no concerns on that score.) "I know how difficult this problem is for you," he added with mounting irony. If he were a dead weight or hindrance to the ticket, Nixon would "get off and take the heat," but some decision would have to be made after the speech. "There comes a time in matters like this when you have to shit or get off the pot. The great trouble here is the indecision."

Those in Nixon's room were flabbergasted, but Eisenhower was unperturbed and said that they would have to wait "three or four days" after a telecast. He concluded jauntily, "Well, Dick, go on the television show. Good luck and keep your chin up." Eisenhower's performance was, at best, ungracious. He should have urged Nixon forward, wished him well, and assured him that he thought that after the telecast it would be resolved. If Nixon had bombed on television, he could have acted accordingly then. As Nixon wrote, "It is one thing to offer to sign your own death warrant; it is another to be expected to draw it up yourself."[35]

Nixon told Chotiner and Rogers to set up the telecast with Summerfield, and then retired to his own room and considered the Eisenhower conversation. He was pleased with it; it was entirely up to him. If Nixon was well-satisfied with his television program, he would stay; if he was not, he would withdraw. He visited Pat, who was unable to sleep under the pressures of the events. She heard his description of the conversation with Eisenhower and said, "We both know what you have to do, Dick. You have to fight it all the way to the end, no matter what happens."[36]

Humphreys and Summerfield arranged through Dewey's advertising agency (headed by Congressman Bruce Barton, of "Martin, Barton, and Fish" fame) a network of sixty CBS television stations and seven hundred NBC and Mutual radio stations. Nixon would speak between 9:30 and 10 P.M., following the very popular Milton Berle show, on Tuesday night, September 23, two days later. He could not be better placed to attract a huge audience. Jim Bassett told the press crew to stand by, because reports were already coming in from St. Louis of the Eisenhower-Nixon telephone call. At 1 A.M., Nixon finally met his press contingent and teased them by announcing, "I am breaking off," which incited thoughts that he was quitting, but with a smile he elaborated that he was interrupting the campaign to go to Los Angeles and speak to the country and lay out the whole story. Senator Harry Cain would fill in for him on the Washington State part of his tour. To questions of what he would do then, he said that he would resume the tour. This built further curiosity about what he would say in his telecast, but he declined to elaborate.

Nixon had finally wrenched control of the crisis away from others and was at least captain of his own fate. One of the great dramas of American political history was at hand. Nixon flew to Los Angeles on Monday morning, on a chartered DC-6. "I had been deserted by so many I had thought were friends but who had panicked in battle when the first shots were fired . . . I had to go for broke. This broadcast . . . had to be a smash hit. . . . I had to launch a political counterattack."[37] Nixon remembered that his children had been given a dog, a cocker spaniel, by a supporter, and he fastened upon the idea of emulating Franklin D. Roosevelt's invocation of his dog, Fala, when a Republican congressional candidate had claimed that he had sent a destroyer to collect his dog on the Aleutian Islands "at a cost to the taxpayers of two or three or eight or twenty million dollars. Fala's Scots soul was furious." The Nixons were met by a crowd of four hundred well-wishers and friendly picketers: "NIXON WILL FIGHT AND WIN," was one of the signs.

Nixon would give no hint to the press or anyone else, except his wife, Rogers, and Chotiner, of what he was going to say. The more fantastic the rumors would become, the better for the size and suspense of his audience. Apart from a swim and a stroll with Rogers, he stayed in his suite all afternoon, evening, and night, while Rose Mary Woods researched figures and facts for him. Chotiner came in excitedly to announce that Stevenson had confirmed that he too had a fund, slightly larger than Nixon's, and that some of the uses of it, while legal, were more doubtful than Nixon's, and Stevenson was a man of inherited wealth.

On Tuesday morning, the reports from Gibson, Dunn & Crutcher and from Price Waterhouse came in, and were completely satisfactory; there was a second Nixon fund of eleven thousand dollars, but that was part of normal election contributions, and there had been no illegalities and no inappropriate uses of money. The rumor mill, as Nixon now intended, went into overdrive as the hour of his speech approached. There was anxiety in the Eisenhower camp, and Dewey, after a good deal of soul-searching, concluded that he would go the distance with Nixon, with, as his biographer wrote, "undeniable misgivings."[38] William Robinson of the *Herald Tribune*, one of the leaders of the Dump Nixon faction, clambered aboard Eisenhower's train, and this caused pro-Nixon congressman Charles Halleck, who was on the train, to call Summerfield in Washington, who dragooned the just-returned Humphreys, and they both took off from Washington and joined Eisenhower Tuesday evening in Cleveland, as the *Look Ahead, Neighbor, Special* had turned east and then north.

When Humphreys arrived in Eisenhower's hotel suite, one of Eisenhower's aides, General Jerry Persons, said that they had heard that Pat Nixon had paid her decorator in cash from the fund. Humphreys debunked that; he had been to the Nixon's house and asked where some of the furniture came from because he liked it, and was told by Pat that it had come from their home in Whittier, and she had made the living room curtains herself.

Despite Humphreys's fine defense, Eisenhower, who was half-sprawled on a double bed during this exchange between Humphreys and Persons, said nothing, and when Humphreys left, he was influenced by the Robinson-Adams line that this was all a frightful burden to Eisenhower. No doubt it was, but it was also a smear job on Nixon, who had received no support at all from the man he had been instrumental in putting across as presidential nominee, and who had asked him to join him in the race.

Eisenhower now took one of the least admirable steps of his generally very admirable career: he asked congressional campaign chairman Leonard Hall to ask Dewey to ask Nixon to resign at the end of his speech, regardless of the strength of the defense he mounted. This was a shameful desertion, altogether unbecoming a man who had led armies with distinction in a noble cause. This was not the caliber of leadership most Americans thought they were buying into with Ike, and delegating the hit to Dewey via Hall was cowardly and dishonorable.

Nixon had slept only about four hours, and had pains in the upper back and neck, which he considered a reassurance that he was "adequately keyed up, mentally and emotionally, for the conflict ahead . . . going through the fire of decision . . . the necessary and even healthy symptoms incident to creative activity."[39] He was something of a philosopher of creative stress. (He generally thought the time of greatest danger was when the crisis was surmounted, and letdown occurred, but not on this occasion.)[40]

Nixon was considering with Chotiner and Rogers how to incorporate Dewey's advice to ask viewers and listeners to communicate with the National Committee, when Dewey's call, requisitioned by Eisenhower via Hall, came in to Rogers. Dewey was put off, and Rogers indiscreetly told Dewey's aide who put the call that Nixon was upset ("crying his eyes out")[41] and couldn't take Dewey's call. The governor insisted; Chotiner took the telephone; minutes went by. Finally, Nixon came on the line. Dewey told Nixon that there had been a meeting of Eisenhower's advisers, and their view, which Dewey did not share but which he had been asked to communicate, was that Nixon should offer his resignation to Eisenhower at the end of his telecast.

Nixon professed to be stunned and asked what "Eisenhower wants me to do." Dewey then waffled and said that he had not spoken to Eisenhower himself but had been asked to make this call by people who appeared to represent him completely. "It's kind of late to pass on this kind of recommendation to me now," Nixon said with admirable self-control, and Dewey completed the bungling of the mission he should never have accepted. Dewey should have told Leonard Hall to tell Eisenhower to make the call to Nixon himself; he owed the vice presidential nominee that, at least.

Eisenhower was just trying to preserve deniability in any scenario, and take for himself a prerogative that resided with the National Committee, to remove or choose nominees after the convention. He had urged Nixon to make his speech "and keep your chin up," two nights before. The National Committee was solid for Nixon, and only it could revoke or replace a nominee now. Nixon had been cleared by independent legal and accounting analysis and could be reasonably assumed to be about to give a fairly vigorous defense of himself. Perhaps Eisenhower had simply become exasperated by the continuing controversy that threatened to derail the *Look Ahead, Neighbor, Special* in all respects except physically, and wanted to make an end of it. Perhaps he was concerned that Nixon would so torque himself up that he would convince himself and the National Committee but not the voters that he should remain and the Eisenhower "crusade" would have Nixon around its neck like an albatross.

Whatever his motives, Eisenhower – always cautious and who, with a buffer of Hall and Dewey, could claim almost anything after the fact – had already given Nixon the chance for a great comeback and it was in his own interest that Nixon succeed. A partial comeback followed by a battle between the nominees over whether Nixon should continue would have achieved what nothing else could: a sixth consecutive presidential term for the Democrats. At this point, Nixon's speech was almost as important to Eisenhower as to Nixon, and Eisenhower should have personally sent Nixon an encouraging message and waited for the address, like the rest of the country.

Thomas E. Dewey now added a double flourish to the low mission he had accepted; he said that not only should Nixon offer his resignation at the end of his speech, which was all Eisenhower had asked Hall to ask Dewey to request of Nixon, he should end by "insisting that Ike accept it." Even after this, the worst was yet to come. On a further spontaneous flight of malignant improvisation, Dewey suggested that for good measure, Nixon resign from the Senate as well, and then win a huge landslide in the special election that would be called to fill the vacancy. (Such a popular verdict could not be forecast with confidence after such a sequence as Dewey proposed.)

That a twice-nominated major party candidate for president and three-term governor of New York would inflict such betrayal and idiocy on a man he had championed for the position of vice president indicated how wise the voters of America had been to pass him over for Roosevelt and Truman. Whatever their failings, they would never have been party to such a shabby task as this. The reflections on Dewey's judgment and ethics, on Eisenhower's political courage, and on the fragility of Nixon's standing with the Republican establishment at this early stage in his career are dramatic and in all cases unflattering.

Another deafening silence settled on the telephone line. Dewey broke it by aggressively asking, "Well, what shall I tell them you are going to do?" At this, the most difficult moment of his adult life, Nixon, almost alone among the prominent Republicans, maintained a sense of the seriousness of what was afoot, of the greater traditions of his party, and an inborn dignity. He resisted what must have been an immense temptation to give an extremely coarse reply about what Dewey should tell Eisenhower and the coven around him to do, and responded slowly, but with gathering speed and volume. He said, "Just tell them that I haven't the slightest idea what I am going to do, and if they want to find out, they had better listen to the broadcast. And tell them I know something about politics too" and slammed down the receiver.

He acknowledged that Dewey had "shaken my equilibrium,"[42] and asked everyone to leave him to his own thoughts. [*] [43] He shaved and showered, "almost in a daze." But he collected his thoughts sufficiently to know that even though Eisenhower and Dewey had turned upon him in the end, it was still between him and the people; there was a chance, but in any case Pat had been right, he had to fight it through to the end. Chotiner reemerged briefly and said that if Nixon were forced out, he would immediately call a press conference and tell everything, in terms that would sink Eisenhower's reputation and the entire Republican campaign. On the evening's performance, that would not have been an unjust result.

Pat came back from a day of rest at the Drownses' home, and they walked together with Chotiner and Bassett behind them down the hotel corridor. Nixon's staff and aides all opened their hotel room doors and stood at them, nodding supportively, as they walked by. Nixon wrote that "It seemed like the last mile."[44]

In Cleveland, Summerfield and Humphreys arrived late at Eisenhower's hotel suite, where another session on Nixon's future was in progress. Senator Carlson cautiously supported Nixon, Robinson of the *Herald Tribune* led the opposition, Summerfield rebutted him; Adams was noncommittal, as

---

[*] In his mid-career memoir, *Six Crises*, Nixon wrote that he discerned that Dewey "did not have his heart in what he told me." In his memoirs fifteen years later, written after Dewey had died, he omitted any reduction of implicit criticism of Dewey's role.

was the candidate. What none of them wished to admit was that Nixon had taken the resolution of the issue away from them. They went to the Cleveland Auditorium, and climbed endless stairs to an upper office to watch Nixon's speech before Eisenhower would address the live audience below.

— v —

Nixon was still consulting his notes during the twenty-minute drive to the NBC El Capitan studio near the corner of Hollywood Avenue and Vine Street. He had insisted that the theater, where the *Colgate Comedy Hour* and *This Is Your Life* were produced, be empty. He was greeted by a group of enthusiastic Young Republicans, including future chief of staff H.R. (Bob) Haldeman, but only managed a wave as he grimly entered the studio. Reporters were separated by a glass partition, and stenographers would transcribe his remarks in a closed-circuit overflow room in the Ambassador Hotel. Nixon would hold his notes and only consult them if necessary; he did not have a text, as was his custom. There was a light makeup session; he wore a pale gray suit, and the set was an average middle-class "GI bedroom den," in current Hollywood parlance. It was a skillful, subtle appeal to the average middle-class American. Nixon insisted on having his wife beside him in a chair. She was wearing a simple dress knitted by Whittier supporters for the Senate campaign. He was carefully coached on how to stand in front of the desk, lean on it, gesture for emphasis.

Rogers asked Nixon how he was going to end and he said that he had not decided, "but you'll know when I'm finished." The Nixons went to the dressing room for a few minutes of solitude, and he told Pat that he didn't think he could go through with it. He didn't mean it; he only meant that the tension was almost unbearable and he needed to know she still had confidence in him. As always, she was not found wanting. The drama, accentuated by Nixon's suspense-building tactics, produced the greatest television audience for a political speech in world history, and what would long remain the greatest number of viewers for any single event in the history of American broadcasting – half of all Americans judged to be capable of viewing it, an astounding sixty million people, almost ten million people more than normally voted in presidential elections, and millions more on the radio.

He began, "My fellow Americans" and said that his "honesty and integrity have been questioned." He said he would not follow the example of the present administration and ignore these charges, that the best answer "to a smear . . . is to tell the truth." He dealt with the eighteen thousand dollars and set up the yardsticks of whether the fund was "illegal . . . morally wrong . . . was secretly given and secretly handled" or bought "special favors." He spruced up his usual denials: "Not one cent for personal use . . . Every penny of it was used to pay political expenses that I did not think should be charged to the taxpayers of the United States." It had never been a secret, all the details of it had been volunteered to the press when they asked, and he had done no favors for any of the contributors in the time he had been a senator.

He explained budgets and spending requirements for senators, and took his usual shot at Sparkman's having his wife on the payroll, in the usual way: "I am not critical of him. You will have to pass judgment on that particular point." He referred to his wife as a "wonderful stenographer" who had "never been on the government payroll," though she had often helped in the office, and the camera moved full face to her briefly. Nixon was not going to take income from "the many deserving stenographers and secretaries in Washington that needed the work." He again offered his rather tired claim about the necessity of additional expenses to enable him to fulfill his task "of exposing this administration, the communism in it, the corruption in it," and quoted from the Gibson, Dunn & Crutcher letter. He was almost halfway through his time and only the very helpful wording of the legal and accounting certifications were new to what he had been saying from the back of the *Nixon Special*. He oscillated between the slick Southern California salesman and Uriah Heep.

Nixon then announced that he was going to give an explanation, "unprecedented in the history of American politics," of "everything I've earned; everything I've spent; everything I owe . . . Our family was of modest circumstances and most of my early life was spent in a store out in East Whittier." He was not histrionic and did not refer to the deaths of his brothers. He spoke of working through university and scrimping a bit when he and Pat were newlyweds, and did not embellish on his war record: "My service record was not a particularly unusual one. . . . I guess I'm entitled to a couple of battle stars. I got a couple of letters of commendation, but I was just there when the bombs were falling."

Moving comfortably along, as if having an earnest talk with a visitor to his own home, Nixon now recited totals of all he had made and spent since he entered politics, and of his and his wife's net worth and composition of assets, down to their bank accounts, mortgage, and 1950 Oldsmobile. "Well, that's about it. That's what we have and that's what we owe. It isn't very much, but Pat and I have the satisfaction that every dime we have is honestly ours. I should say this, that Pat doesn't have a mink coat. But she does have a respectable Republican cloth coat and I always tell her that she would look good in anything."

Then came the most famous lines of the speech: "One other thing I should tell you. . . . We did get something, a gift, after the election. A man down in Texas heard Pat on the radio mention the fact that our two youngsters would like to have a dog. And, believe it or not, the day before we left on this campaign trip we got a message from Union Station in Baltimore saying they had a package for us. . . . It was a little cocker spaniel dog in a crate that he sent all the way from Texas. Black and white spotted, and our little girl, Tricia, the six-year-old, named it Checkers. And you know, the kids love the dog and I just want to say this right now, that regardless of what they say about it, we're going to keep it."

It was pretty maudlin but very effective. He expressed pleasure that "a man like Governor Stevenson, who inherited a fortune from his father, can run for president." But people "of modest means" had to be given a chance too, and he quoted the founder of his party: "Remember Abraham Lincoln – you remember what he said, 'God must have loved the common people – he made so many of them.'" This was a psychological master stroke, aligning himself with America's most admired statesman and with the great majority of his viewers, and slicing out of the public relations equation the fat cats in New York who surrounded and bank-rolled Eisenhower and the effete academics among the Stevenson Democrats.

Nixon was accelerating confidently toward his conclusion: "I would suggest that under the circumstances both Mr. Sparkman and Mr. Stevenson should come before the American people as I have and make a complete financial statement as to their financial history. And if they don't it will be an admission that they have something to hide." Nixon wasn't really aiming at Stevenson and Sparkman, who hadn't much bothered him; he was aiming at Eisenhower, who had received millions for his non-campaign, and would have a good deal more trouble accounting for it, as for other munificences from his wealthy friends, and for his special tax treatment on his book royalties than Nixon had had. It was all legal, but so, everyone conceded, was

Nixon's small fund. The appearances for Eisenhower would have been a good deal less presentable than they were, when examined fairly, for Nixon.

It was at this point that, in the manager's office in the Cleveland Auditorium, that Eisenhower first famously slammed down his pencil in irritation, recognizing at once where Nixon was leading. Others in the room were silent or even weeping softly at the power of Nixon's presentation. Nixon reached his peroration. He had got up from the desk and was moving easily, gesticulating or standing with one hand in his pocket. "Other smears will be made. . . . I have no apologies to the American people for my part in putting Alger Hiss where he is today . . . I love my country and I think my country is in danger." He went again through the "600 million people lost to the communists" and the 117,000 casualties in Korea. Those who "made the mistakes which caused that war and which resulted in those losses, should be kicked out . . . In the Hiss case they [the U.S.S.R.] got the secrets which enabled them to break the American secret State Department code." (There is no evidence of this.) "They got secrets in the atomic bomb case which enabled them to get the secret of the atomic bomb, five years before they would have gotten it by their own devices." (That isn't clear either, though the atomic espionage was certainly dangerous to national security.)

Bassett held up three fingers as Nixon came down to the wire. He read from a letter he had used a few days before in starting out his campaign, from the wife of a marine in Korea, sending him the check for ten dollars, "that I shall never cash." He and Eisenhower were fighting for "prosperity built on peace rather than prosperity built on war. . . .

"I don't believe that I ought to quit, because I am not a quitter. And incidentally, Pat is not a quitter. After all, her name is Patricia Ryan and she was born on St. Patrick's Day, and you know the Irish never quit." This was a straight play for the one-quarter of Americans who were Roman Catholics, most of them habitual Democrats. The facts that Pat was born Thelma Ryan on the day before St. Patrick's Day and had never been a Roman Catholic and was in fact an agnostic were minor liberties compared with some of the lies hurled at Nixon in the last few days. When the camera focused on Mrs. Nixon, she was staring fixedly at her husband with a slight smile, a rigid appearance criticized in some of the media. Her response was that she had had no idea of what her husband was going to say and was listening with interest like the rest of the country.

Finally, what they were all waiting for, especially in Cleveland: "But the decision, my friends, is not mine. I would do nothing that would harm the possibilities of Dwight Eisenhower to become president of the United States. And for that reason I am submitting to the Republican National Committee tonight through this television broadcast the decision which it is theirs to make. Let them decide whether my position on the ticket will help or hurt. And I am going to ask you to help them decide. Wire and write the Republican National Committee whether you think I should stay on or whether I should get off. And whatever their decision, I will abide by it." Whatever happened, he would continue the fight to "drive the crooks and the communists and those that defend them out of Washington. . . ."

The recently hunted victim, clinging by a thread to his nomination and dependent on the general's fickle patronage, had staged a political and moral coup d'état. It was indeed the national committee's decision, and Nixon had almost certainly shored up his position with the committee. Eisenhower now loudly broke his pencil in the silent room above the Cleveland Auditorium.

As he walked toward the camera in the closing seconds of his time, having made his point with Eisenhower, Nixon finished, "And remember, folks, Eisenhower is a great man. Believe me, he's a great man, and a vote for Eisenhower is a vote for what's good for America." The telecast ended before Nixon could give the address of the Republican National Committee, which disappointed Nixon, but this was a much more dramatic ending than the recitation of an address, and Western Union and the U.S. Post Office could be relied upon to find the committee. Nixon, unwinding from the strain, threw down his notes and wiped his face in a stage curtain. He confessed to Pat that he was afraid that he had not made his point. As often with her, and as is often a purpose in a functioning marriage, he was fishing for reassurance. He did not have long to wait for it, from her, or from Rogers and Chotiner, who rushed forward proclaiming the speech a triumph. The cameramen had tears on their cheeks; Nixon, as he would be again in his long career, had been put through the wringer, and then he had put the country through an emotional wringer too.

In Cleveland, as Mamie Eisenhower wept and others were visibly moved,[45] Eisenhower told her that Nixon was a "completely honest man," and he told Summerfield, "Well, Arthur, you sure got your money's worth." The fifteen thousand people below, awaiting the general, had heard the speech on the radio feed. Congressman George Bender, a Taft loyalist, took the microphone and shouted, "Are you in favor of Nixon?" Pandemonium erupted; the gray-haired, well-fed, middle-aged, prosperous Ohioans shouted and screamed their support. The steady chant of "We want Nixon," led by Bender, went up and continued, relentless and thunderous, shaking the little room at the top of the building, where Eisenhower was hastily recomposing his remarks. According to Adams, Eisenhower was "deeply impressed" by Nixon's speech.[46]

Abandoned by everyone except his wife, his mother, Chotiner, Summerfield, Humphreys, and a few others, put right to the wall and verging on nervous and physical exhaustion, Nixon had staged a political version of MacArthur's Inchon landing. He had destroyed his enemies, given the vice presidency a political significance it had never had in 164 years of the history of the office, sacked his judge and the kangaroo court around him and replaced them with his friends in the National Committee, while impeccably restating the greatness of Eisenhower. Dwight D. Eisenhower was, by most measurements, a great man, but his greatness was not in evidence on this occasion, and that was not the description of him uppermost in Nixon's thoughts at this time. The general had now to try to reclaim his hijacked authority within the upper reaches of the Republican Party, while reciprocating, as the occasion demanded, Nixon's generous if tactical, not to say facetious, compliment. In New York, watching in the Roosevelt Hotel, Brownell and Clay thought Nixon's remarks tasteless but brilliant.[47]

At the El Capitan, Nixon quickly regained his composure, thanked the technicians and cameramen individually, posed for some still shots, and had his makeup taken off by an enthusiastic maquettist who told him "there's never been a broadcast like it before."[48] He was told the switchboard in the studio was flooded with supportive calls and said to the waiting press, neutrally, as he got into his car, "It was not an easy speech to make."[49] An Irish setter ran beside his car as it started up, and Nixon said, with the dry and ironic humor that never entirely deserted him, "Well, we made a hit in the canine world, anyway." As he returned to the Ambassador Hotel, the lobby, which had been still and almost empty when he had walked though it ninety minutes before, was jammed with admirers who overwhelmed his security unit, grasping for the Nixons' hands, patting their shoulders, and cheering wildly. The same reception awaited the vice presidential nominee upstairs. The hotel switchboard was jammed. Throughout the country,

Western Union and long-distance telephone exchanges were buried under an avalanche of pro-Nixon activity, almost 100 percent of those who responded to his invitation to "help" the National Committee decide. Among those who did get through to Nixon was longtime supporter and leading Hollywood director Darryl Zanuck, who called Nixon's speech "the greatest production I have ever seen." But the drama was not over yet.

Eisenhower felt the pressure from Nixon's counter-coup, and his response to what had become a rabidly Nixonian audience in Cleveland was, given his sensibilities, a subtle, if not particularly creditable, one. Nixon, exasperated by the exploitation of his vulnerability, having evoked matters to a larger and clearly favorable jury, had left his leader feeling authoritatively underdressed. Eisenhower scribbled the outline of a telegram to Nixon, gave it to Hagerty and asked him to fix it up and hand it back to him while he was speaking, and descended to address the crowd. He set out to distinguish Nixon's fine character from the process of adjudicating the fate of his candidacy and began, "I have been a warrior and I like courage. Tonight I saw an example of courage. When I get in a fight I would rather have a courageous and honest man by my side than a whole boxcar of pussy-footers." Then, astonishingly, he referred to General George Patton's "error" in slapping a serviceman in Italy who had been suffering from battle fatigue, as if that incident, which would have become fuzzy to most of his listeners (unenlightened by George C. Scott's unforgettable film portrayal of Patton fifteen years later), had the slightest relevance to Nixon (though when it did appear it might have amplified his enthusiasm for the film, which he allegedly viewed more than a hundred times).

Patton, Eisenhower told his audience in Cleveland in September 1952, "committed an error . . . [but] he made amends for that error." He spoke of the gravity of Democratic corruption compared to "whatever error of judgment may have been committed by Senator Nixon." Objectively, this was an outrage. Nixon had just made the point to, as it shortly emerged, the great majority of Americans, including apparently almost all of the people Eisenhower was then addressing, that he had not made an error; he had been smeared, and his leader was ambivalent about it. Having extolled courage and decried pussyfooting, Eisenhower followed the latter course.

Ike was trying to keep alive the fraud that there might be something wrong with Nixon's fund in order to maintain his own moral authority over his vice presidential candidate, who had suddenly resurrected himself as a mighty and morally vindictive force in the Republican Party and the country. He would not have found this necessary if he had been more supportive of Nixon earlier, by calling him and getting his irrefutable version of the facts. He might have done this if Nixon had not already acquired an indifferent reputation for campaign ethics. But the source of this attack was the Earl Warren camp, which, if Nixon had not infiltrated it, might have unintentionally produced Robert Taft as the nominee. And Taft had unambiguously supported Nixon when Eisenhower had waffled.

Eisenhower implied that Nixon had committed an error, like Patton slapping a convalescent soldier, but that Ike, the theater commander (which he hadn't been, in fact; the British field marshal Sir Harold Alexander was, though he wasn't responsible for disciplining American army commanders), would be a fair judge of Nixon's error. Having been disconcertingly indecisive about Nixon's fate, as if unaware of the potential damage to his own candidacy and reputation from this controversy, Eisenhower had become a forceful commander in the cause of promoting his own authority. He told the Clevelanders that "he was not intending to duck any responsibility that falls upon me . . . the standard bearer of the Republican Party."

The National Committee chairman was "certain to call upon me." He was, of course, but not necessarily to make that decision, which did not belong to Eisenhower. His decision would be determined not, he assured his confused audience, by "what would get the most votes" or "convenience," but by whether "I myself believe that this man is the kind of man that America would like for its vice president." He could safely have left the determination of whom America liked to the Americans, since they were in an election campaign, but it was "obvious," he said, that he would need more than a "presentation . . . necessarily limited to thirty minutes" to do it.

He was going to meet with Nixon personally, and conceded that he might be "egotistical," but in "critical situations in service to my country I have had to depend on my judgment . . . whether a man was fit to command . . . or . . . whether this man should be saved from the executioner's squad." He would decide as soon as he and Nixon had met, "except for such divine guidance as I may be granted." (This was another sham, because Eisenhower, unlike Nixon, was not a religious man and was even less likely to seek such guidance on this issue than Nixon was to have "prayed about" running for U.S. senator.) The reference to an "executioner's squad" was particularly unfortunate.

He closed the surreal session in the Cleveland auditorium by reading his telegram to Nixon, which the resourceful Hagerty, squatting and kneeling on the floor, had revised and handed up to Eisenhower in mid-speech at the dais: "Your presentation was magnificent. While technically no decision rests with me, yet you and I know that the realities of the situation will require a personal pronouncement, which so far as the public is concerned will be considered decisive. . . . I feel the need for talking to you and would be most appreciative if you could fly to see me at once. Tomorrow evening I shall be in Wheeling, West Virginia. I cannot close the telegram without saying that whatever personal admiration and affection I have for you, and they are very great, are undiminished."

"Undiminished"; with this sign-off, Eisenhower brought the Republican Party to the brink of schism. If Truman, much less Roosevelt, had been the opponent instead of the gentlemanly Stevenson, the Democrats would have pried this open with a crowbar. Nixon took the reports of Eisenhower's speech, as the telegram when Hagerty finally sent it was clogged in the mountains of messages of support to Nixon, as a near declaration of war. This was the point at which Nixon had told Eisenhower three nights before that he had to "shit or get off the pot." Eisenhower had relieved himself, but retained sole occupancy of the water closet. Nixon "exploded."[50] In Nixon's suite, they were celebrating with Nixon playing FDR's old campaign song, "Happy Days Are Here Again," on the piano when news of Ike's speech came.[51] Nixon let his staff know how upset he was, and dictated a letter of resignation to Rose Mary Woods, which Chotiner intercepted and tore up.

Chotiner met privately with Nixon and suggested another tack: instead of forcing Eisenhower to reveal himself as an unclothed emperor by the irretrievable brinkmanship of a purported resignation, which the National Committee would not accept, let us remember that the Democrats, despite recent events, remained the enemy, not fellow Republicans. Chotiner suggested that they wait Eisenhower out as opinion built in Nixon's favor. Nixon should take the position that he was resuming his campaign tour and he would not meet with Eisenhower until the general acknowledged that there was no suspense about whether Nixon should continue as nominee. Nixon agreed readily that this was a better plan.

Nixon sent Eisenhower a reply, when he heard from the media what Eisenhower had telegraphed him, that he could not come to Wheeling, and would not be free to meet Eisenhower until the weekend: "Will be in Washington Sunday and will be delighted to confer with you at your convenience any time thereafter." The Nixon party prepared to leave for Missoula, Montana, as scheduled. The extreme coolness of Nixon's reply was well-noted by Eisenhower and his advisers; the correlation of forces between the nominees had shifted. Eisenhower was still a world-historic figure and a popular hero, and the public had no intimation of the internecine problems that were being played out, but a Nixon blowup at this point would have been a disaster.

Eisenhower was also sixty-two, and this was the climax of his career. This was the same Eisenhower who until six months earlier had been waiting for a draft that did not come. He had been routed out of Paris only by Dewey's spurious threat that MacArthur might be the nominee, and he had been nominated only by dint of Nixon's skulduggery in stampeding Warren's California caucus to help seat Eisenhower's slates of Southern delegates in Chicago. Eisenhower was risking a splendid career; Nixon had effectively cleared his name and was not going to take a fall whatever happened.

The magnificent Humphreys, who had thought all was resolved by Nixon's boffo performance, finally got through to Chotiner, who told him how outraged Nixon was at Eisenhower's antics. Humphreys gave the phone to Summerfield, who was stupefied when Chotiner said that Nixon would not go to Wheeling; he was going, as scheduled, to Missoula. Chotiner then said, "Arthur, we trust you." He explained that Nixon and his many supporters had had as much abuse and condescension as they could take. If Summerfield could promise, on his own word of honor, that if Nixon went to Wheeling, he would be confirmed as nominee without controversy, he, Chotiner, thought he could sell it to Nixon. "I know I can't otherwise. Dick is not going to be placed in the position of a little boy coming somewhere to beg for forgiveness." Chotiner abruptly hung up, and refused Seaton's call when it came through. He said, to general approval from the Nixon inner circle: "Let the bastards wait for us this time."[52]

— VI —

At the last minute before Nixon left for the night charter to Missoula, Bert Andrews (whose publisher, Robinson, had been miraculously converted to the Nixon cause by the candidate's speech), telephoned from the Eisenhower camp. It remains a mystery, and was so to Nixon himself even thirty years later, who prompted him to phone, but most likely Humphreys and Summerfield. Nixon felt he owed it to his ally from the Hiss case to take the call. Nixon said he would not accept Eisenhower's conditions for a meeting, as reported.

Andrews replied with great solemnity and deliberation: "Richard (which no one except his mother now called him), you don't have to be concerned about what will happen when you meet Eisenhower. The broadcast has decided that. Eisenhower knows it as well as anyone else. But you must remember who he is. He is the general who led the Allied armies to victory in Europe. He is the immensely popular candidate who is going to win this election. He is going to be president and he is the boss of this outfit. He will make the right decision. But he has the right to make it in his own way, and you must come to Wheeling to meet with him and give him the opportunity to do exactly that."

Nixon said he would think about it and left for the airport. When he arrived at 11 P.M., there were hundreds of supporters to cheer him. Humphreys had already set up a telephone link with the private terminal where the senator's plane would leave, and he and Summerfield again got Chotiner, who refused to get Nixon off the plane to take another call, even when Summerfield implied he might wake up Eisenhower to talk to him (at 2 A.M. in Cleveland).

Nixon was still keyed up on the flight, happy at times, but tearful at other times, and finally fell asleep. It was about 3 A.M. on Wednesday, September 24, when they landed at Missoula, and the Nixons were given the freedom of the city by the mayor as they stepped down from the airplane. By this time, the inundation of favorable responses to Nixon's speech was clear. Many of more than four million telegrams and letters and millions more of telephone messages had already been received. The great and small newspapers were virtually unanimous in their praise. The headlines were emphatic and flattering, and there was no longer any discernible editorial agitation to ditch Nixon. The *New York Times* reported responses running 200 to 1 in Nixon's favor. It was a tidal wave. Many newspapers had coupons for transmission to the Republican National Committee.

The indefatigable Humphreys and Summerfield called Nixon at his hotel in Missoula and had a rather amiable talk with him, as the tension eased and the proportions of his victory became clear. Nixon stuck to the line enunciated by Chotiner that he wanted an assurance that Ike would confirm him; he was not prepared to go to Wheeling in a state of suspense about the outcome. Summerfield caught up with Eisenhower later in the morning in Portsmouth, Ohio, where the general disembarked from the *Look Ahead, Neighbor, Special* to crowd into a telephone booth with Sherman Adams to take the call. Adams did most of the talking and listening for both of them.

Eisenhower's telegram was public and the general's train was only a few miles from the West Virginia border. Whatever his preoccupation with his own authority, Eisenhower was an astute politician and he had already seen the reaction to Nixon's speech. Summerfield was able to tell him that the National Committee had been flooded with expressions of support, even positive messages from Americans abroad and ships at sea. Eisenhower agreed with the incoming tide of opinion. He had salvaged his authority, Nixon had rescued himself, and the whole episode was shaping up as a net gain for the Republicans. In the light of the morrow, the courses of principle and expediency quickly merged. Summerfield and Humphreys, unsung heroes of the drama, telephoned Nixon, confirmed the understanding, and arranged that after he spent Wednesday in Missoula he would fly into Wheeling that evening to be embraced by Eisenhower.

Tired, but still in good voice and heart, Nixon spoke to four thousand people in Missoula Wednesday morning. "In America, a person from a humble family can run for office. . . . And when enemies attack him, he can go on television and radio, and all he has to do is tell the truth. Politics is a dirty game," but young people should not be deterred from entering it. "The thing to do is go in and clean it up." Nixon received recantatory telegrams from Stassen and Dewey.[53]

The flight to Wheeling was jubilant, with even the cynical reporters joining in singing bawdy songs. The plane stopped at Denver, where Nixon addressed a crowd composed mainly of transient air travelers. In Wheeling, Eisenhower was addressing a crowd about the "attempted smear" of his vice presidential candidate. Then he joined a motorcade to go to the airport and greet Nixon's plane. When it landed, as Nixon was helping his wife with her coat, the general bounded up the steps and into the plane. "You're my boy," he beamed. Nixon wept with emotion.

Eisenhower handled the public ending of the incident with great elegance. They stood together and waved at the crowd of three thousand, and he and Nixon, with Nixon in the place of honor, rode together in an open car to a stadium for yet another speech. It had been just a week since the *New York Post* article had blown up the fund affair, but it seemed longer to all of the principals. On the ride in from the airport, Ike expressed sympathy for what Nixon had been through, but apart from that brief comment, confined himself to other subjects, cheerfully talking about whistle-stopping. Between Pat and Mamie, in the following car, it was a good deal less convivial.

Eisenhower spoke first to the crowd of six thousand. He foreclosed Nixon's time with a lengthy address about a great range of issues, before turning to Nixon, "my colleague," who had been subjected to "a very unfair and vicious attack" but had "vindicated himself" and "stands higher than ever before." Before introducing him, Eisenhower read a telegram: "Dear General, I am trusting that the absolute truth may come out concerning this attack on Richard. When it does, I am sure you will be guided aright in your decision to place implicit faith in his integrity and honesty." It was from Hannah Nixon. Then he read Summerfield's telegram reporting that the National Committee had voted unanimously for the confirmation of Richard Nixon as vice presidential nominee.

Nixon took the microphone and said that there had been two moments in his life when he had been prouder than at any other times to be an American. The first was when he had seen Eisenhower go by in the victory motorcade in Manhattan in the spring of 1945, and this was the other. This was, said Nixon, "the greatest moment in my life." When Knowland congratulated him, Nixon again wept and briefly put his face on Knowland's shoulder.

For Wheeling, this night eclipsed its previous most famous political event of two years before, when Joe McCarthy claimed to reveal the existence of two hundred and five (imaginary) communists in the State Department. The crowd mobbed the candidates and Eisenhower invited the Nixons to join him on his railway car. They did so, and Eisenhower, in an astounding lapse of taste, asked Pat about her decorator and how they had paid for the outfitting of their house. Nixon took over and told Eisenhower that this was a war. "Our opponents are losing. They mounted a massive attack on me and have taken a bad beating." He warned that there would be other smears, and that they had to be knocked down as they arose. Eisenhower didn't pursue the decorator question, but Pat Nixon took a long time to forgive him. This was the last echo of the fund crisis. Nixon refused to comment when the press tried to raise supplementary questions. It died, but in its terrible week of life, it had almost killed Nixon.

Nixon had shown great resilience and durability under tremendous pressure. Eisenhower had flirted with disaster, had shown little loyalty and a martinet's preoccupation with his own rank, which he hid from the press, and had faced political realities with winning cheerfulness in the end. He was a soldier-diplomat even as a politician.

Adlai Stevenson and John Sparkman, though Stevenson claimed not to have seen Nixon's speech, released their tax returns for the previous ten years. It eventually came to light that Stevenson had received $146,000 in a political fund, some of it extracted from state employees, and had made some potentially embarrassing payments, including gifts to reporters, paying the orchestra at a party for his sons, club dues, charitable contributions, and "bowling costumes for girls."[54] Stevenson was irritated at being lumped in with Nixon, and Nixon was outraged at the soft treatment Stevenson received for what was in fact a relatively scandalous state of financial impropriety by the Democratic candidate, ever in the odor of liberal media sanctity.

The six remaining weeks of the campaign were an anti-climax. Polls shortly revealed that Nixon had reaped a new harvest of votes for the Republicans. He had had a greater impact by far than any vice presidential candidate in history, and had carved out for himself a large following of average people. These people were not following the pied piper of a military hero, or an intellectual epigrammatist like Stevenson, or a wily, charming, overpowering aristocrat who had saved the nation like Roosevelt. In Nixon, they were following a younger, better educated, more politically conservative but less natural and confident Truman figure. Where Truman was a plain-spoken, straight-talking man, Nixon was elliptical, awkward, and sometimes diffident. He was also cynical and devious, unlike Truman. But to tens of millions of Americans, he was "one of us." The comparison would have appalled Truman, and not much pleased Nixon either.

Yet to some discerning observers such as Walter Lippmann, Eisenhower had appeared weak and Nixon tasteless and demagogic, and to the Eastern Establishment and the politically influential intelligentsia, Nixon seemed an ogre, a vulgar and distasteful person, even a Manchurian candidate: robotic, fixated, cynical, and manipulative. A joke was that all that was missing was Checkers jumping into Nixon's lap in mid-telecast and licking away his tears.[55] (When the person who gave Checkers to the Nixons died in 2006, the gift of the dog was the entire substance of the *New York Times* obituary. The donor, Lou Carrol, was a retired Illinois salesman.)[56]

A swath of Middle America, however, an army of millions, would follow Nixon throughout his astonishing career, and support him even to and beyond his grave. And a vast number of people would be repelled by him, even when, as happened often in the coming decades, he did things that earned him widespread passing praise. *The Reporter*, an intelligent and generally fair, nonpartisan magazine, wrote just three weeks after what came to be known, generally mockingly, as the Checkers speech: "Somehow, we still cannot work up any great anger at him . . . (but) we cherish the hope that we shan't be bothered with him again."[57] This was what made him durable. The *bien-pensants* would have to "be bothered with him" for another forty years. He personified much of middle America, its qualities as well as some of its vulgarity and, above all, its courage and tenacity. Nixon easily survived *The Reporter* (and did not have to be "bothered with" it). He founded the "Society of the Hound's Tooth" and celebrated the anniversary of the Checkers speech each year. He said he learned that "In politics most people are your friends only as long as you can do something for them or something to them."[58] (He need not have confined the observation to politics.)

Nixon never returned to an easy relationship with the press, and the instant evaporation of most of the goodwill he had built up in the preceding six years of constant political effort aggravated his insecurity, suspicion, and isolation. He developed a particular dislike for columnist Drew Pearson, whom he thought he had saved from being pummeled to death by Joe McCarthy in the Sulgrave Club in December 1950. Pearson falsely accused Nixon of seeking a fraudulent veterans' tax exemption.[59] Pearson retracted under legal threat, three weeks after the election. As with the political campaigns, so with the press; it became obscure which side had first abused the other. But with the liberals, Republican and Democratic, as with the press, the antagonism lingered long after the origins of the problem between them and Nixon were forgotten.

In television, he thought he had the method of avoiding the journalists completely. He had lived to fight another day, and obliterated the public impression that he was the mere beneficiary of Eisenhower's benediction. But he had exacerbated attitudes of his own and attitudes of others that would return at intervals and haunt him for most of the rest of his life.

Emboldened by his successful brush with political eternity, Nixon now chased after the Democrats more strenuously than ever. Truman accused Eisenhower of naively misjudging Soviet intentions at the end of the Second World War, and Nixon called this "gutter politics at its worst." It was, in fact, a fair charge, but Eisenhower wasn't in control of U.S. policy to Russia. Roosevelt and Truman were, and they made a much better job of it than the Yalta Myth and other confections, beloved of Nixon and less respectable Republican orators, allowed. Publicly, Eisenhower defended Yalta, but he descended to partisan Republican cant on January 25, 1954, when he told Republican congressional leaders that at Yalta "our commander in chief didn't have to be so indiscreet and crazy." Eisenhower knew this to be unfounded and gratuitous pandering.[60]

Eisenhower did think he had a particular talent for dealing with the Russians, which arose from his rather convivial visit to Stalin in the spring of 1945, which he did not now emphasize, since good relations with Stalin were not a promising vote-winner in the United States in this autumn of 1952. (Stalin had thought that the Normandy Invasion would be a Dunkirk or Dieppe-style debacle, and was impressed at the smooth success of the Western Allied landings and the crisp clearance of France.) The fact was that Eisenhower, to his credit, thought the anti-communist craze of the United States largely nonsense. He thought that he would have to deal seriously with the U.S.S.R. and not just engage in espionage, Red-baiting, and an endless arms buildup. That he had any particular talent at dealing with the Russians is not clear; probably no more than Truman nor as much as Nixon, but better than his immediate successor. Hitler, briefly, did better dealing with Stalin than anyone else, but Stalin, according to Khrushchev, respected Eisenhower's "decency, generosity, and chivalry," presumably because he did not contest the capture of Berlin with him.[61]

Nixon continued to prey on anti-Red paranoia, on vigilance and fear toward the "Godless, ruthless, realistic, and sinister foe that has infiltrated some of our key institutions."[62] This was the forbidding side of Nixon, which carried politics beyond the hard-hitting but still rather playful methods of Roosevelt, or at least the civilized limits of Truman, and pitched to baser instincts and fears, even if genteel and statesmanlike in comparison with McCarthy and his followers. Thus, Alger Hiss was "the arch spy of our generation." He was nothing of the kind, of course, just a confused and arrogant dilettante. As a spy, he was rather ineffectual and thoroughly out of practice by the time Nixon encountered him.

In Utica, New York, in mid-October, Nixon charged "that Mr. Truman, Dean Acheson, and his associates, whether through stupidity or political expedience, were primarily responsible for the unimpeded growth of the communist conspiracy within the United States . . . that Mr. Truman, Dean Acheson, and other administration officials for political reasons covered up this communist conspiracy and attempted to halt its exposure." And Stevenson had gone "down the line for Alger Hiss." (He had in fact done less for Hiss than John Foster Dulles and Eisenhower himself had.)[63] On October 27, he referred to Truman, Acheson, and Stevenson as "traitors to the high principles in which many of the nation's Democrats believe." This was effectively the end of his civilized relations with Truman, who did not highly appreciate the implication of treason. And on October 30 he referred to "Acheson's College of Cowardly Communist Containment."[64] It was pretty good electioneering stuff, but it was repetitive, superfluous at this point, and bound to come back to haunt him. When he wrote his memoirs in 1978, Nixon regretted the "intensity" of these attacks.[65]

Nixon and Stevenson had, in accord with Eisenhower's desire to be above it all, a main event in the center of the ring. Stevenson said Nixon would "chop down a redwood tree and mount the stump and make a speech for conservation."[66] Nixon said Stevenson was a "weakling, a hustler, a small-caliber Truman" dominated by the Chicago Democratic organization, infested with "mobsters, gangsters and remnants of the old Al Capone gang."[67] As with most caricatures, there was an element of truth in the charges of both men. (The Chicago Democratic machine would eventually do great damage to Nixon.) Only a conviction that this sort of thing would reap political rewards, and a desire for vengeance on the liberal left, which had been tormenting him, could have possessed Nixon to utter such inflammatory excesses. Eisenhower had asked for attacks on the Democrats for weakness toward the communists, but not outright imputations of treason to the president and secretary of state, and of subservience to notorious gangsters to the Democratic nominee for president.

This was more extreme than his strictures against Jerry Voorhis and Helen Gahagan Douglas, and he wasn't attacking a naive, altruistic congressman and a slightly misguided and overwrought senatorial candidate. Nixon would claim that he had not actually charged treason, but this was a distinction without a difference. As in his congressional races, he could claim that the mudslinging started with his opponents, and Truman was more experienced at firing hard balls than Nixon was. Nixon should have stopped trying to straddle between Eisenhower and McCarthy, and steered for less tempestuous waters. He knew that Eisenhower was well ahead in the polls, and as both parties had to cooperate to some extent for effective government, he would be better off showing a lighter, wittier touch. While Nixon slugged it out with Stevenson, Truman attacked Eisenhower and said he didn't know as much about politics "as a pig does about Sunday," and called Ike a "captive" of the Republican fat cats.

Nixon did lighten up sometimes, and was generally cautious and effective in largely Democratic communities like New York City. He could be moderate, and in fact in most of his views was moderate. But in conciliating the moderate and hard-right Republicans, he seriously discountenanced moderate Democrats. The Democrats adjusted to the Southern conservatives and racists in their midst by giving them a share in government and patronage and otherwise ignoring them, as Stevenson ignored Sparkman. With the Republicans, it was more complicated, and Nixon managed Republican relationships well, but he had a cloth ear where nonpartisan, moderate opinion was at stake. He had not forgotten that McCarthy and Taft, whom he had helped to deprive of the presidential nomination, had been loyal to him in his greatest crisis, and that Eisenhower and even Dewey had deserted him. This was another legacy of the fund crisis: Nixon's relative toleration of extremists and distrust of many moderates.

The low point of the campaign for Eisenhower was where he excised a defense of General Marshall from a speech he gave for McCarthy in Milwaukee that particularly disgusted Truman.

On June 14, 1951, McCarthy had harangued the Senate for eight hours with a sixty-thousand-word speech in which he reviewed General Marshall's career and accused him of complete incompetence as chief of staff, envoy to China, and secretary of state and defense, and concluded that Marshall's treachery had produced every communist triumph. It was one of the most inexcusable, egregious, defamatory outrages ever inflicted on the U.S. Congress. McCarthy accused Marshall of "a conspiracy so immense as to dwarf any previous such venture in the history of man . . . so black that, when it is finally exposed, its principles shall be forever deserving of the maledictions of all honest men."[68]

Given Marshall's real merits as, in Churchill's phrase (coined originally for the revolutionary French war minister, Lazare Carnot), "the organizer of victory," and as a brilliant cabinet secretary, support for him should have been solid and bipartisan. Marshall had discovered Eisenhower and promoted him from lieutenant-colonel to theater commander and four-star general in less than three years. Ike's admiration for Marshall was well-known, and he repeated it at his press conference in August 1952, as has been mentioned. When Eisenhower's train went to Wisconsin in early October, he asked for a paragraph in his Milwaukee speech in support of Marshall. Emmett John Hughes wrote, and the general approved, that Marshall had been "dedicated with singular selflessness and the profoundest patriotism to the service of America," and that the charges against him were "a sobering lesson in the way freedom must not defend itself."[69]

In one of the least distinguished episodes of his career, easily exceeding his worst lapses in the Nixon fund controversy, Eisenhower allowed himself to be persuaded not to give his defense of Marshall, after his staff had given the text to the press. Midwest Republican leaders told him it would be too disruptive to party unity to attack McCarthy in this way.

Senator Wayne Morse quit the Republican Party. Members of Eisenhower's staff leaked to the press that they were considering quitting, and Edward R. Murrow attacked Eisenhower on his widely viewed CBS television program, *See It Now*. Even Stassen wrote Eisenhower a censorious letter. Privately, Eisenhower excoriated McCarthy, in their only one-on-one meeting, on October 2, 1952, in Peoria. He allegedly "just took McCarthy apart."[70]

By contrast, Adlai Stevenson, who was admittedly in the other party and had nothing to lose, came to the University of Wisconsin on October 8, just after Eisenhower had steamed out of the state. He told the students that Aristotle had said, "History shows that almost all tyrants have been demagogues who gained favor with the people by their accusations of the nobles. . . . Disturbing things have taken place in our land. The pillorying of the innocent has caused the wise to stammer and the timid to retreat. . . . The voice of the accuser stills every other voice in the land." This was a well-placed shot at Eisenhower, who soon was clearly and rightly ashamed of his performance. He tried to ignore it in his memoirs, and blamed his staff for misleading him about the implications of failing to defend Marshall.[71]

Stevenson referred to McCarthy's attacks on him, without naming the senator, and concluded before a very large audience transfixed by his right-eous eloquence: "If the general would publicly embrace those who slandered General Marshall, there is certainly no reason to expect that he would restrain those who slander me."[72]

Eisenhower's high campaign point was October 24, when he portentously announced, "I shall go to Korea" (with no hint of what he would do there).

Unfortunately, all the pressures were for an escalation of partisan excess. On October 28, the Democratic National Committee charged that Nixon and his parents and brother Donald really were wealthy people, and it vastly exaggerated the family's means. Nixon correctly described these reflections as "despicable treatment of an entire life of [his father's] hard work."[73]

As Jim Bassett recounted, Nixon just kept repeating his speech the press became so bored with him, some stopped covering his speeches, or sent a delegation of their group only "to make sure nobody shot him." Some of his last rallies, in California, were unseemly. He shouted at one heckler: "When we're elected, we'll take care of people like you" and had his security unit eject the heckler. A couple of days later, his people beat up several picketers.[74]

Nixon declined to spend election night with the Eisenhowers, and flew back to California from a one-day speechmaking trip to Boston the day before the election. He spoke around his old district, and on voting day played touch football with Bill Rogers and some marines from Camp Pendleton, at Laguna Beach. By six o'clock California time, it was clear that Eisenhower and Nixon had won easily, ultimately by 6.5 million votes, 55 percent to 44 percent, the biggest plurality since Roosevelt's over Alfred Landon in 1936. And they had brought in narrow Republican majorities in both houses of the Congress for the first time since 1928 (221 to 213 in the House, and Nixon would have to break a 48 to 48 tie in the Senate).

Eisenhower and Nixon both spoke graciously that night, and Adlai Stevenson would joke, quoting Lincoln, "I'm like the boy who said he was too old to cry but it hurt too much to laugh." In his statement, Stevenson, whose regard for Eisenhower had sharply declined during the campaign, graciously said, "General Eisenhower has been a great leader in war. He has been a vigorous and valiant opponent in this campaign." And in his telegram he wished Ike "that you may be the servant and guardian of peace and make the vale of trouble a door of hope."[75] The urbane Stevenson could be relied upon to put a dignified ending on what had been a very destructive election campaign on both sides.

The Nixons took a holiday in Florida with Bebe Rebozo and George Smathers. Nixon's entire family came from California for the inauguration with old friends like Herman Perry, and there was a festive family occasion on the eve of the day. Eisenhower, in his inaugural address, recited a prayer for America – an odd inspiration for a man who did not pray or practice a religion.

Twenty years of Democratic rule by two outstanding presidents were over. Under the Democrats the Great Depression inherited from the Republicans and the prewar isolationism urged by the Republicans were ended, the war was won, and the elements were put in place to assure Western success in the Cold War.

John Foster Dulles was now secretary of state, in place of Acheson, Sherman Adams was White House chief of staff, and Herbert Brownell was the new attorney general. Robert Taft was Senate majority leader, with Knowland as his deputy, facing the Democratic Senate leader, Lyndon B. Johnson. Joe Martin was back again as Speaker of the House of Representatives. Henry Cabot Lodge, having been defeated in his Senate race by the young and rising John F. Kennedy, was named ambassador to the United Nations with cabinet rank.

General Dwight D. Eisenhower had attained the great office he claimed not to have coveted. Next to him stood a man who coveted it every hour of every day. The avuncular but cagey general and the bright, dark young Cassius looked with different thoughts on the future, and eyed each other warily. Their crusade had begun.

PART II

—

The Ordeal of Ambition

1953–1968

Chapter Five

The Chief Apprentice
1953–1956

— I —

NIXON HAD TOILED in the days leading up to the inauguration to clear the backlog of his correspondence. Always a stickler in matters of financial probity, and especially after such a searing campaign, he directed his staff never to introduce anyone, whether a U.S. citizen or foreigner, to any government agency or department, even by telephone. All inquiries about favors or services were to be directed to the California senators (as a parting shot, Earl Warren named Thomas Kuchel, no friend of Nixon's, to fill his unexpired Senate term), and Nixon told his staff to decline to answer any questions, no matter how apparently innocuous, about his own views.

Eisenhower had his cabinet designees for an introductory get-together at the Commodore Hotel in New York on January 12. Nixon and Lodge and Stassen (director of the Mutual Security Agency) were the only members of the group who had ever won an election before (and Lodge and Stassen hadn't won any recently). Eisenhower had chosen the president of General Motors, Charles E. Wilson, as secretary of defense, and as secretary of the Treasury George M. Humphrey, the chairman of the M.A. Hanna Company of Cleveland (an historic Republican name, as Senator Marcus Hanna had been the chief promoter of William McKinley). Eisenhower brought in three of his wartime chums in key positions: General Lucius Clay was counselor, General Walter Bedell Smith, Ike's chief of staff in Western Europe, was undersecretary of state with Dulles, and General Jerry

Persons was congressional liaison. In fact, Nixon did much of the congressional work and wasted no time building up an indispensable position bridging Congress and the administration. The assistant attorney general to Brownell would be Nixon's friend William Rogers.

Nixon, who was always careful of Knowland's sensibilities, though his gestures were little appreciated, was sworn as vice president by the senior California senator, on two Nixon family Bibles. From the start, Nixon's task was to mollify the Southern Democrats, who were the natural allies of the Republicans and were necessary to the achievement of any legislative progress. Lyndon Johnson was a congressional leader of legendary acuity, and there would be no possibility of turning any of his caucus members, other than by negotiation, with a tangible quid pro quo for any cooperation the administration might seek. Eisenhower wanted Nixon to secure the collaboration of the Democrats he needed, but to continue to be the administration's chief partisan, albeit with a little more restraint than in the last few months, now that the election was over and Truman, Acheson, and Stevenson were no longer public servants.

The vice presidency was a legendarily under-fulfilling job. Nixon generally opened each Senate session, waited for the chaplain's invocation and Taft's announcements of the day's business, and then had freshman senators occupy the chair while he worked from a small office nearby, available to cast a tie-breaking vote on a moment's notice. Eisenhower was concerned that Nixon be fully aware of everything important in the administration, as he had been critical of Roosevelt's failure to inform Truman of important developments such as the state of negotiations with Stalin and the atomic program. Eisenhower wanted Nixon fully capable to assume the presidency should that be necessary, and he wanted to give him administrative experience. He started by making him chairman of the President's Committee on Government Contracts. Nixon applied himself with his usual energy to this, and defined the jurisdiction of the committee in the broadest possible way.

Nixon was the informal political and public relations tutor to the whole cabinet, including Eisenhower, and said when they should come physically to Capitol Hill, what television invitations to accept, and how to get publicity for what they were doing. Nixon privately disagreed with Eisenhower's desire to reduce defense expenditures, but told him how to rally congressional support by inviting legislators who were veterans to the White House and taking advantage of his military prestige with them.

Nixon's most important early function in the administration was as shepherd to McCarthy and the almost equally pyrotechnic Senator William Jenner. McCarthy held up Bedell Smith's confirmation because he had allegedly said something flattering about someone in the State Department whom McCarthy had called a communist. He also held up the appointment of Dr. James B. Conant, president of Harvard University, as high commissioner (and then ambassador) to West Germany, because Conant had said that there were no communists on Harvard's faculty. McCarthy concluded from this that Conant must be a communist himself. Nixon, with Taft's help in Smith's case, persuaded McCarthy to let those nominations go through unopposed.

More of a problem arose with Charles E. Bohlen, the State Department's foremost Russia expert, as ambassador to the U.S.S.R. At the confirmation hearings, Bohlen refused to denounce the Yalta agreements. He had been Roosevelt's interpreter in his conversations with Stalin at Teheran and Yalta and was intimately involved in both conferences, and he defended them as the best that could be achieved. This contradicted the holy writ of the far-right Republicans, that FDR had been duped by Stalin. Bohlen authoritatively stated that there was no truth to any such allegation. Even Nixon had been urging Eisenhower to repudiate the Yalta agreement – a nonsensical proposal, as such an act would have no effect, and the problem was not with the agreement, which was favorable to the West. The problem was that Stalin had violated the Yalta agreement. As the fine Roosevelt biographer Ted Morgan wrote, if Yalta had been a bad agreement for the West, "why did Stalin go to such lengths to violate the agreement?"[1]

McCarthy's friends in the FBI leaked to McCarthy suggestions of some homosexual incidents in Bohlen's past (indicating that Hoover was going to be as insubordinate to Eisenhower as he had been to Truman). Nixon could not dissuade McCarthy from speaking against Bohlen's nomination in the Senate, but he did persuade him to make no reference to the FBI's sex-related material. Eisenhower refused McCarthy's demand that the full FBI file be opened to the Senate, but he and Nixon agreed to the compromise that Taft and Sparkman would be permitted to look at the files and give assurances to the Senate based on that examination. Bohlen was confirmed. Smith, Conant, and Bohlen were all excellent nominees against whom there was no possible legitimate complaint.

In February and again in June 1953, Nixon, Persons, and Rogers had McCarthy to Rogers's house for a friendly dinner. The senator had taken to conducting his own foreign policy, by securing an agreement from some Greek shipowners not to ship anything to Communist China, in exchange for being left alone by his Investigations Subcommittee. Stassen, as head of the Mutual Security Agency and a cabinet member in that capacity, publicly accused McCarthy of "undermining" the administration. Eisenhower was outraged at McCarthy's presumption and asked Nixon to sort this out too. Nixon arranged a meeting between Dulles and McCarthy, following which McCarthy promised not to take any further similar initiatives without checking with the State Department, and Dulles issued a statement commending the senator for upholding "the national interest." Eisenhower, at his next press conference, took it upon himself to say that Stassen had meant that McCarthy was "infringing" upon rather than "undermining" the administration.

In the June conversation, Nixon, Rogers, and Persons tried to hose McCarthy down and sell him on the benefits of being less confrontational with the administration. It was cordial, but inconclusive. A month later, McCarthy subpoenaed William Bundy, because he was Dean Acheson's son-in-law, and because he had contributed four hundred dollars to the Alger Hiss defense fund. Bundy was a CIA official and liaison between that agency and the National Security Council. The CIA director, Allen Dulles, forbade Bundy to answer the subpoena and stated that he would not allow any of his officials to give evidence to congressional committees.

McCarthy responded by threatening to investigate the CIA. Eisenhower and Allen Dulles found the prospect of McCarthy sifting through the government's premier intelligence files extremely disquieting, and they asked Nixon to try his hand at this problem. Nixon met with McCarthy and the other Republicans on the subcommittee – Dirksen, Mundt, and Charles Potter. They succeeded in persuading McCarthy to drop his planned investigation of the CIA.

But then in August McCarthy announced that he was about to attack the communists in the Agriculture Department. There were unlikely to be many of them there, since the American farm community and the sections of government that were devoted to its interests were even less susceptible to the seductions of Marx and his Russian espousers than most Americans. Nixon thought there were more loyalty risks in the federal government than there were, though he certainly did not buy into the McCarthy line that Washington was an anthill of Reds. But Nixon also thought that after the Republicans had claimed so noisily that Truman had tolerated the communist penetration of government, and he had walked a long way along this limb himself, that they had to seem to do something. He was opposed to a witch-hunt and the demoralization of the federal civil service, but the country was waiting for a shoe to drop and it should not be disappointed.

As usual, Nixon had covered the political angles in his thinking. He told the cabinet that they could combine the campaign promises to get rid of subversives with Eisenhower's promises of streamlined government, by changing the criterion from "loyalty" to "security." Nixon explained to the politically neophytic cabinet that communists never hesitate to sign loyalty oaths, but that the criterion should be security; i.e., insusceptibility to blackmail, whether for bad habits, sexual deviancy, or subversion. Then, everyone got rid of could implicitly be billed as a security risk and the Republicans could kill the efficiency and security birds with the same stone. It would also take the whole issue back from McCarthy and put the Red question in the more capable and responsible hands of the Republican administration, where Nixon strongly felt it belonged.

Eisenhower was generally in favor of what Nixon proposed, but did not want a mere "numbers game." He was afraid that people let go from government would, under Nixon's proposal, be stigmatized virtually as traitors. Nixon was aware of the problem, but as with his 1948 advice to Dewey and Dulles to promise a crackdown in immigration, he was more concerned with gross political advantage than individual discomfort. Next to his tendency to go for the partisan jugular politically with rich hyperbole, this unconcern of Nixon's for the fate of individuals in his grand political strategies was his most worrisome trait.

When matters were personalized, Nixon was very human and even generous. Bill Brock, the African-American football teammate at Whittier College whom Nixon had befriended, had been an early socialist, but he was now an electrical engineer and a member in good standing of the Republican Party. He had been fired by Howard Hughes's aircraft company because of his ancient socialist affiliation, and he wrote his school chum, now the vice president of the United States, asking for help. Nixon checked with the FBI, who gave Brock a full clearance, and with McCarthy, who had nothing against him, and then sent members of his staff to lobby the Pentagon for a full security clearance that Brock could use to regain his job. This was successful, though it took almost a year. Nixon was, as has often been seen already, a very compassionate man, but when these political questions presented themselves in the abstract, he tended to look upon them in a completely impersonal way and with the sole criterion of ultimate political advantage. This was the source of one of the great incongruities of his life, as those who knew him knew his decency and generosity, but those who knew him only as a public person often took him for an absolutely ruthless political calculator. Up to a point, they were both right, as the public and private Nixon were not always joined very closely.

When he was president-elect, Eisenhower had made the visit to Korea that he had promised during the campaign, and he determined to try to settle the war. But through third-party diplomatic channels he let Mao Tse-tung know that he would use the atomic bomb on the Chinese if they did not start taking the Panmunjom negotiations, which had been going on for many months, seriously. (Dulles so advised Indian prime minister Nehru, who passed it on to the Chinese.)* This came to fruition in July, as a standstill cease-fire along the thirty-eighth parallel was agreed and there was a drastic reduction in violence. Both sides kept threatening attack upon the other, and there were many incidents, but Eisenhower had delivered, early and honorably, on one of his most important campaign promises.

The negotiations would be an immense challenge to human patience, because there were endless provocations from the North Koreans and the Chinese, starting with their bringing in taller chairs than the Americans and South Koreans, so as to look down on them. The Allies put little flags in front of their places, as is standard in international conferences. The communists were back the next day with their own flags, twice as large. The American negotiator Admiral Turner Joy wrote that he resisted the temptation to respond, "which would have led to the 'construction of the two tallest flagpoles on earth.'"[2]

---

* Dulles spoke to Nehru on May 22. On May 7, China had suggested some acceleration of the talks, so some movement may have been afoot already. The war of attrition was onerous to China, and Dulles's reference to atomic weapons would have increased the motivation of the Chinese to end the war.

— II —

On September 29, 1953, Senator Joseph R. McCarthy married his secretary, Jean Kerr, at St. Matthew's Roman Catholic Cathedral in Washington, in what verged on a state occasion. Nixon and his wife attended, the president sent a congratulatory message, and Pope Pius XII sent a benediction. Senator John F. Kennedy was present, his brother Robert having just joined McCarthy's staff. (Joseph Kennedy, the family patriarch, now trying to buy political fortune for his sons, had financially induced McCarthy not to come into Massachusetts during the recent election to assist Lodge against his son.) Allen Dulles, Alice Roosevelt Longworth, General Jerry Persons, and Sherman Adams were among the wedding guests.

Eisenhower was quite conscientious and ingenious in thinking of ways to utilize Nixon and make the vice presidency more useful and more stimulating to him. He decided that Nixon should make an extensive tour of the Far East. He thought that the vice president would be an excellent fact finder and goodwill ambassador, and that it would be broadening for him; and Eisenhower wanted Nixon to carry a personal message of great importance to the South Korean leader, President Syngman Rhee. Eisenhower also shared the MacArthur view that U.S. administrations had been too exclusively Atlanticist and had paid insufficient attention to the Far East.

Nixon selected nineteen countries to visit, plus Hong Kong and Okinawa. He and Pat wrote up their own itineraries, departing from the usual protocol confinements, and insisted on meeting students, intellectuals, labor leaders, opposition personalities, and cultural figures, and, in Pat's case, visiting schools and hospitals and orphanages. They designed a punishing itinerary for themselves, which dismayed the State Department. Nixon worked with his unvarying assiduity to brief himself on the countries he was visiting and the personalities he would meet.

When they sadly said goodbye to their little daughters at Washington's National Airport on October 5, it was for a seventy-day trip, an unprecedentedly ambitious foreign tour for any major American public official. They flew first to New Zealand and Australia, and then to Jakarta, Indonesia. Nixon was thoroughly unimpressed with President Sukarno, the former leader of the independence movement against the Dutch. Nixon found Sukarno, accurately, an egomaniacal, corrupt, vain dissolute, living in Tiberian opulence in a poor country, and evidently preoccupied with using his position to procure the favors of a conspicuous multiplicity of lissome Balinese women. Nixon, Quaker and son of near-poverty, considered it inappropriate that the head of a poor country should have such an ostentatious gold dinner service and should assemble a dinner highlighted by lotuses and candles floating in great numbers on an adjoining lake.[3]

The Nixons went on to Kuala Lumpur and stayed with the British high commissioner, Field Marshal Sir Gerald Templer. Templer was fighting a prolonged communist guerrilla war in Malaya and explained to Nixon at length how the British were enlisting native leaders, embolden-ing them, and empowering them to conduct the counter-insurgency against the communists. Templer explained that most Malayans were not impressed with communists, and that the brutal communist methods were not popular, but that success required that the natives see the war as a communist struggle not against the British, but against their own culture and chiefs, who happened to be assisted by the British. Nixon was impressed. And he made an immensely positive impression on Templer, who wrote that Nixon was "extremely nice . . . anxious to learn and to help . . . with charming manners . . . the very reverse of what one had expected." Nixon had got on "extremely well with the many Asians he met." Templer was "really very impressed with Nixon indeed. He seemed to me potentially a much bigger man than Adlai Stevenson," who had visited Templer a few months before.[4]

Templer suggested that an effort should be made to drive a wedge between China and Russia, and recommended a resumption of trade with China. Nixon agreed with the objective, but doubted that much could be done soon. Stalin had died in March after twenty-nine years as Soviet dicta-tor, and the Kremlin was under an uneasy collective leadership between most of the senior Politburo members – Khrushchev, Malenkov, Bulganin, Molotov, Mikoyan, Voroshilov, and Kaganovich. The only things they could agree on were to get rid of Stalin's personal chief of staff, Poskrebyshev, and then to execute the police minister, Beria, who had terrorized all of them. It wasn't clear what Moscow would do if the Korean conflict started up again, but no one could imagine a more intractable and ruthless leader in the Kremlin than the satanic demiurge that had just departed it. A slightly opti-mistic sentiment persisted that Soviet relations had become less dangerous with the death of Stalin.

Nixon began exploring with Templer the idea of a NATO of the Far East. They agreed that Soviet and Chinese imperialism had to be discouraged in the region and collective security and containment policies would have to be devised.

Nixon went on to French Indochina. This was a country that had already been struggling with a communist insurrection led by Ho Chi Minh for seven years. Ho had been an original Vietnamese leader and Marxist, who had served as a kitchen assistant to the great French chef Escoffier at the Ritz and turned up at the Paris Peace Talks in 1919, in a rented suit, to press an anti-colonialist petition for his people. Woodrow Wilson was in some sympathy with the concept, but Clemenceau and Lloyd George, for obvious reasons, could not accept Ho's argument; in any case, it was academic, since the conference refused to hear unsolicited petitions. (Ho did better than Syngman Rhee, who tried to attend and petition on behalf of Korea, then governed by Japan, and was denied a passport.)

Ho had struggled through the inter-war years, fomenting such revolt as he could, and had made extensive progress with a patriotic resistance movement against the Japanese. Roosevelt had warned privately at several stages during the Second World War that the mere restoration of French colonial rule would not bring peace to Indochina. Roosevelt advocated that most colonies be put in UN-supervised trusteeships designed to prepare them for full independence as soon as possible, and in a nationally disinterested way. This found no more favor with Churchill and de Gaulle than Ho had with Clemenceau and Lloyd George, but it at least recognized the danger of endless wars of independence and the sudden emergence of scores of countries with no aptitude for self-government.

France had purported to set up an autonomous emperor, Bao Dai, an elegant playboy who lounged around Dalat and had no following. In Indochinese matters, anti-American Romantics such as the well-known author Bernard Fall – killed by Ho's army eventually, despite a strenuous intellectual and public relations campaign on Ho's behalf – had proposed an alternate emperor, Duy Tan, favored by de Gaulle, but also killed, accidentally. But the nature of the Indochinese, mainly Vietnamese, conflict was disguised for decades. Ho Chi Minh and his followers wanted absolute power and were not interested in compromises.

With the Soviets and Chinese providing assistance to Ho, only the United States had any possibility of stopping this, and it would have no credibility doing so if it was propping up the French regime, or a successor group of colonial puppets. Obviously, the United States preferred France to those trying to expel the French from Indochina, and the non-communists to the communists in Indochina. But from Roosevelt's time on, certainly with the emergence of Red China, and well before the arrival of Nixon in Hanoi in the autumn of 1953, the issue was how to find the best solution that had any chance of being achieved.

While Bao Dai did not represent anyone, he did make the point to Nixon that there was no point in negotiating with the communists, since that would merely divide the country in two and begin the second phase of the war, in which the communists would try to take the part they had not already seized. He was correct. Nixon went on to Vientiane, Laos, where Prince Souvanna Phouma, the neocolonial ruler, had the same view as Bao Dai: there was no point to negotiating with the communists. Nixon went back to Vietnam, to the capital, Hanoi, and was splendidly received in the French manner, but was concerned by the French high commissioner's dismissive references to the Vietnamese. He contrasted this with Templer's upbeat remarks about the Malayans, and had, from this early stage, misgivings about the imbalance of legitimate motives animating the two sides in the conflict. Nixon donned battle fatigues and went to watch American ordnance being fired at the enemy. The Nixons went on to Phnom Penh, Cambodia, and the inevitable trip to Angkor Wat. Nixon found the Cambodian ruler, Prince Sihanouk, an absurd and neurotic figure in whom no reliance at all could be placed.

He left Indochina still espousing the Truman-Eisenhower view that the French had to be helped until some local leadership could be found that would be a real counterweight to the communists. He was under no illusion that Bao Dai, Sihanouk, and Souvanna Phouma could, holding hands, keep the Chinese- and Russian-backed Vietminh at bay for long, no matter how many shiploads of artillery shells the Americans sent them. It was already a problem that was festering unpromisingly.

It was too late for the French to fight the war the way the British were in Malaya. The non-communist Vietnamese could not win without the French, and the French could not win against authentic Vietnamese nationalists, even communists. Eisenhower and Nixon hoped that France would grant the country independence and try to emulate the British Malayan methods. But it was not the French Fourth Republic style, and the

French Army was trying to redeem itself from the debacle at the hands of the Germans in 1940. Even if the French had been more amenable, it was too late to do what Roosevelt had wanted and give the development of independence to a UN organization, while the French leisurely packed up their hallmarks of civilization from "the pearl of the Orient," as Saigon was known, and departed. A tragedy of thirty years was already well advanced. Roosevelt proposed to Stalin at Yalta a fifty-year trusteeship for Indochina, ending in independence. Stalin agreed, except that he implied that a further fifty-year wait was not going to satisfy the Vietnamese independence party.[5] It would not have, but it would have spared the French and Americans a great deal of tragedy and embarrassment.

Nixon moved on to Taipei, the capital of what was now known as Nationalist China (Taiwan). He had a seven-hour conversation with Chiang Kai-shek, who claimed to be preparing for his reconquest of mainland China. Nixon bore him the unwelcome message from Eisenhower that the United States would not support such an effort. It was, in any case, nonsense. Chiang had been ejected once, and had atrophied in Formosa while Mao Tse-tung extended his control throughout China.

The only point at which Chiang's armies could have been useful was in Korea, where they could have assisted importantly in MacArthur's plan to grind the Red Chinese Army to powder in the Korean peninsula by keeping it constantly engaged, assaulting its communications, and pounding it relentlessly from the air. Chiang's forces, setting out to reconquer the Chinese mainland, commanded by Chiang, and operating autonomously across a wide strait, would be no more successful than they had been the first time round, which is why they were now in Formosa.

Nixon went to South Korea and met with Syngman Rhee. This was the most important part of his program, as he brought a very timely message from Eisenhower that the president did not wish to entrust to any lesser official. Nixon himself still privately favored fighting to victory in Korea – not invading China, but roughing it up from the air and smashing its main armies in the peninsula as a salutary deterrent lesson. This view was widely held by the MacArthur faction of conservative Republicans and by many Southern Democrats, but not by Eisenhower and the moderate Republicans and Democrats. Even Joseph Alsop and Thomas E. Dewey, who were not extremists, thought North Korea was on the brink of caving in when Eisenhower made the July agreement with them.[6] It may have been, but

Red China wasn't. Alsop wrote that the Korean cease-fire was the worst U.S. foreign policy error in many years.[7]

Eisenhower felt that three full years of war in Korea was enough. The United States had held its initial position and he was not prepared to squander American and Allied lives for the geopolitical luxury of a united Korea, so he enforced his settlement. To this end, he entrusted Nixon with the urgent order to make it clear to Rhee that he must not break the peace. Nixon's assignment was to get from Rhee a formal agreement to the Korea settlement. He started by giving Rhee a letter from Eisenhower which stated that the United States would not support South Korea in a unilateral reopening of the war and required a unilateral guarantee from Rhee that there would be no such initiative.

Rhee read the letter, but then tried to ignore it and instead inflicted upon Nixon a lecture about three million South Koreans who were at this point enslaved in the North. In a formula with which Nixon would eventually become painfully familiar, Rhee told him that a divided Korea would inevitably lead to a war that "would destroy Korea and the United States." Nixon would learn that the common denominator of all those seeking U.S. military support was the claim that failure to provide it would lead inexorably to the destruction of both the country seeking America's protection, and America itself.

All Nixon could get from Syngman Rhee was the promise that if there were any unilateral South Korean action in contemplation, Rhee would inform Eisenhower first. This was not what Nixon had come for, but it went better at their next meeting, when Rhee said that it was important for the communists in Korea, China, and Russia to think that Rhee was a madman, capable of unleashing a war to the death at any moment. He gave Nixon a slightly learned strategical lecture on how many troops of the enemy's he was tying down that might more usefully be deployed elsewhere. He said, "Any statements I have made about Korea acting independently were made to help America. . . . In my heart I know that [South] Korea cannot possibly act alone." This mission was accomplished, and the Nixons went on to Japan.

Nixon's trip highlighted the fragmented and centrifugated condition of America's allies and client states in the Far East: embattled Malaya, the unconquered part of Korea, the fugitives from mainland China, whatever could be salvaged from Vietnam. If this assemblage of shards and slivers was to be assembled in a bloc against China and Russia, the major non-communist powers intact would have to be joined to America's effort. The obvious candidate was Japan, one of the world's Great Powers, but so trauma-tized by its defeat, its atrocities, and the atomic bomb, it was a pacifist country. MacArthur, as military governor, had encouraged the constitutional renunci-ation of the use of force, but this was already an inconvenience being invoked by the Japanese as part of the reason why they did not and could not con-tribute to their own defense.

Having unsuccessfully tried to rival the Americans as a military power in the Pacific, Japan now focused entirely on economic growth and abstained entirely from the arms race that engrossed the Western and Soviet blocs. Dulles, who was personally friendly with Nixon, and was closer to his hawkish views than to the president's, had asked Nixon to raise with the Japanese leadership the possibility of Japan's making a representative con-tribution to the defense burden in the Western Pacific. (One of the greatest of Dulles's accomplishments had been the Japan Peace Treaty.) Nixon did do this, at a luncheon with Japanese reporters. He said that the United States had made a mistake in encouraging Japanese disarmament in 1946, because the United States had misjudged Soviet intentions and had not foreseen the rise of Red China. He avoided even implicit criticism of Truman and MacArthur in their different capacities, but said that condi-tions had changed and required adjustment. His remarks made headlines around the world.

Nixon went on to the Philippines, where he was impressed with President Ramon Magsaysay, and to Burma. Here, he was warned of the possibility of an anti-American demonstration. Nixon rejected advice to avoid the demonstrators and walked into their midst, conversing and debat-ing with them. It was the tamest, most elemental form of demonstration, and reluctant protesters holding signs such as "GO HOME WARMONGER" were unable to debate, or even sustain conversation, with Nixon. This would be one of the first of a great many such encounters Nixon would have with demonstrators. They did not always evaporate so easily, but he was always fearless, even when the threat to his safety was very serious. This became part of Nixon's view, first enunciated after the Herter Commission visit to Italy, that all communists respected was strength. In this, as in most other matters, Nixon construed the world as a contest of will.

He and his party went next to India, where he did not like the prime minister, Jawaharlal Nehru. Nehru was accompanied by his daughter, the future prime minister Indira Gandhi, and he found them both viscerally irritating. Nixon claimed that all Nehru wanted to talk about was American aid to Pakistan, and to do so in a soft, imitative English accent, redolent of all the pretensions to piety of motive and purity of character that Nehru attached to all Indian foreign policy, which he represented as sanctified by innate Indian virtue and by the Nehrus' stance of neutrality between the U.S. and Soviet blocs. Nixon found it annoying and incongruous that India, a largely English-speaking democracy, should affect a posture of neutrality between the Western democracies and their enemies. And he found the Nehrus' posture of sanctimony tiresome, given the shambles and corruption of India and its government.

Nixon was unlikely to attach much credence to any purported enactment of Mahatma Gandhi's views in international relations. The Mahatma had advised Britain to surrender to Hitler and Mussolini in 1940, because they could not conquer the "minds or souls" of the British. He had urged the Ethiopians to "allow themselves to be slaughtered" by the Italians in 1935, and the German Jews to accept their fate at the hands of the Nazis with "the strength of suffering given to them by Jehovah," which would lead the Nazis "to an appreciation of human dignity." Richard Nixon was as little susceptible to such appeals, Quaker though he was, as were those to whom they were directed. While the Mahatma's sincerity could be accepted, Nixon considered Nehru and his daughter to be mere hypocrites.[8]

Nixon had a more successful visit to Pakistan and its military leader, Ayub Khan. After very cordial talks, he confirmed to the press that he would favor military aid to Pakistan. This prompted Nehru to call him an "unprincipled cad." Nixon was even more impressed with his host on the last stop of his visit, the Shah of Iran. They seemed to agree on everything, and Nixon predicted that he would evolve into a strong leader. It was only recently that the Shah had been restored to the Peacock Throne by American and British intelligence action, and Mohammed Mossadegh, an alleged neutralist, apparently friendly with local communist elements and an advocate of nationalization of foreign oil interests, had been sent packing. All around the fringes of the great Cold War blocs there were efforts to shore up or destabilize wobbling governments, as the line of demarcation was drawn between the Russo-Chinese and U.S.-Western spheres.

The Nixons returned to a very cordial welcome, including seven senators, at the airport, and a gracious greeting from Eisenhower at the door of the White House. American press coverage had been extensive and uniformly generous. It was obvious everywhere that the Nixons had been extremely well-informed, sensitive to local issues, and energetic in their fact-finding. The rumors from the officials visited were flattering; Nixon had begun his long climb from hardball American politician to world statesman. Eisenhower wrote to Syngman Rhee on January 2, 1954, confirming Rhee's undertaking to Nixon not to restart the war in the Korean Peninsula unilaterally, and extending military and economic aid to South Korea.

Nixon spoke on nationwide television on December 23, 1953, and summarized his trip. He emphasized the necessity of combating the communists in Malaya, Indochina, Burma, Indonesia, and the Philippines. Without using the expression, which Eisenhower coined subsequently, he outlined a form of domino theory, which held that if any of these countries were lost to the communists, others would fall over too and the worldwide balance of power would be tipped. He was privately more worried than he publicly acknowledged. He and Dulles thought that Eisenhower was too concerned about not reescalating the conflict in Korea and not concerned enough to shut down communist expansion right through the Asian landmass and Australasia. He told his television audience that there was no point negotiating with communists, and that the United States had to do the necessary to support local anti-communist forces.

— III —

While Nixon was overseas developing his new vocation as a globe-trotting statesman, his prior chief service to the administration, preventing Senator Joseph R. McCarthy from blowing up, had been missed. During Nixon's trip, McCarthy had made noises about investigating the Atomic Energy Commission, and especially its chief scientist, J. Robert Oppenheimer, who had a number of friends who were ex-communists. Nixon had already publicly defended Oppenheimer, but Eisenhower's chief concern was that McCarthy would completely demoralize the corps of American atomic scientists, just as the government would be relying on them more than ever as the nuclear arms race with the U.S.S.R. accelerated.

McCarthy had also been making threatening noises about the U.S. Army, claiming that the secretary, Robert Stevens, had been only half-heartedly rooting out subversives in the army's communications center at

Fort Monmouth, New Jersey. Eisenhower was not prepared to tolerate McCarthy's tearing his army apart. The president had said at a recent press conference that he did not think communist infiltration of the U.S. government would be an issue in 1954, and McCarthy flatly contradicted him. Truman had attacked McCarthy in a widely publicized speech with his usual refreshing lack of ambiguity, and the main television networks gave McCarthy a right of reply.

Shortly after his return, Nixon was again asked by Eisenhower to try to sort this out, as James Hagerty, the president's astute press secretary, had told the president that McCarthy was trying to hijack the Republican Party from underneath him.

The Nixons and William Rogers flew to Florida for a holiday just before New Year's, and invited McCarthy to join them. Nixon's magic worked again, as he convinced the senator that only the communists would profit from an indiscriminate harassment of atomic scientists and a full-scale assault on the U.S. Army. He and Rogers warned McCarthy of the dangers of being a one-issue politician and said that the country would not believe that both Truman and Eisenhower were soft on the Reds, when McCarthy was perfectly well aware how unfounded the charge was now. They thought they had persuaded McCarthy to go after soft tax deals for Truman cronies in the former administration, and McCarthy made threatening noises along these lines.

It was on this placatory note that 1953 ended and Nixon and his wife and children settled into a pleasant vacation. But McCarthy, having returned to Washington, thought better of it, said that suggestions that he was laying off the communist issue were a "lie,"[9] and continued to paw the ground. Nixon was unlikely to be able to keep the lid on this volcano much longer. Half of Americans, and 62 percent of Republicans, had a favorable opinion of McCarthy, and he seemed determined to have a front-end collision with the administration. McCarthy was a fighting bull with no tactical skill. He had alienated the Democrats beyond any reconciliation. Nixon would rally any waverers behind the president, and whether the voters still liked to chase after communists or not, McCarthy was not going to be able to take on the entire bipartisan political establishment of the country. Nixon had done his best, at Eisenhower's request, to keep him on the reservation, but in late January, McCarthy crossed the Rubicon and began the Army-McCarthy hearings.

A dentist, Dr. Irving Peress, had been drafted into the army and, as a member of the American Labor Party, refused to sign a loyalty oath. He was nevertheless promoted under the Doctors' Draft Law, and McCarthy summoned him before his subcommittee, where he took the Fifth Amendment. The army then gave him an honorable discharge. McCarthy responded in his usual aggressive fashion and summoned the base commander, General Ralph Zwicker (of Camp Kilmer), a much-decorated veteran of the Normandy, Ardennes, and Rhine campaigns, and demanded to know who promoted Peress and what nature of subversive cover-up he had unearthed. He berated Zwicker outrageously, claiming he did not have the brains of "a five-year-old" and was "not fit to wear his uniform." This was pretty rich from "tail-gunner Joe," who had procured an unearned aviation medal through political connections. The army secretary, Stevens, ordered Zwicker not to return to the hearings, and he and, it was authoritatively rumored, the president (with MacArthur and Marshall and Bradley, the highest ranking veteran of the U.S. Army) made it clear that they would not tolerate the denigration of the U.S. Army in this way.

McCarthy summoned Stevens. Nixon was pressed into service again, and again met with Rogers, Persons, Knowland, Dirksen, and now Stevens and counsel. Stevens's plan was to go before the subcommittee, acknowledge an innocuous error in the handling of the Peress matter, and then attack McCarthy for his disgraceful abuse of Zwicker. Nixon told him that since it was McCarthy's subcommittee, he could stack it to any finding he wanted, and that technically only Eisenhower had the authority to tell Zwicker to ignore a subpoena from the U.S. Senate. Nixon set up a luncheon the next day in Dirksen's office with Stevens, McCarthy, Mundt, and others. A compromise was arranged in which McCarthy would stop abusing army witnesses, and Zwicker would return and explain what went on in the Peress matter. Mundt wrote it out, and it was signed, but he omitted to add the McCarthy good behavior clause, enabling the senator to march out of Dirksen's office announcing that he had humbled the administration and its chief supporters in the Senate.

McCarthy was inching closer to a direct confrontation with the president and the serried ranks of the bipartisan establishment. This was the one issue that Eisenhower, Nixon, Dulles, Truman, Acheson, Stevenson, most of the Congress, and almost all the national media could agree on, whatever millions of Americans might think about it. With that said, Eisenhower's own congressional party cautioned him against being drawn into the wrong battle with McCarthy. Senator Leverett Saltonstall of Massachusetts,

Knowland, and even Nixon himself told the president that the army had mishandled the Peress affair.

Hagerty and Ike's other advisers thought that McCarthy was making the big play for leadership of the right in the Republican Party. Robert Taft had died on July 31, 1953, and was succeeded by Knowland as Republican leader in the Senate. But McCarthy was at this point the strongest of the old guard Republicans. This group was irritated, though not surprised, that Eisenhower had not gone for victory in Korea, had done little in Vietnam, had neither cut back taxes, balanced the budget, repealed any significant part of the New Deal, increased emphasis on Asia over Europe, nor given any new encourage-ment for the enslaved people of the European satellite countries, and had not even put the proper fear of the wrathful right into those subversives that many of them thought were still swarming within the administration. Eisenhower had intended to tell a press conference that attacking communism "should not be taken to the extreme of attacking Americanism."

Nixon carefully reviewed the problem. McCarthy would not hear of compromise, and Eisenhower, though sensitive to warnings that the Republican Party could be split, was determined that the McCarthy threat not be allowed to run loose indefinitely. Nixon went over the loyalties of the key Republicans with his own staff the night of the broken McCarthy-Stevens agreement. Finally, he said to his press officer, Jim Bassett, in reference to McCarthy, "It's probably time we dumped him."[10] Nixon had known the time was coming, and had hoped that McCarthy would either join the team or take more rope to hang himself. But matters could not go on as they were. On March 6, 1954, Adlai Stevenson made a nationwide speech and said that the Republicans were divided between Eisenhower and McCarthy, mocked the "New Look" in defense, and said that "the Great Crusade is the great deception." McCarthy demanded the right to reply for the Republicans, who under agreed rules were entitled to equal time. Eisenhower intervened and gave the task of responding for the administration to Nixon instead.

Nixon's task was to hammer the Democrats, defend Eisenhower's foreign and defense policies, which he privately considered inadequately purposeful, and rebuke McCarthy without naming him and without seri-ously splitting the Republican Party. Knowland had been the subject of hostile leaks from the White House, and was threatening to quit as majority leader in the Senate. Eisenhower and the whole cabinet turned to Nixon to try to cooper things back together, and Eisenhower urged him to "smile a little" and "laugh at the Democrats and not hit meanly."[11]

Nixon spoke to a live audience of about ten million on the evening of March 13, without notes, sitting at a desk. He gave such a strong defense of the "New Look" at the Pentagon that it was broadly persuasive, even though Nixon himself did not agree with it. Eisenhower and Wilson were getting better value for money, increasing defense capabilities while spending less, he explained, reasonably plausibly.

Nixon stated that the new administration had discovered that the Kremlin's plan was to exhaust and demoralize America by dragging it into a good many small wars all over the world, and deplete its resources and willpower. Nixon declared that Eisenhower had seen through this and that he would not "let the communists nibble us to death all over the world in little wars . . . [that the U.S.] would rely primarily on our massive mobile retaliatory power which we could use in our discretion against the major source of aggression at times and places that we chose."[12] Nixon was echoing an address given by Dulles in January; both the vice president and the secretary were putting the best face they could on policies that worried them.

They both still wanted to crush the Red Chinese Army in Korea, blast the People's Republic from the air, eliminate North Korea, and ensure that the French, having promised Indochina independence, were not humiliated by the North Vietnamese guerrillas. They loyally did their best for a policy they had argued against. Nixon, if it were up to him, would have brought back MacArthur for his sunset gun as Far East theater commander, with instructions to win decisively. Eisenhower believed that the mountains of North Korea and the jungles of Indochina were not worth, in Bismarckian terms, the bones of one American. (Either policy would have worked better than the catastrophic compromise developed by the presidents between Eisenhower and Nixon.)

Nixon told the country on March 13, 1954, that scaling back the Korean War and some of the conventional defense capacity would save 20 percent off the defense budget, balance the budget, and permit tax reductions. Then Nixon, inevitably, and after over a year of comparative decorum, strayed into Democrat-bashing. It was "wonderful" to have a secretary of state who was not "taken in by the Kremlin," and who would not squander at the conference table what American soldiers "win on the battlefields." In over a year of Republican government, "In not one area of the world have the communists made a significant gain."

Nixon, as cunning in navigating the factional waters as ever in his many decades at it, put rhetorical questions to Stevenson over whether he wanted to send more forces of draftees to Korea, to revive the full-scale war there, and to become engaged in similar wars elsewhere. (The fact that he was prepared to answer all these questions affirmatively himself was beside the point.)

He dealt with McCarthy by expressing thankfulness in the contrast between Eisenhower and the unnamed Truman, rejoicing that the incumbent president "does not engage in personal vituperation and vulgar name-calling and promiscuous letter-writing in asserting his leadership." Without mentioning the senator, he said of him, "Men who have in the past done effective work exposing communists in this country have, by reckless talk and questionable methods, made themselves the issue rather than the cause they believe in so deeply." He asked why such care should be taken in pursuing communists, since communists were like rats whom it was quite in order to shoot. Then he added, "I'll agree they're a bunch of rats. But just remember this. When you go out to shoot rats, you have to shoot straight," and warned of the dangers when you "shoot wildly."

Nixon seized the opportunity to substitute his security criterion for loyalty concerns in the federal civil service, and gave the country the totals of changes that had been effected by the administration. He said that 2,400 people had been dismissed from federal government employment by the administration: 422 for subversive activities or associations; 198 for sexual perversion; 611 for criminal records; and 1,424 for "untrustworthiness, drunkenness, mental instability, or [other] possible exposure to blackmail."

This drew the nettle on the issue, as the Republicans could now claim to have scorched out thousands of undesirables, even though it was a pretty thin harvest of security risks, given the deafening campaign and unstinting demagogy of the preceding five years of Republican oratory. From Eisenhower and Brownell down, the Republican leaders of the administration were afraid of stigmatizing the innocent, but only Nixon, by this pallid claim, prevented the Republicans from being held up to unanswerable ridicule by Stevenson and Truman for producing a completely false Red Scare in the previous years.

It was a very skillful juggling act, and Eisenhower telephoned as soon as it was over and congratulated him on a "magnificent" speech. Nixon was now the indispensable man in keeping the Republican Party, so long out of office, and with Robert Taft now dead, reasonably united behind its leader. Nixon's effort was, however, a palliative. McCarthy, riding high, let it be known that he was "sick and tired of the constant yack-yacking from that prick Nixon."[13] The supreme denouement of the malignant McCarthyite phenomenon could not be long delayed.

— IV —

It was very impetuous for Nixon to have said the communists had made no significant gains, given that the Vietminh were tightening the noose around the French and Eisenhower obviously had no intention of doing anything about it. The French had staked a great deal on the battle of Dien Bien Phu in northwest Vietnam, where they had about fifteen thousand men, only about three thousand of them French, surrounded by the communist Vietminh. The administration was already considering a variety of methods of resolving the problem, as the French showed little aptitude for extricating themselves from an impending encirclement. It would not have been difficult for the United States to assist in airlifting out the French and pro-French Vietnamese soldiers, or smashing up the Vietminh artillery surrounding Dien Bien Phu with heavy air support so the French could make a dignified evacuation. Instead, France, America's oldest ally, was allowed to be severely humiliated before the world. Eisenhower's comrade of ten years before in Algiers and London and Paris, Charles de Gaulle, was brought appreciably closer to a return to power in France by the shambles in Vietnam, but not suffused with increased enthusiasm for the practical uses to France of the American alliance.

Especially after the death of Stalin, there was no possibility of the U.S.S.R. escalating the Korean or Vietnamese wars if the United States had. But since the Cold War was ultimately won and relations with China were eventually normalized, it is hard to criticize Eisenhower for resisting the temptation to commit American forces too flippantly in secondary theaters.

However, since the Nationalist Chinese forces contributed nothing to Western security and great American largesse was lavished on them, they would have been put to better use pushing the communists back to the narrowest neck of the Korean Peninsula, just north of Pyongyang, truncating the primitive tyranny of Kim Il Sung and Kim Jong Il, giving Mao Tse-tung and Chou En-lai a taste of defeat on the ground and a good pounding from the air in key areas, and assisting the French in avoiding embarrassment in Vietnam and trying to set up a British-Malayan type alternative regime there. This could have been done without an over-commitment of American resources.

It appeared to the president an incautious policy at the time. Eisenhower was a distinguished and victorious general, and he ended the Korean War on an acceptable basis and made it clear that he was not prepared to plunge into the Vietnam War on an unacceptable basis. There is room to suggest that his policy options may not have been the very best that were available. But they were also far from the worst.

Ever since his prolonged visit to the Far East, Nixon had been in close and almost constant contact with Dulles. They formed an alliance within the administration to promote as firm a line as they could sell to Eisenhower. A foreign ministers' conference had been convened for Geneva for the spring of 1954, and the U.S.S.R., Britain, France, and China would attend. The United States administration did not wish to be present, but France implored its presence, failing which the government of Joseph Laniel would be apt to fall, and probably be replaced by a government of the democratic left led by Pierre Mendes-France, who wanted France to withdraw from Indochina. Dulles was accordingly committed to go, to try to prop up the French. He consulted Nixon on which senators to invite to accompany him, thinking of Wiley and Green of the Foreign Relations Committee. Nixon recommended Alexander Smith of New Jersey for the Republicans and William Fulbright of Arkansas for the Democrats, and Dulles followed this suggestion.[14] Nixon gave Dulles minute and extensive advice on how to handle individual senators. He also championed his personal hobbyhorses from his Far East trip, a NATO of that region and a South Asian formation to counter the influence of India. Nixon and Dulles suspected Nehru of wanting to lead the entire neutral bloc and align it more closely to Russia than to the West, and Nixon had begun explorations of an arrangement linking the other former components of the British Indian Empire in counterweight to India (Pakistan, Burma, and Ceylon).

Nixon's idea of a Far Eastern NATO was enthusiastically endorsed by the flamboyant American ambassador to Thailand, William Donovan, a Congressional Medal of Honor winner, Republican candidate for governor of New York in 1932, and Roosevelt's wartime intelligence director.[15] On

March 29, 1954, Dulles had called for "united action" in Vietnam, by which he meant Britain, Australia, New Zealand, the Philippines, Thailand, Cambodia, and Laos, joining the United States in coming to the aid of France in a post-colonial effort. The Southeast Asia Treaty Organization (SEATO) was born of this initiative. But this was not Eisenhower's conception; it was his wily method of deferring American action. Once the alliance was up and running, he fell back on the insistence of congressional support for American action in Vietnam, which he knew would not be forthcoming. The president had led a hundred divisions to victory in Western Europe; he was in no hurry to try to replicate that feat in the jungles of Asia.

On April 2, Nixon and Dulles and the chairman of the Joint Chiefs of Staff, Admiral Arthur Radford, met with congressional leaders of both parties and requested approval for the use of American air and sea power in Vietnam. The politicians, of both parties, would not hear of it, the sanguinary mud bath of Korea fresh in their minds. The chief of staff of the French army, General Paul Ely, had been in Washington and had concerted plans for what was called Operation Vulture, a massive American-led air strike against the Vietminh around Dien Bien Phu. There was some flexibility, or more accurately difference of opinion, about whether the bombing would be atomic or conventional. Dulles had no thought of atomic weapons; the service chiefs thought they would be more effective. Nixon thought the threat of use of such weapons, as had served Eisenhower well in getting a cease-fire in Korea, should not be avoided but did not advocate their use. Ely asked for implementation on some basis on April 5. Dulles put it to Eisenhower, who refused point blank, saying that without congressional approval such an effort would be "completely unconstitutional and indefensible." This was not strictly correct, since the commander in chief could do what he chose, constitutionally, but if he effectively plunged the country into undeclared war, that would be another matter.

The fact was that Eisenhower did not believe the Soviet Union was as powerful as the more vocal Cold Warriors believed. He certainly did not think Red China was any imminent threat to the United States, and he wasn't convinced anything in Indochina was strategically worth the cost of keeping the communists out of control of it. He believed that if the United States retained atomic superiority and a containment policy with advanced countries who contributed adequately to their own defense, the West, including allies like Japan, would prevail eventually. Eisenhower had been similarly unimpressed with the domestic communist threat, though he had not been reluctant to sound the foreign and domestic communist alarms in order to take up residence in the White House.

Although he had appointed the head of America's largest industrial corporation, Charles Wilson, as secretary of defense, he was also beginning to question the relationship between the military and their industrial suppliers, which led to his eventual admonition against the "military-industrial complex," as he called it, coining the phrase. He found the resistance to defense expenditure cuts irksome and at times irrational. It is little wonder that the conservative Republicans were disappointed in Eisenhower. He was not an ideologue, was no one's captive, and was in social and economic terms at a midpoint only slightly to the right of Roosevelt and Truman.

Nixon told the National Security Council on April 6 that Eisenhower should not "underestimate his ability" to secure congressional support for what he regarded as being in the national security interest. Nixon proposed sending American equipment and technical advisers to help the French in Vietnam. He agreed with Dulles's "united action" plan, but pointed out that the problem in Southeast Asia was not so much overt aggression, as it was in Europe, but subversion. So something more than NATO was required. Eisenhower was not much moved by this, and Nixon wrote in his diary that he seemed "resigned to doing nothing at all."[16]

Nixon was trying to propel his leader forward into confrontation with the Asian communists by the scruff of the neck and the small of the back. He was no puppet vice president, but Eisenhower was not to be manipulated either. On April 16, Nixon replaced the vacationing Eisenhower before the American Society of Newspaper Editors, and gave an "off the record" talk and answered questions. He knew as well as everyone else there that everything newsworthy he said would be published at once. Nixon warned the editors of the danger of communist domination in East Asia and the possibility of a result at Geneva that would just be a fig leaf for a capitulation to the Reds. Nixon was asked if he favored sending Americans to replace the French if their military pulled out. Nixon said that he did not believe this would occur (though all contingency planning in Washington was on the presumption that the French were heading for the ships and planes to take them out almost as fast as they could). Nixon then said that in that hypothesis, he would favor the commitment of American forces to prevent a communist takeover of Vietnam. "I believe the executive branch of the government has to take the politically unpopular position of facing up to it and doing it, and I personally would support such a decision."[17]

This was an explosive story, and Eisenhower saw at once what his vice president was up to, but was fairly indulgent of him. Hagerty called to ask what he had said and Nixon "played dumb." Eisenhower told Hagerty to have the State Department put out a statement hosing down the controversy but not undercutting Nixon personally. As Eisenhower and Nixon biographer Stephen Ambrose put it: "Eisenhower was willing to protect Nixon, though not to listen to his advice."[18] The basic policy disagreement continued between Nixon and Dulles and others who wanted a hard line, militarily enforced, and Eisenhower, who didn't want to risk much in secondary geopolitical areas. The Southern Democrats tended to side with Nixon and Dulles and the Northern and liberal Democrats with Eisenhower, but Nixon and Dulles were careful never to be publicly offside with the president.

At the weekly White House meeting with the congressional leadership at the end of April, House majority leader Charles Halleck of Indiana said that Nixon's comments about Vietnam had been very damaging. Nixon responded at once that the United States must never show "weakness" to the Russians, nor give them any indication of the limits of actions the U.S. might contemplate.[19] At the National Security Council meeting on April 29, Harold Stassen, in his uniquely impetuous manner, asked for an immediate infusion of U.S. ground forces into Vietnam. Eisenhower said that he could not envision the circumstances that would justify such an action, nor conditions in which the public would support such an expedition, nor conditions in which such an expedition "would not in the long run put our defense too far out of balance." Nixon stated that he thought there was no need for ground troops, that air attacks would be adequate.[20]

Eisenhower and Nixon and NSC specialist Robert Cutler met the next day, and Nixon made it clear that he was not talking about atomic bombs, just the retention of that threat, and that he was not advocating a ground-forces action. Still, Eisenhower would not agree, and declined to do anything, and Dien Bien Phu fell on May 7. The Geneva Conference ended on July 21, with a French withdrawal from all of Indochina, North and South Vietnam divided, and Ho Chi Minh and his Vietminh in charge of the North. Dulles conspicuously refused to shake hands with Chou En-lai, and the United States did not sign the accords, though it did not suggest it would obstruct the settlement, which included the promise of elections on whether to unite the two halves of Vietnam within two years. Dulles was in his bath in Geneva when an aide rushed in to say that the Chinese were prepared to release remaining U.S. prisoners from Korea and normalize relations. Without stirring from the bath, Dulles refused.[21] It is not clear that the United States accomplished much with this long quarantine of China, which Nixon would end.

In France, the Laniel government had fallen and Mendes-France concluded the agreements for France. On the fall of Dien Bien Phu, General de Gaulle announced that he was holding a service of solidarity for the French Army at the Arc de Triomphe. He did not consult anyone about this, but announced it at a press conference, where André Maurois "looked out the window to see if psychiatric orderlies were approaching to detain" de Gaulle. When he arrived at the ceremony he had convoked on his own (informal, or moral) authority, de Gaulle said, "The people are not here." He knew that the Fourth Republic had not yet forfeited the support of the population, but he correctly believed that it could not long retain it, with endless revolving-door governments and a sequence of military humiliations.

It is easy from the comfortable deck chair of hindsight to disparage Nixon's proposals. In fact, he was probably correct about the desirability of helping France disengage gracefully from Indochina, if not (and this is not clear) about Korea. Declining to lift a finger to assist France, when it had pledged to end its colonial occupation, was a shabby treatment of an ally, and it was repaid to the United States manyfold when de Gaulle returned to power in four years, founded the Fifth Republic, and restored France as a power in the world. If the United States had made an aerial intervention and a French-led division had not been compelled to surrender in one of the worst military humiliations in French history, except for 1940 and 1870, France could have negotiated a harder line and it might have been able to organize a combined ground effort, with the United States focused mainly on air interdiction. This would have been infinitely preferable to the debacle that ultimately did occur in Indochina. Eisenhower may have been correct that Indochina was not worth a serious military effort, but conserving the French alliance was worth a few air raids.

Nixon had stuck to his position even when Knowland and the entire congressional delegation – who talked a good game in their clubs and lounges, bourbon in hand – had scurried out the back door into the tall grass after a fleeting glance at the polls. (McCarthy, for all his incandescent

anti-communism, never declared himself on this issue.) Nixon's only supporters were non-elected military and Defense and State Department officials. Nixon always wanted for Vietnam a variation of what the British had
achieved in Malaya (where they and their native allies won against the communist insurgents). He was never for substituting American for local ground
forces, and was always in favor of recourse to massive air power and a full
naval blockade. If Indochina was worth a fight, Nixon had the correct
notion of how to do it, including retention of the notional nuclear threat,
implausible though it became; it had, after all, worked in Korea just a year
before Dien Bien Phu. Eisenhower seems to have been slightly impressed
by Nixon's firmness of purpose, rather than resentful of his independence.
Eisenhower felt, with good reason, that no one advising him knew as much
as he did about what was required in leading a coalition to victory over a
determined enemy in an overseas war.

And once Eisenhower had made his decision, he had no way of ensuring
that subsequent presidents would not reverse it, in hugely more dis-
advantageous conditions. In sum, Eisenhower may have been right about
Vietnam, but he was wrong about France. Nixon may or may not have
been right about Vietnam, but he was certainly right about France. The
presidents who served between them, John F. Kennedy and especially
Lyndon B. Johnson, got every part of the problem tragically wrong.

On April 5, the faculty of Duke University, with 80 percent of the faculty
not voting, narrowly rejected the conferral on Nixon of an honorary
degree. He did receive one from his other alma mater, Whittier College,
though there was a substantial number of graduates who did not wish to
shake hands with him.

— v —

The famous and climactic Army-McCarthy hearings opened before a
nationwide television audience on April 22, 1954. The entire sequence of
contemptible, demagogic, pseudo-patriotic posturing that had animated the
House Un-American Activities Committee, much of the antics of J. Edgar
Hoover and the FBI, and pelagic immensities of political oratory since the
Grand Alliance with the Soviet Union came to an end in 1946, reached its
tawdry apotheosis in these hearings. Nixon leaked to selected senators a

summary of the threats and attempted intimidations launched by McCarthy and his understudy, Roy Cohn, against the army. He and Eisenhower began intensively lobbying Republican senators that McCarthy was a menace to their party and to the country.

Army Secretary Stevens claimed that McCarthy had improperly tried to secure a preferment for one of his protégés, Private G. David Schine, and McCarthy countercharged that the army had tried to dissuade him from pursuing his search for communists in its ranks. McCarthy was not in charge of proceedings as he had been accustomed to being, and the army witnesses were strong, well-represented by counsel, and respectfully received by the other senators. Given the needle constantly, McCarthy, like a blooded fighting bull, writhing and charging from the provocations of the picadors, raged against fellow senators, calling the respected W. Stuart Symington of Missouri, a former secretary of the air force, "sanctimonious Stu," and constantly, tediously intervening with "Point of order."

He upbraided and antagonized everyone and finally threw down the mask and referred to "twenty-one years of treason." Roosevelt, Truman, Eisenhower, a perfect continuum of traitors at the head of the nation through six straight elections; he apologized for having supported Eisenhower in the 1952 election. (He need not have done this; his support was very lukewarm.) This was more than all but a small percentage of Americans could endure. The senator self-destructed, and as the process began, there was no shortage of people to help him on his way.

Eisenhower and Nixon continued to buttonhole senators and congressmen and tell them that McCarthy was mad and a mortal threat to the political credibility of the country and to civil political discourse in America. McCarthy, as circumstances turned against him, instead of cutting his losses and pulling back, throttled right out and purported to subpoena the White House chief of staff, Sherman Adams. This publicly smoked out Eisenhower. He informed the Republican leadership on May 17 that he would not tolerate any executive branch employee being subpoenaed about advice he gave the president, that any who so testified would be dismissed by him the same day, and that the White House would accept and honor no such subpoenas. He took the same position that Truman had opposite HUAC.

This posed a slight problem for Nixon and even Knowland, because of the positions they had taken opposite Truman's administration. Eisenhower was now unconcerned with their discomfort and publicly stated on May 18, "It is not in the public interest that any of [administration members'] conversations or communications, or any documents or reproductions concerning such advice [to the president] be disclosed." This was the strongest version of executive privilege ever formulated in the United States, and the Congress, although McCarthy fumed and ranted, was not inclined to challenge it.

Denied any star witnesses, McCarthy ran out of ammunition. The army counsel, Joseph Welch, became a folk figure by his avuncular but mordant repulses of McCarthy: "Have you no decency, sir?" "I like to think I'm a gentle man," etc. Welch was so effective, he was engaged to play the judge in the award-winning film *Anatomy of a Murder*, in which the contending counsel, each in one of his more memorable performances, were the eminent actors James Stewart and George C. Scott. The country tired of McCarthy's wild accusations and endless "Point[s] of order," which were merely harassments. The subcommittee exonerated McCarthy on the charge of improper influence but did not substantiate any of his charges against the army.

The hearings ended June 17, but McCarthy could not let it rest there. He continued to flail and rave against perceived traitors, and after a holiday announced that he would be holding one-man hearings in Boston. He continued to try to bully subcommittee members, especially Symington. He did not realize for a time how severely his political position had eroded. Polls now showed his approval rating at 34 percent, with a 45 percent disapproval rating and an overwhelming antagonism from more educated people. He still had his friends, but he was bent on a course of self-destructive brinkmanship.

Senator Ralph Flanders, long-standing McCarthy critic, moved a motion of censure. (McCarthy had said that a man should be found "with a net, to take [Flanders] to a nice quiet place." Many senators agreed with McCarthy on that.) Censure motions had succeeded only a few times in the history of the Senate: against Timothy Pickering in 1810 for releasing secret treaty information, two South Carolina senators in 1902 for having a strenuous fistfight on the Senate floor, and Hiram Bingham of Connecticut in 1929 for placing a lobbyist on his staff to help write legislation of financial interest to the lobbyist. Generally, the Senate tried to avoid a rupture with any member. Senator Henry Foote of Mississippi was not censured in 1852 for aiming a loaded pistol at the head of another senator. Lyndon Johnson, Richard Nixon, and William Knowland selected the composition of the committee that would determine whether to censure McCarthy. With Taft dead, Knowland was now an Eisenhower loyalist, and Eisenhower generally acted with the Congress through Nixon. The Republican members would be Arthur Watkins (Utah), Frank Carlson (Kansas), and Francis Case (South Dakota); and the Democrats would be Edwin Johnson (Colorado), John Stennis (Mississippi), and Sam Ervin (North Carolina). Watkins became chairman. McCarthy hired the prominent, soon the legendary, lawyer Edward Bennett Williams as his counsel. Flanders had dished up forty-six charges against McCarthy, who promised Williams that he would behave with exemplary senatorial dignity.

The committee sat from August 31 to September 13, and Flanders had assembled a meticulous record of every slight McCarthy had uttered in the Senate, and there had been many of them. This was droned through at excruciating length, the committee counsel, Wallace Chadwick, growing hoarse and inaudible from the process. Watkins had banned the cameras and klieg lights. McCarthy responded with a dignified statement written for him by Brent Bozell, who with his brother-in-law, William F. Buckley, had written a rather favorable biography of McCarthy.* According to this version, McCarthy's offense had been to call attention to a national danger, even though it was bound to create social disunity. Williams was unsuccessful with an ingenious series of procedural arguments, and the committee did not demonstrate much more respect for due process than McCarthy had when he had been conducting the hearings a few months before, in the same Senate Caucus Room.[22]

This committee had looked at all forty-six charges against McCarthy and produced a forty-thousand-word report in one week. The committee finally recommended censure on two counts only – failing to cooperate with the committee on Privileges and Elections, which had been looking into his personal life and finances, and abuse of the Select Committee to Study Censure. The committee thought he had been "intemperate" to Brigadier General Zwicker when he had appeared as a witness before McCarthy's subcommittee. In fact, the Privileges and Elections Committee

---

* Writer Dwight Macdonald described the book as like "a Covington and Burling defense of a pick-pocket." (Covington and Burling is a prominent Washington law firm where Dean Acheson worked in the twenties.) Macdonald was an ex-communist of whom Leon Trotsky had once said, "Everyone has a right to be stupid, but Comrade Macdonald abuses that right." Trotsky also called him "a petty bourgeois philistine."

had been excessively obtrusive, and Zwicker had himself been a rather obstreperous witness, but the Senate establishment, led by Johnson, Knowland, and Nixon, had determined that McCarthy was a menace, a justifiable conclusion, but rather shabbily arrived at.

The issue was not put to the Senate for a vote until the midterm elections were out of the way. In these, falling farm prices and rising unemployment were expected by the Democrats to restore them to control of the Congress. Nixon masterminded the Republican campaign, which was to ignore the horribly divisive issue of McCarthy himself but continue to take credit for rooting out security risks "by the thousands,"[23] which had accumulated under the Democrats.

Nixon tried to encourage the cabinet, whom he regularly advised on political matters at Eisenhower's request, since none of them knew much about politics (except to a slight degree Lodge and Stassen), to think positively about the off-year elections. He said that there need not be a big setback. Eisenhower's problem was that as his stance was not excessively belligerent abroad nor sufficiently reactionary at home to suit the Republican congressional leadership; he was getting more support from the Democrats than from his own party. He wanted Nixon to conduct the fight for the Republicans, but not to attack his Democratic policy allies. Eisenhower, having failed to be drafted to the presidency, was now acting as if he had been; he was the nonpartisan general above the battle. This made Nixon's role as partisan party leader very difficult.

Nixon gave an address in Milwaukee on June 26 in which he blamed Acheson for the "loss" of China, which had caused the wars in Korea and Indochina. Eisenhower composed a letter to Nixon. "I am constantly working to produce a bipartisan approach, and I rather think that keeping up attacks on Acheson will, at this late date, hamper our efforts."[24] The president decided not to send the letter and asked Nixon to come to see him instead. Nixon said that he did not attack the Democrats, only Acheson. Eisenhower was not buying that sophistry and said that the "loss" of China had occurred when Marshall had pushed Chiang into taking some communists into his government when Marshall had been Truman's special envoy in China. This was an astonishing allegation, which may go some way to explaining Eisenhower's failure to defend Marshall against McCarthy, as this was one of McCarthy's allegations. In fact, neither the inclusion of some communists in the Chinese government nor the two-week cease-fire Marshall urged upon Chiang brought Chiang down (though both were mistakes). The corruption and incompetence of the Chiang Kai-shek Kuomintang government did.

Eisenhower inveighed against McCarthy's "twenty years of treason" charges against Roosevelt and Truman, which the president said were "indefensible," and said that Nixon must not seem to be saying anything similar. Nixon resisted the temptation to point out that McCarthy was now at "twenty-one years of treason" (i.e., including Eisenhower and Nixon) and said that he, Nixon, had never said anything remotely similar to any of that. (Nixon almost always avoided mentioning Roosevelt and danced around treason with Truman.) Eisenhower was concerned that Nixon was becoming confused in the public mind with McCarthy. This too was a bit of a liberty, given what Nixon had done to put McCarthy over the side while Eisenhower snuffled in private. But there was something to Eisenhower's concern for Nixon's public relations: that summer Pat canceled the home delivery of the *Washington Post* because of the frequent caricatures of her husband as a sewer rat by the paper's editorial cartoonist, Herblock.

The Nixon-Eisenhower relationship, which had moved fairly steadily upward from the fund crisis through Nixon's March 13, 1954 national television address, took another nosedive. Nixon felt that his leader had waffled badly with France and Vietnam, had sent the vice president out to do the political dirty work while he himself cavorted with the Democrats, and that he had no interest in strengthening the Republican Party, since he thought he could rely on his own prestige for an adequate level of support. Nixon warned Eisenhower that the Democratic nonpartisanship was a ruse, that they were trying to neutralize him, that there would be no more nonpartisanship in the next presidential election than in the last, and that once the Democrats were in control of the Congress, the Republicans would not accomplish anything legislatively.

The fact was that Eisenhower was not a very activist president, and it did not much matter to him whether he dealt with Republican or Democratic leaders in the Congress. Despite his antagonism to Roosevelt and Truman (both of whom had decisively advanced his career), Eisenhower was happy with the Roosevelt worshippers and Truman cronies who led the Democratic congressional party, Sam Rayburn and Lyndon Johnson. It must be said for Eisenhower that with Taft dead, the congressional Republican leadership was not at all of competitive quality to the Democrats. Rayburn and Johnson were towering parliamentary figures, where Knowland was a blustering mediocrity, lacking courage and judgment, and Joe Martin and Charlie Halleck were pedestrian journeymen. Eisenhower regarded Knowland (his vice presidential nominee in waiting during Nixon's fund crisis) as a dunce. Dirksen was colorful and promising, but abrasive and relatively untried.

Nixon was quiet for the summer, during which a personal highlight for him was the visit to Washington of Prime Minister Winston Churchill, starting on June 25, 1954. Nixon had been dismayed, as a longtime Churchill admirer, when Admiral Radford had visited him two months before to recruit British solidarity against the Vietnamese communists, and Churchill had declined, saying the war could only be won by using the atomic bomb, which he called "that horrible thing."[25] The prime minister had said that if Britain had not been willing to fight for its position in India (to which Attlee had granted independence in 1947), it would not be likely to fight for Indochina. He acknowledged that if Vietnam fell to the communists, Cambodia and Laos probably would too, but doubted that this would lead to the fall of other countries to the communists in Southeast Asia or Australasia. This was odd reasoning, as retaining a colonial empire that was clearly untenable and ready for independence was hardly comparable to joining the United States and France in resisting communist insurgency supported from Russia and China, as Britain was successfully doing alone in Malaya.[26]

In accord with protocol, Nixon and Dulles met Churchill at the airport; the president of the United States only greets arriving chiefs of state and those very rarely. Nixon and Churchill rode together in an open car into Washington, and Nixon engaged the illustrious leader in conversation.[27] Churchill claimed to have read many of Nixon's comments with approval, and they discussed Churchill's memoirs, rolling out in large volumes (for which he received the Nobel Prize for Literature). Churchill gave Nixon his well-prepared theory that Roosevelt was virtually non compos mentis for the last four months of his life, starting a month after the 1944 election, and that Truman had been kept in the dark.

This was, in fact, untrue. Roosevelt's physical powers were declining, but he was at least as alert as Churchill at Yalta, and at least as vigorous in defending Western interests, and for a few weeks less enthusiastic than Churchill in laudations of the Yalta agreements.[28] However, Churchill survived Roosevelt and was writing what for a long time passed as an author-itative history of the period. As has been mentioned, Truman and Eisenhower, when their turn as memoirists came, did not challenge the Churchill version and steered delicately around Roosevelt and each other. Marshall, who declined to write any memoirs, and unlike the others did not seek elective office, gave his official biographer, Forrest C. Pogue, a more exact account of what had happened.

Nixon asked Churchill what he thought would have been the result if his proposal had been followed and the Western Allies had attacked at Trieste and toward Austria in 1944 rather than across the English Channel and into France. Churchill responded that it would have been "handy to have Vienna." Nixon resisted the temptation to point out that it was handy to have Paris and the rest of France too, and that the West would not have had them for an indefinite period, if ever, but for the insistence of Roosevelt, Marshall, and Eisenhower on the cross-Channel landings in France.

There was a small dinner at the White House that evening, and after General Marshall had proposed a toast to Queen Elizabeth, and Churchill had proposed a toast to the president, Eisenhower, making amends for much unpleasantness, proposed a moving and comprehensive toast to Marshall. Marshall, usually the most impassive of men, was visibly affected by the compliment of his protégé, now the leader of his country.[29] Pat sat with Churchill during dinner and asked if he would prefer whisky to wine. She was slightly taken aback when he said that he had whisky at eight-thirty in the morning, sometimes in the afternoon, but enjoyed wine with dinner before moving to champagne and brandy afterward. Eisenhower asked Nixon to join him and Churchill after dinner, and they talked again about Churchill's memoirs, but skirting any controversy. (Churchill preferred to "dictate to a pretty girl than to a machine," and was able to find someone fitting that description to take his dictation between midnight and 3 A.M.)

Two nights later, there was a stag dinner at the British embassy, where Nixon represented Eisenhower and sat with Churchill, who told him, "I always seem to get inspiration and renewed vitality by contact with this great novel land of yours which sticks up out of the Atlantic." Nixon questioned him about the Civil War, which Churchill had studied, and Churchill elaborated on his great admiration for Lee and Grant. Of Grant's magnanimity at Appomattox, he said, "In the squalor of life and war, what a magnificent act."[30]

Nixon finally edged into the issue of containment of the communists, and Churchill defended his record of anti-communism, going back nearly forty years to the Bolshevik Revolution, and denied that he was advocating a "go-slow" policy. It was a policy of "patience and vigilance . . . and strength." In a Washington still seething with the McCarthy controversies, about which Winston Churchill expressed astonishment (though he said that Labour Party firebrand Aneurin Bevan was almost as much trouble to him), patience was in short supply. Nixon and Dulles conducted Churchill to the airport the next day. Nixon wrote, "I was honored to have met one of the world's greatest leaders, but I was saddened by the realization that he would soon be passing from the scene."[31] Nixon offered no opinion on Foreign Secretary Anthony Eden, who had accompanied Churchill and would take his place a year later.

— VI —

In the following autumn congressional election campaign, in what Stevenson called "ill-will visits," Nixon went to ninety-five cities in thirty states, and managed fairly well with McCarthyism without McCarthy – what Stevenson wryly described as "McCarthywasm." Nixon attacked on the theme that the Republicans had discovered Democratic plans to "social-ize" America, at a cost of forty billion dollars. He tried the communist issue in a few places, claiming discovery of a Communist Party memorandum urging support of the Democrats. The number of security risks turfed out of government service, which he had given as about 2,400 in his March 13 speech, skyrocketed to 6,926 by the time he got to Rock Island, Illinois, on October 21.

Eisenhower sent Nixon a note in his convoluted style, usually reserved for the press, on September 29: "Please don't think that I am not unaware that I have done little to lighten your load."[32] Eisenhower remained on holiday in Colorado until mid-October, and then did take to the road, helping moderate Republican candidates in the East. He finally realized that Nixon was correct, that if the moderate Republicans weren't assisted, the Democrats would again be the only electable party, as they had been in Roosevelt's time. It was to deliver the Republicans and the nation from this fate that Eisenhower had been lured into politics in the first place.

Stevenson claimed that the Republicans were as "confused as a blind dog in a meat-house," and had caused economic stagnation, which enabled the Soviet Union to enjoy a higher economic growth rate than the United States. This was nonsense, but Nixon typically went a little over the top in Beverly Hills on October 28, when he accused Stevenson "probably without being aware that he was doing so, of spreading pro-communist propaganda as he has attacked with violent fury the economic system of the United States . . . He is performing a grave disservice to us and the rest of the civilized world." This was the Nixon who was his own worst enemy. Adlai Stevenson was not violent or furious; his positions were often wishy-washy, but he was a civilized, entertaining, and altogether admirable man. Nixon's heavy beard and perspiration, ski-jump nose, and absurdly robust partisanship made him seem sinister, unserious, and immoderate. On October 29 in San Mateo, California, when a heckler shouted, "Tell us a dog story, Dick," Nixon ignored it until the end of the speech and then said this was the only time he had been heckled in two hundred speeches he had given in this campaign, and then told his security unit to eject the heckler, though his speech was over. It was an inelegant performance.[33]

On election eve, Eisenhower and Nixon shared a national telecast. Eisenhower was unexceptionable, but Nixon described a comment of Stevenson's objecting to Eisenhower's statement that the Republicans would bring prosperity through peace, while the Democrats had only managed to do so through war, as "one of the most vicious, scurrilous attacks ever made by a major political figure on a president of the United States." He seemed not to remember many of the comments he had made about Truman. He accused Stevenson of using the Hitler method of "the Big Lie," and said again it was the Democratic objective to "socialize" America and "return to the Acheson foreign policy," as if this were something reprehensible and not the policy of one of the founders of NATO and authors of the Marshall Plan. The contrast between the civilized, measured, if not rivetingly eloquent president and general and the strident, ham-fisted vice president was unflattering to Nixon.

The Republicans lost seventeen House seats and two Senate seats, and Rayburn and Johnson took over the Congress, which they would rule with great dexterity for the rest of the decade. On election day, Nixon flew back to Washington in a depressed mood with Murray Chotiner and claimed to be contemplating retirement from politics at the end of the term.[34] He found the result doubly annoying, because he received little public credit for his efforts on behalf of the Republicans while Eisenhower was cited as the main reason the Republicans avoided an electoral debacle. He had, however, once again incurred the gratitude of a great many rank-and-file Republican candidates and organizers.

Democrats did make less than the usual gains in midterm elections, and smaller gains than had been expected. However, it was the end of the Red Scare as an irrational goad to the voters. In fairness to Nixon, he had been tasked with trying to hang onto the security risk issue while getting the Republicans clear of McCarthy. He had managed a difficult brief well enough, but his preposterous charges against Acheson and Stevenson rankled with many, and his shopworn formula of disclaiming any imputation of bad motive before charging them with heinous shortcomings was wearing very thin. Henceforth, the Cold War would be conducted by the United States in a comparatively rational and civilized way. It was no longer necessary to frighten the living Jehovah out of the whole population to ensure a national consensus for a policy of sane resistance to international communism.

At the first cabinet meeting following the election, Eisenhower asked Nixon to explain the political angles and said that he would be relying on him to help the administration deal with a Democratic Congress. Nixon had snapped out of his election day gloom and said that the swing was so small that it was effectively a draw, and so much less than the ordinary off-year swing that he considered it a moral victory. For this, he gave the credit to "the program and the campaign at the top," by which he meant, without being specific about allocation, Eisenhower and himself. This was doubt-less true. He disparaged Republican candidates and organization. The latter factor must have displeased his ally Summerfield, party chairman and post-master general. "There were just too many turkeys running on the Republican ticket," he said.[35]

He was buoyed by the fact that west of the Mississippi, the Republicans had gained one Senate seat and broken even in the House. He pointed out, which no one else in the cabinet room would have noticed, that with a movement of only a single vote for each precinct in Oregon, Montana, and Wyoming, the Republicans would have a margin of five Senate seats. He said that the Republicans were on their way to building a lock on the West to counter the "Solid South" of the Democrats, and that the West was a much richer and faster-growing region. He concluded his presentation by taking a little toy-soldier drummer out of his pocket and releasing it on the cabinet table. As it marched down the table banging its little drum, he said,

"This is not the time to be depressed, and we have to keep beating the drum about our achievements."[36] Whatever his partisan excesses, Nixon was the indispensable politician in the administration, and the only person who, in party terms, knew what he was doing. Eisenhower was untarnishably popular and respected, but he recognized Nixon's competence, even if aspects of Nixon's personality grated on him.

The Senate moved to consider the censure recommendation on McCarthy on November 8, well before the newly elected senators were sworn. McCarthy might still have made conciliatory or even slightly apologetic remarks. He was only two years into his term and could have reconstructed a role for himself and taken good care of his constituents. Lyndon Johnson worked to ensure that the Democrats remained firm behind the leadership; he was acting for Truman and Stevenson, as well as himself, in this matter. He was concerned at the possible defection of some Dixiecrats or Northern Catholics. His eventual successor as Democratic Senate leader, Mike Mansfield of Montana, a Roman Catholic, was worried at the scattering of nuns in the Senate gallery.[37] McCarthy's friends, Everett Dirksen, Karl Mundt, and Styles Bridges, tried to build some links with Democrats, but the likeliest Democratic ally, Pat McCarran, who had taken over the Mundt-Nixon bill, had died just before the election.

These efforts at heading off the Lyndon Johnson juggernaut died when McCarthy announced that the Watkins Committee was a "handmaiden of the Communist Party." Watkins himself, a frail and ulcerous Mormon from Utah who spoke little in the Senate, at great physical discomfort, held the chamber spellbound with a ninety-minute harangue on the lengthy catalogue of McCarthy's many gratuitous incivilities to his fellow senators.

McCarthy engineered a delay while he marshaled his forces; he went to Bethesda Naval Hospital for treatment of bursitis. This was greeted with skepticism by the Senate, but they would not vote on the censure of a colleague without giving him a chance for reply. Senator Barry Goldwater and Edward Bennett Williams visited him and asked McCarthy to sign letters of mild apology to Watkins and Senator Robert C. Hendrickson of New Jersey (whom McCarthy, in one of his more extreme sallies, had accused of having "no brains and no guts"). McCarthy refused so vociferously that the duty nurse appeared, who called the doctor, who summoned the admiral in command of the hospital, who threatened to summon the shore patrol. Dirksen tried in the same cause, bringing a bottle of whiskey with him, which he and McCarthy went through in quick time. But McCarthy again refused.[38]

While McCarthy was in Bethesda, there were rallies for him in Washington, and one of thirteen thousand people in Madison Square Garden. But a newly elected Senate had seen the erosion of the issue. McCarthy would not retreat, and his opponents would not relent. As judgment day approached, some senators were braver than others. Alexander Wiley of Wisconsin (Foreign Relations Committee chairman) was so desperate to duck the issue that he prevailed upon Dulles to send him to represent the United States in an obscure ceremony in Rio de Janeiro. John F. Kennedy of Massachusetts, who had exploded at a Harvard Club dinner when someone compared Hiss to McCarthy ("a traitor and a patriot," he said), was convalescing from surgery on his back, injured in navy wartime service. He did not pair or register his vote with the secretary of the Senate, as he could have done, but simply ducked the issue. His brother Robert had just left McCarthy's staff and the senator was still a family friend. His conflict was understandable.

The Senate voted 67 to 22 to censure McCarthy on December 2. The Republicans divided evenly, 22 to 22. All Democrats who voted yielded to Lyndon Johnson's intense pressure for censure. Nixon, not wanting to aggravate Republican differences further, took little overt part; McCarthy would not help himself, and so could not be helped. On December 3, Eisenhower publicly invited Senator Arthur Watkins to the White House to congratulate him. In the last headline he would receive before his funeral, McCarthy apologized to the American people for having recommended support of Eisenhower in the 1952 election. What a spiral there had been between them in just over two years since Eisenhower had failed to defend Marshall in Wisconsin. This blast was too much for even his diehard respectable supporters. Knowland, Goldwater, Mundt, and General James Van Fleet, former Korean commander and organizer of a pro-McCarthy petition, all publicly renounced him.

Thereafter, McCarthy descended into suicidal alcoholism and was shunned by virtually everyone. He died on May 2, 1957, aged forty-eight. Even Dean Acheson and Joseph Welch spoke graciously of him. President Truman publicly expressed "sorrow," but privately, famously, said, "He was a son-of-a-bitch and now he's a dead son-of-a-bitch." There was a service at Capitol Hill attended by Richard Nixon (whom McCarthy particularly

blamed for his downfall) and J. Edgar Hoover, and seventy senators. He was
returned to Appleton, Wisconsin, via Green Bay, for burial, and large
crowds lined the route, more curious than mournful, but respectful. The
thoughtful liberal commentator Eric Sevareid said that "Senator McCarthy
had a certain manic brilliance. . . . But the brilliance outran his knowledge,
and his ambition outran them both."[39]

Nixon had, more than anyone, pulled the rug out from under him,
after McCarthy made it clear that he could not be relied upon in any
agreement with the administration and set out to tear the U.S. Army apart.
Nixon helped generate the censure motion that the Republican leadership otherwise could have avoided. A censure in a very close, partisan
vote would not have carried much moral weight anyway. In his memoirs,
Nixon wrote that McCarthy was "personally likable, if irresponsibly
impulsive . . . [but] sincere."[40] Nixon looked upon him, as he looked upon
almost everyone, impersonally, and recognized when McCarthy had
become irreconcilable to any useful end. Nixon repaid McCarthy's
support of him during the fund crisis for as long as he could, but he knew
when the party and national interest required him to act, which he did
with the silent effectiveness of a professional. It was, following his seminal
role in rescuing the Republicans from the isolationist right and helping
vitally to deliver the presidential nomination to Eisenhower, the greatest
feat he had yet performed for his party and country. Joseph R. McCarthy
had been a bright but dreadful meteor who streaked across the American
political sky for only a few years.

— VII —

In July 1954, Eisenhower, who was quite conscientious about finding roles
for Nixon that would help him shed his bad-boy image and play the statesman, sent him to a governors' conference to announce the administration's
plans for an interstate highway system. This was a magnificently grand
scheme that was instantly popular with the states, the public, and industry.
It was proposed that federal funding for roads of all kinds, and especially
highways linking cities and states, be increased from an annual seven
hundred million to nearly six billion dollars, and maintained at that level
for ten years. This was as grandiose as many of Roosevelt's public-works

projects, such as the Tennessee Valley Authority, and encountered no opposition. The private sector could not build such roads and no one could dispute their utility. The U.S. automobile industry had reached the astounding level of selling nearly eight million cars per year, and backed into almost every phase of primary industry and manufacturing.

The impasse in Congress once Rayburn and Johnson were in control was exactly what Nixon had warned Eisenhower would happen. In 1955, notwithstanding the popularity and grandeur of the highway program, the Democrats killed it because they wanted to finance it on the back of the trucking industry, while the Republicans proposed to do so through increased sales taxes on gasoline and automobile tires.

The administration also proposed a billion dollars a year in aid to the states for school construction, but the Democrats obstructed this too. The Southern Democrats were outraged at bipartisan liberal support for excluding states that maintained racial segregation in schools, and the liberal Democrats wanted assistance to teachers' salaries, which the administration considered a state and local matter. This plan did not move in 1955 either, but with schools, as with highways, the Republicans, under Nixon's guidance, had struck the right note with the voters. Eisenhower assisted in this when Hagerty took to releasing film of the president's press conferences, excluding only small parts where his phrasing became too confused. These were telecast the same day and drew large and favorable audiences.

Nixon spent most of February 1955 on his second state visit, to Mexico, Central America, and the Caribbean. He had again prepared carefully. As in his trip to the Far East, Nixon had legitimate diplomatic objectives: to reassure the Cubans about sugar exports to the United States; to pledge assistance to the new government in Guatemala, which the United States had helped to install the year before, replacing a communist-leaning one; and to urge a de-escalation of tensions between the military regimes in Costa Rica and Nicaragua.

He handled these tasks very competently, and at Eisenhower's request reported to the cabinet on his return. He urged greater attention to the region, and said he was impressed by presidents Batista in Cuba, Cortines in Mexico, and Castillo Armas in Guatemala (who had recently replaced President Jacobo Arbenz, thanks to U.S. intervention disguised as a local uprising).[*] [41] His description of Batista as an honest and socially progressive leader and a "voracious" reader is not one that most Cubans would recognize. His concern that the palace of the president of Mexico was more opulent than the White House, although people less than a tenth of a mile away from it "lived in caves," was perceptive. His belief that the United Fruit Company would see to the rising prosperity of Honduras was inexplicably foolish for such a well-qualified observer (that company had led the opposition to the former regime in Guatemala). But his reservations about Rafael Trujillo in the Dominican Republic, and about the desperate poverty of Haiti, were sensible, if not startling feats of observation. He did advocate the gradual incentivization of more democracy in the region, and successfully advocate assistance for the Inter-American Highway. While his trip was a modest success, it did not generate much publicity for him.

There was rising curiosity in 1955 about whether Eisenhower would run again for president the following year, and Nixon was concerned to ensure that he was the second most prominent Republican. Dewey had retired after three terms as governor of New York (and was succeeded by Democrat Averell Harriman in a very close election). Earl Warren had landed solidly on his feet with Eisenhower's successful nomination of him as chief justice of the United States in October 1953. Taft had died, and Knowland and Stassen had no leadership credibility whatever.

The only plausible rival to Nixon was Nelson Rockefeller, Roosevelt's assistant secretary of state for Latin America. Rockefeller became Eisenhower's special assistant in June 1955, and immediately began to generate publicity as he worked on preparations for the first summit conference of leaders of the Great Powers (which were deemed to include Britain and France, as well as the United States and the U.S.S.R.). Walter Trohan, a veteran Washington reporter for the *Chicago Tribune*, warned Nixon's assistant Bob Finch, shortly after Rockefeller's arrival in the White House, that the president's new assistant was ambitious and determined.[42] Nelson

---

[*] This was a morally questionable but successful CIA operation, in which 440 CIA-trained guerrillas, supported by two P-51 fighter-bombers borrowed from Nicaragua's Somoza, panicked the Guatemalan leftist president, Jacobo Arbenz Guzman, into fleeing. Eisenhower concluded Guatemala had become an "outpost of communist dictatorship" when Arbenz bought a small quantity of arms from Czechoslovakia. One of the leaders of the farcical but successful CIA operation was future Nixon election supporter Howard Hunt, already an admirer of the vice president.

Rockefeller was an energetic, photogenic, affable man, who smiled easily and had all the gregariousness and felicity of manner that Nixon lacked, as well as splendid connections and practically unlimited financial resources. Their rivalry as the two leading figures of the Republican Party would extend for more than twenty years, between the retirement of Dwight D. Eisenhower and the elevation of Ronald Reagan.

For the first half of 1955, there had been almost constant tension between the United States and Communist China over Formosa (Taiwan) and the tiny islands of Quemoy and Matsu, which were within artillery shelling range of the Chinese mainland (only four miles at one point). Chou En-lai was regularly threatening to invade Formosa, and Chiang Kai-shek announced virtually every day through this time that war was imminent. Eisenhower considered Quemoy and Matsu to be strategically nonsensical, but was determined to defend Formosa. He felt that if there was to be any viable containment strategy, it had to prevent the Communist Chinese from overwhelming Chiang on the island to which he had fled with the remnants of his army, which the United States had now armed to the teeth. U.S. intelligence kept searching for indications of a Red Chinese buildup for an invasion, and not finding it. Eisenhower decided that "it is time to draw the line," and he did so with the authority of a supreme military commander. On January 24 he had asked the Congress for a resolution that would "clearly and publicly establish the authority of the President as Commander in Chief to employ the armed forces of this nation promptly and effectively for the purposes indicated," which were defined as the defense of Formosa, the Pescadores, and unspecified "closely related localities."

The president was a master of deliberate vagueness and he was explicitly asking for a blank check. This was a more consultative procedure than Roosevelt or Truman had been in the habit of using, and Rayburn and Martin rammed the resolution through the House of Representatives in one hour by a vote of 410 to 3. In the Senate, hearings were demanded, at which General Matthew Ridgway, one of Eisenhower's divisional commanders ten years before, and now army chief of staff, criticized Eisenhower's "New Look" defense strategy, which gave the United States overwhelming nuclear superiority but pared back manpower expenses, reducing the budget deficit and enabling increased domestic spending. (The administration had extended social security benefits, along with unemployment compensation levels and coverages, and had raised the minimum wage by 33 percent; so much for Ike's conscientious dissent from the spirit of the New Deal.) Eisenhower was tempted to sack Ridgway as army chief of staff, but Dulles dissuaded him. The president's military authority and credibility vastly exceeded Ridgway's (or any of the generals' except MacArthur and Marshall, who remained publicly silent and were privately supportive of their former staff member), and on January 28 the Senate passed the so-called Formosa Resolution 83 to 3.

This created the Formosa Doctrine, which essentially declared the inviolability of Formosa and its immediate approaches and gave the president authority to defend Formosa in a wide perimeter, and to do so by any means he chose. It was well known that this included nuclear weapons, which the chairman of the Joint Chiefs of Staff, Admiral Radford, on the heels of his unsuccessful championship of such escalation in Vietnam a year before, had advocated to the president on five separate occasions in the first six months of 1955, all atomic attacks on Red China. Eisenhower declined each time.

Dulles mounted a diplomatic effort, especially with the British, to round up support for taking a strong hand against Red China. Eisenhower wrote to Churchill with the candor of a close ally and an old friend that he was aware that Europeans "consider America reckless, impulsive, and immature" but that he was trying to cope with "the truculent and the timid, the jingoists and the pacifists." (There weren't many of the latter in the United States, unless he considered Adlai Stevenson in that category.) Churchill and Eden didn't see it that way. The British never wanted to provoke the Chinese, because of Hong Kong and Malaya, but Churchill told Dulles the U.S. Seventh Fleet could "drown" any Chinese trying to cross the Formosa Strait, and that the smaller islands weren't worth bothering about. They were for any temporizing and delaying that would cool things out. Britain had interests in the Far East, but it wasn't a Pacific Rim country, as the United States was, and had a very different perspective.

At his March 16, 1955, press conference, in response to a question of whether he would countenance the use of atomic weapons in a Far Eastern war, Eisenhower was more direct than usual: "Yes, of course they would be used."[43] Eisenhower's combination of saber-rattling, obfuscation, and restraining Chiang while promising him landing craft for an invasion of the mainland if conditions seemed propitious finally produced a solution in September. Chiang followed Eisenhower's urging to reduce his excessively large garrisons, totaling about eighty thousand troops, on the tiny islands (which Eisenhower considered to be militarily insane). Chou En-lai announced that his forces would shell convoys resupplying Quemoy and Matsu only on odd days of the month, which would permit unimpeded resupply on even days, and Eisenhower "wondered if we were in a Gilbert and Sullivan war."[44]

It was providential that the United States had at this point a president who had the self-confidence and personal knowledge and stature not to be manipulated by the military high command. Fifty years later, Quemoy and Matsu have assumed a Jenkins's Ear quality, but the danger was real, and Eisenhower handled it with great finesse and judgment. Nixon, after having been the hawk-in-residence over Vietnam, sat Quemoy and Matsu out; he stayed in lockstep with the president and said little about it publicly. The McCarthy crisis had passed and he was happy to conciliate the Democrats, who had loyally backed up the president with the whip-snapping efficiency that Rayburn and Johnson generally exercised over their legislators.

Eisenhower had said in November 1954 that he would be prepared to have a summit meeting with the Russians, as well as the British and the French, if the U.S.S.R. facilitated an Austrian peace treaty. The new Soviet leadership, Nikita Khrushchev as Communist Party secretary general (only the third holder of the post after Lenin and Stalin) and Premier Nikolai Bulganin, agreed to this in May 1955. Austria was evacuated by the occupying powers and recognized as a neutral state. Winston Churchill had retired in April (after fifteen years as Conservative leader, nearly ten of them as prime minister, and nearly thirty years in a variety of cabinet positions). Anthony Eden led the government to reelection in May. The Far East crisis was deemed to have eased somewhat by the late spring. The Austrian treaty was signed on May 13; the four national foreign ministers announced a summit conference on June 13 for Geneva, to begin on July 18.

Eisenhower, Dulles, and Nixon were not optimistic about the meeting. Eisenhower thought that the main problems, the divisions of Germany, Korea, China, and Vietnam, as well as the arms race, were insoluble in the short term, but felt it a duty to try. Marshal Zhukov had emerged as a political power as defense minister of the U.S.S.R., and Eisenhower had had quite a good relationship with him when they had held somewhat analogous positions in 1944–45. He prepared some ideas that would perhaps appeal to the conservative Soviet military mentality, and would start to show the masses of the world some prospect that their leaders were thinking of policy options less forbidding than endless public ruminations about atomic attack and defense. This would be the first such meeting since Potsdam in July 1945, when first Churchill and then Attlee met with Stalin and the newly elevated Truman. As Churchill left, defeated in the general election, Stalin said, "Western democracy must be a wretched system if it could exchange a great man like Churchill for Attlee."[45]

Eisenhower, by the summer of 1955, was able to say that Americans had not had peace and prosperity built on stable foundations since before the First World War, forty years earlier, and that now no one was left behind. It wasn't exactly true, but it wasn't false either. In the middle of 1955, the head of the American Federation of Labor and Congress of Industrial Organizations, George Meany, a chronic Democrat but an American patriot, said, "American labor has never had it so good." Between 1952 and 1955, the percentage of American families owning automobiles increased from 60 percent to 70 percent. Inflation was under 1 percent and the country was booming. This, and his emerging success in settling down the Formosa crisis and disengaging honorably in Austria, gave Eisenhower the moral lift for some interesting initiatives with the U.S.S.R. And in Moscow, the mighty and immovable Stalin had gone and there was now more collective and apparently more reasonable leadership. Under the sunny Ike, benign and golfing, but tough and clever and unflappable, the grim freeze of the Korean and Cold Wars of the Truman times had lifted appreciably. So had the climate of labor unrest, and the problems of cronyism, minor scandals, and supposed communist infiltration.

Eisenhower had reoriented American defense to reduced spending through reduced manpower, while extending America's lead in the quantity, delivery capacity, and sophistication and power of its nuclear arsenal. Now he set out to play poker with the Russians, and grope toward arms control. After ten years of an intensifying Cold War, and six months in which his senior military commanders had almost routinely asked for atomic attacks on China for what proved insubstantial reasons (false fears of an impending attempted invasion of Formosa), the president was prepared to try to de-escalate tensions.

He explained to a news conference on July 6, 1955, that bomber production facilities, landing fields, and extensive missile launching facilities could not be concealed from serious intelligence gathering – especially, though he did not say so at this point, aerial detection. He was familiar with the potential for air surveillance from the Second World War, and aware of radical improvements in aircraft and impending satellite-based photography. He focused on preparing a proposal for assisting each side, by local airfield access, in aerial reconnaissance, while dispersing American nuclear delivery capacity all around its alliance system and accelerating development of an intercontinental ballistic missile (ICBM).

Eisenhower had to deal with intense bureaucratic pressures, especially from Stassen and Rockefeller, who both wanted to take over arms control policy, from Dulles, who wished to retain (and retard) it, and from Radford, who had his misgivings about any clipping of the wings of the American military, even if it was to the country's comparative advantage. Eisenhower enunciated to the nation on July 15, just before he left for Geneva, the objective of improving the international atmosphere. He sent Stassen, Rockefeller, and Radford to Paris, to be available if he needed them in Geneva, with no intention whatever of calling them. They would have a pleasant sojourn in the splendid French capital, waiting disappointedly for the telephone to ring. He asked Nixon to hold a cabinet meeting in his absence, as usual, and act routinely in his place. Nixon strengthened his relationship with Eisenhower by being completely supportive and responsive, and not joining the serried ranks of those jockeying and agitating for place and attention.

Eisenhower set himself the task of finding out who was really the Soviet leader, and quickly established that it was not Zhukov, who seemed to him a much diminished figure from ten years before. He quickly determined that Molotov too had lost influence, that Bulganin was a rather cardboard figure, and that Khrushchev was the strongest member of the group. In his opening remarks he called for a united Germany in NATO, the end to the international communist effort to foment revolutions and insurgencies, and the U.S.S.R.'s adherence to its Yalta promises to respect and promote democracy in Eastern Europe. Then he called for a greater effort in arms inspection and control, unspecifically, and increased cultural exchanges. With Churchill retired, Stalin dead, and de Gaulle still waiting for the Fourth Republic to flounder to an end as he had predicted it would from its inception in 1946, Eisenhower was by some measure the most commanding personal presence at the conference, as well as the representative of the greatest and richest power. He played his role with great skill and on July 21 revealed his "Open Skies" proposal for reciprocal aerial surveillance by the United States and the U.S.S.R., with aerial reconnaissance facilities provided by both countries. The British and the French (now led by the very intelligent Edgar Faure, Mendes-France having lasted about a year) had had no real notice of what was coming, but responded enthusiastically. Bulganin replied positively for the Russians, though non-committally. But Khrushchev came to Eisenhower after the formal session and said that it was just an American espionage effort. It is not clear why, as he must have known that high-altitude aerial and satellite reconnaissance was coming anyway.

Eisenhower spoke in the following sessions of the conference of the need for greater economic and cultural links, and exchanges of people generally. And he concluded with a somewhat upbeat statement on the duty of all of them to preserve the peace and reduce tensions. He created an atmosphere that was easily more relaxed and positive than had existed in the world for many years, and when he returned to the United States, he reassured his countrymen that there had been no breakthroughs but no secret agreements either. Even though he had started the conference by demanding that the Russians live up to the Yalta commitments, he was mindful of the ignition of a new Yalta Myth about Geneva.

Nixon had told Eisenhower that Khrushchev, he felt, now held power in Russia, which proved to be true, and Nixon had conducted a cabinet meeting and meetings with legislative leaders in Eisenhower's absence perfectly competently. Nixon was allowing his public relations to settle down, and watching carefully, as 1956 approached, to see if Eisenhower intended to stand for reelection.

On September 24, 1955, President Eisenhower had a coronary. Hagerty telephoned Nixon to tell him, just after the Nixons had returned home from a wedding and Nixon was reading the newspaper. Hagerty assured Nixon that there was no doubt that it was a heart attack, and it wasn't clear at this point how serious it was. Nixon invited Rogers over, and as reporters massed on Nixon's lawn, he sent his daughter Tricia out to look at the cameras, while he and Rogers snuck out the back door and were picked up by Rogers's wife. They agreed that for as long as possible Nixon should not speak to the press nor be photographed. They got Jerry Persons over to Rogers's house and started to make plans to strengthen Eisenhower's medical team. Eisenhower was in a military hospital in Denver. Nixon called other cabinet members, and all were agreed that for the time being they had to present the appearance of business as usual.

Eisenhower had strengthened sufficiently by the second day to tell Hagerty to tell the cabinet that all meetings should be held regularly under the chairmanship of the vice president. Nixon convened the National Security Council on September 29 and the cabinet the next day. Dulles, at Nixon's invitation, inflicted a rather pedantic foreign policy summary on the group, followed by other cabinet secretaries. Dulles wanted to send Sherman Adams to Denver to prevent "hustlers" from getting at Eisenhower, who, according to early reports, was mentally competent and recovering well. In fact, they wanted to get Adams out of Washington, because he was trying to deny the cabinet a functioning control of the government. It was a quiet period in foreign and domestic affairs. At the end of the September 30 cabinet meeting, Dulles congratulated Nixon on the dignity with which he had handled a delicate situation and graciously concluded that "we are . . . proud to be serving in this cabinet under your leadership."[46] It is universally conceded that Nixon showed poise and exactly the right note, confident but not presumptuous, cool but not flippant, concerned but not overwhelmed.

In the light of conditions, Allen Dulles took Nixon on a tour of the CIA headquarters and gave him a complete maximum security intelligence briefing. Eisenhower invited Nixon to Denver on October 8, followed by all of the cabinet in protocol order, starting with Dulles. Eisenhower expressed his gratitude to Nixon for the very capable and diplomatic way he had handled the problem. He gave Nixon a letter setting out a few things, including the importance of Dulles's speaking with his authority at a resumed foreign-ministers-level session of the Geneva Conference. Eisenhower told Hagerty that Nixon was "a darn good young man." Eisenhower was not convinced that he would not run again, since it was already looking like a very mild heart attack from which he would recover, and which need not recur.

It was a time of intense concern for the health and person of the president. When Dr. Paul Dudley White, a distinguished heart specialist whom Nixon and Dulles and Eisenhower's brother had recruited, examined the president, he told a rapt press conference that "the president's stools are firm" and the stock market rallied sharply. Dwight D. Eisenhower remained an admired and popular leader, and for nearly three years had been a cautious but capable president. He seemed to think that Nixon had everything except perhaps the full maturity needed. He thought Rockefeller "a gadfly" and said that "he was too used to hiring brains instead of using his own."[47] Dulles was outraged at Rockefeller's attempted intrusion into his policy area, and started to squeeze him out of government.

Eisenhower recovered quite uneventfully and very fully, and the prognosis was excellent. As the year 1955 ended, Eisenhower was leaning to running again, ostensibly because he couldn't see a successor, but really because he liked the job he had coveted but had pretended not to seek. He met with Nixon on December 26, having written him a note of thanks for his performance during his convalescence. Eisenhower expressed regret that Nixon's popularity had not come up as he had hoped it would, and staggered Nixon with the suggestion that he might wish to take over a cabinet department in order to gain some executive experience. Eisenhower went so far as to suggest that Nixon might replace Dulles eventually. Nixon said little as the two parted, and Eisenhower left for a Florida holiday.

Almost everyone agreed that Nixon had performed well in three years as vice president. His foreign tours, his party management, especially in getting rid of McCarthy fairly painlessly, his contribution to cabinet, National Security Council, and congressional liaison meetings, his successful advocacy of the setting up of the Southeast Asia Treaty Organization, and his performance during the president's illness, had all been exemplary. But in an eerie rerun of aspects of the fund crisis, Nixon had an uneasy feeling that his leader was trying to dispense with him.

Chapter Six

The Regent and the Striver
1956–1959

— I —

PRESIDENT EISENHOWER HAD NIXON in for a political talk on February 6, 1956. He was awaiting doctors' final tests regarding his fitness to serve another term as president, but was by now confident of the answer. Nixon told him that he need not campaign harder than Roosevelt did in 1940 and 1944. This was a bit misleading, since Roosevelt could rightly claim a war emergency, and did not even appear at the conventions that nominated him in those years. But he did tour war production and military training facilities, in supposedly non-political trips that got him plenty of publicity, and had strenuous speaking tours at the end of both campaigns, which included, most famously, his attack on "Martin, Barton, and Fish," in 1940, and the Fala speech in 1944 that had inspired Nixon's invocation of Checkers.

Where Nixon was accurate was in saying that Eisenhower could campaign on television. He recognized the power of the new medium and told Eisenhower he could give six television speeches and not physically inconvenience himself at all. Nixon kept comparing Eisenhower to Roosevelt, and he was a popular president, but he had nothing like Roosevelt's virtuosity as a public speaker, live or on television.

Eisenhower, whose ego was not appreciably smaller than Roosevelt's, had some astonishing political ideas. He told Leonard Hall, one of the Republican Party's leading organizers and future national chairman, that he was thinking of running as a Democrat, in order to put himself at the head of the Democratic congressional apparatus, as if there were no question that the Democrats would nominate him and there were no policy differences at all between the parties.[1]

The president began a lengthy rumination about Nixon's status, praising him to some degree but expressing reservations. He spoke to both Dulles and Nixon, separately, on February 9, and suggested to Dulles that Nixon become secretary of commerce. Dulles said that Nixon would not accept such a demotion. He argued that Nixon had the aptitude to be secretary of state and offered to hand the position over to him, but Eisenhower said he wished Dulles to remain. As always, Dulles was supportive of Nixon. When Ike met with Nixon the same day, he said that Nixon, if he thought Eisenhower would survive four years, should take over Interior; Health, Education and Welfare; or the Defense Department, but that if he thought Eisenhower might not survive, Nixon might wish to remain where he was. This was an astonishing comment, putting Nixon in the position that if he said he wished to remain where he was, it implied that he didn't think Ike had long to live.[2]

Nixon said he would do what Eisenhower wanted, and was told that it was Nixon's decision. On February 13, Eisenhower met with Leonard Hall and mused about various possible vice presidents, including Earl Warren, Thomas E. Dewey, Frank Lausche, and Milton Eisenhower, as well as his navy secretary, Robert Anderson. Anderson would have been serviceable, although he would have brought nothing to the ticket politically, had never won an important election, and was not well known in the country. Warren would never have traded the life position of chief justice for four years as vice president. Completely out of the question were Dewey, after two tries for the presidency; Lausche, the Democratic (and Catholic, but that was probably manageable) governor of Ohio; and the president's brother, Milton. (One person Eisenhower never mentioned, who at this point had never run for public office, was his ambitious and dynamic special assistant, Nelson A. Rockefeller.)

Hall said that the only position Nixon would take was secretary of state, but Eisenhower wanted to retain Dulles and wondered if Nixon, though he clearly had a flare for foreign affairs, was up to that job. (It would have been a brilliant appointment and Dulles died in mid-term anyway.) Eisenhower told Hall to speak to Nixon, to be "gentle," but to ask him what he wanted to do. Hall did so, though not particularly gently, and Nixon interpreted it as a brushoff from the president. He said, "He never liked me . . . he's always been against me." Nixon reverted to his stance during the fund crisis; if Eisenhower wanted him out, he could ask him to go. Nixon would not fall on his sword on the basis of hints from go-betweens.[3]

It is not clear what Eisenhower's motive was in all this. There was no question that Nixon had performed effectively and loyally as vice president, and Eisenhower could have got rid of him and still been elected, without the rending damage that would have occurred in the fund crisis after Nixon's nomination in 1952. Since the other possible candidates Eisenhower mentioned were completely nonsensical choices, and he was not the political naïf he pretended to be, it seems likely that he was putting Nixon in his place after Nixon's coarse admonition, and the virtual usurpation of position Nixon had staged in the fund crisis. Eisenhower was a subtle operator and this seems most likely to have been his way, on the last best occasion he would have to do so, to remind Nixon of the correlation of forces between them. If they ran together again, they would almost surely win, but from the day after the election on, unless he made a serious error, Nixon would be gathering political strength, and the two-term president, as he approached his compulsory retirement, would be losing it.

There was not, at this point, a great rapport between Nixon and Eisenhower. Ike seems to have found his vice president's "obvious ambition and opportunism, his humility contrasted with hot flashes of political savagery, the sense that his public persona concealed some other man," difficult. For his part, John F. Kennedy said of Eisenhower, "No man is less loyal to his old friends than Eisenhower. He is a terribly cold man. All his golfing pals are rich men he has met since 1945."[4]

Getting rid of Nixon would not be as easy and painless as Eisenhower, and even Hall, seemed to think. Seeing the danger, Nixon, as was his custom, behaved like a porcupine. He redoubled his speaking tour on behalf of party regulars, avoided press conferences, did not reply to attacks from Truman, who again accused Nixon of calling him a traitor, or from Stevenson, who said the vice president "was uniquely qualified by his experience for a campaign at the lowest level."[5] As the identity of delegates to the Republican convention was not difficult to guess in most cases, there being no opposition to the incumbents within their own party, Nixon quietly and efficiently lined up pledges of support from over eight hundred delegates, a substantial majority. Eisenhower could have overturned this, but at the cost of an enormous controversy and the generation of immense ill will within his party, where Nixon's tireless efforts were widely appreciated. Nixon also worked with Ralph de Toledano on a hagiographical book about himself for wide distribution in the early summer of 1956. Among other things, there appeared an elaborate disclaimer of ever having called Truman a traitor. Nixon was finally moving to tone down his quasi-McCarthy image, into which Eisenhower had partly pushed him – a move better made late than not at all.

Presidents running for reelection had switched vice presidents before, but the only recent precedent was when Roosevelt ran for a fourth term and dumped Wallace for Truman in 1944. Then he arranged for the party bosses to take the heat, and Wallace was generally regarded in the higher reaches of the Democratic Party as a flaky, far-left, peculiar man, who had done nothing to build a following within the party generally. Wallace's attempt to keep his job had been very inept, and Roosevelt was so subtle that Wallace never really understood what had happened to him, even years later. Roosevelt had led the country out of the Depression, assisted the democracies against Hitler in 1940 and 1941, and brought the nation from the shambles of Pearl Harbor to the successful invasion of Normandy as the campaign was about to begin, and to the mighty naval victory over Japan at Leyte Gulf the week before the election. In twelve years, he had reduced unemployment from 33 percent of the workforce to less than 1 percent, got rid of Prohibition, electrified rural American homes, guaranteed bank deposits, and uplifted the nation. He could have run with the party's mascot for vice president (instead of Harry Truman) and he would still have won. When he had run for a second term in 1936, Roosevelt had kept his vice president (John N. Garner), though he didn't much like him, as Woodrow Wilson had kept his in 1916 (Thomas R. Marshall), and these were the only two-term vice presidents in over eighty years. The only other reelected president in that time, William McKinley, had to choose a second vice president (Theodore Roosevelt) because the first (Garrett Hobart) died in office. Abraham Lincoln and Ulysses S. Grant changed their vice presidents after one term, but that was too far back to be relevant.

At his press conference on February 29, 1956, the president announced that he would seek renomination and reelection. The first question put to him was about the identity of his running mate. Eisenhower spoke of his "tremendous admiration for Mr. Nixon," but claimed that it was "traditional . . . to wait and see who the Republican Convention nominates." The national press corps wasn't having this canard and pushed Eisenhower into a statement of "unbounded" admiration and respect for Nixon, who had been "loyal and dedicated . . . and successful . . . I am very fond of him, but I am going to say no more about it." All of the press realized at once that Eisenhower was just dangling Nixon over the side, but not necessarily severing him loose.

Outwardly, as in the president's health crisis, Nixon kept cool and behaved with perfect decorum. Privately, he told de Toledano and a few others that he was tempted to quit, but as with such comments in 1952, he really intended to dig in as discreetly and tenaciously as he could, and if Eisenhower wanted to force him out, he would extract the greatest possible penalty to Eisenhower's popularity in his own party for it. Nixon did not have a fraction of his leader's prestige, nor a shadow of his popularity, but he had his supporters, had been a good vice president, had carried a great deal of heavy water for the Republican Party, and was an ingenious, tenacious, and cunning infighter. The porcupine dug into his shelter, extended his quills, and prepared to repel intruders.

It was a completely unnecessary charade, as Eisenhower made a point of his own authority, of which Nixon was already aware; Nixon had the greater grievance over the still raw wounds of the fund crisis, not Eisenhower. Dumping Nixon would be a mistake, but if Eisenhower wished to do it, he had to do it cleanly, not in this sadistic public farce; and the momentary psychic income of humbling Nixon, Eisenhower should have known, could easily be reversed by the younger man with the longer race to run. It was never going to be worth Eisenhower's trouble to purge his vice president, but the demeaning exercise continued for some months. Nixon did not, because of its embarrassing nature, emphasize it in detail in his subsequent book on crises he had faced, or in his later memoirs, other than as an upsetting experience, but this was one of the greatest agonies Nixon had to traverse in his pre-presidential years. Eisenhower, in his memoirs, professed to be astounded to have read in Nixon's first book, about his early "crises," that this episode had been so unpleasant for him.

Eisenhower aggravated matters at his next press conference, March 7, 1956. He was asked to comment on rumors that he had been advised to "dump Nixon" and had suggested that Nixon take a cabinet post. Ike huffed and puffed unconvincingly: "If anyone ever has the effrontery to come in and urge me to dump anybody that I respect as I do Vice President Nixon, there will be more commotion around my office than you have noticed yet."

Everyone knew that was not an answer to the question posed. Eisenhower went on to say that he had not "presumed" to tell Nixon what to do, which all suspected, and he knew, to be untrue, and that he had asked Nixon "to chart out his own course." The supplementary question, as the president must have foreseen, asked if that meant, if Nixon wished to be re-nominated, Eisenhower would be happy with that. Eisenhower lamely replied, "I am not going to be pushed into corners here. . . . I have no crit-icism to make of Vice President Nixon, either as a man, an associate, or as my running mate on the ticket." As in the fund crisis, Eisenhower was start-ing to generate sympathy for Nixon. Nixon appeared loyal, resolute, and put-upon, and Eisenhower, despite his position and prestige, appeared thoughtless and indecisive.

Nixon had been offered the principal position in a large California law firm, and a partnership in a large New York law firm. He was just forty-three, and both positions would be much more popular with his family and better paying than where he was. Apart from secretary of state, which was not on offer, he would not consider a cabinet post (which was what Wallace did, becoming secretary of commerce after being replaced as vice president). He could not but assume that Eisenhower was trying to get rid of him, and let it be known to Vic Johnston of the Republican Senate Campaign Committee that he was going to announce at a press conference the next day, March 9, that he would not seek or accept renomination.

Len Hall and Jerry Persons, informed by Johnston, as Nixon had intended, hastily called upon Nixon and told him that he would be regarded as a "quitter" if he did anything of the kind. This too had reve-nances of the fund crisis; Nixon agreed to defer the decision a couple of weeks. Persons was a close, wartime colleague of Eisenhower's, reporting directly to the president, and this was Nixon's method of raising the ante. Both the president and the vice president were good poker players. The question remains, what possessed Eisenhower to start such a no-win game? The only conceivable answer is that Eisenhower was trying to create the myth that he didn't owe Nixon anything for having got to be president.

Obviously, if Eisenhower had had the least concern about the adminis-trative aptitudes of a vice president, he could have got Dewey to try to find an administrator to undermine Warren's hold on the California delegation and seat his delegates at Chicago in 1952, rather than Nixon. It was a bit late to think of such things now, but Ike, who had proved himself a skilled memoirist, was already starting to recreate the myth of the draft. This would be facilitated by the unlikelihood that Nixon would emphasize the lengths he and Chotiner had gone to, in contemplation of the vice presidential nomination Dewey had told them was awaiting, to hollow out Warren's candidacy and use his pledged supporters to deliver the convention to Eisenhower.

Eisenhower then made Nixon's future the subject of one of his famous stag dinners with his rich friends. Charles Jones, president of Richfield Oil, told Eisenhower that Nixon "has done the hard jobs that many of your other associates have run away from. . . . What does a man have to do to get your support?"[6] There was a view that Nixon should show what he could do as a department head, which Eisenhower heartily endorsed. But Eisenhower was playing another game and the businessmen knew nothing about political realities. Eisenhower had had a heart attack. He would be seventy at the end of his second term, the oldest president in history to that time. Nixon had been the most active vice president at least since Burr and Jefferson, who were opponents of the presidents they served with, and active in that role. If he was pushed out of his position by Eisenhower, he could have no possible confidence that the same fate would not befall him when he served in the cabinet at the president's pleasure, which could be withdrawn at any moment.

On March 13, Eisenhower laid out his reservations for Sherman Adams's deputy chief of staff, Fred Seaton. He said that he was happy with, and happy to be associated with, Nixon, but that he wanted "a bevy of young fellows to be available four years from now. Nixon can't always be the understudy to the star." This was rewriting the 1952 arrangements. Nixon did the dirty work to put Eisenhower in the White House in order to be the "understudy to the star," as the president modestly put it. Eisenhower wanted to give himself freedom to choose another successor, or at least nudge another one forward, and to redact out of history the unspontaneity of some of the 1952 presidential nominating process. To do this, he tried again to sell Nixon on the virtues of voluntarily demoting himself in quest of "administrative experience." (If that had really been a concern, Eisenhower could have delegated mountains of administrative work for him to perform.)

As in 1952, Nixon was calling his hand. Even Ike's friends who bought the nonsense about gaining departmental experience didn't want Nixon fired. Only Adams, and up to a point Brownell, and a very few others wanted that. (Even the Democrats, not that they had a voice, other than slightly through part of the media, wanted Nixon retained, because they thought

they could run against his more outrageously partisan past utterances.)
Nixon agonized, and had attacks of pessimism and a paranoiac but not
unfounded sense of being singled out for unjust punishment, but he was too
clever and tenacious and conscious of his own value, however much he felt
underestimated by others, to, as he put it in September 1952, draw up his own
death warrant.

Immediately after his meeting with Fred Seaton, Eisenhower had
Richard Nixon in for a talk. He blamed the press bitterly for inventing the
malicious falsehood that he, Eisenhower, was trying to get rid of Nixon. He
was particularly annoyed at James Reston of the *New York Times* for propagating the myth that Adams and Brownell were trying to force Nixon out,
that Nixon was a dangerous opponent, and that Eisenhower was dithering –
a reasonably accurate summary, in fact.[7] Eisenhower tried again his tired
football metaphor that Nixon would look like a second-string quarterback
instead of a "halfback in your own right" if he remained in the vice presidency. Nixon said that a change to a cabinet department "could [not] be
sold, because the press would say Nixon is afraid to run again or the president is afraid to have him."[8]

Nixon said that he wanted Eisenhower to canvass the field carefully and
that if there was someone the president would rather run with, he would
stand aside "gracefully." He didn't want to be kept on just out of duty. "We
can't have that type of thing." This was an even more exquisite minuet than
in September 1952. Nixon was almost four years older and more confident,
and there was no allegation of wrongdoing against him, so he could play his
hand with greater panache. The two men agreed that the decision should
be made (in theory by Nixon) at the last possible time. Nixon said, "I think
you ought to decide it at the time, on the basis of what *we* think is the best
thing to do."[9] He then helpfully added that if he left the ticket, "Friendly
columnists will say, 'Nixon has done a good job; it's a terrible thing for the
president to fire him.'" Eisenhower didn't need any help figuring out
whether Nixon himself would be pouring gasoline on that fire.

Eisenhower allowed that he would really like as his running mate "a
good Catholic or an outstanding Jew. I just don't know any good man to fit
the description." (Sectarian diversity was not the president's strong suit;
there was no shortage of such people.) Nixon reinforced the point that a
cabinet position was not on, as his wife did not like Washington and he was
not sure she would agree even to his running again for vice president.

Eisenhower concluded the one-hour meeting by saying that he would tell the press that he would be happy to have Nixon on the ticket and say no more. Nixon said once more that a cabinet post would not work, and Eisenhower said again that he was just trying to strengthen Nixon for four years hence (when he was in fact trying to break Nixon's hammerlock on the 1960 presidential nomination).

With a fine flourish, Ike said that the press was being "silly" claiming there was a difference between them: "It would be like trying to promote a fight between me and my brother." Nixon left. It was a chicken game; Nixon had the advantage, unless he forced the issue, which could cause Eisenhower to pay the punitive cost of proving his superior strength. The porcupine strategy, a discreet, smiling porcupine, albeit a prickly one, was the best strategy. As if to underline the point, the day of this meeting was the day of the New Hampshire presidential primary. New Hampshire senator Styles Bridges, a strong Nixon ally, had made a quiet but comprehensive effort to get Republicans, as they voted for Eisenhower for the presidential nomination, to write in Nixon for vice president. Eisenhower, without opposition, received 56,464 votes, from voters who simply put an X beside his name. Nixon, on a ballot that had nothing to do with the vice presidential nomination, had his name laboriously written in for vice president on over 23,000 ballots. Despite all the bunk about standing aside "gracefully" and an absence of any sense of "duty" as Ike "canvassed" alternatives, Eisenhower must have realized that he would not shake Nixon off, and that all he could do was demonstrate one more time that he was the captain of the team, something Nixon had only slightly challenged once, over Indochina.

On April 9, 1956, having had a Florida holiday, Nixon returned to Washington and met with Eisenhower, who told him that he thought Nixon should take Commerce or Health, Education, and Welfare. Nixon gave his customary demurrals, and they went round the dance floor again. It was Nixon's decision, *but* there was a lot of opposition to him, *but* they could overcome a lot of it.[10]

On April 25, a Senate subcommittee issued a subpoena on Chotiner, looking into the possibility that he had been engaged in influence-peddling with Nixon. Chotiner did not appear as ordered. As all Nixonians knew, this risked a contempt citation. Chotiner was a slippery character, but this had the appearance of a straight, partisan, election-year assault on Nixon by the Democratic majority in the Senate. Chotiner had taken advantage of a few disparagements of him as a Jew to stir up the Jewish press of the country to counterattack on his behalf, waving the bloody shirt of anti-Semitism.

On the same day, the 25th, Eisenhower answered a press conference question about whether Nixon had reported back on the course he was going to "chart" by saying no, he had not. This resolved Nixon to make his move and end the inelegant parlor game. He requested a meeting with the president for the following day, and began it by saying that he agreed with Eisenhower that the matter of the vice presidency should be left open, and that any variety of possible candidates should be encouraged, and that having considered it carefully, he thought that he should remain as vice president. Eisenhower said that in that case, Nixon should go out at once to tell that to the press. Nixon declined and suggested that it was Eisenhower's place to tell the press. A final compromise: Hagerty, who was pro-Nixon, although he warned Eisenhower that there was some anti-Nixon sentiment in the South because of his integrationist and anti-segregationist sentiments, would go out with Nixon and tell the press that Nixon would seek (i.e., receive) the vice presidential nomination, and that Eisenhower was "delighted by the news."[11] Before leaving the president's office, Nixon told Eisenhower about the commotion over Chotiner, but assured Eisenhower that the administration had no connection with the controversy and would not be embarrassed by it.

The press received the news of the vice president's decision without surprise, though they were skeptical at Nixon's explanation that he had been motivated by concern for what was best for Eisenhower. The whole issue had another brief revival when Eisenhower had a two-hour operation for ileitis on June 8. It was not life-threatening, and, though not elective, it was not time-urgent. The president recovered very quickly and on schedule, but there were new fears about his health and doubts about leaving the vice presidency as it was.

The inimitable Harold Stassen, who though no longer the Benjamin of the Republican Party was still widely thought to have some political astuteness, returned from an unsuccessful disarmament conference in London and filled his compulsive need for busy activity by starting a dump-Nixon movement. To this end he commissioned a poll, which revealed, as Stassen had intended it would, that Nixon could cost Eisenhower 6 percent in the election. That still did not endanger Eisenhower's own candidacy, but it would have an impact on congressional races. Stassen informed Eisenhower of the poll when he called upon him on July 20. Eisenhower was concerned, but had to leave almost at once for Panama for a meeting of inter-American presidents, which he had determined to go to, to demonstrate his fitness after his operation the month before.

By this time, Nixon had had a thirteen-day trip to the Far East, which had long been scheduled, from June 30 to July 13. He and Pat were, as always, well briefed and indomitably energetic. They received a great deal of entirely favorable publicity. Instead of participating in pan-Vietnamese elections, as the Geneva Conference of 1954 had foreseen, the foremost South Vietnamese political leader, Ngo Dinh Diem, had held a referendum that removed Bao Dai as emperor, liberating him to go the Côte d'Azur where he was happier, and set up the Republic of (South) Vietnam.

Diem was no great democrat, but he was a fervent Roman Catholic and anti-communist. The United States had not signed the Geneva agreement, but had stated that it would not obstruct its implementation. The Eisenhower administration's support and encouragement for Diem would be cited as evidence of its having obstructed that agreement. However, the agreement provided for genuine elections that would reflect popular wishes, and there was no possibility of that occurring in North Vietnam, where Ho Chi Minh had imposed a heavy Stalinist regime. The issue would have to be settled by force.

By this early date, it should have been as obvious to Eisenhower as it had been to Nixon two years before that it would have been much better to help the French out of Dien Bien Phu (and there would have been no need for Radford's nonsense about atomic weapons to do it), proclaim the united Republic of Vietnam, set up SEATO before the fall of Hanoi to Ho Chi Minh, bring in the allies, and negotiate Geneva to a better deal from that point and defend South Vietnam with greater legitimacy and valuable allies. Dulles did not achieve anything useful in not shaking hands with Chou En-lai either. A deliberate refrigeration of relations with China made no sense if the United States wasn't going to use Chiang's forces in Korea (and that bolt had been shot by 1954), and after McCarthy's fangs had been pulled. By the time of Nixon's visit to Saigon in 1956, a horrible tragedy was already well underway in Vietnam.

SEATO, which at Nixon's behest had been set up in 1954, was already pledged to defend South Vietnam, and Nixon brought assurances of

American support to Diem. Nixon had become the administration's leading Asia advocate. He had even prevailed on Eisenhower to give a very respectful welcome to the Indonesian president, Sukarno, whom Nixon regarded (accurately) as a shabby rake and political scoundrel, when he came to Washington in April. Schoolchildren were given the day off to provide a huge crowd of welcome for a man virtually no one in America had heard of.

The Nixons had a very satisfactory visit with President Magsaysay of the Philippines. Nixon raised eyebrows by saying that America respected neutrality but had no "sympathy" for those who claimed moral relativism between the communist and democratic worlds. In Karachi, Nixon cautioned against accepting economic assistance from the U.S.S.R., because the price was "a rope around the neck."

Nixon returned to a Washington where Stassen had already unleashed his mischief. Stassen sent a special message to Nixon on July 23, including the poll and his request that Nixon withdraw as vice president in the (inevitable) national and party interest, in favor of Christian Herter, the respected but bland and arthritic sixty-one-year-old governor of Massachusetts. Nixon was having lunch with Len Hall and Jerry Persons when Rose Mary Woods brought in the envelope from Stassen, and Nixon read it to them. Stassen claimed that Nixon's greatest problems were with the best-informed and younger voters.

Nixon's own view was that he brought a lot of money, peace in the conservative Republican bloc, and enthusiasm, which made up for his poor standing with independent Democrats. Since Eisenhower was so uninterested in congressional and party matters, it was important to keep the conservative Republicans happy, as they felt generally let down by Eisenhower's neo-Roosevelt-Truman program. Hall and Persons agreed that Stassen's initiative could be a serious problem, though more a public relations negative than a threat to Nixon's renomination. The vice president had the rank and file and the president's endorsement, and if Eisenhower did a U-turn now, especially on the basis of a rigged private poll by the erratic huckster Stassen, it would be a disaster for the Republicans.

On the afternoon of July 23, Stassen called a press conference and announced his support for Herter for vice president. He did not refer directly to his poll, but hinted at it and followed with extensive leaks. Nixon said that he would be happy, as always, to abide by any decision the president and delegates made about the vice presidency, stated his high opinion of Herter, and promised that if Herter were the nominee he would support him wholeheartedly. In Panama, Eisenhower told Hagerty to issue a statement saying that Stassen was free to campaign for whomever he wished, but, in the circumstances, Stassen was going on indefinite leave without pay while he did so. This was not what Stassen had hoped for, but not the ringing endorsement Nixon had sought either.

Eisenhower returned to Washington on July 26 and was greeted by an orchestrated avalanche of official support for Nixon, in particular the signed support of 180 of the party's 203 congressmen. Eisenhower saw that the jig really was up, and with his Byzantine finesse in such matters cut Stassen off at the knees. He had Adams call Herter and say that Herter could be under-secretary of state, and privately would be Eisenhower's choice to succeed Dulles when he retired, probably in about a year. But if Herter chose to run for vice president, that offer was withdrawn. Herter immediately issued a statement asserting that he had no interest in the vice presidency and would not seek it. Nixon would be renominated; Herter would eventually replace Dulles; and Stassen sank virtually without trace. (He did send Nixon another letter, on August 16, asking him to withdraw not only for the benefit of "our country, but in the long run, for your future career."[12] Nixon was staying with the evangelist Billy Graham, in North Carolina, discussing desegregation, and ignored Stassen, with great pleasure.)

At Eisenhower's August 1 press conference, James Reston asked if it was fair to conclude that Nixon was his preference. Eisenhower said that he was happy with Nixon, as he would be with some others, and he refused to express a preference. Merriman Smith of United Press asked if there had been "the commotion" in the president's office Eisenhower had promised if it were suggested that he dump Nixon. Eisenhower said that there had not been, because no one had proposed that he "dump Mr. Nixon. No one, I think, would have that effrontery."

The entire press and public was well aware that Stassen had done just that. Having failed to shake Nixon's likely grip on the 1960 presidential nomination, Eisenhower had at least established that he had tolerated his renomination voluntarily, rather than having the choice made as part of a nomination deal as it had been in 1952, and left for confirmation by the National Committee after Nixon had stampeded the public with a dramatic and fraught speech. This had been an excruciating drama for a very small purpose. As with the events of four years earlier, Nixon came through them looking, then and now, better than Eisenhower.

The Democrats met in the third week in August and renominated Adlai Stevenson, despite an energetic effort by Harry Truman behind the scenes to promote his fellow Missourian Stuart Symington. Stevenson threw the nomination of the vice presidential candidate open to the convention, and a strenuous battle occurred between Senator Estes Kefauver of Tennessee, seeking the semi-traditional Southern place on the ticket, and the thirty-nine-year-old Senator John F. Kennedy of Massachusetts, who was really running for the presidential nomination in 1960. (There was a Southern or border-state vice presidential candidate for the Democrats every election between 1928 and 1960, inclusive, except Wallace in 1940, while the presidential candidates were all from New York, Chicago, or Boston, except for Harry Truman in 1948.)

Eisenhower had spoken privately, including, as has been mentioned, to Nixon, of getting a Roman Catholic running mate. He detected that bigotry had eroded to the point that it would be a positive and not a negative, and the Roman Catholics were now more than a quarter of the population and could be assumed to be influenced in large numbers if one of their co-religionists were a candidate for national office. This had been attempted only once before, with Alfred E. Smith, the Democratic presidential candidate in 1928. But then America was prosperous and sociologically primitive, and Smith was not just a papist; he had loud suits and ties and a brown derby, a florid nose and a broad Lower East Side accent, unleavened by any education beyond Grade Eight, and he was anti-Prohibition. He was too much of an affront to the sensibilities of the Protestant majority, but even then he appreciably raised the recent Democratic vote, especially in the cities. In 1956, Kefauver won the convention vote fairly narrowly, and Kennedy graciously called for the nomination to be made unanimous. But politically astute people could see the Nixon-Kennedy race coming.

The Republicans met on August 19 in San Francisco. Stassen, emboldened by Stevenson's move, wrote to every Republican delegate urging a vote for Herter for vice president. Eisenhower finally did the necessary and overdue, summoned Stassen, ordered him to desist, and told him to give a seconding speech for Nixon, Herter having been recruited as the nominator.

Frank Nixon had suffered a ruptured abdominal artery on August 22, and Nixon was with his father in hospital when he was renominated, 1,323 to 1. Nixon returned to give an acceptance speech that was the usual elegiac in favor of the presidential candidate, amplified in this case to the encomium "man of the century." Nixon returned to Whittier, while Eisenhower accepted renomination and thoughtfully asked for prayers for the vice president's father. They were unavailing, as Frank Nixon died on September 4. Nixon allowed no photographs at the funeral on September 7. Frank Nixon had traveled an extraordinary distance in his seventy-eight years, from orphan and poor unskilled roustabout to a man of modestly comfortable means and father of the renominated vice president and twice-chosen running mate of one of America's greatest heroes and most popular presidents.

Nixon had won again, and now his influence and standing should steadily increase as he got closer to the 1960 presidential nomination. The ascent continued, but as he inched higher, the process became no easier, and more intricate.

— II —

The Republican campaign got under way on September 13, with a picnic at the Eisenhowers' farm at Gettysburg for six hundred party officials and office-holders. Eisenhower had asked Nixon to reply to Stevenson's attacks on the administration and the president personally, but not to be personally nasty to Stevenson. Nixon had so far been very uncontroversial. The communist issue was pretty inactive; McCarthy was an extinct volcano. The country was prosperous; Eisenhower had ended the war in Korea, had not blundered into new wars, and had been firm with the communists while using the Geneva Conference to lighten the general atmosphere. The Republicans had secured passage of their immense interstate highway program in 1956, as well as the almost equally ambitious St. Lawrence Seaway project, which would transform Chicago, Detroit, Cleveland, and Buffalo into ocean ports. The administration had finally managed significant tax reductions, along with extensions to social security and increases in payout levels, and the large minimum-wage increase. Economic and employment and real income growth levels were high and spread throughout the economic system. There was not a great deal for the Democrats to run against.

Nixon struck exactly the desired note in his remarks at the Eisenhower farm. He debunked the theory that the Democrats were the party of the average people and the Republicans the preserve of the rich, called Stevenson's suggestion that the draft could be ended soon "political fakery," mocked Stevenson's claim that the Republican administration was corrupt, and had a good time with the Supreme Court decision ordering school desegregation (*Brown v. Board of Education*), which laid bare a deep fissure that had been in the Democratic Party throughout its history, from the times of Jefferson and Jackson – its ambiguity first about slavery and then about segregation. Eisenhower was pleased with Nixon's light (no question about anyone's patriotism or manhood) but effective touch, and when he spoke, he said that he felt very well, and that "There is no man in the history of America who has had such a careful preparation as has Vice President Nixon for carrying out the duties of the presidency, if that duty should ever fall on him." This was the unqualified endorsement Nixon had been seeking, but not receiving, from Eisenhower for a long time.

Eisenhower showed great consideration in coming to Washington National Airport to see the Nixons off on September 18 as they started their campaign. He urged a moderate campaign and offered a takeoff on Harry Truman's famous "Give 'em Hell" campaign of 1948, and said, "Give 'em Heaven!"[13] Nixon traveled in a DC-6B, with a private compartment for his wife and himself at the back. It carried the largest press contingent that had ever accompanied a vice presidential campaign. While Chotiner was going through his travails, Nixon took his distance from him, and he was not involved in the 1956 campaign. Father John Cronin, with a request to pare back some of the anti-communist comment, was his chief speechwriter, but did not accompany him on campaign trips.

The formula was pretty simple. He would come down the ramp with one arm around the shoulder of his wife, greet the local Republican leadership, ride into town in an open car, unless the weather was very bad, and never in a Cadillac, as that would be unrepresentative of the "cloth-coat" GOP. His speeches extolled Eisenhower and peace and prosperity. Nixon never was informal with the press, but he ran an extremely smooth operation. Schedules were followed exactly, crowds were good. The speeches were numbingly predictable and familiar, but they went down well with the audiences, and there was very little heckling. Even the most hard-bitten press political veterans, including David Brinkley, then of NBC, were impressed.[14] (Brinkley had covered the presidents starting with Roosevelt, considered Eisenhower "a politician in a uniform," and was awed only by Rayburn, General Marshall, and to an extent Roosevelt, and impressed by few. His praise was telling.)

The official positions of the parties in 1956 were not far apart. The Republicans wanted private ownership of electric power. The Democrats favored public ownership of electricity, but not to the point of nationalizing anything, and fixed, as opposed to flexible, parity payments on the original New Deal programs for paying farmers not to grow unusable surpluses that would merely be dumped on the world markets and bring down American farm prices and incomes.

Republicans sought the "progressive elimination" of segregation, while Democrats sought only "equal opportunities," a euphemism for continued segregation. Stevenson had not fully endorsed the *Brown v. Board of Education* decision, because of the dependence of that party on the Southern whites. Neither had Eisenhower, and he had no such excuse. Nixon did agree with the decision, and urged the president and other Republican leaders to get on the integrationist bandwagon, not only because it was the law, and the Republicans were the party of Lincoln and could split the Democrats and pick up a lot of Northern black and liberal white votes, but because it was morally right.

Eisenhower and the others never grasped either the moral issue or the practical opportunity, though they did rather quietly disapprove of the repulsive segregationist oppressions of the Old South. Nixon referred to the problems of African-Americans in almost all his speeches and was an unambiguous egalitarian and integrationist. He referred to African-Americans he had known in Whittier, and was publicly, at least, a good deal more liberal than Stevenson or Eisenhower, or any other prominent national politician, on the race issue.

When Nixon campaigned in Texas, the Democrats put it about that Nixon was a member of the National Association for the Advancement of Colored People, the NAACP, which had been a persecuted organization throughout the South. Nixon acknowledged in his remarks in Texas that he was proud to be an honorary member of the NAACP, and that he supported the goal of equal opportunity for all.

He spoke at the great quadrennial political gathering of New York at the Waldorf-Astoria, the Al Smith Dinner, under the auspices of the cardinal-archbishop, the legendarily influential Francis J. Cardinal Spellman, on October 19. He predicted that the majority would see racial integration in the schools of America, and that he looked forward to the day, and made it clear that he considered this a problem in the North as well as the South. He concluded that the goals of independence and freedom enunciated by the American Revolution had not been fully achieved in the United States and that they would not be fully achieved until they prevailed everywhere in the world.

Nixon pioneered not only whistle-stop campaigning by air but also the multi-link live television news conference. On October 4, he spoke from Philadelphia to newsmen in eight different cities, and in answer to a question from a Nashville editor about desegregation, he said, "America . . . cannot afford the cost of prejudice and hatred and discrimination. We can't afford it morally . . . economically, [or] internationally." He calculated the cost of discriminating against blacks at fifteen billion dollars, "and at a time when we have to keep ahead of the communist world, [this] is a cost we cannot afford." He added that everywhere he went in the world, he found that American racial discrimination was the heaviest burden the United States had to bear and the most powerful anti-American argument the communists possessed.

There was much talk of a "new Nixon." He ignored the attacks of Stevenson and even Truman, who had little else to campaign about. Stevenson, the amiable, witty butt of unfair abuse four years before, became the nasty campaigner of 1956. Stevenson said that Nixon had "put away his switchblade" and had become "an Eagle Scout." On October 27, as time was running out, Stevenson said, "This man [Nixon] has no standard of truth except convenience and no standard of morality except what will serve his interest in an election. . . . Nixonland [is] a land of slander and scare . . . sly innuendo, the poison pen, the anonymous phone call, and hustling, pushing, shoving, the land of smash and grab and anything to win." On November 5, as the sands ran out before the election, Stevenson called Nixon "the little Lord Fauntleroy of the Republican Party [who must] yearn for his old tar bucket and brush." Truman, having grumbled noisily again about being called a traitor, which Nixon again denied, demanded to know, on November 3, "Why is the Republican Party offering us this over-ambitious, unscrupulous, reactionary boy orator as a possibility for president? Why are they imposing this terrible choice on the people?"[15]

Nixon did not respond to any of it, except for explaining calmly to a few reporters that he had accused Truman of complacency about communist infiltration of the government and a departure from some of the principles of Jefferson and Jackson. The country was accustomed to pretty fierce talk from Truman, a crusty septuagenarian. But Stevenson's attacks fell flat and largely backfired. Nixon ignored them and his own public remarks were unvaryingly reasonable and measured.

He was already adjusting to his new status. Stevenson was headed for defeat and would be unlikely to be treated to a third try at the presidency after two defeats. In the whole history of the country, only Henry Clay and William Jennings Bryan had been so honored, and Stevenson was not such a mighty national influence as Clay, nor such a populist spellbinder as Bryan. He was headed for the last roundup; Eisenhower was on his last lap before an honored retirement. There were no serious Republican rivals to Nixon in sight, unless Rockefeller could get an electoral career launched with tremendous velocity in 1958.

Lyndon Johnson might run in 1960, though he was very comfortable in his power in the Senate, and he was unlikely to have more than regional appeal. Symington might try again, but even with Truman pushing hard behind him, he had no traction nationally. Hubert Humphrey was a likely contender, but he was an admirable outsider with no power and only the appeal of the little engine that would try but not make it. The largest cloud on Nixon's horizon was John F. Kennedy, young, attractive, intelligent, facile (and wealthy). This was the same type of person as Robert Logue, who had suddenly arisen and defeated Nixon as student president at Whittier Union in 1929.

There was something inevitable, inexorable, laborious, and therefore apparently boring, about Nixon. It made him vulnerable to the sort of people who put others at their ease and seemed less programmed and striving (though Nixon would have perhaps the least boring career in American political history). Nixon knew this vulnerability, which was one of the reasons he had been such a fanatical assailant of his opponents until he had the laying on of hands from the undefeatable Eisenhower in September 1956.

Yet Nixon, usually so sensitive to this sort of threat, did not see Kennedy in this role. He knew him too well, and knew him to be attractive and intelligent and well-financed, but lazy, completely distracted by satyriasis, and whimsically undermotivated. It was very late before Nixon saw Kennedy as the public would see him. For now, Nixon was winding up his sixth biennial electoral triumph in ten years.

The Democrats threw all the muck they could find at Nixon in 1956, and almost none of it stuck. It was not the nature of Nixon to attract great sympathy, or even empathy, as Stevenson had when Nixon attacked him. But the ability of the Democrats to frighten the country with him had failed. Nixon wrote the Republican National Committee, whose leaders asked him to counterattack, that he would not become "a political Jack the Ripper."[16] He had substantially addressed Eisenhower's concerns about his "maturity." Nixon was the most likely next president; it was no longer necessary to produce a "rocking, socking campaign" as he had, by his lights in 1946, 1950, and 1952.

Nixon looked more relaxed, smiled a lot, and was in newspaper photographs and on television almost every day. In the course of the campaign he wiped out a great deal of the jowly, sinister impression he had created with many when he had torn out after the Democrats as virtual "commies," as well as crooks, in previous years.

The only substantive issues Stevenson could promote in 1956 were the end of the draft and an end to nuclear testing. All he could do was dangle the first, but he made a major push for a moratorium on nuclear testing, starting on October 15. He claimed that the United States possessed nuclear sufficiency, having previously mocked Eisenhower's New Look defense emphasis on nuclear weapons. He also claimed that a ban could be monitored because of the easy detection of atmospheric testing (underground and underwater testing not having been developed), and spoke of the great hazard of radioactive environmental and health dangers. He also, mistakenly but plausibly, claimed that such an initiative would help prevent nuclear proliferation.

Eisenhower said that national security prevented a detailed public discussion of the issue, and Nixon conceded Stevenson's good faith but said that the country should, in defense as in other matters, trust in the general who was commander in chief. The Soviet premier, Nikolay Bulganin, came to the aid of the Republicans by sending Eisenhower a message in midcampaign advocating a test ban, and pointing out that he was agreeing with "certain prominent public figures" in the United States. This enabled Nixon to fluff up his rhetoric a bit, and he happily called Stevenson a "clay pigeon . . . a Neville Chamberlain," who would make war more likely and who was proposing the "height of absurdity and irresponsibility." America, Nixon warned, sounding more avuncular than acidulous, could not afford a "trial and error president."[17]

In the last week of the campaign, two dramatic and unforeseen foreign policy events intruded. Egyptian president Gamal Abdel Nasser had nationalized the Suez Canal earlier in 1956, dispossessing the British-controlled Suez Canal Company. The French were the minority shareholders, and they were almost as annoyed by Nasser's action as British prime minister Anthony Eden was. Months were wasted in international conferences in London of what called itself the Suez Canal Users' Association. (Acronyms kept being devised and abandoned because they were always rude words in one of the languages of the shipping nations, especially Turkish.) The U.S. ambassador in London, Winthrop Aldrich (Nelson Aldrich Rockefeller's uncle), advised Dulles on October 24 that an Anglo-French invasion at Suez, possibly in coordination with the Israelis, would be launched in a few days, according to Walter Monckton, one of Eden's ministers. One of the senior Foreign Office civil servants, Patrick Dean, implied something similar to the London CIA station head a few days after that. There was no official advice to the U.S. government, much less consultation with it, although Eisenhower had made it clear through the autumn talks in London that his country opposed a restoration by force of the canal to Anglo-French hands, or any military assault on Egypt.

A mad conception was devised, in which Israel would invade the Sinai and attack up to the canal but not cross it, and the British and French would, after the briefest lapse, leaving no possibility that their action was not considered premeditated, make an amphibious landing at the Mediterranean end of the canal, secure its western bank, and claim that they were installing a peacekeeping force to separate the Israelis and the Egyptians.

It was, unquestionably, one of the most ill-considered strategic plans ever devised in the long and uneven military history of either Britain or France. No one in the world would believe the bunk about peacekeeping. Launching such an initiative without formally advising the principal Western ally, the United States, was, to say the least, not in the spirit of the Western Alliance; the public of neither country would be impressed by such a ruse. There was no follow-up plan on how to end hostilities and produce an agreed settlement that would achieve anything for the aggrieved former owners of the Suez

Canal. And, surprisingly, though the Israelis executed their part of the plan very crisply, the Anglo-French invasion was a shambles, and they made sluggish progress against a very unimpressive military opponent.

Eisenhower, Nixon, and Dulles were all scandalized by this development. Both Eisenhower and Nixon felt that domestic political considerations, specifically for the presumed pro-Israeli sympathies of Jewish voters (only about 3 percent of the total but packed in big cities and in influential occupations, especially finance and the media, but usually Democratic anyway), should not affect the official American response. The impulse of all three men was to condemn the attackers. Eisenhower telephoned Eden and opened the conversation by saying that he assumed that Eden had become insane. This was a reasonable inference, but it did not contribute usefully to a resolution of the impasse.

Whatever Eisenhower and his closest collaborators thought of the Suez war, the British and French were America's closest and most important allies. When Dulles and Eisenhower in 1954 had refused to give any financial support to Egypt on the construction of the giant Aswan High Dam, and the U.S.S.R. stepped into the breach, Nasser ejected practically all Americans from the country. A deep freeze settled on Egyptian-American relations, which the U.S. stance on Suez did not alleviate until Nixon thawed them dramatically with Nasser's successor more than fifteen years later. The Aswan Dam decision by the Americans undoubtedly contributed to Nasser's determination to seize the Suez Canal. Allowing the World Bank to advance the Aswan Dam money, and then canceling, had to rank as one of the great blunders of the Eisenhower-Dulles foreign policy. Whatever its impact on the Suez question, it drove the Arab nationalists into the arms of the Russians and helped destabilize the friendly regime in Iraq. Less than two years after Suez, Eisenhower was calling Nasser a communist in public.[18]

What was required in 1956 was a creative solution that would convert the imbroglio to a positive outcome without putting unsustainable pressure on the Western Alliance. Instead of any such approach, Dulles fumbled around with the nonsensical Suez Canal Users' Association, which was supposed to take interim control of the canal. How it was supposed to do so, given the armed Egyptian operation of the canal, was not made clear. But to force the British out, and the French with them, Eisenhower directed the destabilization of the British currency by the U.S. Treasury. This was compounding the problem, not curing it, and internecine cabinet politics of the most disreputable variety, to which the prestige of Churchill was immune but to which Eden was vulnerable, now added itself to Eisenhower's pique.

While this was in progress, an anti-communist uprising broke out in Hungary, and a new government headed by Imre Nagy withdrew the country from the Warsaw Pact and asked for UN assistance. The Soviet Union invaded Hungary, suppressed the uprising, and ultimately executed Nagy. The United States, through the Voice of America and Radio Free Europe, had constantly urged the revolt of Eastern Europe, and incited the belief that it would be of assistance should such an uprising occur, but there is no evidence that their urgings had any significant impact on the Hungarians. Nor is there any reason to believe that most Hungarians wanted American military intervention. They sought neutrality like Austria and Finland. Nixon had sponsored a bill in 1951 to prepare a rapid assistance force in the event of just such an uprising, but Truman had blocked it.

Now, distracted by Suez and the U.S. election, Eisenhower did nothing but make unctuous noises. It was, especially after all his and Nixon's and Dulles's vapid posturing about the rollback of communism, liberation of Eastern Europe, and, as Nixon at least would have it, retrieval of Yalta, a serious dual failure of American foreign policy. Stevenson waffled on both matters and would have been no better. (Hungary had been militarily con- ceded to Stalin by Churchill in October 1944, four months before Yalta and against Roosevelt's wishes, but Stalin would have taken it anyway.) Eisenhower had not been overly hawkish, and so was somewhat consistent, but Dulles and Nixon were a disappointment. Dulles was usually long on belligerency and short on imagination, where Nixon usually possessed both, but they both just flimflammed. Nixon at least recognized that U.S. policy was mistaken, but he wasn't sure what alternative to propose.

In his memoirs, Nixon acknowledged that Suez was a failure of foreign policy judgment. Eisenhower should have offered his good offices to both sides in the Middle East, which would have been accepted, advanced Nasser a loan that would have been used to compensate the shareholders of the Suez Canal Company, and secured the withdrawal of the invaders in exchange for a reinforced guarantee of unfettered access to the canal. The British and French could then have claimed to have achieved something. The United States should not have destabilized the British currency. It was an outrageous treatment of a glorious, if momentarily misguided, ally. Eden's health broke down; he was deserted by his party and forced from office, replaced by Harold Macmillan, the chancellor of the exchequer, who had told Eden, probably falsely, that the country could not resist American currency pressures. Eisenhower could not be blamed for the internecine skullduggery of the British Conservative government, but having been shabbily treated by his allies, he overcompensated in revenge. His purpose should have been the conservation of a grand alliance, not petulant vengeance on the principal allies.

The French premier, Guy Mollet, who followed Faure, who had followed Laniel and Mendes-France, was not as shaken by events as Eden was. But France had seen again how little use the American alliance was when it was most needed. The country was now mired in the Algerian war, with several hundred thousand draftees in a savage conflict. The Fourth Republic was clearly not able to command the respect of the country and make France a coherent force in the world. De Gaulle's long-awaited and much foreseen return to effect the changes he had advocated in 1945 and 1946 was now probably imminent, and was in fact only eighteen months away. If Eisenhower had lifted a finger to assist the French in avoiding humiliation at the hands of communists in Indochina and Arab nationalism in the Middle East, its relations with the French Fifth Republic, when de Gaulle set it up, would surely have been much less troublesome. Alliances are, after all, reciprocal matters.

The British and French and Israelis withdrew, and a United Nations force of "peacekeepers" was inserted between Egypt and Israel. The Canadian minister for external affairs, Lester B. Pearson, won the Nobel Peace Prize for proposing this idea. Macmillan sent Eisenhower a telegram including the phrase "Over to you," meaning that Britain would happily let the United States deal with the Middle East almost exclusively. Thus was a powerful and useful regional ally simply dispensed with; yet Eisenhower in his memoirs strongly defends his handling of Suez.

As for Hungary, the desire of the United States to avoid war with the U.S.S.R. is commendable, but there was an opportunity for a useful initiative. At the least, Eisenhower should have proposed a neutral status for Hungary, like that of Austria, or what came to be called "Finlandization," and offered in exchange to the U.S.S.R. some corresponding NATO withdrawal, even if only some force reductions, or the removal of some secondary bases, such as from Greece or Spain. More interesting would have been to supplement this offer with the air landing, by invitation from Nagy, of some airborne forces in western Hungary. In exchange for extracting the Anglo-French from their self-authored debacle at Suez, the United States could have got some of their forces to join them in Hungary, not with a view to war or occupation, but to destabilize the Russian empire and turn up the pressure for compromise. Nagy did eventually ask for the help of the "international community." Sending forces would have been a bold move, but might have been justifiable, if only to redeem the Churchill-Stalin accord of October 1944, which promised the Western Allies a 25 percent sphere of influence in Hungary, to the U.S.S.R.'s 75 percent.

NATO did not possess the ground combat forces or the will to conduct a conventional war with the Soviet Union in Central Europe, and a nuclear war was out of the question. But such a move might have sent the whole of occupied Europe up in flames under the nose of the Russians, and enabled Eisenhower to propose a general withdrawal of the U.S.S.R. and the United States from Western Europe other than Germany. Almost anything short of a direct act of war would have been preferable to the blustering and helplessness that did occur. Truman, Marshall, and Acheson would almost certainly have done better. It must be said that Nixon was not much better than Eisenhower in these crises. He wanted Israel, Britain, and France rebuked, though not so publicly, and said little about Hungary, though he was uneasy about inaction.

The election campaign ended on a particularly undignified note, from an uncharacteristic source, Adlai Stevenson. On election eve, he gave the customary closing address for his party on national radio and television, and this most elegant and civilized of public men plumbed a depth Nixon had never tested. Stevenson said, "Distasteful as this matter is, I must say bluntly that every piece of scientific evidence we have, every lesson of history and experience, indicates that a Republican victory tomorrow would mean that Richard M. Nixon probably would be president of this country within the next four years." He elaborated again on what a disaster that would be, not because Eisenhower would be such a loss, but because of the complete unsuitability of the vice president.

This was a disgraceful, a shameful, and an inexcusable statement. It had the utility, however, of ensuring that in the terrible exchanges of slander and malevolence that Nixon waged over the years with the Democrats, his opponents had scraped the barrel and dug lower than he had. He had been rough with Jerry Voorhis in 1946, but the nonsense about Marcantonio and the CIO PAC was not beyond tolerable limits. He had been rough with Helen Gahagan Douglas in 1950, with the various "pink" charges and innuendos, but no worse than she had been in endlessly calling him "Tricky Dick" and finally a fascist, and she had started it. He had been unacceptably destructive toward Truman and Acheson in 1952, but he had been Eisenhower's hit man, and Truman gave it back pretty well; the former president was one of the most pugnacious politicians in American history and he could take care of himself.

Nixon had gone too far in his attacks on Stevenson in 1952, with the outrageous comments about "Sidesaddle Adlai" and the absurd allegations about his support of Hiss. But in 1956, Stevenson's attacks on Nixon, culminating in his prediction of the imminent death of the incumbent president on the asserted basis of scientific evidence, were more contemptible than anything Nixon had come up with and provided the vice president an unhoped for, and historically little-noted, moral victory. (Eisenhower finished out his second term with only one medical incident and outlived Stevenson by four years, despite being ten years older.)

Eisenhower won the second-greatest plurality in American history up to that time, 9.6 million votes, next only to Roosevelt's in 1936, about 35.6 million to 26 million for Stevenson. The president, and it was certainly a personal victory, despite Nixon's hard and effective work, had taken about 56 percent of the vote, a strong though far from unprecedented showing, quite close to what Hoover had done in 1928 and Roosevelt in 1932, and behind Harding's landslide in 1920 and Roosevelt's in 1936. But the Republicans came back with an unchanged number of senators and three fewer congressmen. Eisenhower was disgusted that, for the first time for a victorious president since General Zachary Taylor in 1848, he had not brought either house of Congress in with him. Eisenhower blamed this setback on "mossback" Republican old guardsmen.

This election night, the Nixons and the Eisenhowers were together at the Park-Sheraton Hotel in New York, and Eisenhower claimed that it was time to start a new party. Nixon remonstrated with him not to include, as he was threatening to do, any such reflections in his comments to the party faithful downstairs. A Gallup Poll just before the election indicated that Eisenhower's approval rating was 76 percent to 8 percent negative and that the corresponding Nixon figures were around 45 percent to 28 percent, but that would not have caused the drag in the congressional voting. This was a Nixon victory also, as he became only the seventh person to win two consecutive elections as vice president – the fifth if the criterion is contested elections – and only the third to win two straight elections running with the same presidential candidate.* Of thirty-three holders of the office of president, Eisenhower was the eleventh to win two consecutive terms, the ninth to win two consecutive contested terms.

Nixon did distinguish himself, at Eisenhower's request, in trying to assist the hundred thousand Hungarian refugees who streamed into Austria, many of them screaming epithets at the United States for its failure to do anything except watch with proverbially folded arms while the masses of Budapest threw Molotov cocktails or rocks at Soviet tanks. At Eisenhower's prompting, Nixon flew to Austria on December 18 to try to help organize support for Hungarian relief and immigration to the United States. Eisenhower favored this but was unable to move the Congress, as Roosevelt had been unable to move Congress to admit more fugitives from Nazi oppression in the thirties.

Nixon went with William Rogers and the ambassador to Austria, Llewellyn Thompson (subsequently ambassador to Moscow), and a congressman, Robert Wilson. After a dinner in his honor given by the Austrian government, he drove to the border and met with some young refugees. He asked them if they blamed the Voice of America and Radio Free Europe for inciting false hopes, and they replied that they did. Nixon wanted to go right to the border, and some of the refugees accompanied him, on a hay wagon towed by a tractor. He was up all night and kept to his scheduled meetings the following day. This trip was not a publicity stunt, though it was favorably publicized (and Nixon generally was kindly treated by the press for his well-modulated election campaign and gracious post-election comments). The vice president returned on December 24, and met the president on December 26. Nixon now regretted his vote in 1952 to override Truman's veto of the McCarran-Walters Act severely restricting immigration.

Nixon wrote up a report of this trip and released it to the press on New Year's Day. He proposed naturalization of temporarily admitted political

---

* After the aforementioned T.R. Marshall and John N. Garner. George Washington's elections with John Adams, and James Monroe's second election with Daniel Tompkins, were uncontested. George Clinton and John C. Calhoun were each elected vice president with different presidents in consecutive elections.

refugees and authority for the president to issue visas above the quotas for fugitives "from communist persecution." There were no votes in it, the country was indifferent, and Nixon tried a hard selling job on Speaker Sam Rayburn, who wouldn't hear of it and complained about unemployment in Dallas. Nixon visited Herbert Hoover, who had organized relief in Europe after the First World War, and asked him how something might be done for the Hungarian refugees. Hoover recommended using agricultural surpluses, as he had done nearly forty years before. Nixon tried, but could not even secure congressional approval for that. With Truman gone and Eisenhower reelected but unable to bring his own party in with him in the Congress, the Democrats did not feel the need to do anything except respond to sluggish local opinion. Nixon did his best, with Eisenhower's full support, and found it very discouraging.

Nixon had again been proved correct when he had warned Eisenhower that Democratic control of the Congress would paralyze the administration, and the appropriate response was not Ike's petulance about founding a new party. If Eisenhower was not prepared to do anything about Khrushchev's taking on the role, as Nixon put it, of "the Butcher of Budapest," he could have foreseen the need to help refugees at least, and put that in his pre-electoral message in dramatic terms. At least he and Nixon could then have claimed that they had a fresh public mandate to be generous to the unfortunate (and gullible) Hungarians who responded to America's invitation to throw out the Russians, and then fled for their lives and nearly starved to death when they were refused any American assistance. In fact, American embassies and consulates, and those of many other countries, were directed to be generous to Hungarian visa applicants and the refugees were quickly resettled.

The United States had become the world's greatest power very quickly. It had managed its entry onto the very center of the world stage with outstanding statesmen, especially Roosevelt, Truman, Eisenhower, Marshall, MacArthur (in Japan), Acheson, and others, including Nixon. But it did not have the natural attitudes of a country with worldwide interests and a population that was especially aware of the world. This was the principal reason why it was necessary to stir up such virulent anti-communist sentiment to maintain a consensus for a containment policy throughout the world. The people responded to communism not as a group of national antagonists, but as if it were a contagion transmitted by contact, or through digestion or inhalation. It was some time before the American people, in their natural generosity, would see the need for consistency and stability in their foreign policy. Their vice president, however, was becoming a steadily more thoughtful and intelligent foreign policy analyst and planner. And he was now, more than anyone else, the coming man.

— III —

After the tumultuous end to the election campaign, and to events in Hungary and the Middle East, the New Year and the new presidential and vice presidential term began very quietly. Nixon bought a new and larger home, a Tudor six-to-eight-bedroom house in Wesley Heights that had formerly belonged to Franklin D. Roosevelt's first attorney general, Homer S. Cummings (whom Roosevelt eventually fired, blaming him for the abortive Supreme Court-packing measure that Nixon used to rail against when first setting out on a public career as a young lawyer). He had hired H.R. (Bob) Haldeman as his special assistant, and Haldeman recommended John Ehrlichman as legislative assistant. Ehrlichman was unable to accept, but he would be back. Nixon's best friends appeared to be Bill Rogers, Bebe Rebozo, and Billy Graham, with whom he discussed a full range of theological and political matters.

Nixon met often with John Foster Dulles, and while they were not friends in the sense of loosening up very much with each other, they were allies and spoke almost every day. Nixon went to lunch at Dulles's home and they agreed to require that Stassen be made directly subordinate to Dulles. Stassen had made such a complete fool of himself in his frenzied dump-Nixon effort that Eisenhower was resistless against this, and Stassen soon quit to run unsuccessfully for governor of Pennsylvania. He vanished off the radar in an endless series of frivolous election campaigns.

Eisenhower and Dulles prevailed upon Nixon to undertake another foreign trip, to Ghana, Liberia, Ethiopia, Uganda, Sudan, Libya, Tunisia, Morocco, and Italy. He traveled with a press group of thirty, more than half of them from what was known as the "Negro press." As most of the countries he visited were not geopolitical powerhouses, he did not achieve great publicity, although he and Pat were, as always, very well briefed and tireless in their exploration of the countries they visited. He had nothing to bring with him to impress or please the Africans, and so his conversations with the leaders he visited were not overly substantive. The new head of Ghana,

Kwame Nkrumah, was so outraged that all Nixon had was an Eisenhower Fellowship for one Ghanaian student that at the official dinner for Nixon he seated him at the back of the hall and put the Red Chinese at the head table with him. Nixon told the press he found it entertaining to be so snubbed (by such a mountebank).

More important was Nixon's meeting with the young American civil rights leader Martin Luther King Jr., the undoubted star of the proceedings in Ghana. King told the press that Nixon should make "a tour of the American South." Nixon arranged to encounter King the next day, had a long talk with him, and asked King to meet with him when they had returned to the United States. The rest of the tour went off fairly uneventfully, although Nixon had good talks with the king of Morocco, the emperor of Ethiopia, the president of Tunisia, and several others. He returned to Washington on March 21 and released a report on his trip, in which he predicted that Africa "could well prove to be the decisive" factor in the determination of the struggle between the West and communism.

He met with Eisenhower, who was not much interested in Africa, and had an exchange with him about the aspirations to independence of the African peoples in particular. Eisenhower felt that the United States had to support the claims to independence of almost all peoples, to maintain consistency with the principles of its own revolution.

Nixon cautioned that the subject had to be approached more carefully, especially in respect of Algeria, officially a department of Metropolitan France and geographically much closer to France than Alaska or Hawaii was to the United States. There was a terrible war in progress in Algeria, where more than 10 percent of the population was French (including the renowned novelist Albert Camus) and, obviously, large numbers of the Muslim population wished to remain part of France. John F. Kennedy gave a speech in July proposing a Senate resolution favoring Algerian independence. Eisenhower was in some sympathy with this, but Nixon seemed to be almost alone in the upper reaches of the U.S. government in taking seriously the sensibilities, as well as the positive and negative potential, of France as an ally. Nixon advocated working with the French for a compromise rather than trying to bulldoze them.

Nixon lost no time meeting with Martin Luther King. The administration, under Nixon's prodding, had produced the first civil rights bill since Reconstruction, and the Southern Democrats had largely emasculated it, especially in the stipulation of jury trials in many matters, which assured the triumph of the segregationists. Dr. King and his chief associate in the Southern Christian Leadership Conference, Rev. Ralph D. Abernathy, came to see Nixon and said that, unlike many black leaders, they believed that the bill, despite its lacerations, should be passed. They thought the bill better than none at all, and King went further and told Nixon that if it did pass, there would be two million African-Americans on the rolls in the South who were not there previously, and implied that they would vote Republican.

King wrote to Nixon after their meeting in Washington of "how deeply grateful we are to you for your assiduous labor and dauntless courage in seeking to make the Civil Rights Bill a reality. This has impressed people all across the country, both negro and white. This is certainly an expression of your devotion to the highest mandates of the moral law." King went on to claim that it was also an indication of Nixon's political sophistication, because "the negro vote is the balance of power in so many important big states that one almost has to have the negro vote to win a presidential election."

This was a slight exaggeration, but it was not chiefly from the political angle that Nixon, for once, was looking at it. This was Nixon the Quaker: brought up to see African-Americans as equals, with blacks often invited randomly in to dinner by his grandmother Milhous, who had had African-American friends at school and as an undergraduate had talked through with his unofficial spiritual adviser, Billy Graham, the moral implications of the racial questions. He did not believe that the United States could retain its moral credibility in the world, or its moral self-esteem, or even its status as a conscientious, largely Christian country, if it did not end the systematic injustice toward black citizens. Nixon sent his daughters to integrated private schools, and he refused to sign a race-restrictive covenant on the resale of his new house.

Nixon also saw the potential for splitting the Democrats, as Lincoln had split them between Stephen A. Douglas of the North and John C. Breckinridge and others of the South, nearly a hundred years before. More than half of the Democrats were more or less in favor of the enhancement of civil rights for African-Americans, but at least a third, in the South, were fervently opposed.

Nixon lobbied hard for the modified Civil Rights Bill. The jury trial amendment would severely dilute its effect, but it was impossible to contest the right to a jury trial in the United States. Nixon warned the Republican leaders in the Congress that if the Republicans held out for more, the Democrats would kill it and claim to be champions of civil rights in the North and West, and of states' rights in the South. The bill did finally scrape through the Congress. Eisenhower, who had done his best to help it through, was urged by Nixon and King to sign it, but by Ralph Bunche of the UN, Jackie Robinson, the first African-American in major-league baseball, and by the dean of black labor leaders, A. Philip Randolph, to veto the bill as insufficient. The president followed Nixon's advice, and the Civil Rights Act of 1957 became law.

During his deliberations about the bill, Eisenhower met with Southern Democratic leaders, including Senator Richard Russell of Georgia. Jackie Robinson and Roy Wilkins of the NAACP came to Nixon and asked him to arrange for the president to see the African-American leaders also – King, Randolph, and the NAACP. Nixon did his best, but Eisenhower, who was ambivalent about African-Americans, declined. This was a shocking decision, considering that African-Americans were 11 percent of the population, it was ninety-four years after the Emancipation Proclamation, and Roosevelt and Truman had regularly met with African-American leaders. Nixon was well recognized as, in civil rights terms, the most liberal and activist senior federal political leader in the country.

Meanwhile, the civil rights movement was approaching one of its dramatic climaxes. The Supreme Court had determined in 1954, in *Brown v. Board of Education*, that segregation of schools was unconstitutional. Eisenhower, though he did not approve of segregation, was no enthusiast of enforcing the court's ruling. Resistance from the white South was fierce, and there were legal challenges to details not exactly specified in the Supreme Court's decision. By early 1957, federal district courts, following the law made by the Supreme Court, were ordering the integration of specific schools and school boards, including Central High School in Little Rock, Arkansas. The confrontation could not be deferred much longer.

The segregation showdown occurred in Little Rock, in the fall of 1957, when Governor Orval Faubus called out the National Guard to prevent the integration of Central High School. In a subsequent meeting between the president and the governor, Eisenhower believed Faubus had assured him that he would not continue his defiance of the federal courts' desegregation orders. But that is what Faubus did, and Eisenhower, recognizing the challenge to the rule of law and federal authority, ordered units of the

United States Army to Little Rock to ensure access to Central High for neighborhood black youths. The world was astounded by photographs of little black girls in crisp, clean dresses being escorted into school by heavily armed paratroopers with fixed bayonets, past braying redneck mobs. Eisenhower did the necessary, and without hesitation, but the whole episode was a public relations disaster for the country.

Nixon was not much involved in the decision-making over Arkansas, but there was no choice and he was a much more strenuous supporter of it than Eisenhower himself had been. He wrote innumerable letters to influential Southerners, which generally included the passage that "the issue is a moral one and is of such transcendent importance that all Americans must face it." Nixon did not try to finesse it with the Southern whites, or sugar the pill. Segregation was immoral and unlawful and it had to end. The carrot he did hold out to the South, then and subsequently, was that these profound changes had to be effected fairly and, above all, the South could not be penalized by being singled out; Nixon was well aware of the hypocrisy of much of the North in the same matters. In straight political terms, he thought the Republicans could take back the African-American and some liberal white votes from the Democrats in the North, and be the party of the future in the South, the party of moderates of both races, whose numbers were certain to grow, leaving the Democrats tied to the sinking barge of the rednecks, not to say the Klansmen.

Little Rock was not the only education issue facing the administration. The demographic bulge created by the baby boom was putting great strains on the local school boards. The Republicans had put through legislation to aid education in 1956, but the subject arose again in 1957. Many Republicans did not want to return any tax money to the states or local school boards. The administration and liberal Republicans wanted federal grants for specific purposes, so segregationist school boards would not misallocate the funds. The Democrats wanted undivided grants, for precisely this purpose, to enable segregationist boards to enjoy federal funding but prolong racial injustice and, as it had been defined, unconstitutionality. But the influential African-American congressman from Harlem, Adam Clayton Powell, had moved an amendment denying funds to any state that retained segregation.

Nixon had an uphill struggle with sluggish congressional Republicans like Charles Halleck and Everett Dirksen. But he hammered both the moral and political arguments and Eisenhower came down strongly on his side. The new education legislation was finally passed in 1958, as the National Defense Education Act, which provided direct grants to states for upgrading science and mathematics programs, and low-interest loans and fellowships to university undergraduates and graduate students.

Nixon chafed in the vice presidency, where there was no executive authority and little of interest to do, apart from being the political guru of the administration and taking the odd foreign trip. He agitated with Dulles and Eisenhower, and the president wrote him an extremely platitudinous letter ("there is an interrelationship between expenditures and taxation, and the domestic economy"[19]) suggesting an unspecific coordinating role between some of the departments, but no one would surrender any jurisdiction, and Nixon could not impose any. Eisenhower should have done what subsequent presidents did – create a range of commissions with important but temporary mandates – and put Nixon at the head of them.

On October 4, 1957, the United States was startled, from the president through the whole population, by the successful Soviet launch of the first space satellite, the Sputnik. A few weeks later, national perplexity increased when an American rocket that was to launch a U.S. space satellite blew up a few feet over the launch pad before the news cameras of the world. Eisenhower downplayed the whole affair and assured everyone that American defense capabilities were more than adequate and far greater in these areas than the Russians'. This was true, and the American public was generally inclined to believe Eisenhower on defense matters because of his impeccable military career.

Nixon had always had his doubts about what he considered to be Eisenhower's rather complacent approach to defense, not so much in absolute terms as in public and political relations areas. Nixon wanted Eisenhower to say to the country that he would recommend paying any price necessary to ensure American military superiority. Instead, the president warned against "hasty and extraordinary effort under the impetus of sudden fear." Eisenhower would never have to face the voters again; Nixon's greatest elections were ahead of him. He could see that the Democrats were going to make defense and space exploration a big issue. The next Democratic presidential candidate would not be such a dove as Stevenson, and Nixon did not have a five-star general's uniform to swaddle himself in, as the incumbent did.

On November 25, 1957, Eisenhower had a stroke. Adams called Nixon, who came in haste to the White house. It did not seem especially serious, but Eisenhower got words garbled. He had to be virtually browbeaten by his wife not to attend a state dinner that evening, and Nixon took his place. Eisenhower was so frustrated by his condition that he was threatening to resign. When Nixon and Adams called upon him the next day he had improved measurably, and the following day he was signing papers and conducting a little business from his bed. Nixon held a press conference, during which he made a very good impression, and assured everyone that the cabinet was functioning well as a team. Thanksgiving Day arrived and Eisenhower insisted on taking his wife to church to be seen by the public, and then they went to Gettysburg for the long weekend.

The country was pretty well reassured by this point, but there were a number of editorial comments that seriously irked Eisenhower. Walter Lippmann thought Eisenhower should make Nixon the acting president, and several others thought he should retire. Drew Pearson called for Ike's retirement and added, to Nixon's merriment, that Nixon was a fine man and would make an excellent president. (Their relations had improved considerably since 1952, when Pearson had mistakenly accused him of tax fraud. This was another dividend of Nixon's new relaxed attitude to the Democrats.) These editorial reflections did galvanize Eisenhower into going back to work on the Monday after Thanksgiving. He recovered energy quickly and went to Europe in December for a NATO chiefs of state and government meeting.

Brownell had retired as attorney general and was replaced by Nixon's friend Bill Rogers, who was consulted about procedures should there ever be a problem with Eisenhower's competence. In February 1958, Eisenhower wrote Nixon a letter, which he handed to him, with a copy to Rogers at the same time, in which he outlined a status of "acting president" in the event of his own incapacity. If Eisenhower was aware of the incapacity, he would hand over to Nixon, and take his office back when he felt well enough. If he didn't recognize it, Nixon could take over anyway, but Eisenhower would still be able to regain the office when he felt equal to it. This wasn't overly practical, as Eisenhower would presumably declare himself competent, if he were unaware of a problem, as soon as Nixon had declared him incompetent. In any case, this was an adjustment to the Constitution, which is ultra vires to two individuals, even the two senior officials of the government.

The letter was announced on February 26, 1958, and greeted with some astonishment by the press, but Eisenhower declined to answer hypothetical questions about it. It was a vote of confidence in Nixon, and the compliments paid to Nixon in the letter were themselves a fine commendation.

— IV —

Dulles and Eisenhower asked Nixon to undertake another trip, this time to South America. Initially it was to be present at the inauguration of Arturo Frondizi, the first democratically elected president of Argentina since before dictator Juan Perón and the generals who had sent Perón packing. The trip was extended to cover every South American country except Brazil, where Nixon had visited in 1956 for the inauguration of President Juscelino Kubitschek, and Chile, whose president would be visiting Washington while Nixon was in South America. It wasn't clear what the purpose of the trip was; Nixon had no messages to deliver, as he had had in his trip to the Far East in 1953, and no concessions or assistance to confer. Nixon did not, for once, particularly want to undertake the trip at all.[20]

Nixon and his party, including Pat, left on April 27 and flew to Montevideo, Uruguay. There was a press party of twenty-five, including Tad Szulc of the *New York Times* and Herbert Kaplow of NBC. Nixon stopped his motorcade unpredictably on the way in from the airport in Montevideo, and with his interpreter (the redoubtable Colonel, later General and Ambassador, Vernon Walters) engaged startled onlookers in conversation, asking about their families and problems. This worked quite well, and when he saw some hostile signs at the university, he decided to return the following day so he could engage the students in conversation. Nixon turned this technique into something of a commonplace, but it was innovative, and enterprising, and at times courageous. And in his position he had other things to do than debate with surly Uruguayan undergraduates. He had a brief and very successful impromptu debate with the head of the communist-dominated student union at National University, and when he left the campus received generous applause, as he did from the press in Montevideo and throughout Latin America the next day.

The party went on to Buenos Aires on April 30. The following day, in a farcical interlude of the kind that traditionally often awaits visitors to Latin America, Nixon arrived, in top hat and tails, ten minutes late for Frondizi's inauguration, which had already occurred when Nixon got to the reviewing stand. This was the chief ostensible reason for his entire trip. The ambassador had misjudged the traffic. It was never explained why there was not a police escort for the most important person at the ceremony, not excluding the new president.

Nixon only stayed for about half the parade and then returned to his hotel, changed into less formal clothes, and went to the picnic of the Municipal Workers' Union, where he joined a barbecue with ordinary workers and again made a very positive impression, on the union members and, through the media, on Latin America and the United States. Nixon went on to the University of Buenos Aires and had another successful visit, without any apparent initial hostility. Pat visited a children's polio hospital and also impressed everyone she met, as she always did on these visits.

They traveled on to Asunción, Paraguay, where they were greeted by the iron strongman of the country, President Alfredo Stroessner. Nixon claimed in his memoirs that the fact that he spent only one day in Paraguay was a clear message of American disapproval of dictators. There is no evidence to support this. The message would have been communicated much more effectively if he had not gone there at all. He plunged into crowds all day, quite convivially, and left the next day for La Paz, Bolivia. He repeated the same process here, and was well received. What Bolivia wanted was lower American tariffs on Bolivian tin imports, but Nixon was not in any position to offer that.

The vice president's party arrived in Lima, Peru, on May 7. From his arrival he was warned that all intelligence indicated that the communists and other local leftists were determined to avoid a Nixon public relations victory at their expense of the kind he had enjoyed elsewhere in South America. The rector of the University of San Marcos and the chief of police of Lima urged him not to go through with the planned visit to the university (the oldest in the Americas) the next day. There were many reports of leftist elements from all over Lima massing at the university to turn Nixon's visit into a fiasco, and possibly a physically dangerous occasion. He was prepared to change to a visit to the smaller and more conservative Catholic University if either the rector of San Marcos or the chief of police would publicly urge him not to come. They were concerned at loss of face if they did so, but privately urged Nixon not to come to San Marcos. He thought about it overnight.

On the next day, Nixon laid a wreath at the statue of General San Martín – next to Bolívar, South America's greatest liberator – and then decided that he would go through with the visit to the University of San Marcos as planned. There were two thousand surly and hostile students awaiting him, some with insulting signs. Nixon stopped his motorcade in front of them and walked quickly toward the most apparently militant of them, right hand outstretched, accompanied by Walters and another aide, Jack Sherwood. He had Walters shout the translation of "I want to talk to you. Are you afraid of the truth?" He asked the police not to push back the demonstrators. Nearby students (if that is what they were) seemed to be impressed by Nixon, but farther back, the demonstrators started throwing fruit, bottles, and stones, one of which glanced off Nixon's shoulder and struck Sherwood in the mouth. Nixon still told the police, via Walters, not to arrest anyone. "Let him go," he said. "I want to talk to him."

At this point, Nixon ordered a dignified retreat, facing the crowd. When they reached their car, Nixon stood on the back seat, raised his arms, and shouted (with Walters again translating), "Cowards! You are afraid of the truth. You are the worst kind of cowards!"[21] According to Nixon and Walters, as the car pulled away, Tad Szulc of the *New York Times*, running alongside, complimented him: "Good going, Mr. Vice President." Fawn Brodie claims that Szulc denies having said that. Szulc is a sometimes sensationalist reporter, and his denial would not be more believable than Nixon's assertion. Fawn Brodie, at least on Nixon matters, cannot be believed about anything. Nixon is not above embellishment, but Walters is an honest and unquestionable source, so it probably happened. Whether it did or not, the Latin American and U.S. press again credited Nixon with a gallant performance.

He went directly, unscheduled, to the Catholic University and intruded on an assembly electing the student council. He improvised an address on the importance of democracy, and then repaired to the university chapel, where he stood in the place of the clergy, beneath the effigy of Christ on the Cross, and answered questions for ninety minutes. He said that the hallmark of a great university was to encourage a "free expression of views."[22] The students were impressed and applauded warmly, even though many of the questions had been hostile.

When they returned to the Hotel Bolivar, there was a thick crowd of demonstrators, so Nixon again determined to walk through them. The police had done nothing to clear a passage for him, and he and Walters and Sherwood walked through the group, Nixon chatting amiably and shaking hands. Pat watched from their suite on the fourth floor and said that she had "never been more proud of him."[23] Again, fruit and small stones came down upon them, as well as spittle; one complainant, with a mouth full of tobacco juice, spat full in Nixon's face. Sherwood cuffed him aside as Nixon kicked his shin ("Nothing I did all day made me feel better."). He later wrote that "spitting in a person's face is the most infuriating insult ever conceived by man."[24]

In the afternoon, Nixon met with senior Peruvian government officials, and then held a press conference, where the local press tried to apologize for what Nixon had been subjected to. He wouldn't hear of it. He told them that the person who spat in his face was "spitting on the memory of San Martin . . . This day will live in infamy in the history of San Marcos University." It was an eloquent statement about the hypocrisy of "those who speak of freedom but deny it to others."

More important to Nixon, Eisenhower sent a telegram praising his "courage, patience, and calmness." Nelson Rockefeller, who had been undersecretary of state for Latin America and spoke Spanish fluently, and had set his sights on Nixon's position as heir to Eisenhower, and many other people, telegraphed their good wishes.

Nixon went on to Quito, Ecuador, where he determined not to visit the university but did meet with a delegation of students, strolled around town, had an unscheduled haircut, and gave a press conference in the barbershop. Quito, and Bogotá, Colombia, which followed, were both successes. Nixon and his whole entourage were now deluged with warnings that the last stop, Venezuela, would be very difficult. There were even rumors of assassination attempts, and Nixon requested assurance of adequate security from the Venezuelan government. This assurance was given. Sherwood tripled Nixon's accompanying security detail to twelve. On the plane from Bogota to Caracas, the American minister-counselor in the U.S. embassy in Caracas told Nixon that there would be large and friendly crowds to greet him, outweighing any leftist demonstrators.[25] Nixon had no reason to doubt this, and the charge that he was needlessly taking risks and taunting the South American left is unjust. (This episode did not raise his confidence in the career foreign service.)

The Venezuelans did have some grievances. The severe dictator Pérez Jiménez had just been driven out, but had been decorated and praised by Eisenhower with the Legion of Merit and the fantastic commendation that he was a "model" for Latin America. He and his corrupt and brutal police minister, Pedro Estrada, had been given temporary asylum in the United States. (Jiménez was eventually extradited back to Venezuela and imprisoned.) Nothing could have prepared the Nixon party for what was about to happen.

When his airplane taxied to a stop at the VIP landing place, it was clear that the large crowd on the observation deck and behind the peripheral fences was hostile. Nixon quickly exchanged greetings with the welcoming party, reviewed the honor guard, greeted some hangar workers, and then started toward the terminal. He dispensed with opening speeches, which would have been drowned out by the crowds shouting obscenities. When he and his wife were almost at the terminal, the band struck up the Venezuelan national anthem. The Nixons stopped and stood at attention, and the crowd on the observation deck spat down upon them in a brown cataract of expectorated tobacco juice. The Venezuelan police and soldiers, in immaculate uniform with gleaming bayonets, stood by motionless, even though some of the projectiles, liquid and otherwise, landed on them.

The Nixons, in a magnificent but strange gesture of implacability, did not move, though the band was barely audible above the howls of the orally incontinent mob. There were further, but lesser, outrages as the Nixons got to their cars. Nixon traveled with Walters, Sherwood, and the Venezuelan foreign minister, Oscar García Velutini, who obsequiously apologized for the disgrace at the airport, and tried to wipe the spit off Nixon's jacket and shirt with his handkerchief. Nixon told him not to bother, as he would burn them when he could. He tried to reinforce the quavering minister, who replied that they must not displease the communists, who were clearly responsible, because they had helped vitally in the overthrow of Pérez Jiménez.

As they approached the National Pantheon, where Nixon was to lay a wreath at the tomb of Simón Bolívar, there was a roadblock, and crowds streamed out from the side streets, in a poor working-class neighborhood. There was a gap in the roadblock through which the motorcade threaded, but they were soon at another, leak-proof blockade, which required the Nixon party to stop. There was a press truck in front, followed by Nixon's car, followed by Pat's car, which closed right up to the preceding vehicle's rear fender. The motorcycle police escort stopped, and remained in place, motionless, while the mob assaulted the official cars on both sides with rocks and pipes. Secret Service men came forward and personally barred anyone from trying to open the car doors. The mob virtually ignored Pat's car.

The car windows were shatter-proof, and so fairly resistant to the onslaught they received, but some glass came through and struck the foreign minister in the eye, which naturally amplified his hysteria. Walters also took a flying-glass wound in the mouth, but Nixon calmly told him to be ready to translate a good deal of Spanish for him later in the day. Sherwood and two of the Venezuelan policemen pulled revolvers, but the Americans prevailed upon the police to put theirs back in their holsters, and Nixon told Sherwood not to draw his gun unless he told him to. The nightmare continued for twelve minutes, and became very sinister when the mob, swollen to about six hundred people, started to rock the car.

A Venezuelan army unit finally appeared and cleared the way, and someone, presumably the somnolent or complicit police, fired a tear gas canister well back in the motorcade (which seriously disconcerted Rose Mary Woods, in the ninth car). The motorcade started forward and went through a breach in the roadblock created by the army. Nixon ordered that they depart the planned route, pass on Bolívar's tomb, and head straight for the U.S. Embassy residence. The foreign minister, Velutini, whose performance on the day must be reckoned one of the great fiascoes of diplomatic history, wailed that they must not be parted from their security escort. Nixon, with the admirable self-control he had exhibited throughout, said that they were better off without such "protection."[26] (There was, in fact, an even larger and uglier crowd at the National Pantheon, and they were wise to disappoint this mob.)

As soon as they reached clear road, Nixon ordered a stop to see how his wife was. Walters reconnoitered and said that she was calm and unharmed. They were in front of a hospital, and let the foreign minister off for treatment to his eye. The injury was not serious, and Nixon was happy to see the back of him. Nixon answered a few questions of American reporters and stuck to his Peruvian line that this was not personal but indicative of communist behavior and an affront to Venezuela itself: the Venezuelan flag had been torn down and trampled, the national anthem jeered and made inaudible, the foreign minister injured, and the country embarrassed.

He showered, took his first afternoon nap in twelve years of public life, met with some local American businessmen, and told a full press conference later in the afternoon that as far as he was concerned the incident was closed. The press of both countries applauded him lengthily. He canceled his schedule for the evening and had his dinner alone with his wife in the embassy residence, determined to leave Venezuela the next day without seeing the ruling junta, and, preferably, without laying eyes on the hapless Velutini again.

The incident was not quite over, however. There had been a break in communication between Caracas and Washington, and Eisenhower was concerned that anarchy had broken loose and that his vice president was in danger of his life. He ordered detachments of the 101st Airborne Division to Puerto Rico and of U.S. Marines to Guantanamo, Cuba, and the Caribbean Fleet, including an aircraft carrier, to Venezuelan waters. Inexplicably, Eisenhower made these movements public, which was unnecessary, and said that he was positioning the forces as he was in case the government of Venezuela requested assistance.

Given that the Venezuelan government had been complicit, or at the very least, grossly negligent, in this shameful incident, it is not clear what coincidence of circumstances the president might have imagined would have caused such a request. When he heard of it, Nixon was horrified, not only because calm had already been restored in Caracas without the marines and 101st, but because he correctly foresaw that this would be seen throughout the continent as gunboat diplomacy of a kind Latin Americans had long been accustomed to from the United States. Nixon issued a statement at nine that evening saying (with no authority, since he really knew nothing about it, and Eisenhower could have been cranking up to invade Venezuela for all he knew) that this was a minor movement of forces within American territories and repeating that the incident of earlier in the day was concluded.

The next day, Nixon declined the junta's invitation to lunch and announced that he would leave Venezuela at once. He was beseeched to stay for lunch, promised maximum safety, and the entire junta of five generals and admirals (the Venezuelan navy had fewer than ten ocean-going ships and an unusually high ratio of admirals to enlisted men) undertook to come to pick him up, take him to lunch, and then take him to the airport. He was escorted by tanks, jeeps, armored cars, and twelve truckloads of heavily armed soldiers. Nixon traveled with the acting president of the country, and their limousine "was an arsenal on wheels," Nixon wrote. "The floor was piled with submachine guns, revolvers, rifles, tear gas canisters, and ammunition clips; there was hardly room for our feet."[27]

They went to the extravagant officers' club, where the food was tasted to assure it had not been poisoned, and the military leadership conducted the Nixons to the airport through the same streets through which they had come in the opposite direction the day before. This time, there were heavy troop contingents all along the route, and as a preventive measure (which would not qualify as populist solicitude, but was effective), the army had heavily tear-gassed the cross-streets. When the vice president's plane got into the air, the whole planeload of reporters and staff applauded. They stopped for the night in Puerto Rico at President Eisenhower's request so he could prepare a proper welcome.

The president, escorting Julie and Tricia, the cabinet, about half the Congress, and fifteen thousand cheering people greeted the Nixons when they arrived at Washington National Airport. (Lyndon Johnson embraced the vice president, whom he had famously once described as a "chicken shit." When asked by a reporter to explain this, LBJ said that it was important to understand that "chicken shit can turn into chicken salad.")[28] Eisenhower had given the civil service a half holiday and large crowds lined the route to the White House; the Nixons rode there with Eisenhower and stayed for lunch. That afternoon, Nixon held a very successful press conference, was loudly cheered at a Women's National Press Club reception, and very warmly received at one of Eisenhower's famous stag dinners with some of his rich friends. Nixon was still on a high after days of acute tension.

Americans were overwhelmingly proud of the sangfroid and poise of their vice president and his wife, and they were right to be. The Nixons possessed, and had demonstrated, remarkable human qualities. Richard Nixon appeared to be without physical fear, and a determined and resourceful and untiringly energetic Cold Warrior. Walter Lippmann and James Reston took nothing from Nixon for courage, but described the trip as a disaster and pointed out that there were substantial problems in relations with Latin America. Nixon said as much in his press conference of May 21, when he asserted that if the corrupt oligarchies and juntas of the past did not give way to reform government, the communists would be a very serious threat. Privately, Nixon had agreed with the timeless J. Edgar Hoover over lunch that the South American junket had made "anti-communism respectable again."[29]

Dramatic events unfolded in France in the spring of 1958. The army was restive that the French government might not fight with adequate determination to retain Algeria as part of France, and there was some insubordination among senior officers. Charles de Gaulle, leader of the Free French, who had refused to accept defeat in 1940, and who had always predicted that the Fourth Republic would end in shambles, was invested with extraordinary powers to govern and to propose a new constitution.

He returned to power at the age of sixty-seven and soon went to Algeria, where he famously told a vast crowd, at the Algiers Forum, composed roughly half of French Algerians and half of Arab independentists, "I have understood you." Both irreconcilable groups cheered. De Gaulle prosecuted the war with redoubled vigor, instituted far-reaching reforms in favor of the Arabs, and entered into secret negotiations with the rebels. He offered what he called a "peace of the brave."

De Gaulle quickly produced a new constitution that was overwhelmingly approved by the country, for a Fifth Republic, which combined France's republican and monarchical traditions by making the president a virtual sovereign with a seven-year term. De Gaulle won about 80 percent of the vote as a presidential candidate, produced a new hard currency, gave independence with continued association with France to almost all French colonies, developed atomic weapons, and quickly revived France as one of the world's most powerful and important countries This would alter the world's geopolitical balance for the next twenty-five years. Next to Franklin D. Roosevelt and Winston Churchill, de Gaulle would be the greatest democratic statesman of the mid-twentieth century. He would be a great inspiration, and ultimately almost a mentor, as well as a trusted friend, to Richard Nixon.

On July 14, 1958, pro-Nasser factions in the Iraq military murdered the entire royal family and the long-serving prime minister, Nuri as-Said, and seized the government. The new regime immediately withdrew from the Baghdad Pact set up by Dulles in 1955, linking Iraq, Iran, Turkey, Pakistan, the United States, and Britain.

On July 15, in response to an out-of-date and garbled request from the Lebanese president, Camille Chamoun, Eisenhower sent a division of marines into Lebanon armed with nuclear-tipped, short-range rockets. Khrushchev and Nasser fulminated, but it was an effective show of strength. The forces were withdrawn after four months, with no combat casualties. But it was almost a rodomontade after four years of misconceived Middle East policy. If Eisenhower and Dulles had maintained support for the Aswan Dam, and kept a common front with Britain and France, Suez would not have occurred and the Iraqi monarchy and the regional alliance might have survived.

— v —

As the 1958 midterm elections approached, Nixon was uneasy, despite his rising electoral status. Eisenhower was so contemptuous of Karl Mundt, William Jenner, Jack Bricker, and his would-be vice president William Knowland, and had been so seduced by Lyndon Johnson and Sam Rayburn, that he was uninterested in the congressional results. Those particular Republicans were members of the contemporary Flat Earth Society, but the Republican Party did have more promising personalities, led by Nixon, and was in any case essential to the functioning of a two-party system. Eisenhower only slightly arose from this torpor when he figured out that a repudiation of the Republicans might be interpreted as a lack of public confidence in him. Eisenhower continued to be popular and respected, but his administration was becoming tired. Ike played golf with his wealthy friends while the Russians appeared to take a lead in space. His response was bland assurances to a country that he had helped to whip into such a fervor of anti-communism that they were busily building bomb shelters all over the country and demanding that their government erase any possible lead the Russians might have in rocketry. In fact, as Eisenhower said, there was no such lead, but cunning Soviet public relations made it seem that there was.

Nixon was also severely exasperated by Eisenhower's robotic insistence on keeping up taxes to reduce the deficit, rather than reducing taxes to stimulate growth, win votes, and, ultimately reduce the deficit through increased economic activity and reduced welfare costs. The Treasury secretary, since July 1957, succeeding George M. Humphrey, was Robert B. Anderson, whom Eisenhower had considered for some time the most capable person in the U.S. government except for himself. Anderson had been a Texas legislator and tax commissioner, had sold Mrs. Lyndon Johnson the famous Austin radio station that became the basis of the sizeable Johnson family fortune, and served as Eisenhower's secretary of the navy. He was an unimaginative fiscal conservative, but Eisenhower was constantly promising to campaign for him if he would run for president in 1960.

He was, with Dulles and Nixon, the strongman of the cabinet, and he supported Eisenhower's Dickensian fiscal humbug. (Anderson left public life with the administration in 1961, but was ultimately convicted of tax evasion and disbarred and imprisoned in 1987. He died two years later.) A recession was again settling on the country, and Eisenhower would neither reduce taxes nor increase public spending on defense, the space program, or the vast interstate highway program (eventually to be named the Dwight D. Eisenhower National System of Interstate and Defense Highways). The administration had suddenly come to look like a group of tired, detached, golfing, rich geriatrics.

Insiders thought Eisenhower was becoming doddery. Joseph Alsop wrote to Isaiah Berlin, the eminent British thinker, that he prayed for the presidency to be transferred to Nixon, an evolution in his thoughts which he acknowledged to be an "odd" turn of events. He said that Nixon had almost asked him a few days before how he could take issue with "a ramolli papa without getting disinherited yourself."[30]

Nixon needed to stand on the Eisenhower record, which he would implicitly try to present as the Eisenhower-Nixon record, while staking out new ground where he disagreed with the president. The jockeying for the 1960 election was already underway, and Kennedy and Nixon were running about even in the polls, somewhat ahead of Stevenson. (A joke was that Kennedy was demanding "equal time" from the Venezuelans, Nixon's visit to them having been such a boost to his poll numbers.)

Knowland had had the final attack of insanity of his public career (though not of his life), as he had determined to quit the Senate, where he had a reasonable chance of reelection, bump Goodwin Knight out of the governor's chair (to which Knight had moved from the lieutenant governorship on the retirement of Earl Warren to go to the Supreme Court), and use the California statehouse as a stepping stone to the presidency. William Jenner, mercifully, would not run again from Indiana; as McCarthy had died, this extreme anti-communist group was fading away.

Nixon became a pioneer in advocating stimulative tax cuts. It was a novel notion to the Republicans, and not fully assimilated Keynesian economics by the Democrats. In September, in a speech at Harvard University, Nixon outlined what became a supply-side blueprint: lower tax rates, especially in the higher brackets, but adjusted to appeal to a majority of taxpayers, and a comprehensive argument for economic growth and deficit reduction through the higher multiplier effect on private sector economic activity. He stated the then rather radical idea that moderate corporate and personal income tax cuts would actually increase revenue.

He presented these as ideas for consideration, and managed the delicate matter of not having cleared it with Anderson or Eisenhower by saying that he was offering food for thought and did not want to "put Anderson on the spot."[31] Nixon wanted a simpler tax system as well as generally lower tax rates. His proposals were ultimately taken up by succeeding presidents, passed in some part by President Johnson, and passed in fairly pristine and radical form by Ronald Reagan and again by George W. Bush. All of these tax reductions were successful. Nixon was, to a considerable degree, the progenitor of post-Depression American tax-cutting.

Nixon endlessly argued for a more positive, less morally deflating comment than the usual Eisenhower-Anderson theory that something desirable, such as increased spending on missiles, is either not really desirable or not affordable. Despite a wide and positive public and business response, and the distribution of hundreds of thousands of copies of his speech, Nixon received no notice at all from Eisenhower, who kept repeating his Dickensian economic catechism that expenditures had to stay within revenues. (In fact, he had an unbalanced budget in all but one year, but never a large deficit.)

The Republicans became further entwined in right-to-work controversies. Organized labor had become relatively well housebroken since Nixon helped put through Taft-Hartley in 1947, but a number of Republicans, especially Knowland in California and Bricker in Ohio, were running for a further assault on the rights of unions. This brought the Democratic union leaders, especially George Meany (AFL-CIO), Walter Reuther (UAW), and even the venerable John L. Lewis (United Mine Workers) out in greater force and ferocity than usual. Nixon calculated that this was an electoral loser in 1958, and ducked the issue completely.

Harder to duck was the problem of Sherman Adams. Adams had been hostile to Nixon, and there was little rapport between them. In fact, Adams had few friends in Washington; his blunt, monosyllabic New England manner was not conducive to the sort of logrolling that builds friendships in the higher reaches of the U.S. government. The origins of the controversy were rather picayune: New England industrialist Bernard Goldfine had given Adams a number of presents, including an about-to-be famous vicuna coat, and had paid for his hotel stops in Boston, to a total of about three thousand dollars over five years. Adams had made some telephone calls to federal agencies on Goldfine's behalf. The Democrats unearthed this at committee hearings and charged an outright case of influence-peddling, albeit on a very modest scale.

Adams was a naturally friendless man. He had no small talk, not even that of a sycophant. When Eisenhower painted a portrait of him, he said only, "Mr. President, you flatter me," and left without a word of thanks for the attentions of the painter, the world's foremost officeholder.[32] Adams had, and cultivated, the reputation of being the most powerful man in Washington except for the president. This was an affectation, as Eisenhower was too clever to be manipulated by anyone. Despite Adams's well-known hostility to Nixon, when the minor favors to and by Adams came to light and the Democrats started to magnify them into a serious issue, Nixon undertook some research on his own He produced a formidable list of presents that the Roosevelts and Trumans had received, including a mink coat and jewels for Eleanor. Nixon was ready to go with a counterattack, but Eisenhower did not want any such revelations, as he had accepted a great number of valuable gifts from his wealthy friends and did not want any comparisons with the Roosevelts and Trumans, who would have appeared rather restrained by comparison with Eisenhower.

It is hard to believe that Nixon embarked on this course wholly innocently. He had a fair idea of the nature of Eisenhower's friendships with many wealthy people. Their activities could have been used to even up the match between the president and the vice president that started in the fund crisis, was equalized by Nixon's Checkers speech, and opened up again by Eisenhower with the preposterous suggestion that Nixon take the post of commerce secretary in 1956. When Eisenhower immediately rejected any thought of a revelation of gifts to his predecessors, Nixon dropped it, having presumably made his point.

Nixon was motivated not by any affection for Adams or even Eisenhower, but by a desire to counterattack the Democrats. Adams was being pounded in the media, a process probably amplified by Nixon's campaign against the "crooks" of the Truman years. Nixon was preparing to run for president, and the condition of the Republican Party mattered a great deal more to him than it did to Eisenhower. He had breakfast with Eisenhower on July 15, 1958. He then met with Adams and urged him to resign because of the damage he was doing to the Republicans. Adams took the familiar Nixon position, with which Nixon could hardly disagree, that if Eisenhower wanted him to retire, he could ask him, but he would not quit at the request of messengers. Eisenhower did not want to ask Adams to quit, because of the many services the governor had rendered, so the problem just festered.

Nixon told Eisenhower in late August that the Republican Party stood to lose from Adams's presence and could not go all out in defense of him without counterattacking the Democrats on receipt of gifts, which Eisenhower forbade Nixon to do. It was an impossible state of affairs and the solution was obvious, but Eisenhower had to take it. When under this sort of a cloud, the suspected person had to take decisive action, as Nixon did with the fund speech. Adams just sat in the White House pretending that he was functioning normally, and Eisenhower sat in the next office hoping Adams would retire but neglecting to tell him that.

Nixon went on holiday with his wife and daughters to The Greenbrier, in West Virginia, on August 24. He had promised his family an uninterrupted holiday, but after one day Eisenhower telephoned and asked Nixon to come back to Washington to get rid of Adams. Eisenhower's loyalty to his long-serving chief of staff was commendable, but his inability to do the necessary, no matter how distasteful, was unbecoming someone who had been one of the world's great figures of command for fifteen years. Eisenhower now adopted the pretense that he and Nixon had agreed that Nixon would sever Adams. This was a feat of the president's imagination, but Nixon, as always, did the dutiful thing. He met with Adams and laid it out bluntly to him. Adams refused to budge and then met with the president and convinced him that he should stay. Nixon had warned Eisenhower that the Democrats would make it a matter of committee hearings in the run-up to the election. Eisenhower asked Nixon to play golf with him and took the specious position that "I can't fire a man who is sincere, just for political reasons. He must resign in a way I can't refuse." It was again astonishing, and perhaps illustrative of the ravages of years and illnesses, that so distinguished a leader had become so pusillanimous. Nixon had done what he could, and returned to West Virginia and his family holiday.

Eisenhower's former ambassador to London, and Rockefeller in-law, Winthrop Aldrich, told Eisenhower that Bernard Goldfine was a crook and that Adams had to go. Eisenhower sent the new chairman of the Republican

National Committee, Meade Alcorn, to deal with Adams. Alcorn said that he was speaking for the president, and Adams called Eisenhower on September 17 to say that he would leave in about a month. Eisenhower read him the pre-prepared statement that he had written up announcing Adams's resignation. Adams finally took the hint and retired a week later, but by clinging to the White House furniture as long as he had, Adams (and Eisenhower) had inflicted further inconvenience on the beleaguered Republican Party.

It was clear that the midterm election was going to be difficult, and almost all the advice Nixon was getting, including from such disparate sources as General Douglas MacArthur and Thomas E. Dewey, was to stay out of the campaign.[33] Nixon was being beseeched by the desperate party regulars to help in many places around the country. He wrote in his memoirs that "there was no one else to do it." This is true, but not the whole truth. Nelson Rockefeller was running against Averell Harriman for governor of New York and could emerge as the Republican rival Nixon was hoping to avoid. However grim the election result might be, this was the time to bank all the goodwill he could with the party regulars, and he again undertook a heavy campaign schedule.

Nixon did not have an easy argument to make. It was hard to run against the Democrats after six years of Republican rule. The administration, in the image of Eisenhower and Dulles, appeared to be old, tired, unimaginative, and repetitive. The country was slipping steadily into recession and Eisenhower and Anderson would not hear of doing anything to defer or ameliorate it.

Nixon focused on the split between Southern Democrats, who favored a strong defense and foreign policy but were civil rights bigots and filibustered anti-lynching bills, and the Northern and Western liberals, whom Nixon painted as extremists, tax-and-spend regulators, stooges of the labor leaders, and appeasers in international affairs. A Democratic congressional sweep, Nixon claimed, would produce a cataract of horrors from left-liberals and the Southern segregationists. It was a far cry from the bloodcurdling shrieks of treason and the Red fifth column with which he had regaled the country in the early fifties. It wasn't entirely believable, either, at least in reference to centrist Democrats like Kennedy, who was running for reelection as U.S. senator from Massachusetts. But it was the best Nixon could do.

Nixon almost turned his raw task into a replication of his Whittier football days, telling audiences that many had advised him against coming out in an unpromising cause, but that it need not be a losing cause; Republicans only had to have faith in themselves, etc. Cabell Phillips of the *New York Times* gives a good depiction of the hustings Nixon of 1958: "The brisk, buoyant march to the head table, the exaggerated hand-shaking with the other guests, follow a ritual pattern not unlike that used to show off a fighter in the prize ring. Mrs. Nixon, fragile and shy, is an important prop in this pageantry. There is always an extra measure of applause when the crowd recognizes her. His platform manner is that of a sales promotion manager pepping up his sales force. . . . His posture is mobile and expressive, and he scowls or smiles or betrays indignation or whips the air with a clenched fist, at precisely the right moment and with good elocutionary effect. His mood is earnest and evangelical and tinged now and then with righteous anger."[34] But Nixon sometimes seemed a "little too stagy . . . the sweep of his arms or the twists of his body or the counting of points on his long fingers seemed ill-timed with his words, as if speech and gesture had gotten out of sync, like a film running a few frames ahead or behind its sound track. Could either speech or gesture, therefore, proceed from genuine emotions or impulse?" He also tended to move sideways, for emphasis, at the podium, in "his Lawrence Welk gestures" (a reference to a well-known dance-band leader at the time).[35] Usually his delivery was successful but occasionally not.

There was a tempest in a teapot over a leak to the *New York Times*, September 27, 1958, that four thousand out of five thousand letters received at the State Department about the U.S. determination not to yield Quemoy and Matsu were negative. Nixon issued a belligerent statement expressing shock that a State Department employee would set out to undercut the secretary and the country's policy, but expressed greater annoyance at the attitude that "the weight of the mail rather than the weight of the evidence" should determine administration policy.

There was a good deal of criticism that he was bullying the unnamed indiscreet official, and talk of the "old Nixon" and not the relatively bonhomous "new Nixon," but it wasn't a very durable controversy. It has never been clear why Nixon thought it was his place, rather than that of Dulles, to issue any statement at all. He later claimed that he was combating State Department officials who were undercutting Dulles and trying to soften U.S. resistance against communist aggression. Even allowing for some degree of lassitude from Eisenhower, it is still not obvious what business the vice president thought he had triggering a public controversy over leaks in the State Department. Dulles had never made any secret of the fact that he didn't want any help running his department.

Unfortunately, Nixon chose to freshen up the election campaign by going after Truman and Acheson again. On October 13 he denounced "the defensive, defeatist, fuzzy-headed thinking which contributed to the loss of China and led to the Korean War. . . . The Acheson foreign policy resulted in war and the Eisenhower-Dulles policy resulted in peace."

The next day Dulles told a press conference that partisan discussion of foreign policy was "highly undesirable." Nixon telephoned Dulles and asserted that when the Democrats attacked his and Eisenhower's foreign policy, somebody had to reply to them. Dulles issued a clarification, but the next day Eisenhower told his press conference, "Foreign policy ought to be kept out of partisan debate. . . . I realize that when someone makes a charge, another individual is going to reply. I deplore that."[36] This was widely seen as a rebuke of Nixon, and was seen by Nixon as a very irritating and gratuitous box on the ear from his leader, whose somewhat dyspeptic foreign and defense policies, as Nixon considered they had become, he was loyally trying to defend.

There was plenty of skepticism still in the dovecotes of the American media about any "new Nixon," and this flushed them all out again, flapping and screeching. There was absolutely no point to this relapse by Nixon, especially as he considered that the administration's policy was not especially distinguished. When Nixon set out on his countless partisan trips, designed to whip up the fighting spirit and ingratiate himself with the party regulars, he seemed to torque himself up to irrational, and tactically ill-considered, utterances.

Nixon told his press conference in San Francisco, on the same day as Eisenhower's press conference, that he was defending the administration against unfair attack, and that he had no quarrel at all with the stance the president was taking and was merely trying to defend Republican candidates. Eisenhower then sent him two telegrams, one summarizing the bipartisan agreement on the main lines of foreign policy, but defending the right to rebut attacks on the administration's implementation of foreign policy and praising Nixon's talent at doing so. The other telegram invited Nixon to call him if there were any misunderstanding between them. Nixon wrote, "His telegram was hardly sufficient to repair the damage that had been done to me." He called Dulles to say that if he didn't get a public statement of support from the president, "I may just have to make a statement about how you and the president wanted me to carry on this attack." This smoked out Eisenhower, who made a supportive statement.[37]

Nixon now went on a peace offensive: "There is no war party in the United States" (a line of Roosevelt's). "All Americans want peace. There is no party of surrender . . . [Truman was] a gallant warrior," whom he praised for the Marshall Plan and resisting aggression in Korea. Nixon even offered to play a duet with Truman at the National Press Club, but Truman wasn't having it. "He has called me a traitor. . . . I've refused to enter the Senate when he was there."[38]

When Nixon came to New York on October 23, Rockefeller did not meet with him at first, and Nixon only briefly mentioned Rockefeller in his remarks at a large rally in Garden City, Long Island, while he referred extensively to Senate candidate Kenneth Keating. Rockefeller had taken his distance from Eisenhower, and had declined even to appear on television with the president. At Garden City, Nixon tailored his remarks to a comparatively liberal audience and was credited with an artful performance.

There was not great ill will between Nixon and Rockefeller, but Rockefeller was angling for the endorsement of the ultra-liberal *New York Post*, which, since the fund crisis, had always led the press antagonism to Nixon. When Dewey and others pressured Rockefeller to meet with Nixon, they had breakfast together, which caused Dorothy Schiff, proprietor of the *Post*, to write that but for his meeting with Nixon, Rockefeller might well have received the *Post*'s endorsement. This was better than an endorsement, as no sane voter would vote against Rockefeller just because he had had breakfast with the chief campaigner of his party and vice president of the United States, no matter what his personal opinion of Nixon. Privately, Nixon and Rockefeller agreed that the administration had bungled the defense issue and blundered into a recession that was quite avoidable.

The result on election night was even worse than had been anticipated. The Democrats gained seven Senate seats and forty-seven House seats, and now had 62 to 34 and 292 to 153 majorities. It would be the supreme height of the Rayburn-Johnson ascendancy. William Knowland was badly defeated by Edmund G. (Pat) Brown, running for governor of California, and Goodwin

Knight, from whom Knowland seized the nomination, went down badly in the California Senate race against Clair Engle. Senator John Bricker, a simpleminded rightist and Dewey's vice presidential nominee against Roosevelt and Truman in 1944, was badly defeated in Ohio. The time of these blowhardish and very limited men was over, and generally unlamented. Knowland's life and career trailed off, and he eventually took to drink and gambling, left his wife, lost his money, and committed suicide in 1974.

The main Republican winners were in New York and Pennsylvania. Nelson Rockefeller defeated Averell Harriman by an impressive 660,000 votes, and Nixon's old Chowder and Marching Society friend, Kenneth Keating, came in with him in the Senate race. In Pennsylvania, Congressman Hugh Scott, who had christened the Fair Play Rule at the 1952 convention, was elected to the Senate. Mark Hatfield, elected to the Senate from Oregon for the Republicans, and the big Senate re-election victory of Barry Goldwater in Arizona, were also bright spots (although Goldwater, a conservative, had frequently criticized Eisenhower). As challenging to Nixon as the big Rockefeller win was John F. Kennedy's reelection in Massachusetts by an astounding 864,000 votes. These three, Nixon, Rockefeller, and Kennedy, with Lyndon Johnson and the unextinguished champion of the nostalgic intelligentsia, Adlai Stevenson, and the irrepressible Hubert Humphrey, were the people to watch coming up to the presidential campaign, which, effectively, had already begun.

Nixon was somewhat saddled with the Republican setback in the media, although the administration had become torpid and boring and Nixon was by far the liveliest person in it. On November 12, Harold Stassen, who had run unsuccessfully for the gubernatorial nomination in Pennsylvania, emerged from a meeting with Eisenhower and announced that Nixon was responsible for the debacle and should be dumped in favor of Rockefeller. He did not claim to be speaking for Eisenhower (who had less use and regard for Rockefeller than he did for Nixon), but some journalists made this inference.

Another casualty was twenty-year House Republican leader and frequent convention chairman Joe Martin of Massachusetts, made famous by Roosevelt, and a patron of Nixon's from when he was first nominated against Voorhis. Martin was reelected, but House Republicans moved for a younger leader. Martin was particularly irritated when Nixon, despite Martin's past favors to him, supported the rebels. The new House minority leader,

Richard Nixon in 1917, aged four. A composed, serious, and diligent child, young Richard Nixon was almost compulsively clean and neat, and brushed his teeth spontaneously several times a day.

First-time congressional candidate Richard Nixon in 1946 with his redoubtable mother, Hannah Milhous Nixon. Contrary to widely believed mythology, Nixon's mother, though not demonstrative, was affectionate, gentle, even-tempered, intelligent, and fanatically devoted to the welfare of her family.

Pat, Tricia, Julie, their dog, Checkers, and the forty-year-old vice president on holiday at Mantoloking, New Jersey, August 15, 1953. Nixon was away from his family a great deal, but they remained close and devoted to one another to the end.

Less than ten years after serving with distinction in the U.S. Navy at Bougainville and Green Island, Vice President Nixon, with Mrs. Nixon, is the honored guest of the Emperor and Empress of Japan, April 1953. Nixon urged Emperor Hirohito and his government to rearm.

Vice President Nixon's disastrous visit to Caracas in 1958 was a political bonanza for him. He and his wife and entourage were in danger of their lives when their cars were stopped and attacked, but Nixon's coolness and composure deeply impressed Americans, even the venerable warrior President Eisenhower.

Nixon always had a good deal of support from celebrities in the entertainment community at a time when there were still many conservatives prominent in Hollywood. Here, he is with Zsa Zsa Gabor in 1959.

Nixon with the seventy-five-year-old Eleanor Roosevelt in 1959. Nixon thoroughly disapproved of most of Mrs. Roosevelt's political ideas, apart from her champion-ship of civil rights, but he respected her as a tireless and courageous woman and had admired the human qualities, strong leadership, and political virtuosity of her husband. Mrs. Roosevelt thought Nixon a distasteful politician who funda-mentally disliked himself.

Nixon with the eighty-six-year-old former president Harry S Truman in 1970. Nixon had come to admire Truman for his talent at tough decision-making and his foreign policy of containment of communism. Truman never forgave Nixon for having implied, as he thought, that Truman had committed treason. This was a slight exagger-ation, but some of Nixon's oratorical flourishes during the great Red Scare of 1947–52 were understandably irritating to Truman.

The vice president reads a line from *Advise and Consent*, a Washington political novel by Allen Drury, whom Nixon knew well, to Senator John F. Kennedy of Massachusetts, whom Nixon already suspected would be his opponent in the presidential election of the following year, 1960.

The last photograph of Dwight D. Eisenhower with Richard M. Nixon, four months before Ike died and a month before the president-elect was inaugurated. Nixon visited his old chief often in hospital. There had not been such a complicated relationship between two American presidents since the days of the founding Virginians, Washington, Jefferson, Madison, and Monroe.

The Nixons campaigning in Chicago in 1968, shortly after the debacle of the Democratic convention in the same city, which dissolved in riots and police repression. Though often shy and even awkward in person, Nixon loved to campaign, at which he was very effective, and enjoyed public speaking all his life.

Nixon mobilized patriotic, socially conservative workers, most conspicuously hard-hats in the construction industry, against the anti–Vietnam War movement. Here he is cheered by, and responds to, construction workers in New York in 1970.

Nixon's visit to President de Gaulle, February–March 1969. The French leader, who had dealt with Nixon's five predecessors in the White House, was, along with Winston Churchill, the contemporary statesman Nixon admired most. Waiting to be presented to their august seventy-seven-year-old host, with visibly different thoughts, are Nixon's "Prussian Wall" or "Siegfried Line," as some wits called them, from left: Bob Haldeman (chief of staff), John Ehrlichman (domestic affairs counselor), and Henry Kissinger (national security adviser), as well as Secretary of State William P. Rogers, whose powers Kissinger and Nixon had largely emasculated.

Nixon and South Vietnamese president Nguyen Van Thieu, at Midway Island, June 1969. These were always difficult meetings, as Thieu suspected Nixon of preparing to desert him, and Nixon found Thieu unreasonably addicted to American military assistance of the kind that produced high casualties and domestic discord.

Nixon visits American soldiers near Saigon, 1969. He believed in defeating the communists and preserving a non-communist South Vietnam, but not by Americans fighting Vietnamese battles for their local allies. Nixon had almost always campaigned in the home cities of the members of the armed forces, and knew something, from memory, of their local sports teams.

It was part of Nixon's bourgeois populism that he loved bowling, and he used to confuse Kissinger with talk of his bowling score. Kissinger thought he was speaking of golf, a sport with which he was equally unfamiliar.

Nixon at Key Biscayne, Florida, circa 1970, with his dog, King Timahoe. Nixon was something of a dog lover, though his detractors, who accused him of almost everything, claimed that his dog could only be induced to come to him if a trail of dog biscuits was laid down first.

C776-11 / Ollie Atkins

E2481-09 / Ollie Atkins

Nixon's ordinariness was not an affectation. Here, in a diner in Houston with a secret service agent, in February 1974, he was genuinely relaxed. Probably the only other presidents elected in the twentieth century who could have carried off such a mundane activity believably were Harding, Truman, and Clinton.

Charlie Halleck of Indiana, was no more dynamic than Martin, and not as cagey. Martin served twenty-one straight terms in the House.[39]

The year ended on a very positive note for Nixon when Eisenhower sent him to London for the dedication of the American Chapel in St. Paul's Cathedral, honoring American servicemen who died while stationed in Britain in the Second World War. Nixon was thoroughly prepared and he and Pat carried it off to perfection. He gave an eloquent speech to the English-Speaking Union at the Guildhall, where Woodrow Wilson and Dwight D. Eisenhower had also spoken. He delivered a moderate and intelligent address, calling particularly for "a great offensive against the evils of poverty, disease, and misery" in underdeveloped countries. He revolutionized British opinion of him. In splendid lunches and dinners, he was received by the prime minister, Harold Macmillan, by Churchill, and by Hugh Gaitskill, the leader of the opposition (the Labour Party); he conversed with, was impressed by, and thoroughly impressed, all of them. The British and U.S. media were unanimous in their praise of the vice president, whom the British media had formerly represented as a rather shabby politician. Drew Middleton of the *New York Times* was typical when he wrote that Nixon had "arrived billed as an uncouth adventurer in the political jungles, [and] departed trailing clouds of statesmanship and esteem."[40]

As 1959 opened, following the election shambles, the London visit put Nixon solidly back into hot contention for the great office that was now almost within reach, and that the American people would fill the next year. The end of Richard Nixon's long, steep, contentious climb seemed to be in sight.

Chapter Seven

Defeat and Endurance
1959–1963

— I —

ALTHOUGH IT HAD RUN only about half its course, the complicated Nixon-Eisenhower relationship was entering a critical phase. Nixon needed Eisenhower's popularity and legitimacy, but also needed a distinct policy identity, amplifying the Eisenhower record but neither refuting nor resting on it.

They were men of similar socioeconomic origins but different ages and career paths. Eisenhower was in the cocoon of the army from 1907 to 1949, with secure pay and employment, and emerged as a world historic figure. He was immediately embraced and revered by the fraternity of America's greatest financiers and industrialists. Nixon and his family, as we have seen, scrabbled desperately through the Depression, and Nixon had had to scheme and scrape and, he believed, sling mud and suffer to be smeared himself for every advance he had made. Eisenhower was rightly proud of his great reputation, earned and maintained in war and in peace. But when he had been Nixon's present age, forty-six, in 1936, he was a junior officer working as a clerk for an eccentric ex-chief of staff (MacArthur) who was trying to create an armed force in the Philippines almost out of whole cloth. Nixon had been U.S. vice president for six years and effectively the acting president twice.

When Eisenhower looked upon the progress of American life over his nearly seventy years, he saw the Depression, much of which he missed in the Philippines, as an unpleasant interlude. He saw the working class become prosperous, and the wealthy numerous. Nixon saw a squeezed middle class, a perception heightened by his realization, which did not bulk heavily with Eisenhower, that this was where Republican votes were. These were the people who appreciated Nixon, identified with him, and would, he hoped, put him in the White House, if Eisenhower and his other collaborators would do the fiscally necessary to encourage them.

The next round in the tug-of-war between them came early in 1959. Eisenhower, with some reason, considered himself an authority on administration, and so did his brother Milton. Milton, the White House intellectual Arthur Flemming, and Nelson Rockefeller, a friend of Milton's and an opponent of Nixon's while he was still in the White House, cooked up a plan for an administrative restructuring. There were various measures that had no chance of being approved by the Congress, such as the line-item veto that all presidents seek to enable them to veto parts of bills without having to strike down the entire bill, and congressional term limits, which the president thought should be applied to the Congress as it was to the presidency.

Nixon knew these were losers, whatever their merit, but more sinister was the Eisenhower-Flemming-Rockefeller plan to create two assistant presidents, one for domestic and one for foreign and national security matters. With no warning, Eisenhower, who pretended not to grasp the implications for Nixon of Rockefeller's sorcery, revealed this idea to an astounded cabinet on January 24, 1959. John Foster Dulles and Nixon were instantly alarmed, and politely stirred up the other cabinet members, as this would interpose unelected people between the cabinet and the president, and render the vice president almost completely redundant. Nixon and Dulles conversed about it by telephone at once and at length, and Nixon said that "many would think" (often a polite expression for his own suspicions) that Eisenhower was just shirking responsibility and lightening his workload even from what it had been. By this time, Eisenhower was not a martyr to the work ethic, though he retained control of almost all authority in important matters for himself.

Nixon kept insisting that the president could not simply reorganize the administration without any recourse to Congress, anymore than he could appoint cabinet officials without getting them confirmed by the Senate. He and Dulles got a committee struck, and Nixon muddied the waters and played for time. But his decisive argument was to warn Eisenhower that the

Democrats would say that he was just ducking his duty, delegating every-thing, and becoming an amiable, geriatric golfer of a president. Once again, Nixon the infighter succeeded in beating off a threat, as the proposal was never implemented. (Ten years later, Nixon would informally enact part of the proposal through his national security adviser, Henry Kissinger, but his secretary of state was not as assertive as Dulles, and his vice president would not be of the same stature in that role as Nixon was.)

The intermittent problem between Eisenhower and Nixon was compli-cated by Eisenhower's regular lapses into the delusion that he was above politics. On June 11, 1959, Nixon had breakfast with Eisenhower and asked him to take some of Nixon's wealthy supporters out on an official yacht and then play a little golf with them. Eisenhower, who did this sort of thing with his own friends frequently, refused.

The debate over administrative reorganization was the last time Nixon would fight shoulder to shoulder with Dulles. The secretary of state was diagnosed with inoperable cancer of the throat and more remote places. He was in Walter Reed Army Hospital from mid-February on, struggling bravely but without hope. Nixon frequently visited. Eisenhower came sometimes, and brought the retired but still active Winston Churchill, eighty-four, to visit. John Foster Dulles died a brave death on May 24; he was seventy-one. When Eisenhower announced his retirement as secretary of state to the press, there were tears in his eyes, and the reporters, respectfully, asked no questions. It was his shortest press conference. As had been prom-ised, Christian Herter succeeded Dulles.

Nixon would miss Dulles's unfailing support and remarkable inter-national knowledge. He had attended as an assistant the Hague Conference of 1907 (as secretary to the Chinese delegation, a position his grandfather arranged for him). Dulles attracted President Wilson's appreciative notice as an expert on reparations at the Versailles Conference in 1919. He was the nephew of Wilson's second secretary of state, Robert Lansing. Dulles was the author of the much-admired Japan Peace Treaty, and invented the concept of brinkmanship, "to get to the verge, but not into war." Nixon wrote an eloquent appreciation of Dulles for *Life* magazine at the request of Henry Luce, and dwelt on his personal graciousness, which was hard to per-ceive in the severe public man. Dulles had built well on the containment strategy, failed to do anything to promote his vision of liberation of Eastern Europe, and had not been successful in the Middle East, where he was largely responsible for the revocation of assistance to the Aswan Dam project and partly to blame for the Suez fiasco. He had a good record in the Far East, with the Japanese peace treaty, his contribution to Korean peace, and his suggestion of sensible assistance to the French to avert disaster at Dien Bien Phu. He was not a public relations genius, but next to General George C. Marshall and the much-maligned Dean Acheson, he was probably the most accomplished secretary of state among John Quincy Adams (1817–1825), Henry Kissinger (1973–1977), and George Shultz (1982–1989). He was a formidable and dedicated and learned man, who presented an implacable exterior (what Churchill called "his great slab face") to the communists. He had been something of a tutor to Nixon in some of the finer points of international affairs, and Nixon would greatly miss his counsel and support.

As the Dulles era ended, there were worrisome perturbations in the world. In Cuba, on January 1, 1959, the long-serving strongman, Fulgencio Batista, an elegant man who had impressed Nixon when he visited there in 1955, was driven out by the leftist and, as it shortly emerged, in fact communist Fidel Castro.

Nixon met with Castro for three hours when he came to Washington to speak at the National Press Club, although Eisenhower had not recognized his government. Nixon and Castro spoke at and past each other, but Nixon reported that it was not clear whether Castro was an unwitting dupe of the communists or an outright communist practitioner. He said he had the most naive economic ideas Nixon had encountered among the fifty national leaders he had met, but that he clearly possessed formidable qualities of leadership. Nixon made no progress trying to sell Castro on the virtues of due process for the large numbers of Batista regime personnel he was publicly executing every day, and Castro was dismissive of free elections, a free press, and other democratic frills, saying that in Cuba they had only led to despotic and corrupt government. Nixon urged that despite the unpromising start, there seemed to be no choice but to try to work with him. Eisenhower ignored this advice, and set upon a policy of quarantine and diplomatic and economic sanctions.

Nixon also met with Soviet deputy prime minister Anastas Mikoyan, a wily Armenian survivor from the Stalin era, when he came to Washington in January, the highest-ranking Soviet visitor to the United States since

Vyacheslav Molotov had come to the founding conference of the United Nations at San Francisco in April 1945. Their conversations were rather superficial. Mikoyan's main official purpose was to try to get some status for East Germany, as the youth of that country was deserting it and streaming into West Germany in great numbers. Nothing was accomplished by his visit, and the problem of how to prop up East Germany, in whose population the puppet satellite government infamously claimed to have "lost confidence" in 1948, remained. Khrushchev said, "West Berlin is a bone in my throat."

Khrushchev sent Mikoyan to America for the real purpose of seeking an invitation to the United States; Mikoyan invited Nixon to open a U.S. trade show in Moscow, hoping it would lead to an invitation to the United States for Khrushchev. This was part of the atmospherics of cultural exchanges that had been approved at Geneva in 1955. Nixon prepared himself massively for his visit to the U.S.S.R., speaking to everyone he knew who had ever met Khrushchev, including Harold Macmillan, Walter Lippmann, and Hubert Humphrey, who had just returned from a highly publicized trip to Moscow and a meeting with Khrushchev, which he claimed had yielded a "Cold War breakthrough, about which he would privately brief" Eisenhower. He did so, and Eisenhower told his cabinet that Humphrey's breakthrough was "thinly sliced baloney."[1]

Nixon had discussed his upcoming trip at length in his last hospital bedside meetings with Dulles. He received very extensive briefings from the CIA, the Joint Chiefs of Staff, and the Soviet specialists in the National Security Council and State Department, and extensive discussions with the president. Eisenhower gave Nixon all the details of Khrushchev's agitation for a summit meeting, and said that he should stick to the precondition of some progress at Geneva on the status of West Berlin. Nixon departed on July 22 with a very large staff and press party, including James Reston of the *New York Times*. The visit took place during what Congress and the president had proclaimed, six years before, to be Captive Nations Week, during which the American people were urged to pray for all those under Soviet subjugation. It is not clear if any Americans actually did so, much less the effect of such supplications, other than that the gesture fulfilled its terrestrial purpose of completely aggravating the Soviet leadership.

The American party received a low-key arrival greeting from deputy premier Frol Kozlov, and the Nixons went to Spaso House, the American embassy (the ambassador was now Llewellyn Thompson, whom Nixon had worked with when in Austria in December 1956, trying to help Hungarian refugees). That night, Nixon was too keyed up to sleep well, and got up at 5:30 A.M., called for his chief Secret Service man, Jack Sherwood (who had earned his spurs with Nixon in South America), and went to the Danilovsky Market to compare it to the Los Angeles produce market where he had worked at the same hour of the day as a boy. Nixon mingled with the people quite amiably, and offered a hundred rubles to people who wanted to come to the U.S. exhibition Nixon would open at Sokolniki Park. They declined the money, saying the problem was availability, not cost, of tickets. The next day, *Pravda* and other Soviet information outlets ran pictures of Sherwood holding out a bank note, and accused Nixon of trying to "bribe and degrade" Soviet citizens.

Following his surprise appearance at the produce market, Nixon went to the Kremlin, a place he would come to know well, and had his first of many meetings with Soviet leaders. While photographs were being taken, Khrushchev was genial and complimented Nixon on his Guildhall speech eight months before about aid to underdeveloped countries and peaceful competition. As soon as Nixon and Khrushchev were alone with their interpreters, the Soviet leader started raving about Captive Nations Week. He lapsed into scatology, and told Nixon: "People shouldn't shit where they eat," an assertion whose context in this case Nixon never understood. "This resolution stinks," Khrushchev yelled at the puzzled Nixon. "It stinks like fresh horse shit, and nothing smells worse than that." Nixon responded, with unsuspected knowledge of the barnyard (from reading that Khrushchev had once been a pig-herder), that "The chairman is mistaken. . . . Pig shit is fouler than horse shit." Khrushchev looked pensive for a moment, then conceded that Nixon was correct, and changed the subject.[2]

The two men drove together to the American exhibition, where a good deal of badinage took place for the cameras. Khrushchev was more self-confident at this sort of thing, embracing a burly Russian laborer and asking rhetorically: "Does this man look like a slave laborer to you?" Nixon unwisely (and inaccurately) conceded that the U.S.S.R. was ahead of the United States in rocketry, but said the United States was ahead in many other areas, such as color television, which was being demonstrated in front of them. They had a further exchange in the model kitchen, and Khrushchev claimed that Soviet houses were better built than American ones and that Nixon had been given a mistaken impression of the U.S.S.R. Nixon criticized the command economy and said that people should have choice and not be told what they liked, in houses or other matters. Khrushchev denounced this as inefficient. Nixon tried to introduce a note of conviviality and said that it was preferable to debate the relative merits of washing machines than of rockets, that both the U.S.S.R. and the United States were great military powers, and that neither should present the other with an ultimatum.

Khrushchev, instead of being placated, pretended that he had been threatened and demanded to know why Nixon was threatening him. Nixon replied forcefully: "We will never engage in threats." At one point, Nixon was reduced to saying that he had worked hard as a youth and that his father was a shopkeeper. Khrushchev responded with the Marxist orthodoxy that "All shopkeepers are thieves." Inane though all this was, it was the first public exchange there had ever been between American and Soviet leaders, and only the fifth time, after Teheran, Yalta, Potsdam, and Geneva, that a holder of national office in the United States had met a Soviet Communist Party chairman. As they jabbed fingers at each other in front of the senior American media, and Soviet officials, including Leonid Brezhnev (who would overthrow Khrushchev in five years), the atmosphere lightened, and it became clear that Khrushchev was enjoying the joust. James Reston credited Nixon with keeping the spirit jovial and generally improving the ambiance, which was the purpose of the exhibition and the vice president's trip. It was clear that Khrushchev was immensely self-conscious about the great wealth and power and international influence of the United States. Nixon could have been a little more relaxed and less earnest, but it was such an astonishing spectacle, he fought his corner reasonably well.

Khrushchev embraced an elderly Russian woman, and then engaged in more repartee with Nixon and William Randolph Hearst Jr., whom Khrushchev already knew, and who was accompanying Nixon. Khrushchev greeted Hearst as "My capitalist, monopolist, journalist friend" and professed to disbelieve Nixon when he said that the United States had a free press. By this time, though the exchange had been absurd and bumptious, the atmosphere was so frivolous, there was no longer anything sinister about it. They returned to the Kremlin and had a sumptuous lunch, joined by their wives, including reciprocal champagne toasts at the end of which they all, following Khrushchev's lead and urging, threw their glasses into the fireplace.[3]

That evening Nixon opened the exhibition officially. Khrushchev had promised that Nixon's remarks would be published unaltered in *Pravda* and

Izvestia. Nixon started with a direct appeal to the bourgeois ambitions of his supposedly communist readers and listeners. He said that 25 million of the 44 million families in the United States had homes as large or larger than the one in the exhibit; and that 31 million American families had their own homes. He said that in America there were 56 million automobiles, 50 million television sets, and 143 million radios. Nixon declared that his country was the closest in the world to the ideal of a generous distribution of wealth in a classless society, and denounced the communist propaganda version of America as a "predatory, monopolistic" country. He then emphasized American freedom of speech, religion, information, internal and external travel, and the right to criticize the government, and concluded by extolling the virtues of peaceful competition. It was an effective address, and was run the next day in the Soviet media as Khrushchev had promised.

Nixon was credited with a major success, putting the American case forcefully, but not undiplomatically, for the first time before the Russian masses. Although he allegedly had several stiff nightcaps when he returned to the embassy,[4] Nixon was again too keyed up to sleep for most of his second night in Moscow, and then had a busy day of meetings and a formal dinner at Spaso House for Khrushchev and the entire Soviet leadership. Khrushchev insisted that the Nixons come with him at midnight to his luxurious forest dacha and spend the night, which they did. It had formerly been occupied by the czar, and was almost as large as the White House, according to Nixon.[5] The next morning they went for a boat ride on the Moscow River and were greeted by swimmers, who it subsequently was established by Ambassador Thompson were party officials, who assured Khrushchev, when he stopped the boat and asked, that they were not "captives." Unfortunately, their boat grounded in the river and the leaders had to transfer to another craft. Nixon put in a plea for the pilot, claiming in his memoirs to have feared for his life.

There was then a five-hour lunch, "under a canopy of magnificent birch trees; the scene could have been out of Chekhov."[6] When Mikoyan spoke to Pat Nixon in English, Khrushchev accused him of trying to be a Romeo though too old for the part: "Now look here, you crafty Armenian, Mrs. Nixon belongs to me." They started with thinly sliced whitefish, which Khrushchev assured his guests was Stalin's favorite dish.[7] They got back to the debate of the first day, though without such coarse metaphors. Khrushchev demanded to know why the United States was encouraging

South Vietnam not to hold elections as promised at Geneva. Nixon demanded to know why the U.S.S.R. was reneging on its promise to promote genuine democracy in Eastern Europe, and especially East Germany. That evening, Khrushchev and Nixon went for the first of a number of famous Soviet-American walks in the woods. Nixon followed Eisenhower's request to try to "break the impasse on Berlin," at Geneva. For once, Khrushchev gave a cautious, equivocal reply.

When Nixon returned to the embassy, he cabled Eisenhower that he had emphasized, as the president had told him to do, the need for progress on Berlin at Geneva and that it was Thompson's and his recommendation that "we probe Gromyko at Geneva for a further period before you send reply to Khrushchev on possible visit." Unfortunately, Eisenhower (claimed to have) discovered that the State Department had not stressed the need for progress on Berlin as it had been ordered to do, and before Nixon returned to Washington, the White House announced that Khrushchev would be making a ten-day visit to the United States, and that Eisenhower would be returning the visit.

The Republican right was outraged, and some blamed Nixon. Senator Goldwater came to his defense, saying that Nixon was "shocked and surprised"[8] that the invitation was extended. Nixon did not deny this and the occasional but recurrent friction between him and Eisenhower again came close to the notice of the public. (It is unlikely that Herter and his officials did anything other than what they were instructed to do in these matters, especially as Eisenhower had so meticulously coached Nixon on the point.)

Nixon toured in the interior of the Soviet Union for five days, going to Leningrad, Novosibirsk, and Sverdlovsk (in the Urals). He tried his traditional methods of taking off into the crowds, shaking hands and asking pointed questions. His hosts were ready for this and had hecklers planted who asked him about racism in America, nuclear testing, and the American military bases all around the perimeter of the Soviet Union. But there was no physical threat as there had been in South America, and Nixon handled the exchanges without difficulty.

Pat Nixon was as indomitable and charming as ever, visiting hospitals, schools, and pioneer camps, and at the official dinners held her own with Khrushchev. When he said he did not know enough to answer a question of the vice president's about solid-fuel rockets, she expressed surprise that there was any subject on which he didn't consider himself an authority.[9]

The Nixons returned to Moscow on July 31, and Nixon prepared his television address to the Soviet people for two days, without, he later claimed, any sleep at all. He was tempted to hold forth on the evils of the police state he had seen, but did not want to run the risk of denying Eisenhower an opportunity to make a similar address when he came to Russia.

His speech was very intelligently crafted. He described Russia as a beautiful country inhabited by fine and brave people, remembered the great Soviet war effort, and expressed sympathy for the many millions of Soviet war dead. He dealt with the hecklers' questions he had encountered. He said that American military bases were entirely defensive, that the U.S.S.R. spent the preposterous sum of 25 percent of its gross domestic product on the military (the real figure was almost twice this; the American figure was then about 7 percent), and that the United States had proposed the internationalization of atomic energy in 1947 and the Open Skies proposal in 1955, and that the U.S.S.R. had rejected both.

He said that the American media faithfully reported Khrushchev's utterances, but the same courtesy was not granted by the Russians to Eisenhower. Nixon proposed that both countries promise to print the speeches of the leader of the other, that they beam television and radio programs directly to each other, and that there be a free flow of periodicals between them. He referred to the incident at the start of his tour when *Pravda* falsely claimed he had tried to bribe Soviet citizens. Nixon's conclusion was that he had seen in all the cities he had visited billboards urging the people to "work for the victory of communism." He had no problem with exhortations to a better life for all the people of the U.S.S.R. But if what is meant is the victory of communism over the United States, "We have our own ideas as to what system is best for us." Nixon asserted that if Khrushchev "devotes his immense energies and talents to building a better life for the people of his own country," he will be one of Russia's greatest leaders. "But if he devotes the resources and talents of his people to the objective of promoting the communization of countries outside the Soviet Union, he will only assure that both he and his people will continue to live in an era of fear, suspicion, and tension."[10] This, in the time, was electrifying.

Nixon later wrote that he knew he had had no impact on Khrushchev and the other Soviet leaders and so left Russia "frustrated . . . and with a sense of depression."[11] This is almost surely an overstatement, because he was well aware that the American audience was a good deal more important to him and that he had played very well at home.

Whatever gloomy thoughts he may have had were dispelled by his stop in Warsaw. Khrushchev had been there two weeks before and the puppet communist occupation regime was unable to generate any enthusiasm for him. Nixon's visit was publicized in advance only by Radio Free Europe, the Voice of America, and the Roman Catholic Church. Hundreds of thousands of people jammed the entire route of the Nixons' open car and motorcade, and deluged them with thousands of floral bouquets. It was the exact antithesis of the debacle in Venezuela. The crowds shouted their enthusiasm for America, Eisenhower, and Nixon, and even the honor guard at the airport applauded and cheered Nixon and his wife. He cabled Eisenhower that it was "the most moving experience I have ever had."[12]

He again returned a hero to the United States. His performance was universally commended, including by the often acidulous James Reston. He appeared on the cover of *Life*, with the towers of the Kremlin behind him. Among those who sent congratulatory letters were Eisenhower, J. Edgar Hoover, and an effusive film actor, undergoing a gradual career change, Ronald Reagan. Ralph de Toledano, who was at this point his leading cheerleader (but who would eventually break violently with Nixon), claimed in *Newsweek* that he might have "changed the course of history" in Moscow. It is not clear what possessed him to engage in such hyperbole, other than hopes of a good position in the event of Nixon's election as president, but it was a fine domestic political success for the vice president, as well as a competent and important exercise in personal diplomacy. He had been to the lion's den, where no such prominent American official had preceded him.

One day after his return, Nixon briefed Eisenhower and told him that Khrushchev was undoubtedly intelligent and forceful, and witty, a conversational bully and filibusterer, with a lively if crude sense of humor but an absolutely closed mind. This confirmed Eisenhower's impression of Khrushchev from Geneva. There was no point arguing the merits of the competing systems with him. Nixon recommended that he be given the maximum exposure possible when he came to the United States, because it would oblige him to do the same for Eisenhower, and because Khrushchev would abuse the access to the Western public and ultimately make a poor impression. It was sage advice.

Eisenhower told his press conference on August 12 that he wanted to take Khrushchev to Camp David by helicopter during a time of congested traffic so the Soviet leader could see the profusion of automobiles and the size and apparent comfort of suburban houses in America. As if this were not banal enough, the president went further and said he wanted to take Khrushchev to Abilene, Kansas, where locals could assure the visitor that Eisenhower had worked hard as a youth. He said he was prompted to wish to do this by Khrushchev's claim to Nixon that Nixon knew nothing of work: "You never worked," Khrushchev had said. "Well I can show him the evidence that I did, and I would like him to see it."

The five-star general and two-term president was apparently even more self-conscious and defensive than Khrushchev had been with Nixon. It is inexplicable that such an able and experienced man as Eisenhower could have imagined that Khrushchev thought that he and Nixon had got to their positions by a life of idleness, and hard to believe that he much cared what Khrushchev thought about either of them personally. It is hard not to think that Eisenhower was feeling slightly upstaged by his vice president and wanted to take back the center of the stage. These were relatively minor abrasions, but they were unfortunate.

Eisenhower went to Bonn, London, and Paris in August and September 1959, before returning to receive Khrushchev. He wanted to square matters with his principal allies before meeting at length with the Soviet leader. He found the West German chancellor, Konrad Adenauer, very worried about the Algerian War and convinced that it was a communist revolt and that if the French were unsuccessful there, all of North Africa would fall to the communists. Since Germany had had practically no political experience of North Africa, and certainly Adenauer had none, he was presumably inspired to say this by de Gaulle, who was a proponent of a historic settlement of grievances between France and Germany, and was exercising some influence on Adenauer. Eisenhower said that he doubted that the independence of Algeria would be quite such a catastrophe and that the West had to be careful aligning itself with colonial forces. He had the same fear that Roosevelt had had that if the United States seemed to support indefinite European colonization, the communists would be the beneficiaries.

He had a warm reception in London and in Scotland, where he had been given a castle for life because of his war service, and had a very successful joint appearance on television with Macmillan. More than a million people cheered him and General Charles de Gaulle as they rode together in an open car from the airport into Paris (this was the inaugural trip for the new presidential aircraft, a Boeing 707, which became Air Force One. It was Eisenhower's first experience of jet travel). De Gaulle had proposed a triumvirate of the United States, Britain, and France as a sort of executive committee of the Western alliance, to coordinate Alliance policy. Eisenhower had rejected that, partly out of concern for the sensibilities of other countries, especially the Germans and Italians, and partly because he did not really consider that France had earned such a status.

Now sixty-eight, de Gaulle was the first person in French history to hold high office in three different republics. He left France for Britain in 1940 to continue the war and denounced those who would make peace with the Nazis, having been associate war minister in the last government that swore allegiance to the Third Republic. After four years as head of the government in exile, he returned in the Liberation of 1944, and resigned in 1946 as head of the provisional government rather than accept what he knew to be a doomed regime of political fragmentation and weak government under the Fourth Republic. And after twelve years of domestic exile, he came back again to head the last government of the Fourth Republic and bring in the Fifth Republic, whose president he now was. A veteran of the Battle of Verdun, and of colonial service in Beirut in the twenties, he had seen and participated in almost as much history as Churchill, and was just now reaching the summit of his astounding career.

As had Roosevelt, Eisenhower underestimated the value of France as an ally and, now that it was led by such a formidable and ingenious statesman, its potential danger as a non-ally. De Gaulle had resented the weakness of France during the Second World War, as one violently opposed to any parley with the Nazis, and had tried to gain the esteem of Roosevelt, both by cooperation and then by obstruction. Churchill had recognized the desirability and the need for a revived France to assist Britain in organizing a counterweight to Soviet influence in central Europe, preferably with a revitalized and democratized Germany and a continued American presence in Europe. But Churchill had always favored the American view over the European. Roosevelt came late to the realization of de Gaulle's qualities, and correctly foresaw that France would not be acting like a Great Power any time soon.

Now the Fourth Republic had come and gone, as de Gaulle had predicted, and the country had a strong presidential system, a strong president, a strong currency, and atomic weapons, and was in all respects an important force, held back only by the Algerian entanglement, which de Gaulle was trying to win militarily at the same time that he liberalized and conciliated the Algerian moderates and conducted secret peace negotiations. Nixon had foreseen the return of de Gaulle when in Europe in 1947. He thought only de Gaulle could restore France, but he noted a legislator's comment that "In political terms, de Gaulle thinks he has a direct telephone link with God."[13] A France fully participating in the Western alliance would be a great further source of strength. A France giving lip service to the Anglo-American alliance but really trying to stir up Western Europe to be less cooperative, and trying to hold and manipulate the balance between the American and Soviet blocs, could be a terrible nuisance, and was. Eisenhower and his immediate successors did not see the problem or figure out how to deal with de Gaulle (but Nixon did).

As years went by, de Gaulle effectively withdrew from NATO, expelled its headquarters from France, vetoed British entry into the European Common Market, opened relations with China, encouraged Quebec to separate from and fragment Canada (a country to which France owed much, including four divisions in its liberation), and incited Arab hostility to the Anglo-Americans. Once scorned, as he considered he had been, de Gaulle demonstrated his superhuman powers of harassment and obstruction. When the two major blocs are perceived to be of approximately equal strength, the potential for the third power is very great. De Gaulle's foreign policy was in large measure an aggregation of confidence tricks, but the times and his prestige and virtuosity enabled him to carry it off with great effect and panache.

De Gaulle personally liked Eisenhower, and although the trip to Paris did not accomplish what had been hoped by either side, as Eisenhower again rejected de Gaulle's "triumvirate" and de Gaulle again rejected the European Defense Community, de Gaulle did describe Eisenhower publicly and movingly as "forever in the minds of the French, the benign and supreme commander of the armies of our liberation."

Khrushchev arrived in Washington on September 14. The leaders started with two days of talks. There was no movement on Berlin and Germany,

Formosa, the Middle East, or arms control and nuclear testing, so all Eisenhower could aim for was atmospheric improvement. They agreed at the outset that neither of them wanted war. Beyond that, their meetings went smoothly but unproductively. Eisenhower did take Khrushchev on a helicopter ride over Washington, and he did see the heavy traffic and the fine middle-class homes but made no comment and was expressionless. (He had presumably read that this was Eisenhower's ambition.)

Henry Cabot Lodge then conducted Khrushchev around the country. Some interpreted this as a snub of Nixon, but Nixon had already told Eisenhower that he should not accompany Khrushchev, as he had not accompanied other world leaders on tours of the country. Khrushchev spoke to the United Nations in New York on September 18, and advocated the abolition, over four years, of all weapons, nuclear and conventional, with no inspection or verification system. If this was not acceptable, and he could scarcely have imagined that it would be, he was prepared to revive discussions of a comprehensive test ban.

He returned to Washington and told Eisenhower that he had noted the traffic congestion but, far from being impressed, found it wasteful. On Germany, he pointed out that a reunified Germany was "the last thing" de Gaulle wanted, and Eisenhower allowed that there might be some truth to that. (Macmillan wasn't very enthused about it either.) The highlight of his trip around the country was the cancellation of his visit to Disneyland for security reasons, and his mockery of the tall fins on the back of the current year's Cadillac. Khrushchev had a media success, and he and Eisenhower both spoke of the "Spirit of Camp David." His visit could be counted a modest success for both leaders and a step forward in relations between the superpowers. After almost thirty years of the sinister, enigmatic, though startlingly intelligent and sardonically witty Stalin, who never left Soviet-occupied areas (apart from Teheran, where he had an immense security detail), Khrushchev was at least a lively human face on Soviet communism, and the world media enjoyed him.

— II —

By the end of the summer of 1959, all attention in Washington was already focused on the approaching presidential election. Nixon's task was becoming steadily more complicated. It would not be possible to go on defaming

Acheson. This election would transfer power from the Hoover-Roosevelt-Truman-Eisenhower generation, who had been junior in the First World War and eminent in the Second World War, to men who had been toddlers in the First World War and junior figures in the Second World War. Kennedy and Humphrey and even Johnson, though he had been an influential congressman and went to the Senate in 1948, could not be identified with the "loss" of China or the origins or conduct of the Korean War.

The election of Rockefeller to an important position ensured that to win the Republican nomination Nixon had to keep both his natural conservative supporters and Eisenhower happy, and not get so far to the right of Rockefeller and the floating voters and centrist Democrats that he couldn't resurrect the winning arithmetic between his nomination and the election. He had to run for the nomination from the moderate right, and then for the presidency from the center, navigating between Eisenhower, Goldwater, and Rockefeller. It still was not clear if Rockefeller was going to challenge Nixon for the nomination.

On June 9, 1960, Eisenhower had to step out of a meeting with congressional leaders to meet the president of Peru. Nixon immediately warned the others that Rockefeller's charge that the United States was becoming a "sitting duck" in defense terms had to be contradicted. He said, "We cannot allow this charge of weakness to stand. Not that the president's judgment is bad, but we just can't ignore Rocky's 'sitting duck' charge."[14] In this way, Nixon was effectively enlisting the Republican leaders in the Congress against Rockefeller, but also in favor of a variance to Eisenhower's political complacency. By this time, John Ehrlichman had been hired to follow Rockefeller and note whom he met with and exactly what he said.[15] The betting from the autumn of 1959 was that Rockefeller would run and take Nixon down to the last primaries, and that Nixon would be the nominee of a divided party. Kennedy was still the Democratic favorite.

In fact, revealing what would prove to be his tactical Achilles' heel, Rockefeller did not run in the early primaries but attempted an upgraded Harold Stassen campaign of polls. He paid for heavy polling, which was suspect because he had commissioned it, that demonstrated that he would run more strongly against the Democrats than Nixon would. This did not move many delegates, and Rockefeller ran out of time and options. By the spring of 1960, his only hope really to shake Nixon was the possibility of Eisenhower's endorsement. It is hard to imagine how he thought

Eisenhower, at this point having failed to dump Nixon when he could have in the last two presidential elections, would desert him now. He telephoned Eisenhower on June 11, 1960, and sidled up to the question. Eisenhower lectured him that he should not "alarm people unnecessarily" about defense. The president said that if he declared now, he would seem like "off again, on again, gone again Finnegan." He should go to the convention in Chicago and make his views known, and if others wanted to nominate him they could, but that he should support Nixon if he was the nominee.

In April 1960, Charles de Gaulle made his first trip to the United States since he had visited President Truman in 1945. He had very satisfactory meetings with Eisenhower "as old soldiers," held out little hope for the upcoming summit meeting, and "told Dwight Eisenhower that whatever happened at the conference, he would carry away the esteem of all on leaving office."[16]

He also held conversations with Richard Nixon, separately, and wrote: "In his somewhat curious post of vice president, he struck me as one of those frank and steady personalities on whom one feels one could rely in the great affairs of State if ever they were to reach the highest office." De Gaulle never wavered in his view that Nixon would attain that office, and that he would distinguish himself in it. He had long been a fascinating figure to Nixon, and these meetings began a relationship that flourished for nine years before flowering briefly when they would both be in their countries' highest offices at the same time.[17] (De Gaulle made his only visit to California, and as his motorcade sped across vast suburbs of Los Angeles, he sat silent for a long time, contemplating what he feared could be the urban future of the West, and then said, to no one in particular: "This will end badly.")

Eisenhower was going to finish the quest for peace of the latter part of his administration with the summit meeting, his trip to the Soviet Union, and then a trip to Japan and a couple of other Far Eastern countries. Unfortunately, in the bumbling manner of the late-Eisenhower era, a high altitude U-2 reconnaissance plane had developed engine trouble over the U.S.S.R. and the pilot, Francis Gary Powers, had bailed out and been captured. He was trotted about before the media of the world like a prize cow. Khrushchev demanded an apology, which Eisenhower declined to give, and the summit meeting in Paris was a fiasco. De Gaulle, as host, visited

Eisenhower, Macmillan (whom he had also known well during the war), and Khrushchev, to see if anything could be done to reconstitute the meeting. After Khrushchev's diatribe in reply, de Gaulle responded, "In that case, Mr. Chairman, do not let me detain you." The summit meeting broke up in acrimony. (De Gaulle, having held his own with Stalin, gave up on Khrushchev and waited for and did better with Brezhnev.)

Eisenhower went on to the Far East, but was asked by the government of Japan not to come to that country, because of communist-led riots. This was another breach of American prestige, and an inexcusable lapse by the Japanese government. There were not many communists in Japan, and the government should have kept order for the visit of so distinguished and important a visitor. The president returned to Washington shortly before the Democratic nominating convention.

Eisenhower was pretty well resigned to the nomination of Nixon by now, but in May 1960 was still touting Anderson, and suggested to his former Health, Education, and Welfare secretary, Oveta Culp Hobby, that she put Anderson forward as a favorite-son candidate in Texas, or, if necessary that she put herself forward in that role. Eisenhower was always interested in promoting women, Roman Catholic, and Jewish candidates, in theory, but never did anything about it. Mrs. Hobby wouldn't touch any of it.

As Rockefeller waited for lightning to strike, Nixon bore down on the Republican organization he had been courting and massaging and building for fourteen years. The Democrats were proposing a lot of mad ideas that Nixon urged his congressional colleagues to force to a vote, in order to get senators Humphrey, Johnson, Kennedy, and Symington on the record. He was not entirely successful. Nixon by this time saw the Kennedy candidacy coming; he was sure by late 1959 that Kennedy was his opponent and knew that religion would be a big winner for Kennedy. He knew that almost all Roman Catholics, about a quarter of the people, would vote for Kennedy and that many Protestants would feel that to be confident that they were not bigots, they would have to vote for him also.

Humphrey and Kennedy were the early candidates for the Democrats, as Johnson, Symington, and Stevenson held back. Nixon was concerned at what appeared to be Kennedy-financed anti-Catholic mailings into Wisconsin, prior to its April 5 primary, in order to arouse both Roman Catholics and fair-minded Protestants. This level of devious and ruthless primary tactics concerned Nixon, not only as a threat to him, but because even he, rough operator though he was, found it ethically offensive.[18] Kennedy won the primary easily and went on to West Virginia, an overwhelmingly Protestant state, which voted strongly for Kennedy in the primary, as Humphrey ran out of money and was reduced to spending his own grocery money to pay campaign workers. (Kennedy's campaign was bankrolled by his father, one of America's wealthiest, if more controversial, industrialists.)

When Roosevelt set up the Securities and Exchange Commission in 1934 and astounded everyone by naming Joseph P. Kennedy as the first chairman, he was asked by the press why he would nominate such a shady stock promoter. Roosevelt, with a toss of his leonine head and a debonair wave of his cigarette-holder, replied, "Set a thief to catch a thief." The press roared with laughter and the appointment was a success, unlike Kennedy's last venture into public life, as Roosevelt's ambassador to Great Britain. In West Virginia, where Roosevelt remained an icon, Kennedy imported FDR Jr., who pointedly asked where Humphrey had been during the war. He had been mayor of Minneapolis and was not in the armed forces.[19]

After West Virginia, Kennedy soldiered on toward the nomination, almost unchallenged. Nixon had predicted this for many months, and he also foresaw that Kennedy would offer the vice presidential nomination to Lyndon Johnson. What was not so clear was whether Johnson, one of Washington's mighty powers along with Sam Rayburn and next only to Eisenhower, as majority leader of the Senate, would take it.[20]

Adlai Stevenson, indecisive to the end, had allegedly been offered the position of secretary of state if he threw in with Kennedy, but was being urged by Eleanor Roosevelt to run outright. At the convention in Los Angeles, Stevenson was the querulous candidate of Mrs. Roosevelt, Symington the unsure candidate of Mr. Truman. Lyndon Johnson was more or less of a Southern and congressional favorite son, and Kennedy won on the first ballot, on July 13. He invited the mercurial, vital, and powerful Johnson, the quintessential congressional deal-maker, to be his vice presidential nominee, and Johnson accepted. He did so despite being told by the other great living triumvir of Texas federal politics, with Rayburn and Johnson, former House Speaker and FDR's first vice president, the ninety-one-year-old John Nance Garner, that the vice presidency wasn't worth "a pail of warm piss," which was cleaned up publicly to "warm spit." Rayburn, as convention chairman, rammed Johnson's nomination through "unanimously," despite loud yelps of protest from a liberal minority.

On the closing night, before more than a hundred thousand people in the Los Angeles Memorial Coliseum, Symington introduced Johnson, who introduced Stevenson, to introduce the presidential nominee. There were Indians (or people dressed up as American Indians, in full head-dresses) snaking around in the middle of the playing field and a number of helicopters buzzing irritatingly about as Stevenson, an inexhaustible wit, was introduced. He stood for almost a minute at the rostrum, waiting for a respite from the cacophony, and began: "I know the helicopters are Republican, but I'm not so sure about the Indians."

Kennedy spoke well and even movingly, quoting everyone from Harry Truman to the Prophet Isaiah, in support of his mission. The politically ambitious and observant actor Ronald Reagan, now a vice president for public and employee relations of General Electric, sent Nixon a handwritten letter, warning: "Under the tousled boyish haircut, it is still old Karl Marx."[21]

Nixon was a sure bet for the nomination, and wondered who he should take for vice president, the only remaining matter of suspense to the Republicans. He thought of a Roman Catholic, an idea sponsored by Eisenhower, who suggested his old comrade, General Alfred Gruenther, oblivious of the fact that the country might have had enough of political generals for a while. Nixon wanted Rockefeller, but Rocky was not interested. Nixon even asked Eisenhower to ask Rockefeller, but the president said, "Nelson would go out and tell it to the world."[22] Eisenhower suggested that Nixon promise to Rockefeller (who was five years older than Nixon), that he, Nixon, would not seek reelection. No one would believe Nixon, and Nixon did not believe in self-nominated lame-duck presidents, and did not follow the advice. Rockefeller might have taken secretary of state in exchange for an all-out campaign effort, pursuant to a promise made in Eisenhower's presence, but Nixon did not pursue it. The president's proposal of a promise to one term was about as absurd as his idea that he might take his brother Milton as vice president in 1956.

Eisenhower had a low opinion of Rockefeller, thought Stevenson a "monkey," Kennedy "incompetent," and Johnson "a small man." Whatever he thought of Nixon's limitations, and he had put him to the tortures of the damned at times over the last eight years, Ike considered him a candidate for Mount Rushmore compared with his rivals.[23]

Nixon met with Rockefeller on July 22 at Rockefeller's Fifth Avenue apartment in New York. They had a pleasant dinner alone, in which Nixon said that he would beef up the vice presidency, with particular responsibility in foreign affairs, and stated that if Rockefeller ran with him unsuccessfully, he would be in line for the nomination in four years. Rockefeller said that he had no interest in being vice president. If Nixon were unsuccessful, Rockefeller would be the front-runner in four years anyway, and either way, he would rather spend the intervening time as governor of New York.

From ten o'clock, when they finished dinner, to about four-thirty, they hammered out a joint statement. Nixon had to bring Rockefeller on board without alienating Eisenhower and the Republicans to the right of him. Nixon would not accept Rockefeller's plan for compulsory medical insurance for the elderly, nor binding arbitration in labor disputes. (These were the notions of someone who had only been in electoral politics for two years.) They agreed a delicate wording on defense: "The United States can afford and must provide . . ." etc. "There must be no price ceiling on America's security."

They were bolting from the Eisenhower view that it was all a lot of hype from partisan Democrats, military-industrial self-serving alarmists, and gullible dupes of communist propaganda, but not directly criticizing the administration. When he heard of the "Treaty of Fifth Avenue," Eisenhower said he found it "somewhat astonishing [from men] who had long been in administration councils and who had never voiced any doubt – at least in my presence – of the adequacy of America's defenses."[24] Eisenhower was correct in all respects except the domestic partisan implications of the defense issue in an election year.

Rockefeller leaked the deal to the press and spun it as a capitulation by Nixon. Eisenhower telephoned Nixon (from Newport, Rhode Island, where he was on holiday) and told him that "it would be difficult for Nixon to run on the administration record if the platform contained a repudiation of it." He also implied that it would be difficult for Nixon to serve in the administration for the next six months if he was disaffected. Nixon assured him that he would ensure there was nothing critical of the administration in the platform, failing which he would repudiate the platform. Eisenhower phoned back the next day, after general publicity of Rockefeller's policy "victory."

Nixon prevailed upon the platform committee and secured Rockefeller's agreement to a substitute defense wording: "The United States can and must provide whatever is necessary to insure its own security. . . . To provide more would be wasteful, to provide less would be catastrophic."[25] It would have been better for Nixon, Rockefeller, and Eisenhower if they had agreed on this formulation at the first try.

Nixon had carved out ground where he, Rockefeller, and Eisenhower could all stand. Nixon went to the convention in Chicago and found the delegates restive and disturbed. He held a press conference and counter-spun Rockefeller's version and then, in a mighty blitz, shook hands and was photographed with all of the twenty-six hundred delegates, individually or in small groups, over the next twenty-four hours.

Nixon's one big decision of the convention, apart from the composition of his acceptance speech, was the choice of a vice presidential nominee. He went through a charade like the one organized by Brownell and Dewey eight years before that had recommended him. He had about twenty party elders together and mulled over candidates, especially Congressmen Gerald Ford of Michigan, Walter Judd of Wisconsin (who had given a fiery, rather far-right, FDR-and-Uncle Joe convention keynote speech), party chairman and Kentucky senator Thruston Morton, and Ambassador Henry Cabot Lodge. It shortly became clear that Lodge was Nixon's choice, which he confirmed at the end of the session.

This was not a good choice, and was the first serious political error Nixon had made since his excessively violent attacks on some of the Democrats earlier in his career. Lodge had been defeated by Kennedy in 1952, was a patrician Bostonian who had no chance of bringing in his own state or any others, and was not an energetic or compelling campaigner. Nixon thought Lodge would be useful as an Easterner acceptable to all sections of the Republican Party, who was familiar to a great many voters by constantly being on television replying to Soviet provocations at the United Nations, where he had been the ambassador throughout the Eisenhower years. This was all right as far as it went. But Kennedy had wrapped up the Roman Catholics, the left, and, with Lyndon Johnson, most of the South, and Nixon needed reinforcements. Lodge proved to be the most lethargic campaigner for national office of modern times.

The voters weren't concerned about the anti-communist credentials of any of the candidates. What Nixon needed was someone to help pull a big swing state for him, and preferably excite the media a little. Everett Dirksen, senator from Illinois, would have been a flamboyant campaigner and almost certainly would have carried Illinois (which, in a dubious count, went, by nine thousand votes out of five million cast, for Kennedy). Senator Kenneth Keating, a Roman Catholic, probably could not have brought in his home state of New York, but would have added a significant scattering of Irish and Eastern votes, and would have made it harder for the Democrats to claim that a Republican vote was an act of bigotry. Senator Hugh Scott of Pennsylvania might have won his state, the third in the country in electoral votes, for Nixon. Keating and Scott were not electrifying on the hustings, though Keating was accomplished and likable, and Scott was unusually intelligent and amusing. Lodge was an impressive-looking man, but he probably did not move a thousand votes one way or another, in an electorate of nearly seventy million.

It is not impossible that Nixon, the common man from Whittier, was making a sociologically balancing move. Facing the wealthy Harvard alumnus Kennedy, veteran of the pre-war debutante parties of London when his father was the ambassador, Nixon reached for the top drawer: first Rockefeller, then the great Boston Brahmin, son of a famous senator and friend of Theodore Roosevelt. This is a wild surmise, but Nixon's judgment in political matters was usually very clear, and he had seen the Kennedy-Johnson ticket coming for many months.

The party's biggest vote-winner, Dwight D. Eisenhower, was not present. He had spoken the night before and gave a very combative and effective speech but did not remain to hear his successor. It is not clear whether he was irritated by the Rockefeller compromise or Nixon wanted the limelight for himself. Nelson Rockefeller introduced Nixon, quite enthusiastically, as "Richard A. Nixon," implying that the candidate had something less than iconic status with the governor, and Nixon gave an out-standing address. Though exhausted, with his mother, wife, and daughters sitting near him, he rose admirably to the occasion. Still somewhat darkly hirsute and complicated, but forceful and dynamic and articulate, he approximately matched Kennedy's fine oratorical effort in Los Angeles of two weeks before.

Nixon praised the speeches of Herbert Hoover, Walter Judd, Eisenhower ("our beloved, fighting president"), Barry Goldwater, and "my friend Nelson Rockefeller." The convention was frequently referred to as being on the one hundredth anniversary of the nomination in the same city of the first Republican president, Abraham Lincoln. Eisenhower was praised for peace, prosperity, and the restoration of integrity and dignity to the nation's highest office. (At least he didn't accuse Truman of treason.) Nixon claimed for the incumbent the greatest full two-term presidency since the founders of the country. This careful choice of words excluded Lincoln and Theodore Roosevelt, the two greatest Republican presidents, and Wilson, because of his illness. No one disputed that Eisenhower was a more capable president than Grant; Cleveland's terms weren't consecutive, so Nixon was really only exalting Ike over FDR's first two terms, which was unwarranted but a forgivable partisan excess.

Nixon accused the Democrats of promising everything with no hint of how to pay for it, and of running America down by holding Eisenhower responsible for the Paris Summit fiasco and the communist-led riots in Caracas and Tokyo, and denigrating American scientists and education.

He promised ever greater and wider prosperity through the private sector, and accused Kennedy, in effect, of trying to promote a cult of youth. Nixon was only four years older than Kennedy, but he praised de Gaulle, Macmillan, and Adenauer, as men of "wisdom, experience . . . and courage," adding that it was not any of them but Kennedy who had suggested that Eisenhower should apologize to Khrushchev for the U-2 overflights. He gave a cogent summary of American domestic and foreign goals, and while there was the usual tedious flag-waving and platitudinous phrases, he attacked racial discrimination, avoided any jingoism, and situated the United States squarely in the world. The communists were referred to unflatteringly, but not demagogically.

Nixon planned a frenetic campaign; he pledged to appear in all fifty states. (Alaska and Hawaii had been admitted as states and Eisenhower took from this the possibility of supranational institutions with Britain, Canada, Australia, and New Zealand.) Instead of pacing himself, and ensuring that when facing such an elegant and alluring candidate as Kennedy, Nixon would look his best and seem relaxed, he emphasized those practices that tended to make him appear haggard, worn, and afflicted by jowly beardedness and excessive perspiration. This unceasing physical activity was his second serious campaign mistake, after the Lodge nomination. He took no advice, not even from Eisenhower, who gave unsolicited advice from time to time.

The Democrats were attacking the Eisenhower administration's defense record, which along with their promised fiscal extravagance, redoubled Eisenhower's partisanship for his vice president. Eisenhower remained a very popular and respected president, although the country felt his government, and he himself, had become rather tired. Eisenhower was so contemptuous of the Democrats, and considered their 1960 nominees to be such an ill-favored pair – Kennedy a debonair and shallow fraud and Johnson a shabby and unscrupulous trickster and con man – that his enthusiasm for Nixon reached unforeseen heights. He was prepared to do almost anything to elect Nixon, but was little used. This underemployment of a magical political weapon in the person of the president was the third principal error of Nixon's campaign.

Either Kennedy or Nixon would be a startling change, in physical and intellectual energy level. (Kennedy suffered from acute backaches and was addicted to various painkilling medicines, as well as to a prodigious amount of conventional sexual activity with a rather indiscriminate variety of ephemeral or serial mates. But the public never saw this, partly because of the lack of curiosity and widespread partisanship of the national media.) Eisenhower was old enough to be the father of either man (he was only two years younger than Kennedy's father, and twelve years younger than Nixon's). This would be one of the rare elections where the age of the president of the country would fall by a whole generation.

Congress had legislated to enable the principal candidates to have free televised political debates. Eisenhower warned Nixon not to get into this. Nixon was better known than Kennedy, and while his grasp of the subject material would probably be at least as strong as Kennedy's, his appearance and manner were less naturally attractive. Eisenhower thought there was nothing in it for Nixon. He always emphasized his comparative experience, and this would be challenged if Kennedy came through more or less as plausibly.

Eisenhower, who was not especially articulate, thought debates were contests of slickness and glibness and revealed nothing of real importance. Kennedy, for obvious reasons, was instantly in favor of debating Nixon. Nixon did not follow Eisenhower's advice, and agreeing to debate Kennedy is generally reckoned his fourth important tactical mistake in the 1960 campaign. It need not have been a mistake; Nixon was a convincing and experienced advocate, and if he had declined, he would have appeared afraid of his youthful opponent, and would certainly have been so accused.

Nixon also declined Eisenhower's offer of his television and lighting expert.[26]

Eisenhower did not assist his protégé by his tepid comments about him at press conferences. Reporters asked Eisenhower to say whether Nixon really was as experienced as he claimed to be at involvement in presidential decision-making. Eisenhower found the persistent questions annoying, perhaps because they implied that he had not entirely maintained his authority, although Nixon never suggested any such thing. Eisenhower, even as he cranked up to help Nixon keep Kennedy out of the White House, was very hesitant to give him the unqualified endorsement he had been seeking for eight years.

Privately, Eisenhower blamed Nixon for not accepting the post of secretary of defense, which, he claimed, would have qualified him much better to be president. This was not only nonsense in itself, but left out the fact that in that case, he would not have been nominated. He could never have retained delegate support from the Pentagon against Rockefeller and Goldwater.[27] The ambivalence between the two men would continue for another eight years, but this year would do Nixon great harm.

On one occasion in August 1960, Eisenhower, when asked if Nixon had initiated any important policies or ideas, snapped, "Give me a week. I might think of one." He immediately realized he had made a mistake, and instead of trying, however awkwardly, to put things right, telephoned Nixon right after the press meeting and apologized. The Democrats and Nixon's press critics had a good time with this regrettable malapropism. As the campaign got under way, Nixon, for all his suspicious wariness and thoroughness, still hadn't identified Kennedy as the menace to his career that he was. Nixon had always liked Kennedy. When JFK underwent a perilous spinal fusion operation in November 1954, Nixon visited him at Bethesda Naval Hospital. As Kennedy's condition worsened, the senator's family and a priest were summoned. When he returned to his car, Nixon wept and said to his Secret Service escort, Rex Scouten, "That poor young man . . . poor, brave Jack is going to die. Oh, God, don't let him die." He returned to see a recovering Kennedy a few weeks later, and Jackie Kennedy wrote: "I can never thank you enough for being so kind and generous and thoughtful. . . . I don't think there is anyone he thinks more highly of than . . . you."[28] Yet Nixon saw the Kennedys as a sleazy family of a corrupt, quasi-fascist patriarch, and Bobby as a mad McCarthyite monk and Teddy as a friendly Irish lush with a gaggle of toothy, frothy sisters. (Nixon always had a high regard for Jackie). Nixon saw Jack as a whimsical, pleasant, bright, lazy man who had simplistic views, had made no contribution to the Senate, and suffered severe withdrawal symptoms if his appetites of a rutting panther were unfulfilled even for a few hours. He did not see Kennedy as the voters saw him: handsome, fresh, natural, cultivated, very intelligent, with a good sense of humor, and a brave man with a glamorous wife and family.

He recognized that Kennedy had been personally friendly with many of the journalists and would be favored by most of them, but he did not see him as the Robert Logue type of effortlessly attractive and apparently not indecently ambitious man who had defeated him for student body president at Whittier Union in 1929. Nixon could not shake his impression of Kennedy as basically a charlatan and was convinced that the more direct competition there was between them, the more the public would see Nixon's comparative solidity and Kennedy's superficiality.

In pursuing this course, he reinforced the public perception that Kennedy was a natural champion and that Nixon was an earnest but hokey striver, or, as the distinguished journalist and historian of modern presidential elections Theodore H. White put it, "one of nature's losers." This was an odd description of a man who had risen as quickly as Nixon had, was politically undefeated, and had been almost the acting president, despite underprivileged origins and a very challenging and severely contested career path. This underestimation of Kennedy, aggravated by his lack of Chotiner-quality expert political advice, may be taken as Nixon's fifth tactical error in the campaign.

— III —

Nixon spent most of August in Washington, while the Congress was still sitting, and he had some senatorial duties. His long-standing and talented supporter, Robert Finch of California, chairman of the Los Angeles County Republican Central Committee (an almost communistic title), became campaign chairman. Herb Klein was the press secretary. H.R. Haldeman became the chief aide, and John Ehrlichman the chief advance man. Frederic Morrow, an African-American, and L. Pat Gray, a former submarine captain and aide to the chairman of the Joint Chiefs of Staff, joined Nixon's staff. Jim Bassett was in charge of scheduling. The redoubtable Rose Mary Woods headed the large corps of secretaries.

The Scholars for Nixon and Lodge group was established, with Lon Fuller of the Harvard Law School as chairman and the former chairman of the Council of Economic Advisers, Arthur Burns, a respected economist from Columbia University, the chief of the economic group. The scholars were an impressive but not a politically practical group, and they bombarded Nixon throughout the campaign with interesting ideas that he referred to policy specialists who invariably explained their unfeasibility.

Celebrities for Nixon was a helpful group that spoke on his behalf and included Elizabeth Arden, James Cagney, Irene Dunne, Freeman Gosden, Jeanette MacDonald, Gordon MacRae, Dina Merrill, Mary Pickford, Rosalind Russell, and John Wayne, with Helen Hayes and Mervyn LeRoy as co-chairs. Supporters, but not declared members, included Bob Hope, Walt Disney, Jackie Gleason, and Ronald Reagan (still a registered Democrat, who yet made some speeches for Nixon).

The Dick Nixon Sports Committee included Ted Williams of the Boston Red Sox, one of baseball history's greatest hitters, and Frank Gifford of the New York Giants, a great football halfback. (Williams told me forty years later that he had "seen enough of the Kennedys in Boston to know I didn't want them in the White House." He added that because of his position he had met every president from Roosevelt to Clinton, and "except for FDR and Ike, Dick was the most impressive." This would have gladdened the heart of the Whittier College football extra, but Williams, apart from his unforgettable baseball-hitting talents, was a very intelligent, if eccentric, man, and his comments were not just the effusions of a well-muscled groupie.)

On August 29, with the opening polls showing the two candidates effectively even, Nixon suffered a jolt of bad luck; after bumping his knee on a car door a few days before, and treating it with hot compresses, he went for a fluid tap test, then was called back and told that if he did not return at once to Walter Reed Hospital, he would be "campaigning on one leg." He had a severe staphylococci infection, and was hospitalized for two weeks, while Kennedy barnstormed the country. Lyndon Johnson and Barry Goldwater graciously visited him and wished him well. So did Eisenhower and Rockefeller (separately), and his wife and daughters visited every day. (When Eisenhower returned from the hospital, he told his secretary, Ann Whitman, "there was some lack of warmth." He mentioned that Nixon had very few personal friends.[29]) Many thousands of cards and telegrams arrived. Nixon rested, wrote speeches, recorded some radio statements, but was tortured by the enforced inactivity and emerged looking gaunt and pallid.

While Nixon was in hospital, his friend the Reverend Dr. Norman Vincent Peale signed a public statement expressing concern over whether a Roman Catholic could be trusted to exercise the office of president without being instructed by the Pope. With such friends, Nixon had no need of enemies. There was no win for Nixon in this. The rabid anti-papists were going to vote for him anyway. The great majority of the Roman Catholics, despite the efforts of Nixon's Catholic friends like Clare Booth Luce and Rose Mary Woods, were going to vote for Kennedy, which must have conferred an advantage of approximately two to one on Kennedy among those who were going to vote on the Catholic issue. Nixon had to prevent open-minded Protestants from stampeding to Kennedy to demonstrate to themselves that they weren't bigots and that they did not subscribe to the sort of nonsense that Peale had just endorsed.

Kennedy played the religious card with tactical genius. A few days after the Peale incident, he addressed a large convention of Protestant ministers in Houston and said that he was "not the Catholic candidate for president. I am the Democratic Party's candidate for president. . . . If this election is decided on the basis that forty million Americans lost their chance of being president on the day they were baptized, then it is the whole nation that will be the loser in the eyes of history."

Kennedy had his foibles, but he was a refined and tasteful man, and he said almost nothing more about the issue. However, his partisans did not leave it alone. Lyndon Johnson and other Democratic spokesmen responded to the anti-Catholic hate literature as if it might have emanated from the Republicans, without ever suggesting that it had, repeating that a quarter of the people could not simply be disqualified in this way; no one had asked Kennedy or his millions of co-religionists in the armed forces what their religion was when they were risking their lives in combat, etc. Congressman Adam Clayton Powell of Harlem, the leading African-American public officeholder, and the AFL-CIO's Political Education Committee both called the election a contest between Kennedy and the bigots, as if the Democratic candidate were really running against a lynch-mob in bedsheets, not the two-term vice president. Billy Graham warned Nixon that Kennedy not only was trying to polarize the vote between all Catholics and tolerant Protestants on one side and bigots on the other, but was trying to disguise the real issues behind the false question of sectarian fair-mindedness.[30]

Nixon handled it as best he could. Utterly devoid of any such prejudice as was being decried from the housetops (and most of the steeples) of America, he left the hospital September 9 and appeared on *Meet the Press* September 11. He stated his certainty that Kennedy would always put the "Constitution above any other consideration," said he had ordered his party to say and do nothing on the religious issue, renounced the support of bigots, and disavowed Peale. He made it as difficult as possible for Democrats to represent that they were fighting religious intolerance.

There was nothing more he could do, but this did not stop low-level Democrats from saying that every time Nixon disavowed religious prejudice, he was raising religion as an issue. Kennedy and Nixon handled a touchy issue with distinction, worthy of the great office they sought and achieved. In lower echelons, in a very close and hard-fought campaign, the Republicans performed more creditably than the Democrats. Both candidates recognized that Kennedy's religion was a political asset to him.

Nixon went over the schedule with Jim Bassett, who urged him to use his hospitalization quietly to cancel his pledge to go into fifty states and avoid those where there was no hope and those that were very safe. It was obviously a close race and the larger swing states would decide it. Nixon, in what became the sixth serious tactical error of the campaign, stuck to his fifty-state campaign plan. The reason for this is obscure. He claimed that having made the pledge, he didn't feel excused from it just because he had spent two weeks in hospital. Perhaps it brought out another aspect of Nixon's fierce tenacity and stubbornness. To a degree, he believed that if he simply did not yield, he would win, and his experience had to some extent justified that conviction. He finally hit the trail on September 12, visiting nine states in three days.

He awakened in the early morning of September 15 with a high fever and chills, and told the doctor traveling with him that he had to speak to the International Machinists' Union five hours later. The doctor, John Lungren, managed to subdue the fever, and Nixon gave the address, to a union that had already committed to endorse Kennedy. In the next day, he went from St. Louis, Missouri, to New Jersey, Virginia, and then back cross-country to Omaha.

The fifty-state commitment was grueling enough, but hop-scotching all across the country like this was just bad scheduling. Ehrlichman had the idea of going by motorcade across Iowa for a day. It was a fiasco, as much time was wasted, the crowds were small, and it was a rather safe state anyway. (Nixon carried nearly 57 percent of the vote in November, and would not have lost a hundred votes if hadn't gone on Ehrlichman's slow car trip.) Nixon had a tantrum in the car, kicking the seat in front of him in frustration, until the occupant of the seat, Don Hughes, who had had nothing to do with the decision to travel by car in Iowa, got out of the car, resigned from the campaign, and started walking across Iowa. Haldeman walked after him and brought him back.[31]

Nixon had earned such a reputation as a nasty campaigner from the Democrats that now, running in his own right for the headship of the nation, he astounded Nixon-watchers by his restraint. There were no references to Kennedy's wealth or the questionable origins of it, the fascist sympathies of his father, his poor attendance record in the Senate, or his peccadilloes. It may seem cynical to claim it, but Nixon made a seventh error running such a soft campaign.

Kennedy's attacks on the defense performance of the supreme Allied commander in Western Europe and founding commander of NATO were outrageous. Kennedy had made a number of ill-considered comments, such as his embrace of the Algerian rebels and his assertion that Eisenhower should apologize for reconnaissance overflights of the U.S.S.R. Nixon did criticize the last, but could have made much more of it. Nixon seemed to have no alternative campaign to "rock'em, sock'em" allegations of communist sympathies, or white gloves gentlemanliness. It was as if he was afraid that his own notoriety would rise up and smite him if he really swung at Kennedy. It was almost as if he had come full circle from the Voorhis and Douglas and 1952 campaigns, and would rather be admired for his sportsmanship than win. To those too young to remember the Nixon of 1946 to 1952, who first became acquainted with him as a public figure in 1956 or later, he did not at all seem the dreadful ogre conjured by the Democrats but rather, as Theodore White wrote, a man "almost pathetic in his eagerness to be liked."[32]

Cuba loomed as an issue through the campaign. Nixon was an enthusiastic promoter of an incipient plan for the invasion of Cuba by exiles, armed by the United States, and the overthrow of Castro. Kennedy was regularly accusing the Eisenhower administration of being excessively tolerant of the continued irritation of Castro, and implied that he would dispense with him. Nixon was then reduced to accusing Kennedy of being a hip-shooter, and an impetuous and potentially trigger-happy president. Considering what was afoot, and what came to pass seven months later in the Bay of Pigs, this exchange was ironic. Eisenhower had approved, in March 1960, a CIA program for training and equipping Cuban exiles "for future Guerrilla action." The training took place in Guatemala, and Nixon was constantly urging it forward and asking about its progress. The initial target date for landings to join forces with indigenous anti-Castro forces was September, but Eisenhower delayed it because the exiles could not agree on an alternative to Castro as leader of Cuba. Nixon's impatience was unwise; given the mortifying failure that befell Kennedy when he implemented the plan developed originally under Eisenhower with Nixon's prodding, if any such thing had occurred as Nixon agitated for incessantly, in mid-election campaign, the Nixon candidacy would have sunk like the battleship *Maine* in Havana Harbor (in 1898).

Nixon told the Veterans of Foreign Wars in Detroit at the end of August that the United States could "throw [Castro] out of office any day that we would choose" but clarified for the press (to hose down Eisenhower and the State Department) that this was "simply out of the question."[33] On September 21, Nixon compared moving on Castro to Khrushchev's invasion of Hungary, an acrobatic stance, given that he was hounding the CIA to get on with injecting the guerrillas into Cuba.[34] Kennedy regularly pointed out that the Republicans had been elected in 1952 on a campaign pledge to "roll back" communism, and now it was only ninety miles from Florida. Castro came to New York for the UN General Assembly session from September 18 to 28, hamming in front of photographers with Khrushchev, who took off his shoe and pounded it on his desk at the United Nations, in mock rage over the U-2 incident.

The first presidential debate was in Chicago on September 26. Nixon prepared the day before and flew to Chicago, touring the wards in a motorcade when he arrived and speaking to the Carpenters' Union in the morning. He studied the issues in the afternoon and arrived at the studio in a light suit with a shirt collar too large, which made him appear drawn and fatigued, as his clothes seemed to hang on him like a bat. He had light makeup only.

Nixon had bumped his knee again as he got out of his car (perhaps if he had not eschewed Cadillacs for reasons of image, he would have had the legroom to spare his knees the severe battering they suffered). He was standing uncomfortably as a result of the bump he had sustained.

Kennedy had prepared in his own fashion, relaxing on a sun deck and enjoying the pleasures of a professional woman procured for him by the specialists on his staff who supplied him in this regard before, during, and after the campaign. Kennedy found it so refreshing, he insisted on the same preparatory therapy for all the debates.[35] As is notorious, Kennedy won the battle of appearances. He wore a dark suit, was tanned and confident, while Nixon seemed haggard and at times a little nervous. Nixon's five o'clock shadow, jowls, dark eyes, and tendency to perspire under television lights were all in evidence. Both candidates knew the material, and the contrast between the 1960 encounters and future presidential debates, which have been sound-bite exchanges circumscribed to superficial treatment of subjects, is striking. Yet they were not so much debating as answering reporters' questions that they had addressed many times before.

They had an unprecedented audience of over eighty million people. Kennedy opened with his "get America moving again" theme. "I am not satisfied, as an American, with the progress we're making." He wanted faster progress on everything from steel production to civil rights to teachers' pay. Nixon replied defensively, but argued that the Eisenhower years had shown a good deal more progress than had the Truman years. The fifties were not slow-motion times, he pointed out, but in fact the greatest years of progress and generally improving living standards in the country's history. Nixon extolled Republican faith in the private sector and unlocking America's creative energies, and only lightly broke out the violins on the issue of the poor, saying that he had been poor himself, but having the taste to avoid saying that Kennedy had not.

Nixon handled very competently the inevitable questions about whether he had really done anything in the administration or just been an observer, referring to the reports he gave on returning from foreign trips, the setting up of the inter-American lending agency, the admission of Hungarian refugees, his role in various foreign exchange programs, and his work on the Cabinet Committee on Price Stability for Economic Growth. To the follow-up question of Sander Vanocur (who was intermittently paid by the Kennedys while working for NBC) about Ike's inability the month before to think of an initiative of Nixon's that he had adopted, Nixon said that Ike was "facetious" and that he had suggested a great many things. "Sometimes my advice has been taken. Sometimes it has not. I do not say that I have made the decisions."[36]

The candidates repeated their positions on a number of issues, Kennedy generally favoring government action to remedy all problems, and Nixon favoring the same ends but through the private sector, incentivized, if necessary, by the federal government. They agreed almost exactly on civil rights.

When Nixon returned to his hotel, feeling fairly good about his performance, he was advised by Rose Mary Woods and others that he had spoken well but looked sick. It quickly became clear that he had lost on appearance but not on content. Those who heard the debate on the radio felt, by a slight margin, that Nixon had won. For television viewers, there was an edge, though not a decisive one, to Kennedy, and this was more a press consensus than a genuine opinion sampling. Republicans who had expected Nixon to eviscerate Kennedy were disappointed, and Democrats were correspondingly happy, but the race was still close and all was still to play for. Henry Cabot Lodge, who was so laid-back that he got into his pajamas after lunch for a nap every day, watched from Texas and said, "That son-of-a-bitch just lost us the election." In the circumstances, even if it had been true, Lodge was in no position to complain. To improve his appearance Nixon put on five pounds by drinking milk shakes, and for subsequent debates he used more makeup and wore shirts with fitting collars.

Both candidates campaigned energetically. Both drew large and friendly crowds and there was no sense that Kennedy was pulling away, though most polls showed him with a slight lead. Pat Nixon pitched in and gave it her all. Jackie Kennedy was pregnant, and because she had had some difficulty bearing children, she was little seen. (At the outset of the campaign she had been asked if it was true that she spent thirty thousand dollars a year on clothes, and not only defused the question but surely picked up some votes when she responded that she could not do that "unless I wore sable underwear.")[37]

The second debate was in Washington on October 7. Nixon did not rest much before the debate, but had the temperature reduced in the studio, arranged for minimal lighting in his face, and wore adequate makeup. His clothes fit properly and he was in sharper form. The whole tenor of the exchange was more aggressive. Kennedy started with the allegation that if the Republicans were going to claim that the Democrats had "lost China," the Republicans had lost Cuba. Nixon denied that it was lost, reminded Kennedy that there was a non-intervention treaty in the Americas (which the United States frequently violated and which had not received much consideration as Eisenhower and Nixon planned the invasion of Cuba by exiles), and said that the Cubans "who want to be free are going to be supported and . . . they will attain their freedom." (Forty-six years later, long after Kennedy and Nixon had passed prominently into history, Castro was still the dictator of Cuba.) Nixon could have mentioned that China had one hundred times Cuba's population, but he didn't.

There were frequent references to Khrushchev. Nixon said that the United States could not allow Khrushchev to point to the mistreatment of black Americans, and debunked Kennedy's claim that American prestige had sunk. When Kennedy was asked why he attacked the administration but not Eisenhower, he replied that he had been given to understand that Nixon was a prominent member of the administration. Nixon pointed out that the Democrats had expended a great deal of effort claiming that he had played almost no role in it.

Kennedy attacked the Quemoy-Matsu policy and said the islands, which were only five miles offshore from China, were militarily useless and should be abandoned. Nixon scored well on this point that the United States must not oblige its nationalist allies to give up territory; "This is the same kind of woolly thinking that led to disaster for America in Korea."[38] Nixon a couple of times emphasized that he did not question Kennedy's sincerity and he hoped that Kennedy would accord him the same courtesy. Kennedy did not respond, and it seemed slightly importunate of Nixon. The press and the polls concurred in Nixon's own judgment that he had done well and had a slight edge. The audience had declined from eighty million in the first debate to sixty million in the second.

Nixon took off to the hustings beating the drums about Quemoy and Matsu: "If you elect me president, I assure you that I will not hand over one square foot of the Free World to the communists."[39]

Lodge did Nixon no favors by pledging in Harlem and again on television that there would be an African-American in the cabinet. This was a reasonable idea, but a foolish pledge, as it did not impress the blacks and alienated many Southern whites. Nixon had Klein issue a statement saying that he would choose the best people possible, and that "race or religion would not be a factor either for or against."[40]

The third debate was on October 13, with the candidates on different coasts: Nixon in Los Angeles and Kennedy in New York. The Quemoy-Matsu policy was again a big issue, as both candidates demonstrated the brilliance of the Eisenhower-Dulles Formosa Resolution and Doctrine, which gave the president authority to use any means he wished to defend Formosa and "closely related localities," a formulation that enabled Eisenhower, a specialist in dissimulation, to play poker with Mao Tse-tung and Chou En-lai.

Kennedy harped on Quemoy and Matsu, saying that Nixon had done nothing about Tibet, Budapest, Laos, Guinea, Ghana, and Cuba. Nixon replied (accurately) that they were hardly comparable. (Kennedy would later claim that Laos was not a communist state.) What the Democratic candidate proposed to do about Tibet, or what he would have done about Budapest, was never clear, and unfortunately, Nixon did not make an issue out of it.

They clashed on domestic issues also, where Kennedy favored health care for the elderly, which he pretended would not be costly. Nixon replied effectively that his opponent was playing a game of "Here it is and here it isn't," and pointed out that Social Security taxes were deducted from people's paychecks and Kennedy was flimflamming the country by pretending that the tax would not increase to pay for higher medical benefits for many millions of people.

Nixon became unctuous when he complained that President Truman had said that Southerners who voted for Nixon could "go to hell." Nixon was at least as coarse in private speech as Truman, and complaining about "bad language" made him seem to many a namby-pamby. Kennedy said, on that subject, with his usual amiable light touch, that he didn't think there was much he "could say to Mr. Truman, that's going to cause him, at the age of seventy-six," to change his vocabulary. "Maybe Mrs. Truman can, but I don't think I can." (Mrs. Truman, though a formidable battle-axe at times, couldn't either.)[41] Nixon might have had a slight edge in the third debate, but the candidates essentially were still even going into the last three weeks. It was like a gripping, matched horse race, with two stallions thundering toward the finish line. The campaign now entered the fiercest and most punishing finale at least since Franklin D. Roosevelt's great battle for a third term against Wendell Willkie in 1940.

The policy differences between the candidates were relatively subtle, and centered on the role of the public sector. Both candidates favored construction of low-cost housing, extension of medical care, and aid to education, but Nixon thought the private sector could be incentivized to deal with the first two and that money should be given to the states to address educational needs. Kennedy was for direct federal government funding and operation of these programs, including supplements to teachers' salaries. In foreign policy, Nixon accused Kennedy of being an apologetic appeaser and Kennedy accused Nixon of being a warmonger. Kennedy claimed the country's defenses were in disarray; both put on an invasion-tease in respect of Castro, and they said virtually the same things about civil rights and stimulative tax cuts.

Kennedy was exploiting Cuba to try to turn the tide on Nixon as a paper tiger, and on October 17, Nixon met with Eisenhower and Undersecretary of State C. Douglas Dillon and urged that something be done about Cuba and that, for political reasons, Nixon be seen to be involved in it. Eisenhower agreed on both counts. While this was being concerted, Kennedy spoke to the American Legion in Miami and accused Nixon of "vicious distortions" over Quemoy and Matsu. Nixon spoke to the same audience the next day and described Castro's regime as "an intolerable cancer" and promised "the strongest possible economic measures." (The Legion was composed of veterans of the armed forces and had about fifteen million members; they tended to be fairly hawkish, and liked both candidates because of their tough stances and distinguished war records.)

The following day, October 19, the United States announced the imposition of a complete trade embargo on Cuba except for medicine and food, and the recall of the ambassador from Havana. Kennedy replied that these measures were inadequate and late, and that there should be stronger sanctions (presumably the cut-off of supplies of medicine), aid to the democratic exiles, and a general aid program for Latin America. This was all very frustrating for Nixon, as he had been advocating such an aid program since his first visits to Latin America, and an outright invasion of Cuba by the exiles.

Kennedy claimed that the exiles were being given no support, even though he had had intelligence briefings from Allen Dulles at Eisenhower's instruction, clearly stating that they were being assisted and prepared. The crowning irony of this exchange came in the fourth and last debate, on October 21, when Nixon gave a brilliant answer to a question about Cuba and excoriated the whole idea of an invasion of Cuba, which he had, in fact, been advocating, and which Kennedy did, in fact, carry out with disastrously humiliating results. Nixon emphasized the problems of violating the 1948 Organization of American States Treaty, which pledged nonintervention in the internal affairs of signatory countries, and predicted that any such course would alienate all of Latin America, open that continent up to the Russians, and probably fail militarily.

As Stephen Ambrose wrote, "In his long political career, Nixon made any number of predictions, some of them amazingly accurate, but never was he more exactly on the mark than in this case. The trouble was, he did not believe a word of what he said."[42] Nixon would have done better, since Castro had publicly predicted an American-sponsored invasion, to state that a variety of options were under consideration, that Kennedy had had a full intelligence briefing, and that he knew as a result that what he was alleging against the administration was dishonest. It could have been a knockout blow.

The other main point of contention was Kennedy's claim that Nixon was suppressing a report showing the decline of American prestige in the world. Nixon said the report referred to was obsolete and that American prestige was in fine fettle, and then tore into Kennedy for "running America down," citing a speech of nine months before when Kennedy had claimed "seventeen million Americans go to bed hungry every night." Kennedy replied that he didn't "need Mr. Nixon to tell me what my responsibilities are as a citizen." He said that he was running down the country's leadership, not the country – regarding, for example, Nixon's statement to Khrushchev that the U.S.S.R. was ahead in rockets and the United States was ahead in color television. "I think that color television is not as important as rocket thrust."

It was an agile use of Nixon's unwise and inaccurate admission in Moscow. At this point, at the latest, General Dwight D. Eisenhower should have given Lieutenant Kennedy a massive, public verbal box on the ear. The United States was overwhelmingly stronger in nuclear forces and delivery systems than the U.S.S.R., and not 5 percent of Americans would have believed Kennedy over Eisenhower in a military debate, and it was Eisenhower's presidency he was attacking.

— IV —

On October 19, Martin Luther King and other civil rights workers were arrested during a desegregation sit-in in a department store in Atlanta. His comrades were released, but on October 25, King was sentenced to four months in jail for violating parole in regard to an earlier charge of driving with an invalid license. John Kennedy telephoned his wife, Coretta Scott King, and Robert Kennedy telephoned the judge and secured King's release.

Nixon, in the eighth serious mistake of the campaign, told Herb Klein, the campaign press secretary, with the same sort of pompous priggishness that caused him to object to Harry Truman saying the word *hell* in public: "I think Dr. King is getting a bum rap, but despite my strong feelings . . . it would be completely improper for me . . . to call the judge." He did speak to William Rogers and ask him if King's constitutional rights were being violated, and Rogers asked James Hagerty to issue a statement, but Eisenhower refused to get involved.

This was a disaster: Nixon's fine record and sincere beliefs about civil rights and his good relations with King went for nothing. Lodge had alienated the white supremacists with his pledge of a black cabinet member, and Nixon ruined many years of assiduous support for civil rights by bumbling in the crisis, where Robert Kennedy moved with the instincts of a masterly political operator, as well as a just man. King had voted Republican in 1956, and Martin Luther King Sr. had already endorsed Nixon, but now he publicly reversed course, endorsed Kennedy, and said he would deliver him "a suitcase of votes." (So he did, as the Democratic share of the African-American vote moved up from 60 percent in 1956 to 80 percent in 1960.)

Eisenhower, in preventing Hagerty from issuing a statement recommended by the attorney general that would have assisted a noble cause and materially helped his vice president in the election, demonstrated that he was starting to lose his judgment and that it was time for him to retire. He might even have made a clinching argument for term limits.

Another bad turn was Drew Pearson's allegation on October 26 that Howard Hughes had received a very valuable tax categorization for his Hughes Medical Institute, and the settlement of an anti-trust suit, just after lending Nixon's brother Donald $205,000. Nixon handled this one well; Finch issued a statement calling it "an obvious political smear," and stating that the loan had come from an old Nixon family friend, and not from

Hughes at all. Rogers issued a further statement the next day that established that the anti-trust suit had been launched after the loan was made,
and that the settlement had been approved by every lawyer in the anti-trust
division. Donald Nixon was a rather unsuccessful hustler, who had
expanded the family business into a complex including a drive-in restaurant
that sold the Nixonburger. The loan was made by a family friend to Hannah
Nixon, but did originate with Hughes, who did receive adequate collateral
– a trust deed on the business. There is no evidence, despite relentless
efforts to turn some up, that Nixon intervened in Hughes's affairs at all, or
that the ruling and settlement in question were in any way improper. The
Democrats and their media friends tried to hype the story, but Nixon's
relaxed response and the absence of evidence cooled it out without noticeable damage. Because of their complicated personalities and extraordinary
careers, relations between Hughes and Nixon have been a hardy perennial
favorite with conspiracy theorists ever since.

Nixon challenged Kennedy to a fifth debate, about Cuba, but Kennedy
declined. Nixon, after his ringing disparagement of any American-sponsored
invasion, tried to hedge his bets by saying that a quarantine had preceded the
overthrow of the communist Arbenz regime in Guatemala. On October 26,
he said that "sooner, I think, than you think, they [the Cubans] will get rid
of [Castro] in their own way" (by waiting for him to die of old age, as it turned
out). Some of the leading columnists turned on Nixon for trying to suck and
blow on Cuba at the same time; Walter Lippmann correctly saw that his
"show of righteous indignation was false and insincere." Less significant,
Arthur Krock, a longtime quasi-employee of Joseph Kennedy, took the
senator's side in the exchange. Kennedy said on *Face the Nation* on October
30 that he was opposed to "naked force." It was, in sum, a shabby display of
posturing and weaseling by both candidates, with Kennedy's abuse of his
advantage from the intelligence briefing more distasteful than Nixon's
clumsy efforts to straddle. In these matters, Eisenhower, the eminent
general, emerges as much the soundest of the three eventual presidents, as
he had serious reservations about both the ethics and the military feasibility
of what was in contemplation.

There was extensive debate about the debates. If it had been expected
that Nixon would win, he lost, because he did not win. But this reasoning is
overused. The two candidates were running neck-and-neck going into the
debates, and they were in the same position at the end of them, so there

cannot have been a great disappointment in Nixon or adherence of new believers to Kennedy. To the extent that neither candidate flattered the other, as Jimmy Carter was deemed to have done with Gerald Ford in 1976, or Ronald Reagan did with Carter four years later, or Bill Clinton did with George Bush Sr. and Bob Dole in 1992 and 1996, both failed and both succeeded. They were very well-informed and articulate candidates, with much greater verbal command of the whole range of the issues than any of their successors, except perhaps President Clinton.

Kennedy's denigrations of the Eisenhower record brought the president out, finally, in the last week of October. He spoke well and had no trouble demolishing the aspersions the senator had heaped on his administration. But he did not at first say much about Nixon. He was much more preoccupied with debunking Kennedy.

President Truman had been having a delightful time energetically campaigning against Nixon. He said in Oakland on October 28 that Nixon would be too young to retire and should set up an amusement park, "Nixonland," where there could be no curses "because of the children there" and where "our prestige would be at an all-time high" and all would be "cleaner than a hound's tooth." Herbert Hoover, though eighty-six, made a few good speeches for the Republicans. It was the only election in the country's history in which six people who were or would be president were prominent in the campaign, and all were effective.

After the shambles with Martin Luther King, Nixon abandoned his reticence about Eisenhower campaigning for him, as the president was drawing larger crowds than any of the candidates or other prominent campaigners. If in the last days he had been deployed to Chicago instead of New York, and Michigan instead of Ohio, it could have been decisive.[43] On October 30, Mamie Eisenhower called Pat Nixon and said that she was concerned that her husband was overstraining himself. Eisenhower's doctor, General Howard Snyder, also called and expressed concern about his patient's planned campaign schedule.[44] Nixon dutifully called on Eisenhower later that day and talked him out of the ambitious schedule that he had, which included barnstorming parts of Illinois and Michigan, states that were very tight. He could have asked Eisenhower to consult his doctor, or scale back his efforts, or just not to overdo it. As so often in delicate personal matters, Nixon bungled the call, which was self-sacrificing and undertaken for the very best of motives. Eisenhower found Nixon mousy and obsequious and almost incoherent, and said that if he had had such an officer in the war he would have "busted" him.

With one week left, Kennedy had the lead, though narrowly. Nixon urged Eisenhower to call for both candidates to make their medical records public, as he had done to counteract morbid Democratic claims in 1956. Eisenhower flatly refused[45] as being an unworthy initiative. This was the correct reaction. Nixon should have published his own medical records early in the campaign and said that he expected Kennedy to do the same, and that he believed Eisenhower had started a useful precedent.* He could have extended it to the vice presidential candidates, as Johnson had had a serious heart attack a few years before. He moved too late, and in the wrong way. If he had done so, Kennedy could have ignored it, or probably have found a doctor, as Roosevelt did in 1944, when he was clearly medically unfit to serve another term, to attest to his good health. It would have been worth a try for Nixon, but probably would not have been decisive. (Roosevelt had retained the enthusiasm of the White House duty doctor who assured the nation of the president's good health, by promoting him to vice admiral and the position of surgeon general of the U.S. Navy.) If real medical records had been released, it might have been a negative event, as Johnson, whose health held through very stressful years ahead, would possibly have been disqualified, cardiologically.

Coming into the last week, Nixon, trailing narrowly, staged an Homeric effort, supplemented by the greatest television blitz in history. The Republican National Committee was rich, and his media advisers, whose creative ideas had been largely ignored until very late in the campaign, came to life in the last days. Nixon had originally planned the "most imaginative use of television ever displayed in a national campaign."[46] He was concerned with being labeled with the opprobrious charge of "Madison Avenue," and as a result his media group moved one block east to Vanderbilt Avenue. For three months they became impatient and grew disaffected, but finally, after the King blunder and Mamie Eisenhower's intervention, Nixon reached for all the weapons he had left, and the television group, at five minutes to midnight in the campaign, sprang into action.

---

* He did release a partial medical report early on, but didn't go further and didn't suggest Kennedy emulate him.

There was a national telecast of a Nixon rally in Cincinnati on October 25, an Eisenhower telecast from Pittsburgh on October 29, an Eisenhower-Nixon-Lodge rally from New York City on November 2, a live Nixon television program at seven o'clock every night for the last week of the campaign, and on election eve a four-hour celebrity telecast from Detroit. It is estimated that one in five Americans saw part of the telethon, and it was followed up by fifteen minutes from Thomas E. Dewey (for some inexplicable reason – Nixon cannot have imagined that Dewey would pull any votes for him). At 11 P.M. on the night before the nation voted, Nixon, Eisenhower, and Lodge all appeared together for thirty minutes. Kennedy's only reply to this television assault was a rather banal election-eve address from Faneuil Hall in Boston.

Despite the overwhelming pressure, there were some things that, as a matter of principle, Nixon would not do. He declined a Billy Graham endorsement in *Life*, and rejected staff advice to claim that Kennedy was practicing "reverse bigotry," although he certainly was. Nixon refused to touch the religious issue. He put out papers saying that Kennedy would destroy Social Security, and that the most politically motivated labor leaders would be running the country, neither of which, to say the least, proved to be accurate, or could have been believable to Nixon himself. But these were not unreasonable end-of-campaign gambits by conventional standards. He avoided anything that would revive the allegations of "Tricky Dick" or match some of the most unseemly Democratic attacks on him from past campaigns.

In the last few days, Nixon put on a final burst of mighty personal energy, sleeping only a couple of hours per day as he campaigned through the West. On November 4, Rose Mary Woods called Eisenhower's ana-logue, Ann Whitman, and said that Nixon wanted to send Eisenhower on a goodwill trip to Eastern Europe. Eisenhower responded, via Hagerty, that he was "astonished" at this effort at "auctioning off the presidency," and thought it a "last-ditch, hysterical, action."[47] This was being a little harsh, and on November 6, Nixon, ignoring Eisenhower completely for the first time, announced on television that he would send Eisenhower, Hoover, and Truman to Eastern Europe to promote freedom, and said that he had discussed the idea with Eisenhower. Eisenhower was enraged, and told Hagerty to issue a public statement repudiating Nixon, but Hagerty per-suaded him to let it go on the day before the election. In the end, Eisenhower, as they were all at the weary end of the battle for his succession, issued a statement congratulating Nixon on his speech, without referring to the three-presidents proposal, which could not have stirred too many votes, and must have flabbergasted Truman. At this point Truman had no more use for Eisenhower than he did for Nixon. (He would only be reconciled with Eisenhower on the grim national occasion of Kennedy's funeral, and with Nixon in the extreme winter of his days when Nixon was trying to execute a bipartisan policy in Indochina.)

All polls showed Nixon narrowing the lead to a statistical dead heat on the last days. He was alone, except for his wife, with defeatism afflicting his staff.[48] The Kennedys were rampaging in their irritating, noisy, physical Irish way, like a caricature of boisterous Boston Southies (except for the elegant JFK himself). Nixon oddly liked to be the underdog, and in any case thought it his destiny, and strove mightily to salvage his supreme life's effort. He flew with his family from Chicago to Los Angeles and had a final campaign rally in the City of Angels at 1 A.M., on election day, and went to the Royal suite of the Ambassador Hotel, which was tarted up in all the vulgarity L.A. could muster, in gold, purple, violet, pink, and red.[49] His wife and daughters stayed a floor above, and his mother one floor above that. Nixon slept only two hours, and then drove with Pat to Whittier to vote. He and a couple of aides drove to Tijuana in an open convertible for lunch, and Nixon took the wheel for the return trip, stopping at the mission at San Juan Capistrano.

He returned to the Ambassador Hotel at 5 P.M., as the polls were closing in the East. Kennedy leapt to an early lead, which shrank as the votes moved west. As in all things, Nixon's tenacity was formidable. The Kennedys and their friends in the media became impatient, but Kennedy's lead, as the last polls had predicted, dropped to almost nothing. At about midnight in California, Nixon and his wife descended to the ballroom to thank the campaign staff. He said that "If the present trend continues, Senator Kennedy will be the next president of the United States . . . and if he does . . . he will have my whole-hearted support." Pat, the strongest, most dignified, most admirable of political soul mates, wept silently and motionlessly. But there was no concession, and none was called for. He expected to win California, and did, as the Golden State voted for him for the fourth time in ten years. If he had won Illinois and Michigan or Minnesota or Texas, he would have won the election. (Lodge, an ineffable defeatist, had prepared his concession statement some days before, though he did not release it prematurely.)[50]

It was only after another two hours' sleep, at 6 A.M. – 9 A.M. in the East – that Nixon learned that he had lost Illinois by 9,000 out of 4.757 million, and Minnesota by 22,000 out of 1.542 million ballots cast. Texas was carried by Kennedy and Johnson by 46,000 out of 2.312 million ballots cast. This appeared on its face to be convincing enough, but the Johnson-Rayburn machine in the state had performed prodigies of electoral mischief. There is little doubt that Chicago mayor Richard J. Daley cheated Nixon out of victory in Illinois, then the country's fourth state in population. The real winner of the 1960 presidential election has never been clear.

The official popular vote was 34.221 million for Kennedy to 34.106 million for Nixon, the electoral vote 303 to 219. Nixon ran five points ahead of his party, and the Republicans gained twenty-two congressmen and two senators. Kennedy's popular margin was, in fact, very doubtful, because the Alabama Democratic vote was partly for electors pledged to Kennedy and partly for Dixiecrat Harry Byrd's electors. A reasonable division of the Democratic Alabama vote would have given Nixon an overall national plurality. The states won with a margin of approximately or less than a one-point swing were: by the Republicans, Alaska, California, Hawaii, and Montana; by the Democrats, Delaware, Illinois, Michigan, Minnesota, Missouri, Nevada, New Jersey, New Mexico, and Texas.

If Daley's almost certain fraud in Chicago were reversed out of the result, and if there were a legitimate 4,500-vote shift in Missouri, or a total in Illinois and Missouri of 9,000 votes out of nearly 6.7 million votes cast in the two states, the election would have gone to the House of Representatives. Here, Johnson (by influencing Senator Byrd) and Rayburn would probably have won it for Kennedy. If another 2,500 votes had shifted in Nevada and New Mexico, out of nearly 420,000 votes in those two states, Nixon would have won. An honest election in Texas could only have helped Nixon, and it was remarkable that he ran as closely as he did in the Johnson-Rayburn fiefdom.

Theodore White, and the Kennedy camp generally, assumed that Nixon was riding into the sunset, and they doffed their hats to a gallant foe. White referred to "the fight that Richard M. Nixon had so valiantly waged, under such personal suffering . . . Nixon's skills in politics were enormous, his courage unquestioned, his endurance substantial."[51] "Substantial," in this case, was to prove one of the great understatements of American political comment.

He had fought a brave struggle, almost alone personally, comparatively undersupported by celebrities, intellectuals, and the media. His frictions with Eisenhower had been in evidence throughout the campaign, from the August 12 presidential request for a week to think of a contribution Nixon made to the administration, through to the small role of Eisenhower in the campaign, and his wife's plea for her husband's health at the end. Nixon said to the author: "Eisenhower told me that his friends, by which he invariably meant his rich friends, would pay for a challenge and a recount. I thought it would be irresponsible to leave the country without a government for six months." Without most of the benefits of incumbency, representing a tired government led by an admired leader with non-transferable popularity, Richard Nixon had run about even against the most naturally attractive Democratic leader, apart from FDR, since Jackson.

The Kennedys, whom British Prime Minister Harold Macmillan compared to a medieval Italian clan taking over a town, and the main, liberal, stream of the national media missed the point. Nixon was only forty-seven. Despite the vast resources of the Kennedys, the immense attractiveness and ability of Jack Kennedy, the larger party membership and greater professionalism of the Democrats, the relative indifference of Eisenhower, the strong biases of the media, the great superiority of Lyndon Johnson over Cabot Lodge, and a series of personal mistakes and unlucky incidents, Nixon had won half the votes, and the election was a draw.

By not campaigning on anti-communist innuendoes, wealth-envy, Kennedy's sexual indiscretions, the Kennedy intelligence scam on Cuba, any pitch to religious prejudice, Kennedy's severe health problems and addiction to painkillers, and finally, the theft of votes on such a scale that JFK was moved to exclaim (of Daley and Johnson): "Thank God for a few honest crooks," Nixon had been so gentlemanly that he shed his image as an insufferable ogre, the Herblock sewer rat. He said to Peter Flanigan, "This campaign has laid to rest forever the issue of a candidate's religion in presidential politics. Bad for me, perhaps, but good for America."[52]

Nixon would be fifty-five eight years later, when Kennedy would have had two terms. The presumptuous Democratic notion that Nixon was finished and would not be heard from again was one of American political history's colossal underestimations. Nixon had had a toss-up election, and lost the toss. Without his affecting the balance in the Republican Party, or Eisenhower playing a role, the party was approximately half divided between Goldwater conservatives and Rockefeller liberals. His party needed him, and so would his country, and Nixon would be back, much stronger and of surer judgment than in this campaign, and almost certainly against a less attractive opponent.

With John F. Kennedy and his family, a mighty legend was born. Lyndon Johnson, too, would prove an epochal figure. But Richard Nixon, whom *The Reporter* magazine had not wished to "be bothered with again" in 1952, would prove the most durable American political leader since Jefferson, leading an army of the awkward, the ordinary, the unflamboyant, silent masses of millions of decent, unexceptional people, through important decades of American history.

A few days after the election, the Nixons went to Key Biscayne and the Kennedys went to Palm Beach. The president-elect's father wanted to arrange a meeting between the candidates and asked Herbert Hoover to call Nixon. "Hello, Chief," said Nixon as he picked up the pay-telephone receiver in the restaurant where he was having his dinner, when he heard Hoover was calling. Hoover proposed the meeting and, with his usual implacable gloom, said, "We're in enough trouble in the world today; some indications of national unity are not only desirable but essential."[53] A few minutes later, JFK himself called (further startling the restaurateur, who was not accustomed to incoming calls on his pay phone from such exalted people).

Kennedy came by helicopter the next day to meet Nixon at the Key Biscayne Hotel, though Nixon had offered to come to Palm Beach, "in view of last Tuesday's results." Kennedy talked about bringing Republicans into his administration, including Nixon, who declined, saying he would be leading "a constructive opposition." Kennedy was probably concerned to assure himself that Nixon wasn't about to launch a full political challenge on the election result, but did not directly ask that question. He did volunteer that "It's hard to tell who won the election at this point."[54] He also asked, "How the hell did you carry Ohio?" (Nixon thought the support of the Ohio State football coach, Woody Hayes, had a lot to do with it.)[55]

Nixon personally signed an astonishing 160,000 letters of thanks to campaign workers, and replied to thousands of personal letters. Eisenhower gently suggested in April that he thank more contributors, from whom he had heard some grumbling, and Nixon did so, taking a year to finish this task.[56] He wrote General Douglas MacArthur that he was prouder, and more confident of the historical vindication, of his speech "castigating Mr. Truman for his action in recalling you from Korea" than of anything else he had said in the Congress. He wrote to every Republican senator and congressman, and to the party elders, such as Dewey.

On January 6, he and Rayburn presided over the joint session of the Congress at which the electoral votes were officially tabulated, with each state reporting in alphabetical order. Nixon amusingly said, after Senator Byrd had picked up some votes from the first state to report, Alabama: "The gentleman from Virginia is in the lead." He spoke with high sportsmanship and eloquence when he announced the result: "In our campaigns, no matter how hard fought they may be, no matter how close the election may turn out to be, those who lose accept the verdict and support those who win. It is in that spirit that I declare that John F. Kennedy has been elected president of the United States." He wished Kennedy and Johnson well, to great applause and media commendation. Rayburn warmly shook hands, and called him "Dick" for the first time in fourteen years.[57]

Dwight D. Eisenhower and Richard M. Nixon handed over to John F. Kennedy and Lyndon B. Johnson on January 20, 1961. It was the only time in the history of the country that such a ceremony involved, as it turned out, four consecutive presidents. It was a measure of America's public capacity that four such talented leaders were in place to follow the great Roosevelt and capable Truman administrations, when the crises of war and peace had been addressed by such commanding figures as Marshall, MacArthur, Nimitz, Acheson, Stevenson, even the Dulleses, and many other outstanding public servants.

The rending partisanship of the early postwar years tended to draw an unjust division between the Republicans and Democrats in this group. A couple of years into his presidency, Kennedy confidant and respected historian Arthur Schlesinger circulated a form among selected historians inviting them to rate America's presidents. The recipients chosen assured a selection that would be indulgent of the Democrats, and Franklin D. Roosevelt came in with Lincoln and Washington in the top group, where Wilson and Jefferson also resided, with Truman and Jackson and Polk and

Cleveland (all Democrats) just behind, and with Theodore Roosevelt as their only accompanying Republican. Eisenhower was outraged to find himself in twenty-second position, with generally ignored presidents like Benjamin Harrison, Franklin Pierce, and Rutherford B. Hayes. This was a gross injustice to a good president. Eisenhower considered Roosevelt an artful but shifty political trickster (true up to a point but hardly an overall judgment of FDR), and Truman an incompetent (a preposterous opinion), and set down his own administration's achievements.

He enumerated the achievements of his presidency to his old friend Bill Robinson (who had tried to dump Nixon during the Fund Crisis): statehood for Alaska and Hawaii; the building of the St. Lawrence Seaway and the greatest highway program in world history; an honorable and satisfactory end to the Korean War, with no further combat deaths; the biggest tax cut in history and first civil rights bill in eighty years; defeat of communist aggression in Iran, Guatemala, Lebanon, Formosa, South Vietnam (this was stretching it, especially in Vietnam); desegregation in Arkansas and the District of Columbia; beginning of federal medical care for the aged and the Defense Education Act; reorganization of the Defense Department; start of the Polaris submarine and other ballistic missile programs; acceleration of the space program; initiation of the Atoms for Peace program (which led to the Nuclear Test Ban Treaty); a Latin American aid program that led to the Alliance for Progress; and the setting up of the Department of Health, Education, and Welfare.[58]

This was a very respectable record, and Eisenhower had been a distinguished president. He could have handled Suez (including Aswan), Hungary, and the French departure from Indochina better, but generally he defended and stabilized the perimeter of communist containment. His became a gray and rather phlegmatic administration that Nixon and to some degree Rogers were trying to energize, but they had been eight years of peace and prosperity under the leadership of an admired and popular man, although one ultimately too much identified with golf, uncertain cardiology, and fiscal humbug. There had been the considerable embarrassments of Sputnik, the U-2 affair, the Caracas riots against Nixon, and the anti-American riots in Tokyo. But America was generally respected in the world.

The "missile gap" was soon exposed as a fraud, which came as no surprise to Kennedy, the author of the canard. Eisenhower had a better knowledge of America's defense needs than any president since Grant, and by the time Grant was president, the nation hardly had any defense needs. Nixon wrote Eisenhower that history would judge his administration as having achieved the highest "standard for honesty, efficiency and dedication . . . The American people, because of your leadership, have enjoyed the best eight years in their history," and added, "Never in this nation's history has one man in public owed so much to another as I owe to you."[59] This was a considerable embellishment, but Eisenhower replied very graciously: "I have always felt a complete confidence in your ability and capacity for taking on the Presidency at any instant." And he added, presciently: "The future can still bring to you a real culmination in your service to the country." The exchange put a nice cap on their official association.

The position of vice president was so nebulous, or as de Gaulle wrote, so "curious," that there were no awards from historians for having acquitted it well. But Richard Nixon was undoubtedly the most successful occupant of the post in history, and the first to be nominated to follow the president whom he served in the highest office since John C. Breckinridge in 1860, or, if Southern particularism is excluded, since Martin Van Buren in 1836. In general, vice presidents presided over the Senate and that was almost all they did. Apart from this mundane function, and a few strong regional leaders, such as Aaron Burr and John C. Calhoun, they were chiefly known for personality foibles – for example, Van Buren's vice president, Richard Mentor Johnson, was generally reckoned the man who killed the Indian leader Tecumseh, and as vice president cohabited in evident intimacy with a black woman, a rather bold social statement in the slave-trading Washington of the 1830s.

Nixon knew exactly how to use the Senate to pick up scuttlebutt, turn the lobbies and cloakrooms into places of information exchange, and build the momentum of a congressional deal. He was instrumental in all the important legislation for which Eisenhower claimed credit. Stephen Ambrose estimates that at the basic task of assembling coalitions, figuring what could be traded between legislators, and always being on top of gossip and the latest events in the home states, Richard Nixon was at least as astute as that long-acknowledged master Lyndon B. Johnson.[60] Eisenhower had made good his pledge to ensure that Nixon was the best-informed vice president in history. It is still not clear who was right, as between Eisenhower and Nixon, on the Korean settlement, but Nixon was almost certainly on better ground in 1954 in Indochina in regard to Dien Bien Phu, and in 1955 over Geneva.

Nixon's inestimable services in bringing the Republican Party out of isolationism and reaction and ending the McCarthy era, and the undoubted value of some of his foreign travel, have been recounted and have no precedent in the prior history of the vice presidency. He conducted most of the administration's reelection campaign of 1956, and he performed impeccably when Eisenhower's indispositions required him to be more or less of an acting president. Nixon effectively succeeded Walter Bedell Smith as "Ike's prat boy," the designated assistant in charge of the dirty work. Nixon performed these odious and thankless tasks admirably, even when Eisenhower sawed off the limbs he had sent him out on, especially the more spirited attacks on the Democrats. Eisenhower rewarded Nixon's loyalty, discretion, efficiency, and suppression of his own dissent with an uneven pattern of appreciation and aloofness.

And Nixon, with almost no assistance from Eisenhower, kept the Republican Party lubricated and somewhat coordinated, and left it in 1961 in reasonably good condition, except that with Dewey and Eisenhower retired, Nixon remained the only possible conciliator of the conservative and liberal wings of the Party. The schism among the Republicans was almost as profound, and slightly more imminent, than that between the Southern Democrats and the liberal Democrats. Richard Nixon and Lyndon Johnson, legendary political operators who had much in common but little rapport, were the indispensable men of their parties, and the vice presidency passed between them at one of American history's turning points.

Eisenhower's farewell address, warning of the dangers of the military-industrial complex, was prescient and insightful, and the most important such leave-taking since General George Washington's admonition to avoid "entangling" alliances in 1797. Eisenhower wrote that the "conjunction of an immense military establishment and a large arms industry is new in the American experience. The total influence – economic, political, even spiritual – is felt in every city, every statehouse, every office of the federal government. We recognize the imperative need for this development. Yet we must not fail to comprehend its grave implications. . . . In the counsels of government we must guard against the acquisition of unwarranted influence, whether sought or unsought, by the military-industrial complex."

Apart from being apposite in itself, this was a final post-electoral response to the "missile gap" allegations.

Roosevelt was one of the nation's and the modern world's very greatest leaders. Truman was an unusually capable president. Eisenhower was an unambiguously good president. Between them, they led America and much of the world for twenty-eight years, from the terrible depths of the Great Depression and a world afflicted by Hitler, Stalin, Mussolini, and the Japanese imperialists to the general peace and great prosperity of 1961. And they led America from the depths of isolation to victory in history's greatest war, to leadership of history's greatest alliance system, which they devised; and from the futile international diplomatic claptrap of the thirties to the challenges of the great American innovations of the United Nations and the atomic age. The nation and the world watched with great curiosity to see how the next generation would continue the work of the last three presidents.

— v —

On January 20, 1961, President Kennedy referred graciously to Eisenhower, Truman, and Nixon, and then gave the most famous of all inaugural addresses except Lincoln's two and Franklin D. Roosevelt's first. He promised that America would "pay any price, bear any burden, meet any hardship, support any friend, oppose any foe, in order to assure the survival and the success of liberty." He recited categories of nations, allies, new nations, poor nations, "sister republics to the south" (given that many of them were corrupt despotisms, it was a motley sorority), the United Nations. And for "those who would make themselves our adversary," he referred to the "balance of terror that stays the hand of mankind's final war." The new president said that "civility is not a sign of weakness, and sincerity is always subject to proof. Let us never negotiate out of fear. But let us never fear to negotiate." To Americans he said, "Ask not what your country can do for you. Ask what you can do for your country.

"And to my fellow citizens of the world: Ask not what America will do for you, but what together we can do for the freedom of man." By using the phrase *balance of terror*, he presaged the abandonment of the Truman-Eisenhower policy of nuclear superiority and massive retaliation for one of accepted equivalence. And with the stirring but open-ended preamble about bearing any burden, he appeared (at least in retrospect) to be more amenable to involvement in the sort of secondary, conventional conflicts that Eisenhower had avoided. In one sense, his remarks seemed to reduce tensions, not only by their optimistic and civil tone, but by stepping back from the previous administration's policy of threatening nuclear war over peripheral issues, specifically including Formosa and Berlin, and possibly, at the president's express discretion, even Quemoy and Matsu.

While Washington celebrated with the Kennedys, Richard Nixon left Washington after nearly fifteen years. He went to a luncheon for senior members of the outgoing administration, held by Admiral Lewis Strauss. Some of those present he would never see again. At the end of Inauguration Day, he was without employment, security personnel, an office, or a driver. In his public career, his net worth had increased from ten thousand dollars to forty-eight thousand, represented by increased equity in the value of his house. He had not profited a cent from the high offices he had held. Before leaving Washington, he returned to the Capitol, as the inaugural balls proceeded around the city, and had a last look at the monumental skyline from that perspective. He had, he later wrote, the sensation, by which he meant also determination, that he would be back, and not as a visitor.

The logical step for Nixon would be to a law firm. A number of people – including Robert Abplanalp of the Precision Valve Corporation (he invented the aerosol can); Walter Annenberg, proprietor of the *Philadelphia Inquirer*, *TV Guide*, and other publications; and Elmer Bobst of Warner-Lambert – offered Nixon rich consulting arrangements. At a law firm, he could make up his own schedule, be selective about clients and cases, and remain as active as he wished in politics. Thomas E. Dewey offered him a place in his firm. Almost any large law firm in the country would be honored to have him, and so would many corporate boards, which he declined as potential conflicts. Despite his recent narrow defeat, he enjoyed a very high stature in the country and much of the world. Though he had made nothing from public life, he had become one of the most prominent people in the country. But what most interested him was righting the electoral setback. He decided not to move to New York as Bobst and others had urged, and returned instead to California, answering Pat's desire to return (though assuredly not to Whittier, and not for the same reasons that motivated his wife).

Nixon, from the start, had an alternative ambition. Pat Brown, whom Nixon regarded as a somewhat bumbling character, would be running for reelection as governor of California the following year. There was no place politically for Nixon in New York, where Rockefeller dominated and both U.S. senators were Republicans. In California, the only prominent Republican was Kuchel, whom Warren had appointed to Nixon's seat in the Senate, to which he had been reelected in 1956. Nixon joined the law firm of his old friend Earl Adams – Adams, Duque, and Hezeltine, in Los Angeles. (Adams had offered him a job in his law firm in 1946, if he had lost to Voorhis.)

Nixon also started writing a newspaper column and said that in his first fourteen months in the private sector, he made more money than he had in fourteen years in Washington. For Hannah Nixon, now living fairly comfortably in Whittier, with one son making thousands of dollars per week and another, having transformed the mean little gas station where she had baked and sold pies into an incorporated complex underwritten by Howard Hughes and selling Nixonburgers, it must have seemed an astounding ascent of fortune. (Unfortunately, Donald's venture was unsuccessful.)

Nixon lived alone in a very modest bachelor apartment on Wilshire Boulevard from February to June 1961 while Pat and his daughters remained in Washington until the end of the school year. Nixon maintained a discreet political silence, observing the normal honeymoon of a new administration, into April, although he did try, unsuccessfully, with Everett Dirksen and others, to get a full examination of the Kennedys' financial interests with Robert Kennedy's confirmation hearings as attorney general of the United States. He arranged a speaking tour starting May 2, and canvassed some prominent Republicans on what they thought might be the best subjects.

The time bomb that Nixon had helped to assemble, and that might have blown up his candidacy if Eisenhower and Allen Dulles had been less cautious, detonated on April 17 with the Cuban exiles' invasion of the Bay of Pigs. It was a debacle and the greatest peacetime strategic humiliation the United States had suffered in its history. Nixon was in Washington and had a prearranged intelligence briefing with Allen Dulles, who said that the landings had failed, and that the reason was the withdrawal of U.S. air strikes that the CIA had said were necessary for the mission to succeed. When Nixon returned home, Tricia had left him a message: "JFK called. I knew it! It wouldn't be long before he would get into trouble and have to call on you for help."[61]

Kennedy asked Nixon to the White House urgently and poured forth his grievances against the intelligence and military personnel, who had misled him. Nixon said the president felt himself "the innocent victim."[62] Kennedy asked what Nixon would do, and he counseled an immediate invasion, invoking protection of American lives and of the base at Guantanamo. (These would have been very thin pretexts.) We should "do whatever is necessary to get Castro and communism out of Cuba."[63] Nixon dismissed Kennedy's concern that Khrushchev would then move on West Berlin. Nixon also urged action in Laos, where Kennedy had accepted the professedly neutralist government, which was in fact a communist puppet state. This was another domino in Indochina, as there would be no possibility of stopping the flow of North Vietnamese soldiers and military supplies through Laos into South Vietnam. Nixon recommended bombing in Laos, and promised he would not make a political issue out of any forceful policy, in Cuba or Laos, but Kennedy had no stomach for any of it.

Nixon repeated the same point in his speaking tour, including to the Executives' Club of Chicago, where he pledged his support for a strong policy and said, to great applause: "We should not start things in the world unless we are prepared to finish them."[64] In Detroit four days later, Nixon said that "some Americans" were advocating an attack or blockade of Cuba. The principal American among them was himself, but he said that he was opposed to such action without "provocation." He didn't say that he had counseled the president to invent the provocation.

At his press conference on April 21, 1961, Kennedy gallantly said, "Victory has a hundred fathers and defeat is an orphan. I am the executive officer of the government." Despite the fiasco, his popularity jumped and he joked that "like Eisenhower . . . the worse I do the more popular I get." Eisenhower had not been responsible for a shambles on this scale, but the public liked Kennedy's frankness in admitting the failure of his policy in Cuba. Kennedy had had an almost unimaginably inauspicious launch as president. It was a poor start for the new generation of American leaders.

The Nixons moved from Washington in June, the former vice president contracting a sore back shuffling cases around. They moved to a rented house in Brentwood while the home they were building, a large ranch-style house on the Trousdale Estate at the edge of Bel Air, was being built. The Teamsters Union was the vendor of the lot where they built, and the *Los Angeles Times* alleged that Nixon had received a seven-thousand-dollar discount. Nixon was outraged and pointed out, as his archives confirm, that he had been offered a number of desirable lots for free, and declined them, as he thought that accepting would be inappropriate.

Nixon played golf with Eisenhower at Walter Annenberg's splendid house in Palm Desert. It was a pleasant reunion. He played a little more golf than he had, and got a hole-in-one while golfing in Bel Air with Bebe Rebozo and Randolph Scott. With his usual hyperbole, in an expression he used too often, he called it "the greatest thrill of my life."* He returned to the Bohemian Grove and had a comic triumph with a mock reenactment of his kitchen debate with Khrushchev.

Nixon embarked on a book in the spring of 1961, and called it *Six Crises*, referring to the Hiss case, the fund controversy, Eisenhower's heart attack, the South American trip (and especially Caracas), the debate with Khrushchev, and the 1960 election. Some of the actual writing was done by Stephen Hess, with an assist from Alvin Moscow, but all from Nixon's recollections and files, and so heavily revised by him that he was the chief author.

Adela Rogers St. Johns, an early backer and tough magazine editor, a gravelly careerwoman before her time, had been the strongest advocate of the book. When Nixon visited Kennedy in April, he had recommended writing a book, for the "mental discipline," and to acquire a reputation as an intellectual. (Ted Sorensen had written most of Kennedy's *Profiles in Courage*, which won the Pulitzer Prize after Joseph Kennedy's intervention with the Pulitzer Committee.) *Six Crises* was a creditable effort, and got fairly good reviews. It was a best-seller, selling more than a quarter-million copies. The Hiss, fund, Caracas, and election parts were the highlights, and did qualify as crises. Eisenhower recovered very quickly from his heart attack and the debate with Khrushchev was too farcical to be a real crisis. Eleven years later, Mao Tse-tung paid Nixon the compliment that he had read *Six Crises* and thought it "not a bad" book. Nixon's description of the constructive tension of crisis, followed by the depressive letdown when the crisis is satisfactorily over, was revealing of him and useful. Much of the narrative was graceful and original writing.

---

* Succeeding, for that honor, his sighting of Eisenhower in the New York victory parade in May 1945; his reconfirmation as vice president at Wheeling, West Virginia, in September 1952; and his reception in Warsaw in August 1959. His next successful election, the moon landing, and the recovery of the *Apollo XIII* spacecraft would join this category.

Kennedy denied that he had been briefed before the election by Allen Dulles about what became the Bay of Pigs, as Nixon claimed in his book, and Dulles also issued a statement claiming that the briefing he had given Kennedy had been more general and did not cover "our own government's plans or programs for action overt or covert." Dulles had been retired by Kennedy after the Bay of Pigs, more or less as a scapegoat, and his successor, John McCone, like Henry Luce, claimed Dulles had told him that he had fully briefed Kennedy on the planned invasion of Cuba by the exiles before the election. It is hardly conceivable that Dulles did not give Kennedy some inkling of what was in contemplation in Cuba, though perhaps not with the precision Nixon claimed.

By mid-1961, Nixon was heavily involved in an excruciating decision-making process about whether to run as Republican candidate for governor of California. He corresponded with an astounding range of prominent and ordinary people, asking their advice. Eisenhower, Dewey, and the inevitable J. Edgar Hoover (the most politicized secret police chief since Beria) thought he should run. Herbert Hoover and Douglas MacArthur thought he should wait for the Senate. Polls indicated he could win against Brown, who was popular and had not made bad mistakes. Nixon didn't like local issues and was quite out of touch with California issues, though he was such a swift learner, he could put that right quite quickly.

He was afraid of the split in state Republican ranks between the hard right and the John Birch Society, which purported to believe that Eisenhower and John Foster Dulles were communists and Nixon wasn't too much better, and the residue of the liberal Republicans of the Earl Warren school. After Nixon visited Eisenhower at Gettysburg in September 1961, Eisenhower reinforced his recommendation that Nixon run for governor. He was concerned that "mossbacks" would take over the Republican Party in the state, and felt that Nixon should position himself to run for president as soon as possible.

Nixon loved to campaign, and hated to be out of the loop. If he were governor of California, he would be the leading Republican, not Rockefeller or Goldwater. There was a danger of the California Republican Party transmuting itself into a politically primitive organization. There was also a danger of losing, but in the end, Nixon thought that if he could draw, countrywide, with Kennedy, he could surely defeat Brown in their home state. There is little doubt that, despite his agonizing decision-making process, a large part of the reason for his coming back to California was to seek the governorship and get back to the front of national politics as soon as possible.

His wife was opposed, and warned him that she thought it a mistake but, with her unvarying selflessness, said that if that was what he wanted to do, she would support him as always. Nixon announced his candidacy on September 27, 1961, pledging that if elected, he would serve a full term and not use the statehouse as a trampoline to go for the White House. He claimed, as in 1952, that he would "clean up the mess," this time in Sacramento, and that Brown was running for president. This was fatuous, as Brown was not running for president and there was no mess in Sacramento. He also said, in an eerie echo of a 1960 error, that he would campaign in every county of the state. This was not such a challenge, as it was just one state and he had over a year to get to them all, but there was a slight air of mustiness and old-hat clichés about his campaign from the start.

Brown immediately said that Nixon was just using California as a "stepping-stone," and former governor Goodwin Knight also attacked him and confirmed his own candidacy for the Republican nomination, which he shortly withdrew for health reasons. Nixon's only Republican primary opponent would be Joseph Shell of the John Birch Society. Nixon said he would not begin campaigning until January, and went to Apple Valley to finish his book, which he did just before year-end.

— VI —

Nixon tried to take the offensive, as he had in all his campaigns, but it was hard; Brown was a soft target, an amiable, pleasant man who was in fact a tough politician masquerading as a gentle person. Nixon couldn't make sarcastic remarks about Kennedy, whose popularity had rebounded quickly after the Bay of Pigs. He was seen as a capable, attractive young president who projected America in the world very successfully, which was nothing but the truth. The *Los Angeles Times* was no longer overtly partisan in Nixon's favor, Norman Chandler having handed over control of it to his son Otis, who was a moderate political independent.

Nixon had the unprecedented experience of running in the primary against a candidate on his right. Nixon had a largely new staff, but Bob

Haldeman, Herb Klein, John Ehrlichman, and Robert Finch were still there, as were Maurice Stans, Herbert Kalmbach, Dwight Chapin, Ron Ziegler, and Rose Mary Woods. Most of these people would go on to fame and controversy with their leader. With Joseph Shell on the right and only the governor's mansion as the prize, fund-raising was very patchy. Nixon campaigned around the state almost on a shoestring, as he had in 1946 and 1950.

The Republican primary was a wild and woolly race. Most of the far right were more interested in the campaign for the Senate nomination. Thomas Kuchel had held Nixon's old seat for ten years, and was challenged in the primary by Howard Jarvis and Lloyd Wright, two men of the right. Murray Chotiner was Wright's campaign manager, and his chief advocate was longtime Democrat and former World Federalist Ronald Reagan. Jarvis was a populist who went on to the famous taxpayers' revolt that he successfully led in California, with a slogan borrowed from the movies: "I'm mad as hell and I won't take it anymore!"

Nixon had to face the John Birch issue and did so at a meeting of the California Republican assembly in March. He recited his anti-communist background, and said that the Birchers' leader, Robert Welch, had called Dwight D. Eisenhower a communist, and that no respectable Republican could endorse this view. Chotiner drafted a motion of condemnation of Welch and this was adopted, despite many Birchite members of the state assembly, and two congressmen.

This put Brown on the defensive, as Nixon had got clear of the far-right group without splitting his party. Brown had his fair share of wild-eyed leftists in his party, California being the catchment for eccentrics that it is.

Nixon won the Republican primary over Shell in June, with about two-thirds of the vote, still a respectable Shell total for an extremist candidate. Despite the delicacy with which he had handled the parting with Welch, many liberal Republicans deserted Nixon, including Goodwin Knight and Earl Warren Jr., both of whom endorsed Brown. And he could not sell communism as a serious problem in California. The issue just would not fly anymore, and the public was not so much becoming more tolerant of communists as harder to frighten with the issue fifteen years into the Cold War. There was a good deal of robust pamphleteering on both sides and unofficially, but this was pretty routine. The Democrats circulated a copy of a restrictive covenant Nixon had signed when he bought a house in

Washington in 1951, promising not to resell it to a black or a Jew. Ehrlichman recommended that he say that he had not read the fine print (which he had not), but Nixon said nothing, as he believed that he would not lose votes on the allegation.[65]

The administration poured in announcements of defense contracts for California, and Kennedy, Johnson, and much of the cabinet came to California and campaigned for Brown. (Nixon expressed private admiration for their professionalism but publicly called them "carpetbaggers.") Nixon responded as best he could, by bringing in Eisenhower, who told a large hundred-dollar-a-plate live and closed-circuit television audience: "I can personally vouch for his ability, his sense of duty, his sharpness of mind, his wealth in wisdom." Nixon replied, probably truthfully, after receiving an endorsement he had aspired to for a decade, that all his efforts had been validated by "these words from the greatest living American."

Nixon could feel his position slipping, with a slightly stale campaign, elusive opponent, and massive federal intervention. He challenged Brown to debate him in any format he chose. Brown resisted for a long time, and finally there was a joint press meeting, at which personal questions were excluded, in San Francisco, on October 1. A question was put, contrary to the agreed ground rules, about a candidate for governor allowing "his family to receive a secret loan from a major defense contractor in the United States." The moderator told Nixon he did not have to answer, but Nixon declared his eagerness to take the question, about the hoary bugbear of the loan from Howard Hughes, through a lawyer, to Donald Nixon. Nixon's brother had recently gone bankrupt, and Hannah Nixon had surrendered the deed to Howard Hughes, who did not accept it, but the income from the property went into an escrow fund.

Nixon said that Kennedy had known about this in 1960 but declined to "make a political issue out of my mother's problems, just as I refused to make an issue out of any of the charges made against the members of his family." He then tore out after Brown, accusing him, with reason, of circulating and amplifying the rumors about the Hughes loan. "All of the people of California are listening. . . . Governor Brown has a chance to stand up as a man and charge me with misconduct. Do it, sir!" Brown fumbled about and said he had not made an issue out of the loan "other than in casual conversation from time to time." Nixon said Brown "cringed and went away like a whipped dog."[66]

Nixon certainly won on the day, and had cowed his opponent. But the national and state press corps took up the loan story. Nixon could labor Brown over it, but the press started demanding answers and did not accept Nixon's claim to have dealt with the issue completely, at the debate or elsewhere. From this point, the campaign descended into a gutter of unseemly accusations. It became a shabby campaign for the leadership of what had become the nation's most populous state. Nixon accused Brown of being bankrolled by a giant, Kennedy-financed slush fund; Brown accused Nixon of aspiring to be a dictator and to decide whether individuals were too communistic to speak at California's universities. Nixon accused Brown of taking free cruises on the yachts of wealthy oilmen. Brown claimed he was "a better American" than Nixon, and one anti-Nixon *Los Angeles Times* reporter found some Republican candidates who claimed that Nixon had taken campaign funds intended for others. There was a flurry of various pamphlets and lawsuits.

Nixon did present a comprehensive program – anti-communist school curriculum, a restriction on communist public speaking, the death penalty for thrice-convicted drug peddlers, and increased funding for teachers' salaries, highway construction, and police budgets. It was a respectable effort (though the anti-communist part was pretty dubious legally and philosophically). He also promised an overall budget reduction.

The famous Caryl Chessman case came up in the campaign. Chessman had been sentenced to death in the gas chamber because of the "Little Lindbergh" law on kidnapping, and had resided on death row for twelve years. He had written four books arguing his case, and among those advocating his commutation were Pablo Casals, Robert Frost, Billy Graham, Aldous Huxley, Christopher Isherwood, Dwight MacDonald, Norman Mailer, and Eleanor Roosevelt. He was finally gassed in May 1960. Brown, who opposed the death penalty, said that his "hands were tied," which was untrue, and Nixon, who favored the death penalty, said with some reason that the episode illustrated the weakness and indecision of Brown.

But the real issue in the campaign was Nixon. Did California want an international figure as governor, or should amiable Pat Brown be allowed to continue and not have his job taken away by a returning interloper with his eye on the White House? As was his custom, Nixon brought his campaign to a final surge in the last two weeks, designed to climax on election eve. Pat came out with him, and even transgressed her normal rule and made speeches for him. Nixon's great closing effort was narrowing the gap, but he was overtaken by international events.

President Kennedy, after a successful visit to Paris and Versailles at the start of June 1961, had gone on to a summit meeting with Khrushchev at Vienna, the seventh between U.S. and Soviet leaders, going back to Teheran. It was not as evident a failure as the Paris meeting following the U-2 incident, but it was unsuccessful. Kennedy, who had mocked Nixon's performance in the kitchen debate in Moscow, privately acknowledged that Khrushchev had "savaged" him and "thinks I have no guts."[67] Following the Bay of Pigs, this confirmed the Soviet leader in the belief that he could make gains at America's expense. In the autumn of 1962, American intelligence detected unmistakable signs of Soviet missile deployment in Cuba. Kennedy recognized this as a supreme test of his credibility, as well as a serious national security threat. Plans were developed by the Defense Department for a surgical air strike on the missile launching sites, which were thought to be likely to be operational within a few weeks, as well as plans for broader air strikes, an outright invasion, and a complete naval blockade. On a few days' reflection, a surgical air strike was thought to be uncertain to eliminate all the missiles, and a blockade would not affect those already in place.

On October 18, Kennedy received the Soviet foreign minister, Andrei Gromyko, for two hours. Gromyko accused the United States of "pestering" Cuba, a little country. Kennedy, playing poker like some of his predecessors, did not mention the United States intelligence about the missiles, but reminded Gromyko of Kennedy's statement of six weeks before warning against the deployment of offensive weapons to Cuba. On October 20, Adlai Stevenson, whose resolution in a crisis Eisenhower and Nixon had questioned in 1952 and 1956, arrived from New York, where he had succeeded Lodge as Kennedy's ambassador to the United Nations, and advocated that a quarantine of Cuba be accompanied by a promise of withdrawal of American missiles in Turkey and abandonment of the U.S. base at Guantanamo in Cuba.

Kennedy acknowledged that at a future date the United States would have to be prepared to withdraw missiles from Turkey and Italy, but not simultaneously with the abandonment of the Soviet deployment in Cuba. On October 21, Kennedy asked former defense secretary Robert Lovett (whom Nixon had briefed on the Hiss case in 1949) if he thought that

Stevenson was capable of negotiating terms with the Russians at the UN. Lovett thought not, and it was agreed to bring John J. McCloy, chairman of the Ford Foundation and former assistant secretary of war and U.S. high commissioner for Germany, into the administration's inner councils to reinforce Stevenson. Kennedy's judgment in these matters was similar to that of Stevenson's former Republican opponents.

At 7 P.M. on October 22, 1962, in a seventeen-minute address to the nation, President Kennedy revealed the presence of the Soviet missiles as well as the deployment to Cuba of nuclear-capable bombers, announced "a strict quarantine on all offensive military equipment" destined for Cuba as one of his "initial steps," and said that any nuclear attack from Cuba against any nation in the Western Hemisphere would be regarded by the United States as an attack on the United States by the Soviet Union "requiring a full retaliatory response against the Soviet Union."

To reinforce his point, he placed all U.S. military forces on a worldwide state of alert, dispatched all missile-firing submarines in port to their pre-assigned war stations, and deployed constant air force interdiction squadrons to the narrow air space between Cuba and Florida – all activity that would have been detected by Soviet intelligence. David Bruce had already secured the support of the British (though there was some wavering and waffling by Macmillan), and Dean Acheson happily emerged from retirement to brief Charles de Gaulle, who declined to look at aerial photographs, saying he was accustomed to accepting the word of U.S. presidents and needed to hear no more. (The next morning, he summoned the Soviet ambassador in Paris and informed him of France's solidarity with the United States. When the ambassador said this could well mean nuclear war, de Gaulle replied, "I doubt it, but in that case, we will perish together" and dismissed him.)

The world endured a week of extreme tension. The Soviet ambassador to the UN, Valerian Zorin, flatly denied on October 23 that there were any such missiles in Cuba, and Stevenson, always a formidable orator and debater, easily won that round before the whole world, probably the finest moment of his long career. There were messages back and forth between Kennedy and Khrushchev, as well as back channels, and Kennedy effectively pledged not to invade Cuba and conceded the removal of the Jupiter missiles from Turkey, while denying this was a quid pro quo.

Robert Kennedy, in his memoirs, claimed that he had told the Soviet ambassador to the United States, Anatoly Dobrynin, that this could not be a straight exchange, but that his brother had wished to remove the missiles from Turkey and Italy for some time. This was a distinction without a difference. This preemptive initiative came from the Kennedys. The Turks made it clear that they wished the missiles retained and their removal was a reciprocal concession, whatever the Kennedys may have called it. This would send the wrong signal to the Europeans about American resolve to defend Europe, and establish a false equivalence between missiles deployed by a defensive alliance in sovereign countries by mutual consent and Soviet deployment of offensive weapons to a satellite state.

The crisis subsided quickly from October 29 on. To the world, Russia appeared to take an initiative and then be forced, rather humiliatingly, to withdraw from it. In the abstract, at the beginning of the problem there were American missiles in Turkey and Italy and no Soviet missiles in Cuba, which the United States had threatened to invade; and at the end, there were no missiles in any of the countries and the Soviets were therefore advantaged. Khrushchev later wrote: "Our aim was to preserve Cuba. Today Cuba exists. So who won? It cost us nothing more than the round-trip expenses for transporting the rockets to Cuba and back." He denied that there had ever been a moment's thought of unleashing nuclear war. These were retrospective views from an unreliable source, but they can't be entirely dismissed.[68]

The American military had mixed views; the navy representative on the Joint Chiefs, Admiral George Anderson, said that "We have been had," and the air force's ineffably hawkish General Curtis Lemay (a colorful third-party vice presidential candidate six years later) wanted to make the agreement with Khrushchev but attack Cuba anyway.

Kennedy certainly kept calm, marshaled administration and public opinion well, kept a coherent policy throughout, succeeded in his basic objective, redeemed the Bay of Pigs debacle and the Vienna misfortune, and generally exhibited high crisis management skills. Whether it was a long-term, unambiguous strategic success was another matter. De Gaulle, who was preparing to try to pry Western Europe away from the Anglo-Americans (except when the Europeans vitally needed them), held this incident out as an example of how the United States put its own hemispheric security ahead of solidarity with Europe. Kennedy could easily have got rid of Castro once and for all, and had the provocation to do so. He was concerned at a counter-blow against West Berlin, but he could have replied to that without precipitating the Third World War. After the end of the Cold War, these are academic arguments. At the time, the American people and the world thought, and they were not mistaken, that President Kennedy had handled the crisis very competently.

While the crisis was in progress, it was difficult for Nixon to campaign as he had wished, and when it subsided, there was a great flow of support to the party and followers of the president, in the aftermath of the national security emergency. And Kennedy had just enough time to make a few midterm pre-election campaign speeches, particularly in Indiana, where he sank the incumbent Republican senator, Homer Capehart, by excoriating "those who wish to send other men's sons to war."

Nixon had loyally supported the administration throughout, but the final slapstick farce of the California campaign came over the absurd but evanescently topical issue of civil defense. As the Cuban Missile Crisis was winding down, Kennedy dispensed to Brown the grandstand opportunity of chairing a governors' conference on civil defense, in a blatant intervention in the California election. On October 24, the civil defense director of Los Angeles, Joseph Quinn, said that in the event of hostilities, Kennedy would probably shut all retail outlets for five days. For a person in Quinn's position, this was as presumptuous and stupid a statement as it was possible to make. Huge and unmanageable lines arose at every supermarket and convenience store and gasoline station. Nixon urged calm and support of the president.

Nixon, now gasping for electoral air, went for Brown's jugular, by claiming that he had incited panic, greed, hoarding, and selfishness, and generally was guilty of "gross negligence that potentially endangers the lives of 17 million Californians." The state was "completely naked" without fallout shelters. Brown scorned Nixon's (political) deathbed conversion to the cause of civil defense.

On the night before the election, Nixon attempted to replicate his success with the 1960 telethon, and appeared for four hours with his wife and young daughters beside him on a sofa, from his home. It was not a howling success. It was stilted and unnatural – Nixon started to say "president" when he meant "governor" – but it was a great deal of exposure.

Nixon and his wife voted at about 7 A.M. and Nixon went to his office and called supporters all day, holding out little hope of victory. Cuba gave him a plausible reason for losing, but it had been a campaign that, as Pat had said, was misconceived, and where every conceivable part of it had gone wrong. Brown was no star, and he wasn't a Robert Logue–Jack Kennedy, effortless, athletic, not overly ambitious, campus hero type of the kind that always had Nixon's number. But he was apparently amiable and unexceptionable, smiling a lot while he kicked hard, and was a perfect underdog to Nixon's cynical, returning political bully. Nixon the world statesman might still have pulled it out by a whisker, but Kennedy, the real world statesman, in the job Nixon might/should have had, stole the show and threw the California roses to Brown.

Nixon lost by 297,000 votes out of six million cast. If allowance is made for the Cuban Missile Crisis, he had probably fought to an approximate draw in the popular vote again, in the nation's premier state, as he had two years earlier in the nation as a whole. Nixon-haters claimed that he had already become a Harold Stassen figure, ludicrous in his Quixotic and futile quest for public office that electorates would not give him. But he was not.

On election night, Nixon determined to let Herb Klein deal with the press, and at 10 A.M. the day after the election he read a perfectly acceptable press statement and telegram of concession to Brown that Nixon had written. Nixon left his suite as Klein started speaking, and was embraced by weeping secretaries and even media people as he walked down the corridor, and after that the record is unclear. Nixon wrote that he saw, on a monitor, snappish questions from the media. Klein wrote that the friends who had picked him up to drive him home told him he could not seem to be chased out the back door of his hotel.

Haldeman, Finch, and a few others were with Nixon as he rode down in the elevator to meet the press after all, philosophically saying that he had been bitten by a mosquito, having been bitten by a rattlesnake two years before. Earlier, he had said that with Cuba, he now understood how Stevenson had felt when Suez and Budapest occurred. (Kennedy had handled Cuba a great deal better than Eisenhower had handled the earlier problems.)

Instead of sticking to such a sportsmanlike tenor of remarks, Nixon marched into the press conference, interrupted Klein, and with out-stretched chin and hands thrust in pockets, said, "Now that all the members of the press are so delighted that I lost . . . I think each of you covered it the way you saw it," and congratulated Brown and wished him well. And then it all went horribly wrong. "I believe Governor Brown has a heart, even though he believes I do not. I believe he is a good American, even though he feels I am not. . . . For once, gentlemen, I would appreciate it if you would write what I say."

Nixon claimed he had been outspent two to one (only true if government defense contracts ostentatiously let in California during the election are included), and claimed a Republican victory on the night with Rockefeller's win, by more than 1.5 million in New York (over Robert Morgenthau, U.S. attorney and son of FDR's Treasury secretary) and the election as governors of William Scranton in Pennsylvania, John Rhodes in Ohio, and George Romney in Michigan. He expressed cautious concern that Kennedy had brought down an Iron Curtain around Cuba.

"We fought a good fight. We didn't win. And I take the responsibility for any mistakes." There were four "One last thing"s, and the last of them ended: "Just think how much you're going to be missing. You won't have Nixon to kick around anymore, because, gentlemen, this is my last press conference, and it will be one in which I have welcomed the opportunity to test wits with you." This was an odd flourish, as he then waved, smiled, and left, with no test of wits.

This was certainly not a premeditated tactic, claiming what he did not believe – that with this reversal, his political career was over at the age of forty-nine. He gave way to the towering and easily flammable resentment that drove him much of his life, before, during, and throughout his public career. But his intuition, momentarily suppressed, perhaps, by his hatred of losing and of those he judged complicit in his humiliation, came to his assistance. By leaving as he did, slamming the door behind him somewhat ungraciously, he confirmed his enemies in their heartfelt hope that they really had finally seen the back and the last of him. But now the Republican Party would be hopelessly split between Goldwater and Rockefeller, the right and the left. One would win over the other; the other would effectively defect, and the apparent winner would be annihilated by the Democrats, evidently by Kennedy. Goldwater or Rockefeller would become, in national terms, a chronic loser, and the other a disloyal spoiler. Nixon would still be there, still relatively young, narrowly defeated twice, by, as Republican orthodoxy would have it, theft of ballots in 1960, and Castro and Khrushchev in 1962. He would become neither a designated loser nor a mere spoiler.

For now, the striver would become the survivor, and he would depart the center of the stage. John F. Kennedy would be a compelling but tragic leader. And neither Nixon's millions of admirers – who identified with him in his lack of glamor, dedication to hard work, old virtues, and home truths, as well as his tactical political cunning, and above all his dogged indefatiga-bility – nor the people who worshipped the new icon of JFK would forget him. He would be back, in one of Roosevelt's famous phrases, "again and again and again." (Boston, October 30, 1940.[69]) He had involuntarily fallen on his sword in an act of political self-purification in 1960, and then been impaled by unbidden misfortune in 1962. But he was, in part, a magician, who had missed a few tricks in both elections, not having been a solo candi-date for ten years. He was also a man of superhuman staying power.

Eleanor Roosevelt, who had disliked both Nixon and Kennedy, died the day after the 1962 elections. All the men who had succeeded her husband as president attended her funeral, and on the presidential aircraft returning from Hyde Park to Washington, President Kennedy and Chief Justice Earl Warren joked about Nixon's political demise. (Kennedy had acknowledged to Ben Bradlee of the *Washington Post* and others that he would have lost to Nelson Rockefeller.)[70]

Nixon's complacent, celebrating opponents were no longer on guard against him. He withdrew and regrouped, but like a hungry, rejected jungle cat, he was prowling not far off and his ambitions had not changed. Now, Republican schism, Democratic errors, and national tragedy would be his allies, and they would be much more reliable allies than most of his pro-fessed friends. Warren would live to see Nixon's revenge; Kennedy would not. Richard Nixon would show his friends and his enemies, the nation and the world, that he was almost imperishable.

Chapter Eight

The Triumph of Survival
1963–1968

— I —

RICHARD NIXON RETAINED HIS ADMIRERS, and there was still no short-age of law firms, corporations, and foundations that sought him out. He was even canvassed about becoming commissioner of baseball.[1] He did not want a position that would prevent him from speaking as a partisan whenever he wished to, although he was going to maintain silence for the proverbial decent interval after his recent setback. There was no longer any purpose to remaining in California, and he determined to move to New York.

Nixon's wealthy friends, Elmer Bobst, chairman of the pharmaceutical company Warner-Lambert, and Donald Kendall, CEO of Pepsi-Cola, used their influence with the firm that handled Warner-Lambert's legal business, Mudge, Stern, Baldwin & Todd, to which Kendall shifted a large part of his company's legal work, to pay Nixon $250,000 per year and leave his sched-ule pretty much to him, as long as he was reasonably available to the firm. Six months after Nixon moved to New York, when he would be eligible to join the bar, he would move from being a consultant to a partner and his name would head the firm name.

Nixon started in February 1963 to stake out his position as Republican Party foreign affairs critic. He appeared in March on a television program hosted by the popular late-night entertainer Jack Paar (who was followed as host of *The Tonight Show* by Johnny Carson and Jay Leno), and called for a blockade of Cuba until all Soviet military personnel had left the island.

He was probably hedging his bets, and angling to be secretary of state in the next Republican administration, if he could not lead it himself.

The Kennedys were not such good sports as they seemed to be, careening around on their lawn at Hyannisport playing touch football. Nixon was subjected to an extremely rigorous tax audit, even though the Treasury secretary was Republican former undersecretary of state C. Douglas Dillon. At the same time, the attorney general, Robert Kennedy, conducted a meticulous probe into the Howard Hughes–Donald Nixon loan that Pat Brown had exploited in the late election. Neither activity yielded anything damaging to Nixon, but it was a tedious, time-consuming dual harassment, clearly politically motivated.

Nixon continued in close touch with Eisenhower, who shared the Nixon and de Gaulle view that Kennedy had sustained a reversal in Cuba. Eisenhower said that if Kennedy had submitted a treaty to the Senate forswearing invasion of Cuba in exchange for removal of the Russian missiles, it would not have passed.[2]

Nixon spoke to the American Society of Newspaper Editors in Washington on April 20, 1963. He joked about his "last press conference," saying that he had taken Truman's advice to "get out of the kitchen if you can't take the heat," but that he was back. He attacked the Cuban settlement as making Castro untouchable and giving the Soviet Union "squatters' rights in our own backyard." Kennedy had managed "to pull defeat out of the jaws of victory . . . We must no longer postpone making a command decision to do whatever is necessary to force the removal of the Soviet beachhead." Nixon, under questioning, did not want immediate or maximum force, and was unspecifically jingoistic. He denied that he would ever again seek electoral office. He used against the administration some of Kennedy's 1960 lines about getting the country moving. Nixon thought Kennedy had "a lackluster domestic record and [a] crisis-prone foreign policy, [but] felt that he was almost certainly going to be reelected."[3] Kennedy's much-ballyhooed "New Frontier" had been a comprehensive reform program of state-sponsored additions to medical care and local education, to which were added tax cuts and civil rights proposals, but no significant part of it had moved through the Congress, despite Lyndon Johnson's expertise in these matters. (Sam Rayburn, after a total of seventeen years as House Speaker and forty-nine years as a congressman, had died in 1962 and was replaced by the long-serving Democratic House Leader John W. McCormack of Boston.)

When asked about Republican candidates for 1964, Nixon suggested Goldwater and Rockefeller. "If Jack and Lyndon can get together, Barry and Nelson can." He knew this to be impossible – if Rockefeller would not run with him in 1960, he certainly would not consider it with Goldwater in 1964, but Nixon was already dusting himself off as the 1968 unity candidate. Although it was not a profound speech, rather in the nature of Kennedy-bashing, Nixon was welcomed back by the media and his remarks were accorded wider coverage than their content deserved, apart from Nixon's sighting shot that the Cuban Missile Crisis had been something less than the triumph portrayed by the Kennedy propaganda machine.

The Nixons found a ten-room apartment at the corner of Fifth Avenue and Sixty-second Street, and sold their Los Angeles home for enough to pay for the Fifth Avenue apartment and its renovation. Nixon's landlady was the former Mrs. Nelson Rockefeller, and the governor and his new wife lived on the twelfth floor of the same building. Nixon claimed this was a surprise, but that is unlikely, as this was the venue for the famous Treaty of Fifth Avenue less than three years before. Rockefeller graciously hailed Nixon's arrival as "wonderful news."[4]

Nixon departed on June 12 for an extended trip to Europe with Pat, Tricia, Julie, Jack and Helene Drown, and their daughter, Maureen. He organized in advance, through the State Department, to meet with the leaders of the countries he visited, and to give a press conference in each capital. In his comments for the press he urged Goldwater to renounce the support of the John Birch Society and supported the Nuclear Test Ban Treaty when it was announced. He urged Republican senators to support it and reminded them that it had been Eisenhower's idea originally.

In Barcelona, Nixon was received by Franco, who seemed to him not "the rigid and unpleasant dictator pictured in the press" but "a subtle and pragmatic leader." The highlight of the trip was a luncheon de Gaulle gave for the Nixons at the Élysées, on a patio behind the presidential palace. Always exquisitely courteous in person, de Gaulle rose to toast the Nixons after lunch and said that "he knew that I had suffered some difficult defeats, but he predicted that at some time in the future I would be serving my nation in a very high capacity."[5]

Khrushchev had sealed off East Berlin in 1961 by building the infamous Berlin Wall, the only such barricade in history designed to keep people in.

Nixon went for an unescorted stroll through the dingy Stalinist streets of East Berlin and made a speech advocating, again unspecifically, in the manner of opposition leaders, the use of American force to bring down the wall.

Nixon was received in Cairo by Gamel Abdel Nasser, in the Egyptian leader's "surprisingly modest" home. Nixon declined to criticize Kennedy, and urged Nasser to focus on economic and social and educational development in Egypt. Nasser wasn't much interested in these mundane goals, and "like Sukarno and Nkrumah, had devoted the best of his energies to revolution." Nixon was impressed by his "superior intelligence, and great charisma . . . [and] dignity, [but] now he was more interested in a grandiose crusade for Arab unity" than in bettering the lot of the Egyptians. The Nixons toured the Pyramids, Luxor, and the dam site at Aswan. "I could see that, despite its terrible poverty, [Egypt] was moving ahead and eventually would exert enormous influence throughout the Middle East." Nixon thought that despite Israel's technological superiority, the Arabs would "defeat them by sheer weight of numbers unless some accommodations were reached."[6] From this time forward, if not before, Nixon recognized that it would be necessary to develop some sort of relationship with the major Arab powers.

The Nixons visited Germany, Athens, Venice, and Rome, and while they were in Rome, President Kennedy came to that city on a state visit. This tour of the president's was best remembered by his famous statement at the Berlin Wall, "Ich bin ein Berliner." One afternoon the telephone rang in the Nixons' Rome hotel suite and it was President Kennedy, just calling to say hello, exchange greetings, and wish the Nixons a pleasant holiday. It was a typically elegant gesture by that most attractive man. Richard Nixon and John Kennedy, elected to Congress together in 1946, were never to speak again.[7]

Nixon started work at what became the law firm of Nixon, Mudge, et al. in August 1963. He was at his office by 7 A.M. and stayed until 6 P.M. He was a prodigious worker and clearly a competent lawyer. The firm's investment in him had been very fortuitous, as its business, especially its new international clientele, flourished. The Nixons enjoyed New York, attending the theater and musical evenings at Carnegie Hall and the Metropolitan Opera House, and Nixon frequently went to big league sports events. He worshipped on Sunday mornings at Norman Vincent Peale's downtown Marble

Collegiate Church, where Peale often sermonized on his favored theme of "the power of positive thinking."

Nixon was always surrounded by well-wishers and autograph-seekers, and he and his wife were a couple much in demand in the highest social circles in the city. It was a happy time (notwithstanding Henry Kissinger's subsequent claim, as someone who did not then live in New York and was not a well-known or received social figure outside a narrow academic circle, that Nixon was shunned on Park and Fifth Avenues).[8]

On August 28, 1963, civil rights moved to the very forefront of American consciousness with an unforgettable, almost Ciceronian oration by Martin Luther King from the Lincoln Memorial to an audience of hundreds of thousands who had come from all over the country, and a television audience of scores of millions. The government had encouraged federal employees to attend. His theme was "I have a dream . . ." (of a time of racial equality and brotherhood). He mixed in lines from the anthem "My Country 'tis of Thee (America)": "Let freedom ring . . . from every village and every hamlet, from every state in every city . . ." and concluded in his thunderous yet sonorous voice that when this was accomplished, "We will be able to say, in the words of the old Negro spiritual, 'Free at last! Free at last! Thank God Almighty, we are free at last!'"

It was twenty-four years since Marian Anderson sang "My Country 'tis of Thee" in the same place, after she had been banned by the Daughters of the American Revolution from singing in Constitution Hall. Eleanor Roosevelt had publicly resigned from the DAR, and organized a concert for Anderson at the Lincoln Memorial. The recollection of that occasion was in the minds of many when King staged his march on Washington, and on this occasion as on the preceding one, the administration favored the cause and the event.

With the famous seated statue of the Great Emancipator in the background, the effect of King's powerful address was electrifying. King was awarded the Nobel Prize for Peace in 1964. The long struggle of African-Americans was entering a new phase, buttressed by the support of scores of millions of conscientious whites who could no longer abide the institutionalization of bigotry and racism in a country that never ceased to proclaim itself the cradle and guardian of man's freedom. The era when Southern Democratic senators could successfully filibuster an anti-lynching bill in the Congress was almost over, one hundred years after the official emancipation of the slaves.

Nixon steadily ran strongly in polls of Republicans expressing a presidential preference, but always said that he was not a candidate for the 1964 nomination. When Eisenhower enumerated for the press ten Republicans that he thought would be good presidents, and left Nixon out, Nixon let his displeasure be known at a fashionable dinner table. He knew this would be reported to Eisenhower, who called the next day and said that Nixon had made his point many times that he was not a candidate. Nixon pointed out that, as reported, Eisenhower was not confining himself to declared, or even likely, candidates, and the former president told a reporter the following week that if there were a "sudden wave of support" for Nixon, he would certainly be qualified. Nixon had had about as much of Eisenhower's condescensions as he could take, and referred to his former boss from time to time as "that senile old bastard," which was in fact the opinion that he had intermittently had of him since the fund crisis thirteen years before.[9] Nixon was aware of Eisenhower's qualities and of his historic status, but it was a relief to drop the mask of exaggerated deference, at least occasionally and in private.

Nixon gave about a speech a week and was always controversial enough to assure a good deal of publicity. In September 1963, he attacked Kennedy's sale of $250 million worth of wheat to the U.S.S.R. and said that the U.S. should not be bailing Khrushchev out of an agricultural crisis. In October, he was in Paris on Pepsi-Cola business, and in a press conference he attacked the Kennedy abandonment of South Vietnamese leader Ngo Dinh Diem. Diem and his regime were under siege from a Buddhist monastic faction around the An Quang Pagoda, as well as trying to deal with an endless flow of communist guerrillas and North Vietnamese regular troops into his country. Nixon presciently warned that the choice was "not between Diem and somebody better, but between Diem and somebody infinitely worse."

Writing in the *Saturday Evening Post* and *Reader's Digest* in October, he implicitly criticized Eisenhower for not helping the Hungarians in 1956. There is no evidence that Nixon himself spoke very forcefully in favor of moving to assist the Hungarians in 1956, and he does not allege in his memoirs, written after Eisenhower's death, that he did, but, as with Suez, he concluded that the administration had bungled the crisis.

November 1963 brought some early portents. Ngo Dinh Diem and his brother, the interior (police) minister, were murdered in Saigon, and there was not the slightest doubt that the U.S. administration was complicit in the overthrow, if not the death, of these men. The ambassador in Saigon was now Nixon's old running mate, Henry Cabot Lodge. His appointment was a sage bipartisan move, like Roosevelt's naming of a Republican governor, John G. Winant, ambassador to Great Britain in 1941. Lodge had bought into the idea that South Vietnam would fare much better with a less autocratic and sectarianly zealous leader than the intense Roman Catholic Diem. In fact, his removal horrified America's East Asian allies and started South Vietnam into its sanguinary, final crisis, which would drag on for twelve horrible years.

In accord with his customary policy, Nixon maintained a public silence about the Diem affair for a while but wrote to Eisenhower that "our complicity in Diem's murder was a national disgrace." Eisenhower, who possibly was losing touch with the world by this time, responded that he did not "believe that any American would approve the cold-blooded killing of a man who had, after all, shown great courage when he took on the task of defeating communism." He further did not believe that "Kennedy would have ordered the murder of a fellow Catholic." The general's faith in the benignity of his countrymen, and especially his successor, was touching but misplaced, and not shared by Nixon.[10] (Subsequent South Vietnamese President Nguyen Van Thieu confirmed to the author on October 1, 1970, that the Kennedy administration, and Lodge in particular, had been entirely complicit in, and had forcefully promoted, the overthrow of Diem, and that while they had probably not asked for the murder of the Diems, they should have known that such a fate was the likely outcome of their policy.)

Diem's reluctance to go through the motions of democracy, along with his appearance of religious intolerance, was an embarrassment, and there was some doubt about whether he could be relied upon to continue the war, or whether the U.S. Congress, in these circumstances, would approve continued support of Diem. But meddling to the point of encouraging military revolt and the assassination of an ally whose inauguration Nixon had attended as Eisenhower's emissary was a mad and immoral enterprise. Lodge, at the least, could have intervened to assure the safe exit of the Diems from the country.

Another distant portent was the Otepka affair. Otto Otepka, a State Department security evaluator, had refused a security clearance to Walt W. Rostow, an economist and Kennedy's deputy national security adviser. Rostow was a hawk on Vietnam, but he was the son of an active socialist, and Otepka denied him a security clearance. This was an eccentric and presumptuous thing to do to a senior presidential appointee, but the Kennedys overreacted. Otepka was demoted, and he leaked documents about some of Rostow's associations to Republicans in Congress. He was subjected to personal surveillance, his telephone was tapped, and he was harassed at work and at home.

The State Department functionaries who had carried out the telephone intercepts lied to the congressional committee that questioned them, and when confronted with evidence, said that the intercepts had been ineffectual, because of static on the line, and they had therefore not really tapped Otepka's telephone. This too was untrue, but the Justice Department never took any action. Nixon wrote to his old HUAC colleague, Senator Karl Mundt, asking him to chase after the administration for this outrage – evident crimes by junior officials against a superior, on orders from even higher up. If the trail had been followed, it would presumably have led far up in the administration. Nothing much came of it, and the controversy, to which the great liberal media responded in pretty blasé fashion, was shortly overtaken by other events.

A year after his "last press conference," Nixon had given fifty more press conferences, and a year before the next election, he was frequently mentioned, including by Rockefeller and Eisenhower, as a possible presidential candidate. (Chastened, Eisenhower described him on *Face the Nation* as "very knowledgeable and very courageous.")[11] Rockefeller invited him upstairs for a drink on September 3, 1963, and said that he intended to run for president. He said that Kennedy had "messed up on all issues." He disparaged Goldwater as uneducated, unworldly, and "just too shallow." He dismissed Romney as someone who "knows too little of the world and is too sure of what he doesn't know." Scranton was competent but wanted a draft, and "there just isn't a draft around with Bill Scranton's name on it . . . Dick . . . What we both have to recognize is that you and I are the only ones qualified on both foreign and national issues to serve as president." This was essentially a correct analysis of all the players, though Kennedy, while somewhat ineffectual, was very popular. What Rockefeller offered was that if Nixon didn't run and the convention deadlocked, he would throw it to Nixon. Nixon thanked him, repeated that he was not a candidate, and said he would not make any deals but wished him well.[12]

— II —

Nixon went to Dallas on November 21, to a meeting of Pepsi-Cola bottlers. It later emerged that a communist drifter, who had taken a shot at General Edwin Walker a few months before and missed, had set out to assassinate Nixon but was restrained by his Russian wife.[13] A month before, Adlai Stevenson had been attacked by right-wing demonstrators, hit by a placard, and spat upon. As the police dragged off one of his assailants, Stevenson said, "I don't want to send them to jail, just to school."

Nixon had his usual press conference when traveling, and urged Texans to give President and Mrs. Kennedy, who were expected in Dallas the next day, "a courteous reception." He always deplored picketing, heckling, demonstrations, and all forms of mob incivility, and had never engaged in it, apart from planting a few relatively polite hecklers in Jerry Voorhis's and Helen Douglas's election meetings. Nixon returned to New York on the morning of November 22.

He took a Yellow Cab from the airport, and someone shouted to the driver at a stoplight that President Kennedy had been shot. When he got to his Fifth Avenue home, his doorman was in tears; the president had died of gunshot wounds, and the governor of Texas, John B. Connally, who had been traveling with him and Mrs. Kennedy in an open car, had been wounded. Nixon was about to sign a book contract to write about the 1964 election as Theodore H. White had written about the 1960 election, but this project was now deferred.* Nixon called J. Edgar Hoover to get the FBI director's take on what had happened, and Hoover said that the assassin was not one of the radical Dallas right but, in fact, a communist.

Television cameras had set up downstairs to get Nixon's, and if he was home, Rockefeller's, reaction. Nixon wrote out a statement tastefully expressing admiration for Kennedy, sympathy for his family, and stating that "The greatest tribute we can pay to his memory is . . . to do everything we can to

---

* So was Nixon's planned golf game with Thomas E. Dewey and the chairman of U.S. Steel, Roger Blough – it was getting pretty cool for golf around New York anyway, in late November.

reduce the forces of hatred which drive men to do such terrible deeds."[14]

Nixon denied that he thought that it could as well have been him who was assassinated if he had been elected, but this would be a natural reflection. He wrote Mrs. Kennedy a very appropriate "Dear Jackie" note of sympathy. He recalled that though they were opponents, he had been friendly with her husband, and had been grateful that JFK had invited the Nixons to his wedding. "Nothing I could say now could add to the splendid tributes which have come from throughout the world to him. . . . The nation will also be forever grateful for your service. . . . You brought to the White House charm, beauty, and elegance as the official hostess for America, and the mystique of the young in heart which was uniquely yours made an indelible impression on the American consciousness." This was nothing but the truth.

She replied, quite promptly: "Dear Mr. Vice President, You two young men, colleagues in Congress, adversaries in 1960 . . . Whoever thought such a hideous thing could happen in this country. I know how you must feel – so long on the path – so closely missing the greatest prize. And now for you . . . the question comes up again, and you must commit all your family's hopes and efforts again. . . . If it does not work out as you have hoped for so long – please be consoled by what you already have – your life and your family." She closed by hoping that "your daughters love Chapin School as much as I did."[15]

Jacqueline Kennedy clearly thought that Nixon was cranking up to run for president. His initial political opinion was that there would be a rending struggle for power among the Democrats between Robert Kennedy and Lyndon Johnson, who was sworn as president on Air Force One just before it took off from Dallas, with the blood-spattered widow beside him, and the coffin of the former president on board.

Nixon underestimated Johnson's ability to move quickly and effectively to solidify his control of the government and the Democrats. But it was hard to foretell the immense mythic quality that would quickly engulf and exalt the Kennedys. Jacqueline Kennedy was the chief author of this legend. On the night of the assassination, she declined to change her suit, gruesomely besmirched with her husband's blood though it was, because "I want them to see what they have done." There was no "they." Although most comment was to the effect that, in Chief Justice Warren's phrase, the late president had been "martyred as a result of the hatred and bitterness that has been injected into the life of our nation by bigots," Lee Harvey Oswald had nothing to do with the right-wing extremists who had assailed Stevenson. Though this crime, made more macabre by the assassination of the apparent assassin by strip-club owner Jack Ruby a few days later, has been the all-time magnet for conspiracy theorists, there is no evidence that Oswald was anything more than a solitary, avowed communist misfit.

James Reston in the *New York Times* struck a resonant note when he wrote under a headline that "Kennedy was a victim of the violent streak he tried to curb in the nation." His title two days later was: "A portion of guilt for all." From the start, the liberal left had trouble accepting that the president had been murdered by an isolated person, especially a communist. Even Jacqueline Kennedy privately expressed regret that he had been killed "by a communist." "Far better, she said, if, like Lincoln, he had been martyred for civil rights and racial justice."[16] Though Oswald was entirely un-American and anti-American in his disaffection, the nation, in its shock and grief and shame, led by much of its liberal media, portrayed the murder of the president as a collective crime of national violence and hatred.

It was a splendid and poignant funeral, in crisp, bright autumn weather, a piercingly sad and crystalline moment in the lives of all of the hundreds of millions of people who watched it on television. Richard and Pat Nixon attended, but were not too noticed among many world leaders, including Charles de Gaulle, the emperor of Ethiopia, the king of the Belgians, and the queen of Greece; presidents of Ireland, Israel, South Korea, the Philippines, Turkey, and West Germany,* and the German chancellor, Ludwig Erhard; the prime ministers of Canada (Pearson), Great Britain (Home), and Japan, and a substantial scattering of secondary royals led by Britain's Prince Philip. Walking close together were the former foes Vice Premier Augustin Munoz Grandes of Spain (who had commanded Franco's Blue Division in Russia in the Second World War) and the U.S.S.R.'s timeless Stalinist veteran, Deputy Premier Anastas Mikoyan. There were many assorted luminaries, including UN Secretary General U Thant; the founder of the European Community, Jean Monnet; and future national leaders Golda Meir of Israel and Olaf Palme of Sweden.

---

* The eighty-three-year-old Eamon de Valera, a veteran of sixty years of Irish politics; Zalman Shazar; Park Chung Hee; Diosdado Macapagal; Ataturk's companion and chosen successor, Ismet Inonu; and Heinrich Lübke.

Elder statesmen Eisenhower and Truman were reconciled when they met for the obsequies. Given the very distinguished service both men had rendered to their nation and its allies, in peace and war, this was the appropriate thing to happen at this very sad national occasion, after ten years of often fierce public animosity. The funeral was suitably solemn and dignified, apart perhaps, from the slightly grating histrionics of the presiding clergyman, Richard Cardinal Cushing of Boston, whose cadences were not sonorous and not always comprehensible, even to those familiar with the ancient, eloquent liturgy.

A week after the death of President Kennedy, his widow gave an interview to Theodore H. White, who was writing a remembrance for *Life* magazine. She told White that Kennedy's favorite tune had been from the Lerner and Lowe musical *Camelot*, specifically the lines "Don't let it be forgot/ that once there was a spot/ for one brief shining moment/ that was known as Camelot." She continued, "There will be great presidents again, but there will never be another Camelot again." Allowance must be made for the terrible bereavement of Jacqueline Kennedy, who carried through the funeral with magnificent poise and dignity, and deservedly won for herself and her two young children the hearts of the whole world. But as a mythmaker, she demonstrated an amazing and instant talent.

White later regretted his role in propagating the *Camelot* canard. Even the normally rather rigorous Samuel Eliot Morison, author of the distinguished fifteen-volume official history of the U.S. Navy in the Second World War (for the writing of which Roosevelt had plucked him from the Harvard professoriate and commissioned him a rear admiral), took this imposture seriously. He concluded his *History of the American People* with an excerpt from the *Camelot* musical score.[17]

There was no recollection of Kennedy's fondness for that production by anyone else who knew him well apart from his wife. The Kennedy administration was bracing and peppy, but didn't really accomplish much, apart from getting the missiles out of Cuba and completing Eisenhower's Test Ban Treaty. In nearly three years, Kennedy did not achieve a fraction of what Roosevelt, Truman, Eisenhower, Johnson, Nixon, or Reagan did or would accomplish in the opening years of their presidencies.

After the geriatric slippages of the late-Eisenhower era, America was ready for something more contemporary, cerebral, and energetic. But the Kennedy style was mainly touch football, sound-bites, quips that were good but not as good nor as spontaneous as Stevenson's, and sophistical gimmickry in speechwriting, such as JFK's "Declaration of Interdependence" on July 4, 1962. The famous dinner for de Gaulle's culture minister, renowned author André Malraux, was attended by an academically rather second-echelon group. When Kennedy conferred honorary American citizenship on Sir Winston Churchill, he announced it with a straight lift from Edward R. Murrow's introduction of his widely sold phonograph record album of excerpts from Churchill's greatest speeches.

John F. Kennedy showed much promise as a president, and he was an immensely attractive public man and private personality. He persevered with great courage and elegance through physical pain from war wounds and the burdens of an overbearing and often misguided father. But his widow, the clever survivor of a rather dysfunctional marriage, created a Brobdingnagianly serene myth, almost overnight, and almost from whole cloth, of his brief administration as the summit of American political and social development, against which American politicians would contend for many years.

The country was persuaded by the liberal media that it was collectively responsible for the death of the nation's youngest elected president (forty-six when he died), and Jackie and her in-laws successfully peddled the bunk about *Camelot*. In these circumstances, it shortly emerged that it was going to be practically impossible to run against the Democrats successfully in 1964. Richard Nixon would be well out of it.

The new president, Lyndon Baines Johnson, was a raw, coarse, overwhelming Texan wheeler-dealer, fifty-five years old, and a veteran of eleven years as a congressman and twelve years in the Senate, six of them as majority leader. He was a genius at organizing congressional votes and coalitions, and was a vehement and strenuous man, an overpowering and crudely colorful personality, assisted in his cajolery and browbeating by his physical stature (six feet, four inches, and about two hundred and forty pounds). Kennedy had said that he reminded him of a riverboat gambler. He was always cutting a deal with someone. He and Sam Rayburn had run Texas like a cornerstore, and had emasculated the powers of the Texas governor to reserve all authority to themselves. Johnson had surprised many by accepting Kennedy's offer of the vice presidency in 1960, but had taken no chances and had himself reelected to the Senate at the same time. If the national ticket lost to Nixon, Johnson would not be leaving the Senate, nor relaxing his control of it.

In policy terms, he was an enigma. He had arrived in Washington in 1932, in the vanguard of the New Deal, as assistant to Congressman Richard Kleberg, of the family that owned the famous King Ranch, America's largest single-family, residential acreage. He had been an enthusiastic New Dealer, but had always played it very close to the wealthy oilmen of Texas. He took good care of their interests, and while he was at it, didn't do badly for himself either. Unlike Nixon, he profited greatly while in public life, most particularly by having his wife receive the television license for Austin, Texas, which she retained for many years, as the only television station in that city, a unique monopoly in the country. He always accompanied his wife, as Senate Democratic leader, to license renewal hearings at the Federal Communications Commission. He was probably the wealthiest person in the history of the presidency, unless all Joseph Kennedy's fortune were attributed to JFK. There was always a financial probity question about Johnson, but it was never really plumbed.

LBJ had shown some movement on civil rights, and claimed to favor the Kennedy program for tax cuts and expanded federal government activity in support of wider health care and welfare benefits. He had been trained as a teacher and briefly was an elementary school teacher (something that requires a good deal of imagination to envision). His heart was thought to be with the poor people of the Texas hill country where he was born and raised, and still lived, albeit on the commodious LBJ Ranch. But no one had much idea what he would do as president.

He took charge promptly and earned widespread, instant respect for the dignity and calm with which he gathered the reins of office into his hands, showing exquisite sensitivity to the Kennedys, but leaving no room for anyone to imagine that the presidency was not fully and purposefully executed. He and Theodore Roosevelt and Harry Truman must rank as the ablest vice presidents ever to succeed to the presidency in midterm. His broad, somewhat common Texas accent and rough manners were a shock to the nation and the world, accustomed to the Ivy League urbanity of his predecessor, a problem that was never fully surmounted. To the Kennedy faithful, Lyndon Johnson would always be a placeman, or even a usurper, though Kennedy would probably not have been elected without Johnson, who had loyally served him as vice president.

Johnson's wife, Claudia Alta Taylor Johnson, but universally known as Lady Bird, was – and at time of writing, on the verge of her one hundredth birthday, remains – a very talented and intelligent, universally admired, woman. Like the Nixons, the Johnsons had two daughters.

— III —

Richard Nixon was called to the bar of New York in December, having written an obligatory essay, "The principles underlying the form of government of the United States." His examiner pronounced it the best of its kind that he had seen in twenty-eight years, and it was widely excerpted in the press. He described the balance between order and freedom, and wrote that "individual enterprise should be allowed and encouraged to undertake all functions which it is capable to perform . . . [the U.S. system] is the most effective safeguard against arbitrary power ever devised by man."[18]

Nixon started back on the speaking circuit in February 1964. He accused "the Kennedy-Johnson" administration of a sequence of foreign policy disasters surpassing anything that had occurred since the Second World War. This was a severe indictment, given what he had been in the habit of saying about Truman. So much for Johnson's political honeymoon in a climate of national mourning, or even restraint. "We no longer contain communism, but are contained by it," Nixon said.[19]

Nixon appeared at Senate hearings on presidential succession early in March and joked that this was the first time he had been on the witness's side of the table in the Senate Caucus Room. He recommended that when the vice presidency becomes vacant, it be filled by a candidate nominated by the president and endorsed by the electoral college that had met after the last presidential election. He spoke for half an hour without pause or notes, and made a very strong impression on everyone. The Constitution was eventually amended to provide for a vacant vice presidency to be filled by a presidential nominee endorsed by both houses of the Congress.

The New Hampshire primary took place on March 10. Henry Cabot Lodge, who was still in Saigon dealing with an endless procession of political factions in the wake of the murder of the Diems, won with 33,400 write-in votes after a campaign on his behalf by his wealthy Boston friends. Goldwater and Rockefeller, who were the official candidates, received only 21,700 and 19,500 votes, respectively, a rather dismal showing. Nixon, who had spent nothing and had not appeared in the state, and repeatedly said he was not a candidate, got 15,700 write-ins, a respectable performance in the circumstances, though he had hoped for more. At a Republican dinner in Newark the following day, Nixon declared that the reelection of Johnson, who had declared his candidacy and was unopposed in his party, would mean "that this country could be in for four more years of wheeling and dealing and influence-peddling unprecedented in" American history.[20]

On March 12, Nixon spoke with Eisenhower's old aide, Fred Seaton of Nebraska, and talked tactics. He was clearly still thinking of offering himself as an unspontaneous draftee, but agreed that Seaton would run a write-in campaign for Nixon in Nebraska, and that Nixon would not declare himself a candidate in any primary.[21] Johnson had declared his "War on Poverty" in January, and brought forward the Civil Rights Act of 1964 and rammed it through the Congress. This law banned racial discrimination in public places, employment, and federally funded programs. It was the most ambitious civil rights legislation in the history of the country. Goldwater voted against. Nixon refrained from public comment.

Nixon favored civil rights as he always had but was opposed to any pretense that this was a problem confined to the South. This was his sharp political calculation – that he could not take the African-American vote from the Democrats, but that he could take a good deal of Southern white votes from the Democrats without alienating Northern moderates and liberal Republicans, who would not abide truckling to southern white supremacists.

Kennedy had sent sixteen thousand American soldiers to Vietnam. Lodge, having enthusiastically encouraged the coup against the Diems, had had to deal with another, though almost bloodless, coup a few months later, as Nixon had predicted. The Saigon government was in shambles and North Vietnam was pouring forces and military supplies into the South along the Ho Chi Minh Trail, an intricate but massive tangle of roads and paths through Laos and into South Vietnam. The issue of what the United States proposed to do about the growing threat to South Vietnam could be dodged, but not for long. Johnson was still claiming that it could be fought with economic and development aid and military "advisers." Nixon said this was untrue and that what was needed was a determination to stop the communists and that that could not be achieved by launching an Indochinese War on Poverty of building schools and bridges in rural Vietnam.

Nixon left on another extensive overseas tour on March 22, 1964 (from New York's John F. Kennedy Airport, as Idlewild had just been renamed). He flew first to Beirut. He was promoting Pepsi-Cola, and said at every stop (Karachi, New Delhi, Singapore, and Bangkok) that he was on business, and would accept a presidential nomination only if the "party leaders ask me to run." This was pretty close to the usual pious claptrap about accepting a draft, but Nixon knew that that was unlikely, and that even if it occurred, the Republican nomination might not be worth much, because of Johnson's good start, the Kennedy mystique, and the looming split between Goldwater and Rockefeller, which, as Nixon long had felt, probably required one of them to vanquish the other and be thrashed at the polls, and the other to be chastised by the party as a traitor. Nixon already foresaw that Johnson's impetuosity in both foreign and domestic issues could create great possibilities for the Republican candidate in 1968.

Nixon moved on to Saigon and conducted his usual extensive private tour. He was appalled at the views of his former running mate, Lodge, who had bought into the groupthink of the academics and theorists around Kennedy and now Johnson, immortalized in David Halberstam's description "the Best and the Brightest." It was about these people, when Johnson effused to the late Sam Rayburn about how intelligent they were, that Rayburn said, "I hope you're right, but I just wish one of them had ever run for county sheriff." The word from Johnson's inherited entourage at this point was that the war in Vietnam could be won with social spending, acts of goodwill, and encouragements to democracy. An inexpressible, unbelievable tragedy, on a new, hideously magnified scale was about to spring, whole, from its Indochinese cradle and be unleashed upon the world.

In Saigon, Nixon said to the press that he hoped Vietnam would not be an issue in the upcoming election, but that it would inevitably become so if administration policy continues to be afflicted with "inconsistency, improvisation, and uncertainty." He quoted General MacArthur, that "in war, there is no substitute for victory." MacArthur, like Eisenhower (and they were the nation's two highest-ranking retired soldiers and had received the unconditional surrenders of Germany and Japan nineteen years before), had urged Kennedy and Johnson not to commit ground forces to continental Asia.[22] (MacArthur died a few days later, April 5, 1964, aged eighty-four.)

Nixon found Lodge even more hopeless and woolly-minded in Saigon than he had been when touring around as a vice presidential candidate.

Nixon was disconcerted to learn from the U.S. military in Saigon that they had been restrained from launching air raids on the North and against the Ho Chi Minh Trail. While completely inadequate as a war-winning strategy, bombing at least had more realistic content than the social-work Vietnamese fairy tale Johnson was about to use as an argument for his reelection.

Nixon flew on to Hong Kong, where he attacked Senator J. William Fulbright for proposing a reexamination of relations with China, and then to Manila; Taipei, where he met with Chiang Kai-shek; and Tokyo, where he was received by the leaders of the government. In Tokyo, Nixon told his inevitable press conference that he favored, along with senior military personnel in Saigon, taking the war to the North, by air. He even used MacArthur's old line about not accepting that the enemy could have a "privileged sanctuary" within his own borders, and was even more explicit when he returned home and warned against a "Yalu River concept in Vietnam."[23]

The danger inherent in what he was saying was that MacArthur had been speaking of Korea, where the United States had deployed a large army and it had a UN cover for its activities and militarily significant allies, and a fixed battle line. Vietnam was a porous country and the only useful allies had been effectively dispensed with eight years before when, against the advice of Dulles and Nixon, Eisenhower had pulled the plug on any effort to assist the French and attempt an orderly, non-communist transition to independence. It was already very late to try to avert an outright communist takeover of Indochina. And nobody in any relevant office in Washington had the remotest idea of how to avoid it.

There remained a thin chance for Nixon to be the nominee in 1964 if he wanted it. What he had foreseen was starting to come to pass with the Goldwater-Rockefeller split of the party. There remained the technical possibility of a hung convention, a saw-off between Goldwater and Rockefeller, and receipt of the call to Nixon to reconcile the factions. Though assiduous Nixon and Eisenhower biographer Stephen Ambrose,[24] as well as a few others, claims that Nixon took this seriously, there is no evidence that he did. He was too astute a reader of political tea leaves not to know how insuperable the Democrats would be with Johnson invoking the memory of Kennedy while promising painless peace in Vietnam through a miniature Marshall Plan and promising to eliminate poverty in America while reducing taxes and promoting civil rights.

The last deadlocked major party convention was that of the Democrats in 1924, between New York's Roman Catholic, anti-Prohibitionist governor, Al Smith, and Sheridan Downey's predecessor as California senator, Woodrow Wilson's son-in-law, William G. McAdoo, candidate of Protestants and Prohibitionists. The last time the Republicans had deadlocked was in 1920, when the impasse was broken by the catastrophic selection of Senator Warren Harding in the original proverbial smoke-filled room, in the Blackstone Hotel in Chicago. The simplification of nominating requirements (a bare majority rather than a qualified one) and the extension of the primary system had made deadlocked conventions almost impossible, and there have been none since the twenties. This was the strategy of Earl Warren in 1952 and, even without the sabotage of Nixon and Chotiner, it was unlikely to have been a success.

Nixon was interested in shedding his loser's image while shadow-boxing and leaving it to Goldwater and Rockefeller to spend themselves against each other before having the honor of being executed by Johnson. Nixon also knew that Johnson was playing with a combustible mixture of issues at home and abroad, and was running a serious chance of getting into real trouble in Vietnam and in the disadvantaged regions of America, black and white.

Nixon had trouble raising money for Seaton's write-in effort in Nebraska; even his wealthy friends were reluctant to contribute to a non-candidate as they had been to contribute to a mere candidate for governor of California in 1962. He had to man the telephone himself to get halfway to Seaton's target of fifty-thousand dollars; life had been easier for those who could buy their elections, like Kennedy and Rockefeller.

On April 27, 1964, Nixon spoke at the annual Gridiron Dinner of the press in Washington: "My friends of the press, if I have any," and said that if he did not, he might be chiefly to blame for it. "I hope a man can lose his temper once in sixteen years and be forgiven for it." He then got into what he claimed to be the mood of the evening by producing a glass of bourbon and asking, What could better express the spirit of the evening "than for Harry Truman to take a drink from Dick Nixon without asking someone else to taste it first?" He handed the former president the drink; Truman, suspicious but cheerful, accepted it and stood and shook hands with Nixon, and the house, containing most of the government, including the president, and the entire national press corps, rose in prolonged applause.[25]

In two articles he wrote for *Reader's Digest* published in the spring of 1964, Nixon outlined some of his foreign policy views. South Vietnam was being lost but was winnable, he wrote. If it went down, Laos, Cambodia, Thailand, Malaysia, Indonesia, the Philippines, Australia, and Japan would follow. This was fantastic nonsense. Assumedly, Nixon, who had heard Eisenhower and Churchill and MacArthur, and probably de Gaulle as well, debunk any such theory, did not believe it. He was clearly staking out a position to the right of everybody else, specifically Goldwater, for tactical reasons. He advocated an immense aerial assault on the enemy's infiltration routes and capability. His views were more sensible than anything else that was on offer, except for those who said simply to cut Vietnam loose and not waste any casualties or resources on it. Nixon at least made it clear that he was militantly opposed to any use of nuclear weapons, as he had not ten years before.

The second article was about Cuba. Nixon revised history and resurrected his opposition to invasion by exiles during the 1960 campaign, the position he was forced to adopt by circumstances. He blasted the Bay of Pigs mission for lack of proper air cover, and accurately said that he had urged Kennedy to find a cover and invade once the action of the exiles had gone horribly wrong. He claimed again that Kennedy had "pulled defeat out of the jaws of victory," by failing to require on-site inspections while adopting a no-invasion, "weak-kneed foreign policy."

On May 12, Nebraska voted 49.5 percent for Goldwater, 31.5 percent for Nixon as a write-in candidate, and the rest was between Rockefeller and Lodge. This was a very respectable showing for a non-campaigning non-candidate who had spent twenty-five thousand dollars only on direct mail and a bit of newspaper advertising. By this time, Rockefeller had little chance of winning the convention, but might be able to stop Goldwater if he won California.

On May 15 in Oregon, where only Rockefeller and Nixon (still a professed non-candidate) were on the ballot, Rockefeller took 93,000 votes to 78,000 for Lodge, 50,000 for Goldwater, and 48,000 for Nixon. Lodge was an aberrant illustration of the Republicans' lack of enthusiasm for the two leading candidates. He would have been an electoral disaster, and not a strong president.

On June 2 in California, Goldwater defeated Rockefeller with 51.6 percent of the vote and clinched the nomination. Rockefeller withdrew and Scranton made a goal-line stand for the moderates, but Nixon's scenario was being followed to perfection: he had largely exhumed his viability as a candidate, repairing press relations, publicly cavorting with Truman, while Rockefeller split the party and Goldwater led it to a complete demolition by an overconfident, swaggering Johnson.

Goldwater had voted against civil rights, the Test Ban Treaty, and federal aid to education. His opposition to graduated income tax and suggestions for making Social Security more flexible were interesting positions, though ahead of their time and not well advocated by him. Nixon said it would "be a tragedy" if Goldwater's platform were not "challenged and repudiated" by the Republicans. Goldwater said he had got most of his opinions from Nixon, who sounded "more like Harold Stassen every day."[26]

Goldwater could enjoy his fleeting hour; he was elevating Nixon as the soul of reasonable Republicanism after the onrushing fatal encounter with the voters. Nixon went for a brief business trip to London, and arranged to speak at the convention in San Francisco after Goldwater had been nominated. He had made his dissentient point and, having gone well to the right on Vietnam and Cuba and encouraging Scranton and Romney to run against Goldwater, did not wish to antagonize the nominee further.

Although he had stood aside, he wrote later that: "I had finally come to the realization that there was no other life for me but politics and public service . . . that if all I had was my legal work, I would be mentally dead in two years and physically dead in four."[27]

The Republicans met at the Cow Palace in San Francisco on July 15. Nixon told the press on arrival that whoever the nominee was, "I, for one Republican, will not sit it out or take a walk," distinguishing himself from Rockefeller. He hinted at the impending problem in his Machiavellian way by saying that he had been disappointed to find in his recent European trip that the press there considered Goldwater "some kind of nut, a jerk, a wild man."[28] What Nixon meant, of course, was that that view was too widely held to be overcome, and was not without merit, though he, as a loyal Republican, would go the distance for the nominee. When Senator Hugh Scott of Pennsylvania proposed an anti-extremism plank against the Ku

Klux Klan (which could not have had more than two thousand members in the whole country by this time, but was a symbol of a shameful past) and the John Birch Society, it was voted down. Rockefeller tried to speak in favor of the motion, and was booed and jeered and prevented from finishing. This disgraceful treatment of a politician who had more popular support than Goldwater provided a second burial for the still-born presidential candidate.

Nixon introduced Goldwater to the convention, and made an eloquent and opportunistic plea for party unity, which he knew would be ignored by millions of habitual Republicans. He introduced the nominee as the implicitly legitimizing voice of the party. Nixon was heavily applauded, took his place, and was flabbergasted at the suicidal tenor of Goldwater's accept-ance remarks. Early in his bombastic address, Goldwater said, "Extremism in the defense of liberty is no vice. Moderation in the pursuit of justice is no virtue." Nixon later wrote that he was "almost physically sick."[29] Nixon arranged a party unity meeting with Eisenhower and Goldwater and himself in Hershey, Pennsylvania, at the end of July. Goldwater moderated his words and Nixon promised to campaign energetically for Goldwater and his vice presidential running mate, outgoing party chairman and congress-man William E. Miller, a likable Roman Catholic (though this was little referred to) lawyer, former Nuremberg prosecutor, and pool hall owner from Lockport, New York.

It was foreordained that when the painful campaign was over, Eisenhower would already be back in retirement, Goldwater would go back to the Senate, never to rise again in presidential terms, and Miller would return to Lockport. Rockefeller could fester in Gotham with his and his party's resentments, and Nixon would be Mr. Republican, with better rela-tions with the major factions than they had with one another. And four years of racial frictions and grappling with Vietnam later, the Democrats would have to do more than pretend that Johnson was the Marlboro Man as guardian of Camelot.

As Johnson's great victory approached, clouds continued to form on the horizon. On July 27, de Gaulle joined with Khrushchev and Ho Chi Minh to advocate a conference in Geneva over the Vietnam War. Johnson rejected this as an attempt "to ratify terror," and announced the dispatch of five thousand more military advisers to South Vietnam, bringing their total to twenty-one thousand. On August 2, the White House reported that

American destroyers in international waters had been attacked without warning or provocation by North Vietnamese torpedo boats. Johnson presented the Gulf of Tonkin Resolution to the Congress, authorizing him to take "all necessary measures . . . [to] repel any armed attack." It emulated Eisenhower's Formosa Doctrine, though the world had moved beyond any contemplation of nuclear weapon use. The resolution passed 416 to 0 in the House of Representatives and 88 to 2 in the Senate, with only maverick Democrats Wayne Morse and Ernest Gruening voting against. Johnson ordered retaliatory air strikes on North Vietnamese military targets. By this action, he had covered his political flank against Goldwater, but he would have to jump into or out of Vietnam shortly after the election.

There has been much controversy about the Tonkin Gulf incident. On August 2, 1964, the U.S. destroyer *Maddox* was attacked by three North Vietnam torpedo boats, and three torpedoes and some machine-gun fire were aimed at the *Maddox*, without effect. A fighter-plane from the aircraft carrier *USS Ticonderoga* sank one of the torpedo boats and President Johnson issued a stern warning to Hanoi. On August 3, *Maddox* and another U.S. destroyer, the *C. Turner Joy*, were again patrolling near the site of the first incident, about eight miles offshore from North Vietnam. Instruments were affected by heavy thunderstorms and the bridge officers on both ships believed that they were again under attack, although there were no sightings of the enemy in the heavy weather. In good faith, they reported the incident. It now seems that the American ships were not attacked on August 3, but Johnson believed they had been when he solicited the resolution from the Congress. Whether they had been or not, it was a slender legal basis for the eventual American effort in Vietnam.

Severe racial disturbances erupted in New York City's Harlem neighborhood on July 18; in Rochester, New York, on July 27; and three weeks later in Philadelphia. On August 4, the bodies of three young white civil rights volunteers from the North were found in Mississippi. This problem was set to explode in much of the country. The pent-up frustrations of generations of African-Americans would not simply evaporate. It would prove providential that Lyndon Johnson was in place to address this problem. His presence as commander-in-chief of the American effort in Vietnam was less fortuitous.

As his own convention approached, with his nomination scheduled for his fifty-sixth birthday on August 27, Johnson should have been in piping spirits, but he was not. As his self-taped conversations, released thirty-five years later, demonstrate, Johnson was haunted by fears of being unseated by the Kennedys and having his party driven by the race issue. He claimed, right up to the convention, to be considering throwing in his hand. (If he had, it would have been an extremely successful presidency, though the third shortest in history, after William H. Harrison and James A. Garfield.)

He had announced his Great Society program, to eradicate poverty and excessive inequalities in America, to a hundred thousand people at the University of Michigan stadium at Ann Arbor, in the spring. It was an ambitious program, and for the first time since Franklin D. Roosevelt the country had a leader who could probably get almost anything he wanted from the Congress. He was clearly headed for a big victory.

The Democratic convention was at Atlantic City, New Jersey. It was a celebration of the historic achievements and recent mythology of the Democratic Party. The only suspense was the identity of the vice presidential nominee. Johnson strung this out, and selected Hubert Humphrey, the widely respected, doughty, and eloquent liberal of the Minnesota Farmer-Labor populist tradition, and a legislative pioneer of civil rights. It was a generally admired choice.

The hall was festooned with pictures of the icons of the party's past: Jefferson, Jackson, Wilson, FDR, JFK, the last three having, in their different ways, given their lives for the country in its highest office. There were three eulogies on the evening before the finale: James A. Farley's of Sam Rayburn; Adlai E. Stevenson's of Eleanor Roosevelt; and Robert F. Kennedy's of his brother, the late president. Farley, FDR's legendary party chairman from 1932 to 1940 (until Farley got the mad idea of running against FDR for the presidential nomination), who allegedly knew twenty-five thousand people by their first names, recalled the glory days of the start of the great Democratic ascendancy. He touchingly concluded his eulogy: "Mr. Sam of Texas, farewell!"

Stevenson said that Mrs. Roosevelt "would rather light a candle than curse the darkness." He received a great, sentimental welcome and congratulated the convention on "nominating my old friends Lyndon Johnson and Hubert Humphrey. This is the seventh time I have been with you in a national campaign, and on two of those occasions, I had the privilege of leading our party in days when its fortunes were less promising than they are tonight."

Robert Kennedy, who had retired as attorney general and was running for senator from New York against Kenneth Keating, although he had not lived in that state and could not vote for himself, received a very emotional, prolonged, and moving ovation. His eulogy was elegantly written and delivered with great self-control, concluding, admirably, from the supreme wordsmith of the language (from the Bard's *Romeo and Juliet*): "Take him and cut him out in little stars, And he will make the face of heaven so fine, That all the world will be in love with night, And pay no worship to the garish sun." It was affecting and unforgettable.

Humphrey gave a good-humored, fighting speech, referring to the Republican convention as "the shambles in the Cow Palace." He began each paragraph in a long litany: "Most Americans believe . . ." and ended each "but not Senator Goldwater." After such a feast of oratory, Lyndon Johnson's acceptance address, though perfectly adequate, was an anticlimax. None could know it, but James Farley, a fixture at Democratic conventions since 1920, Adlai Stevenson, Robert Kennedy, and Lyndon Johnson, all great Democratic patriarchs, would never appear at a Democratic convention again. Only Johnson would even live to watch another quadrennial convention of his party on television (and he would not enjoy what he saw).

Following his speech, President Johnson appeared with scores of the party elders on a balcony overlooking the beach and the ocean. He watched a birthday fireworks display that turned night into day, as in Kennedy's excerpt from Shakespeare, and waved to the tens of thousands below like Stalin from Lenin's Tomb, affectionately, almost paternally. He appeared on that night of his nomination to an almost certain reelection to the highest office within the gift of any people on earth, and of his fifty-sixth birthday, a mighty man, with all the power of a purposeful, idealistic America to dispose. Few sensed, though Richard Nixon was one who did, that the appearance was deceiving, and that the United States was about to enter, next to the Civil War and the Great Depression, the greatest crisis in its history.[30]

Johnson campaigned at a stately pace, and Humphrey was the nightly news highlight, a colorful, combative, but good-natured and likable candidate. Goldwater was a stolid speaker, but like Robert Taft, he had an uncompromising integrity. He spoke his mind without fear of the consequences. After decades of ideological frustration, and leadership of the Republican Party by Democratic look-alikes – at least as the conservative Republicans conceived Landon, Willkie, Dewey, Eisenhower, and Nixon, the last two elevated only, the Old Guard felt, with some reason, by Nixon's and Dewey's chicanery (in 1952) – there was a cause, a dream, and true believers.

Like Stevenson, though for different reasons, Goldwater attracted fervent followers. For Stevenson, it was partly the purity of Eleanor's (and not the crafty Franklin's) liberalism, coupled to Stevenson's magnificent urbanity, culture, intellectual eloquence, and brilliant sense of humor. Goldwater was the opposite; he had none of these qualities, but he upheld a complete reversal of policy, privatization of virtually all revenue-producing public assets, including the Tennessee Valley Authority; ending the graduated income tax and lowering taxes generally; slicing welfare costs, and arming to the teeth against the communists.

There would be no more waffling and pandering. America would go back to its roots: Minutemen, Patriots, rugged individualists, the care of the strong for the weak, and of the lucky for the unlucky; but not the demoralization of the successful by hanging the burdens of all under-achievers on them like a dead weight. The whole process of taking from those who had earned income and giving to those who had not, in order, the Republicans claimed, to buy their votes and hand the invoice to the guilt-ridden lumpen-bourgeoisie, had to be revisited with a sharp knife and pencil. The young George Will – later, and for decades, one of the greatest proponents of modern American conservatism – came back from Oxford to campaign (with his short hair, bow tie, and highbrow vocabulary and syntax) for Barry Goldwater.

Goldwater was a symbol, not the vibrant leader of his movement, as Stevenson, in his absent-minded, gentle, witty way had been. The campaign was not exciting. Unlike four years earlier, when Kennedy and Nixon had run neck-and-neck all the way, Johnson took off with a twenty-length lead and Goldwater never narrowed it. There were no debates.

Nixon embarked on a grueling, thirty-three-day, thirty-six-state tour, giving a formidable one hundred and fifty speeches. As in the previous three quadrennial elections, when he had campaigned all over the country for national office, Nixon was repetitive. This time he avoided excessive parti-sanship. He called Johnson a "chameleon," and Humphrey a "radical," and left it at that. While Nixon was ostensibly campaigning for Goldwater, he was really doing all he could for the local candidates, and for himself.

Nixon the organizer, the same person who had prepared so carefully his election as president of the student body at Whittier College, studied personal details of the candidates for Congress and for state office in each place where he spoke, and gave extensive introductions and commendations of them. While Rockefeller and Romney and Scranton, as he had foreseen, sat on their hands and did nothing for the nominees to national office, Nixon barnstormed the country, but never much connected the national and local candidates in his remarks. He was building a deep reservoir of gratitude and goodwill with people who, win or lose, would be influential at the next Republican presidential convention and would not forget what Nixon had done when they needed help most.

The one unexpected development that came late in the campaign was a widely telecast speech for Goldwater by Ronald Reagan. Reagan was a fine-looking, silver-tongued, mellow-voiced, almost hypnotic speaker. He spoke for low taxes, less government, traditional values, and a firm foreign policy. Reagan stretched it when he implied that a vote for Johnson was "the first step into a thousand years of darkness." But in general, he managed to sell what was a somewhat radical conservative line. He upset Nixon's apple cart of anti-Cuba, Vietnam-hawkish, and otherwise Eisenhower-centrist line, moderated further by proposed tax cuts and deficit-financing. If Reagan got any traction, he could completely disrupt Nixon's strategy of being the indispensable center, acceptable to factions on all sides, that could not abide other factional figures.

Reagan had never run for public office, but this speech caused a sensation, and Nixon was soon aware that Reagan was being approached by some of his own former big backers in California to take on Pat Brown. If he did so successfully, he would be Rockefeller in 1958, in his first two years as governor of a big state, as Nixon entered a presidential nominating convention as the favorite.

On November 3, 1964, Lyndon Johnson won one of the greatest electoral victories in the country's history. He took 61 percent of the vote, equaling Roosevelt's greatest triumph in 1936. Johnson won 43 million votes to 27 million for Goldwater, an unprecedented 16-million-vote plurality, surpassing Roosevelt's previous record of 11 million votes (in an electorate of 43 million, compared with the 71 million votes of 1964). The Democrats won 486 electoral votes to Goldwater's 52, and gained 2 senators and 38 congressmen. They would now have 68 senators and 295 congressmen, against only 32 Republican senators and 140 congressmen. Lyndon Johnson had an immense mandate to implement his Great Society program.

It could not have worked out more conveniently for Nixon. The day after the election, Goldwater, after gracious comments for Johnson and Humphrey, blasted those Republicans who had not supported him. Rockefeller replied at once, and blamed the conservative Republicans for hijacking the party and taking it where no one wished to follow. Nixon claimed to regard this as an attack upon himself, though it was not, and responded that Rockefeller was a "party divider" and spoiler, who had no standing in the Republican Party outside New York.

Rockefeller gained no friends in Republican ranks, after all Nixon had just done for the party in a needful time, when he said that "This kind of peevish post-election utterance has unfortunately become typical of Mr. Nixon." Goldwater, on the other hand, told Nixon at a Republican National Committee meeting in Chicago on January 22, 1965, for all to hear: "Dick, I will never forget it. . . . If there ever comes a time when I can [return the favor] I am going to do all I can."[31] Goldwater, as Nixon had foreseen, though he had a following, had blown up the Republican right's presidential claims. Rockefeller was barricaded into New York and had no currency outside it.

Nixon, just turning fifty-two, was the inevitable candidate, again. He was everywhere, in America and throughout the world, regarded as the leader of the opposition. Everything was in place for an instant further step upward. The huge Democratic harvest of votes and congressional gains of 1964 could not possibly be retained in 1966. Nixon began at once to plan a massive campaign on behalf of the party's more promising candidates in the midterm elections. Goldwater was unwelcome outside conservative circles, and retreated to the Senate; and Rockefeller was persona non grata outside New York City and the Hudson River Valley around his grandfather's estate. Once again, Nixon was the indispensable man.

— IV —

Between the 1964 and 1966 elections, Nixon spoke at over four hundred separate occasions in forty states. His first major address was in New York on

January 26, 1965. He spoke on Vietnam, said the United States was losing the war, and had to "end the war by winning it . . . We either get out, surrender on the installment plan by neutralization, or find a way to win." He called for comprehensive air and naval bombardment. He did not think either nuclear weapons or the infusion of American ground forces was necessary.[32]

He and Johnson were just playing footsie on the use of U.S. troops. All the Goldwaterites were whistling in the dark if they thought Vietnam could be saved from the communists without the use of U.S. ground forces. Johnson famously said in mid-campaign 1964 that he would not send "American boys to do what Asian boys" should be doing – i.e., fighting the North Vietnamese and Vietcong. Nixon was too well-informed to imagine that the reeling Saigon regime could be saved without U.S. intervention on the ground. He was waiting to see if Johnson threw over the whole country, in which case Nixon would claim that he could have saved it without the insertion of troops, by a more aggressive air war; or if Johnson poured in ground forces, enabling Nixon to second-guess every action of the commander in chief, while claiming to support the war effort and promote the interests of the American lads Johnson had promised not to send into the fields and jungles of Vietnam. In this hypothesis also, Nixon could claim that American ground forces were not necessary.

When the enemy attacked a U.S. base at Pleiku, South Vietnam, in March, Nixon supported Johnson's retaliatory air raids, but said there should be more of them. On April 1, Nixon told a press conference (of which he held an astounding number), "The United States cannot afford another defeat in Asia." He was goading Johnson almost every week, and in March, Johnson, still relying on the nebulous Gulf of Tonkin Resolution, started pouring marines into South Vietnam in what shortly became ground combat roles. On April 15, Johnson had two hundred and thirty aircraft drop napalm (a flaming chemical) on Viet Cong emplacements.

Johnson finally revealed in June that he was authorizing commanders in Vietnam to commit U.S. forces to combat, and dispatched another 21,000 men to join a force that he had already raised from 21,000 to 50,000 since the election. In July, Secretary of Defense Robert McNamara announced that the U.S. Expeditionary Force would be raised to 125,000. Johnson was plunging into jungle war, against the advice of most senior military experts, including Generals Eisenhower, de Gaulle, and MacArthur.

It wasn't just Vietnam that was heating up. In August 1965, the worst American race riots in more than twenty years erupted in the poor African-American district of Watts, in Los Angeles. Dozens of people were killed. Nixon denounced the rioters, while maintaining his support for civil rights. Johnson had presented his Voting Rights Bill to the Congress in March. The anthem of the civil rights movement was "We Shall Overcome." The president, in the greatest speech and most inspired moment of his career, said that "It is not just blacks but all of us that suffer from racial bigotry and injustice, and we shall overcome." In the election campaign, in New Orleans, he had said that "All my life all I have heard in the South is 'nigra, nigra, nigra.'"

In passing the Voting Rights Act, Johnson radically altered the politics and sociology of America. He added about five million voters to the rolls, cemented the hold of his party on the African-Americans, but completed the disintegration of the formerly solid white South that since the Civil War (and in fact in all but a couple of elections since Jefferson) had supported the Democrats almost en bloc. It was Johnson's greatest achievement; no one else could have done it, and without it, the racial violence in America would have become much more severe than it did, and so would the country's moral hypocrisy. But the strains of the death throes of segregation would severely disrupt the nation. At the same time, the president poured forces into a war at the ends of the earth on a flimsy constitutional pretext, and without explaining, other than in simplistic invocations of the domino theory, why it was in the national interest to do so (which Eisenhower, the only president who really knew anything about war-making since U.S. Grant, doubted). The role of leader of the opposition became more interesting every week.

Nixon went to Finland for a client later in April, and then went on to Moscow. Khrushchev had been ousted by Brezhnev and others as Communist Party chairman in October 1964. Nixon went to Khrushchev's apartment, but the former party chairman's housekeepers told him that Khrushchev was away. Nixon left a handwritten message, but never received a reply. Khrushchev would die, in obscurity, but unpersecuted, in 1971.

Nixon did lead his train of reporters to Moscow University. He was met at the gate of the institution by the deputy rector, who would not allow Nixon to do his usual foreign university routine and march into a lecture hall and start debating with the students and answering their questions. The Russians knew his methods and would not indulge him. He and the deputy rector had a bit of a debate before the American press contingent. The Klan and the John Birch Society and the Kennedy assassination were bandied about by the Russian, and Nixon responded with references to Beria, the murder of Trotsky, and the suppression of the Hungarian Freedom Fighters in 1956. As before, Nixon was credited with more than holding his own, and there were no preemptive concessions about superior Russian rocketry, as there had been in 1959. The trip generated Nixon a good deal of favorable publicity in the United States, which is why he went to Moscow in the first place – it was entirely a grandstand show. He had no commercial or touristic reason to be there.

Nixon's Vietnam stance was a relatively painless way of pulling conservative support, which he early received from Strom Thurmond, who had rallied to the Republicans when Goldwater was nominated, and William F. Buckley, editor of the *National Review* and undisputed leader of American conservative intellectuals. These people regarded Nixon as rather soggy at the edges on most domestic issues, but solid in national security areas, and all that stood between them and Rockefeller liberals. It was 1968 or never, as Nixon could already feel the hot breath of Reagan, now being strongly pushed as a gubernatorial candidate in California.

Nixon began to assemble a staff, and engaged two speechwriters who would go on to great renown, William Safire and Pat Buchanan. Safire was a moderate Jewish intellectual, and Buchanan a far-right Irish Catholic, and they gave Nixon the speechwriting flexibility he needed to walk the tightrope between the factions to the Republican nomination.

Nixon went on another of his "non-political" trips, to Asia, in August and September, holding press conferences every couple of days. After meeting Chiang Kai-shek in Taipei, he announced that if Red China intervened in Vietnam, the Nationalist Chinese would attack across the Formosa Strait to the mainland. This was a complete fiction, but it was certainly worth a headline. What is not so clear is why Johnson did not use the Nationalist Chinese in Vietnam itself since there were eventually 320,000 Chinese soldiers in support and ground anti-aircraft roles in North Vietnam. In Tokyo, Nixon denounced peace demonstrators in the United States. He moved on to Saigon for three days, and after meeting American and South Vietnamese officials, told the press that Johnson should not speak of negotiations, that such references just made the United States appear weak and would prolong the war. He said that it should be possible to win with 125,000 soldiers in country, within two to three years, as long as the bombing attack and naval blockade on the North were adequately comprehensive. When he returned to the United States, Nixon told viewers of NBC's *Meet the Press* that 200,000 men might be necessary to win, but apart from that, he repeated what he had said in Saigon.

There was some merit in Nixon's military views. While there was an element of rank opportunism in his endless demands of Johnson to fight the war more effectively, this was a legitimate demand. One of LBJ's problems was that he never fought it as an all-out war. He got no credit for restrictions on bombing and only sent the message that the United States was not entirely serious about winning, while making it easier for the North to sustain the war through the Ho Chi Minh Trail and to shoot down American aircraft with a sophisticated ground-to-air missile defense system the Russians were happy to provide.

If Johnson was prepared to undertake the mission at all, he should have got a clear congressional authorization of it, assembled a serious coalition, including sizable numbers of Nationalist Chinese, as well as more South Koreans than the fifty thousand men who were there by 1968, moved much more swiftly to train and equip the South Vietnamese, and absolutely shut down the North as a military supply center by a massive and constant bombing policy and an air-tight naval blockade. And, as Eisenhower had instantly detected, if the war was to be won, the Ho Chi Minh Trail had to be cut. This would require at least seven or eight first-class divisions, and would also require a temporary vacation of the Laos Neutrality Agreement that Kennedy never should have endorsed, and which Hanoi had ignored and Nixon had opposed from the start. All of this could have been done, if Johnson had been prepared to lead, but instead he pretended that the country wasn't really at war at all, that it was conducting a police action while building the Great Society. He maintained this pretense, to mounting outrage and incredulity, even when the United States was losing four hundred draftees in battle deaths most weeks.

There were some resemblances in Nixon's Vietnam policy to the stance Nixon had taken over Korea, but not much resemblance between Johnson's conduct of the Vietnam War and Truman's of the Korean War. Nixon was a partisan of the MacArthur school that "In war there is no substitute for victory." He was right; there wasn't, and it was extremely difficult to convince young draftees that they should be risking or sacrificing their lives for an objective short of victory. By confining the ground war, except for a couple of brief forays into Laos and Cambodia, to South Vietnam, and pursuing an on-again, off-again bombing policy that regularly excluded large and strategic areas of North Vietnam, the United States did enough to lose the war, but not enough to win it. Nixon's criticisms were not entirely partisan and tactical, though there was certainly an element of that in them. He didn't agree with the way Johnson was conducting the war, and he was correct.

The domestic issue Nixon selected as a point of concentration was anti-war protests and disorder on the campuses. Race was too explosive an issue, and he had staked out a position that would collect some support, which would evaporate if he appeared to be trying to exploit the issue. Johnson had won (and earned) the African-American vote. There were third-party threats from the white supremacists. Nixon would get his share of pro-civil rights, anti-violence whites like himself, but there was no advocacy position that was going to gain him any votes. But 90 percent of people resented rioting university students and the left-wing academics who stirred them up. By the autumn of 1965, many of the campuses of America were starting to seethe with protest, partly from antipathy to the draft that loomed on graduation, partly on legitimate principle, partly from the overenergized sanctimony of youth, and partly fueled also by the small indigenous strain of radical left or anarchic sentiment, always stronger in some of the universities than in the country as a whole.

These were perfect foils for Nixon. He divided the country on the issues overwhelmingly in his favor, and those that he was attacking were bound to be even more hostile to Johnson than to him. Supporters of the war effort couldn't fault Nixon for saying he would be a better war leader than Johnson (he was, as it turned out). Opponents of the war effort could hardly shift their fire from the president who plunged them into Vietnam to someone who promised to command the war effort at less cost in American lives.

The majority that still supported the war could back the president while approving Nixon's call for a more effective war policy. And Nixon's attack on the protesters was a good deal better formulated and more disinterested than Johnson's counterattacks on them.

Lyndon Johnson was caught in a tragedy not all of which was of his own making. He had sought the presidency, without much hope of achieving it.

He did so in two steps, by being the only vice presidential candidate in history essential to the election of his running mate (a stronger position than Nixon had had in 1952, when he was important to Eisenhower's nomination but superfluous to his election), and then by succeeding on the tragic death of the incumbent. All his expertise was in the congressional arts, rather than, as Kennedy did to perfection, projecting himself to the country. Johnson never had a large constituency in the people, and always had the Kennedy loyalists, led by Robert Kennedy, relentlessly on his back.

Johnson determined to put through a far more radical program than Kennedy's New Frontier, with his Great Society, and he did so. Johnson had enacted the proposed Kennedy tax cuts, far deeper and more stimulative than Eisenhower's, which had languished after Kennedy proposed them. They were perhaps his greatest legislative success, except for the Voting Rights and Civil Rights Acts. Johnson passed Medicaid, for disadvantaged people, which effectively assured that every American got some level of medical care. He produced welfare enhancements, in fact, subsidized the erosion of the family by assisting single parents and greatly amplified the habit of procreation as a way of opening the window to welfare cheating and dependency. More successful were the Job Corps and many types of aid to teachers and school standards, though they were, again, abused by the teachers' unions. And there were Model Cities (originally "Demonstration Cities" until anti-war and civil rights demonstrations became so militant and widespread that the name became ambiguous) – a measure designed to be the forerunner of massive slum clearance and urban renewal.

Lyndon Johnson was the final, blazing coruscation of the New Deal (Roosevelt), the Fair Deal (Truman), and the New Frontier (Kennedy). He rammed through the measures, and spent and spent until the red ink was ankle-deep, though nothing the country could not handle. As he was doing this, and as he was acting out his apotheosis as the supreme promoter of civil rights, he did what he thought was required in Vietnam, so that he could not be denounced as a weakling by the Republicans.

As a young congressman, he had seen Franklin D. Roosevelt redefine neutrality as making war on Germany in "territorial waters" that extended three-quarters of the way across the North Atlantic, while "lending" the British and Canadians anything they wanted to make war. He heard, though he was not present, of Roosevelt's assurance to Churchill in August 1941 (at their first meeting since 1919) that he would "make war without declaring it." Johnson appears to have surmised that he could conduct a limited war without it interrupting his War on Poverty, led by the Kennedys' brother-in-law, Sargent Shriver, while cutting taxes, making the social safety net leakproof, and advancing civil rights.

In support of this vision, he even adopted, when it was advanced by pundits, the formula *guns and butter*, a phrase, of all unlikely sources for such a liberal inspiration, from Dr. Joseph Goebbels, one of Hitler's closest collaborators. It was as if the Vietnam War was designed to cover his political flank on the right while he made war on poverty and racial injustice. But as casualties mounted toward four hundred dead young Americans a week, and draft calls became more difficult for the middle class to defer or avoid legally, Johnson's coalition started to disintegrate.

Nixon saw almost from the start that it would not work. He shared the interest in civil rights and helping the poor and cutting taxes, and fighting the communists in Indochina. But the cataract of spending programs, spawning bureaucracies of the kind that had repelled Nixon when he served in the Office of Price Administration from 1941 to 1942, was bound to raise hopes and disappoint them. Drafting young men from the ways of peace for short-term tours at the ends of the earth conducting search-and-destroy missions against virtual suicide squads disguised as women and children and innocuous peasants, for an objective short of victory in a mission not clearly connected to the national interest, and on the vague authority of the trumped-up Gulf of Tonkin Resolution, was itself a political suicide mission. Nixon had seen Truman's political position erode in Korea, though it was a clear case of enemy aggression, a conventional war along a defined front, with a serious alliance under UN auspices. Johnson's pretense at merely intervening to get a satisfactory settlement, while not taking America's eyes off domestic social goals, was a prescription for disaster on all fronts.

As long as Johnson was the heir to Kennedy and the alternative to Goldwater, he was safe, despite what many Americans found to be his grating and gauche regionalism. But when Robert Kennedy, who had run as a hawk for the Senate in New York in 1964, became attuned to how the war and opinion were moving, and doubtless developed sincere, as well as opportunistic, reservations, and the alternative was good old Dick Nixon, no longer, in such circumstances, such a bête noire as he had been for the Democrats and independent voters ten and fifteen years before, Johnson's public constituency shrank on both sides. He retained his mastery of the

Congress, at which he was rivaled only by FDR as the greatest genius in the country's history (an especially noteworthy achievement for FDR, given that he had only been a legislator for four years at the end of his twenties, in the New York State Senate).

Nixon needed Johnson to stay where he was, as he would be a much easier opponent than Robert Kennedy, and he needed to play his hard-line anticommunist tune, without the implications of increased casualties, to placate the Goldwaterites, as Reagan began to emerge as a much more formidable leader of the Republican right than Goldwater had been. It was a Byzantine plot, but no one since FDR, the font and master of all modern American political arts, navigated the American political Byzantium better than Richard Nixon.

An issue that arose in the campaign for governor of New Jersey, which, unusually, is held in odd-number years, and fell in 1965, highlighted this point. A self-proclaimed Marxist professor of history at Rutgers University, Eugene D. Genovese said at a teach-in, a particularly tedious phenomenon of the Vietnam era where faculty and students collectively reeducated themselves, that he "welcomed . . . the impending Vietcong victory." The Republican candidate for governor, Wayne Dumont, tried to blow this up into an issue, but his Democratic opponent, Governor Richard Hughes, ignored him, except to make the customary liberal noises about freedom of speech. Eisenhower, Rockefeller, Scranton, Romney, and Rhode Island governor John Chafee, as well as Robert Kennedy, all came to New Jersey and either dodged the issue or, in Kennedy's case, spoke positively of Genovese's right to speak his mind. Nixon saw his chance.

Nixon spoke in New Jersey on October 24, 1965, and showed his tactical dexterity. He addressed the issue squarely, unlike the other Republican heavyweights who had preceded him. He said that every American had a right to any opinion on any subject and, in peacetime, a right to express it. But now, said Nixon, the "United States is at war," and Genovese used a state university, which employs him, "as a forum to . . . give aid and comfort to the enemy." Once again, Nixon had found the majority like a heat-seeking missile.

The United States was not officially at war, but in fact it was, and the fact that it wasn't officially at war merely illustrated Johnson's ineptitude: the hawks thought him half-hearted, and the doves thought him as great and mindless a warmonger as the hawks wanted him to be. Nixon, in attacking Genovese, was championing America's warriors, indicting the commander in chief, and exposing his own rivals as shilly-shallyers. Nixon was largely correct; Genovese had the right to express his opinion, but the unctuous praise of the right to free speech in respect to him by high present and former officeholders, including someone of Eisenhower's military attainments, was tiresome.

Nixon made the same point to a very enthusiastic audience at a New Jersey branch of the American Legion, the same day. He called for the dismissal of Genovese. And, responding to a critical editorial in the *New York Times*, Nixon wrote to that newspaper that "The victory of the Vietcong which Professor Genovese 'welcomes' would mean ultimately the destruction of freedom of speech for all men for all time, not only in Asia but in the United States as well." This was extreme, even for Vietnam-era speeches to veterans' organizations. Nixon certainly did not believe that what he was saying was literally true. Nixon crossed swords with Kennedy, who claimed that what Nixon was saying was like the governor of Mississippi demanding a professor be fired from a state university for advocating integration. This was, in fact, hardly comparable, but Nixon raised the ante, by going back to the philosophical point he had endorsed in debate since high school: "Does the principle of freedom of speech require that the state subsidize those who would destroy the system of government which protects freedom of speech?" Nixon clearly won the exchange with Kennedy, and was a better lawyer than the former attorney general, and a better debater if Kennedy did not have full access to his family's forensic advisers.

Hughes was reelected, but with a plurality six hundred thousand votes smaller than Johnson had carried the state by a year before. The same night, Republican congressman John V. Lindsay was elected only the third Republican mayor of New York in the twentieth century. (The previous one, Fiorello La Guardia, a fusion candidate with reform Democrats, was promoted by Franklin D. Roosevelt as the instrument of his revenge on the Tammany Hall bosses who had bedeviled him for twenty years, and was at best a nominal Republican.) Lindsay ran as a liberal, at least as well to the left as his machine Democratic opponent, Abraham Beame, and the election was enlivened by thirty-nine-year-old editor William F. Buckley, who was the Conservative Party candidate.

Buckley uttered many long-remembered witticisms, including his reply at an all-candidates' debate, when asked to make a brief concluding comment: "No, thank you, I will contemplate the eloquence of my previous remarks," and his response to the question of what would be the first thing he would do if he won the election: "Demand a recount." On election night, Buckley won 13 percent of the vote and made a "victory" statement, saying that "to have won so many votes in the most liberal city in the world is a result that will not go unnoticed in Albany, in Washington, or in Moscow." It was one of America's best-remembered and most intellectually lively campaigns.

Nixon had not uplifted a following as Buckley had, but he had sent a message to millions of receptive Americans. Balancing as always, Nixon went to Salt Lake City and denounced the John Birch Society in the most draconian terms, much to the irritation of his former colleague and Mormon apostle, Ezra Taft Benson (who had been Eisenhower's agriculture secretary). Tacking again, on November 21, on *Face the Nation*, Nixon warned that Vietnam would be an issue in the next election (nearly three years away), and that American military commanders should be empowered to bomb military targets throughout North Vietnam. He opposed Congressman Gerald Ford's call for a declaration of war, as that might increase the possibility of Soviet and Chinese involvement, but he dismissed China as "a fourth-rate military power." (That would have made North Vietnam a sixth-rate military power, but that was not how it appeared to his countrymen who were fighting it.)

Nixon wrote in the December 1965 *Reader's Digest* that North Vietnam had to withdraw from the South, and that South Vietnam's independence had to be assured, and that there should be no negotiation other than to finalize those conditions. He specifically took issue with Senate Foreign Relations chairman William Fulbright, Walter Lippmann, and Martin Luther King, for advocating negotiations. Nixon was again correct. Those people simply wanted withdrawal, and negotiations were a euphemism for pulling out. If that was what America wished to do, it need not negotiate about it. When LBJ asked, in deep frustration, how he could get out of Vietnam, one of his opponents obligingly replied, "By plane and by

---

* Members of the quorum of Twelve Apostles select the head (Prophet) of the Mormon Church.

boat."³³ Nixon warned that if the North won, "The Pacific will become a Red Sea." (He meant ideologically, not geographically.) The dominos were rolled again, including Indonesia; Red China would be "only fourteen miles from the Philippines and less than a hundred miles from Australia." As worldly and well-informed and traveled a man as Nixon must have known that this was twaddle. He could have made his point without recourse to such hyperbole. While Nixon was much more cautious in his comments on his adversaries than in the boiling fugue of his political youth, there were still traces of the Old Nixon. (He and Acheson were joint signatories of a petition calling for supporters of the war to be more vocal.)³⁴

For the first time in ten years, the Republicans appeared to have the upper hand as 1966 opened. They had been lean years for the Grand Old Party since Ike and Dick's reelection in 1956, but after scorching his fingers in California, and as a matter of necessity as well as calculation in 1964, Nixon believed the adage that good things would come to those who wait.

Nixon celebrated the decennial deliverance by starting to campaign for the most promising Republican candidates in January 1966. He selected the districts and states that the Republicans would normally expect to win and that had been lost in the Goldwater rout of 1964. He predicted at least forty gains in congressional districts, which the press, as he had hoped, portrayed as wildly ambitious. He attacked the Democrats as a party divided in Vietnam policy between the ineffectual prosecutors of the war under Johnson, and the appeasers and defeatists, led by people like Fulbright, with the more important Kennedy starting to waffle. Senator Eugene McCarthy of Minnesota was becoming vocally critical of the whole enterprise, and there were stirrings among the friends of Vice President Humphrey, though he was maintaining complete public solidarity with Johnson.

Nixon said the war would be an issue only if Johnson did not fight it vigorously enough, which in effect meant that it would be an issue unless the enemy surrendered or withdrew before the election. Nixon could respond more effectively than Johnson to the anti-war agitators, and could rally the stout-hearted believers in the war more effectively than the president could. The Democrats, said Nixon, were united only in their extravagance and enthusiasm for bureaucracy and overbearing government at home.

He revived traces of the Old Nixon by astonishing allegations. Du Bois Clubs, named after the Marxist black leader W.E.B. Du Bois who had died in Ghana, where he had been living for some years, in 1963, had sprung up around the country and were labeled by the attorney general a communist organization. Nixon was the national chairman of the Boys Clubs of America, and he conceived that the Du Bois Clubs were an effort to subvert and supplant the Boys' Clubs. This revealed imagination, but it also betrayed Nixon's contorted suspiciousness, sometimes verging on paranoia, to imagine that large numbers of people could be duped by mispronouncing Du Bois' name into thinking that his followers were operating boys' clubs. He called it "an almost classic example of communist duplicity and deception." Historian Stephen Ambrose aptly asked, "Who else but Nixon would have seen this particular danger to the Republic?"[35]

For the only time in his life, Richard Nixon pleaded a case before the Supreme Court of the United States in April 1966. He was acting for the family of James Hill, which had been held at gunpoint by intruders, and whose privacy had then been invaded by *Life* magazine. He prepared the case very thoroughly, with the help of Leonard Garment, a less senior lawyer in the firm, and argued it very cogently. He eventually lost the case, *Time, Inc. v. Hill*, 5 to 4, but earned the respect of the entire senior legal community. Appearing as a barrister before the Supreme Court was a feat Bobby Kennedy never attempted. Nixon said he always knew he could not win "a big appeal against the press." He did have the satisfaction of seeing this decision partially overturned in *Gertz v. Robert Welch, Inc.* in 1974.[36]

Nixon was working every corner of an expanding Republican constituency. He spoke in June 1966, at Rochester University, in favor of freedom of speech and dissent, and said that he drew the line in the Genovese affair and generally only at the point where academic freedom was stretched to include overtly favoring an American opponent in a shooting war. It was a respectable position, well formulated in a place where he was not popular.

Eisenhower wrote to him, denying that there were any special rights for academics. Nixon, as usual, and perhaps sensing that he might need Ike one more time after all these years, was too polite to mention that the general could have made these points himself when he spoke in the gubernatorial campaign in New Jersey, when Genovese was an issue. Nixon was the only serious intervener who raised the subject, and Eisenhower, as in dealing with McCarthy and denouncing the Democrats, had left the heavy lifting to Nixon.[37]

A few weeks later, Nixon spoke at a fundraiser for Ronald Reagan, now Pat Brown's confirmed opponent, despite the fact that Reagan accepted financial support from the John Birch Society. He said that he did not "lay down a code of conduct for other candidates" and raised three hundred thousand dollars for Reagan. Of course he did lay down such a code, but Reagan had not offended it, because his own views were not extreme, and attacking the John Birch Society was tactically a free shot; attacking a possible next governor of California and much more servicable successor to Goldwater as leader of the Republican right would be imprudent.

Maurice Stans and Peter Flanigan, an in-law of the Busch family (Anheuser-Busch, the world's largest brewery), helped raise the hundred thousand dollars Nixon needed to conduct his 1966 campaign tour. A few old supporters, sensing they were really starting the ball rolling for the 1968 presidential campaign, chipped in most of the money. Among them were DeWitt Wallace of *Reader's Digest*, Elmer Bobst of Warner-Lambert, and Robert Abplanalp, inventor of the aerosol can. When Abplanalp's check for thirty thousand dollars arrived, one of Nixon's adjutants said, "Let us spray!"[38] William Lear lent Nixon the airplane that had been used in the recent James Bond film, *Goldfinger* (which the villain, after whom the film is named, exited through a window in midair).

He assembled his small team, including John Ehrlichman, a teetotaler, who only joined if Nixon assured him that he, Nixon, did not have a problem with drink.[39] He did, and he didn't. Nixon drank, and sometimes, when tense or tired, had a very limited capacity for alcohol, but he was never a prodigious drinker, and never influenced by it other than slightly and at the very end of the day, when unwinding. He was a man who concentrated fiercely almost all the time, and whose concentration was easily interrupted by alcohol.

— V —

Nixon embarked on another of his highly political overseas trips starting in July 1966. The circuit was familiar: London, Dublin, Paris, Tel Aviv, Karachi, Bangkok, Saigon, Manila, Hong Kong, Tokyo, and Seoul. He held press conferences wherever he went, and in Saigon attacked the anti-war movement in the United States for prolonging the war. Johnson then had 287,000 men in Vietnam, and Nixon now called for 500,000 and, as always, intensified bombing. Johnson obliged a few days later, by blowing up the oil storage depots around Hanoi, begging the question of why he had waited so long.

In the fall, Nixon campaigned in thirty-five states for 105 candidates. He claimed that it was a war for the survival of the Republican Party and the two-party system. He was relaxed, confident, and, with the help of Buchanan and Safire, often amusing. "Anyone who thinks LBJ is a conservative thinks Richard Burton married Elizabeth Taylor for her money." (Since the "pink right down to her underwear" comment on Helen Douglas, Nixon had had a slight trend to verge on salacity, like one of the locker-room boys.) He said that Johnson's "War on Poverty has become a war on prosperity." He still claimed he wasn't running for president again and said that he was "a dropout from the Electoral College because I flunked debating," a good-natured act of unjustified self-deprecation. The word *stoned* had taken on a new meaning with the rise of recreational drug use. This enabled Nixon to convulse audiences all around the country with variants of: "I got stoned in Caracas. . . . It's a lot different from getting stoned at a Jaycee convention."[40] He hammered hard on Vietnam and said that Secretary of Defense McNamara was taking "opium or LSD" if he thought the Vietnam War would be won in a year or two and that Secretary of State Dean Rusk's perception of "light at the end of the tunnel" was an oncoming locomotive. His evaluation of the accuracy of their predictions was correct, even if the imputation of the cause of them was not.

On domestic matters, he cast a wide net for Democrats, advocating the indexing of Social Security payments. He made no compromises on civil rights, never wavering against segregation even in the deepest South. His appeal to the Southern whites was in his insistence that the Northern states cease their hypocritical lecturing of the South, that rioting and violence and crime generally be the subject of a crackdown, and that Vietnam be won with stern measures.

Nixon spoke well, and tailored his remarks to his audiences very artfully. He still had his full share of peculiarities. Political organizer John Sears claimed that Nixon remarked to him, after some far-fetched allegations by Nixon had not gone over especially well with an audience: "I can say things that when the other people say them, they are lies, but when I say them, people don't believe them anyway," presumably meaning that some people disbelieved everything he said. Sears added, "From then on, I realized I was dealing with a very complicated person."[41] Nixon was extremely conversant with every conceivable domestic and foreign issue, but he seemed always more of a tactical than a conviction politician, except sometimes in matters of war and patriotism. The slightly mechanical, stagey way he spoke on most issues left no doubt of his views, intelligence, or determination, but there was always some question about the weight given to simple political tactics in his positions. This is partly unfair, because when he had the opportunity as a policy maker, he was generally not afraid to adopt and stick to unpopular positions.

As Johnson slipped in the polls and Kennedy rose, Nixon greatly amused himself by going around the country rather presumptuously informing audiences that Johnson would dump Humphrey as vice president and replace him with Kennedy. Johnson irritably told the press that he would not be "guided by . . . the predictions of an ex-vice president." Nixon alternately accused Johnson of committing too many resources to Vietnam and mishandling and underusing the resources he had there. Both charges were reasonably well founded.

The administration was having real problems presenting a coherent front. The ambassador to the United Nations, Arthur Goldberg (whom Johnson had talked off the life appointment to the Supreme Court to take the post), said that the United States was prepared to halt the bombing if this was promised to be matched by a "corresponding de-escalation." The Democratic leadership was in a dream world if they imagined that Ho Chi Minh, who had fought for over forty years, and sacrificed the lives of countless countrymen, to lead a united, communist Vietnam, was going to be intimidated by random bombing raids. Nixon demanded that Johnson should "publicly withdraw and repudiate" Goldberg's suggestion, and warned that any such course would be relying on false, communist promises. He was again correct, and exchanged letters with Eisenhower, who wrote him that "The Vietnam War is creating more whimperings and whinings from frustrated partisans than it's inspiring a unification of all Americans in the solution of a national problem."[42] So it was.

Johnson roused the suspicions of almost everyone at the end of September when he announced he was going to Manila to meet with South Vietnamese President Nguyen Van Thieu. Thieu was the plausible leader who eventually emerged after Diem. He had a good record as a general and was a Roman Catholic, though a less publicly militant one than Diem had been. There was no notorious charge of corruption against him and he effectively gathered the fragments of government together without scandal-izing the hypercritical and skeptical American media. The United States was betting on him.

Nixon immediately began publicly to question Johnson's motives in going to Manila at all, and engaged in the traditional ploy of establishing an impossible bar of expectations for an opponent to clear, by urging on Johnson and Thieu a "Pacific Charter" like Roosevelt's and Churchill's Atlantic Charter, which entrenched national sovereignty, democracy, and resistance to the use of international force as universal goals in 1941.

This was pretty far-fetched. No one knew better than Nixon how differ-ent was the stature of Johnson and Thieu to that of Roosevelt and Churchill. And Ho Chi Minh, French master chef Georges Escoffier's former under-study, with his wispy goatee, did not, despite the more robust flourishes of the American Red-baiters, have his hands at the throat of Western civiliza-tion as Hitler had. Nixon suggested that "This is the first time a president has figured the best way to help his party is to leave the country."[43]

Nixon's endless needling did get to Johnson, though much worse was to come. The president replied, of Nixon's predictions of big Republican gains in the midterm elections, that Nixon was "a consistently poor politi-cal prophet," and cited some of his happy public forecasts in the late Goldwater campaign. That Johnson began to engage directly with Nixon was another step toward the former vice president's objective: Johnson effectively recognized him as the leader of the opposition. As Johnson's polls deteriorated, Nixon's own political fortunes, as in a teeter-totter, moved proportionately upward.

On October 13, Johnson again showed how rattled he was becoming by Nixon's relentless harassment. He said in Wilmington, Delaware, that a Republican midterm victory "could cause the nation to falter and fall back and fail in Vietnam." Nixon could not have hoped for more, and replied (again accurately) that the Republicans had given "President Johnson the support for the war that his own party has denied him."[44]

A few days later, Johnson left for Manila and Nixon suggested in his absence that after the elections he should meet with leaders of both parties to map out a bipartisan strategy to win the war "in a year." Apart from the absurd timetable, from someone who was regularly ridiculing the false opti-mism of McNamara and Rusk, this was not a bad idea. Johnson ignored it, which was both a political and a practical mistake. He could have drained a good deal of the partisanship out of the issue, and any input from the Republicans, especially Nixon, would have produced a better strategy than the intermittent escalations interspersed with plaintive requests for negotiations that Johnson did pursue.

Johnson returned from Manila with a peace policy he had agreed with Thieu: if the North Vietnamese withdrew their army from the South and ceased all support for the Vietcong, the United States would withdraw its forces from the South within six months. This was an insane proposal. There was no chance of acceptance, as it did not remotely reflect military realities. If it had been accepted by the North Vietnamese, they would have returned in overwhelming force as soon as the Americans had left. As a pre-election gambit, it was ineffective; the American public had seen enough of false starts and misplaced official optimism.

Nixon waited a week and then had the text of his reply reprinted in the *New York Times* (through Safire's intervention with Harrison Salisbury, the managing editor). Nixon said that mutual withdrawal would "most certainly" lead to communist victory, and asked if Johnson really wanted the South Vietnamese and North Vietnamese to "slug it out" together. Once again, he was right, and the obvious inference was that if that was what Johnson preferred, why not just withdraw over a six-month period and let it happen? From this point on, there was little credence anyone, American or Vietnamese, North or South, could attach to Johnson's war and peace policy.

Nixon's statement was published on November 4. Johnson erupted at his regularly scheduled press conference. He referred to Eisenhower's comment about needing a week to think of an idea suggested by Nixon, and called Nixon "a chronic campaigner" (not an unreasonable charge). Johnson referred sarcastically to Nixon's campaign for governor of California, and to his supposed effort to make himself available for the nomination in 1964.

Eisenhower telephoned Nixon and said, "Dick, I could kick myself every time some jackass brings up that 'Give me a week' business. Johnson has gone too far." Eisenhower could not have doubted what would be made of the gratuitous comment when he said it, and had never retracted or clarified it as emphatically as he should have. The statement he now issued was as good as could be in this strange relationship: "highest personal and official regard . . . one of the best informed, most capable and most industrious vice presidents in the history," etc.[45]

Nixon immediately saw Johnson's outburst as an opportunity, and responded coolly, smilingly, expressing understanding that the president could be tired and irritable after a long trip, but saying that he wasn't going to change his concern for the soldiers and the cause in Vietnam no matter what epithets Johnson hurled at him. At this point, Johnson thought Nixon a weak and discredited challenger. That had been the view of the Democratic leadership since 1962, if not 1960.

Rockefeller, being much closer in policy terms to the Democrats, and a more spontaneous and effervescent personality than Nixon, remained the most formidable opponent to Johnson, as he had been to Kennedy. Robert Kennedy would be a much more dangerous opponent for Nixon than Johnson, and even Humphrey was a more sympathetic figure, a better public speaker, and a less politically damaged figure than Johnson.

The Democrats had been hoping to defeat Rockefeller, now seeking a third term as governor, something only three other New York governors in the century had had (Al Smith, Herbert Lehman, and Tom Dewey). Since his last election, Rockefeller had divorced, remarried, and had a child with his new wife. This was considered extremely controversial at this time. There was a general view, hard though it is to credit, that if he couldn't manage his own life better, how could he run such a large state? Rockefeller's opponent, New York City Council president Frank O'Connor, though a candidate of less personal stature, was a better politician than the governor's previous adversaries, Averell Harriman and Robert Morgenthau.

Rockefeller had spent a great deal of his own money and campaigned with great vigor and determination, and on election day morning, Nixon, despite their rivalry and general lack of rapport, sent Rockefeller a personal note, from one professional politician to another. He wrote: "Win, lose, or draw, you fought a most gallant battle. It took an incredible amount of courage to look at those unfavorable polls early this year and then to make a horse race out of the contest." He praised "that rare ability which you have demonstrated in this contest to fight at your best when the odds were greatest."[46]

The *New York Times* predicted the Republicans would pick up twenty-eight seats in the House and five governorships, with no change in the Senate. Nixon was still judged to have gone well out on a limb predicting forty House seats. As it turned out, the Republicans had one of their greatest nights of the last forty years, gaining 47 House seats, 3 Senate seats, 8 governorships, and 540 seats in state legislatures.

Nelson Rockefeller won by less than a hundred thousand votes. His brother Winthrop was elected governor of Arkansas. Ronald Reagan defeated Pat Brown by over a million votes for the governorship of California, killing the giant-killer, while the giant came back to life. Nixon's close supporter, Robert Finch, was elected lieutenant governor of California with a margin a hundred thousand votes greater than Reagan's. Charles Percy, one of the bright stars of the rising Republicans, was elected to the Senate from Illinois, having been narrowly defeated for governor two years before. George Romney was reelected governor of Michigan by a very large majority. An African-American, Edward Brooke, was elected Republican U.S. senator from Massachusetts by a large majority, under the nose of Teddy Kennedy, and a former municipal official, Spiro T. Agnew, was elected Republican governor of Maryland. It was an unrelievedly dismal evening for the Democrats.

Nixon had not attracted so many votes for the many candidates he supported, most of whom won. But he had attracted increased press attention and funding for them, and praised them all lavishly in front of their electors. He had earned the gratitude of the party as no one else had. In 1966, 70 percent of those candidates for whom Nixon appeared won, and only 45 percent of those for whom he did not appear won.

Rockefeller declared "unequivocally" the day after the election that he would not be a candidate for the presidential nomination in 1968. (No such declaration was believable, especially from him, but it was an indication of his current thinking.) Reagan, not having served a day in elective office, made no such pledge. Both men constituted a threat to Nixon, but Nixon had a long lead for the 1968 nomination. Johnson looked distinctly vulnerable, and there was no reason at this point to conclude that he would not seek reelection, and little chance of Kennedy's taking the nomination away from him if he did. Nixon issued a statement saying the election had been an endorsement of escalation and accelerated victory in Vietnam, and an indication of the revitalization of the two-party system. He said in an interview that "The press are good guys." Much had changed in four years.[47]

Lyndon Johnson determined to intensify the war in Vietnam, believing the optimistic predictions of Robert McNamara and of the commander on the spot, General William Westmoreland, that victory could be had by escalating. Westmoreland called for 100,000 more soldiers, to bring the U.S. total of servicemen in country to 565,000. Johnson promised that he would have them. This mighty effort was still entirely based on the Tonkin Gulf Resolution, which vaguely authorized the president to protect American interests. There was not a significant demand for a congressional upgrade of the authorization process.

Westmoreland began major offensive action, sweeping the Cambodian border areas, attacking the Central Highlands concentrations of enemy strength, and intensifying bombing, both in the Hanoi area and in the approaches to South Vietnam. With such a large number of soldiers in the theater, Johnson became impatient with military bureaucracy, as he never had more than two hundred thousand "trigger-pullers." The rest he deprecated as "Coca-Cola stackers" or "Ban deodorant squads," a reference to the huge PX in Saigon, bigger than all but the largest American department stores, and the colossal supply and recreation operation that accompanied the U.S. effort.

Even with this escalation, the strategy was mistaken. The Soviets and Chinese could still supply the North Vietnamese, and so wide and intricate were the countless trails and jungle roads of what was known as the Ho Chi Minh Trail, so complete was the communist discipline among the population twelve years after Dien Bien Phu that, as Eisenhower had always said, the only way to win in the South was to end infiltration from the North.

To do this, the Ho Chi Minh Trail had to be severed by military action across the trail (hundreds of trails in fact), south of the demilitarized zone (DMZ) dividing North and South, and straight west through Laos to Thailand. The border sanctuaries in Cambodia would have to be got rid of, a full naval blockade of North Vietnam imposed, including the mining of Haiphong and the destruction of all bridges and accesses to the country from China, and it might be necessary to shut down the Cambodian port of Sihanoukville as well. A good deal of the Vietcong military effort was supplied through Sihanoukville, and then through Cambodia to the border sanctuaries of the Vietcong and the North Vietnamese Army, which the hollow and theatrical regime of Prince Sihanouk was powerless to stop, though he would thank the Americans, discreetly, if they could stop it.

The entire air defense network of the North Vietnamese – which enabled them to hurl at American aircraft practically unlimited numbers of SAM missiles, fast-moving surface-to-air missiles the size of telephone poles – would have to be taken out. All the launchers and radars would have to be knocked out and such intensive reconnaissance and aerial bombing maintained to ensure that North Vietnam was defenseless against ceaseless American air attack.

These would be strong measures that would excite controversy at home and opprobrium abroad. There was no real prospect of escalation into conflict with Russia or China, as the United States was only trying to get the North out of the South, not to overrun Ho's regime. Had Johnson determined on such a policy, even at this late date, it might have had a chance of succeeding. His mastery of the Congress was still adequate to assure support, especially as most of the Republicans were pledged to back a tougher war policy.

As the American war effort was escalated, so were domestic protests. Huge and widespread demonstrations built around the country throughout 1967, and especially the march of fifty thousand protesters on the Pentagon on October 21. At the same time, racial disturbances escalated in the country. There were serious riots in African-American areas of many cities, including Harlem (again), Newark, and Detroit, where nearly forty people were killed, and Johnson deployed a third of a division of paratroopers and a number of tanks. These were not image-building snapshots for America the Beautiful, in the eyes of the world or itself.

Though there was little effort to take advantage of it politically in the United States, the domino theory did get a satisfactory workout in 1965, 1966, and 1967. There was an attempted communist coup in Indonesia, the fifth most populous country in the world, apparently with the complicity of the aging dissolute whom Nixon had known for fourteen years, Sukarno. The chief of staff of the Indonesian army, General Abdul Haris Nasution, was almost killed in his home, and broke his ankle jumping a wall, and his young daughter was shot dead. But the general escaped and mounted a terrible counter-coup.

This normally serene and smiling people ran amok, and nearly seven hundred thousand people were massacred, mainly alleged communists, including almost the entire communist leadership, among them the ex-communist leader, D.N. Aidit, dragged from a motor scooter and beaten to death. It was the end of the tiresome pseudo-neutralist Sukarno, and the end of any communist threat to Indonesia also. Sukarno was unlamented in Washington, and Indonesia was a big prize. Indonesian developments were occasionally claimed later (i.e., by Henry Kissinger) to have been a product of America's resistance to communism in Vietnam, but were little mentioned in the United States as they unfolded.

Nixon organized his new presidential bid for office starting shortly after the 1966 elections. He had not stood successfully for election on his own since 1950 and had to erase the "loser" image. He could probably lock up the nomination by continuing to pad around the country schmoozing delegates, much as Goldwater had done, but determined that he had to come through more strongly than as an inevitable benefactor of decades as a party wheelhorse. There were formidable rivals in both parties and the greatest prize could not be had just because it was deemed to be "Buggin's turn." He would run in the New Hampshire, Wisconsin, Nebraska, and Oregon primaries, from March to May. There was no point in California, where Reagan would lock it up.

Nixon also decided to let the "chronic campaigner" rap abate, and pledged to stay out of partisan activity for six months, while touring abroad and trying to seem like a president, as he met foreign leaders with a frequency and apparent seriousness that considerably surpassed the normal activities of a goodwill ambassador for Pepsi-Cola. In successive months he visited Europe, East Asia, Latin America, Africa, and the Middle East.

His tactic would be to build up Romney as a serious opponent, and even a favorite to beat. Rockefeller, as usual, was hanging back in a haze of indecision. Reagan would be premature to throw his hat in the ring at this point. Romney charged ahead, bright-eyed and lantern-jawed, the perfect unwitting foil for Nixon, who doubted that Romney could "hit major league pitching."[48] Nixon was an unlimited storehouse of traditional political turns and tricks. Romney was an energetic and effusive former automobile executive who, as Rockefeller had said, was "sure about what he doesn't know." Nixon would have more trouble selling the national press the notion that Romney was a serious presidential candidate than he would shedding the unjust tag of unelectability hung on him by 1960 and 1962. He was trying to look like a winner by defeating a loser (which Romney was almost sure to be in presidential terms). It was at the borderline, where Nixon often dwelt politically, between fine cunning and mere tricks.

The primaries were still a long way off. There was the perennial charade with Eisenhower, whose endorsement was solicited, and who proclaimed his admiration for Nixon but repeated his "usual custom" of declining to express any preference. In fact, this was not unreasonable at this point; with Reagan and Rockefeller also in the picture, there was no point to Eisenhower's committing himself prematurely. But Nixon was disappointed that so few of Eisenhower's collaborators were prepared to come out for Nixon, the senior member of that administration still active. At this point, Peter Flanigan, Maurice Stans, and Fred Seaton were Nixon's principal organizers.

Nixon left for Europe on March 5. The day before, Bobby Kennedy had called for a bombing halt in Vietnam, and Nixon, at Kennedy Airport, told the press that Johnson was correct and Kennedy was mistaken, that such a policy would mean "prolonging the war by encouraging the enemy."[49] Kennedy had run as a hawk in 1964, and it has never been clear to what extent his change of policy was a sincere reexamination of the war and its effect on America, and to what extent rank opportunism. Many of the bright academics and government service stars that Johnson had inherited from Kennedy, and who had been eager Vietnam participants, were now streaming out the back doors into the tall grass, including, a few months later, Robert McNamara himself, who had said in 1963: "We'll win by '65" and had regularly announced the turning of the corner in Vietnam since.

The CIA refused Nixon a briefing, a churlish act by Johnson, given that Nixon was obviously back as one of the most prominent politicians in the country. Poland refused him a visa, while the U.S.S.R. would allow him to enter but no one of consequence would see him there. Undaunted, he flew to Germany and met with retired federal chancellor Konrad Adenauer, then ninety-one. Adenauer was very fearful of Soviet antics and of what seemed to him the American distraction with Asia. He recommended that the United States seek a rapprochement with China and was concerned that when de Gaulle left the scene, the communists would be a serious threat in France, as they would be also in Italy.

The founder of the Federal Republic and of modern Germany, Adenauer was one of the great statesmen of the postwar world. Arguably the greatest act of statesmanship of the fifty years following the Second World War was Adenauer's rejection of Stalin's offer of the reunification of Germany in exchange for the neutrality of Germany and his success in carrying the West German public with him. Adenauer's suggestions about China had an impact on Nixon. Adenauer had physically embraced Nixon when he arrived; they were not to meet again. The former chancellor died a few weeks later, aged ninety-one. At his funeral, German president Heinrich Luebke seized the right hands of Charles de Gaulle and Lyndon Johnson and thrust them together in an unspontaneous handshake.

Nixon received similar comments from the secretary general of NATO, Manlio Brosio, and from Italian leaders. President Giuseppe Saragat and the foreign minister and sometime premier, Amintore Fanfani, stressed that the United States was too preoccupied with Asia and that the rise of communist sympathies in Western Europe was extremely serious. Nixon's trip to the U.S.S.R. did not achieve much, not only because no one of importance would see him, but also because his attempts to circulate in crowds and engage in candid conversation were foreseen. In Alma Ata, Kazakhstan, as he mingled with a crowd, a bemedalled, uniformed war amputee was pushed forward and debated him about Vietnam. An attempted reenactment of his debate with Khrushchev with an engineer at Sokolniki Park did not really come off.

More successful was his trip to Romania, where the communist dictator, Nicolae Ceauşescu, greeted him very respectfully. Nixon told him that he thought any progress in relations between the United States and China would have to await the resolution of Vietnam and any serious thaw in the Cold War would have to await an opening of relations with China. The Romanian leader expressed interest and doubtless reported the conversation to the Chinese.[50]

Nixon remained only a week in New York before taking to the air again, this time to East Asia. He met with Japanese prime minister Eisaku Sato and other factional leaders in the governing Liberal Democratic Party, who were unanimous in endorsing the American effort in Vietnam. Nixon went on to meet with the eighty-year-old Chiang Kai-shek, whom he described in his memoirs as "a friend and unquestionably one of the giants of the twentieth century." Few would be quite so generous in their evaluation of him. Chiang claimed to be ready at any time to return to mainland China and said the people were ripe for such a thing, as the country was very discontented with communism. Nixon recognized this as unrealistic.

He went on to Saigon and was suspicious of military optimism. He would later write that he "became further convinced that continuation of the administration's policy of fighting a defensive war of attrition would inevitably lead to defeat." The communists "had a total commitment to victory. We had, at most, a partial commitment to avoid defeat."[51] Yet when he returned to New York, he declared that "the defeat of the communist forces in South Vietnam is inevitable. The only question is, how soon?" From Saigon he had urged anti-war Democrats to declare "a moratorium on the kind of criticism that gives aid and comfort to the enemy."[52]

It is difficult to know if Nixon was engaging in revisionism in his memoirs or if he was trying to prop up Johnson opposite Kennedy. He would run more strongly against Johnson, and better against a war leader that could be accused of being ineffectual than against a Democrat not so easily linked to what was widely perceived to be an unsuccessful war policy, one who was proposing to cut and run. If Kennedy were to say the war wasn't worth it and the country should get out, while Nixon was still saying that all Asia would go down if America lost in Vietnam, it would be much less promising than running against Johnson or even Humphrey and saying that he could pursue the war more efficiently. Several Asian leaders told Nixon that it might be time to alter American policy to China, especially now that China and Russia were publicly quarrelling quite vituperatively.

Ray Price, former chief editorial writer for the *New York Herald Tribune* (which had folded, after an industry-wide strike, leaving the quality field in New York to the liberal *Times*), accompanied Nixon. He was an intelligent and discriminating man and he found that Nixon always "spoke extemporaneously . . . and invariably [was] gracious, knowledgeable, and minutely sensitive to the feelings of the host country." When he left the U.S. embassy residence in Tokyo, where he stayed, Nixon shook hands with the entire staff. "They don't vote," he told Price, "but it means a lot to them."[53]

In May 1967, Nixon went to Peru, Chile, Argentina, Brazil, and Mexico, taking Bebe Rebozo with him. This had become a close but strange friendship. Nixon invested with Rebozo in residential real estate acquisitions in Key Biscayne (Miami), and they spent a good deal of time together but didn't seem to speak a great deal. Rebozo was a reliable and caring friend who never asked Nixon for anything, and was a cunning operator in the several businesses where he had made his way from humble origins to some fortune. On this trip, Rebozo doubled as a translator.

There were slightly farcical exchanges when Nixon met with slum-dwellers in Rio de Janeiro. His mixing with the people was a routine that was losing its novelty and wearing thin, like the subsequent Pope John Paul II always kissing the ground when he arrived at a new country. Such things, initially unexpected, once they become expected are rather commonplace. The South American leaders Nixon met said that they were disappointed in Kennedy's Alliance for Progress – that it had raised expectations but not delivered on them. Nixon was rather impressed with the Argentinean president, General Juan Carlos Ongania, who looked for a time like he might be the the de Gaulle of South America. He proved, however, to be rigid and socially antiquated, and though not oppressive by Latin American standards, he had no interest in democracy. At the end of the Second World War, Argentina had had the same standard of living as Canada. Misgovernment, as well as a comparative lack of variety of resources, combined to make Argentina almost a Third World country.[54] Nixon said that "U.S.-style democracy won't work here. I wish it would."

That was the same take-away message from his trip to Africa in June with Pat Buchanan, an even more improbable traveling companion than the enigmatic Rebozo. All the leaders Nixon met asked for more and said that they did not wish to rely on the former colonial powers, but Nixon was uniformly unimpressed with them.[55] He wrote Eisenhower that it would be "at least two generations before . . . anything [Americans] would recognize as freedom" would take hold in Africa.

Nixon went to Israel right after the Six-Day War in June 1967. He had predicted, a week before the war: "In the Middle East, those who want war do not have the power to wage it, and those who do have the power, do not want it." He was correct, as usual in such things, but those who wanted war and didn't have the power to wage it, waged it anyway. Nixon's old friend Nasser convinced himself that he could avenge the Arab world's humiliation at the existence of Israel on what they believed to be Arab land, and redress the military victories of Israel in 1948 and 1956. On incontestable evidence of an imminent attack by Egypt and Syria, Israel struck. Jordan's King Hussein was persuaded by Nasser to enter the war, and Israel cleared the Arab armies out of Sinai and up to the Suez Canal, where they had been eleven years before; out of Jerusalem and the West Bank of the Jordan River; and part of the way to Damascus.

Nixon professed to be impressed, especially after speaking with Yitzhak Rabin, then a practicing general, "by the courage and toughness of the Israeli leaders and people." But he was concerned that this easy and decisive victory had made them overconfident. He claims to have detected "an attitude of total intransigence."[56] He did say that Israel was entitled to keep the territory it had captured until there was a settlement. He had already said, in Athens, before coming to Israel, that there "could be no lasting settlement without the joint guarantee of the United States and the Soviet Union."[57]

Nixon gave the Lakeside Speech at the Bohemian Grove, on the Russian River north of San Francisco, in July. He wrote of the inspiring setting, "a natural amphitheater built up around a platform on the shore of a small lake. Redwoods tower above the scene."[58] It is odd that Nixon, no great outdoorsman, and a very conservative man in habit, not garrulous, soberly dressed at all times, should have found this strange club so bracing. The setting is majestic, and there is an astounding variety of talents grouped at any of their summer weekends. But it is still a superannuated boys' club. (Perhaps this is the key, as Nixon was, as has been mentioned, the chairman of the Boys Clubs of America.) The lavatories are a hike from the bedrooms, almost all of which are dual or multiple occupancy; and trees substitute as plumbing for the most frequent bathroom function. There is virtually no privacy, and the atmosphere of obligatory concelebration, costume farce (known as "Lo-Jinks"), and reciprocal laudatory incantations must have appealed to Nixon precisely because it was so foreign to him. He never enjoyed such unstructured camaraderie at any other time. As with so many other accomplishments of his career, he may have thought that to be fêted as he was, in such surroundings and by such people, was a triumph of his iron will. So it was on this occasion.

Herbert Hoover had given the Lakeside Speech for many years, but had died in 1964, aged ninety. Nixon's address was in his honor. It was a genuine connection, as Nixon had first met Mrs. Lou Hoover as a Whittier College trustee more than twenty-five years before and had often consulted with the former president. He dazzled the audience with his world tour, describing the elements of the crises and prospects of each region and most major countries, and concluded that the United States could certainly lead the world toward a durable peace, if the American people possessed the will to do so. It was very warmly received by this immensely wealthy and influential audience.

Nixon also wrote a piece for *Foreign Affairs*, the journal of the Council on Foreign Relations. He focused on Asia, predicted American victory in South Vietnam, reasonably soon – presumably, again, to encourage the Democrats to favor Johnson over Kennedy. This must be only conjecture, but it conforms to Nixon's always complicated and almost compulsively devious methods. He proposed an expanded successor to SEATO, of which he had been something of a godparent, and thought it might extend "even" to India. He also called again for the end to the self-imposed constitutional restrictions on Japan's recourse to a military capability, as he had when he visited Tokyo as vice president in 1953, and many times since.

The article is best remembered for Nixon's proposal for a new relationship with China, after the Chinese leaders "turn their energies inward rather than outward." Since they were already extremely preoccupied, albeit in very eccentric ways, with internal issues, as the supreme madness of the Great Cultural Revolution stoked up, the message was clear, though few took it in, that Nixon thought it was time to explore a reopening of relations with China after a lapse of eighteen years. Nixon had listened to the recent urgings of Adenauer and Sato,[*][59] and he had also known to discount the ruminations of Chiang Kai-shek, seventeen years after he had inelegantly taken to the boats in the Formosa Strait. The key words were a call to "come to grips with the reality of China . . . We simply can not afford to have China forever outside the family of nations, there to nurture its fantasies, cherish its hates, and threaten its neighbors." He was explicitly not calling for instant recognition of the regime in Beijing.[60]

— VII —

While still at the Bohemian Grove, Nixon started to negotiate with Reagan, who was also there. Reagan had already learned the old Earl Warren canard about running as a California native son to preserve party unity. Nixon had revealed that for what it was in 1952, and didn't bother debating the point

---

[*] Another long-standing influence for opening up relations with China was Nixon's generous backer Elmer Bobst, son of a missionary in China, who had spent much of his youth in that country.

with California's new governor. Other Bohemians present included Texas's Senator John Tower and Florida's Governor Claude Kirk, who warned Nixon that Reagan had a great deal of incipient support in the South.

Ronald Reagan was much disparaged as an ex-actor, as if that were an undignified occupation, especially in starstruck America. It didn't deter the voters of the country's most populous state from ejecting, by over a million votes, an apparently popular governor who had defeated Nixon four years before. And Reagan was clearly a rising political force. He was conservative, but so, increasingly, in response to racial violence, campus unrest, and the Vietnam imbroglio, were tens of millions of Americans. He was a fine-looking man, a familiar and reassuring name and face, having been a prominent actor and television personality off and on for more than twenty-five years. And he was a spellbinding, overwhelmingly persuasive, velvet-voiced orator. Ronald Reagan had no rivals since Franklin D. Roosevelt, and no superiors among prominent American politicians since voices were recorded, in his ability to move and win political audiences by the power of his verbal delivery and manner. Nixon was too knowledgable in these areas not to realize what a factor Reagan could be.

But Nixon had many strengths. He was a good public speaker, spoke from memory, and was an encyclopedia of facts and political sensibilities, unlike Reagan, whose delivery was magnificent but who was never fast on his feet in repartee or responding to probing press questions. Nixon had piled up a bank of IOUs from the party apparatus in every state over twenty years, and he was calling them all in. Reagan could wow the right, but he frightened the center and scandalized the liberal Republicans.

Rockefeller was formidable in all respects. Like Reagan, he was a gregarious and attractive and apparently spontaneous political personality, but he had completely alienated the right of the party. Nixon had to mobilize his strength, rather as he had in his porcupine mode when resisting the caprices of Eisenhower and his entourage during his fight to retain the vice presidential nomination in 1952 and 1956. He had to gather his forces at the center of the Republican Party, extend the center as far as he could to right and left, be the first choice of more delegates than anyone else, and be the second choice over Rockefeller to the Reaganites, and over Reagan to the liberals. He had to ensure that the center was a position of tactical strength, and not a vulnerable, melting mass of ice cream from which both sides could drain support. If he could carry off the theory that George

Romney was a serious candidate, whose defeat by Nixon could solidify the center, so much the better.

Where Nelson Rockefeller was a schismatic Republican, powerful but strangely indecisive, and not popular with party regulars outside the Northeast, Reagan could take the conservatives, if he could delay matters until it would not seem indecently presumptuous for him to make a run at the presidency. Reagan and Nixon agreed that there would be no sarcastic references by them or their partisans to "losers" and "actors" by the one camp or the other, and this was honored. Reagan urged his supporters in the South to defer coming out for Nixon while Reagan settled in as governor and had the time to seek the nomination without being unseemly in his haste.

Nixon set out to defeat the charge of deviousness. What he was really doing was attacking the charge of being unelectable, but he realized that if he said that he was trying to avoid being thought a loser, it would be too tempting to too many people to make him one. A candidate for president of the U.S. campaigning on the theme that he was not a loser was too absurd to be practical. So what Nixon did was claim to be aggrieved that he was still being reviled as "Tricky Dick," though that epithet had not been much used for years. This at least enabled him to take the moral high ground, claim to be an underdog, and continue breathing hope into the barely aerodynamic diversionary balloon of Romney, whom few took more seriously than Nixon did.

Nixon went on a round of interviews, almost indiscriminately, with political journalists. They all went quite well; there was little newsworthy in them, but Nixon projected himself as a pleasant and worldly, unfrightening person. It was toe-curlingly bland treacle, but useful to the last stage of his process of apparently effortless reentry on the great national stage.

On October 18, 1967, Nixon was in Washington and held a reception in the office of the Republican Whip, Leslie Arends, for all those congressmen and senators whom he had supported in the 1966 elections, and other kindred spirits. He was relaxed and confident, and knew a lot about each of the congressmen. Reagan and Rockefeller could not claim any such background of support, or knowledge of the individuals.

Nixon assembled a first-rate group of policy people in domestic areas, and began to outline proposals for tax and welfare reform that would gather strength over the next fifteen or twenty years. Daniel Patrick Moynihan, a florid and colorful personality, and free-thinking Harvard professor, had studied the African-American family and the impact on it of LBJ's Great

Society programs. It shortly emerged that, with the best intentions, Johnson had legislated aid to dependent children as long as their fathers were absent from the home. This was the virtual death-knell of the black family in homes below the middle-class education and income level, which was still a majority of them.

Nixon borrowed from Moynihan and University of Chicago economist Milton Friedman the negative income tax as a welfare supplement. He concluded that sending school buses loaded with children around metropolitan areas to achieve racial balance was insane, educationally, sociologically, and politically; and that the black ghettos had to be improved through the private sector, incentivized by the government. Nixon's policy team furnished him with ample arguments and catchy speech phrases that debunked traditional leveling of slums, population movement, and increased government supervision of growing numbers of the underprivileged. It was clear to Nixon that the key to raising the living standards of the poor was job creation, and the two keys to reducing the crime rate were less unemployment and more police.

He claimed in speeches that were well received throughout the country that the United States had become "the most lawless and violent nation in the history of free peoples . . . Far from becoming a Great Society, we are becoming a lawless society."[61] Parts of the great LBJ domestic program were becoming a terrible albatross to the incumbent.

On Vietnam, Nixon stuck to his line that the war had to be won, and could be won, "in about a year . . . The last desperate hope of North Vietnam is that they can win politically in the United States what our fighting men are denying them militarily in Vietnam."[62] He was trying to bring on Johnson's supporters while discouraging them from defecting to the anti-war movement.

As 1967 drew toward a close, it was becoming harder for Nixon to keep up the pretense that defeating Romney constituted victory over a serious opponent and proof of Nixon's electability against Johnson or Kennedy. Romney had been to Saigon on a fact-finding mission, and came back reinforced in his enthusiasm for the Vietnam effort. But in September 1967, he told a Detroit broadcaster that "I just had the greatest brainwashing that anyone can get when you go over to Vietnam." LBJ commented that he "must have gone quietly into a corner and brainwashed himself." This was the end of Nixon's Romney charade, as the Michigan governor's campaign began to implode. Nixon had predicted that Romney would have trouble with the national press corps, but not that he would hit the wall with the media before he left Detroit. Nixon gamely continued to claim that Romney was a strong opponent.

More fortuitously for Nixon, Reagan's quick-march to a presidential candidacy was delayed by the exposure of a homosexuality controversy in the California governor's staff. Reagan himself was certainly nowhere near it personally, but it was a distraction and slowed his timetable.

Nixon cleverly leapfrogged the candidates by challenging Johnson to a series of debates in 1968. The challenge, which was a bit nervy, was ignored by the president, since Nixon was just assuming the role of leader of the opposition with no authority. The fact that the press did not ridicule this effort indicated how far Nixon had come in establishing himself as the Republican spokesman. Presidential debates, only started in 1960, were legislated to be between the major party, nominated candidates, not aspiring candidates throwing down gauntlets before election year had dawned and before the primaries had even begun.

Hannah Nixon died on September 30, 1967. She had been in a nursing home for two years, unable to recognize anyone, so her death was not unmerciful or surprising. She was eighty-two. The funeral was in the Friends' Church in Whittier, where Nixon had attended and then later taught Sunday school. Billy Graham officiated, and at the end of the service, Richard Nixon, overcome by the flood of memories of his mother and earlier deceased family members, all buried from this church and interred together nearby, briefly lost his composure, as he embraced Graham. His last exchange with his mother was two years before, as Mrs. Nixon was about to undergo an operation. He said to her: "Don't give up." She sat up in bed, a great physical effort in her condition, and said, "Richard, don't you give up. Don't let anybody tell you you are through."[63]

Nixon visited Eisenhower at Gettysburg on October 17. The seventy-seven-year-old five-star general was now much more of a hawk on Vietnam than he had been when in office. He told Nixon that Johnson had been eighteen months late putting in ground combat troops, bombing the North, and setting out to build support for the war. (Inserting ground forces eighteen months earlier would have required giving the order the day after President Kennedy's funeral, which would have been, to say the least, inopportune.)

Nixon agreed with Eisenhower, but put some distance between his former chief and himself after Eisenhower said on November 28 in a television interview that American forces should be authorized to cross the DMZ separating North and South Vietnam and enter Laos and Cambodia to stop infiltration. Nixon, when asked, said that Ike was "absolutely right" militarily, but "From a political standpoint, I would be very reluctant to take action that would be regarded as an invasion of North Vietnam, Cambodia, or Laos."

The war could only be won by the United States militarily, and not politically, and Eisenhower had again recognized that the infiltration from the North had to be stopped, or the war would be endless and unwinnable. Neither Nixon nor the television interviewer asked Eisenhower if Johnson was eighteen months late in his escalations, whether Eisenhower would now like to revisit his decisions about Indochina at the time of Dien Bien Phu and after – whether he believed the United States should have become directly involved in Indochina at all. He had always thought not. Nixon knew that Eisenhower's military view was correct, but was not prepared to enter a political year promising to make Johnson's war policy more effective by invading three more Indochinese countries. Unfortunately, he didn't entirely adopt Eisenhower's recommendation as a post-election strategy either.

At a Republican governor's meeting in Palm Beach in October 1967, Nixon had arranged for the pro-Rockefeller governor of Colorado, John Love, and the quasi-Reaganite governor of Montana, Tim Babcock, each to say Nixon would be an acceptable candidate for president if he could win "the first two or three primaries." This was his plan to drop the "loser" tag, using Michigan governor George Romney as a punching bag, before Rockefeller or Reagan entered the race, and having the formula endorsed by governors of the liberal and conservative wings of the party.[64]

On November 30, the engagement was announced between Julie Nixon and David Eisenhower, the ex-president's grandson. They were an attractive young couple, and the story got wide play. A happy event in itself, it also seemed to strengthen Nixon's lengthy campaign to make himself Eisenhower's legitimate political heir. Eisenhower, when questioned by reporters if this new connection would cause him to endorse Nixon for president, again went on autocue and drearily recited his timeworn formula of praising Nixon but saying that he would endorse the Republican nominee when he was officially chosen.

Nixon claimed at the end of 1967 to have a crisis of indecision about running for president, which he had in fact been doing for the last five (or fifteen, or twenty) years. He consulted Billy Graham, who urged him to run, and had Rose Mary Woods to a family dinner on January 15, 1968, to talk it over. The couple who worked in the Nixon home, Fina and Manolo Sanchez, fugitives from Castro's Cuba, joined the discussion too. Everyone except Pat wanted him to seek the presidency, and Pat kept her own counsel. Nixon wept after his children and most intimate staff said he owed it to the country, the world, and himself to run, and finally said that he had decided to make the race, which could hardly have been a surprise to his dinner companions. It was part of his Quaker heritage and no affectation to consult the domestic staff as complete equals. One can hardly imagine the aristocratic Roosevelt or proud General Eisenhower doing the same. It is not clear whether he went through this as the domestic version of engineering a draft, to generate a bandwagon that his wife could not oppose, or because he required all important decisions to be the product of wrenching emotional catharses. In his own way, he had taken his decision.

It was an irony that Lyndon Johnson, a talented man trying to overcome what Dr. Samuel Johnson had famously called "the disingenuousness of years" of his manipulative political past from the rotten borough of Texas and the teeming lobbies of the Congress, should have embraced all respectable policy options at once, in a combustible mélange. The tax cuts produced revenue increases and a briefly balanced budget, an isolated event in decades of deficits. Civil rights legislation addressed a horrible problem, but the lid could not be removed from the pressure cooker without an explosion at a most unwelcome time. In trying to protect himself on the right by being "tough" with international communism in Vietnam, Johnson stepped, and sank, into a quicksand morass. In trying to limit the war, he made it militarily and politically unwinnable. In trying to alleviate poverty, he promoted welfare addiction and cheating. And in raising expectations by promising everything to everyone, he assured the disappointment of almost everyone.

Possessing the skills of interpersonal, congressional logrolling, he lacked the mass appeal of a Roosevelt or a Kennedy (Jack or Bobby), or even Nixon, much less Reagan. Johnson was a talented and deeply well-intentioned, and in some respects a courageous man, but all he knew about being president came from watching at very close range men with different aptitudes and greater natural public support than he (his four predecessors in that office). The wheels came off his great 1964 coalition in all four directions. Yet he remained a formidable and generally admirable figure to, and beyond, the end of his life.

It would be an advantage to the nation that the beneficiary of Johnson's discomfort was someone who knew and even empathized with Johnson's political problems. And though Nixon exploited them for partisan ends, he was interested in a bipartisan consensus, having toiled for many years, earlier in his career, in the thorny vineyards of factional stridency.

Classical tragedy was afflicting the American presidency. Hoover, a great talent, took office as his skills and experiences became irrelevant, and even a hindrance, to coping with the unprecedented economic and psychological crisis that soon befell the country in the Great Depression.

Roosevelt led the country out of the Depression and through the war, and died on the eve of his supreme triumph.

Truman, of whom not much was expected, proved a distinguished president, who became caught in the coils of Asian war. He passed from the scene in an involuntary spontaneous career suicide pact with another outstanding subaltern of Roosevelt's, General Douglas MacArthur.

Dwight D. Eisenhower, cleverer than he seemed or admitted, and outwardly amiable, came in on a wave of respect and affection he never lost. He dodged the presidential curse, and was, with Coolidge, the only one of the thirteen presidents in the seventy-two years between Theodore Roosevelt and Ronald Reagan (1909 to 1981) to leave the White House voluntarily and in good health and standing with the voters. But Ike gradually became, as British commentator Malcolm Muggeridge later said, "an indulgent nanny putting America to bed." His own grandson, David Eisenhower, wrote to his future father-in-law, Richard Nixon, in January 1968, that Dwight Eisenhower was "now regarded as a simple country bumpkin and a sweet old general."[65]

John F. Kennedy, a Wagnerian Siegfried, cut down beside his wife and before the camera and admiring crowds, was the most obvious tragedy of all.

And Lyndon Johnson, full of energy, ability, and the benignity of the convert to the highest office, was destroyed by forces he did not understand and was not equipped by experience, temperament, or intellect to master.

In the wings now, another potentially tragic figure: Richard Nixon carried a self-destructive apparatus in his campaign knapsack, but like the others, he too would address the problems of his predecessors. Roosevelt cured the Depression, and the once-reviled Hoover survived Roosevelt by many years and became a revered elder statesman. Truman won the peace that Roosevelt engineered, and adapted to the postwar challenge the alliance Roosevelt had created. Eisenhower was an annealing continuator who ended the war that had consumed Truman and MacArthur. All three lived into old age, honored, as they deserved to be honored, as great men of America's and the modern world's history. Kennedy was the allegory of revitalization, and was universally mourned. Johnson enacted and amplified his program. It would be left to Nixon to liquidate the scourge of war that was destroying Johnson's presidency, to complete the desegregation of the African-American, to hose down the seething factions of America, and to create a new foreign policy for a changed world. His successors would deal with the problems that would torment Nixon, and he, too, in his unique, almost incredible way, would become a sage and respected elder statesman.

Thus would America pass from isolationism, laissez-faire economics, and a rather juvenile relationship to the world, in the twenties, to the eminence, earned by painful experience, excruciatingly traced in the lives of its leaders, of a stable and unprecedentedly powerful nation-state, the world's only superpower, sixty years after Hoover's election. The new year would announce one of the five or six stations in this dolorous, but impressive, intense, absorbing progress. It was 1968, which would prove one of the most tumultuous and momentous years of modern times, like 1789, 1848, or 1914.

PART III

—

The Pursuit of Peace

1968–1972

Chapter Nine

Tumult and Victory
1968–1969

— I —

AFTER THE FINAL LAUNCH from his household, Richard Nixon prepared
a basic campaign speech with Buchanan and Safire and a few others, and
took the tompions out of the campaign guns he had been massing for
some time. His organization was in place, and sent out 150,000 letters to
the homes of New Hampshire announcing the unsurprising news that
he was joining Romney in the quest for the Republican presidential
nomination. In the letter, Nixon emphasized his experience and
demurely remarked that over "the past eight years I have had a chance to
reflect upon the lessons of public office. . . . I believe I have found
some answers."[1]

Nixon's candidacy was announced as the letters were delivered to
their addressees in the Granite State, on February 1, 1968. Nixon's
announcement was not featured, because of competing news. The Viet
Cong and North Vietnamese had launched what appeared to be a general
offensive beyond what Westmoreland and McNamara had represented as
their capabilities. An enemy suicide squad had penetrated the U.S.
embassy compound (but not the chancery itself) and fired at close range
at the presidential palace. Intense fighting was underway, in what became
known, after a local holiday, as the Tet Offensive, in almost every city and
town in South Vietnam.

At the same time, McNamara, in a final appearance before the Senate Armed Forces Committee,[*] revealed that in the last year the U.S.S.R. had doubled its intercontinental ballistic missile forces and now enjoyed parity with the United States in this supreme category of military power. McNamara represented this as desirable, because it gave the two sides an equal incentive to avoid war. As Kennedy had somewhat presaged in his inaugural address of seven years before, the United States had deliberately allowed a state of "mutual assured destruction" to emerge, reversing the Truman-Eisenhower policy of retention of clear nuclear superiority with the doctrine of massive retaliation. There had been no serious national debate on this issue; the administration had simply allowed it to happen, and then its outgoing defense secretary proclaimed it a welcome development and a part of the Kennedy-Johnson plan for "flexible response," of which Vietnam was illustrative.

It was completely spurious reasoning; one nuclear device that was deliverable by either country against the other was a perfectly adequate incentive to avoid war and nothing useful was gained by allowing the Soviets equality at the top of the military scale when they already had greater conventional strength. It must be said that this was not the whole story, as the United States retained greater bomber-delivered nuclear capability, and a wide technological advance in putting Multiple Independently Targeted Reentry Vehicles (MIRVs) – i.e., separately targeted warheads – on intercontinental ballistic missiles (ICBMs). But the whole concept of giving away a large part of nuclear superiority and calling it progress while the country was mired in South Vietnam, where every hamlet was aflame, and one of the most opinionated defense secretaries in history skipped out the back door of the Pentagon, was unsettling to the country.

Nixon's candidacy ranked below these stories, and along with Johnson's plan for a 10 percent surcharge on income taxes to pay for Vietnam and the now self-mockingly described Great Society. Nixon launched his campaign

---

[*] McNamara's replacement was the elegant and prominent Washington lawyer Clark Clifford, former counselor to President Truman. Bobby Kennedy said that Johnson "might as well have named Attila the Hun." Kennedy misjudged Clifford, who had already concluded that the Vietnam War could not be won on any acceptable basis. (That is not to say that Attila, if available, might not have been a competent nominee.) Clifford had returned from a trip around East Asia in 1967 with General Maxwell Taylor, concerned at their inability to drum up more support from allies.

in Manchester, New Hampshire, on February 3: "When the strongest nation in the world can be tied down for four years in Vietnam with no end in sight; when the nation with the greatest tradition of respect for the rule of law is plagued by random lawlessness; when the nation that has been a symbol of human liberty has been torn apart by racial strife; when the president of the United States cannot travel at home or abroad without fear of a hostile demonstration, then it is time America had new leadership."[2]

Another omen of the new year had been furnished on January 23, when North Korea had seized an American intelligence vessel, the *Pueblo*, that apparently strayed into North Korean waters and was unprotected. The liberal press, in the United States and elsewhere, irritatingly insisted on calling it a "spy ship," as if there were anything improper about monitoring radio signals from international waters. Johnson huffed and puffed, but nothing happened. The crew of eighty-two was roughly treated and was eventually released in December 1968, but the ship became a museum of American perfidy. The rather trivial episode highlighted the appearances of American sneakiness and impotence.

Nixon had abandoned his former frenetic campaign style of hanging around factory gates and speaking from the backs of cars. He ran a television blitz, based on what became known as the "Hillsboro meetings," where he met with a few followers in front of a camera and was always very effective. His television group excerpted parts of his meetings, as well as of speeches to larger groups, and his amply financed campaign could put them on television. The candidate almost completely avoided the press. Nixon quickly lived down the tag of the "last press conference" and the first 1960 debate, and even the sniggerings of those who had been offended by the kitsch aspect of the Checkers speech, and buried the myth that he was not a capable television exponent. He was immediately superior in this vital skill to Johnson, and as good as Rockefeller and Humphrey. Bobby Kennedy was still almost an unknown quantity as a campaigner, and Reagan would be in a class of his own.

It was a dignified, relaxed campaign, almost like an incumbent with a comfortable lead in the polls. Rockefeller had said again that he would not run, but uttered the most hackneyed cliché of American politics, that he would accept a draft. (The last one was in honor of General George Washington; even the draft of FDR in 1940 to a third term was an unspontaneous hoax executed on instruction by the Chicago Democratic machine.) The campaign slogan, "Nixon's the One," was apt and effective. (Witty opponents produced a poster with Nixon's slogan under a photograph of a heavily pregnant young woman in a Girl Scout uniform.)

Nixon had lived as long as he could on the myth of a viable Romney candidacy. The Michigan governor, floundering after the claim to have been brainwashed, was down to 10 percent in the polls and withdrew at the end of February. His last shot was to challenge Nixon to debates, which Nixon (who would have won the debates easily), declined because he said the only beneficiary of such debates would be Lyndon Johnson.

On the Democratic side in New Hampshire, Senator Thomas McIntyre was a stand-in for President Johnson. The only challenger was Minnesota Senator Eugene McCarthy, who ran a stylish but eccentric anti-war campaign. McCarthy was recruited by Congressman Allard Lowenstein, after General James Gavin, economist John Kenneth Galbraith, and Senator George McGovern of South Dakota had declined. McCarthy was galvanized when Undersecretary of State Nicholas Katzenbach told a Senate committee in November 1967 that the Gulf of Tonkin Resolution had the effect of a declaration of war.[3] He said it had "to be taken to the country," and he did so himself. With Romney's withdrawal, the Republican anti-war vote moved to McCarthy. Johnson had not taken McCarthy's candidacy seriously, as it was assumed that an incumbent president could ignore such a fly-by-night challenge.

It was too late for New Hampshire, but Alabama Governor George Wallace announced at the end of February that he would be the presidential candidate of the American Independent Party. Johnson's position was being attacked from right and left, but he still appeared to be holding the core of Democratic support, and he and Nixon were running about evenly in the polls. The economy was strong; Johnson had earned the African-American voters, a great many of whom owed their right to vote to him. He had cut the nation's taxes and still had the support of about half the people for his Vietnam policy.

The first week of the Tet Offensive had caught the American high command clearly off guard. Westmoreland complained of enemy "ruthlessness," as if that were an unwarlike quality. Finally, as the enemy was beaten back with heavy casualties in every part of the country, though the battle for the old capital of Hue went on for three weeks, Johnson declared victory, but not very convincingly. Westmoreland stated that the kill-ratio was twenty to one in the Americans' and their allies' favor. He was probably correct, but the public was tired of it. They had been assured that after the huge draft calls and the endless body bags returning at the rate of two to four hundred a week (spiking up to over eight hundred during Tet and a thousand in one week in May in post-Tet mopping-up operations), the United States would prevail, and yet it had barely been able to keep the enemy out of its own embassy. It didn't look to the skeptical U.S. media like a victory for the Americans and South Vietnamese, but militarily it was a great victory. Only in the mind of the American public and the world did it not appear to be one, and Johnson did not have the energy or credibility to send the correct message.

Now, Westmoreland asked Johnson for 206,000 more troops. This was politically out of the question. Westmoreland compared Tet to the Battle of the Ardennes in 1944, when Eisenhower had asked for reinforcements, but this was nonsense. The Western Allies were then almost at the Rhine, having cleared France; victory was in sight in a declared war against a mortally dangerous enemy, and Eisenhower asked for nothing more than the two new divisions a week that were already pouring into the Western Front from America, Britain, and Canada. The proportions of Johnson's over-investment in the believability of his military and civilian advisers now came home to him. He had followed the advice of the Kennedy entourage, though not Eisenhower's or MacArthur's, both of whom had warned him against inserting ground forces into Indochina. Kennedy's people, except for Rusk and Rostow, had gone and it was Johnson's war, and he did not know what to do next. While he unconvincingly claimed a victory, Robert Kennedy said the war could not be won. As Johnson announced that he was canceling draft deferments for graduate students, Nixon announced that when the Vietnam War was over, he would abolish the draft. This was a deft and, as it turned out, sincere move.

In his first months as defense secretary, Clark Clifford canvassed a task force Johnson had established to consider Westmoreland's request for 206,000 more soldiers. No one could see any satisfactory end to the war. In fact, even without this force, they could have cut the Ho Chi Minh Trail and that might have ended the war, but no one had any stomach for it anymore.

To salvage his position and his war policy, Johnson would have had to announce not only a victory, but that the enemy had plunged into a trap that had been baited for him, and that it was now possible to begin staged withdrawals and hand the war over to the South Vietnamese gradually. Johnson did not show any such powers of improvisation. He repeated the proportions of the setback to the enemy, but gave the country no assurance that the North Vietnamese would not be back for another such death-dealing assault after a few months of replenishment. The American public understood that large numbers of enemy forces were being killed, but killing Vietnamese communists was not their primary objective; winning and getting out were the twin objectives, and after four years of inflicting horrifying casualties on the enemy, there was no reason to believe that winning and leaving were particularly closely connected to killing enemy guerrillas or regular forces. The North Vietnamese and Viet Cong seemed to be unaffected by casualties.

Nixon essentially dodged the subject of Vietnam until March 5, when he spoke to the American Legion in Hampton, New Hampshire. It was a canard of subsequent invention that he patted his breast pocket and assured his listeners intimately, "I have a plan," or even, according to the more elaborate version, "a secret plan." Nixon said he was not advocating an abrupt withdrawal, but that by "mobilizing our economic and political and diplomatic leadership," the war could be ended. This was pretty fuzzy, but there was a vague feeling that Johnson had not been very creative diplomatically, and that Nixon would probably be fiercer and more effective in his use of air power, since he had been advocating its application in Vietnam for twelve years.

That evening, March 5, Nixon was in Washington and could not altogether avoid the press corps at a large fund-raiser. He opened the "economic and political and diplomatic" kimono a little by saying that there were ways of enlisting the Soviet Union to assist in the pursuit of peace instead of just fuelling the war. His new pledge was to "end the war and win the peace." He said that Johnson had ignored the non-military options available to the United States.

Nixon was still being a little coy, and said, even to Eisenhower, who earnestly wrote asking what he had in mind,[4] that he did not wish to "undercut whatever diplomatic negotiations might be underway at present." And he did not want to squander his own flexibility when he became president. Nixon was using terminology like de Gaulle's in ending the Algerian War. "Peace with honor," said Nixon (a phrase of Disraeli's from the Congress of Berlin in 1878). De Gaulle had said a "peace of the brave." Nixon was not seeking victory, but the repulse of aggression and the preservation of South Vietnam. He invoked the Korea precedent (having, as will be recalled, been an advocate of a more ambitious and victorious peace at the time).

He couldn't go all the way to the nomination on this pablum, and soon started talking about more vigorously preparing the South Vietnamese, many of whose units had performed creditably during Tet, to take over more of their own defense. Costly U.S. "search and destroy" missions would be scaled back. He also repeated his calls for intensified air and sea war, and added the Chinese to the Russians as a power that the United States could recruit to assist in ending the war. These were substantive conceptual changes, little noticed in the fast-paced fury of the developing election campaign.[5] But the only way to force the North Vietnamese to negotiate seriously was to combine overwhelming and relentless air war with a complete severance of the Ho Chi Minh Trail, and Nixon, as he had made clear in his slight public disagreement with Eisenhower the previous October, was not prepared to course toward election calling for the invasion of the three other Indochinese countries.

Vietnam was the overriding election issue, but Nixon got good mileage out of crime and violence as well. He blasted the conclusions of Johnson's Commission on Civil Disorders, chaired by Illinois governor Otto Kerner, which claimed that "white racism" in America was mainly responsible for group violence. Nixon claimed that the commission "blamed everybody for the riots except the perpetrators of the riots." In a nationwide radio address on March 7, Nixon promised to reply to "force with force," and urged Johnson to be ready for those who were threatening and planning violence for the summer of 1968. He said this had more the character of a war than a "spontaneous outburst" of rioting. He was technically correct, but calling for force to be applied so freely in domestic disputes gave pause to many who agreed that the level of violence in the country, and of civil disobedience on campuses in particular, had become intolerable. George Wallace frequently said at political meetings, "You can't even walk in the shadow of the White House less'n you got two police dogs with you."

New Hampshire voted on March 12, and Nixon suffered the ancient curse of having his wishes fulfilled too completely. He won 79 percent of the Republican votes, eighty-four thousand in total. Johnson actually won a remarkable victory, in that Senator Thomas J. McIntyre, a write-in candidate pledged to him, won twenty-two thousand votes to eighteen thousand for Eugene McCarthy, the only surviving anti-war candidate in the race, who had been almost constantly in the state for many weeks and was on the ballot. Johnson had allowed the media to portray any significant McCarthy vote as a defeat for the president, and the primary vote was universally seen as a grave setback to the incumbent. Nixon had buried his loser's image, but he had smoked out a more dangerous enemy. McCarthy could never have wrested the nomination from LBJ, nor even seriously divided the Democrats. But Bobby Kennedy was another matter, and on March 16 he announced his candidacy for the nomination, in order, he said, that the United States not "lose the moral leadership of this planet." Its claim to moral leadership was far from uncontested, even before Vietnam, but neither the Kennedy family nor American voters were expected to know that.

Nixon watched Kennedy's statement on television from a hotel in Portland, Oregon, and said, enigmatically but prophetically, to Ehrlichman that "very terrible forces have been unleashed. Something bad is going to come of this. God knows where this is going to lead."[6] Kennedy was an under-dog, but if Johnson chose to remain in the race, he would almost certainly gain the nomination of a terribly divided party, assuring Republican victory. LBJ's initial reaction was, "Some speculate in gold, a primary metal, and others just speculate in primaries."

Kennedy could trample McCarthy underfoot, but Johnson was too knowledgeable in the political arts to be driven from the party's leadership, for all his problems. But if LBJ decided not to run after all, Humphrey would take his place and would have a harder time defeating Kennedy, who would be a very serious opponent to Nixon in the election. Kennedy would now be running as an anti-war candidate, and Nixon, assuming he won the Republican nomination, would have to pick up a lot of Johnson's support while still being a centrist compared with Wallace. It was all becoming hor-ribly complicated, and the election year had just begun.

Rockefeller was expected finally to plunge into the race, and Nixon was confident he could deal with him. The governor of Maryland, Spiro T. Agnew, had started a Draft Rockefeller Committee on March 18, with the New York governor's blessing, and Rockefeller promised a major announce-ment for March 21. Agnew had some of the Baltimore press into his office to watch Rockefeller's declaration of candidacy, as they assumed it would be, but in fact Rockefeller announced what he called a decision "to reiterate unequivocally that I am not a candidate" for the presidency. He removed his name from the Oregon primary and in doing so signed an affidavit that "I am not, and will not be, a candidate for the presidency."[7] Agnew was naturally very annoyed. It was almost the end of March and the Democrats were in shambles and Nixon was the only declared Republican candidate.

Nixon tentatively scheduled a nationwide television address on Vietnam for March 31, the day before the Wisconsin primary, but deferred it when President Johnson requested air time from the networks for his own national address the same night. That Sunday evening, the president announced the de-escalation of the war, the suspension of all bombing of North Vietnam except just north of the DMZ, and the offer of unconditional negotiations in Paris, to which he had dispatched veteran government official Averell Harriman, whose previous diplomatic posts had been as Roosevelt's ambassador to Moscow, Truman's to London, and Kennedy's ambassador-at-large, including for the Nuclear Test Ban Treaty conclusion.

Then LBJ dropped the greatest bombshell of his long and flamboyant career. After lamenting division in the country, he said, "I shall not seek and will not accept the nomination of my party for another term as your president," and quickly signed off.

Nixon had been in the air, coming from Milwaukee back to New York, and was informed of Johnson's withdrawal at La Guardia Airport by Pat Buchanan. He told the press that it was "the year of the drop-out," and regretted in his memoirs having spoken "flippantly." Yet this too was an aspect of Nixon; though he became very excited about impersonal events,[8] he tended to assimilate the greatest rises and falls in peoples' fortunes, including his own, relatively matter-of-factly, perhaps because he had become so accustomed to crisis and tumult. He declared Kennedy the Democratic favorite, and predicted the early entry of Humphrey into the race, and probably, finally, Rockefeller.

The next day Nixon declared a personal "moratorium" on Vietnam for an indefinite period, so as not to second-guess the White House at a critical time. That evening, the Wisconsin primary delivered him another great victory: 79 percent of the Republicans, and McCarthy defeated the renounced president, 56 percent to 34 percent. Crossovers between parties are allowed in Wisconsin, and Nixon's win was impressive, but the real opponents, Kennedy, Humphrey, Reagan, Rockefeller, and Wallace, weren't there.

Bobby Kennedy came round to the White House and praised Johnson for taking charge of the shaken nation so effectively after the assassination of his brother, and warmly lauded his achievements for civil rights and public education. The men were ancient foes, to the point of reciprocal and probably not unfounded paranoia. Bobby's visit may have been tactical, because the Democratic nominee would need Johnson, but it was at least a gesture. The senator graciously concluded, of the president, "You are a brave and dedicated man." He was; they both were, but it would end badly for one and tragically for the other.[9]

For the rest of the country, the fury of events was bearing it along on a mystery conveyer belt at an accelerating pace, and there was little thought given to the end of one of America's remarkable political careers. From social and economic origins as obscure as Nixon's, Lyndon Johnson had been one of the legendary masters of the congressional arts, with Henry Clay, John C. Calhoun, Daniel Webster, Stephen A. Douglas, Sam Rayburn, and a very few others (including Richard Nixon if he had stayed longer in the Congress). Next to Lincoln, Lyndon Johnson had done more for civil rights than anyone, and at great cost to the white Southern constituency that had launched and supported him.

Many of his education measures, and some of his anti-poverty initiatives, positively affected the lives of millions of disadvantaged Americans. He was the nation's greatest tax-cutter, except for possibly Calvin Coolidge, and its greatest budget-balancer since Coolidge, a scarcely comparable president from an infinitely simpler time. And despite a great deal of what Stewart Alsop called "vulgar snobbery," Lyndon Johnson was one of the most colorful figures in the history of the highest office, as well as of the other great offices he held. As a vital force, and as a unique personality, he would be missed. So would his unfailingly gracious and very intelligent and capable wife.

As Johnson wrote himself, in his memoirs, "The blue collar worker felt that the Democratic Party had traded his welfare for the welfare of the black man. The middle class suburbanite felt that we were gouging him in order to pay for the anti-poverty programs. The black man, having tasted the fruits of equality, began demanding his rightful share of the American promise faster than most of the nation was willing to let him have it."[10]

Unfortunately, Johnson was also leaving a country with 565,000 draftees at the ends of the earth in an undeclared war for uncertain objectives, and after effectively delegitimizing the entire process in his March 31 overture to Hanoi. In Manila seventeen months before, he had been demanding the complete withdrawal of the North Vietnamese and the end to aid to the Viet Cong before the United States would withdraw one soldier. Johnson didn't string the Tet American victory to the unilateral de-escalation, and thus confirmed the American and world impression that Johnson had gambled with the lives of millions of young men in an imprudent cause, had mismanaged the military expedition, lost his nerve, and had incurred a humiliating defeat.

The campuses, as well as the African-American areas, which were grateful for the vote but not forgiving for generations of mistreatment, were seething and eructing, and the president was harassed by hecklers and demonstrators wherever he went. The whole atmosphere was one of revolt. There was no respect for university administrations; the offices of the presidents of Harvard and Columbia were occupied by students, and the faculties scurried under the wing of their militating enrollees. The president of Columbia University could not come to the Columbia commencement exercises in 1968, because he did not want to "provoke" the students. American academia had fallen to this. (It was quite a change from when Nixon and his friends had shinnied into the law dean's office at Duke to get a preview of their results, and then surreptitiously departed, assured that their hard work had been rewarded.)

Oral contraception vastly facilitated premarital sex among young people, relieving their ancient risks and frustrations, and leading to a great deal of sexual exhibitionism, much of it agreeable to most people – thigh-high skirts and exiguous coverage of the most erogenous female areas. Jackie Kennedy and Nixon's and Johnson's daughters did not abstain from tasteful versions of these fashions. The atmosphere was very self-oriented and sharply contentious and antagonistic, accentuated by an unpopular foreign war and heavy casualties (though only about 15 percent of Second World War levels in a much larger population, and still much smaller than annual highway traffic deaths). A hundred thousand draft dodgers or deserters having fled the country, but continuing to stir the political pot from outside, endless racial disturbances, and noisy complaints from young people that most of their elders considered, by their own standards in the Depression and the War, to be vastly overindulged, steadily embattled the social and political climate of the country.

Lyndon Johnson, lion of the congressional caucus rooms, was as incongruous a figure to preside over this seething and turbulent country as could be imagined. But he was a great man in his way, and more care should have been taken by the Washington establishment – politicians and press, including Richard Nixon – to give him the sendoff he deserved. Robert Kennedy had managed to put himself at the head of much of the discontent, Richard Nixon was at the head of much of the resistance to the aggressively discontented, and the surprises were not over. Hubert Humphrey, a campy but admired tribune of the idealism of the forties and fifties, was now coming on stage, the unannounced Reagan and twice-renounced Rockefeller would be heard from, McCarthy and Wallace, like an odd couple of political raccoons, were scouring the edges of left and right.[*] [11] And the great American political football, with its odd shape and unpredictable bounces, had not settled. The nation had not nearly done with tragedy in this early spring of 1968.

— II —

The world was just getting accustomed to the idea of life without Lyndon Johnson in the White House when, on April 4, 1968, Martin Luther King was assassinated in a motel in Memphis, Tennessee. He was only thirty-nine. The country erupted in racial disturbances in many cities, with very severe riots, looting, and arson in Washington, D.C. In the country as a whole, 46 people were killed, over 2,600 were injured, and over 21,000 arrested. There were over 2,600 cases of arson, and Chicago's Mayor Daley ordered his police to "shoot to kill" if they saw an arsonist. Property damage in the country was about forty-five million dollars, and fifty-five thousand soldiers and National Guardsmen were deployed.[12] Robert Kennedy gave the awful news of King's death with gentle eloquence to a largely African-American crowd that had been waiting for him in Indianapolis. He invoked the ancient Greeks and

---

[*] LBJ flew to Chicago on April 1 and was greeted by the city's omnipotent Mayor Richard J. Daley, then in his fourth term. He would be hosting and organizing the Democratic convention. Kennedy, when he entered the presidential contest, said, "Daley's the ball game." When Johnson arrived on April 1, Daley, who had played a middle-echelon role in the renomination of Roosevelt in 1940, when the president supposedly wanted to retire, offered to organize Johnson's renomination. That would have been a tall order even for so formidable a boss, but Johnson declined. He was determined to retire.

urged an effort to "tame the savageness of men and to make gentle the life of this world." He called for a "prayer for our country and our people," though he did not offer one himself.[13]

Nixon visited Mrs. Coretta Scott King and paid his respects to her and her family on April 7, reminiscing about his first meeting with her husband in Ghana in 1955. He returned two days later for the funeral, although he did not walk in the procession, which he thought would be "grandstanding." It would be cynical, though possibly not inaccurate, to guess that there might have been political calculations involved as well.

Martin Luther King had discovered, from Gandhi, the secret to complete the march to African-American emancipation: endless, non-violent confrontation. The white majority could not resist the moral imperative of equality for all. It could crush minority violence if threatened, but not minority rights when not threatened. Elaborating and pursuing this policy, and bringing most of his people with him, was a huge accomplishment for King. He led the liberation of millions of persecuted Americans, and spared the whole country untold bloodshed. He was a courageous and capable leader and a great public speaker. The murder of King fragmented the black leadership and removed the strongest voice for non-violence, making the tragedy of his death not just personal, and tribal, but national. J. Edgar Hoover had made much of King's womanizing. But, though possibly a reflection on his clerical aptitudes, that was not relevant to King's role as a civil rights leader (and the septuagenarian bachelor, Hoover, was as much the subject as the source of imputations of unconventional and unseemly sexual practices). Martin Luther King remains one of America's compelling and honored figures, and is probably rivaled only by Nelson Mandela as the greatest black leader of modern history.

Nixon quickly shifted from kicking Johnson at every chance to courting his support against Kennedy. He spoke to the American Society of Newspaper Editors on April 19. Changing his previous stance, Nixon challenged Bobby Kennedy to a debate, and repeated that he would do nothing to hinder the president's efforts to make progress toward a Vietnam peace settlement. Eisenhower continued to send Nixon effusive letters, though he was skeptical about his promises to end the Vietnam War quickly, which seemed to him "away into the background."[14] David Eisenhower served as liaison between his grandfather and future father-in-law.

The correlation of forces between the two men finally had turned. Eisenhower was a warmly regarded figure of the past, with little power over Nixon now, one way or another, and Nixon was making a strong bid to take the headship of the country with no help from Eisenhower. At this point, Nixon could accord Eisenhower the respect, but, unlike bygone days, no more than the respect, he deserved, and Eisenhower could offer the respect, and, also in a departure from the past, no less than the respect, Nixon deserved.

The general was now seventy-eight, and his cardiological problems were always with him. The long and intricate and sometimes abrasive relationship between the two men was coming to a satisfactory stage as it was about to end, symbolized in the marriage of their descendants.

As Nixon had predicted, Rockefeller announced on April 30 that he was a candidate for president, just forty days after he swore an affidavit for the secretary of state of Oregon that he would not be a candidate. Rockefeller had been advised by Eisenhower in 1960 not to be "On again, off again, gone again, Finnegan." But that was his weakness. Admittedly he withdrew between the entry of Kennedy and the departure of Johnson, but why, if undecided, had he not just waited a few days instead of disillusioning his followers like Agnew? The day of Rockefeller's announcement, he won the Massachusetts primary narrowly, over the pro-Nixon favorite son, Governor John A. Volpe. Rockefeller, in what Nixon described in his memoirs as an "irritating" development, took all thirty-four delegates from Massachusetts.[15]

Nixon was not overly concerned about Rockefeller, although much of his electoral support would probably ultimately go to his fellow liberal New Yorker, Robert Kennedy. Maurice Stans had Nixon very well financed, and Nixon's organizer and law partner, John Mitchell, a municipal bond specialist who knew an astonishing number of local officials because of his legal work, was running a very smooth organization and was vacuuming up delegate votes in small lots all around the country.

On May 3, the North Vietnamese accepted the invitation to peace talks in Paris, where Harriman was awaiting them. This gave Nixon all the pretext he needed to continue his moratorium on discussion of Vietnam; i.e., on his own vague plans to end the war satisfactorily, and quickly, while reducing American casualties and not invading other countries or having recourse to nuclear weapons. Adjusting to the new political landscape, he threaded his way with protected flanks between Rockefeller and Reagan toward the

Republican nomination. He would then run against Kennedy, who would have discontented Johnsonites and even McCarthyites falling off his bandwagon (Hubert Humphrey would rally loyally). Nixon tacked again and produced a pitch for independents and Democrats from a slightly different angle, picking up hawks without losing moderates. McCarthy had told the Oregonians, a relatively well-educated populace, that Kennedy's supporters were "among the less intelligent and less educated people in America."[16] This went down well in Oregon, but not in the country, where it was seen as a callous reference to African-Americans and poor whites.

On May 16, Nixon invoked "the silent center who do not demonstrate, who do not picket or protest loudly." He was offering the African-Americans government tax incentives for small business and home improvements in their existing areas and neighborhoods. He had given up on notions of vast, horribly costly slum clearances and compulsory relocations of people. If standards of living and quality of life could be improved where the people were, all the rest would follow. He was promising a hard crackdown on crime and violence, and objected to the Supreme Court decisions in the Escobedo and Miranda cases, which required that criminal suspects be informed of their right to counsel, and asked that juries be allowed to determine whether confessions were real or extorted. And he had given enough of a hint, at least for a time, of what he would do to end Vietnam, without attacking Johnson's efforts, of which he was, in fact, deeply suspicious.

The night before the Oregon primary, May 27, Nixon appeared on a telethon for two hours, interspersed with clips from his best "Hillsboro meetings" around the country. The famous former university football coach, Bud Wilkinson of Oklahoma, received the questions and sorted them for the candidate. Julie and Tricia Nixon were among the switchboard operators. It was very successful, and Nixon won a huge victory the next day, 73 percent to Reagan's 23 percent and 4 percent for Rockefeller (who had again sworn solemnly not to be a candidate in Oregon less than nine weeks before). As interesting, McCarthy, who had gone from Don Quixote to a Truman-like underdog with a Stevensonian wit against Johnson, defeated Robert Kennedy, 43 percent to 37 percent. This meant the Kennedy-Humphrey contest could be very close, and McCarthy could play a role in it, and the Democratic nominating process went on to California. Coming up to California, most estimates were that Humphrey led, with 1,000 delegates to 350 for Kennedy, 250 for McCarthy, and 1,000 scattered. California would have narrowed Humphrey's lead, but the prospect was a very divided party.[17]

Nixon went to Florida and Atlanta and met with senators John Tower and Strom Thurmond and others, and promised gradual desegregation, the end to singling the South out for racial infelicities, higher cotton tariffs, and continued big defense spending in the Southern states, which the committee chairmen like Thurmond had long been accustomed to. This seemed to be enough to steady the ranks, and Tower and Thurmond promised to resist the depredations of the Reagan forces. It was to this point that the fluid course of events had tumbled, as the polls closed in California, on June 4, 1968.

Robert Kennedy won a close battle with Eugene McCarthy, by a little over 2 percent, with about 10 percent being taken away by the so-called state slate, headed by California attorney general Thomas Lynch and pledged to Humphrey. (Reagan won on the Republican side, unopposed, and led the poles for both parties.) Kennedy spoke to his supporters at the Ambassador Hotel, concluding, "On to Chicago!" It was not to be. As he walked through the kitchen to return via a back elevator to his suite, a lone gunman, a militant Palestinian (Christian) Arab, Sirhan Sirhan, shot him fatally. He died the next day. Robert Francis Kennedy was forty-two.

The country was again severely shocked as it once more witnessed the much-bereaved Kennedy family go through a mighty and tragic funeral with great courage and dignity. President Johnson, Vice President Humphrey, Richard Nixon, Nelson Rockefeller, Eugene McCarthy, George Romney, and the leaders of the government, military and civilian, attended a solemn funeral mass at St. Patrick's Cathedral in New York, on June 8. Senator Edward Kennedy gave a moving eulogy, probably the finest moment in his own public career of more than forty years. His brother was, he said, "a good and decent man who saw wrong and tried to right it, saw suffering and tried to heal it, saw war and tried to stop it." He ended by quoting Bobby: "'Some men see things as they are and say "Why?" I dream things that never were and say "Why not?"'"

Robert Kennedy left his widow and ten children, one of them born a few months later. He remains an enigma. His critics saw him as a happy understudy to Senator Joseph R. McCarthy, an uncritical beneficiary of his father's overbearing ambition and questionable judgment and ethics, and an underqualified attorney general who paid little attention to civil liberties or legal niceties as he persecuted political enemies (like Nixon over his tax returns and the Hughes loan) or when he tapped Martin Luther King's telephone. There was also considerable doubt about his motives in rapidly evolving from an enthusiast for the Vietnam War to the leading proponent of what amounted to a cut-and-run policy. His role in propagating the more far-fetched notions of the great Kennedy myth of canonical benignity, unblemished by human failings, though an understandable gambit, was also often rather grating. (He would speak vaguely of "finishing what President Kennedy tried to do," with no hint of what that had been.)

With all that said, he was a courageous and determined patriot, an idealist who cared passionately about his country, including its moral well-being and particularly the condition of its disadvantaged. By a combination of inheritance and his own qualities, he became a great American political leader in whom tens of millions of largely disaffected people invested their hopes. He was the enforcer of the Kennedys, leaving his elder brother the role of charming America, and there were huge numbers of Americans to whom Robert Kennedy's ten-week campaign for the presidency was a vividly defining moment of their lives. His death was not just a personal and family tragedy; it also probably deprived the country of a brave and indomitable man who could have rendered immense service at a very critical time.

Without knowing precisely what it had lost, America sadly knew that it had sustained another severe blow. If Robert Kennedy had survived, he might have been nominated, but Johnson might then have discreetly thrown the election to Nixon. But Robert Kennedy (not Jimmy Carter) would still have been the next Democratic president and would have had a very great and generally positive impact. The torrent of events rushed on, leaving people with little time or inclination to engage in such conjecture.

President Johnson ordered expanded and round-the-clock security for all candidates. As if in exhaustion at the self-destructive process American presidential politics had become, all candidates informally observed a respectful fortnight of contemplative public inactivity.

Nixon remained the favorite for the Republicans, and Humphrey had moved into that slot on the kaleidoscope of candidates for the Democrats. The polls were volatile, with Nixon, Rockefeller, Humphrey, and occasionally McCarthy in hot contention. Reagan trailed, but was more than just a factional or regional candidate, and Wallace was cutting into everyone else in varying degrees.

— III —

By this time, the United States had been joined in national crisis by another of the world's Great Powers. General de Gaulle's France was demonstrating that ancient French practice of interrupting the luxurious occupancy of their rich country with social and political turmoil. It was as if boredom, or even guilt at their good fortune, stirred the French from enjoying their culture, with its pleasures of food, wine, gift for rationalization, and the feline cynicism of a tired but vigilant nation, to tear up the paving stones and throw them at the police. De Gaulle was absent on one of his rather portentous foreign visits, to Romania's Ceauşescu, whom he was naturally encouraging to throw off the Russian yoke, when a student general strike began in May, about overcrowded campus conditions.

De Gaulle offered a referendum on reorganizing both the universities and local government, but the unrest grew and extended to almost all of organized labor. The more militant unions took to the streets, often waving the symbols of orthodox or even pure-Marxist communists (red and black flags). As always in incipient revolutions, especially in France, the most absurdly unrepresentative characters came quickly to the fore, haranguing public meetings and making outlandish demands as if vested with some instant legitimacy.

Revolutionary movements always migrate to the radical extremes, and France's in 1968 did so with unusual rapidity. De Gaulle had incarnated French resistance to the Nazis when there was little of it in practice, had patiently waited from 1946 to 1958 for the hour of legitimacy, had built France back from a political vacuum of revolving-door governments to be, in the midst of America's distractions and the rising Russo-Chinese dispute, the holder of the world's balance of power. His personal prestige was rivaled in the world only by that of Mao Tse-tung (who admired him), yet he was facing an insolent and dangerous uprising from his rebarbative countrymen. At age seventy-seven, this was not what he had planned. After a few days of silent incomprehension, he rose, one more time, to the requirements imposed by his ungrateful countrymen.

After being informed of the doubtful loyalty of the Paris police (far from an unprecedented situation in French history) a few weeks into the disturbances, as the most preposterous demands were being made by instant popular tribunes on behalf of the workers and academics (from under-graduates to members of the French Academy), de Gaulle visited the French Army in Germany to assure himself of its loyalty. The BBC World Service, ever the slave of its prejudices, began its news report on May 30, 1968, "Day by day, the proud facade of Gaullism can be seen, crumbling into dust." A march of half a million people went up the Champs Élysées, demanding the general's departure. It was widely believed that he would resign.

Finally, at the end of the afternoon, he spoke to the nation, for less than five minutes. Like anyone whose authority depended on a combination of normal legitimacy, moral credibility, the implicit threat of force, and the self-interest of his listeners, de Gaulle had had to judge when the French penchant for periodic bouts of mad rebelliousness would yield to their ancient bourgeois avarice and fear of economic loss and social chaos. The instinct of the great man, one of Nixon's mentors, did not fail him. Television screens had only a still picture of the chief of state, as the technicians of the state network were on strike. It was one of the great speeches of the time, and of French history, and was rendered without frills or preamble, with admirable economy of words. It was scarcely longer than Mr. Lincoln's address at Gettysburg, and less conciliatory in tenor. In translation, it was repeated verbatim on all American news networks and throughout the world.

"As the sole legitimate repository of national and republican power, I have, in the last twenty-four hours, considered every means, I repeat every means, for the conservation of that power. I have taken the necessary deci-sions. In the present circumstances, I will not retire. I have a mandate from the people; I will fulfill it. I will not replace the prime minister, whose value, solidity, and capacity have earned the homage of all. He will propose to me the changes that seem to him to be appropriate in the com-position of the government.

"I have dissolved the National Assembly. I proposed a referendum which would permit the citizens to approve a profound reform in our economy and our universities, and to say whether I retained their con-fidence or not, by the sole acceptable method, popular democracy. I have deferred the date of this referendum, because the present circumstances make it impractical. [A considerable understatement.]

"Legislative elections will take place on the timetable provided by the constitution, unless it is intended to gag the entire French people, and to prevent it from expressing itself, as they attempt to deny it, politically, life itself, by the same means that the students have been prevented from studying, the teachers from teaching, and the workers from working. These means are intimidation, intoxication, and tyranny, exercised at a distance by a party that is a totalitarian enterprise, although it is already fragmenting into even more extreme groups.

"If this condition of force continues, I will, to maintain the Republic, in conformity with the constitution, take other means than the immediate consultation of the people. [This was a direct threat to exercise emergency powers, enforce martial law, and assign the maintenance of order to the Algeria-tested and notoriously heavy-handed French Army.]

"France is, indeed, threatened by dictatorship. There are those who wish to constrain it to resign itself to a power that would be imposed in a state of national despair; the power would be that of totalitarian communism. Naturally, it is colored, at the outset, with the deceiving appearance afforded by the ambition and hatred of discredited politicians. After this service, these people would weigh no more heavily than their merit, which is insignificant. [He was referring to former premier Mendes-France and future president, and his late electoral opponent, François Mitterand.]

"No! The Republic will not abdicate. The people will triumph. Progress, independence, and peace will prevail with liberty. Long live the Republic. Long live France."

The revolutionary movement collapsed; 750,000 people, many of them doubtless from the previous anti-Gaullist parade of earlier in the day, marched back up the Champs Élysées, supporting the general. The workers went meekly back to work, the students and faculty returned to the universities, and the army was not needed. Six weeks later, de Gaulle and his partisans won the greatest legislative electoral victory in 175 years of intermittent republican French history. (He then dismissed the premier, Georges Pompidou, when all pressure to do so had ceased, saying that he placed him "in the reserve of the Republic.")

It was a turning point in this tumultuous year. Enlightened, democratic authority asserted itself, in a way that Metternich could not in 1848 nor Louis XVI or his ministers in 1789, as neither were democratically legitimate and probably neither regime had the will to resist the mobs. In the following election campaign, de Gaulle, who was never reluctant to blame unbidden developments on the United States, claimed that Vietnam was responsible for youthful agitation in France. But he also took a decisive stand for the legitimacy of democratic government, and made the point that the West would reform as its people wished, but that it would not be subverted by communists and wretched dupes of communists frustrated in their desire to achieve office through constitutional means.

This was a harsh designation of Mendes-France, whom de Gaulle actually respected, and even of Mitterand, perhaps the most cynical senior French public official since Talleyrand and Fouché, Napoleon's and Louis XVIII's ministers of foreign affairs and police. But in these dire circumstances, in a country where the Communist Party had been a force to be reckoned with for fifty years, de Gaulle was prepared to use a version of the Red Scare that would have been too much for Nixon at the height of the Hiss case. It was the last great triumph of Charles de Gaulle's career, but it was a decisive victory for Western democracy and a bone-crushing defeat for its enemies, in one of the cradles of republican government – the founding nation, if not the most faithful conservator, of liberty, equality, and fraternity. The implications of de Gaulle's success were very important. Had he been defeated by insurrection, the consequences for the West would have been extremely serious. Richard Nixon lived through these events as if personally involved, praying for, and uplifted by, Charles de Gaulle's overwhelming victory.

Nixon took it as a personal slight that his old opponent, Earl Warren announced on June 21 that he would retire as chief justice. Despite questions of the propriety of filling the position at the very end of his term, Johnson put forward the name of Justice Abe Fortas, formerly and long one of Washington's greatest lawyers, with defense secretary Clark Clifford and the foremost of modern American barristers, Edward Bennett Williams. (The slightly younger Lloyd Cutler and Robert Strauss, who would be in and out of government for decades, would soon join this exalted fraternity in the lawyering and legislating and adjudicating capital of the world.)

Nixon admired Fortas, and did not object to him or to the new nominee for the vacancy on the high court, Homer Thornberry, formerly Johnson's successor as congressman from Austin, Texas, and more recently a competent federal judge. However, Warren would not escape renewed intimacy with Nixon that easily. Fortas was revealed to have accepted consulting fees from a controversial financier, who was ultimately convicted as a felon, and withdrew from consideration as chief justice and retired from the bench.

So the incoming president would fill his and Warren's vacancies. Johnson had set out to influence the court and put his lawyer and Texas protégé on it, and ended up with his lawyer off the bench and his successor poised to change the court. Nixon did wish to do this, as he considered Warren, and Eisenhower agreed, a woolly-headed chief justice (not having been Nixon's favorite governor, either). Nixon, unlike Eisenhower, thought the desegregation decisions right and necessary, but Miranda and some of the court's other nostrums he felt were legally silly and dangerous in their consequences.

Eisenhower was now, apparently permanently, in Walter Reed Hospital. Nixon decided to have one more try at wringing an endorsement out of him. He sent Bryce Harlow to see him and he got the usual flimflam about waiting for the convention. Nixon then sent Admiral Lewis Strauss to the hospital, asking him, rather indelicately, to get the endorsement "before the old man dies." No sale. Ike had his fifth heart attack, and with his usual persistence Nixon appeared in person on July 15 to ask for the endorsement. He was blunter than usual, or probably ever, with Eisenhower. He had virtually sewn up the nomination, the general's health was unstable, and it was, for both reasons, unwise to wait. Eisenhower agreed.

Nixon went away happy, but was soon back with the further indignity of asking Ike to make the announcement before a slew of endorsements came in from prominent current party figures, including Governor Agnew of Maryland, Senator Charles Percy of Illinois, and Governor John Rhodes of Ohio. Eisenhower didn't want to look as if he was just joining a groundswell, and agreed. He was got into his dressing gown and wheelchair, and, in the last direct political intervention of his life, called in the press and gave the emphatic endorsement Nixon had been seeking for sixteen years. Finally, there was none of the claptrap about "well-informed, well-prepared," and so forth. Instead, he prepared and read a statement about "my admiration of his [Nixon's] personal qualities: his intellect, acuity, decisiveness, warmth, and above all, his integrity."[18] Finally, now that he no longer really needed it, but wanted it no less to close out happily a long quest and extraordinary and historic political relationship, Nixon had the unqualified, superlative endorsement of his old chief. (Eisenhower was a perceptive man; he would not have spoken so flatteringly of Nixon's integrity if he did not believe it.)

Nixon was now into pre-convention planning. He did not want to make a mistake choosing a vice presidential candidate as he had in 1960. His greatest concern was losing too much of the South to Wallace, so his greatest need was someone who would steady the reasonable Southern whites without antagonizing the Northern moderates. This had been the traditional role of border state (between North and South) or Southern vice presidential candidates among the Democrats, when that party normally carried the South.* The Republicans had not fared well in the South and did not have to consider such things until now. But in 1968, running against a Northern liberal like Humphrey, there was a chance to squeeze the Democrats between Wallace and Nixon.

What became known as Nixon's "Southern strategy" and has largely been portrayed by liberals as a shameful dispute with Wallace for the redneck vote, was really a refusal to waffle about desegregation and civil rights, and also a refusal to single out the South for its failings while pretending the Northern states were without blemish – a determination to carry out the law but go no further than the law required, and to pitch the Republican message to the emerging and growing moderate factions of the South, white and black. The key was to be closer to the moderate whites than, as he was considered, the ultra-liberal Humphrey and preferable to the blacks over the segregationist Wallace (not a high hurdle).

Considering these factors, Spiro Agnew appeared to be the best candidate. As a defector from Rockefeller, he had some apparent liberal credentials. Maryland is a border state, and when there had been rioting in Baltimore after the death of Martin Luther King, Agnew had summoned the black leaders and squarely blamed them for doing almost nothing to restrain the blacks or point out to them that they were essentially trashing their own neighborhoods and vandalizing the property of their own people. His comments, including his reference to some of his guests as "Hanoi-visiting, burn-America-down hypocrites," were pretty feisty and received wide coverage, much of it hostile in the liberal press.

---

* Thus were chosen Joseph T. Robinson of Arkansas in 1928, John N. Garner of Texas in 1932 and 1936, Harry Truman of Missouri in 1944, Alben Barkley of Kentucky in 1948, John Sparkman of Alabama in 1952, Estes Kefauver of Tennessee in 1956, and LBJ in 1960.

Agnew himself was a centrist on the issues, but earned an instant reputation as a good law-and-order candidate and not someone who fell into the trap of Johnson's race relations commission and blamed everything on the whites, and everyone, in short, except those who were rioting.

When they met, [19] Nixon liked Agnew's big, square-jawed confidence, a sort of smarter version of George Romney, and Mitchell invited him to put Nixon in nomination at the convention. Agnew, irritated by Rockefeller's volte-face, agreed and did a commendable enough job of that. He was the best fit they could get to reassure the voters whom they had a shot at in the South, and he was a new face for the Republicans, a symbol of the party's post-1964 recovery.

Wallace's appeal went further than segregation, which, after Lyndon Johnson's presidency, was no longer a defensible battlement, though there was a terrible amount of foot-dragging in most of the Southern school districts. Wallace was also a populist of sorts, and his slogan now was "Send them a message." "Them" was the Washington bureaucracy and establishment, and Wallace adapted his appeal quite well to the benighted little person. His critics would claim he was pitching his message to white trash, but it was more complicated than that. Wallace, with his mean mouth and eyes and straight slick hair, was like the man who put gasoline in your tank in a Southern filling station – a crisp salute with "Wipe your windshield?" His followers were not just white racists but unpretentious, hard-working people, without a national voice, apt to be drafted to a war that they thought was being commanded with more attention to Fifth Avenue cocktail parties than the infantry fighting it. While unexceptional and uncouth, most Wallaceites were part of the backbone of the nation. Humphrey and McCarthy weren't going to round up many of his supporters, but Nixon had known throughout his political career how to sidle up to that sort of voter without burning his bridges with the more educated and better off, who were his more natural constituency.

Nixon paid careful attention to the Vietnam plank of the Republican Party platform, and foreign affairs generally. He wrote out, from a retreat at Montauk, Long Island, and sent to the platform committee meeting ahead

---

* Nixon's files reveal correspondence with Agnew going back to 1964, when Agnew promised to assist Nixon if he ran for president. Nixon encouraged Agnew to run for governor of Maryland in 1966.

of the convention in Miami, his treatment of Vietnam as a war that "must be ended." To the hawks, he expressed confidence that it could be ended honorably, retaining the independence of South Vietnam. To the doves, he made it clear that he did not favor escalation, but the fastest possible preparation of the South Vietnamese for the task of taking over their own defense. He stressed more than ever the need for comprehensive discussions with the U.S.S.R., and with China. This was a particularly interesting perspective, as the snarling and snapping between the two communist giants was now becoming very animated.

Nixon's call for discussions with Red China attracted almost no notice, though the Democrats said nothing similar, and this was now a recurrent theme with Nixon, alone among leading American politicians. He did not specify what incentives the United States could offer the U.S.S.R. and China to cool down the Hanoi war effort, but the concept was the first new ingredient in this horrible subject since Johnson's big escalation in 1965, and Nixon repeated that he would not undercut American negotiators. (These were now arguing over the shape of the negotiating table, and the status of the Viet Cong and South Vietnamese, each of whom objected to the presence of the other, and in Saigon's case, to the holding of such a conference at all.)

Nixon had had a security briefing from Johnson, Rusk, and Rostow on July 26. Johnson was already bitter at Hanoi's shifting conditions and shilly-shallying. Before the negotiations just beginning were over, the North Vietnamese would establish themselves as among the most exasperating interlocutors in the history of international diplomacy.

Reagan and Nixon both arrived in Miami on August 5. Reagan, demonstrating his acting talent, claimed that he was responding to irresistible pressures to abandon his favorite-son status and go for the nomination. The only hope of stopping Nixon now was if Reagan could peel loose a large chunk of Nixon's Southern delegates. Thurmond, Tower, and others trusted Nixon and they held most of the South in place for Nixon, who was assured on his arrival at his Miami hotel suite by John Mitchell that they had the convention in hand. Nixon spent the day of the 6th touring and receiving delegations, and especially smoothing down the Southerners.

The roll of the states was called starting at midnight on August 7. Nixon was filmed for CBS's new television series *60 Minutes*, in an armchair, keeping score on a pad. His family was on each side of him on sofas. There were no surprises, and he went over the top at Wisconsin. Nelson Rockefeller called very graciously and said he had expected Reagan to do a little better. Richard Nixon was back to the previous height of his career, Republican presidential nominee, but after an astounding comeback, facing a less formidable opponent than the one he had effectively fought to a draw eight years before, and in times much different to the proud, confident dawn of the New Frontier. The country and much of the world were in turmoil. Johnson would not be handing over to his successor the serene, confident, and placid America that Eisenhower had handed over to Kennedy. So far, the post-Roosevelt presidential generation had produced a very rough road.

Nixon apparently considered Robert Finch, his old friend and protégé and lieutenant governor of California, as vice presidential nominee. Finch declined, citing pressures on his young family, the excessive jump from his present position to vice president, cronyism, the likely irritation of Reagan, and the problem of his and Nixon's being from California, though Nixon was now a New York resident. It is not at all clear that Nixon was serious. (Finch would have been a much better vice president than Agnew, but less comforting to accessible white Southern voters.)

In any case, Agnew, for better or worse, was the one, and Nixon announced this to the press at 1 P.M. on August 8 in the ballroom of his hotel. John Lindsay led a liberal revolt and nominated George Romney, but the Nixon forces were now in control, and Agnew was chosen, 1,128 to 186. Nixon asked Agnew nothing about the condition of his finances, perhaps sensitive to the unjust treatment he had received in 1952. The die was cast.

Nixon addressed the convention and the nation at 11 P.M. that night as only the eighth person and second Republican to be renominated to the presidency by a major party after losing his first attempt.* On the way to the podium he answered the question of Kennedy supporter Sander Vanocur of NBC about why he thought he would win in 1968 when he had not in 1960. He thoughtfully replied, "The office seeks the man, and it did not seek me in 1960, but it does now." He opened his remarks, "This time, we're going to win." Then he called on the party to "win this one for Ike."

---

* The others were Thomas Jefferson, Andrew Jackson, Henry Clay, William Henry Harrison, William Jennings Bryan, Thomas E. Dewey, and Adlai Stevenson.

Vietnam was his first priority. "After an era of confrontation, the time has come for an era of negotiation with the leaders of Communist China and the Soviet Union." He was strong on civil rights and assisting African-American capitalism, and firm, but not irresponsible, on law and order. He traced a bowdlerization of his own career in the third person, "He dreams of faraway places. . . . [His] father had to go to work in the sixth grade, sacrificed everything he had so his sons could go to college. . . . a gentle Quaker mother . . . quietly wept when he went away to war." The whole cast was trotted through. The fables of Pat, Tricia, Julie, the clergy, Chief Newman, all unnamed; and only then the mystery subject of the story sprang forth, unbound, though unsuspenseful, as the nominee. As U.S. political conventions go, it was no more tasteless than usual, and Nixon did not refer to his brothers who died young, Harold and Arthur. He did not pull out all the stops, unlike many who preceded and followed him.

The greatest applause came at two lines: "No one will use the American flag as a doormat when I am president," and, "My fellow Americans, the dark, long night for America is about to end." There were a couple of Nixonian lapses into extreme sentimentality, but it was a good and effective speech. The country was in a shocking condition, wracked by foreign war, violence, and assassination. Nixon appeared and sounded realistic but confident, experienced and knowledgeable, firm without being reactionary, and capable of providing change without wild experimentation. He left Miami with more than the usual jump from a nominating convention, and about a fifteen-point lead over Humphrey and more than twenty-five points over Wallace.

Nixon flew to Texas and received another intelligence briefing from Johnson. He suspected Johnson of trying to pull something out of the hat to resolve or de-escalate the war just before the election, but also tried to make the point that he was closer to Johnson's Vietnam policy than the Democrats were likely to be. Johnson promised Nixon he would make no more preemptive concessions.

In the interregnum between the two party conventions, Nixon smoothed down concerns about Agnew and brought Rockefeller, Lindsay, Romney, and other dissidents aboard by promising a moderate policy and reminding them of the disastrous consequences of party disunity in 1964. Maurice Stans continued to lead the fundraising effort. Nixon had spent nine million dollars becoming the candidate and Stans budgeted twenty-four million to get the rest of the way, and anticipated no difficulty raising that amount.

— IV —

All signs were that the Democratic convention in Chicago would be very divisive. The New Left had promised, through some of its most media-prominent spokesmen, to challenge authority and disrupt the convention. Mayor Richard J. Daley did not shrink from the challenge. He put his nine-thousand-member police force on sixteen-hour shifts, and reinforced them with seventeen thousand National Guardsmen and regular army para-troopers. There would be no chance of losing control of the convention hall, with a paramilitary force greater than Washington's Continental Army in the Revolutionary War. But it was clear, as the convention approached, that it was a mighty tinderbox, surrounded and beset by pyromaniacs.

Just before this event, which Nixon eagerly awaited, confident that the fissures in the Democratic Party would be rent open, another world crisis blew up. The Soviet Union had become progressively more upset by the lib-eralizing tendencies of the new leadership in Czechoslovakia, which had virtually granted freedom of expression and assembly to the country, result-ing in a good deal of cautiously stated objection to the communist system. On August 21, the U.S.S.R. landed an unscheduled electronic control plane at Prague airport, and then landed a large military transport plane carrying hundreds of soldiers, every two minutes. The aircraft took off on a neighbor-ing runway and returned from nearby jump-off points very promptly. In this way, the Soviets landed a full airborne division in a few hours, while thir-teen Soviet divisions and one each from East Germany and Poland, 165,000 Warsaw Pact soldiers and 4,600 tanks, entered Czechoslovakia at twenty dif-ferent points. There was no organized resistance and they moved swiftly to occupy all the strategic points in Prague.

There were some scenes reminiscent of Berlin in 1953 and Budapest in 1956, as people threw rocks at tanks and even a few Molotov cocktails, but the heavy hand of Soviet repression strangled what had been known as the Prague Spring in a few days. There were massive protests all over the Western world, and severe criticism from China. There had not been much recent American talk of liberating Eastern Europe, so no one could accuse the United States of inciting this activity, as had been said in 1956, and Alexander Dubček was, after all, something of a communist, albeit a rather democratic one.

In the midst of the great upheavals over Vietnam, the Prague intervention did give the world a taste of communism in action. De Gaulle had played his role of holder of the balance of power between Moscow and Washington, but the involvement of the Moscow-directed French Communist party in the near-overthrow of his own government and of the Republic he founded, and the brutal suppression of an unoffending country only three hundred miles from Paris, reminded the West of the nature of the adversary.

In Chicago, Daley declined the request of the New Left coalitions for a demonstration permit. Because the convention center had burned down after Chicago won the right to hold the convention, Daley moved it to an old building near the stockyards, six miles from where the delegates would be staying, in the Conrad Hilton and other famous hotels on the waterfront. Most of the intervening space was filled by the mayor's home district of Bridgeport, where he had lived modestly all his life. He would not have marches through Bridgeport.

One of the most famous of the demonstration leaders, Abbie Hoffman, said that all should prepare for five days of "energy exchange," and he began in the whimsical manner that marked him as a natural comic talent. He claimed he was holding a "Festival of Fun," with workshops in snake dancing, "non-violent self-defense, underground communications, how to live free, guerrilla theater, folksinging, love-making [there was a good deal of it very publicly], mantras, Yippie Olympics, a Miss Yippie contest, Pin the Tail on the candidate, Pin the Rubber on the Pope, and other normal, healthy, games." Poet Allen Ginsberg went about claiming to be a calming influence by repeating the supposedly placatory noise "Om."

Once the convention started and the demonstrations began, there was a great deal of taunting of the police and a serious lack of disciplined response. By the second night of the convention, the demonstrators, by shouting obscenities at the police, blowing marijuana smoke in their faces, and showering them with projectiles, including excrement, brought forth what the demonstration organizers had sought, a police riot. Television crews recorded the police rampaging through whole sections of the splendid lakefront of the city, randomly clubbing and arresting people. Abbie Hoffman called it "the greatest military blunder since Waterloo." It was a disgusting spectacle that brought shame on all sides in the melee, on the

Democratic Party, on one of America's greatest cities, and on the United States, one more time, in this endless year of horrors and tragedies.[20] The world, as it had for some time, looked on at this latest American debacle, wondering what the great republic of the New World was becoming. So did millions of Americans.

Richard Nixon could scarcely credit his good fortune. Four years before, Lyndon Johnson had seemed omnipotent as he waved from the balcony at Atlantic City. He did not appear in Chicago, but hundreds were injured in his name. Humphrey, who had entered too late to be in any primary, won the convention, over Eugene McCarthy and George McGovern, the candidate of the die-hard Kennedy followers (whom Allard Lowenstein had tried to recruit before Eugene McCarthy, but who had then declined).

In a shambles of a convention and a riot-torn city, its downtown hospitals overflowing with the brutalized veterans of Daley's crowd-control techniques, it was Hubert Humphrey at last. He had the uncommon decency, in his acceptance speech, to express his gratitude to Lyndon Johnson. He was a good man, a sincere liberal, but more dated and caricaturable in his yokel's enthusiasm than Nixon. Some found Nixon sinister, many thought him stiff and even robotic, but no one doubted his seriousness or intelligence. Hubert Humphrey was a well-liked but not especially imposing or serious person. But he was a brave man and would fight a memorable campaign, from a most unpromising start.

Nixon launched his campaign a week after the end of the Chicago Democratic convention, in Chicago, on September 6. He rode in an open car, with his wife and his daughters in the automobile behind him, in a motorcade through downtown Chicago and around the very areas that had been most violently disturbed while the Democrats were there. Daley ordered his police to avoid any possible problems, and gave municipal workers the afternoon off, eager to start rebuilding his city's and his own reputation. About four hundred thousand people lined the streets, a very respectable turnout, and while there wasn't much Nixonmania, or even real enthusiasm, it was a cheerful, polite crowd. There were no incidents, and another unimagined irony – Nixon's campaign was well kicked off by the nation's most powerful mayor, who, more than anyone else, had stolen the presidency from him in 1960.

On September 8, Nixon did his best to detach Lyndon Johnson from the campaign of his Democratic successors, whose convention had so reviled him (though Humphrey himself had remained discreetly loyal, out of principle as well as expediency). Nixon met with his and Johnson's mutual friend, Billy Graham, and asked Graham to deliver a powerful message of support and solidarity to the president. Nixon expressed high respect for Johnson and violent animosity to Johnson's extreme critics, and praised him as the "hardest working president in 140 years" (since Monroe or John Quincy Adams, depending on whether dating back from the start or end of Johnson's term, and neither of them worked a fraction as diligently as LBJ did). Nixon promised never to embarrass Johnson, to seek his advice, to entrust him with important work if he wanted it, and to give him full credit when Vietnam was settled, and a generous place in history, "because [he] deserves it."

Billy Graham read from his notes of this conversation to Johnson, in the White House the next week. He reported to Nixon that LBJ asked that they be repeated and was "touched and appreciative," and said that he would support his vice president, his party's candidate, but that if "Mr. Nixon becomes the president, I will do all in my power to cooperate with him."[21]

It was a rough campaign from the start, as it was bound to be with such a terrible prelude, including the assassination of one of the main candidates and the mob assault of the conventions. The anti-war militants were everywhere, and disrupted the meetings of Humphrey, Wallace, and Nixon. But Humphrey was the most vulnerable, as they were the deserters from his party and were most aggrieved by the outrage in Chicago. Eugene McCarthy egged them on, by refusing to endorse his fellow Minnesotan and former mentor. McCarthy had run an elegant and articulate, even brave, campaign for the nomination, first against Johnson, then Kennedy, and finally Humphrey. But he proved that worst sort of politician, the poor loser – unlike Humphrey, Nixon, and the Kennedys, all of whom had experienced defeat (JFK for the vice presidential nomination in 1956, RFK in the Oregon primary in 1968), and had the taste and intelligence to speak well of their opponents (even Nixon in 1962, who attacked the press but not Pat Brown).

Wallace flourished on hecklers. He had plenty of musclemen in his security unit, who physically expelled hecklers if they gave the governor a real acoustical problem. Short of that, he mocked "pointy-headed liberals" and promised that if any of them lay down before his car, as had happened to Humphrey, that would be their last act. His crowds, usually rough reactionary, working-class groups, loved his ripostes.

Nixon's campaign organization admitted crowds to the candidate's appearances by ticket only, distributed many more tickets than there were places, and screened out longhairs and other doubtful people at the entrances, ushering them down corridors to the street or just turning them back. Young men with short hair and girls in miniskirts abounded, but not the unkempt, surly, randomly hirsute or ostentatiously bra-less; the Nixon campaign was built on the clean-cut of all ages and both (unambiguous) genders. The unassailable David Eisenhower became the active and effective head of Youth for Nixon. He reassured his contemporaries of the candidate's accessibility, a claim that, in the circumstances, was not received with universal credulity. Off-duty policemen, or the serving police, if they were willing, were engaged by Ehrlichman's organization to tear up offensive placards and rough up, but not injure, protesters, and where hecklers did make themselves heard, Nixon had little trouble verbally rebutting them.

Humphrey did not have such a tight organization, nor such an untrusting nature, and in the early weeks, he was frequently prevented from speaking. He and his vice presidential nominee, Senator Edmund Muskie of Maine, a dignified and eloquent campaigner who made a good impression from the start and throughout (a Roman Catholic, but this was no longer much of an issue), soon attracted the support of the average reasonable American. The anti-war movement, which won some support after being brutalized by Daley's police, soon lost it by the relentless and anarchic nastiness of its attacks on the democratic process, and especially on Hubert Humphrey, an evidently decent man.

The vice president was not glamorous or very contemporary, but he had been ahead of his time on almost every issue, as Nixon had written in his newspaper column when he covered Humphrey's first senatorial campaign in 1948. Where had these scabrous, foul-mouthed, dung-throwing young people been when Hubert Humphrey led the Democratic Party to the championship of civil rights twenty years before? By his pluck and eloquence and decency, and demand only for fair play and equal time, Humphrey started to attract support, as the Democratic nominee was almost bound to do.

Nixon presented some imaginative, or at least novel, ideas on the campaign trail. He proposed opening up arms sales to Israel, and said the Middle East military balance had to be "tipped in Israel's favor." He pressed his campaign for assistance to black entrepreneurs, and campaigned widely with Senator Edward Brooke, the African-American Massachusetts Republican, who was at this point the highest elected black official in the country's history. He did not vary the message between black and white and Northern and Southern audiences.

These were interesting approaches to groups where Republicans were habitually chronic minorities. Both major candidates advocated indexing Social Security payments to the cost-of-living increase, and Nixon made broad welfare reform proposals, where Humphrey felt bound by adherence to what he and Johnson had enacted. Nixon emphasized his promise to end the draft when Vietnam was wound down, and said that the Democrats had got the country into that war and had lost their chance to end it, which he would do. Humphrey made the usual Democratic efforts to frighten the country with bowdlerized reminiscences about Herbert Hoover and Franklin D. Roosevelt and the Depression, but a whole generation had gone by, including the unexampled prosperity of the Eisenhower era, and Nixon did not need or accept any lessons from Humphrey on what the Depression had been like.

Nixon declined to debate Humphrey, saying that the real debate should be between Humphrey the former radical leftist and Humphrey the unregenerate Johnson apologist, and that he would debate the winner. Nixon's staff represented Humphrey's call for a debate as mere opportunism, and the presence of Wallace was invoked as a negative argument, since neither side wished to legitimize Wallace, and the law required that Wallace be included.

Nixon referred to Humphrey's antics as "kid stuff" and accused him of trying to promote the Wallace candidacy to take votes from Nixon and push the election into the House of Representatives if there was not a majority in the Electoral College. This was Nixon showing himself, as usual, to be the most tactically astute of the candidates. By representing Humphrey as a Wallace supporter, he debased the political coinage of both Wallace and Humphrey, and shored himself up as the preferable alternative in the eyes of the followers of both men.

Polls indicated that Agnew, though he spoke insensitively of "Polacks" and of a "fat Jap" on one occasion, and was a bit unserious generally, comparing Humphrey to Neville Chamberlain and Nixon to Winston Churchill (pretty obscure or improbable allusions to most of his listeners), was popular with people who might otherwise be tempted by Wallace. He had a similar blunt, hardhat approach, but was at least respectable on race matters and not so sociologically down-market as Wallace.

With five weeks to go to election day, Nixon was still holding a fifteen-point lead, but Humphrey was being heard and considered seriously as an alternative. Nixon was concerned that Johnson would purport to pull the rabbit out of the hat on Vietnam. The country still believed that a negoti-ated peace was possible. The doves were prattling on about a complete bombing pause and a coalition government, which, as Nixon pointed out privately, would give the communists "the whole Goddam country."[22] The prevalence of naivety in the peace camp, the idea that what they were pro-posing was anything less than surrender, made the disaffected Democrats still applying liniment to the physical and policy bruises inflicted in Chicago vulnerable to a last-minute peace move by Humphrey or Johnson, or the two together.

Johnson was just as devious as Nixon, and while he and Nixon had got on not badly over the years, Johnson was an unambiguous Democrat, and he had been Humphrey's sponsor and mentor in the Senate (he called him "my bridge to the bomb-throwers"). He had chosen Humphrey as vice pres-ident, and was instrumental in nominating him in place of Gene McCarthy. He might not be excited by either candidate, but he would not now desert his longtime protégé and the party he had served for forty years. If Johnson and Humphrey could claim the imminence of an apparently honorable, or at least not disgraceful, peace, Nixon's vague promises to end the war by "de-Americanization," intensified bombing, and more produc-tive relations with Moscow and Beijing would not impress either instant peace-seekers or hard-liners.

— v —

In this savage year of 1968, several historic Americans left the scene – most conspicuously Martin Luther King and Robert F. Kennedy, tragically, and Lyndon B. Johnson, at least sadly. The chief new arrival was the most improb-able of all, Heinz Alfred Kissinger. He had long been a foreign policy adviser to Nelson Rockefeller, and was a respected Harvard academic, historian of the Congress of Vienna, and author on Great Power politics in the nuclear age. He had emigrated with his Jewish family from Germany in 1938, and his first job was in a toothbrush factory in lower Manhattan. He was a triple graduate and long-serving faculty member at Harvard, and had served as a sergeant in the Second World War, translating in the American occupation of Germany and assisting in denazification. He built up a foreign affairs seminar at Harvard and co-editorship of the magazine *Confluence* as a springboard to association with the international foreign policy elite, and his relations with Nelson Rockefeller gave him some repute in the wings of the American political community.

His incorrigible German accent, which frequently made him sound like an imagined Groucho Marx imitation of Kaiser Wilhelm (who in fact spoke English almost without an accent), his shadowy activities but irrepressible personality, his talents at closed-door politics and media self-promotion, and his erudition, charm, and crackling wit, made him an instant celebrity, his role reflexively magnified by admirers and opponents. He became almost a Bismarckian omnipresence as soon as he became a presence at all, operating in the void between Nixon and the State Department. His relations with Nixon would be historic, and mythic, and complicated as only two such Byzantine personalities could assure.

Henry Cabot Lodge had known Kissinger on the academic-social-political circuit in Boston, and had asked him to Vietnam when Lodge was ambassador in Saigon. Kissinger spent two weeks in Saigon and around the country in September 1965, and felt that America was committed to propping up a corrupt government and had become boxed into a war strategy that could not succeed. Unless the United States struck decisively at the enemy sanctuaries in Cambodia and the Ho Chi Minh Trail, victory was militarily impossible, but doing so was politically unsustainable. Johnson was consequently on a course that would gradually lose the war and political support for the war. This showed remarkable and swift insight, and was essentially correct. The Johnson policy was, in fact, hopeless.

Kissinger said so at an off-the-record press luncheon before he left Saigon, and when one of the reporters violated the pledge of discretion, Johnson's press secretary, Bill Moyers, rebuked Kissinger, who then engaged in a wide and furious correspondence denying that he had said what he did.

Kissinger, however, publicly and loyally supported the administration, including in a number of academic debates, among them a trans-Atlantic exchange with future British Labor Party leader Michael Foot.

Kissinger was back in Vietnam in July 1966, and three months later got very industriously around the country again. He could not be "brainwashed," as George Romney claimed to have been, and discovered from peasants that even in "pacified" areas the people paid taxes to the Viet Cong. In an article in *Look* magazine in August 1966, he supported the effort and said that although the war could not be won, it must not be lost, and that the United States had to do enough to be able to negotiate for some permanent non-communist state in the South. He had grave fears of the destabilizing consequences of an American failure in this endeavor.

The beginning of Kissinger's diplomatic connection with Vietnam, which would take him to world fame and a Nobel Prize, was when he met a microbiologist, Herbert Marcovich, who had a friend, Raymond Aubrac, who was himself a friend of Ho Chi Minh, at a conference in Paris in June 1967. From this unlikely connection, Henry Kissinger managed, for the first time, to lever himself into the workings of the White House. Aubrac had known Ho when the Vietnamese communist leader lived in France in 1946. Kissinger persuaded the secretary of state, Dean Rusk, to utilize this channel, and the two Frenchmen met Ho and his prime minister, Pham Van Dong, in Hanoi on July 24, 1967.

The North Vietnamese repeated their familiar position that if the bombing of the North stopped, negotiations "could follow."[23] LBJ replied, through the same channel, that the United States would cease bombing if this would "lead promptly to productive discussions," and if the North did not exploit the bombing pause to pour increased war supplies and personnel into the South. This was slight movement by Johnson. On September 10, Marcovitch was advised by the North Vietnamese office in Paris that Johnson's proposal was rejected.

Kissinger tried various reformulations of the message, translating an "assumption" of talks into less than "a condition." He was already skilled at semantic bridging formulas. President Johnson telephoned him at a friend's weekend farm, and authorized "professor Schlesinger," as he called him, to give it one more try, but added, in the coarsest terms, that if it didn't work, the president would castrate the professor (whatever his name was).

Kissinger went to the White House to meet with Johnson, Rusk, McNamara, Clifford, Rostow, Fortas, McGeorge Bundy, and Katzenbach (who had replaced Kennedy as attorney general and then became under-secretary of state). Kissinger championed his microbiologist's channel, against the skepticism of Rusk and Johnson. The president said, "The net of it is that [Ho gets] a sanctuary in return for his consul talking with two scientists who talked with an American citizen."[24] McNamara was now a defeatist, as he sped out of government, and denied that bombing Hanoi and Haiphong accomplished anything that was useful, and so there was no reason not to stop the bombing. He had faced in all directions on this and related issues. Katzenbach was also for continuing with the scientists, but Clifford was still a hawk, and Johnson shut the channel down.

About ten weeks later, the Tet Offensive erupted. In June 1968, Kissinger participated in an academic panel on Vietnam with the other noted academics (the real) Arthur Schlesinger, Hans Morgenthau, Stanley Hoffman, and (still hawkish Vietnam specialist) Daniel Ellsberg. Kissinger was now an avowed defeatist, thinking that all the United States could get was the infamous "decent interval," that South Vietnam was a lost cause, and that it wasn't geopolitically important anyway. He was only concerned about avoiding a collapse of American credibility, by making the interval adequately decent.

When Rockefeller finally kicked off his bumbling campaign for the presidential nomination, on May 1 with a speech to a Philadelphia foreign affairs group, Kissinger wrote the Vietnam section, which showed that he was thinking along parallel lines to Nixon's. He called for handing the war to the South Vietnamese (which was more of a euphemism for a bug-out with Kissinger than it was with Nixon), and he called for exploration of relations with China, and a triangular approach to China and Russia. On this point, Kissinger and Nixon, who had met only once, at the home of Clare Booth Luce for five minutes of reciprocal awkwardness at Christmastime 1967, were now in lockstep.

On July 13, Rockefeller delivered another Vietnam speech written largely by Kissinger, in which he called for a phased, unilateral withdrawal. Kissinger attended the Miami convention with Rockefeller and constantly disparaged Nixon to all within earshot, though he had some discussion with Nixon's foreign policy adviser, Richard Allen, about the Vietnam plank of the party's platform. He was building relations with the nominee's entourage, while telling Rockefellerians, and even the press, that Nixon was "a disaster [who] fortunately . . . can't be elected."[25]

Richard Allen (twelve years later, Ronald Reagan's national security adviser) subsequently claimed that Kissinger had telephoned him in September 1968, offering confidential revelations of the Paris talks. There were allegedly four subsequent calls, all from pay phones, for security reasons. (LBJ and J. Edgar Hoover, who both were addicted to tapping other people's telephones, were as likely to intercept Allen's incoming calls as Kissinger's outgoing ones, and Kissinger's accent would be hard to mistake no matter where the call originated.) There was nothing illegal in what he was doing, so the only risk he was running was to annoy the Democrats and be considered treacherous. Under any believable scenario, given his ineffably devious methods, he was unlikely to escape that opprobrium for long, whether his telephone calls were being recorded or not.

In this first appearance on the Nixon horizon, very sketchily mentioned in the otherwise ample memoirs of both men, and hesitantly recollected by both in later years, Kissinger told Allen that he was advising Humphrey but favored Nixon's election, that he was concerned that something not in the national interest but politically opportunistic for the Democrats might be in the offing, and that he was prepared to provide intelligence to the Nixon camp.

Kissinger claims in his memoirs that both the Nixon and Humphrey campaigns called him during the campaign and that he answered specific questions in foreign policy areas from both. This verges on obfuscation. Nixon supports the Allen account that Kissinger initiated contact and did not reveal anything that was classified, but warned when a bombing halt might come. This account is almost certainly accurate. When Kissinger started calling Allen (whose mental stability Kissinger occasionally questioned and with whom he sometimes bizarrely spoke in German, supposedly to maximize security), he had already thrown in the towel on Vietnam and had no particular objection to a bombing halt. So his motive in warning that one might be imminent could only have been to ingratiate himself with Nixon, who at this point appeared electorally unbeatable.

On September 30 in Salt Lake City, Humphrey called for a bombing halt (including in the small area immediately north of the DMZ but symbolically important to the American voters), saying he was prepared to "take a risk for peace." Humphrey could do this without breaking with Johnson, who, as

Kissinger warned Mitchell in early October, was probably about to announce such a step, combined with a good deal of diplomatic activity in Paris.[26]

Humphrey's move was enough to satisfy the Democratic peace renegades that, however unexciting, he was preferable to Nixon or Wallace, or abstention. McCarthy, who had already spuriously endorsed Muskie for vice president but not Humphrey's presidential candidacy, gave the Democratic candidate an impersonal endorsement. "I'm voting for Humphrey, and I think you should suffer with me."[27] The hecklers deserted Humphrey's meetings, and the race started, slowly, to tighten.

On October 7, Nixon told the editors of United Press that he would be prepared to assist in the reconstruction of North Vietnam, after the "generous peace" that he sought. He compared his position to that of Eisenhower regarding Korea in 1952: that he could make a deal the Johnson-Humphrey administration could not. He implied that he could extract a better deal, and also that he could settle for less, with his frequent, subtle imprecision. All his polls showed Nixon still leading by at least ten points with four weeks left. If Humphrey was to get into hot contention, it was all down to Johnson. The president, like a great, caged bird, afflicted by sadness and disappointment, but formidable and cunning, was not going to relinquish his position quietly to his ancient foe, civilized though their relations now were.

Kissinger's chief contact on the Paris Vietnam discussions was Daniel Davidson, a member of Harriman's staff. To Davidson as to others, Kissinger constantly and gratuitously denigrated Nixon. On October 11, twelve days after Humphrey called for a bombing halt and two days after the North Vietnamese shifted their position in Paris to facilitate one, Nixon warned Allen and Mitchell that a bombing halt was probably imminent. Nixon was already accusing Humphrey and Johnson of using the security of American forces in Vietnam as an electoral tool.

It is not clear what role, if any, Kissinger was playing with the Humphrey campaign. Hubert Humphrey never accused him of infidelity, and continued to be a Kissinger admirer. He often said that if he had had the opportunity, he would have named Kissinger as his national security adviser. So, presumably, Kissinger was, as he wrote, available for consultations when the Humphrey campaign wished them, and sometimes it did. He did tell Davidson in September that he thought that whichever candidate won, he expected to be offered a serious position in the new administration.[28] In such a year of upheaval and acrimony, this was no small political achievement of maneuver by the Harvard professor (who had considered an offer from All Souls, Oxford, almost to the end of the summer).

Kissinger always has been an inexhaustible storehouse of nasty opinions about almost everyone. Only a few extremely powerful or intimate people are exempt from his rather unattractive habit of running down everyone, no matter how congenial he is with the individuals when he sees them. Reviling Nixon was probably reflective of the hostility to Nixon in Rockefeller and Humphrey's camp, and a sincere expression of Kissinger's own views. His truckling to Nixon, via Allen and Mitchell, was not the most admirably consistent behavior, but pretty standard Washington careerism.

Though Kissinger was a pessimist about Vietnam, he did not want the United States defeated or shamed there, and the concern that such a fate might be embraced, wittingly or otherwise, in quest of the White House was legitimate.

— VI —

Nixon hammered hard on the crime rate and attacked the Democrats' surrender of nuclear superiority, justly mocking the Kennedy claims of a missile gap eight years before. The Republicans had resented advertising in the 1964 campaign that implied that Goldwater might blow up the world (a little girl picking the ten petals off a flower, to a countdown, followed by the detonation of a hydrogen bomb behind her). In 1968, the Republicans replied by running, late in the campaign, on popular comedy television programs, footage of violent war scenes, domestic race riots, and chronically poor and ill Americans, interspersed with film of Humphrey laughing and joking and talking about "the politics of joy." Political hardball usually begets harder ball.

On October 16, Johnson arranged a teleconference with the three candidates to tell them that there had been a breakthrough in Paris – that North Vietnam no longer objected to the presence of the South Vietnamese at the conference. On Johnson's orders, Harriman had required that Hanoi also promise to respect the DMZ and refrain from attacking South Vietnamese cities. And Johnson reported that if those conditions were accepted, both the Joint Chiefs of Staff and South Vietnam's president Nguyen Van Thieu would support a bombing pause.

Nixon, who took the call in a cramped little room in the Kansas City railway station, could see the Johnson ruse coming, and stuck to his line that he would not be political about peace, though the issue was now the core of the campaign. He told audiences that a bombing pause would be welcome provided it was not a disguised surrender, reserving to himself the ability to claim just that.

By October 20, his lead over Humphrey had shrunk in some polls to just 5 percent. Wallace's vote was evaporating outside his strongholds of Alabama, Georgia, Mississippi, Louisiana, and Arkansas, as disgruntled supporters of the main parties drifted back to their natural political abodes. A profoundly regional vote might give Wallace those five states in the South, but the Northern Wallace voter was fading, not wishing to waste ballots in what was starting to seem like a possibly tight election.

In these circumstances, there was a real danger of a hung election, with the Electoral College not recording a majority, and the presidential election going to the House of Representatives and the vice presidency to the Senate, where almost certain Democratic majorities would presumably elect Humphrey and Muskie. Nixon began challenging Humphrey to agree that in the event of such a development, both sides would support the candidate with the larger popular vote. Humphrey piously uttered and tiresomely repeated the humbug that he would abide by the Constitution; i.e., logrolling in the Congress, no matter what he had to give away to Southern committee chairmen to get to the White House.

There was an inevitability of drama throughout Richard Nixon's career. His second try for the presidency was shaping up to a gripping climax. The North Vietnamese presumably preferred Humphrey to Nixon, and in any case knew that any de-escalation by the United States would be almost irreversible in domestic political terms. The South Vietnamese, for the same reasons in reverse, preferred Nixon to Humphrey. For Johnson and Humphrey to have any chance of claiming progress toward a satisfactory settlement of the war, both Vietnamese sides had to be roped into the talks in Paris.

Most of the journalists who have written on the next phases of this minuet are not reliable, and there is no documentation, and interviews did not yield much, so the story must be pieced together cautiously. The co-chairwoman, with Mamie Eisenhower, of Republican Women for Nixon, was Anna Chennault, widow of Second World War Far East volunteer air force commander (of The Flying Tigers) General Claire Chennault. She was a friend of Thieu's and served as a contact between Thieu and the Nixon campaign.

Anna Chennault and the South Vietnamese ambassador to Washington, Bui Diem, had gone to New York to meet with Nixon and Mitchell in early 1968. The Chennault conduit to Thieu was established and Nixon impressed upon the ambassador that he would be a more reliable friend of Saigon than his Democratic opponent (who hadn't been nominated, but the choice was Humphrey or McCarthy).

From here, it becomes very tangled. Anna Chennault was a strenuous admirer of Nixon, but was romantically involved with the former chief fixer in Franklin D. Roosevelt's first two terms, Thomas G. Corcoran. Corcoran was a longtime friend of Lyndon Johnson, and Corcoran's law partner, James Rowe, was the co-manager of Hubert Humphrey's election campaign. Corcoran listened on an extension to one of Mitchell's telephone calls with Chennault, and cautioned her against any violation of the Logan Act, which forbids U.S. private citizens from conducting negotiations with foreign governments. Chennault spoke to Diem and to Mitchell very frequently.[29] Diem was a very educated and urbane man whose family owned the *Saigon Post*.

Some combination of phone taps on Chennault and Mitchell, cable interceptions and decoding on the South Vietnamese embassy (despite the status of Saigon as an ally now being defended by 565,000 American draftees), and possible advice from Corcoran to Johnson or Clifford apprised the administration of the Nixon effort to restrain Thieu from becoming an agent in Humphrey's election campaign by being overly credulous or cooperative in an election-eve Johnson peace plan.[30] Mitchell changed his telephone number every couple of days and Diem complained to all sides about telephone and cable intercepts on his embassy.[31] At one point Chennault was overhead in a telephone call to a Saigon government official, urging against an early agreement to a peace plan. When asked if Nixon was aware of her call, she said the he was not, "but our friend in New Mexico" is. Agnew happened to be in New Mexico, so it was mistakenly assumed to be him, and Johnson ordered personal wiretaps on Agnew (who had dusted off the old claim that Humphrey was "soft on communism"). Agnew knew nothing of this and New Mexico was code for someone else.

Thus, Hanoi had an incentive to agree to conditions, and Saigon to oppose conditions, that would lead to a bombing pause. Chennault went to Saigon in the midst of the campaign and was in frequent contact with Ambassador Diem. There is no doubt that Johnson was trying to give himself plausible cover for a peace move and deliver the election to Humphrey, and that Nixon was determined not to be robbed of the presidency by the Democrats again. To this end, Nixon, with no illegal dealings by him or his entourage, assisted Thieu in detecting his own self-interest. The allegations have been made, but not substantiated, that Kissinger played a role in this process in Paris. In the absence of any evidence or any need for what was already being otherwise accomplished, Kissinger deserves the benefit of the doubt his enemies have created about his behavior.

The Democrats were outraged at Nixon, but what Johnson was doing was equally questionable. Nixon's desire not to be the victim again of Democratic electoral trickery is understandable, and there is no evidence that Thieu, a wily and tenacious Vietnamese political general, needed much prompting to discern which side he favored in the U.S. election. Kissinger was playing a fairly innocuous double game of self-promotion, and there was nothing very controversial, at this early stage, in his international contacts.

On October 26, sensing that it was time to interrupt Johnson's inexorable progress toward a peace move, Nixon, who had used the Paris discussions as an excuse not to comment on Vietnam for seven months, decided to reveal a likely imminent bombing halt. His source was a contact of Bryce Harlow's, who was reporting from inside the White House that Johnson was about to make a supreme effort to pull the election out for Humphrey. Nixon asked Mitchell to check with Kissinger, but Kissinger had not heard of anything imminent. Nixon purported in his statement to be confident that what was afoot was not "a cynical, last-minute attempt by President Johnson to salvage the candidacy of Mr. Humphrey." As was often the case with Nixon, what he claimed to disbelieve was what he believed. His suspicions were rarely unfounded and were not misplaced in this case.

The next day, October 27, at a luncheon speech in New York, Johnson denied that any such thing as Nixon had alleged had been agreed, and attacked Nixon as someone "who distorts history" and had made "ugly and unfair charges."[32] That evening, Nixon warned in a nationwide radio address against the evils of a coalition government in Saigon. He was firing blind, because there was no discussion of any such thing at this point, but it was a way of muddying the waters for Johnson and invigorating Thieu's always verdant suspicions.

The same day, Hanoi accepted Harriman's conditions, provided the Viet Cong could also attend the Paris talks. Despite all the jockeying, nearly seven months had passed in Paris with nothing substantive discussed, and nothing, not even participants, agreed, except the shape of the table. It is indicative of American war-weariness and the jumpy nerves of the election candidates and campaign organizers that anyone imagined Vietnam negotiations would proceed quickly.

The American commander in Vietnam, General Creighton W. Abrams, who had replaced Westmoreland a few months before, as Westmoreland became chief of staff, was summoned home and met with the president at 2:30 A.M., October 29, in the cabinet room. He supported a bombing halt. However, by this time, Thieu was balking. He said he would not join negotiations with the Viet Cong. Johnson and Clifford blamed Nixon, via Chennault, but did not want to acknowledge recourse to illegal telephone intercepts or diplomatic cable cracking of the South Vietnamese, which would have been, to say the least, an unseemly admission a week before the election. Johnson told his ambassador in Saigon, Ellsworth Bunker, to put all the pressure he could on Thieu. Thieu would not move, but Johnson, when he felt he could wait no longer before trying to influence the election, made his big play. On October 31, he told the nation in a television address that Hanoi had promised to respect the DMZ and refrain from attacking South Vietnamese cities, and that both the South Vietnamese government and the Viet Cong were, as he delicately put it, "free" to attend the Paris peace conference as participants. This generated great euphoria, and according to some polls, Humphrey pulled ahead of Nixon. Showing iron nerves, fortified by his intelligence about Thieu's likely lack of enthusiasm, Nixon briefly returned to his former policy of saying nothing that would compromise the peace process.

On November 2, three days before the election, Thieu publicly announced that he would not join the talks. Nixon had Finch issue a statement to the press expressing "surprise" that the players were not all in place prior to Johnson's announcement, by which, of course, they meant that the bombing halt was a preemptive concession to the enemy to try to salvage the election for Humphrey.

There was great anger in the Johnson and Nixon camps at the skullduggery of the other side. But Johnson and Nixon themselves, two of the most worldly and cynical political operators in American history, were relatively philosophical. Unedifying though this great poker game seems, it was not completely discreditable. Richard Nixon and Lyndon Johnson, though no sane person would ever accuse either of them of taking political ethics to a fault, were patriotic Americans. But their methods were unusually open to question at times.

Johnson had lost confidence in the military advice he had received, and was politically exhausted. He felt intensely the sorrow of bereaved armed forces families, and could not sleep at night worrying about casualties. He sincerely wanted to move the war toward a solution before leaving office. That such a move would suit his political preferences was desirable and convenient, but to what extent domestic politics predominated in the president's thoughts will never be known. It was nonsense for Thieu to claim that he would not sit at the same table as the Viet Cong. Most South Vietnamese disliked communism, but were more fearful of the VC and its North Vietnamese sponsors than of the Saigon government, which was still in place only because of the exertions of the United States. They needed reassurance that the anti-communists were likely to be the winning side.

On the other hand, Nixon, unlike Humphrey, Kissinger, McNamara, Clifford, and even, to a point, the beleaguered Johnson himself, still thought there was a possibility to salvage a durable non-communist regime in Saigon, and was prepared to try. Thieu could not be blamed for not wishing to facilitate the victory of those who were going to hand his country over to the communists, with or without an interval that might be perceived as decent from the comfortable perspective of Washington. There is no reason to believe that Nixon did more to motivate Thieu than to ensure that he was aware of what was obvious to anyone who carefully followed the 1968 U.S. election campaign.

On November 3, Nixon, after two days' silence, ended his second "personal Vietnam moratorium" and responded to Johnson's maneuver with escalated dissembling. Having approved Finch's insinuation that Johnson had made a misleading and overblown announcement about progress in peace talks for partisan reasons, he said on NBC's *Meet the Press* two days before the election that he and Finch did not agree on the subject, that Nixon gave Johnson the benefit of the doubt but Finch thought the bombing pause was a political trumpery.

Finch had not issued his statement as lieutenant governor of California but as Nixon's joint campaign manager, and this was egregious flimflam by Nixon. Nixon took it a step further, by telling the interviewer that if elected two days later, he would be happy, if President Johnson wished, to go to

Saigon or Paris "in order to try to get the negotiations off dead center." Though outrageous, this was magnificent effrontery, to offer to go to Saigon, once elected, and tell Thieu to accept what he now implicitly urged him to reject. Nixon carried it off with the expressionless sincerity of a consummate actor and poker player.

It was too much for Johnson, who telephoned Nixon and demanded to know who "Fink" was and what he was up to, and asked about Chennault's antics also. Nixon said that Finch had the same freedom of self-expression as any other American, and whatever Chennault did was on her own account and not Nixon's. Johnson persisted in referring to "Fink" – like the father of the narrator in Evelyn Waugh's *Brideshead Revisited*, refusing to accede to facts – but he had little option but to accept Nixon's version of his role. He knew it was bunk, but he knew the vulnerabilities in his own official line too, and there was no gain to him in insisting publicly that it was really Nixon who was accusing him of cynical political manipulations. This would do more harm to the Democrats than the Republicans. Nixon had deftly claimed to believe in Johnson's virtue while his aides did not, and stuck to this charade with perfectly confected earnestness.

In the last full day of the campaign, Nixon continually expressed confidence in Johnson's motives but disappointment that the hopes for peace had proved chimerical. With a doleful expression, he lamented that Johnson had, with good but over-eager intentions, sold the country a false prospectus. Given that Johnson had set out to steal the election, it must be said that Nixon's reply, labored though it was, was a political masterpiece, upon which he embellished to the last moments before the polls opened. In his memoirs, published in 1978, Nixon maintains the same air of simple and impenetrable innocence. Johnson, in his own memoirs, professes complete political disinterest, and adds, of the opposition, "People who claimed to speak for the Nixon camp began encouraging Saigon to stay away from Paris and promising that Nixon, if elected, would inaugurate a policy more to Saigon's liking."[33]

Both candidates had nationwide telethons on election eve. Humphrey had a number of film stars, including Paul Newman, manning his switchboard, and Frank Sinatra introduced him. Nixon was introduced by Jackie Gleason and Bob Hope. In such an unethical campaign, failing to close it in an atmosphere of Hollywood kitsch would have been a deprivation. Both telethons received incoming calls at the formidable volume of over two thousand per minute, for two hours with Humphrey and four hours for Nixon. On this last night, Nixon took a few more liberties, and as he regretted the false start to the dreams of Vietnam peace, he added that he had heard reliable reports of increased North Vietnamese infiltration. This was complete fabrication, and Humphrey branded it as such in the middle of his telethon.

Finally, it was over. On election day morning, November 5, Nixon, who had voted in an advance poll, flew on his campaign plane from Los Angeles to New York with his family. Below him, he saw the lights of America twinkling, as he wondered how the nation would vote. He thought he would win, but acknowledged that it was really too close to call. He went to his suite in the Waldorf Towers and remained alone in it until midnight, after taking a hot bath and trying, unsuccessfully, for a nap.

Nixon took an early popular vote lead that slowly evaporated and became a Humphrey lead of six hundred thousand by midnight. But Nixon retained a narrow advantage in the Electoral College, and after midnight started to eat into Humphrey's plurality. He finally asked for Haldeman, Mitchell, Finch, and the ineradicable Chotiner at 2:30 A.M., but didn't emerge to meet them until three. While all the networks, and news agencies and large newspapers were still calling the election a toss-up, Nixon went over his own calculations and declared to his aides that he believed they had won. The four agreed. Nixon telephoned Agnew, and Nelson Rockefeller, to thank him for his help (of which there had not been much), had a glass of beer and a cigar, and unwound. He credited the choice of Agnew for the margin of victory in a number of Southern and border states, including Kentucky and Tennessee.

His wife and daughters were in a greater state of suspense until he visited them at 6 A.M. and assured Pat, who had vomited at the news that Daley was holding back the Cook County vote again, that he was the president-elect. He told her that it was now beyond even Daley's powers of election-rigging. Pat Nixon, always reserved and calm, determined and supportive, a frequently unsung heroine of Nixon's entire turbulent public career, embraced him fervently and wept with joy and relief.[34] Between eight and nine that morning, the networks conceded Nixon's victory, and foreign news organizations acknowledged, many of them rather wistfully (so rampant was Vietnam-era anti-Americanism), that Wallace would play no role in choosing the president and that the process had produced a winner. At 11:30 A.M., Hubert Humphrey telephoned, and a few minutes later Lyndon Johnson, both very graciously, and the White House prepared a statement acknowledging Nixon's victory and promising Johnson's co-operation. In newsrooms around the world, emergency bulletin bells on news wires rang for a full minute announcing the imminent arrival of a maximum-interest, breaking news item. It came at 11:57 A.M., Eastern Standard Time: "Nixon is elected."

Nixon had polled 31,770,237 votes to 31,270,533 for Humphrey and 9,906,141 for Wallace (43.4 percent to 42.7 percent to 13.5 percent). Other candidates polled just 239,908 (.35 percent). Of the eight largest states, Nixon had taken California, Illinois, Ohio, and New Jersey; Humphrey prevailed in New York, Pennsylvania, Texas (thanks entirely to Johnson), and Michigan. Except for Texas and Washington, and Humphrey's home state of Minnesota, Nixon took everything on the Great Plains, in the Rocky Mountains, and in the Far West. Wallace, as expected, held Arkansas, Louisiana, Alabama, Mississippi, and Georgia. (Strom Thurmond held South Carolina for Nixon, who took the rest of the South.) Humphrey took all the Northeast except New Jersey, Vermont, and New Hampshire. The Electoral College vote was 301 for Nixon, 191 for Humphrey, and 46 for Wallace. Johnson blamed the defeat of his party on the extremists in Chicago and the universities, "who offended the majority of American citizens and pushed them to the right."[35]

The Republicans gained five Senate and four House seats, but the Democrats retained comfortable majorities, 58 to 42 and 243 to 192. Nixon was the first president since Zachary Taylor in 1848 to enter a first term in office without his party controlling either house of Congress (though the same fate had befallen Eisenhower when he was reelected in 1956).

It had been far from the worst American presidential campaign in out-right mudslinging, but in shameless but sophisticated political chicanery, Johnson and Nixon had written a new playbook, and 1968 was the *ne plus ultra* of American elections. The system had worked without recourse to the courts or the Congress, which had been feared. Wallace's overt pitch to racial and social antagonisms failed. There was no violence and no serious suggestion of voting irregularities. In a terrible year and a tormented time,

Americans voted in quite strong numbers (around 62 percent – Johnson's Voting Rights Act had helped). They chose from among a group of very able candidates (Johnson, Kennedy, Humphrey, Rockefeller, Reagan, and Nixon were an unprecedentedly impressive cast of contenders, an encouraging fact in such a desperate year for the country).

Nixon had achieved an astounding comeback from six years before, and had demonstrated an artist's mastery of the American political process. As soon as he was declared elected, as is customary in the United States, he started to look like a president and be treated like one by the media, and there was relief that there would be a change. Even people who disliked Nixon acknowledged that he was intelligent and experienced, and might prove a good leader after all.

It must be said that Hubert Humphrey staged a courageous and principled campaign. A tireless advocate of good and often noble causes for a quarter of a century, he was shamefully reviled by the New Left, and subjected to disgraceful harassment in his early election tours. Squeezed between two of the roughest and wiliest politicians in the country's history, who used the rawest electoral tactics ever resorted to in an American presidential election, and subjected to the snide carping of Gene McCarthy, who owed much to Humphrey, and also to attacks in the low demagogy of Wallace, Humphrey never became ill-tempered or even downcast.

He fought gamely back from a terrible disadvantage after the horrifying fiasco in Chicago, made the election a cliff-hanger, and conceded and conducted himself thereafter with the utmost taste and discretion. Johnson and Nixon (much less Wallace) had not upheld the highest electoral traditions of the country, though they contributed to its political history and folklore. But Humphrey did uphold them, and he did those traditions, and himself, honor.

With his wife and daughters and David Eisenhower, Richard Nixon appeared in the ballroom of the Waldorf-Astoria a few minutes after noon on November 6. He reciprocated the courtesy of Humphrey and Johnson, and pledged to try to "bring the country together." It was a dignified end to a rending struggle. Of the thirty-five men who had preceded Richard Nixon in the nation's highest office, only Abraham Lincoln facing civil war, and Franklin D. Roosevelt inheriting the almost complete economic and psychological collapse of the Great Depression, had taken on such a daunting task as the new president-elect.

The Nixons went home and their daughters made lunch, as their house-keepers, the Sanchezes, were taking their oaths as American citizens. Nixon sat alone in his library and played Richard Rodgers's score of *Victory at Sea* (something of a lift from Wagner's *Ring* cycle, but a suitably upbeat piece).[36] Later in the day, they flew to Key Biscayne, and stayed in a house owned by Democratic Senator George Smathers, next to Bebe Rebozo's. For the first time in the Nixons's lives, the Secret Service and the national press corps were present in strength, and privacy became more difficult than ever.

Hubert Humphrey stopped at Opa-locka, Florida, on his way to a holiday in the Virgin Islands. He and Nixon met privately in a Coast Guard station. Humphrey, an emotional man, wept, and Nixon expressed under-standing, having gone through a similar session with Kennedy eight years before. Nixon offered Humphrey the ambassadorship to the UN, but Humphrey said, as Nixon had to Kennedy, that he would be a loyal leader of the opposition. In his remarks to the press later, Humphrey was upbeat and generous to his late opponent.[37]

Nixon began assembling his administration, with Rose Mary Woods as principal secretary and Bob Haldeman as chief of staff. Where Woods was virtually one of the family, Nixon's relationship with Haldeman was entirely professional. Nixon knew nothing about his family or private life. Nixon was so wary of the press corps, whom he recognized as essentially adversaries, that he named Herb Klein, a loyalist since 1946 who was popular with the press at all levels, as director of communications, a new and undefined position, and the twenty-nine-year-old Ron Ziegler, who did not command the respect of the hard-bitten White House reporters, as press secretary. Klein and Ziegler would have to work out for themselves, without much help from Nixon, a division of tasks between them. John Ehrlichman became White House counsel, but with sizable responsibilities in domestic policy coordination.

Nixon went to a foreign policy briefing at the White House on November 11. He was unaccompanied, and met with Johnson, Rusk, Clifford, Helms (CIA director), and Rostow. Nixon agreed to assist in pushing Thieu to join the Paris talks. Clifford proposed the beginning of troop withdrawals. Nixon was noncommittal to that. When Mitchell called Chennault and asked her to tell Thieu on Nixon's behalf to go to Paris after all, she refused, since she had given the South Vietnamese president the opposite message from the same source just two weeks before. Nixon wrote to Thieu himself.

Nixon was determined to be his own secretary of state, and needed a skillful executant as national security adviser if he wanted to keep control of the main lines of foreign policy in the White House. This course of action has scandalized many observers, but there is plenty of precedent for it. Nixon's treatment of the State Department was less high-handed than that of Woodrow Wilson or Franklin D. Roosevelt. Roosevelt's secretary of state, Cordell Hull, did not attend either of the Big Three meetings (Teheran and Yalta), nor any of the meetings with Churchill, except when they occurred in Washington. He played some role in pre-war negotiations with Japan, but almost none in dealing with the main allies, Britain and Russia. Wilson paid no attention at all to his secretary of state, William Jennings Bryan, a three-time presidential candidate from Nebraska, or to his successor, Robert Lansing, the Dulleses' uncle.

Lodge had recommended Kissinger, and Nixon noted Kissinger's helpfulness during the campaign. Nixon's appointments secretary, Dwight Chapin, called Kissinger out of lunch with Nelson Rockefeller on November 22 to arrange for him to see Nixon on Monday, November 25, at Nixon's transition headquarters in the Pierre Hotel. Kissinger found Nixon nervous, and his conversation somewhat disjointed. They did, however, agree on their skepticism about the competence and loyalty of the State Department staff, and Nixon emphasized the need to cease to be completely preoccupied with Vietnam, to attempt to develop a relationship with China, and to reactivate the European alliance. He hinted that he would like to have Kissinger in his administration, and Kissinger hinted that he would be interested.

On November 23, Nixon told Rockefeller, who thought he might be offered a serious position, that he would prefer him to remain as governor of New York, and Mitchell invited Kissinger to return to see Nixon on November 24. When Kissinger did so, Mitchell asked him if he wanted to be national security adviser, and took him down the hall to see Nixon, who confirmed the offer. Kissinger said that he was flattered and that he would need a few days to organize support for acceptance from his colleagues in the Rockefeller campaign and at Harvard. Nixon strangely acquiesced in this rather cavalier treatment, which Rockefeller himself considered to be discourteous. Nixon "had a strong intuition about Henry Kissinger."[38]

Rockefeller himself thought it an excellent move, for Nixon and for Kissinger, and after a few days of maneuvering, Kissinger had most of his academic friends urging acceptance, despite their reservations about the president-elect. Kissinger telephoned his acceptance on November 29, and Nixon announced the appointment with Kissinger at his side, in the press room of the Pierre, on December 2. Nixon assured everyone that Kissinger would be engaged in long-term planning and would not be a "wall" between the president and the secretaries of state and defense. This was exactly the opposite of what he and Kissinger had agreed, and what they immediately set out to achieve. This was dissembling that would soon prove typical of both of them in office.

Nixon received J. Edgar Hoover at the Pierre at the end of November. Their relations had been generally cordial for over twenty years. Nixon was not always impressed by the FBI, but he had been aware, almost all of his conscient life, of the director's power. Hoover was now lumbering determinedly through his fifth decade in that position. Nixon told him that he would continue Johnson's waiver of the obligatory retirement at age seventy, which Hoover had passed in 1965. Hoover then started to arm Nixon with secrets about his opponents, including that Johnson had had him bug Nixon's campaign plane, as he had bugged Martin Luther King and other civil rights leaders, and even Hubert Humphrey. Nixon was aware that Chennault's and Mitchell's telephones had been tapped, but was somewhat surprised at some of the liberties Johnson had taken. Hoover warned Nixon that he should not make calls through the White House switchboard: "Johnson has it rigged and little men you don't know will be listening."[39] Nixon told Haldeman to get rid of all Johnson's taping equipment, one of many ironies that would afflict Nixon's presidency.

Nixon tried to recruit some other Democrats, besides Humphrey as ambassador to the UN, including Senator Henry Jackson as secretary of defense, but he also declined. He tried John and Robert Kennedy's brother-in-law Sargent Shriver, at the UN, but Shriver, Johnson's director of the War on Poverty and then ambassador to France, wanted an assurance that none of the programs he had administered would be cut. Nixon considered this "intolerable" and looked elsewhere.[40] His efforts to bring in high-level African-Americans were also unsuccessful. Senator Brooke declined the UN position, and Whitney Young of the National Urban League declined Housing and Urban Development.

Nixon did succeed in recruiting Daniel Patrick Moynihan, a Harvard professor who had been a fairly senior maverick intellectual in the Kennedy and Johnson administrations. Nixon had read some of his unconventional criticisms of the Great Society, and they had an excellent meeting. Nixon said he intended to set up an Urban Affairs Council, which would be a domestic version of the National Security Council. He offered Moynihan the leadership of it and Moynihan eagerly accepted.

Nixon created the post of counselor to the president, and gave it to Arthur Burns, an esteemed conservative economist who had served in his 1960 campaign. Kissinger, Moynihan, and Burns were powerful minds and personalities to have in offices proximate to the president, and sent an early message that the White House would be asserting itself across a wide policy range.

Robert Finch became secretary of Health, Education, and Welfare. George Shultz became secretary of labor, and Maurice Stans became secretary of commerce. These were all strong appointments. Shultz, Nixon had learned, had been widely praised for his arbitration decisions in labor-management disputes. Shultz was head of the school of administration of the University of Chicago, and had been a combat officer in the U.S. Marine Corps in the Second World War. He now began one of the longest, most varied, and most distinguished cabinet careers in American history, including over six years as secretary of state (1982–89).

The head of the Continental Illinois National Bank of Chicago, David Kennedy, became secretary of the Treasury, as Nixon wanted someone who was not from Wall Street or Boston, financial communities that he felt considered the U.S. Treasury to be their fiefdom. John Mitchell, after his prodigies during the campaign, became attorney general (though very concerned about the state of his outspoken wife, whose overwrought emotional and nervous condition was a constant worry, and would become a matter of national interest). Congressman Melvin Laird, an astute operator well-regarded in the House of Representatives, became secretary of defense. Nixon had been unimpressed with the graduates to the Pentagon from the automobile industry, Charles Wilson under Eisenhower and Robert McNamara under Kennedy and Johnson.

Conservative University of Michigan economist Paul McCracken became chairman of the Council of Economic Advisers, and Nixon's old friend William P. Rogers became the secretary of state, with no warning from Nixon about what sort of tussle was about to break out between him and Kissinger. Nixon's first choice had been Robert Murphy, who would have been an eccentric appointment. He had been a career diplomat for forty years, including ambassador to Belgium and to Japan. As FDR's representative in North Africa in 1942, he was responsible for the elevation of the treacherous Admiral Darlan and the very limited General Giraud, and was complicit in the underestimation of de Gaulle. He was an interesting journeyman, then seventy-four, with little foreign policy judgment. He was not what was required.

George Romney became secretary of Housing and Urban Development; the governor of Alaska, Walter Hickel, took Interior; Clifford Hardin became Agriculture secretary, and John Volpe got Transportation. (Volpe, the governor of Massachusetts, had stood in for Nixon in the Massachusetts primary.) Winton Blount became postmaster general, even though in the fund crisis of 1952, he had told Eisenhower that "Nixon is as expendable as a Normandy paratrooper, [he's] Humpty Dumpty, no matter what."[41] He had presumably developed a greater appreciation of Nixon's qualities in the intervening time. These and other appointments were generally well received.

The cabinet was composed of moderate, colorless, and self-made men of reasonable apparent competence, representing the strength of the Nixon Republicans in the prosperous executive and professional suburbs of America. Despite the fact that there were no African-Americans, Jews, or women in the group, the media and the Democratic majority in the Senate found all of them well-qualified and all were approved without difficulty. There were no great stars among them (though Shultz became a star), just solid bourgeois Republicans. For the senior foreign ambassadorial position, Nixon named his old friend and generous supporter Walter H. Annenberg, owner of the *Philadelphia Inquirer* and *TV Guide*, one of the nation's most distinguished publishers and philanthropists.

The Nixons enjoyed a pleasant diversion with the wedding of Julie to David Eisenhower on December 22 at New York's Marble Collegiate Church. Norman Vincent Peale presided. General and Mrs. Eisenhower attended by closed-circuit television from Walter Reed Hospital (although the picture failed and only the sound was continuous). Clare Booth Luce, Thomas E. Dewey, and Nixon's wealthy friends and new cabinet members-designate attended.

This and the election were the apotheosis in the eighteen-year seesaw relationship between Richard Nixon and Dwight D. Eisenhower. Now that he was the president-elect, and had made it on his own, and Eisenhower was on his deathbed, Eisenhower was happy to embrace his loyal vice president wholeheartedly as his worthy successor.

In 1952, Nixon had been the sly promoter of Eisenhower, whose services were too shadowy to be acknowledged. Eisenhower, perhaps to emphasize his great prestige and popularity in the country, almost under-indulged Nixon, as if to convince himself that he had not needed Nixon at all, and that Nixon served exclusively at Eisenhower's pleasure. When Nixon finally got the presidential nomination in 1960, he overcompensated for his years of subordinacy and did not seek Eisenhower's help when it was available and could have been decisive. Like everyone else, Eisenhower assumed Nixon was a spent political force, and like everyone else, he had to admire the cunning and determination of his comeback.

One must go back to the earliest days of the country, to Washington, Jefferson, and Madison, to find a relationship between presidents that might have been as prolonged and intricate as that between Eisenhower and Nixon.

Another figure from the early days of the Eisenhower-Nixon relationship was Chief Justice Earl Warren. The lack of rapport between Nixon and Warren was well-known, and it was thought that Nixon might ask for someone else to swear him as president, or that Warren might decline to do it. But Nixon made a point of courteously asking for Warren to perform the ceremony, and the chief justice expressed pleasure in doing so.

It was his last important act as chief justice, but it was another dignified closure to a long and generally rather antagonistic relationship. Warren had been a controversial chief justice, but without his court's impetus to de-segregation, an insoluble problem would have festered and been more of a moral impediment and retardant to national life and progress than it was. This would effectively be his departure too, as it was Johnson's, and Humphrey's, and he left his mark, generally a positive one in human terms, if not always as well reasoned legally as it might have been, and underappreciated by Eisenhower though it was.

Nixon was taking over a country that, whatever its social and political turmoil, was in good economic condition. As in previous wars, prosperity came with increased military expenses. There was full employment (just over

3 percent unemployment), and inflation was about 4.5 percent, creeping up, but far from severe. There was a modest trade surplus, and the federal budget deficit, though larger than Johnson would like, was nothing to worry about. There was some danger of inflation, but economically, the Kennedy-Johnson record had been eight years of unbroken prosperity, a better record, with greater tax reductions, than in the Eisenhower years. Wars do tend to be economically stimulative, providing they are far from the shores of the combatant country, whatever hardships and sadnesses they bring in other respects.

The Nixons went to California for New Year's and were welcomed back to their state as heroes, with a large reception at the Anaheim Convention Center. They attended the Rose Bowl, and Nixon gave some advice to the Ohio State coach, the much-admired, and active pro-Nixon Republican, Woody Hayes. Although the opposing Southern California halfback, O.J. Simpson, was the game's star, Hayes and Ohio won. For Nixon's fifty-sixth birthday, January 9, the Nixons went to Julie's student apartment at Northampton, Massachusetts, where she cooked them a dinner. Julie had returned to Smith College, and David Eisenhower was able to drive to lectures at Amherst.

Nixon finished preparing his inaugural address in Florida. Johnson lent him Air Force One, and when the president-elect and his wife boarded the plane, and thought no one was watching, Nixon hugged his wife, lifted her off her feet, and whirled her around.[42]

On January 20, the Nixons were warmly greeted at the White House by the Johnsons and the Humphreys. Johnson wrote in his memoirs that he considered Nixon "a much-maligned and misunderstood man. I looked on Nixon as a tough, unyielding partisan and a shrewd politician, but always a man trying to do the best for his country as he saw it."[43] The same could be said of Johnson. In fact, since Eisenhower never lifted a finger to help the Republican Party, and Hoover, though much respected in the twenties, had walked off an electoral cliff into the Great Depression in his first year in office, Nixon was really the first Republican president the Democrats had had to take seriously as a political threat to their party since Theodore Roosevelt.

This day marked the painful end of the long public career of Johnson and the temporary retirement and permanent retreat of Humphrey. They had rendered the country conspicuous service. Nixon told Johnson he would be consulting him regularly and wanted a relationship with him like Johnson had had with Eisenhower. He had already told him that he intended to see Vietnam through to a satisfactory conclusion and would see to it that Johnson got his share of the credit. He jokingly asked Humphrey to give the inaugural address for him, and the outgoing vice president instantly replied that that had been his intention but that Nixon had spoiled his plans. In the car to the Capitol, Johnson volunteered that the press had "slobbered" over Muskie but he had delivered only Maine, while Agnew had brought in five Southern states for Nixon.[44] (That had been Nixon's view on election night.)

Pat held two Milhous family Bibles for the swearing-in, and they were opened at Isaiah 2:4, at Nixon's request: "They shall beat their swords into plowshares, and their spears into pruning hooks." Kissinger recorded that Nixon's trousers were slightly too short (often the case with Americans), and that although he extended his jaw purposefully, Nixon seemed "uncertain."[45] Moynihan, Price, and Nixon himself were the chief authors of the address, which strongly emphasized the quest for domestic and international peace. To the African-Americans he said, "No man can be fully free while his neighbor is not. . . . [All must] go forward together. This means black and white together, as one nation, not two." (The one-nation theme was taken from Disraeli.) Nixon had seen his percentage of the black vote go from 32 percent in 1960 to 6 percent for Goldwater, and only back to 12 percent in 1968, but he was determined to work on it. He had never wavered in his commitment to civil rights.

He said, "The greatest title history can bestow is the title of peacemaker" and made a "sacred commitment . . . to the cause of peace among nations." In domestic terms, he said that the country had "suffered from a fever of words." He decried "inflated . . . angry . . . and bombastic rhetoric," undeterred by the fact that he had recently contributed a good deal of each category of it. He struck a resonant note when he said, "We cannot learn from one another until we stop shouting at one another." Nixon kissed Mamie Eisenhower and stood with Johnson, each with an arm behind the back of the other and the other arm waving. Comment on Nixon's address was uniformly positive, and Eisenhower issued a statement expressing admiration for the new president's remarks, from the perspective, he wrote somewhat gratuitously, of "one who has grown old in the service of the Republic."

The parade proceeded from the Capitol to the White House. On the first part of the route, there was an ugly scene of demonstrators who had not taken the president's inaugural spirit to heart. There were anti-Nixon and pro-North Vietnamese placards, and many burned the miniature American flags that had been handed out by the Boy Scouts. The police, supplemented by the Secret Service and a ceremonial but instantly capable military contingent, kept demonstrators out of the street, but at one point Nixon's car was pelted with bottles and refuse. The car quickly emerged into a stretch that was free of demonstrators and Nixon ordered the sunroof opened, and, in defiance of security advice, he and his wife stood for most of the ride, receiving generous applause from the crowds. It had been a shabby incident, but Nixon, in his first presidential decision, had clearly won the public relations contest with the demonstrators.

After the parade and a tour of the inaugural balls, the Nixons and the young Eisenhowers had a party for close friends at the White House, starting at 1:30 A.M. David showed them around and found a note he had left under a rug when his grandfather moved out, eight years before. (In the note, he quoted his grandfather's former commander, MacArthur: "I shall return.")[46] Pat asked that all the lights in the Executive Mansion be turned on, and this was done. The almost simultaneous illumination was a striking sight and gesture.

— VIII —

The greatest immediate issue was Vietnam. Nixon was also concerned about reconstructing the Western alliance, pursuing arms control, exploring a possible relationship with China, activating a peace process in the Middle East, rather than just a reflexive approval of whatever Israel did; and, in domestic affairs, adopting anti-crime measures, ensuring that inflation did not get out of control, accelerating desegregation by sensible means, and reforming welfare, to make it more of a self-help, and less of an addictive and self-amplifying, program. From the beginning, he wanted to make the point that, unlike Johnson, he went where he wished in the country and was well-received by most citizens. Most people were disposed to give the new president a chance and even Herblock, the antagonistic *Washington*

Post cartoonist, ran a flattering caricature of Nixon without his stubbly beard and said everyone is entitled to a fresh start.[*]

The world waited to see what Nixon, who had essentially finessed the issue, proposed to do about Vietnam. The American Army in that country was suffering about three hundred dead a week – a total of thirty-one thousand dead by inauguration day, 1969. Johnson, as has been mentioned, had a completely futile policy after his Manila communiqué with Thieu in October 1966. Once he had promised to withdraw all American forces six months after the withdrawal of the North Vietnamese from the South, there was no chance of a satisfactory outcome for the Americans, unless the offer was rescinded, because if the North Vietnamese ever did withdraw, they would return shortly after the Americans departed, and the Americans would never return.

Though the North Vietnamese losses were horrific, they showed no signs of cracking, and the American high command now believed that Ho Chi Minh and his government were unaffected by casualties, unless they reached such a level that they literally ran out of manpower. Johnson softened the Manila proposal in 1968, on March 31 and October 31, to a complete suspension of bombing of the North in exchange for unconditional negotiations. After seven months, the participants in the negotiations had not been agreed and all that was established was that they would have a round table. Johnson had been unable even to sue for peace. Hanoi effectively insisted that the Americans just get out. (Ho Chi Minh should have accepted Johnson's Manila offer at the end of 1966. The Americans would have been completely out by the end of 1967; LBJ would have been reelected, and Ho would have entered Saigon in triumph, in 1969, six years before his successors did.)

If there was no chance of a satisfactory outcome of the war for the United States, there was no point to fight on in the war, so Nixon had either to implement a new policy with a chance of securing a permanent non-communist state in South Vietnam, or withdraw. He could do either, at least in theory, as he was not bound by what Johnson had done, either in plunging

---

[*] Not quite in this spirit was Tom Wicker of the *New York Times*, eventually a somewhat sympathetic biographer of Nixon, who wrote on January 19 that there was an even chance that Nixon would blow up the world. Nixon still affected some otherwise reasonable people that way.

into Vietnam or proposing possible withdrawal terms. So Nixon could retract Johnson's Manila and 1968 offers and stipulate stiffer peace terms, or withdraw the entire expeditionary force, or anything in between. At this point, the polls indicated that everyone in the United States wanted out of Vietnam, but slightly more wanted to leave by escalating and winning than "by plane and by boat," as the bon mot of the day put cutting and running. Either course – escalation or instant withdrawal – would cause huge political perturbations in the United States, but Nixon would never have greater possibilities for general support than at the start of his administration.

Nixon should have known the Democrats well enough to know that they would wait the minimum period necessary before declaring Vietnam to be Nixon's war and then undercutting him at every opportunity. He also knew, from Eisenhower and his own observations in his visits to Vietnam, as Kissinger did, that the only way to stop the endless infiltration of the South by the North was to cut the entire Ho Chi Minh Trail by moving west from the DMZ in ten-division strength and reinforcing the position with massive and constant aerial bombardment of all land approaches from the North. This would require a limited violation of Kennedy's acceptance of a "neutralist" coalition in Laos, which everyone knew would be a fig leaf for communist Pathet Lao assistance to North Vietnamese infiltration of the South. Nixon had opposed the coalition, when it was agreed in 1962, as "communist victory on the installment plan through the fraud of neutrality" – an accurate description.

More delicate still was the question of what to do about the three hundred and twenty thousand communist Chinese non-combat soldiers in North Vietnam, freeing an equivalent number of North Vietnamese for combat functions. Nixon could have justified the importation of corresponding numbers of Taiwanese into South Vietnam but was concerned about domestic U.S. reaction and sought a new relationship with the People's Republic.

It would also be necessary to get rid of North Vietnam's sophisticated, Soviet-supplied anti-aircraft missile system, to mine and close down Haiphong Harbor, and to apply overwhelming pressure to all logistical and war-making targets in North Vietnam. As this would probably lead to a redoubled effort to supply the war through Cambodia, it might be necessary to blockade the Cambodian port of Sihanoukville, and the North Vietnamese Army/Viet Cong sanctuaries in Cambodia just inside the South Vietnamese border would certainly have to be cleaned out. Under this scenario, a massive overhaul would also have to be made on the South Vietnamese Army to train and motivate and supply it so it could conduct the war within its own borders. But if the Americans could keep the North Vietnamese out, and provide instant close-air support in-country, this might be possible. Much less than this was unlikely to produce a durable non-communist state in the South, and it would be better for Nixon to call the whole enterprise a mistake and go, leaving the Democrats to carry the can for it, than to engage in half-measures. This is not to conclude that the retention of South Vietnam would in itself justify such severe war-making, but the objective was unlikely to be accomplished with a less comprehensive effort.

The complication to this clean choice between massive escalation and almost instant abandonment was that most people and most policy planners couldn't face the political heat that would come with such escalation, and few were prepared to be associated with an outright U.S. military defeat, the first in the country's history. To avoid being dragged down by the war, Nixon had to secure bipartisan support for one policy or the other – presumably, given his views, the victory-by-escalation option – and make it clear that if the Democrats did not sign on to give that policy a reasonable chance, he would pull the plug and put the responsibility for the costly failure of Vietnam on them, where it belonged.

Kissinger, though he cut his suit to fit the cloth of the president's policy, was a decent-interval advocate, as he did not want the United States identified with a military defeat but regarded the war as hopeless. His reasons for seeking an interval were not jingoistic egotism, but concern for a political vacuum and destabilization resulting from American defeat and loss of military and political credibility. This was an arguable view, but it could never be presented in its true colors in the United States, where a conscript army was not prepared, or expected, to risk all for such an inglorious objective.

This might have played a role in Nixon's pledge, which was redeemed, of volunteer armed forces. In the past, the United States had raised land armies for direct national emergencies only. There had been no concept, until the Cold War, of a permanent preventive force deployed abroad. The notion of a draft was acceptable to Americans for unlimited national emergencies. Truman and Eisenhower had threatened recourse to nuclear weapons at any point on the worldwide perimeter of the Western and Communist blocs. Kennedy presaged flexible response in his famous inaugural address, rather than an automatic recourse to the hair trigger of nuclear weapons. The United States then promptly became ensnared in Vietnam, where, obviously, nuclear weapons were out of the question, but it was not clear that the use of twenty-five divisions of draftee forces taking up to fifteen thousand dead a year was justified either.

Nixon adopted, as quickly as he could, the appropriate strategic responses. He transformed Kennedy's professed willingness to "bear any burden" in support of liberty to mean that the United States would help any endangered country bear the burden, and would commit all its forces only in strategically vital areas, such as Western Europe. He would reverse the Kennedy-Johnson-McNamara policy of mutual assured destruction with a policy of nuclear superiority, which he quickly defined in office, more soberly, as "nuclear sufficiency," while pursuing nuclear arms control with the U.S.S.R. from a position of strength.

For some reason, Nixon, so often a pessimist, thought that he could end the Vietnam war within a year. He knew that any recourse to the good offices of Moscow and Beijing, and any improvement in the fighting capacities of the South Vietnamese, would be time-consuming, so it is not clear why he thought he could extract himself more swiftly than he did, without losing the war. He had studied Vietnam carefully and had a good idea of the tenacity of the North. He somehow imagined that he could partly replicate Eisenhower's peace in Korea (although he had disapproved of it at the time). He believed that he could frighten Hanoi by recourse to what he called the "Madman Theory"[47]: that everyone knew that Nixon had suggested the use of nuclear weapons in Indochina in 1954, and possibly against Red China over Quemoy and Matsu, and that he was capable of anything, no matter how draconian, to punish North Vietnam.

He seemed to think that Hanoi would see his election as a defeat of the U.S. peace party, and that he could stabilize American opinion with a substantial peace offer, and rally the United States behind a more comprehensive, but not drastically escalated, war effort that would rely steadily more on the South Vietnamese. He prepared what he considered a fair peace proposal to Hanoi that provided for a continuing U.S. right of enforcement, and effectively revoked Johnson's Manila and 1968 offers of unconditional negotiations in exchange for a full bombing halt over the North, toward full withdrawal six months after the North Vietnamese were out. Nixon seemed to see Vietnam more as policy mismanagement than as an issue that produced a blood-revulsion in the country.

Nixon resolved to make military conditions produce a correlation of forces that would make realistic to the North Vietnamese a peace that was acceptable to the United States. He thus started to carve out a march to peace that was more than the cynical decent interval that Kissinger thought was all that was attainable, but less than the drastic escalation that might have forced Hanoi to negotiate seriously, instead of wasting the lives of tens of thousands of American soldiers, and four years of the time of serious American diplomats (starting with the durable Henry Cabot Lodge, who replaced Harriman and Cyrus Vance) in Paris. It was a very hazardous policy, as there was no assurance that the South could ever, in these circumstances, be made capable of self-defense against the North.

Though his war policy was better than Johnson's, Nixon did not have Johnson's majorities in the Congress. Nixon later claimed not to realize that if he did not get the congressional Democrats committed to a bipartisan Vietnam policy, they would hang the war on him, probably after an indecently short interval. Having implied that he had the key to success in ending the war, he had incited a good deal of impatient partisanship on the opposition benches in Congress, which controlled funding for the war. Months passed, and the Democrats started to edge away from "the president's war."

— IX —

As Nixon was delivering his inaugural address, Kissinger was writing up three memoranda that he brought to the inaugural parade reviewing stand for Rogers to sign. These abolished the Senior Interdepartmental Group, chaired by the undersecretary of state, which had determined what matters would be put before the National Security Council, and replaced it with the Review Group, chaired by the national security adviser. These initial memoranda also enabled the national security adviser to require briefing papers and research from the State and Defense departments. Thus the White House would be able to use the bureaucracy when it wanted to, without involving it in decision-making. Rogers, a cheerful man who had made his way on his legal judgment and intuition and pleasant personality, rather than any skill at bureaucratic maneuver, cheerfully signed away much of the power of his office before the inaugural parade was over.[48]

Nixon came to work on his first full day as president, January 21, 1969, at seven thirty, after only four hours' sleep. He had resurrected the Wilson desk that he had used as vice president, which had been in LBJ's Texas office. (It will be remembered that he had asked for it in 1953, because of his admiration for Woodrow Wilson, but later discovered that it had been the desk of Henry Wilson, Grant's second vice president.) Nixon had stripped out Johnson's taping equipment and his elaborate system of television sets and news tickers, and his immense telephone console with scores of buttons on it. He did require a written daily news summary, of all media, on which he wrote comments and demands for follow-up action every day of his presidency. The White House advisers, Kissinger, Moynihan, Burns, were much stronger than the cabinet, who were, except for Shultz, Finch, and Stans, essentially a group of jut-jawed, unsophisticatedly accomplished Rotarians. The new president's first appointment was with Henry Kissinger at seven-fifty.

This was the official beginning of an astonishing and historic relationship. Both men were devious outsiders, overwhelmingly ambitious, excessively suspicious, and always inclined to fear the worst, mistrust everyone, and impute low motives to virtually everybody. But where Nixon tended to be shy and awkward and only occasionally humorous, Kissinger was gregarious, charming, witty, a great presentational talent, and in all respects a formidable personality. For a time, Nixon was proud of Kissinger, a star, and, in his own thoughts, almost like a son, and his pleasure at employing him was probably augmented by having hired him away from Rockefeller. Where Nixon was generally rather serious, Kissinger was a sparkling wit, and disguised some of his own foibles by mock self-deprecation, frequently responding to compliments or deferences with "You are feeding my megalomania." Kissinger played the press like a violin, awesome in his articulation and knowledge, disarming in his apparent confidences, and often very amusing. (When, as secretary of state, he arrived at a friend's son's bar mitzvah and was asked by a journalist if it reminded him of his own bar mitzvah, in Germany, he instantly replied, "Actually, von Ribbentrop wasn't able to come to mine.")

Though Nixon had less personality than Kissinger, and was a more somber person, he was more confident of America. He had not been chased out of his country as Kissinger and his family had been by the Nazis, and Nixon had, after all, been elected to high public office many times. However unpopular he was in certain circles, however uneasy with himself in some ways, and driven, hesitant, and sometimes even socially inept though he was, he had millions of admirers and the legitimacy of person as well as office that only electoral success can give. And whatever his fatalism and fear that success could only come after unbelievable effort, and was apt to be fleeting, deceptive, or changeable, he was yet a Quaker, a practicing Christian, a Californian exemplar of the American meritocracy, who believed in America's manifest destiny to achieve human triumphs undreamed of by any other nation. He was also a loyal man, who reciprocated favors and was touchingly generous countless times throughout his life.

Kissinger was a much more unambiguous and self-absorbed egotist. An atheist and fugitive, he had monumental confidence in himself but acute insecurity about his circumstances, and no particular or spiritual attachment to his country, or to any faith, culture, or person, except his immediate family. Isolated from matters that could influence his own career, he sometimes showed a fine sensibility as an older man, but mostly, almost always in fact, he gravitated, as if directed by a radar-based guidance system, toward the accretively powerful and away from those in decline, or of no evident importance. Nixon was generally kind to low-echelon employees, where Kissinger was usually brusque and impersonal. But Nixon the politician was vulnerable to the blandishments and counsel of extreme cynics and people of some thuggish mien, like Chotiner and Chuck Colson, where Kissinger the snob took his distance early from suspect characters. Kissinger frequently pandered to the media and social elite's hostility to Nixon by privately disparaging the president whom he served, but played on Nixon's susceptibilities, and perhaps even thought he was atoning for his snide indiscretions, by scraping the barrel in his obsequious memos and asides. Nixon was too astute and well-informed not to know what Kissinger was doing, and tested his adviser by engaging in gratuitously anti-Semitic remarks and other conversational gambits to inflame Kissinger's insecurities.

As Kissinger later put it about that Nixon drank too much and was erratic, and not necessarily sane, Nixon responded that Kissinger was a defeatist, who in a crisis began babbling incoherently about the need for pre-emptive concessions and running around in circles as if his hair were on fire. Both were engaging in caricatures, but the insidious practice of off-the-record denunciation was started between them by Kissinger, and because of his genius for public relations and Nixon's later misfortunes, Kissinger got the better of it for a long time. Some have made rather flippant comparisons with the relations between Woodrow Wilson and Colonel House, or Franklin D. Roosevelt and Harry Hopkins, or even Eisenhower and Dulles, but none of them behaved particularly unusually toward each other. After a brief honeymoon, Nixon and Kissinger were like two scorpions in the same bottle, sometimes friendly, often antagonistic, but almost inseparable.

The relationship survived because Kissinger was the perfect instrument for stripping power from the State Department and the Pentagon, and exercising it efficiently and imaginatively, and Nixon needed him. But Kissinger owed his position to Nixon, not the opposite. What Nixon owed Kissinger fluctuated from day to day.

They had shared strengths, quirks, and weaknesses, and similar methods, but quite different perspectives. But Nixon and Kissinger were unique in the history of their positions. Each was an extremely unusual personality, Kissinger by his unwavering focus as well as his high intelligence and charisma; Nixon by his unpredictability and complexity and moodiness, as well as for his cunning and determination; and both by their sheer improbability as characters. They would achieve a great deal together, and become rivals, in office, and for the attentions and judgment of history. Their personalities are a matter of taste, but in what they would accomplish, there is certainly much to admire and enough for both to share.

Chapter Ten

The Silent Majority
1969–1970

— I —

ALL HIS LIFE Richard Nixon had worked very hard, usually to the point where he became so exhausted he was ineffective. Haldeman became the master of his schedule and provided time for him to take naps, though these were never admitted, other than to Haldeman and Rose Mary Woods. When tense or nervous, Nixon would sometimes take a sedative to sleep, or a drink to relax, but a drink in that condition often had an inordinate effect on him, causing him to slur words and seem impaired. Richard Nixon was a tough and determined man, but he required careful assistance from Haldeman to achieve a maximum work output and stay reasonably clear of his tendency to overreact or become distracted by irritations.

He was an astonishingly profuse source of memos and instructions on every conceivable subject, many of them written on the margins of his daily press briefings, and then written up and passed on, as appropriate, by Haldeman. Despite his conviction that he was now immune to the assaults of the press, Nixon took the comments of the press as his incitement to much of the action he ordered from his staff and even his cabinet. So from the start of his administration, Nixon was largely reacting to the press in determining the tactics, if not the substantive goals, of his government.

Nixon used a two-room suite in the Executive Office Building (adjacent to the White House) for reflection, writing, reading, and snatching a little sleep. He sat most of the time, jacket on and buttoned, in a brown velvet-covered chair that had been in his study in New York, writing on his yellow legal pads. Only Haldeman, Ehrlichman, and Kissinger, and the messengers, would penetrate to this sanctum. Often, Nixon would pull the blinds and curtains, so it was not clear from within whether it was night or day. Because he liked active fireplaces, he sometimes had the fire lit in the stifling heat of Washington summer and balanced it by turning up the air conditioner.

His breakfasts (juice, plain cereal, unbuttered toast, and coffee) and lunches (a pineapple ring with cottage cheese flown in from Knudsen's Dairy in Los Angeles) were taken alone and rarely lasted more than ten minutes. If there was no preempting official occasion, he had dinners with his wife and Tricia, who was living in the White House, but they never took more than half an hour. With these breaks, and perhaps a nap of thirty minutes, he generally worked from between 6 and 7 A.M. until almost midnight, every day.

He allowed for one outside meeting a day, though he sometimes had to be more sociable; but apart from that, only Haldeman, Ehrlichman, Kissinger, and Rose Mary Woods saw him to converse with, supplemented after the first month by Moynihan after he had really enlisted the president's interest in what he was doing. Ehrlichman was the domestic adviser, who coordinated with Moynihan. Kissinger eagerly assumed all the delegated powers of the president and all the expropriated powers of the secretary of state, and took a bite out of the jurisdiction of the defense secretary as well.

Haldeman did what Nixon disliked doing: he cranked out the memos from Nixon's marginalia on the press briefings and further asides, and reprimanded and rewarded as Nixon directed, as well as exercising his own judgment up to a point – firing, hiring, and relieving Nixon of the burden of abrasive or personal and stressful encounters with individuals. There was probably no aspect of the presidency Nixon enjoyed more, not even the official aircraft, than having Haldeman, a brusque, unambiguous, brush-cutted guard dog, all efficiency and no subtlety, to deal with people in confrontational or delicate matters, which Nixon always found abhorrent.

Nixon was constantly telling Haldeman to fire people, cut off all contact with great swaths of journalists, and shake up the entire government. Haldeman generally ignored these demands, and was very effective at giving no hint to the outside world of how irritated the president was much of the time." [1] Nixon was happy to be in the place he had so ardently sought, and he enjoyed the perquisites of his office, but he carried into the presidency a great deal of resentment at previous slights, and all his convictions of the hostility and malice of much of his own party, almost all of the Democrats, and virtually all of the media. He was aware of the support of millions of ordinary Americans, not the most fashionable ones, and was always seeking a direct line to his supporters that could not be distorted by the press.

Nixon took to referring to himself in memos, and sometimes even verbally, as "RN." This was in emulation of de Gaulle, upon whom he professed to be modeling his remoteness and inaccessibility. De Gaulle, in referring to himself in the third person, was imitating Julius Caesar. This was a hazardous road for Nixon to take, and an unfortunate aspect of the general's technique for Nixon to adopt. De Gaulle was the most eminent Frenchman since Napoleon. He had continued, almost alone, French resistance to the Nazis, was now seventy-eight years old, and was in his second seven-year term as president of France, which, under the constitution he designed, was an extremely powerful post. Other than when rebellions broke out, as in 1968 and not infrequently in France, de Gaulle didn't much have to bother with the opposition, the media, or even the public. And in French, use of the third person about oneself does not sound so self-important as it does in English. That Nixon had such early and frequent recourse to this style of self-address was unsettling.

The Urban Affairs Council met for the first time on January 23. Nixon signed the executive order setting it up and introduced Moynihan. Burns, who had thought he would be running domestic policy, asked Moynihan if he would produce an urban policy outline. Moynihan, with the splendid Irish charm that never deserted him, replied that he would be glad to do so, provided that "no one take it seriously."[2] Moynihan's mirthful erudition took the edge off possible abrasions with Burns, and his council got down to serious policy work.

The following day the Cabinet Committee on Economic Policy met, though it was held up while Ehrlichman drafted the enabling executive

---

* What sympathetic biographer Jonathan Aitken called the "Berlin Wall" (Haldeman, Ehrlichman, and Kissinger) was designed not only to keep unwanted callers away from the president, but to contain Nixon's Red Queen, ex cathedra, ill-considered summary orders.

order. The chairman of the Council of Economic Advisers, Paul McCracken, of the University of Michigan, spoke of excellent economic growth prospects. Nixon had an uncertain interest in domestic affairs, apart from possibly radical approaches to welfare reform and completing desegregation. Routine home affairs he referred to as "building outhouses in Peoria."[3] For some reason, Nixon alighted on Peoria, an unexceptionable downstate Illinois city and headquarters of the Caterpillar heavy equipment company, as the symbol of hinterland America, as he would refer sarcastically to "Upper Volta" as representative of unimportant countries (even after it changed its name to Burkina Faso).

Nixon's first presidential press conference was on January 27. Helen Thomas of United Press asked about his peace plan in Vietnam, and he gave an anodyne reply about "mutual withdrawal on a guaranteed basis by both sides," without a hint of how he expected to achieve this, a goal that had completely eluded his predecessor. On inflation, he said that policy "should not be made by off-the-cuff answers at press conferences," but did say that government is the "culprit." This would be his answer to quite a range of matters as time went by. Nixon was never outsmarted by the press, no matter how difficult things became, but they never warmed to him, even on the rare occasions when the press seemed ready to give him credit for a noteworthy achievement. There were normally about 450 journalists at his press conferences. He ended this one prematurely to go to the Rose Garden for a photo opportunity of the Nixon family's new dog, King Timahoe, named after the town of his Irish ancestors.

Hugh Sidey, the longtime Time-Life White House correspondent, had quite a pleasant interview with Nixon in early February. Sidey had been very friendly with Kennedy and had found Nixon a devious, unsociable, inaccessible man, but he now found him comfortable in his great office, "at ease" and altogether a reassuring figure. This was the general impression Nixon created and the honeymoon was off to a good start.

Nixon's second press conference, on February 6, got very high praise from all the networks and major newspapers. There was this strange reluctance on Nixon's part to believe in the sincerity of praise, especially from the press, but to resent bitterly any absence of it. He was not a very companionable person, at least prior to old age, but he could be affable and was always curious, and he was the president.

If he had made a little more effort with the media, and not made it clear at all times that he considered it a relentlessly adversarial relationship, he would never have the press eating from his hand, as Roosevelt and Kennedy did, and would not have been able to exact the same reverential respect as Eisenhower did, or the camaraderie that Truman, a poker-playing, whiskey-swilling, straightforward extrovert, enjoyed, but he could have done much better than Johnson and avoided a good deal of tension. Nixon was not particularly devious with the press, and need not have been perceived by most of the journalists as an enemy, or even a quarry, but that was how he perceived them and himself, and relations developed accordingly.

Nixon was basically right that many of the press were hostile partisans, were lazy, dishonest, and incompetent. Few of them were intelligent, and few were thorough, and most of them couldn't write or speak with any elegance of composition. But there were exceptions, and the press was there and important, and part of the system. Beyond a certain point, most journalists, like most people, are conscientious men and women trying to do a reasonable job, but Nixon's attitude allowed for little of this.

When they wrote or said something nice about him, he thought he had outsmarted them, but knew it wouldn't last. It was not that Nixon disliked himself, or felt despised by the country or the world, as some have gratuitously speculated. He knew that there was always a type of political rival who could vacuum up the support of most of the press, and it was his lot to have to try harder, make do with the constituency of the unglamorous and be on guard against the facile, Kennedy-style rival, who could be lurking at every stage in his career.

He was constantly urging Ehrlichman to generate reams of letters to the press supporting him at every opportunity, and wanted to use the Republican National Committee for such purposes. Such efforts never developed much traction, but they would not be taken seriously, or much appreciated, by the press anyway, as there were always rumors, and it is not difficult to discern the difference between spontaneous and orchestrated letter-writing.

He had amassed over the years a list of ten thousand media people and academics with media access, and whenever anything useful was published, he would order that it be circulated to the whole list. This was certainly reasonable, but Nixon always gave the impression of being convinced that he had no chance of a fair hearing, and so would try to manipulate opinion. This ensured that whatever disposition there might have been with some people to be fair to him was squandered. He ordered the compilation and constant updating of lists of journalistic friends and foes.

He was correct that there was a bias against him, and he had outsmarted the media by winning the presidency, and much of the media was waiting for the opportunity to jump him. But instead of making it easier for them, he should have tried to develop some relationships and some credibility, as a bank to draw on, as Kissinger did (though Kissinger did it in part by slagging off Nixon, off the record). This was not Nixon's way, and to the historian the views of the press don't count for much, but they were an impediment to Nixon.

Eisenhower had said at his last presidential press conference that there wasn't much a journalist could do to a president. Perhaps not, but a swarming mass of hostile journalists could do a great deal of damage. Nixon got to the presidency on a rougher road and in a more difficult time than had Eisenhower. He was not a world historic war hero who could rely on others to do the political dirty work for him. Nixon did that work for Eisenhower, and then had to do it for himself, and that doesn't require the same level of iconoclasm for the working press to defile it. He wrote on his daily press briefing on February 16, beside a piece reporting on the very favorable press the president was receiving, "They are waiting to destroy us."[4]

Nixon met with Soviet ambassador Anatoly Dobrynin on February 17. Kissinger and State Department Soviet specialist Malcolm Toon were present. Kissinger and Dobrynin had already begun a back channel, which Nixon approved after Toon had left them. Dobrynin would come to the east entrance of the White House in an unidentifiable car. This process, about which Rogers knew nothing, became the principal conduit for U.S.-Soviet relations. On February 17, Dobrynin accepted Kissinger's proposals of three days before, suggesting comprehensive discussions on arms control, the Middle East, Berlin, and Vietnam. Nixon made it clear to Dobrynin that if there was not adequate progress, the United States would look to relations with "other powers," which was clearly a reference to the Chinese. He showed less than the usual American presidential interest in a summit meeting.[*] [5]

---

[*] Just before his inauguration, Nixon told a group of journalists that he thought Soviet pressure on Hanoi could produce peace in Vietnam, failing which there would have to be what he enigmatically called "a phased withdrawal."

Nixon telephoned Kissinger four times on the afternoon and evening of February 17, and Kissinger gleefully advised his best media friends that Nixon had asked what Kissinger thought of his performance. There was some of that, but Nixon was also concerned to know what Kissinger thought of the likely progress of the discussions. He was undoubtedly seeking some reassurance, which he should have known was an unwise thing to ask from Kissinger, but he wanted Kissinger's professional evaluation of how to move the talks with the Russians forward. Kissinger's indiscretions to the press were an unattractive feature of this relationship. Nixon and Kissinger had embarked on an imaginative and important initiative to remake Great Power relations, and Kissinger sullied the process from the beginning, and did no credit to himself, by betraying Nixon to his enemies in the press, so often, so self-servingly, and with such adolescent glee. Neither man possessed an emotional maturity equal to his high intelligence. In this they were more like Lyndon Johnson than like Roosevelt, Truman, Eisenhower, or Kennedy.

On February 19, Nixon met the congressional leadership of both parties, four days before leaving for Europe on a tour that the State Department privately advised against, an opinion noisily shared by the Senate Foreign Relations Committee, most columnists, and Dean Acheson. Anti-Gaullist sentiment was expressed, and Nixon said how he would respond if de Gaulle attacked America's pro-Israeli policy: that Israel wanted peace and its enemies wanted vengeance, and Israel had to maintain a military edge. He assured the Republican Senate leader, Everett Dirksen, that he would not attend the Paris peace talks, which he considered an inappropriate activity for an incumbent president. Nixon knew from private visits that relations with the European allies were in need of repair, and he wanted to consult, especially with de Gaulle, before taking new initiatives with China or with the U.S.S.R. on arms control, the Middle East, Vietnam, and Berlin.

Nixon wrote in the margin of a report from the Institute of Strategic Studies asserting that the United States had "lost the desire and ability to be the dominant power in the world" that this was "very important and accurate."[6] But he did not believe that. He thought that it could still dominate, but not without a good deal more diplomatic ingenuity and maneuvering than the country had engaged in since it was lining up support for the American Revolution, when Franklin, Jefferson, Madison, Monroe, and the Adamses were often abroad. He thought he could do something about this perception. He would.

On February 22, Nixon sent Kissinger a memo about the Middle East in which he made the point that domestic political considerations would have no impact on Middle East policy-making, a delicate way of emphasizing that 95 percent of American Jews had voted Democratic; and that the sole determining criterion of U.S. policy would be U.S. security interests. Nixon had William Scranton (who was his second choice for secretary of state after Robert Murphy, but who also declined, leaving the half-drained-by-Kissinger chalice to Rogers) speak about a "more evenhanded" approach to the Middle East. Nixon was convinced, after his visit to Egypt and to Nasser's house in 1963, that Israel had to settle with the Arabs, and was even more convinced after he found the Israelis completely overconfident and inflexible following the Six Day War in 1967.

He sent another memo to Kissinger saying that Golda Meir, the prime minister of Israel, and the Israeli ambassador in Washington, Yitzhak Rabin, had to understand that the United States under his leadership would always provide Israel with an edge, but that Israel had to compromise or the demographic weight of the Arabs, and the extent of the assistance Russia would give them, would eventually become overwhelming. Nixon emphasized that the Israelis must understand that the United States was "pro-freedom" and not just pro-Israel, and that much depended on bringing the sensible Arabs around to their interest in focusing on something other than the endless fixation on Israel. He believed this would be achievable if the United States could make the point that it was pro-peace in the Middle East, while the U.S.S.R. really sought to swallow the entire region and was merely playing upon the Arab preoccupation with Israel for manipulative reasons.

With some reason, Nixon thought that the United States had never really had a Middle East policy except to encourage the Israelis to believe they had a blank check, other than in Eisenhower's rising up against Anthony Eden's mad Suez foray in 1956. He was substantially right, and set about cobbling together a new policy. As with China and arms control and even Vietnam, Nixon was breaking U.S. policy out of a mould and opening up new prospects.

Dulles had been a rigid Cold Warrior, Herter a caretaker, and Rusk an honorable but unimaginative captive of events. Nixon and Kissinger and even Rogers were going to provide a new take on American foreign policy for the first time since the days of Marshall and Acheson, when Nixon entered public life. (At the outset, Nixon thought Kissinger could play no role in the Middle East because he was a Jew. He quickly discovered that the Middle Eastern leaders had no problem dealing with Jews, and expected nothing else from the United States – that the problem wasn't sectarian prejudice but the legitimacy and symbolism of territorial entitlements.)

Nixon's first message to Congress, in mid-February, effectively offered the retention of most of Johnson's anti-poverty programs in exchange for a free hand in foreign policy. Naturally, this could not be made explicit, but it was the line that Moynihan and Kissinger and the White House Congressional Liaison Office gave to the Democratic congressional leadership. Moynihan, an even more inveterate flatterer than Kissinger, and, unlike Kissinger, a personal loyalist who spoke nothing but well of Nixon to the end of his life, had become an early favorite with Nixon, not only because of his flattering blarney but more because of his powerful and novel ideas. Moynihan warned Nixon against a frontal assault on the congressional, bureaucratic, and media welfare establishment, but promised to suggest seductive alternatives.

Moynihan enlisted Nixon to the role of the conservative reformer, and gave him a copy of Robert Blake's newly published biography of Benjamin Disraeli, which was largely based on William Moneypenny and George Buckle's multivolume 1910 biography of the same subject, which had been written from Disraeli's private papers. Nixon had read the original work, and was already a believer in the virtues of Disraeliism, which was why he used the great British leader's famous unifying slogan "One nation" in his inaugural address, in reference to the African-Americans. But he had not thought of himself in such a splendid role before; Disraeli was ethnically Jewish, and only became prime minister for the first time at the age of sixty-four, and not for a full term until he was seventy, having three times been chancellor of the exchequer and leader of the House of Commons. He was rivaled only by Churchill as the greatest wit of all British prime ministers, and surpassed only by Churchill as the greatest conservative prime minister (though Pitt the Younger also had a claim and Margaret Thatcher was yet to be heard from). Nixon read Blake's book and it rekindled his admiration for Disraeli and incited some level of emulation of him.

This allusion tickled Nixon. He liked intellectuals who were not slaves to convention, and felt severely undervalued for his intellectual leanings and attainments. It was a legitimate grievance, compounded by his tendency to slightly know-nothing sloganeering in his earlier days. Nixon never understood the durability of liberal grievances, and expected his opponents to understand that in politics one does as one must. This was especially surprising, as he never forgot or forgave a slight himself.

Nixon had built his public career attacking the liberal intelligentsia that had provided much of the background, horsepower, and political cannon-fodder for Roosevelt, Truman, Stevenson, Kennedy, and Johnson. But he had laid off the soft-on-communism tag by the mid-fifties, partly at Eisenhower's urging, and partly because it no longer had any takers who were politically respectable. As has been recorded, Stevenson was nastier than Nixon in the 1956 campaign, with conspicuous lack of success, and now that Nixon was president, he set out to earn the respect of many of his former adversaries.

— II —

His trip to Europe began at 8 A.M. on February 23, as airplanes carrying his party of three hundred took off from Andrews Air Force Base near Washington. He sat in the front of Air Force One in a smoking jacket reading briefing books, including the comment from the Soviet defense ministry's daily English-language news sheet that compared Mao Tse-tung to Hitler, a promising development from his perspective. Apart from Kissinger, who was called forward briefly to talk about bombing the forty thousand North Vietnamese soldiers squatting in Cambodia just across the South Vietnamese border, as the U.S. command in Saigon requested, and Nixon now ordered, he was alone throughout the trip. The North Vietnamese had launched another offensive, though a much more modest one than at Tet the year before. Nixon wanted a strenuous response, but before Kissinger could implement Nixon's bombing order on Cambodia, Laird and Rogers had indicated their disapproval, from fear of being accused of escalation. Nixon felt that Hanoi, as he had predicted it would, had violated the agreement with Johnson that led to the pre-electoral announcement of talks, but he suspended his order until he returned to Washington. He was irritated by what he considered the shilly-shallying of Laird and Rogers.[7]

The president was met as he descended the steps of his aircraft by Baudouin, king of the Belgians, and delivered an elegant arrival speech from memory. (William Safire, who wrote it, was afraid that Nixon was confusing arrival with departure, but he just deliberately transposed some lines.)[8] Nixon spoke in very appreciated conciliatory terms the next morning to the assembled fifteen NATO ambassadors.

He went on to London and a private dinner at the prime minister's residence, 10 Downing Street. One of the guests was to be the recently named British ambassador in Washington, John Freeman, former editor of the socialist *New Statesman*. Freeman had been an ancient foe of Nixon, regularly writing extremely acidulous comments about him, and it was impetuous of the prime minister, Harold Wilson, to appoint him a few months before the election when it was obviously possible that Nixon would be elected president.

William Safire's wife, who is English, had subscribed to the *New Statesman* and told her husband of some of Freeman's more incendiary anti-Nixon comments, and he prepared a quip for dinner. Haldeman, with his usual heavy-handedness, had tried to have Freeman disinvited, but the ambassador, David K.E. Bruce, one of America's most admired and accomplished diplomats (still in place awaiting the confirmation of Annenberg as his successor), pointed out that it was not Haldeman's place to say whom the British prime minister could have to dinner in his own house.

Wilson toasted the president, who responded very fluently and in an amiably learned and relaxed way, adding that "They say there's a new Nixon . . . and a new Freeman. Let me set aside all possibility of embarrassment because our roles have changed. He's the new diplomat and I'm the New Statesman." The tension was broken, hands patted the table, and Wilson wrote on his menu and handed to Nixon the compliment that "That was one of the kindest and most generous acts I have known in a quarter-century in politics," and that Nixon was a "born gentleman."[9]

Nixon had had an indifferent press in Britain, but he had long known how to impress the British with tasteful extemporaneous eloquence, which they did not generally expect to receive from Americans. His meeting with a group of prominent people from different walks of life, including student leaders, and his visit with Queen Elizabeth were also successful, and he received a generous press in London, amplified in the United States. The most important intelligence Nixon gleaned in London was Wilson's information that Soviet premier Aleksei Kosygin had uttered the most violent insults he had ever heard about the Chinese.[10]

Nixon had briefly attended a British cabinet meeting and, true to his frequent custom of physical awkwardness, spilled the contents of an inkwell, but apart from that made a good impression on everyone. This sort of thing was the bane of Nixon's life. He met Anna Chennault once in Taipei in 1965, and was going to the airport with her: "Then it happened. As Nixon followed me into my car, he cracked his forehead on the door. It was a hard resounding blow that left no doubt about the pain." He pressed her handkerchief against his forehead, but spilled blood on her white dress. He stopped the habit of serving soup at White House official dinners after spilling soup down his vest on his first such occasion, as host for Canada's flamboyant leftish prime minister, Pierre Elliott Trudeau, in March. (Despite their frequent differences, Trudeau retained great respect for Nixon, who considered Trudeau intelligent but frivolous, not an unreasonable assessment.) When he threw out the first ball in the Washington baseball season in April 1969, Nixon actually dropped it, and had to pick it up, with cameras clicking and his friend the new Washington manager and co-owner, and all-time great hitter, Ted Williams, looking on.[11] In mundane physical terms, Nixon was a disconcertingly accident-prone person.

The party went on to Germany, and Nixon received a very enthusiastic welcome in West Berlin, where he made the customary remarks about the sinister Berlin Wall. Then it was on to Rome. The talks with Italian leaders were ceremonious, but Nixon showed great sensitivity to the government in Rome, giving them the same treatment as he had the British, French, and Germans, and leaving Rome and returning for a meeting with Pope Paul VI, as if the Italian government and the Roman Catholic Church were not headquartered in the same city. (The pope has historically overshadowed all modern secular Italian leaders, except, to some degree, Mussolini.)

The highlight of the trip for Nixon was Paris and de Gaulle. As he prepared to disembark from his plane and saw his host at the foot of the steps without an overcoat, Nixon removed his own overcoat and was visibly warmly received by the French leader, who greeted him in English, a language he did not really understand and almost never spoke.[12] De Gaulle had had no rapport with Johnson, and liked but disagreed with Kennedy. His relations with Eisenhower and Truman had been cordial but inconclusive, and they were just warming up with Roosevelt, after a very difficult start, when Roosevelt died. The nadir of his relations with the United States had come when he had requested the removal of NATO bases from France in March

1966 while continuing in the alliance; that is, he would graciously accept an American and alliance military guarantee but act as a Cold War neutral power most of the time. President Johnson told the secretary of state, Dean Rusk, to inquire whether de Gaulle's demand extended to the removal of the graves of the approximately ninety thousand American servicemen who had died in Europe in the world wars and were buried in military cemeteries in France. This was a sorry deterioration of relations with America's original ally. Nixon was the sixth American president de Gaulle dealt with, and this relationship promised to be the most productive and amicable of all.

De Gaulle told Nixon that Russia was now so concerned about China that it was ready for a serious de-escalation of tensions with the West, and that China, though ideologically irreconcilable, could not be isolated much longer. He laid out the standard Gaullist view of the European-American alliance: The Russians realized that the United States would not tolerate them overrunning Western Europe, but also did not believe that the United States would fire its full nuclear arsenal against them, as that would lead to the complete destruction of both countries. But if there were a tactical nuclear exchange, that would destroy Western and Eastern Europe but leave the United States and the U.S.S.R. essentially unharmed, which, though macabre, would be a net gain for the Russians.

De Gaulle preferred, but did not say so, that Moscow and Washington slug it out, if they must, between them, and over Europe's head, each destroying the other. This was always de Gaulle's rationale for his own nuclear force in France, and his argument was a sensible one, never understood by Eisenhower or Kennedy. Nixon responded that the conventional forces in Western Europe had to be strengthened to assure conventional deterrence, and emphasized battlefield tactical nuclear weapons, which would stabilize – i.e., desolate – the front, but not destroy all Europe. Some of the talks were held in the Grand Trianon palace at Versailles, where, de Gaulle claimed, Louis xiv had "ruled Europe." (He did nothing of the kind, and was defeated in the War of Spanish Succession by the Duke of Marlborough and Prince Eugene of Savoy, but de Gaulle had his own interpretations of French and European history.)[13]

De Gaulle urged Nixon to negotiate his way out of Vietnam, but not to go precipitately. Nixon generously assumed that this was a thoughtful solicitude for American prestige, but was aware that continuing to be mired in Vietnam reduced American ability to lead the Western alliance and thus empowered France to manipulate a complicated East-West and intra-Western alliance balance of power. De Gaulle formally acknowledged that France, by not giving Indochina independence promptly enough, was partially responsible for the debacle in Vietnam.

De Gaulle did not believe in having aides at such meetings, so Kissinger attended only one, and then told an incredulous de Gaulle that if the United States withdrew hastily from Vietnam it would impair American credibility in the Middle East.

Kissinger recounted in his memoirs Nixon's excitement at the pomp and ceremony of state visits by a U.S. president, for whom host countries would naturally lay on all they could. And he repeated his constant refrain that Nixon endlessly asked for reassurance that he, Nixon, was doing well. This is not entirely believable, and was denied by Nixon, who was well-accustomed to state visits. It was fifteen years since he had met Winston Churchill at Washington National Airport, and had traveled throughout the Far East as vice president. Kissinger had not been on such a mission before. Nixon probably asked Kissinger how he thought the meetings were going, but that is not quite the same as asking his precocious assistant for a report card on his performance.[14]

It was agreed that de Gaulle would pay a return visit to the United States in January or February of 1970. France's minister of culture, André Malraux, who had known Mao Tse-tung in 1930, and seen him a few times since, told Nixon that Mao had told him the year before that the only difference between the Americans and the Russians was that the Russians were barbarians who came by land and the Americans barbarians who came by sea. It had not occurred to Mao, said Malraux, that the United States did not want to destroy China.[15] De Gaulle paid generous tribute to Nixon, "statesman and man."[16] Nixon was right to be pleased; he had earned the respect of one of the twentieth century's greatest leaders, in the same general category as Churchill and Roosevelt (the twentieth century's greatest, benign, democratic statesmen).

The foreign visit ended with the return to Rome, where Nixon had a very satisfactory visit with Pope Paul VI, who told him how severely mistreated Christians had been in North Vietnam, and urged the United States to stay the course in Vietnam.[17]

Nixon and his party returned to Washington on March 3. His trip was acknowledged to have been a very substantial success. He had a positive meeting with the bipartisan congressional leadership on the morning of March 4, after only a few hours' sleep, and had a one-hour press conference that night exclusively devoted to foreign policy. It was a tour de force. The questions were respectful and apposite, and the answers were exceptionally knowledgeable and articulate.

On Vietnam, he said that he had no plans to withdraw troops in "the near future" but would do so as the South Vietnamese increased their capacity to carry the fight and the level of violence declined. When asked if, in response to the renewed North Vietnamese offensive, he would renew the bombing of the North, he said that "deeds are more effective than words," that he would do so or not, but would not announce it at a press conference. After six weeks in office, Nixon had made an excellent impression on virtually everyone.

Nixon was in Florida when Kissinger telephoned him on March 9, complaining about Rogers having spoken to the Soviet ambassador. Rogers had told Dobrynin that the United States wanted simultaneous political and military talks with the North Vietnamese, which was essentially what Nixon had told de Gaulle and assumed that de Gaulle had transmitted to the North Vietnamese. Kissinger and Nixon required that shelling of Saigon cease, but this could not be stipulated as a condition after what Rogers had said. Kissinger was right that there should be a common policy between the White House and the State Department, but he could hardly insist that Rogers couldn't speak to the Soviet ambassador. Kissinger made one of the first of his countless threats to resign, to Haldeman. Nixon ignored the fracas.[18]

On March 15, Nixon finally ordered the secret bombing of the North Vietnamese positions in Cambodia, and asked Rogers and Laird to see him in his office the next day. Laird favored the bombing, but not as a secret, and Rogers opposed it. Nixon had already ordered the bombing, and the planes were almost in the air, when the two senior cabinet members arrived for what was billed as a debate.[19] At the end of the spurious debate, Nixon announced that he would order the bombing, secretly, rejecting the advice of both Rogers and Laird. In the next fifteen months, 109,000 tons of bombs would be dropped on Cambodian targets near the South Vietnamese border. The air force considered the bombing a success.[20]

As he launched the giant B-52s against the North Vietnamese in Cambodia, Nixon summoned the congressional leaders and gave them a brief advance notice that he was proposing to go forward with a modified version of Lyndon Johnson's anti-ballistic missile (ABM) system. Johnson had proposed in 1967 a comprehensive missile defense for the cities of the United States called Sentinel. Nixon renamed it Safeguard, and confined it to the protection of American intercontinental ballistic missile (ICBM) launching sites.

He explained to the congressional leaders and later to the press that this was primarily a defense against the Chinese once they had a limited nuclear missile attack capability, and against a freak accidental firing. He emphasized that pursuing the Johnson option would give the Russians room to believe that the United States was effectively rebuilding an unanswerable first-strike capability, as the U.S.S.R. would have limited deterrence if America's populated centers were protected in depth. (This was wild scientific speculation, as it would be many years before any of these anti-missile missiles would be tested successfully, and no leader of sound mind of either country would make any significant part of his civil population hostage to the assurance of the impermeability of a missile defense system.) Nixon emphasized that it would be a fool's paradise to repose excessive confidence in a leak-proof anti-missile system, but that what he was proposing was entirely defensive and unexceptionable.

Nixon also explained that Johnson's system would be unsustainably expensive. When Fulbright, who, with Edward Kennedy and Albert Gore Sr., had been leading the senatorial opposition to Sentinel, asked if it would not be easier just to build more Polaris submarine-launched missile capability, Nixon replied that that would achieve precisely what he was trying to avoid, inciting the Russians to think that the United States was seeking an overpowering first-strike capability, and that sea-launched missiles were more expensive than ground-launched ones. They also required greater manpower (full submarine crews) and frequent service (when the ships were in port).

In a package of simultaneous, very skillful initiatives, Nixon publicly announced his desire to pursue arms control negotiations with the U.S.S.R., suspended by Johnson after the Soviet invasion of Czechoslovakia in 1968, and reduce the defense budget by $2.5 billion, the first reduction since one at the end of the Eisenhower-Nixon years (which Nixon had opposed at the time), as he proposed an ABM system designed to satisfy the hawks and perplex the Russians with the specter of enhanced U.S. military sophistication but not arouse them to concern about a threat to their own deterrent power.

He told NBC's Herbert Kaplow – the same journalist he had solemnly assured in November that he and his campaign co-manager, Robert Finch, had quite different views on Johnson's motives in claiming a breakthrough in the Paris peace talks – that Safeguard was not an escalation in the arms race. He added that historically, Russian statesmen and military leaders had always emphasized the defensive, and that what he proposed was not an affront to their strategic concerns. Once again, Nixon was too subtle for Kaplow, but not for the Russians.

This astute and intricate approach required a good deal of coordination between the diplomatic, military, intelligence, Treasury, and congressional liaison groups within the administration. Nixon gave the Russians an incentive to take arms control seriously without enabling them to complain of escalation of the arms race, rescued Johnson's floundering ABM plan by reconfiguring it, pitched to the domestic nuclear hawks and doves at the same time without becoming linked to either, and embraced arms control and stronger defense and fiscal restraint all at once. It was a brilliant stroke and was almost entirely the president's doing in overall conception. (Not even Kissinger, who in his voluminous and elegantly written memoirs is not reluctant to cast a wide net in pursuit of credit for the administration's strategic successes, claims authorship of more than a small part of this artistic ensemble.)[21]

On March 19, Nixon received a visit from Dean Acheson. Much water had flowed over the dam since Nixon had campaigned against him as a pompous, affected, communist appeaser in striped pants who had blundered into Korea. The passage of seventeen years had healed the wounds, and he invited Acheson in order to ask for his advice, beginning the talk with praise of the Marshall Plan as one of the greatest triumphs of statesmanship in American history.

Nixon said that all the old Democratic elites in New York and New England finance and academia, and even business and the big law firms, vocally thought that Vietnam should be "scuttled" at once. He said that that was not his view but he found it an uncommonly difficult problem and asked for Acheson's opinion. Implicit in the invitation and the acceptance of it was that Acheson was now exiled from the contemporary, instant-peace Democratic Party, and that events had placed these two old adversaries on the same side.

Matters had, in fact, evolved further than that, as it shortly emerged that Nixon was an energetic peace-seeker compared with the man he formerly accused of truckling to the communists. Acheson advised simply sticking to it, no negotiations, no compromises, just go on making war. He said that the Chinese had only agreed to peace in Korea after they realized that they could not defeat Matthew Ridgway. He didn't bother mentioning that Eisenhower's threat to use the atomic bomb on China might have helped jog Mao's thinking a little. Acheson did say that he doubted there would "ever" be a political settlement on the Korean peninsula. Nearly forty years later, events had not contradicted him.

When Nixon asked Acheson for advice on dealing with the Russians, Acheson urged the president not to negotiate with the Russians at all. Sixteen years out of office had induced a certain sclerosis in the thinking of the formerly imaginative foreign policy specialist who had first told Roosevelt in 1940 that he could give the hard-pressed British fifty destroyers without congressional approval (in the middle of the election campaign) and had been one of the originators of the Marshall Plan and founders of NATO.

Acheson was impressed with Nixon and wrote to a friend that he found Nixon's views and approach intelligent, orderly, and realistic. The ambiance of the meeting was very cordial and reciprocally respectful, and this was a milestone for Nixon too, as he had not only done the gracious thing in inviting the most distinguished living former secretary of state to the White House, but had clearly earned the respect of his former principal foe. In a memorandum of the meeting, Acheson recorded that he had told the president he had approved of Johnson's decision to inject large numbers of ground forces in Vietnam in 1965 but now thought it a mistake. Nixon made the same admission. From the current commander in chief, this was a telling point.

Acheson strongly supported Nixon's deft ABM plan and spoke publicly in favor of it. Their relationship, though not overused by Nixon as a source of advice, was cordial and supportive to the end of Acheson's life (in 1971).[22]

— III —

Dwight D. Eisenhower died at noon on March 28, 1969. He was seventy-eight. For Richard Nixon, it closed the door of his political nursery forever. His last conversation with Eisenhower had been two days after his return from Europe on March 4. He told Ike that the Pope said he was praying for him, and that de Gaulle and Queen Elizabeth sent their best wishes. He added, "You were absolutely right about de Gaulle."[23] Nixon subsequently explained that he meant Eisenhower had been right in seeing de Gaulle's merit before Roosevelt did in 1942, 1943, and 1944, not that he had been correct in making such short work of de Gaulle's suggestions in 1959 for overhauling NATO.

Nixon had sent his whole cabinet, one at a time, to see Eisenhower in his hospital suite, and had visited him frequently. They were now almost family, as well as a political continuation. When the White House doctor, Walter Tkach, told the president, in the presence of Haldeman, Kissinger, and Laird, that Ike had died, Nixon went to the window, and, as he wrote himself, "could not hold back tears." He said, "He was such a strong man."[24] The bells began tolling across Washington almost immediately. Eisenhower had directed that he be buried in a simple, eighty-dollar soldier's coffin, in his uniform, with no medals. Nixon ordered a state funeral and agreed to Mrs. Eisenhower's request, which her husband had already expressed to Nixon, that the president give the eulogy.

The ingredients of Nixon's feelings for his former leader are hard to calibrate. He certainly admired him, had ardently sought and finally gratefully received his endorsement, and had also resented him. But Nixon seemed to feel that the approval of Eisenhower, once achieved, was the ultimate legitimization, a talisman and a coronet. No matter how disparaged he might be in some circles, no matter what doubts he might have about himself, or what pessimism about his own fate, and despite his disappointment with Eisenhower's withheld approbation for many years, in the end he had received the unqualified laying on of hands of possibly the greatest American, except for Franklin D. Roosevelt, of Nixon's century (though there were rivals, including Nixon's heroes, Theodore Roosevelt and Woodrow Wilson, and Eisenhower's own mentor, General George C. Marshall). Whatever Nixon's accumulated resentments, his grief was certainly not an affectation.

After all their years together, when Nixon was taking leave of him for what he sensed would be the last time, on March 26, he stopped at the door, turned, and said, "General, I just want you to know how all the free people of Europe and millions of others in the world will forever be in your debt for the leadership you provided in war and peace. You can always take great pride in the fact that no man in our history has ever done more to make America and the world a better and safer place in which to live." Eisenhower had been reposing, with eyes closed, but "after a brief moment he opened them and lifted his head from the pillow. With an unusual formality he said: 'Mr. President, you do me great honor in what you have just said.' Then he slowly raised his hand to his forehead in a final salute." Even allowing for Eisenhower's condition, and Nixon's unverified account (although doctors were present who could have contradicted any inaccuracy), this was an astonishingly stiff leave-taking. Nixon had earned Ike's respect, but no relaxation in his reserve, even at death's door.[25]

Nixon always found Eisenhower's penetrating pale blue eyes and his fierce temper intimidating. And he was awed by his prestige and effortless popularity. He was not particularly impressed by Eisenhower's work habits, or even, at times, his judgment. But their relationship had long since become totemistic and barometric, a symbol and yardstick of Nixon's progress. And the general's approbation was the ultimate testimony of blue skies, which was not what Nixon had been conditioned throughout his life to expect overhead.

Nixon gave the eulogy on March 30 at the Capitol Rotunda. He did not dwell on Eisenhower's career other than in the broadest terms. His achievements as a soldier-statesman in blending international armed forces together under a unified command; the successful direction of the greatest military operation in history in the invasion of Normandy; his successful repulse of the final Nazi offensive of the Ardennes; the double-envelopment of the Ruhr; the liberation and prescient filming of the Nazi death camps, thus preventing the world from being taken over by Holocaust deniers; his generous military governance of Germany; his skillful setting up of NATO; and his presidential accomplishments, from ending the Korean War to warning of the military-industrial complex, were not mentioned.

Rather, Nixon spoke of Eisenhower's Guildhall address in 1945, when he said, "I come from the heart of America." He called him "that rarest of men, an authentic hero. . . . Every trust that the American people had it in their power to bestow, he was given. And, yet, he always retained a saving humility. His was the humility not of fear, but of confidence. He walked with the great of the world, and he knew that the great are human. His was the humility of man before God and of man before the truth. His was the humility of a man too proud to be arrogant."

This was perhaps the key to their relations; Nixon admired Eisenhower's equilibrium, his lack of hate, fear, pessimism, or any sense of being persecuted. He exaggerated when he said he said that "for a quarter of a century and to the end of his life Dwight Eisenhower exercised a moral authority without parallel in America and the world." He never had the standing of Churchill or Roosevelt, and was latterly less esteemed in the world than de Gaulle, who thoughtfully attended the funeral in his wartime uniform and saluted the flag-draped casket. But he had a serenity and natural respect that Nixon considered almost superhuman, and sublimely admirable, whatever Eisenhower's failings and lack of consideration at times for him.[26]

Nixon spent all day March 31 and April 1 meeting with world leaders who came to Eisenhower's funeral. He naturally started with a long session with de Gaulle, who told him the "world is waiting" for him to meet the Russian leaders, whom he described as "forthright and frank, and sincere, though that could be a pose."[27] On Vietnam, de Gaulle said that the sooner the United States made it clear that it was leaving Vietnam, the sooner Saigon and the communists would negotiate an agreement. As de Gaulle cannot possibly have believed this, and must have known that there could be no durable agreement without permanent American support for the South, he must have been advocating that Nixon do the necessary to incur an undisguised American defeat, presumably as part of his campaign to reduce American preeminence in the world and enhance the relative importance of third powers, especially France. Despite his admiration for de Gaulle, Nixon was not gulled by this and said only that he might have some announcement of force reductions before the end of the year.[28]

Nixon met with President Bourguiba of Tunisia, who derided the current Arab leaders and asked Nixon to keep an eye out for Tunisia after he, Bourguiba, had gone. (This was an unnecessary precaution, as Bourguiba ruled for another eighteen years and lived on after that for thirteen more, to the age of ninety-six.)

From the prime minister of South Korea, Chung Il-kwon, a tough general and veteran of the hardest fighting of the Korean War, Nixon received refreshingly different advice about Vietnam from that which de Gaulle had given him. Chung said to resume bombing, blockade Haiphong, cross the DMZ, cut the Ho Chi Minh Trail, and let the Chinese know that if they intervened, he would use atomic weapons against them, as the man whose funeral they had just attended had successfully threatened to do in ending the Korean War. Nixon said he would consider this advice, which was a good deal more astute, if no more disinterested, than de Gaulle's on the same subject.

Nixon received many other visitors, including Turkey's prime minister, Suleiman Demirel, and the shah of Iran, and the thirty-three-year-old King Hussein of Jordan, who said he was bearing a message from Egypt's President Nasser.

Since the Arab defeat in the Six Day War of 1967, Hussein said, he and Nasser had concluded that Israel's right to exist could not be challenged. He sought a durable settlement. Hussein was officially representing the Palestinian cause as well as the Jordanian one, as he now had more Palestinian refugees in his country than Jordanian citizens. Israel had occupied all of Gaza and the West Bank of the Jordan River, and had thus taken on the task of overlordship of about two million Palestinians. This would prove a terrible problem, as Nixon had already foreseen.

Hussein said Nasser wished to restore diplomatic relations with the United States, and that the Arab powers wanted a settlement, but not a peace treaty, with Israel. Hussein almost certainly meant that he wanted back all the territory his country and Egypt lost to Israel when they provoked war two years before, without a treaty that constituted real recognition of the State of Israel. The Arab position, from the first days after the Six Day War, was that there must be an immediate reversion to the pre-war borders, as if being aggressor and respondent, and defeated and victorious, were interchangeable positions. Even if what Hussein was offering was probably not as good as it sounded, and no message from Nasser could be taken at face value, this was progress. Nixon liked Hussein, and asked him to prepare some preliminary thoughts about borders. The greatest problem would be Jerusalem, which had been severely divided before 1967, with the Jewish holy site of the Western Wall in Arab hands. Nixon had targeted the Middle East for a creative effort, and had got on well with Nasser when they had met in 1963. Hussein's visit was an unexpected dividend of Eisenhower's funeral.

On April 15, the North Koreans shot down a slow, sophisticatedly equipped electronic reconnaissance plane of the U.S. Navy, a reconditioned Lockheed Constellation, ninety miles off their coast. This was reminiscent of the *Pueblo* incident fifteen months before, but this time the aircrew of thirty-one men was killed. There were radio intercepts that indicated the shooting, unlike the seizure of the *Pueblo*, might have been on local authority only and almost accidental. The plane, called an EC-121, was certainly in international air space, flying a familiar pattern, and the North Korean action was completely illegal.

Kissinger wanted immediate retaliation against the airfield from which the two MiGs that had shot down the EC-121 had flown. Rogers and Laird disagreed, and did not want to do anything. They were afraid of provoking a resumption of the Korean War. The U.S. ambassador in Seoul reported that an air attack on North Korea might be taken as an excuse by either side to invade the other. Kissinger warned Nixon that he would seem a "weakling" if he did not respond forcefully. Nixon's natural impulse was to strike back, but Laird dragged his feet and said, almost surely falsely, that it would take five days to organize an air strike. The United States had an adequate air force in South Korea for such a task, and did not have to move aircraft carriers.

Rogers rather pitifully stated that Johnson had said "we would show them, in Vietnam, and we're still there." Haldeman and Ehrlichman lined up behind Laird and Rogers, not out of any policy consideration, but because of their exasperation with Kissinger, whom they regarded as overbearing, temperamental, and a full-time megalomaniac. In the end Nixon moved two aircraft carriers and escorting vessels to within sight of the North Korean coast and cruised up and down the coast for a few days, with television crews aboard.

Kissinger's advice was better than Rogers and Laird's, though Nixon could have done without his constant schoolyard incitements to macho pugilism. ("The world will see the lack of a response as proof of America's moral decay." Nixon did enough to avoid quite such a climacteric as that.) Nixon found it frustrating to encounter such a swamp of official pusillanimity from everybody but Kissinger, Agnew, and Mitchell, and this was not a field where the vice president and the attorney general had unlimited credibility. Nixon was hamstrung by bureaucratic insubordination. What he did was plausible enough and he put a good face on it by also announcing that he had ordered full fighter escorts for the lumbering EC-121s in future, oblivious of the fact that Laird had taken it upon himself to cancel such flights. When he discovered this, he restored the flights, escorted, a couple of weeks later. The president said that it would "be the practice of this administration to give one warning only," and he had given it to North Korea. As it turned out, what he did do seemed to be adequate. He did not appear weak, but Laird and Rogers did, and while Kissinger had been forceful, he had also been intemperate, hectoring, and over-dramatic. Three months into his presidency, Nixon had lost confidence in his two senior cabinet secretaries, and considered his chief foreign policy adviser an over-flappable and slightly operatic figure, though a brilliant and useful executant if managed. These preliminary judgments proved a bit ungenerous, but not unfounded, and they were worrisome. In his memoirs, Nixon claims that intensified bombing of the North Vietnamese was part of his response, though Hanoi and Pyongyang had nothing to do with each other and Ho Chi Minh and Kim Il Sung were not friendly, and the bombing was secret. He moderates considerably his reservations at the time about the conduct in the EC-121 affair of his chief collaborators.[29]

Up to a point Nixon liked to promote rivalry between his subordinates, but with Kissinger under his roof he got more than he bargained for. He wrote, "Rogers feels that Kissinger is Machiavellian, difficult, egotistical, arrogant, and insulting. Kissinger feels that Rogers is vain, uninformed, unable to keep a secret, and hopelessly dominated by the State Department bureaucracy. . . . Kissinger suggested repeatedly that he might have to resign unless Rogers was restrained or replaced." Though Nixon valued both men, especially Kissinger, he did not suggest that the view either had of the other was inaccurate, and did find the endless abrasions and tantrums tiresome.[30]

Nothing was happening with Vietnam. Nixon had Dobrynin deliver a request for unconditional secret talks, which was relayed to Hanoi within two days. There was no response. Hanoi was unlike any power Nixon had dealt with before. It paid no attention at all to the opportunity to get most of what it was seeking, and an elimination of its current heavy casualties, in exchange for some recognition of the normal prerogatives and right not to be humiliated of the world's greatest power. Even Nixon and Kissinger, astute and insightful and historically knowledgeable of foreign relations though they were, had no idea that it had become Ho Chi Minh's objective not only to take over South Vietnam but to humble and defeat the United States.

This episode confirmed what nonsense previous Johnson, and even tentative Nixon, planning had been. Johnson's intimations of peace talks proceeding anywhere beyond the now hackneyed accomplishment of the shape of the table, and, to date, any notion of the utility of Nixon's madman theory, had been trampled in the dust. Hanoi intended to raise all America in protest against its own government and drive the American armed forces into the sea like the British at Dunkirk, if it couldn't kill them all on their way to the beaches. Nixon's vague plan to create a correlation of forces that would require serious compromise negotiations, much less de Gaulle's breezy encouragement to reach the same end virtually by dialing the telephone, bore no relationship at all to the facts. Nixon's former uncharacteristic optimism that he could end the war within a year, and his and Kissinger's view that Hanoi would respond seriously to a reasonable peace proposal, were evaporating as quickly as Democratic nonpartisan indulgence of the absence of any administration progress to wind down the war.

The country and the world, though impressed with Nixon to date, were becoming very curious about what he proposed to do about the open artery of Vietnam, where American war dead had spiked up to over four hundred per week in the renewed North Vietnamese offensive. And there was no assurance that the Democratic majorities in the Congress would not start meddling in war policy and swaddling themselves in the newfound morality of peacemaking, by which they meant simply scuttling. Dean Acheson, or even Lyndon Johnson, did not speak for much of that party any more.

Student demonstrations and violence were starting up again, including disorderly scenes and building seizures again at Columbia and Harvard, where once more the police were required to reopen them and keep the campuses functioning. Heavily armed African-American students at Cornell seized a building, although they were only 2 percent of the student body, and had been lent the university's aircraft to fly to New York City to buy a bongo drum for the celebration of the birthday of assassinated radical black leader Malcolm X.[31] Nixon sent a message of congratulation to Father Theodore Hesburgh of Notre Dame, who asseverated that students involved a second time in disorderly demonstrations would be expelled. At San Francisco State College, the Japanese-Canadian philologist Samuel Hayakawa faced down demonstrating students, wearing a tartan tam-o'-shanter, and was eventually rewarded with election to the U.S. Senate. Governor Reagan used the National Guard and the state police as necessary to maintain full operations at all campuses of the University of California, including the original hotbed of student radicalism, Berkeley, where Mario Savio and the Free Speech Movement had arisen. As in so many other areas, those who resisted the forces of radical disorder were lionized by the general public; those who conciliated were despised and reviled by all. Kissinger, a recent practicing academic, disparaged the hand-wringing among some of Nixon's advisers. He had a healthy disrespect for the barricades aptitudes of his former students, and grumbled that some of Nixon's entourage acted as if they thought the "French Revolution was breaking out."

Nixon would have no trouble holding majority American opinion against such violent infantilism on the part of those who had gained the most from, and had the least to tell, the society that was paying for what would now have to be only broadly described as their education, but it was polarizing, embittering, unseemly to the world, and an outright encouragement to the North Vietnamese.

Nixon recognized that he had to take serious steps if there were any chance to produce an alternative to massive escalation or outright withdrawal, apart from the attrition that had exhausted the patience of the country, killed thousands of young Americans, and destroyed the previous presidency. On April 27, James Reston in the *New York Times* decried the tendency to anarchy, and the collapse of the university administrations before recourse to violence by students. "Some authority must oppose anarchy," he wrote.[32]

Thoughtful Americans and Americans abroad were distressed. Alistair Cooke, who had made a cottage industry out of interpreting America to his native Britain for thirty-five years, sometimes perceptively, said that the Cornell students reminded him of the Congo and that their shouted threats and slogans reminded him of Nazi students in Germany in the thirties.[33] America's enemies rejoiced. The Chinese, especially, claimed that the overthrow of American capitalist imperialism by the righteous students was imminent. The Americans would handle their problems with rambunctious youth better than China was with the Cultural Revolution, or than it would twenty years later when ostensible students occupied Tiananmen Square in Beijing. (The large crowd that occupied the main square of the country for many weeks began as students, but its composition later became more diverse.)

Nixon recognized, as de Gaulle did, that student unrest was a worldwide phenomenon, and while many blamed it on Vietnam, which was clearly a contributing factor in many places, he sought more profound analyses, though largely from people incapable of producing it, such as the CIA. Nixon made it clear in a public statement on March 22 that the federal government was not going to maintain order on the campuses; the universities had to do that. He reminded the university administrations that "from time immemorial, expulsion has been the primary instrument of university discipline." Of physical intimidation in places of learning he said darkly but accurately that "this is the way civilizations begin to die," and quoted Yeats: "Things fall apart; the centre cannot hold," adding, from Sinclair Lewis, "None of us has a right to suppose that it cannot happen here." He repeatedly urged university administrators to show some "backbone." It was a reasonable request, little heeded.[34] Nixon set the IRS and, even more than it was already, the FBI on surveillance of the radical organizations. They didn't accomplish much, except to harass people ineffectually and arouse legitimate civil liberties concerns.

The political judgment Nixon would make was to what extent to rouse the silent majority he was planning to assemble, and had occasionally referred to, against unruly students; and to what extent to peel off the relatively moderate dissident youth from the hard core by some flexibilities of policy and rhetoric. But these were tactical questions. More important, he understood that if he did not produce progress on Vietnam soon, not only the disaffected youth, against whom he could always mobilize adult opinion, but the whole country would become very restless.

On April 28, Charles de Gaulle abruptly resigned as president of France. He had called another referendum on reforms to local government and the organization of universities. An almost incomprehensible question was posed to the voter, and he had added, quite unnecessarily, that if it were not approved, he would resign. The French were tiring, after eleven years, of the general's threats to resign, and he could safely have claimed that he had won his vote of confidence in the great parliamentary election victory of the year before. It was clear, coming up to the vote, that it would be close, and a rather tired president addressed the nation and said, "The army of those who have supported me, will, whatever happens, hold in their hands the destiny of the nation . . . [and that he would soon], without upheaval or disorder, hand over my official charge to whomever you shall have chosen to assume it after me."

This was accurate, but so cynical a people as the French, when their élan is not stirred and their avaricious bourgeois fears are not excited, become bored with the exhilaration of inspired leadership. One of de Gaulle's brightest protégés, Valéry Giscard d'Estaing, formerly his finance minister, deserted him. And although Georges Pompidou was silent, it is a reasonable assumption that he was not responding to his dismissal as prime minister by urging his large following in the Gaullist movement to prodigies of activity on behalf of the general.

De Gaulle realized he had made a mistake, that the French, whom he had famously described as ungovernable because of having 227 different types of cheese, were ingrates. (He had also said that he loved France, but not the French.) He told Malraux that his home at Colombey would be an object of touristic curiosity for a time, with the sale of postcards and trinkets, and then, "There will be nothing." He lost the referendum very narrowly, and at a few minutes after midnight issued the statement "I shall cease to exercise my functions as president of the republic, effective at noon today." (He had indeed held his last press conference.) He never returned to the Élysée Palace.

What de Gaulle wrote of Churchill, when he was rejected by his electors in 1945 after leading Britain through its darkest days to victory in the Second World War, now applied equally to him: "His nature, identified with a magnificent enterprise, his countenance etched by the fires and frosts of great events, were no longer adequate to the era of mediocrity." The succession of French presidents that followed was a steady descent from de Gaulle's greatness to the depths of the humdrum and the tawdry.

Nixon saw this at once. He released an official message, but also had the U.S. embassy in Paris deliver to de Gaulle's house a personal message, describing de Gaulle's retirement as "a great loss to France, and to the cause of freedom and decency in the world." He invited de Gaulle to come to the United States and added, "In this age of mediocre leaders in most of the world, America's spirit needs your presence." It's doubtful that the rancorous students or still occasionally rioting African-Americans or ever more frequent skyjackers of commercial aircraft would have found much balm in de Gaulle's grandiloquence or erudition, but what Nixon meant was that he would have valued it himself.

When he received the letter, de Gaulle said, of the sender, "He is a true comrade," and wrote his response from his library desk, where he did all his writing, with a view out over the Champagne countryside. He wrote that Nixon's messages "touched me deeply," not just because of Nixon's high office, but "because they are from you, Richard Nixon, and I have for you, with good reason, esteem, confidence, and friendship as great and as sincere as it is possible to have. Perhaps one day I will have the opportunity and honor to see you again; in the meantime I send you from the bottom of my heart all my best wishes for the successful accomplishment of your immense national and international task," and concluded with "the assurance of my feeling of faithful and devoted friendship."[35]

The relevance of this to Nixon and to this narrative is not just that de Gaulle and Eisenhower were the last two front-line participants in the Second World War to pass from the scene (Hirohito and Chiang Kai-shek, both of whom Nixon knew, survived yet, but were not comparable), and that Nixon had fervently sought Eisenhower's approval, and admired de Gaulle at a distance. Both men had now passed, Eisenhower altogether, but not before Nixon accomplished his long ambition of achieving the very high esteem of both. De Gaulle, though an exquisitely courteous man in person, was not an endless font of compliments of the kind he lavished on Nixon in his letter.

It was a sincere and disinterested comment, and like Eisenhower's request that Nixon deliver his eulogy, was immensely gratifying to one who had struggled so long to attract the attention, and then the respect, and finally even, to a degree, the friendship of such exalted and great men. Eisenhower and de Gaulle had known five other American presidents, and at the end they both valued their relations with Nixon more highly than those with any of the others (though de Gaulle was a wary admirer of Roosevelt's genius and physical courage). Nixon would not have years in which to seek and benefit from their advice, but at least he had gained their confidence. No matter what tempests raged in the balance of his career, these were attainments that could not be repealed or impeached.

Richard Nixon and Charles de Gaulle were not to meet again. Georges Pompidou led the Gaullists to victory in the election to replace de Gaulle, who spent the election with eighty-nine-year-old President Eamon de Valera in Ireland. At Winston Churchill's funeral in 1965, de Gaulle had said in answer to a question from Israel's founding prime minister, David Ben-Gurion, that at his funeral "there will be no spectacle for General de Gaulle." On November 9, 1970, two weeks short of de Gaulle's eightieth birthday, Pompidou came on the air and, without preamble, announced, "General de Gaulle is dead; France is a widow." The general had decreed that his funeral be in his parish church at Colombey, that his pallbearers be aldermen of the town. "The neighboring people surround me with their discreet friendship. I know their families; I respect and love them," he had written. Only comrades of the Resistance were welcome from outside. He had renounced any pension as a political officeholder, and had a simple, traditional, Roman Catholic French officer's funeral, and was buried in the churchyard, beside his daughter.

Pompidou organized a mighty memorial service in Notre Dame Cathedral and virtually every leader in the world attended. Nixon was placed in the position of greatest prominence, except for Pompidou himself, in deference not only to the Great Power he led, but to the admiration the deceased had had for him. There had been some parallel in the relations between Nixon and Eisenhower and Pompidou and de Gaulle, and when the two presidents met privately afterward, Pompidou said after a pause, with tears in his eyes, "At last, we are alone." They both understood. There seemed to be a brief hiatus in the torrent and fury of events, and the world stood still for a moment, as great men passed on. Nixon, historically minded, and emotionally susceptible in many ways, saw the significance of these occasions far more than merely ceremoniously.[36]

— IV —

Nixon had considered offering the position of chief justice to Herbert Brownell, Rogers's predecessor as Eisenhower's attorney general, but Brownell had been so emphatic an advocate of desegregation that he would be harmful to Nixon in the South, so Nixon offered the post to Thomas E. Dewey. It would have been a distinguished finale to his career, and he was certainly well-qualified. Dewey declined on grounds of age; he was sixty-six.

Distinguished sitting justice Potter Stewart also declined, saying it would be difficult for him now to claim some ascendancy over the seven colleagues with whom he had been serving as equals. (It might have been even more difficult for a complete newcomer from a lower court or outside the judiciary.) Nixon turned next to Mitchell, who also declined, because he did not think the president should appoint a political friend (though some had, and that had been Johnson's move with Abe Fortas, though he was a much more distinguished lawyer than Mitchell). Mitchell also had some concerns about whether he had the stature for the post, which was not a concern with Brownell, Dewey, and Stewart. All showed a commendable spirit of disinterest.

Nixon eventually settled upon Warren Burger, a judge of the U.S. Court of Appeals, who had been Stassen's manager at the Republican convention in 1952 and had helped put Eisenhower in as nominee, over the political corpse of Earl Warren's candidacy. Nixon took his selection of a nominee to this position very seriously, read articles of Burger's, had him swear some of his nominees, so he could interview him informally, and sent Mitchell to question him closely. Nixon never uttered a word of criticism of Fortas, whom he respected, and sent him a warm message of sympathy when he retired from the bench.[37] Burger was confirmed easily and proved a competent chief justice.

Nixon had two of his most successful social occasions in the White House in the last week of April. On April 24, he had a departure dinner for Chief Justice Warren and his family. It was a tasteful and convivial evening, and Warren wrote the president the next day that "it was the most thrilling social event of my half century of public life."[38] They had had a very strained relationship for more than twenty years, hitting its nadir when Nixon had riddled and honey-combed Warren's California delegation at the 1952 Republican convention in Chicago, persuaded it to back the seating of Eisenhower delegate-slates, and had Chotiner installed as the delegation manager, in which capacity he had left the then governor to pay his own hotel bill. (Chapter 3.) Now, all was forgiven, if not forgotten. The starting president and departing chief justice elegantly closed an unpleasant wound, and it was a tidy end to it.

On April 29, Nixon held Duke Ellington's seventieth birthday party in the White House. It was the first time that African-Americans had predom-inated on a White House guest list, and was a spectacular party, attended by most of America's greatest popular musicians, and went on until after 2 A.M. Ellington kissed everyone on both cheeks, man and woman, when he left, after playing a song for Mrs. Nixon, "Pat," which as Nixon gallantly put in his memoirs, was "lyrical, delicate, and beautiful – like Pat." Nixon played the piano himself at times, but cheerfully gave way to Cab Calloway, Earl Hines, Billy Eckstine, Mahalia Jackson, Richard Rodgers, Dave Brubeck, Dizzy Gillespie, and others. Nixon was determined to show the snippy Washington society writers that the White House was alive socially (they hadn't been too impressed with the Johnsons either, or indeed, apart from the Kennedys, with anyone in living memory). He set out to surpass Kennedy's famous evening for Pablo Casals.

He succeeded, and sent an important message to the African-American community as well. Duke Ellington's father had worked as a part-time butler in the White House. And one departing guest from Los Angeles who claimed to have voted against Nixon seven times, said he would vote for him now "if he ran as Grand Dragon of the Ku Klux Klan."[39]

Nixon was becoming increasingly preoccupied with leaks from his inner councils. Johnson had warned him that these would wreck his administration if he wasn't careful. Far-ranging National Security Council directives were being bowdlerized and published, in the New York Times and elsewhere. Nixon met with J. Edgar Hoover and John Mitchell to discuss how to deal with this. Hoover said all presidents starting with FDR had employed wiretaps, and that they would have to be put on suspects, along with background checks and physical surveillance.

What blew the lid off this story was the report in the New York Times on May 9 revealing the secret bombing of Cambodia. Nixon and Kissinger were in Key Biscayne, and Kissinger brought the president the story. Both men worked themselves and each other into a tremendous rage very quickly. (In fact, the story was based on the personal on-site observations of a British journalist, not on a leak at all, but there had been lots of other leaks, frequent and more important, almost since inauguration day.) Kissinger allegedly raged that the authors "must be destroyed," and used the same words in conversation that morning with the FBI director, according to Hoover's notes.[40]

Kissinger, showing the form that caused him to be regarded in Nixon's entourage as a hothead, got on the phone to summon Melvin Laird off the golf course at the Burning Tree Country Club and opened the discussion about leaks with the defense secretary with "You son of a bitch!" That's as far as it got, as Laird hung up and returned to his game. Nixon told Kissinger to screen his own people. Kissinger did not defend them, but was convinced that Laird and Rogers were leaking against him to force him out of the White House. Nixon was more concerned with national security consequences than with the motives for the indiscretions.

From 1969 to 1971, eighteen individuals were subjected to wiretapping. The principal initial suspect was Morton Halperin, an old Harvard colleague of Kissinger's, who had first devised for Kissinger the plan to have all matters to be submitted to the National Security Council selected by a committee that Kissinger, and not the undersecretary of state, would chair and control. Halperin was with Kissinger and the president's party in Key

Biscayne, and Kissinger walked with him on the beach and said that Nixon was upset about leaks, and that to clear Halperin, he would, for a time, not give him access to highly confidential material. He didn't say anything about wiretaps. While they were walking, the FBI placed the intercepting device on Halperin's home telephone. The next day, Kissinger's military assistant, Colonel Alexander Haig, gave Hoover's office some more names, including Kissinger's assistant, Helmut Sonnenfeldt, and his former Paris peace talks informant, Daniel Davidson.

Other subjects of the taps included Anthony Lake, a member of Kissinger's staff, and eventually President William J. Clinton's national security adviser, and future Nixon biographer, Roger Morris. Both men were partisan Democrats, and Lake was active in the incipient Muskie campaign for the presidency, while Morris was moonlighting for Democratic senator and future vice president and presidential candidate Walter Mondale.

Long after it became clear that there was no possible security justification for tapping their phones, there continued to be transcripts of private conversations, including disparaging references to the president personally, which Kissinger referred to in his conversations with Nixon. (Since Kissinger hired these people, it is not obvious how he thought he was advancing his own interest reporting on such conversations to Nixon, who had warned him, with some reason, in political but not national security terms, about the questionable loyalties of some of his staff members.)

Of more value to Kissinger were the taps on aides to Rogers and Laird. They were completely discreet, but they enabled Kissinger to get a good deal of advance notice of what the two cabinet secretaries intended to say at upcoming meetings and gave Kissinger an edge in the intense bureaucratic competition that was already well under way.

Syndicated journalist Joseph Kraft had written a piece that Nixon considered nasty, though there was no suggestion of a leak, and his telephone was tapped by the security specialist of the Republican National Committee. Nixon acknowledged approving the plan, but not the individual subjects of the taps, apart from Kraft. Kraft's RNC tap was lifted after a brief period, when the FBI was able to justify tapping his telephone while he visited Paris and met with the North Vietnamese.[41]

Kissinger or Haig, it was perpetually disputed between them, approved a tap on William Safire, Nixon's own chief speechwriter, because he had been seen talking to a journalist, Henry Brandon. Safire considered

Kissinger to be responsible, and the excuse of a journalistic contact is a bit rich, as Brandon was a better friend of Kissinger's than of Safire's and Kissinger was frequently at Brandon's home. Again, long after any national security excuse for continuing the tap on Brandon existed, it was retained, assumedly to sweep in conversations between Brandon's companion and future wife and her close friend Joan Kennedy. As is almost inevitable in such cases, the ostensible excuse for imposing the infringement on privacy of selected citizens lapses, and completely illegitimate grounds of interest for keeping them going prevail.

Among the more absurd matters thrown up in this affair was from the tap on Kissinger's assistant, Winston Lord, a man of unquestionable integrity and discretion, as well as high competence (a future assistant secretary of state and ambassador to China). Lord's Chinese wife, the successful novelist Bette Bao Lord, frequently conversed in Chinese with her mother about recipes. The FBI was put to a great deal of inconvenience finding, first translators, and then decrypters, as neither Hoover nor others involved could believe that an exchange of Mandarin recipes was the real subject of discussion.

One of Nixon's close aides, John Sears, and Nixon's brother, Donald, were also tapped. Nixon did not suspect his brother, who lurched from financial crisis to crisis and regularly traded off his brother's name and position in a manner familiar to the families of several presidents. The president was concerned that his brother might just be indiscreet to impress people.

The whole program was shabby and some of it was illegal. When it began, Johnson's Omnibus Crime Control and Safe Streets Act of 1968 gave these intercepts a national security exemption. But it's doubtful if that could have been used to justify continuing the taps for over a year in the absence of anything worrisome, and extending them to family members and circulating transcripts of private calls between untargeted spouses and friends and total outsiders, for the delectation of Kissinger and Haig.

That Nixon and Kissinger would start tapping the telephones of their closest associates is not a flattering reflection on their judgment of the character of those whom they themselves recruited, nor of their own serenity of mind and judgment, or respect for at least the spirit of the law. It is hard to imagine, no matter how nerve-wracking the circumstances, Truman or Eisenhower and his national security adviser, General Goodpaster, conducting such a dragnet, though it is not so difficult to imagine from

Roosevelt and Kennedy. Johnson would probably have gone further, and did, and without the qualms Nixon clearly had, as Nixon urged the early termination of the program.

When this all came to light in 1973, two years after it had stopped, Nixon manfully took the entire responsibility for it and gave it a national security cover. In his private relationships with some of the targets, who knew that Kissinger had had a great deal more to do with choosing the targeted individuals than Nixon had, Kissinger tried a fully gymnastic range of explanations, including that he was doing some of them a favor by enabling them to demonstrate that they were above suspicion. As Kissinger biographer Walter Isaacson pointed out, those upon whom such feeble excuses were inflicted could have found "them as offensive as the spinsters of Old Salem must have found it when the citizens told them they would be dunked in water to prove they were not witches."[42]

The one redemptive and reassuring aspect of the whole tawdry business is that none of the taps turned up anything, only, as Nixon wrote, "gossip and bullshitting." So Nixon's and Kissinger's judgment of people was vindicated, even as their respect for their privacy and the law was not.[43] There was an initial justification for trying to trace the source of leaks, but no excuse for spreading it to extraneous people and keeping it going so long. And while their professional discretion was not at issue, Kissinger must have taken temporary leave of his senses to bring active partisans of Muskie and Mondale onto the National Security Council staff (though Lake and Morris soon quit anyway).

Nixon found the whole wiretapping process more troubling than Kissinger did, never looked at transcripts, at least made noises about ending it fairly soon after it began, and took the entire responsibility for it. Kissinger seems not to have had such scruples, though he wrote in his memoirs that Nixon ordered the wiretaps on Hoover's recommendation and Mitchell's assurance that they were legal, and that "contrary to malicious lore, senior officials did not spend time pruriently reading over lengthy transcripts of personal conversations." According to Hoover's notes, Kissinger said the White House would "destroy whoever did this, if we find him, no matter where he is." Kissinger's own version was that he "went along with what I had no reason to doubt was legal and established practice." They were strained times and Kissinger deserves the benefit of the doubt, though his role is not creditable and some of his jejune explanations of his conduct are not believable. Safire may have been correct when he remarked that

Kissinger was "capable of getting a special thrill out of working most closely with those he spied on the most."[44]

— v —

Nixon knew that Vietnam could not be allowed to continue indefinitely, returning three hundred or more body bags a week to the United States with no end in sight. The North Vietnamese were benefiting from a bombing pause for which they gave nothing in return, not even a response to direct messages from the president of the United States. Nixon launched his effort to extract the Disraeliite ideal of peace with honor in Vietnam in a nationally televised speech of May 14. The core of Nixon's proposal was simultaneous substantial withdrawals from South Vietnam of North Vietnamese and American forces one year after reaching an agreement. There would be international verification of withdrawals and supervision of free elections in South Vietnam. Although there was no practical chance of North Vietnam agreeing to this, it was at least a more realistic proposal than preceding American offers, and, in promising free elections, reconnected the United States to the Geneva Accords of 1954, which it had promised not to disrupt.

Nixon made the point that "reports from Hanoi indicate that the enemy has given up hope for a military victory in South Vietnam, but is counting on a collapse of will in the United States. There could be no greater error in judgment." There were no such reports from Hanoi, or at least no believable ones, but Nixon was right that Hanoi obviously thought the United States would just give up and pull out. He was now determined at least to bring to an end the prolonged insolence of Hanoi's silence to American overtures. But he was still not moving to get the Democratic Congress to sign on to any bipartisan war or peace plan.

As long as Fulbright and Kennedy, Gore, Cranston, and the others were nipping at his ankles, there was no assurance that the home front, in the event of bad news, which Hanoi was capable of generating, and the American media, once the honeymoon was over, would amplify, would not abruptly collapse. Most Americans now thought it had been a mistake to go into Vietnam in the first place and Nixon was moving late and tentatively to cooper up support for a policy of gradual retreat, no matter how he covered it with a fig leaf of tough talk. Nixon announced that he would meet with President Thieu at Midway Island in the Central Pacific in early June.

The speech was quite well received in the United States, but once again there was no response from Hanoi. On the day after the speech, Nixon had the CIA director, Richard Helms, brief the cabinet and National Security Council, which met jointly, on Asian reaction to his speech. Helms referred to Prime Minister Pham Van Dong as the young Ho Chi Minh, and Nixon interrupted, "Oh, he's our Finch," to some merriment. Helms claimed that the message that the United States was not just going to leave was an important one to send.

Nixon had effectively set a deadline of November 1, one year after Johnson's bombing pause, for something useful to happen, and started working to that deadline. There were problems with that concept, as there was no chance that Hanoi would pay any attention to any deadline set by Washington. The North Vietnamese were confident they could dispose of the Saigon regime if the United States wasn't supporting it in great strength, and Nixon was losing the time in which he had at least the notional option to escalate.

Nixon made a few forceful speeches, including one at the United States Air Force Academy, and flew to Midway to meet President Thieu on June 8. The results were prearranged, but the meeting was designed to lend an air of collegiality to them and also to exchange opinions. Thieu, when he found he had been allotted a smaller chair than Nixon in the home of the U.S. commandant where they met (just after the twenty-seventh anniversary of the great aircraft carrier battle that immortalized the islands), Thieu himself carried in a larger one from the neighboring room.[45] It was agreed that there would be an immediate withdrawal of twenty-five thousand American soldiers, and Nixon made the point that the pace of withdrawals would depend on the progress of the South Vietnamese in taking over the war, the restraint of the North Vietnamese, and the progress of peace talks. Nixon claimed that Thieu and Creighton Abrams, his Vietnam commander, were happy with the withdrawals, which was not true, but Thieu gamely held up his end.

Thieu returned to Saigon via Taipei, where he met with the unextinguished Chiang Kai-shek, who warned him that the Americans tried to solve military problems by economic or political means. (After Chiang's inept efforts against the Japanese and the communists, he should have been a little more grateful to the power that had threatened to use nuclear weapons in his defense on Taiwan.) Thieu told Chiang that Nixon had a domestic problem with the Congress, the press, and demonstrating students, and had promised him eight years of strong support, four years militarily and then four more years of economic support and as a military guarantor.[46]

Nixon felt he had gained the initiative, at least opposite the anti-war groups in the United States, by sketching out a more plausible peace plan, envisioning international supervision of the arrangements, promising freedom of choice for the South Vietnamese, and beginning withdrawals, with apparent agreement from Saigon. It was certainly an improvement on anything Johnson had managed, but Nixon was now six months past his election, with a hostile Congress, and in terms of domestic opinion he was chasing a moving target, as support for the war steadily eroded.

Clark Clifford had said that the United States should reduce the troop levels in Vietnam by one hundred thousand by the end of 1970. Nixon told his June 10 nationally televised evening press conference that Clifford had been secretary of defense when troop levels and American battle deaths and casualties reached and remained at their highest point, and he didn't consider him a natural source for such advice. He had had his "chance and did not move on it . . . I would hope we could beat Mr. Clifford's timetable." (He did.)

It was a very strong performance, and Nixon engaged in what would become a drearily predictable habit: telephoning supporters to a late hour asking them how they thought he had done. It is astonishing that a man of Nixon's intelligence would not realize how this demonstrable insecurity, when all he had to do was wait for a few hours and he would learn how people thought he had done, would undermine the confidence of his staff.

He assiduously read de Gaulle's early works on the necessary remoteness of the leader, and had stripped out the television sets Johnson had in the Oval Office, and endlessly and misleadingly put it about that he had no interest in what the media thought of anything. To those who knew him best, he was always on an emotional roller coaster and had a performance anxiety, before and after a major appearance, that made his achievement in successfully pursuing a public career the more remarkable.

He was up early and in a good mood the next day, and walked King Timahoe on a leash around the White House grounds and even along Pennsylvania Avenue. A little exposure like this was good for him and for the public's perception of him.[47]

His next Vietnam move was to write directly to Ho Chi Minh. He did this, and again utilized veteran French diplomat Jean Sainteny as courier. Sainteny came to the White House and Nixon advised him in the strongest terms that he would take drastic measures if Hanoi did not go some way to reciprocate American efforts at de-escalation. His letter to Ho Chi Minh, which Sainteny gave on July 16 to North Vietnamese negotiator Xuan Thuy, who delivered it personally to Ho Chi Minh, acknowledged the difficulty of communicating "across the gulf of four years of war," promised a "forthcoming and open-minded" approach to peace-making, and gave the customary exhortation to move toward a settlement. Sainteny had promised to transmit to Xuan Thuy Nixon's assertion that if there were no progress before November 1, the United States would have recourse "to measures of great consequence and force."

After a few days, the North Vietnamese suggested through the French channel a secret meeting between Xuan Thuy and Kissinger in Paris. This was scheduled for July, when Nixon would be on a world tour, in the midst of which he would observe the splashdown in the Pacific of American astronauts returning from the moon. Kissinger did meet with Xuan Thuy and Mai Van Bo, also a negotiator for North Vietnam, at Sainteny's apartment on the Rue de Rivoli on August 4. The North Vietnamese reiterated to Kissinger their contention that there were no North Vietnamese in South Vietnam, that it was no legitimate concern of the Americans to be in Vietnam at all, and that they should depart and dispense with the Thieu government as they went.

Kissinger, "exercising his tremendous skill," as Nixon fairly stated, laid out to the North Vietnamese what the United States had done to try to demonstrate goodwill and move matters toward peace, but left them in no doubt that failure to respond otherwise than by repetition of their customary inflexible position would, as their propaganda said, make it "Nixon's War. We do not believe this is in your interest, because if it is Mr. Nixon's war, then he cannot afford not to win it."[48]

Nixon observed the astronauts' splashdown from the bridge of the aircraft carrier *Hornet*, pointing and bobbing around slightly excitedly, like the very active young boy he had once been, and as he sometimes still did at sports matches.[*] He went on to Guam, and enunciated what became the

---

[*] As when he went to a baseball game with Herbert Brownell, a few days after his nomination as vice presidential candidate in 1952. (Chapter 4.)

Guam Doctrine, and then, quickly, the Nixon Doctrine. He stated that the United States would uphold all its existing treaty commitments, but would only contract further ones if required by indisputable national interest, and that henceforth it would supply material and economic assistance to countries engaged in self-defense. It was another necessary step backward from Kennedy's extending a blank check in the "Bear any burden" section of his inaugural address. Calling it a "doctrine" and enunciating it after the United States had erased the Sputnik fiasco by sending men to the moon, gave this scale-back the most dignified possible formulation. (Henry Stimson, Hoover's secretary of state and Roosevelt's secretary of war, and Harry Truman had "doctrines" too.)

The moon landing itself, on July 20, had been a scientific and public relations triumph for the United States. "One small step for man; one giant leap for mankind" was a brilliant landing statement by Astronaut Neil Armstrong. Nixon indulged his weakness for hyperbole by telephoning the astronauts in their spacecraft, the *Eagle,* and saying that "This certainly has to be the most historic phone call ever made from the White House." Probably some of Roosevelt's and Churchill's were, but Nixon went further when he then flew to the splashdown site and greeted the returning astronauts in their decompression chamber and declared, "This is the greatest week in the history of the world since the Creation." This was too much even for Billy Graham, who championed Christmas and Easter for that honor. (Nixon rationalized that he was speaking of a week, not a day.)

Hugh Sidey captured something of Nixon's strategy and his nature and his following when he wrote in *Time*: "He has given a voice to the majority that did not know it was a majority. . . . RN who goes to ball games . . . and follows space flights with the enthusiasm of a small boy. He is the president of the Jaycees, the Kiwanis booster, the cheerleader flying around the world, glorying in what Middle America has wrought."[49]

This was a two-edged sword; Sidey was reasonably equable about Rotarian and booster America having a spokesman, after Eisenhower, Kennedy, and Johnson (the great general, the Ivy League multimillionaire's son, and the Texas wheeler-dealer). However, much of the national media, which disliked Nixon for his old Red-baiting campaigns, his awkwardness and lack of companionability, his Checkers kitsch, and his maddening durability, despised his followers and resented his ability to rouse a mighty army of nondescript, or, from the perspective of Nixon's critics, silly, people. Too much of the Washington press corps, and the most influential people in the American media generally, fancied themselves endowed with the right, and even the talent, of H.L. Mencken or Sinclair Lewis to despise the American masses. (And the masses of America had become a good deal better educated and more prosperous since their day.)

One unforeseeable result of the moon landing was that it took the spotlight off Teddy Kennedy's automobile accident at Chappaquiddick, where he drove his car off a bridge and his female passenger, a former member of Robert Kennedy's office staff, the twenty-eight-year-old Mary Jo Kopechne, drowned. Kennedy had disappeared for eight hours, and the circumstances of the accident have never been adequately explained. Nixon assured Haldeman that the Kennedys would not be able to hush this one up, as they had hushed up many other things, because "too many journalists want the Pulitzer Prize."[50] He overestimated the enterprise of the craft of journalism. The tragic incident did, however, permanently remove the youngest Kennedy brother as a viable presidential candidate, and Nixon had expected to face him in 1972. But his private view of Chappaquiddick, apart from a very unflattering construction of the actual events, was: "He ran. There's a fatal flaw in his character."[51]

Nixon flew on from Guam to Manila, Jakarta, Bangkok, and Saigon. There were Filipino and Thai contingents serving in Vietnam, and Nixon wanted to coordinate policy with the leaders of those countries. The American security establishment was still celebrating the overthrow of Sukarno and massacre of the communists in Indonesia, and Nixon's visit there was timely.

Nixon met with Thieu and helicoptered to the U.S. First Army's base at Di Am, about fifteen miles away. He chatted amiably with the soldiers, and always knew something about the towns or counties they came from, as he had campaigned in almost every village and rural area in the country at some point. And he talked about sports, always an encyclopedia of past scores and statistics. Some of the press tended to mock the rather predictable conversational gambits Nixon offered at such times, but the lads appreciated the visit and the solidarity of the commander in chief, and he was moved by their clean-cut courage and sense of duty. With such people, he was much less awkward than he sometimes had been in the salons of New York and Washington. When he was back on Air Force One, he told Haldeman that he never wanted to receive a group of "hippie college boys" again.[52]

He went on for brief stops to speak to the leaders of India in New Delhi, and of Pakistan in Lahore. Nixon took an instant liking to Pakistan's General Yahya Khan, a whisky-drinking, British-trained officer, and concluded that he could be useful in relations with China and Russia. The president went on to Romania, to, as he had put it privately, "needle" the Russians. He wished to demonstrate America's popularity among the countries the U.S.S.R. was illegally occupying or intimidating, and to make more vivid the specter he had already raised with Dobrynin, of opening relations with China. He was the first American president to make a state visit to an Iron Curtain country, and had said to Kissinger that by the time this trip ended, "the Russians will be out of their minds that we are playing a Chinese game."[53]

Nixon and his party landed in Bucharest on August 2, and received an immense welcome from hundreds of thousands of Romanians, organized by Ceauşescu, whom Nixon described in his memoirs as "a strong, independent, leader."[54] Nixon repeated the November 1 ultimatum date in forceful terms, and his host, who had good relations with Hanoi, said he would do anything he could to move discussions along. Two days later came Kissinger's meeting in Paris, and three days after that, Nixon had Henry Cabot Lodge, who had carved out quite a diplomatic career for himself after losing his Senate seat to John F. Kennedy in 1952 and was now the U.S. representative at the Paris talks, make a very vigorous statement saying that the United States had done all it could and it was time for a serious response from Hanoi. When Haldeman told Kissinger that Nixon intended to visit China before the end of his term, Kissinger, according to Haldeman (who was writing retrospectively and must be read with some caution, given the complicated relations involved), said, "Fat chance."[55]

Nixon returned from his round-the-world trip on August 3, and was greeted by thousands of people, including an effusive Edward Kennedy, in a severe downpour at Andrews Air Force Base. The next morning he met the bipartisan congressional leadership and gave another tour de force performance, fielding questions effortlessly, with depth of background but never pedantry. He gave realistic hope of a declining problem

---

* Twenty years later, Nicolae Ceauşescu was regarded as a brutal and incompetent dictator. He and his wife were overthrown and executed by firing squad, without much pretense of due process. Nixon continued to be friendly with him, almost to the end.

in Vietnam and improving relations with all shadings and factions among the communist powers.

He said that if the United States had not intervened in Vietnam, Indonesia would then be communist, an argument only intermittently made, which, if demonstrably accurate, would alter the general assessment of Johnson's strategic capabilities, and of the rationale for the whole Vietnamese venture. He said that Thieu was the "most impressive South Vietnamese leader I have met. That isn't saying a great deal." But it was saying perhaps more than he had intended, given his former admiration for Diem.[56] After the meeting with the congressional leaders, Nixon had a private session with Edward Kennedy, wished him well, and told him never to give up. Nixon said that he had been surprised at how hostile the press had been, but that Kennedy must remember that the press, even when they liked you, were the enemy, because they wanted the story.[57]

Ho Chi Minh's reply came in a few weeks later, and was dated August 25. He wrote that he was "deeply touched at the rising toll of death of young Americans who have fallen in Vietnam by reason of the policy of American governing circles." He demanded the withdrawal of all foreigners from all of Vietnam. It was, wrote Nixon, "a cold rebuff. . . . I knew that I would have to prepare myself for the tremendous criticism and pressure that would come with stepping up the war."[58]

He would, but the questions remain: Why had he waited seven months before getting to this point, and losing his moral ability to enlist the congressional Democrats? And why didn't the North Vietnamese take any of these overtures seriously, as they would have brought victory much more quickly and at much reduced cost in life, and war damage, and indebtedness to the Russians and Chinese?

Nixon claimed he had thought that the Democrats could not desert so reasonable a position as he was espousing, but he was too experienced at partisan affairs and the nature of the other party to have invested too much faith in such hopefulness. The inner workings of Hanoi remain a mystery. Ho Chi Minh died on September 3, and it was not immediately clear if the elevation of Pham Van Dong would have any material effect on Hanoi's stance. Sainteny attended the funeral and reported to Kissinger on September 20 that Pham Van Dong had been, as Nixon put it, "notably unvituperative" about the United States, but didn't trust Washington.[59] Nixon had already announced the withdrawal of another thirty-five thousand soldiers in mid-September, to take place before year's end, and considered this to be the last gesture of goodwill he was prepared to make before the expiry of his November 1 deadline.

He reinforced his position in an address to the UN General Assembly, and had Kissinger make purposeful noises to Dobrynin through their back channel. Nixon told a group of Republican senators, whom he knew would leak it, that he was considering blockading Haiphong and invading the North. It was in print a few days later. He cut off foreign aid to Cyprus and Malta, as two countries with extensive shipping contacts with North Vietnam that refused to reduce them (unlike Singapore and Somalia, which did). And on September 26 he told a press conference that he was aware of protest against the war but that "under no circumstances whatever will I be affected by it." This fuelled a good deal of criticism at home, but was the best he could do to give pause to the post-Ho leadership in Hanoi. This was how matters stood as the fateful deadline approached.

— VI —

Though Nixon was much more interested in foreign than in domestic affairs, he was interested in some domestic problems, and he was interested in politics, which was heavily influenced by the economy and civic conditions generally. He had hammered his anti-crime theme throughout the campaign, and had an ancient prejudice against the Roosevelt-era Washington regulatory and money-handling bureaucracy, going back to his and Pat's days in the wartime Office of Price Administration. He had taken a dim view of Johnson's oversold Great Society programs as he rammed them through a docile Congress, and he was very persuaded by Moynihan's elegantly reasoned and charmingly advocated concept of a radical reform of the welfare system. He knew that he was unlikely to get anything really imaginative through a Congress still crowded with unregenerate New Dealers, Fair Dealers, New Frontiersmen and Great Societalists, sitting like the rings on a tree in the Democratic benches of both houses. But he would try for something, and stake out a position that he would attempt to expand upon in the next two congressional elections, and, at the least, put down a marker for the future.

Aid to Families with Dependent Children (AFDC) was the core of the American welfare system. It dated from the thirties, an era when one third of the country was without income and nearly half the people were in danger of eviction from their homes through mortgage foreclosure. Roosevelt did not want what he called "the pauperism of the dole;" he wanted useful work at modest wages, to occupy the unemployed until the self-resuscitating private sector could take them back into regular employment. To this end, colossal schemes of irrigation, rural electrification (including the Tennessee Valley Authority), drought control, flood control, conservation (from the soil to the whooping crane), and reforestation were carried out; and public works, including much of the Chicago waterfront, the University of Pittsburgh's Cathedral of Learning, New York's Triborough Bridge, the state capitol of Montana, thousands of parks and campgrounds, thousands of miles of roads, hundreds of airports and landing fields, and even the historic and bravely manned aircraft carriers *Enterprise* and *Yorktown*, were built at bargain cost to the taxpayer. At times, as many as six million people were engaged in these projects, but they were always emergency relief.

Unemployment insurance was part of the Social Security system that Roosevelt enacted in 1935, but he had intended it to be insurance against unemployment, on a contributory basis, not a system for making the status of citizen a salaried entitlement. Roosevelt substantially reduced unemployment and, if the emergency relief workers are included, had largely eliminated it by 1937. As the war crisis deepened, he ditched the isolationist liberals of the West and Midwest who had supported the New Deal, in exchange for the Southern Democrats who had opposed it but favored an expanded defense effort and were, for a variety of practical and traditional reasons, favorable to the British and French.

With this new coalition, which obliged Roosevelt to turn a blind eye to aspects of the South that he found nauseating, including the Southern congressional habit of filibustering anti-lynching bills to death, he transferred a great deal of spending from conservation and public works to defense production, and later the first peacetime conscription in the country's history. Unemployment had fallen by over 75 percent when Roosevelt was reelected to a third term in 1940, and it had been completely eliminated when the United States was plunged into the Second World War by the attack on Pearl Harbor and Hitler's declaration of war on America thirteen months later.

After the war, the Truman administration managed a fairly orderly decontrol, and the private sector absorbed about twelve million young men demobilized from the armed forces and perhaps another million men and women released from wartime civilian government employment. Through the Truman, Eisenhower, and Kennedy years, unemployment was moderate, and continued to be with Johnson and Nixon. But AFDC had been altered by the deterioration in the status of marriage and the facilitation of childbirth to single women.

In earlier times, the rigid and unjust stigma of illegitimacy assured that AFDC was covering struggling families. In 1940, 2 percent of America's children were on welfare; thirty years later, in a population nearly a hundred million greater, the percentage was more than five times as great. By LBJ's era as president, the children of unemployed fathers were ineligible for benefit, but the children of unwed parents, or of mothers abandoned by their husbands, were eligible. The welfare system had become an assault on the family, a situation aggravated by Johnson's well-intentioned but imperfectly designed effort to ensure that traditional moralizing did not economically punish innocent victims.

The welfare establishment grew immensely through the postwar years and spiked upwards under Johnson. His pledge to abolish poverty, as Nixon had foreseen at the time, had given employment to a large number of low-level government officials with great powers of intrusion in the lives of the lower economic groups, and had extended greater benefits to categories of African-Americans who had previously been comparatively shortchanged. But it had become hideously expensive, relatively unproductive, and, as has been mentioned, sociologically counterproductive.

It had an insatiable natural cost growth rate. The Johnson program was based on the theory that what the poor needed was skills, and colossal plans were put in place to train them. The Moynihan-Nixon conception was that what they needed was cash. The welter of government programs that Roosevelt initiated to assist the distressed had permutated into a method of taking money from those who had earned it and redistributing it through a vastly expensive government transfer-payment system to people who had not earned it, without adequate regard to merit, presumably in exchange for votes, though this was very rarely explicit.

The great middle class of America, over 60 percent of the population, was handed the tax invoice, to appease the puritanical conscience of America (which inspired the country's founders and has been ineradicable, no matter how large and diverse the population has become). Nixon regarded this process as fraudulent, wasteful, and morally and often financially corrupt. No one doubted the good intentions of successive presidents or even the contemporary congressional leadership and senior federal civil service who had constructed and managed the ramshackle American welfare edifice. But Nixon, aided by Moynihan as cunningly, if less grimly and more benignly, as he was in foreign matters by Kissinger, was determined to try to change the system he had so long despised.

On January 15, five days before he was inaugurated, Nixon asked Moynihan and Finch to come up with a plan that would address what the president-elect was convinced was the "outraged" condition of the voters over the state of the welfare system. They produced a plan for what amounted to a negative income tax, that would top up the incomes of the working poor, end the pressure on low-income fathers to desert their families, and incentivize welfare recipients to get a job. Arthur Burns was opposed, as it would lead to increased welfare rolls, and temporarily cost more. Nixon, when assured by Moynihan that it would drastically reduce the number of government-paid social workers, was, to Burns's astonishment, in favor of Moynihan and Finch's conception, which was called the Family Security System (FSS).

George Shultz, the labor secretary, coined the phrase "the working poor," which FSS set out to assist through what Nixon called, inventing the word, "workfare." This was exactly the constituency that Nixon had directly targeted to lift from the Democrats and George Wallace, and the project combined Nixon's deeply rooted detestation of the federal bureaucracy with his love of the dramatic and surprising, and his quest for political advantage. Moynihan and Finch, two people whom Nixon highly valued in any case, had no difficulty holding the president's attention and gaining his support for such a plan.

Nixon's parents had refused to send their son Harold to a state hospital when he was dying of tuberculosis because they thought it demeaning, and instead Hannah Nixon had moved to Arizona and taken care of other tubercular patients as well as her son. This was the fierce, proud tradition from which Richard Nixon came. While, as a politician, he knew that most people were not cut from such sturdy cloth, he was a partisan of self-help, direct aid, and the reduction of the number and jurisdiction of meddling government officials. Above all, for some reason not based on much personal contact, he hated social workers. He was right that the system required radical reform, and he became the first president, though he claimed his four predecessors (back to Truman) were of the same ambition, to propose the massive reform of the welfare system that finally came almost thirty years later, with a reluctant Democratic president and a crusading Republican Congress.

The president convened the cabinet on August 6 at Camp David to discuss FSS. There was a comprehensive presentation by Robert Patricelli, one of Finch's assistant secretaries, but most of the cabinet was opposed. Agnew and Romney, former state governors, said that almost all the governors would oppose it, and Agnew complained that FSS would add thirteen million people to the welfare rolls. He had to leave early to break a possible Senate tie on Nixon's ABM proposal. (His vote was necessary to get Nixon's measure through and make it usable as a bargaining chip with the Russians. It passed 51 to 50, in a Senate of one hundred members.)

Nixon did not care in the slightest what any member of the cabinet thought, except Finch and Shultz, who had had a hand in shaping FSS (the name of which Nixon changed to Family Assistance Plan, to accommodate Laird's concern that it sounded too much like a New Deal measure). He stopped short of de Gaulle's formula, at the end of cabinet meetings, of saying the ministers would be the first to hear of the government's decision without hinting at what that would be, and said that he had decided to proceed and expected enthusiastic support from all cabinet members.

Nixon spoke to the nation on the evening of August 8. He eviscerated the existing welfare system, trolling through all its shortcomings and excessive costs. He said that all presidents from Roosevelt on wanted to reform it and that this was the time to do so. He proclaimed a New Federalism, in which, instead of the federal government sending money to the states with attached requirements on how it was to be spent, it would simply rebate money, what he called "revenue sharing," with the states free to spend it as they wished, or give it back to their taxpayers. He had not sketched this out to Agnew and Romney, who might have been less vociferous in their opposition if they had heard this aspect of it.

He said that the Family Assistance Plan (FAP) would guarantee a sub-par-income family of four sixteen hundred dollars per year, and promised the same benefit level in every state and the end to discrimination against continuation of marriage and low-income employment, which his proposal would supplement. It was a radical concept and was widely praised. Polls indicated popular support, and the president's usual enemies, such as the *New York Times*, led by Nixon's frequent critic, James Reston, enthusiastically supported him.[60] The idea has been circulated, by contemporaries and historians, that Nixon did not particularly seek passage of the FAP, that he just wanted the praise for original thinking, and was concerned about the short-term costs. There is no evidence of this, and Nixon and Moynihan both denied it. Nixon sought the measure, but as Bryce Harlow told him, just springing it on the Republicans in the Congress was sure to antagonize many of them. Nixon liked the surprise and always thought of welfare reform and the New Federalism as electoral winners in the 1970 midterm elections and in 1972. In March 1971, country and popular singer Johnny Cash, a Nixon admirer, asked the president to reconsider his request that Cash sing "Welfare Cadillac," a song about a Cadillac-driving welfare recipient, at the White House.[61]

On August 9, Nixon left for a one-month holiday with his family in California, at the house that he had bought in San Clemente, between Los Angeles and San Diego, a mile from where he had proposed to Pat nearly thirty years before. Apart from a break in San Francisco for a conference with the visiting president of South Korea, Park Chung Hee, to whom, as he did with all foreign leaders, he uttered a dire warning to Hanoi (Park was probably the last leader in the world, not excluding Thieu, who would be in touch with the North Vietnamese), Nixon remained at La Casa Pacifica, as his house was called.

On August 18, Nixon nominated Judge Clement F. Haynsworth of South Carolina to fill the vacancy created by the retirement of Justice Abe Fortas. Nixon wanted a Southerner, and felt no obligation to maintain the so-called "Jewish seat" on the court, which had been maintained since Wilson's time. Liberals, and most of the national media, were not enthused about replacing a liberal judge with a conservative one. There wasn't much specific comment about sectarian identification, but George Meany, on behalf of the AFL-CIO, objected to an industrial relations judgment of Haynsworth's, and black leaders, including Roy Wilkins of the NAACP, complained of his segregationist judicial past. Almost from the start, it looked like a donnybrook getting the nomination through.

Another flap at this time was the case of the commander of the Green Berets (Special Forces) in Vietnam, Colonel Robert Rheault. He and seven other Green Berets were detained by General Abrams and the U.S. High Command in South Vietnam for murdering ("termination with extreme prejudice" was the CIA jargon for it) an apparent double agent, Thai Khac Chuyen. Nixon did not want Rheault prosecuted, as he had no objection to dealing pretty roughly with double agents, and was concerned that some other apparent excesses of the Special Forces would come to light in a court-martial. But Abrams and Secretary of the Army Stanley Resor locked arms and insisted on a trial. Nixon got Kissinger to pressure Helms to withhold CIA witnesses, and Resor was finally forced, in September, to release Rheault and the others on the increasingly more familiar and versatile ground of national security.

Despite these perturbations, it was a quiet and pleasant August, although there were protesters when he met with South Korean president Park Chung Hee, in Union Square in San Francisco. The president returned to Washington on September 7, stopping at Del Rio, Texas, to open a bridge across the Rio Grande with the president of Mexico, Gustavo Díaz Ordaz, and then inspecting hurricane damage and landing at Gulfport, Mississippi. This had been scheduled to be a ten-minute stop, but approximately fifty thousand wildly cheering Mississippians gathered at the airport and admiringly mobbed the president. He extended his projected ten-minute stop for over an hour to enjoy the excitement of the crowd.

— VII —

As Harlow, Laird, and others had predicted, the campuses started to come to life soon after the return to university of millions of the nation's youth. Two former organizers for Eugene McCarthy – Sam Brown and David Hawk – started what was called the Vietnam Moratorium, a student-based anti-war movement that called for a national demonstration against the war on October 15. Nixon removed the controversial seventy-six-year-old director of Selective Service (the draft), General Lewis Hershey, hated by anti-war groups, and announced a fifty-thousand-man cut in draft calls. On September 20, he had 225 carefully selected university student leaders to the White House. He found the students boring and presumptuous, and left after a little less than two hours to play golf with comedian Bob Hope at Burning Tree.[62] (He had described golf as "a waste of time" when Eisenhower used to summon him to a game, but was warming to it now that he issued the summonses.)

At his press conference on September 26, Nixon objected to moves from members of both parties in the Congress to order a complete retirement of American forces from Vietnam by the end of 1970, saying, as he had in response to Clark Clifford, that he hoped to beat that date. When asked about the Vietnam Moratorium, he said that he would not be influenced by it in any way. The congressional cat was now out of the bag, and Nixon would have great difficulty holding any kind of majority for a policy to stay the course. He had lost all possibility of a bipartisan approach and it now was his war. He could blame the Democrats for getting into the war, but not Democrats who were still in active politics, and those that were would now blame Nixon for staying in the war. The students could aspire to roll over the Congress as many of them had rolled over the presidents of some of the country's greatest universities. There was obviously no movement in Hanoi, and two days before the Vietnam Moratorium, on October 13, the White House announced that Nixon would give a major address on Vietnam on November 3.

The Vietnam Moratorium planned mass demonstrations throughout America, but especially in Washington, D.C., on the ides of every month until the war stopped, or at least American participation in it; the promoters weren't much concerned with what happened to the Vietnamese, they just wanted the United States out. As this stoked up, the Democrats launched a full-force attack on the Haynsworth nomination, and the Republican leadership in the Senate told the president on October 1 that Haynsworth would not be confirmed. He was a shareholder with Bobby Baker, LBJ's protégé as secretary of the Senate, who was forced out because of financial improprieties, and in the circumstances Haynsworth appeared to be tainted.[63]

The national press jubilantly rang down the curtain on Nixon's honeymoon. "Nixon in Trouble," gleefully bannered *Newsweek* magazine, owned by the *Washington Post*. Hugh Sidey, fluttering like a butterfly to the next conventional wisdom, wrote that the calm and sphinx-like unconcern Nixon publicly displayed was "perhaps as alarming as the events themselves."[64]

On October 14, Pham Van Dong purported to address the American public, and commended the peace demonstrators and expressed solidarity between the "progressive people" of America and Vietnam to end "U.S. aggression. . . . May your fall offensive succeed splendidly."

Nixon had Agnew read this message to a press conference, and was appalled that the White House press corps ignored the content of Pham Van Dong's address and skeptically asked if the administration was not using this as a pretext to try to derail the Moratorium.[65] Suddenly, and without any gradual movement, Nixon inherited the weight of the protest against Johnson.

The outrage he expressed in his memoirs was genuine and understandable,[66] but publicly he had done nothing about Vietnam in seven months except the May 14 offer and the announced and partially implemented withdrawal of sixty thousand troops. This certainly offered more hope of progress than Johnson had. But Nixon was almost inviting the post-Johnson Democrats, who weren't all Abbie Hoffman's hirsute armies of guitarists and public lovemakers of Grant Park, and were in fact led by Mike Mansfield (Senate majority leader), Fulbright, and Kennedy, to desert him and identify with the majority of Americans who now thought the country should never have been in Vietnam and should leave at once.

Nixon had lost the option of just leaving, and appeared to have lost the option of winning also, since he was leaving gradually. He had avoided the controversy of the only sort of escalation that could have won the war, but he would receive almost as much opposition from peace groups for continuing the fight at all. In mid-October, it was not clear that he had a viable strategy for which he could muster public support or that he had any chance of achieving anything useful in Vietnam. Polls indicated a deterioration in support for his war policy from about half the country in June, a few weeks after his May 14 offer, to only 35 percent in late September. Whatever Nixon did seemed to shore up his position for a briefer and briefer respite, and his political opponents, including liberal Republicans like New York's Mayor John Lindsay and Senator Charles Goodell, whom Rockefeller had named to fill out Robert Kennedy's term, were swarming in increasing numbers.

He had frittered away his honeymoon in the unfounded belief that negotiations with Hanoi might be possible and might yield something useful. Nixon believed, at the time and afterward, that the demonstrators and peace groups "destroyed whatever small possibility may have existed of ending the war in 1969." It is hard to believe that there was any. Hanoi never showed an interest, under Ho Chi Minh or after he died, in offering any quid pro quo for American withdrawal.

The United States had to make war more effectively or leave, and now Nixon had said he would not be influenced by the demonstrators, had given a lengthy ultimatum to Hanoi that had been ignored, and was going to have to cooper together a policy and sell it, in the teeth of partisan efforts to hang the war on him, to a porous and disheartened public. Kissinger favored escalation to cover withdrawal, which was and had been since the Tet Offensive twenty months before the only sensible policy. Nixon seemed to realize that nothing short of instant abandonment of the whole effort would appease the protesters, so their animosity might as well be endured for a policy that had a possibility of achieving a durable non-communist South Vietnam, though Kissinger himself doubted that was possible. For seven months Nixon had tried to palliate an intractable and sanguinary problem, and now Hanoi and the American peace movement and the U.S. national media had suddenly combined to put him right to the wall.

The American public and apparently even Henry Kissinger[67] did not know about the letter to Ho Chi Minh. And the public knew nothing of the November 1 ultimatum. Nixon was to some degree the victim of his own mysterious methods. He rather ostentatiously put on alert the nuclear-equipped B-52s on Pacific bases, in a manner he assumed would be detected by Soviet intelligence and communicated to the North Vietnamese. This was another stab at the "madman theory," but there was no evidence that Hanoi cared whether Nixon was insane or not.

Moratorium Day went well for its organizers and espousers. There was no violence, with sizable crowds of respectable people asking that peace be given the proverbial chance, a euphemism for ignominy and abandonment of an ally in what now seemed a losing and even ignoble cause. There were twenty thousand demonstrators in Washington, carrying candles after nightfall, fifty thousand in New York. Among those who spoke at anti-war rallies were Coretta Scott King, Senators Gene McCarthy and Charles Goodell, entertainers Woody Allen and Shirley MacLaine, and LBJ's former press secretary Bill Moyers. A small number of the demonstrators were active partisans of the enemy, calling for American defeat, waving Viet Cong flags, burning American flags, and demanding that their country be punished and humiliated for its arrogance and wickedness. Naturally, the media could not resist these people, and they got more play than their numbers would justify. This was fortuitous for the president. Americans never warmed to the spectacle of watching their flag burned, especially by fellow Americans.

It was clear that the national media had almost unanimously abandoned the war effort; all networks gave extensive and favorable coverage to the demonstrators, and set out to confect an impenetrable cocoon of unilateral withdrawal in which to enfold the president. It became a stampede to force the president's hand. Almost his only supporters were former opponents. One was the doughty Hubert Humphrey, who favored an accelerated withdrawal but left a White House briefing saying, "We only have one president at a time," and, "He's on the right track." Nixon told Haldeman to generate at least a hundred telegrams sent to Humphrey commending what Nixon, not very disinterestedly, but fairly, called "his courageous stand."

Dean Acheson and Nixon had now come full circle, and Acheson supported Nixon publicly and told the *New York Times*, "I think we are going to have a major constitutional crisis if we make a habit of destroying presidents."[68] Republican Senators Mathias and Percy differed with the president, and the Republican Party was waffling and shaking underneath him. Otherwise loyal congressional leaders assumed the press clamor for withdrawal would be heeded, and Hugh Scott, the Republican leader in the Senate, proposed a unilateral cease-fire, an utterly inane suggestion from a normally sensible person.

As on other occasions in his career, the most difficult times in the Hiss affair, the fund crisis, Ike's half-hearted attempts to dump him as vice president in 1956, the worst of the 1960 and 1962 campaigns, Nixon began to feel isolated and deserted, but had the seasoned, not uncomfortable feeling that he alone could resurrect his position, and that he was not a bad person to rely on. He began preparing his November 3 speech, and it soon became clear to Safire and Buchanan and Price that he would do it entirely himself, that this was one of the most important addresses of his life.[69]

Nixon set up the Middle America Committee within the White House, whose existence would be known only to its members. He planned a massive pitch to the great, solid, middle of America to reduce the influence on them of the national networks and newspapers, and strike a blow to what he considered the contemptible administrators, seditious faculty members, and overindulged, opinionated students in most of the country's universities. He was moving late, but it was a bold improvisation.

On the committee was a skilled political organizer who had just come on board, Franklyn (Lyn) Nofziger. He was a former press secretary to Governor Ronald Reagan. He and Jeb Stuart Magruder, a small cosmetics company executive also from California, and Charles Colson, a tough-talking Washington lawyer whose methods more than matched his words, were brought in to make a more determined and hardball public relations effort. Nixon's disgust with the White House press as anti-American accomplices of the nation's enemies, lazy, carping critics of their own country and most of its people, and irreducible adversaries of his had completely undermined any effort to get on with the press or win them over.

Now, Nixon would run on the backs of the press and exploit the public's distrust of this, as he saw it, narcissistic, irresponsible elite. Nixon's dislike of the press is understandable. Most of them did not give him a fair chance. But a free press, as Nixon knew, is vital to any democratic society and he had some duty to make a greater effort to have at least a civilized relationship with it. The press had been lied to pretty relentlessly by Johnson and McNamara, though probably unintentionally about Vietnam, and it would have been very difficult to bring them around to his Vietnam policy now.

The opening cannonade on this front had been fired by Agnew, on Nixon's instructions, when Nixon unleashed him on the press in a speech in New Orleans on October 19. Agnew denounced a state of "national masochism [and] an effete corps of impudent snobs who characterize themselves as intellectuals" in academia and the media. He attacked "hard-core dissidents and . . . professional anarchists in the so-called 'peace movement' [who refused to disassociate themselves from Hanoi]. . . . Education is being redefined to suit the ideas of the uneducated." The "generation gap" was an excuse for the obliteration of the lessons of history, and so forth. It was a lively speech, and he scored some clear points on press and academic biases, and liberal attitudes generally. But it was not going to be any balm of Gilead to the national political fissures, and was not intended to be.

It certainly played in New Orleans, but was a mere warm-up to the next night, in Jackson, Mississippi. The New Orleans speech had been largely written by Agnew himself, but for Jackson, Nixon assigned Safire and Buchanan, who became almost irresponsibly playful: "For too long the South has been the punching bag for the . . . liberal intellectuals . . . a glib, activist [group of the] nattering nabobs of negativism . . . snobs who disdain to mingle with those who work for a living." The United States must not "divide over their demagoguery, be deceived by their duplicity, or let their license destroy liberty." It was verging on doggerel, and Buchanan, Safire, and Agnew were being mischievous, but the Mississippians rose in thunderous applause at almost every line, and the national media began to have a slight suspicion of what their president might have in mind. The well-upholstered Walter Cronkite and the elegant but over-sufficient Eric Sevareid of CBS, and their peers in other networks, continued to give

Nixon avuncular advice in the run-up to his much-anticipated speech.

Kissinger was shaken by the Vietnam Moratorium, and had no idea of Nixon's plans for mobilizing Middle America in support of his war policy. Kissinger now changed course and abandoned his long-standing support for the escalation plan Duck Hook, it was called, which consisted of cleaning out the Cambodian sanctuaries with main force ground action, mining Haiphong harbor, intense bombing of all routes of supplies and personnel from North to South, and direct attacks against the Ho Chi Minh Trail.

In a memo of October 17, Kissinger concluded that "no quick and decisive military action seemed attainable, and that there was not enough unanimity in our administration to pursue so daring and risky a course."[70] This too was mere humbug. Of course there was no quick military fix, apart from a nuclear one, which was out of the question. If there were a quick fix, Johnson would have applied it and been reelected, and Kissinger would still be co-editor of *Confluence* magazine at Harvard, and not in the White House. The only way Duck Hook or any other military escalation was going to work was to crush the windpipe of the war in the South by breaking the connection from the North and asphyxiating the Viet Cong. Such a virulent enemy would not die quickly or without terrible death throes. The only available quick and decisive end would be for America to give up.

This was a fateful turn, as Kissinger, by the lucidity of his arguments, and his ability to play on Nixon's macho susceptibilities, might have provided the margin of victory for the heart and mind of the commander in chief. Nixon paid a price for not letting any of his aides see the entire range of relevant factors that had to be considered before a course of action was implemented. Some other presidents, including Franklin D. Roosevelt, had a similar method of operation, but it worked better for Roosevelt, who had a keener intuition than Nixon and unshakable self-confidence, was much more in touch with a wide range of people and officials (he spent most of each day talking to an astonishing variety of people, as did his wife), and completely seduced the working press. He also had complete control of both houses of the Congress.

Nixon was preparing to pitch his message to the country, which knew nothing of his ultimatum or letter to Ho Chi Minh, as well as to Hanoi, which had called his bluff. He had a plan to rally support for his Vietnam policy, but was still determining what that policy would be. He explained in his memoirs that there were three principal reasons that contributed to his decision not to escalate the war after all: sharply lower recent American casualty figures, the death of Ho, which might yet enhance the possibilities of a settlement, and the advice of Sir Robert Thompson, whom he had first met in Malaya in 1953, when he was fighting a guerrilla war against communist insurgents.

Thompson visited the president on October 17 and recommended against escalation because it would risk a "worldwide furor"[71] without determining the central issue, which was whether the South Vietnamese were capable of being made able to defend themselves. Thompson was optimistic on this point and said that he thought victory could be had within about two years, if it was made clear that America would not pull out and the South Vietnamese were given the proper encouragement. Thompson agreed to go to Vietnam and make a report for Nixon, and when asked if he believed in the importance of what the United States was trying to do there, replied that "the future of Western civilization is at stake in the way you handle yourselves in Vietnam."

Not much of this resonates very believably. If Nixon was not going to scuttle the Vietnam effort altogether, the protesters would not be appeased by any policy of continued fighting. If he was mustering the great moderate center of America, he would do it better with a policy that clearly included a credible strategy to achieve the objective of a durable non-communist South Vietnam. If he was going to be afraid of a "worldwide furor," he might as well get out now rather than play for a decent interval and try to retain support for a gradual, as opposed to an instant, bug-out. And if any significant part of Western civilization depended on the American effort in Vietnam, then it had to be fought forcefully to a win, and not by half measures in the context of an inexorable retreat. Whatever chance the South Vietnamese had of conducting their own defense would be raised by an effective American attack such as Duck Hook on the North's war-making ability. In sum, Nixon's and Kissinger's excuses for ditching Duck Hook were feeble and faint-hearted sophistry.

Nineteen years later, speaking on *Meet the Press*, Nixon said that not going for Duck Hook in November 1969 was the greatest mistake of his presidency. It was certainly one of them. As early as January 1973, Kissinger said the same to William Safire: "We should have bombed the hell out of them the minute we took office."[72] What he did do was to prepare a very intelligent appeal for political support, and a plausible exit strategy. The missing ingredient was the fulfillment of his November 1 ultimatum. The North Vietnamese leaders did not care about what they considered the great, flabby core of Middle America. They had been promised actions of "great force and consequence" by Kissinger to Xuan Thuy, speaking for the president, and by the president himself to Ho Chi Minh in his letter, and through the Russians and Ceauşescu and Yahya Khan. No such actions followed swiftly after the expiry of the deadline.

Nixon's explanations for this change of course are not believable either, and could not have been believed by him. "In view of these factors, and recognizing that the Moratorium had undercut the credibility of the ultimatum, I began to think more in terms of stepping up Vietnamization while continuing the fighting at its present level rather than of trying to increase it. In many respects, Vietnamization would be far more damaging to the communists than an escalation, that, as Thompson pointed out, would not solve the basic problem of South Vietnamese preparedness, and that would stir up serious domestic problems in America."[73]

These factors, in resumé, were low casualties due to temporary, relatively light, enemy activity; the death of Ho Chi Minh, the significance of which, for Nixon's purposes, was nil and continued to be nil, and he had seen enough of Ho's successor to know that; and the opinions of a retired British military officer, who had successfully fought a scarcely analogous war fifteen years before.

The British had never had in Malaya more than 10 percent of the military manpower that the United States had in Vietnam, and the Malayan guerrillas weren't an entire country with an open weapons pipeline from Russia and China. Was Thompson, a competent but slightly pretentious old soldier, now the acting commander in chief of the United States? As for the theory that Vietnamization was more a threat to the enemy than escalation, Hanoi had no regard at all for the Saigon regime or its army, and no fear of it. The only way Vietnamization would work would be by the United States reducing the war-making powers of the North and helping to raise those of the South so that there was some balance between them. And that could not be done just by handing over the work of the U.S. military in Vietnam to Thieu's often ill-assured legions.

Nixon claimed to have feared that Laird and Rogers would resign. They would not have done so if Nixon had consulted with them, brought them along, and they saw the results of his trumpet-call to the nation. Solitude and cabinet government aren't entirely compatible. (In any case, he would not have had any difficulty replacing them with better people; a star candidate for secretary of state, and Rogers's eventual successor, was festering and erupting several times every day in the White House basement.) The Moratorium hadn't "undercut the credibility of the ultimatum." It was up to the president to show Hanoi that the Moratorium was irrelevant, by telling his countrymen, whose support he was seeking, about his ultimatum to Hanoi and delivering on it.

Nixon effectively followed de Gaulle's advice, and Kissinger's initial, and most recent, impulse, and went for a decent-interval strategy. He blunted the animosity of the peace party by accelerating the American departure and avoiding escalation. He preserved a chance for Saigon, though a very thin one, if it developed miraculously improved military capabilities and national cohesion.

But to Hanoi, Nixon had promised dire consequences for their "insolence," and these turned out to be handing the war over to Saigon, the fulfillment of Hanoi's most heartfelt ambition. In the eyes of Hanoi, Nixon was as much a paper tiger as Johnson, and less estimable, in that he put on the airs of the dauntless warrior while retreating, where Johnson had had the decency to acknowledge implicitly the failure of his policy, and retire. As has been mentioned, another aspect of the Vietnam quagmire was the presence in North Vietnam of three hundred and twenty thousand Chinese soldiers performing tasks that liberated the North Vietnamese Army in equivalent numbers for service in the South. Johnson had ignored them, and Nixon was set on a policy of reconciliation with the People's Republic of China. Either could have required corresponding forces from Chiang Kai-shek to assist in the South, but both were preoccupied by the doubtful Korean precedent; Johnson gave up, and Nixon began playing for bigger stakes with China.

Soviet ambassador Dobrynin came to see Kissinger and Nixon on October 20, 1969. Dobrynin had an aide-mémoire that he was instructed by his government, presumably the timeless foreign minister Gromyko, who had been at Teheran, Yalta, Potsdam, Geneva, Paris, Vienna, and Glassboro (Kosygin and LBJ in 1967), to give Nixon, which essentially said that for the United States to solve the Vietnam imbroglio by force would be "extremely dangerous," and that any attempt by the United States "to profit from Soviet-Chinese relations at the Soviet Union's expense, and there are some signs of that, [would be] a very grave miscalculation."

Nixon took a yellow legal pad out of his desk drawer, passed it to Dobrynin, and told him to take notes. Nixon reviewed the major policy areas – the Middle East, Berlin, trade – and blamed Soviet "intransigence" and games-playing for the absence of progress. He said that whatever he was doing with China was absolutely not directed against the U.S.S.R. and that if two other sovereign countries developed relations, it was no legitimate concern of the Soviet Union's. "The only beneficiary of U.S.-Soviet disagreement over Vietnam is China. . . . This is the last opportunity to settle these disputes."

He suggested that Johnson had only engaged in the bombing halt because his advisers, Charles Bohlen, Llewellyn Thompson, Averell Harriman, all former ambassadors to Moscow, said the Kremlin could do nothing while the United States was bombing a "fellow socialist country. . . . The bombing halt was then agreed to, but the Soviet Union has done nothing to help. . . . You may think that you can break me. You may think that the American domestic situation is unmanageable. . . . If the Soviet Union will not help us get peace, then we will have to pursue our own methods for bringing the war to an end. We cannot allow a talk-fight strategy to continue without taking action . . . the humiliation of a defeat is absolutely unacceptable to my country. I recognize that the Soviet leaders are tough and courageous, but so are we." With that, Nixon shook hands with Dobrynin and escorted him to the door. Kissinger saw him out, and then returned and warmly commended Nixon on his handling of his visitor.[74] The congratulations from Kissinger were deserved, and the more significant for coming from such an authority on diplomatic history (though an inveterate flatterer of superiors), but Nixon had just reinforced an ultimatum he had decided not to complete. His standing with everyone, except those at the poles of domestic political opinion, would have risen if he had ordered Duck Hook, or announced that the Democrats had overcommitted the country and he was withdrawing, making whatever he judged appropriate out of Vietnamization.

Nixon received a great deal of advice, almost all of it of the wholehearted or thinly disguised withdrawal variety. Senate leader Mansfield wrote to urge a unilateral cease-fire and withdrawal, unnegotiated – that is, an outright bunk on the whole effort (which he had long supported) – because "continuance of the war in Vietnam . . . of dubious origin and purposes . . . endangers the future of this nation." He promised support for a complete break with the "diplomatic and military positions which, unfortunately, were assumed over the last few years." Nixon recognized that Mansfield was offering him the final opportunity to lay it all on Kennedy and Johnson and walk, blaming it on them, and the Senate leader would not bother him for it. Nixon wrote that "it would be wrong to end the Vietnam War on terms I believed to be less than honorable."[75] He was crossing the Rubicon, but not wholeheartedly. He had either to produce a winning strategy or take Mansfield's offer to throw in the towel and blame it on Kennedy and Johnson. If he was going to try to win, he had to act on the November 1 ultimatum. He had to answer Mansfield and Pham Van Dong in the same speech. He half-succeeded.

Finally, at 9:30 P.M., Eastern Standard Time, November 3, 1969, came the man and the moment. Nixon had built the suspense and distributed no advance texts to anyone, nor any hint to anyone, of what he was going to say. He memorized his speech and delivered it live and unaided (no notes, no teleprompter), without pause or slip, to the camera, and to a live viewing and listening audience of many scores of millions of people throughout the world.

"I have chosen a plan for peace and I take responsibility for it." If it succeeded, "what the critics say now won't matter. If it does not succeed, anything I say then won't matter." (This was a paraphrase of Lincoln, a bust of whom was behind him.) He outlined his efforts to achieve peace, his engagement of the Russians, his letter to Ho Chi Minh and Ho's "quite frivolous" reply. The "other side" had not shown "the least willingness to join us in seeking a just peace," and would not "while it is convinced that all it has to do is wait for our next concession, and the next concession after that one, until it gets everything it wants."

He referred to the sharp decline in casualties, the decline in infiltration, the Nixon Doctrine, and the progress of Vietnamization, his plan for handing the ground war to the South Vietnamese and gradually withdrawing U.S. forces while retaining air support in Indochina. He spoke directly to the young people: "I respect your idealism." (He did not in fact; he thought they were cowards and shirkers and incipient draft-evaders masquerading as having moral qualms about the war.) "I want peace as much as you do." (This was undoubtedly true.) He explained that he had signed eighty-three letters that week to parents of servicemen killed in

Vietnam and fervently desired not to have to sign any more such letters.

Then he addressed "the great silent majority of my fellow Americans – I ask for your support. . . . The more divided we are at home, the less likely the enemy is to negotiate at Paris. Let us be united for peace. Let us also be united against defeat. Because let us understand: North Vietnam cannot defeat or humiliate the United States. Only Americans can do that."

As the cameras and special lights were being removed from his office, Nixon told Haldeman to organize the customary deluge of letters complaining about network commentary and "dirty, vicious ones to the *Times* and *Washington Post* about their editorials."[76] The media coverage was very biased. Averell Harriman, who helped deliver Laos to the communists and who had wasted nine months in Paris arguing about the shape of the conference table, complained about Nixon's tone.

But Nixon need not have had any doubts about public response, and for once, there is no indication that he much doubted what it would be. Over eighty thousand letters and telegrams flooded into the White House, almost all of them supportive. Among many thousands of positive telephone messages was one from Dean Acheson. Three hundred congressmen and fifty-eight senators co-authored resolutions of support. The silent majority rallied to the leader of the nation as he had asked. An instant telephone poll showed 77 percent support for the president, and a more profound Gallup poll showed that his approval rating jumped from 52 to 68 percent.

Most Americans would rather hand over the war to the South than hand the South over to the North, if the president promised that Saigon had a chance of survival. Nixon had got at least a decent interval, and he always believed that it might have been more, if circumstances in the next presidential term had been different. He would have the support he needed, at least for a time, and could continue withdrawals. (A few weeks later, he ordered a further withdrawal of sixty thousand men.) He would not have had any less support, or not appreciably less, if he had announced Duck Hook and redeemed his threat to the North Vietnamese, and they would have negotiated seriously nearly three years before they actually did. There was still time. The president could have announced Duck Hook a week after the avalanche of support he received and combined it with his sixty-thousand-man troop withdrawal announcement. For an escalate, withdraw, and win option, this was the last train leaving the station. The president missed it.

Richard Nixon had demonstrated a remarkable ability to rally the people, and had laid a rod on the backs of his media critics. The chairman of the Federal Communications Commission, Dean Burch, required the transcripts of post-speech network comment, and Nixon, after prompting from Pat Buchanan, sent Agnew out for a frontal assault on the media. He spoke at Des Moines, Iowa, on November 13, delivering an address written by Buchanan and edited personally by Nixon. The text was delivered two days before and the White House requested and received live television coverage from all three networks.

"A small group of men," the vice president said, "settle upon the film and commentary that is to reach the public. They decide what forty or fifty million Americans will learn of the day's events in the nation and the world." It was a powerful address and brought Agnew instant national celebrity. Agnew followed up on November 30 with a more good-natured blast in Mobile, Alabama, against the *New York Times* and the *Washington Post*.

Conservative and even reactionary people, such as the House Armed Services Committee chairman, L. Mendel Rivers of South Carolina, started adapting the gestures of the left, dispensing V-for-victory digital signals almost compulsively, an amusing affectation for an elderly, reactionary, frequently drunken, long-haired segregationist. Nixon gave a voice to millions who had not thought that they had any (including L. Mendel Rivers outside his committee and congressional district). The Moratorium gave way to the New Mobilization Committee, and control passed from the McCarthy campaign veterans to Students for a Democratic Society, the Socialist Worker Party, and the Weathermen.

These were radical and revolutionary groups and they reinforced Nixon's authority as spokesman for the country. They had blood-curdling slogans, and the media did not cover up their extreme and anti-American tone. They strenuously sought communist victory in Vietnam, the crushing defeat of the United States, and in many cases overtly advocated the violent overthrow of the U.S. government and its replacement by a Marxist dictatorship.

This was, to say the least, a bridge too far for the very comfortable Walter Cronkite, Eric Sevareid, Dan Rather, and their analogues on other networks. There was no media fawning over the Mobe, as it was called, such as Walter Cronkite and others had accorded the Moratorium, and there were no senatorial endorsements of them. It was like the earlier days of his political career for Nixon, as he squeezed the Democrats between his majority and the forces of anarchy.

Not everything went as he had wished, as the Haynsworth nomination was defeated 55 to 45 in the Senate on November 21. This had its consolations, as he could now exploit Democratic prejudices against the South and name an equally congenial nominee. Seventeen Republicans voted against. This assisted Nixon in deciding to run a fundraising campaign for the 1970 midterm elections parallel to the Republican National Committee, which would be available to loyalist Republican candidates but not dissident ones.

His combative and polarizing instincts were formidable, but he was getting into dangerous waters, where he could find himself with insufficient support from his own party and the Congress to conduct the government effectively. Nixon kept raising the ante, and had no apparent sense of durable reconciliation. It was the equivalent of a national policy of constant combat, which eventually must lead to defeat.

Starting on November 17, there trickled out the disturbing story of what became known as the My Lai Massacre. A hamlet had been declared a free-fire zone because of its infestation by suicide snipers and woman and child grenade carriers, and ultimately 567 apparent civilians were killed and Lieutenant William Calley was court-martialed, with the approval of Secretary Laird and the president himself. The story was broken by Seymour Hersh, McCarthy's campaign press secretary the year before, and it shook the country. The Viet Cong frequently used women and children for lethal purposes, but combat officers were warned against the temptation to designate all civilians as enemies in any affected area.

Nixon gave a universally admired performance at his last press conference of the year, on December 8. He handled the My Lai affair very effectively, saying that almost all of the 1,200,000 Americans who had served in Vietnam had done so with distinction, and had helped the Vietnamese people "in one way or another. . . . This record of generosity, of decency, must not be allowed to be smeared and slurred because of this kind of incident." He promised punishment for anyone convicted of responsibility in the My Lai killings.

Nixon had withdrawn another 50,000 men from Vietnam by year's end, bringing U.S. force levels down 115,000 to 435,000, easily beating Clark Clifford's target of 100,000 fewer by the end of 1970, the level of mid-1967. He had driven the anti-war movement to the political fringe, and no one could say that he was not pursuing a coherent policy in Vietnam, solidly supported in the country.

The first family went to California for the holidays. Nixon had been innovative and effective in many areas and was the undisputed master political tactician of recent American history. His popularity surged after his December 8 press conference to an astounding 81 percent. This was a levitation, certainly, but was more genuine than *Newsweek*'s jubilant banner in October of "Nixon in Trouble."

The silent majority had spoken, and the nation was much quieter than when Richard Nixon was preparing to be inducted into the presidency he had won by a wafer-thin margin a year before. A terrible decade for America, which had started with the sun setting on the tranquil complacency of the Eisenhower era, ended in slowly reviving serenity. The United States had its president to thank for that.

Chapter Eleven

Calming the Nation

1970–1971

— I —

NIXON HAD STABILIZED domestic opinion and outmaneuvered his more radical political opponents and the partisanly hostile sections of the media. But North Vietnam had no incentive to negotiate, and unless Vietnamization were a euphemism for doing a complete bunk, the war was going to go on for at least the two years Robert Thompson had predicted, and probably longer. There would be many challenges to Nixon's place in U.S. public opinion in that time. For the moment, he had the upper hand and the initiative, and was delighted by a Republican National Committee poll in January 1970 that revealed that 73 percent of Americans thought they were part of the silent majority.

On New Year's Day 1970, Nixon telephoned an eclectic group to wish them a happy New Year and decade: Guy Lombardo (orchestra leader), Billy Graham, J. Edgar Hoover, Bob Hope, Bing Crosby, Jackie Gleason, John Wayne, and Paul Keyes.[1]

The president was already hard at work on an electoral strategy that would keep his enemies crowded on to the fringes where his silent majority speech had left them. What he devised was a plan that ultimately produced a mighty triumph. Nixon's first priority was to spread his centrist majority as far as he could in all directions and anchor it as firmly as he could. He wished to dissuade or deter George Wallace from running for reelection or, better still, induce him to run as a Democrat. With Johnson and Humphrey retired, Robert Kennedy dead, and Edward Kennedy disqualified by the Chappaquiddick drowning, the remaining Democratic presidential hopefuls were a very unprepossessing group. Nixon doubted, as he correctly said of George Romney (who was now boring him to tears at cabinet meetings with his loquacity and interruptions), that they could hit "major league pitching." (Nixon had found cabinet meetings under Ike "ineffably boring," and held them as rarely as he could.)[2]

The first point of attack was on desegregation. Nixon knew that he had no chance of challenging the Democrats effectively for the African-American vote, but he wanted to get an increasing share of the rising black middle class and to build up from the 12 percent of the African-American vote he had received in 1968. The Supreme Court had repealed the requirement of the 1954 *Brown v. Board of Education* case for "all deliberate speed" in desegregation, and now demanded immediate implementation (*Greene et al v. County School Board of New Kent County*, 1968). Segregation was rightly seen by the higher courts as institutionalized racism, but, as often happens, the bench had no idea of the legislative or administrative remedy and gave ambiguous signals about ill-considered schemes for using school buses to ship millions of schoolchildren all around metropolitan areas far from their neighborhoods in search of the judicial will-o'-the-wisp of "racial balance."

A less talented political operator than Nixon would have seen this as a hopeless minefield and simply tried to steer around it. Nixon made up in astute and bold political calculation for what he lacked in charisma. (And he wasn't altogether deficient in that area either, when there was a serious issue and he went through his de Gaulle technique of complete isolation, mystery, and suspense-building, as on November 3.)

On desegregation and school-busing, Nixon determined to implement exactly what the court ordered: full and prompt desegregation, which he defined as opening all state schools to all eligible children, regardless of race, color, or religion, but not the impressment and forcible motorized transportation of children against their parents' wishes all over the country to satisfy the capricious meddling of judges. Nor would he tolerate the continued defamation of the South as the sole offender. There was a great deal of Northern hypocrisy in all this, and Nixon required that all sections of the country meet the same standards.

He wrote to Ehrlichman on January 14: "I just disagree completely with the court's naive stupidity. I think we have a duty to explore ways to mitigate it. . . . I don't give a damn about the Southern Strategy. I care a great deal about education, and I know this won't work."[3] A few days later he told his speechwriters that he would have "to carry out this law [desegregation] . . . I can't throw down the gauntlet to the court."[4]

Desegregation would happen, not because Nixon was under any illusions about harvest ng black votes, but because he had never lost his strong views about civil rights; because he was the law-and-order candidate and would do as the courts ordered; because the silent majority was mainly reasonable people who did not want to see Norman Rockwell black children escorted into school by paratroopers with fixed bayonets, as they had been in Little Rock in 1957, and did not want to see peaceful black and white demonstrators attacked by fat policemen with clubs and flesh-rending attack dogs. These were shaming events. Nixon had warned since his first visits abroad as Eisenhower's emissary that this racism was the greatest moral and credibility weakness the United States had in the world.

Nixon the Quaker detested racism, though he was unconvinced that all races were in fact of equal intelligence. He thought the East Asians might be the most intelligent, followed by the Caucasians, the Indo-Asians, and the Africans; but they all had equal rights. He thought assimilation and intermarriage and attitudinal change in the United States might take another hundred years, but that it had to start with desegregation.

While he would enforce desegregation, he forbade Robert Finch and George Romney, the two cabinet secretaries most directly involved, to boast about it. To the African-Americans and the moderate whites, it would be the administration that ended segregation. To the lower-income Southern whites, it would be the administration that ended the baiting of the South and upheld the law, not just the laws against segregation, but those against violent disorder, rising crime rates, and mob rule. To the silent majority of all regions and complexions, it was the rule of law evenly applied, liberalizing in some instances, a matter of enforcement in others.

Nixon also linked desegregation to improving the quality of education. He promised increased federal money for school districts that met court-ordered requirements, and made it clear that the money could not be available realistically to school districts that were still in defiance of desegregation orders sixteen years after an unambiguous Supreme Court decision. He had to compromise with Senator John Stennis of Mississippi, Senate Armed Services Committee chairman, who had tied his support of

ABM to a go-slow on desegregation in Mississippi, but Nixon was over that hurdle and made it clear that it was a one-time-only arrangement.

The Republicans would not compete with heart-on-sleeve, flannel-mouthed leftists like McGovern, but they would not be confused with shabby rednecks like Wallace either. It would occupy the territory between Pat Moynihan and Spiro Agnew, but that was at least 60 percent of the country. Nixon smelled a big win, if he could keep the balls in the air in Vietnam.

In rounding upward the dimensions of his Middle American majority, Nixon ordered careful polling on the Agnew phenomenon. The vice president had spiked up markedly in the polls since Nixon had unleashed him and set Buchanan and Safire to making the oratorical ammunition for him.

He also reached out in very original ways; his (seventeen years) younger brother, Edward, told him at New Year's that car racing was the most popular sport in the United States, most of it jalopies with massively upgraded engines raced by owner-mechanics, and that the two greatest racing-car drivers in the country, Mario Andretti and Andy Granatelli, were outspoken Nixon supporters. This was a sport particularly popular in the South. Nixon directed that receptions be held for winning drivers in the White House and that the administration treat this sport with as much respect as it did baseball and football. The president even started to brush up on it a bit himself, although he wasn't especially interested in cars, and driving them around in circles was not quite the stuff of the lives and legends of Knute Rockne, Chief Newman, Babe Ruth, Lou Gehrig, Joe DiMaggio, and Ted Williams.

The desegregation strategy worked out by the President's Cabinet Committee on Education was based on bringing local black and white community leaders together, district by district, under the aegis of the White House and the president himself, and helping them work out between them how desegregation would come to the South. Agnew was nominally the chairman of the committee but was frightened by the possibilities of destroying his new standing with millions of people who were not desegregationists at heart and left it to George Shultz, the academic but practical labor secretary. As progress was made there, the federal government would use its funding and legal enforcement powers to require equivalent progress, where necessary, in Northern and Western school districts. There was much to be achieved in the North, but also a much-reduced dependence on segregation as a buttress to the socioeconomic system and cultural tradition, steeped in the lore of Southern literature, and a much smaller potential for violence.

The first meeting in this new plan was on June 24, 1970, in the Jefferson Room of the State Department, and was hosted by George Shultz and John Mitchell. Shultz was the chief broker between Warren Hood, the chairman of the Mississippi Manufacturers Association, and Gilbert Mason, a medical doctor who was head of the Biloxi NAACP. Shultz finally vacated the table where he was the host, because his extensive experience as an arbitrator taught him that that was the way to close the deal after it got close: leave it to the parties. They closed and agreed on a way to end the opprobrium on their state, comply with the law, and receive the monies the president, who had received them all at the White House before lunch (including a black pharmacist who had just been released from jail the day before on a spurious civil disturbance charge), wished to distribute in Mississippi. The blacks were apt to be apostrophized as Uncle Toms, and the whites as nigger-lovers, but under the convening authority of the president, and jointly armed with the money earmarked as federal aid to education in Mississippi, and not overly publicized, on the one side or the other; and with the national media only too happy not to amplify a success of the Nixon administration that flew in the face of their notions of the Southern strategy, it was a model for other Southern states, once Gilbert and Hood agreed to promote it in Mississippi.

The Mississippi initiative worked, and desegregation was achieved adequately for the school year beginning in the fall of 1970. Similar biracial committees were set up in all the Old Confederacy states, with the stick of court orders, the carrot of federal money for "quality education," and the facilitator of direct presidential and cabinet involvement. All those attending such sessions had to know that if they did not agree, the imposition of desegregation would be on ham-handed court orders executed by federal marshals with all the subtlety and sensitivity the South had been accustomed to from the North since General Sherman's march through Georgia. This had been celebrated in song, film, mythology, and the long, consequent, corrupt regime of the carpetbaggers.

This program of White House–sponsored, non-mandated, and therefore voluntary, biracial arrangement of desegregation with accompanying federal financial incentives to education was one of the very greatest triumphs of the Nixon administration. In February 1971, the figures supplied by the new secretary of Health, Education, and Welfare (replacing the recently retired Robert Finch), Elliot L. Richardson, were that there were 8.6 million white and 3.2 black million public elementary and secondary school students in the South, for a total of 11.8 million. The percentage of blacks in schools 50 percent or more white had increased from the autumn of 1968 to the autumn of 1970 from 18.4 percent to 38.1 percent. The percentage of blacks in what were effectively all-black schools declined in the same period from 68 percent to 18.4 percent, and the percentage of blacks in schools that were 80 percent or more black declined from 78.8 percent to 41.7 percent, all in the same two-year period.

Nixon, with no fanfare, had done more to break down official racism than any president in history, after Lincoln's abolition of slavery and Lyndon Johnson's enfranchisement of the African-American. It was a great and noble accomplishment, and like a number of Nixon's acts of selfless idealism, such as his refusal to contest seriously the 1960 presidential election, it went largely unrecognized, until historians started to unearth the facts.[5] The conventional wisdom in the United States has not been conditioned to view Nixon as a great friend of the African-American, trailing, in practical terms only Lincoln and Johnson, but he was.

This was a key part of Nixon's silent majority plan: there was to be no braggadocio about what had been achieved in this area, but he could not be accused by liberals of not complying with the law, nor accused of over-complying by varying shades of anti-integrationists.

The issue, from one of raging controversy in almost every city in the country, with utterly disreputable people running for mayor on anti-busing campaigns in dozens of major cities, died almost silently. Legislative and judicial meddlers were left with no more damage to do, proving the value of an enlightened and efficient executive. The Supreme Court did unanimously approve school busing for racial balance on April 19, 1971, aiming at the next scholastic year, beginning in September, but by that time administration-sponsored desegregation and acceptable deferrals had blunted the impact of the Court. To integrationists, the administration was carrying out the law. To non-integrationists, it was doing what the law required as painlessly as possible.

In his singular, unsung way, Richard Nixon defanged and healed one of the potentially greatest controversies of the time. For a country that seemed to have a collective compulsion to ugly disputation, it was a great service of self-rescue to deliver it from yet another potential source of mass discord and probable violence.

To replace the rejected Clement Haynsworth, Nixon nominated to the Supreme Court Harrold Carswell, a rather nondescript Florida judge. This nomination came off the rails quickly too, as Carswell was regarded by his peers, by the American Bar Association, and by the senators that he was trotted around to meet, as a dunce. Most of his decisions were subsequently overturned, and one of Nixon's loyal supporters of him, Senator Roman Hruska of Nebraska, was reduced to saying that not everyone was a genius and that the people of relatively limited intelligence were entitled to representation also.

Carswell had made some rather racist remarks in judgments he had rendered early in his career. But his great problems were that his legal reasoning was often found wanting on appeal. After Bryce Harlow took him around to meet senators, he told Nixon they thought Carswell "a boob, a dummy. And what counter is there to that? He is."[6] On April 8 he was rejected 51-45, despite some personal lobbying by the president. One of the senators he courted, Marlow Cook of Kentucky, was invited to a reception at the White House for Congressional Medal of Honor winners, and concluded, as he was driving back to his office, that Supreme Court nominees had to be exceptional people too, as had been the honorees at the ceremony he had just attended.[7]

Nixon got what he needed, however, out of the Haynsworth and Carswell nominations; he tried to put on a Southerner, and issued a statement that the rejection of both men was a slap in the face to the South by the Democrats, the party that for so long had taken the South for granted. Nixon did not start the politicization of the Supreme Court. This was an initiative of the Democrats and it would continue for decades. After a rocky start, Nixon would hold his own in this rugged arena, but it was a discreditable episode in the long era where the White House and the Congress were in the hands of different parties and each branch of government and party was struggling with the other for apparent control of the judiciary. It was the preliminary round in what would soon become, and long remain, an even more dangerous and destructive game: the criminalization of policy differences.

Nixon also set out to purge the civil rights zealots in Finch's Department of Health, Education, and Welfare, who put desegregation, and more exactly, racial balance – through school busing to distant school districts, in disregard of parents' wishes – ahead of Nixon's desire to desegregate the schools but focus on better education. They also had the tendency to hold forth rather garrulously to the press about their determination to reconstruct education patterns throughout the country, especially in the South. This flew in the face of Nixon's plan to do what the law required, no more nor less, discreetly, evenly across the country, and to fight the long-range use of school buses to seek racial balance.

This also produced a double watershed, as the first target was Leon Panetta, head of the civil rights section in Finch's department, and an able young man. Panetta was dismissed by Ziegler to the press before Finch could tell him, so annoyed was Nixon. This was an inelegant way to treat a talented official who went on to be assistant to New York's Mayor Lindsay, Democratic congressman from California, and President Clinton's well-respected White House chief of staff. A petition of two thousand Health, Education, and Welfare employees who claimed to be "gravely concerned" about civil rights, was publicly sent to Finch. The departure of Panetta was one watershed.

It was also the beginning of the end of the Nixon-Finch official relationship. This was another watershed. Finch was an able man, who had imaginative policy ideas, but he was not cut from the same political cloth as Nixon, and quietly retired from government later in 1970 and pursued an essentially academic life after that (the University of Southern California). He was a star of the Nixon administration, which didn't have many in the cabinet, and was one of the most impressive and constructive of the people that Nixon paid any personal attention to; he would be missed.

The blunderbuss treatment of Panetta led to a wave of resignations and some more firings, as virtually the entire civil rights unit was gutted. Nixon had a policy and a right to enforce it, and taken all in all, it was probably a much more effective and fairer policy than the idealistic young men in the Panetta school of civil rights were advocating, but as so often with Nixon, he delayed the enforcement of his objectives until he became convinced that it was a matter of asserting presidential authority and squashing a virtual attempted coup d'état. Then, grim and without any sensibility at all, the hob-nailed jackboot of impersonal authority was brought down on people who could have been reoriented and continued to be an adornment to an administration that was not awash in original, bright young people.

The clearing out of Finch's civil rights unit led to publicity that did not much hurt Nixon in places disposed to favor him, and surely helped him in parts of the South where he wished to assure that Wallace did not rise again, so the damage was not deep or lasting, but it contributed to the ambiance of a short-haired, bull-necked, buttondown administration that was too friendly to the Southern rednecks. The Pat Moynihan school of original thinking, of which Nixon was himself the principal, received unnecessarily short shrift.

The national media were only too happy to publicize a comment of black Georgia legislator Julian Bond, traveling in Europe, who told Dutch television: "If you could call Adolf Hitler a friend of the Jews, you could call President Nixon a friend of the blacks." This was outrageous, indeed a disgraceful thing to say about a president who had always been a civil rights supporter, but it illustrated the overheated spirit of the time and the inadvisability of agitating it with needless frictions. Through much of his career, Nixon was a man for whom everything was difficult, and controversy, rippling over such an awkward personality, was pandemic. There was no Teflon aspect about Nixon, as there was with Roosevelt, Eisenhower, Kennedy, Reagan, and Clinton. He was a magnet to contestation and bulled his way through a great deal, like a ship always doomed to sail in rough weather.

A further issue arose about a memo of Moynihan's that came to light in mid-March and was seized upon as illustrative of the administration's lack of sympathy for the lot of African-Americans. Moynihan had written on January 16 that African-Americans had made tremendous progress in the sixties, that the income gap between the white and black middle classes had been largely eliminated, and that black college enrolment had risen an astonishing, and almost unbelievable, 85 percent from 1964 to 1968. There were some laggard indices in the South, but the economic and educational progress had been remarkable (and was an immense achievement for Lyndon Johnson). Where Moynihan saw difficulties was in the steady rise of illegitimacy in the black community, where the incidence of illegitimate birth had risen 30 percent and was still rising, inadvertently encouraged, as has been mentioned, by some of Johnson's Great Society legislation. Moynihan concluded that there was a welling-up of black hostility, much of it pent up for a long time and, inevitable, that would peak and fall, but could perhaps best be now treated with "benign neglect," which would become one of the famous phrases of the time.

A particular controversy had arisen over the militant group the Black Panthers. The Panthers had no great currency and were in decline as a small league of angry, violence-favoring blacks when the Chicago police raided their local headquarters at 4 A.M. on December 4, 1969. With the attention to the niceties moderate America had come to expect from the Chicago police, shot two members of the group to death, one the local leader, Fred Hampton, in his sleep. They also shot Hampton's wife, who was eight months pregnant and unarmed. The police, as usual, claimed that they were fired on, but subsequent forensic reports indicated that the Panthers had fired one bullet, to approximately one hundred from Chicago's men in blue. The local (Daley-appointed) judges whitewashed the episode and it became a cause célèbre.

Mrs. Leonard Bernstein, wife of the conductor of the New York Philharmonic, held a party to introduce the Panthers to liberal, high-minded, Fifth and Park Avenue society, including Mrs. Brooke Astor. To author Tom Wolfe, who coined the phrase "Radical Chic" in reference to it, and to Nixon himself, this was the supreme illustration of the inanity of the forces in play.

The Panthers were just a rag-tag band of street toughs, claiming some intellectual pedigree in a radical political platform based in part on the career of Malcolm X. (They gained 40 percent of the vote in a mayoral election in Oakland, California.) Having been brutally assaulted by the police of one of the nation's greatest cities, demonstrating the barbarity of some urban police methods, they had been taken up, as Nixon saw it, by the mindless, hemophiliac, bleeding-heart doyennes of New York society, who in their boredom and vacuity could be induced to attempt almost any sociological enterprise, no matter how asinine. Stokely Carmichael, Huey Newton, Bobby Seale, and Eldridge Cleaver, four of the most prominent radicals associated at one time or another with the Black Panthers, were about as unlikely as any homo sapiens on earth to have a useful relationship with Brooke Astor and her circle. (Mrs. Astor was an admirable woman, who never would have come up with such a fatuous concept as this on her own.) Wolfe's thin book about it was a classic of the era.

Moynihan advised Nixon to ignore the Black Panthers, and most of the rest of the African-American community, and when the memo leaked and the predictable storm of protest went up against the reactionary character of the administration, Moynihan offered his resignation, which Nixon, often awkward but rarely cowardly or disloyal to staff, refused in the most unambiguous terms. On such occasions, he employed to perfection the dignity of his great office, declared his complete confidence in Moynihan, whose job included submitting a variety of suggestions, recommended with varying degrees of emphasis, for the president's confidential consideration, and that the White House would have no further comment, other than that it was proud of the progress the administration was helping to generate in many areas of African-American life.[8]

Nixon gave his first State of the Union message to the Congress and a nation-wide audience on January 22. He had worked more than a week on it and again gave no hint to anyone of what he was going to say. Once again he surprised his opponents (as well as his supporters), but this habit of working intensively on a speech for days on end in secret did not make for efficient management of the presidency. Haldeman remarked, as one who knew: "He spends as much time discussing the problem he has of shortage of time as he does doing the things he says he doesn't have time to do."[9] Haldeman was loyal, useful, and in some ways indispensable, but such an insensitive philistine that there were bound to be combustible abrasions with brilliant and egotistical people like Kissinger and Moynihan and Burns. Nixon probably would have been better with a chief of staff who was a little more able to understand the historic precedents for what he was trying to do, and speak at a higher intellectual plain with his policy advisers. The Prussian guardhouse approach of Haldeman would pedestrianize the administration on the inside, and render it unnecessarily vulnerable to critics on the outside, when the shooting season started in earnest. Haldeman was devoted and efficient, but limited, and his diaries have been overly influential on writers of instant histories of the administration.

Nixon was of the old school that believed in comprehensive knowledge of what he was speaking about. He memorized major speeches, and memorized detailed responses to up to two hundred questions before each press conference. He wished to bulldoze the country and the media with the authoritative nature of his White House public appearances, and usually he succeeded.

To an efficient but rather pedestrian person like Haldeman, he could have done just as well spending each day dealing with trivia of administration, reading his speeches as recent presidents had done, and winging it in press conferences. Nixon knew and possibly even exaggerated the hostility of the media, as questioners or commentators after his speeches, and knew the importance, for his own public standing and the morale of his administration, the necessity of turning each nationally televised encounter into a successful storming of the bastions of the enemy.

In his State of the Union message on January 22, 1970, to the amazement of everyone, friend and foe, Nixon seized the initiative on environmental issues from the Democrats and ran away with it into a secret political rain forest where the Democrats couldn't find or attack him. He had noted that Muskie, who now seemed his most likely opponent in 1972, was a promoter of Earth Day, an environmental event coming up in April, and that his own polls showed that since 1965 the percentage of respondents who cited concern about the environment as a serious issue had risen from 25 percent to 75 percent. He spoke with determination of securing guarantees of cleaner air and water. The Democrats had complacently assumed that Nixon would paddle slowly in circles like a sitting duck while they took aim at him. That was not his way of defending his incumbency.

He foresaw the abolition of hunger, a livable income for every family (FAP), "enormous progress" in housing, "faster transportation, improved health care, and superior education." He went on, "I see an America in which we have checked inflation and waged a winning war against crime." He had already said that the "prospects for peace are far better than they were a year ago," and quoted Jefferson, that "We act not for ourselves alone but for the whole human race." Notoriously anti-Nixon CBS commentator (and Cronkite's successor as anchorman) Dan Rather announced, taking no pleasure in it, that "The President has caught the Democrats bathing and has walked away with their clothes." (This too, like Nixon's "peace with honor," was a quote from Disraeli.)[10]

Nixon gave his critics a rare open goal as a target when British prime minister Harold Wilson arrived at the White House in late January. Nixon had become tired of the "slovenly" White House police, and had them kitted out in white double-breasted uniforms, large gold epaulettes and piping and gold braid, and tall black plastic hats with the presidential seal on them. He must have taken momentary leave of his senses to dress the palace guard of so republican a country in such Ruritanian-Hollywood finery.[11] There was a storm of mockery, and after a brief counterinformation effort ordered by Nixon through Haldeman, the uniforms were abandoned, and not spoken of again. The hats eventually surfaced at a rock concert.[12] It is a trivial matter, but this was Nixon's idea, and one is entitled to wonder what possessed him to order anything so un-American.

He was also always ordering boycotts of writers and television anchors. There was no point to his directed hostility to CBS's Walter Cronkite, NBC's David Brinkley, and *Time*'s Hugh Sidey. They had been in Washington a long time and would still be there long after Nixon left. He was, in Franklin D. Roosevelt's phrase (which he was happy to apply to himself), "the head of the American people." Apart from the indignity of his having dabbled personally in such spiteful activity, it sent a message of how personally vulnerable the president felt, how easily his own attention could be distracted, and how unpresidential, in some ways, his nature was.

Brinkley was an intelligent and discerning man, and no particular opponent of Nixon's (though he was quite friendly with Kissinger), and Sidey was at least an amateur historian of the presidency and well above the normal level of intellect for a White House journalist. Walter Cronkite was as great an icon as Brinkley, though not as intelligent a man – indeed, a rather platitudinous old journalistic warhorse, full of arcane references to his days as a war correspondent, but an amiable and not at all nasty man. He achieved a high national status because of his comforting mustache and country-doctor bedside manner.

Nixon should not have paid a moment's attention to any of them, other than normal courtesies when they met. In terms of antagonism, there were much worse around Washington, but Nixon seemed never to take fully on board the fact that while in office, a president has no peers and has some customary duty to rise above normal media comment. Nixon's lack of self-confidence helped propel him to gain the nation's highest office, but the possession of the office did not seem to do much to alleviate the problem without which he might not have been so demonically motivated to seek the presidency in the first place. There have been many amateur psychoanalyses of Nixon, none of any apparent validity or value, but it remains a mystery why his astounding success, in such a difficult time and against such odds and such an imposing group of rivals, did not confer on him a more relaxed sense of himself. It would come, but only after further horrible and unprecedented wrenchings of his career and in the mellow serenity of the fullness of years.

On February 18, 1970, Nixon released a forty-thousand-word summary of his foreign policy, which he intended as an antidote to what he feared was a trend to rising isolationism. He and Kissinger wrote it, but without a word of input from the State Department. It was well and logically developed, taken seriously by the foreign policy establishment and the upper-brow media, and the *New York Times* ran it entirely as an insert. Nixon did not write a word about "victory" in Vietnam, which he underplayed, and confined himself to the pursuit of a "just settlement." Arms control and the Middle East were represented as the greatest challenges. He sought a durable "framework" or "architecture" of peace, not haphazard arrangements but specific agreements linking the Great Powers and preemptively addressing concerns. "Peace must be far more than the absence of war." He wrote of the removal of the causes of war.[13]

Nixon and the Soviet president, Nikolai Podgorny, had signed, three months earlier, the nonproliferation treaty Johnson had negotiated. Nixon wrote in his foreign policy report that the United States and U.S.S.R. had reached nuclear parity, but in fact it was obvious that the United States still had a greater variety and precision of delivery capacity, even if the throw-weights were now about even. In fact, the multiple, independently targeted (MIRV) warheads would reestablish American superiority, but Nixon had de-escalated the missile rhetoric to a less jangling contest of technological machismo by referring to "nuclear sufficiency" and reigniting the arms control negotiations toward Strategic Arms Limitation Talks (SALT).

The report again expressed the wish for "a normal and constructive relationship with the government in Peking." Kissinger had told Nixon in December that he thought a Soviet invasion of China might be imminent, so severely had the relations between the two countries deteriorated. Diplomatic discussions had begun in Warsaw between China and the United States. Kissinger told Nixon he thought the Russians more dangerous than the Chinese, not only because of their greater military capability but because their leadership was unimaginative and crude, as were most of the Russian public, while China remained a more sophisticated culture, with very intelligent and original leadership. "Real fear in Russia," Kissinger wrote, "is that their Kennedy might emerge, and urge 'Let's get moving.'"[14] (He, Mikhail Gorbachev, did, fifteen years later, and the Soviet Union and the entire communist movement collapsed as a result of the shock.)

There may have been some truth in this opinion, but it was hard to prove on Mao Tse-tung's record of the needless massacre of millions of people, on a scale that surpassed even Stalin and Hitler, and the economic shambles of the "Great Leap Forward" in the fifties, followed by the near-collapse of the entire country under the "Great Cultural Revolution" of the sixties. This was the beginning of what became a rather annoying and durable Kissinger practice of toadying to the Chinese as the far-seeing wise men of the Middle Kingdom. The basic intelligence and historic standing of Mao and Chou En-lai were not at issue, but the lionization of them as oracular visionaries was a confidence trick, largely engineered by Kissinger in his post-government days to inflate his own status as a (well-paid) interpreter to the West of the indiscernible currents and tides of Chinese affairs.

However sophisticated they may have been, the Chinese responded to Nixon's minor overture to better relations in the body of his report by accusing the United States of "hypocrisy" and of being a "pitiable and ridiculous . . . paper tiger."[15]

In late February, Nixon received a report from a commission headed by Eisenhower's last defense secretary, General Thomas S. Gates, that recommended a swift move to all-volunteer armed forces. This was exactly what Nixon was hoping, and was a powerful arm against the anti-war movement, and another plank in his rather radical platform for changing the country, with welfare reform, tax reductions, rigorous desegregation, aid to the environment, revenue sharing with the states, and tough anti-crime measures. The target date for ending the draft was June 30, 1971.

French president Georges Pompidou and his stylish wife made a state visit to the United States in February 1970, the visit Nixon had arranged with de Gaulle a year before. France had recently sold one hundred and ten Mirage fighter aircraft to Libya, while declining to sell fifty of the same aircraft to Israel, and the Pompidous were jeered and even jostled on their tour to Washington, San Francisco, Chicago, and New York. Nixon became incensed at the rudeness and presumption of some Jewish individuals and organizations, as France evidently had the right to sell its aircraft where it pleased. He found it extremely annoying that private citizens would take it upon themselves to inflict such coarse censure on the invited leader of a friendly country, and would embarrass their own president and country in this way.

Like Truman, Nixon was friendly to Israel but did not need a great deal of provocation to toss off rather crude slurs against various ethnic groups, including Jews. To some extent, this was a way of inflicting unease on Kissinger, who was neither a religious Jew, a Zionist, nor a particular partisan of Israel, but it repaid him, Nixon imagined, for Kissinger's snide indiscretions to members of the press and at the high tables on the Georgetown social circuit about Nixon. (Given what would prove their shared talent at de-escalating Vietnam, the arms race, and the Cold War, they should have mastered less unseemly games-playing between themselves.)

The formal presidential talks with Pompidou went well, and when Nixon learned that Rockefeller and Lindsay were going to boycott the U.S. Government's official dinner for the Pompidous in New York, he erupted: "I'm going then, God damn them." While he was at it, Nixon postponed the sale that he had just verbally agreed two weeks before with Golda Meir and her ambassador in Washington, Yitzhak Rabin, of twenty-five Phantoms and eighty Skyhawks to Israel.

In fact, that transaction was not delayed for long, but Nixon was concerned that these demonstrations were to some extent encouraged by the Israeli government. He liked Meir and Rabin, but he was scandalized at the notion that any power thought it could manipulate the United States, and wished to send a message to the American Jews, to whom he owed nothing electorally but who apparently thought they could influence an administration to which 90 percent of them had been ostentatiously hostile.

Nixon, like Pompidou, was greeted by hecklers when he arrived at the Waldorf-Astoria for the dinner in New York, and in his remarks he brought the house down by saying that he "wanted President and Madame Pompidou to see our country as the president of the United States" does. He salvaged the visit for Franco-American relations and sent a clear message to the Arabs and Israel, and most Americans seemed to agree that the president of France and his wife should not have been publicly harassed as they were by demonstrators.

Once launched on this track, Nixon took it further and cut off a lot of federal aid to Lindsay, who was a frequent public critic, and to states where senators or governors, irrespective of party, made a habit of publicly attacking the administration. There was nothing morally wrong with this, and it is a time-honored method of demonstrating the powers of high office. Roosevelt stopped all New Deal projects in Louisiana when the state's boss, Senator Huey Long, deserted him publicly. He did the same in the Texas congressional district of Martin Dies, chairman of the House Un-American Activities Committee, when he attacked Roosevelt's attorney general, Frank Murphy, and did similar things at other times and made no secret of it. But Nixon was not Roosevelt. Nixon's actions were neither unprecedented nor hard to justify, but they did raise the ante with his potential enemies should the occasion ever arise when they had a reason to coalesce against him.

There was a series of bombings in New York and elsewhere in February and March 1970, one of them in New York's West Village, apparently an inadvertently detonated bomb factory. As the extreme, violent elements of the far left seized control of the unofficial opposition, a large number of formerly disaffected people, including many of the country's nearly eight million university students, melted back into the orthodox Democrats or Nixon's silent majority. As casualties and draft calls came down and units were withdrawn from Vietnam, it became easier for Nixon to separate dangerous sociopaths from his large following, and leave the Democrats floundering somewhere between them.

This continued to be the politics of polarization, but he livened it up a bit at the Gridiron Dinner, where the Washington press corps traditionally roast the government and the president replies. On March 14, when Nixon's turn came to respond, the lights dimmed and he went to the other side of the hall, where he and Agnew played a piano duet. Nixon announced he would play some of the favorite songs of former presidents, starting with FDR's "Home on the Range." He had just got into this when Agnew, who adopted a ludicrous Southern accent for the occasion, butted in with a noisy version of "Dixie." Nixon waited for a moment and then went to Harry Truman's "Missouri Waltz." Again, Agnew waited for a bit of it and thundered in with "Dixie." The same thing happened with Lyndon Johnson's "Yellow Rose of Texas." Then they both played Irving Berlin's "God Bless America" and the entire press corps stood and sang with them. There was tremendous applause at the end of it, and Nixon quietly told Haldeman that he was never going to top that and so would not go to another Gridiron. Nor did he, though he had been attending for over twenty years.

In February and March, a new controversy arose over Laos, where the North Vietnamese were keeping the embryonic Lao army at bay while they funneled tens of thousands of men and hundreds of thousands of tons of supplies down the tangled web of roads and tracks of the Ho Chi Minh Trail. Kissinger and his staff prepared a statement for Nixon released in late February stating that there were no U.S. ground forces in Laos and that none had been killed in combat there. All that was public at this point was that there were B-52 raids on the North Vietnamese Army units in Laos.

This story started to unravel at once; it emerged that twenty-seven American servicemen had died in Laos over the years, and that U.S. ground forces had been engaged in that country since Kennedy's Laos Neutrality Treaty, which North Vietnam had ignored, obliging the United States to conduct outnumbered clandestine operations there. Even Walter Annenberg's old *Philadelphia Inquirer* declared that there was a "credibility gap" in administration comments about Indochina.

Nixon became seriously annoyed and blamed Kissinger for submitting to him for release a paper that the media could demonstrate was materially inaccurate. Kissinger blamed Rogers and Laird for feeding him false information, and launched into one of his frequent diatribes against Rogers. Nixon told Haldeman to keep Kissinger away from him for a few days. This was bound to be very upsetting to the hypersensitive Kissinger, and pleasing to the guard dog Haldeman, but it could not last long. Kissinger was indispensable to Nixon also. Temperamental though he was, he grasped Nixon's strategic vision, had a fairly complementary one of his own, knew the major Western powers and the history of diplomacy, and was an extremely skilled negotiator. Whatever the abrasions between them, Kissinger could not have had such an arrangement with anyone except the American president and with no president of recent times except Nixon. All the others except Roosevelt relied on normal channels too much, and Roosevelt would not have delegated as much authority, not even to his chief collaborator, Harry Hopkins.

Rogers was a bonhomous, affable lawyer, but had neither the physical nor intellectual stamina nor the negotiating determination to undertake what Kissinger was doing every week. Most weekends Kissinger would secretly travel on what was billed as an aircraft training mission to a small airport in the middle of France, and there go on Pompidou's own jet to Paris, and then to a house in the working-class district of Choisy-le-Roi, where he would meet Le Duc Tho, a senior North Vietnamese politburo member. (To his own entourage, Kissinger referred to him as "Ducky.")

No one – not Rogers, nor Henry Cabot Lodge at the regular Paris talks, nor anyone except Nixon and a couple of others on the American side – knew what was afoot. Even these talks were not making any progress. Hanoi saw the Americans withdrawing and saw no need to offer them anything to accelerate their withdrawal. Hanoi wanted the United States to dispose of Thieu on the way out, but as the Americans withdrew, it would become less and less complicated for the North Vietnamese to accomplish this themselves.

It was clear from the last meeting of Kissinger and Dobrynin in 1969, just before Christmas, that Nixon and Kissinger had jettisoned the whole notion of "linkage" as a way out of Vietnam, which, along with Vietnamization and increased bombing, was the Nixon election-campaign Vietnam exit strategy. The bombing hadn't happened, and Kissinger agreed with Dobrynin that discussions on Berlin, the Middle East, and arms control could proceed without progress on Vietnam.[16]

Kissinger tried to convince Le Duc Tho at their meeting on February 21 that the United States could break up Soviet-Chinese solidarity in support of Hanoi, but he had no impact. When he referred to Nixon's strengthening of his domestic political position, Le Duc Tho quoted selected poll figures and Senator Fulbright, and Kissinger said that he would hear no more comments on domestic American politics, a subject he had raised.

Kissinger said that the United States could not act on Hanoi's desire that the Americans dispense with the Saigon government while leaving the country, for domestic political reasons: "I'll be realistic about your imperatives, you must be realistic about mine." Hanoi didn't have any, except to win, and Ducky asked how, if the United States couldn't win with five hundred thousand men in South Vietnam, could it "succeed when you let your puppet troops do the fighting?" Kissinger later allowed that "that was also tormenting me." Yet, three months earlier, he had not urged a resumption of bombing, despite having transmitted to Dobrynin most of the threats of dire consequences if there was no movement in Hanoi. How Kissinger proposed to secure a decent interval between American withdrawal from Vietnam and a complete communist takeover is not clear, and it was clear on February 16 that Le Duc Tho and his comrades in Hanoi were not going to lift a finger to create such an interval. The talks broke down in April, though Kissinger tried to convince Nixon that they should be kept going. As he later acknowledged, with commendable candor: "Aware of Nixon's skepticism, I fell into the trap of many negotiators of becoming an advocate of my own negotiations." It was a reprise of the contact with Ho Chi Minh through the French microbiologists and Kissinger to Dean Rusk and LBJ in 1967.

Kissinger had taken over from Rogers all foreign policy except the Middle East, and was only restrained by Nixon's unfounded concerns that a Jew could not deal for America in that region, because of Arab reactions, and that Kissinger could not be a public spokesman for the United States because of his Katzenjammer accent.

Kissinger was increasingly indispensable, as no one else could do this sort of work so quietly and effectively, and maintain the complicated relationship with Nixon, but he was a very high-maintenance colleague. In March, Nixon was suggesting to him that he take a holiday, as Kissinger was constantly announcing that Rogers was "stabbing" him in the back.

In the midst of this operetta, the Cambodians sacked the North Vietnamese and Viet Cong diplomatic buildings in the Cambodian capital of Phnom Penh. This could not have occurred without the approval of the Cambodian government, which for sixteen years had been in the hands of the flamboyant but unpredictable Prince Norodom Sihanouk, who was acceptable to all the powers and factions, and maintained neutrality by not complaining about the military activity of all manner of Vietnamese and Americans on his territory. The heavy American bombing of the North Vietnamese sanctuaries along the South Vietnamese border had drawn the North Vietnamese troops deeper into Cambodia.

Sihanouk had been away from Cambodia since the beginning of January, shuttling between Beijing and Moscow and trying to persuade the two leading communist powers to compel the North Vietnamese to withdraw, at least partially, from his country. Hanoi was no puppet of anyone else, and Sihanouk was not making much progress when his prime minister, General Lon Nol, an old ally of the Americans, started to force the issue. After sacking the North Vietnamese and Viet Cong diplomatic buildings, Lon Nol closed the port of Sihanoukville to any military imports for the North Vietnamese, and ordered the sixty thousand men of the North Vietnamese Army and Viet Cong to quit the country at once.

Cambodia had no possibility of enforcing this order, and Hanoi confined itself to a statement of respect for Cambodian sovereignty. Sihanouk said in a statement from Moscow that what amounted to a CIA plot was afoot. Soviet Premier Kosygin, who did not much care for Sihanouk but was conducting him to the airport for a flight to Beijing, learned just before departure of an apparent coup by Lon Nol. But he didn't mention it to Sihanouk until they got to the airport. It gave Kosygin some evident pleasure to tell Sihanouk that his carnival regime in Cambodia, which consisted largely of doing walk-on parts in movies constantly being filmed at the great and ancient temples of Angkor Wat, was over.

Lon Nol rounded up ten thousand irregulars, students and peasants, had them drilled for a few days on a golf course, and then sent them, semi-armed and semi-uniformed, on Coca-Cola trucks, toward the North Vietnamese troop-concentration areas. The North Vietnamese greeted their arrival with some amusement and then sent them packing by firing a few rounds into the air.

The coup against Sihanouk had not met with universal local enthusiasm either. In the town of Kompong Cham, fifty miles from Phnom Penh, a crowd of Sihanouk loyalists set upon Lon Nol's brother, lynched him, tore out his liver, roasted it, and distributed tender slices of it in the town square. The Cambodians, apparently cheerful people, had some of the manner-isms of the Indonesians, and when violent, they became frenzied. The Cambodians were in no position to resist the North Vietnamese, but they did turn on the Vietnamese civilians in Cambodia killing many thousands of them in the most barbarous manner. The North Vietnamese started to occupy larger and larger sections of the country, and approached the capital. It shortly became clear that Nixon would have to deal with the possible collapse of Cambodia if drastic measures were not taken.

Kissinger finally went to the Bahamas for the holiday Nixon had urged upon him in late March, which facilitated greater contact between the president and Rogers and Laird. Nixon quickly confirmed his suspicions that Kissinger had frequently misrepresented the views of the cabinet secretaries, as a part of his internecine disinformation campaign.[17] A few days later, as Nixon was about to address the nation about Vietnam, April 7, Kissinger was covering his flanks and sent the president a handwritten message: "Free people everywhere will be forever in your debt. Your serenity during crisis, your steadfastness under pressure, have been all that has prevented the triumph of mass hysteria. It has been an inspiration to serve."[18] This was at some variance with the version of their relations that Kissinger habitually retailed to his acolytes in the press and on his energetic and ambitious social rounds.

Kissinger was unfailingly brilliant, but half Iago, half Hagen, denouncing rivals, briefing against his president while fawning over him, sensing plots and resentments everywhere. He was also becoming squeezed slightly from below, as General (as he now was) Alexander Haig, Kissinger's assistant, caught the president's attention and was always happy to fill in for Kissinger. He was not as brilliant as Kissinger, but not as temperamental either. Shultz was now the brightest light in the cabinet, but he didn't have much direct dealing with Nixon.

If Nixon was going to get anything to show for his continuation of the American presence in Vietnam, he would have to get Hanoi to negotiate seriously, and if he was going to do this, he would have to hit them hard and bite the bullet in domestic politics with those who were traumatized at the thought that of any escalation.

The peace movement was now divided between Marxist and anarchist revolutionaries and gentle Hollywood-inspired advocates of withdrawal who, when asked what they thought the United States was doing in Vietnam, stared blankly and suggested that it was better to make love than war, and sensible people who simply thought it wasn't going well and wasn't worth the effort.

Nixon was simultaneously coping with the first Post Office strike in American history and went on television March 23 to announce that he was ordering the armed forces and the National Guard to sort and deliver mail. Priority was to be given to medical supplies, benefit and salary checks, apparently important financial information or notices, and letters to or from Vietnam. The strike was illegal, and Nixon easily gained public support for his refusal to tolerate it. Nixon eventually won a victory of sorts; he got a substantial amount of mail flowing, transformed the Post Office into a corporation and not a government department, and paid a generous make-good settlement to the disgruntled workers. It was a reformist achievement to remove what had long been a sinkhole for patronage run by successive chairmen of both parties and turn it into a corporation making some effort for efficiency.

Nixon spoke about Vietnam to the country three times in April, first on April 7, when he proclaimed the success of Vietnamization, and he astounded the country, which he had conditioned to expect an announced troop withdrawal of about forty thousand men, by announcing a withdrawal of a hundred and fifty thousand men over the next year. Always the master of surprise, and an imaginative policymaker, he successfully represented this to the hawks as evidence of the success of the Vietnamization plan and to the doves as an acceleration of the downsizing of the war effort. It was agile, but it would not impress the North Vietnamese. In between these speeches, Nixon announced that he would not nominate another Southerner to the Supreme Court and submit him to another "character assassination," and proposed instead Chief Justice Burger's fellow Minnesotan and best man at his wedding, court of appeals judge Harry Blackmun. This nomination, though the candidate was thought to be conservative (but proved not to be), went through without difficulty.

And the whole country was distracted by the hair-raising exploits of the space mission *Apollo XIII*. All seemed normal until there was an explosion in an oxygen tank and a small fire aboard, 206,000 miles from Earth. Emergency procedures were skillfully improvised and the damaged craft tumbled back to a perfect splashdown. Nixon, as was his wont, became very absorbed in the drama, called for cigars and drinks when the landing was effected, and jubilantly telephoned the astronauts' homes and spoke to their wives and families. Nixon briefly addressed the country on the rescue of the *Apollo* astronauts, on April 20. He used the overfrequent claim that this was the most exciting moment of his life.

— III —

Immediately after his April 20 speech, Nixon returned from California to Washington. He had determined that he finally had to take a strong position in Indochina and teach Hanoi that he could not be routed by demonstrators or treated by the North Vietnamese as if he were the prime minister of Laos.

Plans were prepared for a joint U.S.-South Vietnamese attack on the North Vietnamese and Viet Cong in Cambodia, and there was a National Security Council meeting to discuss it on April 22, the same day as the Earth Day demonstrations in favor of environmental causes all around the country. As the Cambodian operation was being discussed, Agnew, who regularly irritated Nixon by bothering him with trivial patronage matters, or becoming a thundering blowhard at such sessions as this, did it again by demanding an end to "pussyfooting" and, for good measure, telling Nixon not to be "intimidated" by war protesters and go to his daughter's university graduation (which he decided reluctantly not to do, to avoid an unpleasant campus scene).

Quite unjustly, Nixon took this out on Kissinger, who had nothing to do with torquing up Agnew. This was the sort of relationship that had developed between Nixon and Kissinger. If Nixon had a problem with what Agnew was saying, obviously he should have slapped the vice president down himself, which would not have been difficult. It was not for the national security adviser to do it. Kissinger sometimes claimed to divine the human drama in Nixon, and he respected him in some ways, but they had minimal personal relations. Kissinger considered that there were five Nixon personalities that coexisted sanely but uneasily: one was a chronically nervous and reticent introvert; one a rather nondescript middle-class Southern California suburban; one a clever and devious politician; one a capable Wall Street lawyer; and one an outstanding statesman, comfortable with de Gaulle, Adenauer, or Mao Tse-tung.[19]

Nixon was hovering on the brink of approving the Cambodian incursion, although he knew it would be terribly divisive in the administration and in the country. If he had delayed the April 7 announcement of the withdrawal of one hundred and fifty thousand men from Vietnam until he had decided what he was going to do about Cambodia, and then announced the two dramatic steps together, it would have sugared the pill for the anti-war demonstrators. Nixon was finally facing up to the task of disabusing Hanoi of their view that he was just doing a scuttle and trying to cover it behind bold and purposeful words.

As he inched toward the decision, Nixon watched the splendid film *Patton* with George C. Scott in the title role and Karl Malden as General Omar N. Bradley, and excellent portrayals of British field marshals Alexander and Montgomery and other senior figures. Rebozo was around a lot, usually a sign that Nixon was under intense pressure, and he and the president drank more than Nixon usually did, and more than was good for his diction out of hours at times.

Battle was looming with Laird and Rogers over Cambodia. Laird was scrupulously following Nixon's budgetary orders for a reduction in defense spending, and using these as a pretext for cutting back on B-52 bombing of Cambodia, as if there were nothing else that could produce a saving in such a vast budget. It was a bureaucratic cat-and-mouse game super-imposed on Nixon's apotheosis as subject and author of the madman theory. He would finally give the North Vietnamese a bloody nose and ignore the American anti-war demonstrators, just as Laird was employing tricks to try to hasten de-escalation.

These are the consequences of having senior cabinet officials with whom the president is not in regular, or at least informative, contact. From April 24, there were fairly steady high-level meetings on these issues. Admiral Thomas Moorer, who would soon become the chairman of the Joint Chiefs,[*] [20] attended some of the meetings, but Nixon admonished him that he was there to advise the president and was to say nothing of what went on to Laird. Helms and his deputy, General Robert Cushman, as well as Kissinger, were at the first meeting. The CIA had not provided very reliable intelligence on Cambodia, so Nixon and Kissinger were largely talking to themselves.

Kissinger finally asked Laird for some contingency plans for an invasion of the Cambodian sanctuaries, and Laird started to rise to the scent and said that the Congress should be consulted. Kissinger replied that if anything was to be done, the president would take care of that. On the evening of the 24th, Kissinger – who was coordinating and advising on diplomatic aspects of the invasion – met with his young staff and started to take them into his confidence. Nixon phoned repeatedly, becoming more peremptory and agitated with each call. Kissinger finally said, "Our peerless leader has flipped out." This was the core of the Nixon-Kissinger problem. Even as they steeled themselves to do important and brave things (leaving aside whether it was sound policy or not), Nixon did not act like the president, and Kissinger was snide, indiscreet, and insubordinate. They were both less unattractive without the interaction of the other, but the combination of them undoubtedly raised the historic status of each, especially of Kissinger, who might never have had a senior governmental post but for Nixon.[21]

At one point in this long evening, even Rebozo got on the telephone with Kissinger. ("The president wants you to know if this doesn't work, Henry, it's your ass.") All commanders in chief have their own methods, but this was a long way from the standard set by the most distinguished of Nixon's predecessors.

---

[*] Strongly recommended by Lyndon Johnson.

Kissinger had still not told his staff that what was afoot was more ambitious than a South Vietnamese invasion of Cambodia assisted by U.S. spotter planes. All – Winston Lord, Anthony Lake, Roger Morris, Laurence Lynn, and William Watts – opposed such an action, saying it would be a military disaster and a domestic political shambles as well. Watts refused Kissinger's request that he coordinate NSC staff work on it, and an acerbic exchange followed. Watts, Lake, and Morris all resigned (though Kissinger subsequently claimed he had fired Lake and allowed him to resign, whereupon he publicly resigned, claiming principle).

The ins and outs of Lake's disembarkation are not important. It illustrates the extent to which Nixon and Kissinger were isolated in the administration, apart from Haig and the military. Everyone, from the secretaries of state and defense and the NSC staff down, apart from John Mitchell and Spiro Agnew, who did not qualify as geopolitical thinkers, had given up on Vietnam. None of them believed that the sacrifice the United States was continuing to make had any purpose at all. They were a defeated and resigned command group, offended by the thought of a more prolonged resistance or greater aid to their despised ally.

In some respects, this ennobles the conduct of Nixon, Kissinger, and Haig. The White House was a lonely fortress and the companionship of the military was not so consoling; they weren't hanging out politically, and the former Vietnam commander, General William Westmoreland, now the chief of staff of the army, had so savaged the credibility of the Vietnam command by his own overoptimistic predictions and endless demands for more forces when he commanded there that there were real problems about how much credence to attach to anything the brass at the Pentagon had to say. Certainly Laird didn't believe any of it.[*] [22]

---

[*] Nixon did not have a particularly high opinion of the senior officers as a group. In a telephone conversation with Kissinger on April 7, 1971, he would say that the military were trying to avoid the end of the draft. "Listen, ending the draft gets us breathing space for ending the war in Vietnam. We'll restore the draft later. But God damn it, the military . . . are a bunch of greedy bastards who want more officers' clubs and more men to shine their shoes. The sons of bitches are not interested in this country." It isn't clear whether Nixon's assurance to Kissinger that they would restore the draft later was a sop to Kissinger, who didn't want to abolish it, or an outburst of wishful thinking, or a revelation of rank cynicism. The first is most likely as Nixon cannot have imagined that once abolished the draft could be restored.

Direct meetings between Kissinger and Nixon took up much of Saturday, April 25, at Camp David and on the presidential yacht, *Sequoia*. Rebozo was present but, appropriately, said nothing. As they were now coming right down to the wire, there were no histrionics, posturing, or tantrums. The NSC met on the afternoon of April 26, and Laird and Rogers heard the full story of the Cambodian operation for the first time. Rogers was fully opposed, saying that little would be gained and the domestic political problems would be severe. Laird, cagier and probably recognizing that something useful might be achieved, claimed not to be opposed but warned that American casualties were likely to jump to five hundred dead a week and the protests would be massive.

Nixon seemed finally to have reached, as he usually did in crises, a point of serenity. He had steeled himself to take this plunge. He had known all along that he had waffled when he gave the North Vietnamese to November to make a conciliatory gesture and then allowed his bluff to be exposed. If the United States did nothing to protect Cambodia after the impossible Sihanouk had been given the high jump, and the new government in Cambodia virtually declared war on Hanoi, the United States would be not just a paper tiger, but one made of tissue paper. It was now or never. There had been some private moments of unseemliness getting to this point, but now Nixon was unshakably determined.

Kissinger, too, deserves credit. He was flying in the face of all his former academic peers and social chums. As has already been mentioned, his judgment failed him when he brought partisan Democratic campaign workers close into the top of the NSC, but it must have made participating in such a step even more difficult for him. When the decision was taken, Nixon said to Kissinger that now they must agree that there would be "no recriminations among us, not even if the whole thing goes wrong. In fact, especially if the whole thing goes wrong."[23]

Unfortunately, Kissinger could not cure himself of his predilection for studied leaks and press manipulation, even on the verge of so controversial a step. The president's chief collaborator and confidant sat down with columnist Stewart Alsop and, on guarantees of anonymity, said that he had warned about campus reaction. Kissinger predicted that some universities would actually be burned down. Kissinger quoted Nixon as saying that the United States had to avoid the North Vietnamese takeover of Cambodia and Laos, and that Nixon was detested by the Establishment, which he was, in fact, trying to rescue from its own simplemindedness.

Nixon was in a position that somewhat resembled that of both Roosevelt and de Gaulle. Roosevelt didn't much care for the Establishment either, nor it for him, but he did want to make America safe for people who lived as he did, in a forty-room house on a thousand-acre property. He was trying to channel all the rage and frustration of the Great Depression against imaginary foes, whom he invented but never specifically named – "economic royalists, malefactors of great wealth, monopolists, war profiteers," and so forth, none of whom actually existed – in order to contain that bitterness in a disposable cul-de-sac, and later turn the country's animus against its real enemies, Nazis and Japanese imperialists.

And de Gaulle, some of whose terminology in ending the Algerian War Nixon had already copied, had managed to leave Algeria without that move seeming to be a defeat, by avoiding a military failure and appearing to bestow a just peace and sovereignty on the country. (He was, as Nixon knew and Kissinger said to Alsop, an illusionist, but that was beside the point as far as Kissinger was concerned.)[24] This was what Kissinger thought Nixon was doing, and he told Alsop that. But Nixon was not such a pessimist about America as Kissinger, though he was more pessimistic about his own career than Kissinger was about his. Nixon believed it might still be possible to salvage a durable non-communist South Vietnam, though he was almost the only prominent American civilian who did. But if there was such a chance, it would have to be seized now.

The operation was held up for a day so Rogers could appear before a closed session of Fulbright's Foreign Relations Committee and speak the truth in saying no decision had been reached about Cambodia. At the end of the session, Fulbright told the press that his committee was unanimous in its opposition to sending arms to Cambodia. There was no thought of U.S. forces being involved. A year before, Nixon could have shamed and cajoled many of the Democrats into joining him in a policy that could plausibly be represented as having some prospect of a victorious conclusion.

By allowing Hanoi to string him along to November, and then not acting on his ultimatum, Nixon had very insufficient support in the country. And by conducting his administration as he did, he was down to Agnew, Mitchell, and Kissinger for support. Mitchell's wife was becoming very erratic, drinking heavily, overmedicated, lonely, and loquacious. At this time she telephoned the White House military assistant at 4:30 A.M. and half passed out but stirred herself to bellow down the phone at him, "Don't you go to sleep on me, you little son of a bitch! My husband's the fucking attorney general of the United States of America."[25] The attorney general naturally found it very distracting.

Nixon privately enunciated his theory (to Rockefeller) that political leaders attract as much opprobrium for doing things by halves as for doing them completely, so the United States might as well make a proper job of the Cambodian incursion. It had originally been thought that U.S. forces would only enter one of the sanctuary areas (Parrot's Beak and Fish Hook), but Nixon determined that they might as well be engaged in both.

The president spoke to the nation on the evening of April 30. He did not refer to the heavy bombing the United States had been conducting in Cambodia's border areas, and did not say that the action he was announcing was being welcomed by the Cambodians. He spoke with the aid of a map of Cambodia and reassured his viewers that this was not an invasion, it was an operation to get rid of the North Vietnamese and Viet Cong in Cambodia, following which the U.S. and South Vietnamese forces would withdraw. It was entirely an action to preserve the integrity of Cambodia, not violate it.

Then: "We live in an age of anarchy, we see mindless attacks on all the great institutions which have been created by free civilizations in the last five hundred years. . . . Here in the United States, great universities are being systematically destroyed. . . . If when the chips are down, the world's most powerful nation, the United States of America, acts like a pitiful, helpless giant, the forces of totalitarianism and anarchy will threaten free nations and free institutions throughout the world. . . . I would rather be a one-term president and do what I believe is right than to be a two-term president at the cost of seeing America become a second-rate power and to see this nation accept the first defeat in its proud, 190-year history. . . . It is not our power but our will and character that is being tested tonight." He invoked Woodrow Wilson, Franklin D. Roosevelt, Dwight D. Eisenhower, and John F. Kennedy (referring to the Cuban Missile Crisis, the outcome of which he had criticized, as JFK's "finest hour") and asked support for "our brave men fighting tonight halfway around the world."

It was an effective performance and the initial responses to the White House were quite heavily favorable. Polls in succeeding days all showed the president carrying the country comfortably enough, though opposition to his speech was at or a little above 30 percent. The next day the president underlined his message of supporting the troops by going to the Pentagon, where he was applauded in the halls. In conversation with supporters there, he referred to protesters as "bums" and praised the young men in the armed forces he had seen in Vietnam. At a military briefing, he ordered that further sanctuaries beyond Fish Hook and Parrot's Beak be cleaned out, and when officers commented on likely demonstrations, he said they could leave the political considerations to him. Once embarked on the chosen course, Nixon was resolute, and even inspiring.

On May 2, after a day and evening's disorder in Kent, Ohio, by Kent State University students, including the burning down of the armed forces recruiting and training office, National Guardsmen opened fire on students who pursued them, pelting them with rocks and returning tear gas canisters. The students fled, but four of them were killed and eleven wounded. It had not helped that the governor of Ohio, John Rhodes, had called the student demonstrators "brownshirts." They were irresponsible and annoying, and the Cambodian activity did not justify the histrionics it attracted even on Kissinger's staff, much less the campuses of the country. But the governor of Ohio had no right comparing this university student demonstration to Hitler's SA. And he should have assured that the National Guardsmen had the proper rules of engagement. They should have had rubber or plastic bullets if tear gas wasn't adequate, and if they went to live ammunition they should have fired in the air, or even right on the ground. Student demonstrators are rarely hard to scatter, and there was no excuse for students to die from gunshot wounds.

Nixon asked, "Is this because of me, of Cambodia?" He issued a statement that said that "When dissent turns to violence it invites tragedy." He asked university "administrators, faculty, and students alike, to stand firmly for the right which exists in this country of peaceful dissent and just as strongly against the resort to violence as a means of such expression."[26] Nixon "wrote personal letters to each of the parents even though I knew that my words could not help."[27] There was widespread violence on campuses and large demonstrations in many places, but Kent State was the only scene of fatalities. Most fears of university buildings being burned to the ground did not materialize either. There were demonstrations on 1,100 campuses, and 448 universities and colleges were closed. The Center for Advanced Study in the Behavioral Sciences in Stanford, California, was burned down, which destroyed the life's research of a renowned Indian anthropologist, Professor M.N. Srinivas. Nixon telephoned Srinivas to condole with him.[28]

Two million university students, about a quarter of the total, claimed to be on strike, but the academic year was over, so the gesture was irrelevant. Nixon graciously received a delegation from Kent State and heard them out sympathetically. On October 25, 1970, an Ohio grand jury indicted twenty-five students and university officials and no police or National Guardsmen in the Kent State deaths. The grand jury concluded (i.e., the prosecutor adopted the view) that no one who did the shooting could be charged, because they honestly believed their lives were in danger. (If they did, they were hallucinating or were too cowardly by nature or unsound of judgment to be armed with loaded guns.)

There was also a countermove by the president's supporters. At two sights in New York, near Wall Street and near City Hall, hardhat construction workers attacked student demonstrators carrying North Vietnamese and Viet Cong flags, and forced their way into City Hall and raised back to the top of the mast the flag that Lindsay had had lowered in honor of the dead at Kent State. The workers roughed up some of the students, as the police, indicating fairly clearly which side of the silent majority they worked and lived on, watched passively. The flashpoint on Wall Street was when one of the demonstrators urinated on the famous statue of George Washington. At this, the construction workers charged. The majority of Americans were tired of the antics of the students. They weren't enthused about Vietnam, but they had no sympathy for the North Vietnamese and Viet Cong and were tired of the denigration of America.

The hardhat political movement grew quickly, and with it the phenomenon of the unionized workers of America defecting in large numbers from the party of Roosevelt and Truman to the Republicans. This change had started with Eisenhower, steadied in 1960, rolled back against Goldwater, and vacillated between all three candidates in 1968, but came in a torrent to Nixon and in a cresting flood a few years later to Reagan. On May 20, more than a hundred thousand pro-Nixon demonstrators marched along Broadway to City Hall, led by tens of thousands of helmeted construction workers carrying scores of thousands of American flags and telling

Lindsay to run for mayor of Hanoi. They raised the chant, which resonated powerfully in the country: "America, Love it or Leave it!" (One-third of heavy construction in the United States was undertaken by or assisted by the federal government, and was required by law to be paid for at the top of union wage scales. The hardhats had a natural self-interested disposition to support the president.)

To some extent, Nixon was succeeding in his earliest political gambit, of raising the great majority against enemies whom he caricatured and excoriated. But the anti-war demonstrators were a good deal less blameless than the bedraggled rat-tail of forties and fifties communists and fellow travelers who had first received this treatment from him. On the other hand, there was plenty to complain about in the war, but espousing the cause of the North Vietnamese and the Viet Cong when hundreds of young Americans in the armed forces were being killed or wounded by them most weeks, calling for the Marxist overthrow of the U.S. government or outright anarchy, provoking riots, and blowing up federal government and university buildings was bound to be unpalatable to most Americans.

Reports of lack of enthusiasm for the Cambodian action in parts of the administration inevitably leaked out, but Nixon personally met with the House Armed Services and Senate Foreign Relations Committees on May 5 and walked them through what was already an impressive haul of enemy ordnance and food. The North Vietnamese had retreated farther into Cambodia, so casualties continued to be light, but the seizure of large quantities of war materiel would be a serious inconvenience to them. Kissinger was moved to tell Stewart Alsop that he was "no Nixon idolater, but you have to give him credit for doing what he thought was in the national interest." Kissinger deplored the feebleness of the Establishment, citing Clifford, Cyrus Vance, John Gardner, and McGeorge Bundy, all senior past or future officials in Democratic administrations.[29]

The secretary of the interior, Walter Hickel, sent Nixon a letter on May 6 that was published in the *Washington Star* before it arrived at the White House. Hickel wrote, "Youth, in its protest, must be heard." He accused Nixon of failing the youth of America and referred to Patrick Henry, Jefferson, and Madison as youths, which they were once, but not when they were famous. It was an astounding act of insolence rather than dissent, as it was not accompanied by Hickel's resignation. He apparently imagined that he could have such a public break on such a watershed issue, and advise the public of the difference with the president he served before the president himself learned of it, and soldier merrily on in Nixon's cabinet. Unless political etiquette was remarkably different in the remote fastness of Alaska, where Hickel had been the governor, he must have imagined that Nixon's moral authority was disintegrating.

Nixon's own reaction was typically Byzantine; he punished Hickel by breaking up the tennis court at the White House, of which Hickel was one of the most frequent users. Six months later, after the Cambodia controversy had passed and the midterm elections were over, Nixon disposed of Hickel in another typical Nixonian way. George Shultz supposedly wished to talk to Hickel about some of the estimates for his department. He arrived to meet with Shultz (now the budget director) and was advised that the president wished to see him. He went to see Nixon, who informed him, raising his voice to be heard over a Marine Corps band that was practicing on the White House lawn, that he wished to "make a change." Hickel imagined that this could take effect at New Year's, but Nixon told him it would take effect at once. Hickel, for once, had no comment for the press.

Nixon met the press on May 8, for what was the testiest session he had yet had with them as president. His tendency to perspire reasserted itself, as the natural questions about the incursion in Cambodia, the Kent State student demonstrators, Hickel, and related matters came in. Nixon said that taking out the sanctuaries had unearthed "thousands of rockets and millions of rounds of ammunition" and that the operation had bought six or eight months for ARVN (the South Vietnamese Army) to train and prepare itself for the full defense of the country, so that if the sanctuaries had to be cleared again, ARVN would be able to do it alone.

When asked if he thought the United States was headed for revolution, or the repression of opposition, he answered very calmly that neither was the case. He said that the traditional right of dissent would make any revolutionary thoughts unnecessary, that it was being widely exercised, that his opponents were very active and vocal and often personal, and that he had no complaint with that. Of the students, he said that they claimed to be for peace, for an end to killing and to the draft, and for getting out of Vietnam. "I agree with everything they are trying to accomplish."[30] He asked for some understanding: "I did not send these men to Vietnam." He said he was working eighteen hours a day to bring Americans back from Vietnam. He

clarified that he had not meant to say at the Pentagon on May 1 that protesters were "bums," that he was referring to those who resorted to violence
and vandalism.[31]

Nixon then reverted to his old performance anxiety and made nearly
fifty telephone calls between 9:20 P.M. and 1:20 A.M., all around the country,
asking people what they thought of how it had gone. He spoke seven times
to Kissinger, and then called him again at nearly 4 A.M. He called Hickel,
whose tennis court he was confiscating, Billy Graham, Norman Vincent
Peale, and many others. Most assured him that he had put his case very
effectively. It was already clear that the issue was to what degree to indulge
the students, not whether the country, in policy terms, sided with the president or his opponents – Nixon had won that contest.

Nixon was too keyed up to sleep, so at 4:20 he awakened his butler,
Manolo Sanchez, called for a White House car, and was driven to the
Lincoln Memorial, which was being peacefully occupied by visiting
student demonstrators. The White House night duty officer was Egil (Bud)
Krogh, who took out after Nixon and found him on the steps of the memorial surrounded by about ten or a dozen wild-looking youths. They were
listening politely as the president spoke of his press conference, and his
embrace of all the objectives the students had, of his youth in a poor family,
a Quaker brought up to oppose war, his support as a young man for
Chamberlain over Churchill. He rambled very coherently, if discursively,
on about the virtues of travel, the environment, cities he had visited, his
hopes for relations with China.

The group around Nixon grew to about twenty-five, and one asked him
if he realized that they were prepared to die for their beliefs. Nixon said he
knew that, that he had been prepared to die for his beliefs when he was
their age, and still was, and that the point was to fix up the world so no
American would have to speak in such terms. The sun was rising over the
Washington Monument, and after about half an hour, Nixon said, "Don't
go away bitter. Remember, this is a great country for all its faults." He
stopped on the steps to speak with a few other people and then drove to the
Capitol, to show it to Sanchez. As he drove away, one angry student raised
a middle finger in an obscene digital salute, which it gave Nixon youthful
pleasure to reciprocate.[32]

The myth arose instantly, on the basis of the snide comments of one
student who spoke to the media hours later, that Nixon had been maudlin

or incoherent, or had condescended to the students by talking about football or giving a travelogue. In fact, he spoke very fluently and thoughtfully, replied calmly and effectively even to occasional sharpish comments, had made an important gesture, and made a favorable impression on his astonished interlocutors. The Washington press interviewed the students after the fact and among them all they embellished a version of Nixon's conversation that was inaccurate and unflattering. On this occasion, he would have been better to have had his exchange recorded. As often happened, and as he always expected, he was unfairly treated by the national media.

At the Capitol, surprised night guards opened the House chamber for Nixon and he sat in the place he had first occupied as a freshman congressman twenty-three years before. He asked Sanchez to sit in the Speaker's chair. Nixon autographed a Bible for one of the cleaning ladies, and reminisced briefly about his mother. He had breakfast with Sanchez, Haldeman, Ziegler, and a few others at the Mayflower Hotel, and returned to the White House at 7:30 A.M.

Each day the White House issued new figures detailing the huge cache of supplies that had been piled up. Casualties were running at barely 10 percent of what Rogers and Laird had predicted. After the first couple of weeks, it became clear that the president's opponents had cried wolf and he was gathering strength steadily.

Kissinger was playing his customary double game, doing what he could to push Nixon out on to a limb opposite moderate opinion, urging him to be strong. At the same time, he was saying to groups of students and academics, and in off-the-record press briefings, that none of them could imagine what he was sparing the country in talking Nixon out of wild war-mongering ideas.[33] For his part, Nixon was promoting Haig as another irritant to Kissinger, and sent him to Cambodia in late May to see Lon Nol and determine what he thought of the incursion, and what could be done to shore up the Lon Nol government.[34]

Nixon, having just received loud cheers and applause from eighty thousand people at the stadium of the University of Tennessee, where he appeared with Billy Graham, again spoke to the country on June 4 and showed film of the captured rifles, machine guns, ammunition, and rice. He said, "I can now state that this has been the most successful operation of this long and difficult war."

The press began to play up stories of involvement between Kissinger and actress Jill St. John. Kissinger would assure Nixon on June 25 that the stories were exaggerated. Nixon wasn't much concerned with Kissinger's romantic life, and Jill St. John was an attractive and intelligent woman, but Kissinger insisted the stories made him appear unserious and had been planted by Rogers. Nixon acknowledged that there were frictions between his secretary of state and national security adviser but defended Rogers against the charge of disparaging Kissinger for keeping company with a beautiful woman.

He had partly himself to blame for the incessant backbiting in the higher reaches of the government. Nixon, unlike some more idealistic presidents of the United States, endlessly claimed that the masses of the world were inspired by America, which was partly true, but he suspected almost all foreign governments of trying to pick America's pockets and manipulate it. To deal with such opportunists, Henry Kissinger was a providential figure.

By this time, Nixon had little confidence in his cabinet, except for Shultz and Stans. Finch had relinquished Health, Education, and Welfare in favor of Elliot Richardson, and had become a White House counselor, but was really on his way out of government after the civil rights controversy and the Panetta fiasco. Romney had aggravated the president by turning cabinet meetings virtually into debating sessions, and joined the corral of the irredeemable with Hickel when he issued a press release announcing he would fight inflation by taking a 25 percent cut in salary. Romney was a well-to-do man after his time at American Motors (where he was very successful), and Nixon considered this a silly grandstand move. He felt that David Kennedy was ineffectual at Treasury and that John Volpe had accomplished little at the Transportation Department. Burns had moved to the Federal Reserve, and Moynihan and Kissinger continued to be the stars.

Despite his irritation with Kissinger, and Ehrlichman, who had advised him he had had a public relations setback at the Lincoln Memorial, Nixon distributed blue cloth hearts to "the true blue" – Ehrlichman, Haldeman, and Kissinger – that were sewn for him by Bebe Rebozo's girlfriend.[35]

Nixon had tried unsuccessfully to snuff out any presidential chances for George Wallace. Wallace had served two two-year terms as governor of

Alabama, from 1963 to 1967, and when forced by the state term limits to step aside, had managed to get his wife, Lurleen, elected to the following term while he continued to run the state. Lurleen died of cancer in May 1968, and Lieutenant Governor Albert Brewer became governor. He had been a Wallace loyalist, but once in office was more independent than Wallace would have wished. Wallace had pledged not to run against him but changed his mind, and they contested the Democratic primary in May 1970. Nixon directed that a hundred thousand dollars be given to the Brewer campaign, and this was handed over by Nixon operative Herbert Kalmbach, under an assumed name, in the Sherry Netherland Hotel in New York, in hundred-dollar bills. Nixon also ordered a tax investigation of Wallace's brother and finance chairman and fundraiser, Gerald Wallace, and ordered that the existence of the investigation be leaked to columnist Jack Anderson, former co-author with the late Drew Pearson (who had died in 1969) of the column "Washington Merry-Go-Round."

In the first round of the primary, May 5, Brewer led Wallace by eight thousand votes. It was allegedly partly to strengthen Brewer that Nixon appeared with Billy Graham just across the Alabama border at the University of Tennessee on June 4. He also ordered another three hundred thousand dollars for Brewer. The Brewer messenger, returning from seeing Kalmbach in New York, was so nervous that the plane might crash and the wads of hundred-dollar bills be discovered that, in a singular act of potentially posthumous image management, he pinned a note to his underwear explaining that he was carrying the money for the president of the United States.[36] Wallace ran an old-fashioned segregationist campaign, called Brewer the candidate of the niggers, and won the run-off by thirty-two thousand, not an impressive win, but enough to keep him in the presidential running for 1972. In the spring of 1971, Wallace would decide to run for the Democratic nomination, and the IRS audit of Gerald Wallace would quietly end. The inference that the two events were connected is probably not unreasonable.[37]

On June 5, Nixon met with Hoover, Helms, and the heads of the Defense Intelligence Agency and the National Security Agency and complained that they were not adequately protecting the country from revolutionary elements. He demanded to know why there were skyjackings every day or two and illegal ammunition factories in residential neighborhoods, why the Black Panthers were receiving money from the Office of Economic Opportunity, and why no connection had been discovered between local subversive groups and foreign communist or radical Arab governments. It was a harangue more than a question. He constituted the group the Interagency Committee on Intelligence and used as a working paper a rather draconian document written by Tom Charles Huston, a twenty-nine-year-old aide who took these threats extremely seriously.

From the vantage point of a later generation, it is easy to dismiss these concerns as phantasmagoric paranoia, but strange things were going on in the United States, and some of the radical groups were well-armed, well-organized, and murderous. Huston, who was completely above his station with such prominent people, made several recommendations – including a widespread plan for phone taps, opening of mail, and "surreptitious entries" (i.e., break-ins) – that were illegal, easily surpassing whatever cover was provided by national security exemptions. Hoover, though he had frequently operated more or less as a law unto himself since Eisenhower's retirement (and was no paragon of restraint in the thirty-five years prior to that), drew the line at completely illegal activity, to judge by his record, from tactical rather than ethical motivations. Huston candidly stated that what he was proposing was "illegal," amounted to "burglary," and could lead to acute "embarrassment," but was the most "fruitful" course available.

The intelligence chiefs agreed to the recommendations as long as the president specifically approved actions taken under the plan. Nixon agreed to this on July 14. However, Hoover had further second thoughts and summoned Huston to his commodious office on July 26 and went through his paper. The following day he warned Mitchell that the implementation of Huston's paper would be a disaster – that illegal entries would quickly be discovered and bring in "the jackals of the press," as well as a lot of civil liberties litigation.

He told Mitchell he would respond to direct orders from the president, but otherwise he would not touch Huston's recommendations. This demonstrated that the seventy-five-year-old director, forty-six years in office as FBI director, had retained astute practical judgment. He undoubtedly saved the administration from itself, for a time.

In his memoirs, Nixon wrote, "I knew that if Hoover decided not to cooperate, it would matter little what I had decided or approved. Even if I issued a direct order to him, while he would undoubtedly carry it out, he would soon see to it that I had cause to reverse myself."[38] Nixon was in the classic position of the national leader who feared his own police minister, like Napoleon and Fouché and Khrushchev and Beria.

Haldeman had all copies of the report rounded up, and Nixon rescinded his approval of its recommendations on July 30. No harm had yet been done, but the contagion of lawlessness, a virus transmitted by its enemies, had driven the administration to the verge of febrile self-destruction.[*][39] Even after all these decades, they all still underestimated the immovable director of the FBI.

The Senate gave a foretaste of what was coming with two resolutions, one sponsored by John Sherman Cooper, Republican of Kentucky, and Frank Church, Democrat of Idaho, requiring American withdrawal from Cambodia by June 30, and the other sponsored by George McGovern, Democrat of South Dakota, and Mark Hatfield, Republican of Oregon, requiring a complete pullout from Vietnam by June 30, 1971. Nixon had pledged to withdraw from Cambodia by the end of June, and apart from stating that both bills were unconstitutional, ignored Cooper-Church. It was passed 58 to 37 on June 30, which meant Nixon could have vetoed it, but it was abandoned before it got to the House of Representatives, which was expected to vote it down. The other bill made slow progress, but this opposition was the price of not getting a consensus on war policy when it was still the Democrats' war and he was a new president, fifteen months before.

On June 30, the White House released a report on the Cambodian activity then ending. The United States had suffered only 344 dead and ARVN 818, not the thousands that had been almost universally predicted (including by Rogers and Laird). The report claimed 11,349 enemy killed and 2,328 captured, as well as over 22,000 guns, fifteen million rounds of ammunition, an impressive fourteen million tons of rice, nearly 12,000 buildings and bunkers destroyed, including, Kissinger deadpanned to the

---

[*] On February 12, 1971, Pat Buchanan wrote the president a memorandum urging the immediate retirement of Hoover as a "reactionary" who was alienating the young people of the country and whose moral authority was steadily evaporating. On April 12, 1971, Nixon told Haldeman: "Mitchell says we have Hoover exactly where we want him. Mitchell wants the resignation."

cabinet, "a five-sided wooden building" that was assumed to be the enemy's command headquarters. (There had been much talk early on of finding the enemy's headquarters, so Kissinger gave it a pentagonal shape.)

Doubtless, the action was, as Nixon claimed, a success. But only about a third of the North Vietnamese and Viet Cong soldiers or guerrillas in Cambodia were eliminated. The Soviet Union and China could replace the rifles, handguns, and ordnance in a few months, and the rice harvest of the next year would replace what was removed by the United States and ARVN. Transporting it all down the Ho Chi Minh Trail would be a challenge, but Nixon was right in his press conference that all they had really done was buy six months for ARVN to face the onslaught without its American big brother. Nixon had effectively traded another reduction of the residual support for the war effort in the United States for whatever credibility he might have earned in Hanoi for finally ignoring domestic hostility to the war.

However, at least he had departed from the conveyor belt to oblivion that the U.S. effort in Vietnam had been on since the Johnson-Thieu Manila Declaration of October 1966, and had flatly affronted the domestic forces of instant defeat. He could not really have believed that he had done much more than buy the cover for the already-announced departure of a hundred fifty thousand Americans. This was not the showdown, but it was a hint that while Nixon was not a madman, the showdown with him could be more than Hanoi bargained for.

Whatever the strategic justification for the Cambodian incursion, Nixon had prepared in his own way, including plenty of alcohol and at least ten viewings of the film *Patton*, and he had seen it through and shown courage and resolution in the face of a controversy that would have daunted many. In its way, his was an impressive performance, as originally, if not as nobly, acted out by him as George C. Scott's portrayal of George S. Patton, and Nixon was a man to whom conspicuous courage did not come as easily as it had to Patton, either in life or as dramatized.

Also in early July, Nixon took another important step when he set up the Environmental Protection Agency. Initially, it was a gathering of fifty-six hundred employees and $1.4 billion of annual budget from other departments, especially Interior and Agriculture, but it was directly responsible to the president, not through any cabinet official, and this was a distinct recognition of the importance of the issues. Nixon actually had strong views about the environment, and as in civil rights, tax reductions, welfare reform, and various foreign policy areas, he was something of an avant-garde thinker, if not an outright pioneer. He had resented as a youth the scarcity of public parks where people of modest means could spend holidays, and early adopted a policy of setting up parks wherever practical, from excess federal land as defined by the Property Review Board. His watchwords were to "bring parks to the people" and "when in doubt, make a park out of it." The result was six hundred and forty-two new national parks.[40] He was a friend of industry, and was always interested in job creation, but he was outraged at gratuitous spoliation of the environment.

In one of his many off-the-record press statements, attributable only to a senior official, Kissinger said on June 30 that Indochina was no longer the principal foreign policy concern of the United States, that that honor now fell to the Middle East, because of the Soviet arming of Arab states and the increasing radicalization of some of the Muslims. He went so far as to state the American goal to be to "expel" the U.S.S.R. from the region. Nixon was required to clarify this at a press conference on July 20, and said that there was no thought of a military expulsion, but the establishment and maintenance of a military balance in the region, which the Russians were trying to upset. The Russians had approximately ten thousand advisers and technicians on the ground in Egypt, steadily upgrading Nasser's air defenses and air capability. Egyptian anti-aircraft missiles were becoming as sophisticated as those in North Vietnam, and were starting to knock down advanced Israeli aircraft when they made reconnaissance overflights. Nixon was quietly replacing Israeli losses and assuring that Israel had about forty operational F-4 Phantom fighter-bombers, the most advanced in the world, at all times. Israeli ambassador Yitzhak Rabin, a respected general, told Nixon and Kissinger that Israel's air force was now encountering the most sophisticated Soviet planes, and often Soviet pilots in the planes, bearing Egyptian markings.

Soviet adventurism was in the air, and with Israel on the Suez Canal and more Palestinians than Bedouins in Jordan, and frequent skirmishing between King Hussein's army and the Palestinian fedayeen, the whole region was a tinderbox. The American response was made more complex by the Rogers-Kissinger rivalry. Since Nixon had determined that he did not want the United States represented by a Jew in these matters, Rogers had taken this field for himself and spent part of the summer of 1970 touring around Europe advancing what became known as the "Rogers Plan" for an instant, ninety-day Middle East cease-fire and negotiations under the auspices of the United Nations. The Israelis were regularly knocking out new Egyptian anti-aircraft missile launchers, weapons that they thought would furnish the Egyptians and their Russian allies an advantage; but Egypt, Jordan, and Israel all signed on to the Rogers Plan in July, despite the announcement from the Palestinian Al Fatah leader, Yasir Arafat, from the Jordanian capital, that he would ignore any cease-fire and try to disrupt it.

Any apparent success of Rogers upset Kissinger. Nixon did not want to pander to American Jewish sentiment, and did not want to become embroiled with the Russians while he was still enmeshed in Vietnam, but he would not allow them to lead the subjugation of Israel. It was a compli-cated and dangerous minuet, aggravated, but also made less relentlessly serious, by the more absurd rivalries in Nixon's entourage.

Israel alleged in mid-August that the Russians were continuing to build up the Egyptian anti-aircraft missile capacity, and Prime Minister Golda Meir wanted to come to Washington to warn Nixon about a tilting balance of power in the region. Nixon discouraged her visit but went to Camp David with the secretary of state to talk about it, and thus inadvertently intensified the Kissinger-Rogers problem. Kissinger became so aroused, he expressed direct criticism of Nixon to Haldeman, knowing that this would be repeated to Nixon.

Nixon thought Kissinger was trying to derail Rogers's peace proposal, rudimentary and unpromising though it was, out of jealousy more than any partisanship for the Israelis. Nixon asked Haldeman and Haig to try to settle Kissinger down, but he was at this point on a mission of self-aggrandizement in the White House and responded with his own demands for transmission to the president: "1. Attacks on Henry Kissinger, direct or indirect, must cease. An attack on Kissinger is an attack on the President. 2 All cables with policy implications, including especially the Middle East, must be cleared in the White House [i.e., Kissinger]. 3. All contacts with Dobrynin must be cleared ahead of time." Kissinger left for Paris for a resumption of secret talks with the North Vietnamese. The public talks, now conducted by the respected veteran diplomat David K.E. Bruce, were also about to resume, after a nine-month boycott by the North Vietnamese. (Henry Cabot Lodge had finally retired.)

Obviously Nixon could not allow the Kissinger-Rogers problem to fester indefinitely. He could not accept such an ultimatum as the one Kissinger had given via Haig and Haldeman, but dispensing with Kissinger would be a needless loss of an extremely competent official who was in many ways carefully attuned to Nixon's preferred methods of complete secrecy punctuated by startling surprises.

Nixon was right to have some doubts about Kissinger's ability to choose and control his own staff. (Halperin, the author of the initial memo that had largely emasculated the State Department, had quit in the aftermath of Cambodia.) That policy watershed had shaken out the more partisan Democrats and left Kissinger with less of a straddle between the views of his staff and his preferred academic and social and journalistic milieus, and the president.

The logical move would have been to move or remove Rogers and give his job either to Rockefeller or Kissinger himself. Either would have ended the friction between the White House and the State Department, and enabled the White House to use the resources of the State Department more extensively. Rockefeller could have managed Kissinger, but he was becoming rather a defeatist about Vietnam himself, as his appointment of Charles Goodell to fill Robert Kennedy's term indicated. (Goodell had gone so far off the charts, as far as Nixon Republicans were concerned, that William F. Buckley's brother, James, mounted a serious challenge as a Conservative against Goodell and the liberal Democratic congressman, Richard Ottinger, for the upcoming election.)

If Nixon didn't want to reward Rockefeller, or create a Rockefeller-Kissinger axis right behind his back, he could have found something else for Rogers, who had no particular aptitude for foreign affairs other than a conciliatory personality, and given the job to Kissinger. This was the eventual solution. If Nixon had wanted to make a dramatic move, he would have retired Hoover, replaced him with Mitchell, and Mitchell with Rogers; moved out Laird and replaced him with Shultz, a former marine combat officer in addition to his other attainments; given State to Kissinger with a lecture to desist from some of his more irritating practices; given Finch a serious mandate to turn the new EPA into something important without antagonizing all of American industry; and prepared either Rockefeller or Reagan, depending on which way Nixon wanted to push the party, for the

vice presidency in 1972 and presumed succession to the presidential nomination in 1976. There were plenty of combinations that would work, and
these are just a few of them. Instead, in the unfortunate manner in which
things drifted before events forced Nixon to go into isolation, drink with
Rebozo, watch inspirational military films, and then take draconian crisis
measures bravely, the squabbling of his administration continued. On
September 18, Mitchell was quoted in *Women's Wear Daily* as saying that
Kissinger was "an egocentric maniac." Kissinger made light of it, but in any
sense of teamwork, collegiality, or just normal administration, Nixon's was,
in the upper levels, a dysfunctional government.

Nixon was right not to lose Kissinger; he was possibly the greatest
natural foreign policy talent, rivaled only by Nixon himself, that the U.S.
government had had in an important position for many years, perhaps since
John Quincy Adams. And Adams operated in an infinitely simpler world,
without Israel, the Palestinians, communism, and two Vietnams, when the
United States was far from being a Great Power, and was unable even to
subdue Canada or prevent the White House from being burned down by
the British and the Canadians.

— V —

Nixon launched his campaign for the 1970 midterm elections on
September 16, before a very enthusiastic crowd of fifteen thousand, and
millions live on television, at Kansas State University. He was sharpening
up the cutting edge of his silent majority message, and inching closer to his
old game of uniting the majority against a despised, subversive minority.
He recited a number of recent outrageous crimes, from murders in court-
rooms to the release of a Nobel Prize–winning scientist's experimental
animals. Then he attacked "those who bomb universities, ambush policemen, who hijack airplanes," and went on: "There have always been those
among us who would choose violence or intimidation to get what they
wanted. . . . What is new is their numbers and the extent of the passive
acquiescence, or even the fawning approval, that in some fashionable
circles has become the mark of being 'with it.' . . . There is a growing, dangerous attitude among millions of people that all youth are like those who
appear night after night on the television screen shouting obscenities.

[They] reflect unfairly on those millions of students like those [here] who do go to college for an education."[*][41]

This was the Nixon strategy for the election: to isolate the far left and tie them to the mainstream Democrats, and set himself at the head of an ever-expanding and less silent majority. Most Americans did not believe that the lawless elements in the country were more than a small percentage of the population. They agreed with Nixon's attacks on them, and with his disparagements of the radical chic poseurs of New York, Washington, and California society. But they did not believe that Ed Muskie or even Teddy Kennedy were mollycoddlers of anarchists and bomb-throwers. Nixon was competing now with people who were a good deal more astute than Jerry Voorhis and Helen Gahagan Douglas. But with his approval rating at almost 60 percent twenty months after starting to cope with all the problems Johnson had dumped into his lap, he was not to be underestimated, as he so often had been in his career.

The Rogers Plan, which was not much of a plan as Kissinger had accurately foretold, came apart long before its ninety-day negotiating period expired. On September 6 and 9, a splinter Palestinian terrorist group seized five airliners and forced three of them to land on a deserted airstrip in Jordan. They threatened to kill all the passengers unless a large number of Palestinian detainees were released. Nixon ordered Laird to bomb a number of Palestinian guerrilla camps, but Laird ignored the order, telling Nixon there was bad weather in the Mediterranean.

This was rank insubordination, but Nixon knew better than to imagine that sophisticated American military aircraft could be stopped by inclement weather, so he was indulging his frequent practice of ordering tough countermeasures but not really insisting on them, as he had the Cambodian bombing, and later the Cambodian ground incursion. It was a bizarre method of operation, but senior administration officials, such as Laird,

---

[*] One surprising supporter of his remarks was Hubert Humphrey, who did not remember with nostalgia the extreme left attacks on him early in his campaign. Humphrey wrote to Nixon: "I congratulate you on a message that was needed and one that was stated with clarity, understanding and firmness. It is my view that the basic struggle in our own country today is not between the liberal and the conservative but rather between those few who would destroy our system, and those of us, liberal and conservative alike, who would seek to use it to make it work."

Kissinger, and Haig, had the experience of the president and the worldly confidence and intelligence to know when to take Nixon's orders seriously and when not.

Nixon constantly telephoned people in the middle of the night and demanded that thousands of people be dismissed, and on one occasion ordered Kissinger to have every employee of the State Department submitted to a lie-detector test. When Nixon was serious, he followed up orders and demanded they be executed. Almost all serious leaders engage in this practice to some degree, though Nixon was an overachiever. Franklin D. Roosevelt once ordered that the United States Marines occupy the *Chicago Tribune* building and that its publisher be charged with high treason. Winston Churchill, two nights before the invasion of Western Europe in Normandy, ordered (at 3 A.M.) that General de Gaulle be removed from Britain (the Connaught Hotel in fact) and taken to Algeria, "in chains." Needless to say, neither order was carried out.[42] Unfortunately, some of Nixon's political operatives, such as Colson and Magruder, had neither the confidence nor the conventional respect for proprieties to exercise a comparable discretion. The consequences for the administration would be lethal.

The atmosphere of mystery, suspicion, and backbiting in the senior realms of the government almost paralyzed it at times. The problems were aggravated by having a president who gave orders that were not really intended to be carried out. The ambiance of mistrust and dissembling was pervasive, and went far beyond Nixon and Kissinger tapping the telephones of supposedly trusted subordinates. In September 1970, the Joint Chiefs of Staff sent a stenographer to the National Security Council, Navy Yeoman Charles Radford, twenty-nine, whose real mission was to copy and send back to the Joint Chiefs every document he saw. This was outright espionage by the service chiefs on the president's national security adviser and his staff. It was a surreal and insalubrious atmosphere.[43]

While the United States did not bomb the Palestinian camps, the Palestinian guerrillas and the Royal Jordanian Army engaged in heavy skirmishing and even artillery fire in many parts of Amman, the Jordanian capital. This quickly flared into pitched warfare. Nixon went from his address in Kansas to Chicago, and Kissinger telephoned with news of the actions in Jordan, and Israeli and British intelligence reports that Syrian armor was massed on the Jordanian border. Haldeman did not want to wake up Nixon and took it upon himself to tell Kissinger to act in the president's name until the morning. When Nixon called back at 7 A.M. in Chicago, September 17, and Kissinger gave him the news that the Russians seemed to be encouraging the Syrians, who were encouraging the Palestinians, Nixon cheerfully commented, "There's nothing better than a little confrontation now and then, a little excitement."[44]

The Israelis walked out of the New York talks that were the principal result of the Rogers Plan, complaining about steady forward movement of Egyptian missile launchers. There was artillery fire across the idle Suez Canal. The Rogers Plan was a shambles. King Hussein suppressed the Palestinians and drove them out of Amman. Israel's Prime Minister Golda Meir arrived in Washington September 18, after Nixon had returned from Chicago, and came directly to the White House. She blamed Nixon personally for Israel's entering into a cease-fire that Israel respected but Egypt did not, violating it from the start with movements of missile-launchers into the cease-fire zone. She said that the declared goal of the Rogers Plan, essentially the 1967 borders, was impossible for Israel to accept because of the danger posed by the Golan Heights.

Of course, Israel had lived with those borders for nearly twenty years prior to the Six Day War in 1967, but Golda Meir and Yitzhak Rabin said that the insertion of advanced Soviet weaponry had made the former frontiers unmanageable. Nixon responded that he did not think he could force a withdrawal of Soviet weapons, but he could strengthen Israel's hand with enhanced arms sales and further credits to effect those sales at once. Nixon also agreed to Kissinger's suggestion, without at this point telling the Israelis about it, that Israel should, if necessary, shore up King Hussein against the Syrians.[45]

On September 20, Kissinger telephoned Haldeman, with the president at Camp David, to say that there were strong reports of a Syrian tank invasion of Jordan, but that Jordan seemed to have repulsed it and knocked out up to thirty Syrian tanks. Kissinger was concerned that Rogers, who was in New York, might meet with Dobrynin, or blunder into the UN meetings, and undercut the position Kissinger had, with the president's support, been taking opposite the U.S.S.R. in the Middle East since they all came into office. He was concerned that once Dobrynin got a look at Rogers, he would choose to deal with him rather than Kissinger, as a more malleable interlocutor, a "patsy," as he said. Rogers was certainly not a negotiator of

Kissinger's stature, but the Soviet ambassador would negotiate with whomever the president designated, and he had clearly designated Kissinger.

That evening, Nixon returned early from Camp David, amid reports that two hundred Syrian tanks had entered Jordan, and Kissinger telephoned Rabin in New York and told him that Israel should intervene in Jordan, and that Hussein would welcome that. Rabin was incredulous, with good reason. On September 21, Rabin replied that Israel was ready to intervene, on land and in the air, in Jordan. Nixon told Kissinger to tell the Israelis to do it, but Kissinger hesitated, in the Laird manner. By September 23, Hussein's forces had given the Syrians a good thrashing and chased them out of Jordan. The Syrian Air Force, despite some relatively advanced Russian planes, did not contest Jordanian air space and the Jordanian Air Force knocked out the Syrian tanks like sitting ducks. Hussein made it clear that he did not want Israeli intervention in his country.

These events were further complicated for the United States by developments in Latin America. On September 9, Chile gave Marxist presidential candidate Salvador Allende 36.3 percent of the vote in a three-way race, and eighty of two hundred members of its Congress. He was thus elected, the first communist to win a real national election in history, albeit with the anti-communist vote a split majority. From the start, the U.S. ambassador in Santiago, a ponderous and apocalyptic career diplomat, whom Nixon took for a partisan Democrat, Edward Korry, predicted disaster in rather graphic cables. (Nixon had met Korry in Ethiopia in 1967.) The CIA had contributed a million dollars to opposition activities, but this was a good deal less than the approximately twenty million dollars it had poured into the previous two elections, where Allende had also been the candidate of the left. There was considerable alarm in the White House that Allende could cause terrible problems in Latin America, subsidizing destabilization and promoting solidarity with Cuba throughout the region.

Nixon summoned Helms to a meeting with Kissinger, Haldeman, and Mitchell (who had had clients in Chile) on September 15 and told Helms to develop a plan that would be kept secret from the State and Defense Departments, to prevent Allende from being inaugurated, or to remove him if he was. Nixon said to take ten million dollars as a starting budget and be back to Kissinger by September 18 with a plan of action. The State Department, meanwhile, not apparently under any orders from the White House, was offering bribes to Chilean congressmen to vote against Allende's confirmation as president.

The CIA's initial plan was apparently to incentivize officers to kidnap the Chilean Army chief of staff, General René Schneider, for a few days while a coup d'état, which Schneider opposed, was carried out. At word of this, Edward Korry, who must have been aware of the unsavory bribery of congressmen, became aggressively unctuous and warned Washington that the CIA's antics would lead to a "Bay of Pigs failure . . . an unrelieved disaster."

Korry was summoned back to the United States in mid-October and met with Nixon and Kissinger. Korry told Nixon that he was "dead wrong," and that there were "mad men running around." He wanted to try to work with Allende, as he saw no other acceptable alternative. Korry was intelligent, articulate, and principled but the sort of irritating person who endlessly announces the imminence of the worst possible events and with equal emphasis declares that there is absolutely nothing that can be done about them. Nixon was outwardly calmer than Kissinger, but neither said anything that tipped their hand about their chosen course of action, and Korry was shown out and left to his jeremiads and squalid attempts to bribe congressmen.[46]

The CIA cabled its Santiago station that it was authorized to offer "material support short of armed intervention to the Chilean Armed Forces in any endeavors they may undertake to prevent the election of Allende on October 24."[47] On October 16, the CIA cabled its station chief, Henry Hekscher, that "It is firm and continuing policy that Allende be overthrown by a coup," preferably before October 24, "but efforts in this regard will continue vigorously beyond this date." The necessity for there to be no discernible link to the United States was emphasized.[48] There were kidnap attempts on Schneider on October 19 and 20, and on October 22 Schneider was assassinated in his car in congested traffic in Santiago by five men. Allende's election was confirmed by the Congress of Chile on October 24.

On September 18, Nixon was shown a CIA intelligence report that the Soviet Union appeared to be building a submarine base at Cienfuegos, Cuba. By September 23, with the Jordanians having repulsed the Syrians and the king having reasserted his authority, matters were brightening up, but Kissinger, always heavy-laden with Mitteleuropa rabbinical pessimism except when assured that he would have sole authority over a problem, revealed to Nixon his view that the Russian encouragement of Syria and the missile deployment in Egypt were just a smokescreen for the Russian move into Cuba. The apparent election of Allende added to the appearance of an intercontinental Soviet pincers movement. Kissinger compared it to 1962 and said that it could not be left until after the November election. Kissinger was wielding great authority in the president's name, and with panache and skill. He sent two aircraft carrier groups into the Mediterranean, ostentatiously airlifted military supplies to Turkey, and put the famous 82nd Airborne Division on alert in North Carolina, all to reinforce the dire warnings he had been giving to Dobrynin.[49]

Nixon had ordered complete silence on Cuba, not wishing "clown senators" demanding an invasion or blockade of Cuba (as he had insistently done with Eisenhower in 1960 and with Kennedy in 1962). In fact, he did not believe the Cienfuegos story, did not believe the Russians would risk a complete humiliation in Cuba, and did not think they were so well organized as to attempt the grand scheme Kissinger conjured, hinging on an attempted manipulation of the Middle East powder keg, where their Syrian protégé had, in fact, just been given a bloody nose.

Kissinger was convinced of the Cienfuegos story partly because aerial reconnaissance reported the construction of a football (soccer) stadium, and Kissinger thought the Cubans essentially played baseball, and the football facility would be for Russians. The Defense Intelligence Agency told Nixon that Cienfuegos was too shallow for nuclear submarines. No one told the Defense Department's spokesman that there was to be no discussion of Cienfuegos, and the story was referred to at a Pentagon press briefing on September 25. Kissinger then gave the press a further background briefing, but the major media outlets, after checking around the Pentagon, the White House, the State Department, and the CIA, concluded that the Cienfuegos base story was unlikely.

Dobrynin delivered to the White House a statement on October 6 denying that there had ever been a Soviet plan to build a submarine base in Cuba and reaffirming the commitment of the 1962 Cuban missile settlement. He promised removal of anti-aircraft batteries, suspension of suspicious construction, and confinement of Soviet Navy visits to Cuba to recreational and not resupply purposes. Kissinger gave a press briefing that alleged that the Soviets had backed down on what had been a start at such a base. To hedge his bets, he gave Nixon the credit for this diplomatic victory achieved by showing "unmistakable steel." Nixon had never believed there was a crisis in Cuba on this occasion, and the press wasn't really buying it either, but Kissinger's massive Soviet conspiracy expired in silence.[50]

In his memoirs, Nixon claims that a possible crisis of 1962 proportions was averted.[51] In his memoirs, Kissinger suggests that his and Nixon's quiet diplomacy had enabled the Soviet Union to retreat without public embarrassment, and also implies that a 1962-level crisis might otherwise have occurred. It will be difficult to establish what Soviet intentions really were at Cienfuegos. The port was far from ideal for a naval base, and the construction of such a base is much more time-consuming and difficult to disguise and less immediately provocative and dangerous to the United States than the installation of nuclear-tipped missile launchers was in 1962. (The soccer stadium did, indeed, turn out to be for the Russians. Kissinger, a future member of the World Cup committee, and a strong international football fan, had been correct in his suspicions.) What can be said is that however large a problem it might have become, it did not, and Kissinger and Nixon handled it, as they handled the Jordanian-Palestinian-Syrian crisis, well, and that both ended successfully.

— VI —

President Nixon flew to Rome on September 27 at the start of a European trip. The same day, the last of the hostages taken by the Palestinians on the airliners in Jordan were released and a truce was signed between Arafat and King Hussein in Cairo. Hussein's throne and a Palestinian presence in Jordan were both guaranteed, which ensured that the agreement would not last long, despite being witnessed by all the other Arab leaders.

On the flight to Rome, Nixon, according to Haldeman, asked him if he thought it was time to get rid of either Rogers or Kissinger. Haldeman thought not, and Nixon agreed but added that if one of them had to go it would have to be Kissinger, as he could be replaced by Haig. This was disinformation, intended to be passed back to Kissinger, even if only implicitly, to assure that he understood he was not indispensable. Since a combination of Kissinger's lucidity and relentlessness and Rogers's ineptitude had combined to assure Kissinger's preeminence over the emasculated secretary of state, it was necessary for Nixon to buff up Haig, who was only too happy to be the thrusting ranker for this purpose, as a possible alternative. Haig was an able combat officer, a good, efficient, and brave soldier, and a capable political infighter, but he did not have a fraction of Kissinger's intellectual subtlety or knowledge of the history and geography of the Great Powers. When he eventually became secretary of state three presidencies later, Haig was not successful.

Nixon met first with Pope Paul VI, on a simple courtesy call, and then went to the aircraft carrier *Saratoga* for what was intended to be a fireworks display and a general demonstration of the power of the U.S. Sixth (Mediterranean) Fleet. It was a pleasant sojourn, but the publicity of it was diminished by the sudden death, from a coronary, of Egypt's President Nasser, aged only fifty-two. Though militarily and economically ineffective, he had galvanized Arab opinion by seizing the Suez Canal, surviving the ill-considered British-Israeli-French attack, and starting construction of the Aswan Dam despite withdrawal of American financing for it. He had inspired the Arab masses with a vision of Arab renewal and pride that was more symbolic and embryonic than real. He was succeeded by his vice president, Anwar Sadat, of whom little was known or expected.

Nixon went on to Belgrade, where Tito told him the United States should withdraw from Vietnam, the U.S.S.R. should get out of Eastern Europe, and both should cease to interfere in the Middle East. It was a cordial, but not very productive, interview. The president was very warmly received by the Queen and the new prime minister, Edward Heath, in Britain, and spent a couple of pleasant days in Ireland, where he and Pat looked for evidence of ancestors. The party returned to Washington after a brief stop at Madrid on October 6. The semi-fascist Franco was more malleable and congenial than the old Communist Tito.

The midterm election campaign was reaching its climax. Nixon claimed in his memoirs that he had intended to sit the campaign out, but that when he returned from nine days in Europe, the polls had evaporated and the Republicans were staring down the barrel of a thirty-seat loss in the House and several in the Senate, where they had ambitions to make gains ten days before. He attributed this to the Democrats suddenly waking up to the necessity of pitching to the working class, lower-middle class, and Caucasian ethnics, and suspending their long dalliance with the limousine liberals and anti-American intellectuals. The best-selling political book of the time was Richard Scammon's and Ben Wattenberg's *The Real Majority*, which said that the real Democratic voter was a forty-seven-year-old machinist's wife from Dayton, Ohio.

On his return, Nixon determined to spike up the Republican campaign. No one would know it, but this would be the last time, after nearly twenty-five years, that Richard Nixon would be out on one of his rock'em, sock'em campaigns. They were not the most pristine or edifying manifestation of American political life, but after twelve biennial enactments, they had become a distinct national political institution, an almost folkloric, stand-alone genre of American electioneering.

Nixon's advice was for Agnew and other Republicans to do as he, Nixon, had always done, and praise the sincerity of opponents before consigning them to the category of radicals. "I don't question his sincerity – he deeply believes in this radical philosophy. . . . If the vice president were slightly roughed up by those thugs, nothing better could happen for our cause. If anybody so much as brushes against Mrs. Agnew, tell her to fall down. On the kid thing – strong against bomb-throwing. . . . Let others say that life is hard for the little bastards, that we should listen to them." He urged gestures to the Catholics and complete avoidance of discussion of abortion and Israel. He urged against pandering to the press by devising a new speech at every opportunity. Dewey had told him that people had to hear something at least four times before they remember it. "Lincoln gave the 'house divided' speech a hundred times before Cooper Union. Bryan made the Cross of Gold speech 259 times before the [1896] convention. . . . Fund-raising audiences are the flattest of all. They're rich and fat and drunk and dumb. You want to get on TV with the real people, not those sodden-looking old bastards."[52] This was vintage Nixon; good analysis rather humorously delivered. He could have starred on television programs sending up the reactionary working class and petite bourgeoisie, such as *All in the Family* and, later, *The Simpsons*. (In May 1971, Nixon watched an episode of *All in the Family* and was appalled that that "Arch square type" [Archie Bunker] was made to look bad compared to a homosexual friend of his children. "Is this common on television? Destruction of civilization to build homos?" he asked Haldeman.)[53]

On October 7, Nixon ratcheted up his Vietnam peace offers again and proposed a stand-still cease-fire in place. This did not really have the impact Nixon desired. The instant peace advocates, such as Senator George McGovern, who initially favored the proposal, thinking it was a throwing-in of the towel and outright American departure, turned against it when Nixon made it clear at a press conference the next day that force withdrawals had to be reciprocal with the North Vietnamese. Those who still believed in trying to avoid a communist South Vietnam were skeptical about a cease-fire proposal that in practice would lead to American but not North Vietnamese withdrawal, or, to the extent there was any North Vietnamese withdrawal, a strictly temporary one. Nixon thus got the worst of both worlds.

Hanoi immediately rejected it. Again, it is not clear why the North Vietnamese were unreceptive to all the American offers of the last four years, since Johnson's from Manila at this stage in the 1966 midterm election campaign. To the extent that their goal was not just the conquest and communization of South Vietnam, but also the military defeat and political implosion of the United States, there were two wars. North Vietnam ultimately failed at the second, and made a serious error overreaching to the point of trying to lay low the world's greatest power. In this sense, Nixon was absolutely correct when he concluded his silent majority speech on November 3, 1969: "North Vietnam cannot defeat or humiliate the United States. Only Americans can do that."

In this respect, the decent-interval strategy was a more meritorious strategy than it seemed. It may ultimately emerge that the quid pro quo for the blank check Hanoi received from Moscow and Beijing was to conduct this all-out effort to defeat and destabilize the United States. It is hard to imagine what else would have motivated even a regime as blasé about war deaths and injuries as Hanoi to stretch the war out sanguinary years beyond what would have been necessary to attain their declared objective of the expulsion of foreigners and "unification" of Vietnam. If Moscow and Beijing were behind the inflexibility of Hanoi, the Nixon strategy and the subtly different Kissinger strategy (i.e., respectively, a decent interval with a thin chance of a durable non-communist South Vietnam, and a decent interval with no such chance) are more defensible than they have been generally portrayed. Under any scenario, the Johnson administration exit strategy, to the extent it developed one at all, was an incoherent recipe for escalating disaster.

During the 1970 United Nations General Assembly meetings, Nixon had held White House dinners for Yahya Khan, president of Pakistan, whom he gave further messages for the Chinese that he would like to upgrade relations; and Romania's Nicolae Ceauşescu, whom Nixon cultivated, partly to send messages to the Chinese and partly just to aggravate the Russians.

There were some economic concerns. Unemployment was low, but inflation had risen from 3.3 percent to 5.5 percent under Nixon, and Arthur Burns, who had gone to the Federal Reserve chairmanship in January 1970, was a monetary conservative. Nixon urged him to expand the money supply, as he had urged during the 1954 and 1958 midterm elections, but Burns declined to do so (as Eisenhower had). There was virtually no economic growth through 1970. Indicators started to turn up in October, and there were not severe dislocations, but sluggishness is not the best economic condition for incumbents at election time.

On October 24, Nixon publicly took up the report of Johnson's National Commission on Obscenity and Pornography, which had been handed to him a couple of weeks earlier. The commission concluded that pornography did not contribute to crime, delinquency, or deviant behavior. Nixon thundered, "I have evaluated that report and I categorically reject its morally bankrupt conclusions. . . . Pornography can corrupt a society and a civilization. . . . Smut . . . should be outlawed in every state of the Union. . . . Pornography is to freedom of expression what anarchy is to liberty."[54]

This was the reemergence of the authoritarian Nixon, who had always believed that basic freedoms should be diminished or suspended in reference to anti-democratic movements like communists, and that the president and those acting in his name had a practically unlimited right to protect national security. He was, in these matters, less permissive even than most of his followers. Most Americans disapproved of pornography, but outlawing smut was almost certain to lead to arbitrariness and curtailment of freedom of expression on a scale that would make most Americans uneasy. In any case, there was no chance that what he was suggesting would be judged constitutional. He could have attacked the report, which was pretty naive and idealistic, and even insensitive to traditionalists, without ranting about the suppression of questionable or offensive literature, which enabled his opponents to conjure up thought police, intrusions into homes, book burnings, and so forth. Demagogy on such issues can easily be a two-edged sword.

In the last two weeks of the campaign, Nixon appeared in twenty-three states. He often focused on a few hecklers or wavers of confrontational or vulgar placards, and cited them as illustrative of the sort of intolerance and incivility that he attempted to hang around the neck of the Democrats. This was this year's "rock'em, sock'em" message. On October 29, he went from Chicago to Minnesota to Omaha, and on the next day to San Jose,

California. At the San Jose Auditorium, there were five thousand faithful Republicans, but as many as two thousand nasty and noisy demonstrators outside. "We wanted confrontation," wrote Haldeman, and he added that the president delayed leaving for several minutes to ensure that the demonstrators would be waiting. They were, and Nixon responded by standing on the running board of his car and giving them his outstretched-arms V sign, which brought a cascade of bricks and bottles down on the car. There were a lot of broken car windows and so forth. "Made a huge incident and we worked hard to crank it up."[55] Nixon represented it as the only time in history that a mob had ever attacked a president of the United States.

Nixon ended the day at San Clemente, but in trying to light the fire in his fireplace, he mismanaged the flue and smoke filled the house, setting off detectors and bringing the fire department. The president finally spent the night in his guest house while the main house was aired out. Nixon spoke two days later in an airplane hangar in Phoenix and gave a somewhat demagogic speech about the evils of mob rule. "Those who carry a PEACE sign in one hand and a bomb or a brick in the other are the super-hypocrites of our time."[56] He directed that his speech be excerpted on all three networks on election eve. The Democratic right of reply was given by Muskie, speaking calmly against fear-mongering from a rocking chair in his house at Kennebunkport, Maine. Nixon's Phoenix speech excerpt was not a success. It was grainy film, with poor acoustics in the hangar, and a message that was miscalibrated for the voters. The country was tired of confrontation and detected that Nixon was making more out of the San Jose incident than was justified. They did not approve of throwing rocks and bottles at the president's car, but Nixon would have done better allowing news film of the incident to speak for itself, and then giving the sort of address that Muskie did.

On November 3, the Republicans gained two Senate seats and lost nine House seats, a very respectable performance and certainly a sharp improvement on the thirty-seat loss Nixon claimed in his memoirs impended when he returned from Europe on October 6. John V. Tunney, son of the former heavyweight boxing champion and chum of Teddy Kennedy, defeated former vocalist and dancer George Murphy (who had himself defeated JFK's press secretary, Pierre Salinger, in 1964). George H.W. Bush, son of former senator Prescott Bush of Connecticut, lost to Democrat Lloyd M. Bentsen in Texas. James Buckley, running as a Conservative, defeated Charles Goodell in New York, whom Nixon particularly disliked and considered to be a pest inflicted upon him by Nelson Rockefeller. Two of the Democrats Nixon vividly disliked, Albert Gore of Tennessee (father of the future vice president and presidential candidate in 2000) and Richard Tydings of Maryland were defeated. Adlai Stevenson (son of the two-time Democratic presidential candidate who had died in 1965, aged sixty-five) won narrowly in Illinois. In Minnesota, Eugene McCarthy had not sought renomination, and Hubert Humphrey came back for a fourth term and became the only person in history to hold both Senate seats for any state.

There would now be 55 Democrats and 45 Republicans in the Senate, and a margin of 254 to 181 in the House of Representatives. The Democrats picked up 11 governorships, and would now hold 29 to 21 Republicans. But the two star Republican governors, in the country's two most populous states, Ronald Reagan and Nelson Rockefeller, were easily reelected in California and New York. Reagan defeated the State Assembly speaker, Jesse ("Big Daddy") Unruh, by over a million votes, and Rockefeller did the same against former Supreme Court justice and UN ambassador Arthur Goldberg. It was a respectable performance by the Republicans, but they might have done a little better if Nixon had been a little less discordant. Nixon was confident that in two years the economy would be flying and the country would be out, or almost out, of Vietnam.

Nixon moved fairly promptly to shuffle his cabinet. David Kennedy went quietly from Treasury, having been a tight-money advocate through to the election. In fact, Nixon should have overruled him and he had himself to blame. Burns was immovable at the Federal Reserve and there was not much Nixon could have done about the money supply, but he could have just ordered Kennedy to agree to spend more and sought the funding from the Congress. He was replaced as Treasury secretary by John Connally, the former governor of Texas and protégé of LBJ, who was injured in the assassination of John F. Kennedy. He was the sort of tall, firm-voiced, confident person who always impressed Nixon, provided he actually knew what he was talking about and was not just a blowhard. Connally was a competent and forceful man, as an administrator and a politician. Nixon had been impressed with his performance at the President's Advisory Council on Executive Organization, chaired by Roy Ash, which had set up the Bureau of Management and Budget, now headed by George Schultz.

Walter Hickel, as was described earlier, was unloaded, as the delay fuse from his public letter to Nixon after the Cambodia incursion finally reached the powder keg of Nixon's irritation with him. He was succeeded by the chairman of the Republican National Committee, Rogers Morton. Nixon had determined to name Moynihan ambassador to the UN, and Moynihan had accepted, but the story leaked in the *Boston Globe* after Moynihan advised his Harvard colleagues, and no one had got around to advising the incumbent ambassador, Charles Yost, or Mrs. Moynihan. Yost's friends at the Council on Foreign Relations mounted a campaign against Moynihan as underqualified, and Mrs. Moynihan did not want to live in New York. Moynihan withdrew and Nixon gave the position to his recent senatorial candidate in Texas, George H.W. Bush, and ignored what Yost and the Council on Foreign Relations might think about it. He had offered Bush the position of party chairman, replacing Morton, but Bush wanted the UN and told Nixon there wasn't enough advocacy on his behalf in New York and he could deal with this, officially and socially, and Nixon gave him the job.[57] Senator Robert Dole of Kansas became the party chairman.

More of a problem was George Romney, whom Nixon found time-consuming, tiresome, and overenergetic in trifling matters. Romney refused to go without talking to Nixon, who delegated Mitchell to get rid of him. Romney promised to cease the activities that Nixon said annoyed him, and he hung on. Nixon had begun the task of materially strengthening his cabinet. Connally and Morton were a substantial improvement on Kennedy and Hickel.

On November 21, U.S. helicopters landed twenty miles from Hanoi and soldiers went through the Son Tay prison camp. Unfortunately, it had been evacuated a few days before and no prisoners were rescued. But the United States demonstrated the flexibility of its mobile forces. More important, Nixon, who had personally approved the operation, ordered a covering two-day bombing campaign that penetrated two hundred miles north of the demilitarized zone (DMZ). At his year-end press conference, December 10, in an answer to a question from veteran UPI journalist Helen Thomas, Nixon said that he would order resumed bombing of North Vietnam at any time when it appeared necessary to cover the retirement of American forces and protect the reducing number remaining in South Vietnam as Vietnamization progressed.[58]

On December 15, according to Haldeman, Kissinger visited Nixon and the president suggested that the following April he might go to Vietnam, tour around the country boosting Thieu, and then announce a complete withdrawal. Kissinger suggested this could lead to a South Vietnamese collapse before the 1972 election, and that any such pullout should be held to just prior to the election, to assure that there was no chance of an electoral backlash. When he left, again according to Haldeman, Nixon said of Kissinger, somewhat admiringly, "He's a devious bastard." As always, Haldeman must be read with some caution. Nixon would not have needed Kissinger to warn him of military risks in Vietnam and the political consequences domestically. If Nixon had made any such announcement in April 1971, it would have taken almost to election day to get the men out anyway, so it is unlikely that Kissinger was addressing a real concern, or that Nixon described him so graphically, at least not because of any such opinion as Haldeman recorded.[59]

On December 9, after telling Haldeman that he might have to resign because Rogers had met with Israel's defense minister, Moshe Dayan, without asking him to join them, Henry Kissinger met with the Pakistani ambassador, Agha Hilaly. The ambassador handed over a letter from President Yahya Khan, notes of a conversation he had had with Chou En-lai, in which Chou said that it would be quite in order for a senior American representative to come to Beijing to discuss the status of Taiwan. Yahya added that Taiwan was obviously only a pretext and that the Chinese wanted to discuss a range of issues.[60] Kissinger immediately went to see Nixon, with no talk of resignation, and after an animated conversation, began composing a reply that proposed a discussion of "the broad range of issues between" the two countries.

Kissinger felt that even at this moment, when Nixon could see the likely fruition of his pursuit of a relationship with China, two years into a presidency that had clearly been quite successful and when the president was well-regarded by most of his countrymen and in the world, he had no joy, and seemed conditioned always to be confounded by fate and ultimately defeated by his opponents. This was Kissinger, no mean subject of psychiatric speculation himself, taking liberties. Nixon controlled his emotions, and was always wary, but it was more complicated than Kissinger suggested. Nixon thought that he was doomed to be traduced, double-crossed, unjustly harassed, misunderstood, underappreciated, and subjected to the trials of Job, but that by the application of his mighty will, tenacity, and diligence he would ultimately prevail.

He did not have, as many have presumed to suggest, a death wish, but rather a resignation to setbacks and an implacable determination to surmount them. This is rarer, and Kissinger had only known Nixon for two years, but this was part of the mystery of Nixon: he was rare. He seemed ordinary, and attracted the support of tens of millions of ordinary people, but he was not ordinary. He was extremely intelligent, cunning, aloof, unknowable, and demiurgically determined, all masquerading and lurking behind a somewhat ordinary exterior and often banal or even uncouth articulation.

He was not a happy or mirthful person, and the evening after the December 10 press conference, he wrote letters to editors attacking insolent questioners at his press conference, and told Haldeman to find people to sign and send them. The attacks of the press hurt him deeply, as did many things; he endured endless wounds, and was never assuaged by the great honors and successes he achieved. But this was his view of the world, or at least of the only way he could make his way in the world.[61]

Elvis Presley visited the White House on December 21, 1970, having arrived in Washington and sent over a letter asking for an appointment. In the note, Presley made the point that he was not regarded by protesters and drug-addicted people as a figure of "the establishment, I call it America, and I love it." He offered his help in any way he could assist in combating drugs. Nixon had him invited over and he arrived in a frilly white silk shirt, tight dark-velvet trousers and cape, and sunglasses. Toward the end of their very cordial interview, in which, at one point, they were both rummaging through the president's desk looking for a presidential curio for Elvis, Nixon said that his visitor was rather flamboyantly dressed. The all-time most popular single recording artist and showman replied, "Mr. President, you dress for your job, and I dress for mine." His offer to help with drugs was vague and based on his high acceptance level with people who would be skeptical of the administration. Unfortunately, Elvis was himself a chronic drug abuser, who was said to use a great variety of prescription and illegal drugs. He was not a credible bearer of the message, but his motives were sincere. Nothing came of the meeting, which ended shortly after Elvis hugged the president. The official photograph of this meeting is the most frequently requested of all the innumerable photographs in the National Archives.

The same day, December 21, the administration's official report card on itself was circulated at the cabinet meeting. The highlights were: reduction of force levels in Vietnam by nearly 40 percent, and casualties by nearly 90 percent, real and not oratorical desegregation, and the end of mass urban violence and most civil disobedience and protest. The frequent hijackings of airliners were stopped by placing FBI agents on flights. Nixon was the most effective president of all in combating illegal drug use, and this was later reflected in declining crime figures.[62] Richard Nixon, even while he tried to stir up animosities against groups that he rather unjustly attached to the Democrats in his more florid oratorical moments, had settled the country down a great deal in two years.

The former president, Lyndon Johnson, had not been able to travel in the country without protest. There had been no end in sight in Vietnam, and there was disillusionment with much of Johnson's Great Society. Now there was a substantially executed exit strategy in Vietnam, a draft revenue-sharing plan, a proposal for welfare reform (an idea a little ahead of its time), accelerating desegregation, a serious emerging environmental policy, and the ingredients of a new and comprehensive foreign policy regarding arms control, China, and the Middle East. Richard Nixon was as far from being a serene personality as it was possible for an effective holder of his office to be, but he had largely calmed a feverish nation.

Chapter Twelve

Waging Peace
1971–1972

— I —

ONE OF PRESIDENT NIXON'S first initiatives of the New Year 1971 was to tell Chuck Colson to get out a contradiction of a story in a South Carolina newspaper that he must have set a record among presidents in time spent over the holidays watching televised football games. Nixon was concerned that this would make him appear too much of a jock and inattentive to his job. It is, as so often with him, astounding that he would show concern for anything so irrelevant.

Nixon was steadily spreading his political umbrella, and told Howard K. Smith of ABC News on January 7 that he was a "Keynesian." This, coupled with his Family Assistance Plan for welfare reform and his steady withdrawals from Vietnam, showed a quite different Nixon to the one the caricaturists and rabidly partisan Democrats, in politics and the media, had been portraying for years. Only in some of his law-and-order pronouncements and postures, his pre-midterm-election speech, and the ever more discordant ravings of Agnew (who had clearly reached his sell-by date) did Nixon approach the morbid expectations of his ideological enemies and his more primitive supporters.

Great public relations emphasis was placed on a "reordering of priorities," as the ratio between defense and what was called "human resource spending" changed from 1968 to the projection for 1971 from 32-48 to 41-37.[1] In the Nixon presidential years, federal government direct payments to individual citizens in benefits such as Social Security and Medicare, rose from 6.3 percent of GNP to 8.9 percent of a 25 percent larger GNP; public assistance and aid in food rose from $6.6 billion to $9.1 billion; and defense spending declined from 9.1 percent to 5.8 percent of GNP, even as the United States started to surpass the U.S.S.R. in strategic weapons and moved on arms control. And Nixon's revenue sharing program changed federal-local relationships constructively and sent over $80 billion back to states and municipalities, until the program ended with the tax reform of 1986.[2]

Nixon celebrated his fifty-eighth birthday in San Clemente, and in his State of the Union message a few days later he laid out his New American Revolution, based on welfare reform, revenue sharing, environmental renewal, and improved health care. He was not optimistic about getting much of this adopted in the new Congress but was satisfied that he had laid out an excellent program for reelection purposes; to the extent it passed, it would serve him well, and to the extent it was voted down by the Democrats, it was just as useful electorally. Nixon announced that more than a hundred Great Society programs would be ended, but that sixteen billion dollars in tax revenues would be funneled back to the states to enable them to continue the programs, amend them, or replace them with other spending or debt reduction or tax rebates. With welfare reform as with comprehensive tax reductions, Nixon was ahead of his time, and had been since the Eisenhower era, when he was a voice in the wilderness in both areas.

As Nixon was preparing the annual foreign policy statement, the so-called "State of the World" report, he worked with William Safire on refining it and revealed again, though he did not want to put it in the text, that he was loath to abandon the Vietnam effort for which forty-five thousand Americans had died. He realized that most Americans wanted out on increasingly unconditional terms. Everyone was saddened at the terrible loss of life and hundreds of thousands of casualties the armed forces had sustained, but there was a division between those who thought the sacrifice beyond redemption, like Kissinger, and those, like Nixon, who thought something useful might yet be salvaged.

He said to Safire, after describing certain differences with Kissinger over the Middle East, differences Nixon largely ascribed to the fact that it was still a State Department policy area: "God, I hate spending time with intellectuals. There's something feminine about them. I'd rather talk to an athlete." This was a revealing statement, as Nixon was never a lady's man and generally found women too emotional, sentimental, and unstable.

This is not to say that Nixon was never sentimental himself, but he was unpredictably, almost quirkily sentimental. In April 1971, he read in his news summary, which contained quite a range of esoteric items, of a karate expert who set out to break a world record of 2,056 bricks with one hand, and hoped to raise a dollar for each brick to be contributed to children suffering from kidney illnesses. He broke the bricks, but also broke his hand, and raised only three hundred dollars. Nixon told Haldeman to send him one hundred dollars for his own account personally.[3] As with his handicapped friend at Duke Law School, Fred Cady, Nixon identified with truly disadvantaged people, with people who strove nobly and failed, and often with conditions of pathos.

He considered himself something of an intellectual strictly in terms of knowledge and interests, but not in temperament. Although he was a relatively joyless person, who came alive like a child at moments of celebration of events, like the splashdowns of expeditions to the moon, his moods were fairly steady, if not uproariously buoyant.

From mid-January, Nixon was engaged in planning a move to cut the Ho Chi Minh Trail, by moving west from the DMZ through Laos. Everyone with any military or strategic insight, from Eisenhower to (belatedly) Westmoreland to Kissinger, had realized that this was the only way to produce a satisfactory result in the war. As long as the North was able to pour reinforcements down the trail and didn't have any interest in the extent of its casualties, there was no possibility of a positive outcome to the war.

The Cooper-Church amendment denied congressionally approved financing for any action in Laos, so Nixon accepted a plan in which the United States would serve only in support roles, in South Vietnam. Westmoreland had foreseen using four divisions, and it was one of Johnson's greatest strategic errors that he didn't approve it. The new plan, known as Lam Son, since it had to be conducted by ARVN, was to employ only one division. How anyone imagined that one ARVN division could cut the Ho Chi Minh Trail is completely incomprehensible and illustrates that the high command was suffering from political, if not battlefield, shell-shock. It was an insane plan with no chance of success.

The idea was that the ARVN division would give a good account of itself and that this would prove the merits of Vietnamization. The real rationale for Lam Son was not really to cut the trail permanently, as Eisenhower and Westmoreland had had in mind, but to reduce the flow of supplies sufficiently to ensure that there was no major offensive in the South before the U.S. election twenty-one months away. The American strategy in Vietnam had in fact become essentially a decent-interval gambit, with a concern for the possibility of making a fighting, Dunkirk-like departure. Nixon had nostalgic and uncharacteristically vigorous flights of optimism about ARVN taking over, but it is doubtful whether he, in his more sensible moods, or anyone else, believed it.

Lam Son was divided into four phases – U.S. road construction to the Laotian border and setting up of artillery fire bases on the border; invasion by ten thousand ARVN troops toward the town of Tchepone; the encirclement of Tchepone and destruction of all the supplies and trails nearby; and in phase four, withdrawal after up to six weeks. Admiral Moorer, the chairman of the Joint Chiefs, predicted that the North Vietnamese (NVA) would fight and that American air power could do great damage to them. Even if everything had worked as planned, it would have been only a covering operation to slow down the North Vietnamese while the United States completed its withdrawal. It was not a plan for victory.

Nixon was careful to consult Rogers and Laird. He did not want the sort of evident disunity that afflicted the Cambodia incursion. He also determined that Rogers, who was quite fluent and persuasive with the press, could take the public lead on this operation. The run-up to Lam Son was so prolonged and laborious that there was no surprise at all, in America or Indochina. Nixon finally ordered phase 2, the ARVN invasion, on February 3, when he had Kissinger, Haldeman, Mitchell, and Connally (of whom Kissinger was the only one who had anything to do with Vietnam matters) into the study adjacent to the Oval Office and undressed to his underwear and had a massage from his chiropractor. The discussion continued, and when the chiropractor left, Nixon resumed the chair in his underwear and ordered the launch of phase 2.[4] The fact that it was unleashed by someone so unimpressively accoutered could have been taken as a foretaste of the campaign to come.

Nixon, Kissinger, and Haldeman went to Camp David for the weekend, but Nixon sought solitude, and dined and bowled (his singular recreation at Camp David) alone. It was not obvious what the reason was for inviting the other two, who would have been happy to stay at home. The South Vietnamese finally jumped off on February 8. They made good progress for ten days, but then North Vietnamese withdrawn from nearer Saigon attacked from the south, which had not been expected. Nixon pressured Saigon to commit more forces, and Thieu augmented his troop-strength so he had thirty thousand men facing forty thousand North Vietnamese, but he also had strenuous air support from the United States.

ARVN put up a respectable fight but were outnumbered by the best enemy units and were unable to advance. Nixon himself devised the stratagem of helicoptering some ARVN units forward into Tchepone, which had been leveled by U.S. air strikes, so a claim could be made of a South Vietnamese victory. This was what happened, and the press, for a few days, bought the official version of ARVN success. But then the retreat was launched, and the NVA demonstrated their mastery of the jungles. They played electronic tricks on ARVN and managed to call in American air strikes against them, and shot down two hundred U.S. helicopters. There was extremely embarrassing and unbecoming news film of ARVN, very bedraggled, clinging desperately to the runners of American evacuation helicopters. The American media got a pretty good view of the blood-stained, panic-stricken wreckage of ARVN's expeditionary force as it streamed and ran and straggled out of Laos.

Nixon continued to defend the operation as a success, against a barrage of press skepticism. In their memoirs, both Nixon and Kissinger still defended it as a sensible and reasonably successful effort. In fact, it was a fiasco and had no chance of being otherwise. Moorer should have been sacked and Kissinger excluded from military planning for producing such a hare-brained idea as that the NVA would allow ten thousand ARVN troops to cut their supply line from the north. Vietnam was an uphill fight anyway, since the enemy, as Le Duc Tho pointed out, had held its own while there were half a million American servicemen in Vietnam. It was going to be much harder as the Americans had begun what was obviously an irreversible withdrawal. Prospects could not be helped by committing to offensives that dangled ARVN units in front of the NVA like a fatted calf to a hungry and seasoned predator in the most vital supply route of the theater.

Oddly, there is no evidence that Nixon drew suitable conclusions from this episode. He seems not to have reproached any of the planners, and he blamed the television networks for, as he would have it, harping on ARVN's unrepresentative shortcomings. To the end of his days, he stayed in lockstep with Kissinger, repeating the fiction that Lam Son had succeeded.

The trial of My Lai massacre defendant Lieutenant William Calley ended on March 29, 1971, with a guilty verdict and a sentence of life imprisonment at hard labor. The jurors were all Vietnam veterans, who said afterward that they tried to find grounds for giving Calley the benefit of the doubt. Nixon noted that polls showed the country disapproved the massacre but thought Calley was being unfairly singled out. Nixon immediately ordered Moorer to release Calley from the stockade at Fort Benning and let him stay in his apartment on base while the appeal was being heard. Nixon wanted to send the message that massacres were not tolerable but that officers must be given some leeway, given the nature of the war, where the enemy was hard to identify. On this small initiative, Nixon's own polls showed his personal approval rating climb an astounding thirteen points, back into the mid-sixties.

Nixon said he would personally review the Calley case. The prosecutor, Captain Aubrey W. Daniel, wrote Nixon on April 8 to complain that "many people across this nation have failed to see the moral issue . . . that it is unlawful for an American soldier to summarily execute unarmed and unresisting men, women, and children, and babies." He declared it "more appalling" that political leaders, obviously including the commander in chief, did not grasp those issues.[5] In a taped conversation with Kissinger on the morning of April 8 in the Oval Office, Nixon told Kissinger, "I've now figured the Calley thing . . . the generals are really worried . . . because they realize that what it is, is an animal instinct in this country that they're digging and most of those people don't give a shit if he killed them or not."

There was a division between the military, which felt its honor was besmirched by an officer claiming that his orders that "they're all enemies" was a mandate to massacre unarmed women and children, and much of the country, which felt the whole war was a disaster and Calley was a scapegoat. The military were closer to the truth, and Nixon was correct when he said that over 1.5 million Americans had served without blemish and often with bravery and generosity in Vietnam. His somewhat blasé attitude about the massacre itself is a worrisome comment on what happened to Nixon's moral sense in a war crisis.

The appeal process gradually reduced Calley's sentence and Nixon eventually pardoned him for time served. He was paroled in November 1974. Calley himself was a rather unimpressive little man who did not evidently possess the qualities to be an officer. It is not the task of biographers to try to be unlimitedly Solomonic, but three years of what amounted to house arrest seems a light sentence for such an offense, as life at hard labor seems extreme. But at least the country faced the issue and did not try to sweep it under the carpet. All, including Nixon, did what they thought was best. William Calley returned to civilian life as manager of his father-in-law's jewelry store.

On April 9, Nixon gave another televised address on Vietnam. He announced that he would withdraw another 100,000 men in 1971, reducing the total in that country to 184,000 by the end of the year. He again proclaimed the success of the Laos incursion, saying that it had severely disrupted the NVA supply chain, a complete canard, which enabled him to make the announced withdrawals. He even compared the Laos operation favorably with the Cambodian one, in order to "report that Vietnamization has succeeded." Hanoi had less reason to negotiate seriously than ever, since the U.S. was withdrawing almost as quickly as logistics would allow, and the NVA had shown what its commanders thought of Vietnamization during Lam Son.

As Nixon watched the media treatment of the Lam Son offensive and retreat, and noted the antics of Laird, Rogers, and Kissinger, appropriating credit and dodging blame, he concluded that he had been mistaken in taking out Johnson's taping equipment. So suspicious was the president of his chief collaborators that he wished to record conversations to maintain the historical record. Unlike Johnson, who had had the Army Signal Corps perform this function, Nixon did not want the existence of the system known in the Pentagon, and had Haldeman assign the task to the Secret Service, which installed the system at night and was responsible for storing and changing reels. Recording devices were placed in the president's office and office telephones, in the Cabinet Room, and later on the White House residence telephone and in the main room at Camp David. It was a voice-operated system, and easy to forget that it was in place after it had started to function. This would be, along with the indiscriminate taping policy he would follow and the use he made of the tapes, a momentous decision.

The anti-war movement came back to life in the early spring of 1971. Future senator and presidential candidate John Kerry led Vietnam Veterans against the War, and issued orders and bulletins mimicking and mocking Pentagonese and Nixon's own main speeches on the subject. They announced "an incursion . . . for the limited purpose of severing the supply lines currently being utilized by the illegal mercenary forces of the Executive Branch." Like some of the Chicago demonstration leaders of 1968, they had a sense of humor that was a refreshing contrast at times to the heavy-handed official earnest of the administration.

On April 23, seven hundred of the veterans, one by one, threw away combat medals and ribbons they had won in Vietnam at a site near the Capitol. A new organization, calling itself the National Peace Action Coalition, produced a peaceful demonstration of two hundred thousand in Washington and substantial peaceful demonstrations in other cities. Haldeman claims that on receiving a new White House poll showing support for the war slipping another 3 percent, Nixon, who was hoping to dump Agnew and replace him in 1972 with Connally, said he might "have to crank the vice president up again."[6]

On April 25, a new and more militant group became ascendant among the demonstrators, who had been marching around Washington for ten days, reasonably peacefully but generally making a nuisance of themselves. They had the air of aggrieved people who had taken a lot of trouble to get there and did not feel that they were being taken seriously.

A group styled the Mayday Tribe had announced its intention of "shutting down the government." It was led by Rennie Davis, the thirty-two-year-old former chief organizer of the 1968 Chicago demonstrations. Davis had an unusual career, coming to Chicago from a rural background at the age of sixteen on a 4-H chicken-judging contest. He had an impressive academic background, and joined the Vietnam protest movement, becoming Chicago director of community action for the Students for a Democratic Society, an extreme radical, and frequently violent, organization. (After Vietnam, Davis became a stockbroker, a venture capitalist, and ultimately a successful lecturer in meditation and self-understanding. It was not a unique career trajectory among the radicalized American youth of the Vietnam era.)

By April 27, there were demonstrators dressed as Vietnamese peasants darting through the halls of the Congress, some of them mouthing rather witty slogans and epithets, and the mischief factor was rising. Nixon departed for San Clemente and told a press briefing on May 1: "We are going to see to it that thousands of government workers who have a right to work peacefully are not interfered with by those . . . few militants, who in the name of demonstrating for peace abroad presume that they have the right to break the peace at home."[7]

It was May Day and the federal government was ready for Davis's Mayday Tribe. Nixon gave Mayor Daley an ex post facto lesson in intelligent riot control. The showdown came on Monday, May 3, 1971. Protesters moved in large groups to block the roads and bridges into Washington. They lay down in the automobile lanes and rolled in other obstacles – garbage cans, construction materials, heavy objects of all kinds – to stop traffic. The government had called in employees for 5 A.M., so many were already at their offices and functioning when the scuffles and then pitched battles began on the approaches to Washington. On the roads, seven thousand demonstrators were arrested without charge and taken to the fenced parking lots of Robert F. Kennedy Stadium and detained without food, shelter, or sanitation facilities. In the evening, they were transported under armed guard to the indoor Washington Coliseum. The demonstrators caused the closing of the Capitol building to visitors, but that was all. There were no serious injuries and no use of tear gas.

On the second day of Davis's assault, nearly twenty-seven hundred people were arrested around the Justice Department, with a pipe-smoking John Mitchell looking down expressionlessly from his balcony. That evening, traffic was normal out of the city. Most of the detainees at the coliseum had been released. Davis, Abbie Hoffman, and the politically opinionated baby doctor, Benjamin Spock, were among those arrested. On May 5, there were more than eleven hundred arrests around the Capitol, and demonstrations of some size in a number of other cities – over a hundred thousand people in New York and San Francisco.

The White House won a clear success, although many of the twelve thousand people arrested were arrested illegally. Neither the government nor its more energetic opponents were paying much attention to legalities at this point, a climate of disregard for the law that would ramify very far in the next year or so. Chuck Colson had sent a case of oranges to the detainees at RFK Stadium, with the card: "Best of luck, Senator Edmund S. Muskie."[8] The government was not impaired and the country was not really behind the demonstrators. These were fringe groups and as the casualties and draft calls came down, the nation could not be roused to go to the barricades to scuttle the whole mission and evacuate the remaining Americans in

Vietnam a few months before they would be gone if Hanoi's outrageous terms were accepted. Polls showed that over 70 percent of Americans approved of the administration's handling of the Mayday Tribe and the mass arrests. Despite the results of the November elections, the country wasn't ready to dispense with law and order. They just didn't think that Ed Muskie and most other leading Democrats were soft on mob rule.

— II —

Chou En-lai had visited Hanoi in February 1971 to show solidarity during the Lam Son imbroglio, and the Chinese officially denounced the United States in the usual terms. But on April 6, at the end of the international table tennis championships in Japan, the captain of the Chinese team invited the American team to a week of demonstration competition in China. The man who extended the invitation did not know, any more than the Americans did, that the instruction to take this initiative through this quaint channel came from Mao Tse-tung himself.

Kissinger, who floridly exploited and amplified the theatrical character of the stirrings of Sino-American rapprochement, even beyond their legitimate drama and importance, later wrote of the opening actions that they were "so delicately arranged that both sides could always maintain that they were not in contact, so stylized that neither side needed to bear the onus of an initiative, so elliptical that existing relationships on both sides were not jeopardized."[9] Kissinger settled effortlessly into the world-weary hyperbole of Chinese parlance. He would describe in a memorandum to Nixon his experience of the initial phases of the opening to China as having "had all the flavor, texture, variety and delicacy of a Chinese banquet. Prepared from the long sweep of tradition and culture, meticulously cooked by the hands of experience, and served in splendidly simple surroundings, our feast consisted of many courses, some sweet and some sour, all interrelated and forming a coherent whole."[10]

This was a wild flight of poetic exaggeration. He was describing an eerily secret visit of great geopolitical significance, but the modalities and the stilted dialogue could scarcely have been more mundane. To start with, neither Kissinger nor Nixon much cared for Chinese food.

By the time Mao Tse-tung ordered the invitation of the U.S. table tennis team to China, he had taken note of Nixon's subtle overtures, via

Pakistan, Romania, and in Warsaw, his references to the People's Republic of China (instead of Communist or just Red China), and the various hints he had dropped. Mao had read Nixon's article in *Foreign Affairs* in 1967 and commended it to Chou En-lai.[11] China had received many requests for visas to visit from increasingly prominent Americans, including Senate Majority Leader Mike Mansfield (transmitted by the deposed and exiled Sihanouk). The Chinese never responded to any of it. If they were going to deal with anyone, they would deal with the administration at the highest level. Mao and Chou were old men, who had no interest in the factions of American politics and society.

The Chinese reciprocated the treasure hunt trail of hints at accessibility. Two giants were almost indiscernibly winking and twitching at each other across a crowded and unobservant world. Shortly after the American withdrawal from Cambodia in July 1970, an American clergyman was released after twenty unprovoked years in jail in China. (He was carried to Hong Kong on a stretcher and died before getting any farther.) The timeless Vernon Walters, general, ambassador, and intelligence officer, was now the military attaché in Paris, and carried on a liaison with the Chinese military attaché in Paris, General Fang Wen, who deluged him with dried apricots, a fruit Walters disliked, but put in his safe to avoid a security problem.[12]

On October 1, 1970, Mao had Edgar Snow accompany him on the Tiananmen Square reviewing stand for the birthday of the shared hero of Nationalist and Communist Chinese, Chiang Kai-shek's brother-in-law, Sun Yat-sen. Mao gave Snow an extensive interview, in which he was relatively conciliatory toward the United States. This was too obscure a signal for the Americans; Mao may have regarded Snow as a Westerner, but the Americans considered him a U.S.-born European communist. (Nixon claims in his memoirs that the United States knew about the Snow interview a few days after it had been given, and long before it was published. Kissinger wrote in his memoirs that the United States did not hear about it for several months.)[13]

When Yahya Khan carried the first message to Chou En-lai in November, Chou was impressed that finally the hints and signals had reached the stage of "head to head to head" of the governments involved.[14] These messages via Pakistan were very labor-intensive: the Pakistani ambassador took down the utterances of Chou or Kissinger or Nixon, and gave his notes to Yahya, who had them retranscribed for his ambassador to the other capital.

The invitation to the table tennis team was only sent after Mao first accepted a cautious recommendation of Chou's not to invite the American team, which had, on its own, requested an invitation. As he was dozing off, heavily sedated, and accompanied as he was at that hour of the day by his young female helpers, Mao suddenly sat up in his bed and required that the American table tennis team be invited.[15] The invitation was accepted, and the Chinese allowed a number of American media people to accompany the fifteen team members. These were the first visits of ordinary American citizens to China in twenty years, and of newsmen in over twenty years. The Ping-Pong players met Chou En-lai, who said, "You have opened a new chapter in the relations of the American and Chinese people."

He predicted that both peoples would approve what he called "this beginning again of our friendship." He could certainly speak for his side, and the fact of receiving a group of Ping-Pong players so exaltedly and addressing them as portentously as he did left the watching world in no doubt that something was stirring between the two countries. The Chinese even showed the courtesy of fielding a second team, so they won less one-sidedly than they would have with their very best players, as this was a sport where the Chinese were considerably more talented than the Americans.

A long-haired hippie member of the American team, Glen Cowan, asked Chou what he thought of the hippie movement. Chou managed a rather indulgent comment that youth sought change and did not easily find the ways to achieve it, and Cowan assured him that the hippies were "very deep." Chou responded that it was necessary to harness the spirit to material force, and wound down the exchange. Cowan's mother tried to send Chou flowers, and Cowan tried briefly to continue to reside in China, which he thought "less regimented than the U.S." (He would not have made a very good Red Guard.)[16]

Nixon skillfully answered questions about China at a meeting of newspaper editors at the Shoreham Hotel on April 16, and said that it would take a long time to make any breakthrough in relations with that country but that it was a worthwhile long-term objective. Nixon did well, and did his usual afterpiece of calling people and asking them how they thought his press meeting had gone. Also as usual, Kissinger, Haldeman, Rose Woods, Rogers, and the other usual canvassees volunteered that he had done well. He made the point that one person he called had asked what he thought of when he awakened at 3 A.M., and that while he had said that his thoughts then turned to world peace, the true answer would have been "going to the bathroom."[17]

Three days later, on April 19, Agnew attended the Republican Governors' Conference at Williamsburg, Virginia. Agnew had some of the journalists to his suite afterward and said he was disgusted with all the talk of an opening to China, which he entirely opposed. Agnew was not in the inner councils of the administration, had no idea what the president intended with China, and was not astute enough to read the tea leaves, as much of the world was doing with greater accuracy. The off-the-record session was widely publicized the next day and Nixon told Ziegler to issue a statement that the vice president supported the president's policy and to tell Agnew that supporting the president was the vice president's job.

At the end of April, *Life* finally ran its story based on Edgar Snow's recent visit to Mao and Chou, in which he learned that Nixon would be welcomed to China by Mao Tse-tung, "as president or as a tourist." Pakistani ambassador Agha Hilaly had delivered another note from Chou En-lai: "The Chinese government reaffirms its willingness to receive publicly in Peking a special envoy of the president of the United States (for instance Mr. Kissinger), or the U.S. secretary of state, or even the president himself." At Mao's request, Chou reported to the politburo that the United States had declined in strength since the First World War and was now anxious to get out of Vietnam, and that this opening of relations would either strengthen China opposite its enemies and accelerate its resumption of authority over Taiwan or reveal the cowardice and dishonesty of the Americans.[18]

Nixon was not prepared to go himself without some preparation to assure that the visit would not be a failure, and he did not want anyone except himself received publicly. Despite the Ping-Pong diplomacy, and the comments of Edgar Snow, there was no expectation in the world that anything was imminent, and certainly nothing at the highest level. Nixon saw the potential for an absolutely electrifying coup, and wanted the high-voltage current to be transmitted uninsulated to Moscow and Hanoi, as well as to the American electorate.

Nixon contemplated sending various people to Beijing, including the veteran and very respected diplomat David Bruce, and Nelson Rockefeller. Both would have been perfectly competent for such a task, but neither knew what Nixon really wanted to accomplish with China and the intricate relationship with the Vietnam negotiations, and several aspects of Soviet relations. Kissinger, with his customary thoroughness as an all-encompassing courtier, had already sent a message through Ambassador Hilaly to Chou En-lai that "No one except Kissinger is best qualified to have these discussions as he is the *only* person (repeat only) who knows President Nixon's thinking and his mind and can take decisions on the spot without having to refer back to Washington for advice and instructions."

This was probably true, but it also reveals something of Kissinger's self-interested pursuit of his own betterment through public office. In his account, Kissinger alleged that Nixon even considered Thomas E. Dewey for this role. Dewey had died the month before, while visiting industrialist Dwayne Andreas in Miami. Nixon had written a letter of condolence, in respect for the man who had, more than anyone else, promoted him to national office by recommending him to Eisenhower as vice president, and to whom Nixon had offered the post of chief justice of the United States. Kissinger's assertion that Nixon was unaware that Dewey had died is not, in the slightest, believable.[19] After a few days of keeping Kissinger on tenterhooks, Nixon told him that he should go to China to arrange a presidential visit. As early as April 22, there was argument in the Oval Office about internal credit for the expanding prospects of relations with China. In a taped conversation, Kissinger repeatedly tells Nixon that he is ensuring that Nixon gets all the credit for the coming breakthrough with China: "I'm not going to let State hog this China thing," and "It's absolutely outrageous, Mr. President."

"This is my initiative. Mine period," said Nixon.[20]

On June 2, another reply from Chou En-lai, via Yahya Khan and ambassador Hilaly, his hands shaking,[21] was given to Kissinger. Chou had "reported with much pleasure to Chairman Mao Tse-tung" that Nixon was prepared to visit Peking for direct talks and Mao "welcomes President Nixon's visit and looks forward to that occasion," while "Premier Chou En-lai welcomes Dr. Kissinger to China . . . for preliminary secret meeting."[22] Nixon had hit the jackpot. The day before, he had held a press conference and there was only one innocuous question about China.

Kissinger advised Nixon of the message at the end of a state dinner for the rather discredited president of Nicaragua, Anastasio Somoza (whose father and predecessor was immortalized by Franklin D. Roosevelt as "a son-of-a-bitch, but he's our son-of-a-bitch"). Nixon brought Kissinger to the residence and opened a bottle of brandy. Kissinger thought it "the most important communication that has come to an American president since the end of World War II." It may have been. The two men toasted each other, and a generation of peace;[23] they had both earned this moment. It was agreed that Kissinger would secretly visit China July 9 to 11 to finalize arrangements. When it came, right after Kissinger's trip, the news of Richard Nixon meeting with Mao Tse-tung and Chou En-lai would stun the world.

On June 10, Nixon would quietly end a twenty-one-year embargo on trade with China, and lift all controls on imports from China. In the same action, he ended a requirement that half of all grain sold to the Soviet Union had to be shipped in U.S. flag vessels, clearing the way for a large grain sale to the U.S.S.R., as had been discussed between Kissinger and Dobrynin. Kissinger said: "We have got it all hooked together."[24]

The leaders of the maritime unions, Teddy Gleason and Jesse Calhoun, were militant anti-communists of the George Meany school, and when the U.S.S.R. bought four million tons of U.S. grain in the autumn, they refused to load Russian ships. Kissinger called Gleason, who told him, with a negotiating style little reminiscent of Chou En-lai, whom Kissinger had then met twice, to "Fuck yourself." Nixon assigned the work of dealing with Gleason and Calhoun to Colson, who he thought was temperamentally and culturally better-suited to this sort of task. Colson secured Gleason's agreement in exchange for a pledge of increased government subsidies for maritime construction and a few other legislative favors. Gleason was an early and constant Nixon supporter.[25]

On June 5, Agnew had asked urgently for a meeting with Nixon, and when it was accorded, he told the president he was going to South Korea for the inauguration of a new president and would go to Taiwan also to meet Chiang Kai-shek, and why did he not go on to Beijing while he was in the area? Nixon vetoed Beijing and Taiwan, without any explanation, and the next day asked Haldeman to explore in depth with Connally the possibility of the Treasury secretary replacing Agnew as vice president. Agnew was sent to Africa and the Middle East as a consolation prize.[26]

Relations with the Soviet Union were also moving satisfactorily, now that there was no longer any thought of trying to require Moscow to pressure Hanoi. On May 18, an outline of an arms control agreement was reached and an announcement was prepared of an agreement to limit deployment of anti-missile missiles and offensive strategic weapons. Neither the secretary of state nor the chief arms control negotiator and director of the Arms Control and Disarmament Agency, Gerard Smith, had any idea that there were back-channel discussions between Kissinger and Dobrynin, or any discussions parallel to the official talks in Helsinki and Vienna to resolve these matters.

Smith later wrote that Kissinger had botched the negotiations starting in January and February 1971, by allowing Dobrynin to detach submarine launched ballistic missiles (SLBMs) from the agreement. This is a tenuous claim, almost surely and understandably inflated by sour grapes at his own mistreatment by Kissinger and Nixon. The United States had numerical and technological advantages in SLBMs and it isn't clear what it lost in this regard (though Senator Jackson and his foremost staff member, Richard Perle, later claimed Kissinger had omitted twelve primitive Russian submarines from the eventual agreement).[27] For his part, Kissinger claimed that once it was agreed to put limitations on offensive deployments ahead of an anti-missile defense accord and announce them, Nixon was seized by the fear that Gerard Smith, rather than he, would get credit for the seemingly imminent breakthrough of linking "offensive and defensive limitations." Nixon, he said, "wanted the credit for the initiatives identified with peace."[28] Smith was more aggrieved at Kissinger, as the president had the right to take over any policy field he wished. In this reflection of Kissinger's on Nixon's desire for favorable attention, the national security adviser was the pot calling the kettle black.

Haldeman was delegated to tell Rogers and Kissinger to tell Smith, as there would be a joint announcement from Washington and Moscow the next day. Rogers offered Haldeman his resignation and said he would be a "laughingstock," not an altogether inaccurate interpretation. Smith considered that the announcement was really an agreement to keep talking. Kissinger told him the Helsinki and Vienna sessions, seventy-four in total, had been vital to the national interest. Haldeman and then Nixon, whom Rogers called as soon as Haldeman left him, told the secretary of state that arms control cut across several departments and that the breakthrough had come suddenly with a letter from Soviet leader Brezhnev. (There was no such letter, and Rogers apparently did not ask to see it.)

Rogers and Smith loyally held to the party line, as did Laird, when they all met the cabinet and the congressional leaders the next morning, and the whole group stood to applaud the president at the end of his one-hour presentation. He made it clear in his public announcement, as he had to the cabinet and the congressional leaders, that this was not a treaty at this point, but a "commitment at the highest level" to reach a detailed agreement on pre-agreed lines.[29]

The day before, May 19, Senate Majority Leader Mansfield's amendment to the Selective Service Act reducing American troop strength in Europe was rejected by the reassuringly heavy vote of 61-36. Nixon had had his rediscovered friend Dean Acheson, John McCloy, and General Lucius Clay (who had tried nearly twenty years before to dispense with him as Eisenhower's vice presidential nominee) to the White House and asked them to lobby the Democrats in the Senate against Mansfield's rider. They did so very effectively, and Nixon wrote them that they had been "present at the creation [the title of Acheson's autobiography]" when the institutions of the Cold War, NATO and the Marshall Plan, were set up, and that they were "present at the resurrection" also.[30]

On June 20, another amendment of Mansfield's requiring the withdrawal of all forces from Vietnam within nine months if U.S. prisoners were released would pass 57-42. Nixon had Mansfield and House Speaker Carl Albert to the White House separately the next day and warned them of what he was negotiating with the U.S.S.R. and Vietnam, and said that if they persisted he would revive the bombing campaign and recall Ambassador Bruce from Paris and blame it squarely on the Congress. Despite his other preoccupations and the desire of all Americans to pretend they had no further interest in what happened in Vietnam, Nixon still was trying to preserve a slender possibility of survival for the Saigon government.[31] Mansfield's effort fell short in the House, and was still ten votes away from a veto override in the Senate.

Nixon was now very focused on the following year's election, and laid out points he wanted emphasizing his own contribution to the agreement with the Russians. His whole entourage and family were now busily pouring out interviews and anecdotal evidence of the president's warm humanity, sparkling sense of humor, generous nature, and lack of interest in fluctuating opinion (the last, one of the most ambitious falsehoods of his entire career, which was replete with challengers for that status).

Well-known novelist and journalist Allen Drury (*Advise and Consent*, etc.) interviewed Pat Nixon, who met Drury armed with a memo from "RN" setting out his ideas. She hued to the line: "He is so thoughtful of all of us. He is always planning little surprises and little gifts for us. . . . Dick has a marvelous sense of humor. . . . The children gathered round him and put their arms around him [at the Christmas party, where he played the piano]. Children know." Pat Nixon was an independent-minded and straight-forward woman, and even if most of this was true, and she was certainly happy to be helpful to her husband, she may have found delivery of this unspontaneous treacle tedious.[32]

On June 12, Nixon's elder daughter, Tricia, married Edward Cox, a rather blue-blood New York law student at Harvard and former Ralph Nader helper. Nixon liked him and it was a happy occasion, marred only by inclement weather. Tricia was an attractive young woman, with her father's ski-jump nose, composed and pretty, with an admirable, always well-kempt long blonde mane. She had avoided all public attention after she wrote a supportive letter to Georgia governor Lester Maddox, an Atlanta restaura-teur who had refused to serve African-Americans and distributed axe handles to sympathizers, and ultimately closed his Pickrick Restaurant rather than integrate it.

Tricia and her father wanted an outdoor wedding, which had never occurred at the White House before. Nixon kept consulting the air force, which told him there would be a fifteen-minute break in the rain at 4:30 P.M. He had the chairs wiped off, ignored protocol, and with a first come, first seated plan, they all went crisply through the ceremony between 4:30 P.M. and 4:45 P.M. Approximately sixty million people watched on television. At the reception, Nixon danced with Pat for the first time in public and with both his daughters and a few others, including Lynda Bird Johnson, whose husband, future senator Charles Robb, was absent in the armed forces (as was David Eisenhower). The president appeared happy and even carefree. It was a very convivial occasion.

The next day, June 13, the New York Times began the publication of what became known as the Pentagon Papers. This was a 2.5-million-word history of the American involvement in Vietnam, classified as top secret, which meant that they were in fact accessible to about seven hundred thousand people in Defense and other departments and among private contractors. Nixon took it fairly casually at first, as he was scarcely mentioned, and Kennedy and Johnson were raked over the coals for blundering into the war without having the remotest idea of the task they were undertaking.

At first, Nixon thought the leak must have been the work of the project director, Leslie Gelb. Kissinger at first thought it might be the work of Laird, as an effort to further ingratiate himself with the press, an activity at which Laird was one of Kissinger's few peers. But when he learned that it was not just a few pages but the entire report, Kissinger concluded that it had to be his former student, Daniel Ellsberg. Ellsberg, after having attracted Kissinger's attention and graduated, became a marine captain in Vietnam and then served as a civilian assistant to the legendary General Edwin Lansdale, model for the Graham Greene novel *The Quiet American*, as well as for William Lederer and Eugene Burdick's *The Ugly American*.

Ellsberg had set out to copy the papers, all seven thousand pages, surreptitiously and at night, in 1969 when he saw the refusal of the army to prosecute Robert Rheault for the murder of the double agent Thai Khac Chuyen. (Chapter 11.) Given how remote Ellsberg was from these papers, as he did not have one of the fifteen copies, but only out-of-hours access to a copy at the Rand Corporation, it is not clear how Kissinger knew at once that Ellsberg was the culprit. But his intuition was correct. Kissinger, from the start, reviled Ellsberg as a sick though brilliant man, a drug abuser and sexual pervert, and described what he represented as examples of Ellsberg's bizarre sexual habits. Nixon was concerned with politics, not sex gossip. He was no more interested in Ellsberg's sex life than he was in stories about the Kennedys, including current reports of unsuccessful overtures by Teddy Kennedy to Christina Ford and Candice Bergen at the opening of the Kennedy Center.[33]

Kissinger was in California preparing for his secret trip to China, and warned Nixon in his usual terms not to appear "a weakling . . . These leaks are slowly and systematically destroying us. . . . If other powers feel we cannot control internal leaks, they will not agree to secret negotiations."[34] This was nonsense. The papers came up to the week before Nixon's inauguration and in all of their seven thousand pages there was little about still-sensitive diplomatic matters. Other powers might not be delighted with this new self-inflicted wound of the American government as the country struggled with the coils of Vietnam, but they would not cease to deal with the U.S. administration. It must be said, and would be clearer with the China bombshell about to drop, that Nixon's secretive methods, whatever strain they placed on relationships in the White House, the State Department, the Department of Defense, CIA, FBI, NSC, and Joint

Chiefs, at least maintained discretion and didn't misplace much classified information, other than by design by Nixon and his aides.

Kissinger bellowed at Colson and Haldeman: "We might just as well turn it all over to the Soviets and get it over with."[35] He was concerned that his own role as adviser to the Johnson administration would not emerge well, and perhaps that he would seem a dove compared with Ellsberg as he had been a couple of years before. In fact the Pentagon Papers were not very damaging to Kissinger.

Pressed by Kissinger, Nixon told Mitchell to proceed against the *Times*. This was a mistake; the Pentagon Papers reflected discredit on Kennedy, Johnson, and McNamara. By interposing himself, Nixon was bound to look like he was complicit in the shortcomings of their policies and an opponent of the public's right to know. Nothing was accomplished by seeming to try to suppress the papers, which presented Nixon, implicitly, in a comparatively favorable light. Nixon was in fact hoping that the papers contained confirmation of Kennedy's role in the assassination of Diem, and Johnson's motive to defeat Nixon in the 1968 election in the October 31, 1968, bombing pause.

The government did get a restraining order from a New York court, and the *Times* said it would suspend publication pending adjudication. The Justice Department told the court it was considering espionage charges against the newspaper and persons unknown. While the parties waited for that action to come to court, the *Washington Post* received the continuing material and started printing it on June 18. The following day, the New York judge, Murray Gurfein, a Nixon appointee, who had described the *Times* as "unpatriotic" during the oral arguments, found for the *Times* and said the freedom of the press and the public's right to know must take priority over the government's desire for secrecy. Nixon at this point, stirred up by Kissinger (yet consolable at any besmirching of his Democratic predecessors) and curious about the contents of the papers, was claiming that he would argue the government's case himself when it got to the Supreme Court.

The initial hearing in Washington was in the court of another Nixon appointee, Judge Gerhard Gesell, who found for the *Post* and said that the government had not made its national security case. He was overruled a few hours later by the Court of Appeals, but by this time the *Post* had printed for the next day and distributed its contents throughout its features syndicate.

The following day, the Appeals Court in New York also overturned Gurfein, but by now the papers had been distributed like a chain letter to other newspapers, which would publish as in a relay race, taking the torch from whichever newspaper was prohibited by the courts from publishing. The *Boston Globe* was next, followed by the *Los Angeles Times, Philadelphia Inquirer, Chicago Sun-Times, Detroit Free Press, Miami Herald, Christian Science Monitor,* and *St. Louis Post-Dispatch.*

Ellsberg had been identified as the prime suspect, but he traveled from city to city distributing his papers, despite being sought by the FBI. He appeared on the CBS news and was interviewed by Walter Cronkite, and appeared on a television special on the subject, and still the FBI professed to be unable to find him. Kissinger had induced Nixon to enter what quickly became a slapstick, Keystone Kops farce. Nixon should have ignored it, as was his initial inclination. But the stance he did take, apart from making the government appear ridiculous, did Nixon no harm. He made the point that he was personally disinterested and won general agreement for his opposition to "stealing classified documents and publishing them in the newspapers." It also afforded Nixon and Kissinger a splendid improvisation for explaining to Rogers when the time came why he had not been informed of the China discussions: Chinese concern that if they dealt through the State Department, it would be published prematurely, like the Pentagon Papers – a complete fabrication.[36]

Ellsberg finally gave himself up in Boston on June 24. Since he anticipated a negative decision by the Supreme Court, Nixon thought better of his idea that he would argue the government's side of the Pentagon Papers case himself. On June 30, the Supreme Court decided against the government 6-3. There was nothing for it but to print and publish the Pentagon Papers. This was done, but once the attempt to suppress the report was abandoned, there was relatively little interest in it. Its revelations were not especially startling. (To Nixon's disappointment, it did not connect Kennedy to the Diem murders, nor explore Johnson's motive in the October 31, 1968, Vietnam bombing halt.)

Nixon complained to his innermost staff that there was now a counter-government, including the Supreme Court, and that it had to be resisted. He compared Ellsberg to Alger Hiss and told Mitchell he had to prosecute Ellsberg as he had prosecuted Hiss, and proudly said that he had convicted

Hiss in the press. He had indeed, as he now happily said, leaked constantly to the press in the Hiss case, despite solemn promises that he would not and despite the illegality of doing so, much of the time. (Chapter 2.)

Nixon seemed not to realize that in 1949 the press was very hostile to communism, and especially domestic communists and any hint of treason. In 1971, the country was hostile to the Vietnam War and would give conscientious claims, such as Ellsberg would make, a sympathetic hearing, especially as the Supreme Court had upheld the right to publish. The comparison was inexact, and what did Nixon care whether Ellsberg was prosecuted or not? Ellsberg meant nothing to him. (Also, Nixon didn't prosecute Hiss, the Justice Department did, and barely won a conviction, despite Nixon's perfervid efforts.)

This absurd episode, tilted by Kissinger into a test of Nixon's manhood, at the approach of Nixon's greatest successes, revealed the degeneration of the president's always precarious sense of due process and the rights of dissent. He became preoccupied with the Brookings Institution and ordered that it be broken into and its files rifled.[37] He was telling this on June 30 to Haldeman and Mitchell, who normally had the intelligence to ignore Nixon's more extreme suggestions. But if Colson heard any such incitements, he would take them seriously. "Do you think, for Christ's sakes, that the *New York Times* is worried about all the legal niceties?" Nixon said. "Those sons of bitches are killing me."[38]

Nixon told Ehrlichman: "If we can't get anyone in this damn government to do something about leaks, then by God we'll do it ourselves. I want you to set up a little group right here in the White House. Have them get off their tails and find out what's going on and how to stop it."[39] Ehrlichman handed this off to Bud Krogh (who entered this narrative when he pursued Nixon to the Lincoln Memorial at 4:30 A.M. on May 9, 1970). Since they were trying to stop leaks, Krogh and his colleagues called their group the "Plumbers." Colson quickly learned of it and enlisted, promising to expose what Nixon called the "counter-government" in all its lurid treachery. The administration was edging toward very dangerous practices – illegal, probably unethical, acts with little possible reward and vertiginous risk, being executed by under-supervised scoundrels full of a dashing zeal but unencumbered by judgment or moderation.

Nixon had been propelled by the provocations of his enemies to the point where he thought he was under siege; he reckoned "96 percent of the bureaucracy are against us,"[40] as well as both houses of the Congress, the Supreme Court, and most of the media. Despite all the lamentations that would be uttered in the next few years about an imperial presidency, Nixon felt himself an underdog, surrounded, besieged, and harassed, supported only by the silent majority of the people. Some aspects of this perception were true, some were exaggerated, and some were neurotic, but the combination was dangerously fissionable.

— III —

Henry Kissinger left on his Asian trip July 1 with, as he later wrote, Nixon's "invariable hard-line rhetoric with which he sent me off on every mission," including the instruction to be "somewhat enigmatic" about Taiwan ringing in his ears. Nixon wanted the release of all American reconnaissance pilots shot down and detained by the Chinese over the years before he went there.[41] Because the presidential aircraft were all in use, Kissinger took a refitted jet-tanker, with a large bedroom and sitting room for himself, but somewhat cramped accommodation for his entourage. It lumbered off runways so that, as Kissinger wrote, "On take-off, one had the feeling that the plane really preferred to reach its destination over land." Kissinger emerged from time to time in his dressing gown, and the scene reminded one of his staff of a "Roman galley, with the captain commanding imperiously from the stern, and the rowers laboring uncomfortably."[42]

Kissinger went to Saigon, Bangkok, New Delhi (for a very difficult dinner with Prime Minister Indira Gandhi, daughter of the late prime minister, Nehru), and then Pakistan. On July 9, his press party in Islamabad was told that he had stomach influenza and would remain in bed for a day or perhaps two, in the cooler air of northern Pakistan. Yahya had promised that he would make "absolutely foolproof arrangements,"[43] and he was as good as his word. Kissinger left the state guest house furtively at 3:30 A.M., wearing a large hat and sunglasses in the pre-dawn darkness, and went to the airport in a nondescript car driven by the Pakistani foreign minister himself. He flew on a requisitioned Pakistani commercial aircraft to China.

Yahya claimed that Kissinger was nervous and asked him to accompany him. This is not believable. Kissinger may well have been nervous, and that was the initial impression of the Chinese, but he would not have asked the president of Pakistan to be his companion. Yahya offered to send a Pakistani general on the plane with him. Kissinger carried out his historic mission with his customary sangfroid, despite wearing oversized shirts borrowed from one of his officials because his own aide had forgotten to pack his. There were Chinese officials, including Mao Tse-tung's own interpreter, on board. A stringer for a London newspaper saw him, but when he filed a story that Kissinger was seen, in disguise, boarding a Pakistani International Airways plane for China in the middle of the night, his editor spiked the story as too implausible and probably the product of journalistic drunkenness at the newspaper's expense.[44]

Chou En-lai was then seventy-three, descended of an academic and bureaucratic family, a graduate of Tientsin University, and a student nationalist and radical politician. Here he met his future wife and remained faithful to her through a seven-year engagement, including 1920 to 1923, when he was in Paris, with side visits to London and Germany. On returning to China in 1924, he was still a nationalist and not yet publicly a communist, though he had helped found the Chinese Communist Party of Europe in 1922, and ran the Kuomintang Military Academy for Chiang Kai-shek, then trying to unify the country on a nationalist, anti-communist program, taking over from his brother-in-law, Sun Yat-sen. Chou went through the severities of the Long March, ordered executions, and did not hesitate to dip his elegant hands in blood. He always retained his sense of humor, and once told an American diplomat that China could not export with its standard of workmanship – revealing, as an example, that his winter long underwear protruded beneath his trousers and above his socks.[45]

The substantive discussions between Kissinger and Chou were the subject of much speculation, until their record was released. Ambrose was one of those who thought that Kissinger might have made dishonorable promises about Taiwan, a fear of the American right and left.[46] These fears and allegations were without foundation. In effect, he undertook the withdrawal of American forces in Taiwan in exchange for a Chinese promise not to invade. With the American Seventh Fleet nearby and no Chinese use of force, there was no need for American forces in Taiwan. Kissinger said that progress would have to await the end of American involvement in Vietnam. Chou refused to promise anything opposite Hanoi, and the U.S.S.R. and Japan were scarcely mentioned. Kissinger accepted the principle of a single China, but said that it could not be enunciated by the United States at that time. Chou promised not to admit any of the many American politicians who had asked to be received in China until after Nixon's visit. (James Reston of the *New York Times* was put on such a slow train from Canton that he only arrived in Beijing after Kissinger and his party had left. Of course he wasn't a politician, but as far as Nixon was concerned, he might as well have been.)[47]

Kissinger gave Chou sophisticated American intelligence, including aerial reconnaissance photographs and cable intercepts, on Soviet military activities on the Chinese border. The initial Chinese wording of the communiqué portrayed Nixon as a supplicant and asserted that the visit would be about Taiwan. Kissinger rejected this, and Mao himself approved a very fair compromise. The Chinese had wished to defer the meeting until after Nixon's anticipated visit to Moscow, but as Kissinger was aware that that trip had been postponed by the Russians, he pushed for an early trip to China, partly as a spur to the Soviets, and he was successful in this.[48]

Flattery is a large part of Kissinger's repertoire with any person except subordinates, and he laid it on with a trowel on this occasion, endlessly engaging Chou in a flattery competition, and concluding that he was greatly impressed by the "idealism and spiritual qualities of you and your colleagues."[49] Kissinger won the competition with that game-ending, towering act of ingratiation, which left Chou without riposte, except a suggestion they go to lunch. Kissinger told Nixon that Chou, because of his courtesy and subtlety, was a joy to deal with compared with the blustering, bullying, Soviets. Chou subsequently acknowledged that Kissinger was "very intelligent." It was a completely successful visit. Kissinger did not exaggerate when he told the U.S. ambassador in Pakistan: "I did a beautiful job." Even his critics have never accused him of taking modesty to a fault. The ambassador, Joseph Farland, to help maintain Kissinger's cover for the China sidetrip, assured Kissinger's press party that "the stupid ass is in the bazaar arguing about . . . a rug."[50]

By prearrangement, if his talks with Chou En-lai met the criteria he and Nixon had established to justify a presidential visit to China, he would send the signal "Eureka" on his return to Islamabad. On July 11, Haig telephoned Nixon and said that a message consisting of the single word *Eureka* had just been received from Kissinger. (The message was through the CIA from Tehran, where Kissinger went after Islamabad, on a maximum security line.) Nixon and Eisenhower biographer Stephen Ambrose wrote that Kissinger, in his memoirs "devotes a fifty-five page chapter to loving detail about the trip [to China] mainly emphasizing what a great man Chou was, and how remarkable a man the author was to deal with him as an equal." This is unduly censorious, but not completely unjust.

Two days after Kissinger left China, Chou went to Hanoi and then Pyong Yang to reassure the North Vietnamese and the North Koreans. The visit to Hanoi did not go well and relations between the two countries began to degenerate from that point, but the Chinese did not withdraw any of their large support force, which Kissinger had not mentioned, from North Vietnam. The Stalinist leader of Albania, Enver Hoxha, was outraged at Chinese "shamelessness."* [51]

At 7:31 P.M., July 15, 1971, President Nixon made an unscheduled announcement on all network radio and television outlets in the United States and, after a brief preamble, read a statement for about ninety seconds. An identical statement was made in Beijing. The communiqué said that Kissinger had visited China (despite Nixon's warning to Kissinger to keep his own name out of the communiqué;[52] Kissinger wrote that "Reality took care of this problem," but in fact, as Nixon feared, Kissinger took care of it by inserting his own name in the release).[53] It stated that President Nixon had "expressed [a] desire to visit the People's Republic of China," whose leaders were pleased to invite him, and that he had accepted their invitation for a visit prior to May 1972. Normalization of relations and a full exchange of views were cited as the objectives of the president's visit. Nixon added a paragraph to the joint communiqué and assured the Taiwanese, Japanese, and Russians: "Our action . . . will not be at the expense of our old friends. It is not directed against any other nation." He said that "all nations will gain from a reduction of tensions and a better relationship" between China and the U.S. and concluded: "I will undertake a journey for peace."

Opinion in the United States was thunderstruck and generally very positive. "In a single stroke, the president had confounded all of his enemies: the Soviets, the North Vietnamese, the press, and the liberal Democrats."[54] One of the American network commentators was speechless for nearly ten seconds after Nixon concluded his brief remarks.[55] The

---

* Mao, who admired Stalin but not his successors in the Kremlin, could have reflected on Stalin's comment to Churchill and Roosevelt at Yalta in February 1945, on learning that all states would have equal votes in the United Nations, that "the Soviet Union has not endured what it has in this war in order to have a voice in the councils of the world equal to Albania's."

Democrats were uniformly favorable and only the most conservative Republicans were hostile, though some, like Goldwater, were too perplexed to express a declarative opinion. In the world, the West was elated and impressed at Nixon's imagination and flexibility, and the stylish execution by him and Kissinger. In the Soviet camp, stupefaction quickly gave way to misgivings. Taiwan was evidently concerned. It was a huge story that took away the breath of Nixon's critics, exhilarated most of his supporters, and left a few disconcerted, but after all these years with Nixon they would give him the benefit of the anti-communist doubt. (The secretary of state, Rogers, was briefed very extensively by Nixon several days before the announcement, and was given the task of informing Haig. He took it in good part and generously congratulated Kissinger when he returned from Asia.)

William F. Buckley led a conservative group that gratuitously "suspended" support for the president, including leaders of the Conservative Republican Human Works, the New York Conservative Party, Young Americans for Freedom, the Southern Industrial Conference, the American Conservative Union, and the Conservative Book Club. Pat Buchanan, a fellow Catholic conservative, described Buckley as much the most important of all these people, and had urged Nixon all year to placate him. The grievance of this odd assortment of people and groups included possible abandonment of Taiwan, inadequate response to the Soviet arms buildup, and an insufficiently energetic response to Germany's flirtation with Eastern Europe.[56] Buchanan had already warned on January 6, 1971, that most competent cabinet secretaries or officers such as Finch, Schultz, and Donald Rumsfeld (counselor to the president and director of the Economic Stabilization Program), stirred up a good deal of needless conservative antagonism.[57]

Despite what the agreed communiqué said, Chou En-lai represented to his politburo that Nixon had "eagerly presented himself like an over-dressed whore at China's door."[58] But China's leaders were not so sublimely composed. The supposed successor to Mao, Lin Piao, had become a reclusive morphine addict, frightened by the sound of laughter and the thought of meeting people. He was reduced to retrieving himself from the grip of morphine by inhaling fumes from a motorcycle he kept in his house.[59] On September 12, 1971, two months after Kissinger left China, Lin Piao fled China in an airliner his son had requisitioned. They were denounced by

Lin's daughter and the plane crashed, or was shot down, in Mongolia. Being Mao's designated heir was a hazardous position.[60]

Mao Tse-tung and Chou En-lai were both the subject of an immense mystique in the West. In the twenty-two years they had ruled the world's most populous country, they had not set foot in the non-communist world, other than Chou's trip to Geneva in 1954 when Dulles famously declined to shake hands with him. The Western countercultures had adopted both men, as they had Ho Chi Minh, as icons. Mao's oracular style, which would have been regarded as dementia if adopted by any Western leader – claiming to have swum for nine miles in the Yangtze River, styling himself as the Great Helmsman, and issuing little red books full of his epigrams – added to his legend. Few of those who venerated Mao in the West had read many of his writings, and it was difficult to make much out of them anyway. (Even he would disparage his writings to Nixon and Kissinger as of little merit.)

Chou had met enough Westerners that there were many serious and believable people in the West who spoke admiringly of his charm and shrewdness. He had the air of a 1940s Hollywood casting studio's Macao casino operator, a slight touch of the West in his facial features and hairstyle, and a more elegant Mao suit than most Chinese leaders. (Nixon unembarrassedly recommended to Kissinger that in briefing the press he strike the note that Chou and Nixon had similar qualities, and then he enumerated them: "Came up through adversity;* best in a crisis; tough, bold, willing to take chances; takes the long view; philosophical, works without notes; steely, subtle, almost gentle." Understandably, this suggestion seems not to have caught fire with the national security advisor, who did not regard himself as a paid flak for CREEP.)[†][61]

The two Chinese leaders had ruled almost a quarter of the world's population for over a fifth of a century, and were men of mystery. The facts that their government had had a series of economic disasters and was a human rights monstrosity and that they were both steeped in the blood of the innocent, including their own families, counted for little in the liberal West. They had held their own in Korea, were on what appeared to be the winning

---

* Chou, from a family in the Mandarinate, had a more advantageous socioeconomic launch than Nixon.
† Committee to Re-elect the President.

side in Vietnam, made an atomic bomb, and were standing up to the Russians. And China was – at the birth of the United Nations, as Roosevelt had predicted when he sponsored China as one of the world's five Great Powers, against the skepticism of Churchill and Stalin – a very important country in the world. It was not at all the Sick Man of Asia that Chiang Kai-shek had ineptly tried to govern.

It is generally reckoned that the most important statesmen of the twentieth century (considering Lenin a revolutionary and Gandhi a prophet and neither of them really a statesman) were Churchill, Roosevelt, and de Gaulle for the democracies, and Stalin, Hitler, and Mao Tse-tung for the totalitarian powers. Mao was the survivor of this great cast of characters.

And Richard Nixon, though not of the stature of the earlier group of great democratic leaders, was now the West's most eminent statesman, by right of seniority in high office and attainments as well as the incomparable office that he held. His domestic opponents still gloried in accusing him of anti-communist excess, and now he was the invited guest of the leader of orthodox communism, who reviled the Kremlin for heresies and ideological treason against Marx. It was an epochal event, and it did change the world. In an unforeseen way, Vietnam may have facilitated it, as that war enervated the United States to the point where it had to seek alliances and combinations more imaginative than earlier in the Cold War, much less in the one hundred and sixty years of American quasi-isolation. And the Vietnam War conferred on the Soviet Union a comparative appearance of power that alarmed the Chinese. Complicated though the sources of this amazing development were, it was unnatural for two such Great Powers to have no relationship, and Nixon deserves the credit he has generally received, even from his enemies, for this initiative. Chou En-lai prepared for Nixon's visit by reading *Six Crises* and watching *Patton*.[62]

— IV —

After this dramatic news, Washington settled down for a while to routine and relaxed summer activity. Nixon was very preoccupied by disloyalty and indiscretions in the government. When the *New York Times* downplayed a dramatic decline in unemployment figures and cited a Labor Department official, Harold Goldstein, as the source for such an opinion, Nixon had Goldstein transferred and went into one of his periodic rants against the evils of Jews. He made a point of exempting Kissinger, Safire, Burns Leonard Garment (assistant counsel and a former law partner of Nixon and Mitchell's from New York), and others, but demanded to know how many Jews there were in Goldstein's section of the Labor Department. It was true that most Jewish-Americans were anti-Nixon, and his irritation with their rather reflexive hostility is understandable, but ethnic slurs delivered against millions of Americans by their president are, to say the least, distasteful.[63]

Nixon had the presidents of CBS, Frank Stanton, and of NBC, Julian Goodman, to the White House in June and July, and expressed, very calmly and courteously, his disappointment at the biases of their news coverage. He understood that individuals – and he named Roger Mudd and Robert Pierpoint of CBS and David Brinkley and John Chancellor of NBC – were biased and they were entitled to their views, but there was no effort to counteract that bias, to edit it down or to get an alternative view. Stanton was rather obsequious and Goodman quite apologetic. Neither made any effort to deny the biases the president objected to, and both promised to try to make their reporting fairer.[64] When Nixon discovered that the Public Broadcasting Corporation would have a weekly political news hour co-anchored by former Kennedy part-time employee Sander Vanocur (whose independence from the Kennedys had not been beyond question), Nixon ordered a reduction in funding of PBS.[65]

On July 21, Ehrlichman made a preliminary report to Nixon on his anti-leakage activities and told him about the Plumbers. He had offered the job to Buchanan, who declined, and then Ehrlichman had rejected Colson's candidate, E. Howard Hunt, as just too wild and woolly (a considerable distinction in such a group), and only then Krogh. They were starting with an investigation of Ellsberg, and of leaks generally. The Plumbers were in the basement, had a wall-safe and telephones that could not be tapped, and had hired as their first operative G. Gordon Liddy, a former FBI agent and prosecutor. Liddy was apparently being pushed out of the Treasury Department because he had given a speech to the National Rifle Association criticizing the administration's (rather permissive) gun control policy. He was advertised to be a fearless and somewhat uncontrollable character. He would prove one of the most colorful, irrepressible, and, in his way, principled, figures of the middle and later Nixon years. He would shortly produce a fantastic plan, known as Gemstone, for invading or destroying a number of designated enemy citadels, including the Brookings Institution. Gemstone was not approved or enacted.

On July 27, the FBI reported that Ellsberg's psychoanalyst, Dr. Lewis Fielding of Los Angeles, had refused a request for an interview (quite properly under rules of professional discretion that applied also to lawyers and clergymen). Even if the FBI had had a warrant, which they did not, they had no right to question Ellsberg's doctor about his patient. The Plumbers had no respect for the privilege of professional discretion, painfully established and well-recognized over centuries of common law. Hunt and Liddy proposed breaking into Fielding's office to get their hands on Ellsberg's records, explaining that they had had plenty of experience with official break-ins (Hunt in the CIA, Liddy in the FBI; perhaps unfortunately, they had).

On August 6, Ehrlichman told Krogh that the president said for him to do whatever he thought was necessary "to learn what Ellsberg's motives and potential further harmful action might be." On August 8, Krogh sent Ehrlichman a follow-up memo expressing disappointment in a CIA psychological study of Ellsberg and asking authority for a break-in and seizure of Ellsberg's records as a psychoanalytic patient. (Psychoanalytic records, as there are frequent sessions of streams of the patient's consciousness and no comment from the analyst or any prescribed medicine, rarely are very informative, unless it's a unique case.) Ehrlichman checked the box for approval and added, "If done under your assurance that it is not traceable."[66]

On September 8, 1971, Ehrlichman reported to Nixon that a minor Plumbers operation in Los Angeles had been aborted, that it was better Nixon not know about it, and that a few unspecified "dirty tricks" were under way that might produce something. When shown some snapshots of what had been done in Fielding's office, which was ransacked on the night of September 3, in the "minor operation," Ehrlichman came to his senses and said that this operation should be "terminated . . . finalized, stopped." He went on to propose to Nixon on September 10 that documents placed in the National Archives by Morton Halperin, Leslie Gelb, and Paul Nitze should be extracted. Nixon felt the National Archives were accessible to the president on a national security cover and approved that.

Nixon also demanded vengeance for the IRS harassment of friends of his, including John Wayne and Billy Graham. (Graham visited the White House in September and referred to a Biblical category of "Satanic Jews," whose modern continuators, the evangelist thought, were certain IRS agents. Neither Graham nor Nixon engaged in wholesale anti-Semitism, only a rather unseemly selective version.) Nixon told Ehrlichman to ensure that Muskie's and Humphrey's tax returns were carefully scrutinized: "Hubert's been in some funny deals." (Nixon knew this from their mutual friend, Dwayne Andreas of Archer Daniels Midland, who had complicated financial arrangements with a great many politicians, including Humphrey and Nixon and Andreas's late friend Thomas E. Dewey.)

Hunt, with Colson's agreement, finally responded to Nixon's frustration at not finding any evidence of Kennedy's involvement in the murder of Ngo Dinh Diem and his brother in 1963, by forging a cable implicating the Kennedy administration. Not much use was made of this creative effort,[67] but it was outrageous, though it still did not involve the president directly in crimes.

In the terms of a future controversy under another president, all this retained "plausible deniability" for Nixon, but only by a thread. Ehrlichman had given a provisional authorization under Nixon's general guidance that was based on national security considerations. Nixon believed that he was covered by a national security criterion that it was the president's right to invoke. But he should have understood that allowing people like Hunt and Liddy to go about breaking into people's offices was, as Hoover had warned, almost certain to be discovered and would be something the "counter-government" would leap on with justification, like famished leopards.

Apart from that, Nixon the Quaker, Nixon the lawyer, and Nixon the former quasi-psychological patient should have recognized that this was unethical. And Nixon the president should have seen that, whatever Ellsberg's offenses, and whatever the cataract of provocations that rained down on the country's constitutional leader, breaking into a psychoanalyst's office was an act unworthy of the head of the American people. Nixon greatly admired and respected the traditions established by Washington, Jefferson, Lincoln, Theodore Roosevelt, Wilson, and Eisenhower, in particular. None of these men would have entertained such an act for an instant.

The same cannot be said with such certainty about Kennedy and Johnson. And Nixon believed that he was facing an unprecedented assault on the presidency and the traditional rule of law. He was slightly overstating his problem, when it is compared to Lincoln's dealing with an insurrection in which seven hundred fifty thousand Americans died, but his concern is certainly understandable. What is not understandable is why he did not address it by the means that had always prevailed in the United States: use the presidency as a platform to persuade and lead the people. He had quite successfully done this already, until he went too far and implied in October 1970 that the leaders of the Democratic Party were a gang of lawless advocates of mob rule, as he had formerly suggested that previous Democrats (whose advice he now sought and received, like Dean Acheson) were a gang of communist appeasers, if not traitors. That gambit had not succeeded in November 1970, but Nixon had only sustained a slight disappointment, not a public rejection.

Unfortunately, tragically, Nixon was by this time straining at the leash of ethical judgment, legal prudence, and presidential decorum. It is hard not to sympathize with his outrage at the hypocrisy and vitriol of many of his tormentors, and to understand the depth of his concern. But it is also hard to understand why he responded in such a dangerous and indefensible way.

A fairly good technical argument could be cobbled together that all he had done to this point was authorize subordinates to do what they thought the national interest required, and that he had a national security cover for it. He had not committed an impeachable offense. But he was on the slippery slope toward one. Yet there was not now any *mens rea*. Nixon thought he was defending himself legally in unique circumstances. That view can be logically challenged, but that is what he believed. And as his late opponent Hubert Humphrey said when Nixon invoked the silent majority, "We only have one president at a time, and some respect [but not infinite indulgence] is due to the person who is ultimately responsible for the security of the nation."

It was clearly understood from the start that the activities of the Plumbers would often be illegal matters that the FBI and CIA declined to touch, and that they would be carried out without direct presidential instruction. And Ehrlichman, instead of humoring his leader and ignoring the letter of what he said, or lecturing the president on his own self-interest, if not the undesirability of law-breaking, was recruiting inexperienced young people or known adventurers and unleashing them on the administration's enemies. Any intelligent person with any detachment should have seen that it was a recipe for disaster.[68]

For Nixon not to have any idea of the terrible inferno he might be entering is only explicable by an impairment of his moral senses under the pressures of his office that, contrary to the later accusations of his enemies,

735

had no precedent in his career. Nixon could endure enormous pressure, and steeled himself to paroxysms of courage and determination, feats in which the best was still to come. But as he became fixated on his objective, his sensitivity to means evaporated.

His personality was susceptible to a solitary narrowing of perspective that blinded him to secondary issues as he focused entirely on the main threat. He did not have the philosophical nature, easy relationship with friends or family, or ability to take his distance from his official problems even for a weekend that might have enabled him to weigh the consequences of some of the actions he condoned almost without thinking. It was as if he relieved tensions, and gloried in the office he had striven so hard and so long to win, by pretending that he was above the law. He then spoke almost reflexively, or with momentary, ill-considered bravura, addressing subordinates with no reliable capacity of independent judgment. "Fire them . . . force them to take lie-detector tests," and so forth. These weren't real orders; they were self-administered therapy. But Nixon should have known that in so powerful an office, and with some of the people he was instructing, disaster could ensue.

A harbinger of terrible things to come was provided on July 1, 1971, when Nixon told Haldeman in an Oval Office conversation: "I want you to find me a man by noon . . . who will work with me on this whole situation. . . . I mean, I can't have a high-minded lawyer like John Ehrlichman or Dean." (The only time Dean was so-described.) "I want a son of a bitch who's just as tough as I am, for a change, as tough as I was with the Hiss case. . . . Shake them up and get them off their God-damn asses . . . we're up against an enemy, a conspiracy using any means. We are going to use any means. Is that clear? Did they get the Brookings Institute last night?" Haldeman: "No." Nixon: "Get it done. I want it done. I want the Brookings safe cleaned out and have it cleaned out in such a way that it makes it look like somebody else did it."

In the opinion of this author, this exhortation is a more deadly smoking gun than any that was ultimately turned up. Nixon could produce technical legal and national security arguments about individual incidents. Even allowing for momentary and understandable annoyances, this illustrates the disintegration of the president's moral and political judgment. Any such mission against one of the country's leading think tanks would have been a criminal outrage and a political suicide mission.[69]

From this point on, unless Nixon recovered his steady moral sense, or Mitchell or Ehrlichman, or even Hoover if he could be mobilized, or Pat

Nixon if she had been told anything about these things, remonstrated with him, then Nixon, and the presidency and the country with him, were destined to a horrible catastrophe, somewhere, sometime, soon. Nixon temporarily lost his judgment. Mitchell and Ehrlichman, who didn't have the keenest moral sense, let him down. Hoover, who had little moral sense but was a brilliant political survivor, wasn't consulted. Pat Nixon, a clear-headed, brave, ethical, and unwavering spouse, who had seen a lot in thirty years as Mrs. Nixon, wasn't told. It was a cruel confluence of circumstances. It was all now on a hair trigger.

— v —

With Vietnam slowly winding down and no demonstrations since the federal government won the battle of May 3, and the arms control and China announcements, foreign policy was taking shape well. On August 5, Kissinger and Nixon had worked out and given Dobrynin a letter for Brezhnev, who was just emerging after seven years as the principal post-Khrushchev Soviet leader over Kosygin. Nixon proposed a summit meeting in Moscow in the spring of 1972. The reply came back with unheard of promptness, after only a few days, on August 10, that Brezhnev would be glad to receive Nixon in Moscow in May or June. Kissinger told Dobrynin to tell his government to ignore anything they heard from Rogers or the ambassador to Moscow, Jacob Beam, and deal with him about the arrangements. The China success had not prompted any abatement in the administration's idiosyncratic methods. (It is a wonder that people of the stature of Rogers and Beam and Gerard Smith and other senior officials continued to serve under these conditions.)

In domestic affairs, there had been no racially based rioting or any sky-jackings for many months. The only cloud now on the administration's horizon was the economy. Unemployment was not at worrisome levels, though it remained 5.5 percent. But inflation was accelerating and was reported to have made the startling monthly jump of seven-tenths of a percent in July alone. Polls indicated that Nixon was not considered to have done well with the economy, and a majority of Americans, with the usual national weakness for the quick fix, wanted wage and price controls.[70]

On August 4, Nixon held a press conference with no television cameras, and the majority of questions were on economic subjects. Burns was a tight-money Federal Reserve chairman, and David Kennedy, who had been rather unimaginative, had given way to Connally, a big-talking Texan with no obvious qualification to be Treasury secretary, but a sure sense of the politics involved. Connally was brought in to get the economy pointing toward Nixon's reelection and to cease to be a weapon of abuse in the hands of his adversaries. Kissinger later wrote, doubtless with some accuracy, that "Connally's swaggering self-assurance was Nixon's Walter Mitty image of himself. He was one person whom Nixon never denigrated behind his back." (Historian Stephen Ambrose aptly added: "Which was one more than the number on Kissinger's list." And Kissinger had his own transcultural Walter Mitty displacements.)[71]

Nixon had noted that the Republican leaders in the Congress were now very preoccupied by the economy. The press and the official opposition had begun discussion of wage and price controls, generating a modest degree of public awareness of the issue and an enthusiasm for a concept that had not been explained to the public or much thought out by its espousers. They were secure in the confident belief that Nixon would never consider such an option, and that his many dismissals of such controls made this a chimerical salvation that there was no chance of his embracing.

As so often happened throughout his career, Nixon's enemies underestimated him. When he was secure in his position, as he was as head of the administration, his suspicious nature led him to excesses of vigilance and counter-skulduggery against enemies. When he was operating in a broader arena, where he could not simply assert authority and command activity regardless of its ethics and legality, he relied on his wits, and often produced the diametrically unexpected. Doubtless, the Chinese were as surprised to hear of his desire to visit China as the Democrats were to hear that he was making the visit.

At his August 4 press conference, one of the reasons the television cameras were excluded was to not tip his hand when Nixon repeated his opposition to "permanent wage and price controls." There had never been in the history of the world such a thing as permanent wage and price controls, and no sane person would advocate such a thing. Once again, as Nixon calculated, the White House press corps was not sufficiently rigorous to note the inclusion of the redundant adjective "permanent," had no great curiosity about why there were no television cameras allowed, and had no inkling that Nixon might be cranking up, feeling slightly cornered yet again, to pull another gigantic rabbit out of the hat.

In hindsight it is easy to recognize the symptoms of the surprise to come. There was a conventional wisdom of an intractable problem for Nixon. The vultures in the press and the Democrats were assembling. Nixon was deemed to be trapped between deteriorating economic figures, a Federal Reserve chairman who did not believe in raising the money supply, and his own long-standing opposition to controls. All was in place for another of Richard Nixon's dramatic surprises.

In 1944, the Western countries had agreed at Bretton Woods, New Hampshire, on a new international currency arrangement, based on the U.S. dollar and the backing of the dollar by the gold reserves of the United States. There was gold in the Treasury of the United States to redeem about one-quarter of the outstanding currency, and there were fixed exchange rates with other major currencies, especially the British pound. This system had worked well for twenty-five years, but now U.S. gold reserves had declined (from $25 billion to $10.5 billion), Europe was back on its feet, Japan was much more powerful economically than it had ever been, the United States was on the verge of running its first trade deficit in over seventy-five years, and gold was clearly under-priced as a commodity, as the dollar was overpriced as a currency. Gold played an obsolescent and impossible role now because there were at least six or seven other important hard currencies.

Manufacturing in Japan and Western Europe was now extremely competitive, partly because the necessity to rebuild from the rubble of the war had produced more modern factories, and partly because the terrible poverty and devastation that afflicted Japan and most of Europe in 1945 had resulted in lower wages and an enhanced work ethic.

In April 1971, a new recruit to the administration, Pete Peterson, who had followed Senator Charles Percy as head of the camera and photographic equipment manufacturer Bell and Howell, and had become head of Nixon's newly created National Commission on Productivity, produced a paper for the president on the incipient trade deficit. He pointed out the advantage that Japan and Europe had achieved as a result of American largesse at the end of the war, and American acceptance of foreign imports while the dollar became progressively more overvalued as gold reserves dwindled. Peterson was an advocate of orderly devaluation, to prevent the

United States from becoming the victim of what amounted to dumping by its overseas allies and protégés. (Peterson would serve as Nixon's commerce secretary and later became an outspoken opponent of Ronald Reagan's and George W. Bush's tax reductions and budget deficits. He started in government in 1971 as an unorthodox figure, but spent most of the rest of his career as a rather convent onal alarmist, warning of the most dire consequences if something close to Dickensian economics were not followed.)

But as the U.S. market was penetrated by foreigners, and even as more and more American women went to work, taking advantage of lower birth rates and enhanced daycare facilities, American unemployment did not rise appreciably. The U.S. economy was gradually transformed into tertiary industry: services, research, technical expertise, and transactional activity. U.S. income rose, unionization declined in absolute numbers, and in relative numbers plummeted, and foreign economies prospered on exports to the U.S. Foreign countries became greater holders of dollars and the Gross Economic Product of the developed world multiplied manyfold from 1945, when the U.S. had had half of the world's economic activity.

Bretton Woods had become a sacred cow, and when Nixon was prodded hard enough by improvident events, he steeled himself to slay it, and to do the unthinkable, to confound his enemies who thought, once again, that he was cornered. Once steeled, Nixon would do it properly, since, as he said in the Cambodian crisis, he would arouse the same controversy for a half measure as for a profound strategic reform.

There was a truism in the political community of the United States that Richard Nixon, because of his revulsion at controls, arising from his days as an Office of Price Administration regulator, could never devise a system of controls that would not mortally offend him philosophically or that would impress the voters. There was a parallel attachment of the conventional wisdom to Bretton Woods, even though a little perspective would demonstrate that that was an obsolescent arrangement.

These were precisely the circumstances that called Nixon out of his den of wary isolation and melancholy suspicion, and transformed him into an agent of radical change. Connally, on the advice of his undersecretary for international monetary affairs, Paul Volcker, proposed a ninety-day wage and price freeze, the detachment of the dollar from convertibility into gold, the end of fixed exchange rates, a devaluation of the dollar on the free market, and a 10 percent tariff on all imports into the United States. Nixon considered that the best course was to refine the plan and await more unfavorable economic news, stirring demand for remedial measures and inflating the customary overconfidence of his enemies that he was trapped between events and inflexible positions he could not alter or abandon.

On August 12, Nixon told Haldeman to round up thirteen men to come the next day to Camp David, including Connally, Burns, Volcker, McCracken, Peterson, and Shultz. All polls and indices showed increasing concern about the economy. These were the laid-back days of deep summer. Now, thought the president, was the time to strike. It was time for something radical. Nixon arrived at 3 P.M. on Friday, August 13, and opened discussions almost at once. He began by saying that conditions had changed and that no one should be "bound by past positions." Certainly, he would lead the way in this direction. He said that there were to be no telephone calls out of Camp David and that there must be an absolute embargo until Monday. He intended to speak to the country on Sunday night.

Volcker had warned on Thursday, and did so again, that it was too risky to wait before removing the threat of a run on America's remaining gold reserves, that a tidal wave of gold redemptions could come as early as Monday. Shultz thought the present gradualism was working. Connally sounded the political note that the United States had carried the world on its back for long enough, that the dollar should float freely like other currencies, that the 10 to 15 percent import tax Nixon was already contemplating should be imposed, that a 10 percent investment tax credit should be reintroduced, and that the automobile industry should be assisted with the abolition of excise taxes, provided the savings were passed directly to the consumer. Connally also proposed a wage and price freeze until January 1972. Burns said the freeze would obviate the need for closing the gold window. He thought such dynamic action would stop any run on the dollar. Connally warned that the British had asked the transmission into gold of all their dollar reserves, $3 billion. He said the country was completely exposed to the world, and when Burns referred to the "goodwill" of allies, Connally interrupted: "We'll go broke getting their goodwill."[72]

Nixon had already made up his mind to do what Connally had recommended, and, as has been remarked, the program had been in place for two months. The administration would utilize powers granted it under the Economic Stabilization Act of 1970, which the Democratic Congress had passed to embarrass Nixon, since they were sure he would not avail himself of those powers. Only the elimination of excise taxes was new. Nixon said that the wage-price freeze would end when labor balked and called a major strike. He outlined to Safire what he wanted in the speech he intended to give on Sunday night. He told Safire not to bother trying to explain the gold window very much. "Let experts speak to experts." He said the country would like the freeze, until they realized that it applied to them, but Safire must hammer at inflation, as the greatest menace to the working man. "He's on a treadmill," said Nixon, who had been pitching for the treadmill-walker's vote for twenty-five years, and had been on it himself in his early years.

He said the country would like the import tax. "The country doesn't like foreigners." He told Safire to wind it up with the question of whether the United States was determined to remain "Number One." Nixon said the message must be to labor to back the freeze, to business to invest, and to the whole country to shape up in a proper crisis spirit of determination. He said that if the press asked why no one had told them what was coming, the answer was "You dumb bastards, if we had told you, you would have told the world and we would have lost all our gold."[73] Connally was the only other person in the room who had ever run for office, and Connally had been Johnson and Rayburn's apprentice in the governorship of what was then the one-party state of Texas. For the others, Nixon's assured, crisp comments were a quick lesson in political realism, not to say cynicism.

With that, the meeting broke up after a little over three hours and Nixon had his dinner alone. He was up at about 3:15 A.M., starting to make notes for his speech on one of his yellow pads. He emerged from his cabin shortly after 4 A.M., startling a navy duty officer coming out of the sauna, and gave him some dictabelts to go to Rose Mary Woods, who was ready to type. Safire brought her his draft at shortly after 6 A.M., when she had already begun typing. Nixon began by claiming that the winding down of the war required that the problems of peace be addressed, which included more jobs, reduction in the cost of living, and repulse of the assault of international currency speculators. His partial draft was a model of the best-defense-is-a-good-offense school of leadership. Nixon went back to bed.

Nixon refined his text Saturday afternoon, determined to avoid or debunk all thought of devaluation, and again dined alone on Saturday evening. He had Haldeman, Ehrlichman, and Caspar Weinberger (Schulz's undersecretary) over to his cabin after dinner, and before a blazing fire mitigated by the air conditioner on the hot August Catoctin night, he told them that he wanted to lift the spirits of the country, as the Roosevelts had done.[74] The group met again on Sunday morning, and everyone left except the president, who remained alone with his thoughts until mid-afternoon.

The White House had reserved up to half an hour for 9 P.M. Eastern Time on all networks. The president spoke for twenty minutes, beginning with a call to a generation of peace and generalized prosperity. He aimed at more and better jobs, an end to the rise in the cost of living, and protection of the dollar from "international speculators." (This was as good as Franklin D. Roosevelt's inveighings against "war profiteers," of which there were none in the United States in the mid-1930s.)

What he outlined was a broader program than had originally been envisioned: There would be a one-year, 10 percent investment tax credit for new plant and equipment, settling to 5 percent after the first year; abolition of the twenty-nine-year, 7 percent excise tax on new automobiles; a one-year advance of fifty dollars of income tax credit for every American from January 1973 forward to January 1972; a 5 percent reduction in the number of federal government employees and a postponement of all federal employee pay raises; a 10 percent cut in foreign aid; a one-year postponement in the Family Assistance Plan (which had not been approved) and a three-month postponement in revenue sharing; a ninety-day wage and price freeze; creation of a Cost of Living Council that would devise a stabilizing mechanism after expiry of the freeze; suspension of the gold convertibility of the dollar; and a temporary 10 percent tax on all imports.

It was, and was seen by everyone to be, a bold program. Those among "the overwhelming majority of Americans who buy American-made products in America" would suffer no loss of value of their money, he said. "The American dollar must never again be a hostage in the hands of international speculators. . . . Government . . . does not hold the key to the success of a people. That key . . . is in your hands. Every action I have taken tonight is designed to nurture and stimulate that competitive spirit to help us snap out of self-doubt, the self-disparagement that saps our energy and erodes our confidence in ourselves. . . . Whether the nation stays Number One depends on your competitive spirit, your sense of personal destiny, your pride in your country and yourself."

Richard Nixon had done it again. The Democrats were generally supportive but nonplussed. Once again, he had astounded them. They were chasing not only a moving target, but one moving with the agility of a gazelle and the cunning of a cat. Almost all editorial comment was favorable, including that from perennial critics such as the *New York Times*. George Meany, chairman of the AFL-CIO, objected that it was a rich man's money grab at the expense of the working man. But that did not resonate as well as Nixon's call for national pride and purpose, repulse of speculators and foreign dumpers of finished goods, and tax incentives and reductions, and his generally bold leadership. The New York stock market, and Nixon's standing in the polls, rose sharply. All polls indicated overwhelming support for the program, the speech, and the man.

Phase II of the plan was ready by October 4, and was announced by Nixon in a television address on October 7. The core of Phase II was a Cost of Living Council, a tripartite Pay Board, an Interest and Dividends Commission chaired by Arthur Burns, and a Commission on Prices, Costs and Profits, composed only of members of the public not identified with business management or organized labor. This was rightly assumed to be a sufficiently confusing structure to muddy the waters well into election year. After a bit of to-ing and fro-ing, George Meany joined the Pay Board. He thought it was nonsense and hostile to the working man, but the country was supporting the president and he did not want to be left behind.

Europe and Japan, accustomed to working both sides of the street, exploiting a high dollar with cheap exports while undermining the dollar by exploiting its convertibility, were in panic. Currency markets temporarily shut down, and there were widespread cries of protectionism. All the foreign agitation confirmed the administration view that Nixon was acting in the national interest. Renowned economist Milton Friedman, despite the best efforts of his former University of Chicago colleague George Shultz, predicted the complete failure of the freeze, a view Nixon personally did not greatly dissent from, but he privately felt the whole issue could be dissembled and finessed.

He told the author, nearly twenty years later, that he was modeling himself to some extent on FDR, and producing a mixed bag of policies that would be so amorphous no one could really figure it out, while giving tangible incentives to investment and job creation and generally raising the country's morale. Nixon recognized, as Roosevelt had, that much of economics is psychology, and that most economists don't really know what they're talking about. Nixon jumped in the polls, and the Democrats had that sinking feeling that Nixon had taken them over the barrel again, as he did with welfare reform, desegregation, arms control, China, and even, up to a point, Vietnam.

— VI —

In Germany, the Social Democrats under former West Berlin mayor Willy Brandt had finally won the government and opened their Ostpolitik with the Soviet bloc, flirting with neutralism in the Cold War in exchange for a more liberal regime in their relations with the U.S.S.R. and East Germany. The United States agreed that West Germany would not seek the formal inclusion of West Berlin in the Federal Republic, and that the GDR (East Germany) and the U.S.S.R. would assure easier contact between West Berlin and West Germany. This was rightly perceived in the world as a breakthrough, and Brandt won the Nobel Prize.

On October 12, Nixon announced that he would be going to Moscow in late May for a full summit meeting with a broad agenda of all important outstanding matters. It was only sixteen years since Eisenhower was given carte blanche by Congress to use atomic weapons to defend worthless islands four miles off the coast of China (Quemoy and Matsu) and eleven years since Nixon scored against Kennedy for entertaining the abandonment of those islands. The large grain sale to the U.S.S.R. was announced on November 5. On the same day, in Moscow, it was announced that Jewish emigration from the U.S.S.R. to Israel, which had been only a thousand in 1970, had risen to about fifteen thousand in 1971 and would continue to increase steeply. The Cold War was clearly in a full thaw.

On September 17, the retirement of two more Supreme Court justices, Hugo Black (FDR's first appointment to that bench) and John M. Harlan, was announced. On October 14, the *New York Times* floated six names of possible replacements for Black and Harlan, including Democratic Senator Robert Byrd of West Virginia, a former member, as Nixon happily informed his entourage, of the Ku Klux Klan (as Hugo Black had been). There were also, at Pat Nixon's insistence, two women on the list, Mildred Lillie and Sylvia Bacon, as well as the attorney for Arkansas in its unsuccessful anti-segregation efforts in 1957. Gestures to the South were still in contemplation.

Chief Justice Burger telephoned Attorney General Mitchell that evening and said if these people were put on the Court, he would resign. When this was reported to Nixon the next morning, the president used rather extreme expletives, including "F___ the ABA [American Bar Association]." This leaked in the *New Republic*, and Ehrlichman wrote that magazine a letter denying that Nixon said any such thing and claiming he had never heard Nixon use that word. Not only were these complete false-hoods, Ehrlichman was the most likely source of the leak in the first place.[75] The current head of the ABA, Leon Jaworski of Texas, moved to improve relations by sending Nixon an article he had written in the association's *Journal*, praising Burger and comparing him to Chief Justices Marshall, Taft, and Hughes.[76] Nixon acknowledged the letter appreciatively. His rela-tions with Jaworski and Burger would take some strange twists in the next few years.

Nixon considered a range of alternative nominees and gave up on Mitchell as a source of such advice because of his failed record at it to date. He consulted Ehrlichman instead, and came up with Lewis Powell, a sixty-four-year-old Georgia Democrat and former president of the ABA, and Tennessee Republican senator (and son-in-law of Senator Everett Dirksen, who had died in 1969) Howard H. Baker. Baker was considering the offer and called back with his answer half an hour after he said he would on the morning of October 21, to accept. By this time, Nixon had changed his mind and decided to nominate Assistant Attorney General William Rehnquist, forty-seven, instead. Baker, having so narrowly missed the Supreme Court, went on to be Senate Minority and Majority Leader, White House chief of staff in emergency conditions, and ambassador to Japan.

The president again addressed the country on television on the evening of October 21, and presented his two nominees. He had again outsmarted his critics; neither had been mentioned in speculation, and neither was exceptionable. He emphasized their demonstrated professional excellence, and it was clear from the response of the ABA and the media that although Powell and Rehnquist were both relatively conservative, there was no possi-ble legitimate opposition to them. Nixon claimed to believe that he would not have got them through if the Senate had not already been blooded by the Haynsworth and Carswell battles. This was an informed but partisan judgment that cannot be verified. Both were confirmed without difficulty and served with distinction, Rehnquist ultimately following Burger as chief justice and holding that position until he died, after thirty-four years on the Supreme Court, nineteen as chief justice.

The military draft, the Universal Military Training and Service Act of 1951, had come up for quadrennial renewal in September 1971. Nixon proposed pay and benefit increases as a start toward volunteer armed forces, and sought only a two-year renewal. The anti-war factions of both parties leapt on this as an opportunity to deprive the president of the manpower even to carry out his phased withdrawal from Vietnam. Conservatives, who generally opposed a volunteer military because they thought it would soften youth and lead to ethnic anomalies in the forces (i.e., too great a reliance on African and Hispanic Americans), supported this bill to ensure the president could carry out his plans in Vietnam. Liberals, who favored the volunteer military, largely opposed the bill as a way of strangling Nixon out of Vietnam on an accelerated timetable. Nixon attacked frontally, starting at his September 16 press conference, and said that failure to pass the bill would certainly make the United States the second greatest military power in the world and gravely impair its ability to keep the peace. In the end, his congressional opponents were resistless against this kind of pressure, and the draft was renewed as Nixon wished.

An election campaign was almost under way in the United States, and by the autumn of 1971 preparations were well along. Democratic chairman Larry O'Brien, a veteran of the Kennedy and Johnson and Humphrey campaigns, and possibly the greatest organizer that party had ever had, surpassing even Roosevelt's James A. Farley and Edward J. Flynn, was staring with disconcertion at the Democrats' nine-million-dollar deficit and the ease with which Nixon could raise money. He devised the idea of having the government pay for the major parties' campaigns, and calling it a reform. He would have the Democratic congressional leaders attach to a tax cut bill a rider favored by Nixon that would furnish $20.4 million for each party, provided it received nothing else, and could persuade enough people after the election to check one dollar each off their taxes to that purpose. Either party could decline the money and rely on its ability to raise funds from its own sources.

Nixon recognized at once this effort to piggyback on one of his bills and saddle the taxpayers with the fundraising efforts of the Democratic Party. It was a devious stratagem from the Democrats' most accomplished tactician, but Nixon had been around the political traps more than anyone, since the retirement of Lyndon Johnson (with whom he had been in a dead heat for fifteen years as America's canniest and most cunning national politician). After the bill went through the Senate with O'Brien's amendment on it, Nixon had a heart-to-heart talk with the chairman of the House Ways and Means Committee, Wilbur Mills, long one of the most powerful men in the Capitol. Nixon pried Mills off the O'Brien line, using unknown presidential inducements, and O'Brien's amendment was accepted – but it was not to take effect until the 1976 election. Nixon didn't care how the Democrats raised their money after he had retired.

Congress was also working on an amendment to the notoriously porous Federal Corrupt Practices Act of 1925 (from the piping days of the Coolidge administration, when much of what was subsequently called corruption was not regarded as overly un-American). The Democrats wanted more exact disclosure of sizable political contributions. Nixon managed to arrange the legislative timetable so that there was a golden window between the expiry of the Coolidge statute on March 10, 1972, and the entry into law of the new one four weeks later, on April 7. In this period of no obligatory disclosure of political contributions, the Republicans received astounding sums – over $20 million, as it turned out – and the only record of the large donors was kept by the faithful and vigilant Rose Mary Woods. The list was known around Washington as "Rose Mary's baby."* [77]

Kissinger returned to China in late October for another secret trip, though the fact of it, replete with front-page newspaper photographs of Kissinger and Chou En-lai at a dinner in the national security adviser's honor, was released right after it ended. They parted with Chou saying in English: "Come back soon for the joy of talking."[78] While this was circulated, and Kissinger climbed another rung as a worldwide personality, a development that left his leader unenthused, the United States finally lost control of the China-seating process at the United Nations. There was an irritating amount of jubilation when, despite the best efforts of Ambassador George Bush, the Nationalist regime in Taiwan was deprived of its seat on the Security Council, thrown out of the General Assembly, and replaced by

---

* The title of a rather gruesome movie in the sixties.

the People's Republic. The press play given Kissinger's second visit to Chou did not make Bush's task easier.[*] [79]

At a news conference on November 12, Nixon announced the withdrawal of another 45,000 American military personnel from Vietnam by February 1, 1972, which would reduce the troop level to 139,000, the level it had reached on the way up, at the end of 1965. He said that if he could not negotiate a peace with North Vietnam, he would leave a residual force of approximately 40,000 men in South Vietnam. (From the standpoint of conserving a non-communist South Vietnam, this would have been preferable to any negotiated settlement that was conceivable, or that materialized, if he had been able to assure funding for such a force.) He said that he had delivered on all his election promises and expected to deliver on his promise to end the war, and was doing so. He said that he would not grant amnesty to draft dodgers who had fled the country, or to deserters.

The claim had been made that Hanoi was amenable to free elections in the South to determine who should represent and govern that country.[80] There has never been a shred of evidence to support this conclusion. Nixon never wavered from his position that the South Vietnamese could decide for themselves in internationally supervised free elections who was their government, and that if the communists came anywhere close to winning, they could have the country. The United States was sincerely championing free elections, and was happy to abide by whatever government emerged from the application of that criterion.

— VII —

A crisis had been brewing for a long time between India and Pakistan. These two countries had been the two largest components of the British Indian Empire, along with Burma and Ceylon (Sri Lanka). They had been divided more or less along religious lines, Hindus in India and Muslims in Pakistan. But Pakistan was divided into East and West Pakistan, which were separated by a thousand miles of Indian territory – a configuration that made governing the country very difficult. There were strenuous separatist tendencies in East Pakistan (Bengal), which came to the surface when there

---

[*] Chou En-lai was only lukewarm about agreeing to accept the invitation to join the bourgeois UN, but Mao insisted that China take its place there at once.

was a free election in December 1970, and 97 percent of the votes went to the Awami League, which sought an independent East Pakistan. When the Awami League and its leader, Mujibur Rahman, captured 167 of East Pakistan's 169 parliamentary seats, and of the 310-seat federal parliament, Nixon's friend Yahya Khan, president of Pakistan, felt moved to try to save the country.

Mujib took it upon himself to declare the independence of East Pakistan, for which he clearly had a mandate. Yahya deployed an additional forty thousand soldiers to East Pakistan (bringing his force strength to seventy thousand), and an attempt at brutal suppression of over 75 million people ensued. The U.S. consulate in Dacca, the main city of East Pakistan, warned the State Department that acts of great barbarism were under way. The entire staff had already complained of American inaction in the face of Yahya's opening acts of repression; the consul was recalled and reassigned and most of the signatories to the original complaint, who knew nothing of the Pakistani government's help in the Chinese opening, were gradually cycled out or retired.[81]

The Pakistani Army arrested Mujib; U.S. information was that a hundred thousand East Pakistanis were killed in the first three days of Yahya's campaign of repression. The U.S. ambassador in New Delhi (India), a former (Republican) U.S. senator from New York, Kenneth B. Keating, was reporting genocide to Washington, and urged that the Pakistani brutality be decried officially. Yahya cleared the journalists out of East Pakistan and redoubled his effort to resolve the crisis by direct action.[82] Yahya knew that Britain had governed the whole subcontinent with never more than a hundred thousand British soldiers and administrators in the vast Indian empire of hundreds of millions of people. Their methods, however, were a good deal more civil, efficient, and morally irreproachable than the brutal attempted subjugation in which Yahya was now engaged.

Nixon liked Yahya personally and felt considerable loyalty to him as an ally and for his help in opening up the channel to China. But there were limits on how far the United States could go in associating itself with repression on this scale. By mid-November, hundreds of thousands of East Pakistanis were thought to be dead, and millions had fled to India. Yahya acknowledged that three million East Pakistanis had fled, and India claimed it was ten million. Most of the world, including the American public, saw this as a contest between Pakistani barbarity and the autonomist instincts of a separate people, supported by a legitimate, if often tiresomely self-righteous, democracy, India.

Nixon and Kissinger, engrossed as they were in triangular Great Power relations, thought Moscow was inciting India, and that India was encouraging Dacca against the ally of both China and the United States. The validity of this perspective was undercut by Yahya's unrealistic and barbarous notions of what he could accomplish in trying to maintain the territorial integrity of Pakistan by brute force. Yahya put Mujib on trial for treason, a capital offense.

Nixon resented what he considered the duplicitous activities of the Indian government. He had Kissinger warn the Indian ambassador against the lobbying effort he was conducting with Democratic senators, and he took note of the timing of a twenty-year "Treaty of Peace, Friendship, and Cooperation" with the Soviet Union, in the midst of the Pakistani crisis. Kissinger had inflated Yahya's hopes by telling him on his return from China in July that Chou En-lai had pledged Chinese support in any dispute in which India was involved. People, especially when hard-pressed, believe what they want to believe, and Chou's statement to Kissinger that China "would not be an idle spectator and would support Pakistan," was garbled in transmission, with the result that either Kissinger told Yahya, or Yahya thought he had, that China would intervene militarily directly against India. Yahya also persuaded himself that the United States would be an active ally.

India was a much more powerful country, militarily, than Pakistan, and the U.S.S.R. was much more powerful than China. Only the United States could redress these imbalances, and Kissinger could not possibly have told or implied to Yahya that the United States, as it painfully extricated itself from Vietnam, was going to go to, or even over, the brink of war with Russia and India to suppress the right to self-determination of seventy-five million East Pakistanis. Kissinger tried to reason with Yahya, and received assurances of greater warrior capabilities of Muslim soldiers (not completely implausible, but India had three times as big an army and five times as large an air force as Pakistan). Nixon sent Yahya messages urging restraint.

Indian prime minister Indira Gandhi came to Washington in early November. When Kissinger was on his second trip to China, Nixon had told Haig to tell the Indians the United States was cutting aid to India. This was a questionable judgment, as the aid was humanitarian assistance to a country that had suffered terrible droughts, floods, and tropical storms, as well as the arrival of millions of destitute East Pakistanis. Kissinger had heard, and thought believable, reports from inside the Indian government that India sought not just the dismemberment of Pakistan, but the destruction of West Pakistan. Gandhi told Nixon that India sought stability and the avoidance of war and chaos, and absolutely did not seek the destruction of West Pakistan.

The Indian side in discussions that were carried on at both the head of government and ministerial levels (for the United States by the capable Joseph Cisco of the State Department) made it clear that if it came to war, India meant to make short work of Pakistan, and that all the refugees must eventually return. Nixon did not believe a word Indira Gandhi said, and portrayed her privately rather gratuitously as "a bitch [and] a whore." She, for her part, claimed to regard Nixon as a puppet of Kissinger's. When each heard of the other's views of the lack of rapport these interviews generated, it did not bode well for the positive outcome of the Indian leader's trip to Washington. Gandhi was a pompous woman, with all the presumption of Nehru's daughter and of an Oxford alumna among the castes of India. But she was a strong and capable leader and not an unattractive person, socially and physically, when she made any effort to be so. Richard Nixon did not bring out her more sociable instincts, but he was no one's puppet. They judged each other harshly, but Nixon was closer to the truth, the allegation of whoredom being entirely political.

Nixon was right that Gandhi's intentions were not so placatory. She was preparing to intervene in East Pakistan. In fairness to her, convenient though it was for her, East Pakistan sought its independence and slaughter was going on in that country, which was not only unacceptable in itself but was pushing millions of helpless refugees on to the Indians. A bifurcated Pakistan had been an artificial creation of the rather chaotic British departure from India in 1947 (for which neither the then British prime minister, Clement Attlee, nor the last viceroy, Lord Mountbatten, have been held properly to account). The division of Pakistan into two sovereign units was inevitable. The government in West Pakistan should have prepared for it sensibly.

Yahya was contemplating attacking India from West Pakistan if India intervened in East Pakistan. This was an insane initiative, but he thought that he might at least be able to resolve the issue of Kashmir (the region bordering India, Pakistan, and China, and claimed in part by all three nations) in his country's favor, and produce Chinese and American assurances in support of his truncated nation. He found such a course preferable to standing by helplessly while India amputated more than half his entire population. The Chinese were no more prepared to go to war for Pakistan against India than the Americans were, and the Russians were not pawing the ground eagerly either.

In the last week in November, East Pakistani guerrillas, armed and trained by the Indians, started to enter East Pakistan in serious numbers, and units of the Indian Army advanced a few miles inside East Pakistan. Yahya described this as an all-out invasion on November 22. It was not that, but it was less innocuous than the spontaneous Pakistani combustion India claimed to detect. India said it had been invited into East Pakistan by local authorities to help restore order. Gandhi was mendacious and Yahya was delusional, and both were planning recourse to force. It was an unpromising combination of people and circumstances.

On December 3, Yahya acted on his deranged contingency plan, and launched an ineffectual sneak air attack on the Indian Air Force, and there was some skirmishing in Kashmir. This gave Gandhi, with her own Pearl Harbor to complain about (though the raids were at mid-day on secondary airfields, and ineffectual) added to Yahya's enormities in Bengal and ancient Hindu-Muslim antagonism, all she needed. She could now justify an outright invasion in East Pakistan, to liberate that benighted province, and a partial invasion of West Pakistan. The Indian response was on the entire West Pakistan Air Force, and when the two air forces disengaged, the Indians returned with a second wave that decimated the Pakistanis on the ground while they refueled, as the U.S. air attaché at the embassy in Pakistan, General Chuck Yeager, had predicted. Yahya withdrew forces from the border with China, and invited the Chinese to enter Kashmir, but they did not. Pakistan's war effort in the west was in parlous condition after one day. The Indian army was knifing through East Pakistan to the relief of the population, having invaded it from three points of the compass in overwhelming strength.[83]

On December 5, Nixon issued a statement blaming Pakistan for the start of hostilities but blaming India for the escalation of the problem to a major crisis. On December 6, Nixon sent a letter to Brezhnev accusing India of seeking to "dismember the sovereign state of Pakistan" and the Russians of being complicit in it. Brezhnev replied at once and in conciliatory manner that Russia was urging restraint and was publicly calling for a cease-fire.[84] Nixon was convinced that Gandhi was trying to justify the shattering of West Pakistan and that Russia was on the verge of giving them cover. Kissinger's view was that the United States and China could not have an ally of theirs destroyed by an ally of the U.S.S.R. This was an oversimplified opinion. Pakistan was now unsustainable in its present form, with a clear majority of the entire East Pakistan population wishing to secede, and restrained, if at all, only by the imposition of barbarous measures.

There was no clear-cut moral winner in the long India-Pakistan dispute, but Pakistan was crumbling, India was a much stronger country, and in this engagement held all the moral, military, and diplomatic cards. India was succoring millions of destitute refugees, while Pakistan was slaughtering scores of thousands of its own innocent civilians. It was geopolitically unfortunate for the United States and China, and Indira Gandhi was a condescending hypocrite and in many ways an odious woman, but in a phrase applied to Disraeli in another Eastern Question, Nixon and Chou En-lai were "backing the wrong horse." So they didn't back Yahya very far.

Also on December 6, NBC film crews were in the White House, shooting "A Day in the Life of the President." Nixon arranged for lots of Pat and family, friends calling, and so forth, and staged various committee sessions, which gave an extremely bowdlerized version of South Asian events. Toward the end of the day, Kissinger informed Haldeman that he was resigning, the efficient cause, according to Haldeman, being the extent of air time given on the NBC taping to William Rogers. Nixon may well have downplayed Kissinger and featured Rogers in order to slap Kissinger down for all the publicity he took for himself on his second trip to China. Haldeman may have been exaggerating or simplifying in his account, as he resented Kissinger's brilliance and prominence. But there is no reason to doubt that some absurd egocentric juvenilism provoked at least a feint at resignation, which Kissinger said could be announced at once and would take effect right after the trip to China in February. Haldeman reported this to Nixon, who calmly replied that he preferred that Kissinger stay, but that if he was going, he was going now, at once, and not clinging on for "hob-nobbing and a photo op" in China. (Nixon's words to the author, June 23, 1992.) There was, unprecedentedly from

Kissinger, a letter of resignation as well, and Nixon became concerned that Kissinger was tired.[*][85]

Haldeman and Haig thought that he had misjudged the India-Pakistan imbroglio, and was self-conscious and upset about it. Certainly, he seemed at times to think war might be imminent involving the world's Great Powers (and six of its seven or eight most populous countries). That does not seem ever to have been a real possibility. No more was heard of the thought of Kissinger's departing for some time.

On the evening of December 9, the Soviet agriculture minister, Vladimir Matskevich, who was visiting Washington to develop relations following the large recent grain sale, met with Nixon. Nixon gave him a message for Brezhnev, which was that the disintegration of Pakistan was a fait accompli, but that if India moved on West Pakistan, which he, Nixon, suspected the Soviets of encouraging, the United states would intervene. A cease-fire must take hold at once and Indian attacks on West Pakistan had to cease. Nixon made it clear that the United States would not tolerate an Indian assault on West Pakistan even if this led to an outright confrontation with Moscow. He did not claim to be speaking for the Chinese.

On December 10, Nixon moved an expanded aircraft carrier task force, centered on the nuclear-powered fleet carrier *Enterprise*, to the Bay of

---

[*] The Rogers-Kissinger struggle had sputtered and flared throughout 1971. On February 14, Kissinger visited Nixon talking of resignation because he was being attacked by the State and Defense Departments and "liberal senators." "Who, which ones?" asked Nixon. "Fulbright, Simon," Kissinger replied. Nixon asked if they had "done anything against us." "Well, it's coming," was Kissinger's reply. "I don't think so," was Nixon's, who couldn't take these sulks of Kissinger's very seriously. On February 23, Nixon told Haldeman, "Henry is clearly more valuable to me than Rogers is, but if Henry wins the battle with Rogers, I'm not sure he's going to be livable with afterward. Henry's irreplaceable. . . . I think Bill is out of the game. When you ask him, he always says, 'I can't talk about it now.'"

On December 24, 1971, Nixon was explaining to Ehrlichman that Kissinger "can't keep it all in perspective. He's too concerned about what Joe Kraft [syndicated columnist] thinks," when Kissinger entered, as in a Harold Pinter play. Nixon: "Hello, come in, come in. I was just giving John the rundown." Kissinger didn't stay long, and as the door closed behind him, Nixon said, "He's dysfunctional, you know. . . . He is indispensable at this time because of the China trip. . . . We cannot have Henry have an emotional collapse. He's on the point of an emotional collapse."

None of the principal players was exuding unwavering stability of mind and judgment. The astonishing fact is how much good and imaginative government this menagerie managed to generate.

755

Bengal. Nixon later claimed that the United States was threatening "to go to nuclear war with the Russians." Kissinger said it was "the first decision to risk war in the triangular Soviet-Chinese-American relationship."[86] This is a bit dramatic, as these carrier groups all have a nuclear capability and move around often. There was nothing to justify a thought of imminent Russian military invasion, and certainly nowhere near the Bay of Bengal. Nixon took this step with absolutely no consultation with anyone, military or civilian, which makes it unlikely it constituted a war threat.

It was a timely show of strength in an unstable theater, and it may be taken as a gesture of reply to the Indian blockade of the East and West Pakistani seacoasts, as well as a method of underlining his message to Brezhnev via Matskevich. But it was not so much a message to the Russians as to the Indians, who were massively affronted by this U.S. entry into the Bay of Bengal, and embarked on a thirty-year program to expand their navy, somewhat as the Russians did after the Cuba missile crisis. The task force was dispatched to discourage India from attacking West Pakistan, not to deal directly with the Russians. Its mission was successful.

The Russian threat was against China, and there is no evidence that it was accentuated in this period. China sent the United States no such messages. Also on December 10, Kissinger met with the new Chinese ambassador to the UN, Huang Hua (whom he had met on his first trip to China in July) at a CIA apartment on the Upper East Side of Manhattan. (Obviously, the Pakistani channel would no longer be practical for Sino-American relations.)

Kissinger handed over a full sheaf of aerial reconnaissance photographs and other intelligence about Soviet military dispositions along and near the Chinese-Soviet border. Kissinger told the ambassador that the United States was secretly encouraging the shipment of military equipment from Jordan, Iran, and Turkey to Pakistan, which the United States would then replace with the donor countries. This was a sensitive matter with the Congress, as U.S. arms sales always carried restrictions about their on-sale to third parties.

Kissinger said that U.S. intelligence indicated the Indians meant to smash the Pakistani army in West Pakistan and take all of Kashmir, and that the United States would not accept any such result. The Chinese ambassador was grateful for the intelligence package, but offered no strong views about what the Indians or Russians might be doing. China was a good deal less alarmed about these developments than the United States was.

Nixon also activated the hot line with Moscow and directly reiterated his concern for West Pakistan. East Pakistan was proclaimed the new state of Bangladesh (Bengal Nation). Kissinger sardonically saluted the birth of the world's fifth most populous country with the comment that "It's a basket case, but it's not our basket case."

Finally, on December 16, the Pakistani commander in East Pakistan surrendered his seventy-thousand-man army to an overwhelming Indian force. (Both the Indian and Pakistani commanders were British-trained, had formidable handlebar moustaches, and spoke in the clipped accents of British officers, with a somewhat humorous overlay of their native inflections; they sounded and looked like Peter Sellers characters.) The Indians declared a cease-fire, and began withdrawing from their modest incursion into West Pakistan. Yahya, still delusional, said the war would continue, but the following day he accepted and honored a cease-fire. Two days later, he resigned, and was replaced by former prime minister Zulfikar Ali Bhutto. Bhutto, a graduate of the University of California at Berkeley, had been a noisy anti-American for some years, but recent events had changed his view. Nixon met with him on December 18 at the White House in a very cordial interview.

Indira Gandhi sent Nixon a scorching public letter holding the United States responsible for the war that had occurred. This was unjust; the United States had urged Yahya not to attack India. Nixon and Kissinger believed to the end that Gandhi had sought the complete humiliation and dismemberment of West Pakistan as well as the secession of Bangladesh. This is not improbable. That there was a real danger of war with the U.S.S.R. is less clear, and is unlikely. There was no sign of imminent adventurism on the Sino-Soviet border, and it is inconceivable that the Kremlin would have interfered with America's rendering heavy-duty assistance to West Pakistan if that country were under dire threat from India. Kissinger became a good deal more rattled in this emergency than Nixon did, and chucking in his resignation in the middle of it, while wishing to accompany the president to China more or less as a tourist two months later, was conduct unbecoming a national security adviser.

The principal local players in the drama ended badly. Mujibur Rahman, the George Washington or Mahatma Gandhi of Bangladesh, was murdered, with his family and even household pets, in a coup, in 1975. Bhutto, the prime minister of Pakistan, was ousted in a coup by General Zia-ul-Haq and was hanged for alleged conspiracy to overthrow the government in 1979. His daughter was, for a time, the prime minister of Pakistan but was overthrown and chased out of the country. Zia-ul-Haq was assassinated when his aircraft was blown up in 1988. Indira Gandhi was assassinated in 1984. Both her sons became prime minister, but one died in an airplane crash and the other was also assassinated. It is a difficult and unforgiving part of the world.

— VIII —

As the crisis in South Asia was unfolding, Nixon made a tactical foray into the camp of one of his enemies, the AFL-CIO. He spoke at the biennial convention in Bal Harbor, Florida, on November 19. He was, as he said, Daniel in the Lion's Den. He had a very ordinary speech written up, which he would then discard and deliver an apparently spontaneous, impassioned speech on the patriotic qualities of the American workingman. Nixon wanted either to win organized labor over in the wake of the hardhat movement, or be antagonistically treated by the leadership, in a way that would irritate the country, which dislikes disrespectful treatment of the president (especially by a bunch of plumbers and plasterers).

Meany did not like Nixon, but recognized that he had put himself skillfully, several times, back at the head of public opinion during his nearly three years in office. Meany removed the band, so there would be no playing of "Hail to the Chief" for his arrival, and Nixon was not prominently seated on the platform. When his turn came, Nixon held up his speech but then delivered a "man to man" speech supposedly ex tempore. In fact, he was tired from having been up most of the night memorizing it. "I know from the last three years that when the chips are down, organized labor is for America." He referred gratefully to the support he had had from demonstrating workers during the Cambodian controversy, and in a brief reference to the wage-price freeze, said that if they did not believe food prices had been frozen, they should consult their wives, who did the grocery shopping.

Meany had packed and disciplined the audience pretty well. The president's reception was polite, but the audience never warmed to his working-man's pitch. As soon as Nixon had left the hall, Meany said, "Now for Act II," a line that drew much laughter and applause. In general, Nixon was pleased at the following day's press treatment. Nixon told Haldeman to be sure the press noticed that Meany was raising his own pay from seventy thousand to ninety thousand dollars and he allegedly wrote out an outrageously self-serving panegyric of adulation that he wanted one of the Republican plants at the labor convention to read from the floor. Nixon on Nixon had him as "one of the most considerate, honest men I have ever had the privilege to know . . . a fair man, a decent man [who] will go down in history as one of America's great presidents."[87] The authenticity of this document is contested, but it is not altogether implausible. This raised one of Nixon's least attractive characteristics: he was sometimes chronically unsure of himself and desperately sought praise as what he aspired to be, to the point of confecting it himself.

In fact, there was a generally negative reaction to Meany's boorish manner. Hugh Sidey, preparing for Nixon's standing as *Time*'s "Man of the Year," a coveted award (although post-Henry Luce, *Time* was a declining middlebrow magazine) wrote of Meany's "pathetic insults." Nixon need not have written out such nauseating self-praise; he could, as on so many other occasions of needless anxiety, trust the people.

On December 12, Nixon flew to the Azores to meet with France's President Georges Pompidou. Rogers and Kissinger were in full debate with each other in the morning, and continued on the president's aircraft on the way to the Azores. When the sessions began in the Azores, Kissinger declined to enter the hall, but stayed just outside, convinced that Nixon would call for him. Nixon and Pompidou were discussing the fallout from Nixon's economic program and Kissinger knew nothing of economics. (Rogers didn't know much about it either.) Connally had met with the leading industrialized countries and there had been progress toward an abolition of the 10 percent U.S. import tax in exchange for revaluation of currencies. France was the sticking point, as it sought a revaluation of gold. (This had been one of de Gaulle's preoccupations, under the advice of gold-bug economist Jacques Rueff.)

Kissinger sat in vain waiting for the call that did not come. After two and a half hours, Rogers, who had stayed out of the sessions also, and largely to avoid Kissinger, discovered Kissinger sitting grumpily at the door. Kissinger raged at Haig in his frustration, and uttered a number of injudicious things about George Bush, who was in fact performing admirably at the United Nations. Haldeman, who had warned Kissinger not to "press [his] luck," reported all these developments to Nixon, who was indulgent as always, and no stranger to the vagaries of temperament, but was disconcerted at the churlishness that seemed to be escalating in his entourage. (When he returned to Washington and then to Key Biscayne, Nixon told Haldeman he didn't want any telephone calls from Kissinger or Rogers, which had a further unedifying impact on the national security adviser's equilibrium.[88] The secretary of state was less addicted and accustomed to telephone conversations with the president.)

After two days, Nixon and Pompidou reached quite a comprehensive agreement, to be worked out in detail between a committee of representatives of advanced industrial countries, that would revalue currencies and dispense with the import tax. (This was confirmed in Washington on December 18: the U.S. dollar was devalued 8.7 percent against a basket of hard currencies, and the import tax was officially repealed.)

Nixon's economic program at this point had been a clear success. The American party returned to Washington on the afternoon of December 14. On the plane, Kissinger briefed the press pool of five and gave them to understand that Nixon had threatened the Kremlin with cancellation of the May 1972 summit if Moscow did not stop encouraging Indian aggression against Pakistan. This was the day that Dacca fell to the Indian Army and Pakistani resistance in the east collapsed. Kissinger was over-egging this pudding, and when Nixon saw the press coverage of his remarks, he told Ziegler to flatly repudiate Kissinger's statement, without naming him. Nixon entered the White House through the underground entrance to avoid the annual Christmas party for the members of the Congress, whom he had no desire to see.

He did meet the congressional leaders on December 15 and gave a very upbeat report on the Azores meeting. Nixon went to Bermuda for a brief meeting with British prime minister Heath, and a few days later West German Chancellor Brandt came to meet with Nixon at Key Biscayne. These meetings, and the one with Pompidou, gave him the opportunity to emphasize the American shift back from Pacific and Vietnam-based concerns to the traditional Atlantic alliance, which Nixon thought Johnson had allowed to deteriorate into a serious state of disrepair.

To Pompidou, Heath, and to some extent Brandt (whose Ostpolitik dalliances with the Soviet bloc Nixon mistrusted), Nixon laid out his vision of the Atlantic alliance. The problem between Europe and America had festered since the war and some – first the French Gaullists and now the

West German Social Democrats – were picking at it like a scab. Western Europe needed the United States to deter Soviet aggression against Western Europe, and the three hundred thousand American soldiers in Western Europe made it clear that the U.S. would fight for Western Europe if the U.S.S.R. forced the issue. But Europe feared that Soviet land force superiority would force the defenders in such a struggle to have recourse to nuclear weapons, which, as Pompidou said to Nixon, would produce a theater nuclear exchange that would stop the Russians but be of little comfort to the Europeans "in their cemeteries."

The logical antidote to this was for the Europeans to strengthen their own conventional forces, which they had the wealth and population to do. Senator Mike Mansfield presented bills or amendments every year calling for withdrawal of American forces from Western Europe, because he thought the Europeans were not pulling their weight. There was some truth to this, but it was a completely irresponsible position for the majority leader of the U.S. Senate to adopt.

The Europeans acknowledged that the United States was doing most of the burden sharing, but claimed they were doing most of the risk-sharing, and advanced the quaint notion that because their risk was greater, it was right that the United States should bear most of the burden. The Europeans never put it this way, but they wanted any nuclear exchange to be between the U.S.S.R. and the United States directly, and not on the heads and in the laps of the Western Europeans. In fact, any nuclear recourse would probably have been battlefield, tactical weapons only, which certainly would have incinerated some towns and caused some radiation, but would not have turned all Europe into a charnel house.

The French developed their own nuclear deterrent to have some leverage on the Russians and the Americans, and match the British. After the Cold War ended, it became clear that the Soviet Army was not as strong as had been feared, and it is not clear that it could have swept NATO ground forces aside as easily as was widely assumed in the sixties and seventies. The Europe-North America alliance was essential to both and, as Nixon said to all three Western European leaders, the United States would not have a viable world without Europe. Nixon felt that the five geo-strategic points with the potential industrial, technological, and military strength to influence the world were the United States, Western Europe, Japan, the U.S.S.R., and China. As head of one, he was concerned to strengthen his alliance with Japan and Europe, detach China completely from Russia, and then negotiate de-escalated tensions and a reasonable working relationship with the U.S.S.R.

The United States would maintain its presence in Europe, whatever Mansfield thought of it, and would conduct its policy with the U.S.S.R. as chairman of an alliance and not unilaterally, and would try to reduce tensions for all Europeans as well as North Americans. He agreed with Pompidou that, as it had been since the Thirty Years' War, the key to Europe was Germany. Germany was apparently a western country, and the settlements at the end of the Second World War had facilitated the westernization of Germany, when its entire eastern population was moved to the west as the Soviet and Polish frontiers were shifted west. Millions of Germans moved west by foot and in ox carts to stay ahead of the Soviet Army.

But there remained sixteen million Germans under Soviet occupation in East Germany, and these "hostages," as Nixon called them, would always be used by the Russians to entice Germany toward neutrality, as Stalin had tried unsuccessfully with Adenauer. The Western Europeans and Americans would have to make the most constant efforts to ensure that West Germany was locked into the West, economically, culturally, and militarily. Nixon and Pompidou agreed that Brandt's Ostpolitik was dangerous, because it incited the Russians to tempt the Germans out of the Western alliance. Nixon said that it was the sort of thing that could win a Nobel Prize, which it had, but it risked relations with "old friends" for the pleasure of a mortal and ancient enemy, Russia.

With Heath, Nixon emphasized the same points, but also the need for Britain to be in the European Common Market and to play as great a role as it could in keeping Europe in a functioning Western alliance. Nixon, as Americans generally did during the Cold War, saw Britain in terms of what it could do to shore up the alliance, put metal up the backbone of the Europeans to make them better Cold Warriors, and prevent the French from alienating or, alternately, disaffecting and conspiring with, the Germans. What was best for Britain, as a country that would, in the event of European unification, be giving up admirable for experimental political institutions, was not given too much consideration.

This was fine with Heath, who had conducted negotiations on behalf of the Macmillan government for Britain's entry into Europe, which had been vetoed by de Gaulle. Heath was an enthusiastic Euro-integrationist, but not for reasons congenial to Nixon; he was very anti-American and wanted Europe to assert its independence of the U.S. Heath and Pompidou would accomplish the entry of Britain into the European Economic Community. Heath would also achieve what Nixon had thought impossible: he made Harold Wilson and Nixon good friends.* Nixon urged Heath to have Britain play as great a role in the world as it could afford, and he expressed frustration and disappointment at the comparative decline of Britain's position in the Middle East.

With Brandt, Nixon stated that he did not support Ostpolitik but had determined, as a good ally, not to try to obstruct it. Brandt and Pompidou both gave Nixon their views of the Soviet leaders, whom Nixon had not met. They considered that Kosygin was dour and anti-German, where Brezhnev was jovial, upbeat, and relatively positive, though overbearing. Brezhnev had largely shouldered Kosygin aside. Both men thought Russia feared China, and, according to Brandt, showed it by denigrating China as a land of peasants who "tilled the land with their bare hands" and where even the mandarinate traveled on bicycles. Pompidou thought the Russians feared the Germans only marginally less than the Chinese, and the Americans less than the Germans, and that it would be possible for Nixon to reach agreement with the Russians in a number of important areas. Brandt felt the Russians knew they could not occupy Eastern Europe indefinitely, and agreed with Pompidou that the Russians would like to reach an accommodation with the United States.

Nixon told Heath that he was retreating slowly from Vietnam to show that the United States was not prepared to do anything exorbitant to end the war. He said the question would soon arise of what the United States would pay to avert a war.[90]

Just before the year ended, the Plumbers had a modest and completely legal success. A column of Jack Anderson's inexactly named the ships in the task force with USS *Enterprise* in the Bay of Bengal, and the Plumbers discovered that the source must have been the Joint Chiefs spy in the NSC, Yeoman Charles Radford, who confessed that he had been copying information to the JCS but denied he had leaked anything to Anderson. Nixon, when he heard that Admiral Moorer had been conducting espionage on Kissinger,

---

* Conversation of Nixon with author.

was relatively unperturbed. Radford was transferred to Oregon, but Nixon declined to authorize a tap on Anderson's telephone.[90]

When Kissinger was briefed on the JCS espionage on him, he, who had been pretty insouciant about tapping the telephones of his supposedly most trusted subalterns, went into one of his vintage paranoiac rages, of the kind that fueled the unsuccessful attack on the publication of the Pentagon Papers. There were some stormy scenes as Kissinger warned that Moorer had to be fired and that Nixon's tolerance would come back to haunt him.

When Nixon sent Mitchell to interview Moorer, the admiral said he thought Radford was furnishing material that was just part of a routine information process. This was untrue, but Nixon was now, for the first time, generally satisfied with the performance of the military high command, and did not want to stir up controversy with a shakeup there, which would inevitably lead to unpleasant and informed speculation in the press.

Nixon's last newsworthy act of 1971 was a commutation of sentence for James R. Hoffa, the former Teamsters' Union president who had served four years of a thirteen-year sentence for jury-tampering, having been the chief target of Attorney General Bobby Kennedy. Nixon assured the reelection of his friend and supporter, Teamster president Frank Fitzsimmons, and then had Hoffa released, provided he did not engage in union activities for eight years, appeasing Hoffa's followers in his union but assuring Fitzsimmons's position. This had the additional benefit of a symbolic affront to the Kennedys, and a direct irritation to AFL-CIO chairman, George Meany.

With the leaders of organized labor, as with the bemedalled chiefs of the armed forces, all was politics, and Nixon was trying to divide and conquer. It wasn't a particularly admirable sequence of events, in the one case or the other, but, contrary to subsequent mythology, Nixon did not inherit a pristine system of presidential disinterest in the fermentation of American life, in all its creative and cynical spontaneity, that bubbled and erupted beneath him. And John Kennedy and Lyndon Johnson weren't saints either.

In the five days after Christmas, there was a fairly comprehensive resumption of bombing in the southern part of North Vietnam. As U.S. forces thinned out, Nixon was replacing ground forces with air power to retain some leverage on Hanoi. The year, a good one for Richard Nixon, the best he had had in the White House, ebbed away, and an election year began.

Like Thomas E. Dewey, Dean Acheson did not see it out. They were two of the elderly advisers Nixon valued. With Eisenhower dead and the absence of a good relationship with Truman, they conveyed much of the wisdom of the traditional, moderate Republican Party and the Roosevelt-Truman Democrats. As has been mentioned, Dewey died in March, aged sixty-nine. Dean Acheson died on October 12. He was seventy-eight.

Nixon gave a one-hour interview to the generally unfriendly Dan Rather of CBS News on January 2, 1972. He claimed not to have decided whether he would seek reelection, but implied that if he did, Agnew would be his running mate. He privately considered Agnew an oaf, but he wasn't sure that he would not need him to help repulse Wallace again. His plan had been Connally, whom he continued to be rather pixilated with as a colleague. The Kissinger-Haldeman theory of displacement, that Connally was all that Nixon wished Nixon had been himself – confident, facile, physically imposing – is overdone. Though there may be some truth to it, there is also probably some disgruntlement at the arrival of this formidable new contestant for the president's time.

However, Haldeman surely exaggerated when he wrote that Nixon was so enchanted with Connally that he was pleased to catch a cold from him, having established that as he had not been outside, it must have been virally transmitted, and Connally was the only cold-sufferer he had encountered in several days.[91]

Removing Agnew for Connally, though Nixon could have effected it if he had insisted, as Roosevelt had in changing vice presidents in 1940 and 1944, would have created problems with the Southern Republicans, whether Wallace was running or not, and Connally, as a former vigorous partisan Democrat, was less popular with the Republicans than he was with Nixon. It was an impractical idea. Republican conservatives were somewhat disaffected anyway, partly as a result of the China overture. William F. Buckley was still "suspending" support of the president, pending the outcome of the visit to China and other developments. Nixon liked and respected Buckley, a brave spokesman for the intellectual Catholic right and an elegant man, but he was irritated by the condescensions of a man who had gone further than Nixon thought appropriate in support of Joseph R. McCarthy.[92]

Nixon also confirmed to Rather that he expected the United States to be completely out of Vietnam by the election, ten months away, subject only to release of American prisoners of war. He said that he would not hesitate to resume bombing, as he had in the previous week, if it would help cover the continued withdrawals, or was needed to protect remaining American forces. This was the beginning of a relentless emphasis on the POWs, a policy that had its hazards, as it steadily raised the value of their currency as hostages in the hands of Hanoi. He referred to Vietnam as a "desperately difficult" war.

— IX —

Three days after telling Rather he had not decided whether to seek reelection, Nixon accepted to have his name on the ballot for the New Hampshire primary and effectively announced his reelection bid. This was unsurprising, but a more ambitious undertaking than it seemed. Only Wilson, FDR, and Eisenhower, of twentieth-century presidents, had been reelected, to that point. Taft and Hoover had been defeated, Truman and Johnson would have been if they had tried, Harding and Kennedy had not survived their first terms, and TR and Coolidge had declined to run.

The Committee to Re-elect the President was set up, named by Safire, which Mitchell was about to take over, after retiring as attorney general. It was meant to be styled the CRP but quickly became known, and was then immortalized, as CREEP. The emphasis on the president rather than his party was designed not only to assure that he was amply funded, but to exploit the fact that his popularity was greater than the Republican Party's. This was short-term thinking. If Nixon was going to have any chance of getting a serious program through the Congress as a reelected president, he would have to get hold of at least one house of Congress.

As 1972 opened, he was running ahead of Senator Muskie, the leading candidate for the Democratic nomination, by about 5 to 7 percent in the polls, but with economic numbers improving and the China and Moscow visits ahead, Nixon looked like a winner. Nixon did not think either Muskie or Senator George McGovern, who was assumed to be running second to Muskie, could take the heat of a presidential campaign. The Nixon campaign had already begun relatively innocuous harassment activities such as distributing bumper stickers falsely identifying Muskie with school busing. But if Nixon took the campaign money for himself, and made no effort to pull Republican candidates in behind him, he would be facing Democratic congressional majorities again and with a very shallow reservoir of goodwill from his own party in the Congress.

The Congress was now a seething mass of Democratic resolutions to force the United States out of Vietnam, cut off funding, and cut and run, the Democrats having suffered a merciful attack of amnesia that prevented them from recalling how the country originally became involved in Vietnam. McGovern had met with the North Vietnamese Peace Talks delegates in Paris in September, and they had told him they would release the American POWs when Nixon committed to a date for a complete American withdrawal. The Democratic peace groups were complaining that easy solutions were available and that Nixon was avoiding them.

Nixon prepared another of his surprises that so bedeviled the Democrats. He would announce further troop withdrawals in mid-January, wait for a few days to draw out the Democrats, and then reveal the secret talks and the proposals he had made that the North Vietnamese had rejected, exposing the Kennedy-McGovern-Fulbright Democrats as the witless dupes of Hanoi that, on this issue, they largely were. Nixon announced a reduction of seventy thousand American servicemen from Vietnam for May 1, which would leave sixty-nine thousand men, and no complete ground combat units. The remaining force, only about 12 percent of the number of American armed forces personnel in Vietnam when Nixon entered office three years before, would be advisers, logistical support, and some air force units.

The CIA and Pentagon anticipated another NVA-VC offensive in the early spring, and Nixon had unlimbered the bombers in the last week of 1971 in part to try to arm himself with some level of deterrence. With no remaining American ground combat units in the country, the enemy might be tempted to try to roll ARVN over and throw the detritus of the great American army in Vietnam into the sea. Nixon would have to reply with an air war that would probably bring out the demonstrators again.

Nixon made his force reduction announcement in a brief statement in the White House press room on January 13. He spoke only about thirty seconds, then departed, leaving Laird to take questions. After a few days, the White House announced the president would address the country on January 25. McGovern dutifully charged into the trap Nixon had baited, and said that Nixon "knows it is not true that our negotiators in Paris have ever discussed with the North Vietnamese the question of total withdrawal from Indochina in conjunction with the release of our prisoners."

The run-up to January 25 was filled with sorting out the president's allies to ensure that no one who should have known of the secret negotiations and didn't, blew up after the disclosure. Haldeman was delegated to tell Rogers and there was a brief softening up procedure for Thieu, who was sufficiently suspicious to have imagined such discussions were underway with Hanoi anyway. Kissinger, ever the protector of his own negotiations, although they had accomplished nothing in twenty-nine months (through no fault of his) and not having to deal with domestic political realities, did not want the secret talks disclosed.

The problems with Rogers and Kissinger continued unabated into the New Year. Rogers assimilated this news of secret talks about to be revealed with his customary good humor, but when Haldeman then spoke to Kissinger, the national security adviser erupted and inflicted a prolonged, syncopated tirade on the chief of staff. He fulminated about Rogers, whom he accused of telling the *Washington Post*'s publisher and editor, Katharine Graham and Ben Bradlee, that he, Rogers, was responsible for the administration's foreign policy successes. Kissinger called Rogers a "psychopath," which is one charge of which Rogers was innocent. Nelson Rockefeller told Mitchell that Kissinger was on the brink of resigning.

Nixon became alarmed at this new outburst of infighting, having treated the many incidents of 1971 pretty casually, and considered whether Kissinger should be eased out. Nixon told Haldeman that Kissinger had leaked to them in 1968 and so he could do the same for the Democrats in 1972. It was fantastic and disconcerting that there was no trust at all between Nixon and Kissinger, despite their intimate association in great diplomatic initiatives. This was the ultimate public sector American union of convenience. Nixon did not regard Kissinger as indispensable, especially as he expected to end the Vietnam involvement, was normalizing relations with China, and was on the brink of an arms control agreement with the U.S.S.R. But he regarded him as uniquely qualified to execute what he, Nixon, was trying to do.

Nixon's political plans came to some fruition in January as well. On January 12, the Internal Revenue Service announced that it was concluding a tax investigation of Governor George Wallace's brother, Gerald, and other people close to the governor. The following day, George Wallace announced that he would enter the Florida Democratic presidential primary as a candidate for that party's presidential nomination, rather than run again as an independent.

The Democratic field now included Muskie, McGovern, Humphrey, Lindsay (who had deserted the Republicans finally), and Senator Henry Jackson, as well as Wallace. Wallace had carried most Florida counties, though not the state as a whole, against Nixon and Humphrey in 1968. He would almost certainly win it in the Democratic primary. He would create havoc among the Democrats but not be their nominee, and leave most of his hard-core 10 or 12 percent of the national vote behind for Nixon. It was widely assumed at the time by Nixon's enemies on the left, and also by many of his admirers, that a deal was cooked up to drop the IRS investigation in exchange for the Wallace relaunch as a Democrat. This cannot be proved, but the purity of the coincidence of the two announcements on adjoining days is improbable.

Financial controversy lurked around the reelection campaign also. Nixon's relations with Howard Hughes were a hardy perennial. As far as can be established, Nixon never did anything for Hughes, so the eccentric billionaire's campaign contributions and loan to Donald Nixon don't seem to have bought him any favors, not even his request for an end to underground nuclear testing in Nevada, where Hughes lived and was a large casino owner. On January 24, the *New York Times* published that, as attorney general, Robert Kennedy had commissioned an investigation of the Hughes-Nixon loan. Nixon privately called Bobby Kennedy "a ruthless little bastard. He wanted to bring criminal charges against my mother."[93] The same day, Jack Anderson ran a story that Rebozo had been a conduit between Hughes and Nixon, as the financier advanced him a hundred thousand dollars. This story evaporated, because there were no violations of disclosure rules and no favors that could be identified as connected to Hughes's donations.

More complicated was the saga of ITT. This former international telephone utility had become one of the country's leading conglomerates, plunging into a great variety of businesses. The Justice Department's aggressive anti-trust chief, Richard McLaren, attacked three of the ITT's acquisitions – Hartford Life Insurance Company, the Grinnell Corporation (a fire alarm manufacturer), and Canteen Corporation (a vending machine company). Nixon considered most anti-trust actions just harassment of successful businessmen by whining, uncompetitive rivals or meddlesome, envious regulators. He ordered that the attack on ITT end, and "If that's not understood, McLaren's ass is to be out of there within an hour," he had told Haldeman and Ehrlichman on May 13, 1971. The president implied in the conversation that ITT, already a substantial contributor to Nixon, might do more.[94]

Anderson jumped on this one too, and had published in February 1972 the allegation that ITT had received a soft settlement (it kept Hartford and disposed of Grinnell and Canteen) in exchange for a four-hundred-thousand-dollar contribution to the Republican Party. Mitchell was retiring as attorney general to take over the reelection campaign, and Richard Kleindienst was going through the Senate confirmation process. Kleindienst had handled the ITT case as assistant attorney general, because ITT had been a Mitchell client in private practice. Kleindienst insisted on reopening his hearings to rebut Anderson. This was not a public relations success, because of the sensational media treatment of it, but the settlement was not overly favorable to ITT. Kleindienst testified he was given no guidance by the White House, Nixon confined himself to ordering that McLaren not be allowed to challenge what had been agreed, the four hundred thousand dollars was really only a hundred thousand, which went to the City of San Diego to defray expenses related to the Republican convention, which in the end was moved to Miami anyway. It was not much of a controversy and not at all a scandal, but Anderson and some other sections of the media played it up rather irresponsibly. Kleindienst was confirmed.[*] [95] To Nixon, the bête noire in the Hughes and ITT episodes was Democratic chairman Larry O'Brien, who also had a financial relationship with Hughes, but was constantly inciting the press to harass Nixon on both points.

Safire was in New Orleans on January 16 watching the Super Bowl when the public address system identified him and asked him to call his office. Many people watching the game in person or on television knew who Safire was and that his office was in the White House, so the announcement was conspicuous and was commented on in the news media. When he telephoned

---

[*] On March 16, 1972, in what proved a foretaste of some adventures to come, former CIA operative Howard Hunt, now working with Colson in White House special operations, entered the hospital room in Denver of the convalescing lobbyist who had signed the memo that gave rise to the Anderson story. Wearing a red wig and claiming to be "Edward J. Hamilton," Hunt gained a signed statement from the lobbyist Dita Beard that the memo that caused the controversy had been a forgery. This was the end of it. Hunt carried out his mission very successfully, which may have excessively emboldened him and Colson.

he was asked to return as soon as possible and go to work hammering into a speech what Kissinger had provided as a record of the secret Vietnam talks.[96]

The White House went through the customary buildup of suspense prior to the president's address on the evening of January 25, 1972. "Some Americans who believed what the North Vietnamese led them to believe have charged that the United States has not pursued negotiations intensively." He debunked all that his Democratic opponents had been claiming and made the point that some were being incited by the North Vietnamese to accuse the administration of not offering what the North Vietnamese had not only been offered, but had rejected. It was a devastating blow to the leading Democratic peace advocates.

Nixon revealed that Kissinger had offered, in May, August, and September 1971 an American and allied pull-out, a cease-fire, and release of POWs. All these proposals were rejected and the North Vietnamese insisted that the United States "overthrow" Thieu on the way out of South Vietnam. Nixon described the latest American offer: a full withdrawal of all non-South Vietnamese forces six months after agreement, a cease-fire throughout Indochina during this period, a complete prisoner exchange, and free, internationally supervised elections in South Vietnam, with Thieu stepping down as president one month before the election, so he could contest it on a basis of equality with anyone else.

The president said that "the only reply to our plan has been an increase in troop infiltration from North Vietnam and communist military offensives in Laos and Cambodia." Nixon said, "We are being asked publicly to set a terminal date for our withdrawals, when we already offered one in private. . . . If the enemy wants peace, it will have to recognize the important difference between settlement and surrender."

Fulbright waffled that it might be necessary to offer more to Hanoi, glossing over his own gullibility, and McGovern claimed that Nixon should not have opposed the McGovern-Hatfield amendment, since he was apparently secretly offering something similar. This was a fraud, and was widely seen to be a fraud, since there is a distinction between a government freely offering something (that was in fact quite distinguishable from McGovern-Hatfield) and being forced by legislative handcuffs to offer it. More reasonable Democrats like Hubert Humphrey spoke favorably of the president's speech. The North Vietnamese, caught flat-footed in their lies to credulous American peace Democrats like McGovern, accused Nixon of election tricks.

This was a brilliant stroke by Nixon, as Hanoi had been given to understand by both Johnson and Kissinger that the United States set a great premium on negotiations. By first resuming the bombing of the North for a few days at year's end without provoking much controversy, and then blowing up the secret talks, Nixon was sending them a message that was not the submissive importunity they sought and sometimes received from Americans.

The press was, as usual with Nixon's surprises, impressed, but it responded in a way he had not foreseen, by creating a dashing super-secret agent out of Kissinger. Nixon watched with unrecorded, but easily imaginable, sentiments as Kissinger suddenly was brought forward as a regnant genius and boulevardier. Hugh Sidey, always pretty reliable at riding a Washington trend, breathlessly informed readers that at a cabinet meeting, Kissinger's "intellect fills the room . . . [He] is fanatical about being fair to every department [a startling revelation to the cabinet department heads involved] . . . [All were] overwhelmed by facts and intellect," including the person for whom Kissinger worked, and whom *Time* had just proclaimed a few weeks before to be the "Man of the Year."

There is no question of Kissinger's intellect and thoroughness and personality, but this was just idolatrous puffery of a kind Sidey had not engaged in since the piping days of JFK. A new pattern had started, that would be followed for many years, of an unequal distribution between Kissinger and Nixon of the credit due to both of them for the foreign policy achievements of what was, after all, the Nixon administration.

Nixon was discreet in his memos and comments to his entourage, but a tug-of-war had already begun between Nixon and Kissinger for history's attention. It continues yet. President and Mrs. Nixon and a large entourage, including Kissinger and Rogers, left from Andrews Air Force base near Washington on the trip to China in the late morning of February 17, 1972, starting what Nixon would call, without hyperbole for once, "a week that [would] change the world."

Having fought his way against more adversaries and inhibitions than afflict most American leaders, all the way up the rickety stepladder of U.S. public life, and having been inducted into its highest office in the most daunting circumstances, Nixon now appeared to have the opportunity to become one of the great figures of modern history. It was a gratifying and amazing prospect.

PART IV

The Indestructible
Man and Myth

1972–

President Nixon receives Canadian prime minister Pierre Elliott Trudeau. Nixon found Trudeau's infatuation with communist regimes, and what he regarded as his trendy posturing, tiresome, but he did find him intelligent and personally respectful. Trudeau was impressed by Nixon's intelligence also, and by his evident expertise and long experience in foreign affairs, and found him quite congenial.

Nixon folk dancing with Romanian communist dictator Nicolae Ceauşescu (right) in Bucharest, July 1969. Ceauşescu assisted in opening relations between the United States and China, and Nixon remained friendly with him right up to his overthrow and execution in 1989.

C4644-27A / Byron Schumaker

Nixon visiting the venerable quasi-fascist Spanish dictator Francisco Franco in 1970. After their motorcade finally reached the palace where Franco received important visitors, Franco and Kissinger both fell asleep in their chairs, leaving Nixon to converse with the Spanish foreign minister. Nixon was little concerned with the niceties of other leaders' domestic affairs and dealt with foreign leaders according to their potential utility to the United States.

5364-17 / Ollie Atkins

Pictures of Elvis Presley's visit to the White House on December 21, 1970, are the most requested of all the photographs in the national archives. When Nixon, eventually commenting on his visitor's brown velvet suit, said, "You're rather flamboyantly dressed," Elvis replied, "Mr. President, you dress for your job and I dress for mine." Elvis was a long-time Nixon supporter.

Christmas dinner in the White House, 1970. From left: Pat Nixon, David Eisenhower, Julie Nixon Eisenhower, Mamie Eisenhower, who always had an excellent rapport with Nixon, the genial host, and Tricia Nixon.

Nixon often went to Camp David in poor weather and seemed to enjoy an almost Wagnerian Valhalla quality in it. Here, in 1971, he is strolling with British prime minister Edward Heath, a man whose election he welcomed but with whom he had little rapport. Heath's proposal that they go to a first-name basis was greeted with stony silence.

February 21, 1972, Beijing Capital Airport. Nixon completes the handshake Chou En-lai had unsuccessfully offered to John Foster Dulles at Geneva in 1954. Nearly twenty years later, Chou still called Dulles's rebuff "a dirty act."

A photograph that astounded the world. Mao Tse-tung always professed admiration for Nixon and offered him asylum in China at the end of his presidency. He even telephoned Nixon in hospital in Long Beach, California, when Nixon almost died of phlebitis in November 1974, dumbfounding the hospital switchboard. For Nixon, long one of the fiercest Cold Warriors, it was an amazing trajectory of events.

Nixon's massive preparations for the trip to China included lessons in the use of chopsticks. At the same dinner, Secretary of State William Rogers regaled the Chinese foreign minister with stories of his favorite golfer, Sam Snead, but the minister was uncertain what golf was.

Pat Nixon at a reelection telethon in New York with Senator Jacob Javits and four-term governor Nelson Rockefeller, in 1972. Nixon respected Rockefeller's competence, confidence, affability, and wealth, but thought him politically erratic. Rockefeller never knew what to make of Nixon, acknowledging his intelligence, political cunning, and determination, but he was amazed by his stylistic lapses and personality foibles. Nixon had no use for Javits, which was reciprocated.

Nixon at the Grand Ol' Opry in Nashville, in February 1974, as part of his final effort to drum up support in the country during the Watergate crisis. Nixon was a talented pianist but never read music, and at one time had memorized hundreds of compositions, including full concertos and the piano sections of symphonies.

More than a million Egyptians cheered Nixon when he arrived in Cairo in June 1974. More than six million cheered him as he rode with President Anwar Sadat the next day in an open railway car to Alexandria. It was the first time an American president had ridden in an open car since the assassination of President Kennedy. This was the last great foreign policy breakthrough of Nixon's presidency.

At Riyadh, on the same trip, Saudi King Feisal (right) was more guarded. This was still a spectacular breakthrough in the Middle East, as Sadat had expelled the Russians, who were no longer able to exercise great influence in the area.

The end is nigh. The congressional leadership bearing bad news about Watergate in August 1974. From left: House Speaker Carl Albert, Republican House Leader John Rhodes, Senate Majority Leader Mike Mansfield and Deputy Leader James O. Eastland, the president, and Republican Senate Leader Hugh Scott.

On August 8, 1974, in a mighty feat of self-control, Nixon delivers his resignation speech with composure, dignity, and good taste to a live television and radio audience of many hundreds of millions. As always, he spoke without notes or teleprompter and delivered the speech flawlessly from memory. In its way, it was a tour de force, admitting mistakes but not illegalities.

Unyielding to the end, Nixon's farewell to the senior administration and White House staff on August 9, 1974, mixed perfect aplomb with heavy sentimentality (Julie and David at left, Tricia and Ed Cox at right). He reminisced about his parents, quoted from Theodore Roosevelt, made a few jokes, reduced many to tears, promised to be back, and received a huge ovation. He would now begin his greatest comeback of all.

Chapter Thirteen

The Pinnacle

1972

— I —

RICHARD NIXON HAD PREPARED very carefully for his trip to China. He had always been a man to brush up on any subject where he would be tested, but on this occasion, which he recognized as the greatest of his life to date, he was massively briefed.

Nixon and Kissinger were still hoping that the relationship with China would loosen up Hanoi. Kissinger took it as a "significant" omen when he was advised by Vernon Walters on February 14 that the North Vietnamese had invited Kissinger to lunch on March 17. Haldeman claimed that Kissinger was "ecstatic" and announced that there "would be no major North Vietnamese offensive as we had been fearing." Nixon thought he was reading too much into a luncheon invitation. He was (even allowing for Haldeman's tendency to exaggerate Kissinger's mood swings).¹ Walters, learning North Vietnam's Le Duc Tho would be in Beijing when Nixon would be there, was invited to propose a meeting between them, but the Chinese declined.²

Also on February 14, Nixon had received Senator James Buckley, representing essentially the view of his brother, William Buckley, and other conservatives who had "suspended" support for the president. Nixon had at first stated that he would not deal with "the nuts." Though he didn't put the Buckleys in that category, he had always been uneasy about Bill Buckley's overlong dalliance with Joseph R. McCarthy, but was also dazzled by his intellectual and polemical genius and suave self-confidence. James Buckley enunciated the fears of his brother and their group that Nixon had, or would, compromise the security of Taiwan and South Korea. Nixon assured him, in total honesty, that this was not the case, but Buckley departed unconvinced. These conscientious, persevering, and articulate conservatives were admirable, but they were also exigent, high-maintenance supporters, for all the support they ever really provided.

Even more presumptuous, though much more positive, was the visitor on February 14 – former French culture minister, renowned author, and friend of de Gaulle's, André Malraux. Malraux's attempt at profound circumlocution prepared Nixon for what he was about to get from the Chinese leaders. Sitting before the fireplace in the White House residence, Nixon stoked Malraux's aerated taste for the epochal by quoting Lincoln and invoking explorers. Malraux said absolutely nothing that was of any assistance to Nixon in evaluating Mao and Chou, but he was flattering and, in the manner of much of French literature, spoke in allegories. (He had a facial tic that Nixon and Kissinger found very distracting.)

Thus, Mao had had "a fantastic destiny. . . . You may think he will be addressing you, but in truth he will be addressing Death. . . . There is something of the sorcerer in [Mao]. He is a man inhabited by a vision, possessed by it. . . . No one will know if you succeed, Mr. President, for at least fifty years. The Chinese are very patient." This was becoming surrealistic claptrap. Then came the ultimate imprimatur, posthumously provided, as Nixon saw Malraux to his car: "I am not de Gaulle" (a fact on which his host did not require enlightenment), "but I know what de Gaulle would say if he were here. He would say: 'All men who understand what you are embarking on salute you.'"[3]

In between, in the Oval Office, Malraux (whom Nixon called "André" at one point) told Nixon and Kissinger that when China had nuclear weapons, Japan would defect from the American alliance. Nixon demurred, and of course was correct. Nixon was familiar with Malraux's argument in his *Anti-Memoirs* that as the United States was the first power to become a Great Power "without attempting to," as Nixon summarized it, "that's why we always waged war so well, and peace so badly." This was typical French intellectual grandiosity and condescension, and the United States had waged peace extremely well through most of the Cold War. The White House foreign press adviser and future ambassador to the UN, John Scali, said he had been "listening to the views of a romantic, vain old man who was weaving obsolete views into a special framework for the world as he wished it to be."[4]

After Malraux left, Nixon made the point to Kissinger that when Malraux said Mao would be impressed by Nixon's youth, "That's a commentary on the leadership of the world these days. It's all too damn old." Kissinger volunteered that Mao would have thought Kennedy "a total lightweight. . . . Mao would have had total disdain for Kennedy. He would have felt about him the way de Gaulle did. De Gaulle had absolutely no use for Kennedy. These historical figures can't be bluffed and they won't fall for pretty faces." (In fact, de Gaulle professed considerable esteem for Kennedy, as did Malraux, as Nixon knew, and there is no reason to imagine that Kissinger had any idea what de Gaulle or Mao might have thought of JFK.)

This odd exchange ended on a familiar note. Kissinger: "I thought your questions were very intelligent." Nixon: "I tried to keep him going." Kissinger: "Well, you did it very beautifully."[5]

Malraux had pitched right into the cult and cottage industry Nixon and especially Kissinger had already started to build, though Malraux had been one of the founders of the genre – of the surpassing, overarching, quasi-mysticism of the Chinese connection. So great was the void that existed between the United States and China, so great the mystique of Mao and Chou, so desperate was the world for some new dimension, some *deus ex machina* in its affairs, that they could all get away with this fraud that they were in the footsteps of Marco Polo (the code name of the Kissinger visits) and were going to a magic place, if not, like brave pioneers, another planet. Indeed, Nixon almost affected to be emulating the astronauts he had sent to the moon.

It was an imaginative diplomatic initiative of great geopolitical consequences, carried out with great singleness of mind and professionalism by Nixon and Kissinger. But to the extent it was sold, then and subsequently, as a combination of Columbian exploration, Bismarckian diplomacy, and Jesuitical missionary work, it was a confidence trick to reelect the president, pad the cv's of the two explorer/diplomat/pilgrims, and garnish the post-governmental wallet of Kissinger.

Nixon, always hovering between realism, cynicism, and pessimism, with only the rarest outbursts of exuberance, kept a better sense of proportion than Kissinger. He wrote in his diary, "As Henry and Bob [Haldeman] pointed out, there was almost a religious feeling to the messages we received from all over the country. . . . It was really a question of the American people being hopelessly and almost naively for peace, even at any price. [Henry] felt that perhaps there was also some ingredient of excitement about the boldness of the move, and visiting a land that was unknown to so many Americans."[6]

Nixon had been briefed for over forty hours by Kissinger alone, and on the airplane confronted a stack of briefing papers from him four feet high. Kissinger wrote that Mao and Chou "have been surmounting towering internal and external obstacles for some fifty years. They take a long view. They see history on their side." To the extent they did, it was half Han Chinese racism and half a pose, but oracular comments on China and its leaders were now oppressively in vogue.

The trip was broken by two nights and a day in Honolulu and a day in Guam. The accompanying entourage was about three hundred people, including a hundred journalists. When Nixon went over the list of the reporters, news anchors, executives, and cameramen, he asked, "[Are there] any non-Jews here?"[7]

As they proceeded across the Pacific, Kissinger continued to crank out memos. He warned that if the Chinese did not think the Americans serious, "They could then deal with us like the North Vietnamese do – inviting in opposition politicians, dealing with unfriendly private groups, appealing to hostile journalists, lambasting us in the United Nations. . . . We can be certain that they would be extremely skillful at this game; we would pay a double price at home and abroad for our alleged naivety at trying to deal with these people in the first place."[8]

The *Spirit of '76*, as Nixon had renamed Air Force One, landed at Beijing's Capital Airport at 11:32 A.M., Monday, February 21.* [9] On the East Coast of the United States, it was thirteen hours earlier, and the arrival was carried live on television in the United States and throughout the world. (Nixon had placed heavy emphasis on applications for television journalists to accompany him, as opposed to the columnists Kissinger favored.) Nixon foresaw that this could be a mighty television drama, and he detested most of the opinionated columnists. The evening events would be live to breakfast television in the United States, and the morning events live to evening television at home.

---

* There had been some concerns that Chiang Kai-shek would try to shoot down Nixon's plane with warplanes bearing People's Republic markings.

When the aircraft taxied to a stop, Nixon emerged into 34⁰F (1⁰C) winter weather and descended the gangplank. Mrs. Nixon was several paces behind him, and Haldeman blocked the way for anyone else until the Nixons had arrived and been greeted. Chou En-lai awaited them on a red carpet at the bottom of the steps. When Chou began to applaud, Nixon, in the approved Chinese matter, applauded in return. As he set foot in China, Nixon ostentatiously thrust out his hand to Chou, reciprocating the handshake Chou had unsuccessfully offered John Foster Dulles at Geneva eighteen years before (an act Chou described in the ensuing discussions as "false and dirty," indicating how effective a snub it was).[10]

Chou En-lai introduced a number of officials and then stood on Nixon's right, at attention, as the national anthems were played. To Nixon, "'The Star-Spangled Banner' had never sounded so stirring . . . as on that windswept runway in the heart of communist China. The honor guard was one of the finest I have ever seen. They were big men, strong looking, and immaculately turned out. As I walked down the long line, each man turned his head slowly as I passed, creating an almost hypnotic sense of movement in the massed ranks."[11] Chou had greeted Kissinger in English as "old friend."[12]

At his residence, Mao's chief doctor, Li Zhisui, who headed a team of nurses (who probably performed other even more intimate services for him as well), had "never seen him so excited."[13] Mao had been ill, and there was some concern about whether he would be well enough to receive Nixon. At one point, a few weeks before, when Mao had seemed too infirm to be able to receive visitors, the usually unflappable Chou En-lai became so upset he had lost control of his bladder and bowels.[14] Mao had the Hunan peasant's suspicion of doctors and medicine and generally refused antibiotics, though he took huge amounts of sleeping pills.[15] But when he contracted pneumonia, apparently at the funeral of his old comrade Chen Yi, in January, Li and his medical team were brought in again. They used the oxygen tanks and respirator that had been sent in advance for Nixon in case a medical problem befell him. (Chen Yi said he had approved receiving Nixon on the same basis on which Stalin had made peace with Hitler.)[16]

Chou and Nixon rode together in a curtained car, at the head of a long line of old Russian limousines, into central Beijing. There were only a few people on the streets, as the route had been sealed off. When they reached Tiananmen Square, where crowds of five hundred thousand were routinely whipped up to greet obscure visitors such as Haile Selassie (whom not ten thousand people in all China had heard of before his arrival), there was no one. The immense, empty square was Orwellian in its eeriness. Madame Chou greeted the president and his party when they arrived at the official guest houses. Nixon was preparing to have a shower when Kissinger entered to say that Chou had returned to fetch them, as Mao Tse-tung wished to meet Nixon at once.[17] (The ailing but monumental chairman had had his first shave and haircut for months, an unknown but singular honor. He had, in certain habits, almost become an Oriental Howard Hughes.[18])

This was very encouraging, as it left no doubt of high Chinese hopes for the meetings, and it would be clear to all, in China and out, that Mao himself was the promoter of the rapprochement. Nixon, Kissinger, and Winston Lord, who spoke some Chinese, and a Secret Service agent, crowded into the car with Chou En-lai and they drove to the official resi-dential area, the Zhongnanhai,[*] [19] which was separated from the Forbidden City, the ancient complex of palaces and courtyards of the Chinese emper-ors, by two man-made lakes.

Nixon and Chou's car came through the gates and went for a mile past pleasant, but not grand, walled houses and small groves of trees, and arrived at the front door of a house not easily distinguishable from the others.[†] [20] This was the home of the ruler of more people than anyone else in the world, generally reckoned the most intriguing personality in the world. There was a Ping-Pong table in the lobby,[21] and Dr. Li ushered the guests on into the chairman's study. One of Mao's pretty young multipurpose assis-tants helped him shuffle toward the president of the United States, and they shook hands warmly and lengthily as the flashbulbs of official Chinese pho-tographers popped.[22]

The group sat in a semicircle of large armchairs, Nixon and Mao in the middle. All translating was done by Mao's interpreter, Nancy Tang, who had accompanied Kissinger from Pakistan on his first visit in July 1971. She had lived in Brooklyn as a child, and spoke exemplary English, but was also

---

[*] The deposed Prince Sihanouk of Cambodia, no more to conduct visitors around Angkor Wat and now an unhappy resident of the Beijing official quarter, departed in protest at the arrival of the Americans.

[†] Initially, Mao had relieved himself outdoors in this compound, squatting in the peasant manner, but Chou had eventually persuaded him of the virtues of a squatting toilet in his bedroom. Prior to that, he had been followed around the grounds by an aide with a shovel, like a Fifth Avenue dog.

an expert at interpreting Mao's often slurred diction and heavy Hunanese accent. The interview had originally been scheduled for fifteen minutes, but continued for over an hour. The ambiance of the talks was cordial throughout. Mao spoke in short bursts of verbosity, and the Americans presumed that he was convalescing from a stroke.

Mao reached over the end of his armrest and wordlessly seized Nixon's hand again, and held it for a full minute, a gesture of welcome that impressed the Chinese as much as the Americans present. Kissinger had Lord cropped out of the official photograph so as not to offend Rogers, a noteworthy act of consideration by the national security adviser, for a rare recipient of such consideration.

The room was lined with bookcases, and there was a number of books open on the tables beside Mao. Nixon complimented him on his library and his writings, which Mao deprecated. Nixon said they had changed the world, and Mao responded that they had perhaps changed a few places in the vicinity of Beijing but that that was all. Mao generously commended Nixon's *Six Crises*, "not a bad book," and said, "I voted for you in your last election. I like rightists."

Nixon tried to get into legitimate current issues, but Mao referred him to "the premier." Mao added with evident amusement that "our mutual old friend, Chiang Kai-shek, does not approve of our meeting." One point no Chinese leader could resist making for long was that China was never an aggressor, and Mao said, "You will want to bring home some of your troops. Ours do not go abroad." Nixon made the point that the Chinese would rather have U.S. forces in Japan than a remilitarized Japan. Chou En-lai diplomatically changed the subject. Nixon referred flatteringly to Kissinger's ability to travel clandestinely to Paris and Beijing, undetected except by "a few pretty girls." Kissinger said that he used them as a cover, and Mao, whose sex drive had apparently made less compromise with age and infirmity than the rest of his body, expressed appreciation of that. (He had written, showing faulty hygiene, but not false bravura, "I wash myself inside the bodies of my women.")[23]

The Soviet Union was barely mentioned, and Taiwan was acknowledged to be a problem that would require some time to resolve. Nixon made a final effort to reach at least a shared perspective with his host by saying that neither China nor the United States sought to dominate the world or each other, and that they should be able to reach an understanding where each could develop in its own way without bothering the other, though the same could not be said "of some other nations." Mao heard him clearly enough, but did not take the bait, and said that China did not threaten Japan or South Korea, and turned to Chou, who had been consulting his watch, and asked, "Do you think we have covered enough today?"

Stalin had resented Mao's failure seriously to engage the Japanese in the Second World War, and Mao resented being kept waiting by Stalin in Moscow for two months from December 1949 to February 1950, with nothing to do except, as he put it, "eat, sleep, and shit."[24]

Nixon was not going to break off without another try at fishing out some lapidary addendum to *The Little Red Book*. Quoting Mao that we must "seize the hour, seize the day," he said that both he and Mao had taken chances to set up this visit and that he, Nixon, never said "something I cannot do. And I will always do more than I can say." Mao joked that Nixon should pay no attention to China's calls for the overthrow of reactionary governments, and that he, Mao, hoped that Nixon would not be overthrown. Mao praised Pakistan's Yahya Khan for promoting their meeting and said that he had not been "happy with your former presidents, from Truman through Johnson." (Mao had courted Roosevelt, as best he could from northwest China, even sending congratulations on his reelection in 1944.)[25] Mao concluded with almost indecipherable comments about the utility of discussions even if they did not lead to instant results. Mao volunteered to Nixon that he had not been well, and Nixon assured him that he looked fine. There was a further round of handshakes and photographs, and the Americans departed.

Mao told his doctor, Li, that he had been impressed by Nixon, that he was forthright, unlike the leftists and the Soviets. He later told British prime minister Edward Heath that he thought Nixon "a man who knows what he stands for, as well as what he wants, and has the strength of mind to get it." Mao disliked courtiers, and was suspicious of the Kissinger type: "Just a funny little man. He is shuddering all over with nerves every time he comes to see me." This was the unjust snobbery of the totalitarian dictator,[26] possibly amplified by the misanthropic raconteur (though Heath insisted to the author that his account was accurate).

The Americans had hardly got to the end of Mao's long driveway before they began the reinterpretation of their host's anodyne, geriatric remarks into Confucian proverbs virtually written on giant tablets of the rarest marble. Thus, Nixon wrote of Mao's "remarkable sense of humor," and a mind that moved "like lightning." Kissinger, as usual, took the lead in establishing their participation in another of the greatest moments since the Creation: Mao was a near-superman. "I have met no one, with the possible exception of Charles de Gaulle, who so distilled raw, concentrated will power." (He had seen even less of the general than he had of the chairman.) But Winston Lord moved this ball forward with even more energy than his leaders. He and Kissinger both became fond of the explication that if they entered a "cocktail party, they would have instantly grasped that Mao was the most important man in the room." It is doubtful that Mao had attended a cocktail party in his seventy-eight years, and few Western institutions were so likely to repel him, but given that he was invariably cosseted by aides and lackeys, his attendance would be, to say the least, conspicuous. Only Charles de Gaulle's great height would keep him in contention in the "raw concentrated will power" sweepstakes such an improbable forum would induce.

Winston Lord discovered, on reading his own notes, that Mao had outlined the Soviet position on Taiwan, Vietnam, and the Soviet Union, after all, "in just a few sentences, sometimes directly, sometimes in an allegorical way." Kissinger found Mao's remarks like Wagner's motifs, sprinkled through a composition and taken up later. Afterward, Kissinger demonstrated his skill at this sort of magnification: "As I comprehended better the many-layered design of Mao's conversation, I understood that it was like the courtyards in the Forbidden City, each leading to a deeper recess distinguished from the others only by slight changes of proportion, with ultimate meaning residing in a totality that only long reflection could grasp."

On the basis of what he actually said, Mao Tse-tung could not have imagined that his rather casual and breezy comments would attract any such intense and apparently rewarding scrutiny. The meeting between Mao and Nixon had great significance, but it would not have been less important or revealing if they had recited telephone books or the alphabet or risqué stories to each other, or just stared and held hands. The substantive talks would be with Chou En-lai, to whom Mao explicitly entrusted them in the presence of the Americans.

— II —

At the opening plenary session that followed, Nixon got into the spirit of things by speaking in Maoist and Chouist phrases he had memorized. After another ceremonial handshake across the table in one of the meeting rooms in the Great Hall of the People, Nixon launched the talks by saying, quoting Chou himself, "The helmsman must ride with the waves or he will be submerged with the tide." This self-important, affected, aphoristic style took like the measles among the Americans, and rendered parts of the exchange quaint, not to say incomprehensible. They agreed on how to organize their talks and then adjourned to a reception and a formal banquet. Chou said, "The gates of friendly contact have finally been opened," and recited China's familiar five principles of respect for sovereignty and territorial integrity, mutual non-aggression and non-interference, and peaceful coexistence. He went round the room with a mao-tai, slightly bowing to each American and clinking glasses. He was an elegant and exquisitely polite man.

Nixon had memorized his toast, and it included excerpts from Mao's works. His interpreter, Charles Freeman of the State Department, knew that Nixon had memorized his remarks, and he wanted the text, which Chapin, Haldeman's assistant, refused. Freeman responded, "If you think I'm going to get up and ad-lib Chairman Mao back into Chinese to this audience, you're out of your mind." It was agreed that in this case the Chinese would provide the translation. Nixon pointed out that more people were watching this reception than any event in the history of the world, and paraphrased Lincoln at Gettysburg when he said that the world would not note what they said but would remember what they did there. (Of course, Lincoln's speech is even better remembered than the battle.) He quoted Mao: "So many deeds cry out to be done, and always urgently. . . . [Inevitably] Seize the Day. Seize the hour." Then: "This is the hour, this is the day for our two peoples to rise to the heights of greatness which can build a new and better world." He too circled the room, sipping and clinking and slightly bowing to the seventy Chinese.[*][27] It was a gracious start

---

[*] Veteran CBS newscaster Walter Cronkite was not expert with chopsticks and accidentally fired an olive at a neighboring table. Secretary of State Rogers regaled the Chinese foreign minister with stories of his sporting hero, renowned golfer "Slamming Sammy" Snead. This wasn't a success, as the minister wasn't sure what golf was.

to the conference, carried live by all American networks almost without comment for four hours. The Beijing *People's Daily* was sold out for the first time anyone could remember.[28] Nixon's visit to China registered the highest U.S. public recognition of any event in the history of the Gallup poll.[29]

Nixon and Chou En-lai got down to serious business the next morning, with a smaller group of aides. Nixon started by emphasizing the very small number of Americans who would see the transcript or receive summaries of the discussions. He warned that there were opponents to his policies in the American bureaucracy, and that it was subject to even benign indiscretions, and he wanted the Chinese to know that the only way of assuring the security both sides sought was to confine information to the very tight circle he designated. He accepted Chou's invitation to speak first, and said that he would deal with Taiwan first. Dean Acheson had not included Taiwan (or South Korea) in his famous 1949 assertion of America's defensive perimeter, but Eisenhower had been very explicit on this point in 1955. Taiwan was an ally, and Nixon had sent Ronald Reagan to reassure Chiang Kai-shek of this (with no great success) in October 1971. The president spoke about Taiwan for ninety minutes without pause, consultation of notes, hesitation, or repetition. It was a tour de force. He outlined a policy that came as news to his aides, and contradicted his rhetoric and even convictions going back almost to the start of his public career twenty-five years before.

Nixon said that it was understood that Taiwan was a part of China and that there was only one China. This was not so controversial, because it was the official Taiwan position also. He said, as his second main point, that the United States would not support independence for Taiwan. His third point of emphasis, dealing with a concern of the Chinese, was that, to the extent it was able to do so, the United States would discourage Japan from establishing a presence in Taiwan as the American forces withdrew from the island. His fourth principle was that the United States would support any peaceful solution to the Taiwan question. This made it clear that it would oppose a military solution imposed by the People's Republic.

He sought normalization of relations with China, and said that two-thirds of American forces on Taiwan were connected to other American activities in the Far East, and would be withdrawn as the Vietnam presence continued to be wound down, and that the rest would be withdrawn as conditions permitted.

Nixon explained the complexities of his domestic position: "The problem, Mr. Prime Minister, is not in what we are going to do, but in what we are going to say about it."[30] He said the left in America, because of its deference to the Soviet Union, wished his trip to China to fail. The far right wished it to fail because of Taiwan, and there were pro-Indian and pro-Japanese factions across the political spectrum in the United States who also wished it to fail. He described the challenge both sides faced in finding language they could agree upon that would give China what it wanted but would "not stir up the animals" in the United States.

Nixon made a strong statement that he didn't much care or consider it his concern what China said publicly, and he understood that the Chinese leadership might believe that their best interests were served by all the rhetoric about supporting the forces of liberation and so on, but China should realize that a continued U.S. military presence in Europe, the Pacific, and the Far East was necessary to the conservation of peace. He went further and said that it was necessary to restrain the Soviet Union and prevent a nuclear-armed Japan. He said that the sort of American withdrawal that Chou and Mao had privately recommended, and that their government was endlessly demanding, would imperil China. Nixon concluded that he would try to reduce tensions with the U.S.S.R., to reach an arms control agreement, and to reduce tensions and dangers in the Middle East, but that nothing he did with the Russians would be at the expense of the Chinese and that he would keep China fully informed of developments with the Russians, as the two countries were already cooperating in intelligence matters.

Chou En-lai said, in English, "Thank you. Shall we recess for ten minutes?"[31] As a cooperative gesture, Nixon signed a legislative bill enacting a compulsory settlement of a dock strike, and tried to present the pen to Chou En-lai. The premier, suspicious, declined, saying it might be deemed interference in U.S. affairs.[32] When they resumed, Chou said that China was like the United States after the expulsion of the British in 1783 – that the Americans and Russians had left China, and the Chinese themselves had filled the vacuum.* [33] He went on to heap abuse on President Harry Truman.

---

* Chou had already accused Kissinger on a previous visit of conducting American foreign policy in the manner of Metternich after the Napoleonic Wars and trying to bottle up progressive forces. Chou presumably knew of Kissinger's great expertise in the field, and Kissinger behaved with his customary forbearance when dealing with eminent interlocutors.

He blamed Truman for provoking China in the Korean War by putting the Seventh Fleet in the Formosa Strait and approaching the Yalu River.

(Chou En-lai inadvertently made a case for the MacArthur-Nixon, as opposed to the Truman-Eisenhower, view of how to deal with China in 1950. These conversations might have taken place ten years earlier if MacArthur had used Chiang's forces and a less restricted air campaign, especially in Manchuria. Chou made it clear that they had been getting no help from Stalin.)

Chou essentially accepted the Taiwan deal: one China but no reunification by force, and American forces withdrawn from Taiwan on a reasonably timely basis. The Seventh Fleet, whose presence so excited them in 1950 (and still controlled the Formosa Strait fifty years later), was not mentioned.

On Vietnam, Chou said China could not promise anything with the North Vietnamese and that China was bound to continue to support them.[34] Nixon said that the Democrats had tried to claim that Nixon had come to China to resolve Vietnam, in order to represent his visit afterwards as a failure. The Chinese leader rather flippantly said, "You went there by accident. Why not give this up?" Nixon instantly said, "We are not going to walk out of there without an agreement. [Otherwise] the U.S. would be a nation that would . . . deserve nothing but contempt before the people and nations of the world, whatever their philosophies." He did not raise the presence of the three hundred and twenty thousand non-combat Chinese armed servicemen in North Vietnam. Their withdrawal would have seriously inconvenienced Hanoi, and their presence at least justified the threat of the importation of Taiwanese forces in analogous roles in South Vietnam, but Nixon judged that raising this would have blown up the discussions.[35]

The time for playing such a card had passed. The Korean War left the American leadership with a fear of again blundering into war with China, and Nixon judged a relationship with the People's Republic more important than any marginal activity in South Vietnam.

In his reply, Chou envisioned a mad scenario of the U.S.S.R., the United States, India, and Japan all joining in an attack on China. Such a far-fetched idea prompted Nixon to invite China to become a stronger military power so that the United States could spend less on defense. Nixon was the star of the session, and although Chou En-lai had a beguiling charm and obviously high and urbane intelligence, it is not clear where the legend arose, in Kissinger's mind especially, that he was such a talent at Great Power negotiation. He had spent most of his diplomatic career on the second-string communist circuit with the likes of Ho Chi Minh and Kim Il Sung and Albania's Enver Hoxha. Nixon was a good deal better-traveled in the diplomatic big leagues than Chou was.

That evening, President and Mrs. Nixon sat on either side of Mao's estranged and belligerent wife, Chiang Ch'ing, at a performance of the propaganda ballet *The Red Detachment of Women*. It was pretty puerile stuff, the peasants against the ruthless landowners. It reminded Nixon of the ballet *Spartacus*, which he had seen in Leningrad in 1959.[*][36]

The next morning, Rogers and Kissinger each called on Nixon to complain about the other. The president had awakened early and made notes, concluding, as if to Chou En-lai himself, "Your people expect action on Taiwan. Our people expect action on Vietnam. Neither can act immediately. But both are inevitable. Let us not embarrass each other." In fact, the people of China probably expected more terror and starvation, and received it. But the reference to Vietnam and the description "inevitable" could be taken to mean that Nixon was veering toward the decent interval again, though that was certainly not the spirit of his riposte to Chou the day before.[37]

In the afternoon session with the principals, they were essentially waiting for a draft of the joint communiqué that Kissinger was negotiating with one of Chou's officials, Chiao Kuan-hua. At one point, Chou told Nixon that Rogers had asked the Chinese foreign minister to include him, Rogers, in the drafting of the communiqué. (Nixon had no explanation of this disarray in American ranks.)

The leaders fell to reminiscing, Nixon about how Syngman Rhee wept when Nixon conveyed to him Eisenhower's message, in 1953, that the United States would not support a South Korean attack on the North. Chou trumped this with the story that during the worst of the border incidents with the U.S.S.R. in 1969, Kosygin picked up the hotline to speak to Mao. The Chinese operator had refused on the grounds that Kosygin was a revisionist. The Soviet premier then asked for Chou En-lai, but the precocious Chinese telephone operator gave the same reply.

---

[*] Chiang had a great liking for the film *Gone with the Wind*, but this ballet would bear little resemblance to it. Chiang was sentenced to death after Mao died and allegedly hanged herself in prison, by her trouser belt, in 1977, but was as likely executed.

That night, the Nixons had an entirely American dinner in their guest house, and then went to a night of gymnastics, badminton, and Ping-Pong, before eighteen thousand people in a closed stadium. Each section was filled with people of different-colored uniforms. The lights came on one section at a time and the section began cheering wildly. Nixon was impressed by their perfect drilling, if not by their spontaneity as sports fans.

The media contingent was becoming intensely bored with the pap fed them by the Chinese, and the absolute silence on substantive matters enforced by Nixon and Chou En-lai. When Nixon went to the Great Wall on February 24, and told some journalists that "I think you would have to conclude that this is a great wall," they printed this truncated platitude. Instead, they should have noted the rest of his comment: "and that it was built by a great people. A people who could build such a wall have a past to be proud of and a great future."[38] Bill Buckley (who was on the tour, despite having "suspended" support for Nixon), James Michener, and Theodore White started touring around with Pat Nixon, on the theory that they might get more out of her. That didn't work either.[*] [39]

Walter Cronkite and Eric Sevareid, two of the journalists who had gained some additional renown for themselves because they had walked through the great squares of Western Europe in their trench coats in the wake of Eisenhower's armies in the forties, were reduced to astonishing reflections on television. Cronkite thought it unlikely that American women would consent to sweep the streets and sidewalks of American cities with brooms, as swarms of Chinese women did. But he felt that Nixon was probably doing well, as there appeared to be what "we used to call in England during the war, a Hitler moon," apparently meaning a rather full and illuminating moon, which assisted nighttime bombing of Germany. It wasn't clear what Cronkite was talking about. Almost none of these American journalists knew anything about China and they were not accustomed to the rigors of a totalitarian treatment of the press.[†] [40]

---

[*] When Pat visited a pig farm and asked what breed of pigs they were, one of her female press contingent interjected, "male chauvinist."
[†] Many of the journalists stayed in the Nationalities Hotel, where the wooden toilet seats had just been relacquered, making them very adhesive when used. The resulting painful condition of torn skin was known in the press party as "baboon bottom." Cronkite had the further problem of erratic electric socks, which, rather than warming his feet, as was their purpose, jolted him unpredictably.

Nixon and Chou went through the draft communiqué that Kissinger and Ch'iao had been up late at night working on, word by word. Chou accepted fairly flexible wording about Taiwan, but this took grueling days of negotiation. Nixon pointed out that Chou was getting what he wanted, while the Americans, who most wanted some assistance in Vietnam, were not getting anything. Chou asked about the Middle East, and Nixon warned that Israel was just a pretext and that the Soviet Union was trying to take over the entire Mediterranean.

Kissinger's stamina was astonishing, as he bore on indefatigably. After forty hours of talks, Nixon was flagging, and he began to be suspicious that the Chinese were trying to wear him down. Departing from the Kissinger practice of finding every word uttered by the Chinese premier a new demonstration of Chou's worldly subtlety, he began to tire of Chou's company. On the morning of February 26, as they sat in armchairs in the VIP lounge of Beijing Capital Airport and Chou described a group of paintings on the wall, Nixon listened exhaustedly for a while and then said, "What the hell are you talking about?" On the plane to Hangchow, one of the great beauty spots of China, Nixon sat with Haldeman, and when they arrived, Chou went for a walk by himself. It had been a punishing schedule. On February 27, the party moved on to Shanghai.

Nixon received a news report from home that described Senator Muskie breaking down in tears in front of a small crowd but also television cameras, in Manchester, New Hampshire, over a reference in the cantankerous local newspaper (*The Union Leader*) accusing his wife of being emotionally unstable and him of being anti-Franco-American. Nixon never believed Muskie could politically survive a presidential campaign.* [41] Muskie had been running almost even with Nixon before the president's economic message in August, and was still only five to seven points behind when Nixon revealed the secret Vietnam negotiations in January. Now the wheels came off Muskie's campaign at the same time as Americans supported their president's impressive performance in China.

---

* Nixon further muddied the waters by getting Colson to set up a committee of "Democrats for Muskie and Busing," a spurious enterprise that sent out a hundred thousand pamphlets falsely identifying Muskie with the unpopular, court-ordered policy of transporting school children out of their neighborhoods in school buses to promote racial "balance."

The final communiqué was agreed in Shanghai, and Rogers contributed to it also. It was two thousand words, and polemical in some places, but intricate in others. Both sides reaffirmed their support for democracy in one case and revolution in the other. The "U.S. side" emphasized that it placed "the highest value on its relations with Japan," while the "Chinese side" reaffirmed its support "for the peoples" of Indochina. They agreed on the desirability of normalization of relations between them, which they said would be "in the interest of all countries," and expressed their shared opposition to any other country seeking "hegemony" in the Pacific. This was a clear rebuke to the U.S.S.R. (Nixon had told Chou he would "turn like a cobra" on the Soviet Union if it attacked China.[42])

China stated that Taiwan was a province of China, and that all U.S. forces must be withdrawn from Taiwan. The United States agreed that all Chinese, "on either side of the Taiwan Strait," agree that there is only one China and that Taiwan is part of it. The United States "reaffirms its interest in a peaceful settlement of the Taiwan question by the Chinese themselves," and endorsed "the ultimate objective" of full American military withdrawal.

This was an acceptable formulation from the American perspective. Taiwan would prosper and remain independent, for thirty-five years at time of writing, and the United States would occasionally interpose the Seventh Fleet in the interceding strait to deter any sequel to Chinese saber-rattling. Allegations of dishonorable concessions against Nixon and Kissinger were unfounded. Nixon's comments were a good deal weightier than Chou's in their long sessions together, no matter how much hidden meaning the swooning Sinophiles divined in Chou's words. The Chinese premier was a suaver and more relaxed personality than Nixon, but not a more informed or articulate one. Kissinger said little while Nixon, the undoubted virtuoso of the intense week, was around, but he negotiated with invincible stamina and ingenuity and was chiefly responsible for crafting a communiqué that both sides could celebrate. Rogers's intervention had been useful, as he opposed a reference to the U.S. alliances with Japan and South Korea but not Taiwan, and reminded Nixon of Acheson's misfortune with Korea left outside the U.S. protective perimeter he enunciated before the Korean War. The communiqué was altered to refer unspecifically to U.S. allies.

At the banquet that night, February 28, Nixon said that they had been in China for a week and that it was "the week that changed the world." It would shift the world balance of power and start a flood-tide of western-ization in China. Nixon and Chou En-lai had a most cordial farewell. There was almost universal agreement that the dramatic visit had been an unqualified success.

The only dissenters to that, apart from the Soviets and Taiwanese, were the American right. Bill Buckley wrote, "Veni, vidi, victus." (I came, saw, and was conquered.)[43] Pat Buchanan wanted to resign, but Nixon did not accept that. It was hard to fathom at the time, and is even more so thirty-five years later, what Buckley was upset about. Taiwan could not seriously claim to be the government of China; the Taiwanese themselves never ceased to proclaim themselves the rightful government of China, and Nixon had extracted an enforceable (by the Seventh Fleet) promise not to invade from the People's Republic. It was useful, as a matter of obvious fact, for the United States and China to have some relationship, and it was already helpful in improving Soviet responsiveness to the United States. Of course Mao's was an odious government. It had committed disastrous errors, and squandered or deliberately extinguished the lives of tens of millions of innocent Chinese. But it was a strong regime in a country that was already the third most important in the world.

Nixon and Kissinger had conceived and executed a clever strategic stroke. The domestic complainers were unjustly alarmed. The best antidote to the evil Maoist tyranny was to open the country up to the West, which gradually happened in succeeding decades. The cult of Mao and Chou, of which Kissinger was the high priest and Winston Lord the altar boy, was certainly tiresome, but beside the point.

The Buckley-Buchanan element was uttering yet another lamentation in echo of the faded and discreditable China Lobby. This movement, which assembled in support of greater aid to Chiang Kai-shek during the war, and then claimed that Truman, Marshall, and Acheson had "lost" China, were part authentic Sinophiles, including many ethnic Chinese (like Anna

---

* Buckley also wrote, "The effect was as if Sir Hartley Shawcross [the British prosecutor at the Nuremberg Trials] had suddenly risen from the prosecutor's stand . . . and descended to embrace Goering and Goebbels and Doenitz and Hess, begging them to join with him in the making of a better world." (China had not been at war with the West and was not a con-quered country, and Goebbels committed suicide and had his corpse burned before he could be captured, so Sir Hartley could not have embraced him at Nuremberg.)

Chennault); part anti-communist militants, some of the Joe McCarthy stripe; part genuine civil rights advocates (though Chiang was an improbable beneficiary of their attentions); and part sincere Christians, some with a missionary tinge.

Sinophilia, anti-communism, support of civil liberties, and Christian beliefs are all respectable, and, for the most part, commendable adherences. But the China Lobby had always been a gang of meddlesome, self-interested zealots, often lacking equilibrium of judgment. It was regrettable to see William Buckley, already the greatest intellectual conservative spokesman in the country, as he would long remain, an admirable, courageous, highly intelligent and charming man, embark on this undeserving cause. (Buchanan was not such a heavyweight, but was a pleasant and loyal and fearless man.) Buckley was not and would never again be comfortable with Nixon. That was a more understandable position than his overinflated championship of the corrupt and discredited Chiang regime.

Japan was more important, and Nixon and Kissinger had had a rather unproductive meeting with the timeless Emperor Hirohito at Anchorage, Alaska, in September, and with Prime Minister Eisaku Sato in Washington in February.

Once back in Washington, both Nixon and Kissinger played up the personal qualities of Mao Tse-tung and Chou En-lai in a way that was both unseemly and unrigorous. Implicit in their exaggerated comments about them was the elevation of themselves as worthy interlocutors. It was a little like the endless praise of the command qualities of German Field Marshal Erwin Rommel by British Field Marshal Bernard L. Montgomery, who ultimately defeated him (with overwhelming superiority of forces).

It was unsubtle self-praise masquerading as fawning adulation in Kissinger's case, and merely excessive deference in Nixon's. They were both entitled to praise, but they should have allowed it to come more spontaneously. Nixon told his cabinet, "There is no leader I have met who exceeds Chou En-lai's ability to conduct a conversation at the highest level"; i.e., with Nixon. He then inflicted on his cabinet his comparison of the similarities between Chou and himself. Nixon was parched for kudos, as he had been most of his life.

Beyond that, Nixon retained a reasonable sense of himself, his position, and his country. He didn't take courtesy to the point of obsequiousness. He wanted recognition for innovative Great Power diplomacy, but he didn't set up a Mao-Chou admiration society. The fact is that the Chinese leaders were not morally distinguishable, nor personally more impressive, accomplished, or sage, than Hitler or Stalin, and the lyrical invocations of fine architecture and Wagnerian symphonies in respect of Mao's garbled outpourings of peasant aphorisms and senescent maunderings were both nauseating and comical.

Kissinger, especially, vastly exceeded any minimal deferences Roosevelt paid to Stalin, whose country had endured twenty million dead, and fire and sword over half its population, fighting a common enemy. (Yet both Nixon and Kissinger subscribed, for a time, to the Yalta Myth that Roosevelt had been duped by Stalin.) Stalin had, involuntarily, been indispensable to the defeat of Nazi Germany. All Mao Tse-tung and his premier had done was to receive two eminent and very polite American visitors who confirmed China's ultimate entitlement to reunification with (and absorption of) an American ally. Kissinger should have been a little less deferential, and the Americans should have used their own interpreters. Instead they allowed their preoccupation with security to cause them to use Chinese interpreters.[44]

Nixon had an inspired idea and followed it through very effectively. Kissinger was a skilled executant. The cries of alarm from the American right were unjustified. And the implicit claim by Kissinger virtually to have transcended human culture and become an instant authority on the sacred wonders of the Middle Kingdom, conciliating heaven and earth, were an entertaining fraud. They were carried out with his usual energy and style. But in this case, the imposture was so ambitious, the imagery so overdone, that his presentational talents, based on his Strangelove accent and Teutonic syntax, almost caused him to stumble in his leap for immortality. But he did later become a flourishing China expert in the private sector, and Chinese-American relations took on a fairly positive life of their own.[*] [45] It was a turning point in history, and, in their different ways, all the principals said so and all the commentators recognized it.

---

[*] The Chinese found the small contingent of U.S. Marines attached to the American mission that was set up in Beijing irksome, "and were particularly annoyed by the boisterousness and raucous behavior at their bar: The Red Ass Saloon."

President Nixon returned to the early political season in all its mundane pandering and jockeying. The New Hampshire primary was on March 7, Florida's on March 14, and school busing, the timeless irritant and fatuity of all three branches of the U.S. government, would not go away. On March 7, Nixon took a little over 70 percent of the Republican vote in New Hampshire, against Congressman Paul McCloskey of California on the left and Congressman John Ashbrook of Ohio on the right. It was a solid victory that indicated that Nixon certainly held unassailably the great center of his party. The silent majority had room to grow. And the Democratic results indicated that the Democrats would help him find it. Muskie won with 48 percent, a slip in the polls, and McGovern jumped to 37 percent. Wallace wasn't on the ballot.

A week later, in Florida, Nixon carried 87 percent of the Republican vote against the same two opponents as in New Hampshire, although McCloskey had withdrawn. Nixon would be renominated unopposed. Wallace reduced the Democrats to chaos, as Nixon had planned. He took 42 percent of the vote against ten opponents. Muskie got 14 percent and was finished. McGovern had not campaigned in Florida, which was his only excuse for receiving just 5 percent. Wallace took away seventy-five delegates, and the anti-busing amendment on the ballot was passed by 1,096,000 votes to 384,000 against.

Nixon had to return to the school-busing issue and summoned Safire to write him a speech about it. He said that he had to emphasize that he had always opposed mandated busing of children to achieve court-ordered racial balance in schools, and had always opposed segregation. He wanted to get it across that it was wrong to force an eight-year-old child onto a school bus for a long ride who was doing well in a school that was a five-minute walk from home. He told Safire to make the connection that the purpose of desegregation was better education; busing lowered the quality of education, and busing and segregation had the same effect on education, so desegregation had to be pursued without busing.

Nixon spoke to the country on March 16 about education, and announced he was sending the Equal Education Opportunities bill to the Congress the next day, including $2.5 billion that was already destined to education in other channels but had been reassembled for emergency assistance to the neediest school districts. The bill would seek a moratorium on local school-busing orders. The confusion would now be intensified, as the tangle of conflicting authority between the courts, school boards, and local, state, and federal legislators would consign the entire vexed subject to a new round of court interpretations. One of the many areas of Nixon's expertise was his intimate knowledge of public administration law, and how to muddy the waters and reduce any subject to inter-jurisdictional chaos. This is more or less what happened, as the poorest school districts were slowly improved.

The long-awaited North Vietnamese-Viet Cong offensive to try to crush the Saigon government and drive the U.S. forces into the sea after an 85 percent reduction in their levels, began on March 30.[*][46] An entire North Vietnamese Army (NVA) armored division, with two hundred new Soviet tanks, attacked directly across the DMZ. A whole army attacked from Laos and northern Cambodia eastwards into South Vietnam, and the enemy concentrated a large force in the South and attacked toward Saigon, surrounding the provincial capital of An Loc, sixty miles from Saigon. About a hundred and fifty thousand NVA soldiers were moved into the South. The U.S. Air Force and Naval Air Force said that the weather was too cloudy and stormy to support the ground forces with any precision. There was some high-level bombing from B-52s, but it was not very accurate or effective.

Nixon quickly reached his crisis mode, raging at Haldeman that "the bastards have never been bombed like they are going to be bombed this time." He accused the Joint Chiefs of cowardice and defeatism and said, "The air force is not worth a shit." He suspected the service chiefs of doing their own flake-out in South Vietnam. The South Vietnamese Army (ARVN) put up a respectable resistance for the most part, though some units scattered and fled. The South Korean division near the DMZ, as always, fought well.

---

[*] News of the offensive came in just after Nixon had concerted with Haldeman an abbreviation of his schedule for an upcoming visit to Canada. Nixon was happy to have dinner with the Conservative governor general (Roland Michener), as "all governors general are good guys." He didn't want to have to sit with Trudeau, so on the second night he went to the National Arts Centre, stood in a receiving line, and after a few minutes ducked out of the buffet that followed. He was not attaching a high priority to the trip, but found the thought of spending much time with Trudeau (whom he considered a doubtful Cold War ally) especially unappetizing.

Nixon was determined this time to hammer North Vietnam in the manner he had been advocating since the war began in earnest seven years before. He steeled himself to any domestic protests, to canceling the Moscow summit, to any consequences rather than suffer military defeat. Kissinger, who was planning to go to Moscow secretly and replicate some of the drama of the China trip, was speaking of the possibility of defeat in Vietnam. Nixon would not hear of it, and now felt more alone than ever.

Privately, he feared that the communists had an advantage in their military proxies in the world, that their satellites were more highly motivated. He was afraid that arming American's allies to the teeth made them soft.[47] These were difficult times for Nixon, whose credibility opposite the Chinese, Russians, and his own voters was at stake in Vietnam. By April 6, the weather was clearing and Nixon delivered on his promise to send the North Vietnamese a message from the air such as they had not imagined.

He had ordered a massive air and sea buildup. He had increased the number of B-52s in theater from forty-five to a hundred and thirty; two fleet aircraft carriers were deployed off shore; and the number of air force and navy combat aircraft was increased in the first ten days of April from nearly six hundred to almost a thousand. On April 16, the United States appeared in overwhelming strength over North Vietnam, bombing the harbor at Haiphong and selected targets in the Hanoi area, attacking the air defense missile system. Four Soviet ships in Haiphong Harbor were damaged, and Nixon left no one in any doubt, in the higher ranks of his administration and the Congress, and on a wide diplomatic circuit, that he accepted the NVA-VC challenge and would teach them a painful lesson. The bombing intensified each day and close air support for the ARVN defenders throughout South Vietnam was constant and precise, while the bombing of the North was conducted round the clock against any plausibly militarily useful target.

While the press and the left in the Congress speculated that the Soviet Union would cancel Nixon's visit and defer an arms control agreement, and Nixon was half-resigned to such an occurrence, there was no sign of it. Dobrynin told Kissinger that Moscow had known nothing of the North Vietnamese offensive, and reaffirmed the invitation to Nixon, and to Kissinger to precede him. The Kremlin was determined not to be a minor event compared with the massively publicized trip to China.

The North Vietnamese attack strained relations between Nixon and Kissinger. The president delayed his adviser's departure for Moscow for two weeks while he applied the full force of his bombing reprisals. The air force and navy were under no orders to be careful about Soviet ships or other targets in North Vietnam of interest to the U.S.S.R., and Nixon finally let Kissinger go to Moscow on the night of April 20, having told him to return at once if the Russians would not undertake to try to restrain the North Vietnamese. He would have no hesitation in canceling his summit meeting and had put domestic political considerations out of mind.

In fact, polls indicated general support for the president's position; the great majority of Americans recognized that Nixon was trying to get out of Vietnam on reasonable terms and had largely wound down the war, and that what the North Vietnamese were doing was a challenge to the integrity of the United States and an outrage in international law. Hanoi could have had no goal other than the abject humiliation of the United States; otherwise, they could have remained quiet and facilitated the American withdrawal.

Richard Nixon was determined that he was defending the credibility of the United States, and that his office would not be worth holding if he were chased out of Vietnam by the communists, who had treated his every conciliatory gesture with insolent contempt for more than three years. Now they had gone too far.

The ambiance between Nixon and Kissinger was aggravated by the presence of Haig. Nixon promoted Haig, partly on his merits as a dedicated and staunch combat officer, and partly as a bit of a counterweight to Kissinger. Nixon was exasperated by Kissinger's publicity-seeking and his ambiguous loyalty to the administration and the president personally, opposite the media, academic, and Washington social communities he frequented. Haig became the conduit for messages between the two when Kissinger was in Moscow, and Nixon, promoting the cover for his national security adviser, went to Camp David, supposedly with Kissinger and other top aides.

Kissinger reported from Moscow that Leonid Brezhnev ardently sought a summit, fervently denied any foreknowledge of the NVA offensive, and didn't care how violently Nixon hammered the North Vietnamese. There seemed to be a good deal less support for Hanoi in Moscow than there had been in Beijing. The first indications were that the opening with China had startled Moscow into a strong desire to shape up its relations with Washington, and that the direct contact with Brezhnev had been tactically astute, because he was taking over foreign policy and shouldering Kosygin aside.

Nixon had Haig tell Kissinger that he did not believe a word the Russians were telling him about not knowing in advance about the NVA activity – that they had to have known and were obviously doing nothing to moderate the NVA offensive, which they could stop by reducing supplies. He ordered Kissinger back to Camp David after a two-day visit. Kissinger replied with "astonishment" and said, "I do not believe that Moscow is in direct collusion with Hanoi. . . . We are approaching a successful culmination of our policies."

Kissinger wrung another day from Nixon and ignored his order not to pursue arms control by doing just that with the aging foreign minister, Andrei Gromyko. The two quickly reached a tentative agreement on two anti-ballistic missile (ABM) sites each, one for each capital and one for protection of intercontinental ballistic missile (ICBM) launch capacity; on a ceiling on submarine-launched missiles;* and a five-year limit on employment of offensive missiles. Kissinger cabled back that "the most important arms control agreement ever concluded" was imminent. Nixon, who had never believed in arms control, other than as a sop to domestic opinion, because he thought the other side cheated and the United States had the advantage in any arms race (not unreasonable convictions), replied that such an agreement would interest only "a few sophisticates." He transmitted Rebozo's regards, which Kissinger took as a sign that Nixon was drinking heavily and in one of his *Patton*-watching modes of unrestricted belligerency.

Kissinger arrived at Camp David on April 25, and after a frosty start he and the president quickly resumed their usual good face-to-face rapport. Kissinger had great and natural charm, and a clear idea of what pleased Nixon. The president had torqued himself up to unrestrained war-making, and in that state, to avoid the intolerable emotional and psychological roller coaster of believing in early ameliorations of the crisis, banished all peaceful thoughts. Kissinger, once in his presence, without Haig playing his slightly ambiguous role as interpreter and rival, could persuade Nixon to broaden his horizon to make peace and war simultaneously, to disquiet the Chinese slightly by improving relations with Moscow, administer another heavy blow to his critics with an arms agreement that was at worst innocuous, and to lock up another immense satchel of votes in election year while

---

* This was the area Gerard Smith claimed Kissinger had botched in February, 1971 (Chapter 12).

giving the North Vietnamese a long-delayed and richly deserved pummeling to his heart's content.

Kissinger was correct. Nixon had the right response to the initial crisis, and he was correct in insisting on the military defeat of North Vietnam from the air. To the extent that Kissinger had proposed moderating that response, and he had suggested it, he was mistaken. But Kissinger was right that Hanoi and Moscow could be separated and the United States could win simultaneous military and diplomatic victories.[48]

President Nixon again addressed the country about Vietnam on the evening of April 27. He said that the communists had failed to win over South Vietnam "politically." And "General Abrams believes that they will fail in their efforts to conquer South Vietnam militarily." He said that Abrams had advised that "some battles will be lost, others will be won by the South Vietnamese." He then announced the withdrawal of another twenty thousand American servicemen in the next two months.

Hard-pressed, balancing between his national security adviser's optimistic views of the designs of the Soviets and his own suspicions as one who had been fighting the Cold War since Kissinger was a graduate student, Nixon had, yet again in this year of brilliant presidential leadership, struck the right note. Except for George McGovern and the dregs of the American demonstrative left, no one could dispute the president when he pulled another 30 percent of American forces out of Vietnam on the professed authority of the theater commander. Very few Americans were particularly exercised about what American bombing did to the North Vietnamese, and he was steadily painting the Democrats into the corner of unconditional surrender of a war that might still, even now, be won, and into which, they, try as they might to induce amnesia among the electorate, had precipitated the country.

On May 1, the city of Quang Tri fell to the North Vietnamese. Kissinger was about to leave for a long-scheduled meeting with Le Duc Tho in Paris. Abrams had cabled that it was possible that the South Vietnamese had "lost their will to fight" (three days after Nixon had quoted Abrams to the country as believing that South Vietnam would prevail and twenty thousand U.S. soldiers could be withdrawn). Nixon read Abrams's cable carefully and said that whatever happened, Kissinger must not concede anything to the North Vietnamese. "They'll be riding high because of all this, so you'll have to bring them down by your manner. No nonsense. No niceness. No accommodations." He said again, lest Kissinger imagine that he had been uttering bravura in the presence of Rebozo between reruns of *Patton*, that there was a chance the United States could lose in Vietnam. What was unfolding was a dress rehearsal for the postwar settlement: a full-scale land invasion by the NVA and a massive air campaign in return by the United States.

As Kissinger was about to leave for the meeting with Le Duc Tho, Nixon had delivered to him a memo telling him to ignore the domestic reaction (which was generally favorable anyway). "We have crossed the Rubicon and we must win – if possible, tip the balance in favor of the South Vietnamese for battles to come when we no longer will be able to help with major air strikes. . . . [Tell them] Settle or else!"

Kissinger's meeting with Le Duc Tho was completely unproductive. As had been foreseen, Ducky was more haughty and insulting than ever, and Kissinger had no difficulty returning the insults. North Vietnam would accept American surrender, a cease-fire while the United States evacuated, and that was all. Kissinger returned promptly, still in favor of the Moscow summit taking place, and counseling moderation in the escalation of the bombing that Nixon was about to order. Nixon announced that he would again speak to the country on the evening of May 8. He now had over a thousand combat aircraft available for North and South Vietnam, and against Kissinger's advice, on the belief that it might well lead to cancellation of the Moscow meeting (which private polls indicated 60 percent of the American people favored), Nixon ordered the closing of Haiphong Harbor by the dropping of aerial mines, comprehensive destruction of all legitimate military targets in Hanoi, and close bombing of the country's rudimentary railway system.

As always before critical speeches, Nixon ate a bowl of wheat germ and took a cold shower, and met with congressional leaders at 8 P.M. to give them some notice of what he was about to announce. He explained to Fulbright, "They spit in our eye in Paris. We brought home more than half a million men. It was a very difficult decision. If you can give me your support, I would appreciate it. If you cannot, I will understand."

The speech was blunt and direct. He briefly summarized the Kennedy-Johnson escalation and the many offers that he had made to try to end the war, culminating in the total failure of the latest meeting in Paris following the massive, outright invasion of the South by the North. He then said that all North Vietnamese ports would be closed and that that country's transportation network would be destroyed, and "our military forces will have instructions to cut off supplies to the enemy in every way." He said that this level of air war would continue without interruption until the North Vietnamese had handed over American prisoners of war and there was an internationally supervised cease-fire throughout Indochina, and that American forces would withdraw within four months after that.

Buried unspoken in the speech was the fact that he was no longer requiring the withdrawal of the North Vietnamese from the South. This was an important concession, but as a practical matter it was obvious that the United States would not be able to maintain domestic support for a continuing campaign in Vietnam until the North withdrew. Even the previous requirements for such withdrawal, going back to Johnson in Manila in 1966, were a fraud, because if the NVA had withdrawn, they would merely have awaited the American departure and then returned. Nixon was pledged to disband the draft; the United States would never plunge into an undeclared war with draftees on this scale at the ends of the earth again, so Nixon's unspecified concession on this occasion was a minor one.

The mines dropped in the harbors were timed to activate themselves in two and a half days, giving foreign flag vessels time to leave North Vietnamese ports. Nixon sent a memo to Haig and Kissinger castigating the lack of imagination of American military commanders, referring to Patton and MacArthur (on whose staff Haig had served in Tokyo), and considering a tank attack into North Vietnam. He wanted some unconventional thinking from the military, of the kind he frequently engaged in himself as a politician and statesman.[49] "Needless to say, indiscriminate bombing of civilian areas is not what I have in mind."[50]

The following month, June, the Red River at Hanoi would crest about thirty feet above the level of the city, sustained in its banks only by an elaborate system of dikes. There had often been discussion of the vulnerability of the dikes to air attack. Nixon could certainly have assured terrible damage to central Hanoi, and drowned many thousands of civilians, if he had wished. He could even have issued an evacuation warning, to spare civilians, and then flooded out the North Vietnamese capital if he had wished. There is no evidence that he seriously considered such an option (and he told the author that it would not have achieved anything useful).

Polls indicated a massive 77 percent approval of the president's position. The anti-war movement tried one more time to intimidate the government and dazzle the media with the size of its demonstrations, but they fizzled. They were unable to get more than three thousand demonstrators out, even in New York, Washington, and Chicago. Twenty-nine Democratic senators denounced Nixon's "escalation," and the *New York Times* called for unconditional and immediate withdrawal, while the *Washington Post* gave its presidential election endorsement six months early, to anyone the Democrats nominated. But it was clear that the silent majority was solid and Nixon had won the war on the home front. It was no small achievement. If ARVN could hang on while U.S. air power pulverized the northern war-making capacity, the United States could yet make an honorable exit, militarily undefeated and with a Saigon government that might have a chance of survival if the United States retained the will to reimpose this level of air attack when the NVA launched new future offensives.

The national media unanimously assumed that the Moscow summit would be canceled, and informal comments from the White House didn't contradict that, as Nixon thought Kissinger had been gulled by Moscow's eagerness and that the Kremlin was really trying to set him up for a cancellation in the most politically damaging manner.

The Soviet trade minister, Nikolai Patolichev, was visiting Washington to accelerate and expedite grain purchases, and Dobrynin suggested to Kissinger that Nixon receive him. Dobrynin continued to assure Kissinger that Brezhnev was looking forward to the summit, and Nixon agreed to receive Patolichev. The White House press corps gathered at maximum strength to await confirmation from the Soviet minister when he emerged that the invitation to Moscow was retracted. The interview was very cordial, and lasted over an hour. When he emerged to face a battery of microphones, Patolichev was asked if the president's trip to Moscow was on. "Have you any doubts?" he asked. "We never had any doubts."[51]

Precise preparations for the president's visit, the first of an American president to Moscow, began in earnest. Nixon had mobilized domestic opinion, stabilized prospects and relations with Russia, and was delivering on his promise to pound North Vietnam with undreamed-of thoroughness. ARVN was holding, at An Loc and Kontum. American helicopter gunships concentrated on flushing out the enemy where prearranged carpet bombing from B-52s could mow them down. Even the skeptical Saigon American press corps acknowledged that ARVN was fighting with some distinction. The usual hyperbole was mobilized, and An Loc was billed as "South Vietnam's

Verdun." Gradually, the NVA and VC were beaten back. The rains came, military activity declined; Richard Nixon had won again, bucking his way through a crisis in which even Kissinger had defected to the camp of the Vietnam defeatists. This episode added a large cubit to the stature of the unflinching General Alexander Haig in the eyes of the commander in chief.

On May 2, while Kissinger was meeting with Le Duc Tho, Attorney General Kleindienst advised Haldeman that J. Edgar Hoover had died in his sleep the night before. At age seventy-seven, after forty-eight years as director of the Federal Bureau of Investigation, he had achieved his final ambition of dying in office. Nixon was relieved to be rid of the obstreperous old man, who was less cooperative than Nixon had hoped and expected in the White House counter-intelligence activities. Nixon ordered that all Hoover's files be brought to the White House, but Hoover's secretary had already removed them.[52]

(Though Nixon probably did not appreciate it at this point, Hoover had almost certainly spared the administration terrible problems with the Huston plan in July 1971. He had not known about the Plumbers after Nixon resolved that "we will do it ourselves," but he might have been able to mitigate that too, had he lived.)

Nixon ordered that Hoover's body lie in state on a catafalque in the Capitol Rotunda, only the twenty-first time for such an observance. The president gave the eulogy at the National Presbyterian Church on May 4, 1972. Nixon took more than the usual eulogist's liberties with the facts on behalf of the deceased. Thus, he had made the FBI the "incorruptible defender of every American's precious right to be free from fear." For "nearly one-fourth of the whole history of this Republic, [Hoover] has exerted a great influence for good in our national life. . . . [He] has helped to keep steel in America's backbone and the flame of freedom in America's soul. He personified integrity . . . honor . . . principle . . . courage . . . discipline . . . dedication . . . loyalty . . . patriotism." He made a pitch against lawlessness and disorder, and closed with a quote from the Bible, which, he claimed, Hoover regarded as his "guide to daily life."[53]

Hoover had been a formidable leader of the FBI, and was apparently financially incorruptible. His finest hour had been his opposition to the internment of Japanese-Americans on the West Coast after Pearl Harbor in 1942. He had run the bureau very autocratically, and it probably did an adequate, if overpublicized, job of fighting famous gangsters in the twenties and thirties, and did well infiltrating fascist and communist organizations in the thirties, forties, and fifties. Hoover had been effective in civil rights matters, once Johnson ordered him to become involved, though Hoover disdained most African-Americans. The advice he gave about Nixon White House plans for countering press leaks and the official and unofficial opposition had been prescient.

But he was far too indulgent of unjustified FBI-sponsored violence, as in the invasion by the Chicago police of the Black Panther house in Chicago in 1969. His disrespect for due process and individual privacy, and his prurient preoccupation with the private lives of people, such as Martin Luther King, were notorious and unseemly. He had files on almost everyone in politics and was a cagey and unscrupulous political maneuverer.

He was widely presumed to be a homosexual. Twenty years later, Richard Nixon gave the author his opinion of Hoover: "a good police chief." He added that "Edgar had a lot of files, but I had a lot of files too, and there was nothing in them about Edgar in a red dress" (referring to widespread rumors that Hoover was privately a transvestite). Nixon thought that, considering the power Hoover had, especially in his last ten years, he behaved relatively circumspectly. He thought him "asexual, like Ted Heath" (the British prime minister at the time Hoover died).

On May 15, George Wallace was shot several times at close range in the chest and abdomen while campaigning in Laurel, Maryland. Nixon expressed perfunctory concern about Wallace, who was expected to recover but had lost the use of his legs. Nixon was more preoccupied with the political leanings of the would-be assassin. He and Colson repeatedly called senior FBI officials to see if the gunman had political affiliations. Nixon was concerned that he might lose ground electorally if the shooter proved to be a right-wing extremist. In all of the circumstances, it is understandable that Nixon wasn't overcome with solicitude for Wallace, but his preoccupation with the political implications was tasteless. He expressed the hope that McGovern literature would be found in the gunman's apartment. The FBI went to the assailant's residence in Milwaukee, and waited outside, as they had no warrant to enter, while Milwaukee police talked the building superintendent into letting them in. A shouting and pushing match ensued between the two groups of peace officers. The FBI was looking less professional without J. Edgar Hoover already.[54] When asked by Nixon whether it was clear if the man who shot Wallace, Arthur Bremer, was of the left or right, Colson replied with his usual sinister wit, "He's going to be a left-winger by the time we get through."[55]

The day after the shooting, Wallace won absolute majorities in the Michigan and Maryland primaries, leading McGovern by twenty-five points in Michigan. He was now well ahead of the other candidates in primary votes received, but McGovern had chaired a commission that allocated delegates according to an affirmative action plan giving fixed weight to different ethnic groups and both genders. By this method, he had effectively gerrymandered the convention for himself, and although he was 1.2 million votes behind Wallace and half a million behind the splendidly inextinguishable Hubert Humphrey, he was well ahead in delegate support.

It was working out as well as Nixon could have hoped. The far left was taking control in an undemocratic and hypocritical manner, and Wallace was exposing the Democrats as a party largely infested by rednecks and reactionaries who longed to throw down the mask of the permissive, self-indulgent, unpatriotic left. More and more the Democrats were starting to resemble Eisenhower's description of them as "extremes of right . . . and left, with corruption and political chicanery shot through the whole business." (And he was only speaking of Roosevelt, Truman, Stevenson, and Rayburn. What he would have thought of the factionalism and cynical tactics of George McGovern, George Wallace, and Jesse Jackson challenges the imagination.) Nixon moved serenely toward his party's nomination at the head of his immense silent majority, as stately as the great liner *Queen Mary* entering Long Beach Harbor (which she had recently done, to be moored there permanently. This was the ship that had taken Nixon and the Herter Commission to Europe in 1947.).

Nixon visited Wallace in hospital on the 19th and was impressed by his wife. "She has great verve," he wrote, and added that he appreciated Wallace's Southern patriotism, despite the fact that he was a "demagogue." He stayed twenty minutes and had a pleasant visit.

— IV —

Nixon and Kissinger briefed congressional leaders on the Russian trip that afternoon. Nixon was hopeful of substantive arms control agreements.

Kissinger said that the Soviets might be aiming at "softening up the United States and then pushing us out of Europe," but that whatever their motive "we should not be afraid." He and the president intended to give them an incentive for restraint. The next day, with everything flowing heavily in his favor, from Beijing to Saigon to the American political landscape, President Nixon and a very large party enplaned for Moscow, via Salzburg.

To leave no doubt about his policy in Vietnam, he ordered that bombing of the North be increased to at least twelve hundred sorties per day during his visit to the U.S.S.R.[56] This was in contrast to his trip to China, when he had ordered that there be no bombing north of the DMZ. He and Kissinger were embarrassed to be informed by Chou En-lai that there had been some bombing of North Vietnam during their visit, and Nixon fired the air force general responsible. He was accustomed enough to insubordination, but was not prepared to be embarrassed in front of foreign leaders by officers of a service that he usually found expert at devising reasons not to do anything. All was in place for another stunning triumph of Nixonian diplomacy.

The *Spirit of '76* landed at Moscow at 4 P.M. on May 22 and the president of the United States was greeted with great ceremony. A fifty-car motorcade conducted the Americans to their lodgings, President and Mrs. Nixon in the Grand Kremlin Palace. An American flag flew over the Kremlin, alongside the hammer and sickle of the U.S.S.R. Leonid Brezhnev, successor to Lenin and Stalin and Khrushchev as general secretary of the Communist Party of the Soviet Union, asked to see the president shortly after he arrived. They met and had tea for two hours. Brezhnev made the usual pro forma complaints about U.S. policy in Vietnam, which Nixon politely brushed off, but they moved on to the quest for a new relationship. Brezhnev said that Franklin D. Roosevelt was still a hero in Russia, and Nixon said that he would be happy to have the sort of relationship that existed between Stalin and Roosevelt and Churchill. Brezhnev endorsed the prospect. (Implicit comparison of themselves with such gigantic historical figures would not have been unpleasing to either of them.)

Nixon asked Brezhnev to propose a joint declaration of principles, which had already been largely worked out by Kissinger and Dobrynin, because he didn't want to embarrass Rogers. This was a preposterous request to make of the leader of the Soviet Union on first meeting, baring the fissures in the highest ranks of the administration. Brezhnev took it up like a good sport and proposed such a declaration at the first full session the next day. Rogers, who was languid and did not have a work ethic like Nixon or Kissinger, was not a fool and complained to Nixon that obviously everything had been prepared, and he "might as well go home."[57]

At the end of the first full day, Brezhnev spirited Nixon away to his dacha, where he and Kosygin and the president of the U.S.S.R., Nikolai Podgorny, complained at length and in relays about U.S. action in Vietnam. They claimed that Thieu was an illegitimate president, and Nixon asked who had elected the president in Hanoi. Nixon mainly listened, convinced that this was just an effort to build a record, a transcript to send to Hanoi. He did not become riled but rejected their concerns quite simply and briefly at intervals. After about three hours, the Russians had had their say, and they adjourned to a rather bacchanalian rout of many courses and toasts. In this, at least, they emulated some of the dinners that Roosevelt, Churchill, and Stalin had at Teheran and Yalta. (The dacha was pleasant, about seventy-five feet above the Moscow River, and reminded the Americans of Camp David.)

Later that evening, while lying on a massage table having a rubdown, Nixon told Kissinger, who had stepped out of arduous negotiations with Gromyko, to make no more concessions and feel no compulsion to settle that week. Kissinger wrote, "Nixon took a heroic position from a decidedly unheroic posture."[58]

The official arms control negotiations were being conducted in Helsinki, where the American delegation was led by the much-upstaged Gerard Smith, who was an extremely well-qualified arms control specialist. He became convinced that he was being kept away from Moscow by Kissinger so that Nixon and Kissinger could take the entire credit for an agreement. From the United States there were rumblings of discontent from the right. Both Barry Goldwater and Democrat senator Henry Jackson were informally expressing concern at what was afoot in Moscow. The liberal press, reduced to desperation by Nixon's long sequence of victories and impressive surprises, and by the increasing likelihood of a doomed McGovern candidacy, was reduced to accusing Nixon of giving the store away to the Russians in arms control negotiations.

This was one of the many ironies of Nixon's long career; the former Red-baiting, Cold Warrior super-hawk was arraigned by the *New York Times* for conceding military superiority to the Kremlin. The charge was nonsense, in the same tradition as the "missile gap" of 1960. The U.S.S.R. had more inter-continental ballistic missiles, but the United States had a larger bomber force, more submarine-launched missiles, and technological superiority, and was close to mounting up to ten independently targeted warheads on each missile. Nixon had cleverly devised a strategy for seizing the benefits of nuclear parity while assuaging Soviet neuroses, and for indulging the fol-lowers of the McNamara theory of the value of mutual assured destruction while retaining the benefits of nuclear superiority, or, as he had cleverly rechristened it early in his administration, "sufficiency."

Nixon was not a numbers freak in arms control matters. He knew that both sides possessed massively over-adequate deterrence, and the possibility of either side using nuclear weapons against the other deliberately was zero. As was mentioned in Chapters 5 and 6, there was some loose talk of nuclear exchanges in the Eisenhower-Khrushchev era, and Eisenhower had relied on "massive retaliation" even over Quemoy and Matsu, and threatened it to gain the peace in Korea.

Kennedy had stepped back with his "bear any burden" inaugural while McNamara had the United States sit on its nuclear hands and allow the U.S.S.R. effectively to catch it. Nixon was left to make good the short-comings of both the Truman-Eisenhower and Kennedy-Johnson policies. He could not responsibly threaten the use of nuclear weapons for any reason except a mortal threat to the strategic interests of the United States: mainly North America, Western Europe, Japan. Nixon was, with great finesse, extracting the United States from Vietnam, he would have been both mad and not credible if he had claimed that the United States would commit forces where it did not already have them, or go further than the Nixon Doctrine, which called for doing what he intended to do with Vietnamization: help other countries resist aggression.

He had rolled back both nuclear and conventional military adventur-ism. Now he would treat the Russians as nuclear equals in limiting numbers of launchers but retain or restore superiority, which had a psychological value, as well as overstraining the ramshackle Soviet command economy by steadily applying technology to give the United States an edge beyond ostensible parity in launchers. These were complicated calculations, as the United States had more warheads but throw weights were about equal. When Smith tried to walk Nixon through some of the arcane details, the president said, "Bullshit." He knew that they could haggle about the numbers, as long as they got to some sort of equal offset, but that the United States must retain its multiple warhead advantage (MIRVs) and ensure that the Soviets did not get a lead in anti-missile defenses.

The arms race was going to bankrupt Russia eventually, and moving to volunteer armed forces would assure that the U.S. military became very highly educated. To the extent, if at all, that the percentage of ethnic minorities in the U.S. armed forces came to surpass their share of the whole population, the military could perform the double service of reducing the burden of racial inequalities by educating the ranks. In these matters, as in many strategic and political questions, Nixon went by intuition and has been proved farsighted.

He considered arms control agreements to be largely unverifiable. He knew that arms control had begun after the First World War with naval construction limitation agreements on the construction of battleships and aircraft carriers, large ships that required years to build. And he knew that even then, everyone cheated. (The American Washington class, British King George V class, French Richelieu class, German Bismarck class, and Italian Littorio class battleships all exceeded their allowed thirty-five thousand tons.)

Most of the money spent in military budgets, when excessive amounts were not being spent on draftees or munitions, was reasonably productive economically, especially regarding the more technological aspects. Nixon recognized the importance of placating domestic political demand for reduced defense spending, but in arms control terms he was not really a seeker of anything more ambitious than a cap on a runaway arms race.

Kissinger and Gromyko toiled until 3 A.M. on May 26, and then adjourned. The Politburo would decide in the morning which of the American demands could be met (agreeing what Nixon was prepared to agree, and not what he wasn't). At 11:15 A.M., the Politburo communicated its agreement with virtually the entire American position.

Gerard Smith and the other American negotiators were summoned from Helsinki to Moscow after a ceremonial signing had been scheduled for the U.S. ambassador's residence, Spaso House, for eleven that evening. Inadequate ground transport was provided for Smith and his party, who arrived in central Moscow fuming that there had been no discussion at all on the American side before agreement of terms. He said that at least the Russians had to show the terms to the Politburo, but Nixon and Kissinger reserved all power to themselves. Smith's was understandable, but not substantive, pique. The treaty would have to be reported out by the Foreign Affairs and Armed Forces Committees and ratified by the U.S. Senate. Nixon and Kissinger were not arms control specialists, but they were very astute negotiators, and Kissinger secured important concessions from the Russians. And the president of the United States has his rights; he is not bound to follow those who serve at his pleasure, as Smith acknowledged when he learned that his formal Helsinki negotiations had been a sideshow a year before.

The ceremony on the evening of May 26 celebrated a treaty, restricting both sides to two hundred ABMs at two sites, and prohibiting development or deployment of more such systems. There was also an executive agreement that restricted the number of land- and sea-based missiles to those then deployed or being constructed, with specified, equal numbers. MIRVs and long-range bombers, in which the United States also possessed a substantial advantage, were left out.

The cavalier treatment of Smith so rankled that when he and Kissinger held a joint press briefing, it had to be suspended because they began disagreeing on the treaty's terms. Kissinger became apoplectic, and as was now his custom with almost any complaint on any subject, he blamed the press fiasco on Rogers, who was, for once, innocent. Nixon had been meeting with Brezhnev and was unaware of the overheated spirits in his entourage. He understood Smith's grievance, but thought him presumptuous in imagining that the president had to entrust all such negotiations to the Arms Control and Disarmament Agency.

Nixon thought Smith had a sadistic attachment to microscopic precision, and that what was called for, and all that was attainable within any useful negotiating time, was an agreement on ABM and nuclear-strike-launch numbers, and a cap on deployed long-range missiles. This wasn't arms reduction, as new missiles, already being constructed, would be deployed; but it was arms control. On absolute grounds, Gerard Smith's objections were not well-founded.

Despite the *New York Times*'s astonishing and unfounded grumbling about the terms that had been negotiated, it was another big success for Nixon. A month before, the entire national liberal media of the United States had predicted that Nixon's trip to Moscow would be scuttled because of his excessive belligerency in responding to the North Vietnamese invasion of the South. He returned with the most comprehensive arms control arrangements in history, as Kissinger had predicted when Nixon was skeptical that the visit to Russia would even take place. And the North Vietnamese had been repulsed.

The Nixons toured Leningrad on May 27, visiting the Piskarevskoye Cemetery, where hundreds of thousands of victims of the Nazi siege of Leningrad (1941–43) are buried. On the 28th, a Sunday, the Nixons attended Moscow's only Baptist church, and were impressed at the number of young people at the service. That evening, Nixon gave a television address to the Soviet people, which was carried almost everywhere in the world. He was conciliatory and hopeful, and his remarks were uniformly well received. He concluded with a reference to his visit to the cemetery in Leningrad, and resolved to do all he could "that your children and ours, all the children of the world, can live their full lives together in friendship and in peace." It was a tasteful and even moving address; Brezhnev told Nixon he had been moved to tears. It was a sharp contrast to Khrushchev's response to Nixon's address to the Soviet people on his visit in 1959.

Kissinger and Gromyko hammered out the declaration of principles that Nixon had got Brezhnev to claim to have sponsored. It was a fairly anodyne, not to say platitudinous, effort, but it pledged the two countries to honor their obligations under the United Nations Charter, to exercise restraint in their relations, to do their utmost to avoid military confrontations and prevent nuclear war, and to resolve disputes between themselves peacefully.

In their last meetings of the trip, Brezhnev and Nixon became very cordial, and Brezhnev offered to send a very senior Soviet official to Hanoi to see if anything could be done to move negotiations along. Nixon accepted, and Nikolai Podgorny did go, a few weeks later, to Hanoi, with no apparent effect. Apart from during Podgorny's visit, Nixon maintained the full air war on North Vietnam to the last week of October, just before the U.S. election.

Brezhnev had asked Nixon about Mao, and the president replied that he was still astute mentally, though not well physically. Brezhnev said that Mao Tse-tung was a philosopher and not a practical person, and that he found the Chinese in general to be incomprehensible.

Nixon was impressed by the increased prosperity of Moscow and Leningrad since he had first visited in 1959, and he was quite impressed with the Soviet leaders. He believed that his informants had underestimated them. He thought Brezhnev was intelligent and forceful, not at all without emotions, and much less self-conscious and abrasive than Khrushchev. Kosygin he found a less affable personality, a more self-important and reserved character, but very well informed. Podgorny was like a "mid-western senator," Brezhnev like an Irish-American labor leader, or even a Mayor Daley, "with no affront intended to either."[59]

Nixon represented the ABM Treaty as a curtailment of a defensive arms race that could have become hideously expensive, and the offensive missiles cap as the beginning of a slowdown and reversal of strategic weapons that would be reinforced in subsequent agreements. He was correct, and they were important breakthroughs, but they were also extremely valuable in domestic politics in an election year. Not having been a great champion of arms control before, Nixon recognized, as Ronald Reagan would, that a defensive arms race might some day be the last straw to the Russian economy's ability to sustain its worldwide challenge to the United States.

Nixon went on to Kiev (on a Russian plane, after the initial Russian plane aborted its takeoff when an engine failed. Kosygin and Podgorny, who had just bade Nixon farewell, clambered back aboard and asked what punishment Nixon wished inflicted on the pilot. Nixon thought they were serious, and assured them that the pilot had handled the emergency skillfully.). He went from Kiev to Teheran for a meeting with the shah, and promised him practically unlimited access to advanced American weaponry. Using his burgeoning oil revenues, the shah would arm Iran to the teeth.[60] This would be another fortification of the American alliance system, for a time. The president then was received with great enthusiasm in Warsaw, as he had been in 1959.

Nixon returned to Washington on June 1, and the media, the polls, incoming correspondence at the White House, and the reception from congressional leaders all showed overwhelming support for the president's conduct of foreign policy. He came directly from Andrews Air Force Base to the Capitol, dramatically mounted the main staircase of the Capitol building alone, was announced to a joint session of Congress that awaited him, was very generously applauded, and spoke eloquently of the first visit by an incumbent American president to Moscow.

There seems little doubt that Nixon emphasized the anticipated advantages of arms control with what might charitably be called the grace of conversion, as well as the force of opportunism, seizing on the upbeat spirit of the time. Rarely has a dove of such unusual historic plumage been so attentively listened to by an audience so recently and profoundly afflicted by skepticism. Nixon, who was no mean brinksman in the Dulles era, revived (for the purpose of taking credit for subduing it) the great nuclear fear that he said had gripped the world since 1945, for the whole lives of 60 percent of the world's population. He said that, the week before in Moscow, "We witnessed the beginning of the end of that era." (An era through most of which he had been rivaled only by Khrushchev and a few others as the world's most blood-curdling saber-rattler.) Despite the doubts of many, then and historically, he spoke prophetically; the arms race did enter an inexorable decline. Even the Reagan buildup in the eighties was largely of defensive weapons, and did bring the end of the great U.S.-Soviet arms race (and the end of the Soviet Union and the Cold War and communism as a serious threat).

Nixon had made no effort to transfer his political weight from the moderate hawk community he had long led to straddle the centrist doves for whom he had delivered, and so both groups were somewhat incredulous at what they took to be a sudden lurch to the center-left. His old supporters thought he had gone a little overboard in conviviality with the Russians (and the Chinese), and the doves could not, even by rubbing their eyes and pinching themselves, groggy as they were after the China visit, believe that they were hearing the Richard Nixon they had known and disapproved of for twenty-five years. Adlai Stevenson had sarcastically described Nixon as "the man of many masks." After all the talk of a "new Nixon," he had certainly sown confusion in the ranks of all his opponents and many of his supporters, but he had broadened his silent majority to a mighty expanse of popular support.

Nixon's persistent and now somewhat disoriented critics gamely mustered around the theory that he was making rhetorical gestures to the left with the ABM Treaty and Stategic Arms Limitation Talks (SALT), but delivering an arms buildup to the right. Nixon imposed his arms-control tightrope walk throughout the relevant parts of his administration: without SALT, defense costs would skyrocket to pay for an escalating arms race, but his modest buildup was necessary for the country's defense needs and would place it strongly to negotiate a better SALT II. These were not senseless arguments. In such matters, Nixon's cunning as both a domestic politician and a geopolitician, but a patriotic American in both roles, conjoined.

Nixon and Kissinger met with congressional leaders in what was supposed to be a secret briefing, on the morning of June 2. Nixon said that the superiority of the American economic system should not cause people to be overconfident about what the Russian people could achieve, that dictatorships of all kinds can be very attractive, however unappealing to Americans. He sold his arms control position as a response to the U.S. desire to have adequate deterrence and response capability but not more, since the United States was not trying to conquer or intimidate anyone, and as one that enabled it to broaden its lead as clearly the superior system to communism for its inhabitants. He said that the U.S.S.R. feared an arms race it could not win against such a powerful economy as the United States, and had to pay some attention to improving living standards and public services. This was somewhat the theme he had tried to sound in his debate with Khrushchev in Moscow thirteen years earlier (rockets and color television). He said that both sides recognized that an unlimited arms race could increase the chances of nuclear war eventually.

Kissinger gave the congressional leaders a more detailed historical summary, saying that the U.S.S.R. had originally tried to promote discord between Western Europe and the United States, by their adventurism in the Middle East and Cuba. He said that it was fortunate for all that the Syrian invasion of Jordan was such a failure in 1971, as otherwise, a Middle Eastern war could have erupted that neither Washington nor Moscow could have controlled. He said that there was an increasing realization that adventurism for very marginal gain was not justifiable because of the steadily rising risk of third powers triggering responses by the Great Powers with ever more dangerous weapons. Though most of his congressional listeners would not have grasped it, this was Kissinger, an eminent historian, explaining the sunset of the sort of chain-reaction dangers that led to the First World War.

Nixon concluded that the Soviets, for their own reasons, were becoming more responsible, as the United States had always wished, and that while their motives might not be entirely or even largely altruistic, it was an important and promising change. American national interest as well as the international interest, said the president, recommended in favor of the qualified positive response he had made. None of his listeners was minded to disagree.[61]

A measure of his success was the anger of the North Vietnamese, who accused both Moscow and Beijing of deserting the cause of world revolution for their own narrow, short-term interest, of favoring "peaceful co-existence over proletarian internationalism." In effect, Moscow and Beijing had abandoned North Vietnam in the second of its wars, the war to humiliate and militarily defeat the United States. This was the second war that Nixon had disentangled from the Vietnam controversy and highlighted in his silent majority speech of November 1969. The *New York Times* and the *Washington Post* didn't grasp the significance of the distinction between a North Vietnamese defeat of the South Vietnamese, and of the United States, but the American public did.

Both major communist powers were now satisfied that defeat of the United States was not achievable, and that supporting Hanoi in such an obdurate course would not serve their own interests, especially as China and Russia contemplated each other in a complete absence of comradely solidarity.

They continued to support North Vietnam's right to "unite" Vietnam, but thought it no longer had any right to expect their aid in endlessly provoking the United States. This was a considerable achievement by Nixon, who managed it by pulling largely out without enabling the North to overrun Saigon, and maintaining a draconian air interdiction of the North without reviving the American peace movement. Nixon would win the second Vietnam War, but everyone, including Nguyen Van Thieu, knew that his chances of winning the first Vietnam War, for South Vietnam itself, remained slim.

The decent-interval advocates, like Kissinger, would probably prevail, but the outright defeatists, like McGovern, had not. The issue would long be debated, and still is, with an unclear conclusion, but there is, as will be explored later, a very arguable defense for Nixon's policy, despite the sad and predicted ultimate fate of the American effort in Vietnam.[62] Nixon met no serious opposition in Congress to his arms control proposals and left on the afternoon of June 2 for a holiday in Key Biscayne.

On June 10, McGovern defeated Humphrey in the California primary and effectively clinched the Democratic nomination. Nixon had never wavered in his view that McGovern was "a Goldwater of the left," and completely unelectable. Nixon's polls showed him winning by thirteen points over McGovern if the partly paralyzed George Wallace ran as an independent, and by nineteen points if Wallace did not run at all. For the first time since he had been the candidate of both parties in the Twelfth Congressional District of California in 1948, Nixon looked electorally impregnable. In the past year, he had stopped inflation; almost entirely evacuated U.S. forces from Vietnam, not in the hopeless manner the Democrats had proposed, but, by his will almost alone, by defeating North Vietnam's lunge for military victory there;

opened relations with China; brought relations with the U.S.S.R. to their highest point since 1945; and agreed the greatest progress toward control and reduction of armaments in history. He had conceived and conducted his political and diplomatic strategies with great skill and, on occasion, courage, and it was an infinitely happier and calmer country than the turbulent nation whose headship he had so narrowly won four years before.

On June 11 Nixon met again with Republican congressional leaders and attacked what he called "jackass amendments" to cut off the effort in Vietnam, and McGovern's proposals for mandating a reduction in the defense budget. Without making a direct connection to what he considered to be the habitual political antics of the Jewish community, he compared them with amendments that were regularly passed supporting Israel, usually without debate. He pointed out that cutting the U.S. defense budget really cut American credibility, and that, with the rough fluent eloquence of many of his private geopolitical reflections, if "U.S. credibility collapses, the Jews can check out of Israel and go back to Germany."[63]

— v —

The formidable political edifice that Nixon had built suffered a tremor that weekend. The long series of spectacular and astute moves President Nixon had taken to assure that he was reelected with a crushing majority, and was enabled to have a productive second term, began to play against a subtle and distant backdrop of unease. At a level where Nixon had paid scant attention, it all started to go horribly wrong.

Nixon spent most of the weekend with his friend Robert Abplanalp on a private island in the Bahamas. He met Haldeman at the airfield in Florida on Monday evening, who told him that an attempted break-in at the Democratic National Committee (DNC) headquarters in the Watergate complex, near the Kennedy Center, where several prominent Republicans, including Rose Mary Woods, lived, had been foiled three nights before. Halderman said that someone on the payroll of the Committee to Re-elect the President (CREEP) had been among those arrested.

The Liddy-Hunt unit, which was not the Plumbers but a more freelance outfit, had broken into the same offices on May 27 and installed taps on the telephones of party chairman Larry O'Brien and his secretaries. There had been an attempted return visit, which had to be aborted when the office was occupied by volunteers all night. But Liddy had ordered another return because the O'Brien bug wasn't working, and all they got from the secretaries was gossip and chit-chat about office romantic life. Mitchell, according to his CREEP deputy, Jeb Magruder, demanded a new tap on O'Brien.[64] The subsequent cross-allegations of those implicated in this affair must be read with extreme caution, as they are almost impossible to disentangle and evaluate.

Hunt brought together a group of Cuban-Americans – Bernard Barker, Virgilio Gonzalez, Eugenio Martinez, and Frank Sturgis – as well as James McCord. Effecting the break-in required taping open a door lock, which McCord did in a clumsy manner that enabled a security guard to see what he had done, arousing the guard's suspicions. They waited until 1 A.M. for the last person to leave the DNC office, and then, finding the tape had been removed (which should have warned them against proceeding), had to pick a lock to enter the building, again taped the lock open, and entered the DNC office by taking a back door off its hinges.

A lookout saw plainclothes policemen answer the Watergate night guard's call after the discovery of the taped-open lock, but he didn't realize they were policemen until he saw them coming through the building from the top story down with flashlights and drawn guns. He tried to warn the intruders, but Barker had turned off his walkie-talkie because the static was loud and might arouse suspicion. The policemen bagged McCord and the Cubans, without resistance.

Barker told Hunt and Liddy on his reactivated walkie-talkie that they had been apprehended. Hunt and Liddy left their hotel with suitcases containing most of their electronic equipment. But they left behind them thirty-two hundred dollars in new hundred-dollar bills, two address books with Hunt's name and White House telephone number in them, and a check payable to Hunt's country club. The police discovered all this the next day. The amateurish fashion in which the White House counter-insurgency operation collapsed indicates how pathetically shabby, poorly thought-out, absurd and demeaning the whole mad enterprise was. Though when Nixon said, "By God, we'll do it ourselves," it was not clear what legal boundaries he had in mind, he certainly didn't intend an orgy of illegal amateurism, but he did nothing to ensure that that was not what would occur.

Obviously, the police would quickly be on to Hunt, and there was no reason to believe that McCord and those arrested with him would walk the plank without implicating higher-ups. This was going to back into the

White House at an accelerating pace, and the challenge was to put down a firewall that would protect the president and his principal collaborators, without jeopardizing what now appeared to be a won election.

Given Nixon's strength, the wisest as well as the most honest course would have been for him to cut these people loose, say it had nothing to do with him, and let the chips fall, chopping off CREEP personnel as necessary, as the investigation proceeded. A combination of natural insecurity, loyalty to people who would risk everything for him, and painful recollections of Eisenhower's obsession with his own clean hands opposite Nixon in the fund crisis, and even in the case of the loyal but unsympathetic Sherman Adams, prevented Nixon from doing the right and sensible thing. Triumph and tragedy were now proceeding on parallel tracks.

To some degree they would be trading time for later legal problems. The progress of the investigation could perhaps be retarded so that nothing relevant to the election occurred, but that might require either perjury to grand juries or obstruction of justice from some relatively senior White House people. No self-confident or ethical presidency (not a category that includes all of the preceding ones) would have entertained such an exchange for a minute. It is unimaginable that Harry Truman or Dwight D. Eisenhower could have been endangered by such a development, or fostered the ambiance for it or hired the type of people who would have had anything to do with such down-market derring-do. As in many other things, and as both Truman and Eisenhower had sensed, Nixon was a bit different.

Even more obviously, Nixon should have handed control of it, as soon as the problem came to light, to someone of high public standing, completely clear of it, with instructions to make sure it came nowhere near the president, no matter what the electoral consequences. In the circumstances, there was no chance the country was going to throw out Nixon to bring in McGovern, unless Nixon had burgled the Watergate himself looking for pornographic literature for his own delectation and then resale to children whom he had molested. McGovern had taken his stand for clean air and water whatever the cost in jobs; higher income taxes for everyone above the average income level; drastic defense cuts; immediate, unconditional withdrawal from Vietnam; unlimited busing of school children for racial balance; a guaranteed income for every American; and immediate amnesty for all draft-dodgers and deserters. Add to that, McGovern had a monotonous voice and forgettable countenance that was a cross, visually and acoustically, between Mr. Peepers and Mr. Magoo. It was a kook candidacy that could not possibly win, and especially not against a president who achieved so much in four years as had Richard Nixon.

But even if that were not the case, or if Nixon believed he might lose the election, there is no disgrace to losing an election. Putting the presidency itself on the wrong side of the law in a grubby matter like this would be, and ultimately was, both a shame and a tragedy.

At this point, Nixon was legally unassailable enough. All there was against him was his demand that something be done about leaks: "By God, we'll do it ourselves." That was on tape, though he could dispose of the tapes if he wanted to, without legal problems, though there was no need to for reasons of self-protection. Nixon's position was entirely salvageable, but he had minimal margin for error. Nor is there any reason to believe that at this point Nixon himself had ever had criminal intent. He was terribly exasperated that his opponents committed crimes like the theft and publication of the Pentagon Papers and won Pulitzer Prizes for it, and that there was never much of a comeback on his own side.

Yet he was a respecter of the law, a legitimate, if sometimes demagogic, upholder of law and order. He had not known anything about the Watergate break-in, though he had helped to create a shoddy and cynical atmosphere in the White House and was aware that some operations of very doubtful legality, depending on a slender thread of national security cover, were under way. This was mitigated to some degree by the intense times, and by the sometimes lawless behavior of his immediate predecessors and of his unofficial opponents (to whom the Democrats gave sympathy and shelter while coyly keeping their official distance). But the break-in was not excusable. That Richard Nixon possessed the intention of committing crimes, or what he had good reason to believe were crimes, at least at this early stage, has not been proved, despite huge efforts to do so. It was all to play for, but unfortunately, it wasn't played well.

The arrested men appeared in court at 3:30 P.M. on the day of their arrest. When asked their occupations, only one responded, and declared his to be that of an "anti-communist." McCord stepped up to the bench and whispered, as if in automatic self-exoneration, "security consultant, retired from government service," and when asked which service, replied that it had been the CIA. Liddy and Hunt were at CREEP shredding documents. Colson ordered the destruction of White House files recording Hunt's presence, an utterly foolish step, while Magruder was at home burning copies in his own fireplace of Liddy's former Gemstone suggestions.

The whole do-it-yourself White House subversive effort, the most extreme formulation of which had been Liddy's Gemstone plan, which included ransacking the Brookings Institution, was thrown into reverse gear. When this came to light, as it was bound to do, the comedy and the perfidy of it joined. Nixon could have escaped the second, since he wasn't involved in it, but escaping the comedy of the ridicule would be harder, because he did create the atmosphere that spawned these mutations, although Mitchell vetoed Gemstone three times.

Liddy burst into the dining room of the Burning Tree Country Club and told the attorney general, Richard Kleindienst, that Mitchell wanted the arrested men released. Liddy was a lawyer and knew that, as the arrests were municipal, and had already been recorded, Kleindienst could not do anything about it, that if he had tried the repercussions would have been disastrous, and that it was improbable that Mitchell would have made any such request through Liddy, or at all.[65]

The White House and CREEP were in such terrible disarray, with Nixon blissfully sunning himself in the Bahamas, that it reinforces the Nixon defense that he knew nothing about it until well after the fact, and after some of those acting in his name had had a chance to make fools and delinquents of themselves. White House counsel John Dean, after the *Washington Post* reported that there appeared to be a White House connection (Hunt) to the "bugging suspects," had Hunt's White House safe searched and found a Colt revolver, live ammunition, and, in his briefcase, electronic gear, a teargas canister, CIA comments on Ellsberg, extracts from the Pentagon Papers, and the forged cables claiming President Kennedy had ordered the assassination of President Diem and his brother. Dean claimed that Ehrlichman told him to "deep six" the briefcase and that he did so. Whether this last flourish was true or not, this shambles of fumbling and preparatory obfuscation was a very unpromising start.

The role of White House counsel John Dean has been one of the great sub-controversies of Watergate. Nixon would have served himself much better if he had had a more serious lawyer in that position. Dean had met Nixon only three times, briefly, at this point, on secondary issues. But he figured out, and this is a discredit to the president, that the way forward was to sponsor partisan intelligence gathering and disinformation.

This is inexcusable behavior for the White House counsel, but it was not discouraged. Dean had set up his own investigation unit and had caused the investigation of the call-girl ring associated with the "Happy Hooker," Xaviera Hollander, but this achieved nothing useful, as there were as many Republicans as Democrats in it, an unsurprising revelation. Dean also, on his own initiative, was the first of White House figures to compose an "enemies list," of people to be persecuted by the Internal Revenue Service and other agencies.

That the White House counsel, unknown to the president, was the commissioning agent for these initiatives was shaming – to Dean, but also, since President Truman was right about where the buck stops, to Nixon too. How could the president, who went to the Forbidden City and to the Kremlin and came away heavy-laden with political advantage, have been responsible, indirectly, for inciting such tawdriness, or have engaged such an unsuitable counsel? In the end, the world would wonder.

As it was only a local police story, the *Washington Post* initially assigned to it only two young reporters in their twenties, Robert Woodward and Carl Bernstein. The early response of the principal media, so often on the edges of their seats expecting a Nixon pratfall, was that so slick an operator, a Houdini, as the president could not possibly be involved, even at a distance, in so improbable and ludicrous a story.

On June 20, the DNC filed a million-dollar lawsuit against CREEP for invasion of its privacy and violation of its civil rights. That day had begun with an 8 A.M. meeting between Haldeman, Ehrlichman, and Mitchell, in which Mitchell enunciated the rule that, above all, the president must be protected. This was reasonable, and it would not, at that point, have been difficult to do. It has been claimed, but not substantiated, that Mitchell urged that investigations be stopped, as they might lead to what he called the White House "horrors" – Segretti's dirty tricks on Democrats, wire-taps, the Ellsberg psychoanalyst's break-in, and surveillance of leading Democrats, including Senator Kennedy.[66] This was unsavory, but most of it was legal, arguably justifiable under a national security cover, or mere mischief, and none of it led to the president.

At this early point, three days into what became the Watergate era, Nixon was basically unaffected by it, but he began a series of one-on-one meetings about it, starting with Ehrlichman, and then Haldeman, whose notes suggest that Nixon wanted to dismiss the episode as a prank and to counterattack the Democrats for their own misdeeds. Haldeman claimed to believe that Nixon surmised that Colson had ordered the break-in and wanted Haldeman to ensure that he, Nixon, knew nothing about it. All the evidence, fragmentary as it is, is that Nixon knew nothing about it and was only asking to be kept in willful ex post facto ignorance – again, not a very dignified posture for the holder of such a great office, but nothing people are impeached for either.

There was an eighteen-and-a-half minute gap in the Oval Office tape of the June 20 conversation at the Watergate stage of the conversation with Haldeman, and we only have Haldeman's notes to go on. Rose Mary Woods later took responsibility for this accidental erasure, as she described it, but given her loyalty to Nixon, and general efficiency, her account was widely disbelieved.

At four-thirty on the afternoon of the 20th, Nixon had another meeting with Haldeman at his hideaway office in the Executive Office Building. The tape of this meeting is extant, and reasonably comprehensive. Haldeman told Nixon about the DNC lawsuit, which they saw as a clever way to take discovery evidence from leaders of CREEP, such as Mitchell. Nixon asked if Haldeman knew what the legal delays were. Dean had told Haldeman that it could probably be stalled to the election, and said that Hunt could disappear "if we want him to." Neither Nixon nor Haldeman was aware whether Hunt worked for CREEP, the White House, or whomever.

Neither Nixon nor Haldeman thought that Colson was directly responsible for the Watergate break-in, contrary to Haldeman's notes of the meeting that morning. It seems clear that they were both still groping around. Nixon knew that he must keep his distance from it, but he couldn't seem to contain his curiosity and wanted to ensure that it wasn't botched. Given the Keystone Kops performance of his aides while he had been in the Bahamas, this was an understandable concern.

Nixon referred to the taping machines, which Haldeman said only a few people knew about. There was no talk of destroying the tapes, or shutting down the system, though Nixon showed no sign subsequently of speaking with any consciousness of being recorded. He could have jammed their tapes with self-serving talk if he had wished, but rarely had recourse to such talk. Nixon concluded the discussion by saying that he didn't consider the DNC "worth bugging." This was not an edifying statement, but it is a somewhat self-exculpatory one.

On June 21, starting again with Haldeman at 9:30 A.M., Nixon stuck a toe into the quagmire by talking about how the story might develop. The night before, he had called Haldeman and said that the involvement of the Cubans could lead to a discussion of what a mess Kennedy had made of the Bay of Pigs. In the morning, Haldeman laid out a scenario of Mitchell's that Liddy would take the rap and say that he had organized it to advance himself in the Republican organization. Later, Haldeman told Nixon that Liddy was an aspirant to the status of the Revolutionary War hero Nathan Hale. ("I regret that I have only one life to give for my country.") Liddy claimed to believe that Dean was behind the Watergate break-in, but this is very unlikely and Dean has successfully sued over the allegation.[67]

Nixon said that it was a Washington matter only, that the country assumed that everybody was bugging everyone else, and – as a joke presumably, though not absolutely certainly – that perhaps their people should bug themselves and leak the contents to make it seem the Democrats had done it. This was the sort of expatiation Nixon regularly inflicted on his entourage, which had no sequel. This wasn't very comforting about the high-mindedness of the president.

Nixon then met with Colson. For someone who wanted to be distanced from the Watergate break-in, which Ziegler had referred to as a "third-rate burglary," Nixon was showing an unhealthy curiosity in the matter. Colson, whom Kissinger regarded as a thug, and who was a rather outrageous partisan at times, suggested dismissing it all as a CIA operation. How he could have imagined that the Cuban intruders, who had had nothing recently to do with the CIA, could be so represented, and the CIA leadership could have been persuaded to accept responsibility for breaking into the headquarters of the majority political party in the country, was not explained by Colson and not asked by the president. This, at the latest, should have been, to use a famous phrase of Jefferson's, "a fire-bell in the night" to Nixon not to get any closer to something that still need not scorch him.

But it wasn't. The next morning, Haldeman was pleased because the money that the burglars were carrying could not be traced (but this pleasure reversed itself the next day when the FBI did trace the money to a larger amount Liddy had given Barker, some of which had come via a Republican fund-raiser from Dwayne Andreas). Haldeman took pride, or at least amusement, in telling Nixon that a rumor they had planted that it was all a Jack Anderson move to bug the DNC had started to resonate. Again, this was mad.

There were arrested suspects caught in the act who had nothing to do with Jack Anderson. What could Haldeman or even Nixon have been thinking?[68]

Nixon held a press conference on June 22, and there was only one Watergate question, which he dealt with by citing Ziegler, that "this kind of activity has no place whatever in our electoral process, or in our governmental process . . . and the White House has had no involvement whatever . . . ," etc. So far, so good, but the president was circling the abyss.

On June 23, Haldeman reported that Mitchell had suggested that Richard Helms and Vernon Walters, the director and deputy director of the CIA, ask L. Patrick Gray, the acting director of the FBI since Hoover's death, to have the FBI stay out of it as a matter that could embarrass the CIA. Nixon replied that that could be requested, as "we have protected Helms from a lot of things," and "this involves these Cubans, Hunt, and a lot of hanky-panky that we had nothing to do with ourselves." He thought it could be represented as possibly leading back into the Bay of Pigs debacle of eleven years before.

They discussed to what extent Mitchell knew about it, and Haldeman thought that he knew generally, but not the details. Nixon asked who was responsible, and guessed at Liddy. Nixon clearly seems not to have known much about it at this point, nearly a week after the break-in, and said, once again, "I'm not going to get that involved." Haldeman replied, "No sir, we don't want you to."[69]

Gray had called Helms and said that he thought they had arrived in the middle of a CIA covert operation. Helms thought not. Helms said he would try to be helpful, but wanted a written instruction and explanation of the reason. As it turned out, the prosecution was not being conducted by the FBI, but by Earl Silbert, an assistant U.S. attorney for the District of Columbia.

The tapes of these June 23 conversations were released on August 5, 1974, and became known as the "smoking gun," but they are not as damaging as they seemed when presented two years after the fact as a sort of last straw. Gray had expressed a concern, denied by Helms, about a CIA covert operation. Helms told Halderman and Ehrlichman that he would cooperate if given written instructions and an adequate explanation, by which he clearly meant that there would have to be an adequate reason to ask the FBI to desist. No such instructions were given; no such request from the CIA was made, though Walters spoke again to Gray. The FBI did not desist, and didn't principally have carriage of the matter anyway. It appeared two years later, and was represented by the press, as an attempt to obstruct justice, and it would have been if it had been pushed, but it wasn't pushed.

It was a discreditable idea for shutting down an investigation, but it wasn't pursued and justice was not obstructed. What was missing was any sense of trying to treat it as a legitimate law enforcement matter rather than just a political inconvenience, and any sense of outrage that the White House and the world's greatest secular office should be connected in any way to anything so sleazy and contemptible. There was not only no righteousness, in the expressed thoughts of the president and his immediate entourage, there was very insufficient embarrassment.

On June 26, Nixon and Haldeman discussed the possibility of Mitchell's retiring from CREEP and accepting ultimate responsibility for the break-in. His wife was becoming so erratic, telephoning people at all hours and raving and screaming allegations in all directions, that he might not be able to see it through anyway. It may be that responsibility for this fiasco ultimately did belong with Mitchell. Haldeman advised Nixon that there may have been other "black bag operations," but that he wasn't sure. If he wasn't sure, Nixon certainly knew nothing of them. This should have been all the more reason for Nixon to ensure that the matter was put in the hands of disinterested investigators and kept away from him. Instead, he was almost constantly involved in it, taking a break only to record in his diary that Kissinger had told him that the publisher of the *Washington Post*, Katharine Graham, had told columnist Stewart Alsop, "I hate" Nixon, "and I'm going to do everything I can to beat him." (Graham denied to the author that she had ever said she hated Nixon, and professed some respect for him at that time and later in his life, but acknowledged that she did not favor his reelection.)[70]

On June 28, Nixon concluded that Mitchell had to go, that his wife was now a potential suicide case. Haldeman was detailed to convey this news to Mitchell, which he did. And Haldeman reported to Nixon that Mitchell was ready to retire from CREEP. Nixon engaged in a lot of atmospherics about the Duke of Windsor (retiring as king for the woman he loved, and so forth). Haldeman also asked the White House counsel, John Dean, to get some money for the Watergate defendants. This activity has generally been regarded as a second smoking gun. That is not so clear either.

For the reelection committee to pay the legal costs and living expenses of part-time and full-time employees is quite in order. It has been assumed that this was "hush money," payments made in exchange for silence about CREEP or White House involvement. In all the voluminous material, it is not clear that was even the implicit intended nature of the payments, at least at the outset. As time went by, what amounted to blackmail was attempted by some of the defendants, and some was paid. But it is not clear that submitting to blackmail constitutes obstructing justice. It was, however, both shaming and demeaning to the presidency.

John Dean met with California CREEP fund-raiser Herbert Kalmbach on June 30, and Maurice Stans gave him $75,100 in cash at his hotel, to start paying the defendants' legal costs. Nixon had a televised press conference on the evening of June 30. There was not a question about Watergate. It was still not conceivable to the national press corps, especially after the mighty winning streak Nixon had built up, that there could be any serious White House involvement in anything so fatuous.

From early on, Watergate was handled by the administration as a sleazy and embarrassingly down-market bit of nonsense, not as a really sinister assault on democratic government, and not as a disgrace that should have been excised at once, taking out whoever had any real attachment to it.

On July 1, Nixon invited in Congressman Clark MacGregor and asked him to take over CREEP in place of Mitchell. MacGregor agreed, conditional on the truth of the assurances he had been given that CREEP had had nothing to do with the Watergate break-in. Nixon said, "That's the line you should take. I know the White House had nothing to do with it." This was a bit disingenuous. Haldeman had mentioned Liddy, whom Stans had ostensibly fired. Haldeman advised Nixon that Liddy was prepared to fall on his sword and say that some of the money he had received was apparently not a legal contribution, as it came in after the reporting deadline, but that he had, on his own authority, decided to say that he had applied it to covert operations. Nixon said, "A true believer." (In the famous June 23 conversation, he had called Liddy "an asshole.") "We'll take care of him. . . . It's good to have some people like that." In his diary that night, Nixon wrote, "I am satisfied that nobody in the White House had any knowledge or approved any such activity, and that Mitchell was not aware of it as well."[71]

— VI —

President Nixon left on July 1 for a holiday at San Clemente, advising his political operatives that there was no need to take counter-measures against McGovern, who would "sink himself."[72] Given his accurate forecast of the McGovern campaign's likely grip on the voters, it is particularly astounding that he wasn't more careful about where Watergate might ramify. His last significant act before leaving Washington was to approve a 20 percent increase in Social Security benefits, and the indexing of them to cost-of-living increases. He had disapproved the bill, as he thought the increase inflationary, but he was a precursor of supply side economics, in that he supported the cushioning of fixed-income earners against inflation through indexing benefits to cost-of-living increases. He allowed his enthusiasm for indexing to prevail over his distaste for inflationary spending increases, perhaps not unmoved by the fact that he was only four months away from an election.

Even though he was three time zones behind in California, Nixon had trouble keeping awake for the nomination of his Democratic opponent in Miami, on July 13. The convention was a shambles; thirty-nine candidates were put forward for vice president, including Archie Bunker (a fictitious character), Mao Tse-tung (ineligible as a foreigner), and Martha Mitchell. McGovern got his (Warholian) fifteen minutes of world fame and addressed the convention that had selected him, at 3 A.M., Eastern Time, July 14.

John Connally and his wife were the Nixons' houseguests in California, Connally having retired as secretary of the Treasury and become head of Democrats for Nixon, whose bulging ranks were vastly increased by McGovern's self-destructive performance on this night. Connally couldn't bear to watch it, and the president and Pat watched it alone.

The credentials committee had taken away Mayor Daley's place and put Jesse Jackson, the rutting panther of an African-American nonconformist clergyman and racial militant, in his place holding the standard for Illinois. Nixon could scarcely believe the spectacle of electoral self-destruction that unfolded before his eyes. He later wrote that the convention "had the air of a college skit that had gotten carried away with itself and didn't know how to stop."[73] As one who had fought the formidable succession of the memory of Roosevelt and then Truman, Stevenson, Kennedy, Johnson, and Humphrey, great or at least formidable men, the thought of facing McGovern was almost unimaginable. George Wallace dramatically spoke to the convention from his wheelchair. He got a polite reception, more out of deference to his injury than to his person or policies, but he was not well enough to run again for president. He confirmed this a few weeks later, after visits from Billy Graham and John Connally on Nixon's behalf.

The Nixon campaign paid for Wallace's campaign staff to the end of the year. Nixon sent Wallace a copy of *Sunrise at Campobello*, the film story of FDR's recovery from polio, with Ralph Bellamy as FDR, and a partly deglamorized Greer Garson (brilliant as always) as Eleanor. He also sent Alexander Haig to give Wallace national security briefings.

Kennedy and other prominent Democrats declined McGovern's invitation to join him on the sinking ship as vice presidential candidate. McGovern chose Senator Thomas F. Eagleton of Missouri. But on July 25, after the press had unearthed the fact that Eagleton had been hospitalized three times in the sixties for mental problems, and twice had undergone electric shock therapy, McGovern announced that he had not known that, but that if he had, he would have selected Eagleton anyway. There was a good deal of controversy about the vice presidential candidate's mental health, and finally, on July 31, he withdrew at McGovern's request.

A new charade began, as McGovern cast publicly about for a candidate, and after being semi-publicly rejected by his first five or six invitees, eventually came up with R. Sargent Shriver, former ambassador to France and head of the Peace Corps and Office of Economic Opportunity, and a Kennedy in-law (the only reason he held any of these posts, though he acquitted them adequately). The DNC confirmed Shriver on August 9. His chances of riding the nomination to victory were not great.

Nixon sent a handwritten letter to Eagleton's thirteen-year-old son Terry, after seeing him on television. He wrote that Terry's father had "fought a terribly difficult battle . . . [and had] won the admiration of foes and friends alike because of the courage, poise, and just plain guts he showed against overwhelming odds." Senator Eagleton telephoned the White House and expressed his gratitude to Pat Buchanan. Nixon did not publicize his letter; the Eagletons did. It was a vintage Nixon gesture; he always identified with people who suffered serious setbacks, as he had with Teddy Kennedy after Chappaquiddick. (A few years later, Eagleton addressed a national mental health organization convention and began by saying that, contrary to widespread belief, he did not begin each day by standing in front of a mirror with a straight razor in his hand and saying, "Well, Eagleton, how's your mental health today?")

As he chose Eagleton, McGovern dispensed with Larry O'Brien as party chairman. This was another insane decision that he would, like his vice-presidential choice, soon rescind. McGovern did well to select a woman as O'Brien's replacement, Jean M. Westwood. But after about a month, O'Brien was called back to manage the campaign. Even O'Brien, exceptionally capable though he was, could not make a big difference in this election, but McGovern needed any professionalism he could find. (O'Brien would go on to be a very successful commissioner of the National Basketball Association.)

As O'Brien's departure was being announced, Nixon was introducing Connally to the press in San Clemente as head of Democrats for Nixon. Connally told Nixon he had already spoken with a number of Democratic senators who were trying to avoid endorsing McGovern, and with President Johnson. LBJ said that he was in much closer agreement with Nixon than with McGovern, that he would vote for his party's nominee, but that he would not try to discourage other Democrats, including his own daughters, from supporting Nixon. He said the same thing when Nixon called him, at Connally's urging. He told Billy Graham that Nixon should just ignore McGovern, as he had ignored Goldwater, and that Watergate would be no problem at all. It need not have been.[74] The silent majority was growing by giant Texan strides.

When Nixon returned to Washington on July 19, Ehrlichman told him that Magruder would have to "take the slide . . . to take responsibility for the thing. They're not going to be able to contrive a story that indicates that he didn't know what was going on." Nixon asked, "Did he know?" He did. The version that was extant when Nixon left for California, that Liddy would carry the can for it, had faded because Magruder had been too closely connected to these activities through his CREEP role. Nixon did not, at this point, know who was involved, and delivered a little homily, basing it on his pursuit of Alger Hiss: "If you cover up, you're going to get caught. And if you lie, you're going to be guilty of perjury."[75]

There was a criminal grand jury, and the DNC lawsuit, and the Democrats had hired Washington's (and America's) leading barrister, Edward Bennett Williams, whom Nixon had known since he represented Senator Joe McCarthy in 1954. Grand juries, instituted by the Fifth Amendment of the Constitution as a guarantee of citizens' rights, had long since become a rubber stamp of prosecutors, and habitually indicted anyone the prosecutors took against. In both proceedings, there would be efforts to take the inquiry as far up the chain into and through the White

House as possible, from Magruder to Mitchell to Haldeman and, unspoken, to the president.

In fact, Nixon was still clear, almost five weeks after the break-in. On July 20, Haldeman told him, "It will be messy." But Nixon was now confident that there would be no trials until the election. He and Haldeman were amused that Howard Hunt was using all the civil libertarian procedural delays that Nixon had long objected to in his law-and-order campaigns.[76] If Nixon had cut the whole tangled knot loose at this point, Haldeman and Ehrlichman might have felt the need to resign spontaneously, or with a nudge from the president, but not under a greater cloud than Sherman Adams had in 1958. The damage to Nixon would have been minimal.

This was the time when Nixon should have dissolved CREEP, combined it with the Republican National Committe, and distributed its massive resources around the party, buying the gratitude and goodwill of his party, and trying to get control of at least one house of the Congress. Apart from assisting him in building his domestic record in a second term, this would have been the very best insurance policy against excessive congressional hectoring of Nixon over Watergate or anything else. Congressional gains would also have retained his deterrent strength opposite Hanoi.

The great North Vietnamese offensive of March 30 had been defeated on the ground by the South Vietnamese Army, a distinct accomplishment, though massive American bombing was essential. The secret Paris discussions continued desultorily through the summer. Kissinger went from one of the Paris meetings to Saigon on August 15, and wrote to Nixon that he thought a negotiated peace might be near. Nixon had no faith in the negotiations. If he could be confident of congressional support for it, he would have been happy to continue to smash the North Vietnamese from the air indefinitely. Certainly, Kissinger shortly discovered, this was Thieu's preference.[77]

Hanoi now realized that Nixon was unbeatable and that he had outmaneuvered the domestic peace movement. They may have hoped for the reelection of a Democratic Congress that would cut off funding for the bombing, but they were by now wary of trying to interpose themselves between Nixon and the U.S. public, as they successfully did with Johnson. And North Vietnam could not endure twelve hundred bombing sorties a day indefinitely, while the United States warmed up its relations with China and the U.S.S.R. The North Vietnamese leadership knew, better than did most Americans, what a skillful game Nixon had played with the communist powers.

The most interesting international news this summer was Egyptian President Anwar Sadat's sudden expulsion of all twenty thousand Soviet advisers and military personnel from his country. Allegedly, Kissinger had not thought Sadat would last,[78] or if he did that he would accomplish much. He was emerging as a historic figure in the Middle East. This sudden step created an immense opportunity for Nixon to send the Russians packing from much of the Middle East, and greatly added to the U.S. position in the correlation of forces between the super powers in that region.

Nixon's approval rating was over 60 percent, and he was leading McGovern by about fifteen points. Nixon convinced himself that because Connally and CREEP were canvassing for him and not the Republicans, and he was careful to campaign against McGovern and not the Democrats, he could not campaign hard for Republican congressional candidates.[79] In fact, he had worked his heart out for the Republican Party for twenty-five years and he was tired of it. He also claimed to believe that he would bring a large number of candidates in on his coattails, but he had taken such distance from his party, this was unlikely.

Nixon had a convivial round of golf with George Meany on July 27, shortly after the AFL-CIO executive committee voted almost unanimously to be neutral in the presidential election, for the first time in its history. Meany said he would not vote for either candidate, but that his wife and two of his daughters would vote for Nixon. The abrasions of the AFL-CIO convention at Bal Harbor, Florida, eight months before were forgotten. Despite their differences, Nixon had a better view of Meany than of most businessmen, whom he considered to be slothful, self-indulgent, and greedy cowards. Businessmen, he frequently said, in one of his more common formulations, were "not worth a shit." He liked the unpretentious patriotism of the labor leaders, and of the union membership. Philadelphia's Democratic mayor, Frank L. Rizzo, noisily defected to Nixon, and Chicago's powerful mayor, twice the host and honorary chairman of Democratic conventions, did not greatly appreciate being bounced for Jesse Jackson by McGovern's stooges in the credentials committee. Mayor Daley wouldn't bolt his party, where he habitually controlled the Illinois delegation at Democratic conventions, but he, who had been instrumental in winning the 1960 election for Kennedy, would not lift a finger for McGovern.

At his press conference on July 27, Nixon said that a precipitate departure from South Vietnam would cause a bloodbath. He was now dealing with the desperate ambition of the Democrats in the Congress to cut what was left of the U.S. mission in Vietnam at any price, and no matter what happened to the American POWs.[80]

The media were friendly, but Nixon did not mistake their motives or constancy. He wrote in one memo, of *Time*'s Hugh Sidey and NBC's John Chancellor: "As long as we appear to have a rather substantial lead in the polls, the Sideys and even the Chancellors will suck around. . . . Play them as suckers, not as friends."[81] In the end, Nixon received the endorsements of 213 major market newspapers, to twelve for McGovern (included among the twelve were the *New York Times* and the *Washington Post*, though both acknowledged that Nixon had had some noteworthy accomplishments).

On August 2, Nixon, Haldeman, and Kissinger had rather entertaining conversations in the Oval Office about the peccadilloes of leading Democrats. Kissinger referred to Teddy Kennedy's current rumored affair with a wealthy socialite; Haldeman asserted that LBJ used to impose himself sexually on his secretaries; and Nixon referred to the alleged physical relationship between Jackie and Bobby Kennedy (after JFK's death), but credited them with being "a hell of a lot more discreet." (News of that arrangement would have been a disaster for both of them.)[82]

McGovern just kept bumbling along. On August 16, he declined Nixon's offer of national security briefings from Kissinger, saying that he could learn as much from reading the newspapers. Three days later, he said that Watergate was the "kind of thing you expect under a person like Hitler." He was confusing "a third-rate burglary" with "the night of the long knives" (in Germany in 1934, in which many hundreds of people were murdered), or even the Holocaust, in which twelve million people, including six million Jews, perished.

The Republican convention was a completely orderly, clockwork-coordinated affair, as unlike the last two Democratic conventions as it was possible to be. The only visible dissent was from the three thousand long-haired, shabbily dressed, counter-cultural denizens of the People's

Liberated Zone of Revolutionary Living. A heavy pall of marijuana smoke hung over their tent city, whose main street was Ho Chi Minh Trail. A few miles away, at the Nautilus Junior High School, was the headquarters of Young Voters for the President, well-scrubbed, polite young people wearing Bermuda shorts and helping out around the convention. The two groups never encountered each other en masse, and may not even have been aware of each other's presence. There was little doubt which better represented the mood and wishes of the country.[83]

Richard Nixon was renominated on August 22, by 1,327 to 1, after his name had been put forward by Barry Goldwater, Ronald Reagan, and Nelson Rockefeller. It was the fifth time his party selected him as a candidate for national office, an honor he shared only with FDR in the whole history of the country.[*] In his quest for consensus (i.e., Democratic votes), Nixon, in his acceptance speech, cited FDR, Truman, JFK, and LBJ, as well as Ike, in his opposition to isolationism. He did not refer to McGovern or the Democrats, but debunked their platform as cowardly, divisive, and dishonest. He called for victory in the election campaign, for the achievement "of a hope that mankind has had since the beginning of civilization . . . a peace that our children, and all the children of the world, can enjoy for generations to come."

Nixon flew to Chicago to give the American Legion a rousing speech about patriotic values and the rule of law in America and the world. The almost delirious reception given him left everyone in little doubt how most of the nation's twenty million veterans would be voting. The president continued to Michigan and San Diego, before spending the night at San Clemente. Post-convention polls showed him leading McGovern by more than thirty points, now just two months before the election.

There were three important tactical questions to be determined: how to handle the campaign, Watergate, and the Vietnam negotiations, and they were all related. On September 15, the grand jury in Washington returned indictments against the Watergate burglars. The Justice Department issued a statement that "we have absolutely no evidence that anyone else should be charged." The Cubans gave anti-communist homilies and pledged that they had no higher-ups to denounce. Attorney General Kleindienst said the

---

[*] Only George Bush Sr. would be nominated to national office by serious parties four times.

investigation was one of the "most intensive, objective, and thorough" in many years.[84] Dean told Nixon the FBI had had more agents on Watergate than on the Kennedy assassination. Nixon considered demanding an apology from the Democrats for their allegations and severe (unspecified) revenge on Edward Bennett Williams.[85]

Nixon asked Haldeman if the line was now set, that everyone would "stonewall." He had watched the news summary and found the perform-ance of the Cubans hilarious: "I thought I'd die. It was so funny. They sound very believable, the Cubans, don't they?" Nixon was plumbing a new depth of cynicism in this fetid affair. The Cubans had been recruited by his cam-paign officials, had been told that they were accomplishing something in the struggle against the worldwide communist enemy that had been oppressing their country for the last thirteen years, and were the victims of an illegal and stupidly planned and executed operation that had nothing to do with communism, and the president was laughing because of their fidelity and discretion. His laughter, wholly inappropriate as it was, would be brief, hollow, and mocking.

The ability to maintain such a fiction as this through two trials under questioning from the likes of Edward Bennett Williams should have been seen to be unlikely, especially as Nixon had been warned that Magruder would have to "take the slide." (Williams had added Stans, Sloan, and Liddy as defendants.) At this point, a little more than two months after the break-in, Nixon could have claimed not to know that his campaign funds were being used to pay for a false version of events. He could still consider the payoffs to the accused to be compassionate support for their legal bills and their families. And he could still claim that the anti-communist line was a sincere revulsion at McGovern.

But there is, here, a glimpse of the Nixon who thought he had got away with a scam; and it is a more unattractive Nixon than the intense, brooding Nixon who genuinely felt he was being tormented and unjustly assaulted, who has so often appeared in this narrative, and is shortly to reemerge.

If Nixon had not decided to avoid campaigning, to let the Republicans do what they could for themselves, and to keep all the vast amounts of cam-paign money for his own virtual non-campaign, he could have developed a fiercely partisan support group in the event of a serious challenge to the conduct of his campaign officials, including Watergate. And he could have turned the election in part into a referendum on whether to continue bombing North Vietnam until the NVA was withdrawn from the South.

The fate of the 1972 spring NVA offensive (which Kissinger thought might not come, because he had been invited to lunch on March 17 by Ducky) had created a stasis that provided a final chance for a non-communist South Vietnam. ARVN could hold with that level of U.S. air support. It might e/en, over time, have been possible to endow the South Vietnamese with enough air power to do much of it for themselves.

Kissinger, engrossed in his negotiations, which he had undoubtedly conducted with impossible interlocutors with great skill, wanted to bring off peace before the election, to strengthen the president in the vote and run no risk of a congressional cut-off of funds for the bombing after the installation of the new Congress in January. He did not expect South Vietnam to last, but thought the decent interval had been worth fighting for and spared the United States excessive humiliation.

Nixon had always wanted to win a durable South Vietnam, but had oscillated between pessimism and cautious hopefulness that, with support, South Vietnam could be viable. The only hope for his desired option lay in continued American heavy bombing indefinitely, and the only method of achieving this would be to call what was shaping up as a landslide election, a referendum on not deserting the South Vietnamese while the NVA was in strength in the South. This would have had the added benefit of strengthening the U.S. negotiating position opposite Hanoi. All these factors increase the mystery of why Nixon sat on his hands for almost all the election, did not campaign for his party, which he said was afflicted by "lousy candidates," and pursued a "Rose Garden strategy" – that is, he sat in the White House Rose Garden. He recognized part of the problem, as he said he wanted the campaign conducted for him to emphasize hard-line Vietnam policies, but only he could sell such policies, and transform the election into a mandate for those policies.[86]

As for Watergate, Nixon should have known that the trials would eventually follow the thread as far as it went, and he should have had the necessary research undertaken by an adequately highly placed and credible person (a category that, it turned out, did not include John Dean). All who would not be able to hold their offices after the facts were known should have been given temporary leave, with financial support, as long as it was understood that they were being paid to tell the truth. Magruder, the already departed Mitchell, Colson, and the Plumbers would have been in this group. Nixon could probably have held the national security line for Ehrlichman's approval of the Ellsberg-Fielding break-in, and Haldeman doesn't seem to have crossed any double lines at this point, though everyone, including Nixon, was getting close. The departure of Ehrlichman and Haldeman might have been advisable, but not necessarily inevitable.

Such a move would not have reflected personally on Nixon, and would not have been overly nastily publicized if Nixon had got clearly out in front on the issue while he was on the campaign trail hammering McGovern for his many policy inanities.

The mighty Nixon electoral juggernaut proceeded inexorably toward victory, but the opportunities to use the election to draw the sting of Watergate and strengthen the president's hand in Vietnam were lost. Nelson Rockefeller, who was intimately briefed by Kissinger, in particular, about goings-on in the White House, was concerned that Nixon might be cracking under the stress and behaving irrationally. Though Nixon became somewhat morose and more reclusive than usual, and seemed to be strangely insouciant about the dangers of Watergate, there is no reason to believe that Rockefeller's analysis was accurate. No president had been impeached except Andrew Johnson, and that was a wildly partisan assault that failed in the end (albeit by a single vote in the Senate), more than a century before. Nixon is to be excused for believing, as he proceeded toward a colossal election victory, that he need not think in such terms.

— VII —

While the Cubans were entertaining the president with their televised pleas, Kissinger was meeting again with Le Duc Tho. He reported publicly that there was little progress, but he told Nixon that the North Vietnamese were prepared to end the American participation in the Vietnam War on the last-stated American terms. The two sides (in the so-called secret talks, now instantly public) had tentatively agreed on an October 15 peace agreement. Nixon had had Haig cable Kissinger just before the meeting that Nixon was no longer prepared to settle on the former basis. Kissinger virtually ignored this and agreed on a Council of National Reconciliation and Concord, which would modify the constitution and supervise elections and be composed in equal parts by Thieu's government, the VC, and others.

Thieu was not reassured by Kissinger at their last meeting, in August, fearing that the United States would trade the POWs for continuation of the NVA presence in the South. His nightmare scenario was that the Americans, while not pushing him out (he took Nixon at his word on that), would impose coalition government, which would be a slightly delayed version of the same thing. He thought the National Council was perilously close to that. Nixon thought the correlation of forces had changed, because polls indicated that Americans favored, by a margin of five to three, continued heavy bombing of North Vietnam, and 74 percent thought it important that South Vietnam not fall to the communists. The United States had already started a massive buildup of the South Vietnamese air force, planning eventually to Vietnamize that part of the war also. (South Vietnam would have technically the world's fourth largest air force.) If he had plunged into the election campaign even at this late date, as Roosevelt did in his last two elections, Nixon could have claimed a mandate to enforce the peace agreement in Vietnam.

He was tempted to start raising the ante, having lowered it for several years. But when Kissinger and Le Duc Tho reached agreement on military points in Paris, September 26 and 27, Nixon sent Haig to Saigon to try to sell it to Thieu.

This meeting was not successful. Thieu wept as he expressed his objections to every clause of what Kissinger and Le Duc Tho had agreed. He was prepared to fear the worst from a Council of National Reconciliation with unspecified powers. This was too much for Thieu, who clearly represented the non-communist majority in the South, and whose army had lately given a very respectable account of itself. Nixon felt moved to write the South Vietnamese president, promising him that any political arrangements would be made only after they had been agreed with Thieu personally. Inexplicably, and with a stupefying lack of taste, Nixon ended by urging Thieu to take every measure to avoid the development of an atmosphere that could lead to events "similar to those which we abhorred in 1963." (The assassination of the Diems.)

This was the last train leaving the station for Nixon's Vietnam policy. If he had reached agreement with Hanoi before the election and demanded that all candidates for Congress be judged on their determination to support the president's use of air power in the event of North Vietnamese violations of the agreement, he might have been able to enforce it. If he wasn't prepared to campaign for Republican congressional candidates or turn the congressional part of the election into a plebiscite on a peace agreement, he would be at the mercy of anti-war Democratic majoritites in the Congress, even without the controversies that soon distracted his administration.

At the beginning of October, Gromyko came to Washington and Camp David for post-ratification SALT treaty signing. Nixon warned him that what Kissinger was about to propose to Le Duc Tho was an absolutely final offer.[87] Nixon told a press conference on October 5 that he would not be emulating Johnson's 1968 election-eve bombing halt, which he criticized while emphasizing his respect for the former president. He said he would avoid "artificial deadlines." Kissinger returned to Paris on October 8, bringing Haig with him, so he could not in Kissinger's absence, exercise, as Kissinger imagined, a Mephisophelean influence on Nixon. Kissinger reported back steady progress, but without specifics. He told the ambassador in Saigon, Ellsworth Bunker ("Blow Ellsworth out of his bunker!" had been one of the chants of the peace movement), to tell Thieu that a cease-fire might be imminent and that his ground forces commanders should take all the strategic areas they could, at once.

Kissinger was negotiating largely on his own account at this point, without specific direction from or precise information to his president. He was aware that there was nothing stopping the North Vietnamese from releasing to the public anything that had been offered by them, and they had already met the terms Nixon told the nation in January, when he revealed the secret talks, they had rejected. Kissinger cabled on October 10 his intention to remain another day. He later wrote that when he felt he had reached an agreement with Le Duc Tho, "it was my most thrilling moment in public service."[88]

On the evening of October 10, McGovern gave a nationwide telecast on CBS and promised to withdraw every American and all support of all kinds from South Vietnam on inauguration day, unconditionally. Even James Reston in the *New York Times* and Joseph Kraft in his syndicated column thought this was going too far. Kraft wrote that McGovern was "prepared to accept worse terms than the other side is offering." McGovern had already declared Nixon's the most corrupt administration in history, and his Vietnam policy the worst crime since the Nazi extermination of the Jews.

The same day, October 10, Woodward and Bernstein broke a story about Donald Segretti's dirty-tricks division of CREEP. The stunts revealed were unseemly, though some were amusing ("If you liked Hitler, you'll love

Wallace. Vote For Muskie"). None seemed to be illegal. Also on this day, tapes and Haldeman's diaries indicate that the deputy director of the FBI, Mark Felt, was identified as the possible leak on Watergate stories to the *Post*. Nixon wondered if it was the kinship of Jews. Felt was Jewish, and Katharine Graham, the *Post*'s publisher, daughter of Albert Meyer, was ethnically half-Jewish, but in fact a practicing Episcopalian. As was not uncommon to people of his generation, Nixon had absurd ideas about the solidarity and conspiratorial proclivities of people with any Jewish ancestry.

Kissinger and Haig returned to Washington on October 12 and went at once to see the president in the Executive Office Building. Nixon was skeptical at first but listened attentively and warmed to Kissinger's message. There would be a stand-still cease-fire in place, followed sixty days later by full American withdrawal and an exchange of prisoners. Thieu's government would remain, and the Council of National Reconciliation and Concord, though composed of representatives of Saigon, the VC, and neutrals, would determine the country's future unanimously, meaning it would agree on, and accomplish, nothing, and be a mere talking shop.

Nixon knew the North Vietnamese would violate the agreement and Thieu would object to it, but it was, he thought, a respectable arrangement; he ordered dinner and some excellent wine for his visitors and himself. The next day he cut bombing over the North from twelve hundred sorties to two hundred. He had feared that Kissinger was rushing headlong to an agreement because he wanted to take the credit for reelecting Nixon (an outrageous imputation).[89] Now, however, he was leaning toward closing a deal, but sent the North Vietnamese delegation in Paris a message that he would require clarification of the role of the Provisional Revolutionary Government (PRG) of the Viet Cong and the Council of National Reconciliation and Concord. He received a negative reply. Kissinger returned to Paris on October 17, and then went to Saigon for a difficult three-day session with Thieu.

Kissinger handed over a letter from Nixon stating that he had "no reasonable alternative but to accept this agreement." Thieu was seething, but controlled. He was aware in advance of the key ingredients, because a near-copy of the agreement was captured from the Viet Cong two days before in a VC offensive, as part of a general order to take more territory from the government. He asked for a Vietnamese translation, which the Americans had forwarded to Saigon. Kissinger had used North Vietnamese interpreters in

Paris, and the Americans were oblivious of the fact that the Vietnamese version of the agreement referred to "Vietnam," not two Vietnams, to the Americans themselves as "pirates," the South Vietnamese as "vassals," and the National Council as a "structure" or "form" of "government." Naturally, Thieu, an intelligent, courageous, and cunning man, read these words with unease. He told his aides he felt like punching Kissinger's face. (It would have been a novel diplomatic initiative. Vietnam had produced almost every other form of drama imaginable.)[90]

In Washington, Haig and Westmoreland were warning Nixon that Thieu would reject the agreement as worded (which Kissinger claimed was not what Haig was telling him when he was part of the American team in Paris). And Westmoreland warned that if the agreement appeared to be imposed on Thieu, he would be overthrown.[91] Kissinger read Thieu a telegram from Nixon saying that if Thieu balked, he would have difficulty continuing "support for you and for the government of South Vietnam." Thieu would not be moved, accused Kissinger of chasing a Nobel Prize, and told him he would not sign, even after Kissinger said the United States would go it alone and that he would not be returning to Saigon.

In cables to Nixon on October 22, Kissinger revealed that Thieu required the complete withdrawal of the NVA and a guarantee of the DMZ. "His demands verge on insanity." (Seeking survival is not normally equated to insanity.)[92] Kissinger had a brief meeting with Thieu the next day and told him how committed many in the United States were to the defeat of South Vietnam, especially much of the media and intellectual community. He would do his best to negotiate his desired changes, but Washington and Saigon should both understand U.S. political realities (as Hanoi did).[93] He feared that he saw "opportunity slipping away. This is why I leave with such a sense of tragedy."

He took it upon himself to send a message to Pham Van Dong in Hanoi asking for a further meeting to adjust terms, and then a message offering a bombing halt in exchange for another meeting, and signed them both "President Nixon." He did so without authorization. Hanoi declined.[*][94]

---

[*] Ehrlichman wrote that Haldeman and Haig considered this evidence that Kissinger was cracking under the strain, and claimed Haldeman said that Kissinger had been "under care." There is no evidence to support any such alarmist conclusion. Haig had strongly advised against the messages to Hanoi.

Kissinger returned to Washington, and on October 24, Thieu spoke by television and radio to the South Vietnamese for two hours, saying that a cease-fire might be imminent, and restating his demand that the NVA withdraw from South Vietnam. The same day, the *Washington Post* reported that Hugh Sloan, CREEP's treasurer, had revealed to the grand jury that Haldeman controlled a fund of seven hundred thousand dollars that was being used to pay the expenses of the Watergate accused. In fact, Sloan had not mentioned Haldeman, and there was nothing wrong with CREEP helping these people with their expenses, as long as it wasn't a bribe to suborn perjury, though it was not an image-building association. Once more, Nixon should have recognized the danger of the related issues, rather than, as he did, telling Colson that he might be able to cancel the *Post*'s television licenses in revenge for the story.[95]

On October 25, the *New York Times* and other media reported that the English, French, and Vietnamese versions of what Kissinger and Le Duc Tho had agreed had been read on Radio Hanoi, which expressed the expectation that it would be signed on October 31. Nixon decided to unleash Kissinger on the audio media at last, despite his accent, and the national security adviser gave his first televised press conference on the morning of October 26. He said that "peace is at hand," a statement that electrified the world. It became a universal truism that the war was about to end. In urging Kissinger into the national media, Nixon not only created an instant superstar, as the media liked his accent and was susceptible to his wit, charm, and intellect. Nixon also created such expectations that he would come under greater pressure than he would appreciate to end the war promptly, even if he had to ditch Thieu completely. Nixon felt Kissinger had reduced their negotiating room with the North Vietnamese.[96] Kissinger was also conducting a private campaign of press briefings, vigorously touting his own role and blaming the elusiveness of a Vietnam settlement on the president and other members of his entourage. He even accused Nixon of anti-Semitism to a Jewish journalist.[97]

On November 4, McGovern feebly said that if reelected, Nixon would quite possibly commit the country to four more years of war "to keep his friend, General Thieu, in office." Nixon ignored him, canceled the rest of his light, late campaign schedule, and went to San Clemente. He voted there, dropping the ballot in the voting place with his usual awkwardness, and stooping to pick it up, to the delight of cameramen. He returned on election day to Washington. On the plane, Haldeman suggested that he and Ehrlichman and Kissinger all retire. Nixon declined. He should have parted with Haldeman and Ehrlichman then, swept out anyone associated with the Watergate affair, and reconstructed his staff and government. He would shortly be doing so, under much less favorable circumstances.

On November 4, Kissinger gave a rather astonishing interview to the Italian journalist Oriana Fallaci, in which he compared himself to the "American cowboy, alone astride his horse. . . . This romantic, surprising character suits me. . . . Independence . . . is very important to me and in me.

"I've by no means decided to give up this job yet. . . . When one wields power, and when one has it for a long time, one ends up thinking one has a right to it."[98]

The interview was only published a couple of weeks after the election, in the *New Republic*. When it appeared, it caused a great deal of scorn and ridicule. Kissinger had his customary recourse to claiming to have been misquoted, but unfortunately for him, Ms. Fallaci had taped the interview without telling him, a timely irony, and released the tape.

When Nixon returned to the White House, he found a note from Kissinger on his pillow. His adviser praised the president for resolving America's differences, ending its hesitations, and giving it new purpose. "It has been an inspiration to see your fortitude in adversity, and your willingness to walk alone. For this, as well as for the unfailing human kindness and consideration I shall always be grateful."[99] Since there was as little human kindness between these two men as there was suspense about the election, Kissinger was presumably providing an anticipatory palliative to Nixon's take on the Fallaci interview.

Henry Kissinger and Richard Nixon were very considerable men, and they rendered great service. In some ways their natures were complimentary, and Kissinger was right to refer to their desire to "walk alone." But in other ways, they brought out each other's worst qualities, especially paranoia, amorality, an unquenchable desire for praise and recognition, and, in Kissinger's case, the obsequiousness of the courtier. It has become a truism of modern American history that they were almost symbiotic, despite their lack of personal rapport.

It is idle conjecture, but Kissinger might have done better with a president of greater rectitude, like Truman or Eisenhower (as he did with Gerald

Ford). And Nixon might have been better served by a talented but less devious adviser, such as Acheson, of all people.

Nixon dined with his wife and daughters and their husbands, and then retired to the Lincoln Sitting Room to watch the election results alone, while listening to Richard Rodgers's *Victory at Sea*. Richard Nixon, in his last election, gained the greatest plurality in American history, eighteen million votes, 47,170,000 to 29,173,000, and won forty-nine states, all except Massachusetts, and the District of Columbia. He had almost 61 percent of the total vote, almost as great a total as Roosevelt's in 1936 and Johnson's in 1964. Yet the Republicans had actually lost two senators, but gained twelve congressmen, and those houses now had Democratic majorities of 57 to 43 and 243 to 192. If Nixon had made a serious effort, he might have made the House a closely contested chamber.

For the former loser, whose national career had barely survived the fund crisis twenty years before, and Ike's attempt to disembark him in 1956, and the defeats in 1960 and 1962, who had scraped into office four years before, "one of nature's losers," as the now sycophantic Theodore H. White had called him, this should have been a very sweet moment.

Nixon being Nixon, there is little sign that it was. He stayed up until four, but was into his office early, and read the news summary, unstinting in praise and respectfulness. Nixon predicted that the journalistic interpretation would be not that he had won it but that McGovern had lost it, that the slightly low turnout showed a lack of enthusiasm for either candidate (54 percent of voters voted, down from nearly 62 percent in 1968 and 64 percent in 1960), and that Nixon had failed his party. There was some comment to this effect, and Haldeman warned Nixon that there would be problems with the party. The president replied that they should "start pissing on the party before they begin pissing on me. Blame bad candidates and sloppy organization." The candidates and organization were no worse than usual, and he had worked like a beaver for a Republican Party of deadbeats many times. Furthermore, he was the party's leader; if he had taken an interest in these matters, and spread some of the campaign funds around, the quality of the candidates could have been better and the results could have been quite different.

In a final, astonishing, and notorious Nixonian touch, Nixon met with the White House staff in the Roosevelt Room at 11 A.M. on November 8. He received a warm, standing ovation, circulated for a few minutes, spoke somewhat incoherently about Disraeli, and then left Haldeman to address the group. Haldeman announced that the renewal of the administration required everyone to offer their resignations, and he distributed forms detailing official documents in everyone's possession. The resignations would have to be in by the end of the day, and all would know within a month if they were being retained or not. Safire whispered to Kissinger that many would have been better off if McGovern had won; at least then they would be employed up to inauguration day.

At one point in this period, Nixon said to Colson and Kissinger, "One day we will get them on the ground where we want them, and will stick our heels in, step on them hard and twist . . . crush them, show them no mercy." These were not the magnanimous sounds of a gracious winner.

Richard Nixon was now only the tenth person to win two consecutive contested elections to the presidency of the United States. He was a widely admired and even popular figure, and he had the satisfaction of knowing that he had, by any measurement, been a very effective president. He was personally a sensitive, and often generous man, and he understood the loyalty of the White House staff. But his somber and morose nature took possession of him, especially when it would have seemed that he had a right and reason to celebrate. He cheered up in crises, was let down by victory, and the few things that excited him caused him childlike pleasure. His best friend was a man with whom he exchanged few words, and his love of solitude was extreme, especially for one of the most energetic and durable politicians in the country's history. All these factors made his achievements as a public man the more remarkable. Very strange things were about to happen, but Richard Nixon was already a very considerable president and statesman.

Chapter Fourteen

The Precipice
1972–1973

— I —

THE DAY AFTER THE ELECTION, November 8, 1972, Nixon flew to Key Biscayne. Four days later, after striking Washington a glancing blow, he moved into Aspen Lodge at Camp David. Nixon left Watergate to Dean (a mistake, as Dean had little integrity or judgment[*][1]) and sent Haig to Saigon with a stern letter for Thieu.

Nixon remained at Camp David, planning to reconstruct the administration. He hoped to keep the State, Defense, Justice, and Treasury departments, and condense the other departments into Economic Affairs, Human Resources, Natural Resources, and Community Development – a massive consolidation of departments and agencies, with the four new cabinet officials in the White House. He wanted to construct a "new establishment." It was an ambitious plan.

Kissinger and Haig came to Camp David on November 13. Haig had delivered Nixon's letter to Thieu, which Kissinger had written, putting

---

[*] Gordon Liddy, an idiosyncratic figure but in his way a man of integrity, vehemently insisted that Watergate was Dean's idea. Dean litigated over the allegation, and the end result was a confidential settlement. The truth of the matter will probably never be known. Dean is the most slippery of all the main players. He told Nixon on March 13, 1973, that Haldeman's assistant, Gordon Strachan, had had prior knowledge of the Watergate break-in. He reversed this in their conversation of March 17 and in his appearance at the Senate Watergate Committee, but repeated the allegation of Strachan's involvement in his memoirs.

acceptance of what Kissinger had negotiated in Paris on a personal basis between Thieu and Nixon. Nixon didn't like the letter but told Ehrlichman that Eisenhower had once said to him, "A true executive can sign a poor letter without changing it."[2] (Neither Nixon nor apparently Eisenhower explained why he would want to.)

Haig told Nixon that Thieu had asked him, as a fellow general, if he had ever heard of a situation in which the invader was allowed to remain in the country he had invaded and it was considered a successful peace. Nixon wrote a conciliatory message to Thieu, replacing Kissinger's threatening letter that Nixon had signed and Haig had delivered. Nixon guaranteed that if North Vietnam did not honor its obligations under the proposed agreement, he would "take swift and severe retaliatory action."

Despite the huge reelection victory and the polls that supported his war policy, Nixon was already concerned that when the new Congress was installed on January 3, it would cut off funds for the war, now that North Vietnam had accepted terms that he had previously offered. He was going to have to sign off on this war within a few weeks, no matter what Thieu thought of it.

Further, Thieu had to realize that the United States had done its best for him. There had been serious errors in the conduct of the war, but Thieu was not the most salable ally, nor ARVN the pluckiest battlefield comrade. Johnson never should have committed forces as he did; and having decided to do so, he should have sought a distinct authority to conduct the war to a victorious conclusion. Nixon should have sought the same authority. But fifty-seven thousand Americans had died in Vietnam and staggering amounts of American money had been dispensed, and peace terms had been agreed that gave Thieu a chance of survival. Even if he had no chance, the United States owed Thieu no more and would not do any more. Nixon had made the point that North Vietnam could not "defeat or humiliate the United States." If he had to make the point that the southern half of Vietnam could not do that either, he would.

The president and his principal domestic advisers were holed up in Camp David for weeks, as personnel and an organization were chosen for the purpose of ensuring that the administration was run from the top down. It was explained to the succession of candidates for retention or engagement by Haldeman, in his humorless, mechanical manner, that cabinet secretaries would not have unlimited or even assured access to the president, that the personnel of their departments would be chosen by the president and his staff and not by them, and that they would owe their loyalty to the president and not to their departments. (It is not immediately clear why any serious person would consent to serve on this basis.) Clumsily executed though it was, Nixon at least had a radical notion of how to turn the government upside down and give the bureaucracy a tremendous shake-up.

Kissinger was back in Paris, trying to get some of Thieu's sixty-nine specified concerns addressed, when the *New Republic* published Oriana Fallaci's interview with him, on November 20. Haig aspersed Kissinger's mental stability, and Nixon wondered if Kissinger was trying to associate Nixon with failure in Vietnam. An indication of Nixon's complicated psychology was his tendency to impute evil motives even to those with whom he worked closely. He considered telling Haldeman to tell Kissinger that he had a taped record of all their conversations, such was his level of mistrust of Kissinger, but he thought better of enlightening his national security adviser about that.[3]

Henry Kissinger was a devious man with a colossal and vulnerable ego, and was almost without sentiment in anything involving his career and position, but he would certainly not have wished Nixon to be the premier figure in a dreadful Götterdämmerung. That Nixon even considered such a thought sheds further dark light on this sociopathic but fecund relationship.

Nixon thought Kissinger had unlimited faith in any negotiation he was conducting himself. He had set some store by the microbiologist friends of Ho Chi Minh's in 1967. He had thought that a luncheon invitation in March 1972 from Le Duc Tho indicated that there would be no NVA spring offensive. He had gone well beyond his authority in October in Paris, and then pushed the whole administration to the end of the limb with "Peace is at hand." He had made promises to Le Duc Tho on behalf of Thieu that he could not now wring from Thieu, even after writing a threatening letter on Nixon's behalf that Nixon had signed, albeit with misgivings (having to quote Eisenhower to himself to do so). From Saigon, he had without authority sent messages to the leader of the North Vietnamese and put Nixon's name on the bottom of the cables. It had been a remarkable performance, but it hadn't closed the deal and ended the war.

Nixon knew time was closing in on Thieu and himself. He hated the North Vietnamese, and mistrusted both Thieu and Kissinger, but he was prepared – recognizing that the bombing was working and was all that had worked, and that he should have resorted to it years before – to give it one final try for the South Vietnamese. He cabled Kissinger to be ready to break up the talks if the North Vietnamese did not make more concessions.

On November 24 he sent a further cable to Kissinger that his strongest supporters in the Senate would not approve going beyond February 1 to get more for Thieu than Nixon and Kissinger had already obtained for him. Yet again in his career, Nixon, the skilled poker player, was prepared to gamble. He was going to intensify the bombing beyond any previous level, but Thieu was going to have to understand that this was the last throw of the dice. Whatever, if anything, they could get from this was all that could be had. Thieu was presumably as well informed of the drift of political events in Washington as any foreign leader, and he must have known more or less what was possible. There was no sympathy whatever for the view that the United States owed him anything more than it had already given. Kissinger considered Thieu's supplementary demands "preposterous."[4] (This was a mild reproof, considering that he had regarded Thieu's previous terms as "verging on insanity.")

After a weekend with his family in New York, Nixon returned to Camp David on November 27 and addressed the press in his helicopter hangar. He said he would be staying another two weeks (having been there almost three already). He announced the retirement of Melvin Laird as defense secretary and George Romney from Housing and Urban Development. The press did not really understand what Nixon was doing in this rustic place in the winter, and were not much enlightened by his claim that by sitting "on top of a mountain, it is easier to get on top of the job."

Announcements of changes began the next day and came in twos and threes for weeks. Nixon had offered Defense to Rockefeller, but he would only accept State. Rogers was going in June, but Kissinger opposed Rockefeller, not only because he wanted the job himself but because he didn't want to be working for Nixon and Rockefeller at the same time. Kissinger knew that Rockefeller would not respond in the laid-back manner of Rogers as Kissinger trespassed endlessly in his domain. Despite all he owed the Rockefellers, loyalty stopped at the perimeter of Kissinger's authority.[5]

Elliot Richardson replaced Laird at Defense (a strange choice given his placatory nature, though he was a well-decorated D-Day veteran). Caspar Weinberger replaced Richardson at Health, Education, and Welfare, and the chief adviser on government reorganization, Roy Ash, replaced Weinberger as director of Management and Budget. Nixon named one of his hardhat leaders as secretary of labor, Peter Brennan.

George Shultz remained as Connally's successor at the Treasury, and was further elevated as an adviser to the president, with oversight of Commerce, Labor, and Transportation. Nixon told Shultz, "The IRS was a walking disaster under Ike and me. . . . [Its agents were] biased against our friends . . . [and there were] too many Jews." He wanted the IRS to stop bothering wealthy people needlessly and to look into some of the liberal foundations, starting with Ford and Carnegie. He also told Schultz he wanted aid to private education, both to raise standards and to reduce the busing controversy, and wanted property tax relief for the middle classes. He wanted most of Johnson's Great Society dismantled.[6]

John Volpe was relieved of Transportation and became ambassador to Italy. Pete Peterson, whom Nixon had found rather bumptious, was replaced at Commerce by South Carolina businessman Frederick Dent. James Lynn, undersecretary of commerce, took over Housing and Urban Development from Romney. Lynn became the overseer for Community Development, as Shultz did for Economic Affairs, Weinberger for Human Resources, and agriculture secretary Earl Butz for Natural Resources. It was as far as Nixon could go reallocating responsibilities without sending it to the Congress.

Robert Finch, Chuck Colson, and Donald Rumsfeld all left the White House. (Nixon delayed Colson's departure to March, because he did not want it to appear that he had been roughly treated.[7]) Finch and Rumsfeld were a loss, and if Finch had been retained he might have spared Nixon much difficulty. He would have been a good replacement for Haldeman. Helms went from the CIA to be ambassador to Iran, indicating, as Nixon had told Chou En-lai, the importance the United States attached to the shah. Helms was replaced by James Schlesinger, former head of the Atomic Energy Commission. Nixon packed loyalists into the departments: Kenneth Rush and William Casey at State, and Bud Krogh, chief Plumber, at Transportation. Whole swaths of officials were removed from Justice and Health, Education, and Welfare, with anyone who had not adhered to the president's line on school busing automatically eliminated. Robert Bork became the solicitor general. George Bush replaced Robert Dole as Republican Party chairman, and was replaced at the UN by John Scali.

Anne Armstrong, a Texan member of the RNC, was appointed counselor to the president.

Nixon was the first Republican candidate to take more than half the Roman Catholic vote, and he admired the comparative patriotism and traditionalism of the Catholics. Scali was appointed on condition that he make a spectacle of his Italian Catholicism and publicly take the sacraments in New York regularly.[8] In his papaphilic zeal, Nixon imagined that Shultz was a Roman Catholic. He was not; his wife was, as was his new deputy secretary, William E. Simon, a star bond trader from Salomon Brothers in New York.

It was a comprehensive change of offices, and the incoming people, while apparently meeting the Nixon loyalty test, were at least equal to those they replaced. Connally was offered State but declined it, as he wished to make some money in Texas. Nixon would have done better to give Nelson Rockefeller the post. He could have managed Kissinger, which he was accustomed to doing, and would have been a distinguished secretary. The president could have chosen between the secretary and the national security adviser, depending on the issue, which wasn't really possible with the relatively incapable William Rogers. And instead of the tussle with Kissinger over media attention, there would have been a triangular contest in which Nixon would have had a natural advantage, because he could have apportioned tasks and credit between the others and with himself.

As it was, whatever the media could withhold from Nixon, Kissinger eagerly took. Nelson Rockefeller had the suavity and self-assurance of one of the world's greatest families, and could have set an example of stylish and confident behavior that would have been a wholly benign influence in such a furtive and neurotic administration. The White House announced on December 2 that Kissinger would be remaining for the second term as national security adviser. Rogers should have been given carte blanche to deal with the Watergate carbuncle, which he would have done amicably and honestly, while it was still manageable.

Kissinger and Haig returned to Paris on December 4 to receive, as expected, the complete rejection by the North Vietnamese of all of Thieu's sixty-nine proposed changes to the agreement. The points at issue concerned wording ("three Indochinese countries" was clearly unacceptable, and so was reference to the famous Council of National Reconciliation as "an administrative structure"); at least some NVA withdrawal from the South; and cease-fires in Laos and Cambodia (where North Vietnam claimed small influence on conditions). Thieu wanted the DMZ recognized as a national boundary, which the North would obviously not do.

Kissinger informed Nixon on December 6 that the talks were almost certain to fail. Nixon felt Kissinger was "a weak link" as a negotiator, having boxed the administration in with the "Peace is at hand" statement. Nixon claimed to believe that he thought Kissinger was a potential suicide case and told Haldeman to prepare a thorough memorandum on Kissinger's psychological condition. Haldeman was not qualified to write any such memorandum, and Kissinger would not have been a more evidently deserving candidate for such an analysis than a number of other senior administration figures, including Nixon. The reference to him as a potential physical danger to himself was more of a comment on Nixon than on Kissinger.

Rockefeller, who got much of his information about Nixon from Kissinger's constant indiscretions, thought Nixon was cracking up mentally. Nixon's relations with Rockefeller were pretty strange too. He published in his memoirs an odd story of having a dream about Rockefeller taking his place in the middle of a public speech during the 1972 election campaign.[9]

The administration was really boxed in, not by Kissinger's "peace is at hand," but by the North Vietnamese revelation that they accepted what had been the administration's – i.e., Nixon and Kissinger's – peace terms. As Kissinger said to the president, he was now in the position of threatening the North Vietnamese that if there was no agreement with them, the United States would continue and intensify the war, and of threatening the South Vietnamese that if there was not an agreement with them, the United States would quit the war and leave the South to fend completely for itself. Kissinger had undergone the grace of conversion, and now favored Nixon's long-threatened "mad-bomber" attacks on North Vietnam.[10]

Showing his astounding intellectual and physical stamina, Kissinger met with the Chinese ambassador to Paris, Huang Chen, in between the arduous and unremitting sessions with Le Duc Tho. Kissinger played the Soviet card, and in a midnight session with Huang on December 7-8, said that if the Vietnam War was not ended, it would be difficult for the United States to assist China against "the hegemonical desires of others" (i.e., the U.S.S.R.).[11] With energy, ingenuity, and relentless persistence, Kissinger pushed every button he could.

His efforts were not unavailing. On December 23 the Soviet ambassador in Hanoi, Ilia Scherbakov, told Pham Van Dong, after hearing out and joining in a lengthy complaint about American bombing (which was distinctly audible and physically perceptible as they spoke), that North Vietnam should express its willingness to resume talks, implicitly on American terms. And on December 29, the world's supreme communist, surpassed historically only by Stalin, Lenin, and Marx himself, Mao Tse-tung, received the PRG (Viet Cong) foreign minister, the daunting (to almost anyone but Mao) Madame Nguyen Thi Binh, and told her that those who opposed talks with the Americans were "so-called communists . . . [and] bad guys."[12]

On March 6, 1982, North Vietnamese foreign minister Nguyen Co Thach told the Amsterdam newspaper *De Volkskrant* that Mao had told Premier Pham Van Dong, shortly after Nixon's visit to China, that "his broom was not long enough to sweep Taiwan, and ours was not long enough to get the Americans out of South Vietnam. He wanted to halt reunification and force us to recognize the puppet regime in the South. He had sacrificed Vietnam for the sake of the United States."

Nixon felt that Kissinger had returned to Paris and been "slapped in the face with a wet fish" by the North Vietnamese. So had they all, but this time it was not the North Vietnamese who had shifted the goal posts, and on the American side it was Nixon, and not Kissinger, who had done so. Nixon finally returned to the White House from Camp David on December 11, not only to try to resolve the horrible and endless war by February 1 but also to deal with a revival of the momentum of Watergate. These were both crises that he had convinced himself were fading away.

Howard Hunt's wife, Dorothy, had been killed in a commercial plane crash on a flight from Washington to Chicago, and crash investigators had found ten thousand dollars in new hundred-dollar bills in her purse. Haldeman and Ehrlichman informed the president that she had been a conduit from CREEP and the White House for two hundred thousand dollars to the Watergate defendants, including her husband. The money had been left for her in airport lockers by a former New York policeman, Anthony Ulasewicz, who had been hired by Ehrlichman as a campaign irregular and was being paid out of funds donated to the presidential campaign. Nixon asked about the traceability of the money, which Dean was working on, and expressed concern that he remain able to assure the press that no one in the White House had anything to do with Watergate. He lamented that Mitchell "had not been handling it" at the time.[13]

That Nixon and his advisers had any idea that White House or CREEP money could be paid to the defendants without the source of their money becoming known is an indication that they had all taken leave of both their moral and practical senses. There was, as has been remarked, nothing wrong with helping these people with their legal and living expenses, as long as it wasn't an effort to suborn perjury. But there was absolutely no chance of withholding from the prosecutors or judges the source of their money. They were all people of modest or limited means, engaging expensive counsel. It isn't clear exactly what terms were agreed for the advancement of this money, but no one acting in the president's interest had ensured that what was being done was not an obstruction of justice by suborning perjury. It is not clear that Nixon himself was involved at this point, but everyone should have seen the danger.

There was now absolutely no alternative but for Nixon to amputate this gangrenous limb, contemporaneously with liquidating the Vietnam War, trading the recognition he would gain for the second for cover for the first, and making sure that he have no involvement in Watergate or any other of the questionable activities that his people had engaged in. He could lay down a national security cover for some of it, and there were relatively few illegalities at this point.

Nixon had detected danger many times in his presidency, when his opponents thought they had him cornered, over Vietnam, the economy, and even Supreme Court nominations. He had outsmarted them every time. On this issue, he seemed to be blind to its legal implications, and to the horrible indignity that the proximity of any such sleazy behavior inflicted on the great office to which he had just been returned by the largest margin in the nation's history.

The failure of his usual defensive instincts to warn and guide him is inexplicable. All his career he had had a sixth sense of danger. It had not deserted him in Vietnam matters, where he was about to move, with the deft and bold instincts of the brilliant poker player he had long been, to extract himself from the present impasse. Perhaps some combination of the distraction of the final Vietnam crisis and the confidence generated by his landslide reelection dulled his survival instincts, but they were now starting to fail him, potentially catastrophically.

Henry Kissinger returned to Washington on December 13. The media greeted his return as indicative of an imminent end to the war in successful negotiations. He and Le Duc Tho had agreed to meet again on January 8, but at this point he reported to the president that the talks had broken down, and that his interlocutors were "tawdry, filthy shits."[14] He said they made the Soviets seem like reasonable negotiators, as the Soviets made the Chinese seem reasonable. His scatological description of Le Duc Tho and negotiator Xuan Thuy was accurate, and applicable also to the regime they represented.

The fact that the criminal, corrupt, Stalinist regime in Hanoi was applauded in the West as much as it was reflected immense discredit on the media and collective judgment of the Western elites. The United States had its failings, and its policy in Vietnam had been insufficiently considered and then often unwisely executed. The Thieu regime was not a liberation movement like those of George Washington, Simón Bolívar, or Benito Juárez, but most South Vietnamese did not wish to be governed by communists, and the United States was defending it against communist aggression. The Hanoi regime was odious and brutal. It failed in every respect except warmaking. It deserved none of the kudos it was accorded in the salons and editorial rooms of the West. In some respects, the cognoscenti of Moscow and Beijing knew better.

On December 14, Kissinger asked Haldeman's advice on how to improve his relations with the president, which appeared to have deteriorated. Haldeman suggested that he stop telling the press, as he had the anti-Nixon reporter of the *New Republic*, John Osborne, that he didn't know where he left off and Nixon began.[15]

Nixon found Kissinger's pursuit of a personality cult in the press tiresome in itself. He believed that 90 percent of the accredited White House correspondents had been declared McGovern supporters. Given his deep animosity to the press in the abstract, and his not unfounded conviction that the press was largely hostile to him, Nixon was bound to think that Kissinger's courting of the press was a deliberate usurpation of the credit due to the president for what even Nixon's enemies had to concede were foreign policy achievements.

Kissinger in fact implicitly claimed that the breakthrough with China, the SALT agreement, and, should it finally happen, peace in Vietnam were his doing. He was never so crude as to deny that Nixon deserved any credit for these accomplishments. But he was the perfect antidote to the conundrum posed by the antagonism of the press to Nixon, yet the necessity of their acknowledging the administration's foreign policy successes. They could just give the credit to Kissinger.

Nixon was too astute and his instincts of victimization too well-exercised for him not to realize that Kissinger was using the press, and allowing the press to use him, to redistribute media and public recognition from the president to the national security adviser. With Oriana Fallaci, as with John Osborne and many others, Kissinger was brazenly exploiting the president's long-running lack of rapport with the national political press.

This was the supreme moment of the career of the man who had plucked him from the Rockefeller entourage and enabled him to be a historic figure and a media star. Henry Kissinger had performed brilliantly, most of the time, and Richard Nixon was not an easy master, but he owed Nixon a higher degree of loyalty, and he was too worldly and hungry for applause to play the ingénue believably. He and the press had the same victim, Richard Nixon, but all three parties knew the game, the objective, and the consequences.

Nixon compounded the problem by trying to monitor and curtail Kissinger's contact with the press. He was justifiably aggrieved, but when he asked Haldeman to devise a method of cutting off contact between Kissinger and the press through the White House switchboard, he again demonstrated that he was not in all respects a well man. This was a mad notion. He should have reprimanded Kissinger, or even dismissed him, not try to retain him but curb his right to free speech with whomever he wished to talk on his office telephone. It is impossible to imagine any other modern U.S. president behaving like this, driven by anger and resentment but paralyzed by insecurity. Unattractive though it is, it puts in relief Nixon's accomplishment in achieving so much in a free society despite his sometimes neurotic personality. Kissinger's conduct was often sleazy; Nixon's was becoming intermittently deranged; Haldeman's was generally robotic. It was a disconcerting and sordid fusion of misapplied talents.

— II —

Nixon returned to the Vietnam poker table on December 14, and ordered the re-mining of Haiphong Harbor and the intensive bombing of Hanoi. He explicitly threatened to remove Admiral Moorer and the Joint Chiefs if they didn't carry out his orders effectively.[16] An unprecedentedly massive air assault on North Vietnam began on December 18. (Nixon told Haldeman and Kissinger that he didn't want to start on Sunday, December 17, because he didn't want a church service in the White House while he was bombing.)[17] The United States lost three aircraft to a new anti-aircraft missile system that the Americans suspected was operated by Russians. Ziegler was told to reply to press questions, after the North Vietnamese started howling like wounded animals through their propaganda apparatus about the bombing, that it would continue until American conditions were met securing the release of POWs and a cease-fire.

Nixon dispatched Haig to Saigon with another stiff letter. Thieu disliked and distrusted Kissinger (who would never return to Saigon) but had a soldierly relationship with Haig. The letter stated, "You must decide now whether you desire to continue our alliance or whether you want me to seek a settlement with the enemy which serves U.S. interests alone."[18] Haig told Thieu that Nixon would absolutely not accept a right of veto over a peace agreement by Saigon. Thieu replied that this was not going to be a peace at all. There would be a comparative abatement while the Americans withdrew, and then a resumption of the war at whatever level it could be sustained without bringing American air strikes on the North as reprisals. He was accurate, but after all this the United States felt no obligation to do any more.

There was widespread criticism, in the U.S. media and among politicians of both parties, of the severity of the bombing. There were reports of damage in civilian areas of Hanoi, and the embassies of Cuba, Egypt, and India had been hit indirectly. (The United States had no relations at all with Cuba and Egypt, and frosty relations with India. Nixon was probably not displeased to have smashed up the Cuban and Indian embassies.) Nixon ordered a thirty-six-hour bombing pause for Christmas, which President and Mrs. Nixon spent in Key Biscayne. But it began again at maximum levels on the day after Christmas. The United States had lost fifteen planes in ten days, out of more than a thousand that were swarming in North Vietnamese skies, but they were hammering North Vietnam with an effectiveness that would soon become unendurable. There were over two thousand civilians killed in Hanoi, and about as many injured.

Between them, Nixon and Kissinger had pulled out all the military and diplomatic stops. Something was going to give. Kissinger had favored peace on the terms available in October, no matter what methods were necessary to impose them on Thieu. It has never been entirely clear why Nixon decided to assault Hanoi before turning the screws on Saigon, as there was some risk in doing so, given the determination of the Congress to stop the war once the president's last public terms were met by Hanoi. Nixon was concerned not to have a break with Saigon, though he was equally determined not to allow Thieu to bring down the negotiations at this stage.

Kissinger had felt that there were two options – to escalate the bombing and suspend the talks, or to strip down the sixty-nine changes in the agreement to a relative minimum and state it as a final offer. Nixon felt that the second would probably quickly lead to the first, while the first could be tailored into the second. But there is also a sense, in some of his subsequent comments, that Nixon wanted to make a gesture to the South, for all it had suffered at the hands of the communists; and even more, that he wanted to kick the North Vietnamese with what Haldeman called "brutal unpredictability." He had been brandishing the "mad bomber" theory almost throughout his time as president, and he had deeply resented, for his country and himself, the belligerent insolence of the Hanoi regime. He would send them a parting message. They might win their war to conquer South Vietnam, but they would fail decisively in their war to defeat and militarily humiliate the United States.

As Nixon was considering the last stage of the end game, President Harry S Truman died, on December 26, aged eighty-eight. Nixon had never enjoyed a relationship with him, though he had come to admire him. He had made certain that anything the former president wished, in briefings or information, was available, but after all that had disturbed their relations, and after what they had said about each other, he was not going to chase after the former president's approval. As time passed, Truman's cronyism was forgotten and his capacity for tough decisions and his unpretentious manner were ever more fondly remembered.

He was ultimately admired for all the difficult decisions he made, dropping the atomic bomb, the Berlin airlift, going into Korea, firing MacArthur, as well as for the Marshall Plan and NATO. He was a man whom it was almost impossible not to admire – courageous, unaffected, colorful, and highly effective in an office that he did not seek and that he filled unself-consciously following the death of Roosevelt, an overwhelming and grand incumbent. Nixon issued a gracious statement, declared an official state of mourning, and facilitated and participated in a state funeral. (When the plans for his funeral were shown to him, Truman had said, "Looks splendid; too bad I won't be able to enjoy it.")

Nixon received word on December 29 that the North Vietnamese had essentially accepted the revised American terms and were returning to Paris on January 3 in preparation for the January 8 resumption of talks. Nixon scaled back the bombing of Hanoi and Haiphong, ending the loss of air-craft and most of the civilian casualties on the ground, but continued it elsewhere over the country.

Once again, his gambling instincts seemed to have been vindicated. Far from being chased out of Vietnam by the unholy alliance of the communists and the domestic peace movement, the United States had extracted (minor) concessions from the enemy and was departing militarily undefeated, though bruised politically.

He was in Camp David alone. His wife had left on the 30th to preside over the Rose Bowl in Pasadena, the premier event of the annual university football season. The president thoughtfully gave the staff New Year's Eve off and ate a simple meal prepared by Manolo Sanchez. It had been an aston-ishing year.

Kissinger, in his usual ineffable manner, had been busy assuring Reston (before the bombing resulted in concessions from Hanoi) that he had opposed the bombing on the scale that it had been conducted. Once peace really was at hand, his opposition to the bombing was retroactively reduced to matters of degree. (He had opposed it prior to favoring it.[19]) Nixon had the telephone logs checked and told Colson to demand to know what Kissinger was doing speaking at such length with Joseph Kraft. Kissinger said to Colson that he "wouldn't speak to that son of a bitch."[20] It was an absurd state of affairs for the president to monitor his national security adviser's tele-phone calls, and unacceptable for the adviser to lie about them. Kissinger should have declined to comment on the identity of people with whom he spoke, and resigned if pushed (which he would not have been).

On January 3, Nixon and Haldeman explored Watergate matters again. Haldeman shocked the president when he said that Colson and Mitchell had both committed perjury at the grand jury by denying that they had known anything about the Watergate break-in. Mitchell had left the government and the reelection committee, and Colson would be going in a couple of months. But the flames were licking closer to the Oval Office all the time. Still, even as Vietnam appeared to be headed for formal resolution, Nixon failed to take decisive action. Howard Hunt, whose wife had died in the airliner crash, was demanding assurances of executive clemency to plead guilty at the trial of the Watergate intruders, which would begin on January 11. On January 8, Dean reported that with evidence that Johnson had bugged Nixon's campaign plane in 1968, the hearings could be expanded to 1968, which would largely shut them down. Hard evidence of Johnson's bugging wasn't to hand, though it certainly happened.

Nixon said that Hunt could be built up as a sympathetic character, because of his bereavement and a permanent injury to one of his sons. Nixon confidently announced that "we'll have Buckley write a column." (William F. Buckley was a godparent to three of Hunt's children.) He was still not thinking of doing the necessary to ensure he was not dragged down by Watergate, and was only speaking of the cynical elevation of a man who had served him illegally.

This was the last, best time to move on Watergate, coming up to reinauguration and masked by the end of Vietnam as an American problem. Kissinger cabled on January 8 that the North Vietnamese appeared to have accepted all of the American conditions, and wording of a final agreement was being worked out. Nixon received this welcome news on his sixtieth birthday, January 9.

The Watergate trial opened on January 11, 1973, in front of an Eisenhower-appointed judge and one-time friend of Joe McCarthy, Judge John J. Sirica. Hunt pleaded guilty to six counts of conspiracy, burglary, and wiretapping. Sirica questioned him in open court about orders from higher officials, and Hunt denied knowledge of any. He told journalists that whatever he had done he had thought was in "the best interests of my country." On January 16, Sirica would put the same questions to the Cuban defendants, all of whom took the same line, even when the judge asked them if they knew who was paying their legal fees and living expenses. Each in turn said he did not. Sirica said, "I'm sorry, but I don't believe you."

At this point, at the latest, Nixon should have fired Dean and anyone else remotely connected to this hare-brained, dishonest, and disgraceful sham. How any sane person could have imagined that these people could have withstood the pressures that would be asserted by a federal judge to find out who was paying them hundreds of thousands of dollars escapes comprehension. The judge was certain to demand to know the source of the money, and to find it out, even if the defendants didn't know themselves. Since there was a Nixon campaign connection from the start, the money should have been paid over candidly; deserving people should have walked the plank, and Nixon should have sanitized himself. He could have saved some of his senior aides, but it was high time the Haldeman-Ehrlichman cast-iron cocoon around Nixon was dispensed with anyway, for the president's own good.

Ehrlichman, apparently forgetting that he had authorized the break-in at the office of Dr. Fielding (Ellsberg's psychoanalyst), urged Nixon to get rid of anyone "who had even the appearance of wrongdoing." "I would never take this approach, because of the human equation," wrote Nixon.[21] Nixon still bitterly remembered how Ike had treated him in the fund crisis and how he had disposed of Sherman Adams, whom Nixon did not like but sympathized with, in 1958. He would not follow the same path.

While this was going on, the incomparable Spiro Agnew appeared in Nixon's office and volunteered to go to the Middle East and meet with Egyptian president Sadat and begin a peace process. Nixon was so thunderstruck at this suggestion that he was momentarily speechless, but then told Agnew that the prestige of so exalted an official should not be put at stake in so risky a venture. He began to be concerned that Agnew could be construed as his successor, and told Haldeman that Rockefeller and Connally were the only people capable of doing the job.[22]

While he was clearing away the coils of his first term, Nixon quietly allowed his wage and price control regime to expire, claiming that it had successfully reduced inflation by half. It had – not for long, but long enough for him to achieve his real objective, which was to help reelect him.* [23]

---

* He had some discussion with McCracken's successor as chairman of the Council of Economic Advisers, Herbert Stein, about a second freeze, which led to one of Nixon's best jokes. Stein said, "You can't step into the same river twice." Nixon instantly replied, "You can if its frozen."

Kissinger returned secretly from Paris to Florida, via Andrews Air Force Base, where he collected Haig. Nixon awaited them, and they arrived just after midnight on January 14. They spoke for over an hour, and Nixon told Kissinger the country was "indebted to him." He wrote in his diary that "it is not really a comfortable feeling for me to praise people so openly."[24] Kissinger replied that it could not have happened without Nixon having the "courage" to order the carpet bombing of December 18, and wrote later that he felt "an odd tenderness" toward his leader. This was the upside of this complex relationship. They were both right. Kissinger had negotiated with his usual ingenuity, stamina, and determination, after Nixon, as was customary with him too, had steeled himself to a final raise of the ante. Their compliments and flickering of affection were not misplaced.

The interregnum had not achieved much, as the accepted changes were subtle ones, but they had facilitated Thieu's acceptance. Haig, who had just been named vice chief of staff of the U.S. Army (promoted over 243 senior candidates for the post), was dispatched from Key Biscayne to Saigon, bearing yet another letter from Nixon. It declared that Nixon was "irrevocably" determined to initial and sign the Paris agreement. "I will do so, if necessary, alone. In that case, I shall have to explain publicly that your government obstructs peace. The result will be an inevitable and immediate termination of U.S. economic and military assistance." But if Thieu acceded, the United States would make it clear that his was the only legitimate government in South Vietnam, "that we do not recognize the right of any foreign troops to be [in South Vietnam and] that we will react strongly in the event the agreement is violated."[25] Nixon had two of Saigon's most powerful senatorial supporters, Barry Goldwater and John Stennis, warn Thieu publicly that he was risking losing any further U.S. assistance if he blocked the agreement.

Peace finally really was at hand. On January 16, Ziegler announced in the president's name a complete suspension of the bombing of North Vietnam, and referred to progress in the peace negotiations. On January 17 and 18, Nixon and Thieu exchanged cables of the familiar tenor: Thieu would not sign, and Nixon would cut off all aid and sign for the United States alone if he did not. Thieu had played out his string and had no bargaining position. On the 18th, Ziegler announced that Kissinger and Le Duc Tho would meet on January 23 to finalize arrangements.

Thieu's own version of this was that the Americans had muscled their way into the war and taken it over. "Kissinger treats both Vietnams as adversaries. . . . The Americans let the war become their war. . . . When they liked the war, they carried it forward. . . . When the Americans wanted to enter, we had no choice, and now when they are ready to leave, we have no choice." This was devious, Vietnamese distortion. If the United States had not intervened forcefully in 1965, the communists would have overrun all Indochina by 1966.

The Americans never wanted anything to do with Vietnam. Eisenhower and Kennedy did the least they could. Johnson plunged in because he felt the worldwide struggle with communism required it. He and his country-men did so without enthusiasm. Johnson did not mobilize domestic opinion; did not obtain an unambiguous mandate from Congress; did not adopt the strategy, when there was broad domestic support for what he was doing, that had the only possibility of winning, that of cutting the flow of supplies and men from North to South.

Johnson then effectively caved in in 1966, in a futile effort to soften the setback the Democrats would take in the midterm elections. Finally, he threw in the towel and allowed Ho Chi Minh to chase him from office. A scruffy little goateed, Stalinist dictator in Hanoi emptied the chair of Washington, Jefferson, Lincoln, and the Roosevelts. The North Vietnamese had come close to winning both Vietnamese wars: against the South Vietnamese and against the Americans.

In Nixon's first term, there were twenty thousand American and eighty thousand ARVN dead, and at least two hundred thousand NVA and VC dead and as many civilians of indeterminate loyalties. Nixon had given Thieu a chance. If Thieu had run a better and cleaner and more heroic gov-ernment, he might have succeeded. He had no standing to complain of the performance of the Americans, under Johnson or Nixon. The United States made a heroic and generous effort on behalf of a non-communist Vietnam.

Nixon had won the Vietnamese war he had to win. He had defeated the North Vietnamese effort to humble the United States. He had outbid Hanoi for the attentions of both Beijing and Moscow, and made a Swiss cheese of communist solidarity. He had conducted an orderly withdrawal, and ARVN, the "puppets," had shown a resilience the international left had claimed was impossible. He had enforced acceptance of his latter condi-tions, and when these were accepted, for good measure, he had gone back to the air war and hammered Hanoi into accepting further indulgence of the "puppets."

There is room for legitimate debate about every phase of this ghastly, uncommonly vicious war, and there was already an Ozymandian air about the American presence, even before its vast physical apparatus was handed over to the South Vietnamese. If Nixon was going to redeem the second Vietnam War, that between Hanoi and the United States, he should have won the first war, by blocking the Ho Chi Minh Trail, but because he was brought into office to end an unpopular war, he hesitated to escalate it. He should then have resorted to heavy bombing of the North as he announced Vietnamization. Within reason, the American public didn't care what happened to the North Vietnamese; they were concerned about being mired in an unwinnable war. To have a real chance of winning the peace, even without the scandals that were already surfacing, he had to bring in more congressional Republicans behind him, or transform the election into a referendum on upholding his peace terms. He did neither.

Withal, Nixon had done his best. He took over a desperate state of affairs, won the more important war, and preserved what would have been a chance in the second war against Saigon if he had been able to maintain the political integrity of his administration. Thieu's complaints were unjustified. More accurate were his statements that "we have an absolute guarantee from Nixon to defend the country. I am going to agree to sign and hold him to his word. . . . He is a man of honor. I am going to trust him."[26] Whatever aspersions might be cast on his integrity as an American politician and officeholder, Richard Nixon was by some margin, indeed, the most honorable of all the prominent players in the horrible tragedy of Vietnam.

He should have made more of an issue about the presence of the three hundred and twenty thousand Chinese military personnel in North Vietnam releasing more North Vietnamese for the war in the South. But by the time the Allied side was commanded with any imagination,s the will was not to win but to withdraw in as unembarrassing a way as possible. This is understandable, since the United States should never had become so involved in Vietnam in the first place, but it created a confusion about war aims that was never resolved. In the circumstances that obtained after he failed to act on his November 1969 threat to punish Hanoi as if he were a "madman," Nixon did as well as anyone could.

President Nixon took the brief presidential oath of office for the second time on the steps of the Capitol at noon on January 20, administered this time by a chief justice whom he had appointed (Warren Burger). He improvised on Kennedy's famous theme of twelve years before, and said, "Let each of us ask not what government can do for me, but what I can do for myself." He called for "civility and decency . . . and the rights of one another. . . . We shall answer to God, to history, and to our own conscience for the way in which we use these years." Unfortunately, both he and his opponents would have a lot to answer for.

On January 22, 1973, Lyndon Baines Johnson died of a coronary at his ranch in Texas. He was only sixty-four. He had not taken very good care of himself since he had left office; he was overweight and had ignored doctors' warnings about diet and exercise. As his friend Senator Lloyd Bentsen told the author many years later, "He was waiting to die." The terrible controversy over Vietnam had demoralized him. And it has obscured Johnson's achievements as the greatest champion of civil rights since Lincoln, the author of Medicare, the country's greatest tax-cutter between Coolidge and Reagan, and a giant of congressional history on the scale of Henry Clay and Daniel Webster, and his own patron, Sam Rayburn. He had had a crowded and colorful life.

Nixon referred to him on national television as a "great American," which was nothing less than the truth, and the president participated in the Washington obsequies, saluting his flag-draped casket as it was carried past him. Lyndon Johnson was eulogized in the Capitol Rotunda, where he had been a powerful figure for a quarter century before he became president, by his protégé, Austin congressman Jake Pickle: "Mr. President, we take you home now to the Texas hill country where you were born and are loved, where people fear when you're ill and grieve when you die." Billy Graham conducted the burial service on the bank of the Pedernales River, on the LBJ Ranch. Lyndon Johnson would permanently repose under what he had often wistfully called "the tattered skies of Texas." There were now no living ex-presidents.

President Nixon spoke to the nation and the world at 10 P.M. Eastern Time on the evening of January 23 on all radio and television networks. On this occasion, there was no question of partisanship, nor any request from the Democrats for equal time. He announced that "we today have concluded an agreement to end the war and bring peace with honor to Vietnam and

Southeast Asia," and that a cease-fire would go into effect at 7 P.M., Washington time, on January 27. Within sixty days all of the 23,700 Americans left in Vietnam would be withdrawn and all American prisoners of war would be released.

He referred generously to President Johnson, whom he had promised he would credit when peace came.[*] [27] He was as good as his word, and said that he had spoken to Johnson the day before he died and told him the war was ending. With Mrs. Johnson's agreement, he directed that all flags on federal lands and buildings, at home and abroad, which had been lowered in honor of the late president, be raised in observance of the end of hostilities and imminent return of the prisoners of war, whose release would start on February 12. (Nixon, after Haldeman started wearing an American flag in his lapel, because he had seen it in the anti-patriotic movie *The Candidate*, took to wearing one himself, and let it be known that others should. The fashion caught on.[28])

On February 12, Captain Jeremiah Denton, a subsequent Republican senator from Alabama, emerged from an airplane at Clark Air Force Base in the Philippines and said, "We are honored to have had the opportunity to serve our country in difficult circumstances. We are profoundly grateful to our commander in chief and to our nation on this day. God Bless America." Nixon ordered corsages, at his own personal expense, for the wives of all POWs. When the longest detained prisoner, navy pilot Everett Alvarez, was asked what most surprised him after eight years in prison, he replied, to the pleasure of everyone, male and female: "Miniskirts."[29]

Others spoke even more admiringly than Captain Denton did of Nixon, and the ranking officer of the first wave of released POWs, Colonel Robinson Risner, after seven years as a prisoner, four of them in solitary confinement, called the White House and said to Nixon, "This is Colonel Risner reporting for duty, sir." Nixon was meeting with California governor Ronald Reagan when Risner telephoned. Nixon became emotional, and after the call, said to Reagan, "Compare these fine men with those sniveling Ivy

---

[*] Nixon wrote to Mrs. Johnson, "I only wish Lyndon could have lived to hear my announcement of the Vietnam Peace Settlement tonight. I know what abuse he took – especially from members of his own party in standing firm for peace with honor. Now that we have such a settlement we will do everything we can to make it last, so that he and other brave men who sacrificed their lives for this cause will not have died in vain."

Leaguers." Nixon believed that Ivy Leaguers "played with each other in frilly sports – squash and crew."[30]

It was an emotional time for the whole country, and Nixon (at the suggestion of black, Jewish, ex-Democrat entertainer Sammy Davis) held one of his most successful social occasions for the POWs at the White House (May 24). They were practically unanimous and highly vocal in their view that Nixon had handled the war and the peace superbly. Their voices have weighed less heavily than they should have in evaluating Nixon's Vietnam performance.

Nixon telephoned Kissinger at midnight on January 23 and reminisced with him, but it was really a discursive monologue. He wondered if they would get any break from the anti-war media and intellectuals. To ask the question was virtually to answer it. After what the commander in chief had been through, he was entitled to ruminate aloud for a few minutes with his national security adviser. Kissinger had just returned from Paris and was in his office. It had been a very long and arduous struggle, for both of them.

Vietnam had been the longest and most unsatisfactory war in American history. In seven years, probably more than two million Americans had served there, and 58,151 had died there, as well as more than two million Vietnamese on both sides, military and civilian, often a difficult distinction in a guerrilla war. In addition to the massive American military budgets, the United States had provided nearly $150 billion of military and economic assistance to South Vietnam.

It will long be debated how Nixon should have dealt with the intractable Vietnam problem that he inherited from Johnson. If there was a legitimate hope of salvaging a non-communist South Vietnam while winding down the war, Nixon's decision to pursue it is defensible. Nixon chose an optimistic variant of the decent-interval option, and withdrew gradually while handing over to Saigon, and covered the latter phases of the withdrawal with, as one experienced Washington journalist put it, "the most massive air raids in history without a word of explanation to anyone."[31] (In fact, the air raids on the major cities of Germany and Japan in 1944 and 1945 were much more devastating, as they were designed to kill as many civilians as possible.)

Thieu was right to trust Nixon, and not Kissinger, who told Ehrlichman that he thought South Vietnam would last "a year-and-a-half."[32] What could not be foreseen was the erosion of the moral and executive authority of the administration.

The Vietnam debate cannot be resolved here. What is beyond debate is that Richard Nixon inherited one of the most horrible crises in the nation's history and withdrew the country from it, if not with unanimously conceded honor, at least without dishonor. Those who bustled into the war and then scurried out of the Johnson administration, leaving their tragic president to do his own scuttle (while trying to throw the presidential election to his vice president), are in no position to utter moral disparagements of Richard Nixon and Henry Kissinger on this issue. Nixon, especially, had earned the gratitude of the nation, and for the most part he received it, briefly.

— III —

On the day President Johnson died, the Supreme Court produced the long-awaited decision on abortion in *Roe v. Wade*. It decided 7 to 2, with Nixon's nominee, Justice Harry Blackmun, writing the majority decision, that legislating against abortion was unconstitutional, on the grounds of a woman's right to privacy and the belief that the government should interfere as little as possible with the lives of citizens.

Unfortunately, the Congress, which should have addressed the issue, had not, leaving it to the courts, and the Supreme Court did not address the real issue, which is when the unborn assume the rights of people. Some say at conception, others at birth, and most believe at some date in between, but by taking refuge in the notion of privacy, the Supreme Court invited endless controversy between "pro-life" and "pro-choice" factions, which in fact believed in the first instance that abortion was murder, and in the second that it sometimes had no more moral significance than throwing out a dishrag.

The Supreme Court compounded the cowardice of the legislators in ducking the issue of the rights of the unborn by trying to bury it in the comparative legal undergrowth of individual privacy, even though the justices had life tenure and were relatively immune to popular agitation. The view that the state should not have or seek the right to impose childbirth on a woman who does not want to have a child is a strong argument, but it was not arrived at for the right reasons. The *Roe v. Wade* decision intensified, rather than damped down, the abortion debate. Most of the country favored abortion rights, but most who did not were Republicans, so Nixon made a non-committal statement about the decision, opposing abortion as a means of birth control.

Nixon read Kissinger's congressional briefing on January 26, executed with Kissinger's usual didactic mastery, a formidable command of facts and arguments delivered with wit, but without flippancy or condescension. The president noted that Kissinger had referred only three times to Nixon, where in a previous briefing when agreement seemed impossible, he had referred fourteen times to the president. He was also miffed by Kissinger's avoidance of his preferred phrase "peace with honor," and by his failure ever to refer to the enemy as "communists."

Nixon told Haldeman to tell Kissinger to plug the president's "lonely courage" and other such self-serving themes. He told Colson, who was finally about to leave the White House, and whom Nixon had been advised had already perjured himself, to organize a campaign of writing letters to Kissinger complaining that he was giving inadequate credit to the president.[33] To such a worldly and egocentric cynic as Kissinger, nothing could be better suited to reduce his respect for his leader. Nixon was endlessly citing de Gaulle, and to a lesser degree Churchill, as models of leadership, and they were certainly worthy subjects of his admiration. He could not have imagined them (or Truman or Eisenhower or Kennedy, or even, for all his insecurities, Johnson, presidents whom he knew) ever engaging in such juvenilism as he suggested to Colson.

Despite Kissinger's lack of servility, Nixon now stood at the commanding height of a 68 percent poll approval rating, and two respondents out of three in the polls believed that he had achieved peace with honor, though only about a third of people thought the peace would hold. Now was the time for Nixon to conduct his own offensive with the press. The way to counter Kissinger's endless (and certainly not completely unwarranted) self-aggrandizement was for Nixon to be more accessible and give his version of the facts, not to send the ultimately unsuitable messenger of Haldeman, the former Southern California manager of the Sani-Flush advertising account, to beseech Kissinger to become a mindless public idolater of the president, or to delegate a dodgy character like Colson to generate a phony chain letter. There have been two general reactions to these foibles of Nixon's: revulsion that a president of the United States could be reduced to such things; and wonder that a man so hobbled by self-doubt could achieve the office and conduct it as successfully as he did.

On January 27, Nixon delivered his budget, which announced the end of the Office of Economic Opportunity, of Johnson's Model Cities program, of Nixon's own Family Assistance Plan, and of a good deal of other programs, and their replacement by increased block grants to states and municipalities, to spend or rebate to taxpayers as they wished. He was also refusing to spend $12 billion the Congress had already appropriated for various programs in areas where Nixon felt the federal government had no business. This was known as "impoundment" and became an instant cause célèbre.

The Watergate trial ended on January 30. On January 23, Sirica had put his own questions to one of the witnesses, Hugh Sloan, outside the hearing of the jury. Sloan – who had not been invited to perjure himself, and would not have considered doing so – when asked, said that he had given Liddy $199,000 for campaign intelligence operations, with the approval of both Mitchell, then the attorney general, and Maurice Stans, CREEP's finance chairman. Sirica was starting to lift the lid that should never have been closed on the operation.

On the 30th, the prosecutor, Earl Silbert, called Liddy the chief criminal of Watergate. The jury deliberated ninety minutes and returned guilty verdicts against McCord and Liddy, who faced forty-five- and thirty-five-year jail sentences. Sirica ordered them jailed while he considered bail, and said that he did not believe the court had heard the truth. He urged the Senate to inquire into the whole Watergate question. In conversations with Colson, on February 3, there was still no indication that Nixon had any idea what a storm was building up. He was pleased that any Senate Watergate committee would be headed by Sam Ervin, a conservative Southern Democrat and strict constructionist on the Constitution.[34]

Liddy saluted as he was led out of the court. (Shortly after he was jailed, he beat up a fellow prisoner for taking his toothbrush.) He never wavered in his loyalty to Nixon and the cause.

On February 7, the Senate took up Sirica's invitation, 77 to 0, and set up a Watergate Committee. Nixon thought it unfortunate that it would be televised, as the media were finally beginning to realize that they might be on to something. But Nixon and Haldeman believed that this would soon bore the country. With mortal danger almost on top of them, they were still slumbering contentedly. It was a complete aberration in Nixon's character and career to have no idea of impending danger.

On February 22, Howard Baker, whom Nixon had almost appointed to the Supreme Court, now the senior Republican on Ervin's Watergate Committee, came round the White House for a confidential chat. Nixon told him the Democrats and "the press are after bigger fish. . . . The main thing is to have no damn cover-up. That's the worst thing that can happen."[35]

It is generally assumed that this was just Nixonian dissembling, to build up a group of witnesses who would say that he warned against a cover-up, and perhaps even to have a taped record of having taken that position. He made similar comments to a number of people. Like so much else in the Watergate drama, this is murkier than it first appears.

Nixon certainly knew and approved CREEP's paying legal fees and living expenses for the Watergate defendants. He cannot have been unaware that the defendants were claiming an anti-communist motive, which was, broadly speaking, sincere, though misguided. (Larry O'Brien was almost as Machiavellian a political trickster as Nixon, but he was no communist, and even McGovern, for all his inanities, easily cleared that test also.) But it is not clear that Nixon thought that giving them money in exchange for discretion, as opposed to false testimony, was a cover-up. This is a tenuous thread, and it is inexcusable that he would have put himself and the presidency of the United States in such a demeaning position, but his idea of a cover-up was the outright suborning of perjury on substantive matters.

As has been mentioned, it is inconceivable that any experienced person of sound mind could have expected that the defendants would come through the trial and its sequels without the source of their money being identified. If the money was advanced conditionally on the source being withheld, and the defendants, whatever their suspicions, were unsure of the ultimate source, and the money was not advanced to suborn perjury on the facts of the case, the offense, though not the stupidity of the offense and its aftermath, is mitigated. The defendants who were caught in the act pleaded guilty, and acknowledged what they were doing. Insofar as there was a cover-up at this point, it was either on concealment of where their orders came from, and in Liddy's case he acted voluntarily, or on the secondary issue of where their defense funds came from.

Nixon may still not have been aware of the details, but he knew that his aides were still trying to keep CREEP and the White House out of Watergate, while paying the defendants. Every day that passed without his severing the official links with those who were directly involved in some level of obstruction of justice brought him closer to disaster. And he should by now have been thinking of the ambiguity of some of the taped record, and of the likelihood that its existence would come to light and a demand be made for production, over executive privilege, which would be hard to maintain in a criminal case.

He had attacked President Truman's use of executive privilege in loyalty cases, but this was a distinguishable matter. He was going to have great problems keeping White House personnel from having to testify at the Senate, or before a serious Justice Department investigation, if one came. Nixon had been a very competent lawyer and should have seen these storm warnings also. The sky was darkening and the thunder was not distant.

The possibility that Nixon did not commit "high crimes and misdemeanors" in the terms of the constitutional requirement for removal of an officeholder has been almost ignored.

As he delicately stated in his memoirs, "At the time of my reelection I had known that for almost five months we had done everything we could to minimize the impact of the Watergate break-in. . . . As certain as I was that we had done everything we could to contain the scandal, I was equally as confident that we had not tried to cover it up."[36] Dean had described Segretti's activities to him as "standard political mischief [like hiring a plane to tow a sign over the Democratic convention in Miami that read 'Peace Pot Promiscuity Vote McGovern'] . . . But he crossed the boundaries of pranks when he sent out phony letters on stationery from different Democratic campaign offices claiming that two of the Democratic candidates had records of sexual impropriety and that another had a history of mental instability." In acknowledging these excesses, of which he undoubtedly only became aware later, Nixon "felt that an element of double standard was at work in the media."[37] This was undoubtedly true; over his career, the Democrats had thrown almost everything at Nixon, and as Pat pointed out, "No one said anything when they broke into our headquarters" (in 1946) or when Bobby Kennedy had the IRS harass him (in 1961).

Nixon asked Dean for public statements in early December, to dispel the notion that the administration was trying to hide something, "but nothing happened." Nixon blames his failure to chase up on this on his absorption in government reorganization in the five weeks after the election, and in the Vietnam peace effort in the five weeks following that. "By the beginning of January, the ground began to shift." He referred to Howard Hunt's despair following the death of his wife, and wrote that "implicit in [it] was a threat to start talking, although I was never sure exactly about what."[38]

As February came, "There was little we could do. Whatever our suspicions, we did not actually know who was responsible, and I was not going to force someone to change his testimony just to solve a public relations problem for me. . . . As I said to Colson: 'We're not covering up a damn thing.'"[39] In his diary note of February 14, Nixon blames Mitchell and Magruder for authorizing the Watergate break-in, and writes that the whole matter should be resolved quickly and "we should take our lumps." But then he writes that the best method might be simply to "delay as long as we can and let it drag on and on."[40] That is not the usual definition of taking one's lumps.

It is at this point that Nixon's credibility starts to collapse. He seems to have been entirely focused on the break-in, and not at all on the connection of the intruders with his campaign organization. There was no cover-up of the break-in, and the half-hearted suggestion that the CIA tell the FBI to stay out of it was not appropriate, but it wasn't obstruction of justice either. Nixon seems to have recognized that they couldn't, and should not have sought to, hide the intention to bug O'Brien's telephone, nor the fact that this was being done by Republican supporters, sponsored by people close to or even in the reelection effort.

To a man of Nixon's astuteness and political experience, the fact that Dean refused to give a public statement in December, however busy he was, should, and must, have been a warning of more serious problems than he had thought. In acknowledging that "we didn't actually know" in February, he acknowledged he had failed in his duty to find out whose conduct had been unacceptable or illegal, and he was leaving it to prosecutors and the Democratic Senate to find out for him. He should have guessed where that could lead.

In writing on February 14 that "we should take our lumps . . . [by deciding to] delay as long as we can," even if he was trying to build a record, Nixon was accepting that he was bound hand and foot to a scandal that he had to try to suppress. If he held to this course, he was doomed.

Nixon must have had some idea what Howard Hunt was threatening to disclose, and he should have had an inkling of what the Democratic Senate, opposition prosecutors, Edward Bennett Williams, and his dear friends in the media would make of it.

Of course the Democrats and some of the media were guilty of hypocrisy. Arthur Schlesinger and Henry Steele Commager, distinguished but partisan historians, revered the strong presidencies of Franklin D. Roosevelt, Harry S Truman, and John F. Kennedy, but found Nixon, facing a hostile Congress, "imperial." As Nixon pointed out in a memo to Haldeman, Kennedy had impounded more funds, installed more wiretaps, and engaged in more illegal surveillance than he had; and Truman had pushed the theory of executive privilege beyond anything he had done. Bobby Kennedy had bugged the Kennedys' own vice president, Lyndon Johnson, who duplicated that liberty with his vice president, Hubert Humphrey.[41] But they hadn't meddled with criminal prosecutions as Nixon was doing, especially not prosecutions involving their own staff and campaign workers.

The War Powers Act, which the Congress was considering in early 1973, and did pass, was a massive assault on Nixon. The Congress had not tried to curtail Roosevelt's powers as commander in chief, even when he had ordered acts of war against Germany. They had voted Eisenhower, almost unanimously, authority to use nuclear weapons in defense of Quemoy and Matsu or anything he wanted in the Formosa Strait. These were eminent men with great moral authority.

However, it was Nixon's misfortune to be on watch at the White House when the Congress came to reconsider the carte blanche it had given Lyndon Johnson on Vietnam. The War Powers bill was presented in early February, as well as a vote by the Senate to confirm the budget director, now called the director of the Office of Management and Budget. Nixon attacked farm subsidies on February 13. There was a great deal of further legislative posturing, with Nixon demanding greater economy and law enforcement, and providing many examples of Great Society waste and demanding stiffer drug penalties.

Nixon engaged in a little humanization in February, visiting his old patroness Alice Roosevelt Longworth on February 7 with Pat. TR's daughter had not been able to attend the presidential inaugural for the first time since 1900. On the 13th, the Nixons went to a pre-Valentine's dinner – strolling through

Lafayette Park, chatting with passersby, and going to Trader Vic's in the Statler-Hilton Hotel. Pat had a cigarette after dinner, something she almost never did in public. When the National Women's Political Caucus met in Washington and the voluminous and bombastic left-wing New York politician Bella Abzug read Nixon's greetings and then called him "the nation's chief resident male chauvinist," Nixon aptly, if unchivalrously, commented to Ehrlichman, "Is it wise to throw pearls before swine?"[42]

Nixon had what he thought were satisfactory discussions with John Dean on February 17, 27, and 28. In the first of these meetings, Dean told Nixon that the Watergate accused would keep quiet no matter what sentences Sirica threw at him. This was an unfounded confidence that Nixon should have known better than to believe and in any case should not have sought.[43] Nixon was at this point impressed with Dean, and assured him that he, Dean, could not be called before the Watergate Committee, because he enjoyed an absolute privilege as the president's counsel. Their meetings continued into March almost every day.

L. Patrick Gray had bungled his confirmation hearings as Hoover's successor as director of the FBI, and had frequently referred to John Dean in his testimony. The Democrats let it be known that they would not confirm him without hearing from Dean. Nixon and Dean agreed that he would give sworn, written answers to questions, but would not appear before the Committee. He agreed with Dean that he would "finesse other Watergate questions by reasserting our intention to cooperate with the Ervin Committee's investigation. . . . We have furnished information. We have nothing to hide." Obviously, they had a good deal to hide.

Nixon was still fixated on the alleged truism that there had been no White House awareness of the Watergate break-in, as if that were the only issue. He and Dean agreed that Haldeman and Mitchell were the targets. Nixon professed to be "stunned" that Haldeman aide Gordon Strachan had known about the break-in. Dean had operated a form of confessional in the White House counsel's office, and almost everyone above the secretarial level had dropped in and expressed concern about what was going on.

Hugh Sloan described to the author many years later how it gradually dawned on him that Dean was completely aware of the level of involvement of everyone, and was giving thoroughly self-interested advice as he weighed whether he was better off to stick with the president or jump to the other side and trade incriminating evidence he had claimed to receive as counsel for immunity or a minimal sentence for himself.

Dean confirmed to Nixon that Magruder had been aware of the break-in; that Colson had not; and that Mitchell had known about "intelligence-gathering" (as if that included breaking into the office of the opposition political party) but not specifically about Watergate. He acknowledged that he had sent Liddy to CREEP, but claimed he had done so only in Liddy's capacity as a lawyer. Nixon was now aware that his long-standing assertion that there had been no White House involvement in the break-in was hanging by a thread: that Strachan had heard of it only after the fact. "In any case, my first instinct was not to accuse or even criticize, but to consolidate." This was a memoirist's euphemism for a last-ditch, desperate struggle to patch together a defense of lies, evasions, and lame excuses. He and Dean agreed that it was "too late to go the hang-out road." It wasn't, and deliberately selecting a route of concealment was insane and dishonorable.

Dean was a malignant influence. Nixon was taking advice from him as Dean was cranking up to trade the attempted incrimination of Nixon for a soft landing for himself. Nixon had undoubtedly, under any version of events, come late to any realization of the proportions of the rot created by Watergate and the syndrome that gave rise to such conduct.

He and Dean had agreed that the Senate and media would claim a connection between Watergate and Segretti's antics and any funding irregularities they could find.

At the decisive moment of his entire career, Nixon made the wrong, as well as the timid, decision. As the recently deceased Harry Truman could have reminded him, the decision-making stopped with him. His instinct was to astound his critics and do the brave thing, but the brave thing here was an admission that many of his aides and campaign advisers had been engaged in sleazy behavior. If he did not move very soon, it would be impossible to disentangle himself from those who had committed felonies. Unfortunately, his counsel was one of them, and his advice had nothing to do with what was best for the administration and the president and the country. Nixon, a preternaturally suspicious man, seems to have been late grasping any idea of this.

At his press conference on March 15, Nixon faced a barrage of Watergate questions, which came with "a passion that I had seen only in the most emotional days of the Vietnam War. It was during this conference that for the first time I began to realize the dimensions of the problem we were facing with the media and Congress regarding Watergate . . . I also knew immediately that our current approach to Watergate was not going to work."[44]

Nixon claimed he confronted Dean on March 16 and 17, and that it was agreed that Dean did not have a criminal involvement, but that Chapin, Colson, Magruder, Mitchell, and possibly Haldeman did. Dean then told him that Ehrlichman had a problem because of his authorization of the break-in at the office of Dr. Fielding, Ellsberg's psychoanalyst. Nixon claimed, probably accurately, that this was the first he had heard of this.

Dean described how Liddy and Hunt had borrowed cameras from the CIA and taken photographs in Ellsberg's psychoanalyst's office, and Hunt had taken a picture of Liddy in front of the office, and then left the film in the camera when it was returned to the CIA. Nixon was incredulous at the sheer absurd amateurism of it all. "What in the name of God . . . " he exclaimed, repeating that it was the first he had heard of any of it.[45]

Nixon is believable when he wrote that only at this point did he realize the proportions of the problem. To the extent that he was now harboring people in his administration who he knew had probably committed felonies, he was complicit in offenses that could be impeachable. By this time, there were two possible escape routes: sack or suspend everyone who was suspect, pending clarification of responsibility; or destroy the tapes, draw the line where he thought it defensible, and form a solid wall with the most respectable and reliable of his staff and dispose of the rest of them. The first was much the more honorable and credible course. It was also, with this group, hard to know who would adhere to a pre-agreed position. At the end, Gordon Liddy was the only one, apart from Nixon himself, who didn't flee and blame everyone else.

Nixon was now about to cross the legal Rubicon, or not. He was still well-regarded by the people, as the polls showed. He could have saved himself and done the honest and virtuous thing. It would have been humiliating, but he could have survived it.

Unfortunately, not only was Nixon not receiving sensible advice from a disinterested lawyer, he was becoming more sociopathic than ever. He decreed that all trips on the *Spirit of '76* had to begin in Florida or California, so he would not have any obligation to invite senators or congressmen along (although he could travel completely separated from them).

Aspen Lodge at Camp David was closed to everyone but him; he cut back meetings, and even tried to exempt himself from receiving the letters of credence of ambassadors, until advised that it was a constitutional duty that could not be delegated.[46]

When he met the Republican congressional leaders, Hugh Scott in the Senate and Gerald Ford in the House, he dismissed the complaints of their caucuses. Scott said they needed more access to the president. He responded, "Bring them down for cookies? . . . Our senators are nothing but a bunch of jackasses. . . . We can't count on them. Fuck the Senate! . . . No one gives a shit what the Senate does or how the Senate votes." He told Haldeman to demand IRS audits of all members of Congress.

This was not the optimal perspective for facing and coming through this new crisis, in which the goodwill or malice of senators and congressmen would be decisive. Nixon was aggrieved that the Senate was balking at his promise, in the Paris Vietnam agreement, of reconstruction aid for both Vietnams. He felt that this conferred a little leverage on the conduct of the North Vietnamese and that the Senate was nitpicking and undercutting him. It was a legitimate grievance. He was also irritated by the 77 to 0 vote on setting up the Watergate Committee. It was obvious to him that the Democrats were going to throw as much muck as they could at him and tear down his administration if they could. He did not understand why the Republicans seemed to be supporting that committee.

It was as if all the years Nixon had spent as a striver, an outsider, seeking the scraps and crumbs of Eisenhower's patronage, running desperately against the rich and glamorous Kennedys, appearing to be washed up, coming back by a hair's breadth despite all the skullduggery of Johnson, enduring four years of media hostility and Washington society condescension, had created, with his immense reelection, the desire to rule like de Gaulle. He seemed to wish to ignore almost everyone except the abstract American People, and be a monarch, and not a constant seeker of support and trust. He had been sideswiped by an event he was just starting to understand when it was almost too late to address it.

He made both bad and weak decisions, but it is hard to withhold sympathy from him entirely. He had not misused the FBI as Johnson and Kennedy had, and he had been subjected to intense and unjustified hostility as he soothed the savage breast of the nation. He was interested mainly in protecting subordinates. But he lacked any sense of

Lincolnian forbearance. Unlike Lincoln, he was always angered rather than saddened.

— IV —

On March 21, Dean, who was concerned because a number of White House personnel were now consulting criminal lawyers, told the president that "we have a cancer within, close to the presidency, that's growing daily." He walked Nixon through the problems, starting with the fact that they were being blackmailed and that perjury was going to be committed soon and by many people if something wasn't done.

Dean said that Hunt was demanding money, and Nixon asked how much would be required. Dean thought the group of defendants would cost a million dollars over the next two years. Nixon said that this could be found, and certainly contemplated at length the possibility that the best course might be to buy silence through the whole process. It is not possible to consider this otherwise than as at least contemplation of obstruction of justice. He did suggest paying Hunt at once: "It seems to me we have to keep the cap in the bottle that much, or we don't have any options."[47] Some have claimed that Nixon expressly ordered large blackmail payments, but neither the tapes nor the transcripts reveal that.[48] But Nixon was prepared to consider paying blackmail to prevent the denunciation of subordinates, not himself. Throughout these endless discussions, he expressed concern to protect his loyal supporters, and deplored what Eisenhower had done to Sherman Adams.[49] It was mad, tawdry, demeaning, and even disgraceful. But it is not clear that it was what the authors of the Constitution meant to be an offense that justified removing someone from office.

In the same conversation, Nixon said that there was no end to blackmail and paying it was out of the question. Almost all these conversations were rambling and discursive. It is disappointing that Nixon contemplated any of these indignities, especially with portraits of Washington, Wilson, and Eisenhower, presidents he admired, none of whom would have contemplated such a thing for an instant, staring down on him, but no clear intent emerges, just a terrible lassitude, and a vacuum where moral sense should have been.

Hunt was paid off that evening. Nixon sent Dean to Camp David to write him a report that Nixon could claim to believe, to the effect that no one in the White House was involved in the Watergate break-in or a cover-up.

879

Dean and his wife (their sex lives having, Dean revealed, been interrupted by the Watergate distraction) drove to Camp David as Nixon flew to Florida. Meanwhile, Judge John Sirica sentenced Liddy to serve from six years, eight months, to a maximum of twenty years in prison, Hunt to thirty-five years, and the four Cubans to forty years each. The judge described the sentences as "provisionary," meaning that he would shorten them if the defendants came clean and cooperated with prosecutors. It was obvious that, except for Liddy, they would all crack.

Sirica also read the court a letter from McCord, which stated that "political pressure was applied to plead guilty and remain silent; perjury occurred during the trial;" that others involved in the Watergate break-in who should have been identified were not; and that it was not a CIA operation, although the Cubans may have been misled into believing that it was.

Earl Silbert announced that he was reconvening the Watergate grand jury. Ehrlichman greeted Nixon with this when he landed in Florida. The whole absurd scheme was blowing up, as anyone should have seen it would. Nixon could still probably have saved himself if he had thought about it clearly. With J. Edgar Hoover and Thomas E. Dewey dead, the only person who might have had enough access and experience to help him think straight, assistance he obviously needed, was William Rogers, or even perhaps Nelson Rockefeller. Nixon was no longer close to Rogers, who had been devalued in his long and unsuccessful tug-of-war with Kissinger, and Nixon was envious and mistrustful of Rockefeller, who bore him no great goodwill in any case. Connally, though accustomed to taking corners on two wheels himself, could have been a useful counselor.

Even Kissinger, though not a legal mind or a politician, could at least have advised him to do the ruthless thing and get rid of the human baggage he was carrying. When isolated from the high-pressure close-in politics of his career, Kissinger was capable of humanitarian action. He and Nixon didn't much like each other, but there was a peculiar, intermittent spark of community in their relations. Kissinger would have been a useful counselor, especially if the salvation of Nixon was the road to becoming secretary of state. If Nixon had hired a more serious lawyer and told him the truth, it would have helped. His entire, often brilliant, career was now on a knife edge. (On March 26 Walter Lippmann, who had been commenting on presidential matters for more than fifty years, commended Nixon for the skill and wisdom with which he had managed "to liquidate, defuse, deflate, the exaggerations of the romantic period of U.S. imperialism and inflation."[50])

The Watergate Committee counsel, Sam Dash, a Georgetown University law professor, revealed that he had been talking to McCord for two days and now had the names of more Watergate participants. The press reported that Dean and Magruder knew in advance of the Watergate expedition, and Magruder resigned as undersecretary of commerce. Hunt manfully denied to the grand jury on March 27 that he was aware of the involvement of more exalted people in the Watergate affair.

These were naturally not the most encouraging circumstances for John Dean to write his report assuring Nixon that no one in the White House had had anything to do with Watergate. In fact, Dean had defected and was preparing with his own counsel to meet with Dash and testify before Silbert's grand jury. Nixon called for a report from Ehrlichman, since Dean wouldn't produce one. It was obvious that Ehrlichman was in no position to write a disinterested report, but he might be able to tell Nixon what had actually happened.

Watergate was now a huge story and the committee hearings would be televised live. Nixon finally met with Rogers on March 27. Rogers had rightly asked, "Why did we get into a cover-up if we didn't know what the real story was to begin with?" He pointed out that any attempt at a cover-up made all claims of White House non-involvement unbelievable. Nixon told Rogers that he thought Mitchell broadly approved intelligence gathering, that Dean had rejected the Watergate idea, but that Magruder had subsequently approved it.

Nixon managed a slight diversion with an address to the country on March 29, announcing that the last American military and prisoners had left Vietnam. He reviewed his whole foreign policy record. He vowed that the United States would not join the ranks of those countries "which fell by the wayside at the height of their strength and wealth because their people became weak, soft, and self-indulgent, and lost the character and the spirit which led to their greatness."[51] In the middle of the speech, he shifted to domestic matters and said that he was freezing the price of meat (beef, pork, and lamb).

Nixon then went to California until April 9. On March 31, there was a dinner for the veteran film director John Ford. He received an American Film Institute award, and then the president gave him the Medal of Freedom. Ford responded by quoting the returning POWs from Vietnam a few weeks before.

He told the audience, packed and adulatory in the Hollywood manner, that as he saw the POWs emerge, he had said a prayer with his rosary, and then said "a simple little prayer that was the prayer millions of Americans said in their homes: 'God bless Richard Nixon.'"[52] Even the Nixon antagonists in Hollywood were moved by this call to loyalty to the nation's leader by one of the film industry's greatest and most talented and beloved icons.

Nixon met Thieu, who arrived at San Clemente on April 2. Thieu's nephew and chief adviser, Hoang Duc Nha, "the egregious Nha," in Kissinger's memoirs, claimed that Kissinger acknowledged that he had been mistaken in pressing for peace in October.[53] Thieu was reassured by Nixon's promises, but Nha warned him that Nixon had no legal authority to enforce the peace, or even, insofar as economic and military aid was concerned, to honor it. Nixon had assured Thieu that, if necessary, he would bomb the North Vietnamese from Thailand. Thieu did note that Nixon was very distracted. The South Vietnamese leader went on to Washington but got a frosty reception, with Agnew as his host and the new, neo-hardhat labor secretary, Peter Brennan, as the only other cabinet member who met him. It was pretty shabby treatment of an ally with whom America had gone through seven years of war.

The nomination of Patrick Gray as FBI director was withdrawn (after Ehrlichman elegantly suggested that he be left "twisting slowly, slowly in the wind"). Nixon returned to a Washington, where his administration appeared to be starting to disintegrate. Agnew advised Haldeman that he, Agnew, was implicated in evidence given a grand jury in Baltimore regarding construction payment kickbacks. He protested his innocence but acknowledged that it wouldn't look good. He asked Haldeman to intervene with the brother of the U.S. attorney in Baltimore, who was one of Maryland's U.S. senators, J. Glenn Beall. In the circumstances, with everything closing in on him, Haldeman said he couldn't do anything. Haldeman and Nixon had little use for Agnew anyway at this point.

Kissinger claims that he told Haldeman that Nixon was constantly asking him if he should get rid of Haldeman. Haldeman claims that Kissinger said that if Nixon dumped Haldeman, he, Kissinger, would go too, in solidarity, and because "he would refuse to serve in a White House which would permit such a thing to happen."[54] It is unlikely, but not impossible, that Kissinger made such a promise, and if he had, Haldeman would be too intelligent to take it literally.[55]

Ehrlichman, who had scarcely been mentioned in any Watergate context up to this point, produced the report Nixon had asked of him when Dean went AWOL, which he had been working on for three weeks. He found the president was suffering from a short attention span and kept interrupting him when he tried to hand it over on April 14. Ehrlichman said the problem was bubbling up and growing in all directions every day and "you can't just sit here." Nixon agreed, and asked Ehrlichman to read his report to him, which he did despite frequent interruptions.

Ehrlichman confirmed that Liddy had proposed radical activities to Mitchell, Magruder, and Dean, in early 1972. This was Gemstone; and Dean had objected that the plan was "improper and even illegal." Then Liddy and Hunt complained to Colson that Magruder would not authorize the funds for what Colson wanted them to do. The "intelligence" Haldeman and Colson wanted was relatively inoffensive information about the movements of Democratic candidates, but what Hunt and Liddy had in mind was illegal activity of the kind that Hoover had vetoed in the Huston plan and Dean and possibly Mitchell had vetoed in Gemstone.

Here was the core of the problem. This different definition of the word "intelligence," according to Ehrlichman's surprisingly thorough analysis, was at the root of much of the difficulty. Following discussion between Magruder and Liddy, a list of activities was prepared for approval by Mitchell, who did so on condition they be small operations well removed from CREEP. Magruder then told Sloan to give Liddy the funds. Mitchell was agreeing to "intelligence gathering" that was undistinguished, but not illegal, or at least not more serious than the misdemeanor of trespass. When Liddy received funds, it was intended for Mitchell's category of work, but Liddy, in good faith, believed it was for his definition of "intelligence gathering," of the Huston plan or Gemstone variety.

Liddy claimed to Hunt that Mitchell insisted on a reentry of the DNC headquarters at the Watergate. There is no evidence of this. Mitchell asked Dean to help pay expenses for the defendants. Haldeman, Colson, and Ehrlichman became aware of this effort. Liddy prepared a synopsis of the little information the bugs had revealed, and gave it to Magruder, who gave it to Strachan, who gave it to Haldeman. The government of the greatest nation in the world was imperiled by the tiniest mousetrap.

Ehrlichman thought Magruder and Hunt and Dean were about to tell the prosecutors and Dash everything, and that Magruder would implicate Mitchell, Dean, and Strachan, while Dean would bring down Mitchell and Magruder. Nixon asked Haldeman to invite Mitchell to come from New York, and Ehrlichman to try to secure Mitchell's agreement to fall on his sword and take the rap for the whole mess.

Again, Nixon funked. He wanted Ehrlichman to tell Mitchell that he, the president, cared so much for Mitchell that he could not bear to give him this message himself. Nixon told Kissinger it might be time for "brutal measures." Mitchell arrived and told Ehrlichman that he had done nothing wrong and would not take the rap for anything. Mitchell at least confirmed that Hunt and Liddy had asked Colson to obtain funding from Magruder. This is the core of what happened: Mitchell presumably thought he was approving funds for something less dangerously illegal and insane than what Liddy was planning.

There was more discussion, and it was in this discussion that, as they circled round again between the stonewall and the hang-out options, that the inimitable Watergate phrase "a modified, limited hang-out" arose.[56] If Nixon had simply designated Mitchell, Magruder, and Dean as wrong-doers, probably mitigated by respectable intentions, and put them publicly over the side, he might have salvaged more of his administration than he did. But he could never cut the painter. He kept waiting for voluntary, clean-cut confessions, and this was not the sort of imbroglio, nor these the type of people, who yielded such a solution.

Mitchell flew back to New York, and sat next to Daniel Schorr on the commercial flight. Schorr was a CBS reporter whom Mitchell had had investigated. He told Schorr that he knew nothing of Watergate.[57]

Nixon went to the annual White House Correspondents' Dinner, which he detested and had sworn the year before he would not attend again. He arranged to arrive after Woodward and Bernstein had received their awards for their Watergate stories. He looked relaxed and jovial, another considerable feat of self-control, and got extensive laughter for some of his lines. He began by saying, "It is a privilege to be here. [Pause] I suppose I should say it is an executive privilege."

The attorney general, Richard Kleindienst, after attending the dinner, returned home at 1 A.M. Assistant Attorney General Henry Petersen, head of the criminal division, telephoned and said that he and Earl Silbert, the Watergate prosecutor, and Harold A. Henry Titus, the U.S. attorney for D.C., wanted to see him at once. They came to his house and stayed to 5 A.M., describing what had occurred in the Magruder and Dean interviews. Kleindienst called Nixon at 8:30 A.M. and said he had to see him. Nixon invited him to the White House church service and said that they could talk after that.

They met in Nixon's office in the Executive Office Building at 1 P.M. Kleindienst told Nixon that Magruder had provided enough information to secure the indictments of Mitchell, Haldeman, and Ehrlichman. Kleindienst recused from the case, because of his long and close association with Mitchell. Petersen would be reporting directly to the president. On April 16, Petersen, a forthright and refreshing man, told Nixon that Magruder and Dean were seeking full immunity before testifying. Dean had told prosecutors that unless he received full immunity, he would inculpate the president in the cover-up, as well as in the bugging of the telephones of journalists in 1969.

Dean had already told Silbert that Haldeman and Ehrlichman were involved.[58] The tapes and transcripts of these endless Watergate meetings and conversations are farcical, as with the addition of each new participant, there is a slightly different explanation of who knew what, and the new arrival would be the last informed. Nixon could never get a consistent story, until Ehrlichman, who fancied himself relatively immune (having apparently forgotten that he had authorized the break-in at the office of Ellsberg's psychoanalyst and joined in suggesting the CIA deter the FBI from pursuing the investigation), produced a plausible explanation for why, apart from simple convenience, no two people's accounts of the proceedings coincided.

Dean's threat to inculpate the president if he did not receive full immunity was a demonstration of his lack of tactical skill. The inculpation of the president was exactly what the prosecutors wanted (and what he would shortly be offering); he should not, for his own questionable purposes, have been threatening to withhold it. Tapping the journalists' telephones, while unseemly, was not a serious offense, and Nixon would have had no difficulty invoking a national security cover for it.

That evening, April 16, Nixon had Dean in for almost the last of their many conversations. It lasted about an hour. Dean claimed that he had been about to tell the president what Peterson had just told him. Nixon told him that national security matters, including the wiretaps, were privileged, and Dean agreed. Nixon added, as the meeting broke up, "That mention I made to you about a million dollars and so forth as no problem; I was just joking of course when I said that." Nixon had at least recollected his principal vulnerability, but he cannot have imagined that anyone would believe he raised such an idea as a joke. His sense of humor was less than rollicking, but it was not so perverse as that. Dean replied that "I'm not even getting into those areas. You can be assured of that." Nixon knew how much credence he could attach to that assurance.

The next morning, he called for Dean again and asked who he thought had to leave the White House. Dean replied Dean, Ehrlichman, and Haldeman. Nixon handed him two draft letters, one tendering his resignation, in consideration of "my involvement in the Watergate matter," and the other asking for indefinite leave, "in view of my increasing involvement in the Watergate matter, my impending appearance before the grand jury and the probability of its action."

There was then a rather laborious back and forth for the record. Nixon asked Dean to say that he, Nixon, had said there was no privilege to cover wrongdoing, that "I could have told you to go to Camp David and concoct a story. . . . And you never heard that said, have you?" Dean took the credit for assembling the pieces. "I put everybody's feet to the fire because it just had to stop." Nixon asked Dean to say that once Dean started, Nixon had done the necessary to get to the bottom of everything. They were now contending for the honor of having opened up Watergate. Of course, this was preposterous, and Ehrlichman had had more to do with it than either of them, albeit at Nixon's request. But as enemies of the cover-up, they were not quick or selfless starters.

Haldeman, Ehrlichman, and Nixon then met and agreed on the new line, that Nixon got the "tip-off" that Dean did not have clean hands when he came back from Camp David without having done anything. Ehrlichman then went to work, and they got through to the core of the matter quite quickly.

There was still dithering, as Dean came back with a wording of his letter to Nixon that hinged his departure to Ehrlichman's and Haldeman's. Nixon was not quite ready to push out the other two, though he was almost, finally, resigned to it, and he didn't want to declare war on Dean. So at the end of the afternoon, he went to the White House briefing room and said that the administration had reached agreement with the Watergate Committee on the invocation of executive privilege, and that he, the president, "can report today [as a result of his own efforts], there have been major developments in the case concerning which it would be improper to be more specific now, except to say that real progress has been made in finding the truth." He said that he had told the attorney general that no immunity should be offered to any official in exchange for his testimony. This was a preemptive strike on Dean, whose enthusiasm to try to trade incriminating testimony for immunity was by this time incandescent. Ziegler famously told the press that previous comments on Watergate by the White House were now "inoperative."[59]

Nixon was finally coming to his tactical senses; his moral senses, which were not always quickly out of the starting blocks at the best of times, were still trailing behind, exhausted and confused. On the evening of April 17, after a state dinner for the seven-time prime minister and six-time foreign minister of Italy, Giulio Andreotti (a confidant of consecutive popes, who would himself be accused, and acquitted, of complicity in murder), Nixon telephoned Kissinger. He was very upset at the thought he might have to get rid of Haldeman, as Petersen and Leonard Garment, who was now pinch-hitting for Dean as the president's counsel, had urged.

Kissinger sagely said, "The major thing now . . . is to protect the presidency and your authority."[60] In other words, never mind Haldeman or anyone else (or what he had said to Haldeman five days before about quitting if Haldeman were axed); it was time to save the presidency, and every man for himself. Despite being an outsider to the Watergate shambles, Kissinger saw it plainly from the start, and the game was already in the middle.

Nixon talked of "throwing myself on the sword." Kissinger was horrified and said that could not happen, that it would do no one any good, that it would be a terrible injustice, and that Agnew would be a disaster. Kissinger had just been at a dinner where Agnew had told him that Ehrlichman and Haldeman were finished and that Nixon would have trouble saving himself. (This was bold talk from someone who was a good deal further down the well with a grand jury than Nixon was.)

Kissinger said to Nixon, "You have saved this country, Mr. President. The history books will show that when no one will know what Watergate means." This was a noble thought and not mere flattery, but a third of a century later, it had not become an accurate prediction.[61]

Kissinger was concerned at how completely absorbed in Watergate Nixon had now become, and how inattentive he was to his old foreign policy fields of specialty. The Vietnamese shoe was now on the other foot: intelligence estimated that the North Vietnamese had sent thirty-five thousand soldiers into the South since the peace, and Kissinger and the Joint Chiefs were clamoring for massive bombing of the Ho Chi Minh Trail. Nixon agreed but said that he would await the release of the POWs. When this had been completed at the end of March, a serious bombing campaign was scheduled for mid-April, but by then Nixon could no longer focus on Vietnam. It didn't happen.

Leonard Garment was a former partner of Nixon and Mitchell, and a plainspoken, humorous man who liked jazz and, in moderation, martinis. He had filled in in odd roles in the first Nixon term. He was suddenly catapulted to great importance as the ranks thinned in the Watergate debacle. He had brushed up the subject somewhat when Ehrlichman asked him to be acting White House counsel on April 9. Garment said he would do it, but only if the client, Nixon, asked him.

Later that day, Nixon asked for him, and Garment went to the president's Executive Office Buiding office. "He was, as in the past, slouched in his old brown easy chair (from New York), with his super-shined black wingtips aloft on the ottoman, scratching away on the inevitable legal pad. That schoolboy intensity. The unwieldy head. The strange pull of his personality. . . . I told him . . . that I thought his survival depended on removing every official who was actually or potentially implicated in any aspect of the scandal (including, I said, illogically, me)."[62] Garment was so emphatic and disarming, Nixon did not entirely take him seriously, but engaged him anyway.

At this time Pat Moynihan, who in his amiably eccentric career had now fetched up as ambassador to India, wrote Nixon that "it has not really been evil that has brought on the present shame, but innocence. What struck me most, and alarmed me most, about the almost always decent men who came to Washington with you was how little they knew of government, and especially of standards of personal behavior required of men in power." Moynihan blamed academia for insufficient teaching of ethics. This was a refreshingly original view, but was unlikely to placate the Ervin Committee or the grand jury.[63]

— v —

On April 18, Nixon told Haldeman to gather up all the tapes and move them to an outside location. On April 9, he had told him that he did not want any preserved record "of discussions we've had in this room on Watergate."[64] Finally, Nixon's survival instincts were starting to resurface. (Many months late, the activation on the taping system in the Oval Office was changed from voice to a manual switch in the president's desk.)

Also on April 18, Petersen called Nixon and told him of the discovery, from Dean, of the break-in at Dr. Fielding's office. Petersen and the judge then hearing the Pentagon Papers case against Daniel Ellsberg, Matthew Byrne of Los Angeles, were the prime candidates to succeed Hoover and Gray at the FBI. Ehrlichman had interviewed Byrne at San Clemente without a hint that there could be a real surprise in the Ellsberg case. Nixon told Petersen on April 18 to stay clear of the Fielding matter, as it was a national security question. Petersen so informed Silbert, who accused his boss, in effect, of being a White House fixer. They appealed to Kleindienst, who heard them out but declined to take a position because of his previously declared conflicted position.

When Ehrlichman saw photographs of how Liddy and Hunt's Cubans had ransacked Fielding's office, he said, "This is far beyond anything I ever authorized." This is probably true, but it was the break-in that was more inexcusable than the disruption of papers. Ehrlichman shouldn't have authorized any aspect of it. And Nixon, after the fact, wrote, "Given the temper of these tense and bitter times, and the peril I perceived, I cannot say that had I been informed [of the Fielding break-in] beforehand, I would have automatically considered it unprecedented, unwarranted or unthinkable."[65] This is a commendably honest but very worrisome admission concerning Nixon's ethics and judgment.

On April 19, it came to light that Mitchell was about to testify to the grand jury and that he had heard of the Watergate bugging three times before it was carried out, although it was not alleged that he had approved it. Dean issued a self-important comment that "some may hope or think that I will become a scapegoat in the Watergate case. Anyone who thinks this, does not know me, know the true facts, nor understand our system of justice." It was certainly true that anyone who thought Dean was going to take a hit voluntarily, regardless of the facts, didn't know him.

On Easter Sunday, April 22, Nixon inexplicably called Dean to wish him the compliments of the day, and Dean telephoned the *Washington Post* and *New York Times* to say that Nixon had told him: "You're still my counsel."[66] On April 23, Nixon was reduced to getting Ziegler to call Haldeman from Florida, where Nixon had spent the weekend, and telling him on the president's behalf that he had to go. The vagaries of Nixon's personality, the indirectness, aversion to straight talk, and addiction to endless internecine minuets, all became more accentuated and potentially damaging as the crisis deepened.

On the morning of April 25, Nixon discussed with Haldeman and Ehrlichman the possibility that they would both have to go. Ehrlichman did not think that was a good idea, as Dean was capable of generating an impeachment bill against Nixon. This apparently astounded Nixon, and Haldeman thought he had not contemplated this possibility, and "never recovered from this statement."[67]

Kleindienst came to see Nixon on an urgent basis on April 25, and told him that Judge Byrne had to be advised of the Fielding break-in. When Nixon objected that that was a national security matter, Kleindienst replied that it would be leaked to the press within a few days and would be construed as a cover-up if it wasn't revealed to the judge at once. The attorney general said that Dean was the source of the information, and that it was part of his effort to trade inculpation of the president for immunity. Kleindienst said that he had told Petersen to tell Dean to "go fuck himself. You're not going to blackmail the government of the United States and implicate the president in the Ellsberg matter."[68]

Nixon spoke frequently with Petersen, assured him again that he had nothing to do with paying Hunt (close to an outright falsehood), and asked for a summary of the case against Haldeman. Petersen and Kleindienst (who was staying in pretty close touch with a case from which he claimed to have recused) had interviewed Gray, who supported Ehrlichman's version over Dean's about who had told him to destroy the files found in Howard Hunt's safe after the Watergate break-in and arrests. Gray said Dean had, and that Ehrlichman had said nothing. This was a direct contradiction of Dean. Nixon said that Gray really had to go as acting director of the FBI, and Kleindienst recommended Mark Felt, the deputy director, as replacement. Nixon rejected this choice the next day, April 27. This would be a colossal double-irony, as became clear years later.

Nixon flew with Senator John Stennis to Meridian, Mississippi, on April 26 for the dedication of a naval air station. They circled flood-damaged areas, and Nixon was very generously cheered by more than ten thousand Mississippians at Meridian and strongly praised by Senator Stennis. (Nixon no longer found the Senate so insignificant, any more than he still considered the Cuban Watergate intruders to be hilarious.)

On the way back to Washington, Ziegler told reporters that Gray was leaving the FBI and that the president's nominee to replace him was William Ruckelshaus, former head of the Environmental Protection Agency.

On returning to the White House, Nixon was told by Haldeman that he had listened carefully to the tape of the March 21 conversation with Dean, and that Nixon did not specifically tell Dean to pay off Hunt. This was technically true, but he hadn't discouraged it either, and after the Democrats and the media had hammered opinion a little further, Nixon would not get the benefit of whatever slender doubt Haldeman professed to detect.[69] It was at this point that Nixon made the thoroughly demeaning statement that he hoped Dean had not had a pocket tape recorder on March 21 when Nixon made his comments about the possibility of getting money for Hunt. Except for Johnson, it is hard to imagine any previous president since the invention of recording devices uttering such a discreditable hope.[70] In his memoirs, Nixon primly records of the March 21 tape that "I had not finally ordered any payments be made to the defendants, and I had ruled out clemency."[71] He passes over the fact that in the course of the conversation he had twelve times said that such money could be found.

On April 26, Nixon told Haldeman that it should not get out that there had been a tape machine in the office, but if it did, it should be represented as having been used for national security matters only. He ordered Haldeman never to reveal the contents of the March 21 tape to anyone. He was planning to have the tapes destroyed. Even Nixon's enemies have never understood why he did not destroy the tapes at once; Haldeman could have incinerated them in an hour or two.[72]

Judge Byrne, in Los Angeles, had made it clear, on hearing of the Fielding fiasco, that the charges against Ellsberg were about to be dismissed. Byrne was no longer a candidate for director of the FBI, even if Ruckelshaus did not get the job. Nixon was talking with Ehrlichman and Haldeman about the possibility of it all leading to impeachment proceedings when Kleindienst, who had warned about the Ellsberg trial blowing up, telephoned to confirm that that was what had happened. This could not have been a surprise to Nixon, but he was "ashen-faced as he hung up the phone."[73]

He returned to the unremitting subject of his own impeachment when the telephone rang again and he was informed that the *New York Times* was about to go with the story that Pat Gray had burned the documents from Hunt's White House safe. Nixon turned to Haldeman and Ehrlichman and said they had to take a leave of absence. "The shit has hit the fan with this one." So it had, more than ten months after the Watergate break-in.

There were further circular discussions, but the same paralysis by analysis that had consumed and wasted the last ten months continued to immobilize the president's efforts. Haldeman resisted the idea of resigning, because he said it would just be more raw meat to the beasts that were trying to devour Nixon. He and Nixon went endlessly over the March 21 discussion with Dean, which jumped from one feeble interpretation of what Nixon had said to Dean to the next: a stonewall, a refusal to pay blackmail, money for legal fees and living expenses only, money for Hunt in respect of the Ellsberg matter only, to protect national security. Nixon never settled on a version of events and never did anything to get rid of the tapes. He was scarcely functioning at all; he was immobilized.

Nixon later that day told Ziegler, "If we went in sackcloth and ashes and fired the whole White House staff . . . that isn't going to satisfy those goddamn cannibals." This was probably right, but the questions that remain hard to answer are why Nixon took so long to figure it out, and why he effectively cooperated with his enemies. He asked Ziegler to ask Ray Price to start writing a speech for him about personnel changes and went to Camp David, arriving just before midnight.

On the morning of April 28, Nixon called Haldeman and confirmed with him that he and Ehrlichman were coming to Camp David and would be leaving the White House. Tricia Nixon Cox came to Camp David unscheduled and told her father, on behalf of "Julie, David, and Mama as well," that Haldeman and Ehrlichman had to go. "I never thought that the way they handled people served you well."

Haldeman and Ehrlichman arrived on Sunday morning, April 29. Woodward and Bernstein had reported in the *Washington Post* that Dean was about to swear that he had given regular reports to the president's two Camp David guests on what was now universally known as the Watergate cover-up. The presidency was in tatters and Nixon was naturally depressed. He professed to be thinking of resigning. He told Haldeman, whom he saw first, and then Ehrlichman, that he prayed on his knees every night, as his mother had taught him to do, and that the night before, he had prayed that he not awaken. Nixon, a man of great self-control, even with his closest associates, wept. He said it was "like cutting off my arms." He offered Ehrlichman money, but Ehrlichman declined and said that would make matters worse.

Nixon told Price to add his own resignation to his draft speech if he felt like it. Price thought him so ravaged, he feared that he might be a danger to himself. Nixon saw Ehrlichman and Haldeman to their helicopter, and said, "I wish I were as strong as you. God bless you both." He later wept with Ziegler too, and said he could not go on. Nixon then summoned Kleindienst to Camp David and told him he had to go, that suspicion had to be cleared away and he could not have someone who was unable to act as attorney general because of his proximity to Mitchell. He then called Secretary of Defense Eliott Richardson to Camp David and invested him as attorney general. He was an establishment figure, as he explained to Kissinger, a Harvard Law alumnus. Nixon returned the next day to the White House. When he encountered an FBI guard at the door of what had been Haldeman's office, he pushed him aside and said, "What the hell is this? These men are not criminals."[74] He later apologized to the guard.[75]

The president spoke to the country at 9:30 P.M. on April 30 and announced the resignations of Ehrlichman and Haldeman, "two of the finest public servants it has been my privilege to know." He also announced that Kleindienst was retiring and that he had nominated Richardson to replace him. He said he was giving him full authority in Watergate matters, including appointment of a supervising prosecutor if he wished. He also announced Dean's resignation.

It was meant to be the equivalent of previous dramatic speeches he had given as president, such as the silent majority or the Cambodia address, the announcement of the visit to China or the economic message of 1971, the existence of secret peace talks or the intensified bombing of North Vietnam a year before. But he had not worked as hard on this speech, and it was neither authoritatively worded nor the decisive stroke, the slicing of the Gordian knot, of the others. He didn't take the initiative and astound his critics.

It was a resigned speech of retreat delivered by a subdued president. Yet afterward he managed a surprise appearance in the dimly lit White House press room, and said to the few reporters present, "We have had our differences in the past, and I hope you give me hell every time you think I'm wrong. I hope I'm worthy of your trust." It was a game effort, but not an electrifying one. He was fighting for his political life and had left many hostages with his enemies.

He should have announced the new chief of staff, counsel to the president, director of the FBI, Rockefeller as secretary of state, Rogers rather than Richardson as attorney general, and other changes, and given his administration an altogether new look, as prime ministers do with cabinet shuffles, rather than merely a series of painful and unsightly amputations. Rogers was just as respected as Richardson, had more political sense, was a stronger character, and owed more loyalty to Nixon. Robert Bork should have been promoted; he and Rogers would have directed Justice well and fairly and not allowed it to degenerate into the howling lynch mob it quickly became under Richardson and his deputy, Ruckelshaus. Rockefeller would have effortlessly absorbed and reduced much of the emotional stress in the vital and productive relationship with Kissinger.

Alexander Haig, when he was announced, was a well-received and competent chief of staff. If Petersen had taken over the FBI and Bork his position at Justice, and a couple of the country's leading lawyers had joined the team, it would have seemed more like an advance than a retreat, a strengthening of the fort rather than an opening of the gate to the enemy. When Agnew's problems consumed him a few months later, Nixon could have promoted Rockefeller to vice president, or put in Reagan, and, in either case, brought back Connally in a senior role. With Shultz, Simon, Richardson, and Weinberger, it would have been seen as a very strong administration, and Nixon could have practiced a little collegiality, something he had done at times in the past successfully, instead of barricading himself into a bunker and throwing out one grenade for every ten thrown in on top of him.

The president should also have followed through on his plan earlier in the month to get rid of the tapes. Now it would be more complicated, as no one of any seniority was aware of them. Haldeman had his limitations, but he was an efficient delegate. If all this had been done, Nixon would have had nothing to hide from anyone, his word would have prevailed over anyone else's in the areas Dean was exploiting to try to complete his own desertion. It would have been chastening for those who had exceeded their positions, an object lesson for future administrations, and a happier outcome for the presidency, the country, and all the dramatis personae than the gruesome Shakespearean hecatomb to which they were all now proceeding under a lowering, grim shroud of tragedy.

The theory has arisen, largely confected by the media mass assassination squad, that the Nixon administration and Nixon himself were so iniquitous they had to be torn down and destroyed, whatever the impact on the political life of the nation, its foreign policy, and its institutions. This is a self-glorifying fraud. There were sleazy people, and a paranoid, nasty, backbiting atmosphere in the White House. Illegalities had been committed, usually on the basis of misplaced bravura, political mischief that got out of hand, and obstruction of justice in the interests of friends and subordinates. But it wasn't a coup d'état, or even an imperial presidency. Paranoia, especially when it was not unprovoked, and empire are not the same condition. (The distinguished Scottish writer Muriel Spark wrote a parody of the whole Watergate controversy, called *The Abbess of Crewe*, about the theft of a thimble in a convent. In the novel, the efforts of Nixon's enemies to fabricate a constitutional crisis are exaggerated.)

It is not clear that Nixon was motivated by criminal intent, and if he broke the law, it was in submitting to blackmail by people who were threatening to incriminate his subordinates. None of this was acceptable, much less salutary. But it wasn't an administration unique for its moral turpitude either. The best course would have been to frighten it into a sense of tactical probity that would endure for future administrations, not to decapitate and disembowel the government, and engage in a totemistic massacre of the head of the people. What would happen now would be the darkest hour in the history of the American presidency, and not, as has been endlessly bandied into a shibboleth, the finest hour of the American media.

Richard Nixon, in his complicated way, was complicit in it, but he was far from the sole author of the accelerating disaster toward which the chief victim, the United States government, and the national media were now proceeding with a quickening step.

— vi —

The departure of the leaders of the president's staff and the attorney general bought only the briefest respite. Instead of being satiated, the Democrats and their allies smelled blood, Nixon's blood, the most intoxicating scent of all, and only a few months after his crowning victory. There were already questions on the floor of the House of Representatives about whether impeachment proceedings should be instituted. The majority leader of the House, Thomas P. "Tip" O'Neill, of Boston, said such suggestions were "premature." Barry Goldwater, reciprocating little of the loyalty Nixon had shown him as he led the Republican Party to disaster in 1964, spoke of impeachment as a distinct possibility,* and Illinois senator Charles Percy moved a resolution calling for a special prosecutor to be approved by the Senate. The motion passed.

Alexander Haig, on Haldeman's recommendation, was confirmed as chief of staff, though Kissinger only agreed on the condition that he would never have to go through his former aide to see the president. Rose Mary Woods allegedly told Kissinger "to behave like a man" after he told her he would resign rather than take orders from his former understudy.[76] Woods had more traditionally manly qualities of character than most of the men prominent in the administration.[77] As Nixon had foreseen, and doubtless desired, skirmishing between Haig and Kissinger was almost continuous, though they generally collaborated on important matters. Haig would prove very competent and determined, but he knew nothing of Watergate matters and was not a lawyer, and so was of limited use in strategic planning for those problems. He did have the corresponding virtue of having had no part in any of it and was at least able to give disinterested advice.

Richardson announced, without consulting Nixon, that the president couldn't count on him for advice, and Nixon brought in J. Fred Buzhardt to join Leonard Garment as co-counsel. Clarence Kelley, the chief of police of Kansas City, became director of the FBI, and James Schlesinger, director of the CIA, became secretary of defense, replacing Richardson. William Colby, who had been deputy director, and prior to that was associate ambassador in Saigon with Ellsworth Bunker, took over the CIA. These were all good appointments, but where strength appeared to be added was in the appointments of Melvin Laird, Bryce Harlow, and

---

* The year before, Goldwater had extensively discussed with Nixon the possibility of becoming ambassador to Mexico, which greatly interested him for a time. Goldwater was thinking of retiring and asked if he could serve "my country in the country to the south that I know and love so well."

John Connally as counselors to the president (unpaid, in Connally's case).

The negative publicity poured in during the days after the announcement of the White House departures. The fact came to light that Byrne was talking to Ehrlichman about the FBI position while the Ellsberg trial was under way and the break-in at Dr. Fielding's office was being concealed. There were instant and lurid rumors whenever anyone went to the grand jury or was interviewed by Sam Dash. Segretti, the head of the dirty-tricks department at CREEP, was indicted, and Bud Krogh, co-founder of the Plumbers, resigned as undersecretary of commerce. Ron Ziegler was mistrusted by the press, and his deputy, Gerald Warren, handled most of the press briefings. The administration Nixon had so painstakingly reconstructed in his long sojourn at Camp David in November and December was falling apart.

Nixon gave a fighting speech to a large fund-raiser in Washington on May 9, which Goldwater conspicuously refused to attend. On May 11, the *New York Times* revealed the 1969 National Security Council wiretaps. On May 14, Missouri's Senator Symington revealed that General Vernon Walters had told a closed hearing of the Senate Intelligence Committee that Haldeman, Ehrlichman, and Dean had attempted to involve the CIA in a Watergate cover-up.

On May 15, Nixon proposed a bipartisan congressional commission to consider a single, six-year presidential term, and a change in the term of a congressman from two to four years. Democratic National Committee Chairman Robert Strauss of Texas dismissed this rather ungraciously as "another delaying tactic and whitewash effort."[78] Nixon also acknowledged that he had ordered thirteen administration and four media wiretaps in 1969 on national security grounds.

Martha Mitchell was uncontrollably telling the media that there was a conspiracy to make her husband the fall-guy of Watergate and that Nixon should resign. Richardson ensured that the investigation would be as partisan and destructive as possible by nominating Archibald Cox as special prosecutor. Richardson's confirmation was held up until Cox's identity was known. This was a completely inappropriate appointment. Cox had been solicitor general under Kennedy and Johnson, and Kissinger had known him as a fellow faculty member at Harvard, and told Nixon he was a rabid Nixon-hater. Cox was a friend and admirer of the Kennedys, and invited Robert Kennedy's widow, Ethel, and Teddy to his swearing-in. Seven out of

Cox's eleven senior appointees had worked for the Kennedys, thirty-four out of thirty-seven were declared Democrats.

Richardson gave Cox an open-ended mandate to investigate anything that he thought an offense "arising out of the 1972 election" and anything else Richardson might assign him. There was no limit to Cox's parameters of investigation, time to act, ability to indict, or budget. His staff quickly became a proliferating hotbed of Nixon-hating zealots. Nixon's gesture in trying to satisfy the Eastern establishment by naming Richardson to the Justice Department was already clearly a disastrous error; Richardson had handed the investigation of Nixon over to the president's most fanatical enemies with a complete immunity to persecute him any way they wished for as long as they wanted.

Against Cox's army, Nixon had only Buzhardt, Garment, and Charles Alan Wright (whom Nixon had tried to have fired from the University of Minnesota twenty-five years before for writing an article in defense of Alger Hiss in a law journal [Chapter 2]), and half a dozen juniors.

Nixon again pressed the self-destruct button when he told Haldeman that he wanted to give him all of the White House tapes, to make it easier for Haldeman to get a commission from *Reader's Digest* to begin work on an official account of the Nixon presidency. Haldeman did not take this up, but the fact that Nixon made the offer shows that however comatose his own sense of self-preservation, he sincerely thought himself guiltless. On May 22 he moved to preempt John Dean's imminent televised testimony before the Watergate Committee with a seven-point declaration.

The president declared that he had no prior knowledge of the Watergate break-in (true); had no knowledge of or participation in any attempt to cover it up (very tenuous); neither authorized nor knew of any offer of clemency for the Watergate intruders (arguably true); did not know, until his own investigation, of any effort to provide the Watergate defendants with funds (not true); did not authorize or attempt to involve the CIA in Watergate (not true); did not know, until his own investigation, of the Fielding break-in, and he authorized that Judge Byrne be informed of it (true, though Kleindienst had to insist that Byrne be informed); neither authorized nor encouraged subordinates to engage in improper or illegal campaign tactics (tenuous). Nixon also justified the 1969 wiretaps on national security grounds.

So vulnerable a statement was not going to serve as a defensible perimeter for the president, not with most of his former aides now singing like canaries to investigators and trading any damage they could do to him for reduced penalties for themselves. If he had kept it to asserting that he lacked prior knowledge, didn't participate in a cover-up or offer clemency, thought funds for the defendants were unconditional aid for legal fees and living expenses, sought only an assurance that a proper investigation would not embarrass the CIA, knew nothing of the Fielding break-in or campaign dirty tricks, he might have been able to hold the line, if he had disposed of the tapes. He would not then have been entirely truthful, but there is plenty of presidential precedent for that, and at least he would have spared the country the emasculation of its highest office.

Commentators noted that in August 1972, Nixon had said there had been no White House involvement in any Watergate matter; in April 1973, he said that if any White House employee was involved, he would be discharged; and on April 30, 1973, he had dismissed the three senior White House staff members. His opponents' blood was up, and with a steady cataract of negative news about campaign tactics and funding, perjury, collusion in possible obstruction of justice, there would be a massive effort to destroy the credibility of Nixon in a war of a thousand cuts, to make his position impossible, even if there were no smoking gun, as it would shortly be called, linking him to an impeachable offense. To stop it, Nixon would have to put an unbreachable wall between himself and the metastasizing crisis. He could not do it with assailable accounts of his innocence, from which he would shortly have to retreat. In a sports metaphor he would have appreciated, he was inside his own twenty-yard line, and the opposition was moving the ball.

On May 24, he held his grand reception for the released POWs, with the help of Sammy Davis, Bob Hope, and John Wayne. It was a splendid occasion, but was overshadowed in the press by news that Magruder would be trying to inculpate a number of his former workmates in the White House. Nixon asked his daughters if they thought he should retire, but they would not hear of it. There was no one to give him the tactical advice he needed. Buzhardt and Garment didn't know the facts, and didn't have the stature such a crisis required. And on the tactical, political side, Connally and Laird, as well as Rogers, could have been useful, if Nixon had used them more. The advice they did give was sensible.

In May, the Congress effectively cut off any bombing in Vietnam, and cut down funds for Vietnam to $25 million, dooming the last, slender chance

Thieu had of retaining a non-communist South Vietnam. It was an illustration of the anti-communism of the South Vietnamese that they managed to hang on for two more years. It had only been a month since Nixon was promising undying assistance to Thieu in California.

Congressman O'Neill declared that Cambodia was not worth the life of an American flier, and on June 4 the Senate cut off all aid to the Cambodian government of Lon Nol. This was a lamentable desertion by the Democrats in the Congress, abetted by many Republicans. They knew that they were helping to kill Nixon's peace in Indochina, and they knew they were deserting allies who had relied on the United States, at a heavy human cost.

They could not have known that the result would be the infamous Pol Pot's Khmer Rouge regime, which achieved a macabre record by murdering 40 percent of the Cambodian population. Hitler, Stalin, and Mao Tse-tung were gentle rulers in comparison. The fact that the Democratic leadership could not have known exactly what would happen does not excuse it from what did happen. On June 21, Nixon would write to the Speaker, Carl Albert, asking his support and warning of the consequences if no bombing in Cambodia were approved, following a preliminary shutdown vote. Albert said he would do what he could but was, as usual with this rather ineffectual and frequently bibulous man, not very hopeful.[79]

The House would vote to cut off funds for bombing in Cambodia on June 25, and Nixon vetoed the bill on June 27. His veto was sustained, but he finally felt compelled to accept a compromise and agree to a cutoff on August 15. The interim contained some good ordnance drops, but it was ending. The Democrats had plunged into the war on the flimsy and largely fraudulent pretext of the Gulf of Tonkin Resolution in 1965. Nixon had tried to save it for the country and its designated allies, and now, as they tormented him over an amplified domestic issue, the Democrats scuttled the entire Indochina effort, and masqueraded as the party of peace against a warmongering president. Kissinger accused the Congress of being "vindictive, cheap," and it was. It was also geopolitical inexperience, as well as a manifestation of the country's terminal aversion to Indochina, now that America's forces were out and its POWs were home. This impulse was understandable but unwise. Kissinger thought Nixon would never have acquiesced in it had not Dean's "testimony drained all his inner resources" (when he appeared at the Ervin Committee). This is almost certainly true also.[80]

The next irritant to be thrown at Nixon was the charge that his San Clemente home had been improperly acquired with illegal campaign funds. He shot that down with the revelation that he had borrowed from his friend Robert Abplanalp to make the acquisition. The press then started harping on improvements at the taxpayers' expense. They were all unsightly security and communications requirements that added nothing to the value of the house, but Nixon had to endure this for a time.

Then came a new press offensive on Nixon's taxes, and malignant Nibelungen within the Internal Revenue Service happily leaked confidential information to the media. He had avoided tax on the sale of his New York home by applying the proceeds to his new principal residence in California. He was then attacked because his principal residence was the White House, but he was clearly referring to the San Clemente home as an ultimate principal residence and principal owned residence, where he was not a temporary tenant, as he was in the White House. There was more controversy over his elimination of tax by donating his vice presidential papers to the archives and receiving a suitable deduction for them. All presidents engage in this sort of activity and there is nothing wrong with it, but the press badgered and implied chiseling at every turn, fed by leakers who were committing illegalities and fireable offenses by brown-enveloping Nixon's tax records to the media. It was an ugly spectacle of harassment, and even of lèse-majesté.

There were widespread concerns about rising inflation, and Nixon went on television on June 13 to give a very calm and persuasive comment about the economy that reassured those concerned that Watergate and attendant problems were completely distracting him. Nixon ordered a sixty-day freeze on all consumer prices except unprocessed agricultural products, where he hoped to encourage increased supply, and rents. He also sought authority to reduce tariffs and an immediate start on the Alaska pipeline to alleviate a possible oil shortage.

Except for William Proxmire, a Wisconsin Democrat, and Ronald Reagan, who were generally supportive, most politicians were unhelpful or hostile to Nixon. Charles Percy was a frequent source of self-righteous, hectoring platitudes, and Goldwater was ostentatiously unsupportive. Nixon wanted to reveal the illegal activities of Kennedy and Johnson, including evidence that JFK had bugged even his brother Bobby, and Martin Luther King and Bernard Baruch; and that LBJ had bugged Humphrey, Nixon, and

Bobby Kennedy. Nixon's aides objected and Nixon did not have the concentrated will to overcome them. He should have. There was a sense with Garment, and even slightly with Haig, that Nixon now had to be Mr. Clean, and could not evoke the bad old days of political skullduggery that had prevailed for many years up until a few weeks before. They were inadvertently tightening the noose around Nixon's neck by assisting the media in their campaign to represent him as a uniquely corrupt president.

Despite periodic statements from Cox agreeing with White House complaints about leaks from his office and all the investigations, the leaks continued and there was nothing that could be done about them. Nixon would have done better with a more credible and substantial spokesman than Ziegler, but as Haig pointed out, there were not a great many qualified people eager to be Nixon's press secretary at this time. (Pat Buchanan might have been more effective, but most press encounters would have become boisterous shouting matches.)

General Walters expressed skepticism to the Senate Intelligence Committee that there had been any real national security concern in the approach to the CIA to ask the FBI to leave Watergate alone. He was right, but all the juice should have been squeezed out of this orange already. Nixon authorized the call on Haldeman's recommendation, but did not push the point. It was a shabby idea but made a pretty feeble case for obstruction of justice.

On June 3, the heavy batteries of the anti-Nixon press (apart from CBS), the *Washington Post* and the *New York Times*, wrote that Dean had met forty times with Nixon to discuss a cover-up. Nixon was very "discouraged" when he read this and asked Haig if he thought he should resign. Haig said no, but he should use the tapes as an "unassailable defense" against these charges. Haig had no idea how ambiguous the tapes were in places. Nixon found that there were thirty-four tapes in all, and "an uneasy feeling came over me as I wondered what we might have talked about in all those conversations."[81] After some conversations with Haldeman, Nixon expressed pleasure at having kept the tapes, and confidence that they would prove his innocence.

On June 4, Nixon himself listened to tapes for eight hours. He was worried about the March 21 tape (money for Hunt and "cancer on the presidency"), but otherwise optimistic. Nixon was apparently placing his confidence in a technical defense, and not recognizing the terrible damage that his enemies would do to him with the steady undermining of his credibility in all directions.

By mid June, Nixon was remorseful that Ehrlichman and Haldeman had not come to him about the cancer on the presidency, and had left Dean to do it, very late.[82] This was a legitimate complaint, but he should have shown a good deal more determination to have a disinterested party like Rogers get to the bottom of it early on and move decisively – at the latest, right after the election.

Chuck Colson told the *New York Times* on June 9 that Nixon was completely innocent, and that he would bet his life on it. Haldeman said the same thing.[83] The Ervin Committee had started up with small fry but was now building toward the higher drama, which Dean was expected to provide. On June 14 Magruder appeared, said that he had lied to the grand jury, and that Colson had asked for the funding of Liddy's plans, including the Watergate break-in. From now on, the hammering on television every day was very damaging and almost without letup. The frightened revisionists trotted out contrite and well rehearsed and outdid each other in piling blame onto others higher and higher up in the White House. The revulsion against the welter of allegations of ethical decay in the senior ranks of Nixon's government had almost destroyed the president's moral authority before any evidence was adduced against him. This was Nixon's greatest problem. The question of whether he was involved in crimes remains murky, but his administration was revealed as steeped in sleazy practices, and the new broom of aides didn't want any revelations of the often equally tawdry behavior of the Kennedy and Johnson regimes.

Nixon met with Agnew on June 14. The vice president, although he had serious legal problems with the grand jury in Baltimore about kickbacks when he was governor, wanted a new role, and suggested energy czar. Nixon wouldn't hear of that, reminded him that his job was to defend the administration, and told him to get out and do it. Nixon was aware of Agnew's problems, and he would have done better to get rid of him as vice president and bring in Rockefeller or Reagan, or even now Richardson, so he could put in Rogers or Bork as attorney general, and have an untainted vice president take up the cudgels for him.

Kissinger had been agitating to be secretary of state, and had developed the novel idea of retaining the position of national security adviser at the same time. The correlation of forces between Kissinger and Nixon had been altered, and Kissinger's star was so bright with the media – who, eager to deprive Nixon of any credit for the administration's foreign policy successes, poured it all on him – that his presence in the administration was clearly necessary, as he was now the administration's most prestigious figure.

Leonid Brezhnev, Andrei Gromyko, and their party arrived in the United States on June 16. Nixon arranged for them to spend two days in Camp David to absorb jet lag before serious talks began.

Brezhnev had written Nixon in February that he was hoping to sign an agreement on non-use of nuclear weapons and completion of SALT II; trade, science, health, nuclear technology, and economic agreements; and agreements on the Middle East, Mutual and Balanced Force Reductions in Europe, and Germany. Shortly after, Senator Henry Jackson of Washington added to the matters for discussion by proposing, with seventy-three co-sponsors in the U.S. Senate, a bill linking Most Favored Nation (MFN) status for the U.S.S.R. to liberalized Jewish emigration from the Soviet Union.

At the time of the February communication, George Shultz was meeting with Brezhnev in Moscow, and the Soviet leader agreed to open up emigration and not to collect the departure tax, but not to change the law, which he considered a demeaning submission to American legislators. Nixon submitted the Trade Reform Act of 1973 to the Congress in April, including MFN for the U.S.S.R. An unholy alliance of arch-anti-communists and ultra-liberal Jews objected to the president's proposal.

Nixon received a delegation of Jewish leaders and told them that the U.S.S.R. was too proud and powerful a country to be humiliated, and that Jewish emigration had increased from five thousand in the first three years of his presidency to over thirty thousand the previous year to over forty thousand in the current year. Ultimata were not the way to open it further. Nixon got the formal suspension of the exit tax, but Jackson now demanded an easing of emigration visa restrictions for everyone in the U.S.S.R. and not just Jews. Nixon was outraged and declined to take such a position.

Kissinger had gone to Moscow to prepare the summit agenda. He proposed a ceiling on ICBMs, SLBMs (submarine-launched ballistic missiles), and bombers (with a maximum of 2,350), and a suspension of further testing and deployment of MIRVs (multiple independently targeted warheads on each missile). Since the United States had already MIRVed its ICBMs, and the U.S.S.R. was well behind in this area, Brezhnev naturally rejected this. Instead he proposed a suspension of the testing and deployment of any new strategic systems, which Kissinger and Nixon saw as directed against the U.S. Trident submarine, which was almost ready to go into service, and they rejected this. The logical thing to do would have been to try to trade a lower number of Trident submarines against a lower level of MIRVing by the Russians, but in fact SALT II was essentially dead for 1973.

A Prevention of Nuclear War (PNW) agreement was reached, but it was mere puffery of the Kellogg-Briand Pact variety. (This agreement purported to outlaw war in 1928.) The United States would not agree on no first use of nuclear weapons, so there was a good deal of sophistry about no premature first use. As Brezhnev arrived, the summit meetings were not expected to achieve much.

Though it audibly pained them to do so, like fox hunters in hot pursuit suddenly reining in, the Democratic congressional leaders agreed to suspend any Watergate hearings while the Soviet leader was in the United States. Nixon knew he couldn't sell much to his conservative loyalists in the Senate, so he agreed with Brezhnev to try to arrive at SALT II by the end of 1974, in exchange for signing the meaningless PNW agreement. There was an elaborate signing of PNW in the East Room of the White House, and then the Soviet leaders, Brezhnev and Gromyko, flew in *Spirit of '76* to San Clemente, where they stayed in the compact and frilly bedrooms of Nixon's daughters (to the amusement of Kissinger and Nixon).[84]

Nixon, Kissinger, and Brezhnev met on June 23, and the Soviet leader launched into a violent attack on the Chinese. Nixon suggested that Brezhnev was exaggerating, and changed the subject to Cambodia, which Brezhnev blamed on China. Nixon had a reception for the Soviet leaders to which a few Hollywood stars that Nixon could tolerate were invited, and everyone retired early, wearied by the transcontinental travel. At ten-thirty, Nixon was reading in bed when a Secret Service agent delivered a message from Kissinger that Brezhnev wanted to speak. Nixon had the faithful Manolo Sanchez light a fire in the library, and he and Kissinger met with Brezhnev and Gromyko and Ambassador Dobrynin. A three-hour discussion ensued, largely about the Middle East.

Laird had proposed secret talks with Sadat after the Egyptian president had expelled the Russians, but the only sequel was the visit to Washington of Sadat's national security adviser, Hafiz Ismail, who asked for American assistance in recovering territory lost to Israel in the 1967 Six Day War. Kissinger did not take it as seriously as Nixon, who saw an opportunity to negotiate a lasting agreement. Nixon was prepared to be a lot friendlier to the Arabs than the U.S. Jewish community was accustomed to. Sadat had been threatening war throughout the year, and although he was starting to seem slightly absurd, obviously something had to be done. Nixon sensed that opportunity might be knocking, but he wanted to await the Israeli elections in October 1973, as well as Kissinger's replacement of Rogers at the State Department, given the fiasco of the Rogers plan.

Now Brezhnev proposed a compulsory Israeli withdrawal to the 1967 borders, the end of the state of belligerency, and a guarantee of all frontiers by the super powers. This was not a frivolous proposal, but the United States could not deliver Israel like a satellite, and Nixon did not accept the sanctity of the 1967 borders, which the Arab powers had departed to unleash unsuccessful aggressive war.

The imaginative thing would have been to revive SALT II with a trade-off of reduced Trident and MIRVing for some Soviet rollback, tied in to what Brezhnev proposed in the Middle East but with the later concept of territory swaps in place of restitution. Israel could not be asked to go back to a severely divided Jerusalem with the Western Wall in Muslim hands. A special arrangement for the Temple Mount would have had to be worked out, and the West Bank made narrower, as Israel could not go back to being nine miles wide, in exchange for a deepening of the Gaza Strip. The super powers could have agreed on the rights of the Palestinians, as Brezhnev was urging. A Mutual and Balanced Force Reductions (MBFR) agreement in Europe and an MFN trade agreement with liberalized migration could have been added to it all, and it would have been a major diplomatic achievement and political victory. Brezhnev appeared to be ready for more than came from his distracted American hosts.

The following day, Brezhnev proposed that Mutual and Balanced Force Reductions in Europe begin with a symbolic reduction of ten thousand Soviet and American soldiers. Nixon said he would have to speak to his allies. There was nothing stopping Nixon from having consulted them before this and agreeing a larger reduction. It would have had an important symbolic effect and greatly stimulated America's European allies. Nixon was not as imaginative as usual, and Kissinger was strangely passive.

Brezhnev was impulsive and far from reliable as a negotiator, but there was room for more to come out of this meeting.

The Soviet party flew from El Toro Marine Corps Air Station near San Clemente. There were a number of lesser agreements on transportation, agriculture, aviation, oceanic studies, and civilian atomic energy. Nixon, as the Soviet leaders prepared to fly off, emphasized the PNW agreement. He also stressed the personal rapport that had allegedly arisen between Brezhnev and himself. It was a modest success, and détente was still intact, but nothing like the extravaganza of the year before. Richard Nixon was very preoccupied with other things.

— VII —

Well he might be. The day after Brezhnev and Gromyko departed, the Ervin Committee finally heard from John Dean. Goldwater had written Nixon on his own portable typewriter that the president was isolated and had to become better acquainted with his own party's leaders in the Congress. It was a well-intentioned letter from the Arizona senator, and it was good advice, but Nixon, more isolated than ever without Haldeman and Ehrlichman, ignored it. While Dean, the ultimate turncoat cooperating witness, fired an endless series of accusatory torpedoes at the derelict hulk of the administration he had just deserted, Nixon sat, torpid and shell-shocked in San Clemente.

Dean gave a 245-page opening statement that required an entire day to read to the committee, with his wife sitting demurely behind him. He claimed to have been a restraining influence on the Huston plan (only Hoover had prevented its implementation), and revealed that he had been a double agent for many weeks between the Nixon White House and the prosecutors. He said Nixon had had some idea of the Watergate cover-up early on, and had discussed with him the possibility of clemency and the payments to the defendants. There was nothing wrong with talking about clemency, and Nixon seems to have been reasonably circumspect here. There was room for disagreement whether the payments were hush money or compassionate, unconditional support. Dean claimed that Ehrlichman and Haldeman were the orchestrators of the cover-up and that he had bolted when he saw that they were trying to set him up. He claimed that

Mitchell had made cover-up payments to Hunt, and that Nixon had tried to blame everything on Mitchell.

There were some elements of what Dean said that were thoughtful and not just a scramble for cover: Nixon "did not realize or appreciate at any time the level of his involvement. . . . The Watergate matter was an inevitable outgrowth of a climate of excessive concern over the political impact of demonstrators, excessive concern over leaks, an insatiable appetite for political intelligence, all coupled with a do-it-yourself White House staff, regardless of the law." This was a reasonable insight, though Dean himself was one of the eager participants in it at the time.

Nixon rebutted Dean's testimony in his memoirs, calling it, accurately, "an artful blend of truth and untruth, of possible sincere misunderstandings and clearly conscious distortions." He recognized that the "real issue had already changed. It no longer made any difference that not all of Dean's testimony was accurate. It only mattered if any of his testimony was accurate." The president, for the first time in the country's history, was accused by his own counsel of complicity in a felony, and this occurred before tens of millions of television viewers and was plausibly and fluently delivered by Dean, an attractive and articulate young man. No one seemed to be much concerned about the normally inadmissible practice of a man's attorney giving evidence against his former client. Procedurally, it was an outrage.

Dean had produced no tapes or documents to support his charges. Nixon was still in possession of the tapes, but if he used them selectively, they would have to be produced entirely. He was now paying the price for not having done what he should have done and what most presidents would have done, and for not having condemned the entire sequence of sleazy events as soon as he became aware that some of his wild exhortations had been put into action. It was the ultimate tragedy: the impetuous utterances of a lonely man, tormented by unfair opponents, having been translated into inept action by loyalists, attracted the leader's compassion for well-meaning helpers at the expense of his instinct for self-preservation. Nixon wrote, accurately, "In the end it would make less difference that I was not as involved as Dean had alleged than that I was not as uninvolved as I had claimed." The believability of the chief of state and head of government was involved, and it had sustained a deep wound.

On June 27, Fred LaRue, a junior-level CREEP official, admitted to taking part in the destruction of incriminating documents and misleading the FBI and grand jury, and to paying over more than three hundred thousand dollars to Watergate intruders in exchange for their silence.

The same day, Nixon's counsel, Fred Buzhardt, managed a spirited comeback, sending a letter to Hawaii senator Daniel K. Inouye (the second-ranking Democrat on Ervin's Committee) which asserted that Dean "knew of . . . the [Watergate] break-in . . . was the principal actor in the Watergate cover-up . . . [and is] the principal author of the political and constitutional crisis that Watergate epitomizes." Buzhardt managed a blockbuster ending (presumably with Nixon's encouragement): if the facts had come out shortly after June 17, 1972, it would have been "the kind of embarrassment that an immensely popular president could easily have weathered. The political problem has been magnified one thousand-fold. . . . because the White House has been led to say things about Watergate that have since been found untrue. These added consequences were John Dean's doing."[85]

Dean responded by releasing the White House enemies list, which was not evidently connected in any way to Nixon but did include the names of many prominent media personalities. This is not exceptionable; they were enemies, and their shrieks of moral indignation, made more piercing by their joy at being so recognized, had an impact on current opinion, but should not influence history.

Nixon and Buzhardt now used some of the tapes to write up near verbatim rebuttals of Dean, without referring to the existence of the tapes. Dean ended his testimony on June 30, and the committee recessed for the July 4 holiday. David and Julie made a very effective and persuasive appearance on the popular *Tonight Show* with Johnny Carson on June 29. Nixon made it clear to Ervin in a letter of July 7 that he would not respond to a subpoena for his own appearance or for White House documents, and he appeared to be on strong precedented ground, invoking Jefferson, Lincoln, Truman, and Eisenhower. Ervin sent a letter in reply, asserting what he claimed to be his committee's rights to what it sought.

John Mitchell appeared as a witness on July 10 and solidly supported Nixon, and thoroughly debunked Dean. On the night of July 11, Nixon came down with what his doctor diagnosed as pneumonia. Every breath was painful, but he took a telephone call from Ervin and said that he had read Ervin's letter to him in the newspapers before it arrived. Ervin gave the customary assertion (as Nixon had done in the Hiss case) that he had no idea how the press got hold of the letter before the addressee did. Nixon said that he would not just open up his files for Ervin's committee to paw through and that it was obvious from the hearings to date that the committee majority's objective was to destroy the president and that he would not cooperate with that. Ervin denied any such objective.

By July 16, Nixon seemed to be recovering from his pneumonia and was able to eat normally and get out of bed for a time. One of his legal aides, Richard Moore, had testified at the Watergate Committee and rattled off astoundingly authoritative recollections of parts of conversations. The committee was almost sure to demand the documentation on which such precise recollections were based.

On that day, Alexander Butterfield, head of the Federal Aviation Administration, former chief administrative aide to Haldeman, and an old friend of Haldeman's from university, under close preparatory questioning in camera, revealed the existence of the White House taping system. Nixon had assumed that the few people who knew about it would invoke executive privilege before admitting to its existence.

When this came to light, Nixon discussed with Haig the advisability of destroying the tapes. Haig recommended that he speak to his counsel first. Nixon had Buzhardt send a letter to Ervin explaining that there was such a system, as there had been with Kennedy and Johnson. Arthur Schlesinger and Joseph Califano spontaneously and violently denied that the presidents they served had done anything of the kind, although they presumably knew that they had.[86]

John Connally strongly urged that the tapes be torched on the White House lawn in full sight of the White House press corps.[87] The tapes were the president's property; they had not been subpoenaed, and there was a national security justification for destroying them. It would be controversial, but not much of an escalation from where they were, and thereafter Watergate would inevitably run out of steam. Nixon would limp to the end of his term and might yet be able to achieve something, especially in foreign policy. Haldeman said their tapes were their "best defense," and Agnew and Garment said that destroying them would seem to be an admission of guilt. Nixon apparently did not imagine that they could be judicially wrenched completely out of his hands and the most damaging parts of them highlighted by his enemies while the exculpatory parts (more numerous, in fact) were downplayed or ignored.

Many of the president's entourage were audibly hedging their bets. Agriculture Secretary Earl Butz criticized the anti-inflation program. Labor Secretary Brennan criticized the wiretaps. Laird was balky generally. And Kissinger, whose propensity to run for cover when a friend was under attack was an irrepressible reflex (of which he never cured himself), called any dissimulation about the Cambodian bombing in 1969, which investigative reporter Seymour Hersh had just brought to light, and of which Kissinger was perfectly well aware, "deplorable." Ehrlichman and Haldeman spoke powerfully in support of the president and themselves at the Watergate Committee at the end of the month. Ehrlichman, combative and well-briefed, fully held his own with his questioners, called Dean a liar, and supported the president. Haldeman, courteous, deferential, and equally well-informed, also made a strong, as well as personally favorable, impression, and also supported the president unreservedly. Haldeman finished testifying on July 31.

If Nixon had moved earlier on the tapes, he could have had the best of both worlds, editing out damaging sections, claiming national security or whatever he wanted, and keeping the many exculpatory and also the generally neutral parts. It was too late for that. Instead, he got the worst of all options. Ervin wrote to him on July 17 asking for all "relevant documents and tapes," and Nixon took a week to reply and then declined. He acknowledged that people of different perspectives could interpret the tapes differently, and said that there were "a great many very frank and very private comments" that could be unnecessarily harmful. Archibald Cox quickly chimed in that he wanted to piggyback on Ervin's request. So, shortly, would Judge Sirica.

Ervin signaled a compromise: he and Baker and Cox alone would go over the tapes and edit out anything not relevant to what they were examining. This would have allowed Nixon some ability to splice and finesse the relatively few worrisome passages and appear to be in overwhelming compliance, and a great deal of material that was not probative but would eventually be splashed about to his embarrassment – expletives, ethnic slurs, gratuitous comments of the kind a man makes in his office to his closest colleagues at tense moments – would not have come out. Nixon eventually declined Ervin's request, though there was discussion of a number of compromises. The tapes would determine the fate of the president.

Richard Nixon's presidency had already reached an extremity only approached by Andrew Johnson more than a century before. Johnson had been an accidental and not overly important president who was the victim of post-Civil War partisanship and the residual bitterness of that horrible conflict, following the assassination of Abraham Lincoln.

Nixon was a very considerable president who had achieved much and been massively endorsed by a grateful electorate. Not only his presidency hung in the balance. This most suspicious, morose, generally joyless of men knew that he was now facing an existential crisis. His health, no less than his hold on his office, was under siege. He was, as always in supreme crises, alone. His family was present and supportive, but unable to share or reduce the burden. His standing in the polls had declined from 68 percent to 40 percent in six months. His enemies, numberless and rabid, were in full cry. His incumbency was threatened, certainly, and beyond it, within himself, his survival as a self-respecting moral being. The public and private crises of Richard Nixon were now unfolding together in pitiless, relentless, unpredictable sequence. The world's most powerful officeholder, so resoundingly reaffirmed in his power and dignity nine months before, was fighting for his official, moral, and physical life as events tumbled pell-mell upon him.

The drama, both awesome and squalid, would hypnotize the world. A president could be unmade, but the man who was president could also remake himself. The world would have to wait for the solitary, awkward, brave, distant figure at the center of the colossal tumult. For the most part, his enemies were not his peers, and there was no useful precedent in American history. All eyes, hostile, curious, or admiring, now and for a long time, would be on the mysteriously, deceptively, apparently ordinary figure of Richard Milhous Nixon. All sensed that a mighty political drama was occurring, and with it, a great human drama also.

Chapter Fifteen

The Inferno
1973–1974

— I —

THE RELENTLESS POUNDING of the president continued through the summer. The Ervin Committee gave great and undeserved credence to the theory that Nixon might have poured millions of dollars of public money into the improvement of his homes in California and Florida. It revealed that a number of large corporations had made illegal contributions to CREEP, though none of this had any direct connection to the president. By early August, his approval rating had sunk to 31 percent, less than half of where it had been six months before. Nixon wrote a public letter to the Democratic leaders of the Congress warning them of the consequences of their abandonment of Cambodia to the communists. It had no effect.

A large boulder in the rockslide of unbidden events now crashed down on Nixon, as the Agnew problem with the Baltimore grand jury abruptly blew up. At the end of July, Richardson told Haig that there was an unanswerable case against Agnew for taking bribes and kickbacks on at least forty occasions while governor of Maryland. Nixon knew that in state government, leading contractors were often large contributors and that sometimes these arrangements were just coincidental. Having been savagely defamed himself, he was not prepared to be complicit in the same treatment of his vice president, though he was not surprised by suggestions that Agnew had had his snout in the public trough (one thing, almost the only thing, that was never alleged against Nixon). He sent Buzhardt and Garment to meet with

Richardson and go over the evidence. They agreed with Richardson that this was a very strong case, and that Agnew should resign.

Nixon met with Richardson again and asked for an independent assessment by Henry Petersen. Agnew was popular with the conservatives Nixon would need in his own struggle, but his popularity might not survive much airing of the evidence in this case. Cynically, if Agnew had gone through full impeachment proceedings, it would have delayed any Watergate action for up to nine months and probably over a year to install a new vice president, which was the procedure when that office became vacant, following adoption of the Twenty-fifth Amendment to the Constitution in 1967.

Nixon did not wish to mire the government in any such controversy, and on August 6 told Haig and Harlow to tell Agnew he should resign, without seeking to hear Agnew's side of the story. Agnew demanded a face-to-face meeting with the president, which took place on August 7 and lasted ninety minutes. Agnew said Richardson was conducting a vendetta and that he was innocent. Nixon said he would ask Petersen to conduct an independent review, as if he had not already requested this, and did allow that he had reservations about Richardson himself. Nixon did not ask for Agnew's resignation.

The vice president met the press, as rumors of the grand jury findings had already been published, and he militantly denied everything, calling the allegations "false and scurrilous and malicious, [and] damn lies." It was effective, and elicited many expressions of support for Agnew, but Nixon's information was that Agnew's customarily belligerent stance would not stand the official assault that was coming. Nixon determined not to ask Agnew's resignation, nor to stick his neck out for his vice president. He had enough problems of his own. The administration was now in a shocking condition, with both national officeholders fighting for their positions against strong imputations of prior illegal conduct.

The Watergate Committee wound up on August 7. Nixon had said that he would comment at the end of its hearings. And he went to Camp David with key staff members to prepare a response, of which much was expected. He spoke on national television and radio on August 15. He appeared somewhat drawn, and confined himself to his usual disclaimers of prior knowledge of the Watergate break-in or any participation in any cover-up. He accepted "full responsibility," but it was not clear for what since he acknowledged that there had been wrongdoing and denied any knowledge or toleration of it at the time or subsequently. He made a number of assertions that the tapes would contradict, especially the March 21 references to money for Howard Hunt, and the June 23, 1972, acquiescence in inviting the CIA to shut down the FBI's investigation.

Nixon believed that the tapes established his innocence, and they were a stronger argument for the defense than the prosecution, as a whole, but he also seems to have been confident that he would not have to hand them over. He seems not to have had any notion of his own guilt, which is a comment in his favor, but seems also not to have taken into account that the country had been whipped into a frenzy on the issue and there was little chance that the courts would agree to a stonewall on the tapes. Nixon said that lawlessness became a fad in the sixties as people routinely took the law into their own hands. He found it "deplorable" but not surprising that some people in his own administration, in response to those people, had emulated their tactics. He asked his supporters of the year before "for your help to ensure that those who would exploit Watergate in order to keep us from doing what we were elected to do, do not succeed."[1]

The Republican National Committee generated an avalanche of letters and telegrams of support, but the Democrats, and even the inconstant Barry Goldwater, dismissed the speech, as did most media comment. Almost the only prominent officeholder who was unambiguously positive was Ronald Reagan, as most Republicans ducked. Polls indicated that a very large number of people watched or listened to Nixon, nearly 80 percent of Americans, but that less than 30 percent found Nixon "convincing." However, almost 70 percent agreed with him that it was time to leave Watergate to the courts, and by a margin of two-to-one, Americans still preferred Nixon to McGovern.[2]

On August 18, Nixon was very well received by the Veterans of Foreign Wars in New Orleans, but the press understandably highlighted an incident in which he seized Ziegler by the shoulders, turned him around, and told him to keep the press away from him. Nixon flew to San Clemente and gave an outdoor press conference live to television for the first time in fourteen months. The questions were hostile; Nixon slurred a few words, was somewhat antagonistic in some of his answers, and was not entirely persuasive on such matters as why he had let Haldeman listen to the tapes and why he had not asked Mitchell exactly what had gone on at the Watergate. After thirty minutes, Nixon complained that there had not been any questions on any subject except Watergate, and he accused some people, including unspecified members of the press, of trying to repeal the results of the 1972 election.

His annoyance was understandable, as the press highlighted negative aspects of the press conference and were clearly hostile, even bordering at times on disrespect. But he had left a trail of partially, or implausibly, answered questions and he could hardly expect the press to leave Watergate aside. No matter what controversial or illegal things Kennedy or Johnson might have done, the press had a job to do. If Nixon had had a clearer and more defensible record over Watergate, instead of a tangled one that could only be evaluated by listening to tapes that he declined to release, and if he had been better humored about the questions, admittedly a challenge to anyone, the bias of the press would have been more evidently distasteful. He had to stop muddling a technical defense with self-righteous posturing that was not supported by his reluctance to release all the evidence, and stop attacks on his opponents in the media and previous administrations. It was never clear if he was saying that he was absolutely, or technically, or just relatively blameless, so he brought much press skepticism on himself.

By this time, Kissinger was so impatient to be done with Rogers that he was again threatening to resign if Rogers was not let go. Kissinger had cultivated an immense cult of popularity in the press, most of it earned by his undoubted competence, imagination, and stamina, augmented by his wit and charm and personal attention to key journalists, but also by the widespread desire of the national media to tear down Nixon. Nixon now had no choice; he could not even bring in Rockefeller if he wanted to; he could not have the defection of Kissinger, for reasons of both domestic politics and continuity in foreign affairs.

Rogers, having been advised by Haig that Nixon thought it was time for him to go, met with Nixon on August 16 and handed him an unrancorous letter of resignation. Nixon told Kissinger on August 21 in San Clemente, while floating in his swimming pool, that he would advise the press the following day that Rogers was retiring and that he would nominate Kissinger to replace him. Rogers exacted a minor revenge on Kissinger by publicly deploring the wiretaps that Kissinger had instigated, forcing the Senate Foreign Relations Committee to ask the nominee something about them. They were pretty soft questions, and Kissinger's great prestige and facile confidence brought him through the hearings completely unscathed. He was now the undisputed star and strongman of a very beleaguered administration.

He was confirmed 78-7 by the full Senate on September 21 and sworn by the chief justice the next day. Nixon made only the most perfunctory appearance at the ceremony and his remarks included the assertion that Kissinger was the first secretary of state since the Second World War who did not part his hair. (Rusk, not having much hair, had not parted his either; nor did Nixon, but this was presumably a manifestation of Nixon's peculiar sense of humor.) Nixon did not attend the reception afterward, and Pat Nixon did not even join the receiving line after the swearing-in. Nixon did the necessary, but the estrangement between the Nixons and their new secretary of state was greater than ever.

On August 27, Nixon had released a deluge of information about the acquisition of his house in San Clemente, and identified Bebe Rebozo and Robert Abplanalp as the lenders. The press, which should have been satisfied with a full and uncontroversial disclosure, generally responded with snide innuendos and suggestions that there was more than met the eye to the transaction.

On August 29, as Sirica issued a court order for seven of Nixon's tapes, the president's lawyers accused the Ervin Committee of conducting a "criminal investigation and trial." Nixon refused Ervin's and Sirica's demands for tapes. Nixon could simply stonewall, and say that he would not accept a judicial finding on the issue, or he could accept Sirica's invitation to appeal, implicitly accepting that the Supreme Court would decide. The White House announced on August 30 that Nixon would appeal Sirica's order, and the process, on which everyone seemed to understand the fate of the administration depended, started through the courts.

Nixon met with Agnew on September 1, and Agnew said that he was being crucified in Baltimore, but he wanted an impeachment, by members of the Congress, who knew more about political campaign funding and would be less righteous about it than Baltimore jurors would. He thought that if an impeachment were in progress, an indictment could not be launched, but Richardson had a differing opinion. Nixon should not have been in a hurry to part with Agnew, because his presence was an argument to most Americans to keep Nixon where he was.

The press continued to publish rumors about Agnew's activities through September, and Agnew met with Nixon on September 20 and said that Richardson had laid down completely unreasonable grounds for a settlement. Agnew was prepared to plead nolo contendere and resign in exchange for an absolute immunity, but Richardson was requiring admission of the government's case. Nixon had Buzhardt and Haig tell Richardson that he could not subject the country to the uncertainties of a trial by taking too inflexible a position. Petersen had confirmed the Richardson view that it was a very strong case against Agnew, and with Buzhardt's and Haig's efforts, a deal seemed very close. This was a statesmanlike approach by Nixon, as he could have benefited, in a completely cynical way, as has been mentioned, from a prolonged struggle involving the vice president.

When the press broke the story of Agnew's plea bargaining on September 22, in part by the *Washington Post's* quoting Petersen, Agnew broke off discussions and prepared to demand an impeachment proceeding, as he informed Nixon on September 25. Agnew met with House Speaker Carl Albert that afternoon to request an impeachment proceeding and expressed his view that he could not be subject to a trial while in office. Half an hour earlier, Richardson had announced that he was submitting evidence to the grand jury, and would clearly be seeking an indictment. Nixon could have intervened and required an impeachment proceeding for Agnew, as he had the power to pardon him, but in the circumstances, that would have been extreme brinkmanship.

He chose not to do anything except issue a statement pointing out that Agnew was entitled to a presumption of innocence and had served for four-and-a-half years as vice president with "dedication and distinction."[3] Discussions continued sporadically for another two weeks. At one point, Agnew tore out after Petersen and accused him of bungling the Watergate investigation, a reflection Nixon could have done without. Finally Agnew agreed to a ten-thousand-dollar fine and three years' probation for not filing a complete income tax return. He informed the president of this on October 9 and resigned later that day. Nixon heard him out sympathetically enough, promised him his friendship, and shook hands lengthily. They never spoke again.

While the dismal dénouement of Spiro Agnew's career unfolded, there was no shortage of other activity in, and involving, Washington. On September 10, Nixon warned about an impending energy "problem." He called again for a new natural gas pipeline from Alaska, increased incentives to drilling, gas deregulation, increased use of coal and nuclear power. He was absolutely right in seeing the problem and suggesting solutions, but more than thirty years passed with nothing useful happening in energy conservation or alternate sourcing. As in a number of other areas, Nixon was prophetic, but at this point, the country was preoccupied with more mundane issues about his presidency.

In the previous few days, Nixon was accused by the *Washington Post* of having tapped the telephone of his brother Donald, because of his commercial relationship with Howard Hughes. This was greatly amplified throughout the media. The White House dissembled. The *New York Times* reported that Nixon had paid no income taxes in 1970 and 1971, had backdated a gift to the national archives of his vice presidential papers, and had reserved for himself most of the best items in what was rather arbitrarily valued as a five-hundred-thousand-dollar gift. Nixon had followed the same practice as other politicians, including Dwight D. Eisenhower and Hubert Humphrey, but this was a damaging revelation as much of the media continued a campaign to exhaust any reservoir of sympathy for Nixon personally. In addition to Reagan, Republican Party chairman George Bush, John Connally, and a few others were still publicly speaking on Nixon's behalf, but the climate continued to deteriorate.

On September 14, Nixon's brief to the U.S. Court of Appeals was filed, and he had made a sizable contribution to it himself. The court unanimously urged a compromise: that Cox and Nixon's jurisconsult, Charles Alan Wright, go through the tapes together and decide what it was appropriate to give the grand jury. This would have been better than some fates, including the decision to hand over everything, which the media was endlessly pushing public and juridical opinion toward. But Nixon wouldn't hear of it. He would fight it all the way out in the courts, even as the media steadily built the belief, not without reason, that Nixon was more concerned to hide something than to establish the principle of executive privilege.[4] His only way to avoid releasing everything would have been to accept one of the several compromises that were available in earlier stages.

The Ervin Committee had reconvened and was taking testimony from secondary figures and not receiving much publicity. The senators were visibly disappointed that they were overshadowed now by the courts and the special prosecutor, and in their efforts to generate a little publicity, they called Pat Buchanan on September 26. They got a good deal more than they bargained for. Clean cut, direct, articulate, humorous, likable, and armed to the teeth with facts about previous administrations, Buchanan was Nixon's greatest spokesman. As has been mentioned, though pugnacious, he would have been a more effective press secretary than Ziegler.

Buchanan turned every question into a soaring speech and recited chapter and verse of the iniquities of Democrats at every echelon. It was a disaster for the committee, and Sam Dash dismissed the witness before he had had a full chance to give all the Democratic senators a full mauling for what he considered, often with reason, their hypocrisy and grandstanding. Most of the media played it down as best they could, but at least five million Americans saw the spectacle live as Buchanan eviscerated the president's unctuous accusers. When he returned from the hearings, President and Mrs. Nixon invited him straight to the residence for champagne and Pat had a dance with him. It was quite a contrast with the frostiness that had settled on the relationship with Kissinger.[5]

The Chilean political cauldron blew up in September 1973. Chile was a country largely reliant on copper exports for its income, and the copper price was at the lower end of the cycle when Allende squeezed in with about 37 percent of the vote in 1970, his fourth run as presidential candidate. (See Chapter 11.) Inflation was then at 30 percent and unemployment at about 15 percent. Malnutrition was a problem with an alarming number of young people. Allende's policy prescription was the usual Marxist one, with the usual results. He seized large rural estates with minimal compensation and redistributed the land among his rural followers in a rather random fashion that quickly reduced agricultural production; nationalized the copper and banking industries, again with minimal compensation; decreed a 40 percent wage increase throughout Chilean industry, while freezing prices.

Utter chaos ensued. There was also intimidation of anti-government media and members of parliament, where the government was a minority, and far-reaching measures were forced through parliament by excluding groups of opposition members or simply miscounting the votes on division. A 37 percent vote for president and the election of 40 percent of the congressmen was not a mandate to turn Chile into a Marxist dictatorship, and violence rose steadily. Allende had been confirmed as president after he signed a "Statute of Constitutional Guarantees" pledging not to violate the Chilean Constitution. The Congress and the Supreme Court determined that he had grossly violated his oath, and by September 1973, if there had not been a coup d'état, the country would have descended into civil war.

The role of the United States in these developments has been a matter of considerable controversy ever since. There is little doubt that the United States let it be known that it would not oppose a coup d'état that removed Allende. The United States seems not to have directly subsidized such an effort after Nixon's original effort to bar Allende's election in 1970, but Nixon and Kissinger remained concerned at the impact in the Americas of a communist regime, for that is what it was, apparently seeking to consolidate its minority position into totalitarian rule in the manner of Czech and Polish communists after the Second World War.

The Chilean armed forces high command seized the strategic targets around Santiago on September 11, occupied the Congress, the radio stations, and the railway terminus, and imposed martial law. There was a good deal of skirmishing and running gun battles, but the military almost entirely followed the orders of their officers rather than the government, and the battle for the streets of Santiago was very unequal. There were actions by groups of tough miners, irregularly armed, but they were no match for the Chilean Army, perhaps the only one in South America that was not flabby, overloaded with bemedalled Ruritanian officers, and incapable of serious combat.

Tanks approached the presidential palace, where Allende was barricaded in with his die-hard followers, and after Allende refused to come out, the palace was attacked by armor and infantry, and everyone within was killed or captured. According to Allende's doctor, the president committed suicide with a machine gun given to him by Castro and inscribed "To my good friend Salvador Allende from Fidel Castro." The facts have been contested and it is possible that he was shot in action or simply murdered.[6]

It was a sanguinary business, and skirmishing and heavy-handed mopping up continued for several weeks as the military imposed control on all parts of the country. There were many assassinations and seizures of people on both sides with no semblance of due process, and probably several thousand people were murdered, many after being tortured in a particularly disgusting manner. As many as thirty thousand others were detained and interrogated brutally. The victorious armed forces, led by General Augusto Pinochet, committed many more of the outrages than the communists, but the attempt to place all the blame on Pinochet and portray Allende and his followers as innocent social democrats has been a very tiresome exercise in myth-making.

Once securely in office, Pinochet governed more successfully than any national leader in Latin America in strictly economic terms, and handed the economy over to a group of young Chilean followers of George Shultz's colleague from the University of Chicago, Professor Milton Friedman. Almost everything was denationalized and deregulated, taxes were lowered, union powers were reduced, and investment flowed in. He gradually restored a regime of laws and a democratic congress, and finally stood for election in 1988, with all opponents from left to right grouped against him in a simple referendum on the extension of his presidency for a further eight years; Pinochet lost 55 percent to 42 percent, though he would almost certainly have defeated any individual candidate. He handed over to a democratically elected Christian Democrat in 1990, though he continued as commander-in-chief of the armed forces and life senator for another eight years.

The Senate confirmation hearings of Kissinger as secretary of state were in progress when Pinochet seized power, but Kissinger received only slight questioning about it. After more than thirty years, no evidence has come to light in either country that the United States played a direct role in the overthrow of the Allende government, but it was certainly a geopolitical bonanza for the United States, as Allende was cavorting with Castro with a particularly irritating relish. It was ultimately good for Chile also, as unexampled prosperity was produced by Pinochet, and he ultimately restored what seems at time of writing (when a moderate socialist, single mother has taken office as president) a stabler democracy than Chile ever enjoyed before.*

In sum, the Nixon-Kissinger Chile policy was broadly successful by all criteria except short-term human rights outrages in perturbed conditions, and there is nothing connecting the U.S. administration to those. In geopolitical terms, it was another clear-cut Nixon victory.

---

* Pinochet himself would be detained for sixteen months in Britain in 2000 and 2001 on a questionable warrant from a (communist) Spanish judge and then released, at the age of eighty-six, on compassionate and humanitarian grounds. There were further legal problems for him in Chile, and the principal message of the Pinochet experience to dictators is not to surrender office or democratize, as he did. Unfortunately, the example of Franco or Castro, to hang on to a belated death, commends itself. Pinochet died in 2006, aged ninety-one.

— II —

Thus came the fateful month of October 1973. Nixon was in Key Biscayne, working on edited transcripts of some of the tapes he expected to be ordered to hand over, when Egypt and Syria abruptly attacked Israel on October 6, the Jewish holy day of Yom Kippur, as Kissinger told him after a three-hour delay. American and Israeli intelligence were taken completely by surprise. The Syrians cleared the Israelis off the Golan Heights and the Egyptians crossed the Suez Canal, pierced the Bar-Lev Line that Israel had represented as virtually impenetrable, and advanced a short distance into Sinai. Brezhnev's warnings at San Clemente in July had been accurate and Sadat's endless threats to make war had not been the hot air that Nixon and Kissinger had thought they were. The Arab powers were far more militarily capable than ever before and the scale of fighting vastly exceeded anything seen in the Middle East since Montgomery and Rommel were engaged in the Battle of Egypt. The Israelis had assumed that a brief war, as in 1967, was all that need be provided for, and they went through aircraft, tanks, and ordnance with worrisome speed.

Nixon presciently saw both the threat of a victory by Soviet arms, and the possibilities for progress toward a durable solution. Although Sadat had expelled the Russians, Russia was the chief arms supplier, and was trying to reenter the region. Nixon knew that to keep them out, American arms in Israeli hands would have to defeat Russian arms wielded by the Arabs. He also recognized at once that the first Arab military successes against Israel since the founding of that state in 1948 might create the conditions in which the Arabs could make an honorable peace on a basis of having proved their military point opposite the Israelis.

While Nixon sought these objectives in the region, he did not want to jeopardize détente with the Russians. It would be a delicate operation, defeating the Russian clients without removing their sense that they had preserved their honor and created the possibility of peace; repulsing the Russians without impairing the developing U.S.–U.S.S.R. relationship; and assisting Israel enough to assure its success without transforming conflict into another crushing humiliation of the Arabs. Complicated though it was, Nixon always liked foreign crises, and it was probably a welcome relief from the dismal audition of Watergate tapes.

Nixon returned to Washington on October 7 and told Kissinger that the United States would give Israel what it needed to win on condition that it finally negotiate seriously to a durable agreement. Israel could not "get away with just having this thing hang over for another four years and have us at odds with the Arab world. We're not going to do it anymore."[7]

Nixon was largely preoccupied with the vice presidential crisis for several days, but on October 13 he was informed by Haig that the Soviets, in an act of what Kissinger described as "pure insolence," were accusing the United States of sending excessive supplies to Israel. In fact, the United States had not supplied Israel at all. James Schlesinger, the new defense secretary, was concerned about arousing the Arabs and Russians, and especially about a cut-off in oil supplies. He was only offering to Kissinger to send three transport aircraft, though a stop-off had already been arranged with the Portuguese in the Azores, so there was no practical impediment to deploying the full, massive U.S. airlift capacity. Part of the problem was the hostility to Israel of the chairman of the Joint Chiefs, Admiral Thomas Moorer.[8] Intelligence demonstrated that the Soviets had been heavily resupplying Egypt and Syria for several days, while masking their actions with complaints to the United States.

Nixon went into action and told Schlesinger, an energy expert, that he, Nixon, would take responsibility for any oil boycott from the Arabs and to begin a major air resupply of Israel at once. When informed a few hours later that there were still disputes about what types of planes to use, he told Kissinger to use "anything that can fly." He accurately enunciated his principle that they would get as much blame for "three planes as for three hundred," and the policy of assuring Israel's security would be carried out at maximum efficiency. A contest of airlifts was waged from October 13 to October 20, which the United States easily won with five hundred and fifty arrivals of large, fully loaded transport aircraft. Within this period, the Israeli Army had crossed the Suez Canal in two places, almost encircled the Egyptian Army that had crossed into Sinai, and pushed the Syrians back from the Golan Heights almost to Damascus.

The American action had the desired effect, and on October 19 Brezhnev wrote Nixon urgently, proposing a cease-fire in place and an immediate visit to Moscow by Kissinger to work out a more durable agreement to be sponsored (i.e., imposed) by the superpowers. Nixon and Kissinger stalled for a day, in order to assist Israel in making the point that U.S. arms would prevail over Soviet arms in the Middle East. Kissinger prepared to leave for Moscow at the very end of the 19th, after a conversation with Nixon in which they disagreed. Nixon saw the possibility of a comprehensive peace and wanted to seize it. Kissinger thought a cease-fire was all they should attempt at this point. The next day, Nixon sent a letter to Brezhnev through the Soviet embassy expressing a determination to join the Soviet leader in seeking a comprehensive peace. He added a handwritten postscript sending personal greetings from his wife and himself to Brezhnev and his wife. Some have interpreted this as an insurance policy that Kissinger would not try to tamper with the letter. That Kissinger might have had such an impulse is understandable, and that Nixon would have suspected him of such high-handedness is believable, but it is not clear how he would be able to intercept a letter delivered directly from the White House to the Soviet ambassador and forwarded through the Soviet diplomatic fast channel on to Brezhnev.[9]

Nixon wrote to Brezhnev that Kissinger had "full authority" to negotiate comprehensive agreements that there would be "a firm commitment from both of us . . . to provide the strong leadership which our respective friends in the area will find persuasive."[10] Nixon sent Kissinger a closely reasoned follow-up cable on October 20 proposing a full and durable settlement, which he thought possible. Nixon sensed that Israel had been frightened, and understood that as time went by, it could be vulnerable, and the Arabs believed they had recovered their military honor with a respectable battlefield performance, and the Russians realized, after being expelled by Sadat, that this was their last chance to be anything like a co-equal player with the United States in the Middle East. Nixon was right in these perceptions, which makes Kissinger's desire to confine discussions to a cease-fire the more mystifying. Kissinger's explanation of his performance to the author was based entirely on what he thought practical. His skepticism is understandable; his insubordination is not.

In his October 20 cable to Kissinger, Nixon wrote that Israeli inflexibility, unrealistic Arab views, and the influence of Jewish elements on American policymaking had made an arrangement impossible up to now. He believed the first two had changed and he assured Kissinger that he would pay no attention to the political agitation of American Jews. He told Kissinger to point out to Brezhnev that, unlike MFN status, this was a matter of executive authority for the U.S. president and he would not have to refer any agreement they made to the Congress.[11]

Kissinger disagreed with all this and thought that Nixon under-estimated the difficulties of reining in the Israelis. Nixon thought Kissinger was failing to notice opportunity knocking as it never had before in the Middle East. Nixon now became overwhelmingly preoccupied with events in Washington, as will be described, and Kissinger safely felt that he need not take Nixon's instructions too literally.

On October 20, Saudi Arabia announced it was stopping all oil supplied to the United States. This was presumably something Sadat and the Syrian leader, Hafez Assad, had had up their sleeves. Nixon was not taken by sur-prise, and hoped that it might cause his complacent countrymen and the more slothful or partisan elements in the Congress to take his advocacy of self-sufficiency in energy more seriously. Kissinger wanted to let the Israelis make more military progress, as the Egyptian army in the Sinai could be forced to surrender within a few days, for lack of supplies. Brezhnev wanted a cease-fire for the inverse reason. Nixon, and to some extent, Kissinger, were in partial agreement with Brezhnev, as the Arabs could not make a real peace if they were severely humiliated, and Israel would be less disposed to compromise than ever if, after a rocky start, they completely humbled the Arab powers again.

Kissinger was more indulgent of Israel than Nixon was at this point, and excused himself from the Moscow talks to go to Israel to try to coordinate with the government of that country. He told the Israelis that they could have a "slippage" while he flew back to Moscow, and he would keep the UN out of it, as everyone regarded their "peacekeepers" as a nuisance and an irrelevancy, but he lowered the boom on Nixon's behalf that a cease-fire in place had to begin imminently. The UN Security Council adopted Resolution 338, jointly moved by the United States and U.S.S.R. at 12:52 A.M. on October 22, mandating a cease-fire. There was still some movement, but the cease-fire took after a few hours. The Israelis quickly moved to complete the encirclement of the Egyptian army in Sinai.

On October 24, the Egyptian position became so desperate that Sadat asked the sponsoring super powers to send ground forces to the Middle East to enforce their cease-fire. Nixon was not prepared to do this and said that such a step "would introduce an extremely dangerous potential for great power rivalry in the area."[12] Dobrynin offered to work out a plan for joint intervention with ground forces and to introduce a resolution proposing it at the UN. Kissinger said the United States would veto such a resolution. In the evening of October 24, a message came in from Brezhnev, making the same proposal and going further and adding that if the United States did not choose to participate in such a proposal, the U.S.S.R. would commit the necessary forces to impose the cease-fire unilaterally.

There is some unnecessary confusion about the sequence of events after this. Nixon and Haig agree that Haig told the president of the message and that he told Haig to meet with WSAG, the Washington Special Action Group, chaired by Kissinger and including the defense secretary, the chairman of the Joint Chiefs, the national security adviser (now General Brent Scowcroft), the CIA director, and anyone else Kissinger invited, and to advocate a heightened military alert on the president's behalf. The president did not normally attend these meetings. Kissinger met with WSAG at 2 A.M. and Haig presented Nixon's views, which were an order, unless there was such dissent that Kissinger wished to consult the president directly. There was no dissent and it was agreed to issue an upgraded state of alert order to U.S. military forces. The aircraft carrier *Franklin D. Roosevelt* and its task force were ordered to the eastern Mediterranean; the *John F. Kennedy* and its task force were ordered from the Atlantic into the Mediterranean. An airborne division was put into a state of readiness for immediate departure. Sixty B-52s from Guam were ordered back to the United States to join the Strategic Air Command (i.e. for potential attack on Russia), and the strategic nuclear forces were moved to a higher, but not a full, state of alert.

The next morning, Nixon and Kissinger met with congressional leaders and Nixon gave a lengthy history of Soviet communism that did not impress everyone as relevant to the Middle East.

The myth has arisen that Nixon, under the pressures of Watergate problems, had retired in a water-logged and drink-taken condition and that Haig and Kissinger acted in his name on a consensual basis. Both men, and Nixon himself, refute this. Nixon was exhausted by the pressure of events, did not normally attend WSAG meetings, and left it to Haig to represent him.[*] In his eulogy of Nixon twenty-one years later, Kissinger mentioned that Nixon had "dared a confrontation [with the U.S.S.R.] in 1973 . . . in the midst of the greatest crisis of his life." There was some controversy at the time that Nixon had exaggerated the problem to take attention away from the latest Watergate

---

[*] Unfortunately some historians have given some credence to this version of events, including the generally fairly rigorous Stephen Ambrose.

eruption. Kissinger reacted angrily to such insinuations, and the circumstances of the decision make it clear that that charge is unfounded.

Whether it was an appropriate response or not, it worked. The U.S.S.R. made no further reference to deploying ground forces to the region. The Security Council adopted a third resolution, now "demanding" return to the October 22 positions, and Kissinger intervened rather heavy-handedly, but with the president's full concurrence, to require Israel to give up its ambition to capture the entire Egyptian army in the Sinai.

Kissinger got his cease-fire and handled the crisis well. The question remains of whether an irretrievable opportunity was lost in not seeking a broader settlement with the Russians. After this, the Russians would not have enough influence to compel much Arab compliance, the Palestinians would be steadily less susceptible to the influence of King Hussein, and agreements could only be made by agreement between the parties in the region. This would prove much more difficult than agreement between Moscow and Washington, reasonable powers compared with some of those in place, whose fate Nixon wished to try to settle in absentia.

Nixon had adopted the principle of assuring that U.S. arms prevailed, and had resupplied the Israeli Air force with warplanes in the middle of the combat. He was not surprised by the Arab oil embargo, as it became, and upheld political and strategic principles in the teeth of dissent in his administration, terrible domestic pressures, threatened Soviet impetuosity, and a serious economic threat from the oil exporters (the Arab members of the Organization of Petroleum Exporting Countries reduced production on October 17). He, too, had performed with distinction, to a successful conclusion, despite his subsequent requests of Kissinger to build him up in the press and urge American Jewish leaders to be less hostile to him, which may, as Kissinger later wrote, have been "pathetic," as unbecoming for a president of the United States.[13] It is more understandable in the context of the political crisis Nixon was facing and does not, in any case, detract from the efficacy of Nixon's response to the constellation of foreign policy challenges he faced in this freighted month (as Kissinger affirmed).

— III —

While the Yom Kippur War and its aftermath were playing out, there was great drama in Washington. First, Agnew abruptly resigned right after the war started, on October 9. The natural curiosity about his replacement was heightened by the widespread view that Nixon would not be completing his term, and that the next vice president was also the next president. If Nixon had wished to be Machiavellian, as has been mentioned, he could have engineered an impeachment of Agnew, as the former vice president had wished. In the same spirit, he could now have achieved something almost as time-consuming, while serving his own preference, by nominating John Connally. There would have been a prolonged battle getting him confirmed, as the Republicans didn't trust such a friend of Johnson's and Rayburn's, and a veteran of the Kennedy administration, and the Democrats did not appreciate his defection to the Republicans.

As always where the national interest was at stake, as in the issue of contesting the 1960 election, Nixon put the country first. He dutifully consulted the cabinet, the Republican congressional leaders and delegations, and the Republican National Committee members. The most obvious candidates were Nelson Rockefeller, Ronald Reagan, Elliott Richardson, Gerald Ford, Melvin Laird, and Hugh Scott, though many others were mentioned, including Warren Burger and George Bush. Nixon met with Ford and said to him, as he did to others, that the person selected should meet three tests: competency to take over as president, continuity in foreign policy, and likely swift confirmation by Congress.

The RNC responses, canvassed by Bush, gave 56 votes for Reagan, 51 for Rockefeller, and 47 each for Connally and Goldwater, with no one else above ten. The cabinet had four votes for Rockefeller, three for Rogers, two each for Reagan and Ford. The Senate, polled by Scott, had six for Rockefeller, five for Goldwater, four each for Connally and Reagan, and the rest widely scattered. In the House, naturally, Ford led, with 80 votes, followed by 35 for Rockefeller, 23 for Reagan, and 16 for Connally (Ford's own choice, he has said, was Connally). Nixon had all these results in hand in the course of October 10. On that day, shortly after the meeting with Ford, Speaker Carl Albert came to see Nixon and said that Ford was the only one of the mentioned contenders who would be confirmed quickly.[14]

The fact is that any of the leading contenders, except possibly Connally, would have been confirmed, and there was no reason for Nixon to pay any attention to what Albert said. Most serious political experts were as concerned about Albert's becoming president – as he would have if anything had happened to Nixon with the vice presidency vacant – as they had been about Agnew. Albert was a mousy little Oklahoman, lacking the magisterial presence of Rayburn or McCormack, and he had a substantial problem with alcohol, having recently driven his car through a shop window while thoroughly drunk.

Rockefeller and Reagan were well qualified and would have been approved (as Rockefeller was a year later, admittedly after unnecessarily prolonged and acerbic hearings). They were clearly more formidable leaders than Ford, which has led to a widely held view that Nixon was hoping to choose a vice president who would not be an encouragement, by his stature, to the impeachment of the incumbent president. Nixon vehemently denied this and told the author that choosing between Reagan and Rockefeller would have forced the party on to one side or the other of the Republican spectrum and been divisive. He said Richardson was never considered – that he had been an incompetent attorney general – and would have been a worse president, had no support in the Republican Party, and had as severe a problem with alcohol as Albert. This begged the question of Nixon's motives in offering Richardson the post of secretary of defense and attorney general. Nixon said he envisioned Richardson as placating the Eastern, Ivy League establishment, while being adequately loyal to him, but that he had misjudged and overrated Richardson.

It is now clear that if he had gone with Reagan, Nixon would probably have spared the country the dreary Carter interlude and Reagan would have served at a younger age than he did, which would have made him a more effective president in his second term than he was. But Nixon could hardly be expected to foresee that. And it may also be that to win as he did, taking the Senate with him and receiving a mandate to reconstruct the nation's morale, cut taxes, and win the Cold War, Reagan had to run against what came to be seen as the ineffectuality of Carter. Again, Nixon was trying to fill a vacancy with an uncontroversial but adequate person, and not map out the country's political future. For, he claimed, these reasons, he chose Gerald Ford.

Ford was unexciting but solid and well liked, of unquestioned integrity, loyal to Nixon (still a legitimate consideration), and would be confirmed without difficulty. He was no world-beater, then or subsequently, but he could, and did, provide what George Orwell called, in another time and country, "a government of decent men." It was a perfectly defensible choice and Gerald Ford, as he had throughout his twenty-five years in

Congress, served with competence and dedication in national office. Sometimes, especially after such immense contestation as Nixon habitually generated, a nation does well with a solid plough-horse. Nixon announced his selection on the evening of October 12 to general approval and Ford was confirmed without difficulty on December 6, by 92-3 in the Senate and 387-35 in the House.* [15]

On the day of the Ford announcement, October 12, the U.S. Circuit Court of Appeals decided, 5 to 2, that Nixon had to hand over to Sirica the seven tapes demanded by Archibald Cox. Nixon knew that Cox would now be back for all the tapes. He recognized Cox's partisanship and animosity, but he does not seem to have recognized his own vulnerability. Having said that he knew nothing of a cover-up, knew nothing of paying Watergate defendants until late on, and never of paying them to remain silent, and knew nothing of trying to involve the CIA in discouraging the FBI to discontinue its investigation, he could be proved by his own tapes to have lied. Presidents lie quite often and aren't impeached for it, but some of what he lied about was or may have been felonious behavior.

Much of the media had systematically assaulted the administration, nibbling around the edges with malicious and usually inaccurate stories about Nixon's taxes and improvements to his homes at the government's expense. There had been unflattering exposure of a discreditable range of political dirty tricks, which were not linked personally to Nixon but helped to besmirch him. Growing numbers of his former subordinates were being indicted, and some had been convicted. Nixon had placed his hopes in a technical defense against having committed "high crimes and misdemeanors," the constitutional criterion for removal of a federal office-holder.

He may have had such a defense, but his partisan and media opponents, with his unwitting cooperation, had set him up. His fate would depend on the Congress, and Congress, beyond a certain point, would follow public opinion. Public opinion did not believe that he was withholding his tapes for entirely disinterested reasons of the constitutional right to privacy. He had pledged to the country that he knew a good deal less about

---

* For some reason, Clare Booth Luce, a longtime Nixon admirer, suddenly wrote to Nixon on October 30, 1973, and proposed pulling Ford as vice presidential nominee and replacing him with Rockefeller.

the post-Watergate shenanigans than he did. The second highest court in the country had ordered him to hand over the tapes, and he had just nominated a replacement president whose confirmation would eliminate an obstacle to the removal of the incumbent.

He wrote that "firing Cox seemed the only way to rid the administration of the partisan viper we had planted in our bosom."[16] It would also be a brinkmanship step. If he was going to go that far, and was now concerned with doctoring or withholding evidence, he should have removed the relatively few damaging parts of the tapes and handed them over in that modified condition, claiming national security or whatever he wanted, had necessitated the cuts, which need not have been more than a few minutes in many hours of tapes.

This would have led to immense and obviously well-founded skepticism, but not necessarily to the Congress's uprooting Nixon from the White House and banishing him from the presidency. He was now down to only a few turns and none of them was a very pleasing prospect. But if he got rid of Cox, he had no reason to believe that there would not be continued demand for the tapes, judicially upheld, and when they were audited, the erosion of what was left of his credibility would be too severe for the normal test of a reasonable doubt about the commission of a crime. The test would be one of public trust and confidence and Nixon would be too far down the well to hold his support in Congress. And there was no assurance that a Cox replacement would be much of an improvement.

Nixon described Cox accurately enough, but instead of attacking Cox, he would have had a better chance dealing with inanimate evidence while purporting to comply with 95 percent of what the courts required and offering the most plausible reason he could for his 5 percent non-compliance. It might not have worked, but it was more promising than what he did do. A more dignified alternative would have been nominating whomever between Rockefeller and Reagan he respected more, in place of Agnew, appealing the Circuit Court decision while his choice was confirmed, and then destroying inconvenient parts of the tapes and resigning. That would have spared the country and himself a horrible indignity. It would not be as clear as it became that he had misled the country, and even his enemies would have had to admit that he had paid a heavy price for whatever his involvement had been in the legal issues that imperiled him.

(On the Reagan-Rockefeller question, Nixon thought Rockefeller was more intelligent and presidential and worldly, and that Reagan was too much dominated by his wife, but that Reagan was more courageous, and sounder in policy terms, and he liked him better. Reagan proved, as all the world now knows, to be an outstanding, if idiosyncratic, president. Rockefeller, a capable governor and vice president, would probably have been a capable president as well.)

Nixon, in discussion with Haig and to some extent Ziegler (the ranks of White House advisers had thinned dramatically), worked out a plan to offer transcripts of the tapes instead of the tapes themselves and to invite the seventy-two-year-old Senator John C. Stennis of Mississippi to verify that the transcripts conformed to the tapes. Stennis was in his fifth term and was chairman of the Armed Forces Committee and a former circuit judge. He was a segregationist, but was, in the manner of better Southern senators, a man of great experience and integrity. He had been a hawk on Vietnam, but was also co-sponsor of the War Powers Act, which limited to only sixty days the president's ability to deploy forces to combat or possible combat areas without congressional approval. (Nixon would veto this measure as "unconstitutional and dangerous," which it was, as well as imprecisely written, on October 24, but both houses of the Congress overrode his veto and future presidents had to live with it. The constitutionality of the War Powers Act had not been challenged.)

Stennis was somewhat hard of hearing, but in practice he would have had his staff do the verification. Stennis attended one of Nixon's White House church services on October 14, and Nixon asked him if he would be prepared to verify the Watergate transcripts by checking them against the tapes. He said he would. If he had offered it earlier, when he had a greater bargaining position, there might have been a chance of success – not with Cox, but with public opinion; so non-compliance need not have been fatal politically.

Nixon made his proposal to Richardson. Richardson claimed that on October 10 Nixon had said to him, "Now that we have disposed of [Agnew] we can go ahead and get rid of Cox."[17] Nixon denied having said anything of the kind, and is more believable in this than Richardson. There has never been agreement on exactly what Richardson's position was with Stennis. Nixon believed that Richardson had accepted the arrangement and that Cox would be told he could not sue for any further tapes, and that if he dissented, he would have to resign and Nixon would not need to fire him. Richardson claimed that he was thinking about it and had not committed himself. Richardson claimed that only later did he realize that the Stennis compromise wasn't real and was just devised as a pretext for getting rid of Cox.[18] Any of the compromises that were proposed would have been preferable to the showdown that finally occurred. While Richardson's performance was indecisive, Nixon's conduct had prolonged and amplified this crisis, and it was his responsibility to solve or de-escalate it. Firing Cox was certain to achieve the reverse.

Nixon had Ervin and Baker in and laid it out to them. Again, there is no agreement on their response, and they gave different versions after the fact as years went by. Nixon thought they had agreed. They have generally claimed that they would discuss it with their committee. This is one occasion when it is regrettable that Nixon did not tape the conversations, with the two senators and with Richardson. It would have been piquant if he had been able to produce tapes confirming his version of events, and it might have tipped public opinion in his favor on this compromise.

On the evening of October 19, Nixon issued a statement outlining the Stennis compromise and stating that Ervin and Baker had agreed to it. Nixon went a step beyond and said that he was ordering Cox, as "an employee of the executive branch," to desist from further efforts to lay hands on the tapes or other records of the conversations. Nixon was like an excited football player celebrating a touchdown that could still be called back because of an infraction; he contacted the cabinet and the White House staff, and a mood of celebration briefly took hold. Cox issued a short statement of demurral saying that he would not desist and was not taking his orders from Nixon. (This was unfolding at the most critical moments of the Middle East crisis, and Nixon, despite apparently false suggestions of his allegedly water-logged condition at the end of October 24, turned in a fairly impressive performance of stamina and creative management through almost a whole month of relentless crises.)

Cox held a press conference at the National Press Club at midday on Saturday, October 20. As Nixon wrote, Cox adopted "the air of a modest and even befuddled professor," denied he was hostile to Nixon, and professed to fear that he had become "too big for his britches" or even yielded to "vanity" in resisting the president.[19] Kissinger was in Moscow in intense negotiation with Brezhnev and Gromyko. Ervin, Baker, and Richardson had not publicly responded to Nixon's statement of the previous evening, indicating that they were not rushing to contradict the president's version of their conversations with him. Cox rejected the Stennis compromise. He did not criticize Stennis, but gave a technical, rather professorial objection, essentially that he could have what he wanted and did not have to compromise and that anything less would be devaluing the rule of law.

If Nixon had not ordered Cox to desist from pursuing the tapes further, he might have been able simply to declare an impasse. He possessed the tapes and he could claim that he had proposed a compromise that the attorney general and the leaders of the Watergate Committee had accepted, and that as far as he was concerned that was compliance by the co-equal executive branch with the courts, with the concurrence of the third (legislative) branch. He could then have given the transcripts and the tapes to Stennis. The courts might have reinforced their order, and Richardson and Ervin and even Baker might have started waffling, as they did anyway, but it is not at all clear that the Congress would have impeached Nixon for offering and implementing a compromise that centered on one of the most eminent members of the Senate, and that appeared to have been accepted by the attorney general and the Committee leaders.

But Nixon was outraged. His outrage is understandable, but his failure to grasp the realities of the political and public relations problem is not. It was at this point that Kissinger had decided to ignore Nixon's direct order to try to explore a comprehensive settlement with Brezhnev in the Middle East. When Nixon repeated the order, Kissinger telephoned Haig and started to tell him rather testily that Nixon wasn't being realistic. Haig responded rather snappishly and said he had other matters to take care of. When Kissinger asked what could the problem be in Washington on a Saturday evening in October, Haig briefly summarized what instantly became known as the "Saturday Night Massacre."

Following Cox's press conference, Nixon told Haig to call Richardson and order him to fire Cox. Richardson requested a meeting with the president and this was set for 4:30 P.M. Despite the insubordination of Kissinger and Richardson, and the outright defiance of Cox, Nixon was composed. He said a little of the problems with the Russians, but allegedly added that "Brezhnev would never understand it if I let Cox defy my instructions." Almost nothing of Richardson's account of these matters rings very true, and such a comment by Nixon would be uncharacteristically absurd. Richardson explained that he had promised the Senate that he would not countermand the special prosecutor, and that he could not fire Cox for that reason. Instead, he would have to resign. Nixon asked him to defer that because of the foreign policy emergency. Richardson refused and handed over a written resignation, despite Nixon's appeal to him to consider the public interest. This was not a distinguished performance by Richardson, though he shortly basked in the glory of a martyr of the Nixon despotism and soaked it for all it was worth. He was being asked to remain, without firing Cox. By insisting on resigning, Richardson ensured that Cox would be axed too. If he had agreed to Nixon's request to defer his resignation there might have been a chance of settling the controversy down and salvaging something of the Stennis compromise.

William Ruckelshaus automatically became acting attorney general, and Nixon told Haig to tell him to get rid of Cox. Ruckelshaus also declined and sent over his resignation. Nixon refused to accept it on the grounds that he had made no such promises as Richardson to the Senate, and he told Haig to inform Ruckelshaus that he had not resigned, he had been fired. This made the solicitor general, Robert Bork, the acting attorney general. He attended upon Nixon, and Nixon told him to fire Cox. Bork had no doubt Cox could be fired by the president, which was undoubtedly true, as it is true of any employee of the executive branch of the Federal Government. The abrupt departures of Richardson, Ruckelshaus, and Cox were the events of which Haig advised Kissinger when he called from Moscow to complain of the obduracy of Nixon's orders about the Middle East.

What had occurred proved to be a disaster for Nixon, but he cannot be accused of indecisiveness in these intense days. His Middle East initiative for a general settlement was worth a try, and it is regrettable that it was not tried. Once progress in that region depended on direct talks between the Israelis and Palestinians, and especially after a radical Islamic Iran started to assert an influence, all chances of a settlement effectively vanished for decades. Nixon believed he had an arrangement with Richardson and that Richardson had floundered out on his word. He believed he had a compromise that the relevant leaders of the Congress had agreed with, and they did nothing to indicate otherwise in the full day between Nixon's announcement and the high tide of the "Massacre," not even after Cox had publicly objected.

As has been mentioned, Nixon would have been better off to come to this arrangement earlier, before the court order was out, or when the court urged a compromise. Having arrived at it when he did, he would have been better off not to comment publicly on ordering Cox to desist as "an employee of the executive branch," to just leave Cox and Richardson and Ruckelshaus in place and say that he had reached an agreement and would not move from it, and to implement that agreement by sending the tapes to Stennis.

At 8:22 P.M. on October 20, twenty-four hours and seven minutes after Nixon's announcement of the Stennis compromise, Ziegler told the press that Richardson had resigned and that Ruckelshaus and Cox had been fired and that the office of special prosecutor had been abolished and that the investigation would be conducted by Petersen. On Nixon's ultimate orders, the FBI sealed off the offices of the departed officials. Richardson rather histrionically wrote, "A government of laws was on the verge of becoming a government of one man." Nixon told the author that he had been so offended by the insertion of FBI agents at the offices of Haldeman and Ehrlichman, he was engaging in tit for tat. There was, in any case, no danger of unilateral government, as the Congress shortly made clear. But it had not been a very well-functioning government of laws under the Richardson-Cox regime or in the untrammeled pre-Watergate days of Nixon (or Johnson and Kennedy), either.

Archibald Cox was a distinguished law professor, though a rigid and highly partisan one. The special prosecutor's office functioned well in many ways, but it was a libel-and-slander operation staffed by rabid Nixon-haters. Cox himself was an eccentric zealot. Fifteen years later he wrote to every member of Congress effectively urging the impeachment of President Reagan over the Iran-Contra Affair. No impeachment motion was introduced. The United States was just entering an era of generally Republican presidents and Democratic congresses, and was starting down the slippery slope toward criminalization of policy differences. The antipathy to Nixon in liberal circles, and the ease with which the media could stir up antagonism against him, as much as the legal and ethical failings of his own conduct, made this a very serious problem for him. But the allegation that he was trying to subvert the Constitution and arrogate undemocratic authority to himself was unjust. The Watergate cover-up was illegal and ineffectual, but it wasn't an attempted coup d'état.

Nixon clearly had no idea what a tempest he would unleash. The universal media reaction was that it was a putsch and that there was a constitutional crisis that threatened the rule of law and democratic institutions.

Early polls indicated at least three-to-one support for Cox over Nixon. Nixon should have stood his ground and gone on a public relations campaign in favor of his compromise. There was a torrent of impeachment resolutions; he would have been better to assert, in reasonable tones, that he had negotiated a reasonable settlement and that if the Congress wanted to transpose itself into a cat's paw for a ravingly partisan law professor who had never been elected to anything, it could, but he would not move. Tempers would have cooled down, his enemies would have had their impeachment trial on the wrong issue, and Nixon might have survived.

Instead, in the face of endless comparisons with the Nazis (e.g., from Senator Robert Byrd) and what he called a climate that was "almost hysterical," Nixon backed down. He wrote, "I was taken by surprise by the ferocious intensity of the reaction. For the first time I recognized the depth of the impact Watergate had been having on America. I suddenly realized how deeply its acid had eaten into the nation's grain." It has never been clear why this came as such a revelation to him. Watergate bombshells had been falling like confetti for six months. The media was obsessed with it and it was a legitimate and fascinating, steadily expanding story. And large parts of the Congress were simply a presidential lynch mob. It was not in Nixon's nature to try to charm his enemies, and there would be a serious credibility gap if he tried now. He had to find the highest ground still available and take his stand there.

Bork said that the Justice Department would vigorously pursue the existing Watergate investigation, and he accepted Cox's proposal to extend the grand jury for six months. Nixon met the press for a nationally televised news conference on the evening of October 26. He appeared calm and rested, opened on the Middle East, and handled a wide range of difficult questions very fluently and capably. Even James Reston in the New York Times credited his appearance and command of the facts. He artfully dodged traps that had been set for him, and kept his apparent good humor.

They got to him eventually, however, and he referred to "outrageous, vicious, distorted . . . frantic, hysterical reporting." This was, again, not completely inaccurate in some cases, but not a wise gambit. A few moments later, when asked by a CBS reporter, rather disingenuously, what had the media done "that has so aroused your anger?" he replied, after a little more fencing, "You see, one can only be angry with those he respects."[20] This was an understandable reaction to the relentless attacks on Nixon, but it was not understandable coming from so seasoned a public figure.

He knew that the media is best dealt with by standing up to the hostile ones, answering calmly, keeping cool, maintaining a sense of humor, and rising above it. Many journalists are extremely biased and destructive, but most of them are just doing their jobs like anyone else. A free press is an essential part of democracy and the public expect the press and the leader of the country to treat each other with respect. On this occasion, Nixon snatched a public relations defeat from the jaws of the victory he had won by his intelligent answers to all the substantive questions.

Nixon did promise a new special prosecutor. Bork said that no "reputable" person would take the job without the ability to subpoena the White House. Nixon put up Senator William Saxbe of Ohio as attorney general. He was a very independent Republican, and was assured of confirmation. He would be stronger than Richardson and less prone to allow the special prosecutor to be so obviously partisan as Cox had been, but he would not spare the administration anything. The new special prosecutor, at Haig's suggestion, was Leon Jaworski of Texas, a friend of Lyndon Johnson and John Connally. Nixon was again warned that Haig had got it wrong, that Jaworski was a leftist and would cause all the problems he could.[21]

He could have been scrupulously fair, and in fact was a less obviously antagonistic person than Cox, but now Nixon was further down the well than before. It was agreed Jaworski could only be fired with the approval of the majority and minority leaders and judiciary committee chairmen and ranking members of both houses of the Congress. Nixon might have marginally less abrasive people to deal with than under Cox, but he knew that Jaworski and Ervin, and Sirica and other judges, would now come swarming after the tapes, and there was no chance of any compromise.

Nixon had a pretty good recollection of what was on the tapes, and he knew that it had all been set up that if there was anything on them about Nixon asking the CIA to get in the way of the FBI's investigation of Watergate, or urging the purchase of the silence of witnesses, his political capital would be vaporized. He might have a technical defense against a criminal charge, but he would not be able to govern. He had no room left for anything confrontational: destroying or withholding the tapes, sacking the prosecutor, producing a Stennis-like compromise. He had no ability to do any of it. The media, with Nixon's unintended cooperation, had poisoned the wells. About a quarter of the people still profoundly admired Nixon and would never desert him, but they weren't the most influential people and they were very outnumbered.

In time, the Muriel Spark view that Watergate was like the theft of a thimble in a convent would win adherents. Watergate had resulted in no theft, no injury, no property damage, no useful espionage, and it would be seen in perspective eventually, but not until after the investigators had run out of evidence to adduce that could still embarrass the administration. Nixon had perhaps not committed an impeachable offense. He certainly believed he had not. He had rendered great service as president, but he had allowed a minor problem to become a symbolic issue of great importance. And he had allowed his ability to continue in office to depend on assertions he need not have made, that could be disproved by evidence he was trying to withhold, against the wishes of the courts, and for stated reasons the country did not believe. His fate was almost sealed.

It was an unimaginable state of affairs, but Richard Nixon was an unimaginable character leading an incredible career. And although it appeared that his career might be almost over, that too was not as it seemed, and Richard Nixon's most astonishing achievement might still lie ahead.

Several senators, including James Buckley and African-American Republican Edward Brooke of Massachusetts, the *New York Times, Time* magazine, and finally the excitable Leonard Garment all suggested that Nixon resign, some more politely than others. (Garment was disillusioned because Nixon had claimed to Cox that he had, first, a recording of Dean exculpating him in April, then a dictabelt of his recollections of a conversation with Dean in April, both of which Cox subpoenaed, and finally had said to his own counsel that he had nothing, but since the dictabelt had been subpoenaed, why not make one up now?) The entire Watergate attack was striking at Nixon's most vulnerable point, a lack of probity, and slapdash, sleazy reflexes in secondary matters not involving national security. The underlying problem was that Nixon had always had a rather authoritarian view of law enforcement, that repression was justified to fight subversion; and he had always had a rather cynical view of political mores. At this point, American Puritanism was in the air, the highest office in the American state appeared morally decrepit, and Nixon saw nothing wrong with making up a fake, self-serving dictabelt, ex post facto, to satisfy a subpoena. He wasn't standing on the law and wasn't upholding a recognizable principle in resisting the application of the law. Thus did an apparently trivial matter become a great crisis.

He had not always been like this, but had been through such a rough political career and had been so tormented by unsportsmanlike adversaries, and had such a propensity to feel victimized, not always without reason, that his ethical standards had slipped. They had not disappeared, or even become unprecedentedly bad, but they were inadequate to his position in these times, and now his opponents had found his weakness. Like a trapped, wounded animal, he struggled as his remorseless and, for the most part, not particularly ethically exalted enemies closed in on him. It was a horrible spectacle.

Rabbi Baruch Korff, chairman of what was called the National Citizens' Committee for Fairness to the Presidency, took out a full-page advertisement in the *New York Times* declaring that the media had "scandalized . . . brutalized . . . savaged [Nixon] day after day and night after night, and now they have come to bury him, draped in infamy." Fantastic charges were being hurled back and forth.

Nixon's conduct was blameworthy, but the response to it was extreme. He was the chief, but not the sole, author and victim of the unfolding tragedy.

— IV —

The president spoke to the country about the energy crisis, which had been severely aggravated by the Arab oil boycott, on the evening of November 7. He explained the origins of the problem in almost Rooseveltian Fireside Chat terms. He stated that there had been a looming energy shortage, and that as a result of the Arab embargo, the United States was now two million barrels of oil per day short of its normal needs, or about 10 percent. He pointed out that he had been warning for two years of impending problems and trying to persuade the Congress to act. With commendable irony, he allowed that the "Congress has been distracted in this period by other matters."[22]

Nixon again trotted out his energy plan and added a few domestic flourishes. He called for increased use of coal and nuclear power, reduced commercial aviation flights, a fifty-mile-per-hour speed limit, construction of the Alaska Pipeline, relaxation of some environmental regulations, and car-pooling and turning down thermostats to between sixty-five and sixty-eight degrees. He invoked the Manhattan (atomic) Project and the Apollo

Project (moon exploration) and announced Project Independence, which aimed at making the United States self-sufficient in energy by 1980. At time of writing, he was the last president who took energy problems seriously, as the country became steadily more addicted to energy provided by increasingly unfriendly countries.

Nixon concluded by observing that it was the anniversary of his reelection, and that he was proud that in that year he had extracted the United States from Vietnam, secured the return of the POWs, ended conscription, and reduced unemployment and inflation. He referred to the "deplorable Watergate matter" and debunked any thought of resigning. This was the point that was most publicized the next day. He might have been better off to conduct business as usual and ignore the recent controversy.

He conducted a blitz in the succeeding days, meeting with all congressional Republicans and many of the Southern Democrats, and trying to shore up his position. Many supported him, but many others felt that it was a bit late to be courted by a president who had ignored them and taken all the campaign funds for himself and had not lifted a finger to help them share in his big victory of a year before. Nixon embarked on a speaking tour in the Southern states that was extensively publicized and covered, which he handled well, including a pretty candid question-and-answer session with editors. He told the Associated Press Managing Editors association, in among the most memorable lines of his career, "I am not a crook," responding to a question about his taxes, which the hostile media had whipped into a controversial issue. The line backfired and was so unprecedented a comment by a president of the United States that it became a favorite with late-night television hosts, stand-up comics, and political foes, and has endured, like Marilyn Monroe's sung birthday greetings to President Kennedy, a national American cultural moment.

The problem created by the "I'm not a crook" statement was compounded when he told an audience in Memphis there would be no more bombshells, a day before Buzhardt had to tell Sirica that there was an eighteen-and-a-half-minute gap in the tape of June 20, 1972. Rose Mary Woods had said that she must have taken her foot off the pedal while she reached for something, which led to a good many mirthful jokes about the "Rose Mary stretch," but this was when it was thought that the gap was only five minutes. At over eighteen minutes, new doubts were deluged on the president's credibility.

Sirica called witnesses to explain the gap. It was a sorry performance. Rose Mary Woods gamely did her best, and surmised that she had accidentally pressed the record button while speaking on the telephone, but thought she had only spoken for five minutes. Alexander Haig joked somewhat chauvinistically, it seemed to some, about women who think they have spoken for five minutes when they have really talked for an hour, and then told Sirica and his court that a "sinister force of energy" had erased the tape. No one has ever discovered what happened to the tape. If the same extent of gaps had been inflicted precisely on other tapes they would have caused Nixon no greater problem and spared him a great deal of difficulty. As it was, this was another public relations setback. "I'm not a crook," the "Rose Mary stretch," and Haig's "sinister force" were not going to get him clear of the problem. Haldeman's notes of the June 20 conversation are fairly innocuous, so a completely benign explanation cannot be ruled out.

Nothing useful had happened in response to his energy address on November 7, partly because he had brought Watergate into it, so Nixon was back on national television on November 25 with a more radical plan of action. He again asked for a reduction of the speed limit to fifty m.p.h., fifty-five for diesel-fueled trucks and buses. He was reducing the flow of gasoline from refiners to retailers by 15 percent and asking all service stations to close voluntarily between 9 P.M. Saturday and midnight Sunday. He cut jet fuel for commercial flights by 25 percent, domestic heating oil by 15 percent, and commercial heating oil by 25 percent, and he was asking Congress for a legislated rollback in commercial lighting. He would set an example by not lighting the White House Christmas tree. It was a sensible program that had teeth in it, and contained something of a spirit of sacrifice. He refused the recommendation of his energy task force chief, former Colorado governor John Love, of gasoline rationing, and Love resigned. But his program was taken seriously. Rationing gasoline would have been a practical and political disaster.

Jerry Ford was installed as vice president in the Capitol on December 6. Nixon presided and was warmly applauded and carried off the ceremony with confidence and dignity. Ford struck exactly the right note in his remarks, declaring himself "a Ford, not a Lincoln." He rejoiced that "our great Republic stands strong upon the bedrock of the Constitution," and made a very favorable impression in his new role.

Nixon issued a comprehensive financial statement as a rebuttal to the financial allegations that had been made against him. He released all his figures and assets, which indicated that he had made $200,000 in a real estate venture with Bebe Rebozo, and had about $430,000 in the bank. There was nothing illegal in his transactions, nor anything as questionable as some of Eisenhower's fiscal planning, much less Lyndon Johnson's. Nixon thoroughly debunked the theory that he had used public money to enhance the value of his homes in San Clemente and Key West. It was not a public relations image-builder that he had paid $5,971 in taxes in the years 1970 to 1972 combined, on income of $794,000. It was completely legal and Americans don't generally resent a person outfoxing the IRS legally, but this was not the message that Nixon needed to send at this time.

William Saxbe was confirmed easily by the Senate as attorney general on December 17, and the House Judiciary Committee retained John M. Doar, a nominal Republican who had served in the Kennedy and Johnson administrations, as special counsel to head the impeachment probe that had been unleashed after the Saturday Night Massacre.

As Christmas approached, Nixon was closely watched at social events to see if he seemed to be showing the strain. Goldwater thought him almost incoherent at a small White House dinner on December 19, and Harlow assured him there was nothing to worry about, as Nixon had only had too much to drink. On December 22, at a business session with the Joint Chiefs, Admiral Elmo Zumwalt thought him overwrought but far from "the haggard, palsied, drunken wreck" social Washington was gleefully talking about.

The Nixons flew to California for the New Year holidays on December 28, on a commercial plane to save energy. Nixon circulated in the economy-class section and was warmly applauded, though his fellow first-class passengers never took their eyes off him.[23] It wasn't a brilliant holiday; the weather was cold, the house was not heated, and there was a good deal of rain. He only got to play golf twice. When Nixon went to the San Clemente Presbyterian Church on January 6, there were hecklers and picketers when he emerged. Gallup reported his popularity at 29 percent, not surprising considering the buffeting he had suffered, though still better than Truman's worst figures.

Nixon was disbelieved by most people, and once his spell was broken, and he no longer had the stature he had enjoyed as an almost magic political operator in his first term, seeming to pull one rabbit after another out of the hat after his opponents thought they had cornered him, his stiffness and predictable phrases and gestures aroused derision. He appeared so unspontaneous he became a comically sinister figure to many. The only way to deal with it was to appear relaxed, be good-humored, and simply weather it. These were not the times, and he was not the man, for the implementation of such a formula. In between purposeful statements of his determination to remain and serve out his term, there were clear signs of moroseness and even depression.

John Wayne came to dinner, and John Connally telephoned on his birthday, January 9, but told him of a conspiracy of Southwestern Republican congressmen to try to force him out as president in the summer. It was probably good intelligence, but an infelicitous birthday greeting.

Nixon had Weinberger release a plan for a federally sponsored backstop system of medical care for all Americans, showing himself once again to be a pioneer in domestic policy, as he had been with welfare reform, revenue sharing, desegregation, the environment, energy, and tax cuts. A great deal more publicity attended his rejection of the Ervin Committee's subpoena of 492 tapes. Nixon gave his usual explanation of defending presidential privacy. He would have done better to hand over all the tapes after the fiasco with Cox, instead of allowing the media to create such a morbid ambition to find the proverbial "smoking gun" that anything slightly hinting of complicity in questionable actions would eliminate his support in the Congress. Once the Circuit Court of Appeals had decided that he had to hand over the tapes, he could not have been in much doubt of how the question would be decided by the Supreme Court. Nixon was living as president on borrowed time.

The oil price had risen nearly 400 percent in a few months, and this was creating chaos in international financial markets and severely affecting many oil-importing countries. The U.S. inflation rate was naturally increasing again and there were recession fears as well. The Democrats in Congress, like Nixon's former energy adviser, wanted to ration gasoline, which Nixon again (correctly) refused to consider. There were lineups at service stations throughout the country and food prices were increasing sharply as well, the result of a freakishly poor wheat crop.

More positively, Henry Kissinger achieved a remarkable and personal feat in negotiating the disengagement of the Egyptian and Israeli armies. This was announced on January 17, and followed a period of what Kissinger called "shuttle diplomacy," as he moved back and forth between Cairo and Jerusalem. Kissinger demonstrated, even more convincingly than he had before, his stamina and subtlety as a negotiator, and gained the trust of both Golda Meir and Anwar Sadat. He had won, with Le Duc Tho, the Nobel Prize for Peace, of which Nixon would have been a worthier recipient, but his efforts in the Middle East were entirely his own initiative. He continued his shuttle diplomacy to try to disengage the Israeli and Syrian armies. (In Indochina, fighting had reverted to pre-armistice levels, but it had been Vietnamized, and the American media didn't much cover it.)

Kissinger responded to the reversals his leader suffered, and to his own promotion as secretary of state, with more frequent public praise of Nixon and a more generous attitude generally, which improved relations between them. This was part of the Kissinger personality too; when the rivalry between them subsided as a result of Nixon's ordeal, a magnanimous side of Kissinger emerged, not unbound, but less inhibited by the requirements of his own ego and ambition. So gifted and ruthless a man was not without his human instincts.

Nixon had appointed James St. Clair of Boston as his chief counsel. St. Clair had been an understudy to Joseph Welch, who had won the great match with Senator Joe McCarthy in the Army-McCarthy hearings. Jaworski was convinced, from listening to tapes that had been handed over, that Nixon was guilty of urging and suborning perjury, that he had committed crimes of obstruction of justice, and that he had to be removed from office. He had reached the point where Cox had left off (which was probably also where Cox started as special prosecutor) after only a few weeks of initiation.

The House Judiciary Committee, chaired by Peter Rodino of New Jersey, made it clear it would be exercising a virtually unlimited power of subpoena. Nixon could stonewall the courts up to a point, but the House of Representatives initiated impeachment proceedings, and could not be just straight-armed. Jaworski told St. Clair he wished to take evidence from the president, and St. Clair told him that was out of the question. John Ehrlichman, who wished to call Nixon as a witness in his trial in California for authorizing the break-in at the office of Daniel Ellsberg's psychoanalyst, received the same answer. This was a contemptible effort by Ehrlichman. Nixon had not asked for or approved a break-in at the office of Ellsberg's psychoanalyst. Those demanding sworn evidence and original documents from Nixon were multiplying and becoming steadily harder to withstand.

Murray Chotiner died on January 30, 1974, as a result of an automobile accident a week earlier. Nixon issued a statement praising him as an ally and friend through the most difficult moments of his career. Chotiner had earned a niche in American history as an agile political tactician, and almost the only significant political influence on one of the most prominent and durable politicians in the country's history.

That evening, Nixon delivered his State of the Union message to the Congress and the nation. He entered the House chamber with a spring in his step, though he had feared hostile demonstrations from congressmen. He began with a recitation of the achievements of his administration, and a contrast of the present relative serenity with the besieged, war-weary and strife-torn condition of the country five years before. He gave his energy proposals another airing and presciently called for energy self-sufficiency, something the United States had enjoyed until recently. When he got to the end of his prepared remarks, he announced that he would conclude with a few extemporaneous words on the "so-called Watergate affair." He effectively said that he would give nothing more to Jaworski, and that he would cooperate with the House Judiciary Committee, which, he recognized, had "a special responsibility" (because of the impeachment hearings), but that he would "never do anything that weakens the office of the President."

This brought a mixed, but not impolite, reception. He made his usual statement of determination to finish his term, which brought to their feet his wife and Julie and David and Haig in the gallery, and a good number of Republican stalwarts and some Southern Democrats, nodding and clapping, but left the Democratic majority as still and unenthused as gargoyles. He had drawn the battle lines, but his opponents had the constitutional forces, the better part of the legal argument, the regicidal lust of most of the national media, and ultimately, as much as they needed of the facts.

In the tense circumstances, as the various investigators and prosecutors prepared for the legal battles over the tapes and the trials of some of his former subordinates, Nixon abandoned the solitude he had sought for his second term. He embarked on a vigorous schedule of public appearances, from the peculiar American institution of the prayer breakfast to the peculiar American institution of "Honor America Day," when he addressed twenty thousand people in Huntsville, Alabama, accompanied by Governor George Wallace. He elaborated on his universal Medicare proposal in an address at Cedars of Lebanon Hospital in Miami, where there were competing pro- and anti-Nixon demonstrators. He easily made himself heard and dealt effectively with the hecklers.

On February 25, Nixon held another nationally televised press conference. He opened with a prepared statement on the energy crisis and the Middle East, linking the two together with a prediction that Kissinger would produce a disengagement agreement between Israel and Syria and that the Arab oil boycott would then end. He warned the Arabs that the United States would not be "blackmailed." He handled the Watergate questions skillfully and without a hint of loss or shortness of temper.

At his medical checkup the same day, Nixon's doctors pronounced him in excellent condition, though they wished that he would get a little more sun and sleep.

The comparative tranquility of February was broken by the clash of battle on March 1 when the grand jury brought indictments in Sirica's court against Ehrlichman, Haldeman, Colson, Mitchell, Mardian, Strachan, and Kenneth Parkinson (of CREEP) for conspiracy (with others "known and unknown"), suborning perjury, arranging hush money and offering executive clemency, destroying documents, ordering illegal wiretaps, and lying to various investigators. Mitchell and Stans were already accused in New York of violating campaign financing laws.

John Dean was the chief informant against this new group of accused, having pleaded guilty to one charge of conspiracy, accepted a soft sentence, and ratted out his former colleagues. Connally was being scrutinized by a grand jury in Texas over the relationship between contributions from, and preferments to, milk producers. (He was ultimately tried and acquitted.)

Nixon held another news conference on March 5 to deal specifically with the implications of these charges. He gave an extensive explanation of the March 21 conversation with Dean, but one that was at some variance with what the tape of the conversation would reveal. Nixon acknowledged that listening to the tape could produce "different interpretations, but I know what I meant and I know also what I did."[24] Hunt was paid, but while it is probable, it is not clear, that Nixon knew this was for altered testimony, though his detractors have created an ironclad historical consensus that that was his clear meaning. It is clear that he did not approve promises of clemency in exchange for a line of testimony, and said that doing so would be "wrong."

At the news conference he said that he "never at any time authorized the payment of money to any of the defendants," and that it was determined that the best policy was one of "full disclosure." An objective audit of the tape does not sustain those assertions. The president was not under oath when talking to a press conference, but the country was listening and he must have known that if there was too great a gap between his emphatic statements of innocence and the ambiguity of the tape, he would suffer terrible damage in public and congressional opinion if the tape was released. He presumably, then, still believed that the tape would not be released, though how he could have believed that is a mystery.

The following day, March 6, Nixon sent Haig a memo saying that "the law case will follow the p.r. case. St. Clair sees it too much as a trial, not a public relations exercise."[25] He was correct, but he was tightening the rope around his neck, unless he assumed either that he would not have to hand over the tapes, either by judicial decision or by withholding them whatever the Supreme Court said.

The House Judiciary Committee left little doubt of the malevolent intent of the Democratic majority when, in mid-March, Rodino revealed that the impeachment inquiry was examining domestic surveillance and wiretapping and other "intelligence activities"; campaign dirty tricks; partisan misuse of government agencies; Nixon's finances; the secret bombing of Cambodia; and the impoundment of congressionally voted funds.

This was such an exercise in partisan hypocrisy, the committee did leave Nixon some room to challenge its seriousness. There was no evidence connecting Nixon to any domestic intelligence activities except some wiretaps, which, though possibly unethical, had a legitimate national security cover. Pursuing these would require impugning Kissinger and would invite examination of the less justifiable acts of Johnson, the Kennedys, and Roosevelt. There was no evidence connecting Nixon to campaign "dirty tricks," and these had a long history in the United States and had never been judged a potentially impeachable offense before. The same could be said of partisan direction of government agencies. Several of his Democratic predecessors had been much more egregious in these areas than Nixon, and as chief executive, he had some prerogative to direct them as he wished. He was clean on his finances, unlike Johnson, and a good deal cleaner than Eisenhower, and had broken no laws in this area. This was just a smear job.

As commander in chief, he had the authority to bomb Cambodia, which the Congress had funded for eight years. The reference to impoundment was nonsensical. Rodino and his Democratic colleagues were going beyond a partisan attack on the president; they were trying a partial coup d'état by stripping the presidency of much of its authority and upsetting the constitutional balance between the three co-equal branches of government.

All sides were now dipping their hands in the blood of national tragedy. Members of the administration had committed crimes. The complicity of the president in obstruction of justice was a matter of legitimate suspicion, bordering on high likelihood. Even if it could not fairly be proved beyond a reasonable doubt, and whether it was in these circumstances a constitutionally impeachable "high crime or misdemeanor" or not, it was an irresponsible and disgraceful derogation from his duty that he tainted his office with such conduct. His lapse was perhaps mitigated somewhat by his apparent absence of criminal intent and by his reasonably benign motives of loyalty to subordinates, but it was still, and at the least, reprehensible.

Few representatives of the television networks and leading publications did not join, often with undisguised and sanctimonious glee, in the pursuit of the president, once his shifty and bizarre behavior facilitated it.

The Congress, led by its Democratic majority, but with an indecent sprinkling of opportunistic Republican fellow-travelers, aggregated the assault on Nixon into the rape of the executive, the enthronement of the party that had been routed in the presidential election a year before, and the temporary reformulation of the constitutional balance of power between the executive and legislative branches.

Evaluating the performance of the courts would require a very long analysis of legal minutiae. It is not so clear that the courts were on good legal ground requiring production of Nixon's tapes, given Fifth Amendment rights of due process, and ambiguous precedents. But in general, the judiciary seems to have been the guardian of the rule of law, after the other two branches had failed or compromised it, and the media had whipped public opinion (doubtless including, to some immeasurable extent, judicial opinion) into a moralistic frenzy. Few of the main participants would emerge from this awful drama with much credit: the president's family, Gerald Ford, Haig,

Kissinger, Buchanan, Sirica, and most of the judges, but very few members of the Congress. No interest and few involved individuals revisit this awful chapter in American history with clean hands.

— v —

Part of Nixon's strategy, and in all respects probably the best part, was to be a constant source of intelligent policy initiatives. On the heels of his championship of revenue sharing on a scale that he grandiloquently described as "The New Federalism," his founding of the Environmental Protection Agency, his universal health-care proposal, and his advocacy of energy self-sufficiency, Nixon presented himself, somewhat improbably, as the nation's chief proponent of campaign financing reform.

On March 8, in a national radio address, he proposed an imaginative package of reforms, including shorter campaigns, with summer primaries and conventions in September; a legal prohibition on designated dirty tricks; the requirement that all contributions above fifty dollars be by check; and caps on individual contributions of three thousand dollars for congressional candidates and fifteen thousand dollars for presidential candidates. Nixon did reject public financing of election campaigns, as "taxation without representation," because it would use the public's money for the support of candidates regardless of the public's wishes. The Republicans gave Nixon's proposals a rougher ride than the Democrats, but as usual, nothing except elevated verbosity resulted. As with Medicare and energy (but unlike welfare reform and tax reductions) more than thirty years later, despite much posturing by presidents and Congresses of both parties, little progress had been made.

Henry Kissinger achieved remarkable success in his prolonged visit to the Middle East. The Arab oil embargo was unconditionally lifted on March 18. Egypt and the United States formally reopened full diplomatic relations after a lapse of seven years and nearly a decade of frosty relations before that. Nixon had provided some guidelines and agreed with what his secretary of state was doing, and intervened usefully in the Israeli-Syrian talks, but the credit for these developments, and for the Syrian-Israeli disengagement that followed, on May 29, after more than a month of intensive effort, belongs to Kissinger. Together, and with Anwar Sadat, Nixon and Kissinger had virtually bundled the Soviet Union out of the Middle East. It was a remarkable success, and a harbinger of what was possible now that the United States was free of Vietnam, if Watergate did not make a durable shambles of the administration.

Nixon took to the road in mid-March, to Chicago; to Nashville, where he dedicated an extension of the Grand Ole Opry and played several songs on the piano, including "Happy Birthday" for his wife; and to Houston, where he spoke to the National Association of Broadcasters. At the question-and-answer session in Houston, Nixon fully held his own with Dan Rather of CBS, generally reckoned the most antagonistic of Nixon's interviewers, and the next day was well received at the Johnson Space Center. In Chicago, there had been some competing pickets, for and against the president, but Nixon had no difficulty winning the day with such crowds. The Southern crowds were friendly, and it was a gallant performance.

But he continued to refuse demands for tapes and documents from Jaworski, Rodino's Committee, and the courts. Republican Senate Leader Hugh Scott warned him that continued refusal to respond to Rodino's subpoenas would lead to a citation for contempt of the Congress and would in itself be a ground for impeachment. Other leading Republican senators, including Howard Baker, urged him to hand over the tapes.

Nixon obviously knew that the tapes would be embarrassing, and potentially lethal, if released, but he believed they would exonerate him in a fair judicial trial, so he kept endlessly stating that he was protecting the presidency, and kept repeating that Jaworski had said he already had all he needed, even as Jaworski subpoenaed him for more tapes and documents. It was natural that the press and most of the public assumed that if the tapes really would clear him, as he had claimed, Nixon would release them, with whatever contemporaneous gestures he wanted to take to show that he was not setting a precedent. By digging his heels in on this issue, he assured that any "ambiguity" on the tapes would be fatal to him. And there was plenty of "ambiguity."

As it was, there were endless damaging leaks, amplified by the press and denied by Ziegler, but Ziegler had made too many "inoperative" statements, and few people believed him. Nixon gave an impressive speech on Vietnam Veterans' Day, March 29, at Fort McNair in Washington, D.C. He was now advocating an elaborate and imaginative domestic program, which included supplementary grants to facilitate access to higher education by financially disadvantaged people, and heavy emphasis on mass-transit improvement, including the country's dilapidated railways, as part of his response to the energy crisis.

He continued to push for universal private health care, energy self-sufficiency, welfare and campaign financing reform, and lower taxes. In many of these areas, Nixon was absolutely sound and far ahead of his time, but the media and the country considered anything he did a mere distraction from the real issue of Watergate. Liberals had their chance to enact many reforms they had sought and would long claim to espouse. They preferred to destroy Richard Nixon. Their chance as reformers would not come again. Conservative Republicans would reduce taxes and enact welfare reform.

Conservatives, including conservative Democrats, feared that Nixon would try to distract the country with foreign policy extravaganzas. George Meany, referring to the fact that Kissinger was now in Moscow, said on April 2 that he prayed "every night that Henry Kissinger won't give the Russians the Washington Monument – he's given them every God-damn thing else."[26]

In early April 1974, the Internal Revenue Service determined that Nixon owed $432,787 in unpaid taxes. This was a political assault, and it was made more irritating to Nixon by a campaign of leaks out of the IRS insinuating he was a tax cheat, though there was no suggestion of evasion or a false tax return. Further, though the deduction for his vice presidential papers was disallowed, the National Archives kept the papers. This was outrageous mistreatment of Nixon, but he paid the assessed tax and did not contest the ownership of the papers.

French president George Pompidou died on April 2, and Nixon attended his funeral on April 5. He remained in Paris for three days, meeting with other world leaders who attended the funeral, which replicated the memorial service for de Gaulle in the same place (Notre Dame Cathedral). Despite his domestic problems, Nixon was evidently respected in the world and was by far the most eminent figure in Paris. All those with whom he met expressed admiration for his grasp of all subjects discussed and his apparent imperviousness to political controversy. Even Canada's Prime Minister Pierre Elliott Trudeau, a social democrat and very balky NATO member with long-standing anti-American tendencies, said Nixon had great presence and stature and was very widely respected by other national leaders. The puritanical spirit of America had been roused against him and regarded any positive evidence of Nixon's competence as a statesman as a diabolical trumpery designed to throw the righteous off the trail of justice.

On returning to the United States, Nixon continued to travel around the country, pulling large and friendly crowds. He was unsuccessful in trying to help a Republican candidate in a special congressional election in Michigan, but this period of tireless physical activity and one of the greatest reform legislative programs presented in the country's history, surpassed in scale (and not in soundness of policy) only by FDR and LBJ, remains a tour de force of Nixon's iron determination and perseverance. The lessons learned with Chief Newman at Whittier were applied again.

The House Judiciary voted the subpoena of forty-two tapes and required a response by April 25, when St. Clair had assured the committee that his client would provide what was needed, without specifying what it would be. Nixon preferred to stonewall, but Buzhardt and St. Clair told him that was impossible. He would be impeached for contempt of Congress and of the courts (Sirica had issued a subpoena at Jaworski's request for sixty-four more tapes, on April 18). Nixon was rather contemptuous of the Congress and was not convinced that he would actually be removed from office by the Senate if he followed this route.

Buzhardt and St. Clair, having a more roseate view than was justified of what the tapes would reveal (not having any direct knowledge of their contents), told Nixon he had to seek an accommodation. It was agreed to hand over transcripts, with deletions of irrelevant, unintelligible, or coarse material. The expression *expletive deleted* entered the language and became instantly notorious. The man who had scolded President Truman for telling opponents to "Go to hell" in 1960 scandalized some of his straight-laced followers with the frequency of blasphemies and recourse to scatological vulgarity. Nixon was not as crude, but nowhere near as original or amusing, in his vulgarity as Lyndon Johnson had been. He was a good deal less prone to this sort of language than Truman, Eisenhower, or Kennedy also. In fact he was relatively prim, not referring to sexual intercourse or female body parts. These were routine comments, and absurd prudishness was shown in deleting any reference to God or "damn" or "hell" or elemental bodily functions. The result was a tremendous sequence of such announced deletions that made Nixon seem like a foul-mouthed fishmonger spewing forth billingsgate. He claimed to be concerned that if his mother had heard him, she would be horrified. (If Hannah Nixon's spirit were then conscient, she would know of Richard's un-Quakerish language, whatever was deleted.)

On April 28, Mitchell and Stans were acquitted on the campaign financing charges, implying that Dean's testimony was not credible. The next evening, Nixon spoke to the country, with twelve hundred pages of tape transcripts in folders on his desk. He said he was handing over some conversations that had not been requested, and was providing the full record, which would establish his truthfulness once and for all. He gave his version of the March 21 conversation ("cancer on the presidency" and the money for Hunt) and claimed that "I did not intend the further payment to Hunt or anyone be made." Implicit in Nixon's remarks was the fact that he was again trying to stop the endless demands for more information. Rodino and the ranking House Judiciary Republican (Edward Hutchinson) could come to the White House to verify the tapes. In his peroration, he quoted Lincoln. It was a solid performance.

John Dean accused the president of misrepresentation the following day, and John Doar claimed that Nixon had altered the tapes. The Judiciary Committee voted on almost straight partisan lines, 20-18, that Nixon had not complied with their subpoena. He could have held the line on this if it were the only problem. The House might vote impeachment on straight party lines, but the Senate would not provide a two-thirds majority for conviction on any such basis.

There was an absence of a smoking gun, and while large tracts of the transcripts were published, and read avidly, and many were shocked at Nixon's rages, dislike of many people, cynicism, and vulgarity, he had not apparently lost much ground to the impeachers. But his enemies now attacked on a new line: Nixon was morally inadequate to his office. Hugh Scott called the tapes "deplorable, disgusting, shabby, immoral." Even Bill Safire defected and described the tapes as "sleazy." Eric Sevareid called them "a moral indictment without known precedent." The country was inundated with unction and sanctimony. The tapes and transcripts were frequently unedifying, but that is not a "high crime or misdemeanor." No one could have imagined that LBJ's raucous and extreme outbursts of vulgarity would have sat well with Washington, Jefferson, or Lincoln. But this was just another aspect of the great smear: not having found a club to beat the president with in the matters under investigation, even his own supporters, in a country where the civil tort of defamation was about to be abolished and pornography was deemed virtually not to exist, shrieked with outrage at the low moral tone of the president's private conversations. It was another her-niating levitation of pandemic hypocrisy.

Nixon's latest tactical problem was that those who tended to be most loyal to him were those who were most affronted by the contents of the transcripts. While they were widely republished in the press, the most salacious excerpts were naturally highlighted, and the long hours of nondescript conversation were passed over. The impression was sewn and fertilized that Nixon was morally unsuitable to his office and was a moral embarrassment, not by his conduct but by his foul mouth and naughty thoughts. It was like child Richard being disapproved by Hannah and thrashed by Frank. But it was pseudo-pious drivel.

Polls indicated that two Americans of three did not agree with Nixon about what the transcripts showed, and the partisans of impeachment had now reached 58 percent. If this were the high-water mark, he could still have survived it, but with an unprecedentedly wounded presidency at the end of it. And there was every reason to believe that the momentum of events had not stopped.

On May 5, Jaworski offered Haig a deal: the grand jury had named Nixon as an unindicted co-conspirator, but Jaworski was prepared to suppress that and reduce his demand from sixty-four to eighteen tapes. This was outright blackmail by the special prosecutor, but Nixon was inclined to accept it. It would at least be the end of the demands for tapes and materials.

Haig urged acceptance, St. Clair feared a Jaworski double-cross. Jaworski shortly told Connally, who passed it on to Nixon, that the president has "no friends in the White House."[27] Nixon listened to the tapes before making his own decision. It is alleged, but is not certainly confirmed, that when he got to the June 23, 1972, tape with Haldeman, he decided that it was time to stonewall. This was the last crossing of the last Rubicon. The Supreme Court was certain to decide in favor of Jaworski, and if he decided to ignore a Supreme Court order, he was certain to be removed from office. Having got this far, he would have been better off to hand over the eighteen tapes and try to put the best spin he could on the one from June 23.

Nixon pushed his universal health-care proposals, though no one was listening. The economic news was very unfavorable, though he dismissed it as aberrant: because of the oil-price spike, an inflation rate in the first quarter of 1974 of over 14 percent, and an absolute decline in the GDP. The country was not listening, though the fact that he had not said anything incriminating in the hours of transcripts that he had handed over was gradually sinking in, despite the pious handwringing of many commentators. Dwight Chapin was sentenced by Judge Gerhard Gesell, whom the Nixon White House had first encountered in the Ellsberg fiasco, to ten to thirty months in prison. Nixon wrote him a very gracious letter, promising Chapin the prayers of the White House staff.[28]

Nixon was holding his own, but it was all now coming down to the June 23 tape. The final crisis was going to be resolved by the Supreme Court's decision on whether he had to hand it over. After so much foreplay, the puritanically reinvigorated American public would not be easily hosed down. Nixon stonewalled Jaworski, Rodino, and Sirica. In its peculiar way, it was rather impressive. There was something deeply annoying about Nixon's psychopathic enemies and a D.C. federal judge insisting on trying to hoist Nixon on his own petard. Nixon was discouraged by the fact that the Ervin Committee had very damaging evidence on the campaign financing techniques of Lyndon Johnson, Hubert Humphrey, and many of the Democratic members of the House Judiciary Committee, and, apart from a few leaks, wasn't doing anything with it.

Nixon's plucky and generally very popular daughter, Julie Eisenhower, had gone out speaking in support of her father. She invariably made a very good impression, and even Norman Mailer acknowledged that his demonized view of Nixon did not allow for loyal and attractive daughters.

As the moral disillusionment with the revealed tapes started to wear off, Nixon announced that he would be traveling in mid-June to Egypt, Syria, Jordan, Saudi Arabia, and Israel.

In early June, Judge Gesell arose again in Nixon's life. Ehrlichman and his lawyer were demanding access to Ehrlichman's notes of his meetings with Nixon, to use in his trial. St. Clair had advised Gesell that a compromise might be in the offing, but Nixon still favored complete non-cooperation. In the face of St. Clair's placatory noises, Nixon agreed to hand over those items that he thought were relevant to Ehrlichman's trial.

On June 9, Nixon spoke at Rabbi Baruch Korff's dinner, the ultimate pep rally of Nixon's last-ditch, dyed-in-the-wool, suicide-squad defenders. Only Earl Butz of the cabinet members and Carl Curtis of Nebraska, among the Republican senators, came to it, but Nixon gave the war cry of final resistance to his most determined followers. Nixon's main point at such moments was his undoubtedly sincere and probably accurate belief that world peace depended on a "strong American presidency." There was certainly an element of completely self-serving hokum in his claimed defense of the presidency and its prerogatives, but Nixon was absolutely right that if the liberal Democrats were able to storm the crenellated walls of the presidential jurisdiction, they would take over foreign policy as well as social policy, and the president would be a constitutional eunuch in continual fear of the criminalization of policy or even personality differences, if he strayed from the straight and narrow laid down by congressional leaders.

This proved intermittently prophetic in the twenty-five years following Nixon, as the presidency was an enfeebled office for six years, revitalized somewhat by Reagan's inspirational qualities and control of the Senate, reduced again with the controversy about Iran and the Nicaraguan Contras, and then with the unjustified impeachment of President Clinton, largely over sexual peccadilloes.

Nixon knew that he was now down to about two months before the Supreme Court decided the issue of the tapes. If it upheld the lower courts on a split decision, Nixon could claim there was not a "definitive" judgment of the Supreme Court, and try to maintain his stonewall, or release the tapes and have one more try at reconciling his version of events with the apparent meaning of the tapes, or he could resign. He was determined to do the best he could for as long as he could, but seems to have pretty well recognized how heavily the odds were now stacked against him.

The trip to the Middle East gave Nixon the opportunity to demonstrate that he and not Kissinger was in charge of foreign policy, and that he was an esteemed leader in the world. Kissinger's status was also altered by the first unpleasant controversy of his career, which he did not relish. He had been jauntily backgrounding many of the president's most acidulous enemies in the press, and suddenly found himself under attack for his role in the 1969–1971 wiretapping of reporters and his own NSC staff. The *New York Times* had run an editorial accusing Kissinger, in effect, of lying and suggesting that he might be a good candidate for prosecution.

The presidential party stopped at Salzburg, Austria, so they could break the jet lag. Nixon had phlebitis in his left leg and had been advised by his doctor to keep off his feet as much as possible, and wrap it in towels several times a day. Nixon did not pay much attention to this advice, which caused subsequent psycho-biographers, who have swarmed around Nixon like bees around lavender, to claim he had a death wish. If he had had any such ambition, he could have made it happen without an overtly suicidal act. All evidence is that Nixon was preparing for the supreme challenge of his life and career; he might be hounded from the presidency, but he would not be broken as a man.

He had been counted out before, though not as thoroughly or spectacularly as he would be if forced to give up the White House, and he would soon be thinking of the greatest comeback of all. If he had a subconscious drive, it was not a death wish, it was a wish for a flirtation with, and possibly the occurrence of, disaster, and then a breathtaking recovery. This was the pattern of his life, and it is much rarer than traditional rises and falls in prominent careers.

Ignoring Nixon's advice that "A *Times* editorial isn't a charge," Kissinger came steaming off the airplane in Salzburg and threatened to resign as secretary of state if his integrity was going to be impugned. He denied that he had anything to do with the wiretaps, certainly as unambiguous a lie as any that Nixon had inflicted on his Watergate listeners, and said that he would not "leave to history a discussion of my public honor."[29] Kissinger said he was "shattered" by the unkind press and found Nixon's reassertion of himself in the Middle East "disconcerting, even painful." His threat to resign at Salzburg, though it was widely thought to be excessive and histrionic, cooled out the criticism of Kissinger. The national press were not prepared to be distracted from their pursuit of Nixon, and the unspoken plan was to leave Kissinger not only as the catchment for the credit for all the achievements of the Nixon-Kissinger foreign policy, but as the stable continuator of that policy in the eyes of the world.

Nixon and his party arrived in Cairo on June 12, and he and Sadat stood in the back of an open car, something American presidents had not done since the assassination of John F. Kennedy (but Sadat, who was himself assassinated in Cairo seven years later, guaranteed that there would be no safety problem). They drove through wildly cheering crowds, totaling more than a million people, on their way to the presidential palace. It was a spontaneous crowd and demonstrated the desire of Egyptians for peace, and to have good relations with the West again and not dependent be on the Russians for assistance and for international allies. Nixon, buoyed by the mighty welcome, ignored his phlebitis, his doctor's advice, and the heat of over a hundred degrees Fahrenheit, and responded to the cheers of the crowd. Whatever his countrymen thought of him, in the premier Arab country, with which the United States had had no relations for many years, Richard Nixon was welcomed as a peacemaker.

The talks between Nixon and Sadat were very satisfactory. Nixon was impressed by Sadat's reasonableness, and they enjoyed a few shared disparagements of the Russians. Sadat said he expelled the Russians because he "just gave up on them."* [30] Sadat did not rail against Israel but emphasized the need for rights for the Palestinians, the restoration of most of the occupied territory, and some new status for Jerusalem. On June 13, they went in an open railway carriage to Alexandria, and as many as six million people greeted and cheered them as they passed. The two presidents held a press conference, at which Nixon said that peace would have to be approached on a step-by-step basis. The era of an imposed settlement by the two superpowers, Nixon's proposal of just nine months before, was over. Russia no longer brought enough to the party for that. Sadat did not foresee direct discussions between Egypt and Israel, "not yet."

On June 14, Nixon and Sadat agreed a widespread series of secondary accords strongly revitalizing Egyptian-U.S. relations. Nixon was generally elated at the reception he was being given, but he knew that domestic matters were closing grimly in on him almost every day.

Nixon and his party went on to Jidda, Saudi Arabia, where King Faisal emphasized the need for the return of the Israeli-occupied territories, a new status for Jerusalem, and a homeland for the Palestinians. Nixon urged Faisal to strengthen King Hussein's hand as a possible returned champion of the Palestinians. Faisal was lukewarm about this, but more positive when he told Nixon he would try to reduce the world oil price.

Nixon went to Damascus to restore relations with the Syrian president, Hafez al Assad, a brutal but cunning and rather engaging man. He had violently attacked Nixon as a lickspittle of the Zionists and was Russia's only remaining supporter in the region, but he, too, sought a normalized relationship with Washington, and this was agreed within a few hours of Nixon's arrival in Damascus. Assad was opposed to a separate Egyptian-Israeli peace and peppered Nixon with questions about what precise steps he had in mind

---

* Gromyko, for his part, asserted to Kissinger that Sadat was a "paper camel." (Told to the author by Henry Kissinger.)

in his graduated approach to peace. Nixon kept it quite vague. Nixon was impressed with both Sadat and Assad, and thought Assad an uncommonly quick and intelligent leader.

Nixon went on to Israel, where there was less official enthusiasm for the peace process than there had been in the Arab countries. His reception in Israel was cool, despite the huge assistance he had given the country in the Yom Kippur war the year before. As he drove from the airport, the crowds were sparser and less enthusiastic than they had been in the Arab countries, and as Israelis were better informed about American politics, there was no shortage of irritating Watergate signs.

Golda Meir had retired as prime minister in favor of Yitzhak Rabin. At the dinner tendered to him, Nixon went to unusual lengths to praise Golda Meir, who felt moved to respond to him as "a great American president."[31] Nixon met with Rabin and told him that the United States would no longer give Israel a blank check. Whether Rabin believed him or not, the stock Israeli response, after thirteen years of everything they wanted instantly provided, was to call the bluff. It wasn't, as it never was with Nixon, a bluff.

Nixon went from Israel to Jordan and had a very positive meeting with Jordan's astounding survivor, King Hussein. Nixon told him that the United States now considered him, Hussein, the key to finding a settlement that would satisfy the Palestinians. This had been the first visit of an American president to all the major countries of the Middle East, and was a harbinger of what was to come as American efforts to promote progress to peace in the region continued intermittently under presidents of both parties for decades.

Nixon returned to Washington on June 19 and went the next day to Camp David. His phlebitis was aggravated by the strain and heat of the trip, and his wife and his daughter Julie, who had been virtually barnstorming the country, were exhausted too. The president's medical condition was revealed on June 24 by Dan Rather of CBS, and the theory of a possible suicide exit was openly spoken of in the national media.

Watergate was approaching its climax. On June 21, Gesell sentenced Colson to from one to three years and a five-thousand-dollar fine for obstruction of justice in the Ellsberg affair. Colson, who, true to character, had been the most militant defender of the Nixon reelection effort, had suddenly had a religious conversion and claimed to be as able to "serve the Lord" in prison or out. There was some evidence that Colson would be saying things useful to the prosecution of others, including Nixon. The various committees and courts were continuing to subpoena for more tapes and materials and the White House routinely issued statements reiterating its refusal to denude the presidency of its privacy and constitutional position. Doar had completed a six-week summary of evidence that had been adduced by the Watergate Committee. One of Nixon's friends on the committee, Joe Waggoner, a Louisiana Democrat, said he thought it would be close on the committee, but that no such vote would pass the full house unless Nixon were in contempt of the Supreme Court.

The Supreme Court was expected to be heard from in about a month. In the meantime, Nixon would be in Russia and would continue to be as visibly undaunted by the endless Watergate preoccupations as possible.

— VI —

The outlook for the trip to the Soviet Union was unpromising. It was difficult enough to negotiate with the Russians at the best of times. These were the worst of times. Apart from the endless Watergate publicity, which almost no foreigners could understand, the liberal Democrats and the conservatives of both parties were concerned that Nixon might try to salvage some political gain for himself by making even an unfavorable agreement with the Soviet leaders. Senator Henry Jackson was demanding more Jewish emigration from the U.S.S.R., even though it had increased a hundredfold. Defense Secretary Schlesinger did not want a MIRV agreement, because he thought the United States would be giving away more than it achieved. He wanted to limit the number of MIRVed missiles, but not the number of warheads. There was no possibility the Russians would agree to that, though they did want their own version of a MIRV agreement and also a Threshold Test Ban treaty, limiting non-atmospheric testing. Admiral Elmo Zumwalt, chief of naval operations, always had a tendency to insubordination and was a strenuous opponent of even a Threshold Test Ban agreement. The American public agreed with sensible arms control in principle, but U.S. opinion was now completely distracted. Gaining any sort of domestic consensus to support any agreement beyond tokenistic cultural or meteorological or space cooperation protocols would be a challenge.

Nixon and his party left for Moscow on June 25, stopping first in Brussels for the twenty-fifth anniversary of NATO. Nixon made a determined effort to show no sign of phlebitis and to be as relaxed as possible. He mingled with crowds, and was entirely affable. Watergate was not mentioned, but, as Kissinger wrote, he was accorded "the solicitude shown to terminally ill patients."[32]

Nixon arrived in Moscow on June 27 and received the grandest and most ceremonious welcome the Kremlin could lay on. At the end of the red carpet were Brezhnev, President Podgorny, Premier Kosygin, Foreign Minister Gromyko, and Ambassador Dobrynin. There were cheering crowds, addresses of welcome, a motorcade to the Kremlin, and a state dinner in the Grand Kremlin Palace. In his toast, Nixon recounted all the agreements that had been reached between the two countries in the last two years, and ascribed this progress to the personal relationship that had developed between Brezhnev and himself. Their relations were cordial, but observers from both countries considered this a rather obvious claim for indispensability.

Nixon wrote that Kissinger was "depressed" because of the wiretapping allegations, while Kissinger attributed the same condition to Nixon because of the relentless and looming Watergate climax. They were probably both correct.[33]

Nixon and Kissinger kicked around the idea of a comprehensive test ban, but Nixon felt that this was another subject that would have to be pursued step by step; since it offered no decisive breakthrough, the subject lapsed. The next day the conference moved to Yalta. Brezhnev and Nixon met for an hour alone in a lookout with a fine view of the Black Sea. (They were only a few miles from where Roosevelt and Stalin and Churchill had met in 1945.) Brezhnev's latest idea was a mutual defense pact, which Nixon treated cautiously because he saw it as obviously directed at China. Nixon asked for something more on emigration, so he could see off Jackson. He warned Brezhnev that if détente failed in the United States, the hawks would be in the ascendant, an accurate warning whose significance Brezhnev would forget. Brezhnev swore again that he had tried to do everything he could to restrain the Egyptians and Syrians in the autumn of 1973.

They went for a convivial boat ride, and danced around the issue of MIRVs, but apart from the usual small agreements and a very pleasant atmosphere, there was no breakthrough. Nixon's domestic enemies, who had been on the edges of their chairs, about to proclaim that he had sacrificed national security for personal political gain, now slumped back in their chairs and expressed disappointment that Nixon was coming home almost empty-handed.

Nixon returned to the United States on July 3 and was graciously welcomed home by the vice president at Limestone, Maine, where his plane refueled. Armed forces families cheered him, and he flew on to Key Biscayne for the holiday weekend.

Nixon now braced himself for the ultimate crisis. There would be no more uplifting foreign visits. He would await the Supreme Court. He had, he wrote, "a sinking feeling" in his stomach and was prone to severe sleeplessness. Whatever happened, though he had committed both ethical and tactical errors, he had fought bravely and energetically in circumstances that would have defeated or killed the great majority of people. And his family had slogged along with him: Pat, strong, supportive, and uncomplaining; Julie, whom everyone liked, out speaking for her father. Tricia was less of a public person but was fully supportive within the family and was shamefully jeered by Eastern Airlines employees as the president's daughter when she traveled on the shuttle between New York and Washington.[34]

James St. Clair argued Nixon's case before the Supreme Court starting on July 8. He claimed an absolute immunity for the president in responding to demands for his own tapes and documents. Jaworski replied that such immunity could not be claimed in criminal matters; otherwise, the president would be able to suppress evidence of crimes, and any president could commit certain crimes with impunity.

This was a telling argument, but all there was was the allegation of crimes. Where the immunity existed in civil cases, as Truman demonstrated in the Hiss case, all the president's accusers had to do was allege crimes to strip the president of executive privilege. (Hiss was convicted of perjury, but that had nothing to do with the challenge to executive privilege.) Virtually the only evidence against Nixon even at this advanced point was from John Dean, who never should have been allowed to breach lawyer-client privilege as the president's counsel and testify against Nixon, and wasn't very credible anyway. These were knotty problems, but the crisis had to end, and unless Nixon could prove his innocence, any further ambiguity was apt to be hailed as the long-sought smoking gun, just to be done with him and conclude the unbearable crisis and tension. This was the problem of a political, rather than a judicial, trial.

On July 9, the Judiciary Committee released its own versions of eight Nixon transcripts, exposing significant differences between the Nixon and reaudited versions. Doar's four thousand pages of evidence were released, and in the manner of sensational accumulations of opinions from a hostile perspective, they were another public relations jolt for the beleaguered president. St. Clair's direct confrontation with Dean at the Judiciary Committee didn't yield a victory for Nixon's counsel. Dean stood his ground and it was an unedifying standoff, though St. Clair's impugning of Dean's motives should have been effective before a less partisan committee majority.

The Ervin Committee, still gamely contending for its share of the Watergate accusatory publicity, released its report, and Senator Ervin elbowed his way back into contention for headlines by saying that his committee had unearthed such wrongdoing that it called the legitimacy of the 1972 presidential election result into question. This was preposterous. Nothing any of these investigations had produced could have changed more than a few thousand votes in an election Richard Nixon had won, on his record, and almost without campaigning, by 18 million votes.

Polls indicated that the most worrisome problem for the voters was inflation, though trust and corruption in government was a matter of concern to a quarter of the people. Nixon determined to focus on inflation as best he could, and adhere to his policy of doing his job while awaiting escalating events. In his more hopeful moments, he seems to have thought that he would lose at the Supreme Court by 5 to 3, which he could represent as something less than definitive, and then he could "abide by" the verdict, as opposed to obeying it, by handing over more (no doubt lightly bowdlerized, transcripts). It was unutterably humiliating to almost all Americans that the headship of the government was now dangling by such a thin and undistinguished thread.

On July 12, John Ehrlichman was convicted of perjury and civil rights violations against Ellsberg. It was depressingly and bitterly ironic to Nixon that Ehrlichman was about to be imprisoned while Ellsberg, who had violated serious laws, was not only free, but something of a lionized hero. Rabbi Korff released a book of interviews he had done with Nixon, in which Nixon spoke with great and violent emotion of the unjust treatment he and his staff had received, and doubted that any of them could get a fair trial anywhere in the United States. This was probably true and was probably an element in the conviction of Ehrlichman.[35]

Korff printed three hundred thousand copies, and the president's supporters, who, even after all he had been through, were between a quarter and a third of the people, found it the fair and anguished cry from the heart of a leader who had been badly mistreated. Most people, including almost all the press, whom Nixon excoriated in his talks with Korff, found in it more self-pity, obfuscation, evasion, and mealy-mouthed rationalizing. With perspective, the president's supporters' reaction is partly justifiable, but as was often the case with Nixon, especially when he was overwrought, there are a good many artless tirades of self-pity and unsubstantiated allegations against vague groups. The tactics that had served him well when he was one of the more responsible invokers of the Red Scare twenty-five years before were ineffective for his defense now.

On July 19, John Doar threw down the paper-thin mask of impartiality* and made an impassioned speech in favor of the impeachment of the president for his "enormous crimes," in particular "the terrible deed of subverting the constitution." Nixon may have flown off the handle when talking to Korff, but Nixon's enemies were the unchallengeable champions of hyperbole. Even if Nixon may have sanctioned obstructing justice in favor of his followers, it may possibly have been an impeachable offense but did not deserve to be spoken of in terms similar to the atrocities of Hitler and Stalin, and vastly exceeding Jefferson's inflammatory attacks on the supposed despotism of poor old King George III.

Nixon and his enemies both believed they were fighting an assault on the entire American system of government. Nixon went in mid-July to California, and on July 21 was the guest of honor at a sumptuous and glamorous Hollywood dinner hosted by Budget Director Roy Ash in his home, which was formerly owned by comedian W.C. Fields. Rabbi Korff was leading a three-day vigil of prayer and fasting at the Capitol.

The Judiciary Committee was going to hold televised hearings on the impeachment votes starting on July 24. On the 23rd, conservative Republicans and Democrats Nixon had counted on started to peel off. Nixon called Governor Wallace to ask him to lean on one of the Alabama congressmen, but Wallace politely declined to do so. As he hung up from Wallace, Nixon said to Haig, "There goes the presidency." Nixon telephoned his friend Joe Waggoner, who had promised fifty Southern Democrats in the House on a

---

* According to his companion and staff member, the respected author Renate Adler, Doar had advocated Nixon's impeachment well before there was any official thought of it.[36]

full vote, but he now thought he could hold only thirty-five of them, which would send the issue to the Senate for a full trial, but where a two-thirds majority was required.

The biggest and longest-awaited bomb of all fell on the morning of July 24. Chief Justice Burger wrote the decision and reasoned it very fairly and without any gratuitous references to the president. He expressed respect for the principle of executive privilege, but said that it could not be imposed absolutely on criminal cases. The court voted 8 to 0 to require the president to hand over the subpoenaed tapes. (Rehnquist recused as a former employee of the Justice Department.) It was "definitive." Nixon could respond fully, stonewall and be impeached and removed, or resign. He was down to final option selection; there was no room for editing transcripts, deleting "irrelevant" material, "Rose Mary stretches," or any of the other stratagems or misadventures that had so irritated the media and the public already.

Nixon asked Buzhardt to listen to the June 23, 1972, tape, which was the only one that Nixon thought could be a problem. Readers will recall that that was when Haldeman told Nixon of Dean and Mitchell's plan to suggest that the senior officials of the CIA be invited to tell the acting director of the FBI to stay out of the Watergate investigation because it might blow up an intelligence operation and back into the Bay of Pigs fiasco of eleven years before. Nixon had said: "All right . . . fine . . . Good deal. Play it tough . . . Don't lie to them . . . Just say this is sort of a comedy of errors." Buzhardt listened to the tape and called Nixon back and said that this was the "smoking gun"; both Haig and St. Clair thought it was manageable, though neither, unlike Buzhardt, had actually heard it.

As a public and political relations judgment, Buzhardt was almost certainly right. Nixon had repeatedly denied any involvement in or knowledge of a cover-up until March 21, 1973. The fact that he had entertained such an intervention nine months earlier would be very embarrassing. The whole subject had been carefully teased and sculpted by the media so that if there was anything questionable in the tapes, Nixon's destruction would be jubilantly completed. But this was the only matter in all the material involved that was a serious problem. Nixon had approved a plan to suggest that CIA officials be encouraged to make a request of the FBI that would certainly have been an obstruction of justice if it had been a successful intervention and shut down the investigation. Haldeman and Ehrlichman, it will be recalled, met with Helms, and he and Walters declined to make any such request of Gray, so there was no obstruction of justice. From Nixon's standpoint, there was, at worst, acquiescence in a suggested obstruction of justice. This, on its own, could not reasonably be considered as grounds for removing a president from office.

Of course, it wasn't going to be considered on its own. It was the last straw, and when the media and the Democrats (not entirely separate groups) got hold of it, what was left of Nixon's political capital would evaporate. But then there would be the period necessary to put the impeachment votes through and prepare for a Senate trial. Public indignation had subsided after the revelations of the president's unwholesome language in the transcripts. (He would have been better off to release the tapes rather than the transcripts; then the broadcasters would have had to delete the expletives and the country would at least hear that the president's tone of voice was one of concern, and not the imperial overconfidence generally and unfairly imputed to him.)

As when he refused to contest the questionable 1960 election and when he declined to destroy the tapes, now Nixon would not consider giving himself a pardon, would not consider seeking asylum in France, China, Chile, Egypt, or any of the many other countries that would have been happy to accord it to him. And he determined not to put the country through an impeachment trial in the Senate. It may be that his motives were not entirely altruistic, as, had he been removed, he would have lost his pension and any perquisites of an ex-president. Instead, Nixon prepared a statement, promised full compliance, and had one last try at explaining away his regrettable lapse of taste and propriety. St. Clair read Nixon's statement and said that it could take up to a month to break out the subpoenaed tapes and index them and prepare a commentary on them. (Both Richard Helms and Vernon Walters, the director and deputy director of Central Intelligence, told the author that they did not consider what Nixon had said on June 23 justified his removal from office.)

The Judiciary Committee began its impeachment debate on the evening of June 24, naturally before the full glare of television cameras, and with up to forty million American viewers. Nixon's description of the antics of the Democratic members as "demagogic theatrics" was exact. A number of congressmen, including Charles Wiggins from Nixon's old California district, made the point that no specific crime had been alleged and that it wouldn't do just to waffle on about the sanctity of the Constitution. Many of the Democrats recited "We the people . . ." and a few succeeding phrases, and Barbara Jordan, an African American from Texas, led the committee and the country through the progress of her people toward their rights, as if this had anything to do with what they were debating. (Slave-holding was almost the only crime Doar had not alleged against Nixon, the great desegregationist.)

Article I of impeachment alleged that Nixon had "made it his policy" and acted "directly and personally through his close subordinates and agents, to delay, impede, and obstruct the investigation of the [Watergate break-in], to cover up, protect and to conceal the existence and scope of other unlawful covert activities." Even allowing for the usual laborious and righteous overkill of prosecutors, this was a rather extreme rendering of Nixon's conduct. He had authorized Haldeman to waste half an hour of Helms's and Walters's time, and authorized payments to defendants, where it is a reasonable inference that he thought some of the money was going to protect subordinates but not himself, since he had had no direct connection with the Watergate break-in, or the rest of the madcap gambits in Colson's and Segretti's bags of tricks. He and St. Clair had focused on the fact that he had a good legal argument against these charges. What Nixon only realized very late was that a good legal argument wasn't adequate. He needed a spirit of public and political forgiveness, such as subsequent president Bill Clinton benefited from when he was impeached on rather nonsensical sex-related charges.

The South, which owed much to Nixon, especially for liberating it from racial opprobrium while desegregating it as quickly and painlessly as possible, largely abandoned him. Much of the Republican Party, for which he had not done much in the last two years, but to which he had rendered more assistance than any man since Abraham Lincoln, largely abandoned him also. Loyalty is a scarce resource when it is unfashionable.

Nixon gave a nationally televised address on inflation at the Century Plaza Hotel in Los Angeles on July 25. On July 26, Kissinger brought the West German foreign minister, Hans-Dietrich Genscher (a slippery quasi-neutralist, who impatiently asked Kissinger how long Watergate could go on) to meet Nixon. The president was calm and composed, but clearly shaken by events and pallid. Kissinger and Haig now took it upon themselves to push the line that the country could not endure an impeachment trial. It could have, as was demonstrated twenty-four years later in the Clinton case. It was not their place to make such a decision in any event.

The Judiciary Committee hearings ended on July 26, an indelible monument to orotund posturing and scene-stealing. The Harris Poll indicated that the percentage of people favoring impeachment against those who opposed it had increased from 53 to 40 to 66 to 27 in just four days. Nixon was still, however, holding his bedrock support, and if June 23 could be absorbed, he would conceivably have a chance if Nixon wished to fight it out and the senators finally had to vote on a proper legal criterion. In fact, we now know from his diary entries, he had determined to resign, either before or after the House voted impeachment but before it went to the Senate. He was convinced that he was innocent of an impeachable offense, but was preparing to remove himself from the impeachment slaughterhouse, gather his physical and emotional strength, and plan yet another comeback – the greatest and most ambitious of all.

On July 27, the Judiciary Committee voted the first article of impeachment 27 to 11, with six Republicans and all the Southern Democrats joining Nixon's habitual enemies. On July 29, the committee voted 28 to 10 to adopt Article 2 of impeachment, which claimed Nixon had "endeavored" to misuse the IRS (not that he actually had misused it as some of his predecessors had), had not fulfilled his oath faithfully to execute the laws, and had violated the constitutional rights of other citizens, citing the Plumbers, wiretaps, and abuse of the CIA and FBI. This was a disgraceful vote and an unjust charge. Nixon had a reasonable national security cover for what he ordered, and tapping a few telephones while there is a real security problem with leaks is discreditable but not an impeachable offense. If it had been, Franklin D. Roosevelt, J. Edgar Hoover, the Kennedys, Lyndon Johnson, and Henry Kissinger would all be among the illustrious Americans who had offended as much or more than Nixon had and should have shared his fate. The Judiciary Committee had descended to rank hypocrisy.

On July 30, the Judiciary Committee voted by 21 to 17, the Republicans returning to the fold, in favor of Article 3 of impeachment, which was the allegation of impeding the impeachment proceedings by non-compliance with eight committee subpoenas for 147 tapes. This was nonsense and would not have passed the whole House without a smoking gun to put it through. Even this committee had the judgment to vote down Articles 4 and

5, 26 to 12. Article 4 claimed that Nixon had usurped Congress's power to declare war by the Cambodian bombing in 1969, but it was an outrage that it attracted even twelve votes. Article 5 was the equally fatuous charge over Nixon's taxes and improvements to his homes. The pious fraud about impoundment didn't even make it to a vote.

On July 31, Haig listened to the June 23 tape and discussed it with Kissinger. They, as well as St. Clair and Buzhardt, were of the view that the game was over. (Haig and St. Clair having previously said it was manageable.) Haig told Nixon that when it came out, "the staff won't hold, and public opinion won't hold either."[37] Even Ziegler thought it was hopeless. Nixon informed Haig on August 1 that he had decided to resign. Now, only the president's family and Rebozo wanted to fight on. Nixon told Haig to tell Ford that he was considering resigning, that Ford must keep this absolutely secret, and that if delegations of Republican members of Congress or members of the National Committee started agitating for his resignation, he would fight to the end.[38]

The inevitable swarms of conspiracy theorists claim that Haig brokered a pardon for Nixon from Ford. Both Haig and Ford deny this and have done so in identical and strenuous terms for over thirty years at time of writing. It is very unlikely that any of them – and especially Ford and Haig, neither of whose integrity has ever been questioned – would have been a party to such a scheme, and Nixon would have had no confidence that it would be followed through if it were agreed. There is no reason to believe the idea was ever raised. And after Ford was installed as vice president, Nixon had no bargaining position; he had nothing to offer Ford in exchange for a pardon, since Ford was going to be president soon enough anyway. Further, Nixon considered himself a wronged and tormented man; he was not seeking anything that would imply admission that he had done anything that justified his present legal condition.

He would similarly not consider pardoning himself or anyone else. (On July 31, Ehrlichman was sentenced to between twenty months and five years for conspiracy, the fourteenth official of the Nixon administration to be convicted of criminal offenses.) It is more likely that Nixon made no indirect requests and Ford realized that he could evaluate the merits of a pardon later, but that he must be in a position where it could not possibly be asserted that he had made a dubious trade to accelerate his assumption of office. While Nixon, unlike Ford and Haig, was not a man of unblemished integrity, he always put the national interest above all other considerations.

On the evening of August 1, Nixon and Rebozo went for a cruise on the *Sequoia*. Rebozo extracted from Nixon a promise not to throw in the sponge without giving it one more try to rally opinion. On August 2, Sirica sentenced John Dean to from one to four years for conspiracy. Gerald Warren, speaking in place of the rather tarnished Ziegler, repeated each day that the president would not resign.

Haig and St. Clair gave a transcript of the June 23 tape to Congressman Wiggins, a member of the House Judiciary Committee, who said after reading it that the president's supporters on the committee "had been led down the garden path." Wiggins made it clear that he thought it was over. When advised of this, Nixon resolved to tell his family and get on with it. Wiggins told St. Clair that if he didn't hand over the tape to the Judiciary Committee promptly, St. Clair and Wiggins himself, now having a transcript of it, could be accused of obstruction of justice. St. Clair promised that it would be given to the committee soon.[39]

On August 3, Nixon told his family, starting with Julie. He gave the June 23 transcript to Julie and her husband, and to Tricia and her husband, and they went to nearby rooms to read it separately. Pat refused to read any transcript but urged her husband to fight on. The young people correctly thought the June 23 was subject to different interpretations, which was true, other than in the climate that had been created. Generally, his family felt he underestimated the level of his support in the country and should continue. Nixon changed course again, and, adhering to what he had promised Rebozo, said that he would release the June 23 tape and an explanation. Pat Nixon discreetly started to pack her belongings and prepared to leave the White House.

Others had changed course also. St. Clair had convinced himself that a Senate trial was necessary, so the act of removing a president did not become routine. This was the problem of the criminalization of policy differences. The fact was that after June 23, there was nothing more to come out that would damage Nixon. His support never descended much below 30 percent, and if Nixon could mount a spirited campaign of legal and political self-defense, pointing out that despite all the pyrotechnics and sanctimony, the CIA had not tampered with the investigation; that money had been paid for defendants' legal fees and living expenses but it could not have been hush money, because all the defendants except Liddy sang their hearts out; and that Nixon had only really been involved, if with any of them, with Hunt, a compassionate case because of his wife's death, then he might conceivably have survived. Howard Baker thought the Senate would not, in the end, have voted to remove Nixon.[40]

Nixon could have argued that nothing had been stolen; that no one had been hurt ("No one drowned in the Watergate" was a frequently seen bumper sticker, referring to Teddy Kennedy); that there had been no obstruction of justice by the president, and justice had taken its course; and that he, Nixon, had been pilloried by a partisan press after rescuing the country from the horrible problems of 1968. The iniquities of the Kennedys and Johnson and FDR could have been trotted out, and not every member of the House Judiciary Committee was, in Ike's old phrase, as "clean as a hound's tooth," either. He could have left Ford as a sort of acting president, as Nixon had been when Eisenhower had a heart attack.

If Nixon, with nothing more to come out to embarrass him, having already debunked the lies about his taxes, residential improvements, and the Cambodian bombing, had been prepared to fight it out on this basis, with all the moral squalor and evidentiary indignity of a petty larceny criminal court, his support would have firmed up to some degree in the country. It would almost certainly have gone back over 30 percent, which, if reflected in the Senate, would have secured his acquittal.

Much of the support for impeachment was the result of endless media attacks on the general sleazy ambiance of the administration, and its use, and then abandonment, of "inoperative" explanations: "I'm not a crook." "Operation Candor," one of Nixon's many false starts, proved not to be very candid, because he could never chin himself on anything more candid than "a partial, limited hang-out." Now that everything had been dragged out, the total hang-out wasn't as bad as the devious and tenacious resistance to it had been. Most Americans who favored Nixon's removal from office had no idea what offense he had supposedly committed.

As there had not been an impeachment for over a century, there was a horror of it that Nixon, unlike Clinton when his turn came, shared. It was assumed by Haig and Kissinger that the presidency couldn't function, because the staff was scarcely taking the president's orders anymore; as Ray Price wrote, the White House was "a rumor factory," with many of the staff conducting espionage much of the day and "frantically gossiping" the rest of the time.[41]

— VII —

Preparing a statement for the president as he released the June 23 tape created a new problem, as he claimed that he had not heard the June 23 tape until late May 1974, and then had missed its significance. There was a belief on Nixon's staff that he had listened to it on May 5, following Jaworski's offer of eighteen tapes in exchange for his not revealing that the grand jury considered Nixon an unindicted co-conspirator. If this were the case, Nixon had lied to Haig, St. Clair, and other intimates. He had listened to some of the tapes, but only he knew which parts of which tapes. They insisted that his statement reflect the alleged fact that he had listened to the controversial part of the tape on May 5 and not told them about it. St. Clair was afraid that otherwise, his advocacy before the Watergate Committee later in May could be construed as obstruction of justice.

Nixon's aides were, like their predecessors, defending themselves and not him. With this, exhausted and depressed, Nixon gave way. He should have issued whatever the strongest arguable statement he could make was, and St. Clair be damned. As it was, he couldn't carry the battle anymore. He had to get clear of it, and try to relaunch himself from wherever he fell to, whenever and as best he could.

What was released, on the afternoon of August 5, was an unnecessarily disastrous version of the June 23 tape transcript. Nothing was deleted, so a number of gratuitous and cynical comments were left in about, for example, Jews and the Italian currency ("I don't give a shit about the Lira," an inelegant but not unreasonable formulation). He was going to deal with Middle America by having his daughter "ride a bus for two hours; do the cancer thing; do a park in Oklahoma." This was cynical political talk, and rather entertaining in its way, and certainly not more offensive than many private comments by other presidents, but it was unnecessary to release it, and terribly damaging at this point.

Nixon's aides browbeat their exhausted leader into approving a statement that said that he had listened to some of the tapes in early May, and that he "recognized that these presented potential problems. I did not inform my staff or my counsel of it, or those arguing my case, nor did I

974

amend my submission to the Judiciary Committee in order to include or reflect it . . . As a result, those arguing my case, as well as those passing judgment on the case, did so with information that was incomplete and in some respects erroneous. This was a serious act of omission for which I take full responsibility and which I deeply regret. Portions of the tapes of these June 23 conversations are at variance with certain of my previous statements."

Nixon did give some explanation of the CIA-FBI issue, and almost 90 percent of the way through the statement, after he had bailed out all his entourage, he finally began to defend himself. He had ordered the FBI to investigate Watergate thoroughly, and it had done so. "I insisted on a full investigation and prosecution of those guilty. . . . I am firmly convinced that the record, in its entirety, does not justify the extreme step of the impeachment and removal of a president. I trust that as the constitutional process goes forward, this perspective will prevail."

The Nixon presidency could not now take a self-inflicted salvo of this explosive force and not capsize. The fact that Nixon agreed to it indicates not only that he had given up, but that it was probably true. He had, in May, committed another terrible tactical error at a time when it was far too late for any more mistakes. That does not excuse St. Clair and the others for their pusillanimity. Once Nixon was disposed of, no court was going to find them guilty of obstruction. Had they needed to defend themselves, they could have; they were, after all, completely innocent.

But that Richard Nixon, who had brought so much on himself, might be spared nothing, his own counsel and inner staff, including Price and Ziegler, forced upon him an explicit self-inculpation to avoid for themselves embarrassing but easily answerable questions. With a singular lack of courage and absence of loyalty, they put their own convenience, for that is all it was, over what little dignity and credibility remained to the leader of the country, who had promoted them all. Jaworski, Ervin, Sirica, and probably even Doar and Archibald Cox, might have handled it with greater style and human sensitivity. (All of the principal players, including Nixon himself, would have profited from reading Portia's speech on mercy from *The Merchant of Venice*.)

Nixon did not wish to see the evening newscasts, nor have his family see them, and they all went on a cruise on the *Sequoia*. His family hated these cruises, as they were leered at by passersby on bridges and from the shore and other boats, and now helicopters. The news reports were calamitous. All

Republicans who had supported Nixon on Article 1 of the impeachment vote at the Judiciary Committee now deserted him.

Nixon claimed in his memoirs that he had gone through this charade of seeking a reaction because he wanted to give Republicans a chance to take their distance from him coming up to the midterm elections. This was a good improvisation; it is more likely that he hated to resign, couldn't convince his family and Rebozo that he should, and went along with this formula in order to spare himself the need to convince them that he must do what he hated doing. He should have resigned before or when he handed over the tapes and ignored the sensitivities of St. Clair and the others.

The cabinet met on August 6. Gerald Ford stated that he had made some statements that appeared now not to have been accurate and was now maintaining silence on these matters for the time being, that he was a party in interest, but he was proud of the administration's foreign policy and its fight against inflation. George Bush was present as party chairman and said that the party was facing a disaster if Watergate did not end. He all but told Nixon he had to retire. It was a tense meeting, and since no two accounts of it agree in more than general terms, not much of the recollections of participants can be believed.

Kissinger accompanied Nixon back to the Oval Office and urged him to retire in the national interest. He argued that an impeachment trial would "paralyze" foreign policy and "obsess" the country, and "demean" the presidency. Nixon claimed that he had agreed, though he told the author that he was not convinced that Kissinger's motives were disinterested. Kissinger wrote that Nixon only said he would take his views seriously.[42] In fact, a Senate trial would not have taken more than three months and Kissinger and Ford could have functioned fairly autonomously.

Kissinger and Haig, as events closed in on Nixon, sent out an instruction to the military that no military orders from the president of any national security significance were to be acted on unless countersigned by one of them. This was an excusable presumption in the circumstances, but quite unnecessary, as Nixon had no thoughts of misusing his powers as commander in chief and there was nothing in his behavior to justify such fears.

Goldwater had become almost violent in his sense of betrayal and hostility to Nixon. He told Haig that there were only twelve votes left in the Senate for Nixon. This merely bears out that when initial reactions subsided, if

Nixon had mounted a fighting defense on the facts, the animosity of most of the press, the hypocrisy of many of the Democrats, and the precedent of former presidents, he might have clawed his way back to a chance of finishing his term. But Nixon's courage was not like Harry Truman's; it depended on being alone, on feeling entirely deserted, on going to ground and then surprising the adversary with a dramatic speech or initiative that brought instant redemption: Checkers, the silent majority, Cambodia, the economy in 1971. Any defense now would be based on winning nasty arguments day after day for months. Nixon had supporters, tens of millions still in the silent (former) majority, but the leaders and peers who would help him tended to be shadowy figures like Rebozo, or eccentric celebrities like Ted Williams (the retired baseball star, who called to urge Nixon to remain), and Sammy Davis Jr., the African-American/Jewish entertainer. This was not Nixon's kind of fight. If there was any chance to continue, it could not be his kind of lonely fight with a quick turnaround; it would have to be Nixon and his followers and supporters repulsing libel, slander, and partisanship for a long battle, with a very uncertain outcome. There had been too much petty law-breaking, sloppy legal bungling, shabby compromise and evasion, and too little loyalty in the inner circle for that. It was over and it only remained to make as dignified an exit as possible, and then try to rebuild, as after California in 1962.

Nixon told Haig he would speak to the country, without rancor, on the evening of August 8. Price started work on a draft. It was on Nixon's desk when he came in on the morning of August 7, accompanied by a note from Price that he was "proud to have been associated with you, and to have been and remain a friend. God bless you; and He will." Crowds outside the White House were singing "Jail to the Chief." Nixon returned a telephone message from Haldeman. The former chief of staff asked him to give everyone a blanket pardon over Watergate on his way out, and to cover it with a pardon for Vietnam draft-evaders. This was a dubious idea in all respects. Nixon's aides had brought him down, not the other way round, and any attempt to connect a pardon for the Watergate offenders to Vietnam War evaders would have been seen as completely cynical. Haldeman was asking Nixon to pardon everyone in any politically related legal problem, from right to left, and take the fall for all of them himself – for those who had failed him, and for those who had opposed him, as well as anyone he might have misled or let down. This was asking a great deal and from his former alter ego, at

977

this daunting climax of his life, it was an oppressively poignant and piercing intrusion. Nixon was non-committal to Haldeman personally, but rejected the idea as completely unacceptable.

Senators Byrd (whom Nixon had considered naming to the Supreme Court) and Mansfield wanted to introduce legislation to proceed with an impeachment trial in the Senate even if Nixon resigned, such was the dementia of the Democratic blood-lust. Some Republicans were contemplating legislated amnesty in exchange for resignation. Nixon told Haig to discourage that. He would not plea bargain and would take his chances in court. He added, with the dark, ironic, recondite cynicism that was often one of his most attractive qualities: "Some of the best writing in history has been done from prison. Think of Lenin and Gandhi."[43]

Nixon had invited Goldwater, who had been venomous in his unhappiness, to visit him on the afternoon of August 7, and asked him to bring Republican Senate and House leaders Hugh Scott and James Rhodes (Arizona) with him. For months the press had said that the dénouement would come with "the long row of limousines." This would be the arrival of the congressional leadership telling Nixon he had to go. In the end, there were just these three men, invited by their host.

They were seated in the Oval Office when Nixon came in from his private office, where he had been going over his speech draft. Nixon sat down at his desk without shaking hands and said that he had committed no crimes, had been poorly served, had made mistakes, and had been deserted by a great many people in both congressional houses, many of whom would not have got there and stayed there without him. He understood how the world functioned and would deal with the political facts as they were, but he left them in no doubt of the low opinion he had of many of his detractors. He had had his feet on his desk, but abruptly sat upright and turned in his swivel chair toward Scott, who turned to Goldwater. Even at this late stage, Goldwater, despite his former volubility, was muted in Nixon's presence. He did not utter a censorious word, only "Things are bad." Nixon inquired if his support had sunk below half a dozen senators. "Ten at most," said Goldwater, who gratuitously added that he was personally undecided. Scott thought fifteen.

Nixon said he had no interest in a pardon, and would decide what to do on the single criterion of the national interest, without tears. "I have not cried since Eisenhower died." (He had, in fact, over the departure of

Haldeman and Ehrlichman, less worthy subjects of tears than Eisenhower, but nothing to be ashamed of.) He added that whenever he left office, "I will have no ex-presidents to pal around with." (Ultimately, he would have more ex-presidents to fraternize with than anyone in American history.)

When they emerged, the three congressional leaders were besieged by scores of reporters. Goldwater said the president was concerned only with the national interest, and that no decisions had been taken. Immunity was not raised, Goldwater added. "We were fond old friends talking over a very painful situation." Scott said that he was impressed that the president had raised no question on any point except the country's interest, and was "in entire control of himself. He was serene and he was most amiable," in what Scott described as a "very distressing situation." The meeting had been arranged because Goldwater had told Haig that Nixon had lied to him once too often. It ended with all three men impressed by Nixon's composure and objectivity. Rhodes was asked about the House proceeding with impeachment if the president resigned. He replied that "No useful purposes would be served by that." Mansfield and Byrd would have to look elsewhere to satiate their political necrophilia.

In its final phase, Watergate was assuming a drama and a dignity it had not had before. Nixon, at the dreary end of this horrible episode, was determined to finish it in a way that did not damage the dignity, nor ultimately the virtue, of the American Republic. However sleazy the actions that produced the crisis; however tawdry the response of Nixon and some of his opponents; however wronged he felt himself to be and savage the backbiting that preceded and followed the supreme act Nixon was about to commit, the American state would continue serenely.

Nixon called for Kissinger and said that he must notify foreign governments and tell them that there would be complete continuity of foreign policy, and remain and "help Jerry. Just as there is no question that I must go, there is no question that you must stay." Their rivalry, for the time being, was over. Kissinger was essential. Kissinger's human tendencies took charge and for the only time in their relations, he put his arm around the president's shoulder and told him that history would judge generously the talented and successful president that he had been.[44] He said that if Nixon were persecuted, he, Kissinger would resign. Nixon appreciated the comment but rightly attached no more credence to it than Haldeman had to Kissinger's promise to resign if Haldeman were forced out of the White

House. (Haig told the author, more than thirty years later, "When Watergate was at its worst, Henry could never be found.")

Nixon returned to the residence and was instantly surrounded by the affection of his family, indefectible as always. He had called for the official photographer, and pictures were taken of all the Nixons and the sons-in-law smiling. A family dinner followed, almost in silence. After dinner Nixon invited Kissinger back and he stayed for about ninety minutes, though in his memoirs he thought it had been about three hours. They reminisced, and had a glass of brandy from the bottle they had opened when the break-through with China had been achieved three years before. (Nixon was not a frequent brandy consumer.) Kissinger again assured Nixon that he would be treated with respect historically. Nixon responded that it depended who wrote the history. Kissinger summed it up admirably: "At the close of his political career Nixon was left with one associate about whom he was the most ambivalent, who made him uneasy even while counting on him to embody the continuity of his achievements."[45]

There ensued a bizarre incident that tied together the sentimentality and principle of Nixon, the comradeliness and vanity of Kissinger, and the unbearable strain of the occasion. As Nixon walked with Kissinger past the Lincoln Bedroom, he revealed that every night, he uttered a silent payer, kneeling, in that room. He realized that they were of different religions and that neither of them was ostentatiously religious, but he thought that they were both, in their ways, believers, and asked Kissinger to join him in a silent prayer. The secretary of state did so, but was unable to recall in his memoirs whether he "actually knelt." Nixon had used Lincoln's bedroom as an informal chapel all through the difficult years of his presidency. At this darkest, last hour, he sought the solidarity, in the deepest terms, of his closest and most talented associate in government, in the bedchamber of his most illustrious predecessor.

Kissinger the historian, colleague, and decent man complied. But his vulnerable ego and chronic love of gossip and disparagement (from which only Mao Tse-tung, Chou En-lai, Adenauer, and de Gaulle, of all those he had met, however briefly, were spared), caused him to imply that he had not committed the indignity, as if there would have been any in such circumstances, of kneeling; and further caused him to babble garrulously forth to his aides about what had happened as soon as he returned. Nixon called Kissinger about half an hour after he had left to ask that the prayer remain a secret. Kissinger's tongue had already outdistanced his judgment as a historian, his solidarity as a colleague, and even the wonders of telephony. Nixon was about to be ridiculed, graphically, for dragooning Kissinger into Christian attitudes of prayer. Whatever one's view of Nixon, he should have been spared this, above all from this source.

Nixon continued to call Price until after 5 A.M. and emphasized that, as in his greatest speeches in the past, no one was to see it except them. He didn't sleep and after changing, went to the Oval Office and vetoed an agriculture subsidies bill, appointed some judges and other officials, and sent a routine message to Congress.

Nixon met with Ford at 11 A.M. He expressed confidence in Ford and described Kissinger as "indispensable." He called him a "genius," and thought he would be loyal but said, "you can't let him have a totally free hand." Nixon suggested Rockefeller as the new vice president, and recommended the retention of Haig as chief of staff.

Nixon's family requested to be in the Oval Office when he spoke, as a sign of solidarity. He rejected this, as he would not be able to retain his composure if they were present.[46] He met with the congressional leaders at 7:30 P.M. and informed them officially of his decision. He attempted a rapprochement with Mansfield, who ungraciously confined himself to nods, a grunt, and puffing on his pipe. Nixon thought Senator James O. Eastland of Mississippi the only one of them "who seemed really to share my pain." That Nixon could carry off such a meeting at all without any lapse of self-control was a stupefying feat.

Nixon met next with a group of his strongest congressional supporters and a few aides, including Haig, in the Cabinet Room. There were thirteen Republican and four Democratic senators, seven Republican and ten Democratic congressmen. A dozen other invitees had declined to attend. It was clear that Nixon was under great nervous strain, and he had to pause a few times to avoid excessive visible emotion. He spoke of the loyalty of his family and his gratitude for the support of those present, and said that he concluded after the events of the last few days that the country had to have a full-time president and a full-time Congress. Many wept openly; House Republican Whip Les Arends put his face in his hands and, seeing this, Nixon himself wept silently as he finished. "I hope you won't feel that I let you down," he concluded and went to the side office beside the Oval Office and then for makeup.[47]

Those who had just met with him, including Haig, could hardly believe that he would manage to address the country live without breaking down. That was also the fear of the makeup person, Lillian Brown, who performed this service for every president from Kennedy to Carter. As she readied him, he visibly steeled himself to the supremely challenging task of his life. Never in all history had the United States been so focused on one person. His audience would be the largest in history, 150 million in the United States alone; his address was carried simultaneously virtually everywhere in the world. He began at 9:01 P.M., Eastern Time, August 8, 1974.

"This is the thirty-seventh time I have spoken to you from this office," he began. He had always spoken in the national interest and through "the long and difficult period of Watergate," he had believed it his duty to preserve the presidency and complete the term to which he had been elected. But in the past few days, it had become clear "that I no longer have a strong enough political base in the Congress to justify continuing that effort." He no longer could justify bringing the constitutional process to completion. "I now believe that the constitutional purpose has been served and there is no longer a need for the process to be prolonged."

Despite the wishes of his family and the fact that resignation in midterm "is abhorrent to every instinct in my body . . . I shall resign the presidency effective at noon tomorrow." (The last phrase was a direct line from Charles de Gaulle's terse retirement statement in 1969.) He asked for support for President Ford and said that he hoped his own action would assist in the process of national healing that was necessary. "I regret deeply any injuries that may have been done in the course of the events that led to this decision. I would say only that if some of my judgments were wrong – and some were wrong – they were made in what I believed at the time to be the best interest of the nation . . . I leave with no bitterness toward those who have opposed me," and conceded their good motives. He recited a number of achievements of his administration, including the opening of relations with China and the major Arab powers, a new relationship with the U.S.S.R., a strong beginning to arms control and a Middle East peace process, the end of the Vietnam War, the abolition of the draft, a decline in the domestic crime rate, and enhanced prosperity.

He quoted Theodore Roosevelt on the virtues of being "in the arena," of he who "knows the great enthusiasms, the great devotions, who spends himself in a worthy cause, who at the best knows in the end the triumphs of high achievements, and who at the worst, if he fails, at least fails while daring greatly." He pledged to fight for the rest of his life for what he had devoted his public career to, and especially world peace, and felt that the world "is a safer place today" because of his efforts. "May God's grace be with you in all the days ahead."

Nixon's farewell address was a masterpiece. Its effectiveness only slowly dawned on observers, though even hostile commentators acknowledged that he had spoken with surpassing dignity. His enemies, having achieved their goal of driving him from office, could not fail to claim a glorious and delicious victory. They could not diminish their pleasure by reflecting that Nixon had acknowledged no wrongdoing. What was intended to be an unprecedented humiliation for any American president, Nixon converted into a virtual parliamentary acknowledgement of almost blameless insufficiency of legislative support to continue. He left while devoting half his address to a recitation of his achievements in office (which none could dispute).

By leaving so quietly and without recriminations, he had made it temporarily unseemly to all but the nastiest Nixon-haters to speak too ill of him. Most important, and most subtly, he had taken in hand his opponents' terrible, swift sword. The great puritanical conscience of America, irrepressible no matter how overlaid by the mawkishness, cynicism, and pecuniary baseness and vulgarity of some parts of American life, had been roused to end his presidency. He had already mustered it anew to revisit the issue of Richard Nixon himself, the patriot more sinned against than sinning, even before he had handed over his office.

His achievements had been great. He had stolen nothing, physically threatened no one, obeyed the law after some hesitation, gone quietly from office, loved his country, and been singled out unjustly as a uniquely opprobrious president, which, in fact, he was not. It's not clear that Nixon had any criminal intent. He had gone, the hate would fade away, and the subject of the hate would become a matter first of forgetful indifference, then mystery, then guilt. It would take time, but America had punished Richard Nixon, one of its unique and most devoted sons, and he, by clinging to his mother's "peace at the center" and her Quaker turning of the other cheek, no longer being able to return blow for blow, as was his natural impulse, would punish America. He would torment the national conscience that had tormented him and that had been roused to an Old Testament destruction of his career.

Kissinger awaited Nixon after his speech and walked back to the residence with him. His family embraced him with inexpressible emotion. They had been magnificent from beginning to end. He telephoned around for awhile and went for his last night's sleep in the White House, perhaps five hours. Haig entered his breakfast room the next morning, August 9, with apologies, and the one-sentence letter of resignation, addressed, by constitutional practice, to the secretary of state. Nixon signed it and the two men reminisced amiably for a few minutes. Nixon shook hands with every member of the residence staff. He had always been considerate to these people and was universally popular with them; he had never forgotten that he had once held less exalted positions than they.

The six members of the Nixon family made their way to the East Room for the final farewell to the White House and Executive Office Building staff, the cabinet, and other insiders. When President and Mrs. Nixon, Mr. and Mrs. Cox, and Mr. and Mrs. Eisenhower were announced, the packed room stood and applauded strongly, building to a mighty and emotional crescendo as Nixon stepped to the podium. Many wept and all, even the most jaded, shared in the intensity of the moment. Kissinger professed to be "moved to tears, and outraged at being put through the wringer once again, so that even in his last public act, Nixon managed to project his ambivalence onto those around him."[48] But this was the key to Nixon, all through these years and for many years to come; he never really went away. His admirers clung to him; his enemies were never really done with him; he never gave up and first the man, and then the legend, were ineradicable.

Nixon spoke to the camera, partly to avoid the many weeping faces before him, but mainly to speak to his tens of millions of loyal followers all through the land. He said it was not "good-bye" but "au revoir, we will be back." He thanked the staff – each was "indispensable" – and praised his cabinet and all who had served in his administration. Then he reminisced about his father. "They would have called him sort of a little man, a common man . . . But he was a great man, because he did his job, and every job counts." Of course there was no "they," no one disparaged his father or commented on him at all, apart from people who had known him. But he was referring to his father in a way that would remind his followers of themselves. This was FDR's "great voice of America," the indefatigable "People" of John Steinbeck's *The Grapes of Wrath*.[49]

This was sophisticated and subtle populism. He moved on to the subject of his mother, "a saint," and recounted how she had cared for four tubercular patients, including her own son, and had seen them all die. This was unabashed sentimentality as only Nixon could serve it up. He was without makeup, perspiring heavily, shaking occasionally, but delivered his message in a clear and moving voice.

He read from a book about Theodore Roosevelt, a passage about the death in childbirth of TR's first wife (giving birth to Nixon's patroness Alice Roosevelt Longworth, whose ninetieth birthday he and Pat had attended a few months before). The passage concluded that when his young wife had died, "the light went from my life forever."

It was at this point, at the latest, that he should have mentioned all Pat had done for his career, but he only drew the lesson that Roosevelt, of course, had been mistaken, that the light never goes out while life remains. "We think that when we lose an election or suffer a defeat, that all is ended. Not true. It is only a beginning, always. . . . Only if you have been in the deepest valley can you ever know how magnificent it is to be on the highest mountain. Always give your best, never get discouraged, never be petty. Always remember, others may hate you, but those who hate you don't win unless you hate them, and then you destroy yourself." He repeated his gratitude and bade the audience farewell. It was a unique mixture of Hannah Nixon's forbearance, Chief Newman's perseverance, TR's public spiritedness, rolled together as vintage Nixon: homespun, bordering on maudlin in places, but eloquent and revealing, behind his ordinary proverbially slightly awkward appearance, a primeval force. Kissinger, his most brilliant collaborator, saw it first: "Our hearts in the end went out to this man who transcended his extremity by refusing to act as if he were defeated."[50]

The Nixons were prodigiously applauded as they left and went to the Diplomatic Reception Room, met the Fords, and walked with them to the South Lawn, and then along a red carpet past a mixed services honor guard to the presidential helicopter. There were warm leave-takings with the Fords, and David and Julie Eisenhower stayed behind to complete packing. Pat Nixon and the Coxes and some of the household preceded Nixon. When the departing president reached the top step, he turned, managed a broad wave, and then his famous double victory sign and a broad smile. It was a mighty act of will and no one who witnessed it could fail to salute Nixon's indomitable spirit, the more so given his well-known tendency to moroseness.

The end was carried off with exquisite dignity. Ziegler, who accompanied the Nixons, remembered when LBJ had lent Air Force One to the president-elect at the end of 1968. When they thought no one was watching, after boarding it, Nixon hugged Pat and whirled her around.[51] (Chapter 9.) The same aircraft returned them now to California, as Nixon began to plan his greatest and most ambitious career move. At noon, Gerald R. Ford took the presidential oath and declared, "Our long national nightmare is over."*

Literally, he was correct, but the consequences of the combined mass- and self-destruction of the Nixon presidency would burden the country for a long time. And the great protagonist, as he had promised, would never really go away.

---

* He also graciously asked for a prayer for "Richard Nixon and for his family. May our former president, who brought peace to millions, find it for himself."

Chapter Sixteen

The Transfiguration
1974–1994

— I —

RICHARD NIXON SAT ALONE in his airborne office on the flight to California, his wife in her own, adjoining compartment.[1] He disliked parting with the president's airplane almost as much as giving up the White House. They landed just before noon in California at El Toro Marine Base, and were greeted by a very friendly crowd of about five thousand. Nixon spoke briefly before he and his family helicoptered to the Coast Guard station next to his house, and he completed his journey, as he always had, in a golf cart.

He stayed in his house for some days, virtually in seclusion. He asked Haig to send all his voluminous papers and tapes to San Clemente. This was the custom; presidents were traditionally entitled to their papers, and none of the materials he was asking for were under subpoena. Some cartons of documents that had been packed up under the supervision of Rose Mary Woods had accompanied him on the airplane to San Clemente, and as much as a hundred tons of papers followed, until press questions and Jaworski's expression of interest caused Ford to impose a stop and await a determination of rightful ownership of Nixon's papers.

The ex-president was at first in a state of shock, which soon gave way to inert, almost catatonic, sadness. Nixon had not given much thought to what would immediately happen after he left office. He assumed and demanded the same treatment as other ex-presidents, having done everything possible himself to be helpful to Truman, Eisenhower, and Johnson. Saxbe, asked for an opinion by Ford, said the papers belonged by custom to Nixon. On August 20, Ford telephoned Nixon to tell him that he had decided to nominate Nelson Rockefeller as vice president. This had been Nixon's recommendation and he commended Ford on the choice and thanked him for his courtesy.

Nixon had other problems; he had almost no money, as his liquid resources were going to pay back taxes (which he had been unfairly assessed). And there was the open question of his legal status. Polls indicated that a majority of Americans wanted Nixon indicted and tried, such was the public anger at his alleged abuse of his office.

Despite his dignified exit, the moral outrage of the country was just reaching its crest. The House Judiciary Committee reported out on August 22 and accused Nixon, on the basis of what it called "clear and convincing evidence," of thirty-six different instances of obstruction of justice. This was Doar's wild exaggeration, which the Republicans on the committee had no interest in contesting at this point, ten weeks from an election. The report was adopted by the whole House by the astounding vote of 412 to 3. There was evidence of Nixon's obstruction of justice, and it was, of course, a very shabby and in some respects disgraceful record, but there was not "clear and convincing" evidence of the probative value a court is supposed to require, of anything like thirty-six offenses.

Before leaving office, Nixon had jauntily said he would take his chances in court. That did not now seem so appetizing, and his physical and mental health were not robust. Nixon called Senator Eastland about two weeks after leaving Washington, and Eastland reported to Jaworski that the ex-president was "in bad shape."

At Ford's first presidential press conference, on August 28, there was a question about a possible pardon of Nixon, which Ford parried. Hugh Scott and Rockefeller had both said publicly that Nixon had endured enough and should not be pursued further. Ford said that he agreed with Scott and Rockefeller, but that there was no judicial process under way and he thought it inappropriate to comment further. The press took this to mean that Ford would pardon Nixon after a trial but not before. Despite the orgy of Watergate righteousness, there didn't seem to be many people who actually thought Nixon should be incarcerated, even if he could be convicted.

On August 29, Ford requested $850,000 from the House of Representatives for Nixon's transitional expenses. This was standard for presidents, and not an exceptional sum, but in a singularly nasty act, the House voted by 321 to 62 a few weeks later to cut that figure to $200,000. Also on August 29, the flamboyant literary agent Irving Paul "Swifty" Lazar met with Nixon and agreed to represent him in seeking a book contract. He thought he could get $2 million from a publisher as an advance. When he returned to Los Angeles, Lazar was asked fantastic questions by the press about whether Nixon had let his hair grow to his shoulders, had elongated fingernails like Howard Hughes, and was unshaven, disheveled, and incoherent. Lazar dismissed the questions with great aplomb. (If Nixon's hair had grown to his shoulders in three weeks, it would have been an astonishing physical achievement.)

In Washington, Haig had spoken to Nixon and been bombarded with calls from his daughters and sons-in-law expressing concern about Nixon's health and morale. David Eisenhower called President Ford on August 28 and made the same point with him. Jaworski advised Ford that he was not planning to ask for an early indictment against Nixon, but a grand jury might prefer one, and that it would take at least nine months to get a trial started. No one seriously thought it would be possible to empanel an impartial jury anywhere in the United States in such a case, and the timetable Jaworski outlined would have the trial of the former president rolling into and through the election year of 1976.

Ford told his counsel, Philip Buchen, to tell Nixon's new lawyer, Herbert Miller, who had replaced St. Clair, that he was considering a pardon, but that he wanted a statement from Nixon that would be an act of contrition. Buchen and Miller reached a tentative agreement on presidential papers and tapes. The papers would be shipped to a facility near San Clemente and then retained there in the joint control of Ford and Nixon, accessible to subpoenas, and to Nixon and his agents. After five years, they would revert entirely to Nixon. The tapes would remain in the hands of the government for five years, though accessible to Nixon, who could order them to be wholly or partially destroyed after five years.

A lawyer who had been on Ford's vice presidential staff, Benton Becker, flew with Miller to San Clemente, and they were met by Ziegler. With minor concessions to Nixon, the papers and tapes agreement was concerted. Becker and Ziegler then tried to work out a statement Nixon would be prepared to make following a pardon. There were four drafts, mainly composed by Nixon, who refused to acknowledge any guilt, but was prepared to express some remorse. Throughout this process, Nixon remained in his spare little office and Ziegler shuttled between rooms.

Becker finally requested to see Nixon, so he could report to Ford on his condition. He found the ex-president shockingly diminished in the month since he had left Washington. He was jowly, pallid, almost shrunken, and had a limp handshake and a distracted manner. Becker reported to Ford that Nixon was severely depressed and he doubted if he would live more than another couple of months.[2]

On Sunday, September 8, Ford went on television and radio, explained that he wished to put Watergate behind the country and the terrible divisions it had created, and read his proclamation of a "full, free, and absolute pardon" for Nixon. In San Clemente, Ziegler released Nixon's agreed statement: "I was wrong in not acting more decisively and forthrightly in dealing with Watergate. . . . No words can describe the depths of my regret and pain at the anguish my mistakes over Watergate have caused the nation and the presidency, a nation I so deeply love and an institution I so greatly respect." He hoped that Ford's "compassionate act" would ease "the burden of Watergate." He was aware that some thought he had committed illegalities, and that his "mistakes and misjudgments" might seem to confirm that, and mishandling Watergate was a "burden I shall bear every day of the life that is left to me."

The state of opinion was so febrile that Ford's popularity dipped in a month from his honeymoon 70 percent to about 50 percent. The country was not impressed with Nixon's statement either. So convinced was the public of Nixon's guilt, it was outraged that he had confessed no guilt. He felt none, and would not, even if he went bankrupt, was indicted, and died, confess any. Both presidents behaved with some distinction. Ford did the decent and compassionate thing, and also the right thing for the country. Nixon had paid a terrible price for his mistake or offense; trying him a year or two later, or holding that prospect over him all that time, would either kill the ex-president or lead to a very divisive trial. Once hysterical emotionalism had subsided, it is still not clear that he would have been convicted if he received a fair hearing. If he had been acquitted, the backbiting in the country would rise and crest again. If he were convicted, nothing useful would be accomplished.

Nixon, despite his very debilitated condition, clung to principle, and preserved the integrality of his comeback argument: as he said on leaving office, he had made mistakes. That meant, as he confirmed in his pardon statement, that he admitted no illegalities. The spark of doubt about Nixon's guilt, and therefore the whole question of the treatment he had received at the hands of the media, the Congress, and the courts, had survived. Now Nixon would slowly fan and coax the spark into a fire.

When President Ford came on television and radio to announce the pardon, the Nixons were on their way to Palm Springs to stay in the splendid estate of his friend and ambassador to Britain, Walter H. Annenberg. The Annenbergs were not there, and the weather was extremely hot, though dry, and the press was much in evidence, including hovering overhead in irritatingly persistent and noisy helicopters. Nixon told his wife that this was the "most humiliating day of my life." His initial reaction was that he had gone some distance to conceding guilt by accepting a pardon, and that was a widespread reaction at the time, though Nixon's most vociferous enemies howled with outrage that he had not confessed.

In fact, though exhausted, except for "the will to . . . hold on,"[3] and though it took him a short time to realize it, he had, by a final, almost Kiplingesque triumph of "heart and nerve and sinew," saved inviolate his ability to deny wrongdoing. And he had spared himself an unsustainable ordeal. That he managed, sitting in a bare-walled little cubicle in California, depressed and ill and disgraced and abandoned by most of the prominent people who had long courted and attended upon him, to face down the demand for a confession by implicitly stating that he would prefer to die, was a remarkable achievement. Many people in Ford's position, possibly including some of the alternatives mentioned to replace Agnew, might have accepted that choice. That Ford did not was a great credit to the human decency of the new president, a quality that Nixon had rarely seen for many months. It was also, imperceptibly at first, the signal that finally, Nixon's luck had turned.

He had had no means to resist the demand for a confession except his preference for death before complete dishonor. And as Becker reported to Ford, he would almost certainly have died; he was dying, if he was pursued any more by his enemies. He had been forced to the final extremity of the warrior and the victim, death or moral self-destruction. In choosing death, he put himself in the hands of an unusually compassionate man for a long-serving veteran of American national politics. Ford was accused and suspected of consummating a deal with Nixon, the vice presidency for a pardon. This is a canard. Nixon was pressed to the limits of endurance, and Ford, on hearing Becker's report of his predecessor's condition, did what was in every respect except short-term personal political expediency, right. Nixon had gambled all he had left – his life – and that he won, he soon saw as a turning point.

He told the author, eighteen years later, that he had felt as Franklin D. Roosevelt had when his polio started to immobilize his hands (before it receded and he recovered full control of his hands and bowels), that he was being forsaken by God. He would be reassured that this was not the case, but not until a direct, physical crisis of life and death had been met. On the evening of September 8, the day of the pardon, Nixon was seized by a pain in his lower left abdomen, and his left leg had swollen to nearly three times its normal size. His doctor, John Lungren of the Long Beach Memorial Hospital, was called, and he urged Nixon to go to a hospital at once to deal with what he thought was a dangerous embolism. Nixon unconditionally refused.

Lungren gave him a massive prescription, applied a support to the leg, and told him to keep his leg up and not to put any weight on it. Nixon remained in Annenberg's house in this condition, depressed and inert. After three days, his sons-in-law, presumably with the approval of their wives, told the media that Nixon was unwell. The media had generally assumed that he would be celebrating his pardon, and Ed Cox and David Eisenhower set the minds of the press straight on that score.

The Nixons managed to make an undetected return to San Clemente on September 12, as the Secret Service were able to decoy the press, but on arrival, the swelling was worse and Pat Nixon called Dr. Walter Tkach, the White House doctor, who was an air force general. He flew to Los Angeles, checked with Lungren, and told Nixon he had to go to hospital. Nixon was sitting sullenly at home, in severe pain, refusing to wear the support Lungren had given him. Tkach returned to Washington and, in what would normally be judged a completely unprofessional manner, held an almost continuous news conference about the state of Nixon's health. He stated for the record that Nixon was in "critical" condition and had "lost the will to fight."

The ex-president's inner circle seemed to think they were doing Nixon a favor by spreading indiscretions in the press about his physical and psychiatric condition. The apparent objective was to damp down press hostility to the pardon and cool out the ambitions of litigants and the courts to drag Nixon into court as a witness. Jaworski subpoenaed Nixon for the Ehrlichman-Haldeman-Mitchell trial, as had Ehrlichman, and Nixon had received subpoenas in civil cases as well. Sirica, although he had granted a three-week delay in the main Watergate trial after the commotion over Nixon's pardon, declared from the bench that he expected Nixon to respond to the subpoena. Nixon had no intention of doing anything of the kind, no matter what the state of his health.

There was the usual psycho-media speculation that Nixon was attempting a novel form of suicide, generally communicated in a neutral way, effectively confirming that if Nixon had any excuse for his nefarious conduct, it was mental instability, if not insanity. Nixon's state of mind was not at all unstable, though it was generally depressed. Kenneth Clawson, Herb Klein's successor as White House communications director, came to visit Nixon a few days later, and Nixon gave him his familiar theory that he was chased out by the establishment soft left in the media and the Washington establishment, who realized that Nixon posed a mortal threat to their continued domination of national affairs. This had been the long-standing fall-back position for Nixon when he experienced a setback at the hands of those he considered the Establishment. In his own mind he was always an outsider and a victim. He reminisced about how he had steeled himself to endure terrible punishment as a rather inept athlete, and declared that he would not leave his house, no matter what happened to his leg, even if the blood clot were to "reach the end zone." Then he gave his Kipling address: "You've got to be tough. You can't break, my boy, even when there is nothing left. You can't admit, even to yourself, that it is gone." These were partial quotes from Kipling's poem "If." He would not "stand in the middle of the bullring and cry mea culpa . . . while the crowd is hissing and booing and spitting on [him]."[4]

Concerned by Clawson's report that Ford was displacing all his people in and around the White House, Nixon telephoned Ford and urged him to do all he could to retain Kissinger, especially for arms control talks with the Russians. Ford said he was doing just that.[5]

Lungren was back at Nixon's house on September 16 and discovered serious deterioration. Nixon's leg was so swollen he had trouble putting on his trousers. Lungren explicitly stated that if he did not go to the hospital, he would die. Nixon relented and went to Lungren's Long Beach Memorial Hospital, where it was discovered that a clot from his leg had fragmented and part had gone to his lung. He was put on a noisy anti-coagulant intravenous apparatus. Pat sat with him for five days, both of them dozing only occasionally, and watching television.

Nixon remained in hospital until October 4. When he left, Lungren told the press that he would have to have at least a month of completely relaxed recuperation, and three months after that of avoiding any prolonged period of sitting or standing. Going to Washington was out of the question, and he could not even sit at home for a deposition for at least three weeks. Swifty Lazar had sold Nixon's book to Warner for $2.5 million. The advocates of an imminent Nixon suicide quickly complained that he was faking an illness to dodge testimony, and that it was indecent for him to be making millions while his aides were on trial for their liberty. Few of them seemed to be able to recall that Richard Nixon's memoirs would encompass more than Watergate.

The press finally got a look at Nixon as he was wheeled out of the hospital in Long Beach on October 4. He was thin, jowly, and aged, and his clothes hung on him precariously, but he claimed that he felt "great." The day of his release, the Senate, by a vote of 56 to 7, replicating the nastiness of the House in shrinking the transition payments to Nixon, purported to instruct the president to retain control of all Nixon's papers and tapes, abrogating the agreement Ford's and Nixon's lawyers had worked out. Work had already begun on the storehouse for the papers near San Clemente (at Laguna Niguel), where it had been intended to lodge the material, presumably until Nixon, like all the presidents starting with Hoover, had a presidential library to hold them. The Senate thus began a long legal battle that Nixon would finally, after many years, win decisively, in one of the great moral victories of his life. Nixon sued the General Services Administration on October 17 for specific performance of his agreement with Ford's counsel.

Nixon convalesced, while Pat gardened energetically at La Casa Pacifica. Sirica released the pre-trial filings of Ehrlichman and Haldeman. They had turned completely on Nixon and alleged a series of "unrecorded" meetings and telephone conversations with the former president, which, if they had been recorded, would miraculously clear them and make it clear that Nixon was the author personally of every bit of skullduggery that the prosecutors might mistakenly imagine had anything to do with these defendants. The American prosecutorial system encourages a system of suborned or intimidated perjury, or at least spontaneous clarity of recollection, to move upwards in the inculpation of officials in any organization where wrongdoing is alleged. Plea bargains are negotiated by threat and financial strangulation and reduction of penalties, as lower echelons roll over in sequence blaming higher-ups.

It is a questionable system, which led decades later to the installation of the "whistleblower" – i.e., the squealer – as one of the central figures in American commerce. This process is topped out with the "allocution," as the plea-bargainer denounces himself like the tortured victim of Stalin's show trials. Since the purpose of the plea bargain, for the confessant, is to reduce his sentence, the United States at least avoids the splendid Stalinist flourish of the accused demanding the swiftest possible imposition of the death penalty on himself as a minimum punishment for the abominable crimes of these almost always innocent (at least of what they were admitting, people).

In this case, the denunciations seemed less obnoxious than usual, because Nixon had a pardon, having declined Haldeman's request for one for his subordinates, so no punitive harm could come to Nixon. But it was, all the same, a contemptible spectacle as Ehrlichman, who had cheerfully authorized the break-in at the office of Ellsberg's psychoanalyst, as long as "it is not traceable," as if that made it less criminal; and as Haldeman, who had told Nixon they were "beautifully" placed to urge the CIA to shut down the FBI Watergate investigation, dumped everything in Nixon's lap.

Nixon had wept when they left him at Camp David in April 1973, and said that it was like cutting his own arms off to part with them, and told the country they were "great Americans." One expects from the former leaders of the White House staff a higher standard of probity than to invent conversations and falsely accuse their president of matters in which there was almost no possibility of his involvement. Ehrlichman and Haldeman were teetotal, desiccated Christian Scientists, a lawyer and an advertising man, who had shown some organizing ability and had been plucked and lifted from obscurity by Nixon. It is true that except for Johnson and, to some extent, Kennedy, the ethical climate around the Oval Office was lower under Nixon than in the time of any president since Harding. But it is hard to imagine the closest aides of any other modern presidents (or their succes-sor with Nixon, General Haig) betraying their leader as these men did. It was only a few months since they had both last sworn under oath that Nixon was innocent of any wrongdoing.

Their conduct reflected poorly on the man who elevated them, and the general atmosphere of sleaze in the upper reaches of the White House cer-tainly afflicts the president most of all. Rose Mary Woods, Kissinger, Haig, Safire, and most of the less senior people were eminently respectable, if not in some cases paragons of selflessness. Nixon was a cynic, certainly. This came from his defensive and pessimistic nature, and because he was so accustomed to struggle and betrayal and because of his resentment of the hypocrisy of the falsely pious, even though he emulated them at times. But he was a courageous man. He fought through Watergate longer than almost anyone else could have endured.

For his shortcomings, he had paid an unprecedented price in the history of his former office. But he was prepared to die before he admitted guilt. He did not ask for a pardon, and was ashamed when he had to accept one. The "great Americans" were unexciting servitors at their peak, and venal self-seekers and liars when they fell.

While Sirica and Jaworski and the defendants demanded Nixon's presence at the trial, Lungren returned to see his patient at San Clemente on October 23. He was concerned to find the swelling had started again and, over strenu-ous protests from Nixon, brought him back to the hospital in Long Beach. He found serious vascular blockages and a danger of gangrene in his left leg, and of blood clots breaking loose and going to the heart or brain. Anti-coagulants were again injected but were not successful, and the chief of surgery at UCLA Medical Center, Dr. Wiley Barker, examined Nixon. He found one of the largest blood clots he had ever seen, eighteen inches long, in a vein leading to the heart, and he told Nixon that surgery was necessary if he wanted "to go on living." This time there was no argument. Since Barker said the blood clot made medical history and that he would like to use the venogram of it in his medical teaching, Nixon said that he was unable to keep anything secret and to go ahead.

The operation, in the early morning of October 29, lasted ninety minutes and seemed to be a success. But Nixon was so pale and feeble that Pat called her daughters and asked them to come at once to California.

Nixon fainted and almost fell out of his bed. Nurses caught him, but he fell into a coma and emergency resuscitation was attempted, including four blood transfusions in three hours. He had suffered severe internal bleeding and his blood pressure had almost collapsed. At one point a nurse had briefly revived him by lightly slapping his face, and calling "Richard!" – the only person to so address him since the lapse of his mother into insensibility. When he recovered, he was full of foreboding and dictated reminiscences and comments for six hours to Pat and Ziegler and another aide, Frank Gannon, a final reflection on aspects of his career. Pat and their daughters, who arrived later in the day, stayed with him at all times and he gradually revived.

President Ford came to Los Angeles on a campaign trip and there was speculation in the press that he might visit Nixon. His staff advised against it on political grounds. Ford instantly replied, "If there's no place in politics for human compassion, there's something wrong with politics." He said he would offer to Pat to visit her husband. She told him when he called on the night of October 31 that she couldn't think of anything that "would help Dick more."[6]

The incumbent president visited the only, and barely, living ex-president for ten minutes the next morning. He was shocked by his appearance: loose jowls, ashen face, vacant eyes, and thin arms, one stuffed with intravenous tubes. "Hi, Jerry," Nixon gamely greeted him in a feeble voice. They talked about politics and when Ford got up to leave, having predicted a midterm election result that would not be too bad, which he knew to be untrue, Nixon made the effort to speak more distinctly and said, "Mr. President, this has meant a lot to me. I'm deeply grateful." Ford said, "Be well," and told waiting reporters that Nixon was "obviously a very, very, sick man, but I think he's coming along."[7]

As Nixon was convalescing in hospital, he received a telephone call from no less a well-wisher than Mao Tse-tung, who hoped for a speedy recovery and said he thought Nixon was one of the great statesmen of world history. It was a generous gesture by the Chinese leader, who was not much noted for such human consideration, and Nixon consoled himself that the respect of such a man, like that of de Gaulle, outweighed the braying of many less prominent critics.

The election was a heavy setback for the Republicans, who lost forty-three congressmen and three senators. Miller gave Sirica an affidavit attesting to Nixon's inability to do anything that would require any significant concentration or physical exertion for at least two to three months. Sirica, whose implacable hounding of Nixon was becoming oppressive, announced that he was appointing a panel of three doctors to determine if Nixon was medically unable to attend the trial. Sirica had outdistanced Jaworski as the personification of retribution against Nixon, and was starting to seem like the former friend of Senator Joe McCarthy that he had been, eagerly working with Stassen and others to undermine Taft in the 1952 convention, and receiving consequential preferments from Eisenhower. He was an honest judge, but he had never tempered justice with mercy in these matters, and put his own brand on Watergate with the proprietary efficiency of a soft-drink bottler.

Sirica's medical team arrived at San Clemente on November 19, five days after Nixon's return from hospital, and concluded that he would not be able to give a deposition before early January, or come to Washington before mid-February. Over the protests of Ehrlichman's counsel, Sirica dispensed with Nixon and ordered that the trial proceed.

Though it had been a harrowing experience, this crisis was further confirmation that Nixon's luck, which had been so bad so often in his life after his swift rise to the vice presidential nomination, was aggregating into a winning streak. He had not only survived, but avoided the main Watergate trial, and the ghastly spectacle of having to refute the incriminating allegations of his former chief collaborators. Though Nixon had certainly not become a sympathetic figure, there was now no doubt about the seriousness of his illness, and there was widespread suspicion of the invocation of "unrecorded conversations" that inexplicably had escaped the defendants' previous recollections under oath. Nixon was starting to put Watergate behind him at last, and his medical and juridical deliverances were providentially concurrent. His illness had been a well-disguised blessing.

— II —

Bebe Rebozo and Robert Abplanalp, loyal always, came to see Nixon on November 26 to help along his recovery and advise on his financial condition, which was only a little less parlous than his physical state. They proposed to buy from him his Key Biscayne properties for a little less than a million dollars. This would enable him to pay his back taxes of $225,000 and current and early anticipated legal expenses of about $500,000. It would also pay his medical bills of about $25,000, since no one had thought to enlist him in a medical insurance plan in the confusion of leaving the presidency. (If Congress had taken his universal medical coverage plan seriously, it would not have been necessary.)

Nixon maintained a pretense of business as usual as best he could. He put on a suit and tie and was driven in his golf cart every day to the pre-fabricated building where his staff worked, as if he had a good deal to do there, and even held a simulation of a White House strategy session. Nixon's outward appearance of purposeful activity continued to irritate his enemies, some of whom were starting to realize that he was a more durable presence in the country than they had hoped. Few could yet imagine the proportions of the return that he had in mind.

True to its recent vindictive pandering to Nixonophobia, the Congress had cut his transition staff allocation down to sixty thousand dollars annu-ally, which was very discriminatory. Nixon used volunteers from the Orange County Republican Association to help deal with the more than one million items of mail he had received since he had retired, the great major-ity of them favorable. Thousands of Nixon's habitual supporters were sending him small amounts of folding money as tokens of their solidarity, but contributions of this kind, though personally affecting, were not going to pay for the main-force legal effort that would be necessary to regain his papers and repulse those still snapping at his heels.

In December, the Congress passed the Presidential Records and Materials Act of 1974, which didn't dispute that Nixon owned his papers and tapes, but required the Archives to keep and protect them and open them at their own discretion to the public to reveal the "full truth . . . of the abuses of governmental power." Nixon challenged this act and in June 1977, the Supreme Court, by 7 to 2 (with Burger and Rehnquist in dissent), upheld the act, but Nixon continued with extraordinary ingenuity and per-severance and legally prevented the intended purpose of the act from being effected. Once the hysteria against him had fully subsided, the courts could not sustain a different treatment of him compared with other presidents, and his literary executors eventually won control of the materials, but the struggle was still unfolding more than thirty years after he left the White House. Again, the post-presidential Nixon would have the best of the dispute: his right to his documents was upheld, and his executors ultimately have a greater level of ownership of his materials than would any other modern president. Nixon's legendary tenacity did not abate in his life and did not die with him.

The Watergate jury came in on the afternoon of New Year's Day 1975 and found the defendants guilty, as expected. Ehrlichman was vituperative in blaming it all on Nixon, Haldeman and Mitchell announced they would appeal. The verdict further depressed Nixon, who had Ziegler issue a statement of solicitude for the defendants. He took no public notice of Ehrlichman's apostasy. It was a difficult Christmas, but Pat, who again had been a mighty source of strength for her husband, organized a surprise birthday party with Rebozo, Abplanalp, and Victor Lasky, and it was a rather festive occasion, on January 9. Nixon was gratified to receive birthday greetings from Chou En-lai, who had also written a letter of concern over his illness, and from President Ford and from Ronald Reagan, who had just retired as governor and was preparing to challenge Ford for the Republican presidential nomination.

Henry Kissinger and Barry Goldwater were among those who came to visit, and Goldwater told reporters that Nixon would be back as a party spokesman when Watergate had receded, as it quickly would. Billy Graham and Frank Sinatra, who had felt betrayed by the Kennedys (having been a carousing chum of Jack and Bobby), were other reasonably frequent visitors. The six-month anniversary of his retirement as president came on February 9, and he had to part with Ziegler and most of the rest of his staff. The prefabricated buildings that had been the operating venue of the Nixon staff and had been alleged by Doar and some of the Democrats on the House Judiciary Committee to be illicit improvements to Nixon's property at the public's expense, and were in fact an eyesore, were disassembled. The extensive communications unit, including the direct line to the White House, was removed.

On February 19, the Nixons returned to Walter and Lee Annenberg's splendid estate house at Sunnylands, where Nixon's health crisis had arisen in October. Walter Annenberg was a brilliant publisher and philanthropist, and latterly a very well-regarded ambassador in London. Lee Annenberg would be U.S. chief of protocol in a subsequent administration. They had returned from London, as they considered that they were personally serving the former president, and their place was taken, improbably, by Elliott Richardson, and then, more successfully, by Anne Armstrong, whom Robert

Dole had wanted to elevate in place of Agnew. (Richardson then became Ford's secretary of commerce.)

The Annenbergs held a dinner for the Nixons, attended by the Reagans, Frank Sinatra, Bob Hope, and a sprinkling of the California rich. Walter Annenberg's father, Moses Annenberg, owner of the *Philadelphia Inquirer* and the *Daily Racing Form*, had been persecuted, and ultimately imprisoned until a month before he died, by Franklin D. Roosevelt, in one of that president's most sordid acts. They knew the nature of official and public opprobrium, and continually advised Nixon that "Life is a ninety-nine-round fight. Just keep punching." No friends were truer or wiser. On this occasion, Nixon spoke after dinner and offered a toast to the Annenbergs. He said that he too had lived in a big house. "When you are on top, it is filled with all your friends. After, you don't need a house so large." He assured the party that he was in good and improving condition.[8]

After scorning golf for decades as a preoccupation for lazy minds (implicitly including Eisenhower), he took to the sport, and played almost every day with marine colonel Jack Brennan at Camp Pendleton, where a refugee camp was set up for fugitives from what became, in April 1975, the collapse of the independent, non-communist government of South Vietnam. Nixon made no public comment on the fall of Saigon, as he didn't wish to criticize the present administration, or even the Congress at this time. But he later wrote, "Every time we drove by their camp, I was saddened by the thought that had I survived in office, they might not have suffered this tragic fate."[9] Nixon's opening score as a golfer was 125 (so his games with Eisenhower must have been exceptionally painful, more embarrassing than anything at Whittier College), but he quickly broke 100, and his old competitive instincts came to the defense of his game.

As Saigon was falling, Bill Safire was visiting him and wrote in the *New York Times* that "the haunted, hunted look" was gone and that he was in apparently good health and spirits. The collapse of the South Vietnamese state was inevitable once the Congress cut off all aid to it. Having blindly voted the funds for a colossal buildup in Vietnam, the Democrats in the Congress, after they were confident they could hang the war on the Republicans, strangled it and left the American allies and interests in Indochina with no chance of survival. The prevailing view was that Vietnam had been a disaster for America, and the United States simply had to be cut loose from it, whatever the consequences locally.

It is generally thought that no amount of politically sustainable American assistance could have saved South Vietnam. Nixon's view was that if the Congress had acquiesced in the level of support given to South Korea after the Korean War, the Saigon government could have survived. This would have required retention of two divisions of Americans in country, and preparedness to deploy up to a thousand warplanes in intensive interdiction of North Vietnamese infiltration, as had been involved in the repulse of the great North Vietnamese offensive in April 1972. Korea had been his model, and Eisenhower's early settlement was what he had ambitiously hoped to replicate, but the situations were not very comparable, as the thirty-eighth parallel was a fixed border across the Korean Peninsula, and the demilitarized zone and the Laotian and Cambodian borders were a sieve through which Hanoi funneled an endless war effort.

Once Watergate wounded Nixon's presidency, the Democrats completed the disaster they had begun: they never should have entered the war. Nor should they have capitulated as they wished Nixon to do. Nor should they have ensured America's strategic defeat once the American ally could be maintained at a fraction of the human and material cost of the escalation of the war for which the Johnson Democrats were responsible.

By the spring of 1975, Nixon's physical, mental, and financial health were stable and improving. He no longer took his golf cart three hundred yards to the Coast Guard station where his office was located. He walked the route, each day, in his dark suit, white shirt and tie, and black, laced shoes. He generally worked on his memoirs with his skeleton staff. But like de Gaulle when he was at his home at Colombey-les-Deux-Eglises from 1946 to 1958, waiting for the call as the Fourth French Republic floundered to an end, Nixon saw himself, however modest and confined his circumstances, as a "capital of sovereignty." He did not, unlike de Gaulle, question the legitimacy of the present government of his country, but he saw himself as the head of a large, minority block of opinion, and the personification of the unjustly wronged victims of the regnant political establishment. He would build carefully from this modest defensive perimeter to which he had retreated, battered and bleeding (literally), and launch an unsuspected enfilading movement against his ancient foes, serene as they were in their confidence that this time they had driven a silver stake through his heart. He told Pat, "I just get up in the morning to confound my enemies."[10]

Nixon had received invitations for visits from Mao Tse-tung, Brezhnev, the shah of Iran, and King Hussein, all of whom considered Watergate to be incomprehensible nonsense, probably disguising some far-fetched political conspiracy. He was carefully waiting for a sequenced, calibrated return. His friends, including Rebozo and Abplanalp, were urging him to move back to New York, where he would be much less of an exile, and all his plans could be facilitated. He had already begun to call leading politicians around the country, and did his best to shore up Ford against Reagan.

He and Reagan had been friendly, and Nixon was aware that Reagan was a good deal more formidable politically than Ford. (Ford had won thirteen terms as congressman in the safe district of Grand Rapids; Reagan had won two landslides as governor of the nation's most populous state.) But Ford had been Nixon's choice; he had been very thoughtful to Nixon, and Nixon was nothing if not a loyalist. He had been betrayed so often, he put a higher premium on loyalty than most politicians, a quality he shared with, and admired in, Ford.

Apart from that, Reagan was running his big attack on Ford on foreign policy. This was largely Nixon's foreign policy. Reagan was skeptical about arms control and unenthused about relations with China, and regarded the recent European Security Conference in Helsinki as a sellout to Brezhnev, who should not, Reagan felt, have been allowed at any conference discussing human rights. Reagan was scandalized at any thought of giving up the Panama Canal: "We built it; we own it; it's ours, and we'll keep it." He particularly promised to get rid of Kissinger. Reagan's view was that the Watergate-battered Republican administration was defeatist and unaware of America's strength. He regarded Kissinger as a sly, devious maneuverer, with a disposition to defeatism. Reagan didn't question Kissinger's patriotism. But he didn't think Kissinger had the remotest idea of how much stronger than the U.S.S.R. the U.S. really was. He thought him talented if given the right instructions, but prone to give away the store when acting autonomously.[*]

Nixon was naturally concerned to maintain continuity in foreign policy. He had warned Ford not to give Kissinger a blank check, and knew that Ford didn't know enough about foreign affairs to counteract Kissinger's persuasive advocacy. But he didn't think Reagan knew anything about

---

[*] Conversation with author, May 1989.

foreign affairs. He shared some of Reagan's Californian confidence in America, and was less world-weary and resigned to the immutability of problems than Kissinger, the fugitive from the pogroms and moral bankruptcies of the Old World. But he would stick with Ford, who had stuck with him, without uttering a word of criticism of Reagan, whom he liked and whose political power he respected. (Reagan had, after all, defeated, by 1.5 million votes, the governor, Pat Brown, who had defeated Nixon for the same office by three hundred thousand votes four years before.)

On the first anniversary of his retirement as president, Nixon met with British commentator David Frost, and they shortly agreed on a series of interviews for which Frost would pay Nixon six hundred thousand dollars. There was the predictable moralistic sniping from the eastern left (the *New York Times* in particular) that Frost shouldn't be receiving and paying for information that Nixon had declined to give to the Congress and courts. It was as if Frost had the same powers to swear evidence and compel answers as a court, and as if, after the Congress had stolen his property and sliced away his just allowance, Nixon had no right to earn a living and had also forfeited the right to freedom of speech.[11]

When Nixon appeared at a charity golfing day in Carlsbad, California, in September 1975, the same media took out after him because he had played the course with the Teamsters Union president, Frank Fitzsimmons. It is true that there were some other senior Teamsters there of controversial reputation, and it was an odd choice for a return to the public eye by an ex-president, but the Teamsters had supported Nixon, and he had not surrendered his right to play golf with whomever he wished. He had been oppressed by the forces of self-canonized respectability; it is understandable that he might enjoy the golfing company of a few rough-and-tumble labor leaders. (Jimmy Hoffa, the longtime former leader of the union, had disappeared, and presumably been murdered, less than three months before.)

In October, Kissinger was in Ottawa and was commenting to his companions at a table at an official dinner, unaware that the microphone was open and that his remarks were being heard and recorded in the press room. Kissinger described Nixon as "very unpleasant . . . nervous . . . artificial," and expressed amazement that he had pursued a career in politics at all, given his social awkwardness. He credited him with great insight in foreign affairs. William Safire reported that at the recent summit meeting with Brezhnev in Vladivostok, Kissinger had compared Nixon unfavorably with Ford. Kissinger telephoned Nixon and apologized profusely, but their relations continued to be strained, as they would to the end of Nixon's life, but at least they did continue.

Ford went to China in November, and David and Julie Eisenhower made a private visit there at the end of the year, and had a private meeting with Mao Tse-tung, an unheard of honor for private visitors. The venerable helmsman of China invited Richard Nixon emphatically to visit China, and had already sent him a written invitation. Nixon felt that now that Ford had been to China and Russia, he could go to both countries.

Kissinger came to see Nixon at San Clemente on February 2, 1976, for a foreign policy discussion, but also to mend fences after the Ottawa indiscretions. Nixon said he would like to visit China, but gave no hint that he was planning to leave imminently. On February 5, the Chinese government announced that Nixon would be coming on a specially dispatched Chinese airliner on February 21, as the personal guest of Mao Tse-tung. (Chou En-lai had just died – in part, it emerged, because Mao denied him proper medical treatment for cancer, because he did not wish to predecease him.) This was, again, an unprecedented mark of respect by the Chinese leadership, but it discountenanced Ford and Kissinger and the senior White House staff.

Haig would become SACEUR, military commander of NATO, and had been replaced as White House chief of staff by Dick Cheney, early in a distinguished career that would take him to two terms as vice president. Kissinger for a time had continued as national security adviser while secretary of State, but eventually relinquished that post to air force general Brent Scowcroft.

The Chinese trip was seen by the administration as an untoward action by Nixon. He called Kissinger to say that the Chinese had given him only thirty-six hours' notice of their plan to send an airliner, which was not true, as Kissinger knew. Barry Goldwater, who in most respects was a fairly stable personality, was reduced to extreme volatility by Nixon, and fumed on the floor of the Senate that Nixon might be violating the Logan Act (a private citizen conducting the foreign policy of the United States), and suggested he not come back. Even William Buckley, who was rarely a Nixon admirer, referred to Nixon as a "pariah" in the *National Review*. It offended him, as a friend of Howard Hunt in particular, that Nixon would be fêted in China while Hunt "rotted in jail."[12]

Even Buckley bought into the line that all those who got carried away in the run-up to Watergate were doing so at the instigation of Nixon. Whether Nixon dragged down his subordinates, or was dragged down by them, is not clear, and eventually almost everyone lost interest. There was a barrage of press and political protest, again, as if Nixon had somehow lost the right of foreign travel, especially at the invitation of foreign leaders. He replied with great moderation through an interview with Bill Safire that was published in Safire's column the *New York Times*.

Thirty years later William Buckley wrote that Nixon was possessed by "derangements." He was certainly complicated, and sometimes neurotic, and he did produce derangements in otherwise reasonable people. Buckley wrote that the opening to China had achieved nothing, and effectively blamed Nixon for the loss of South Vietnam, for an alleged Soviet lead in strategic weapons (which they did not in fact possess, and never achieved, despite the ineptitude of the administration that followed Ford's), and for having "dismembered the NATO alliance," which did not happen.

Nixon had a very successful trip, which was well publicized in the United States and elsewhere in the world. He met the new premier, Hua Kuo-feng (who didn't last long) and other officials, and had a pleasant meeting with Mao, who now really was on his last legs. (He died six months later.) "Whatever one may think of him," Nixon wrote, "no one can deny that he was a fighter to the end."[13] There were lavish dinners and toasts, and Nixon lapsed into the portentous symbolism of Chinese-speak. In Canton, where he and Pat were cheered by tens of thousands of people (presumably on the government's orders), he had needed assistance pedaling a driver-powered thresher, and made much of the importance of pedaling with the assistance of a Chinese factory laborer. For many years, prominent American visitors to China seemed to think that they had to try to sound like Confucius imitators. Nixon's general theme in China was that relations between the United States and China had to be accelerated, which was widely taken as a criticism of Ford and Kissinger for not doing more, though Nixon did not utter a word about them that was not wholly respectful.

The Nixons returned to the United States on March 29. A few days later, Kissinger telephoned and asked for a full report on Nixon's impressions of the Chinese leadership and the bilateral issues. Nixon wrote up a detailed report. The criticism of his trip and the imbecilities about the Logan Act and the iniquity of Nixon traveling farther than the neighboring

Coast Guard station while former government employees were in prison were not heard again.

On February 24, Ford had narrowly won the New Hampshire primary over Reagan, and the former governor of Georgia, Jimmy Carter, won the Democratic primary and emerged as the front-runner for that party's nomination. He was an unprepossessing and obscure figure, exploiting the sudden evaporation of serious talent in his party. He had been a racially liberal but otherwise not overly distinguished governor of a medium-sized state, an unimpressive speaker, evidently religious in the evangelical Southern manner, and an outsider, running against Washington and the post-Watergate perception of corruption in the capital. Carter's main rivals were the shop-worn Edmund Muskie and former astronaut John Glenn, whom Nixon considered unintelligent even before he "spent too much time in a weightless condition." (Conversation with the author, June 23, 1992.)

Nixon's only known advice to Ford through the race to the nomination was given to Bill Gulley, director of the White House military office, who still traveled between Washington and San Clemente from time to time. Nixon had heard of a snide comment Betty Ford had made about Nancy Reagan, and told Gulley to tell Ford that Nancy Reagan was a "bitch" but a domineering woman who "runs Ronald Reagan," that Ford would need Reagan in his camp after the convention, and that he would not get him if Nancy Reagan was alienated. As usual in matters of practical American politics, Nixon's tactical advice was correct.

Nixon was planning to speak in Yorba Linda, the town where he was born, in favor of Congressman Wiggins, who had stuck with him most of the way on the House Judiciary Committee, though he joined the great diaspora when the smoking gun was discharged. Wiggins represented Nixon's old district around Whittier. Nixon's return to Republican politics was scheduled for July 12.

On July 7, Pat Nixon suffered a small stroke. Nixon called for an ambulance, which conveyed her the forty miles to Lungren's hospital in Long Beach. He visited her every day and showed a prodigious devotion and tenderness, of a nature that was never obvious in public. On the announcement of her indisposition, an astonishing total of more than one million letters and telegrams of good wishes arrived, and Nixon read to her from some of them each day. The speech for Wiggins was deferred. Pat steadily recovered in the implacable Nixon manner, and returned home on July 27.

The Democrats nominated Carter, with Minnesota's Senator Walter Mondale as vice presidential candidate. Nixon quickly came to regard Carter with outright horror, as a naive, moralistic yokel, who thought America's internal problems and any foreign abrasions could be addressed with an avalanche of Southern Baptist goodwill. He thought the U.S.S.R. could run rings around Carter and take the lead in the Cold War.

Nixon maintained a scrupulous neutrality in the race between Reagan and Ford. The former California governor made a tremendous charge and pushed Ford to the last extremity. He was a hypnotic public speaker and had a simple but plausible program – a greater defense budget and lower taxes – which he claimed would actually so stimulate the economy it would produce higher revenues for the federal government. Nixon did not think an incumbent president could be denied renomination. The last time it had happened had been to the undistinguished Chester A. Arthur in 1884.

Ford did win narrowly at the convention in Kansas City, but Reagan, the consummate actor, even if he had played mainly in B movies, made the party wait restlessly before he appeared at the end to speak to the convention that had chosen his opponent. He spoke brilliantly of the evils of the Democrats and the prospects for America, and politely about the nominee, but was coy about the level of his support. If Ford did not win the election, and Reagan, who was then sixty-five, did not age excessively, he was almost the sure nominee in 1980. At the Republican convention, Nixon, who had been a nominee to national office at five of the last six conventions, was not mentioned once.

Nixon became very active in promoting his old protégé John Connally for vice president, calling party wheelhorses all around the country. He telephoned Ford, but Ford, in an uncharacteristic lapse of courtesy, did not take his call, and chose Senator Robert Dole of Kansas for vice president. Ford had been so shaken by the Reagan challenge that he had announced many weeks before that he would not be urging the nomination of Rockefeller.

He should have stuck with Rockefeller. It might have complicated his own renomination, but with Rockefeller, and possibly even with Connally, though he had legal problems, he would have won the election. Dole was a fine senator and later a distinguished Republican Senate leader, of the majority and the minority, but he wasn't a particularly effective candidate for national office, then or subsequently, and Kansas was a small state from a region the Republicans were sure to sweep no matter whom they nominated.

Nixon, through Gulley, gave Ford extensive advice on how to handle television, whom to use for organization in each state, how to allocate his time. Ford used the wrong organizer in California, and although Nixon warned him that New York was a lost cause because Carter would come in on the coattails of Senate candidate Pat Moynihan, Ford ignored the advice, though he did do as Nixon suggested in some areas. Leaving Kansas City, Ford and Dole were trailing Carter and Mondale by nearly thirty points. Nixon assured Ford that this was a levitation, and as Ford doggedly campaigned, the polls steadily narrowed.

Kissinger had started to try to promote a settlement between whites and blacks in southern Africa. Nixon advised: "Kissinger's talking too much about Black Africa. It's pissing off the rednecks. The Negro vote's lost. Don't let it lose you the white vote. The Democrats have the Negroes and the Jews. Let them have them. In fact, tie them around their necks."[14] This was vintage Nixon, but it was not the way Jerry Ford approached politics.

In one of the debates, the first since 1960 between presidential candidates, Ford denied that there was "Soviet domination of Eastern Europe." This was the most serious mistake of the campaign. Ford was not only carrying the Watergate baggage and the pardon; the oil-price spike had stampeded inflation and interest rates were at the highest level in the history of the Federal Reserve, well into double digits.

On election day, Carter won almost as narrow a victory as Nixon's over Humphrey and Kennedy's over Nixon, 40.8 million votes (50.1 percent), to 39.1 million votes (48 percent). The third-party candidates included the Independent Party's increasingly quixotic former senator Eugene McCarthy, who polled 757,000 votes, and Carter's predecessor as governor of Georgia, the axe-wielding redneck, Lester Maddox (American Independent Party), who failed as a spoiler with only 171,000 votes. Carter won the electoral vote 297 to 240, so if Ford had gained another one-quarter of 1 percent of the vote, carefully distributed, he would have won. If he had kept Rockefeller, or followed more of Nixon's advice, or if he had not forgotten the presence of the Red Army's jackbooted heel on the neck of Eastern Europe, he probably would have won.

There was a good deal of comment after the election that if Ford hadn't pardoned Nixon, he would have won. If he had not, and Nixon survived his phlebitis, his trial would have been under way more or less during the campaign, and Ford would have lost by a much wider margin. There was also comment that Nixon had generated bad publicity for Ford by going to China, demonstrating ingratitude. He highlighted his foreign policy, which was still generally respected. And talk of ingratitude to Ford was a little excessive. He owed Ford a good deal, but Gerald Ford would never have made it to the White House other than for a congressional reception, but for Nixon's selection of him. He would have remained there for four more years if he had followed Nixon's advice on how to do so. Years later, when asked if he would have pardoned Nixon if he had had the decision to make again, Ford, ever the decent man, said that he would.

— III —

The early part of 1977 was taken up with Nixon's public relations comeback effort. Woodward and Bernstein had become entrepreneurs of a Watergate industry. The film version of their *All the President's Men* came out just before the publication of their *The Final Days*. The first was pretty far-fetched. But *The Final Days*, an account of Nixon's fall, was an outrage – one that was debunked at least in large part by every responsible person around Nixon from his daughter Julie to Kissinger. Pat Nixon was falsely and maliciously portrayed as a drunkard and a recluse. She had been reading the book three days before her stroke, and the Nixons thereafter believed that the scurrilous attacks on her had helped bring on the stroke. A luridly absurd and nasty version of the Nixon-Kissinger prayer in the Lincoln Bedroom the night before Nixon's resignation was one of the highlights.

Much of Woodward and Bernstein's historical writing has really been journalism, and *The Final Days* was partisan, tabloid journalism. No sources are revealed, all is under the Dartagnanesque cover of "investigative journalism," so mere gossip and bilious antagonism are uniformly presented, along with real triumphs of journalistic enterprise. The book had a tremendous sale, ultimately about half a million copies in hardcover, but it stimulated interest in Nixon's side of the story. The fact that he was writing his own memoirs was amply publicized.

Nixon was working almost full-time on his memoirs, but he interrupted this to prepare for the interviews with David Frost. Frost was a very experienced and thorough interviewer, and since he was putting himself out financially for the interview, Nixon could be sure that it would be a no-holds-barred session. Nixon asserted that the tapes were basically exculpatory and generally contradicted John Dean, and that the excerpts that had damaged him had been taken out of context. This is certainly true of the smoking gun of June 23, 1972, about involving the CIA. The money-for-Howard-Hunt issue on March 21, 1973, is more ambiguous, but on a worst case it is not necessarily a "high crime or misdemeanor" either.

Frost boxed Nixon into the position that money had been paid to Hunt, but, said Nixon, not as a result of the March 21 conversation, and not as blackmail, and Nixon cited the generally ignored statement that he had made in the same exchange with Dean about clemency, that granting it to anyone in exchange for altered testimony "would be wrong." Nixon denied criminal action by him because he denied criminal intent, *mens rea*. Nixon also stuck to his argument that he had made mistakes, especially in trying too hard to protect subordinates. These were familiar arguments, but were stronger in this very civilized format with a knowledgeable British interviewer, embedded in twenty-six hours of interviews skillfully but fairly edited by Frost and his team.

These exchanges brought Watergate somewhat back to what Nixon and St. Clair had sought: a technical legal argument with proper rules of proof and evidence. The real problem had been the endless smearing of the president, the war of a thousand cuts over taxes, Cambodia, CREEP financing, dirty tricks, home improvements, aides making belligerent noises and then plea bargaining and having religious conversions (Magruder became a Presbyterian minister). The public had wanted done with a malodorous administration. As emotionalism subsided, Nixon's argument of absence of guilt was inching forward, creeping up on the Great American Puritanical Conscience like a spider in the night.

Nixon placed squarely on the Congress the loss of Indochina, through the War Powers Act, the Cambodia bombing cutoff, and the outright betrayal of Saigon by refusing Ford's request for assistance at the height of the final NVA offensive. He didn't get into the strategies pursued in Vietnam by Eisenhower and Kennedy and Johnson, or the strategic errors he made himself. "The Congress lost it. That's the tragedy and they have to take the responsibility for it."

The Democrats did not take the responsibility; rather they locked arms with the media that Vietnam and Watergate were triumphs of the free press and the loyal opposition. Frost did not contradict him, and his allegation has never been comprehensively answered. In both Vietnam and Watergate, the press rendered a great service in exposing a great many government lies and much misinformation. Elements of the press went too far – whitewashed the North Vietnamese and initiated unjust suspicions of Nixon. As usual in such huge controversies, the truth is hard to get at and the heroes and villains are more ambiguous than they seemed.

When Frost asked if Nixon was in a sense the last casualty of Vietnam, Nixon said that he might be so described, and "if so, I'm glad I was the last." Frost asked about covert operations and Nixon restated the well-settled fact that the president has wide latitude in those matters: in national security questions, "When the president does it, that means that it is not illegal."

Nixon believed that the greatest concentration of power in the country was in the television networks and big newspapers and that it was excessive and would have alarmed the authors of the Constitution. When asked about his wife's condition, he said that she was almost fully recovered but that reading *The Final Days* had been a large part of the problem. He professed to be unable to remember the names of the authors but said, "I will never forgive them. Never! . . . I didn't want her to read it, because I knew the kind of trash it was, and the kind of trash they are."[15]

The interviews reached a climax when Frost suggested that Nixon go beyond the admission of mistakes, and when the interviewee asked what he had in mind, Frost took it upon himself to speak for the American people, in responding to what he called "that heart-stopping question," to say that he thought the country wanted to hear that there had been "wrongdoing," that Nixon had abused his office, that he had put the American people through two years of agony, and that he apologized for it. He added, somewhat presumptuously, that if Nixon did not answer as his countrymen wished, "You're going to be haunted for the rest of your life."

Nixon responded thoughtfully and with great intensity of emotion. He described his "mistakes" as "horrendous" and "not worthy of a president . . . And for all those things, I have a very deep regret. . . . People don't think it was enough to admit mistakes. Fine. If they want me to get down and grovel on the floor, no. Never. Because I don't believe I should. I brought myself down. I gave them a sword. And they stuck it in. And they twisted it with relish. And I guess, if I'd been in their position, I'd have done the same thing."[16]

Nixon had succeeded again in preserving and expanding the flame of his innocence and victimhood. He had carved out a new tortuous area of "horrendous mistakes unworthy of a president" – an area between mere mistakes and crimes. Frost had dangled "wrongdoing" before him, but Nixon did not take the bait. He made the point that he had been assassinated, but denied his enemies the ability to accuse him of self-pity or even a right of reply, because he had given them the sword, and he would have done the same thing himself. They could all agree, they had assassinated him, but "I impeached myself, by resigning."

As so often with Nixon, his evident awkwardness in facial expression, body language, and syntax, disguised the extreme cunning of the point he was making. The issue wasn't whether he would have done the same to his enemies; he had not. The issue was what he had done, and what they had done to him. And he had committed "horrendous mistakes," and even acknowledged that "a reasonable person could call that a cover-up" (but he did not admit to participating in one, or to any wrongdoing). "I let the American people down, and I have to carry that burden with me for the rest of my life," still not a crime. The moral high ground wasn't easy to find, in this deep moral valley. Nixon concluded that whatever the future might hold, "I will still be fighting."

It was a grueling experience, but he had held and expanded the beachhead of his moral argument and public constituency in what was flamboyantly billed as "the only trial Richard Nixon will ever face." Of course, it was not a trial, but it was a much better forum for Nixon than a court or congressional committee room. The opening program on May 4, 1977, pulled an audience of about fifty million, and subsequent programs were less, but very widely, watched. It was, on balance, a victory for Nixon, not over Frost, who performed very skillfully and also made money on the venture (Nixon made $540,000), but against Nixon's most vociferous enemies.*

He had given his case in the best possible circumstances, with nothing held back. He had held his own and started to force his enemies to face the allegation that they had unjustly tormented him, were guilty of hypocrisy, and had needlessly damaged the institution of the presidency and the national interest, including bringing down on America the only loss of a war in its history. The playing field was leveling, the correlation of moral forces was narrowing, and Nixon served notice that his return to the forefront of affairs had just begun.

---

* Nixon became, among so many other firsts, the only president ever to win an Emmy: "the best spoken word award" for the album made from this interview.

At this point, Nixon's life had settled into a three-track approach to his ambitious objective of a return to an eminent position. He had enough money to conduct the endless battle with the U.S. government over ownership of his papers, though the Supreme Court struck down his constitutionality argument (again with Burger and Rehnquist dissenting), but in the litigious American manner, he started again on another line of legal argument. He was working through most of 1977 for most of every day on his memoirs, and had a manuscript of 1.5 million words, when Warner, his publisher, paperback specialists, sold the hard-cover rights to Grosset and Dunlap, who produced experienced editors. Nixon proved to be cooperative and not overly touchy about proposed changes. This was going to be his answer to the immense volume of work generated by his critics, and he approached it with great care. In the early evenings, he telephoned around the country and kept in touch with a wide range of people.

The Carter administration was a boon to Nixon. Its well-intentioned effort to conquer the Russians with goodwill just led to more Soviet provocations in Angola, which had become almost a Soviet satellite during the Ford administration because of the stinginess and righteous isolationism of the Democratic Congress, and in Central America, and finally in Afghanistan, which the U.S.S.R. simply occupied. The version of SALT II negotiated by the Carter administration was so severely criticized by serious people in both parties as the entrenchment of Soviet military superiority, it was never ratified (though it was generally adhered to by both sides).

Carter deserted the shah of Iran, who was deposed in Iran by religious extremists led by the Ayatollah Ruhollah Khomeini, who routinely referred to the United States as "the Great Satan," and approved the seizure of the U.S. embassy in Teheran and the detention of its occupants as hostages for over a year. This was a sharp acceleration of the rise of militant Islam, and it had a disastrous impact on the position of the U.S. in the Middle East. Carter did have the very important success of the Camp David Agreement, by which Egypt and Israel exchanged embassies, Israel withdrew from the Sinai, and the Suez Canal was reopened.

In domestic affairs, the economy staggered under what became known as stagflation; the rates of inflation and unemployment climbed toward double digits, and interest rates were ratcheted up to over 20 percent by the end of the Carter term. Reagan was the clear front-runner for the

Republican nomination, and although sophisticated eastern opinion refused to take him seriously (a mere Hollywood actor), Nixon knew better, and as the failure of the bold experiment of government by well-intentioned Washington outsiders became clearer, Nixon looked better and better.

Almost the only people from outside Georgia that Carter had known were people he had met in an international conference group, the Trilateral Commission, where there are always a few governors as members. As a result, his administration was stuffed with Trilateral Commissioners, leading to speculation in the conspiratorial left-wing press that this was a secret organization that ruled the world. Carter had as his secretary of state Johnson's Paris peace negotiator, Cyrus Vance; but the most notable figure in the upper ranks of the administration was Kissinger's old Harvard rival, Zbigniew Brzezinski (whom Kissinger had vetoed as inadequate to advise the Rockefeller presidential candidacy, such as it was, in 1968). Brzezinski was a voice of reason and strength in a rather ambivalent administration.

There was a brief revival of fears of Soviet naval activity at Cienfuegos (Cuba), which were unacceptable for several weeks, and then acceptable. NATO would fit the neutron warhead for months of political and scientific preparation, and then Carter suddenly discovered, as if by divine revelation, that it was a morally unacceptable weapon. (It would kill people but not necessarily devastate hard structures.) Aircraft carrier task forces were dispatched with great fanfare but turned around before they reached their destination.

Nixon celebrated his sixty-fifth birthday on January 9, 1978, at a restaurant in San Juan Capistrano that he had frequented and liked for many years. Pat, Julie and David, his aide Jack Brennan, who had retired from the Marine Corps to work with Nixon, and Robert Abplanalp were in the party and it was a very pleasant occasion, much the happiest birthday celebration Nixon had had since at least 1972. Hubert Humphrey, whom he had known for thirty years, always cordially, and who had been suffering from cancer, called to wish him well. Nixon was distressed at the weakness of Humphrey's voice and touched by the gesture.

Two days later, Humphrey died. Nixon had a discreet inquiry made of Humphrey's widow; he took Humphrey's call as more or less an invitation to his funeral, as well as a fond farewell, but he wanted to be sure he would be welcome. Muriel Humphrey responded that she would be "honored if President Nixon attended." There were press and pickets (the usual fatuous

Watergate signs, as if taken out of the attic after four years) at Dulles Airport, but Brennan's arrangements had been so carefully made that Nixon completely eluded them. Carter had accorded Nixon no consideration, so he stayed with a friend in northern Virginia, beyond the reach of his journalistic pursuers.

Nixon dreaded it at the end, and even told Brennan to call Senator Howard Baker, in whose office the VIPs were to meet before the service at the Capitol Rotunda, as after the deaths of John F. Kennedy, Dwight D. Eisenhower, Harry S Truman, Lyndon B. Johnson, and J. Edgar Hoover, and tell Baker that Nixon would go to the service directly. But Baker wouldn't hear of it and insisted that Nixon come to the earlier occasion. Accompanied by Brennan and by his daughter Tricia, no less shapely and attractive with her long blonde hair than when she had been in the public eye, Nixon duly arrived. President Carter, President and Mrs. Ford, former vice president Rockefeller, and Henry Kissinger were already there. There was a moment of awkward silence, but, typically, Gerald Ford broke the ice by advancing with outstretched hand and engaged Nixon and his daughter in conversation, which soon extended to everyone except Carter, who was correct but stand-offish.

It was a moving service. The eulogist was Vice President Walter Mondale, who had succeeded Humphrey in the Senate when Humphrey became Johnson's vice president. Mondale reviewed Humphrey's career and concluded: "He taught us how to live, and in the end, he taught us how to die."

Nixon stood and sat without a glance to either side, and was ramrod straight throughout. He spoke to Mrs. Humphrey at the end and then left via a side door, again eluded the media, and returned at once to California. The *New York Times* reported that "He was indisputably the celebrity of the morning."[17] The fact was that the American public was more interested in him now than they ever were while he was an active politician. His position was unique in American history, and the effort to consign him to figurative sackcloth and ashes was already crumbling after four years.

— IV —

The next stage in Nixon's relaunch was publishing his memoirs. He would not hear of the possibility of respectful reviews, even from his publisher's most experienced experts. He insisted that there would be a concerted effort to sandbag his account of his life, but that he would bull through it (no one could doubt that). In fact, trimmed down to a still not diminutive six hundred thousand words, his *RN: The Memoirs of Richard Nixon* had a fine launch, got quite generous reviews, sold well, and enabled Nixon to get around the country on a book tour that took him out of the seclusion he had been in before he left the White House. He had a launch party at his home on May 20. The book was dedicated to Pat, Tricia, and Julie, who received the first three copies.

The memoirs are at least as well written as those by Truman and Eisenhower (they were both quite good writers), putting them, among American presidents' memoirs, in a solid second tier behind U.S. Grant's, ahead of Lyndon Johnson and others. Nixon doesn't shed much new light on the relationship with Eisenhower, beyond his cautious and unspontaneously affectionate portrayal of their relations in *Six Crises* sixteen years before. Mamie Eisenhower was still alive and David Eisenhower had been a fierce supporter, and Nixon would not have judged that this was an appropriate time to express his resentment of the way Ike had handled the fund crisis or the prospects of running for reelection with Nixon in 1956. There isn't much that is new until his presidential section, which includes interesting pictures of foreign leaders and handles all the main foreign policy issues well and fairly, except Vietnam.

On Vietnam, as has been mentioned (Chapter 10), he gives a lame explanation of why, having promised terrible things if Hanoi did not show some flexibility by November 1, 1969, he waffled and just handed over to Saigon, heading for the exit. He regrets that he didn't enter Cambodia earlier, but doesn't explain why he did not sever the Ho Chi Minh Trail when he had the forces to do it, or why he did not move early to enlist the sensible Democrats in Congress, like Henry Jackson, John McClellan, and others to long-term support of a bipartisan policy, before enough time passed to enable the Democrats (except those two and a few others) to slither out the escape hatch, posturing about "Nixon's war." These shortcomings are no more serious than Truman's and Eisenhower's shilly-shallying in their memoirs about why they didn't occupy more of Germany in April 1945, or Ike's flimflam about his handling of the Suez and Hungarian crises of 1956, but they do involve more American casualties and a much more difficult and ambiguous state of combat.

On Watergate, which absorbed an inordinate number of pages, Nixon gave his now well-tried line but didn't bring anything new to the argument. He left it to the reader to pose the question of whether it was all worth the controversy, and again laid the fall of South Vietnam, the Cambodian bloodbath, and the Angolan civil war squarely on the Democratic Congress. In sum, where Nixon's record was strong, the book was strong. Where his record was vulnerable, it was evasive and sometimes devious, especially in his lawlessness, cynicism, and endless threats of illegal vengeance on enemies. But it is a serious and well-written memoir, and it is probably true that Nixon is the only U.S. president whose memoir, thirty years after he left the White House, remained the best book on his career.

On May 27, on the fourth anniversary of the release of the Vietnam POWs, he had a party at his home for three hundred POWs and their families. He gave each an autographed copy of his memoirs, and their spokesman, air force general John Flynn, said his comrades and he had "a debt of eternal gratitude" to Nixon.[18]

Nixon now started traveling around the country on various pretexts. He went first to Hyden, Kentucky, population five hundred, on July 2, 1978, for the dedication of the Richard Nixon civic recreation center, built with revenue-sharing funds, a Nixon program. Four thousand people gathered in the summer heat and were uniformly enthusiastic. He gave the sort of speech, emphasizing his familiarity with the state, that he had given thousands of times in his career. Current Kentucky officials stayed away, but the state's most famous politician since Henry Clay (except possibly for Alben Barkley, former Senate majority leader and Nixon's predecessor as vice president), A.B. (Happy) Chandler, senator, governor, and commissioner of baseball, greeted him warmly.

He returned to New York in September to deliver a eulogy for Elmer Bobst, one of his earliest, most generous, and most loyal backers, who had first spoken to him of the possibilities of opening up China. The press was alerted, and Nixon spoke with them quite amicably. The Camp David talks were in progress with Egyptian president Anwar Sadat and Israeli prime minister Menachem Begin (who had been the opposition leader for twenty-nine years before becoming head of the government). Nixon wished them well and made only positive comments about Carter's efforts. He stayed in the Waldorf Towers (where General MacArthur and Herbert Hoover had lived) and was accompanied everywhere during his stay of four days by a large press and Secret Service contingent.

In November, he went to Dallas, Shreveport, and Biloxi and was received with huge enthusiasm, as he long had been in the South. Thousands jammed into the Mississippi Coast Coliseum in Biloxi to hear him blast the Carter administration's weakness in foreign policy, which almost recalled some of the things he had said about the Truman, Kennedy, and Johnson administrations, fifteen and thirty years before. He recalled that he had visited the area in 1969 after it had been hit by a hurricane, and had said that "You can come back . . . and I'll come back to see what you've done." The applause was prolonged and thunderous when he added, after a slight pause: "You've come back, and I've come back."

His next venture was to France and Britain at the end of November. He appeared on France's most popular weekly television news program, *Dossiers de l'Écran* (*Screen Files*), for nearly four hours. There was a forty-minute documentary about his career that was very respectful and that scarcely mentioned Watergate, which the French had always regarded as a mélange of misplaced American Eagle Scout naivety and a malignant Washington conspiracy to force a coup d'état. It was too apparently trivial for any foreigners, except some of the Anglo-Saxon and Scandinavian countries, to take seriously. Nixon took calls, with the help of an interpreter, for three hours. Almost all the questions were friendly and respectful; they covered a very wide range of subjects and every response was a tour de force. The leading newspapers, *Le Figaro* and *Le Monde*, were stentorian in their laudations. If Carter hadn't completely exhausted the patience of Americans, he had thoroughly underwhelmed discerning foreigners. Nixon stayed four days in the Ritz, and received visitors, including the supreme NATO commander, General Alexander Haig.

Nixon spoke at the Oxford Union on November 30. There were several hundred demonstrators when he arrived. The audience was friendly inside the hall, but the crowd outside could be heard chanting, "Nixon go home!" The president of the union introduced him somewhat apologetically, and Nixon said, "I feel right at home." He handled two hours of questions very deftly, and concluded a Watergate answer by saying that he had made a mess of it, and paid a heavy price for that, but "You'll be here in the year 2000 and we'll see how I'm regarded then." On Cambodia, he said that accusing him of "invading" North Vietnamese-occupied Cambodia was like accusing

Eisenhower and Montgomery of "invading German-occupied France."[19]

Former prime minister Harold Wilson and Sir Alec Douglas-Home, and the leader of the opposition, Margaret Thatcher (a year before embarking on eleven years as Britain's leader), and the Speaker of the House of Commons, George Thomas, greeted Nixon very warmly. The current prime minister, James Callaghan, and former prime ministers Edward Heath and Harold Macmillan, who had showered Nixon with deferences when he was president and vice president (in Macmillan's case), avoided him. Macmillan even offered the ineffably pompous excuse: "I couldn't face it . . . I was too fond of Jack."[20]

He returned to New York, where Pat joined him and they stayed almost two weeks in the Waldorf-Astoria. Nixon gave a series of interviews to generally sympathetic journalists, and criticized Carter's compulsive championship of human rights. He asked if we were going to tell the Saudis we wouldn't buy their oil "until you unveil the women," and if relations with China would be suspended until their human rights record had improved.

He warned that no SALT II would be better than a bad agreement, and supported the development of the MX multiple-warhead missile. Carter's softness had pushed Nixon to the right, and the right was responding to him. William Buckley wrote approvingly of him for the first time in six years, and he was closing up with Ronald Reagan, who was not only the likely candidate, but a very likely winner to anyone not traumatized by having an actor as president. (FDR had famously said to Orson Welles, "Orson, you and I are the two best actors in this country." Roosevelt certainly was right about himself.)[21] Nixon was returning to his original anti-communist electoral base. Despite his relations with the Chinese and Russian leaders, he had never lost his conservative political support, because, unlike Carter, who was showering the world with almost indiscriminate goodwill, Nixon had always carried his constituency with him in the belief that what he was doing was in the U.S. national interest.

Bob Haldeman, who had never plea-bargained and fought all the way, was released from eighteen months in prison on December 20, 1978. Nixon telephoned him and they had a pleasant conversation. Nixon completely overlooked the book Haldeman had co-authored in confinement, *The Ends of Power*, in which he claimed Nixon had ordered the break-in at the office of Ellsberg's psychoanalyst, had prepared the Watergate cover-up plan himself, and had erased personally the eighteen minutes of the tape, generally attributed to Rose Mary Woods. These were all falsehoods that Haldeman subsequently recanted and put to rights, and he had a cordial, though distant, relationship with Nixon hereafter, unlike Ehrlichman, with whom Nixon retained no contact. With Mitchell, who had never turned on Nixon, it remained completely amicable throughout, and Nixon did what he could to help Mitchell, and Haldeman.

The Nixons spent Christmas at San Clemente, but he returned to Washington in January, and to the White House, for a state dinner for the new Chinese leader, Deng Xiaoping. He was invited at the insistence of the Chinese, to the disconcertion of Carter and other prominent Democrats, especially Speaker and Mrs. O'Neill, whose lack of affection Nixon requited. (Mrs. O'Neill had said she would not attend unless assured that she would not be seated with Nixon.) Nixon sat with Brzezinski; the ambassador to China and former head of the United Auto Workers, Leonard Woodcock; the assistant secretary for Asian Affairs, Richard Holbrooke; and a Chinese deputy premier, Fang Yi, who jocularly suggested that Nixon admired Chiang Kai-shek as much as he admired de Gaulle and Mao.[22]

Nixon met privately with Deng for two and a half hours. It was not yet clear to the world, but Deng was going to be one of the most important statesmen of the century, as he was determined to reconstruct China's economy along capitalist lines, while retaining authoritative, if not totalitarian, powers in the hands of the Chinese Communist Party, whose leadership he had assumed after the death of Mao in August 1976. It will long be debated what influence Nixon's opening to China had on the decisive lurch of China at least toward a Western economy after Mao died. It was certainly clear that Deng held Nixon in as high regard as Mao and Chou had, and Nixon's office and the Chinese government simultaneously announced that Nixon would revisit China, as an honored official guest, that summer.

Nixon returned to California and was hard at work on another book, realigning himself with the reasonable Republican right and accusing Carter of allowing the U.S.S.R. virtually to achieve strategic superiority. His concern was to bring Reagan a little closer to the center, and do what he could to elect him over Carter, not only for partisan reasons, and because of Carter's numerous slights to him, but because he feared that if the present trend continued, China would repair its relations with Russia, as the more promising contestant in the super power competition.

The Nixons also decided that it was time to take the next step in his stately procession back to the center of events, and move to New York. San Clemente had served well as an exile home, but he was leaving exile, and New York was a much more central and stimulating environment for him. He sold his San Clemente home for about $2 million, stirring up a new hornets' nest with the left, who had already been grumbling about his social and speech-making activities while some of his former subordinates were still in custody. The implication was that they had all been in it together, probably at Nixon's behest, and Nixon was only spared because of his position, his medical condition, and Ford's generosity. These were factors, of course, but Nixon's enemies were starting to have to live with the implications of the fact that he had not been convicted of anything. The media had moved on to other objectives than the endless destruction of Nixon, and the revival of his moral reputation was, to some extent, inexorable.

The Senate, on September 6, passed a non-binding resolution seeking recovery of money spent at San Clemente for a flagpole, railway signal, landscaping wiring, and an elemental heating system. Nixon returned the shot decisively the next day. He sent a check for the flagpole and claimed to require the government (General Services Administration) to remove everything else it had installed within sixty days and restore the property to its former condition. This was Nixon's first outright, knockout victory over his tormentors, a small start (like a Ping-Pong match with the Chinese) but a refreshing result for him.

Nixon's first efforts to buy in New York, on Madison and Fifth Avenues, at a little less than half the proceeds from the San Clemente deal, were rejected for a combination of concerns about press and security and tourists, and snobbery and prejudice. He bought a townhouse on Sixty-fifth Street, between Lexington and Third Avenues, beside David Rockefeller, backing on Arthur Schlesinger, and across Sixty-fifth from the side of the upmarket (Dominican) St. Vincent Farrar Roman Catholic Church. The house had formerly been owned for fifty years by the renowned Circuit Court justice Learned Hand. His new home had generous reception rooms, a small garden, four bedrooms, seven bathrooms, and a paneled library.

He went to Cuernevaca, Mexico, on July 13, to visit the exiled shah of Iran, and blasted Carter to the press for his shabby treatment of America's former ally. Referring to the shah and ousted Nicaraguan leader Anastasio Somoza Garcia, Nixon said: "You don't grease the skids for your friends. If the United States does not stand by its own friends we are going to end up with no friends." He warned of a Castroite regime in Central America, which, to a large degree, is what occurred (although it was eventually defeated in a democratic election).

On Labor Day, the Nixons held a party for old White House friends and supporters, including virtually everyone from Mitchell, whom Nixon particularly praised, down through the ranks, excepting only Ehrlichman, Haldeman, and Dean. In mid-September, Nixon left for China with his son-in-law, Ed Cox, and Jack Brennan. The ceremonies for him were less elaborate than they had been, but very deferential all the same, and he had long meetings with Deng Xiaoping, which he declined to describe, even in the broadest terms, to the press. His enemies busied themselves with unfounded insinuations that he was trying, at great personal profit, to promote the interests of American oil companies in China. Nixon was in fact extremely circumspect financially. He refused even to accept payment for speeches, unlike his successors.

His next book, *The Real War*, was published on May 1, 1980; it received polite reviews and sold very well in North America and Europe. It was something of a pastiche of hortatory calls to stay the course in the Cold War. Carter's erratic and uninspiring leadership did give cause for concern, as the Soviet Union had obviously returned to expansionism, and the appearance of American impotence was made vivid, and prolonged, by the seizure of the American embassy in Teheran and the imprisonment in isolation of Americans within it.

Nixon was rallying the moderate center to Reagan, and Reagan toward the center. He was also taking his distance from Kissinger, who was identified with the setbacks of the Ford presidency – the fall of Saigon and of most of Angola. In his artful fashion, Nixon was redefining détente as a new and enhanced level of containment, but with the Chinese detached from the Soviet equation, and specifically praised as the inevitable "great people," with more distinguished leaders than the Russians. The Russians were a great people also. Tolstoy and other great Russian authors and composers had not been writing about an undistinguished nationality, but Nixon was concerned with politics not social anthropology, so many of his distinctions and some of his Cold War history were unrigorous. (Nixon was very knowledgeable about some Russian authors – in particular, Tolstoy, about whom he held forth to his entourage.[23])

Nixon and Kissinger were already competing as authors, as the first volume of Kissinger's memoirs had just come out. Kissinger would win the critical sweepstakes, with his massive and elegantly written three-volume work (stylistically modeled on de Gaulle's), which would appear over more than twenty years. But Nixon, by producing more frequent and less challenging volumes, kept in closer touch with the tides and currents of American opinion, which had never much interested Kissinger, a retired, unelected official. (With his talent as a droll raconteur, Kissinger has often told the author that for many years, when the leaders of the New York State Republican Party became desperate, they would ask him, around Labor Day in an election year, if he wanted to run for U.S. senator from New York.)

Nixon seized the occasion of his book to, once again, pin Vietnam squarely on his liberal Democratic enemies. "The best and brightest," having spent "years fighting the war the wrong way and losing," gave up, and enforced defeat needlessly on the country and the millions of long-suffering Vietnamese. This had become, for Nixon, a novel form of pin the tail on the donkey. The liberal bias against Nixon and the Vietnam effort was such that this criticism was not effectively addressed, but Nixon knew that eventually, historically, it would have to be faced.

He poured it on with the venom of a man who had suffered the tortures of prolonged attack without the ability to defend himself. "Arrogant even in defeat, with the guilt-ridden carping they poisoned an already disillusioned American public and frustrated all the military and political efforts we made in Vietnam to win the war. Now, shocked by the bloodbath in Cambodia [Pol Pot's Khmer Rouge had murdered 40 percent of the entire population] and the tragic plight of the boat people fleeing from 'liberated' South Vietnam [as many as a million wretched souls fled on rafts and other unseaworthy craft], they frantically thrash about trying to find someone to blame. All they have to do is look in the mirror."[24] It is a stern and not easily answerable indictment.

Nixon, unlike Reagan, had little notion that the U.S.S.R. could be close to the end of its endurance as a rival to the United States. At the end of *The Real War*, Nixon prophesied that the Cold War would continue for a very long time. "Victory in this struggle will come through perseverance, by never giving up, by coming back again and again. . . . It will come through the kind of leadership that in one crisis after another raises the sights of the American people from the mundane to the transcendent, from the immediate to the enduring. If we determine to win, if we accept no substitute for victory, the victory becomes possible. Then the spirit gives edge to the sword, the sword preserves the spirit, and freedom will prevail."[25]

Nixon projected his own experience onto the conflict of the super powers, illustrating the way with a sprinkling of aphorisms from everyone from Napoleon to Hugh Sidey. It is not a masterful, Clausewitzian strategic analysis, but it's a lively, bracing, popularly accessible read, and it was a fine success. It left out the great question of whether the West should have fought the Cold War at all, other than in places of undoubted strategic importance such as Europe and even Korea. President Eisenhower used to say: "The cost of victory in the Cold War is high, but the cost of defeat is everything." So it seemed, and posterity should be cautious about criticizing those statesmen who successfully brought the West through a very challenging time.

The book enabled Nixon to go on another very ambitious book tour around the United States and Western Europe, and he was a frequent interviewee on the television screens of many countries, always speaking with insight, articulation, and good taste, careful not to be too critical of Carter in foreign policy matters, especially when he was abroad. He had completely shattered the bonds of his former exile to perdition, and even the *New York Times* had stopped its censorious condescensions.

The shah died in Cairo on July 27, 1980. A close and valued ally of the United States for more than thirty years, he had been disgracefully treated by Carter and, as was alleged at the time, virtually thrown out of office by the United States "like a dead mouse." The State Department issued an impudent statement that amounted to another plea for the release of the American hostages. There would be no official American presence at his funeral, so Nixon determined to represent the United States himself, and flew to Cairo on commercial aircraft, with the leg of the trip from Paris to Cairo in economy class, a challenge to his circulation, as well as his ego.

Nixon walked beside President Sadat in the funeral procession, and told the media that Carter's handling of the shah had been shameful, where Sadat had been "an inspiration" (an accurate assessment in both cases).

Reagan had swept most of the primaries and was easily nominated to the presidency by the Republicans. He was sixty-nine but looked and seemed a good deal younger. He was a benign demagogue of galvanizing oratorical talents, whom his detractors tried to minimize with the grudging acknowledgement that he was a "good communicator." Kissinger was in evidence at the Republican convention in Detroit, and referred to Reagan as "the trustee of our hopes," in a convention address. Reagan wasn't having it; he regarded Kissinger as slippery and politically amoral.

When Kissinger and Alan Greenspan became the emissaries for the idea of Gerald Ford being nominated as vice president, a position Ford did not aspire to, Reagan briefly indulged it, but when the discussion reached the point of some sharing of presidential powers with the vice president, Reagan shut it down and gave the nomination to his distant runner-up in the primaries, former party chairman, CIA director, ambassador to the UN, representative to China, and congressman George H.W. Bush. Thus was launched one of America's great, and improbable, political dynasties.

After Reagan had locked up the nomination, Bush was winning some primaries, but his campaign manager, James A. Baker, suggested he pull out and endorse Reagan. Bush did so, making himself the natural candidate for the vice presidential nomination and the succession to Reagan, and Baker became Reagan's campaign manager and chief of staff, and went on to head the Treasury and State Departments.

The Republican platform proposed tax reductions, a defense buildup, and a return to containment of the U.S.S.R., and opposed abortion and Carter's draft of SALT II. The Democrats tried to represent Reagan as a radical moron, who had hit his stride as the lead actor in the forgettable film *Bedtime for Bonzo*.

Carter had beaten off a challenge from Senator Edward Kennedy, and had broken the Kennedy mystique that had been over the land for twenty years. That mystique had defeated Nixon and terrified Johnson. That it should fall to so comparatively unaccomplished a political leader as Carter was an ironic turn of events. Kennedy's campaign against an incumbent president had been a good deal less spirited and formidable than Reagan's against Ford four years before.

Reagan led the polls through the fall, but the Democrats had convinced themselves that he was not adequately intelligent for a presidential campaign, much less the office itself. Nixon wrote a letter to the *New York Times* praising Reagan and listing the international missions he had skillfully carried out for him when he had been president.[26] In interviews throughout the campaign, Nixon spoke supportively and persuasively about Reagan, though his most widely seen interviews were an entire week in September on NBC morning television with the inevitable Theodore White, who had been on every side of Nixon in the past twenty years. Nixon, as a guest political analyst, made dispassionate observations, but predicted Reagan's victory, and accurately predicted every state Reagan would win, a remarkable achievement.

When he said that he would be happy to give Reagan any advice he wanted, a Reagan aide said to the press that Nixon was "hallucinating." Reagan called Nixon to apologize, and said he had demoted the aide. Nixon said not to be too severe, that such things happened in campaigns.[27]

Nixon had been quietly winding down dozens of lawsuits, and carefully avoiding court appearances. But when two senior FBI officials, Mark Felt and Edward Miller, were accused of criminally violating the privacy of members of the radical Weather Underground, by authorizing break-ins in their homes, he determined to intervene. The trial was in Washington, D.C., and the defendants' lawyers thought Nixon's testimony might not be useful with a largely African-American jury.

There was doubtless another reason. Nixon offered his help, and had personally contributed to help the defendants pay their legal costs, although he suspected Felt had been "Deep Throat," the chief source for Woodward and Bernstein in their Watergate reporting. It emerged, in 2005, that Felt was Deep Throat, and he presumably had the decency not to accept Nixon's support, having done so much to undo his presidency. This did not deter Nixon, who required the prosecutors to call him, although he promised he would testify that he had not ordered Hoover or Patrick Gray to conduct the Weather Underground break-ins. He appeared on October 29, 1980, amid demonstrators outside the court, and hecklers within, who were forcibly removed by U.S. marshals on the orders of the judge.

Under cross-examination by defense lawyers, Nixon made a strong case for national security justification for "warrantless searches." He pointed out that in his first year as president, there had been forty thousand bomb scares and thirty-two hundred bombings that killed twenty-three people, injured hundreds, and caused property damage of over $20 million. He defended his own actions, including his initial support of the Huston Plan, as well as that of the defendants, as necessary to try to save the lives of innocent people. Felt and Miller were convicted, but pardoned by Reagan, and Nixon sent them a bottle of champagne and a celebratory note. In his co-authored autobiography, Felt is extremely ungracious, and makes no mention of Nixon's offer of support, his premeditated helpful evidence, his recommendation to Reagan of a pardon, or his congratulatory notes and gifts to defendants.

When Felt came out of the Watergate closet as Deep Throat twenty-four years later, the U.S. national media made almost no reference to Nixon's appearance, at considerable inconvenience to himself, at Felt's trial. The coronation of Felt as the mystery man who had assisted in the great media triumph of Watergate showed that the ancient proprietary press attitude to Watergate as the greatest victory of American democracy since the Battle of Midway, and the ineluctable bias against Nixon, had not abated to the point where Nixon's services to his most damaging accuser could be acknowledged. Woodward and Bernstein and some other reporters showed commendable enterprise in Watergate, but in the coverage of the self-identification of Deep Throat the fairy tale of national salvationist journalistic virtue in Watergate was perpetuated, and the limitations of the notion of journalism as history committed suicide yet again.

Reagan held his lead through the campaign, and the Democrats gambled everything on a single debate. To their astonishment, Reagan won the debate, holding his own as a knowledgeable candidate and saying "There he goes again," as Carter caricatured the Republican platform or Reagan's views. In the summation, Reagan, with interest rates over 20 percent, inflation in double digits, and the fifty-three American hostages in Teheran about to observe their first anniversary in helpless captivity – invited the voters to consider "if you and your family are better off than you were four years ago."

Ronald Reagan brilliantly combined the glamor of Hollywood and the virtues of the unpretentious, decent American. Because it was genuine and not a pose, Reagan combined equably in his own person the ideals of patriotic, straight-talking, God-fearing, decent America with the glitz and vulgarity of the image-making and hyper-selling industries where he worked all his adult life until he became a full-time politician. He was real Hollywood tinsel, and not bothered or made to feel inferior by the Kennedys and Rockefellers or Kissinger or anyone else. He was confident, optimistic, and never awkward. Even a bullet in his chest would prove an opportunity for brave and clever one-liners. He was an unvaryingly charming man, with no frailties of nastiness or sleaziness. He was a likeable and overwhelmingly eloquent politician.

The Republicans had run a slick campaign, with saturation advertising in the last week, claiming Carter had brought on an economic depression and imperiled world peace by a policy of systematic weakness. "The time is now for strong leadership. If not now, when? If not us, who? Vote Reagan." It was very effective, and Reagan swept Carter out of the White House by 8.45 million votes on November 4, only the third defeat of an incumbent president in nearly ninety years (after Taft, whose party was split by Theodore Roosevelt in 1912, and Hoover, in the Great Depression of 1932).

Reagan won forty-three states and 43.9 million votes for 489 electoral votes, to seven states and the District of Columbia, 35.5 million votes, and forty-nine electoral votes for Carter. Liberal Republican congressman John Anderson of Illinois ran as an independent and received 5.7 million votes. The Republicans gained an astounding twelve Senate seats and took control of that chamber for the first time in twenty-six years, and gained thirty-three House seats, leaving O'Neill as Speaker but with a Republican-Southern Democratic conservative ideological majority on many issues. Nixon's old friend Howard H. Baker of Tennessee became Senate majority leader.

The day after the election, the New York Stock Exchange responded rather favorably with very heavy volume. The election confirmed that Nixon had not been an exception to the presidential rule of the Democrats that began with Roosevelt, but that Carter was an exception to the era of Republican presidential rule that began with Nixon. (The Democrats won seven out of nine presidential elections from 1932 to 1964. The Republicans would win seven of ten elections from 1968 to 2004.)

It was the culmination of a great American odyssey for Reagan. Born of a Catholic father, an alcoholic and impecunious shoe salesman, compared to whom Frank Nixon was a captain of industry and punctilio, and Protestant mother, Reagan was an alumnus of Eureka College in central Illinois. He held only six jobs in his life: lifeguard at Tampico, Illinois, baseball announcer in Des Moines, then California-bound in the Great Depression, film actor (including six terms as head of the Screen Actors Guild), vice president for personnel and public relations of General Electric Corporation, governor of California, and president of the United States. He would be one of the most popular and successful presidents in American history.

— v —

Reagan would telephone Nixon quite often and treated him respectfully, but they were never intimates. They were the twin giants of California political history, the only presidents from that state, but they were very different personalities, and had rather different views. Nixon had tacked to the right in the last couple of years, but Reagan, after he deserted the Democrats in the fifties, was much more a Goldwater than a Nixon Republican. He was well on the way to becoming the greatest vote-winner in the party's history, and would take it and the country well to the right of where they had been, the most ideologically significant president since Roosevelt.

Nixon conducted an energetic campaign on behalf of the appointment of General Alexander Haig as secretary of state, to which Reagan agreed. Nixon may have played some role in the choice, and Haig refused at his confirmation hearings to criticize Nixon or Kissinger. Though impressive in all his former occupations, Haig proved not to be a successful secretary. (He claimed that his problem was that he had fallen afoul of Nancy Reagan.) Reagan changed him for George Shultz after less than two years.

During the eighties, Nixon settled into a pleasant regime in New York. He arose every day at five, took a brisk two-mile stroll on Third Avenue, and went every day, including the weekends, to his office in Federal Plaza in Foley Square, beside the courthouse where he had first become famous in the Hiss case, a third of a century before. He had a very active life on the speaking circuit, before top-drawer groups, always pro bono, and his remarks were always exceptionally well prepared and delivered. He was frequently interviewed on television and was never questioned abrasively, or less than an interesting guest, and he wrote frequently in a wide range of influential publications, including the *New York Times* and the *Washington Post*.

Nixon traveled to all manner of obscure places, and his business connections were, as always with him, shadowy, but nothing has ever arisen to suggest that he did anything except write letters to acquaintances in foreign governments recommending friends, such as John Mitchell and Jack Brennan, who was now in business with Mitchell. Nixon was in no position to dispense government influence and he was free to deal with whomever he wished. Stephen Ambrose implausibly claims that Nixon played a role in the manufacture in Romania and sale to Iraq of $181 million of uniforms. At Romanian wage rates, even allowing for the graft of the Ceauşescu and Saddam Hussein regime, that would buy enough clothing to kit out every uniformed person in the world for the balance of the twentieth century, but there is nothing improper in it. As so often with Nixon, it is so improbable, part of it could be true.[28]

The Nixons had a very active social life with a wide range of prominent people in different fields. They now had three grandchildren (Tricia had a boy and Julie a boy and a girl), and Nixon was a delighted, patient, and attentive grandfather. Always a master of surprise, he loved playing with his grandchildren, as he had so lovingly with his little brother Arthur, nearly sixty years before.

The rivalry with Kissinger became friendlier, as they were both out of public office and the stakes were less important, but the rivalry intensified. The more idealistic foreign policy community, which had so disliked Nixon that it redistributed all credit for what he and Kissinger had accomplished in foreign policy to Kissinger, now recognized that Nixon would never be back in public life, but that Kissinger could be, and began reapportioning it more evenly. Kissinger privately fumed, when Nixon appeared in publications that had long pilloried him, that "He is a prison camp inmate that has fallen in love with his guard." (To the author many times) Kissinger and his former chief were in a historical wrestling match.

Kissinger was, on balance, more generous to Nixon in his memoirs than Nixon was to him. Kissinger recounted Nixon's foibles, and many of his vignettes were far from charitable, but Nixon emerged as a "not inconsiderable" president. Nixon described Kissinger as "Machiavellian, deceitful, egotistical, arrogant, and insulting," but in conversation, Nixon was consistent with what he wrote, while Kissinger, as he was on the subject of almost everyone, was relentlessly scornful of Nixon, apart from the admission that he possessed a reluctant, intermittent courage.

In the late summer of 1981, the Nixons moved to Saddle River, New Jersey, to a comfortable but unpretentious house in a four-acre property. This was the twentieth and final principal residence they had had in forty years of married life together. They sold the Sixty-fifth Street house for $2.6 million to the Syrian government for its mission to the UN. This was more than triple what they had paid two years before. Nixon was now rolling up a tidy nest egg, a far cry from the dire financial straits of 1974 and 1975.

Nixon had considered setting up a presidential library at the University of Southern California, but that did not work out. The president of Duke University, former North Carolina governor Terry Sanford, approached him in mid-1981 with a proposal for a library at his university. Nixon was favorable, but the Duke Academic Council, with a purblind self-righteous stupidity common in academic circles, voted thirty-five to thirty-four against the proposal. As in many other matters, Nixon was going to do it his way, and he had relaunched litigation to retrieve his papers.

The president of Egypt, Anwar Sadat, was assassinated on October 6, 1981, and Reagan, having been advised not to attend the funeral for security reasons, asked Nixon, Ford, and Carter to go as special representatives, with Defense Secretary Caspar Weinberger, Kissinger, and a congressional delegation. Nixon met with Reagan, Carter, and Ford at the White House, and the ex-presidents departed and traveled together. Nixon was the subject of great attention at the funeral (where he wore a bullet-proof vest) and flew on to meet with the kings of Saudi Arabia, Jordan, and Morocco, and the president of Tunisia (Habib Bourguiba). He was everywhere received with great respect and deference, and he went on to Paris, where he issued, through the U.S. embassy, statements of opinion about arms sales in the Middle East and other matters.

Nixon had now perfected the technique of the private-sector state visit. He had developed this in the sixties, but then he was just an ex-vice president, though prescient people such as de Gaulle recognized that he might be destined to higher things. Now, Ford and Carter were not as knowledgeable or accomplished in world affairs as he was, nor generally as articulate, and not the intriguing political personality that Nixon was. His decades of relentless controversy and his durability had given him a timelessness. He was only sixty-eight, but with Mao and Chou and de Gaulle and Truman and Eisenhower and Adenauer dead, all at full ages, he was in some respects the world's elder statesman. (He was actually two years younger than Reagan, but Reagan had started late in politics and had the gift of perpetual youth, and was less interested in foreign affairs than Nixon was.)

Kissinger and David Rockefeller were pretty good at the private-sector state visit also, but Nixon after all had been a two-term U.S. president and had been on the Marshall Plan fact-finding trip to Europe more than twenty years before Kissinger came to Washington. David Rockefeller was the long-time head of the Chase Manhattan Bank and one of the leaders of an immensely wealthy family, but he was not a foreign policy specialist like Nixon or Kissinger.

Nixon's fourth book, *Leaders*, was published in the autumn of 1981. It was a series of sketches of foreign statesmen Nixon had known, except for General Douglas MacArthur, who shared a chapter with Japanese prime minister Shigeru Yoshida. The other subjects were Churchill, de Gaulle, Adenauer, Khrushchev, Chou En-lai, though many other leaders were mentioned. It was a reasonably interesting volume, largely written by Ray Price and a staff of young helpers, but polished and edited by Nixon. It didn't say much that specialists on the men described didn't already know, and it was, in fact, largely about Nixon. It was another device in his self-promotion, as it emphasized great men he had known, and much of the wit and wisdom of his subjects was as communicated to, and recollected by, Nixon himself.

Eight years after he left the White House, Nixon was a thoroughly re-habilitated figure, still disparaged by many but generally respected, much sought after as an adviser, a commentator, author, speaker, and dinner guest. He had not made much of a dent on the general conviction in the United States, guarded and protected by the media like the gold of Fort Knox, that he was an unindicted criminal. His pardon now extended to a sizable percentage of the American people, but his efforts at exculpation were just beginning. He couldn't move them faster, because he had stated his case for absence of criminal intent, and had to wait for the jailers of his reputation to yield to new people, and for history to be written by historians and not partisans.

Reagan was far preferable for Nixon to Carter, who had never stopped prat-tling on about the "shame of Watergate." But Reagan was so popular, he didn't need Nixon. In a tight political race, Nixon could be important, because his followers were still there and his influence could weigh in the balance. Reagan was a beloved president, and he was adopting a sterner line with the Russians than Nixon thought appropriate.

Nixon tacked again, and went from emphasizing his concern that the Chinese would give up on the United States because of its weakness under Carter to expressed concern that Reagan was being unnecessarily confrontational toward the Russians. With his usual dexterity, Nixon managed it without alienating his own supporters, and his antediluvian foes on the left once more embraced this ever-changing but unceasing political presence they had tried so hard and often to exterminate or at least ignore. The great liberal media outlets showcased his gently formulated reservations about Reagan's policies. The Democrats had not had a successful foreign policy since Kennedy, if not Truman, and they had no credible spokesmen, except, to some degree, Brzezinski, who had usually been in dissent in the Carter administration. Like many Poles, he was skeptical of the Russians, and in this regard was more perceptive than his old rival, Kissinger.

In international affairs, Nixon and Kissinger were chess players, and Reagan was a poker player. Nixon did not realize how parlous the U.S.S.R. had become. Kissinger, a balance-of-power historian, had little notion of the power of economics, and even less the power of moral political values, to disturb the apparent correlation of forces between nations. Kissinger was a prodigious intellect; Nixon was a serious intellect and a remarkable politician. Reagan was a cunning old peasant, masquerading as a loveable and simple man. Nixon the cynic shared some of Kissinger's detachment from moral factors, but being a Californian rather than a fugitive from Central Europe, he had some of Reagan's optimism about what America could accomplish.

Nixon had delivered the United States from Vietnam, pried China apart from Russia, and reinforced America's alliances. After Carter had cured the American public of the idea that the Cold War was a fraud and that there was no real Russian threat, Reagan was ready, with the Polish Pope, John Paul II, and the new Conservative British prime minister, Margaret Thatcher, to shake the ramshackle Soviet edifice to its foundations. Reagan had not much appreciated what Nixon and Kissinger had accomplished, while they were accomplishing it. Nixon and Kissinger were skeptical about what Reagan was attempting.

Nixon and Reagan were more successful at devising and implementing policy than at critiquing the performance of each other. They were both essential and successful. But Nixon's subtle differences with Reagan had the added benefit to him of anesthetizing his enemies on the left. He was approaching the end of his fourth decade as a prominent American public figure. His last decade would be one of his most enjoyable.

In the late summer of 1983, he published, initially at his own expense, and distributed advance copies to seven hundred influential people of his latest, shortest, best-reviewed book, *Real Peace*. It was only a hundred and seven pages, and was a Nixonian classic, as it appeared to take issue with Reagan's hard line against the U.S.S.R., but also approved much of it in detail. He approved, as he often had publicly, Reagan's defense buildup and intolerance of further Russian expansionism. He was back to Achesonian demography – a hundred million people had fallen to communism since he had left office (Indochina, Angola, Afghanistan).

He was pitching to the anti-Reagan media, who had almost no one else of any foreign policy stature to recruit, while endorsing Reagan's goals. Essentially, he was saying that a deal could be struck with the Russians now, because the United States was dealing from strength again. Brezhnev had died in 1982. His successor, Yuri Andropov, died in February 1984, leaving the Soviet Communist Party headed by the doddering Konstantin Chernenko, so wracked by respiratory problems that he could not finish a sentence without pausing and gasping for breath. He was an allegory of the Soviet Empire.

Reagan had cut taxes and induced a mighty economic boom, and had played his high card with the Russians. He had unveiled a proposal for a defensive anti-missile system, the Strategic Defense Initiative (SDI), a shield of space-launched, satellite-guided, anti-missile missiles. The unctuous and gullible left of the West went berserk with alarm and ridicule, calling it Star Wars (after a popular-science fiction movie). Earnest groupings of scientists caucused and declared it to be technically impractical.

Reagan smiled serenely and said it was a non-nuclear, completely defensive system that would protect against an accident, and that he would be prepared, under certain circumstances, to share the technology with the Russians. It was a stroke of genius, the supreme moment of the Cold War. The Russians did not have the self-confidence to wait for Western opinion to form against Reagan, or to allow the technical problems and exorbitant costs to accumulate unacceptably and erode Reagan's political support for the program. Even so experienced a foreign policy specialist as Gromyko, who had come to Washington as ambassador in 1943, started complaining about an American effort to make the Soviet defense buildup "obsolete."

The American Sovietologists calculated that the U.S.S.R. was spending 25 percent of its GDP on defense, and that it was cracking under the strain. The real number was almost twice that and the strain was greater than even Reagan imagined. The Soviet leaders now, unlike Stalin, Khrushchev, and probably Brezhnev in his prime, had no idea how to deal with America rampant. Reagan was the silver-tongued optimist, who smiled as he said conventionally hair-raising things, and allowed America to be America, and was just building a defensive system for the good of everyone. (When the air controllers of America struck, and he fired them, he had blandly said: "I didn't fire them; they quit." Military air controllers temporarily took over, and commercial air traffic was only slightly and briefly interrupted. The public was grateful to the president, and no one could have imagined Carter handling it so efficiently.)

The Russians stammered incoherently about SDI, geriatric mummies now, suddenly strangely weak and palsied. The Western Europeans widdered and havered, as most of them since Churchill, except for Adenauer, de Gaulle, and Thatcher, usually did. Trudeau, finally nearing the end of his long term in Canada, waffled and bustled around the lesser capitals of the Iron Curtain – Bucharest, East Berlin – fussing and proposing conferences. Nixon realized at once the potential for Reagan's stroke. To the Democrats, he seemed more sensible every day, compared with the incumbent. To the Republicans, he supported the president but urged that he close with the Russians and negotiate a major de-escalation in the Cold War. As he told *Time* magazine in a long interview in 1985: "The rivalry with the Soviet Union can be managed but not eliminated. That's the kind of world we live in."[29] Reagan thought otherwise, and Reagan was right.

Reagan, by his popularity and oratorical powers, effortlessly carried the country. He had all the power and he did not need Nixon, but he recognized that Nixon was useful in siphoning off much criticism that could otherwise be quite militant and troublesome. Nixon also advised key cabinet members who had been in his administration, Cap Weinberger at Defense, and George Shultz at State.

The 1984 election was never in doubt. "Morning in America" was the Republican slogan. Reagan had produced inflation-free, low-tax, full-employment prosperity with his tax reductions, and by his confident but kindly manner and great eloquence had conveyed a positive mood to the country, battered in the previous twenty years by assassinations, riots, Vietnam, Watergate, and the inanities of the Carter era.

Carter had complained of a national malaise, and Reagan had convinced most Americans that the chief symptom of it was Carter's presence in the White House. When there had been an assassination attempt on Reagan in March 1981, and he received a bullet in the chest, which punctured a lung and lodged an inch from his heart, Reagan had walked unaided into the operating room in the George Washington University Hospital Trauma Center, and, seeing twenty doctors and nurses awaiting him anxiously, said, "I hope you're all Republicans." He won the hearts of the nation again and again by his human qualities, as felicitous as Nixon had been awkward. He spoke with overpowering grace and spirit to the Congress ten days after the attempt on his life and was accorded what veterans of the Capitol believed the greatest, most whole-hearted applause ever furnished by a joint session to any president – rivaled, if at all, only, and of a very different character, by the war messages of Woodrow Wilson in 1917 and Franklin D. Roosevelt in 1941.

Walter Mondale, Carter's vice president, was the Democratic candidate. He did his best, but his promise of tax increases was not popular. In the debates, when asked if age was an issue, Reagan, seventy-three (an unheard of age to contest the presidency), had replied, "No and I will not try to exploit my opponent's comparative youth and inexperience." Reagan swept forty-nine states, leaving Mondale only his home state of Minnesota, which he won by only ten thousand votes, and the District of Columbia. Reagan won by fifteen million votes and the Republicans retained control of the Senate.

On May 9, 1984, Nixon spoke to the American Society of Newspaper Editors in Washington. It was his first encounter with such a group since the "I'm not a crook" fiasco in 1973. He spoke for forty-five minutes without a pause or a note, in perfect sequence, and called for a new relationship with Russia. It was the civilized and reassuring side of the Peace Through Strength message for which Reagan was beating the drums.

He demonstrated an encyclopedic grasp of dates and personalities and details, opened with witty pleasantries about his relations with the press, and closed with an eloquent summary of the great strategic and diplomatic opportunity. The hall, the serried ranks of his most vocal and relentless critics, rose and gave him a prolonged and stirring ovation.

The tenth anniversary of his resignation received a good deal of press attention, but very little of the vitriol of previous comment. Personally, it passed as unremarked as had his seventieth birthday the year before.

Nixon was a very successful self-promoter. Also in 1984, he sold a video-taped memoir of thirty-six hours, unedited, to CBS, the most critical of the networks toward him during his career, for a million dollars. In 1985, he published *No More Vietnams*, one of his more successful books, that again made the case for the Democratic responsibility for the entire dreadful tragedy from beginning to end. It was a very powerful, well-worded case.

He concluded with quotations from Jefferson, Lincoln, Theodore Roosevelt, and Woodrow Wilson. And then: "It is vital that we learn the right lesson from [Vietnam]. We tried and failed in a just cause. 'No more Vietnams' can mean that we will not try again. It should mean that we will not fail again."[30]

By this time, the U.S.S.R. had finally moved to a younger leader, Mikhail Gorbachev, who gave some promise of something better than the Old Bolsheviks had been able to conceive. Margaret Thatcher, already the British leader most revered in the United States since Churchill, had pronounced him "a man we can do business with." Reagan was interested in meeting him, and sought Nixon's advice. Nixon warned against a "get-acquainted" summit meeting and suggested a serious working agenda be organized in advance. Part of the press alleged that Reagan suggested a meeting with all the ex-presidents, but that Nixon had made himself available only when Ford and Carter were not.[31] This is unlikely, the others would not have been particu-larly informative, and Reagan could meet with them separately if he wished.

Nixon was now the world's preeminent authority on summit meetings and Reagan followed his advice carefully. His meeting with Gorbachev at Geneva in 1985 was cordial and promising, and further meetings were planned to advance a wide range of bilateral issues. Reagan had escalated the Cold War, but it was now being sharply scaled down.

Truman and Marshall and Acheson's containment policy, and Nixon's triangulation with the Chinese, had succeeded, and now Reagan's arms buildup, and especially SDI, had forced real arms control on the Soviets. Gorbachev was also making serious reform noises. "Perestroika" (broadly speaking, "reform" or "restructuring") and "Glasnost" ("openness") became household words in the West. It soon became clear that Gorbachev, in the exactly opposite sequence of the Chinese, was going to democratize the U.S.S.R. before he dismantled and capitalized its command economy. American Sovietologists, in government and out, could hardly believe their eyes and ears, and quietly predicted the complete disintegration of the Soviet state if Gorbachev took this course too far. These three presidents, Truman, Nixon, and Reagan, would contribute more than anyone else to the satisfactory end of the Cold War.

In April 1986, Nixon again spoke to the American Newspaper Publishers' Association. It was a masterly address on how to wind down the Cold War. Nixon's delivery and content were superb, witty, constructive, authoritative, self-deprecatory at the start, and never pedantic. As Katharine Graham told the author, "He knocked our hats off." It was one of Nixon's greatest performances. "He's Back" was the headline for the cover story in *Newsweek*, and they ran, an unusual gesture of reconciliation, a photograph of their proprietor, Katharine Graham, and Nixon laughing warmly as they shook hands. It did not wash clean the record, but it was a sweet moment in a career that had had much bitterness, especially in the last ten years, since he left the White House.

Nixon visited Moscow in July 1986, and had a long and far-ranging meeting with Gorbachev. He gave Reagan a twenty-six-page memorandum on Gorbachev, and where he thought there were opportunities for the fastest and most useful progress. He said that Reagan could almost write his own ticket on arms control, and extensively flattered Reagan in his recitation of what he had told Gorbachev of Reagan's popularity. Nixon's insights into Gorbachev's personality and bargaining position were astute.

Reagan went to a second summit with Gorbachev at Reykjavik in October 1986. They tentatively agreed on the complete abandonment of nuclear weapons and delivery systems over ten years, but everything came unstuck because of Gorbachev's insistence on the abandonment of SDI. This was a nonsensical proposal, and the talks collapsed, though not acrimoniously. The strength of the SDI card was confirmed, and Gorbachev, for all his energy and dynamism, was no match as a poker-playing cardsharp for Reagan, for all his avuncular abstractedness. Nixon, with what Len Garment called his "school-boy intensity," had missed the great reality: the Russians were stretched beyond their limit. They could not match the American defense effort; their economy was a shambles; and they could not loosen anything without the Soviet Empire disintegrating in separatist fragmentation.

The next month, the Democrats regained control of the Senate, and Reagan, like Nixon and Ford and, for six of his eight presidential years, Eisenhower, was facing two hostile congressional houses. It was not long before the Democratic temptation to criminalize policy differences returned, with a controversy about Iran and aid to the Contras in Nicaragua, the guerrilla enemies of the communist Sandinista government in that country. In contravention of intermittent congressional prohibitions on aid to the Contras, armaments had been sold for on-shipment to the Contras, and the transactional profit was paid as ransom money to liberate American hostages of Iranian-sponsored terrorist organizations in Lebanon. It was a farcical plot, and it never seriously embarrassed Reagan personally, though Weinberger, quite unjustly, was briefly indicted by another overzealous special prosecutor.

Reagan was now less invulnerable politically and Nixon's support was of more importance to him. Nixon routinely and accurately dismissed the Iran-Contra affair, which took up a good part of 1987, as a "sideshow," and the joint Senate-House investigative committee was routed by the counsel of one of the chief witnesses, Edward Bennett Williams's successor, Brendan V. Sullivan, acting for Colonel Oliver North, a sometime CIA operative. It blew over without too much difficulty. The country was not prepared to indulge another constitutional crisis, and only the most perfervid journalists and politicians, including Woodward, Archibald Cox, and a couple of Democratic congressmen, were enthused by the prospect. It did raise serious issues, but tearing the government apart to get at them, with less tempting evidence than Oval Office tapes, and less vivid partisan figures involved than Nixon, never aroused adequate media or public interest.* [32]

---

* Nixon, as had become something of a habit of his, sent an extensive letter to incoming Defense Secretary Frank Carlucci (who had served Nixon with distinction as ambassador to Portugal and in the CIA), giving his advice on how to deal with post–Iran-Contra and other problems.

On his seventy-fifth birthday, January 9, 1988, Nixon finished his next book, *1999: Victory Without War*. He predicted a very difficult time for the Russians in continuing their occupation of Eastern Europe over the next decade; and said that it would take them at least twenty years to consolidate the occupation of Afghanistan.

However, he still had not glimpsed the epochal vision: "We must recognize that there are no permanent victories in the American-Soviet struggle," he wrote, though he advocated the continued pursuit of Cold War victory. He urged relentless effort to defeat the Soviets and their agents in Afghanistan and Nicaragua. Nixon's nuances were sometimes so subtle, they reduced him almost to humbug. Nixon was impressed by Gorbachev's forceful personality, and simply could not imagine that Gorbachev would allow the whole Soviet communist enterprise to collapse. His book was a good guide on how to fight the Cold War, and his failure to grasp how close victory was resulted from his inability to believe that so formidable a figure as Gorbachev, brought up in the party of Stalin, Khrushchev, and Brezhnev, would commit the terrible strategic mistakes that he did.

Nixon embarked on an extensive, countrywide book promotion tour and was constantly on television through the year and the election campaign. The candidates for the Republican nomination were his two protégés, George Bush and Robert Dole, and Bush won. The Democratic candidate was Governor Michael Dukakis of Massachusetts. For the fourth consecutive time, Nixon was not mentioned at the Republican convention. Bush was very polite to Nixon, and was grateful for his help in assuring that the hard-core Nixon supporters, whom Nixon called the "Nixon-nuts," were onside. Bush won the election safely enough, but became, with Nixon, the only president since Zachary Taylor in 1848 elected without his party's controlling either house of the Congress. Bush was the first vice president since Martin Van Buren in 1836 to finish his term as vice president and be elected to succeed the incumbent president, as Nixon had narrowly failed to do in 1960.

In 1989, the Soviet empire imploded. The Berlin Wall was opened; the U.S.S.R. withdrew from the so-called satellite countries and Afghanistan, and opposition to the Communist Party of the Soviet Union suddenly sprang up in great strength. Nixon had been one of the world's leading anti-communists for more than forty years. He had demanded the destruction of the Berlin Wall when it was put up by Khrushchev in 1961. He was one of the first sponsors of the Captive Nations Resolution and had accused Khrushchev publicly of enslavement of peoples across twelve time zones. In personal terms, it somewhat devalued him, as a great Cold Warrior, but as a public man who had battled all through the Cold War against the Red menace as it evolved, it was a delightful consummation.

It was clouded, from Nixon's standpoint, by Chinese developments. In June of 1989, the Chinese government set out to put an end to a "student" demonstration that had occupied the main square of the country, Tiananmen square in Beijing, for two months. It is understandable that no country could tolerate such a state of affairs indefinitely, any more than de Gaulle did in 1968, or than Nixon accepted the shutting-down of Washington in 1971. But what shocked the world was the gratuitous brutality of the clearance of the square. Instead of fire hoses and plastic bullets and truncheons, the Chinese attacked with tanks and bulldozers, and killed dozens or scores of people. It was a disgusting scene, and a public relations debacle for Deng Xiaoping, whose economic reforms had attracted widespread admiration and generated startling economic growth. The Chinese were determined to avoid the mistakes of Gorbachev, who had allowed liberalization to undermine his regime, but they went to completely unnecessary and, for a serious country, unacceptable extremes.

There was a demand in Congress for a severance of relations, which Bush essentially ignored; he sent his national security advisor, General Brent Scowcroft, secretly to Beijing to try to start a rebuilding job. Progress was sluggish. The seventy-six-year-old Richard Nixon saw his chance, and made his fifth post-presidential trip to China in October 1979. He had extensive meetings with the leadership, including Deng, and warned them that a severe crisis now afflicted Sino-American relations. Left more or less unspoken was that the crumbling of the U.S.S.R. gave China a good deal less leverage than it had previously enjoyed with the U.S.

On his return, Nixon met with Bush and wrote an extensive report for congressional leaders of both parties. He warned that the Chinese would not back down and would not accept to be humiliated in what they considered an internal matter. He said there was "an unbridgeable gap" on the question, but that a functioning relationship between the two countries could not be sacrificed over such an issue. He had not pulled any punches in China, stating publicly that the Tiananmen massacre was an outrage. He was equally blunt in stating geopolitical realities on his return. He probably played some role in the restoration of normal relations, the elimination of economic sanctions, and the retention of World Bank and other incentives to deal with China.

Nixon closed his New York office in 1989 and took a new one in New Jersey, within walking distance of his house. He had already discontinued government security, saving the taxpayers $3 million per year, and he spared himself two hours a day commuting. He went to New York when necessary, and to visit the Coxes, but most days he walked to work in suburban New Jersey. His office was another Nixonian classic. It was reached by walking through a large travel agency on the ground floor of a building on a suburban boulevard, then taking an elevator up two floors, opening a box with a bronze eagle on it, and announcing oneself on the telephone receiver within. A person would materialize at the door and conduct the visitor to a windowless room whose walls were almost entirely covered with photographs of Richard Nixon with almost every famous public officeholder in the world since the death of Stalin, and many other celebrities as well. Nixon would arrive promptly and was a courteous and discursive host.

Nixon glided effortlessly into the nineties, and was finally sought after by senior Republicans. He stepped fully into the role of elder statesman, and was – combining his roles as author, world traveler, and visitor to foreign leaders, and commentator – probably the most successful ex-president of all time. Early in 1990, he produced another book, *In the Arena: A Memoir of Victory, Defeat, and Renewal*. It was a strange pastiche of themes and subjects, though quite interesting in places. It started with a memoir, a digest of what he had already written, followed by thirty short chapters on completely unconnected subjects, such as reading, enemies, speaking, and so forth.

The largest single focus was on Watergate. He was trying to parlay his new standing as a respected former president into another assault on the reputational prison walls of Watergate. In this, he was not successful. He went further than ever, and even rolled his admission of "mistakes" back from what he had admitted to David Frost. Thus, he never deliberately lied to the public or the press about Watergate matters. (If he had not, he would have been the first president at least since George Washington not deliberately to

mislead the press.) He attacked again on his main fronts: he had not authorized hush money and had not tried to obstruct the FBI.

The critics concentrated entirely on Watergate and continued the great
American disappointment that he had not confessed, alleviating their concerns that he might have been mistreated and misjudged, and permitting
the country to forgive him. He would go to his grave unconfessed and un-
forgiven, but suspecting strongly that a posthumous victory awaited him. No
president of the United States had studied the lives of his predecessors as
closely as Nixon had (Truman was probably his closest rival), and he knew
how a president's historical reputation could evolve.

On March 8, 1990, Nixon came to Washington to speak to the House
Republican Conference and meet with Republican senatorial candidates.
The corridors of the Capitol were packed with young congressional aides
and secretaries and he was cheered and applauded as he went through the
building. Countless congressmen and senators asked to have their pictures
taken with him. He gave his hosts a memorable address, rendered without
notes as always, and was generously applauded and thanked. At a news conference afterwards, he demonstrated again the end of his former war with
the press. The questions were courteous, the answers relaxed and often very
informative. He had nothing to hide and they had nothing to tear down. On
this basis, Richard Nixon was articulate, intelligent, and even humorous
and rather charming.

Nixon had already launched the next phase of his great war for personal
recognition. He had raised $25 million for what was called a library, but was
in fact a Nixon Museum, at Yorba Linda. He was still litigating over his
papers and tapes, and successfully blocking access to them for the public or
even designated scholars. As so often before in his career, he turned necessity into a virtue, and claimed, as with Secret Service protection and his
former house at San Clemente, that he had saved the taxpayers millions. He
intended to gain possession of his presidential and vice presidential materials
eventually, or at least his literary executors would, and his library would be
operated without money from the U.S. government, and without the bureaucratic dead weight, and possible antagonism, of the National Archives.

Once again, Richard Nixon did it his way, and eventually, once again, he
was vindicated. His literary executors would have the pleasure of receiving all
the papers and would control them, by an arrangement finally implemented
in the second half of the first decade of the twenty-first century. For a man who

had risen so quickly, Richard Nixon had developed immense tenacity, and it was perceptible in his heirs and executors. He probably honed this tendency in his experiences with the Chinese, and their concentration on long-term perspectives. Not for Nixon the impulsiveness and impatience of a Lyndon Johnson. He was a contemplative, ruminative man, and he fought for every-thing and surrendered nothing, and to nothing – above all, not to despair. He transformed his melancholia into singular motivation.

The grand opening of the Nixon Library was on July 19, 1990, and it was a mighty occasion. President Bush and Presidents Ford and Reagan were present, as were secretaries of state Rogers, Kissinger, Haig, and Shultz. It was the first time in history four U.S. presidents appeared together in public. Almost all his old entourage, including Haldeman, were present, except for the unreconciled and uninvited Ehrlichman and Dean. It was Pat Nixon's first public appearance in ten years. She had been suffering from arthritis and emphysema. There were many celebrities, including Bob Hope, Billy Graham, and Norman Vincent Peale, and a thousand journalists, and the opening was nationally televised. Nixon's birthplace had been moved and reconstructed and placed on the property, and the museum was a very inter-esting and imaginative treatment of his life, essentially repeating the party line on Watergate, that there was a semblance of wrongdoing, but that it was really a partisan effort to repeal the results of the 1972 election. There were effigies of famous statesmen Nixon had known, and the whole effect was impressive and persuasive.

All the presidents spoke, and the incumbent, George Bush, introduced Nixon, who was treated to a tremendous and very moving ovation by thou-sands of his admirers. He spoke tastefully and fluently, and not immodestly or overlong. "I believe in the American Dream, because I have seen it come true in my own life. . . . It is sad to lose [but] always remember that only when . . . you are involved in a cause greater than yourself, can you be true to yourself." Tens of thousands of balloons were released, the band played, and the large crowd lustily sang "God Bless America." He appeared on the cover of *Time* magazine, amazingly, for the sixty-seventh time, another quaint Nixon record.

The following year, 1991, Nixon took another step toward permanence, by setting up the Nixon Center in Washington. This was a think tank and conference center, and he inaugurated it with a speech of his own, and a discussion involving many of the leading foreign policy experts of the

United States and some foreigners, and again, President Bush gave it his full and distinguished patronage. The Center was well-financed, and some years after Nixon died, it acquired the respected foreign affairs quarterly, *The National Interest*, founded by the renowned neo-conservative Irving Kristol.

Nixon continued to write and comment and travel, and maintained relations with the new leadership of major countries, including Boris Yeltsin of Russia, after the Soviet Union collapsed and Gorbachev retired, and the emerging adjutants of Deng in China. He never slowed down, and neither his stamina nor his intellectual faculties flagged. He was asked by the Major League Umpires Association to mediate their salary and working conditions dispute with the commissioner, and he did, with his usual efficiency, satisfying all sides.

His eightieth birthday, on January 9, 1993, was the occasion for general goodwill, and was cordially remarked even in the columns of his formerly bitterest media adversaries. He was now a genial and intelligent and dignified former president, controversial in his time, but one who had unquestionably rendered great service to the nation, and to the West. In his latter years, Milton's phrase seemed to be applicable to him: "his soul serene, all passion spent;" all passion except his determination to continue and build his historical standing and enjoy his grandchildren. He told the author, and doubtless others, that he felt, given his origins, he had had an interesting career, that he had rendered some service and made and paid for some mistakes, but that the service endured, and taking it all in all, he had done quite well. There seemed to be peace, at the last.

A few days after Nixon's eightieth birthday, William Jefferson Clinton was inaugurated as Nixon's fifth successor as president, with the result that there were now more living presidents than had existed at any time since 1862 (and then John Tyler had declared for the Confederacy and was technically in a different country, or at least an insurgent territory). Although Bush had violated his pledge of "no new taxes," he had led the country with great distinction in the Gulf War, undoing Iraq's military aggression against Kuwait. The War Powers Act was honored and after intense and very intelligent debate in both houses of the Congress, the military action was authorized, and a vast international alliance was assembled by Bush and his capable secretary of state, James A. Baker (Reagan's former chief of staff and Treasury secretary). But then Bush seemed to fritter away his support. Nixon advised him occasionally to watch his political flanks, but Bush, a war hero and distinguished public servant, had never had a great electoral talent. He had had a safe congressional seat in Texas, had lost twice for the Senate from that state, and had stood on the magic carpet of Reagan's coattails thereafter.

A third-party challenge from billionaire Ross Perot arose and the Democratic candidate, the five-term governor of Arkansas, Bill Clinton, was a facile debater and astute tactician, much harder to pillory as an un-representative leftist than had been McGovern, Carter (once the country got a look at him), Mondale, and Dukakis. Clinton's wife, Hillary Rodham Clinton, had been on the special prosecutor's staff during Watergate, but Clinton treated Nixon very courteously.

On March 8, 1993, Nixon had a long and very cordial meeting in the family residence of the White House with President Clinton. The next day, he spoke to the House of Representatives, as the guest of the bipartisan leadership, after an absence from that House, other than at joint sessions, of nearly forty-three years. He spoke relatively informally from the well of the House, rather than the podium, and referred to his last speech there as a congressman in 1950, summarizing the Hiss case. He said: "Who would have thought that I would be back in 1993, talking about a democratic Russia? I was a congressman when General MacArthur spoke here. 'Old soldiers never die; they just fade away.' Old politicians sometimes die, but they never fade away." He was warmly received, generously applauded, and given a prolonged ovation by the congressmen when he finished.

Nixon the historian and contender for a better place in history than recent conventional opinion had given him, had well-developed views of the other presidents he had known. He regarded Herbert Hoover as a much wiser man politically than people generally thought, and mentioned that Hoover had said just before he died, in 1964, that Goldwater was a good thing for the Republicans, to "get the party's extremism out of its system." (This was a man who had accused Roosevelt of treason.) Nixon now admired Truman and regretted that he had never been forgiven by Truman, as he had been by Acheson. Having achieved his great goal of Dwight Eisenhower's approval and unqualified endorsement, he rarely spoke of him. He considered Eisenhower a great man, but a cold and calculating one, and not an exceptionally interesting president.

He was sensitive to the charge of envying John Kennedy. He believed that the dividend of the tragedy of Kennedy's death was a pass on serious historical evaluation. He got on well with Ambassador Joseph Kennedy, the father, who he claimed had said he would support Nixon against anyone but his own son, but Nixon regarded the ambassador as a financially and morally dishonest man. He thought Bobby smarter than Jack, but both of them rude to subordinates like restaurant waiters and hotel and household staff, an unpardonable offense to Nixon, who had once performed those functions himself, out of economic necessity. He thought the Kennedys were uninterested in civil rights until they saw votes in it, and oblivious of civil liberties such as privacy from arbitrary telephone intercepts.

Nixon respected JFK's con job on the press and public, and got on well with him personally, but thought him a mediocre president and an historical confidence trick. He detested Bobby as a vindictive hypocrite and fanatic. He thought Teddy Kennedy a weak character of no particular talent who would be on skid row but for his father's money and his brothers' political success (the second chiefly dependent on the first). He noted with disdain what he considered the propensity of all of them to betray their admirable wives and behave "like oversexed pigs" (comment to author).

He considered Lyndon Johnson an admirable tragedy, a cynical politician who had the courage to plunge into war when, Nixon thought, abandoning South Vietnam was politically unthinkable, and achieving what only a Southern master of the Congress could in civil rights, a cause of which, Nixon often pointed out, he was a much earlier advocate than Kennedy or Johnson.

Nixon liked Gerald Ford but was disappointed in what he considered his "selling of the presidency" by taking large fees to speak. He said that Hoover, Truman, Eisenhower, Johnson, and he had never accepted a cent to give a speech as an ex-president, and that Ford's conduct was undignified. Further, he asked rhetorically, "Who would listen to him?" Jimmy Carter was, he thought, an incompetent president, but probably a decent man. He thought that Carter's efforts to "build outhouses in Central Asia" with his evangelical co-religionists was more creditable than Ford's endless golfing, but he found Carter's sanctimony insufferable.

Nixon liked and admired Ronald Reagan, though he thought him hag-ridden and intellectually limited and naïve. He regarded him as almost a pixie who had led a charmed political life, without defeat or serious embarrassment, who would get the credit for what Truman, Eisenhower, and Nixon had prepared for him at the end of the Cold War. With that, he admired Reagan's devotion to principle, courage, genius as a public speaker, and personal integrity, and had great empathy for his decline in his eighties as an Alzheimer's sufferer.

George H.W. Bush he had always thought a "good man with good intentions." But he had "no discernible pattern of political principle . . . no political rhythm, no conservative cadence, and not enough charismatic style to compensate." He had appreciated him at the UN and when he rode his bicycle around Beijing as the U.S. representative there, but thought he only reacted in the Gulf War when Margaret Thatcher told him he had to, and he was very disappointed in Bush's platitudinous address at the opening of the Nixon Center in Washington in 1992.

Richard Nixon regarded Bill Clinton as a "waffler," a clever campaigner and media manipulator, but morally a weakling in all respects. He was grateful for Clinton's attention to him personally, and for the key role he played in Nixon's substantial rehabilitation, but regarded him as a morally empty political operator of great talent but no substance. He considered Hillary Clinton a subversive robot. She professed to be grateful for Nixon's original championship of universal health care, but he thought that even the way she applauded was "mechanical." When her universal health-care proposals were presented to the Congress, he blamed the Republicans for serving "softballs at her when they should have been aiming for her head."[33]

On June 22, 1993, Pat Nixon, who had been unwell for many years, died. She had been through the wringer of fifty-two years of marriage, and whatever abrasions there may have been were very discreetly confined to the family. She had been invaluable in the greatest crises, moving to be nearer to Nixon during the war, encouraging him through the fund crisis, unflinching as crowds spat on her in Caracas, enduring the California campaign in 1962, and suffering through Watergate and her husband's near-terminal illness. She bore through everything with magnificent dignity, and the decorum and stability of their daughters must reflect to some extent on their mother. The effort of some Nixon-haters to portray her as a Stepford Wife, a robot, Betty in Pleasantville, was not the least of the many outrages inflicted on the Nixons.

Pat Nixon was eighty-one. Her funeral was at the Nixon Library, and for the only time in his adult life, at the end of the ceremony, Richard Nixon broke down in convulsive sobs and had to be assisted inside the building to recover his repose of manner. He quickly did recover and then gave the funeral guests a tasteful and touching tribute to his wife, to whom he owed so much.* He met and spoke with all the guests and seemed to Leonard Garment "to have passed some finish-line of his own, taking a slow cooling-off trot around the track after the race was run . . . His hair had finally gone gray. Up close, his features seemed larger, rounder, softened by age. I never saw him quite so loose and at ease." Some thought that without Pat, Nixon would not last a year. They were right.[34]

Nixon continued to write and travel. He had given the annual Atlantic Richfield Dinner address in London in the autumn of 1992, and dazzled the most eminent dinner audience that city could produce with a brilliant one-hour, ex tempore summary of Anglo-American relations, beginning with his recollections of British leaders whom he had known, starting with Churchill and Attlee (and former prime ministers Heath and Thatcher, as well as Ronald Reagan, were at his table). He concluded with a lengthy and appo-site quote from Lord Curzon, whose first wife was an American, and without pedantry, gave an original turn to a much-discussed subject. He managed to work into his remarks, as was his custom, a number of people in his audi-ence, including philosopher Isaiah Berlin.

It was an astounding tour de force, and the packed ballroom of Claridge's Hotel rose to him with more than usual enthusiasm. His daugh-ter Julie watched from behind a curtain, and was relieved and pleased that it had gone so well. He mingled with the audience for thirty minutes or so. The author introduced then Prime Minister John Major's press secretary to him, and Nixon, almost reflexively, said, "Don't trust the bastards!" but now in a rather jocular way, showing none of the lowering countenance of earlier times when referring to the press.

He had just returned from one of his many meetings with Russia's President Yeltsin, and seemed not to have slowed down or to have lost the efficacy of his endless, high-level, personal diplomacy.

— VII —

In April 1994, Nixon was working on a new book, *Beyond Peace*, which *Life* was going to serialize. He went to the wedding of Robert Abplanalp's daugh-ter, Marie, in New Jersey on Saturday, April 16. On April 17, he wrote

---

* Truman Capote, in 1981, had rated Pat Nixon the woman he would most like to meet.[35]

the foreword to *The Day Elvis Met Nixon*, a book by Egil (Bud) Krogh (the former White House Plumber). The next day, he was working at home with his chief of staff, Cathy O'Connor, on the excerpts from *Beyond Peace*, when, just before dinner, some paralysis set in, and he could not speak properly. An ambulance was called and Cathy O'Connor went with him to the New York-Cornell University Hospital. He was conscious but unable to speak. and his sight was impaired. The initial prognosis was hopeful.

Tricia and her husband arrived after a few minutes, and Julie and David Eisenhower a couple of hours later. They and Cathy O'Connor stayed through the week. New York mayor Rudolph Giuliani and Henry Kissinger visited to pay their respects to the former president's daughters and wish them well. Kissinger told the press, as he told Jay Leno (who had succeeded Jack Paar and Johnny Carson on *The Tonight Show*) on his television program the next night, that if unlimited determination and courage could overcome the medical problems, his old chief would be back.

Brian McDonnell, who had conducted a hunger fast in Lafayette Park across from the White House during the Cambodian incursion of 1971, called Kissinger's office and asked that Kissinger tell President Nixon that he, McDonnell, was praying for him. Complications began on Wednesday, April 20. On Thursday, Nixon sank into a coma and hope faded. There was a vigil around the main door of the hospital, as his followers, whom he had led over the hurdles of a very long and tortuous career, did not desert him now. On Friday evening, at 9:08, April 22, 1994, Richard Milhous Nixon died peacefully. He was eighty-one, and exactly one week older than Pat Nixon had been when she had died, the year before.

Obituarists were reasonably generous, though Watergate got the obligatory, and not always very well-proportioned, airing. Richard Nixon was flown for the last time on Air Force One to California; the funeral was at the Nixon Library and Birthplace in Yorba Linda, and the burial was beside Pat. President Clinton declared it a full state occasion and all flags on U.S. federal buildings, installations, and ships were lowered, for the first time since the death of Lyndon Johnson in 1973. There was a good turnout of Nixon's old friends at Yorba Linda, including Spiro Agnew, who had had no contact with the deceased since he left government twenty-one years before. All those who had succeeded him as president were present, with their wives; there had never been such a gathering of presidents. The Fords, Carters, Reagans, Bushes, and Clintons sat together, beside the Nixon family.

The governor of California, Pete Wilson, who had been an advance man for Nixon when he ran for that office in 1962; the Republican leader in the Senate, and apparent party leader, Robert Dole; and, according to custom, the incumbent president, all gave ex officio remembrances. Wilson praised his perseverance, Dole his indomitable rise from humble origins, Clinton his statesmanlike qualities, emphasizing that it was on these, and not mere controversies, that he must be judged. All were gracious and eloquent.

But the real eulogy, from the person who worked most closely with him on his greatest projects, was delivered with great feeling and effect by Henry Kissinger. He "imagined how [Nixon] would have reacted to the tide of concern, respect, admiration, and affection evoked by the last great battle, in his astonishing life," and quoted Shakespeare that "I shall not look upon his like again." He touched on Nixon's gruff exterior, which masked a man of frequent gentleness and sensitivity, and credited his political success in a field where he did not have a natural tendency to be gregarious. He recalled that Nixon said he would take the same abuse for doing partially something that was unpopular as for doing it fully, so that such things should be done thoroughly. He mentioned that "He had risked a confrontation with the Soviet Union in the midst of the worst crisis of his life" (in 1973). "He held fast in the face of wrenching controversy to his basic theme that the greatest free nation in the world had a duty to lead and no right to abdicate. Nixon's greatest accomplishment was as much moral as it was political: to lead from strength at a moment of apparent weakness, [laying] the basis for victory in the Cold War."

At this critical moment, all rivalry between the two men finally vanished, and Kissinger's own best instincts came naturally to his eulogist's task. His voice broke slightly at one point, when he referred to hearing "the final news, by then so expected but so hard to accept, [when] I felt a deep loss and a profound void." [He told the author that he felt that "part of me died with him."]

Kissinger recounted what Nixon had done to end a war in which more than half a million draftees were "as far away from the United States as it was possible to be"; to open relations with China, and the major Arab powers; to start a peace process in the Middle East, arms control arrangements with the Russians, and the discussion of human rights across Europe. He said Nixon "would be so pleased that President Clinton" and his other successors were here, indicating that "his long and sometimes bitter journey had concluded in reconciliation."

No one who heard the peroration to his brief address that day will ever forget it: "So let us now say goodbye to our gallant friend. He stood on pinnacles that dissolved into precipices. He achieved greatly and suffered deeply. But he never gave up. In his solitude, he envisioned a new international order that would reduce lingering enmities, strengthen historic friendships, and give new hope to mankind – a vision where dreams and possibilities conjoined.

"Richard Nixon ended a war and he advanced the vision of peace of his Quaker youth. He was devoted to his family. He loved his country and he considered service his honor." After a reception, the crowd dispersed and the world moved on, without one of its most prominent citizens of the last forty-five years.

A man who was in his cradle when Nixon conducted his investigation of Alger Hiss was now nearly fifty years old. Only Franklin D. Roosevelt was nominated as often by a major party to national office (five times), and no American has served as long as Nixon did in national office – over thirteen and a half years. No president except Thomas Jefferson has been so long and prominently at the forefront of national affairs, as Richard Nixon was, over forty-five years.

Nixon had been instrumental in taking the Republican Party away from the isolationists and country-club plutocrats that had led it to disaster again and again against Roosevelt and Truman. He had played a decisive role in the restoration of functioning two-party government and in creating a bipartisan internationalist foreign policy. He was one of the first and most persuasive advocates of the U.S. national interest in containing communism in Western Europe and East Asia. He, more than anyone else, engineered the downfall of Joseph R. McCarthy.

Nixon was, with Reagan, the chief builder of the modern Republican Party, and he was the supreme Cold Warrior – from champion of the Red Scare in the forties to inventor of détente in the seventies.

He had been the most effective vice president and the most successful ex-president in the country's history. Kissinger's recitation of his foreign policy accomplishments as president was fair. He was, with Truman, and Reagan, the most important person in conducting the Cold War to a victorious conclusion. The opening to China assisted in the exit from Vietnam and the success of arms control with the Russians, and it made some contribution to the eventual reorientation of China as a capitalist country.

He and Kissinger did not have the absolute success they hoped for in the Middle East, but they virtually expelled the Soviet Union from the region and started what was always bound to be a very long and exacting peace process. At least, at time of writing, there have been no full-scale wars involving Israel for a third of a century, after four such wars in the first twenty years of Israel's history.

He came into office in the most daunting circumstances that faced any new president except Lincoln and Franklin D. Roosevelt. He withdrew from the Vietnam War. The riots and assassinations and skyjackings stopped. He quelled inflation, until the oil cartel spiked it up again. He abolished the draft and reduced the crime rate, made serious inroads on illegal drug use, decentralized government through revenue sharing, and practically ended school segregation throughout the country.

He took a terribly divided and angry and demoralized country and solved its principal problems, before new ones arose. He was reelected by the greatest plurality in American history, not only because of the ineptitude of the Democratic candidate, and not at all because of the deranged and lawless antics of some of his supporters, but because he was a very competent and successful president who dealt decisively with all the problems he faced.

He was a pioneer in the environment. He had been a pioneer in advocating stimulative tax reductions in the Eisenhower administration. It took until Reagan's presidency for this to be given a full trial, and it worked. He was an early champion of welfare reform. Only Robert Dole and other Republican congressional leaders finally forced it through in the Clinton administration, and it, too, has had a promising start. Nixon was also prophetic in campaign finance reform, universal private-sector medical care and catastrophic health insurance, and energy self-sufficiency. Not much was achieved in these areas in the thirty years after his presidency, but when it is, he will be remembered.

Certainly the two greatest controversies of Nixon's presidency were Vietnam and Watergate. Nixon inherited a horrible tragedy in Vietnam. It is not clear why he imagined that the North Vietnamese would respond seriously to a peace offer that constituted less than victory for Hanoi; that is all they had been prepared to accept from Johnson. It won't do to say, as Nixon did in *No More Vietnams* and elsewhere, that he inherited Johnson's bombing pause.

The way to win the war was to Vietnamize the internal war in South Vietnam, use the U.S. and South Korean forces to seal the demilitarized zone and shut the Ho Chi Minh Trail, and intensify bombing of the North to a point that North Vietnam would eventually make substantive concessions to reduce the bombing, and not just send an insolent delegation to Paris to debate about the shape of a table. Nixon could have got bipartisan approval of a serious plan to strengthen the South Vietnamese, and attack North Vietnamese war-making potential, while gradually pulling down U.S. force levels in Vietnam, if he had moved early. He did not.

The alternative way to liquidate the problem was to declare that it had been misconceived in the first place and that it was not worth the effort, and leave. There was no Dien Bien Phu. The United States had not been militarily defeated, and it could have been presented as the wise move strategically.

Perhaps Nixon had found another means to achieve a sustainable settlement in 1972: building up ARVN and supporting it with a thousand warplanes on a massive bombing and mining mission in the North, and maintaining this pressure as long as there was any activity on the Ho Chi Minh Trail. That was what he promised Thieu, and if he had made a serious effort to elect more Republicans to Congress in 1972, and not blundered into the Watergate debacle, it might have been possible to carry it out, and it might have worked. It would have had to be sustained for about fifteen years, before international communism collapsed.

At least it must be said, Nixon inherited an utterly hopeless war, which Johnson had given up on to the point that he could not even extract serious concessions from Hanoi in exchange for departing the country. And Nixon withdrew the United States without a defeat and while preserving a tenuous possibility of the survival of a non-communist South Vietnam.

He won the second Vietnam War; Hanoi's war against America, and prevented the military and domestic political humiliation of the United States itself. He inherited and improved upon the worst of all possible policies from the former administration. It is a passable record despite the prolongation and bloodshed and ultimate failure and it was executed with great courage at times.

The story of Watergate is too infamous, and has been too lengthily elaborated here, to justify another long summary. Most of the vast Watergate literature is self serving claptrap. Nixon had no prior knowledge of it. It was never "imperial" or an assault on the Constitution, or a serious conspiracy. Nixon was guilty, as he admitted to David Frost, of, at least, a "horrible mistake unworthy of a president." In a fair proceeding it would not have been easy to prove that he had committed a crime that justified his removal from office.

Watergate reached the point it did because Nixon allowed the media and the more partisan Democrats to create an atmosphere of hysteria, and he became the reluctant revealer of tapes and transcripts of his own conversations. These revealed an unedifyingly sleazy and cynical ambience in the White House. His political capital evaporated and he lost the moral authority to discharge his office. This would not have happened if his conversations with one of his lawyers, Dean, had enjoyed the normal legal privilege and if his private conversations, which were not necessarily much more scandalous than similar exchanges involving some other presidents, had been governed by the usual rules against self-incrimination. After so much foreplay, the great puritanical conscience of America could not be appeased other than by the downfall of the president, however the normal rules of evidence might be suspended to achieve that end.

In a sense, Nixon executed a radical strategic evacuation like the two great leaders he seemed to admire most of those whom he knew (except for Winston Churchill, whom he did not know well), and who admired him. Like de Gaulle tearing himself loose from the crumbling French state and removing to Britain in 1940 where he, as he put it, "assumed France" and continued, in his own person, the personality and ambitions of a great nation; and like Mao Tse-tung disengaging from the Chinese Civil War and undertaking the three-thousand-mile Long March of 1934 and 1935 to a more defensible fastness, so Nixon relinquished the presidency and began to build a legend, reconstruct his moral standing, and revise popular history.

By showing no contrition, but regret at errors committed, and carefully laying out his version of the facts, with some remorse, but no guilt or confession of crimes, Nixon gradually seized control of the national puritanical conscience that had assaulted him. All indications are that ten years after he died, Americans were more interested in Nixon than in any political leader in their history, with the sole possible exception of Lincoln.

In fact, as the nation has come to fear, Nixon was mistreated. He was partly responsible for it himself by his own mishandling of Watergate, but he was viciously and unfairly attacked by the media, the Democrats, and some of his own partisans. He was not a uniquely sleazy president, but was treated as one.

There is room for debate over whether he dishonored, or merely demeaned, the presidency. It is beyond debate that he fully paid for his misdeeds, and that he was a very competent president. His legal and ethical shortcomings kept him out of the small group of great presidents generally deemed to comprise Washington, Lincoln, and Franklin D. Roosevelt, with some argument to be made for Jefferson and Reagan. Nixon is rather in the category of unusually talented presidents who are just beneath the very greatest American leaders, with Jackson, Polk, Theodore Roosevelt, Wilson, Truman, and possibly Eisenhower (it being understood that Jefferson and Eisenhower were world historic figures before they even became president). More than that, Richard Nixon has become a mighty and mythic figure.

He had two incomparable achievements: he made a virtue of his own unglamorous unease to mobilize an immense, informal army of ordinary people whom he led for decades. And he subtly nettled the righteousness of America that had slain him, until it was intrigued by, and addicted to, Nixon, and its implacable hostility had given way to uncertainty and even remorse.

By his inexorable pursuit of his goal of being always at the center of events, decade after decade, and his constantly recalibrated self-promotion as the champion of the average person, the decent toiler, the silent majority, Nixon led a perpetual revolt against the stylish, the facile and fashionable, the well born, all those, from the Roosevelts to the Kennedys and Rockefellers, even to the Buckleys and Bushes, and in a sense to Kissinger, for whom things seemed to come easily.

He was almost never overt about whom he was running against, other than in elections. But all those scores of millions of Americans who identified with the awkwardness, the persevering courage, the endless struggle of Nixon, who never deserted him, who envied but could not identify with the wit of an Adlai Stevenson or the grace of a Jack Kennedy, gave him an immense following that continued to grow after he retired, and long after he died.[*] To them, Richard Nixon was an inspiration, an ordinary man of superhuman determination and perseverance, indomitable, indefatigable,

---

[*] As formerly anti-Nixon journalist Tom Wicker of the *New York Times* at least partially recognized in his biography, *One of Us*.

almost impervious to the vicious attacks of the privileged, the press, the academics, the abusive prosecutors.

Nixon knew how to generate sympathy, because he was frequently plagued by self-pity. He knew how to surmount crises, because he never gave up, and when defeated, he just stole away and attacked toward his objective from another angle, while his opponents were prematurely celebrating the demise of his career.

And when he died at the full age of eighty-one, he had already perpetuated himself, the unconquerable little man, the ordinary but great man, the reassurance of the triumphant power of the common man. He was anything but common in his intelligence and courage and endurance, but he seemed common to those who really were common; he turned leftist playwright Arthur Miller's tragedy about an insignificant person upside down; his was *Life of a Salesman*.

Nixon was the people. He was the representative inhabitant of what Jack Kerouac called the "great unwashed body of America." He was laborious but effective, eloquent but not hypnotizing, cynical but compassionate and patriotic. He got where he did by climbing, falling, climbing again, and never ceasing to struggle. Kennedy and Rockefeller seemed to be born in high places, and Reagan was a popular deus ex machina who came from afar but made the transition quickly.

Richard Milhous Nixon achieved as much as any American political leader since Abraham Lincoln, except for Franklin D. Roosevelt, and perhaps Dwight D. Eisenhower, and he did it against his own unusually troublesome anxiety and limitations and awkwardnesses. He was often his own enemy, because of his complex personality, and he attracted legions of constant conventional enemies. He fought successfully all his long life, and when he died, he was acknowledged to be a unique and, in his way, a great American. His enemies fell away, and he slipped the surly bonds of mortal combat and became the embodiment, the allegorization, of generally well-intentioned determination, not less than human in his failings, but almost superhuman in his strengths. And he had begun to gnaw at the conscience of the nation.

Nixon had said, "You've got to be a little evil to understand those people out there. You have to have known the dark side of life." He probably met both those criteria. He also told Chou En-lai that he wanted a "life in which

I have just one more victory than defeat."[35] He was more successful than that.

He was, for better and worse, the personification of a large section of the American people, and they never forgot it. In the years since his death, his legend seems to have grown more quickly than his memory has receded. Richard Nixon will linger in the American consciousness for a very long time.

Notes

Chapter One

1. Earl Mazo, *Richard Nixon: A Political and Personal Portrait*, p. 20.
2. Roger Morris, *Richard Milhous Nixon: The Rise of an American Politician*, p. 16.
3. Jonathan Aitken, *Nixon: A Life*, p. 47.
4. Morris, p. 28.
5. Benjamin F. Arland and Artilissa D. Clark, *History of Whittier*, p. 28; Morris, p. 29.
6. Edwin P. Hoyt, *The Nixons: An American Family*, p. 102; Morris, p. 34.
7. Aitken, p. 14.
8. Morris, p. 49 (interview with Mary E. Rezo).
9. William Safire, *Before the Fall: An Inside View of the Pre-Watergate White House*, p. 555.
10. Morris, p. 68 (interview with Mrs. Cecil Pickering).
11. Henry Kissinger, *Years of Upheaval*, p. 1184.
12. Morris, p. 70 (interview with Earl Chapman).
13. *Los Angeles Times*, 9/7/70.
14. Bela Kornitzer, *The Real Nixon: An Intimate Biography*, p. 57.
15. Morris, p. 84.
16. Ibid.; Fawn Brodie, *Richard Nixon: The Shaping of His Character*, p. 90.
17. *Whittier Daily News*, 7/28/55; Morris, p. 99.
18. Conrad Black, *Franklin Delano Roosevelt: Champion of Freedom*, p. 25.
19. Aitken, p. 35.
20. Black, pp. 23–24.
21. Richard Nixon, *RN: The Memoirs of Richard Nixon*, p. 19 (after referred to as Nixon, *Memoirs*).
22. W.E. Leuchtenburg, *Franklin D. Roosevelt and the New Deal*, p. 39 (Agnes Meyer diary, 2/25/33).
23. Aitken, p. 53 (interview with Edward Nixon).
24. Kornitzer, p. 238.

25. Nixon, *Memoirs*, pp. 16–17.
26. Aitken, p. 34 (interview with Ola Jobe).
27. Mazo, p. 43.
28. *Whittier College Acropolis*, 1934; Stephen E. Ambrose, *Nixon*, vol. 1, *The Education of a Politician, 1913–1962*, p. 64 (after referred to as Ambrose, vol. 1).
29. Ambrose, vol. 1, p. 71; Earl Chapman interview, California State University at Fullerton.
30. Mollenkopf to Nixon, 3/27/59, Vice Presidential Papers, Duke University Friends File.
31. Ambrose, vol. 1, p. 76.
32. Brodie, p. 131; Morris, p. 72.
33. Aitken, p. 76; Morris, p. 180.
34. Stewart Alsop interview with Nixon, 1958, Stewart Alsop Papers, Library of Congress; S. Alsop, *Nixon and Rockefeller: A Double Portrait*, p. 195.
35. Jessamyn West, "The Real Pat Nixon," *Good Housekeeping*, 2/71.
36. Brodie, p. 154.
37. Black, pp. 150–51.
38. Morris, p. 198.
39. L. Wallace Black interview, California State University at Fullerton.
40. Aitken, p. 91.
41. Lester David, *The Lonely Lady of San Clemente: The Story of Pat Nixon*, p. 60.
42. Aitken, p. 580.
43. Ibid., p. 93.
44. David, p. 62.
45. Aitken, p. 94.
46. Black, p. 593.
47. Mazo, p. 37.
48. Doris Kearns Goodwin, *No Ordinary Time: Franklin and Eleanor Roosevelt: The Home Front in World War II*, p. 42.
49. Julie N. Eisenhower, *Pat Nixon: The Untold Story*, pp. 72–73.
50. Milton Viorst, "Nixon of the OPA," *New York Times Magazine*, 10/3/71.
51. Benscher to S. Alsop, 25/4/58, Alsop Papers, Library of Congress; Morris, p. 241.
52. Nixon, *Memoirs*, p. 26.
53. Kornitzer, pp. 139–40.
54. Aitken, p. 99.
55. Jerry Szumski, "When the Nixons lived in Iowa," *DesMoines Register*, 2/8/70; Morris, p. 246.
56. Aitken, p. 401 (interview with James Stewart).

57. Hoyt, pp. 233–36.

58. Ibid.

59. Nixon, *Memoirs*, p. 29.

60. Ambrose, vol. 1, p. 108.

61. Nixon, *Memoirs*, p. 29.

62. Edward McCaffrey to Nixon, 2/24/50, Vice Presidential Papers; Donald Jackson, "The Young Nixon," *Life*, 11/6/70; Ambrose, vol. 1, p. 114.

63. Nixon, *Memoirs*, p. 30.

64. Aitken, p. 187.

65. Julie N. Eisenhower, p. 84.

66. Richard Gardner, *Fighting Quaker: The Story of Richard Nixon*, Whittier College Special Collections, p. 208.

67. Black, p. 1121.

68. John Sullivan to Francis Matthews, 1/21/46; Morris, p. 266.

69. Black, p. 519.

70. James MacGregor Burns, *Roosevelt: The Soldier of Freedom*, p. 165.

71. Nixon, *Memoirs*, p. 34.

72. Arthur M. Schlesinger, *The Age of Roosevelt*, vol. 3, *The Politics of Upheaval*, pp. 117–21.

73. Leuchtenburg, p. 281; *New York Times*, 2/11/38.

74. Drew Pearson, 7/27/40; Morris, p. 260.

75. Nixon, *Memoirs*, p. 35.

76. Morris, p. 274.

77. *Alhambra Post-Advocate* (California), 11/13/68.

78. Ambrose, vol. 1, p. 120.

79. Julie N. Eisenhower, p. 86.

80. Jerry Voorhis, Oral Histories, Claremont Colleges, 5/61; Morris p. 284.

81. Aitken, p. 75.

82. Mazo, pp. 45–46.

Chapter Two

1. Jerry Voorhis Papers, 4/16/46, Claremont Colleges; Ralph de Toledano, *One Man Alone: Richard Nixon*; Richard Nixon, *RN: The Memoirs of Richard Nixon*, pp. 49–50 (after referred to as Nixon, *Memoirs*).

2. Personal and Family Papers, Richard Nixon Library and Birthplace, Yorba Linda.

3. W. Earl Emick to Voorhis, 5/2/46, Confessions of a Congressman File, Jerry Voorhis Papers.

4. Bela Kornitzer, *The Real Nixon: An Intimate Biography*, p. 160.

5. Jerry Voorhis, *Confessions of a Congressman*, p. 333.
6. Stephen E. Ambrose, *Nixon*, vol. 1, *The Education of a Politician, 1913–1962*, p. 131 (after referred to as Ambrose, vol. 1).
7. *San Francisco Chronicle*, 10/14/46.
8. *Covina Argus-Citizen*, 10/11/46.
9. League for Good Government letter, 9/30/46, Campaign File, Jerry Voorhis Papers.
10. Jerry Voorhis, Oral Histories, 5; 65–66, Claremont Colleges; Morris, p. 327.
11. Morris, p. 330.
12. *San Gabriel Sun*, 10/30/46; Morris, p. 331.
13. David W. Reinhard, *The Republican Right Since 1945*, p. 15.
14. Nixon Private Archives cited in Jonathan Aitken, *Nixon: A Life*, p. 129.
15. Voorhis, p. 347 et seq.
16. Nixon, *Memoirs*, p. 44.
17. Roger Morris, *Richard Milhous Nixon: The Rise of an American Politician*, p. 342.
18. John T. Balch, Richard M. Nixon vs. H. Jerry Voorhis for Congress, 1946, p. 56.
19. Congressional Record, 2/18/47, vol. 93, pt. 1, pp. 1129–30.
20. Fawn Brodie Research Collection, University of Utah; Morris, p. 347.
21. Ibid.; Morris, p. 358.
22. Morris, p. 349.
23. David McCullough, *Truman*, p. 548.
24. HUAC Hearings, 3/26/47, p. 47.
25. Maurice Isserman, *Which Side Were You On?: The American Communist Party During the Second World War*, p. 244.
26. Eric Bentley, *Twenty Years of Treason: Excerpts from Hearings Before the House Committee on Un-American Activities, 1938–1968*, pp. 110–53.
27. Tom Wicker, *One of Us: Richard Nixon and the American Dream*, p. 117.
28. Nixon, *Memoirs*, p. 48.
29. Ibid., p. 51.
30. Morris, p. 375.
31. Walter Goodman, *The Committee: The Extraordinary Career of the House Committee on Un-American Activities*, p. 275.
32. Adolf A. Berle, *Navigating the Rapids, 1918–1971*, pp. 249–50; Ladislas Farago, Fawn Brodie Research Collection, University of Utah; Morris, pp. 387–88.
33. Ovid Demaris, *The Director: An Oral Biography of J. Edgar Hoover*, p. 115.
34. Allen Weinstein, *Perjury: The Hiss-Chambers Case*, p. 361.
35. Morris, p. 398.

36. FBI Report to President Truman, Harry S. Truman Library, 5/23/49; Morris, p. 489.
37. Whittaker Chambers, *Witness*, p. 555; Ambrose, vol. 1, p. 171.
38. Hiss letter to Dulles, 8/5/48, John Foster Dulles Papers, Princeton University; Morris, p. 494.
39. Robert E. Stripling, *The Red Plot Against America*, p. 116.
40. Morris, p. 405.
41. Richard Nixon, *Six Crises*, p. 15.
42. Chambers, p. 558.
43. Ibid., pp. 792–93.
44. Nixon, *Six Crises*, p. 31.
45. HUAC 1, Commodore Hotel Testimony, p. 975 et seq.
46. Weinstein, *Perjury*, p. 39.
47. Chambers, p. 618.
48. *New York Times*, 8/21/48.
49. HUAC 1, 8/25/48, p. 1075 et seq.
50. Ibid.
51. Chambers, p. 709.
52. Ibid., p. 722.
53. *New York Times*, 1/19/49.
54. Weinstein, *Perjury*, p. 469; Earl Mazo, *Richard Nixon: A Political and Personal Portrait*, p. 66; *New York Times*, 7/13/49.
55. Morris, p. 446.
56. FBI memo, Nichols to Tolson, 9/20/48; Alger Hiss Papers, Harvard Law Library; Morris, p. 447.
57. *Whittier Daily News*, 10/25/48.
58. William A. Arnold, *Back When It All Began: The Early Nixon Years*, p. 36.
59. Geoffrey C. Ward, *American Originals: The Private Worlds of Some Singular Men and Women*, p. 24.
60. Nixon, *Memoirs*, p. 72.
61. Stripling, pp. 140–41.
62. Allen Weinstein, *Nixon v. Hiss*, p. 147.
63. Wicker, p. 65.
64. Nixon, *Six Crises*, pp. 48–49; Weinstein, p. 190.
65. Morris, p. 472.
66. Weinstein, *Perjury*, pp. 272–73; Nixon, *Six Crises*, pp. 54–56; Stripling, pp. 148–50.
67. FBI memo, Ladd–Hoover, 12/8/48; A. Hiss Papers, Harvard; Morris p. 479.
68. HUAC hearings, 12/5/49.
69. Goodman, p. 282.

70. FBI memo, Nichols to Tolson, 6/28/49; A. Hiss Papers, Harvard; Morris, p. 491.
71. Weinstein, *Perjury*, p. 469; Mazo, p. 65; *New York Times*, 7/12/49.
72. Goodman, p. 311.
73. Weinstein, *Perjury*, p. 510.
74. Matthew 25:36; Dean Acheson, *Present at the Creation: My Years in the State Department*, p. 360.
75. Ambrose, vol. 1, p. 129.
76. Mazo, p. 59.
77. Morris, p. 507.
78. Nixon Press Release File, 3/12/51, Vice Presidential Papers.

Chapter Three

1. Carey McWilliams, *California: The Great Exception*, p. 21.
2. *Hollywood Citizen-News*, 12/17/48.
3. Robert Caro, *The Years of Lyndon Johnson*, vol. 3, *Master of the Senate*, pp. 141–45.
4. Helen G. Douglas, *A Full Life*, p. 254.
5. *Los Angeles Times*, 1/29/50.
6. *San Francisco Chronicle*, 4/16/50.
7. *New York Times*, 5/11/50.
8. Stephen E. Ambrose, *Nixon*, vol. 1, *The Education of a Politician, 1913–1962*, pp. 239–40 (after referred to as Ambrose, vol. 1).
9. Thomas C. Reeves, *The Life and Times of Joe McCarthy: A Biography*, p. 245.
10. Richard Nixon, *RN: The Memoirs of Richard Nixon*, p. 77 (after referred to as Nixon, *Memoirs*).
11. *San Diego Journal*, 5/6/50; William A. Arnold, *Back When It All Began: The Early Nixon Years*, pp. 12–13.
12. *Santa Monica Evening Outlook*, 5/18/50.
13. Douglas, *A Full Life*, p. 314.
14. *New York Times*, 11/1/50.
15. Earl Mazo, *Richard Nixon: A Political and Personal Portrait*, p. 81.
16. Roger Morris, *Richard Milhous Nixon: The Rise of an American Politician*, p. 589.
17. Douglas, pp. 303–304, Rayburn allegedly referred to Nixon's "chinkapin eyes" and said he had "the cruelest face" he had seen; Morris, p. 307; Alfred Steinberg, *Sam Rayburn: A Biography*, pp. 279–80.
18. Congressional Record, 8/29/50.
19. Nixon, *Memoirs*, p. 74.
20. Nixon Campaign File, Nixon speech, 9/18/50; Helen Gahagan Douglas Papers, University of Oklahoma; Morris, p. 584.

21. *San Francisco Chronicle*, 11/4/50.
22. Julie N. Eisenhower, *Pat Nixon: The Untold Story*, p. 109.
23. Helen Gahagan Douglas, Oral History Project, University of California at Berkeley, Evie Chavoor.
24. *Los Angeles Times*, 10/25/50.
25. Ibid., 11/3/50.
26. Ibid., 11/5/50.
27. Jonathan Aitken, *Nixon: A Life*, p. 191. Aitken interviews with David Astor, 11/91.
28. *New York Times*, 6/29/51.
29. Morris, p. 628.
30. Richard Nixon, *Leaders*, p. 99.
31. Douglas MacArthur, *Reminiscences*, p. 361.
32. Nixon, *Leaders*, p. 93.
33. Ibid., p. 99.
34. Leo Katcher, *Earl Warren: A Political Biography*, p. 266.
35. Nixon to Harriman, 4/28/52, Harriman to Nixon 5/21/52, Vice Presidential Papers.
36. Nixon to David Lloyd, 3/22/52, HST Library, Lloyd Papers; Ambrose, vol. 1, p. 244.
37. Morris, p. 641.
38. Patricia R. Nixon, "I Say He's a Wonderful Guy," *Saturday Evening Post*, 9/6/52.
39. *Los Angeles Times*, 1/13/51.
40. Harry S. Truman, *Memoirs*, vol. 2, *Years of Trial and Hope*, p. 492.
41. Nixon, *Memoirs*, p. 82.
42. William Costello, *The Facts About Nixon: An Unauthorized Biography*, p. 92.
43. Blanche Wiesen Cook, *The Declassified Eisenhower: A Divided Legacy*, p. 77.
44. Dwight Eisenhower, *Diaries*, p. 372.
45. Ibid., p. 373.
46. Ibid., pp. 371–73.
47. Ibid., p. 374.
48. Ibid., p. 375.
49. David McCullough, *Truman*, pp. 888–89.
50. Stephen E. Ambrose, *Eisenhower*, vol. 1, *Soldier, General of the Army, President-Elect*, p. 522.
51. McCullough, p. 889.
52. Eisenhower to General Lucius Clay, 4/6/51, Personal Papers, Dwight D. Eisenhower Presidential Library.
53. Herbert Klein, *Making It Perfectly Clear*, p. 138.

54. Earl Warren, Oral History Project, University of California at Berkeley, Keith McCormac, III; Morris, p. 676.
55. Ibid.
56. Mazo, pp. 82–83.
57. *Los Angeles Times*, 11/15/51.
58. Ibid.
59. Ibid., 5/19/52.
60. Earl Warren, *The Memoirs of Earl Warren*, p. 253.
61. Nixon, *Leaders*, p. 90.
62. *Hilo Tribune-Herald*, 4/5/52.
63. Henry Cabot Lodge, *The Storm Has Many Eyes*, p. 99. There were not the thirty thousand people Stephen Ambrose imagined (Ambrose, vol. 1, p. 679).
64. Geoffrey Perret, *Eisenhower*, p. 402.
65. Richard Norton Smith, *Thomas E. Dewey and His Times*, p. 584.
66. Nixon, *Memoirs*, p. 84.
67. Morris, p. 686.
68. Nixon, *Memoirs*, pp. 84–85.
69. Richard Norton Smith, photo cut-line following p. 290.
70. Ibid., p. 587.
71. Mazo, p. 93; Costello, pp. 87–88.
72. Earl Warren, Oral History, University of California at Berkeley, Mellon 8; Morris, p. 715.
73. *Independent Review*, 10/31/52.
74. Drew Pearson, *Diaries*, p. 216.
75. Morris, p. 729.
76. C.L. Sulzberger, *A Long Row of Candles*, p. 772.
77. Nixon, *Memoirs*, p. 86.
78. Julie N. Eisenhower, p. 115.
79. Nixon, *Memoirs*, pp. 86–88.
80. Lester David, *The Lonely Lady of San Clemente: The Story of Pat Nixon*, p. 95.

Chapter Four

1. Earl Warren Oral History, Hotchkiss, p. 45.
2. William Costello, *The Facts About Nixon: An Authorized Biography*, p. 7.
3. Jonathan Aitken, *Nixon: A Life*, p. 206.
4. Roger Morris, *Richard Milhous Nixon: The Rise of an American Politician*, p. 738.
5. Aitken, p. 343.
6. *Los Angeles Times*, 7/29/52.
7. Costello, pp. 96–97.

8. Thomas C. Reeves, *The Life and Times of Joe McCarthy*, pp. 430, 436.

9. *New York Times*, 9/4/52.

10. Morris, p. 751.

11. *Los Angeles Times*, 9/18/52.

12. Nixon, *Six Crises*, p. 74; Earl Mazo, *Richard Nixon: A Political and Personal Portrait*, p. 97.

13. Peter Lyon, *Eisenhower: Portrait of the Hero*, p. 454.

14. *New York Herald Tribune*, 9/19/52.

15. Richard Nixon, *Six Crises*, pp. 82–83; Morris, p. 769.

16. *New York Times*, 9/24/52.

17. "Nixon's Employment at OPA," Lloyd Papers, HST Library; Stephen E. Ambrose, *Nixon*, vol. 1, *The Education of a Politician, 1913–1962*, p. 295 (after referred to as Ambrose, vol. 1).

18. Morris, p. 774.

19. Nixon, *Six Crises*, p. 87.

20. Lyon p. 455; Richard Norton Smith, *Thomas E. Dewey and His Times*, p. 600.

21. Morris, p. 785.

22. *New York Times*, 9/21/52.

23. *Los Angeles Times*, 9/21/52.

24. Humphreys & Adams Papers, Dwight D. Eisenhower Presidential Library; Morris, p. 790.

25. *New York Times*, 9/21/52.

26. Richard Nixon, *RN: The Memoirs of Richard Nixon*, p. 96 (after referred to as Nixon, *Memoirs*).

27. Tom Wicker, *One of Us: Richard Nixon and the American Dream*, p. 96.

28. Nixon, *Memoirs*, p. 111.

29. *New York Times*, 9/21/52.

30. Dwight D. Eisenhower, *Mandate for Change*, pp. 65–66.

31. Ibid.; Morris, pp. 798–99.

32. Bela Kornitzer, *The Real Nixon: An Intimate Biography*, pp. 192–93.

33. Humphreys & Adams Papers, Dwight D. Eisenhower Presidential Library; Morris, p. 805; Eisenhower, *Mandate for Change*, p. 67.

34. Nixon, *Six Crises*, pp. 99–101; *Memoirs*, pp. 97–99.

35. Nixon, *Six Crises*, p. 102.

36. Nixon, *Memoirs*, pp. 98–99.

37. Nixon, *Six Crises*, p. 102.

38. Smith, p. 602.

39. Nixon, *Six Crises*, p. 107.

40. Ibid., pp. 37–38.

41. Ibid., pp. 109–111; *Memoirs*, p. 102; Smith, p. 601.

42. Nixon, *Six Crises*, pp. 109–111.
43. Ibid., and Wicker, p. 97.
44. Nixon, *Six Crises*, p. 112; *Memoirs*, p. 103.
45. Aitken, p. 219.
46. Wicker, p. 103.
47. Aitken, pp. 218–19, based on Aitken-Brownell interview.
48. Nixon, *Six Crises*, p. 117.
49. *Los Angeles Herald Examiner*, 9/24/52.
50. Edwin P. Hoyt, *The Nixons: An American Family*, p. 270.
51. Ambrose, vol. 1, p. 291.
52. Herbert Klein, *Making It Perfectly Clear*, p. 138.
53. Morris, p. 845.
54. John Bartlow Martin, *Adlai Stevenson of Illinois*, pp. 693–703.
55. Shanley diary, 9/26/52, p. 516, Bernard Shanley Papers, Dwight D. Eisenhower Presidential Library; Morris, p. 854.
56. *New York Times*, 5/12/06.
57. *The Reporter*, 10/14/52.
58. Nixon, *Memoirs*, p. 110; Mazo, p. 137.
59. *Los Angeles Daily News*, 10/30/52; Nixon, *Memoirs*, p. 109; Julie N. Eisenhower, *Pat Nixon: The Untold Story*, p. 127; Morris, pp. 862–63.
60. Wicker, p. 199.
61. President Kennedy's meeting with Soviet Communist Party General Secretary Khrushchev in Vienna in June 1962 was so unsuccessful it helped to precipitate the Cuba Missile Crisis in the autumn of that year. Richard Reeves, *President Kennedy: Profile of Power*, p. 172. The excerpt from Khrushchev's memoirs is cited on p. 383 of Stephen E. Ambrose, *Nixon*, vol. 2, *The Triumph of a Politician*, and refers to a comment Nixon made on his News Summary on December 1, 1970: "Not a compliment."
62. *New York Times*, 10/5/52.
63. *Los Angeles Times*, 10/23/52.
64. Ibid., 10/28/52.
65. Nixon, *Memoirs*, p. 119.
66. Porter McKeever, *Adlai Stevenson: His Life and Legacy*, p. 230.
67. Costello, p. 117.
68. McKeever, p. 232.
69. Ibid., p. 234.
70. Wicker, p. 165.
71. McKeever, pp. 236–37.
72. Ibid., p. 239.

73. Nixon, *Memoirs*, pp. 108–109.
74. Drew Pearson, *Diaries*, p. 227.
75. Adlai E. Stevenson, *Major Campaign Speeches, 1952*; pp. 319–20.

Chapter Five

1. Ted Morgan, *FDR: A Biography*, p. 735.
2. Turner Joy, *How Communists Negotiate*, p. 8.
3. Richard Nixon, *RN: The Memoirs of Richard Nixon*, p. 121 (after referred to as Nixon, *Memoirs*).
4. John Cloake, *Templer: Tiger of Malaya*, pp. 296–97.
5. Conrad Black, *Franklin Delano Roosevelt: Champion of Freedom*, p. 1060.
6. Dewey to Nixon, 11/9/53, Nixon to Dewey, 12/1/53, Vice Presidential Papers.
7. *New York Herald Tribune*, 11/9/53.
8. Larry Collins and Dominique Lapierre, *Freedom at Midnight*, p. 58.
9. *New York Times*, 12/31/53, 1/1/54.
10. Fawn Brodie, *Richard Nixon: The Shaping of His Character*, p. 297, from the James Bassett diary.
11. Nixon, *Memoirs*, pp. 145–46.
12. Text of Nixon's address, Vice Presidential Papers, 3/13/54; Stephen E. Ambrose, *Eisenhower*, vol. 2, *The Triumph of a Politician*, p. 172.
13. Thomas C. Reeves, *The Life and Times of Joe McCarthy: A Biography*, p. 578.
14. John Foster Dulles Papers, notes of telephone conversation, 3/29/54.
15. Stephen E. Ambrose, *Nixon*, vol. 1, *The Education of a Politician*, p. 342 (after referred to as Ambrose, vol. 1). (C.D. Jackson to Nixon, 1/4/54, Jackson Papers.)
16. Nixon, *Memoirs*, p. 151.
17. Ibid., pp. 152–53.
18. James Hagerty diary, 4/17/54, cited in Ambrose, vol. 1, p. 345.
19. Nixon, *Memoirs*, p. 153.
20. NSC Minutes, 4/29/54, cited in Ambrose, vol. 1, p. 345.
21. U.S. Foreign Affairs Oral History Collection, Kreisberg, cited in Margaret MacMillan, *Nixon in China*, p. 105.
22. David M. Oshinsky, *A Conspiracy So Immense: The World of Joe McCarthy*, p. 480.
23. Ibid., p. 483.
24. Ann C. Whitman diary, 6/29/54 (Eisenhower's private secretary, cited in Ambrose, vol. 1, p. 349).
25. Tom Wicker, *One of Us: Richard Nixon and the American Dream*, p. 145.
26. Nixon, *Memoirs*, p. 152.

27. Martin Gilbert, *Winston S. Churchill*, vol. 8, *Never Despair, 1945–1965*, pp. 997, 1010.

28. Black, pp. 1042–90.

29. Nixon, *Memoirs*, pp. 156–57.

30. Ibid., p. 158.

31. Ibid., p. 159.

32. Ambrose, vol. 1, p. 356.

33. *New York Times*, 11/2/54.

34. Nixon, *Memoirs*, p. 163.

35. Minnich, Cabinet notes, 11/5/54; Ambrose, vol. 1, p. 358.

36. Ibid.

37. Oshinsky, p. 484.

38. Ibid., pp. 487–88.

39. Ibid., p. 505.

40. Nixon, *Memoirs*, pp. 149–50.

41. Wicker, pp. 140–44.

42. Finch memo to Nixon, 6/4/55, Vice Presidential Papers.

43. Dwight D. Eisenhower, Presidential Papers, 1955, pp. 332–33.

44. Dwight D. Eisenhower, *Waging Peace*, p. 304.

45. George McJimsey, *Harry Hopkins: Ally of the Poor and Defender of Democracy*, p. 372.

46. Minnich, Cabinet notes, 9/30/55; Ambrose, vol. 1, p. 375.

47. Hagerty diary, 10/10/55; Ambrose, vol. 1, p. 378.

Chapter Six

1. Ann C. Whitman diary, 2/7/56 and 2/10/56, cited in Stephen E. Ambrose, *Nixon*, vol. 1, *The Education of a Politician*, p. 386 (after referred to as Ambrose, vol. 1); Dwight D. Eisenhower, *The White House Years*, vol. 2, *Waging Peace*, p. 294.

2. Ann C. Whitman diary, 2/9/56, cited in Ambrose, vol. 1, p. 387.

3. Ibid., 2/13/56; Fawn Brodie, *Richard Nixon: The Shaping of His Character*, pp. 350–53.

4. Arthur Schlesinger, *A Thousand Days: John F. Kennedy in the White House*, p. 18.

5. Ambrose, vol. 1, pp. 388–89.

6. Richard Nixon, *RN: The Memoirs of Richard Nixon*, pp. 170–71 (after referred to as Nixon, *Memoirs*).

7. *New York Times*, 3/11/56.

8. Ibid.

9. Ibid., (italics added).
10. Ibid., 4/19/56.
11. Nixon press conference, 4/26/56, Vice Presidential Papers.
12. Stassen letter to Nixon, 8/16/56, Vice Presidential Papers.
13. Nixon, *Memoirs*, p. 177.
14. David Brinkley to Leonard Hall, 10/19/56, Vice Presidential Papers; Author conversation with Brinkley.
15. Brodie, p. 357; Nixon letter to Bertha Bourke, 9/17/56, Vice Presidential Papers; Ambrose, vol. 1, pp. 414–15.
16. William Costello, *The Facts About Nixon: An Authorized Biography*, p. 161.
17. Ambrose, vol. 1, p. 419.
18. Stephen E. Ambrose, *Eisenhower*, vol. 2, *The President*, p. 462.
19. Eisenhower to Nixon, 9/3/57, Dwight D. Eisenhower Presidential Library, Ambrose, vol. 1, p. 441.
20. Tom Wicker, *One of Us: Richard Nixon and the American Dream*, p. 207.
21. *Los Angeles Times*, 5/8/58; Nixon, *Memoirs*, p. 188.
22. Ambrose, vol. 1, p. 469.
23. Ibid.
24. Richard Nixon, *Six Crises*, p. 204.
25. Ibid., p. 212.
26. Ibid., p. 220.
27. Nixon, *Memoirs*, p. 192.
28. Ambrose, vol. 1, p. 481.
29. Nixon letter to Chotiner, 6/23/58 Vice Presidential Papers.
30. Alsop to Berlin, 4/30/58, J. Alsop Papers, Library of Congress, with thanks to Michael Beschloss; Ambrose, vol. 1, p. 485.
31. Nixon to Charles McWherter, 9/5/58, Anderson File, Vice Presidential Papers, Ambrose, vol. 1, pp. 486–87.
32. Ambrose, *Eisenhower*, vol. 2, *The President*, p. 467.
33. MacArthur to Nixon, 3/27/58, Vice Presidential Papers; Nixon, *Memoirs*, p. 199.
34. Cabell Phillips, "Nixon in '58," *New York Times Magazine*, 10/26/58.
35. Wicker, p. 23.
36. Costello, p. 170.
37. Nixon Private Archives, Box 28, p. 162; Jonathan Aitken, *Nixon: A Life*, p. 255.
38. *New York Times*, 10/26/58 and 10/29/58.
39. Bela Kornitzer, *The Real Nixon: An Intimate Biography*, p. 163; Wicker, pp. 51–52.
40. *New York Times*, 11/30/58.

Chapter Seven

1. Minnich, Cabinet notes, 4/22/5; Stephen E. Ambrose, *Nixon*, vol. 1, *The Education of a Politician, 1913–1962*, p. 515 (after referred to as Ambrose, vol. 1).

2. Richard Nixon, *RN: The Memoirs of Richard Nixon*, pp. 206–207 (after referred to as Nixon, *Memoirs*).

3. Ibid., p. 209.

4. Tom Wicker, *One of Us: Richard Nixon and the American Dream*, pp. 221, 393. Allegedly, Ambassador Llewellyn Thompson is the source.

5. Nixon, *Memoirs*, p. 205.

6. Ibid., p. 210.

7. Ibid.

8. *London Daily Telegraph*, 9/20/59.

9. Nixon, *Memoirs*, p. 211.

10. Richard Nixon, *Six Crises*, p. 280.

11. Ibid., p. 281.

12. Nixon to Eisenhower, 8/4/59, Dwight D. Eisenhower Presidential Library; Ambrose, vol. 1, p. 532.

13. Jonathan Aitken, *Nixon: A Life*, p. 145.

14. Minnich, Cabinet Notes, 6/9/60; Ambrose, vol. 1, p. 536.

15. Ehrlichman's "Notes on Rockefeller's North Dakota Trip," 6/4/60, Vice Presidential Papers.

16. Charles de Gaulle, *Memoirs of Hope*, p. 244.

17. Ibid.

18. Aitken, p. 268; ACTI HVT, Folio 9, 62–63.

19. Carl Solberg, *Hubert Humphrey: A Biography*, p. 209.

20. Nixon to Dillon Anderson, 7/60, Vice Presidential Papers.

21. Reagan letter to Nixon, 7/15/60, Vice Presidential Papers.

22. Ann C. Whitman diary, telephone call notes, 7/19/60; Ambrose, vol. 1, p. 547.

23. Ambrose, vol. 1, p. 547.

24. Dwight D. Eisenhower, *The White House Years*, vol. 2, *Waging Peace*; p. 595.

25. Ibid., p. 596.

26. Ellis Slater, *The Ike I Knew*, pp. 230–31.

27. Whitman diary, 10/4/60; Stephen E. Ambrose, *Eisenhower*, vol. 2, *The President*, pp. 601–602.

28. Jacqueline Kennedy letter to Nixon, 12/5/54, Vice Presidential Papers; Aitken, p. 137.

29. Whitman diary, 8/30/60; Ambrose, vol. 1, p. 564.

30. Graham letter to Nixon, 9/24/60.

31. H.R. Haldeman, *The Ends of Power*, p. 75.
32. Theodore H. White, *The Making of the President, 1960*, p. 300.
33. Ambrose, vol. 1, p. 569.
34. *New York Times*, 9/22/60.
35. C. David Heymann, *A Woman Named Jackie*, p. 242.
36. Sidney Kraus, ed., *The Great Debates: Kennedy vs. Nixon, 1960*, p. 357.
37. Ambrose, vol. 1, p. 576, widely quoted but originally from the *Women's Wear Daily*.
38. Kraus, pp. 387–88.
39. Notes, F.A. Seaton Papers, Dwight D. Eisenhower Presidential Library; Ambrose, vol. 1, p. 580.
40. Ibid., Nixon Statement, 10/18/60.
41. Kraus, p. 397.
42. Ambrose, vol. 1, p. 592.
43. White, p. 310.
44. Nixon, *Memoirs*, p. 222.
45. Whitman diary, 11/5/60; Ambrose, vol. 1, p. 601.
46. White, p. 312.
47. Whitman diary, 11/8/60; Ambrose, vol. 1, p. 602.
48. White, p. 319.
49. Ibid., p. 317.
50. Aitken, p. 283 (ACTI, Margery Acker interview, 1990).
51. White, p. 314.
52. Aitken, p. 280 (ACTI, Flanigan interview, 1991).
53. Wicker, p. 253.
54. Nixon, *Six Crises*, p. 407.
55. Wicker, p. 254.
56. Ambrose, vol. 1, pp. 601–602; Eisenhower to Nixon, 4/25/61, Dwight D. Eisenhower Presidential Library; Nixon to MacArthur, 1/15/61, Vice Presidential Papers.
57. Wicker, p. 262.
58. Geoffrey Perret, *Eisenhower*, p. 606; Eisenhower letter to William Robinson, 10/12/66.
59. Nixon to Eisenhower, 1/15/61, Dwight D. Eisenhower Presidential Library.
60. Ambrose, vol. 1, p. 610.
61. Nixon, *Memoirs*, pp. 233–35.
62. Ibid.
63. Ibid.
64. *New York Times*, 6/6/61.

65. John Ehrlichman, *Witness to Power: The Nixon Years*, p. 31. (This must be read with caution, as Ehrlichman, when he wrote this book, was very antagonistic to Nixon.)
66. *Los Angeles Times*, 11/6/62.
67. Richard Reeves, *President Kennedy: Profile of Power*, pp. 172, 166 (JFK allegedly said this to the ubiquitous James Reston).
68. Andrew Roberts, *A History of the English-Speaking Peoples Since 1900*, p. 455.
69. Conrad Black, *Franklin Delano Roosevelt: Champion of Freedom*, p. 595.
70. Reeves, pp. 435, 655–56, and photo cut-line before p. 321.

Chapter Eight

1. Stephen E. Ambrose, *Nixon*, vol. 2, *The Triumph of a Politician, 1962–1972*, p. 16 (after referred to as Ambrose, vol. 2).
2. Nixon to Eisenhower, 3/18/63, and Eisenhower to Nixon, 3/25/63, Dwight D. Eisenhower Presidential Library.
3. Richard Nixon, *RN: The Memoirs of Richard Nixon*, p. 250 (after referred to as Nixon, *Memoirs*).
4. Ambrose, vol. 2, p. 22.
5. Nixon, *Memoirs*, p. 248.
6. Ibid., pp. 249–50.
7. Ibid., p. 248.
8. Henry A. Kissinger, *White House Years*, p. 20; Ambrose, vol. 2, p. 25.
9. Author's conversation with Nixon; Ambrose, vol. 2, p. 27.
10. Eisenhower to Nixon, 11/11/63, Dwight D. Eisenhower Presidential Library; Ambrose, vol. 2, p. 31. Nixon "declined to deny it," but said that was not a "durable opinion" (conversation with author, 6/23/92).
11. Jules Witcover, *The Resurrection of Richard Nixon*, p. 58.
12. Nixon, *Memoirs*, p. 251.
13. Ibid.
14. *New York Times*, 11/24/63.
15. Nixon, *Memoirs*, pp. 253–55.
16. James Piereson, "Lee Harvey Oswald and the Liberal Crack-Up," *Commentary*, May 2006.
17. Samuel E. Morison, *The Oxford History of the American People*, p. 1122.
18. *New York Times*, 12/7/63.
19. Ibid., 2/11/64.
20. Ibid., 3/12/64.
21. Ambrose, vol. 2, p. 41.
22. *New York Times*, 4/2/64.
23. Witcover, p. 77.

24. Ambrose, vol. 2, pp. 43–47.
25. *New York Times*, 4/28/64.
26. Ibid., 6/14/64.
27. Nixon, *Memoirs*, p. 265.
28. Witcover, p. 97.
29. Nixon, *Memoirs*, p. 260.
30. Personal recollections of the author, who attended the convention on behalf of the Canada-United States Interparliamentary Group.
31. Nixon, *Memoirs*, p. 266.
32. *New York Times*, 1/23/65.
33. Nixon, "Why Not Negotiate in Vietnam?" *Reader's Digest*, 12/65.
34. *New York Times*, 11/29/65.
35. Ibid., 3/9/66.
36. Leonard Garment, "The Hill Case," *New Yorker*, 4/17/89.
37. Eisenhower letter to Nixon, 6/13/66.
38. Jonathan Aitken, *Nixon: A Life*, p. 323.
39. John Ehrlichman, *Witness to Power: The Nixon Years*, pp. 37–38; H.R. Haldeman, *The Ends of Power*, p. 45.
40. Witcover, p. 37. Nixon often began by saying that he got on well with Nelson Rockefeller, who had recommended he visit Caracas as "a fun town. He was right," etc.
41. Aitken, p. 323 (based on an interview with John Sears).
42. Nixon to Eisenhower, 10/4/66, DDE PL; Eisenhower to Nixon, 10/7/66, Dwight D. Eisenhower Presidential Library.
43. *Chicago Tribune*, 10/7/66.
44. *New York Times*, 10/15/66.
45. Nixon, *Memoirs*, p. 276; Eisenhower to Nixon, 11/5/66, Dwight D. Eisenhower Presidential Library.
46. William Safire, *Before the Fall: An Inside View of the Pre-Watergate White House*, p. 33. Safire thought Rockefeller never replied to this message.
47. Witcover, p. 152.
48. Ambrose, vol. 2, p. 105.
49. *New York Times*, 3/6/67.
50. Nixon, *Memoirs*, pp. 281–82.
51. Ibid., pp. 282–283.
52. Ambrose, vol. 2, p. 109.
53. Raymond Price, *With Nixon*, pp. 21–25.
54. Nixon, *Memoirs*, p. 283.
55. Ibid.
56. Ibid.

57. Ambrose, vol. 2, p. 113.
58. Nixon, *Memoirs*, p. 284.
59. Wicker, p. 17.
60. Richard Nixon, "Asia after Vietnam," *Foreign Affairs*, 10/67.
61. Nixon, "What Has Happened to America?" *Reader's Digest*, 10/67.
62. *Chicago Tribune*, 10/28/67.
63. Nixon, *Memoirs*, pp. 287–88.
64. Witcover, p. 223.
65. Nixon, *Memoirs*, p. 293.

Chapter Nine

1. Stephen E. Ambrose, *Nixon*, vol. 2, *The Triumph of a Politician, 1962–1972*, p. 133 (after referred to as ambrose, vol. 2).
2. *New York Times*, 4/2/68.
3. Tom Wicker, *One of Us: Richard Nixon and the American Dream*, p. 295.
4. Nixon to Eisenhower 3/17/68, Dwight D. Eisenhower Presidential Library. Ambrose, vol. 2, p. 143.
5. William Safire, *Before the Fall: An Inside View of the Pre-Watergate White House*, pp. 47–48.
6. John Ehrlichman, *Witness to Power: The Nixon Years*, p. 40.
7. *New York Times*, 3/22/68.
8. Richard Nixon, *RN: The Memoirs of Richard Nixon*, p. 300 (after referred to as Nixon, *Memoirs*).
9. Lyndon B. Johnson, *The Vantage Point: Perspectives of the Presidency, 1963–1969*, p. 542.
10. Ibid., p. 549.
11. Adam Cohen and Elizabeth Taylor, *American Pharaoh: Mayor Richard J. Daley, His Battle for Chicago and the Nation*, p. 451.
12. Wicker, p. 325.
13. Ibid., p. 327.
14. Eisenhower to Nixon, 4/23/68, Dwight D. Eisenhower Presidential Library, and Eisenhower file NL.
15. Nixon, *Memoirs*, p. 302.
16. Wicker, p. 333.
17. Ibid., p. 348.
18. *New York Times*, 3/19/68.
19. PPF Box 20, RMW File A, Folder 1.
20. Mark Kurlansky, *1968: The Year that Rocked the World*, pp. 272–80.
21. Ambrose, vol. 2, p. 184.
22. Safire, p. 78.

23. Walter Isaacson, *Kissinger: A Biography*, p. 121.
24. Ibid., p. 123.
25. Ibid., p. 127.
26. Nixon, *Memoirs*, pp. 323–24.
27. *New York Times*, 10/30/68.
28. Isaacson, p. 131.
29. Anna Chennault, *The Education of Anna*, pp. 173–77.
30. Nixon, *Memoirs*, pp. 326–27.
31. Chennault, p. 175.
32. *New York Times*, 10/28/68.
33. Johnson, p. 548.
34. Nixon, *Memoirs*, p. 335.
35. Johnson, p. 549.
36. Nixon, *Memoirs*, p. 335.
37. Wicker, p. 390.
38. Nixon, *Memoirs*, p. 341.
39. Ambrose, vol. 2, p. 235.
40. Nixon, *Memoirs*, p. 338.
41. Roger Morris, *Richard Milhous Nixon: The Rise of an American Politician*, p. 811.
42. Richard Reeves, *President Nixon: Alone in the White House*, pp. 601–602.
43. Johnson, p. 548.
44. Nixon, *Memoirs*, pp. 365–66.
45. Henry Kissinger, *White House Years*, p. 3.
46. Ambrose, vol. 2, p. 245.
47. H.R. Haldeman, *The Ends of Power*, p. 83.
48. Isaacson, pp. 154–55.

Chapter Ten

1. Jonathan Aitken, *Nixon: A Life*, p. 414.
2. Richard Reeves, *President Nixon: Alone in the White House*, p. 32; Safire memo to Haldeman, 1/24/69.
3. Reeves, p. 33.
4. Ibid., p. 40.
5. Tom Wicker, *One of Us: Richard Nixon and the American Dream*, p. 415–16.
6. William Safire, *Before the Fall: An Inside View of the Pre-Watergate White House*, p. 152.
7. Presidential Papers (1969), pp. 183–84; Stephen E. Ambrose, *Nixon*, vol. 2, *The Triumph of a Politician, 1962–1972*, p. 257 (after referred to as Ambrose, vol. 2).

8. Safire, p. 124.
9. Reeves, p. 50; Ambrose, vol. 2.
10. *New York Times*, 3/3/69.
11. Anna Chennault, *The Education of Anna*, p. 169; *New York Times*, 4/8/69.
12. Richard Nixon, *RN: The Memoirs of Richard Nixon*, p. 37 (after referred to as Nixon, *Memoirs*).
13. Ibid., p. 373.
14. Henry Kissinger, *White House Years*, p. 39.
15. Reeves, pp. 54–55.
16. Nixon, *Memoirs*, p. 374.
17. Ibid., pp. 374–75.
18. Haldeman diaries, 3/9/69.
19. Walter Isaacson, *Kissinger: A Biography*, p. 175; Nixon, *Memoirs*, pp. 380–81; Henry Kissinger, *White House Years*, pp. 245–47; Seymour Hersh, *The Price of Power: Kissinger in the Nixon White House*, pp. 61–64.
20. Isaacson, p. 175.
21. Nixon, Presidential Papers, pp. 210–11; Ambrose, vol. 2, pp. 258–59; Reeves, pp. 60–61.
22. Anderson's notes of meeting, Acheson Collection, Princeton University: Ambrose, vol. 2, p. 260.
23. Nixon, *Memoirs*, p. 375.
24. Ibid.; Haldeman diaries, 3/28/69.
25. Nixon, *Memoirs*, p. 380.
26. Richard Nixon, *Four Great Americans: Tributes Delivered by President Richard Nixon*, pp. 13–21.
27. Haldeman diaries, 3/31/69; Reeves, p. 65.
28. Reeves, p. 65.
29. Nixon, *Memoirs*, pp. 384–85.
30. Ibid., p. 433.
31. *New York Times*, 4/20/69–4/24/69.
32. Ibid., 4/27/69.
33. USA Special Report, 5/13/69; Safire Papers, Library of Congress; Reeves, p. 74.
34. *New York Times*, 4/30/69.
35. Nixon, *Memoirs*, p. 386.
36. Ibid.
37. Ibid., p. 420.
38. Warren letter to Nixon, 4/25/69; Nixon Papers, College Park.
39. *Washington Post*, 5/1/69.
40. Reeves, p. 75.
41. Nixon, *Memoirs*, p. 389.

42. Isaacson, p. 26.
43. Hersh, p. 96.
44. Isaacson, p. 227.
45. Nguyen Tien Hung and Jerrold L. Schecter, *The Palace File*, p. 32.
46. Ibid., pp. 34–35.
47. John Osborne, *The Nixon Watch*, pp. 79–83.
48. Nixon, *Memoirs*, p. 396.
49. Reeves, p. 104.
50. Safire, p. 149.
51. Haldeman diaries, 7/19/69–7/20/69.
52. Ibid., 7/30/69.
53. Kissinger, p. 156.
54. Nixon, *Memoirs*, p. 395.
55. H.R. Haldeman, *The Ends of Power*, p. 91.
56. Reeves, p. 107.
57. Haldeman diaries, 8/4/69.
58. Nixon, *Memoirs*, p. 397.
59. Ibid., 398.
60. *New York Times*, 8/10/69.
61. Ibid., 3/20/69 and 3/31/69.
62. Haldeman diaries, 9/20/69.
63. Ibid., 10/6/69.
64. Nixon, *Memoirs*, p. 401.
65. Ibid., p. 402.
66. Ibid.
67. Kissinger, p. 304.
68. *New York Times*, 10/10/69.
69. Safire, p. 172.
70. Kissinger memo to Nixon, 10/17/69; Isaacson, p. 248.
71. Nixon, *Memoirs*, p. 404.
72. Isaacson, p. 248.
73. Nixon, *Memoirs*, p. 405.
74. Ibid., p. 407.
75. Ibid., p. 409.
76. Haldeman diaries, 11/3/69.

Chapter Eleven

1. PPF Box 16, File 1, Telephone Calls.
2. Tom Wicker, *One of Us: Richard Nixon and the American Dream*, p. 396.
3. Richard Reeves, *President Nixon: Alone in the White House*, p. 158.

4. Ibid., p. 159.
5. Wicker, p. 487.
6. John Ehrlichman, *Witness to Power*, p. 126.
7. *Time Magazine*, 4/20/70.
8. *New York Times*, 3/6/70.
9. Haldeman diaries, 4/15/70.
10. Reeves, p. 163.
11. *New York Times*, 1/28/70.
12. According to David Brinkley, in conversation with the author, 1/17/92.
13. *New York Times*, 2/19/70.
14. Haldeman diaries, 1/8/70.
15. Stephen E. Ambrose, *Nixon*, vol. 2, *The Triumph of a Politician, 1962–1972*, p. 329.
16. Walter Isaacson, *Kissinger: A Biography*, p. 250.
17. Haldeman diaries, 3/30/70, 4/1/70.
18. Kissinger letter to Nixon, 4/7/70; PPF Box 10.
19. Conversation with author, first printed in Conrad Black, *A Life in Progress*, p. 139.
20. Letter from Lyndon B. Johnson, 15/4/70, PPF Box 9, File 34, Lyndon & Lady Bird Johnson.
21. Reeves, p. 199.
22. White House telephone tape, Nixon Presidential Materials Project, College Park, 4/7/71, 10:21 to 10:27 P.M.
23. Richard Nixon, *RN: The Memoirs of Richard Nixon*, p. 451 (after referred to as Nixon, *Memoirs*).
24. Reeves, p. 203.
25. Ibid., p. 204.
26. Nixon, *Memoirs*, pp. 455–57; Reeves, p. 213.
27. Nixon, *Memoirs*, p. 457.
28. Ibid., p. 455.
29. Reeves, p. 215.
30. Nixon Presidential Press Conferences, 5/8/70, pp. 98–107.
31. Ibid.
32. Wicker, p. 635.
33. Seymour Hersh, *The Price of Power: Kissinger in the Nixon White House*, p. 196.
34. Nixon letter to Lon Nol, 5/19/70, personal collection of author.
35. Nixon, *Memoirs*, p. 466; Haldeman diaries, 5/18/70.
36. Dan Carter, *The Politics of Rage*, pp. 391–92.
37. Reeves, p. 324.

38. Nixon, *Memoirs*, pp. 474–75.
39. PPF File H3, 4/12/71.
40. John Aitken, *Nixon: A Life*, p. 398 (quote from the Hofstra Conference).
41. 7/70 PPF Box 9, File 27, H. Humphrey File.
42. Black, pp. 742, 941.
43. Kissinger memo to Nixon, 8/17/70; Reeves, p. 244.
44. Isaacson, p. 294.
45. Ibid., p. 299.
46. Reeves, p. 259.
47. Ibid.
48. CIA cable to Santiago chief of station, 10/18/70 (Reeves, p. 260).
49. Herb Klein to Richard Reeves; Reeves, p. 257.
50. Isaacson, p. 310.
51. Nixon, *Memoirs*, p. 489.
52. Reeves, p. 266.
53. Nixon memo to Haldeman, 4/28/71.
54. *New York Times*, 10/25/70.
55. Haldeman diaries, 10/29/70.
56. *New York Times*, 11/1/70.
57. Haldeman diaries, 12/7/70.
58. Nixon Presidential Press Conference, 12/10/70, pp. 130–41.
59. Reeves, p. 288.
60. Nixon, *Memoirs*, pp. 546–47.
61. Nixon memo to Haldeman, 12/11/70 (Reeves, p. 285).
62. Wicker, p. 406, based on letter from Moynihan, 8/17/88.

Chapter Twelve
1. White House Year End Review, 1970; Richard Reeves, *President Nixon: Alone in the White House*, p. 294.
2. Tom Wicker, *One of Us: Richard Nixon and the American Dream*, p. 567; Barry D. Riccio, *Richard Nixon Reconsidered: The Conservative as Liberal*, cited in Wicker, p. 8; Herbert Stein, *Presidential Economics: The Making of Economic Policy from Roosevelt to Reagan and Beyond*, p. 206.
3. Reeves, p. 314, from Rose Mary Woods and Herbert Klein.
4. Haldeman diaries, 2/3/76.
5. Ibid., 4/2/71 and 4/7/71; *New York Times*, 4/11/71; Reeves, pp. 306–10.
6. Haldeman diaries, 4/23/71.
7. *New York Times*, 5/2/71.
8. Tom Wells, *The War Within: America's Battle Over Vietnam*, pp. 504–505.
9. Henry Kissinger, *White House Years*, p. 187.

10. Margaret MacMillan, *Nixon in China: The Week that Changed the World*, p. 196.
11. Ibid., p. 163.
12. Vernon A. Walters, *Silent Missions*, pp. 534–38, 529–30; MacMillan, p. 170.
13. Richard Nixon, *RN: The Memoirs of Richard Nixon*, p. 547 (after referred to as Nixon, *Memoir*); Kissinger, p. 702–703.
14. F.S. Aijazuddin, *From a Head Through a Head to a Head: The Secret Channel Between the U.S. and China Through Pakistan*, pp. 42–43; MacMillan, p. 172.
15. Chen Jian, *Mao's China and the Cold War*, p. 261; MacMillan, p. 175.
16. Chen, p. 262; MacMillan, p. 177.
17. Nixon recordings, White House telephone conversations, 4/16/71.
18. Chen, pp. 264–65; MacMillan, p. 180.
19. Kissinger, p. 715.
20. Oval Office tapes, 9:41–10:41 A.M., 22/4/71.
21. Kissinger, pp. 706–707; Nixon, *Memoirs*, pp. 551–52; Haldeman diaries, p. 295.
22. Nixon, *Memoirs*, pp. 551–52; Kissinger, pp. 726–27.
23. Nixon, *Memoirs*, p. 552.
24. Kissinger, p. 716.
25. Seymour Hersh, *The Price of Power: Kissinger in the Nixon White House*, pp. 346–48; Stephen E. Ambrose, *Nixon*, vol. 2, *The Triumph of a Politician, 1962–1972*, p. 479 (after referred to as Ambrose, vol. 2).
26. Nixon, *Memoirs*, pp. 504–508.
27. Gerard Smith, *Doubletalk: The Story of SALT I*, pp. 222–28; Conversations of Richard Perle and Henry Kissinger with author.
28. Kissinger, pp. 814–15.
29. A joint meeting with the cabinet and congressional leaders; MacGregor memo to Nixon, 5/20/71, PDF Box 85.
30. Nixon to Acheson, 5/23/71, Acheson Papers, Yale University; Ambrose, vol. 2, p. 444.
31. Haldeman diaries, 6/23/71.
32. Allen Drury, *Courage and Hesitation: Notes and Photographs of the Nixon Administration*, pp. 226–34; Reeves, p. 312.
33. Reeves, p. 336; White House tapes, 6/23/71.
34. H.R. Haldeman, *The Ends of Power*, p. 110.
35. Charles Colson, *Born Again*, p. 57.
36. Haldeman diaries, 6/22/71.
37. White House tapes, 6/30/71; Haldeman, *The Ends of Power*, p. 115.
38. Ibid.
39. Haldeman, *The Ends of Power*, p. 112.

40. Haldeman diaries, 6/29/71.
41. Kissinger, pp. 735–36; MacMillan, p. 186.
42. John Holdridge, *Crossing the Divide: An Insider's Account of the Normalization of U.S.-China Relations*, p. 52; MacMillan, p. 187.
43. Aijazuddin, pp. 102–105; MacMillan, p. 184.
44. MacMillan, p. 188.
45. Ibid., pp. 40, 44, 46, 235.
46. Ambrose, vol. 2, p. 452.
47. NSA, Electronic Briefing Book, No. 66, Doc. 35, pp. 18, 20; MacMillan, p. 193.
48. MacMillan, p. 195.
49. NSA, Electronic Briefing Book, No. 66, Doc. 38; MacMillan, p. 196.
50. MacMillan, p. 197.
51. Enver Hoxha, *Reflections on China: Extracts from the Political Diary*, vol. 1, 1962–1972, pp. 560, 577; MacMillan, p. 200.
52. Walter Isaacson, *Kissinger: A Biography*, p. 346.
53. Nixon, *Memoirs*, p. 550; Kissinger, pp. 717, 734.
54. Isaacson, p. 346.
55. Ibid.
56. PPF, Buchanan N6.
57. Ibid.
58. Chen, p. 268; Kissinger, pp. 751–53; NSA, Electronic Briefing Book, No. 66, Doc. 37, 1 & 2.
59. Michael Schoenhals, "The Central Case Examination Group, 1966–1979," *China Quarterly*, p. 145, March 1996, p. 111; MacMillan, p. 201.
60. Jung Chang and Jon Halliday, *Mao: The Unknown Story*, pp. 580–83.
61. Nixon memo to Kissinger, 7/19/71.
62. MacMillan, p. 203; Joseph Kraft, *The Chinese Difference*, p. 18.
63. Reeves, pp. 343–44; Frederick Malek memo to Haldeman, 7/9/71.
64. Haldeman diaries, and Colson memo to Haldeman, 7/20/71.
65. Nixon News Summary, 9/23/71.
66. Reeves, p. 353; J. Anthony Lukas, *Nightmare: The Underside of the Nixon Years*, p. 93.
67. Nixon tapes, 9/14/71, 9/17/71, 9/18/71; Reeves, p. 370.
68. Reeves, pp. 348–49; Lukas, pp. 72–87.
69. Oval Office tapes, 7/1/71, 8:45–9:52 A.M.
70. Allen J. Matusow, *Nixon's Economy: Booms, Busts, Dollars, and Votes*, pp. 112–17, 146–49.
71. Kissinger, p. 951; Ambrose, vol. 2, p. 457.
72. William Safire, *Before the Fall: An Inside View of the Pre-Watergate White House*, p. 514.

73. Ibid., p. 518.

74. Haldeman diaries, 8/14/71.

75. John Osborne, *The Third Year of the Nixon Watch*, pp. 162–67; John Ehrlichman, *Witness to Power: The Nixon Years*, p. 275.

76. Nixon to Jaworski, 11/30/71, Nixon Papers, College Park.

77. Lukas, pp. 136–39.

78. Henry Kissinger, "Memorandum for the President from my October China Visit," Kissinger, p. 782–84.

79. Isaacson, p. 352.

80. Ambrose, vol. 2, p. 463.

81. Reeves, p. 390.

82. Kissinger, pp. 894–902; Hersh, pp. 454–60.

83. *New York Times*, Dec. 3 et seq., 1971.

84. Nixon, *Memoirs*, p. 527.

85. White House tapes, pp. 464 et seq., 2/23/71, 10:05–11:30 A.M.; EOB 309, 12/14/71, 12:00–1:37 P.M.

86. Kissinger, p. 905.

87. Nixon memo to Colson, 11/20/71; Reeves, p. 394.

88. Haldeman diaries, 11/11/71.

89. *New York Times*, 1/3/72.

90. Ehrlichman, p. 306.

91. Reeves, p. 385, quoting Haldeman.

92. Conversation of Nixon with author, 6/23/92.

93. Michael Drosnin, *Citizen Hughes*, p. 425.

94. Oval Office tapes, 5/13/71; Lukas, pp. 130–32.

95. Nixon, *Memoirs*, p. 582; Ambrose, vol. 2, pp. 502–503.

96. Safire, p. 398.

Chapter Thirteen

1. Jussi Hanhimäki, *The Flawed Architect: Henry Kissinger and American Foreign Policy*, p. 190.

2. Vernon A. Walters, *Silent Missions*, p. 546; Margaret MacMillan, *Nixon in China: The Week that Changed the World*, p. 259.

3. Richard Nixon, *RN: The Memoirs of Richard Nixon*, pp. 558–59 (after referred to as Nixon, *Memoirs*).

4. MacMillan, pp. 20–21.

5. Oval Office tapes, 14/2/72, 4:09–5:28 P.M.

6. Nixon, *Memoirs*, p. 559.

7. Haldeman notes, 2/17/72; Richard Reeves, *President Nixon: Alone in the White House*, p. 434.

8. Kissinger memo to Nixon, 2/19/72; Reeves, p. 436.
9. MacMillan, p. 290; Walters, p. 546.
10. MacMillan, p. 260.
11. Nixon, *Memoirs*, p. 561.
12. Marvin Kalb and Bernard Kalb, *Kissinger*, p. 267.
13. Li Zhisui, *The Private Life of Chairman Mao: The Memoirs of Mao's Personal Physician*, trans. Tai Hung-Chao, p. 563.
14. Ibid., p. 560.
15. MacMillan, pp. 93–94.
16. MacMillan, p. 142.
17. Nixon, *Memoirs*, p. 560.
18. MacMillan, p. 23.
19. Ibid., p. 47.
20. Li, p. 99.
21. MacMillan, p. 72.
22. Ibid.
23. Jung Chang and Jon Halliday, *Mao: The Unknown Story*, p. 346.
24. Philip Short, *The Dragon and the Bear: China and Russia in the Eighties*, p. 42.
25. Conrad Black, *Franklin Delano Roosevelt: Champion of Freedom*, p. 1023.
26. Edward Heath, *The Course of My Life*, p. 495.
27. MacMillan, pp. 146–47.
28. Reeves, p. 443.
29. MacMillan, p. 312.
30. Reeves, p. 444.
31. Ibid., p. 446.
32. Henry Kissinger, *White House Years*, pp. 1071–72.
33. Memorandum of Conversation, 10/24/71; MacMillan, p. 208.
34. Memorandum of Conversation, 2/24/12, 5:15–8:05 P.M.; NSA, Nixon's Trip to China, Doc. 3, pp. 16–23.
35. MacMillan, p. 258; Conversations with Nixon and Haig.
36. Nixon, *Memoirs*, pp. 569–70; MacMillan, p. 322.
37. Richard Nixon note, 2/23/72, China Notes Folder, PPF, Box 7.
38. Kissinger, p. 1067 (Kissinger included only the abbreviated form); MacMillan, p. 277; Joseph Kraft, *The Chinese Difference*, p. 31.
39. MacMillan, p. 271.
40. Ibid., pp. 147, 153, 277.
41. Jonathan Aitken, *Nixon: A Life*, p. 415.
42. Stephen E. Ambrose, *Nixon*, vol. 2, *The Triumph of a Politician*, p. 515 (after referred to as Ambrose, vol. 2).
43. MacMillan, p. 157.

44. Memorandum of Conversation, 2/21/72, 4:15–5:30 P.M.; Nixon, Presidential Materials Project, NSC files; MacMillan, p. 328.
45. MacMillan, p. 315.
46. Oval Office tapes 698–99, 5:32–6:11 P.M., 30/3/72.
47. Haldeman notes, 4/7/2; Nixon, *Memoirs*, p. 588.
48. Walter Isaacson, *Kissinger: A Biography*, pp. 407–16; Nixon, *Memoirs*, pp. 590–94.
49. Haldeman diaries, 5/28/72; Nixon memos to Kissinger, 4/30/72, 5/9/72; Nixon memos to Kissinger and Haig, 5/15/72; Nixon, *Memoirs*, pp. 602–606; Kissinger, p. 1199.
50. Nixon memo to Kissinger, 5/9/72.
51. Kissinger, p. 1194.
52. John Ehrlichman, *Witness to Power*, pp. 167–68.
53. Richard Nixon, *Four Great Americans: Tributes Delivered By President Richard Nixon*, pp. 53–57.
54. Haldeman diaries, 5/16/72; Colson memo to file 5/16, Colson Box 18, SMOF; Reeves, p. 480.
55. Haldeman diaries, 5/16/72; Reeves, p. 480.
56. Nixon memo to Haig, 5/20/72.
57. Haldeman diaries, 5/23/72.
58. Kissinger, p. 1233.
59. Nixon, *Memoirs*, p. 619. (On his first meeting with Churchill in twenty-two years in 1941, Roosevelt wrote his cousin Margaret Suckley and compared the British leader to New York mayor Fiorello La Guardia, letter dated 8/15/41, personal collection of the author.)
60. Ambrose, vol. 2, p. 595.
61. Memo of congressional leadership meeting 6/2/72, PDF, Box 88.
62. Nixon News Summary, 6/23/72; *New York Times*, 6/29/72.
63. Haldeman diaries, 6/13/72.
64. J.S. Magruder, *An American Life: One Man's Road to Watergate*, pp. 229–30.
65. Reeves, p. 501.
66. Ibid., p. 503.
67. Aitken, p. 471.
68. Nixon tapes, 6/22/72.
69. Ibid., 6/23/72.
70. Nixon, *Memoirs*, p. 684; Nixon tapes, 7/1/72; Reeves, p. 501; Katharine Graham conversation with Conrad Black, 1/2/00.
71. Nixon, *Memoirs*, p. 646.
72. Reeves, p. 513.

73. Nixon, *Memoirs*, p. 653.
74. Nixon memo to Connally, 7/20/72; Nixon, *Memoirs*, pp. 673–74.
75. Nixon tapes, 7/19/72, 12:45 P.M.; Reeves, p. 515.
76. Nixon tapes, 7/19/72, 12:45 P.M., and 7/25/72, 11:14 A.M.
77. Nixon memo to Haig, 8/15/72; Reeves, pp. 522–23.
78. Reeves, p. 515.
79. Ibid., p. 522.
80. Public Papers of the President, 1972, pp. 747–49.
81. Nixon memo to Haldeman, 8/12/72.
82. Oval Office conversations, pp. 759-2 & 5, 8/2/72, 10:25–11:47 A.M.
83. *New York Times*, 8/22/72.
84. *Washington Post*, 9/16/72.
85. Nixon tape transcript, NPMP, 9/15/72.
86. Theodore H. White, *The Making of the President, 1972*, pp. 209–36.
87. Nixon, *Memoirs*, p. 689.
88. Kissinger, pp. 1345–46.
89. Seymour Hersh, *The Price of Power: Kissinger in the White House*, pp. 581–82.
90. Nguyen, Tien Hung and Jerrold L. Schecter, *The Palace File*, pp. 85–106.
91. Haig memo to Nixon, 10/20/72; Meeting with General Westmoreland and General Haig, POF, Box 40.
92. Isaacson, p. 457.
93. Nguyen and Schecter, p. 105.
94. Ehrlichman, p. 314.
95. Nixon tapes, 10/25/72, 12:29 P.M.
96. Robert Schulzinger, *Henry Kissinger: The Doctor of Diplomacy*; Ambrose, vol. 2, p. 643.
97. Hersh, p. 603.
98. Ibid., pp. 608–609.
99. Nixon, *Memoirs*, p. 115.

Chapter Fourteen
1. Jonathan Aitken, *Nixon: A Life*, p. 47, based on Liddy interview.
2. Ehrlichman notes, 11/14/72, Ehrlichman Files, SMOF; Richard Reeves, *President Nixon: Alone in the White House*, p. 545.
3. Haldeman diaries, 11/19/72.
4. Henry Kissinger, *White House Years*, p. 1417.
5. Reeves, p. 549.
6. Ehrlichman notes, 11/28/72, 12/7/72, NPMP.
7. Colson, Oral History, NPMP.

8. Reeves, p. 550.

9. Stephen E. Ambrose, *Nixon*, vol. 3, *Ruin and Recovery, 1973–1990*, p. 35 (after referred to as Ambrose, vol. 3).

10. Reeves, p. 526, based on his interviews with Nelson Rockefeller from 1970 to 1972; Richard Nixon, *RN: The Memoirs of Richard Nixon*, p. 686 (after referred to as Nixon, *Memoirs*).

11. Memoranda of conversations between Kissinger and Hian Chan, 11/24/72, 12/7/72, and 12/8/72; Jeffrey Kimball, *Nixon's Vietnam War*, p. 363.

12. Jussi Hanhimäki, *The Flawed Architect: Henry Kissinger and American Foreign Policy*, p. 255, and Reeves, p. 750 (endnote for p. 446).

13. Nixon tapes, 12/11/72, 11:07 A.M.

14. Nixon, *Memoirs*, p. 133.

15. Haldeman diaries, 12/15/72.

16. Nixon, *Memoirs*, p. 734.

17. Haldeman diaries, 12/15/72.

18. Nixon, *Memoirs*, pp. 736–37.

19. Haldeman notes, 12/31/72.

20. Seymour Hersh, *The Price of Power: Kissinger in the Nixon White House*, p. 630.

21. Nixon, *Memoirs*, p. 774.

22. Haldeman diaries, 1/25/73.

23. Herbert Stein, interview with the scholars at the Miller Center, University of Virginia, cited in Tom Wicker, *One of Us: Richard Nixon and the American Dream*, p. 559.

24. Nixon, *Memoirs*, p. 756.

25. Nguyen Tien Hung and Jerrold L. Schecter, *The Palace File*, p. 148.

26. Ibid., pp. 145–55.

27. PPF Box 9, File 34, Lyndon and Lady Bird Johnson File, 1/23/73.

28. Ambrose, vol. 3, p. 24.

29. Reeves, p. 572.

30. Ambrose, vol. 3, p. 20.

31. Mel Elfin, *Newsweek*, 1/22/73.

32. John Ehrlichman, *Witness to Power: The Nixon Years*, p. 316.

33. Haldeman diaries, 1/27/73; Reeves, p. 565.

34. Haldeman diaries, 2/7/73.

35. Nixon tapes, 2/22/73, 4:04 P.M.

36. Nixon, *Memoirs*, p. 773.

37. Ibid., p. 774.

38. Ibid., p. 776.

39. Ibid., p. 777.

40. Ibid., p. 778.
41. *New York Times, The White House Tapes*, pp. 69–92.
42. News Summary, 2/12/73.
43. *New York Times, The White House Tapes*, pp. 69–92; Ambrose, vol. 3, p. 70.
44. Nixon, *Memoirs*, p. 783.
45. *New York Times, The White House Tapes*, pp. 126–31.
46. Haldeman diaries, 12/7/72.
47. *New York Times, The White House Tapes*, p. 146.
48. Reeves, p. 578.
49. Transcript, 3/22/73, NPMP.
50. News Summary, 3/26/73.
51. *New York Times*, 3/30/73.
52. Haldeman diaries, 3/31/73.
53. Nguyen and Schecter, 161–64; Kissinger, p. 1326.
54. Haldeman diaries, 4/12/73.
55. Haldeman diaries, p. 634.
56. Transcript, 3/22/73, NPMP.
57. Reeves, p. 586.
58. *New York Times, The White House Tapes*, pp. 607–15.
59. *New York Times*, 4/18/73.
60. Nixon tapes, 4/17/73, 4/18/73, 11:45 P.M.
61. Ibid.
62. Leonard Garment, *Crazy Rhythm: From Brooklyn and Jazz to Nixon's White House, Watergate, and Beyond*, pp. 253–54.
63. Moynihan to Nixon, 4/22/73, NPMP.
64. Nixon tapes, 4/9/73, 9:47 A.M.
65. Nixon, *Memoirs*, p. 514.
66. *Washington Post*, 4/23/73.
67. H.R. Haldeman, *The Ends of Power*, p. 268. (This book was written in Haldeman's anti-Nixon phase, from which he recovered, and must be read with caution.)
68. Nixon tapes, 4/25/73, 3:14 P.M. and 3:25 P.M.
69. Haldeman diaries, 4/26/73.
70. Transcript, 4/25/73; Haldeman, *Ends of Power*, pp. 272–75 (Nixon did add, "If worse comes to worst, we have one too.")
71. Transcript, 4/25/73; Nixon, *Memoirs*, p. 843.
72. Transcript, 4/25/73.
73. Ambrose, vol. 3, p. 130.
74. Herbert Klein in *New York Times*, 5/2/73.
75. Ibid., and Haldeman, *Ends of Power*, p. 296.

76. Aitken, p. 493, based on his interview of Rose Mary Woods.
77. Ambrose, vol. 3, p. 141.
78. *New York Times*, 5/16/73.
79. Timmons to Nixon, and Nixon's notes on it, 6/21/73, NPMP.
80. Henry Kissinger. *Years of Upheaval*, p. 359.
81. Nixon, *Memoirs* p. 874.
82. Transcript, 6/4/73, printed in *Washington Post*, 7/21/74.
83. *New York Times*, 6/8/73 and 6/10/73.
84. Nixon, *Memoirs*, p. 882; Kissinger, *Years of Upheaval*, p. 294.
85. Nixon, *Memoirs*, p. 893; *New York Times*, 6/28/73.
86. *New York Times*, 1/17/73.
87. Haldeman, *Ends of Power*, p. 205.

Chapter Fifteen

1. Presidential Papers, 1973, pp. 691–97.
2. *New York Times*, 8/17/73.
3. Presidential Papers, 1973, p. 822.
4. *New York Times*, 9/14/73, 9/16/73.
5. Julie N. Eisenhower, *Pat Nixon: The Untold Story*, p. 378.
6. Andrew Roberts, *A History of the English-Speaking Peoples Since 1900*, p. 503.
7. Henry Kissinger, *Years of Upheaval*, p. 468.
8. Jonathan Aitken, *Nixon: A Life*, pp. 504–5.
9. Kissinger, pp. 547–48; Richard Nixon, *RN: The Memoirs of Richard Nixon*, p. 933 (after referred to as Nixon, *Memoirs*).
10. Ibid.
11. Kissinger, p. 551.
12. Nixon, *Memoirs*, p. 938.
13. Kissinger, pp. 598–99.
14. Jerry Hartmann, *Palace Politics: An Inside Account of the Ford Years*, p. 19.
15. PPF, Watergate, Rockefeller File.
16. Nixon, *Memoirs*, p. 929.
17. Elliot L. Richardson, *The Creative Balance: Government, Politics, and the Individual in America's Third Century*, p. 38.
18. Ibid., p. 39.
19. Nixon, *Memoirs*, p. 933.
20. Presidential Papers, 1973, pp. 896–905. Mrs. Nixon and Julie Eisenhower were upstairs in the White House, and upset by this response (Julie N. Eisenhower, p. 385).
21. Rose Mary Woods to Nixon, 11/1/73, NPMP.
22. *New York Times*, 11/8/73.

23. Stephen E. Ambrose, *Nixon*, vol. 3, *Ruin and Recovery*, p. 286 (after referred to as Ambrose, vol. 3).

24. Presidential Papers, 1974, pp. 229–40.

25. Nixon, *Memoirs*, p. 990.

26. *New York Times*, 4/3/74.

27. Nixon, *Memoirs*, p. 1001.

28. Nixon to Chapin, 5/15/74, NPMP.

29. *Washington Post*, 6/12/74; Kissinger, p. 1125.

30. Nixon, *Memoirs*, p. 1011.

31. Ambrose, vol. 3, p. 360.

32. Kissinger, p. 1161.

33. Nixon, *Memoirs*, p. 1027; Kissinger, pp. 1163–64.

34. Nixon, *Memoirs*, p. 1059.

35. Ambrose, vol. 3, p. 387.

36. Nixon, *Memoirs*, p. 990, and conversation of Ms. Adler with the author.

37. Nixon, *Memoirs*, p. 1057.

38. Ibid., pp. 1057–58.

39. Ibid., p. 1059.

40. Aitken, pp. 525–26, Aitken's interview with Howard H. Baker.

41. Raymond Price, *With Nixon*, pp. 327–30.

42. Kissinger, pp. 1205; Nixon, *Memoirs*, p. 1066.

43. Nixon, *Memoirs*, p. 1080.

44. Kissinger, pp. 1206–1207; Nixon, *Memoirs*, p. 1073.

45. Nixon, *Memoirs*, pp. 1076–77; Kissinger, pp. 1207–10. In his memoirs, Kissinger made an elegant effort to present this experience with respect and dignity.

46. Nixon, *Memoirs*, p. 1080.

47. Aitken, p. 521.

48. Kissinger, p. 1213.

49. Conrad Black, *Franklin Delano Roosevelt: Champion of Freedom*, p. 597.

50. Kissinger, p. 1213.

51. Richard Reeves, *President Nixon: Alone in the White House*, p. 601.

Chapter Sixteen

1. Julie N. Eisenhower, *Pat Nixon: The Untold Story*, p. 429.

2. Gerald R. Ford, *A Time to Heal: The Autobiography of Gerald R. Ford*, pp. 168–72; Stanley I. Kutler, *The Wars of Watergate: The Last Crisis of Richard Nixon*, p. 562.

3. Rudyard Kipling, *If*.

4. Kenneth Clawson, *Washington Post*, 9/9/70.

5. *New York Times*, 9/24/74.

6. Julie N. Eisenhower, p. 436.

7. *New York Times*, 11/1/74.

8. Robert Anson, *Exile: The Unquiet Oblivion of Richard M. Nixon*, pp. 99–100.

9. Richard Nixon, *In the Arena: A Memoir of Victory, Defeat, and Renewal*, p. 31.

10. Julie N. Eisenhower, p. 439.

11. *New York Times*, 8/12/75.

12. Anson, pp. 126–27; *National Review*, 3/19/76.

13. Richard Nixon, *Leaders*, p. 239.

14. Bill Gulley, *Breaking Cover*, p. 264.

15. David Frost, *I Gave Them a Sword: Behind the Scenes of the Nixon Interviews*, p. 193.

16. Ibid., pp. 266–69.

17. *New York Times*, 2/19/81.

18. Stephen E. Ambrose, *Nixon*, vol. 3, *Ruin and Recovery*, p. 517 (after referred to as Ambrose, vol. 3).

19. *New York Times*, 12/1/78.

20. Jonathan Aitken, *Nixon: A Life*, p. 546.

21. Ambrose, vol. 3, p. 522; Conrad Black, *Franklin Delano Roosevelt: Champion of Freedom*, p. 316.

22. *New York Times*, 1/30/79.

23. Richard Nixon, *RN: The Memoirs of Richard Nixon*, p. 15; Ambrose, vol. 3, p. 385.

24. Richard Nixon, *The Real War*, pp. 96, 114–15, 122.

25. Ibid., p. 315.

26. *New York Times*, 7/17/80.

27. Anson, p. 230.

28. *US News and World Report*, 6/4/90.

29. *Time Magazine*, 7/29/85.

30. Richard Nixon, *No More Vietnams*, p. 237.

31. *Newsweek*, 5/19/86.

32. Nixon letter to Carlucci, 11/6/87; Aitken, p. 561.

33. Monica Crowley, *Nixon Off the Record: His Candid Commentary on People and Politics*, pp. 15–34, 172; *New York Times*, 3/10/93.

34. Lawrence Grobel, *Conversations with Capote*; Leonard Garment, *Crazy Rhythm: From Brooklyn and Jazz to Nixon's White House, Watergate, and Beyond*, p. 384.

35. Tom Wicker, *One of Us: Richard Nixon and the American Dream*, p. 686; Nixon, *Memoirs*, p. 573.

Bibliography

The primary sources are in the Nixon Presidential Materials Project at College Park, Maryland, and in the Richard Nixon Library and Birthplace at Yorba Linda, California. Almost all Nixon papers are gradually being centralized at President Nixon's Library and Birthplace, in one of the great posthumous victories of his life, after decades of litigation. Most such documents and tapes are now available, and contrary to anticipations do not much change the impression created from what was available ten or fifteen years ago. The newly released tapes do not remove previous ambiguities, and, as Henry Kissinger has accurately stated, Richard Nixon is much better understood reading what he wrote than listening to the idiosyncratic and inconsistent flow of what he said to his subordinates.

Other presidential libraries, especially President Eisenhower's, and other collections, were used as referenced. But the facts of Richard Nixon's career that can be indisputably established by documents must be supplemented by interpretations based on a wide and fair variety of criteria, including evaluations of his goals and the views of his contemporary confidants, insofar as he had any. Richard Nixon was the most inaccessible and unfathomable of all important presidents. Franklin D. Roosevelt, as I can attest, was an open book compared to him. The best judgment of what he intended is what he did, and what he did was not necessarily very closely connected to what he said, which was often unintelligible tactical dissembling, or spontaneous and inconsequential outbursts of consciousness. I have read, heard, and recorded it here, in the measure that it seemed, as fairly as I could judge, relevant.

Articles from periodicals that are cited in the footnotes are listed after the books. In fact, there is a practically unlimited number of identifiable sources on this subject, but going further to identify them did not seem useful.

Books

Abrahamsen, David. *Nixon vs. Nixon: An Emotional Tragedy*. New York: Farrar, Straus, and Giroux, 1977.

Acheson, Dean. *Present at the Creation: My Years in the State Department*. New York: Norton, 1969.

Adams, Sherman. *Firsthand Report: The Story of the Eisenhower Administration*. New York: Harper and Bros., 1961.

Agnew, Spiro. *Go Quietly . . . or Else*. New York: Morrow, 1980.

Aijazuddin, F.S. *From a Head Through a Head to a Head: The Secret Channel Between the U.S. and China Through Pakistan*. Karachi: Oxford University Press, 2000.

Aitken, Jonathan. *Nixon: A Life*. London: Weidenfeld & Nicolson, 1993.

Alsop, Stewart. *Nixon and Rockefeller: A Double Portrait*. New York: Doubleday, 1960.

Ambrose, Stephen E. *Eisenhower*. Vol. 1, *Soldier, General of the Army, President-Elect*. Vol. 2, *The President*. New York: Simon and Schuster, 1983–84.

——. *Nixon*. Vol. 1, *The Education of a Politician, 1913–1962*. Vol. 2, *The Triumph of a Politician, 1962–1972*. Vol. 3, *Ruin and Recovery, 1973–1990*. New York: Simon and Schuster, 1987–91.

Andrew, Christopher. *For the President's Eyes Only: Secret Intelligence and the American Presidency from Washington to Bush*. New York: HarperCollins, 1995.

Andrews, Bert, and Peter Andrews. *A Tragedy of History: A Journalist's Confidential Role in the Hiss-Chambers Case*. Washington: R.B. Luce, 1962.

Anson, Robert. *Exile: The Unquiet Oblivion of Richard M. Nixon*. New York: Simon and Schuster, 1984.

Arbatov, Georgi. *The System: An Insider's Life in Soviet Politics*. With an introduction by Strobe Talbott. New York: Times Books, 1992.

Arland, Benjamin F., and Artilissa D. Clark. *History of Whittier*. Western Printing Corp., 1932.

Arnold, William A. *Back When It All Began: The Early Nixon Years*. New York: Vantage Press, 1975.

Asselin, Pierre. *A Bitter Peace: Washington, Hanoi, and the Making of the Paris Agreement*. Chapel Hill: University of North Carolina Press, 2002.

Beck, Kent M. "Necessary Lies, Hidden Truths: Cuba in the 1960 Campaign." *Diplomatic History*, Vol. 8, Winter 1984, pp. 37–59.

Bell, Coral. *The Diplomacy of Détente: The Kissinger Era*. New York: St. Martin's Press, 1977.

Bentley, Eric. *Thirty Years of Treason: Excerpts From Hearings Before the House Committee on Un-American Activities, 1938–1968*. New York: Viking, 1971.

Berle, Adolf A. *Navigating the Rapids, 1918–1971*. Edited by Beatrice Bishop. New York: Harcourt, Brace Jovanovich, 1973.

Berman, Larry. *No Honor, No Peace: Nixon, Kissinger, and Betrayal in Vietnam*. New York: Free Press, 2001.

Bernstein, Carl, and Bob Woodward. *All the President's Men*. New York: Simon and Schuster. 1974.

Beschloss, Michael. *Mayday: Eisenhower, Khrushchev, and the U-2 Affair*. New York: Harper & Row, 1986.

Black, Conrad. *Franklin Delano Roosevelt: Champion of Freedom*. New York: Public Affairs, 2003.

———. *A Life in Progress*. Toronto: Key Porter Books, 1993.

Blake, Robert. *Disraeli*. London: Eyre & Spottiswoode, 1966.

Bradlee, Benjamin. *Conversations with Kennedy*. New York: Norton, 1975.

Brigham, Robert K. *Guerrilla Diplomacy: The NLF's Foreign Relations and the Vietnam War*. Ithaca: Cornell University Press, 1999.

Brodie, Fawn. *Richard Nixon: The Shaping of His Character*. Cambridge: Harvard University Press, 1983.

Bullock, Paul. *Jerry Voorhis: The Idealist as Politician*. New York: Vantage Press, 1978.

Bundy, William. *A Tangled Web: The Making of Foreign Policy in the Nixon Presidency*. New York: Hill & Wang, 1998.

Burke, Vincent J., and Vee Burke. *Nixon's Good Deed: Welfare Reform*. New York: Columbia University Press, 1974.

Burns, James MacGregor. *Roosevelt: The Soldier of Freedom*. New York: Harcourt, Brace Jovanovich, 1970.

Burr, William, ed. *The Kissinger Transcripts: The Top Secret Talks with Beijing and Moscow*. New York: The New Press, 1999.

Cannon, Lou. *Reagan*. New York: Putnam, 1982.

Caro, Robert A. *Master of the Senate*. Vol. 3 of *The Years of Lyndon Johnson*. New York: Vintage, 2003.

———. *The Years of Lyndon Johnson: Means of Ascent*. New York: Knopf, 1990.

Carr, Robert K. *The House Committee on Un-American Activities, 1945–1950*. Ithaca: Cornell University Press, 1952.

Carter, Dan T. *The Politics of Rage: George Wallace, the Origins of the New Conservatism, and the Transformation of American Politics*. New York: Simon and Schuster, 1995.

Castle, Timothy N. *At War in the Shadow of Vietnam: U.S. Military Aid to the Royal Lao Government, 1955–1975*. New York: Columbia University Press, 1993.

Chambers, Whittaker. *Witness*. London: André Deutsch, 1953.

Chang, Gordon H. *Friends and Enemies: The United States, China, and the Soviet Union, 1948–1972*. Stanford, Calif.: Stanford University Press, 1990.

Chang, Jung, and Jon Halliday. *Mao: The Unknown Story*. New York: Random House, 2006.

Chen Jian. *Mao's China and the Cold War*. Chapel Hill: University of North Carolina, 2002.

Chennault, Anna. *The Education of Anna*. New York: Times Books, 1980.

Chester, Lewis, Godfrey Hodgson, and Bruce Page. *An American Melodrama: The Presidential Campaign of 1968*. New York: Viking Press, 1969.

Clifford, Clark, with Richard Holbrooke. *Counsel to the President: A Memoir*. New York: Random House, 1991.

Cloake, John. *Templer: Tiger of Malaya*. London: Harrap, 1985.

Cohen, Adam, and Elizabeth Taylor. *American Pharaoh: Mayor Richard J. Daley, His Battle for Chicago and the Nation*. Boston: Little, Brown, 2000.

Colby, William, with James McCargar. *Lost Victory: A Firsthand Account of America's Sixteen-Year Involvement in Vietnam*. Chicago: Contemporary Books, 1989.

Collins, Larry, and Dominique Lapierre. *Freedom at Midnight*. New York: Avon, 1976.

Colodny, Len and Gettlin, Robert. *Silent Coup: The Removal of a President*. London: Victor Gollancz, 1991.

Colson, Charles. *Born Again*. Grand Rapids, Mich.: Chosen Books, 2004.

Cooke, Alistair, *A Generation on Trial: U.S.A. v. Alger Hiss*. New York: Knopf, 1950.

Costello, William. *The Facts About Nixon: An Authorized Biography*. New York: Viking, 1960.

Costigliola, Frank. *France and the United States: The Cold Alliance Since World War II*. New York: Twayne Publishers, 1992.

Craig, Gordon, and Francis Loewenheim, eds. *The Diplomats, 1939–1979*. Princeton: Princeton University Press, 1994.

Crowley, Monica. *Nixon Off the Record: His Candid Commentary on People and Politics*. New York: Random House, 1996.

David, Lester. *The Lonely Lady of San Clemente: The Story of Pat Nixon*. New York: Crowell, 1978.

Davis, Nathaniel. *The Last Two Yeas of Salvador Allende*. Ithaca: Cornell University Press, 1985.

de Gaulle, Charles. *Memoirs of Hope*. New York: Simon and Schuster, 1976.

Dean, John W. *Blind Ambition: The White House Years*. New York: Simon and Schuster, 1976.

Demaris, Ovid. *The Director: An Oral Biography of J. Edgar Hoover*. New York: Harper's Magazine Press, 1975.

de Toledano, Ralph. *One Man Alone: Richard Nixon*. New York: Funk & Wagnalls, 1969.

Dietrich, Noah, and Bob Thomas. *Howard: The Amazing Mr. Hughes*.
 Greenwich, Conn.: Fawcett, 1977.

Divine, Robert A. *Blowing on the Wind: The Nuclear Test Ban Debate,*
 1954–1960. New York: Oxford University Press, 1978.

Dobrynin, Anatoly. *In Confidence: Moscow's Ambassador to America's Six Cold*
 War Presidents. New York: Times Books, 1995.

Donovan, Hedley. *Roosevelt to Reagan: A Reporter's Encounters with Nine*
 Presidents. New York: Harper and Row, 1987.

Douglas, Helen G. *A Full Life*. Garden City, NY: Doubleday, 1982.

Drew, Elizabeth. *Washington Journal*. New York: Random House, 1975.

Drosnin, Michael. *Citizen Hughes*. New York: Holt, Rinehart and Winston, 1985.

Drury, Allen. *Courage and Hesitation: Notes and Photographs of the Nixon*
 Administration. Garden City, NY: Doubleday, 1971.

Edwards, Anne. *Early Reagan: The Rise to Power*. London: Hodder & Stoughton,
 1987.

Ehrlichman, John. *Witness to Power: The Nixon Years*. New York: Simon and
 Schuster, 1982.

Eisenhower, Dwight D. *The White House Years*. Vol. 1, *Mandate for Change,*
 1953–1956. Vol. 2, *Waging Peace, 1956–1961*. Garden City, NY: Doubleday,
 1965.

Eisenhower, John S.D. *Strictly Personal*. Garden City, NY: Doubleday, 1974.

Eisenhower, Julie N. *Pat Nixon: The Untold Story*. New York: Simon and
 Schuster, 1986.

Ellsberg, Daniel. *Secrets: A Memoir of Vietnam and the Pentagon Papers*. New
 York: Viking, 2002.

Ewald, William B. *Eisenhower the President: Crucial Days, 1951–1960*.
 Englewood Cliffs, NJ: Prentice-Hall, 1982.

——. *Who Killed Joe McCarthy?* New York: Simon and Schuster, 1984.

Foot, Rosemary. *The Practice of Power: U.S. Relations with China Since 1949*.
 New York: Oxford University Press, 1995.

Ford, Gerald R. *A Time to Heal: The Autobiography of Gerald R. Ford*. New York:
 Harper & Row, 1979.

Fosdick, Dorothy, ed. *Staying the Course: Henry M. Jackson and National*
 Security. Seattle: University of Washington Press, 1987.

Frost, David. *I Gave Them a Sword: Behind the Scenes of the Nixon Interviews*.
 New York: Morrow, 1978.

Gaan, Narottam. *Indira Gandhi and Foreign Policy Making: The Bangladesh*
 Crisis. New Delhi: Patriot Publishers, 1992.

Gaddis, John. *Strategies of Containment: A Critical Appraisal of Postwar American*
 National Security Policy. New York: Oxford University Press, 1982.

Gaiduk, Ilya. *The Soviet Union and the Vietnam War*. Chicago: Ivan R. Dee, 1996.

Gardner, Richard. *Fighting Quaker: The Story of Richard Nixon*. Whittier College Library, n.d.

Garment, Leonard. *Crazy Rhythm: From Brooklyn and Jazz to Nixon's White House, Watergate, and Beyond*. New York: DeCapo Press, 2001.

Garment, Suzanne. *Scandal: The Culture of Mistrust in American Politics*. New York: Random House, 1991.

Garthoff, Raymond L. *Détente and Confrontation: American-Soviet Relations, from Nixon to Reagan*. Washington: The Brookings Institute, 1985.

Gates, Robert M. *From the Shadows: The Ultimate Insider's Story of Five Presidents and How They Won the Cold War*. New York: Simon and Schuster, 1997.

Gilbert, Martin. *Winston S. Churchill*. Vol. 3, *The Challenge of War: 1914–1916*. Vol. 4, *World in Torment 1917–1922*. Vol. 5, *The Prophet of Truth, 1922–1939*. Vol. 6, *Finest Hour 1939–1941*. Vol. 7, *Road to Victory 1941–1945*. Vol. 8, *Never Despair 1945–1965*. London: Heinemann, 1971–1988.

Gill, William J. *The Ordeal of Otto Otepka*. New Rochelle, NY: Arlington House, 1969.

Golan, Matti. *The Secret Conversations of Henry Kissinger*. New York: Battam, 1976.

Goldwater, Barry. *With No Apologies*. New York: Morrow, 1979.

——, with Jack Casserly. *Goldwater*. New York: Doubleday, 1988.

Goodman, Walter. *The Committee: The Extraordinary Career of the House Committee on Un-American Activities*. New York: Farrar, Straus, and Giroux, 1968.

Goodwin, Doris Kearns. *No Ordinary Time: Franklin and Eleanor Roosevelt: The Home Front in World War II*. New York: Simon and Schuster, 1994.

Graubard, Stephen R. *Kissinger: Portrait of a Mind*. New York: Norton, 1974.

Green, John Robert. *The Limits of Power: the Nixon and Ford Administrations*. Bloomington: Indiana University Press, 1992.

Green, Marshall, John H. Holdridge, and William N. Stokes. *War and Peace with China: First-Hand Experiences in the Foreign Service of the United Sates*. Bethesda: Dacor Press, 1994.

Greenstein, Fred I. *The Hidden-Hand Presidency: Eisenhower as Leader*. New York: Basic Books, 1982.

Griffith, Robert. *The Politics of Fear: Joseph R. McCarthy and the Senate*. Lexington: University Press of Kentucky, 1970.

Grobel, Lawrence. *Conversations with Capote*. New York: New American Library, 1985.

Gulley, Bill, with Mary Ellen Reese. *Breaking Cover*. New York: Simon and Schuster, 1980.

Haig, Alexander, with Charles McCarry. *Inner Circles: How America Changed the World*. New York: Warner Books, 1992.

Haldeman, H.R., with Joseph DiMona. *The Ends of Power*. New York: Times Books, 1978.

Haldeman, H.R. *The Haldeman Diaries: Inside the Nixon White House*. New York: Putnam, 1994.

Hanhimäki, Jussi. *The Flawed Architect: Henry Kissinger and American Foreign Policy*. New York: Oxford University Press, 2004.

Hartmann, Jerry. *Palace Politics: An Inside Account of the Ford Years*. New York: McGraw-Hill, 1980.

Heath, Edward. *The Course of My Life*. London: Hodder & Stoughton, 1998.

Helms, Richard, with William Hood. *A Look Over My Shoulder: A Life in the Central Intelligence Agency*. Foreword by Henry A. Kissinger. New York: Random House, 2003.

Hersh, Seymour. *The Price of Power: Kissinger in the Nixon White House*. New York: Summit Books, 1983.

Heymann, C. David. *A Woman Named Jackie*. Secaucus, NJ: Carol Communications, 1989.

Hoff, Joan. *Nixon Reconsidered*. New York: Basic Books, 1994.

Holdridge, John. *Crossing the Divide: An Insider's Account of the Normalization of U.S.-China Relations*. Lanham, Md.: Rowan & Littlefield, 1997.

Hoxha, Enver. *Reflections on China: Extracts from the Political Diary*. Toronto: Norman Bethune Institute, 1979.

Hoyt, Edwin P. *The Nixons: An American Family*. New York: Random House, 1972.

Hughes, Emmet John. *The Ordeal of Power: A Political Memoir of the Eisenhower Years*. New York: Atheneum, 1963.

Hyland, William G. *Mortal Rivals: Superpower Relations from Nixon to Reagan*. New York: Random House, 1987.

Isaacs, Arnold. *Without Honor: Defeat in Vietnam and Cambodia*. Baltimore: Johns Hopkins University Press, 1983.

Isaacson, Walter. *Kissinger: A Biography*. New York: Simon and Schuster, 1993.

Isserman, Maurice. *Which Side Were You On?: The American Communist Party During the Second World War*. Middletown, Conn.: Wesleyan University Press, 1982.

Johnson, Lyndon B. *The Vantage Point: Perspectives of the Presidency, 1963–1969*. New York: Holt, Rinehart & Winston, 1971.

Joy, C. Turner. *How Communists Negotiate*. New York: Macmillan, 1955.

Kalb, Marvin, and Bernard Kalb. *Kissinger*. Boston: Little, Brown, 1974.

Karnow, Stanley. *Vietnam: A History*. New York: Penguin Books, 1984.

Katcher, Leo. *Earl Warren: A Political Biography*. New York: McGraw-Hill, 1967.

Kaufman, Robert G. *Henry M. Jackson: A Life in Politics*. Seattle: University of
    Washington Press, 2000.
Keith, Ronald C. *The Diplomacy of Zhou Enlai*. London: Macmillan, 1989.
Keogh, James. *This Is Nixon*. New York: Putnam, 1956.
Kimball, Jeffrey. *Nixon's Vietnam War*. Lawrence: University of Kansas Press, 1998.
———, ed. *The Vietnam War Files: Uncovering the Secret History of Nixon-Era
    Strategy*. Lawrence: University of Kansas Press, 2003.
Kissinger, Henry. *White House Years*. Boston: Little, Brown, 1979.
———. *Years of Upheaval*. Boston: Little, Brown, 1982.
Klein, Herbert. *Making It Perfectly Clear*. Garden City, NY: Doubleday, 1980.
Korff, Rabbi Baruch. *The Personal Nixon: Staying on the Summit*. Boston: Fairness
    Publishers, 1979.
Kornitzer, Bela. *The Real Nixon: An Intimate Biography*. Chicago: Rand McNally,
    1960.
Kraft, Joseph. *The Chinese Difference*. New York: Saturday Review Press, 1972.
Kraus, Sidney, ed. *The Great Debates: Kennedy vs. Nixon, 1960*. Bloomington:
    Indiana University Press, 1962.
Kurlansky, Mark. *1968: The Year that Rocked the World*. New York: Ballantine,
    2003.
Kutler, Stanley I., ed. *Abuse of Power: The New Nixon Tapes*. New York: Free
    Press, 1997.
———. *The Wars of Watergate: The Last Crisis of Richard Nixon*. New York:
    Norton, 1990.
Landau, David. *Kissinger: The Uses of Power*. Boston: Houghton Mifflin, 1972.
Lang, Gladys Engle, and Kurt Lang. *The Battle for Public Opinion: The President,
    the Press, and the Polls During Watergate*. New York: Columbia University
    Press, 1983.
Lankford, Nelson D. *The Last American Aristocrat: The Biography of Ambassador
    David K.E. Bruce*. New York: Little, Brown, 1996.
Larson, Arthur. *Eisenhower: The President Nobody Knew*. New York: Scribner, 1968.
Lasky, Victor. *It Didn't Start with Watergate*. New York: Dial Press, 1977.
Leuchtenburg, William Edward. *Franklin D. Roosevelt and the New Deal,
    1932–1940*. New York: Harper & Row, 1963.
Levitt, Morton, and Michael Levitt. *A Tissue of Lies: Nixon vs. Hiss*. New York:
    McGraw-Hill, 1979.
Liddy, G. Gordon. *Will: The Autobiography of G. Gordon Liddy*. New York: St.
    Martin's Press, 1980.
Li Zhisui. *The Private Life of Chairman Mao: The Memoirs of Mao's Personal
    Physician*. New York: Random House, 1994.
Lodge, Henry Cabot. *The Storm Has Many Eyes*. New York: Norton, 1973.

Lukas, J. Anthony. *Nightmare: The Underside of the Nixon Years*. New York: Viking Press, 1976.

Luu Van Loi and Nguyen Anh Vu. *Le Duc Tho-Kissinger Negotiations in Paris*. Hanoi: Gioi Publishers, 1995.

Lyon, Peter. *Eisenhower: Portrait of the Hero*. Boston: Little, Brown, 1974.

MacArthur, Douglas. *Reminiscences*. Greenwich, CT: Fawcett Publications, 1965.

MacMillan, Margaret. *Nixon in China: The Week that Changed the World*. Toronto: Viking Canada, 2006.

Magruder, J.S. *An American Life: One Man's Road to Watergate*. New York: Atheneum, 1974.

Martin, John Bartlow. *Adlai Stevenson of Illinois*. New York: Doubleday, 1976.

Mathews, Christopher. *Kennedy and Nixon: The Rivalry that Shaped Post-War America*. New York: Simon and Schuster, 1996.

Matusow, Allen J. *Nixon's Economy: Booms, Busts, Dollars, and Votes*. Lawrence: University Press of Kansas, 1988.

Mayall, James, and Cornelia Navari, eds. *The End of the Post-War Era: Documents on Great Power Relations, 1968–1975*. Cambridge: Cambridge University Press, 1980.

Mazlish, Bruce. *In Search of Nixon: A Psychohistorical Inquiry*. Baltimore: Penguin Books, 1972.

———. *Kissinger: The European Mind in American Policy*. New York: Basic Books, 1976.

Mazo, Earl. *Richard Nixon: A Political and Personal Portrait*. New York: Harper, 1959.

———, and Stephen Hess. *Nixon: A Political Portrait*. New York: Harper & Row, 1968.

McCullough, David. *Truman*. New York: Simon and Schuster, 1992.

McJimsey, George T. *Harry Hopkins: Ally of the Poor and Defender of Democracy*. Cambridge: Harvard University Press, 1987.

McKeever, Porter. *Adlai Stevenson: His Life and Legacy*. New York: Morrow, 1989.

McWilliams, Carey. *California: The Great Exception*. Santa Barbara: Peregrine Smith, 1976.

Meir, Golda. *My Life*. London: Weidenfeld & Nicolson, 1975.

Miller, Merle. *Plain Speaking: An Oral Biography of Harry S. Truman*. New York: Putnam, 1974.

Morgan, Ted. *FDR: A Biography*. New York: Simon and Schuster, 1985.

Morison, Samuel, E. *The Oxford History of the American People*. New York: Oxford University Press, 1965.

Morris, Roger. *Haig: The General's Progress*. New York: Playboy Press, 1982.

———. *Richard Milhous Nixon: The Rise of an American Politician*. New York: Holt, 1989.

———. *Uncertain Greatness: Henry Kissinger and American Foreign Policy*. New York: Harper & Row, 1977.

Murphy, Bruce Allen. *Fortas: The Rise and Ruin of a Supreme Court Justice*. New York: Morrow, 1988.

Nelson, Keith L. *The Making of Détente: Soviet-American Relations in the Shadow of Vietnam*. Baltimore: Johns Hopkins University Press, 1995.

New York Times. *The White House Tapes*. New York: Viking, 1974.

Nguyen Tien Hung and Jerrold L. Schecter. *The Palace File*. New York: Harper & Row, 1986.

Nitze, Paul, with Ann M. Smith and Steven L. Rearden. *From Hiroshima to Glasnost: At the Center of Decision*. New York: Grove Weidenfeld, 1989.

Nixon, Richard. *Four Great Americans: Tributes Delivered By President Richard Nixon*. Garden City, NY: Doubleday, 1972.

———. *In the Arena: A Memoir of Victory, Defeat, and Renewal*. New York: Simon and Schuster, 1990.

———. *Leaders*. New York: Simon and Schuster, 1990.

———. *1999: Victory Without War*. New York: Simon and Schuster, 1988.

———. *Real Peace: No More Vietnams*. New York: Simon and Schuster, 1990.

———. *The Real War*. New York: Warner Books, 1980.

———. *RN: The Memoirs of Richard Nixon*. New York: Grosset & Dunlap, 1978.

———. *Seize the Moment: America's Challenge in a One-Superpower World*. New York: Simon and Schuster, 1992.

———. *Six Crises*. Garden City, NY: Doubleday, 1962.

O'Brien, Lawrence F. *No Final Victories: A Life in Politics, From John F. Kennedy to Watergate*. Garden City, NJ: Doubleday, 1974.

Olson, Keith W. *Watergate: The Presidential Scandal that Shook America*. Lawrence: University of Kansas Press, 2003.

O'Neill, Thomas P., with William Novak. *Man of the House: The Life and Political Memoirs of Speaker Tip O'Neill*. New York: Random House, 1987.

Osborne, John. *The Nixon Watch*. New York: Liveright, 1970.

———. *The Third Year of the Nixon Watch*. New York: Liveright, 1972.

Oshinsky, David M. *A Conspiracy So Immense: The World of Joe McCarthy*. New York: Free Press, 1983.

Oudes, Bruce. *From the President: Richard Nixon's Secret Files*. New York: Harper & Row, 1989.

Parmet, Herbert S. *Jack: The Struggles of John F. Kennedy*. New York: Dial Press, 1980.

———. *Richard Nixon and His America*. Boston: Little, Brown, 1990.

Pearson, Drew. *Diaries, 1949–1959*. Edited by Tyler Abell. Holt, Rinehart and Winston, 1974.

Perret, Geoffrey. *Eisenhower*. New York: Random House, 1999.

Powers, Richard Gid. *Secrecy and Power: The Life of J. Edgar Hoover*. London: Collier Macmillan, 1987.

Price, Raymond. *With Nixon*. New York: Viking, 1977.

Public Papers of the President (1969–1972). Washington, D.C.: Government Printing Office.

Rather, Dan, and Gary Paul Gates. *The Palace Guard*. New York: Harper & Row, 1974.

Reeves, Richard. *President Kennedy: Profile of Power*. New York: Simon and Schuster, 1983.

——. *President Nixon: Alone in the White House*. New York: Touchstone, 2001.

Reeves, Thomas C. *The Life and Times of Joe McCarthy: A Biography*. New York: Stein & Day, 1982.

Reinhard, David W. *The Republican Right Since 1945*. Lexington: University Press of Kentucky, 1985.

Richardson, Elliot L. *The Creative Balance: Government, Politics, and the Individual in America's Third Century*. New York: Holt, Rinehart and Winston, 1976.

Roberts, Andrew. *A History of the English-Speaking Peoples Since 1900*. London: Weidenfeld & Nicolson, 2006.

Sadat, Anwar. *In Search of Identity: An Autobiography*. New York: Harper & Row, 1977.

Safire, William. *Before the Fall: An Inside View of the Pre-Watergate White House*. Garden City, NY: Doubleday, 1975.

Schell, Jonathan. *The Time of Illusion*. New York: Vintage, 1976.

Schlesinger, Arthur M. *The Age of Roosevelt*. Boston: Houghton Mifflin, 1958.

——. *A Thousand Days: John F. Kennedy in the White House*. New York: Crown, 1983.

Schoenebaum, Eleonora W., ed. *Profiles of an Era: The Nixon/Ford Years*. New York: Harcourt, Brace Jovanovich, 1979.

Schulzinger, Robert. *Henry Kissinger: Doctor of Diplomacy*. New York: Columbia University Press, 1989.

——. *A Time for War: The United States and Vietnam, 1941–1975*. New York: Oxford University Press, 1997.

Sevareid, Eric, ed. *Candidates 1960: Behind the Headlines in the Presidential Race*. New York: Basic Books, 1959.

Shawcross, William. *Sideshow: Kissinger, Nixon, and the Destruction of Cambodia*. New York: Simon and Schuster, 1979.

Short, Philip. *The Dragon and the Bear: China and Russia in the Eighties*. London: Hodder & Stoughton, 1982.

Sirica, Johan J. *To Set the Record Straight*. New York: Norton, 1979.

Slater, Ellis. *The Ike I Knew*. Self-published (Ellis D. Slater Trust), 1980.

Smith, Gerard. *Doubletalk: The Story of SALT I*. Garden City, NY: Doubleday, 1981.

Smith, Richard Norton. *Thomas E. Dewey and His Times*. New York: Simon and Schuster, 1982.

Snepp, Frank. *Decent Interval: An Insider's Account of Saigon's Indecent End*. New York: Random House, 1977.

Solberg, Carl. *Hubert Humphrey: A Biography*. New York: Norton, 1984.

Sorensen, Theodore. *Kennedy*. New York: Harper & Row, 1965.

Spalding, Henry D. *The Nixon Nobody Knows*. Middle Village, NY: Jonathan David, 1972.

Stans, Maurice. *The Terrors of Justice: The Untold Side of Watergate*. New York: Everest House, 1978.

Stein, Herbert. *Presidential Economics: The Making of Economic Policy from Roosevelt to Reagan and Beyond*. New York: Simon and Schuster, 1985.

Stern, Paula. *Water's Edge: Domestic Politics and the Making of American Foreign Policy*. Westport, Conn.: Greenwood Press, 1979.

Stevenson, Adlai E. *Major Campaign Speeches, 1952*. New York: Random House, 1953.

Stripling, Robert E. *The Red Plot Against America*. Drexel Hill, Pa.: Bell Publishing, 1949.

Sulzberger, C.L. *A Long Row of Candles: Memoirs and Diaries, 1934–1954*. New York: Macmillan, 1969.

———. *The World and Richard Nixon*. New York: Prentice-Hall, 1987.

Thompson, Kenneth W. *Portraits of American Presidents*. Vol. 4, *The Nixon Presidency*. Lanham, MD: University Press of America, 1987.

Tiger, Edith. *In Re Alger Hiss: Petition for a Writ of Error Coram Nobis*. New York: Hill & Wang, 1979.

Truman, Harry S. *Memoirs*. Vol 1, *Year of Decisions*. Vol. 2, *Years of Trial and Hope*. Garden City, NY: Doubleday, 1955, 1956.

Voorhis, Jerry. *Confessions of a Congressman*. Garden City, NY: Doubleday, 1947.

———. *The Strange Case of Richard Milhous Nixon*. New York: Popular Library, 1972.

Walters, Vernon A. *Silent Missions*. Garden City, NY: Doubleday, 1978.

Ward, Geoffrey C. *American Originals: The Private Worlds of Some Singular Men and Women*. New York: HarperCollins, 1991.

Warren, Earl. *The Memoirs of Earl Warren*. Garden City, NY: Doubleday, 1977.

Weinstein, Allen. *Perjury: The Hiss-Chambers Case*. New York: Knopf, 1978.

Wells, Tom. *The War Within: America's Battle Over Vietnam*. New York: Henry Holt, 1996.

West, Jessamyn. *Hide and Seek: A Continuing Journey*. New York: Harcourt, Brace Jovanovich, 1973.

Westmoreland, William C. *A Soldier Reports*. Garden City, NY: Doubleday, 1975.

White, Theodore H. *Breach of Faith: The Fall of Richard Nixon*. New York: Atheneum, 1975.

——. *The Making of the President, 1960*. New York: Atheneum, 1961.

——. *The Making of the President, 1968*. New York: Atheneum, 1969.

——. *The Making of the President, 1972*. New York: Atheneum, 1973.

Wicker, Tom. *One of Us: Richard Nixon and the American Dream*. New York: Random House, 1991.

Wills, Garry. *Nixon Agonistes: The Crisis of the Self-Made Man*. Boston: Houghton Mifflin, 1970.

Witcover, Jules. *The Resurrection of Richard Nixon*. New York: Putnam, 1970.

Woodward, Bob, and Carl Bernstein. *The Final Days*. New York: Simon and Schuster, 1976.

Wyden, Peter. *Bay of Pigs: The Untold Story*. London: Jonathan Cape, 1979.

Zumwalt, Elmo R. *On Watch: A Memoir*. New York: Quadrangle, 1976.

Articles

Baldwin, Hanson. "Managed News." *Atlantic*, April 1963.

Bullock, Paul. "Rabbits and Radicals: Richard Nixon's 1946 Campaign Against Jerry Voorhis." *Southern Quarterly*, Fall 1973.

Clawson, Ken. "A Loyalists Memoir." *Washington Post*, September 9, 1979.

Garment, Leonard. "The Hill Case." *The New Yorker*, April 17, 1989.

Jackson, Donald. "The Young Nixon." *Life*, November 6, 1970.

Nixon, Richard. "Asia after Vietnam." *Foreign Affairs*, October, 1967.

——. "What Has Happened to America?" *Reader's Digest*, October, 1967.

Todd, William. "The White House Transcripts." *Discovery: Research and Scholarship at the University of Texas*, Vol. 1, No 2, December, 1976.

Woods, Rose Mary. "Nixon's My Boss." *Saturday Evening Post*, December 28, 1957.

Index

Note: the following abbreviations have been used: GWB: George W. Bush; JC: Jimmy Carter; WC: Winston Churchill; DDE: Dwight D. Eisenhower; GF: Gerald Ford; LBJ: Lyndon B. Johnson; JFK: John F. Kennedy; RFK: Robert Kennedy; MLK: Martin Luther King; HK: Henry Kissinger; RMN: Richard M. Nixon; RR: Ronald Reagan; NR: Nelson Rockefeller; HST: Harry S Truman

Index